THE POSTMODERN *BEOWULF*:

A CRITICAL CASEBOOK

EDITED BY
EILEEN A. JOY
MARY K. RAMSEY

WITH THE ASSISTANCE OF
BRUCE D. GILCHRIST

WEST VIRGINIA UNIVERSITY PRESS
MORGANTOWN 2006

West Virginia University Press, Morgantown 26506
© 2006 by West Virginia University Press

First edition published 2006 by West Virginia University Press
Printed in the United States of America

13 12 11 10 09 08 07 06   9 8 7 6 5 4 3 2 1

ISBN 1-933202-08-4 (alk. paper)

Library of Congress Cataloguing-in-Publication Data

The Postmodern *Beowulf*: A Critical Casebook / Eileen A. Joy and Mary K.
Ramsey, eds.

    lxviii, 704p.   23cm.
    1. Beowulf. 2. Epic Poetry, English (Old)–History and criticism. 3. Civilization,
    Anglo-Saxon, in literature. 4. Literature, Medieval–History and criticism.
    5. Reading. I. Title. II. Joy, Eileen A. III. Ramsey, Mary K.

IN PROCESS

Library of Congress Control Number: 2005937640

Printed in USA by Bookmobile
Book Design by Than Saffel

We were saddened to hear of the death of Nicholas Howe as we were completing the final editing of this collection. Because his scholarship has been one of the primary influences in the development of our project, we wish to dedicate its publication to his memory. From his work on the Old English catalogue poems, to his groundbreaking Migration and Mythmaking in Anglo-Saxon England, *to his more recent writings on place and travel in both medieval Europe and contemporary America, Nicholas Howe was always at the intellectual and imaginative forefront of the field of medieval studies, which is now greatly impoverished by his untimely loss. He was also a steadfast and generous mentor to his students, who will miss greatly his advice, humor, and support, and more importantly, his friendship, which he gave freely.*

Mary K. Ramsey
Fordham University

Eileen A. Joy
Southern Illinois University Edwardsville

Thus Beowulf *(like the Old Testament, but unlike the classical epics) has its deep silences—so much is left unsaid!—in which we can hardly help but read our selves, and out of which we draw our interpretations. . . . We await a postmodern* Beowulf; *for surely, poised between holocausts as we sometimes feel ourselves to be, our more complete disillusionment is bound to discover itself in those same poetic silences even more forcefully.*

James W. Earl, "*Beowulf* and the Origins of Civilization"

CONTENTS

I. PREFACE

After Everything, *The Postmodern "Beowulf"*....................XIII
Eileen A. Joy

II. INTRODUCTION

Liquid *Beowulf*...XXIX
Eileen A. Joy and Mary K. Ramsey

III. HISTORY/HISTORICISM

Critical Contexts

The World, the Text, and the Critic.................................1
Edward Said

In Transit: Theorizing Cultural Appropriation in Medieval Europe......25
Claire Sponsler

"Beowulf" Essays

Beowulf and the Ancestral Homeland 49
Nicholas Howe

Writing the Unreadable *Beowulf*.................................91
Allen J. Frantzen

Locating *Beowulf* in Literary History 131
John D. Niles

IV. ETHNOGRAPHY/PSYCHOANALYSIS

Critical Contexts

Ethnicity, Power and the English 163
John Moreland

Landscapes of Conversion: Guthlac's Mound and
Grendel's Mere as Expressions of Anglo-Saxon Nation-Building 199
Alfred K. Siewers

"Beowulf" Essays

Beowulf and the Origins of Civilization 259
James W. Earl

Enjoyment of Violence and Desire for History in *Beowulf* 287
Janet Thormann

The Ethnopsychology of In-Law Feud and the Remaking of
Group Identity in *Beowulf:* The Cases of Hengest and Ingeld. 319
John M. Hill

V. GENDER/IDENTITY

Critical Contexts

The Ruins of Identity. 345
Jeffrey J. Cohen

Regardless of Sex: Men, Women,
and Power in Early Northern Europe. 383
Carol J. Clover

"Beowulf" Essays

Men and *Beowulf*. 417
Clare A. Lees

Beowulf's Tears of Fatherhood. 439
Mary Dockray-Miller

Voices from the Margins: Women and
Textual Enclosure in *Beowulf* 467
Shari Horner

VI. TEXT/TEXTUALITY

Critical Contexts

What is an Author? 501
Michel Foucault

The Textuality of Old English Poetry 519
Carol Braun Pasternack

"Beowulf" Essays

Swords and Signs: Dynamic Semeiosis in *Beowulf*. 547
Gillian Overing

Hrothgar's Hilt and the Reader in *Beowulf*. 587
Seth Lerer

"As I Once Did With Grendel": Boasting and
Nostalgia in *Beowulf* 629
Susan Kim

VII. POSTSCRIPT: PHILOLOGY AND POSTCOLONIALISM

Post-Philology 655
Michelle R. Warren

VIII. AFTERWORD

Reading *Beowulf* with Original Eyes 687
James W. Earl

PREFACE:
AFTER EVERYTHING,
THE POSTMODERN
BEOWULF

It is the very fact that we cannot live in the present—that the present for us is always part of an unfinished project—which converts our lives from chronicles to narratives. . . . We cannot choose to live non-historically: history is quite as much our destiny as death.—Terry Eagleton[1]

Now that theory is supposedly irrelevant, "over," and "dead," and has even inspired an "anthology of dissent," is the time finally propitious for the belated arrival of *The Postmodern "Beowulf"*?[2] Are we really belated and is theory even really dead? I would say, yes and no—to *both* questions. As Allen Frantzen has remarked, scholars working in Old English studies who engage contemporary, poststructuralist criticism often find themselves "challenged as intruders, as strangers on the beach, not unlike the way Beowulf and his retainers rouse the coastguard's suspicion as they arrive in Denmark."[3] Scholars working in contemporary literary studies do not often look to the field of Old English for enlightenment or direction on the subject of critical theory, and within the field of Old English itself, the resistance to theory, in general, has been strong, and occasionally mean-spirited. But here is not the place to go over old debates, for as Gillian Overing stated more than ten years ago at the 1991 convention of the Modern Language Association, "*we are changed* by this new work," which "has, indeed, arrived."[4] While Theory, with a capital *T*, already has a long history, which some trace to Plato and others to 1966 when Jacques Derrida presented a paper, "Structure, Sign, and Play in the Discourse of the Human Sciences," at a conference at Johns Hopkins University, it has not, in fact, exhausted itself and was never and can never be just "one thing" (or "empire," as recently argued) to be either embraced or rejected without equivocation. As reported in *The Chronicle of Higher Education*, theory is not "a unified kingdom," but is rather "a loose federation of states with permeable boundaries, no universally recognized constitution, and not much in the way of a lingua franca. It looks less like a superpower . . . and more like the fractious and ever-expanding European Union."[5] And whether conceived of as empire or fractious union, as Terry Eagleton reminds us, "[w]e can never be 'after theory,' in the sense that there can be no reflective human life without it. We can simply run out of particular styles of thinking, as our situation changes."[6] Theory will always be with us, if we prefer the examined life (and how could we not?), although some theories will, of historical necessity, eventually become useless (except as chapters in our intellectual history).

Styles of thinking have, indeed, changed as particular situations—social, cultural, political, historical, institutional, and otherwise—have changed, and this is why, for example, we already have first-, second-, and third-wave feminist critique, and even post-feminist critique. A first-ever anthology of critical essays on *Beowulf* that represents scholarship influenced by postmodern thought—which is what we offer here—does, in fact, arrive somewhat belatedly to a set of discourses long in session in the American university and already famous for pronouncing their own enervation, but I would argue that it is precisely in its "after-ness" that *Beowulf* scholarship of a certain postmodern bent is so timely. It is partly due to the fact that the reception of theory in Old English studies has been less than welcoming that those scholars wanting to carry the water to our field of newer analytical models have been so measured and careful in their approaches that they almost never take foreknowledge for granted and have thereby bequeathed to us a great gift—they have *taught* us theory while also practicing and revising it, and they have not neglected in the process what is generally understood to be the great strength of traditional medieval studies: an attention to philology, history, and cross-disciplinary contexts. Indeed, because of our focus on literature within its manuscript context, we should hold open the question of our "after-ness" to theory since, as Roy Liuzza writes, the "poststructural recognition of the enigmatic contingency of the text, as well as the cultural critics' attention to the social circumstances of literary production" already has its parallel in Old English studies, where critics, for a while now, have already been questioning "the authority of the text, the propriety of stylistic criticism, the means and circumstances of reading and reception, [and] the nature of literary creation and transmission."[7]

Paul Strohm has observed that "Postmodern theory has always needed us," mainly as "a necessary foil to an argument for an emergent modernity" and as a repository of a supposedly socially "static" world, but "[o]ur retort must be that our period, no less than any other, is the plagued and proud possessor of motile signs, category confusions, representational swerves and slippages, partial and competing and always irreconcilable narrations."[8] Strohm is correct, I believe, in suggesting that postmodernism is ultimately involved in a project in "which any good medievalist would describe himself or herself as engaged: the attempt to restore complexity to our understanding of the past."[9] This is similar to Lee Patterson's argument some years ago that medieval scholarship has an important role to play in instructing "postmodern criticism in the historical complexity and concreteness of cultural forms."[10] And this means, too, I would argue, that medieval studies have a critical function to perform in refashioning contemporary theoretical models, through a rigorous historicism, that helps to extend and deepen the explanatory power of those models.

The attempt to restore historical complexity to our understanding of the past and its cultural forms, and to also show how Old English studies both practice and reformulate theory, suffices as a description of the project of *The Postmodern "Beowulf,"* which was initially born out of a desire to provide for students an anthology of "the best of" contemporary critical approaches to the poem and then later developed into a casebook that we hope more than amply demonstrates the ways in which Old English scholarship has debated, elucidated, practiced, historicized, and even developed theory in relation to the critical analysis of *Beowulf.* The book is divided into four sections—"History/Historicism," "Ethnography/Psychoanalysis," "Gender/Identity," and "Text/Textuality"—that have been designed, not as much to represent specific movements within theory (such as deconstruction, new historicism, postcolonialism, Lacanian analysis, queer studies, and the like), as to offer broad contextual *fields* of inquiry within which certain questions regarding history, culture, identity, and language have perdured over time (and in response to which questions the more narrowly-defined theoretical "schools" have arisen). This is not to say that specific theoretical approaches are not purposefully highlighted in this volume, because many of them are, but it was also our concern to select essays that took up more than one narrowly defined approach and that also combined approaches (both traditional and more contemporary) in strikingly innovative ways. So, for example, we selected James Earl's "*Beowulf* and the Origins of Civilization" because it utilizes Freudian analysis (especially in relation to Freud's ideas regarding identification and the superego), but also because what is being psychoanalyzed is not what we might at first expect (i.e., the characters in the poem), but rather, the *readers* of the poem, both the present-day readers (ourselves) as well as one of the poem's probable Anglo-Saxon readers, Byrhtnoth, the "real life" hero of the tenth-century Old English poem, *The Battle of Maldon*. At the same time, Earl also analyzes his own dreams about the poem, thereby drawing himself (and more generally, the Old English scholar) under the rubric of his theoretical model. And because his analysis of one of those dreams is also an attempt to understand the ways in which the poem almost demands a certain kind of masculine identification with a particular Anglo-Saxon heroic ethos, Earl's essay also investigates the tensions between gender and ethnography in relation to the process of reading the poem *in our present moment*. Ultimately, Earl creatively interweaves Freud with reader reception theory and even with an imaginative new historicism (how might Byrhtnoth have read *Beowulf*?), and he also provides a glimpse of what "the personal is theoretical" might look like.

In addition to including essays on *Beowulf* here that we feel represent the most innovative uses and refashionings of multiple critical methodologies—both traditional and more theoretical—we decided to also include within each section essays which address more broadly ranging theoretical issues (grouped under the heading "Critical Contexts"), so that the *Beowulf* essays can be read and discussed in the classroom in relation to, not only other essays on *Beowulf* (both within and outside of this book), but also to these broader arguments. These are essays that represent a diverse spectrum of academic fields, from cultural criticism (Edward Said, "The World, the Text, and the Critic") to Old Norse studies (Carol Clover, "Regardless of Sex: Men, Women, and Power in Early Northern Europe") to ethno-archaeology (John Moreland, "Ethnicity, Power and the English") to continental philosophy (Michel Foucault, "What Is an Author?") to medieval studies more generally (the essays by Claire Sponsler, Alfred Siewers, Jeffrey Jerome Cohen, Carol Braun Pasternack, and Michelle Warren). Each section of the books contains five essays: three essays that directly address *Beowulf* (arranged in chronological order, by earlier to later publication date), preceded by two "Critical Contexts" essays that were chosen either because they propose critical paradigms that are reflected upon and articulated in the respective *Beowulf* essays, or because they offer analyses and arguments that broaden the depth of the critical field within which the *Beowulf* essays that follow them can be evaluated. The main objective in doing things this way is to both show the development of certain theoretical lines of thinking within *Beowulf* scholarship and to also create areas of critical tension that would ideally lead to further debate in the classroom. So, for example, in the "History/Historicism" section of the book, we have included two "Critical Contexts" essays—Edward Said, "The World, the Text, and the Critic" and Claire Sponsler, "In Transit: Theorizing Cultural Appropriation in Medieval Europe"—that both advocate (albeit in different ways) a criticism that would be attentive to the ways in which a cultural text, whether a poem or symphony or painting, *performs* in the particular world(s) in which it circulates, and also to the manner in which cultural objects are always being "appropriated" by different groups in different times and places, where meaning becomes as much a question of the environment of the work's reception as of what might be called an original authorial intention.

The essays that follow Said and Sponsler—Nicholas Howe, "*Beowulf* and the Ancestral Homeland"; Allen Frantzen, "Writing the Unreadable *Beowulf*"; and John Niles, "Locating *Beowulf* in Literary History"—all seek to understand what *Beowulf*, as a cultural text, and also as a myth of origins, might have meant in particular places to particular groups. For Howe, that means exploring how the Anglo-Saxons might have composed the poem as a kind of epic of a myth of ancestral migration from continent to island, which "gave the English as a *folc* a common identity by teaching them that they were descended from those who had made the exodus of the mid-fifth century," and therefore the poem might have had a critical function in an emerging proto-national identity. Niles's essay (which explicitly acknowledges, as does Frantzen's essay, the influence of Said's thought) argues for *Beowulf*'s status as "a socially embedded poetic act" that "responded to lively tensions, agreements, and disagreements in the society from which it came." More specifically, Niles sees the poem as responding to "a mixed and somewhat turbulent [post Viking invasions] Anglo-Scandinavian society," and he argues that the poem is ultimately "the projection of two great desires: (1) for a distinguished *ethnic* origin that would serve to merge English and Danish differences into a neutral and dignified pan-Germanism, and (2) for an *ethical* origin that would ally this unified race with Christian spiritual values." Taking the idea of the poem's social utility even further, Frantzen's essay looks at *Beowulf*'s role in nineteenth-century positivist philology, in modern translations, and also in the twentieth-century literary anthology and literature survey classroom, thereby giving us an invaluable (if selective) reception history of the poem that also shows us how the multi-vocality of the text has often been silenced in favor of supposedly authoritative and authentically historical editions. Frantzen also helps us to see, through a careful attention to the text of the manuscript itself and its cruces, "not how *Beowulf* was created, but how we have created it, making and remaking not just its literary meaning but its language." Because Frantzen undertakes a close analysis of the intratextuality and syllepsis of the words *writan* ("to write") and *forwritan* ("to cut through" or "to carve") in the poem, as they relate to the inscription (textual? runic?) on the hilt of the magic sword that Beowulf retrieves from Grendel's underwater mere, and which Hrothgar "reads," Frantzen's essay also practices a Foucauldian exploration of the linkages between writing and death, while also demonstrating "that the illusive and allusive nature of writing and reading in *Beowulf* discourages us from acts of closure, and indeed prevents those acts of interpretation, of 'cutting through,' sought by conventional criticism." The *Beowulf* essays in the first section of the volume, then, all explore in various fashions how the story and text of *Beowulf* have been appropriated for various historically-situated ideological and ontological ends, while Frantzen's essay also delineates how the text of the poem will always resist our desire to read, translate, present, or interpret the poem in narrowly defined, totalizing ways.

Similar to the "History/Historicism" section, the "Text/Textuality" section of the book begins with two "Critical Contexts" essays—Michel Foucault, "What Is An Author?" and Carol Braun Pasternack, "The Textuality of Old English Poetry"—that together formulate a line of thinking clearly influential upon the *Beowulf* essays that follow. Both Foucault and Pasternack call attention to the importance of the structure of language, as well as of its gaps, omissions, and silences, in determining meaning in any text. They also urge a reading of literary texts (what Foucault calls a "typology" or "historical analysis" of discourse) that sets aside the idea of an author, or what Pasternack calls a "poet-figure," in order to understand literature as a cultural "intertext" that is composed and recomposed over time and is always open to multiple interpretations by readers who, more so than authors, are the real producers of the text. The articulation of texts within socio-historical relations is exactly the focus of the three *Beowulf* essays in this section, although the essays are also markedly different from each other (in other words, they do not share a programmatic approach or thesis, although all three are concerned with the ways in which the language of the poem constructs and is constructed by social meanings that are always, to a certain extent, *in flux*). In "Swords and Signs: Dynamic Semeiosis in *Beowulf*," Gillian Overing explores the "nonteleological, nonhierarchical coexistence of the metaphoric and metonymic modes" in the poem, specifically through the use of Charles Sanders Peirce's semiotic theory of the "triadic production of meaning," in order to demonstrate how the poem "invites a challenge to assumptions about the possibility and desirability of a structural overview" and essentially resists any attempts on the part of the critic to limit or totalize what is, ultimately, the text's "infinitude." For Seth Lerer, in "Hrothgar's Hilt and the Reader in *Beowulf*," the main objective is to analyze scenes of reading in *Beowulf*, especially with reference to the engraved sword hilt Beowulf retrieves from Grendel's mere, as a means of reflecting upon "the reader's own relationship to texts, to authors, and to Christian culture generally," art as "a public and social act," and also upon how *Beowulf* "represents a move from presence to absence as it dramatizes differing forms of literary communication and response." With reference to "forms of speaking" in *Beowulf*, as well as in ancient Greek and Arthurian literature, and in Scandinavian runology, Lerer also ruminates on "[w]hat may be called the 'literacy' of *Beowulf* . . . the way in which it imagines its own reading public—the way in which it shows us that to read the legends of the past is to read by ourselves." In her essay, "'As I Once Did With Grendel': Boasting and Nostalgia in *Beowulf*," Susan Kim "locates the poem's representations of linguistic performance in the context of early medieval linguistic theory" and "treats the engagements with linguistic performance as negotiations of concepts of personal identity." Because, according to Kim, "language works by difference, by alienation of the sign as thing and the sign as meaning, but also of sign from sign, the very process of identification in language inscribes alienation within human identity," and on one level, "this is the alienation of the self understood as the body and the self represented in language." More specifically, Kim looks at the ways in which this alienation is "literalized" in Beowulf's identification with Grendel and in Grendel's severed arm as a "sign" of that identification, and she also looks at the ways in which nostalgia functions in the poem as a source for "the potential for an identity not understood as dislocated or alienated from itself." Ultimately, all three of the *Beowulf* essays in this section are interested in the questions posed at the end of Foucault's essay, "What are the modes of existence of this discourse? Where has it been used, how can it circulate, and who can appropriate it for himself? What are the places in it where there is room for possible subjects? Who can assume these various subject-functions?"

Because there is no essay in the entire book that addresses, explicitly, a postcolonial approach to *Beowulf*, perhaps because this is an area that is just beginning to be explored in Old English studies,[11] we have also included, as a "postscript" essay to this section, Michelle Warren's "Post-Philology," which calls for the creation of a new alliance between philology, postmodern critique, and postcolonial studies, and we leave it to our readers to imagine how this might be accomplished, along the lines Warren illustrates, in *Beowulf* studies.

Some of the "Critical Contexts" essays also enlarge (and occasionally problematize) the critical dialectic of the readings that follow them. In the "Ethnography/Psychoanalysis" section, John Moreland's "Ethnicity, Power, and the English" and Alfred Siewers's "Landscapes of Conversion: Guthlac's Mound and Grendel's Mere as Expressions of Anglo-Saxon Nation-Building" both attend to subjects that are not a direct concern of the essays that follow, but which nevertheless create productive critical tension with some of the cultural-historical assumptions of those essays, while also broadening the theoretical horizons within which those essays can be read and appraised. Moreland argues against the idea of the early English as a stable or natural ethnographic category in his essay, where he provides a thorough overview of the latest findings in archaeology, anthropology, and sociology, in order to show that Migration Period groups, such as the Angles, Saxons, and Jutes of Bede's *Ecclesiastical History*, were characterized more by their fluidity, heterogeneity, and overlapping identities than traditional accounts would allow. At the same time, Moreland admits that "it would be a debilitating step to move from the rejection of a direct and inflexible link between ethnic identity and material culture to argue that there is *no* relationship." Siewers's essay combines eco-criticism, Augustinian "sign theory," and Julia Kristeva's theory of abjection (as it applies to western medieval theology), in order to highlight a certain "process of cultural differentiation" in Anglo-Saxon England, where "constructions of nature relate to [the] development of a new kind of performative subjectivity for cultures and people," and this is a subjectivity that, of political necessity, required "a defining of the Welsh and other non-English cultures as Other" as well as a dehumanizing of the native British landscape. Siewers's and Moreland's essays are included in the "Ethnography/Psychoanalysis" section, partly because they both attend to the archaeology and material culture of early England, which is not as fully addressed anywhere else in the volume and which we see as integral to thinking about early English ethnography, and partly because they both attend to the heterogeneous and messier aspects of a so-called Anglo-Saxon identity that are not as fully addressed in the essays here by Earl ("*Beowulf* and the Origins of

Civilization," described above), John Hill ("The Ethnopsychology of In-Law Feud and the Remaking of Group Identity in *Beowulf*: The Cases of Hengest and Ingeld," which argues that the poem's narratives of feud, dismaying to some critics in their violence, are actually "socially acute meditations on the prospects for settlement" and for "accomplished and extended community"), and Janet Thormann ("Enjoyment of Violence and Desire for History in *Beowulf*," which analyzes, through Lacan, the "crisis" of history occasioned by feud in *Beowulf* and also includes an analysis of Anglo-Saxon law codes in relation to that crisis). Likewise, in the "Gender/Identity" section, the "Critical Contexts" essays by Carol Clover ("Regardless of Sex: Men, Women, and Power in Early Northern Europe") and Jeffrey Cohen ("The Ruins of Identity") raise important questions that are intimately related to (yet not always directly addressed by) the essays that follow by Clare Lees ("Men and *Beowulf*"), Mary Dockray-Miller ("*Beowulf*'s Tears of Fatherhood"), and Shari Horner ("Voices From the Margins: Women and Textual Enclosure in *Beowulf*"). For example, if the "principle of sex" was not so "final or absolute" as we assume it was in early northern Europe, and "gender" was not necessarily predicated upon "sex," as Clover argues (following Thomas Laqueur's "one-sex" or "one-flesh" model of sexual difference that he argues obtained in the classical world and in premodern Europe), how does that affect our ideas regarding how masculinity and violence (Lees) or homosociality (Dockray-Miller, whose essay actually responds directly to Clover's) or women's spaces (Horner) are constructed in *Beowulf*? And if, as Cohen argues, "to be fully human is to disavow the strange space that the inhuman, the monstrous, occupies within every speaking subject," how does this affect our ideas regarding how identity—gendered or otherwise—is represented in the poem? This is a question that Susan Kim actually addresses in great depth in her essay (described above) in the "Text/Textuality" section of the book, which brings us to: how to read this book in the classroom, exactly?

The Postmodern "Beowulf," we believe, would be an ideal text with which to introduce students to theory, as well as to *Beowulf*. The four sections of the book—again—represent broad contextual *fields* of inquiry to which certain, more narrowly defined questions and theories of history, culture, identity, and language pertain. The first section, "History/Historicism," covers "cultural history" most broadly, and more narrowly, new historicism, cultural appropriations theory, Foucault's archaeological method, reading reception theory, Said's "worldly criticism," deconstruction, and in the case of Frantzen's essay, the intellectual history of *Beowulf* scholarship. The second section, "Ethnography/Psychoanalysis," attends to anthropology, archaeology, sociology, and eco-criticism; Freudian, Lacanian, and Kristevan analysis; and what can be called, following the work of Georges Devereux, ethnopsychoanalsys.[12] "Gender/Identity," the third section, comprises sexuality and gender studies, feminist critique (of both the Anglo-American and French varieties), psychoanalysis (Freud and Lacan), and queer studies. Finally, the "Text/Textuality" section of the book includes philology most broadly (in its more traditional and more poststructural conceptions), sign theory (or, semiotics), deconstruction, Lacanian analysis, Kristeva's theory of intertextuality, and orality studies. In addition, we have added, as bookends, an introduction (Eileen Joy and Mary Ramsey's "Liquid *Beowulf*") and an afterword (James Earl's "Reading *Beowulf* with Original Eyes") that both take up the question, in different ways, of the poem's relevance to our current historical moment (and to modernity and postmodernity more generally).

Merely listing the theoretical concerns (or, approaches) for each section runs the risk of oversimplifying the diverse hybridity of critical approaches represented in each essay and also obscures somewhat the very rich connections that are present—both explicitly and implicitly—among the different sections of the book. So, while it may be useful to teach the contents of the book section by section, there are many ways in which the contents can be reassembled to create new and critically productive groupings. For example, since Frantzen's essay engages in a close analysis of the text of the giant sword hilt in the poem, it can be read alongside the essays by Overing and Lerer, which take that same sword hilt and its inscribed text as one of the primary focuses of their essays. Likewise, since Kim's essays takes up the question of how monstrosity functions in the construction of Beowulf's identity, her essay can be read alongside Cohen's (whose essay Kim explicitly addresses) in the "Gender/Identity" section. Thormann's essay, because it not only addresses a Lacanian analysis of violence in the poem but also looks at how the poem attempts to foreclose, through language, a particular kind of violent history, could easily be read within the "History/Historicism" or the "Text/Textuality" section. Because Earl's essay directly addresses the issue of how the poem requires a certain gendered identification, and because Lees's essay directly confronts his argument, as does Dockray-Miller's, these three essays could form a grouping unto themselves—one could also add to this group Earl's "Reading *Beowulf* With Original Eyes," since he provides there a linguistic analysis of Hrothgar's emotions upon Beowulf's leaving of Daneland that is strikingly different (yet connected to) the reading that

Dockray-Miller provides for the same scene. Certain essays that concentrate on the issue of violence—Thormann's, Hill's, Cohen's, and Lees's—could form another grouping. Essays that center upon the poem's role in constructing a specific cultural (or "national") identity—Howe's, Niles's, Siewers's, Cohen's, and Lees's—form yet another possible arrangement. How the poem figures loss, absence, and alienation—linguistic, personal, and more broadly social—is also the concern of the essays by Frantzen, Earl, Thormann, Kim, and Lerer. Because the field of Old English studies, and of *Beowulf* studies especially, is somewhat intimate, the readers of this book will quickly discern how often the authors included here reference, concur with, and argue with each other's work, providing a valuable set of critical cross-references that, we would argue, will lead to combinatory readings that even the editors have not yet anticipated.

Ultimately, this book cannot deliver a neatly programmatic or even a whole view of "the state of theory" in *Beowulf* studies at present, for we are still living and working in this moment—a moment, moreover, of constant and continual theoretical upheaval and change, and into which we place *The Postmodern "Beowulf"* as a selective representation of the "first stage" of an ongoing conversation and critical debate among Old English and other scholars over the late modern interpretation of the poem. To the question of what *Beowulf* might have meant to its original audiences, and what it might mean to those of us reading it and trying to understand it today in this place we call modernity (or, postmodernity), the essays collected together in this volume offer a diverse and wide-ranging set of possible answers, while also raising important questions for future research and discussion. History, *the things that actually happen*, as Leopold von Ranke would have said—not only the history of the so-called Middle Ages, but also our own history, both personal and intellectual—is always a more messy business than we would like it to be, more random and chaotic than the structure and order we want to perceive in it (and often invent for it), and despite the schematic organization of this book, we would again urge also reading *against* that schematic, too. Only in that way can connections between the essays *not yet thought* be discerned and new paths of inquiry opened.

In a recent conversation between the two documentary filmmakers Errol Morris and Adam Curtis, where they discussed the Vietnam War and 9/11 (the subjects of their two most recent documentaries—*The Fog of War* and *The Power of Nightmares*, respectively), Morris asked, "[I]s history primarily a conspiracy? Or is it just a series of blunders, one after the other? Confusions, self-deceptions, idiocies of one kind or another?" To which Curtis replied,

"History is a series of *unintended consequences* resulting from confused actions, some of which are committed by people who may think they're taking part in a conspiracy, but it never works out the way they intended."[13] Curtis continued by arguing that what really affects the outcome of history are *ideas* themselves (a notion he credits to Max Weber): "People have experiences out of which they form ideas. And those ideas have an effect on the world . . . [e]ven though it doesn't actually ever work out the way the person who had the idea intended."[14] Such would be an apt description of the development of a theoretical history, whether it begins with Plato or Derrida, and wherever it continues to circulate as a stream of literary consciousness, whether in the study of the Victorian novel or Old English poetry. Foucault could not have guessed, when writing "What Is An Author?", how his argument that the disappearance, or *death*, of the author necessitates the tracing of certain textual "gaps and breaches" in order to locate "the openings this disappearance uncovers" might have been taken up by Carol Braun Pasternack in her discussion of the textuality of Old English poetry, whose authors were always already missing long before Nietzsche or Roland Barthes or Foucault declared them so and called the resulting situation "modern." Such is the inherent transformative power of an idea let loose in the world.

The most valuable intellectual life, I believe, is one that allows for and actively embraces the infinite play and tension between differing ideas and systems of thought, and that desires the always-open question over the statement that supposedly closes the debate. How could our future—never mind the past—be thought otherwise? Yes, some ideas will always be better (more ethically worthy, let's say) than others, and we cannot entirely escape the responsibility of critical judgment if we believe there is something ultimately at stake in the reading, interpretation, and teaching of a poem like *Beowulf*, although the question of whether or not poetry matters, and *how*, is one of those open questions to which I believe the continued study of *Beowulf* could matter a great deal. And it is a question, moreover, in which something—the future of the study of literature within the public university, for example—really *is* at stake. Ultimately, whether we take the more positivist or the more poststructural approaches to the poem, what we are after is *meaning*. We want the poem to mean something because, even in postmodernity, there has to be some kind of answer to the eventual non-being of everything. The poem itself was likely written out of such a desire. There is no one definitive way to read *Beowulf*, either as an artifact that can tell us something about that foreign country we call Anglo-Saxon England or as a poetic narrative somehow relevant to the concerns of contemporary thought and life, and if *The Postmodern "Beowulf"* is read in the manner we have intended it to be read, it will hopefully demonstrate the benefit of an open-ended *pluralism* of theoretical approaches to the poem, as well as the ways in which the poem itself is inexhaustibly productive of the *question* of its own meaning. We learned this from theory.

NOTES

1   Terry Eagleton, *After Theory* (New York, 2003), p. 209.

2   On the supposed irrelevance and death of theory, see Emily Eakin, "The Latest Theory is Theory Doesn't Matter," *New York Times*, 19 Apr. 2003: D9; and Stephen Metcalf, "The Death of Literary Theory: Is It Really a Good Thing?" *Slate.com*, 17 Nov. 2005, available at http://www.slate.com/id/2130583. For a spirited debate over the question of whether "the great era of theory is behind us" and the future of critical inquiry in general, see W. J. T. Mitchell et al., "The Future of Criticism— A *Critical Inquiry* Symposium," *Critical Inquiry* 30 (2004): 324–479. As to theory's counter-movement, see *Theory's Empire: An Anthology of Dissent*, ed. Daphne Patai and Wilfrido H. Corral (New York, 2005).

3   Allen J. Frantzen, "Who Do These Anglo-Saxon(ist)s Think They Are, Anyway?" *Æstel* 2 (1994): 1–43.

4   Gillian Overing, "Recent Writing on Old English: A Response," *Æstel* 1 (1993): 135–49. See also T. A. Shippey, "Recent Writing on Old English," *Æstel* 1 (1993): 111–34, to which Overing's essay is a response. For an excellent historical overview of "the state of theory" (as of 1994) in Old English studies, see Roy Michael Liuzza, "The Return of the Repressed: Old and New Theories in Old English Literary Criticism," in *Old English Shorter Poems: Basic Readings*, ed. Katherine O'Brien O'Keeffe (New York, 1994), pp. 103–47. For an excellent survey of the most important developments in Old English manuscript and literary studies *in general*, see Katherine O'Brien O'Keeffe, ed., *Reading Old English Texts* (Cambridge, 1997).

5   Jennifer Howard, "The Fragmentation of Literary Theory," *The Chronicle of Higher Education*, 16 Dec. 2005: A12–13.

6   Eagleton, *After Theory*, p. 221.

7   Liuzza, "The Return of the Repressed," pp. 129, 130.

8   Paul Strohm, *Theory and the Premodern Text* (Minneapolis, 2000), pp. 158, 160.

9   Strohm, *Theory and the Premodern Text*, p. 153.

10   Lee Patterson, "On the Margin: Postmodernism, Ironic History, and Medieval Studies," *Speculum* 65 (1990): 106.

11 See, for example, the essays by Nicholas Howe and Seth Lerer ("The Afterlife of Rome: Anglo-Saxon England and the Postcolonial Void" and "'On fagne flor': The Postcolonial *Beowulf*, from Heorot to Heaney," respectively) included in *Postcolonial Approaches to the European Middle Ages: Translating Cultures*, ed. Ananya Jahanara Kabir and Deanne Williams (Cambridge, Eng., 2005).

12 See Georges Devereux, *Ethnopsychoanalysis: Psychoanalysis and Anthropology as Complementary Frames of Reference* (Berkeley, 1978).

13 "Adam Curtis Talks With Errol Morris," *The Believer*, April 2006: 60.

14 "Adam Curtis Talks With Errol Morris," p. 61.

ACKNOWLEDGMENTS

T o begin, the editors would like to thank two groups of graduate students from the spring term of 2004. Through their close attention to the texts and their willingness to engage the ideas of more experienced scholars, these students were instrumental in helping to develop the contents of this volume. Students at Université Laval enrolled in Bruce D. Gilchrist's course, "*Beowulf*, Culture, Criticism," included Claudine Auger, Sarah Barclay, Jason Beaulieu, Sonia Bédard, Andrea Beverley, Pierre Dolbec, Maika Dubé, Myriam Dulude, Anas Kabbaj, Andrea Mueller, and Joshua Parlett. Eileen A. Joy's "*Beowulf*, Cultural Memory, and War" course at Southern Illinois University Edwardsville included James Bosomworth, Casey Cooper, Sarah Drake, Patricia Heyen, Sara Kollbaum, Denise Krisinger, Chia-Hui Liu, Janella Moy, William Rable, Benjamin Schrimpf, Justin Smith, Josephine Turbe, and Eric Zelasko.

Further, the editors thank Coastal Carolina University—especially Sara Sanders, the chair of the Department of English, and the College of Humanities and Fine Arts—for helping defray the costs of the cover photo and for generously granting Eileen Joy release time in fall 2005 to work on the book. Thanks also to the English Department of Georgia State University for helping defray the costs of the cover photograph. In addition, many thanks to Southern Illinois University Edwardsville, especially the College of Arts and Sciences, for providing funds to defray reprint permission costs, and the Graduate School's Office of Research and Projects for a generous summer research fellowship in summer 2004 that facilitated the initial planning for the book. Further thanks to the National Endowment for the Humanities for funding Eileen Joy's participation in Cambridge University's summer institute on "Anglo-Saxon England" at Trinity College in the summer of 2004, where she was able to get critical feedback on the initial plan of the book.

Because little is accomplished in the university without their help, we owe many thanks to departmental administrative assistants, who facilitated paperwork relative to production of the book and travel related to the book: Linda Jaworski-Moiles of Southern Illinois University Edwardsville and Laura Barr of Coastal Carolina University. Thanks also to work-study student Amber Welch of Georgia State University, whose tireless and meticulous formatting saved the editors many grueling hours.

For their generous conversations about and critical suggestions for the book as it developed, we thank Roy M. Liuzza, James Earl, Bruce Gilchrist, and Janet Thormann; the editors are deeply grateful for the extended community of medieval scholars in which we work, and we thank them for their encouragement and support. For his very warm and generous stewardship of the book through the West Virginia University Press, but more importantly, for his friendship and mentoring, we thank Patrick Conner.

Finally, Eileen would like to thank the owner, Adam Pashea, sommelier, Rob Harper, and the two barkeeps, Curtis Giberson and Andrew Pastor, of Erato Wine Bar in Saint Louis, for providing her with a "second office" and quiet table at which to work. And both Eileen and Mary would also like to thank the BABEL Working Group—especially Betsy McCormick, Kimberly Bell, and Myra Seaman—for their soul-bracing support, Hello Kitty paraphernalia, and hedonistic joie de vie.

Eileen A. Joy
Mary K. Ramsey

INTRODUCTION: LIQUID *BEOWULF*

EILEEN A. JOY AND MARY K. RAMSEY

The illusion of historical truth and perspective, that has made Beowulf *seem such an attractive quarry, is largely a product of art. The author has used an instinctive historical sense . . . of which* Beowulf *is a supreme expression; but he has used it with a poetical and not a historical object. The lovers of poetry can safely study the art, but the lovers of history must beware lest the glamour of Poesis overcome them.* —J. R. R. Tolkien[1]

What is truly historical—rather than merely mimetic—about a work is inseparable from what within it exceeds its history. —Gerhard Richter[2]

Modernity is the time when time has a history. —Zygmunt Bauman[3]

I n 1904, W. P. Ker remarked, "The fault of *Beowulf* is that there is nothing much in the story."[4] This comment did not appear fair to J. R. R. Tolkien in 1936 when he wrote that it seemed "improbable" that the poet "would write more than three thousand lines (wrought to a high finish) on matter that is really not worth serious attention."[5] But recalling what Tolkien also referred to as Ker's "potent" criticism allows for some reflection on how it is so many have found so much to say and write about the poem, and whether, similar to Achilles' anger, Oedipus's hubris, and Hamlet's angst, this Old English poem might not also be inexhaustibly productive of discussion. The beginning of this century looks promising: from Kevin Kiernan's CD-ROM *Electronic "Beowulf,"* Seamus Heaney's award-winning translation, and Elliot Goldenthal and Julie Taymor's opera, *Grendel*, based on John Gardner's 1971 novel of the same name, the poem continues to assert itself in richly varied cultural productions.[6] For all the talk of the supposed marginalization of Old English studies within the American and British academies,[7] *Beowulf* continues to fascinate students, scholars, and artists alike. Possessing an uncertain provenance covering hundreds of years and written anonymously by one or more authors (or copyists?) in a language both familiar and yet also forbidding, ravaged by fire and by misguided attempts to arrest its deterioration, and, thanks to neglect and mishandling over the years,[8] bereft of thousands of its original letters, the poem could be said to stand as a test case of what literary criticism is capable of saying and doing, and further, of whether or not we need criticism at all, or even poetry, and to what end. How, and why, does *Beowulf* continue to cast its spell on us? Or framing the question somewhat differently, why should *Beowulf* continue to matter at all?

In his review of Heaney's translation, literary theorist Terry Eagleton judges Heaney's refashioning of the Old English poem "magnificent" as well as a "marvelously sturdy, intricate reinvention," but he also argues that *Beowulf*, a poem "both subtle and savage," ultimately retains its pride of place in English studies mainly due to its function, from the Victorian period forward, as the cultural tool of a troubling nationalist romance with an archetypal and mythological past.[9] Indeed, intellectual histories of Old English studies such as Allen Frantzen's *Desire for Origins* have shown this to be partly the case,[10] and it is difficult to deny, as Nicholas Howe reminds us, that "the texts and contexts of Anglo-Saxon England are essential, even originary, to a racist, anti-semitic, and fascist politics in the United States."[11] The occasion for Howe's comment was receiving in the mail a book catalog that included Icelandic sagas, *Beowulf*, Bede's *Ecclesiastical History*, and scholarly works such as Dorothy Whitelock's *The Beginnings of English Society*, alongside Adolf Hitler's *Mein Kampf* and books denying the Holocaust. Although most Old English scholars would be appalled at such an alignment of texts, somewhere out there beyond the academy, Old English poetry and scholarship, unmediated by the sharp knife of criticism, have become part of the spiritual heritage and profane history of fascism. Frantzen and Howe would never dispense with *Beowulf* as an object too tainted for study, but they have certainly challenged us to consider the ways in which Old English scholarship might be related to larger theoretical debates within the university and to the politics of the world in which we live. Moreover, they have asked that we consider how Old English studies might be refashioned as a type of cultural studies that would focus, as Frantzen writes, "on the political nature of the structural, structuring effects of the relationship between scholars and their subjects,"[12] and also, as John Niles writes, on how a poem like *Beowulf* can be seen to have "a relation to the discourses of power of a society whose institutions were very different from our own."[13] Long before Eagleton's review of Heaney's translation, Old English scholars like Frantzen, Howe, and Niles have argued for situating Old English studies within contemporary theoretical paradigms that would help us to investigate how, in Niles's words, literary works such as *Beowulf* "shape the present-day culture that calls them to mind as past artifacts."[14] In other words, Old English studies have not required Eagleton's notice of the socio-historical dimensions of its canon and disciplinary practices in order to acknowledge and investigate those dimensions.

But Eagleton takes his resistance to *Beowulf* one provocative step further when he argues that even as a piece of poetic literature, *Beowulf* may no longer be relevant to us because "we no longer believe in heroism, or that the world itself is story-shaped, and we ask of literature a phenomenological inwardness which is of fairly recent historical vintage," and the epic poem, "as Marx once observed, requires historical conditions which the steam-engine and telegraph put paid to."[15] Eagleton's sentiments here resonate with those of the historian Dominick LaCapra, who argues that, in the post-Holocaust period in which we live,

> traditional religions, Hegelianism (seen in stereotypical ways), and any form of thinking that seems to redeem the past and make it wholly meaningful through present uses no longer seems plausible. . . . It's what Lyotard calls the incredulity or disbelief about grand narratives: we no longer seem to take seriously these grand narratives that make sense of everything in the past—narratives that at certain points seem to appeal to people very much.[16]

LaCapra's statement that grand narratives "at certain points seem to appeal to people very much" creates some slippage in Eagleton's notion that *Beowulf* can no longer appeal to modern audiences, and indeed, we might well ask, who is this "we" Eagleton argues no longer believes that the world is story-shaped? Is it the public at large, including our students, who daily consume grand narratives in the form of video games, comic books, television programs, movies, self-help gurus, religion, patriotism, and bourgeois family values, or is it a certain faction of the elite humanities intelligentsia who have devoted so much of their careers to dismantling and demystifying traditional narrative ontologies that they are effectively impervious to the lure of traditional stories and can only desire instead the chaotic (and beautiful) interiority of a James Joyce, and after all of this "phenomenological inwardness," where to next? Eagleton may believe that we no longer believe that the world is story-shaped, but understanding the self, human experience, and history, and even being able to *turn inward*, as it were, is not possible without narrative constructs, and grand narrative constructs at that. As the philosopher Alasdair MacIntyre argues,

> Just as history is not a sequence of actions, but the concept of an action is that of a moment in an actual or possible history abstracted for some purpose from that history, so the characters in a history are not a collection of persons, but the concept of a person is that of a character abstracted from a history.[17]

Further, MacIntyre writes, "Man is in his actions and practice, as well as in his fictions, essentially a story-telling animal. He is not essentially, but becomes through his history, a teller of stories that aspire to truth."[18] In the field of historiography, Peter Munz reminds us that, "In order to do justice to time, it must be described in a narrative form. Any other form of description fails to take account of the fact that the past bears the mark of the arrow of time," and narrative "is the only literary device available which will reflect the past's time structure."[19] As is well known, the debates among contemporary historians over the "literariness" (and therefore, of the possible "fictionality" or "falseness") of the historical enterprise have been fierce and contentious;[20] nevertheless, as Munz also reminds us, in history, there can never be anything *but* stories:

> The problem [of recording history *as it was*] does not simply consist in the fact that the past is not readily remembered or frequently insufficiently recorded. . . . If this were the case, one would presume that people at any stage of the past knew what was happening to them and that the reason why we do not know is that records or traditions were lost. But the point is that even the people who were alive at any stage of the past had either little knowledge or perception of what was happening; or that such perceptions as they had were widely influenced by their personal interests and abstractions and therefore were in no sense "correct" perceptions. They themselves had no knowledge of *res gestae* but, at best were making up stories about it

and constructing *historiae rerum gestarum*. Which goes to prove the truth of an old saying . . . that "stories only happen to people who have an ability to tell them."[21]

Within medieval studies, Caroline Walker Bynum's work, especially with corporality, identity, and metamorphosis, has shown us how the stories of the past, when read properly, reveal profound ways of thinking about processes of self, identity, and history—processes, moreover, that fascinated medieval audiences as much as they continue to fascinate modern ones. In her analysis of werewolf stories in the classical, medieval, and modern traditions, Bynum concludes that we read the stories of the past, "not in order to understand the tradition (an academic enterprise) but in order to understand—through the tradition and its artful refigurings—ourselves."[22] It may be that literature, especially in its most fabulist forms, gets at something deep in the historical psyche that conventional history, or even theory, cannot get to, and therefore, stories, especially of a certain mythic variety—whether in the form of epic poetry, Arthurian romance, J. K. Rowling's *Harry Potter* novels, *Superman* comic books, or the animated films of Hayao Miyazaki, such as *Spirited Away* and *Howl's Moving Castle*—will continue to play a critical role in how a culture perceives itself and articulates its deepest desires, fears, and questions of *knowing*.

MacIntyre argues, "I can only answer the question 'What am I to do?' if I can answer the prior question 'Of what story or stories do I find myself a part?'"[23] And Emmanuel Levinas once wrote that the whole of his ethical philosophy sometimes seemed to him to be "only a meditation of Shakespeare."[24] Ultimately, "to narrate" means "to know," (from the Latin *gnarus* and *gnaritus*, "knowing" and "knowledge"), and as Mark Turner has written in *The Literary Mind*, "*Story* is a basic principle of mind." We interpret "every level of our experience by means of parable," which is the "root of the human mind—of thinking, knowing, acting, creating, and plausibly even of speaking."[25] In the fields of neurobiology, artificial intelligence, psychology, and cognitive science, there has been amazing consensus on the importance of narrative-like data sequences in the brain, and research in these fields has generally overturned the notion that individuals possess a "single, definitive 'stream of consciousness,'" because there is no central Headquarters, no Cartesian Theater where 'it all comes together' for the perusal of a Central Meaner." Nevertheless, there *are* "multiple channels in which specialist circuits . . . in parallel pandemoniums" create "fragmentary drafts of 'narrative,'" or what Daniel Dennett calls "Multiple Drafts."[26]

So the question is not really whether or not conventional narratives (fabulist or otherwise), even in postmodernity, contribute in very important ways to various meaning-making processes—they may, in fact, constitute *mind* itself—but rather, *which* particular narratives might best answer to our present condition? In this regard, it is precisely Eagleton's gesture toward the conditions of modern life—social, historical, psychic, and otherwise—that raises what we feel is the important question of whether or not *Beowulf*, as both an antique cultural object and ancient poem, might have anything to tell us about the conditions of our modernity, or even, our postmodernity. We contend that *Beowulf* has a great deal to tell us about these conditions, and further, that the poem is not, as some might claim, a coherent and comforting grand narrative that makes sense of everything in the past—nor, strictly speaking, is it even an epic. Rather, *Beowulf* comprises a series of not always synchronic and digressive narratives within narratives that reconfigure historical time in multiple dimensions, and the poem practically brims over with "parallel pandemoniums" of language and situation.[27] As Gillian Overing notes in her essay "Swords and Signs: Dynamic Semeiosis," reprinted in this volume, the poem is "a continuum, an echo chamber, where we experience a continual crisscrossing of temporal-spatial values and relations," and

> The narrative progression of the poem foils logical or linear attempts to sum up, to stand back and conclude that *this*, after all, meant *that*. The poem is essentially nonlinear, describing arcs and circles where persons, events, histories, and stories continually intersect. . . . *Beowulf* is a text that invites a challenge to assumptions about the possibility and desirability of a structural overview. The quicksilver nature of its structure, where individual elements persist, dissolve, and expand in a continuum of resonance and association, questions the notion of textual boundaries as a form of resolution and suggests instead the infinitude of the text.[28]

As James Earl has shown, many passages in the poem are also characterized by ambivalence and "deep, uninterpretable silences," and the figure of Beowulf himself is like the enigmatic and radically ambiguous blank mask of Greek tragedy, all of which "invites a meditation on the unconscious themes of our own individual and cultural origins."[29]

Beowulf does not make sense of the past so much as it calls the supposed coherence of the past (and of conventional narrative) into question. It also calls into question and unsettles how we (and likely the Anglo-Saxons as well) have traditionally defined and understood the relationships between past and present, language and meaning, heroism and monstrosity, justice and violence, nation and *gens*, freedom and necessity, "same" and "Other," and history and memory—relationships, moreover, that form the very center of many current theoretical debates. As one of the poem's more recent translators Roy Liuzza writes, "[T]his unruly poem, like the manuscript in which it survives, does not stay within the framework of our generic expectations. Moreover, the poem itself is a monumental exercise of the historical imagination, poetically re-creating a past which is itself multilayered and temporally complex,"[30] statements that call to mind LaCapra's caution that history can never be construed as a "pure, positive presence that is not beset with its own disruptions, lacunae, conflicts, irreparable losses, belated recognitions, and challenges to identity."[31] Even to its original, let's say tenth- or eleventh-century audiences,[32] *Beowulf* was also already past, a work of artistic *looking back* that, by its very nature, speaks to the desire to have the past, however *fallen* and *over*, to speak to the present moment and be relevant to it. There is hardly a moment in the poem itself when the characters and the narrator are not voicing their anxious concern that the past be remembered in a way that is fruitful for the present and future—Hrothgar's admonishment to Beowulf to learn from the story of Heremod, a former Danish chieftan who was apparently pathologically violent (*blodreow*, "blood-ravenous," line 1719a)[33] and greedy, as well as a "harm" to his people (lines 1709b–23b), is one example among many. At the same time, in its almost manic and looping digressions regarding past, present, and future feuds, the poem points to the inescapable historical fact that even though Grendel and his dam, the dragon, and human aggressors such as Heremod are dead, their children are ceaselessly at play on the killing fields of history. Even Beowulf himself, when he returns to Geatland after journeying to Daneland to clean up, as it were, Hrothgar's hall and help him put his kingdom back in order, acknowledges to Hygelac that "seldom anywhere after the death of a prince does the deadly spear rest for even a brief while"[34] ("Oft seldan hwær / æfter leodhryre lytle hwile / bongar bugeð," lines 2029b–31a). There is always a tension in the poem, then, between the hope, articulated in narrative (in all the stories within the story), that a certain kind of remembering will secure a better future, and the more historical reality that with each shift in the structures of power, the specters of inhumanity always return from their brief periods of exile to wreak havoc and death. In this sense, the poem speaks to a very modern (and disquieting) set of questions regarding history's relation to time, language, and social communities struggling with traumatic and cataclysmic events.

Just as *Beowulf* is decidedly *not* the comforting grand narrative that, perhaps, critics such as Eagleton believe it to be, following Liuzza's statement above, it is also not entirely the literary animal we would expect from the aesthetic traditions of its own time—traditions of which we can never have what might be called a whole history, given the fact that the existing corpus of Old English poetry is scattered, incomplete, fragmentary, and full of maddening cruces. But among what does survive—the elegies, maxims, riddles, charms, religious verse, and battle poems—there is nothing even close to *Beowulf*. One of the hallmark dictums of modernism was summed up in Ezra Pound's famous statement "Make it new," and it is not difficult to make the argument, as Joseph Harris does, that *Beowulf* "presents a unique poet's unique reception of the oral genres of the Germanic early Middle Ages; like the *Canterbury Tales* it was retrospective and comprehensive, *summa*-rizing a literary period in a literary form so new and so masterful that it apparently inspired no imitators."[35] That *Beowulf* is "new," "multilayered and temporally complex," subversive of generic expectations, and humming with discursive and historical ambiguities as well as with various cultural anxieties is beautifully illustrated by many of the contributors to this volume, but before we can begin to fully engage the question of *Beowulf*'s relation and relevance to our contemporary world, we must also ask, what *are* the supposed conditions of modernity (or, postmodernity) to which Eagleton and other scholars of more contemporary periods believe *Beowulf* cannot be related, and how might these conditions matter in our readings of the poem?

The term "postmodern" has become endemic in descriptions of the contemporary academic landscape, its objects of study, and its critical methodologies, as well as of the social and political conditions outside the university proper. Because of this, we cannot see our way around the term, although we wonder if, somewhere up ahead in the future, it will be decided that our "postmodern turn" was primarily a strategy to stake out a place of ground within which to critique a modernity to which we felt we could no longer belong, partly because its technologies and vocabularies of progress and liberation led inexorably and fatally to genocide and the gulag, and also valorized a bureaucracy capable of enacting these horrors. It might be best to say that "postmodernism" is a critical term (and a state of worldly affairs) still seeking a fully-developed definition and even a history, and that it is beneficial to leave open the question of what distinguishes the postmodern from the modern. But we would also say here that we agree with the social theorist Zygmunt Bauman, who argues, "The society which enters the twenty-first century is no less 'modern' than the society which entered the twentieth; the most one can say is that it is modern in a different way."[36]

Following the thought of his fellow social theorists, Ulrich Beck and Anthony Giddens, Bauman believes that we are in a "second," "late," or "accelerated" modernity. For Bauman, this is a "fluid" period of modernity in which, thanks to new "liquid" and "light" technologies and hypertrophied time/space arrangements, such as wireless communications, "smart" missiles, and *maquileros* factory zones, the "heavy" arch-metaphors of an earlier phase—empire, Jeremy Bentham's Panopticon, and the Fordist factory—have given way to a period in which "the prime technique of power is now escape, slippage, elision, and avoidance, the effective rejection of any territorial confinement with its cumbersome corollaries of order-building, order-maintenance and the responsibility for the consequences of it all as well as of the necessity to bear costs."[37] Also being melted are the bonds that, historically, have connected individuals to each other in relation to the state, and therefore, whereas in the past modernity first emerged as the era of territorial conquest and "feverish nation- and nation-state-building," by contrast, in modernity's more liquid phase, the contemporary global elite

> can rule without burdening itself with the chores of administration, management, welfare concerns, or, for that matter, "bringing light," "reforming the ways," morally uplifting, "civilizing" and cultural crusades. Active engagement in the life of subordinate populations is no longer needed (on the contrary, it is actively avoided as unnecessarily costly and ineffective)—and so the "bigger" is not just not "better" any more, but devoid of rational sense. It is now the smaller, the lighter, the more portable that signifies improvement and "progress." Traveling light, rather than holding tightly to things . . . is now the asset of power.[38]

It will be countered by some that certain political powers still engage in cumbersome order-building (witness the present situation in Iraq) and that contemporary life is rife with the gigantic and the heavy, from mega–shopping malls to multinational corporations to super-jumbo Airbus jets to personal armored vehicles to the "bling" and Bentleys of celebrities, but it could also be argued that some of these are points of backlash and resistance to the disembodiments and dislocations of modern life, as well as attempts at securing monumental fortifications against, and even at capitalizing upon, the friability of a too-fluid and fractured world. In political life, under the lengthening shadows of the supposed eclipse of the nation-state, we have also witnessed the backlash, often with deadly results, of the fortress-like "isms" of the past: tribalism, territorialism, nationalism, parochialism, and fundamentalism, although it might be argued, as Bauman does, that these "isms" are always "brittle" and "endemically precarious," since they are subject to a world in which the globalization of the economy, the "privatization of self-formation," and the fragmentation of political sovereignties makes it increasingly difficult for any kind of collective identity-building to secure anything but temporary strongholds.[39] At the same time, precisely because all "grand certitudes" have dissipated, they have also "split in the process into a multitude of little certainties, clung to all the more ferociously for their puniness."[40] With liquid modernity's cutting loose of the heavy structures of the past, then, there are also the pockets (and sometimes huge waves) of tenacious resistance, as well as, one would assume, a lot of personal and cultural and political anxieties over the tenuousness of everything.

According to Giddens, late modernity carries with it a certain "existential anxiety." Whereas, in premodern cultures, "time and space merged with the domains of the gods and spirits as well as with the 'privileging of space,'" in time and space have since become separated and social relations are now "lifted out" of local contexts and have to be articulated "across wide spans of time-space, up to and including global systems."[41] Further, late modernity "breaks down the protective framework of the small community and of tradition, replacing these with much larger, impersonal organizations."[42] Thanks to satellite communications; accelerated processes of the production, consumption, and "dumping" of material goods; the "disembodied labor of the software era"; and the globalization of everything, "space and time, once blended in human life-labors, have fallen apart and drifted away from each other in human thought and practice."[43] Also contributing to the anxieties of living in the late modern age, as Kenneth Gergen has written, are "[t]he dramatic expansion of the range of information to which we are exposed, the range of persons with whom we have significant interchange, and the range of opinions available within multiple media sites [that] make us privy to multiple realities," such that "the comfort of parochial univocality is disturbed" and "we do not know where to limit ourselves" in a world in which "protean being" is privileged over the "palpable self."[44]

We can see the protean nature of things in Beowulf studies, partly, through the example of The Electronic "Beowulf", a CD-ROM facsimile "image-based" edition of the Nowell codex of the Vitellius A.vx manuscript, a joint venture of Kevin Kiernan and his assistants at the University of Kentucky and Andrew Prescott and his assistants at the British Library in London.[45]

Using powerful medical imaging technology and fiber-optic lighting, *The Electronic "Beowulf"* includes a comprehensive collection of images of the entire Nowell codex (which includes, in addition to *Beowulf,* the fragmentary *Life of St. Christopher, The Letter of Alexander to Aristotle, Wonders of the East,* and *Judith,* all in Old English), as well as linked images of readings previously hidden by the paper frames used to rebind the manuscript in 1845, digital facsimiles of the complete transcripts of *Beowulf* made by Grímur J"nsson Thorkelin in the late eighteenth century, as well as of his 1815 edition of the poem, and also of John Josias Conybeare's and Frederick Madden's early nineteenth-century collations between Thorkelin's edition and the original manuscript (made in 1817 and 1824, respectively), "image maps" that offer the reader-user the capability to zoom in on particular letters, a glossarial index (with hyperlinks to the University of Toronto's *Dictionary of Old English* project), search facilities that provide access to new comparative research tools, and finally, a new edition and transcription of *Beowulf* itself. Obviously, *The Electronic "Beowulf"* provides a means for reintegrating the *membra dissecta* of the manuscript and, as Prescott has written, "A user will not only have at his fingertips all the key evidence for the history of this text but will also be able to juxtapose them in ways which would be impossible even if all the volumes were assembled in one room."[46] That same user might also beware, however, since collapsing all of the *membra dissecta* of the *Beowulf* manuscript into two CD-ROMs that can only be viewed on monitor screens (albeit with some split-screen capabilities) means that the physical space of textual scholarship on the poem has also been collapsed to an extent that will likely bring about a certain amount of cognitive dissonance when reading the various texts, whether side by side, enlarged, or in multiple windows with scrolling annotations.

In the heavier modernity, where time and place were, indeed, more tied to each other, a scholar had to possess the means and ability to travel to libraries in England and Denmark to view all of the material now available on two slim pieces of digitized plastic, and she would have had to transcribe the transcriptions, so to speak, with lead pencil, and then carry those transcriptions with her from library to library and back home again, where she would have had to physically arrange all of the material on her desk in such a manner, with various printed editions of the poem and dictionaries and concordances also at hand, that she could begin to read everything, again, in order to arrive at something obscured in the original manuscript, or in the interstices between the manuscript and its multiple facsimiles and editions. Conversely, the present reader-user of *Beowulf* sits in a cyber café in front of her laptop, on which she has loaded the light and portable electronic edition of the poem, clicking from verso to recto, from mapped covered readings to magnified and digitally enhanced letters, jumping in an instant from folio 130 to folio 172, or from line readings in the manuscript to line readings in the transcripts to word entries in the *Dictionary of Old English*, and all this without having to navigate the heavy interfaces of airports and buildings and stern curators, manuscripts and pages and pencils. Ultimately, the earlier scholarly experience—simultaneously visual and tactile, and even olfactory—of physically handling the original, three-dimensional manuscript gives way, with the electronic edition, to a kind of floating encounter with a simulacrum that is not so much an actual "palpable" edition as an ephemeral, "protean" representation of one. We might consider what of "the human" (if we still believe in such a thing) also "gives way" when we work with digitized texts. With the advent of new types of wireless technology and miniaturization, one can imagine the *Beowulf* scholar of the future sitting on a bench in the piazza of a crowded city and wearing PC-powered eyeglasses and a jacket in which transmitters, chips, speakers, microphones, and wireless technology have been woven into the fabric. To each passerby, she is just a woman sitting on a bench, when in fact she is downloading, viewing, and annotating folios of the *Beowulf* manuscript with voice-activated software and wearable hardware. She will be both *inside the book* and yet also *outside, in the world*, and if she likes, she can also feed the pigeons.

One can only guess at the phenomenological vertigo possibly attendant upon such a situation. In this scenario, *Beowulf* is as liquid and supple as the scholar's identity, and both text and human body touch the other's skin. Moreover, the manuscript has been freed from the confines of the library and has the ability to move, in pixellated waves or in the form of zeroes and ones, from server to server, or satellite to satellite—Grendel will come stalking, not only through moor and fen, but also through time and cold space—and the text of the poem will be far more susceptible to being written upon and tampered with (and, frankly, to being "deleted") than the original manuscript that is somewhat protected in its glass case at the new British Library at St. Pancras, because, as Roger Chartier writes, "In the universe of remote communications made possible by computerized texts and electronic diffusion, texts are no longer prisoner of their original, physical existence."[47] We might ponder all the ways in which a "liquid *Beowulf*" also helps to usher in some of those existential anxieties that Giddens and other social theorists believe are a hallmark of the late modern experience, where individuals feel increasingly unmoored from place, and as a result, also from other individuals who were once supposedly collective with them.

Bauman would argue that this disintegration of social bonds is not just the outcome or side-effect of late modernity's various dislocations and globalizing forces, but is also their very condition, for "it is the falling apart, the friability, the brittleness, the transience, the until-further-noticeness of human bonds and networks"[48] which allows particular asocial forces to flow unchecked. Bauman argues further that, in the realm of personal relationships, "The advent of virtual proximity [via various electronic networks] renders human connections simultaneously more frequent and more shallow, more intense and more brief."[49] The end result is a "separation between communication and relationship."[50] We might investigate how Bauman's picture of modern society differs (or does not differ) from the society depicted in *Beowulf*, described by John Hill as a "non-centralized, notably martial, face-to-face, aristocratic world," where "kinship structures are largely bilateral; where there is customary settlement of grievances through revenge and feud; where gift giving matters; where myths and legends are ancestral and incorporating; [and] where the sense of time is genealogical and not deeply historical, mechanistic, and alienating."[51] The Anglo-Saxon hall is, according to Hill, "more than a place or center; rather it becomes a fundamental mode of organization, cutting across kinship lines and creating a hall kinship— a kinship-band (*sibbegedriht*)—that . . . encompasses both private and public activities, both secular and sacred ones."[52] To assume, however, that the Anglo-Saxons *only* understood social relations within local or face-to-face contexts, might be not to understand fully how much of their culture was also "global," in relation to the ways in which they imagined, remembered, and also traversed their northern European history and geography, as Nicholas Howe explains in his essay, "*Beowulf* and the Ancestral Homeland," included in this volume.[53] We would argue, moreover, that in Beowulf's physical movements across broad expanses of land and water, as well as in his narrations of his own and others' histories (past, present, and future—his speech to Hygelac, lines 2000–2151, is a chief example), the social relations of the poem are constantly being lifted out, as it were, of local contexts and are articulated and rearticulated across wide tracts of time and space. Nevertheless, Hill's ethnographic approaches to *Beowulf*, as is well known, highlights what might be called the social unities of a highly localized—and, to Hill, anthropologically coherent—world in such a way as to redeem it from readings of the poem (such as Clare Lees's) that see in that same world a "deliberately ambivalent" attitude toward "a particularly conflicted set of male relationships."[54] Regardless of whether we judge the cultural world represented in *Beowulf* to be socially coherent—where, for example, its violence is part and parcel of what Hill terms its rational system of "jural feud"[55]—or fraught with ambivalence and tension over issues of violence and aggression, it may be that its face-to-face relationships were not necessarily more solid than our supposedly more friable and "liquid" arrangements, nor more natural, for as Bauman writes,

> No variety of human togetherness is fully structured, no internal differentiation is all-embracing, comprehensive and free from ambivalence, no hierarchy is total and frozen. The logic of categories [such as Victor Turner's *communitas* and *societas*] ill fits the endemic variegation and messiness of human interactions. Each attempt at complete structuration leaves numerous "loose strings" and contentious meanings; each produces its blank spots, underdefined areas, ambiguities, and "no man's" territories lacking their official ordnance surveys and maps.[56]

Much of the recent scholarship on *Beowulf*, as represented by many of the essays in this book, is quite intent on revealing the deep ambivalences, ambiguities, and "loose strings" of the social relations in what Hill calls the poem's "cultural world" and Earl calls "the world of the poem." Earl actually argues that the poem is not really a world at all but an "infinitely magnifiable imaginary map" whose "semiosis is unlimited," partly because our mental associations "run along numberless roots under the vast fields of memory," and therefore, we might approach the poem "as if it were a dream—even as if we had dreamed it ourselves."[57]

Michael Winterbottom's film *Code 46* (2004) provides another interesting avenue for thinking about *Beowulf*'s relation to our modernity, and it also illuminates those vast fields of memory and dream to which Earl refers, partly because the story is based on the classical Oedipus myth whose branching tendrils run deep within the modern psyche. The film also provides a picture of the future that is really the present in disguise, and therefore gives another means (albeit through fiction and not social theory) for answering the question posed by Earl, "What kind of present are we in, anyway?"[58]—a question we need to confront if we want to make the case for *Beowulf*'s relevance to our present moment. A romance set in a near dystopic future but shot in the contemporary locales of the modern cities of Shanghai and Seattle, and also in the deserts of Dubai and shanty towns of Jaipur, *Code 46* utilizes present-day landscapes unaltered by special effects to inscribe a dichotomy between the "inside" of the technologically sleek and antiseptic cities and the "outside" ("afuera" in the film) of the squalid developing-world villages and desert. The cities are home to transnational workers who speak a kind of Esperanto and whose movements are controlled by "papelles"—papers that function like visas and travel insurance combined and are issued by a corporation called The Sphinx. More than one reviewer has pointed out the film's prophetic qualities, not because of its vision of the supposed future, but because all of the ways it pictures forth the present we already inhabit, while also making that present seem uncanny—both strange and familiar at once. According to once critic, by setting the film "in the sterile fluorescence of ultramodern airports and hotels and in impoverished outlying regions," Winterbottom "delineates a time of global mobility, extreme inequality, and radical loneliness, distilling the fugitive moods of contemporary life into an ambience of muted, abstracted longing."[59]

Because *Code 46* retells the story of Oedipus, albeit with some modifications involving human cloning (the main character, William, unwittingly sleeps with a younger clone of his dead mother, Maria), the film simultaneously updates the past and also reads the future against the grain of the structures of belief that persist in time.[60] More specifically, Winterbottom's film plays out certain classical and mythological themes regarding fate, desire, and taboo within the context of a future in which biology has replaced divine prophecy (while also retaining the inescapable mandate of a certain determinism), yet basic human passions and sexual sins remain the same. No one in the film ever really moves forward into the future but is stuck perpetually in a modernity, or "middle present," similar to our own time. And yet, much like *Beowulf*, the film also articulates old concepts that are both alive and dead at once, and we could "do worse than [to] define historical epochs by the kinds of 'inner demons' that haunt and torment them."[61] And if these inner demons have a long history—as both Winterbottom's film and *Beowulf* more than amply demonstrate—what better way to investigate these long histories than through our most ancient literatures?

Winterbottom's film and Bauman's and other social theorists' conceptions of the present as modernity's second, late, or liquid phase cannot, by themselves, answer the question of whether *Beowulf* is relevant to our present moment, nor do we even have to agree with these conceptions of the times in which we live, but they can at least help us to *begin* to sketch out a provisional plane of an ideation, or set of pictures, or narrative, of the present upon which we can play out various notions about where we think we are, and more fully pose the question, what is Oedipus to Winterbottom or *Beowulf* to us? The critical anxiety surrounding this question may, at times, be palpable, for as Howe writes, "the desire to historicize our literary and cultural practice suggests our uncertainty that there is a workable connection between past and present," which results in the "haunting anxiety that the past, even if it can be reimagined or recovered, will be mute when we press it to speak to our moment."[62] As Edward Said reminds us, however, it may not be that we have to press *Beowulf* to speak to our present moment, for "texts have ways of existing that even in their most rarefied form are always enmeshed in circumstance, time, place, and society—in short, they are in the world, and hence worldly," and the "closeness of the world's body to the text's body forces readers to take both into consideration."[63]

But it is also *we*, the critics, who "embody in writing those processes and actual conditions in the present by means of which art and writing bear significance," and we therefore have a special responsibility to describe the processes by which a text expresses both "historical contingency" and the "sensuous particularity" of each moment in which it is read.[64] And Old English scholars, we would argue, have already begun to do this. For example, in his essay included in this volume, "Writing the Unreadable *Beowulf*," Allen Frantzen describes how, at various times in its reception history, *Beowulf* has answered to the particular desires of its different editors, translators, and critics, and Frantzen thereby historicizes "the function of the poem as a version of English history," while he also delineates the ways in which the language of the poem itself comments on the intertextual processes of reading and writing in such a manner as to reveal to us some of the poem's "inner" and "dialogized" history,[65] an inner history which, in Seth Lerer's view, may have something to do with "the poem's own conception of the [emerging] role of literature in culture and in the nature of poetic response."[66] And in his essay "*Beowulf* and the Origins of Civilization," Earl engages in a daring thought experiment where he imagines what the poem might have meant to one of its possible earliest readers—Byrhtnoth, the hero of *The Battle of Maldon*—while he also explores, through his personal dreams, his own unconscious reactions to a poem that he believes plucks "the deepest chords of ambivalence within us."[67] Earl's statement in the same essay that, "The system of relations—of us to *Beowulf*, of *Beowulf* to the Anglo-Saxons, and of the Anglo-Saxons to us—constitutes the meaning of *Beowulf*,"[68] opens up an important critical space within which we can begin to trace the ways in which the poem invokes, not an actual Germanic or Scandinavian or northern world, but an imagined world that likely needed to be *dreamed* in a specific place and at a specific time. In a particular present—tenth- or eleventh-century England, let's say—Beowulf's story, and all of the other stories attached to his narrative were desired and set into textual motion. But for what reasons? And how might those reasons still matter to us? We would say that one provisional answer might be that it is precisely in its ambiguities, ambivalences, circularities, and appositive tensions[69] that *Beowulf* clearly questions certain values and ideologies that we are still questioning and struggling with today, in relation to violence, heroism, honor, masculinity, tribalism, loyalty, demonization of the Other, and idealization of the past. In relation to these values and ideologies, the poem does not so much answer the questions as leave them open and conflicted in each present in which it is read.

Niles characterizes *Beowulf* as "a site of ideological conflict" that "represents a broad collective response to changes that affected a complex society during a period of major crisis and transformation"—more specifically, to his mind, "in the period of nation-building that followed ninth-century Viking invasions."[70] As a result, the poem is a "a socially embedded poetic act" that does not so much provide "a clear window on early Germanic social institutions" as it responds to the "lively tensions, agreements, and disagreements in the society from which it came."[71] Further, the poem is "a polyphonic work whose messages are contingent and sometimes contrary."[72] In his essay reprinted in this volume, "Landscapes of Conversion: Guthlac's Mound and Grendel's Mere as Expressions of Anglo-Saxon Nation-Building," Alfred Siewers likewise views *Beowulf*, through an ecocritical and psychoanalytic perspective, as a poem that reflects a certain expression of an emerging cultural identity for Anglo-Saxon elites—a cultural identity, moreover, that is formed out of a "creative tension between Augustinian otherworldiness and secular nation-building."[73] Siewers detects in the poem's treatment of Grendel and his mother and the dragon, and the topographies they inhabit, "stand-ins for residual 'native' Celtic populations in areas such as the fenlands" who might have stood in the way of an emerging, seventh- to eighth-century "Mercian hegemony" that wished to exorcise "pagan ancestral associations from earlier cultural landscapes" through an Anglo-Saxon identity myth, personified in Beowulf, of supra-landscape authority.[74] It is not only in the events or the landscapes of the narratives, but also in the poem's language, as Carol Braun Pasternack argues, that we can begin to detect, through deconstruction, the "cracks," "fissures," and "slippages" in the contradictions between an older "oral-heroic social formation" and an emerging "written-Christian formation" struggling against each other for expression in the poem.[75] Even earlier than Niles or Siewers or Pasternack and other scholars included in this volume who take similar poststructuralist approaches to the poem, Roberta Frank took note of the fact that literary works, like *Beowulf*, with a "sufficiently intense concern for history," cannot help but comprise "a series of projections inevitably focused by the particular anxieties of the writer."[76] Further, "the vision of the *Beowulf* poet seems to derive from contemporary concerns, from a need to establish in the present an ideological basis for national unity."[77] Beowulf himself could be characterized as a *novus homo* (Frank's phrase)[78] in the middle of history who travels back and forth between the "inside" of a proto-Christian social milieu (Heorot) and the borderland "outside" of a condemned and lawless past (Grendel's and the dragon's country but also, importantly, Geatland and its martial outposts).

In Beowulf's heroic exploits and ritualized death scenes we can see the cultural tensions that always inhere in the incommensurability between the ways in which the figures of the past, in Walter Benjamin's words, are always striving by "a secret heliotropism . . . to turn toward the sun which is rising in the sky of history"[79] and the ways in which those in the present (the author and the poem's tenth- or eleventh-century readers, but also we, its modern audience) are resurrecting the dead only to bury them again with different rites and under a different sky. At the same time, the poem speaks to historical contiguities and moments of uncanny recognition between the "familiar" present and the always "Other" past. In the poem's digressive asides regarding future episodes of violence, such as the wars between the Swedes and the Geats, or the enmity between Hrothgar and his in-laws, every heroic action Beowulf undertakes to vanquish monstrous enemies is undercut by the social reality that, in the end, war is always inevitable and ongoing, both in Beowulf's time, the time of the Anglo-Saxons, and our own time, and this calls into question the nature of heroism itself—what, finally, is it good for? Moreover, in Beowulf's encounters with the so-called monsters—Grendel, Grendel's mother, and the dragon—which themselves have deep roots in Old Testament and other mythological traditions,[80] we can begin to trace the inner demons that lie just beneath the more overtly political and ideological conflicts expressed in the poem, and also glimpse the contours of the exiled stranger-Others who reside in the margins not only of Beowulf's world or of Anglo-Saxon history, but also of our own cultural psyche, where they expose what Jeffrey Cohen has described as "the *extimité*, the 'extimacy' or 'intimate alterity' of identity."[81] And regardless of what appears to be the poem's definitive foreignness—partly because of its language and structure, partly because of the tribal culture it represents—as Earl reminds us, "*Beowulf* both reveals and disguises some surprisingly familiar structures of our cultured Germanic, Anglo-Saxon, English-speaking minds—our antifeminism, for example, our repression of affect, our materialism, and our denial of death."[82]

Because of the endless ways in which different presents and different pasts encounter each other through the text of *Beowulf*, and the multiple tensions and varieties of *frisson* that inevitably result from such encounters, the "medieval," as enclosed (and represented) within the poem, becomes what Cohen has described as "a site of infinite possibility . . . an uncanny middle that can derail the somber trajectories of history and bring about pasts as yet undreamed."[83] The poem might even be said to speak to a kind of crisis of temporality that inheres in the often vexed relationship between history and memory and the artist who desires to bring to a standstill, through representation, the always fugitive and ghostly presences of the past. What Gerhard Richter writes about the work of the contemporary German artist Anselm Kiefer, whose monumental paintings and other multimedia works, much like *Beowulf*, plumb the depths of a dark mythological Germanic past as well as the terrors of a haunted and conflicted political present, could apply, we believe, with equal force to our readings of *Beowulf*—that they return us

> again and again to a series of open questions. What is history? What will its relation to presentation have been? What are the links between strategies of aesthetic figuration and the politics of memory and counter-memory? . . . Does the presentation of history necessarily imply a search for lost former presences, fugitive moments of temporality that were once simply themselves and transparently comprehensible? . . . What does it mean that the historical presents itself not as a former presence but rather in the space of intersecting traces that inscribe its genealogical shifts and movements, and that, by extension, the historical was always already—even at the time of its retroactively projected former presence, the fiction of its anteriority—a network of traces and relays?[84]

Tolkien was right that "the main foes in *Beowulf* are inhuman," but he may have missed the mark in arguing that the poem "stands amid but above the petty wars of princes, and surpasses the dates and limits of historical periods,"[85] for it may be that it is precisely "the historical"—however we might define that, through Leopold von Ranke or Michel Foucault—that

the poetry attempts to surpass, but never *can* surpass, and the dragon, ulti-
mately, is not the figure of a particular myth, or mythical force, but history
itself in mythological drag. The answer to whether or not *Beowulf* speaks
to our modernity may lie precisely in the ways in which the poem, much
like Kiefer's art, "offers us a series of conceptual and figurational dilemmas
without which the historical can hardly be thought."[86] And the poem's con-
tinuing attraction, for modern critics as well as the more general public, will
likely have something to do with how the poem poses a certain psychoana-
lytic problem of memory—in Charles Shepherdson's words, "what does it
mean to say that in dredging up the past, repeating it, going back across the
river to see where the ancestors lie buried, one is concerned, not so much
with what really happened—with what Leopold von Ranke called 'the past
as it really was in itself'—but rather with intervening, rewriting the past,
producing a shift in the symbolic structure of the narrative that has brought
us to the point where we are now?"[87]

There has been an explosion in recent years in various humanities disci-
plines in "history and memory" studies, especially with regard to the prob-
lem of trauma in relation to major historical events, such as the Holocaust
or the Rwandan genocide. These studies are especially intent on interrogat-
ing "the historical" in relation to real-world events (or, actual *lived* experi-
ence) and to the aesthetic figurations of those events and experiences, as
well as all the ways in which the two can rarely be untangled.[88] The prob-
lem of memory's relationship to history is especially acute at the end of the
twentieth century, when we consider, as Jacques Le Goff writes, the critical
importance of collective memory:

> Overflowing history as both a form of knowledge and a public river, flowing
> uphill as the moving reservoir of history, full of archives and documents/
> monuments, and downhill as the sonorous (and living) echo of historical
> work, collective memory is one of the great stakes of developed and devel-
> oping societies, of dominated and dominating classes, all of them strug-
> gling for power or for life, for survival and advancement.[89]

In Old English studies, Niles draws attention to the force of collective
memory when he writes that, if a full history of Anglo-Saxon England could
ever be written, "it would read as the story of a series of appropriations [ma-
terial, linguistic, or intellectual] of greater or lesser magnitude," and further,
"Anglo-Saxon England is *nothing other than what it has been perceived to be*
by historically grounded human beings, from the time of the Anglo-Saxons

to the present moment."[90] The historical present, Niles argues, is formed on the ground of a past that is not *out there* somewhere, but is rather *in here*, as a part of our cultural consciousness, which cultural consciousness, moreover, is a kind of *bricolage* that has been formed out of the scavengings and pillagings of the artifacts and remnants of the past—linguistic, geographic, architectural, literary, etc. In the end,

> it no longer matters what "really happened" in history. What's done is done. The victors of former struggles are now wrapped by the same earth that covers their victims. What does matter greatly is what people believe happened in history, what they say happened, for such beliefs and claims can have a passionate relation to rivalries of which the outcome is still in doubt.[91]

In her essay, "In Transit: Theorizing Cultural Appropriation in Medieval Europe," reprinted in this volume, Claire Sponsler writes that the verb *appropriate*, "to make one's own," points to "a system of objects within which valued artifacts circulate and are given meanings and underscores the way in which appropriation is an act of possessing—of ideas, objects, texts, beliefs."[92] In Sponsler's view, medieval studies has tended "to approach their task as one of salvage," and this "has privileged the 'artifact' as the focal point of study rather then the 'process' of cultural creation and transmission."[93] As a result, we do not always recognize that meaning moves continually between different locations in the world, just as cultural objects do—nothing is ever static and everything is "flowing" all the time. *Beowulf* itself opens with the statement *we gefrunon*, "we have heard," and therefore the poem begins with an appropriation of a story from *somewhere out there* that the poet is obviously going to refashion for his own concerns, while also putting on the pretense of only "telling" (i.e., "recording") something not only already *heard*, but more elliptically, already *known*. We would argue that *Beowulf* is an ideal text—both as an artifact and as an act of aesthetic figuration—for interrogating the *process of cultural creation and transmission*, as well as *the flow of meaning through places and over time*, and many of the essays included in this volume do exactly that. A literary text like *Beowulf* that speaks of and points toward a traumatic and violent history—part real, part wholly unreal—so far removed from us in time that we could easily feel emotionally disconnected from it, and for which there are no recognizable memory sites (other than the manuscript itself, there is no real Heorot or Geatland we can visit, although we often strive mightily to create memory sites for ourselves, as we have with Sutton Hoo), and whose composition history is fraught with so many unresolvable aporia (thereby continually unsettling our ability to historically situate its provenance with absolute precision), would seem to provide an ideal site through which to explore the always compromised relationships between memory, history, and art.

Since its first English edition in 1833,[94] *Beowulf* has operated in critical circles less as a purely poetic text from which we want to discover something about meaning—whether local and *past* or more global and transhistorical—and more as an historical *lieu de memoire*, or "memory site," that can aid us in the construction (or deconstruction) of a collective and commemorative English or Germanic- or Nordic-inflected past.[95] This dismayed Tolkien, of course, who believed that some of the earlier dismissal of the poem, such as W. P. Ker's, mainly had to do with the "disappointment at the discovery" that the poem "was itself and not something that the scholar would have liked better—for example, a heathen heroic lay, a history of Sweden, a manual of German antiquities, or a Nordic *Summa Theologica*."[96] Although Tolkien's commentary certainly opened the way for some brilliant aesthetic criticism—Edward B. Irving's *A Reading of "Beowulf"* (New Haven, 1968) and *Rereading "Beowulf"* (Philadelphia, 1989) being two gorgeous examples—a concern for the supposed real history hidden behind the poem's story, or its production and reception, or our relation to it over time, has remained predominant in *Beowulf* studies, perhaps because, as Howe writes, "As they interpret the remains of a past culture, all works on Old English language and literature are historical in method and intent."[97] Howe also reminds us that even Tolkien was somewhat of a historicist—not in wanting to use the poem as a "quarry" for specific cultural facts (a scholarly approach Tolkien condemned), but in recognizing the poem "as a sustained meditation on the past's richly subtle senses of its own past."[98] And the ultimate conclusion of this sustained meditation, for both the characters within the poem and the scholars outside of it, may be that the past, for all of its vibrant materiality *at one time*—can only ever be invented, partly as a hedge against the chaos of time, partly as a hedge against death and nothingness. When we consider the image of the women of Beowulf's tribe, in line 3019, bereft of their possessions, "oft nalles æne elland tredan" ("treading a foreign path, not once but often"), or even the refugees of our present world living along the borders between Chechnya and Georgia, Sudan and Chad, or outside the walls of Fallujah in Iraq, we may believe initially that what we are seeing are the losers of history—those who are utterly bereft of all *we* have built up and retained through knowledge, place, and possessions—but what we are really seeing is the truth of what has, perhaps, always been our own historical

L

condition: our rootlessness and fugitive wanderings,[99] as well as our naked vulnerability to what Tolkien called our "inevitable overthrow in Time."[100]

Vulnerability to an overthrow in time is also Beowulf's historical condition, a condition he strives mightily to displace in three significant places: when, upon returning from Daneland, he constructs his own narrative of his exploits there and also predicts the future destruction of Hrothgar's court in a speech to Hygelac (lines 1999–2151); when, before fighting the dragon, he explains to his retainers the sorrow of Hrethel over his family's fratricide and son's execution, and also points to the bloody and unredeemed history of Ravenswood (lines 2425–2509), a story that sheds some light on the supposed origins of the long-standing feud between the Swedes and the Geats and that Wiglaf's herald will continue narrating after Beowulf's death (lines 2923b–98); and last, when he relates very specific instructions, while dying, regarding how he wants the dragon's treasure to be used (as insurance against enemies) and how he wants to be buried—which is to say, how he wants to be remembered (lines 2794–2816). Strikingly, these three episodes, when taken together, show Beowulf placing himself all over the chronological map (past, present, and future) in order to not only tell his own story, but to also fix that story within a history that has already been sealed within a beginning and a middle, with himself as the sufficient end. Yet the very ending Beowulf wants to write for himself—warrior-vanquisher, peacemaker, and never-forgotten king—is undermined by Wiglaf's decision to bury the treasure with him, and also by the fact that the very mission that he designed to initially fashion himself as a forward-looking hero (traveling to Daneland to take on Hrothgar's monsters, who are also Hrothgar's personal demons) cannot, and by Beowulf's own admission, will not hold, due to the always percolating enmity of Hrothgar's court. According to Janet Thormann, Beowulf's speech before dying, as well as Wiglaf's herald's speech to the retainers afterward (lines 2900–3027), are both personal and cultural memories *and* attempts at representing history during moments of profound crisis and anxiety over the temporariness of material bodies, but we must also remember that,

> No history is ever more than a symbolic construction, more than language relating only to other language, nor may history be ethical before it recognizes itself to be only language and hence acknowledges its limits. Only in language does the vulnerable body appear, not the real, indestructible enjoying body or the imaginary, fortified ego of the young warrior, but the subject without certainty, absolute control, or secure foundation.[101]

In Beowulf's speech before fighting the dragon, especially in his expression of his nostalgic desire that he wishes he could know how, other than with a sword, he "wið ðam aglæcean elles meahte / gylpe wiðgripan, swa ic gio wið Grendle dyde" ("against that terror might otherwise grapple, according to boast, such as I did with Grendel," lines 2520–21), Susan Kim likewise sees an attempt at writing and fixing in time a personal memory that, at the same time, carries the burden of a larger history:

> Beowulf's desire here is explicitly the nostalgic longing for a past moment of origin, which is full, is fixed, and can be held on to in the way that Grendel could be and which is thus experienced only within the nostalgic narrative of loss. . . . Beowulf thus positions himself in a present moment defined by the loss of a past moment; he knows, by the very gesture of its evocation as already an old story, that this is an impossible origin, a self-conscious narrative rather than a lived experience.[102]

Because Beowulf's fight with the dragon and its outcome is linked at a very intimate level with the ensuing Swedish incursions against the now leaderless Geats that Wiglaf's herald will predict in gory detail to Beowulf's "folk" after Beowulf has died (lines 2999–3027), as Kim points out, "Beowulf carries the burden of history within the poem,"[103] and this is a history, moreover, that is continually being foreclosed in language, and in language's fictionality. Indeed, because the poet himself tells us in the first one hundred lines of the poem, before Beowulf is even introduced as a character, that "ne wæs hit lenge þa gen" ("it was not long yet") before the great hall at Heorot is consumed by hostile fires due to the violence of *ecghete*, "sword-hate" (lines 83–84), Heorot is therefore destroyed before Beowulf even enters its horn-gabled doors in order to secure it against Grendel's attacks. Because of the multiple tenses implied in "it was not long yet"—it has already happened and is also about to happen—before Beowulf can undo Grendel and his kin, Beowulf's warrior work has already been undone. Moreover, when he crosses the sea to Daneland he hurries, as it were, toward an absence that trembles with the last traces of its once more vibrant materiality. Beowulf's command, when dying, for his retainers to build a memorial in his honor, both as reminder to his people as well as a marker for seafarers (lines 2802–08)—which seafarers can only come to Beowulf from a future that is now forever out of his grasp—indicates that Beowulf understands the absences and ambiguities of history all too well, and fears his own disappearance there. For all of the poet's labors to complete Beowulf's story with funerary encomiums, with every reading of the poem, Beowulf is awakened, then put back to a rest that is never really a rest, which is why one of his last statements to Wiglaf, "ne mæg ic her leng wesan" ("I can be here no longer," line 2801), becomes a pregnant irony. At the same time, as the poem also shows us, in the end, Beowulf is only smoke, as well as, in Kim's words, "the remains" that "fill the language" of his tribe's lamentations.[104]

Bodies (both dead and alive), history, and language, and all of the fiercely tangled relations between them—what do the dead want from us, what might we want from each other at any given moment, and how might we sufficiently record our past and present histories in order to lend some kind of meaning and ethical content to what some of us fear, deep down, is a kind of unscripted chaos? How, further, can the past inform our future in a way that is ethically and socially constructive? These are the questions that resonate throughout *Beowulf* and also modern life. However insufficient some of Ker's commentary on *Beowulf* might seem to us today, some of his remarks on *Beowulf* in his 1904 book *The Dark Ages* strike us as smartly sensitive to the issue of what might be called *Beowulf*'s historicity, and to the ways in which the poem speaks, not of history itself, but of the anxiety of being undone by history, of being erased in its ever-shifting currents and concerns, of being outright torn apart and killed by it and then consigned to oblivion, to a place where no one remembers anything at all. Following the thought of Richter on Kiefer's art, *Beowulf* "presents itself in the strange figure of a singularity that meets in unforeseeable ways with the generality of its historical and philosophical structure,"[105] and long before many other scholars were willing to concede the matter (and some will still not relinquish it), Ker recognized that the history contained in early epic poetry is always already transformed by a unique artistic sensibility (what Ker called the epic, or heroic, imagination) which, having admitted that the actual history of war and warriors is itself too politically complex for poetry, "turns by preference to adventures where the hero is isolated or left with a small company, where he is surprised and assailed in a house by night, as at Finnesburh, or where he meets his enemies in a journey and has to put his back to a rock. Ultimately, the poet's "subject matter is not purely material; it has been idealized more or less before he takes it in hand."[106] Further, "the actual world, so infinitely more complex than the world of heroic poetry, was nevertheless occupied in the Dark Ages with the heroic ideal."[107] So, even before history is turned into poetry, it already *is* poetry, and the artwork, whether *Beowulf* or *The Battle of Maldon*, is a singular expression of a narrative imagination "concerned with the Sisyphean task of *working through* history and its imbrications in the mythical: to attempt to come to terms with their ghostliness, but also to employ them as the vexed prime material out of which a thought may flow into artistic form."[108] In this sense, the "historical"—whatever that may mean—is not recoverable in the poem, and even when we labor to locate analogues for historical figures and events (and for historical concerns) within the poem, as Michel de Certeau would remind us, "the historical figure is only a dummy," and "the past is a fiction of the present."[109] But what *is* historical about "heroic poetry" is the way in which it reveals, following Ker, what might be called a cultural occupation with that moment when the idealized hero *has to put his back to a rock*. In all times and places, whether under threat of violence and extinction—by Vikings or the Khmer Rouge— or under the obligation to either rush into the breach or out of the foxhole, such heroes are dreamed, and also killed off. Perhaps the poem relates to our present moment, finally, not because it either is or is not a comforting grand narrative, is or is not a story about things that might have really happened, is or is not a type of window, however opaque, upon a past related to us through genealogy and a "desire for origins," but because it expresses some of the wish fulfillment, and also the anxieties, of a human memory troubled by history—in the same way that *we* continue to be troubled by history and our relation to its silences and blank spots, its dark fissures and violent effacements, its holocausts and other zones of devastation.

At the opening of the House of Literature in Stuttgart in 2001, the late writer W. G. Sebald, who grew up in the aftermath of Germany's destruction during World War II, gave a speech in which he ruminated how, as an author of fiction, he had devoted his life to "adhering to an exact historical perspective, in patiently engraving and linking together apparently disparate things in the manner of a still-life."[110] He recalled that, as he was riding the S-Bahn train into Stuttgart in 2001 on a winter night, he could not help himself from thinking, when he reached Feuersee Station, "that the fires are still blazing above us, and that since the terrors of the last war years, even though we have rebuilt our surroundings so wonderfully well, we have been living in a kind of underground zone."[111] Likewise, he found himself imagining how the "network of lights glittering in the darkness" of Daimler Corporations's new administrative complex

> was like a constellation of stars spreading all over the world, so that these Stuttgart stars are visible not only in the cites of Europe and on the boulevards of Beverly Hills and Buenos Aires but wherever columns of trucks

with their cargoes of refugees move along the dusty roads, obviously never stopping, in the zones of devastation that are always spreading somewhere—in Sudan, Kosovo, Eritrea, or Afghanistan.[112]

What, Sebald finally asked, in such underground zones and (paraphrasing the poetry of Hölderin) in "the dark of an all too sober realm where wild confusion prevails in the treacherous light," is literature good for? Sebald's answer was that "[t]here are many forms of writing; only in literature, however, can there be an attempt at restitution over and above the mere recital of facts, and over and above scholarship."[113]

We would like to argue that, similar to the poetry of *Beowulf* or a work like Sebald's novel of post-Holocaust experience *Austerlitz*, scholarship can also be a "restitution," as well as an artistic (even poetic) intervention into history that engraves and links things together in the manner of a still-life in order to "grasp the ways in which [history's] images flash up only in the fleeting moment that illuminates . . . a field of endless relations that cannot be reduced to any realist or literalist concern."[114] And this is why we chose for the cover of our book the Peter Turnley photograph from the first Gulf War of a dead Kuwaiti soldier's hand resting flat in the sand of the desert—a hand, moreover, that has been partially carbonized by unimaginable heat, and on the third finger of which a gold wedding ring is clearly visible. Why this photograph? According to Bruce Gilchrist, who found the photograph first and brought it to our attention,

> It speaks in the synecdochic language of the associative violence of war, the traumatic effect of violence and the frank horror it creates in us as witnesses; it is only a wrist and hand, partially ruined by fire, as is the *Beowulf* manuscript, as is Beowulf's pyre, as is the Finnsburg pyre on which the heads and helmets of Hildeburh's beloved husband and son burn and collapse together in a harrowing metonymic embrace. And yet, that same wrist and hand also bear an intact material object that will outlive its bearer: the gold ring. Similar to the necklaces, the heirloom swords, the rune-carved sword hilt made by giants, and the gold cup (the theft of which awakens the sleeping dragon whose fury will be Beowulf's ultimate undoing), this ring sets up the possibility of story, of inscription, and of the renewal of violence in the urgency for revenge.[115]

Like the photograph, the poem of *Beowulf* "is a cultural response that, as testimony, overcomes the historical gap, its lostness and pastness, with a power to reconfigure our understanding of the present world and our present selves."[116] And it overcomes that gap, of course, through language, in the same way the photograph crosses over the space that separates the middle Eastern desert from our Western shores through the metonymy of the visual. We do not see the work of criticism as belatedly *secondary* to the poem, or to the photograph, or to any work of art (literary or otherwise), for as Said writes, "rather than being defined by the silent past, commanded by it to speak in the present, criticism, no less than any text, is the present in the course of its articulation, its struggles for definition."[117] Ultimately, the job of the critic is similar to the job of the poet, who, in the words of Wallace Stevens, is always confronted, not with *things as they are*, but with *things seeming*, and both scholar and poet are "the artificer[s] of subjects still half night."[118]

We are indebted to the generosity of Roy Liuzza, John Hill, Bruce Gilchrist, and Janet Thormann, all of whom read through earlier drafts of this essay and offered invaluable suggestions for correction and revision; any remaining errors are entirely our own.

NOTES

[1] J. R. R. Tolkien, "*Beowulf*: The Monsters and the Critics," *Proceedings of the British Academy* 22 (1936): 245–95, reprinted in *An Anthology of "Beowulf" Criticism*, ed. Lewis E. Nicholson (Notre Dame, 1963), p. 54.

[2] Gerhard Richter, "History's Flight, Anselm Kiefer's Angels," *Connecticut Review* 24 (2002): 114.

[3] Zygmunt Bauman, *Liquid Modernity* (Cambridge, Eng., 2000), p. 110.

[4] W. P. Ker, *The Dark Ages* (1904; reprint London, 1955), p. 252.

[5] Tolkien, "*Beowulf*: The Monsters and the Critics," p. 61.

[6] See *The Electronic "Beowulf*," ed. Kevin S. Kiernan with Andrew Prescott et al., version 2.0 (London, 2003), and Seamus Heaney, "*Beowulf*": A New Verse Translation (New York, 2000). It should be noted here that 2000 also marks the year of Roy M. Liuzza's verse translation of *Beowulf* for Broadview Press, a translation, moreover, that Frank Kermode has written "can be matched with the famous one [the Nobel laureate Heaney's]" ("The Modern Beowulf," in Frank Kermode, *Pleasing Myself: from "Beowulf" to Philip Roth* [London, 2001], p. 11. In addition, 2005 saw the publication of the anthology of Gareth Hinds's *Beowulf* comics *The Collected "Beowulf"* (published by thecomic.com), and Eric A. Kimmel and Leonard Everett Fisher's illustrated children's book *The Hero*

"*Beowulf*" (published by Farar, Straus and Giroux). In the area of performance, 2005 also marked the release of the Icelandic director Sturla Gunnarsson's film *Beowulf and Grendel*, the performance of *Beowulf* as a "twenty-first century ritualistic rock opera" by the Irish Repertory Company, and the announcement of Robert Zemeckis's plans to make a *Beowulf* movie using "digital capture technology," as he did in the film based on Chris Van Allsburg's children's book *The Polar Express*. And finally, Goldenthal's and Taymor's opera *Grendel* premiered in New York City at the Lincoln Center in July of 2006.

[7] For an overview of the debate of the last fifteen or so years over the marginalization of Old English studies, see Allen J. Frantzen and Robert F. Yeager, "A Recent Survey of the Teaching of Old English and its Implications for Anglo-Saxon Studies," *Old English Newsletter* 26.2 (1992): 34–45; Allen J. Frantzen, "By the Numbers: Anglo-Saxon Scholarship at the Century's End," in *A Companion to Anglo-Saxon Literature*, ed. Philip Pulsiano and Elaine Treharne (Oxford, 2001), pp. 472–95, *Desire for Origins: New Language, Old English, and Teaching the Tradition* (New Brunswick, 1990), pp. 1–26, and "Who Do These Anglo-Saxon(ist)s Think They Are, Anyway?" *Æstel* 2 (1994): 1–43; Annette di Paolo Healey, "Old English Language Studies: Present State and Future Prospects," *Old English Newsletter* 20.2 (1987): 34–45; John P. Hermann, *Allegories of War: Language and Violence in Old English Poetry* (Ann Arbor, 1989), pp. 199–208; Nicholas Howe, "The New Millennium," in Pulsiano and Treharne, *A Companion to Anglo-Saxon Literature*, pp. 496–505; Peter Jackson, "The Future of Old English: A Personal Essay," *Old English Newsletter* 25.3 (1992): 24–28; Gillian R. Overing, "Recent Writing on Old English: A Response," *Æstel* 1 (1993): 135–49; Fred C. Robinson, "Anglo-Saxon Studies: Present State and Future Prospects," *Mediaevalia* 1 (1975): 63–77; T. A. Shippey, "Recent Writing on Old English," *Æstel* 1 (1993): 111–34; James Simpson, "The Enjoyment and Teaching of Old and Middle English: The Current State of Play," *Old English Newsletter* 25.3 (1992): 29–31; Joseph Tuso, "The State of the Art: A Survey," in *Approaches to Teaching "Beowulf,"* ed. Jess B. Bessinger Jr. and Robert F. Yeager (New York, 1984), pp. 33–39; and Robert F. Yeager, "Some Turning Points in the History of Teaching Old English in America," *Old English Newsletter* 13.2 (1980): 9–20.

[8] As regards the mishandling of the manuscript over time, as well as the various attempts to restore it, see Kevin Kiernan "The State of the *Beowulf* Manuscript, 1882–1983" *Anglo-Saxon England* 13 (1984): 23–42, and *"Beowulf" and the "Beowulf" Manuscript*, rev. ed. (Ann Arbor, 1996), pp. 65–169; and Andrew Prescott, "'Their Present Miserable State of Cremation': The Restoration of the Cotton Library," in *Sir Robert Cotton as Collector: Essays on an Early Stuart Courtier and His Legacy*, ed. C. J. Wright (London, 1997), pp. 391–454.

[9] Terry Eagleton, "Hasped and hooped and hirpling: Heaney conquers *Beowulf*," *London Review of Books*, 11 Nov. 1999: 16.

[10] See Allen J. Frantzen, *Desire for Origins: New Language, Old English, and Teaching the Tradition* (New Brunswick, 1990), and the essays collected in Allen J. Frantzen and John D. Niles, ed., *Anglo-Saxonism and the Construction of Social Identity* (Gainesville, 1997). Also in this vein, see Alfred David, "The Nationalities of *Beowulf*," *Old English Newsletter*, Subsidia Series, 31 (2002): 3–21; T. A. Shippey and Andreas Haarder, eds., *"Beowulf": The Critical Heritage* (London, 1998); and E. G. Stanley, *The Search for Anglo-Saxon Paganism* (Cambridge, Eng., 1975). For the same argument in Middle English studies, see David Matthews, *The Making of Middle English, 1765–1910* (Minneapolis, 1999).

[11] Nicholas Howe, "Historicist Approaches," in *Reading Old English Texts*, ed. Katherine O'Brien O'Keeffe (Cambridge, Eng., 1997), p. 96.

[12] Allen J. Frantzen, "Prologue: Documents and Monuments: Difference and Interdisciplinarity in the Study of Medieval Culture," in *Speaking Two Languages: Traditional Disciplines and Contemporary Theory in Medieval Studies*, ed. Allen J. Frantzen (Albany, 1991), p. 22.

[13] John D. Niles, "Introduction: *Beowulf*, Truth, and Meaning," in *A "Beowulf" Handbook*, ed. Robert E. Bjork and John D. Niles (Lincoln, Nebr., 1997), p. 9. For an exemplification of how Niles himself would situate *Beowulf* in relation to the discourses of power of the society that might have originally committed the poem to parchment, see his essay, "Locating *Beowulf* in Literary History," *Exemplaria* 5 (1993): 79–109, and reprinted in this volume. For a further elaboration upon how Niles conceives of what Frantzen terms the "structural, structuring effects" of the relationship between the practitioners and subjects of the discipline of Anglo-Saxon studies, see his essay "Appropriations: A Concept of Culture," in Frantzen and Niles, *Anglo-Saxonism and the Construction of Social Identity*, pp. 202–28.

[14] Niles, "Introduction: *Beowulf*, Truth, and Meaning," p. 9.

[15] Eagleton, "Hasped and hooped and hirpling," p. 16.

[16] Dominick LaCapra, *Writing History, Writing Trauma* (Baltimore, 2001), pp. 154–55. See also Jean-François Lyotard, *The Postmodern Condition: A Report on Knowledge*, trans. Geoff Bennington and Brian Massumi (Minneapolis, 1984). One could argue that by using the Holocaust as a temporal border whereby he can mark off the period "before" (when "grand narratives" made sense) from "after" (when they no longer do), LaCapra privileges a historical event that is itself knowable only as a "grand narrative," or, as the Shoah Project suggests, as a collage of "stories," in much the same way that *Beowulf* presents its own version of heroic history as a collage of interlocking narratives. Of course, in contrast to the stories related in *Beowulf*, the Holocaust is very much a real and deeply traumatic and

cataclysmic event that, because its main actors performed actions that, prior to that point, were unthinkable and unprecedented, blew apart many of the most cherished beliefs of those caught up in its maelstrom, but in coming to grips with that event, those who experienced it firsthand have had a profound need of what might be called conventional narrative devices in order to make sense of what happened to them. LaCapra himself is very much concerned in much of his work with what might be called the ethico-psychology of "remembering" traumatic events and of the narratives—testimonial, artistic, and otherwise—of that remembering. See, for example, his *Representing the Holocaust: History, Theory, Trauma* (Ithaca, N.Y., 1994) and *History and Memory After Auschwitz* (Ithaca, N.Y., 1998).

[17] Alasdair MacIntyre, *After Virtue: A Study in Moral Theory* (Notre Dame, 1981), pp. 201–02.

[18] MacIntyre, *After Virtue*, p. 201.

[19] Peter Munz, "The Historical Narrative," in *Companion to Historiography*, ed. Michael Bentley (London, 1997), p. 852.

[20] For a brief overview of the recent debates in historical studies over "objectivity" and "narrativity," and all the critical and ethical problems attendant thereupon, see the essays included in Brian Fay, Philip Pomper, and Richard T. Vann, eds., *History and Theory: Contemporary Readings* (London, 1998).

[21] Munz, "The Historical Narrative," p. 854.

[22] Caroline Walker Bynum, *Metamorphosis and Identity* (New York, 2001), p. 188.

[23] MacIntyre, *After Virtue*, p. 201.

[24] Emmanuel Levinas, *Time and the Other*, trans. Richard A. Cohen (Pittsburgh, 1987), p. 72.

[25] Mark Turner, "Preface," *The Literary Mind* (Oxford, 1996), p. v.

[26] Daniel Dennett, *Consciousness Explained* (Boston, 1991), pp. 253–54. For other studies in cognitive science and philosophy that also explore the narrative structures of the mind, see Antonio R. Damasio, *The Feeling of What Happens: Body and Emotions in the Making of Consciousness* (New York, 1999); Joseph LeDoux, *The Synaptic Self: How Our Brains Become Who We Are* (New York, 2002); and George Lakoff and Mark Johnson, *Philosophy in the Flesh: The Embodied Mind and its Challenge to Western Thought* (New York, 1999).

[27] In an encyclopedia entry for *Beowulf* in *British Writers*, Supplement IV (ed. Jay Parini, [New York, 2001]), Paul Bibire describes the organizing principle of *Beowulf* as "non-linear parallelism and variation" (p. 37). And in his essay "*Beowulf* and Perception," Michael Lapidge also makes an argument for the "non-linearity of *Beowulf*ian discourse," and the idea that the *Beowulf* author was deliberately experimenting with narrative strategies for which "there is no

satisfactory model in antecedent Western literature" (*Proceedings of the British Academy* 111 [2002]: 62, 76). Further, Lapidge sees parallels between *Beowulf* and the "multiple internal focalization" and preoccupation with epistemology of the modern novel.

28 Gillian Overing, *Language, Sign, and Gender in "Beowulf"* (Carbondale, 1990), pp. 47, 35. In their essays, both reprinted in this volume, both Frantzen and Shari Horner speak to the inter- and intratextuality of *Beowulf*. See Allen J. Frantzen, "Writing the Unreadable *Beowulf*," *Desire for Origins*, pp. 168–200, and Shari Horner, "Voices from the Margins: Women and Textual Enclosure in *Beowulf*," *The Discourse of Enclosure* (Albany, 2001), pp. 65–100.

29 James W. Earl, "*Beowulf* and the Origins of Civilization," *Thinking About "Beowulf"* (Stanford, 1994), pp. 162, 150–52, 188. This essay is reprinted in this volume.

30 R. M. Liuzza, "Introduction," *"Beowulf": A New Verse Translation*, trans. R. M. Liuzza (Ontario, 2000), p. 16.

31 LaCapra, *History and Memory after Auschwitz*, p. 24.

32 The dating of *Beowulf*, as a work of either oral or textual art, or some kind of hybrid between the two, has a long and contentious history that we do not wish to address here. For the purposes of this introduction, we assume a readership (or audience) consistent with the most probable date of the manuscript itself, which everyone agrees is ca. 1000 CE. For those interested in the dating controversy, see Colin Chase, ed., *The Dating of "Beowulf"* (Toronto, 1981); Roy Michael Liuzza, "On the Dating of *Beowulf*," in *"Beowulf": Basic Readings*, ed. Peter S. Baker (New York, 1995), pp. 281–302; and Kiernan, *"Beowulf" and the "Beowulf" Manuscript*, pp. 13–63. Regarding the probable monastic context of Beowulf's écriture, see Patrick Wormald, "Bede, Beowulf and the Conversion of the Anglo-Saxon Aristocracy," in *Bede and Anglo-Saxon England*, ed. Robert T. Farrell (Oxford, 1978), pp. 32-95.

33 All citations of *Beowulf* are taken from Fr. Klaeber, ed., *Beowulf and the Fight at Finnsburg*, 3rd ed. with supplements (Lexington, Mass., 1950); all translations are by the authors, unless otherwise noted.

34 This translation is from Liuzza, *"Beowulf": A New Verse Translation*, p. 115.

35 Joseph Harris, "*Beowulf* in Literary History," *Pacific Coast Philology* 17 (1982): 16.

36 Bauman, *Liquid Modernity*, p. 28.

37 Bauman, *Liquid Modernity*, p. 11. See also Ulrich Beck, *Risk Society: Towards a New Modernity*, trans. Mark Ritter (London, 1992); Ulrich Beck, Anthony Giddens, and Scott Lash, *Reflexive Modernization: Politics, Tradition and Aesthetics in the Modern Social Order* (Stanford, 1994); and Anthony Giddens,

The Consequences of Modernity (Stanford, 1991) and *Modernity and Self-Identity: Self and Society in the Late Modern Age* (Stanford, 1991).

38 Bauman, *Liquid Modernity*, pp. 12–13. We should point out here that Bauman is well aware that much of his description of late modernity applies mainly to the elite elements of society, and that many individuals and groups, due to their location and/or poverty, are effectively "left out." On this point, see Zygmunt Bauman, *Wasted Lives: Modernity and Its Outcasts* (Cambridge, Eng., 2004).

39 See Zygmunt Bauman, *Postmodern Ethics* (Oxford, 1993), pp. 138–44, 229–35.

40 Bauman, *Postmodern Ethics*, p. 239.

41 Giddens, *Modernity and Self-Identity*, pp. 27, 20.

42 Giddens, *Modernity and Self-Identity*, p. 33.

43 Giddens, *Modernity and Self-Identity*, p. 33.

44 Kenneth Gergen, "The Self: Death by Technology," *The Hedgehog Review* 1.1 (Fall 1999); available at http://www.virginia.edu/iasc/hh/THRtoc1-1.html.

45 For more information on *The Electronic "Beowulf,"* see Kevin Kiernan's Web site devoted to the project, available at http://www.uky.edu/~kiernan/BL/kportico.html. Included on this Web site is the original 1993 project prospectus, an overview of the project's early history, a detailed description and complete "help" guide to the 2003 edition (version 2.0), as well as articles written by Kiernan, Prescott, and others about the genesis and execution of the project.

46 Andrew Prescott, "The Electronic *Beowulf* and Digital Restoration," *Literary and Linguistic Computing* 12 (1997): 185–95; available at the project Web site, cited in n. 45 above, under "Articles."

47 Roger Chartier, *The Order of Books: Readers, Authors, and Libraries in Europe between the Fourteenth and Eighteenth Centuries* (Stanford, 1994), p. 89.

48 Charter, *The Order of Books*, p. 14.

49 Zygmunt Bauman, *Liquid Love: On the Frailty of Human Bonds* (Cambridge, Eng., 2003), p. 62.

50 Bauman, *Liquid Love*, p. 62.

51 John M. Hill, *The Cultural World in "Beowulf"* (Toronto, 1995), pp. 4, 5.

52 Hill, *The Cultural World in "Beowulf,"* pp. 6–7.

53 Nicholas Howe, "*Beowulf* and the Ancestral Homeland," *Migration and Mythmaking in Anglo-Saxon England* (1989; reprint Notre Dame, 2001), pp. 143–80.

54 Clare A. Lees, "Men and *Beowulf*," in *Medieval Masculinities: Regarding Men in the Middle Ages*, ed. Clare A. Lees (Minneapolis, 1994), p. 142. This essay is reprinted in this volume.

55 In his essay reprinted in this volume, Hill argues that what we might want to believe are "dismaying" episodes of violence in the poem, such as the digressive

asides recounting blood-soaked feuds between in-laws, are, rather, "socially acute meditations on the prospects for settlement, for accomplished and extended community, between groups who bring histories of past strife to their efforts at composing a feud," and they are also positive "meditations on the dynamic of group reformation" ("The Ethnopsychology of In-Law Feud and the Remaking of Group Identity in *Beowulf*: The Cases of Hengest and Ingeld," *Philological Quarterly* 78 [1999]: 97). This stands in stark contrast to Lees's idea that *Beowulf* "dwells on death and lingers on the tearing of vertebrae, the severed arm, the burnt body," and that the masculinist heroic ethos represented in the poem not only desires blood, but demands it ("Men and *Beowulf*," p. 143).

[56] Bauman, *Liquid Love*, p. 73. Hill himself would agree, and writes that, "To describe a social world of face-to-face relationships does not commit one to a frozen system. In fact, no social world can stay the same for ever or even for some very long time; as agents interact they of course usually do not seek change, given that their understanding of the rules, the arrangements, the relationships provide them with ways to advance themselves, manipulate the system, and compete. . . . Yet changes enter in; even a studied attempt to keep everything the same changes the social scheme of things" (e-mail communication from John Hill to Eileen Joy, 27 Feb. 2006).

[57] Earl, *Thinking About "Beowulf,"* p. 11.

[58] James W. Earl, "Reading *"Beowulf"* With Original Eyes," in this volume.

[59] A. O. Scott, "A Future More Nasty, Because It's So Near," review of *Code 46, New York Times*, 6 Aug. 2004.

[60] The title of the film, *Code 46*, is a reference to the fictional international law within the film that states, "Any human being who shares the same nuclear gene set as another human being is deemed to be genetically identical. The relations of one are the relations of all. Due to IVF, DI embryo splitting and cloning techniques it is necessary to prevent any accidental or deliberate genetically incestuous reproduction."

[61] Bauman, *Liquid Modernity*, pp. 6–8, 27.

[62] Howe, "Historicist Approaches," p. 82.

[63] Edward Said, "The World, the Text, and the Critics," *The World, the Text, and the Critic* (Cambridge, Mass., 1983), pp. 35, 39. This essay is reprinted in this volume.

[64] Said, "The World, the Text, and the Critic," pp. 53, 39.

[65] Frantzen, *Desire for Origins*, pp. 175, 181.

[66] Seth Lerer, "Hrothgar's Hilt and the Reader in *Beowulf*," *Literacy and Power in Anglo-Saxon England* (Lincoln, Nebr., 1991), p. 193. Lerer's essay is reprinted in this volume. Michael Near has also written about *Beowulf* as a poem that

is concerned with an emerging "literacy," and he argues that, "implicit in the poem's involvement with language is a marked and persistent hostility toward the epistemological foundation underpinning the practice of literacy" ("Anticipating Alienation: *Beowulf* and the Intrusion of Literacy," *PMLA* [1993]: 321).

[67] Earl, *Thinking About "Beowulf*," p. 188.

[68] Earl, *Thinking About "Beowulf*," p. 168.

[69] On the subject of the poem holding in balance, through its appositional structure, two opposed worldviews—paganism and Christianity—see Fred C. Robinson, *"Beowulf" and the Appositive Style* (Knoxville, 1983).

[70] Niles, "Locating *Beowulf* in Literary History," pp. 81, 95. The date of *Beowulf's* composition, as mentioned previously, has long been a contentious issue among scholars, but Niles believes the most plausible time period is the century preceding the date of the manuscript, which can be dated on paleographical grounds to ca. 1000 CE, where the poem can be seen as relevant to "the period of nation-building following the ninth-century Viking invasions," as well as a "response to the two great sources of tension in English culture during the late sixth through early tenth centuries: the integration of Germanic culture and Christian faith into a single system of thought and ethics, and the integration of all the peoples living south of Hadrian's Wall and east of Offa's Dyke into one English nation ruled by the West Saxon line" ("Locating *Beowulf* in Literary History," pp. 95, 106).

[71] Niles, "Locating *Beowulf* in Literary History," p. 80.

[72] Niles, "Locating *Beowulf* in Literary History," p. 81.

[73] Alfred K. Siewers, "Landscapes of Conversion: Guthlac's Mound and Grendel's Mere as Expressions of Anglo-Saxon Nation-Building," *Viator* 34 (2003): 3.

[74] Siewers, "Landscapes of Conversion," p. 33.

[75] Carol Braun Pasternack, "Post-Structuralist Theories: The Subject and the Text," in O'Keeffe, *Reading Old English Texts*, p. 185.

[76] Roberta Frank, "The *Beowulf* Poet's Sense of History," in *The Wisdom of Poetry: Essays in Early English Literature in Honor of Morton W. Bloomfield*, ed. Larry D. Benson and Siegfried Wenzel (Kalamazoo, 1982), pp. 61–62.

[77] Frank, "The *Beowulf* Poet's Sense of History," p. 63.

[78] Roberta Frank, "Germanic Legend in Old English Literature," in *The Cambridge Companion to Old English Literature*, ed. Malcolm Godden and Michael Lapidge (Cambridge, Eng., 1986), p. 98.

[79] Walter Benjamin, "Theses on the Philosophy of History," *Illuminations: Essays and Reflections*, ed. Hannah Arendt, trans. Harry Zohn (New York, 1968), p. 255.

[80] On the biblical, mythological, and other "roots" of the Grendelkin and the dragon in the poem, see Martin Puhvel, *"Beowulf" and the Celtic Tradition* (Waterloo,

1979); Ruth Mellinkoff, "Cain's Monstrous Progeny in *Beowulf*: Part I, Nochaic Tradition" and "Cain's Monstrous Progeny in *Beowulf*: Part II, Post-diluvian Survival," *Anglo-Saxon England* 8 (1979) and 9 (1980–81): 143–62 and 183–97, respectively; and Michael Lapidge, "*Beowulf*, Aldhelm, the *Liber Monstrorum* and Wessex," Studia Medievalia, 3rd ser., 23 (1982): 151–92, and "*Beowulf* and the Psychology of Terror," in *Heroic Poetry in the Anglo-Saxon Period: Studies in Honor of Jess B. Bessinger, Jr.*, ed. Helen Damico and John Leyerle (Kalamazoo, 1993), pp. 373–402.

[81] Jeffrey Jerome Cohen, "The Ruins of Identity," *Of Giants: Sex, Monsters, and the Middle Ages* (Minneapolis, 1999), p. 4. Cohen's essay is reprinted in this volume.

[82] Earl, *Thinking About "Beowulf,"* p. 168.

[83] Jeffrey Jerome Cohen, *Medieval Identity Machines* (Minneapolis, 2003), pp. xxiii–xxiv.

[84] Richter, "History's Flight, Anselm Kiefer's Angels," p. 113. For critical appraisals of Kiefer's career, especially in relation to his treatment of German myth and history in his art, see, in addition to Richter's essay, Andreas Huyssens, "Anselm Kiefer: The Terror of History, the Temptation of Myth," *Twilight Memories: Marking Time in a Culture of Amnesia* (London, 1995), pp. 209–47, and Lisa Saltzman, *Anselm Kiefer and Art After Auschwitz* (Cambridge, Eng., 1999).

[85] Tolkien, "*Beowulf*: The Monsters and the Critics," p. 87.

[86] Richter, "History's Flight, Anselm Kiefer's Angels," pp. 114–15.

[87] Charles Shepherdson, "History and the Real: Foucault with Lacan," *Postmodern Culture* 5 (1995).

[88] For an overview of some of the most important work in this vein, see Cathy Caruth, ed., *Trauma: Explorations in Memory* (Baltimore, 1995); Shoshana Felman and Dori Laub, *Testimony: Crises of Witnessing in Literature, Psychoanalysis, and History* (New York, 1992); Patrick Hutton, *History as an Art of Memory* (Hanover, N.H., 1993); Saul Friedlander, *Memory, History, and the Extermination of the Jews of Europe* (Bloomington, 1993); Dominick LaCapra, *History and Memory After Auschwitz* and *Writing History, Writing Trauma*; Jacques Le Goff, *Histoire et mémoire*, (Paris, 1988); Pierre Nora, ed., *Les lieux de mémoire*, 3 vols. (Paris, 1984–92); Eric Santner, *Stranded Objects: Mourning, Melancholia, and Film in Postwar Germany* (Ithaca, N.Y., 1990); Jay Winter, *Sites of Memory, Sites of Mourning: The Great War in European Cultural History* (Cambridge, Eng., 1995); and Edith Wyschogrod, *An Ethics of Remembering: History, Heterology, and the Nameless Others* (Chicago, 1998). In medieval studies, some significant works in "history and memory" studies are Mary Carruthers, *The Book of Memory: A Study of Memory in Medieval Culture* (Cambridge, Eng., 1990);

Janet Coleman, *Ancient and Medieval Memories: Studies in the Reconstruction of the Past* (Cambridge, Eng., 1992); James Fentress and Chris Wickham, eds., *Social Memory* (Oxford, 1992); and Patrick Geary, *Phantoms of Remembrance: Memory and Oblivion at the End of the First Millennium* (Princeton, 1994). There is also an interdisciplinary academic journal devoted to the field—*History and Memory*, published by Indiana University Press.

89   Jacques Le Goff, *Memory and History*, trans. Steven Rendall and Elizabeth Claman (New York, 1992), pp. 97–98.

90   Niles, "Appropriations: A Concept of Culture," pp. 208, 209.

91   Niles, "Appropriations: A Concept of Culture," 220. We would point out here, however, that we do quibble a bit with Niles's notion that "it no longer matters what 'really happened' in history." We think it matters a great deal, especially to the historian who might believe, along with Walter Benjamin that "[t]here is a secret agreement between past generations and the present one. Our coming was expected on earth. Like every generation that preceded us, we have been endowed with a weak Messianic power, a power to which the past has a special claim. That claim cannot be settled cheaply" ("Theses on a Philosophy of History," p. 254). Niles's statement is a fairly safe one to make when discussing a past for which no forms of "living memory" or living witnesses exist, whereas if one were to apply the phrase "what's done is done" to something like the Holocaust or the Rwandan genocide, or even to World War I, we might be appalled at its insensitivity, while still recognizing the general truth of the statement. Inevitably, this raises the question of the *ethics of remembering*, which is especially acute with respect to very recent traumatic events, such as the 9/11 World Trade Center attacks or the incidents of torture in the prison at Abu Ghraib in Iraq. With respect to events such as these, when perpetrators and victims alike are, so to speak, still "at large," the question of "what really happened" matters very much, indeed. With respect to *Beowulf*, we would say that the text, however we might want to rearticulate it in relation to present concerns, and regardless of its "fictionality," is also always and irrevocably an historical artifact—"a gift of the past to a present affected with futurity" that is inscribed with "the *vouloir dire* of a people that has been silenced, of the dead others" (Wyschogrod, *An Ethics of Remembering*, p. 248). In this sense, the question of an "ethics of remembering" should also be examined in relation to how we read and understand *Beowulf*.

92   Claire A. Sponsler, "In Transit: Theorizing Cultural Appropriation in Medieval Europe," *Journal of Medieval and Early Modern Studies* 32 (2002): 18.

93   Sponsler, "In Transit: Theorizing Cultural Appropriation," p. 19.

94   John Mitchell Kemble, ed., *The Anglo-Saxon Poems of "Beowulf," the Traveller's Song, and the Fight at Finnesburh* (London, 1833).

[95] We are borrowing the term *lieu de memoire*, or "memory site," from the work of the French historian Pierre Nora. According to Lawrence Kritzman, Nora coined the term to denote the "'memory places' of French national identity as they have been constructed since the middle ages," and memory must be here understood, not in its literal sense, but in its "'sacred context' as the variety of forms through which cultural communities imagine themselves in diverse representational modes" ("Foreword," in Pierre Nora et al., *Realms of Memory: The Construction of the French Past*, Vol. 1: Conflicts and Divisions, ed. Lawrence D. Kritzman, trans. Arthur Goldhammer [New York, 1996], p. ix). Memory places in French culture cover a broad variety of "sites," including the prehistoric caves at Lascaux, Joan of Arc, the Eiffel Tower, Versailles, the films of Truffaut and Godard, Gitanes cigarettes, just to name a few, all of which, in Kritzman's words, are ultimately "the result of an imaginary process that codifies and represents the historical consciousness of 'quintessential France'" ("Foreword," p. x).

[96] Tolkien, "*Beowulf*: The Monsters and the Critics," p. 54.

[97] Howe, "Historicist Approaches," p. 79.

[98] Howe, "Historicist Approaches," p. 88.

[99] Much recent work in history has begun to question the standard historical narrative of a late antiquity/early medieval Europe as having been shaped by a long period of Germanic expansion and migration, often referred to as the Migration Era. According to Walter Goffart, recent studies of migration by demographers, archaeologists, economic historians, geographers, and social scientists have shown that migration has been a "ubiquitous" and "continuous phenomen[on] embedded in the social and economic framework of human organizations" ("Does the Distant Past Impinge on the Invasion Age Germans?" in *On Barbarian Identity*, ed. Andrew Gillett [Turnhout, 2002], p. 29, n. 32]). Migration is not the unique exception but rather the rule of thumb of human history. See also *Migration, Migration History, History: Old Paradigms and New Perspectives*, ed. Jan Lucassen and Leo Lucassen, International and Comparative Social History, vol. 4 (Bern, 1997).

[100] Tolkein, "*Beowulf*: The Monsters and the Critics," p. 67.

[101] Janet Thormann, "Enjoyment of Violence and Desire for History in *Beowulf*," in this volume.

[102] Susan M. Kim, "'As I Once Did with Grendel': Boasting and Nostalgia in *Beowulf*," *Modern Philology* 103.1 (2005): 19. This essay is reprinted in this volume.

[103] Kim, "'As I Once Did with Grendel,'" p. 20.

[104] Kim, "'As I Once Did with Grendel,'" p. 27.

[105] Richter, "History's Flight, Anselm Kiefer's Angels," p. 115.

[106] Ker, *The Dark Ages*, pp. 85, 84.

[107] Ker, *The Dark Ages*, p. 85.

[108] Richter, "History's Flight, Anselm Kiefer's Angels," p. 115.

[109] Michel de Certeau, *The Writing of History*, trans. Tom Conley (New York, 1988), pp. 9, 10.

[110] W. G. Sebald, "An Attempt at Restitution," *The New Yorker*, 20 & 27 Dec. 2004: 112.

[111] Sebald, "An Attempt at Restitution," p. 112.

[112] Sebald, "An Attempt at Restitution," p. 112.

[113] Sebald, "An Attempt at Restitution," p. 114.

[114] Richter, "History's Flight, Anselm Kiefer's Angels," p. 128.

[115] Bruce D. Gilchrist, "'What am I supposed to do with this gobstopper?' Metonymy and Trauma in *Beowulf*," unpublished essay.

[116] Gilchrist, "'What am I supposed to do with this gobstopper?'"

[117] Said, "The World, the Text, and the Critic," p. 51.

[118] Wallace Stevens, "Description without Place," *The Palm at the End of the Mind: Selected Poems and a Play*, ed. Holly Stevens (New York, 1972), p. 276.

THE WORLD, THE TEXT, AND THE CRITIC

EDWARD SAID

Since he deserted the concert stage in 1964, the Canadian pianist Glenn Gould has confined his work to records, television, and radio. There is some disagreement among critics as to whether Gould is always, or only sometimes, a convincing interpreter of one or another piano piece, but there is no doubt that each of his performances now is at least special. One example of how Gould has been operating recently is suited for discussion here. In 1970 he issued a record of his performance of Beethoven's Fifth Symphony in the Liszt piano transcription. Quite aside from the surprise one felt at Gould's eccentric choice of the piece (which seemed more peculiar than usual even for the arch-eccentric Gould, whose controversial performances had formerly been associated either with classical or contemporary music), there were a number of oddities about this particular release. Liszt's Beethoven transcription was not only of the nineteenth century, but of its most egregious aspect, pianistically speaking: not content with transforming the concert experience into a feast for the virtuoso's self-exhibition, it also raided the literature of other instruments, making of their music a flamboyant occasion for the pianist's skill. Most transcriptions tend on the whole to sound thick or muddy, since frequently the piano is attempting to copy the texture of an orchestral sound. Liszt's Fifth

From *The World, the Text, and the Critic* (Cambridge, MA, 1983), pp. 31–53; reprinted with permission of Harvard University Press. The only alterations to the original have been to remove references Said makes in the body of the essay to other sections of the book in which this essay originally appeared.

Symphony was less offensive than most transcriptions, mainly because it was so brilliantly reduced for the piano, but even at its most clear the sound was an unusual one for Gould to be producing. His sound previously had been the clearest and most unadorned of all pianists', which was why he had the uncanny ability to turn Bach's counterpoint almost into a visual experience. The Liszt transcription, in short, was an entirely different idiom, and yet Gould was very successful in it. He sounded as Lisztian now as he had sounded Bachian in the past.

Nor was this all. Accompanying the main disc was another one, a longish, informal interview between Gould and, as I recall, a record company executive. Gould told his interlocutor that one reason for his escape from "live" performance was that he had developed a bad performing habit, a kind of stylistic exaggeration. On his tours of the Soviet Union, for example, he would notice that the large halls in which he was performing caused him to distort the phrases in a Bach partita—here he demonstrated by playing the distorted phrases—so that he could more effectively "catch" and address his listeners in the third balcony. He then played the same phrases to illustrate how much more correctly, and less seductively, he was performing music when no audience was actually present.

It may seem a little heavy-handed to draw out the little ironies from this situation—transcription, interview, and illustrated performance styles all included. But it serves my main point: any occasion involving the aesthetic or literary document and experience, on the one hand, and the critic's role and his or her "worldliness," on the other, cannot be a simple one. Indeed Gould's strategy is something of a parody of all the directions we might take in trying to get at what occurs between the world and the aesthetic or textual object. Here was a pianist who had once represented the ascetic performer in the service of music, transformed now into unashamed virtuoso, whose principal aesthetic position is supposed to be little better than that of a musical whore. And this from a man who markets his record as a "first" and then adds to it, not more music, but the kind of attention-getting immediacy gained in a personal interview. And finally all this is fixed on a mechanically repeatable object, which controls the most obvious signs of immediacy (Gould's voice, the peacock style of the Liszt transcription, the brash informality of an interview packed along with a disembodied performance) beneath a dumb, anonymous, and disposable disc of black plastic.

If one thinks about Gould and his record, parallels will emerge with the circumstances of written performance. First of all, there is the reproducible material existence of a text, which in the most recent phases of Walter

Benjamin's age of mechanical reproduction has multiplied and remultiplied so much as to exceed almost any imaginable limits. Both a recording and a printed object, however, are subject to certain legal, political, economic, and social constraints, so far as their sustained production and distribution are concerned; but why and how they are distributed are different matters. The main thing is that a written text of the sort we care about is originally the result of some immediate contact between author and medium. Thereafter it can be reproduced for the benefit of the world and according to conditions set by and in the world; however much the author demurs at the publicity he or she receives, once the text goes into more than one copy the author's work is in the world and beyond authorial control.

Second, a written and musical performance are both instances of style, in the simplest and least honorific sense of that very complex phenomenon. Once again I shall arbitrarily exclude a whole series of interesting complexities in order to insist on style as, from the standpoint of producer and receiver, the recognizable, repeatable, preservable sign of an author who reckons with an audience. Even if the audience is as restricted as oneself and as wide as the whole world, the author's style is partially a phenomenon of repetition and reception. But what makes style receivable as the signature of its author's manner is a collection of features variously called idiolect, voice, or irreducible individuality. The paradox is that something as impersonal as a text, or a record, can nevertheless deliver an imprint or a trace of something as lively, immediate, and transitory as a "voice." Glenn Gould's interview simply makes brutally explicit the frequent implicit need for reception or recognition that a text carries even in its most pristine, enshrined forms. A common form of this need is the staged (or recorded) convention of a talking voice addressing someone at a particular time and in a specific place. Considered as I have been considering it, then, style neutralizes the worldlessness, the silent, seemingly uncircumstanced existence of a solitary text. It is not only that any text, if it is not immediately destroyed, is a network of often colliding forces, but also that a text in its actually *being* a text is a being in the world; it therefore addresses anyone who reads, as Gould does throughout the very same record that is supposed to represent both his withdrawal from the world and his "new" silent style of playing without a live audience.

To be sure, texts do not speak in the ordinary sense of the word. Yet any simple diametric opposition asserted on the one hand between speech, bound by situation and reference, and on the other hand the text as an interception or suspension of speech's worldliness is, I think, misleading and largely simplified. Here is how Paul Ricoeur puts this opposition, which he says he has set up only for the sake of analytic clarification:

> In speech the function of reference is linked to the role of the *situation of discourse* within the exchange of language itself: in exchanging speech, the speakers are present to each other, but also to the circumstantial setting of discourse, not only the perceptual surroundings, but also the cultural background known by both speakers. It is in relation to this situation that discourse is fully meaningful: the reference to reality is in the last analysis reference to that reality which can be pointed out "around," so to speak, the instance of discourse itself. Language . . . and in general all the ostensive indicators of language serve to anchor discourse in the circumstantial reality which surrounds the instance of discourse. Thus, in living speech, the *ideal* meaning of what one says bends towards a *real* reference, namely to that "about which" one speaks . . . .
>
> This is no longer the case when a text takes the place of speech . . . . A text . . . is not without reference; it will be precisely the task of reading, as interpretation, to actualize the reference. At least, in this suspension wherein reference is deferred, in the sense that it is postponed, a text is somehow "in the air," outside of the world or without a world; by means of this obliteration of all relation to the world, every text is free to enter into relation with all the other texts which come to take the place of the circumstantial reality shown by living Speech.[1]

According to Ricoeur, speech and circumstantial reality exist in a state of presence, whereas writing and texts exist in a state of suspension—that is, outside circumstantial reality—until they are "actualized" and made present by the reader-critic. Ricoeur makes it seem as if the text and circumstantial reality, or what I shall call *worldliness*, play a game of musical chairs, one intercepting and replacing the other according to fairly crude signals. But this game takes place in the interpreter's head, a locale presumably without worldliness or circumstantiality. The critic-interpreter has his position reduced to that of a central bourse on whose floor occurs the transaction by which the text is shown to be meaning x while saying y. And as for what Ricoeur calls "deferred reference," what becomes of it during the interpretation? Quite simply, on the basis of a model of direct exchange, it comes back, made whole and actual by the critic's reading.

The principal difficulty with all this is that without sufficient argument Ricoeur assumes circumstantial reality to be symmetrically and exclusively the property of speech, or the speech situation, or what writers would have wanted to say had they not instead chosen to write. My contention is that worldliness does not come and go; nor is it here and there in the apologetic and soupy way by which we often designate history, a euphemism in such cases for the impossibly vague notion that all things take place in time. Moreover, critics are not merely the alchemical translators of texts into circumstantial reality or worldliness; for they too are subject to and producers of circumstances, which are felt regardless of whatever objectivity the critic's methods possess. The point is that texts have ways of existing that even in their most rarefied form are always enmeshed in circumstance, time, place, and society—in short, they are in the world, and hence worldly.[2] Whether a text is preserved or put aside for a period, whether it is on a library shelf or not, whether it is considered dangerous or not: these matters have to do with a text's being in the world, which is a more complicated matter than the private process of reading. The same implications are undoubtedly true of critics in their capacities as readers and writers in the world.

If my use of Gould's recording of the Beethoven Fifth Symphony serves any really useful purpose, it is to provide an instance of a quasi-textual object whose ways of engaging the world are both numerous and complicated, more complicated than Ricoeur's demarcation drawn between text and speech. These are the engagements I have been calling worldliness. But my principal concern here is not with an aesthetic object in general, but with the text in particular. Most critics will subscribe to the notion that every literary text is in some way burdened with its occasion, with the plain empirical realities from which it emerged. Pressed too far, such a notion earns the justified criticism of a stylistician like Michael Riffaterre, who, in "The Self-Sufficient Text," calls any reduction of a text to its circumstances a fallacy, biographical, genetic, psychological, or analogic.[3] Most critics would probably go along with Riffaterre in saying, yes, let's make sure that the text does not disappear under the weight of these fallacies. But, and here I speak mainly for myself, they're not entirely satisfied with the idea of a self-sufficient text. Is the alternative to the various fallacies *only* a hermetic textual cosmos, one whose significant dimension of meaning is, as Riffaterre says, a wholly inward or intellectual one? Is there no way of dealing with a text and its worldly circumstances fairly? No way to grapple with the problems of literary language except by cutting them off from the more plainly urgent ones of everyday, worldly language?

I have found a way of starting to deal with these questions in an unexpected place, which is perhaps why I shall now seem to digress. Consider the relatively unfamiliar field of medieval Arabic linguistic speculation. Many contemporary critics are interested in speculation about language in Europe, that is, in that special combination of theoretical imagination and empirical observation characterizing romantic philology, the rise of linguistics in the early nineteenth century, and the whole rich phenomenon of what Michel Foucault has called the discovery of language. Yet during the eleventh century in Andalusia, there existed a remarkably sophisticated and unexpectedly prophetic school of Islamic philosophic grammarians, whose polemics anticipate twentieth-century debates between structuralists and generative grammarians, between descriptivists and behaviorists. Nor is this all. One small group of these Andalusian linguists directed its energies against tendencies amongst rival linguists to turn the question of meaning in language into esoteric and allegorical exercises. Among the group were three linguists and theoretical grammarians, Ibn Hazm, Ibn Jinni, and Ibn Mada' al-Qurtobi, all of whom worked in Cordoba during the eleventh century, all belonging to the Zahirite school, all antagonists of the Batinist school. Batinists held that meaning in language is concealed within the words; meaning is therefore available only as the result of an inward-tending exegesis. The Zahirites—their name derives from the Arabic word for clear, apparent, and phenomenal; *Batin* connotes internal—argued that words had only a surface meaning, one that was anchored to a particular usage, circumstance, historical and religious situation.

The two opponents trace their origins back to readings of the sacred text, the Koran, and how that unique event—for, unlike the Bible, the Koran is an event—is to be read, understood, transmitted, and taught by later generations of believers. The Cordovan Zahirites attacked the excesses of the Batinists, arguing that the very profession of grammar (in Arabic *nahu*) was an invitation to spinning out private meanings in an otherwise divinely pronounced, and hence unchangeably stable, text. According to Ibn Mada', it was absurd even to associate grammar with a logic of understanding, since as a science grammar assumed, and often went so far as to create by retrospection, ideas about the use and meaning of words that implied a hidden level beneath words, available only to initiates.[4] Once you resort to such a level, anything becomes permissible by way of interpretation: there can be no strict meaning, no control over what words in fact say, no responsibility toward the words. The Zahirite effort was to restore by rationalization a system of reading a text in which attention was focused on the phenomenal words themselves, in what might be considered their once-and-for-all sense uttered for and during a specific occasion, not on hidden meanings they might later be supposed to contain. The Cordovan Zahirites in particular went very far in trying to provide a reading system that placed the tightest possible control over the reader and his circumstances. They did this principally by means of a theory of what a text is.

It is not necessary to describe this theory in detail. It is useful, however, to indicate how the controversy itself grew out of a sacred text whose authority derived from its being the uncreated word of God, directly and unilaterally transmitted to a Messenger at a particular moment in time. In contrast, texts within the Judeo-Christian tradition, at whose center is Revelation, cannot be reduced to a specific moment of divine intervention as a result of which the Word of God entered the world; rather the Word enters human history continually during and as a part of that history. So a very important place is given to what Roger Arnaldez calls "human factors" in the reception, transmission, and understanding of such a text.[5] Since the Koran is the result of a unique event, the literal "descent" into worldliness of a text, as well as its language and form, are then to be viewed as stable and complete. Moreover, the language of the text is Arabic, which therefore becomes a privileged language, and its vessel is the Prophet (or Messenger), Mohammed, similarly privileged. Such a text can be regarded as having an absolutely defined origin and consequently cannot be referred back to any particular interpreter or interpretation, although this is clearly what the Batinites tried to do (perhaps, it has been suggested, under the influence of Judeo-Christian exegetical techniques).

In his study of Ibn Hazm, Arnaldez puts his description of the Koran in the following terms: the Koran speaks of historical events, yet is not itself historical. It repeats past events, which it condenses and particularizes, yet is not itself an actually lived experience; it ruptures the human continuity of life, yet God does not enter temporality by a sustained or concerted act. The Koran evokes the memory of actions whose content repeats itself eternally in ways identical with itself, as warnings, orders, imperatives, punishments, rewards.[6] In short, the Zahirite position adopts a view of the Koran that is absolutely circumstantial without at the same time making that worldliness dominate the actual sense of the text: all this is the ultimate avoidance of vulgar determinism in the Zahirite position.

Hence Ibn Hazm's linguistic theory is based upon an analysis of the imperative mode, since, according to this, the Koran at its most radical verbal level is a text controlled by two paradigmatic imperatives, *iqra* (read or recite) and *qul* (tell).[7] Since those imperatives obviously control the circumstantial and historical appearance of the Koran (and its uniqueness as an event), and since they must also control uses (that is, readings) of the text thereafter, Ibn Hazm connects his analysis of the imperative mode with a juridical notion of *hadd*, a word meaning both a logico-grammatical definition and a limit. What transpires in the imperative mode, between the injunctions to read and write, is the delivery of an utterance (*khabar* in Arabic, translated by Arnaldez as *énoncé*), which is the verbal realization of a signifying intention, or *niyah*. Now the signifying intention is synonymous not with a psychological intention but exclusively with a verbal intention, itself something highly worldly—it takes place exclusively in the world, it is occasional and circumstantial in both a very precise and a wholly pertinent way. To signify is only to use language, and to use language is to do so according to certain lexical and syntactic rules, by which language is in and of the world; the Zahirite sees language as being regulated by real usage, and neither by abstract prescription nor by speculative freedom. Above all, language stands between man and a vast indefiniteness: if the world is a gigantic system of correspondences between words and objects, then it is verbal form—language in actual grammatical use—that allows us to isolate the denominated objects from among these massively ordered correspondences. Thus, as Arnaldez puts it, fidelity to such "true" aspects of language is an ascesis of the imagination.[8] A word has a strict meaning understood as an imperative, and with that meaning there also goes a strictly ordained series of resemblances (correspondences) to other words and meanings, which, strictly speaking, play around the first word. Thus figurative language (as it occurs even in the Koran), otherwise elusive and at the mercy of the virtuosic interpreter, is part of the actual structure of language, and part therefore of the collectivity of language users.

What Ibn Hazm does, Arnaldez reminds us, is to view language as possessing two seemingly antithetical characteristics: that of a divinely ordained institution, unchanging, immutable, logical, rational, intelligible; and that of an instrument existing as pure contingency, as an institution signifying meanings anchored in specific utterances. It is exactly because the Zahirites see language in this double perspective that they reject reading techniques that reduce words and their meanings back to radicals from which (in Arabic at least) they may be seen grammatically to derive. Each utterance is its own occasion and as such is firmly anchored in the worldly context in which it is applied. And because the Koran, which is the paradigmatic case of divine-and-human language, is a text that incorporates speaking and writing, reading and telling, Zahirite interpretation itself accepts as inevitable not the separation between speech and writing, not the disjunction between a text and its circumstantiality, but rather their necessary interplay. It is the interplay, the constitutive interaction, that makes possible this severe Zahirite notion of meaning.

I have very quickly summarized an enormously complex theory, for which I cannot claim any particular influence in Western European literature since the Renaissance, and perhaps not even in Arabic literature since the Middle Ages. But what ought to strike us forcibly about the whole theory is that it represents a considerably articulated thesis for dealing with a text as significant form, in which—and I put this as carefully as I can—worldliness, circumstantiality, the text's status as an event having sensuous particularity as well as historical contingency, are considered as being incorporated in the text, an infrangible part of its capacity for conveying and producing meaning. This means that a text has a specific situation, placing restraints upon the interpreter and his interpretation not because the situation is hidden within the text as a mystery, but rather because the situation exists at the same level of surface particularity as the textual object itself. There are many ways for conveying such a situation, but what I want to draw particular attention to here is an ambition (which the Zahirites have to an intense degree) on the part of readers and writers to grasp texts as objects whose interpretation—by virtue of the exactness of their situation in the world—*has already commenced* and are objects already constrained by, and constraining, their interpretation. Such texts can thereafter be construed as having need at most of complementary, as opposed to supplementary, readings.

• • •

Now I want to discuss some of the ways by which texts impose constraints upon their interpretation or, to put it metaphorically, the way the closeness of the world's body to the text's body forces readers to take both into consideration. Recent critical theory has placed undue emphasis on the limitlessness of interpretation. It is argued that, since all reading is misreading, no one reading is better than any other, and hence all readings, potentially infinite in number, are in the final analysis equally misinterpretations. A part of this has been derived from a conception of the text as existing within a hermetic, Alexandrian textual universe, which has no connection with actuality. This is a view I do not agree with, not simply because texts in fact are in the world but also because as texts they place themselves—one of their functions as texts is to place themselves—and indeed are themselves, by soliciting the world's attention. Moreover, their manner of doing this is to place restraints upon what can be done with them interpretively.

Modern literary history gives us a number of examples of writers whose text seems self-consciously to incorporate the explicit circumstances of its concretely imagined, and even described, situation. One type of author—I shall be discussing three instances, Gerard Manley Hopkins, Oscar Wilde, and Joseph Conrad—deliberately conceives the text as supported by a discursive situation involving speaker and audience; the designed interplay between speech and reception, between verbality and textuality, *is* the text's situation, its placing of itself in the world.

The three authors I mentioned did their major work between 1875 and 1915. The subject matter of their writing varies so widely among them that similarities have to be looked for elsewhere. Let me begin with a journal entry by Hopkins:

> The winter was called severe. There were three spells of frost with skating, the third beginning on Feb. 9. No snow to speak of till that day. Some days before Feb. 7 I saw catkins hanging. On the 9th there was snow but not lying on the heads of the blades. As we went down a field near Caesar's Camp I noticed it before me *squalentem,* coat below coat, sketched in intersecting edges bearing 'idiom,' all down the slope:—I have no other word yet for that which takes the eye or mind in a bold hand or effective sketching or in marked features or again in graphic writing, which not being beauty nor true inscape yet gives interest and makes ugliness even better than meaninglessness.[9]

Hopkins' earliest writing attempts in this way to render scenes from nature as exactly as possible. Yet he is never a passive transcriber since for him "this world then is word, expression, news of God."[10] Every phenomenon in nature, he wrote in the sonnet "As Kingfishers Catch Fire," *tells* itself in the world as a sort of lexical unit: "Each mortal thing does one thing and the same: / Deals out that being indoors each one dwells; / Selves—goes itself; *myself* it speaks and spells, / Crying *What I do is me: for that I came.*"[11] So in the notebook entry, Hopkins' observation of nature is dynamic. He sees in the frost an intention to speak or mean, its layered coats *taking* one's attention because of the idiom it bears toward meaning or expression. The writer is as much a respondent as he is a describer. Similarly, the reader is a full participant in the production of meaning, being obliged as a mortal thing to act, to produce some sense that even ugliness is still better than meaninglessness.

This dialectic of production is everywhere present in Hopkins' work. Writing is telling; nature is telling; reading is telling. He wrote to Robert Bridges on May 21, 1878, that in order to do a certain poem justice "you must not slovenly read it with the eyes but with your ears, as if the paper were declaiming it at you . . . Stress is the life of it."[12] Seven years later he specified more strictly that "poetry is the darling child of speech, of lips and spoken utterance: it must be spoken; *till it is spoken, it does not perform*, it is not itself. Sprung rhythm gives back to poetry its true soul and self. As poetry is emphatically speech, speech purged of dross like gold in the furnace, so it must have emphatically the essential elements of speech."[13] So close is the identification in Hopkins' mind among world, word, and the utterance, the three coming alive together as a moment of performance, that he envisages little need for critical intervention. It is the written text that provides the immediate circumstantial reality for the poem's "play" (the word is Hopkins'). So far from being a document associated with other lifeless, worldless texts, Hopkins' own text was for him his child; when he destroyed his poems he spoke of the slaughter of the innocents, and everywhere he speaks of writing as the exercise of his male gift. At the moment of greatest desolation in his career, in the poem entitled simply "To R. B.," the urgency of his feeling of poetic aridity is expressed biologically. When he comes to describe finally what it is he now writes, he says:

> O then if in my lagging lines you miss
> The roll, the rise, the carol, the creation,
> My winter world, that scarcely breathes that bliss
> Now, yields you, with some sighs, our explanation.[14]

Because his text has lost its ability to incorporate the stress of creation, and because it is no longer performance but what in another poem he calls "dead letters," he now can only write an explanation, which is lifeless speech "bending towards a real reference."

It was said of Oscar Wilde by one of his contemporaries that everything he spoke sounded as if it were enclosed in quotation marks. This is no less true of everything he wrote, for such was the consequence of having a pose, which Wilde defined as "a formal recognition of the importance of treating life from a definite reasoned standpoint."[15] Or as Algernon retorts to Jack's accusation that "you always want to argue about things" in *The Importance of Being Earnest*: "That's exactly what things were originally made for."[16] Always ready with a quotable comment, Wilde filled his manuscripts with epigrams on every conceivable subject. What he wrote was intended either for more comment or for quotation or, most important, for tracing back to him. There are obvious social reasons for some of this egoism, which he made no attempt to conceal in his quip, "To love oneself is the beginning of a life-long romance," but they do not exhaust the speaking in Wilde's style. Having forsworn action, life, and nature for their incompleteness and diffusion, Wilde took as his province a theoretical, ideal world in which, as he told Alfred Douglas in *De Profundis*, conversation was the basis of all human relations.[17] Since conflict inhibited conversation as Wilde understood it from the Platonic dialogue, the mode of interchange was to be by epigram. This epigram, in Northrop Frye's terminology, is Wilde's radical of presentation: a compact utterance capable of the utmost range of subject matter, the greatest authority, and the least equivocation as to its author. When he invaded other forms of art, Wilde converted them into longer epigrams. As he said of drama: "I took the drama, the most objective form known to art, and made it as personal a mode of expression as the lyric or the sonnet, at the same time that I widened its range and enriched its characterization." No wonder he could say: "I summed up all systems in a phrase, and all existence in an epigram."[18]

De Profundis records the destruction of the utopia whose individualism and unselfish selfishness Wilde had adumbrated in *The Soul of Man Under Socialism*. From a free world to a prison and a circle of suffering: how is the change accomplished? Wilde's conception of freedom was to be found in *The Importance of Being Earnest*, where conflicting characters turn out to be brothers after all just because they say they are. What is written down (for example, the army lists consulted by Jack) merely confirms what all along has been capriciously, though elegantly, said. This transformation, from opponent into brother, is what Wilde had in mind in connecting the intensification of personality with its multiplication. When the communication between men no longer possesses the freedom of conversation, when it is confined to the merely legal liability of print, which is not ingeniously quotable but, because it has been signed, is now criminally actionable, the utopia crumbles. As he reconsidered his life in *De Profundis*, Wilde's imagination was transfixed by the effects of one text upon his life. But he uses it to show how in going from speech to print, which in a sense all of his other more fortunate texts had managed somehow to avoid by virtue of their epigrammatic individuality, he had been ruined. Wilde's lament in what follows is that a text has too much, not too little, circumstantial reality. Hence, with Wildean paradox, its vulnerability:

> You send me a very nice poem, of the undergraduate school of verse, for my approval: I reply by a letter of fantastic literary conceits . . . . Look at the history of that letter! It passes from you into the hands of a loathsome companion: from him to a gang of blackmailers: copies of it are sent about London to my friends, and to the manager of the theatre where my work is being performed: every construction but the right one is put on it: Society is thrilled with the absurd rumors that I have had to pay a huge sum of money for having written an infamous letter to you: this forms the basis of your father's worst attack: I produce the original letter myself in Court to show what it really is: it is denounced by your father's counsel as a revolting and insidious attempt to corrupt Innocence: ultimately it forms part of a criminal charge: the Crown takes it up: the Judge sums up on it with little learning and much morality: I go to prison for it at last. That is the result of writing you a charming letter.[19]

For in a world described by George Eliot as a "huge whispering gallery," the effects of writing can be grave indeed: "As the stone which has been kicked by generations of clowns may come by curious little links of effect under the eyes of a scholar, through whose labors it may at last fix the date of invasions and unlock religions, so a bit of ink and paper which has long been an innocent wrapping or stop-gap may at last be laid open under the one pair of eyes which have knowledge enough to turn it into the opening of a catastrophe."[20] If Dr. Casaubon's caution has any purpose at all, it is by rigid secrecy and an endlessly postponing scriptive will to forestall the opening of a catastrophe. Yet he cannot succeed since Eliot is at pains to show that even Casaubon's tremendously nursed *Key* is a text, and therefore in the world. Unlike Wilde's, Casaubon's disgrace is posthumous, but their implication in a sort of worldly textuality takes place for the same reason, which is their commitment to what Eliot calls an "embroiled medium."

Lastly, consider Conrad. All of Conrad's work is really made out of secondary, reported speech, and the interplay between appeals to the eye and the ear in his work is highly organized and subtle, and is that work's meaning. The Conradian encounter is not simply between a man and his destiny embodied in a moment of extremity, but just as persistently, the encounter between speaker and hearer. Marlow is Conrad's chief invention for this encounter, a man who is haunted by the knowledge that a person such as

13

Kurtz or Jim "existed for me, and after all it is only through me that he exists for you."[21] The chain of humanity—"we exist only in so far as we hang together"—is the transmission of actual speech, and existence, from one mouth and then from one eye to another. Every text that Conrad wrote presents itself as unfinished and still in the making. "And besides, the last word is not said,—probably shall never be said. Are not our lives too short for that full utterance which through all our stammerings is of course our only and abiding intention?"[22] Texts convey the stammerings that never ever achieve that full utterance, the statement of wholly satisfactory presence, which remains distant, attenuated somewhat by a grand gesture like Jim's self-sacrifice. Yet even though the gesture closes off a text circumstantially, in no way does it empty it of its actual urgency.

This is a good time to remark that the Western novelistic tradition is full of examples of texts insisting not only upon their circumstantial reality but also upon their status as *already* fulfilling a function, a reference, or a meaning in the world. Cervantes and Cide Hamete come immediately to mind. More impressive is Richardson playing the role of "mere" editor for *Clarissa*, simply placing those letters in successive order after they have done what they have done, arranging to fill the text with printer's devices, reader's aids, analytic contents, retrospective meditations, commentary, so that a collection of letters grows to fill the world and occupy all space, to become a circumstance as large and as engrossing as the reader's very understanding. Surely the novelistic imagination has always included this unwillingness to cede control over the text in the world, or to release it from the discursive and human obligations of all human presence; hence the desire (almost a principal action of many novels) to turn the text back, if not directly into speech, then at least into circumstantial, as opposed to meditative, duration.

No novelist, however, can be quite as explicit about circumstances as Marx is in *The Eighteenth Brumaire of Louis Bonaparte*. To my mind no work is as brilliant and as compelling in the exactness with which circumstances (the German word is *Umstände*) are shown to have made the nephew possible, not as an innovator, but as a farcical repetition of the great uncle. What Marx attacks are the atextual theses that history is made up of free events and that history is guided by superior individuals.[23] By inserting Louis Bonaparte in a whole intricate system of repetitions, by which first Hegel, then the ancient Romans, the 1789 revolutionaries, Napoleon I, the bourgeois interpreters, and finally the fiascoes of 1848–1851 are all seen in a pseudo-analogical order of descending worth, increasing derivativeness, and deceptively harmless masquerading, Marx effectively textualizes the random appearance of a new Caesar. Here we have the case of a text itself providing a world-historical situation with circumstances otherwise hidden in the deception of a *roi des drôles*. What is ironic is how a text, by being a text, by insisting upon and employing all the devices of textuality, preeminent among them *repetition*, historicizes and problematizes all the fugitive significance that has chosen Louis Bonaparte as its representative.

There is another aspect to what I have just been saying. In producing texts with either a firm claim on or an explicit will to worldliness, these writers and genres have valorized speech, making it the tentacle by which an otherwise silent text ties itself to the world of discourse. By the valorization of speech I mean that the discursive, circumstantially dense interchange of speaker facing hearer is made to stand—sometimes misleadingly—for a democratic equality and copresence in actuality between speaker and hearer. Not only is the discursive relation far from equal in actuality, but the text's attempt to dissemble by seeming to be open democratically to anyone who might read it is also an act of bad faith. (Incidentally, one of the strengths of Zahirite theory is that it dispels the illusion that a surface reading, which is the Zahirite ambition, is anything but difficult.) Texts of such a length as *Tom Jones* aim to occupy leisure time of a quality not available to just anyone. Moreover, all texts essentially dislodge other texts or, more frequently, take the place of something else. As Nietzsche had the perspicacity to see, texts are fundamentally facts of power, not of democratic exchange.[24] They compel attention away from the world even as their beginning intention as texts, coupled with the inherent authoritarianism of the authorial authority (the repetition in this phrase is a deliberate emphasis on the tautology within all texts, since all texts are in some way self-confirmatory), makes for sustained power.

Yet in the genealogy of texts there is a first text, a sacred prototype, a scripture, which readers always approach through the text before them, either as petitioning suppliants or as initiates amongst many in a sacred chorus supporting the central patriarchal text. Northrop Frye's theory of literature makes it apparent that the displacing power in all texts finally derives from the displacing power of the Bible, whose centrality, potency, and dominating anteriority inform all Western literature. The same is no less true, in the different modes I discussed earlier, of the Koran. Both in the Judeo-Christian and in the Islamic traditions these hierarchies repose upon a solidly divine, or quasi-divine, language, a language whose uniqueness, however, is that it is theologically and humanly circumstantial.

15

We often forget that modern Western philology, which began in the early nineteenth century, undertook to revise commonly accepted ideas about language and its divine origins. That revision tried first to determine which was the first language and then, failing in that ambition, proceeded to reduce language to specific circumstances: language groups, historical and racial theories, geographical and anthropological theses. A particularly interesting example of how such investigations went is Ernest Renan's career as a philologist; that was his real profession, not that of the boring sage. His first serious work was his 1848 analysis of Semitic languages, revised and published in 1855 as *Histoire générale et système comparé des langues sémitiques*. Without this study, the *Vie de Jésus* could not have been written. The accomplishment of the *Histoire générale* was scientifically to describe the inferiority of Semitic languages, principally Hebrew, Aramaic, and Arabic, the medium of three purportedly sacred texts that had been spoken or at least informed by God—the Torah, the Koran, and, later, the derivative Gospels. Thus in the *Vie de Jésus* Renan would be able to insinuate that the so-called sacred texts, delivered by Moses, Jesus, or Mohammed, could not have anything divine in them if the very medium of their supposed divinity, as well as the body of their message to and in the world, was made up of such comparatively poor worldly stuff. Renan argued that, even if these texts were prior to all others in the West, they held no theologically dominant position.

Renan first reduced texts from objects of divine intervention in the world's business to objects of historical materiality. God as author-authority had little value after Renan's philological and textual revisionism. Yet in dispensing with divine authority Renan put philological power in its place. What comes to replace divine authority is the textual authority of the philological critic who has the skill to separate Semitic languages from the languages of Indo-European culture. Not only did Renan kill off the extratextual validity of the great Semitic texts; he confined them as objects of European study to a scholarly field thereafter to be known as Oriental.[25] The Orientalist is a Renan or a Gobineau, Renan's contemporary quoted here and there in the 1855 edition of the *Histoire générale*, for whom the old hierarchy of sacred Semitic texts has been destroyed as if by an act of parricide; the passing of divine authority enables the appearance of European ethnocentrism, by which the methods and the discourse of Western scholarship confine inferior non-European cultures to a position of subordination. Oriental texts come to inhabit a realm without development or power, one that exactly corresponds to the position of a colony for European texts and culture. All this takes place at the same time that the great European colonial empires in the East are beginning or, in some cases, flourishing.

I have introduced this brief account of the twin origin of the Higher Criticism and of Orientalism as a European scholarly discipline in order to be able to speak about the fallacy of imagining the life of texts as being pleasantly ideal and without force or conflict and, conversely, the fallacy of imagining the discursive relations in actual speech to be, as Ricoeur would have it, a relation of equality between hearer and speaker.

Texts incorporate discourse, sometimes violently. There are other ways, too. Michel Foucault's archeological analyses of systems of discourse are premised on the thesis, adumbrated by Marx and Engels in *The German Ideology*, that "in every society the production of discourse is at once controlled, selected, organized and redistributed according to a certain number of procedures, whose role is to avert its powers and dangers, to cope with chance events, to evade its ponderous, awesome materiality." Discourse in this passage means what is written and spoken. Foucault's contention is that the fact of writing itself is a systematic conversion of the power relationship between controller and controlled into "mere" written words—but writing is a way of disguising the awesome materiality of so tightly controlled and managed a production. Foucault continues:

> In a society such as our own we all know the rules of *exclusion*. The most obvious and familiar of these concerns what is *prohibited*. We know perfectly well that we are not free to say just anything. We have three types of prohibition, covering objects, ritual with its surrounding circumstances, and the privileged or exclusive right to speak of a particular subject; these prohibitions interrelate, reinforce and complement each other, forming a complex web, continually subject to modification. I will note simply that the areas where this web is most tightly woven today, where the danger spots are most numerous, are those dealing with politics and sexuality. ... In appearance, speech may well be of little account, but the prohibitions surrounding it soon reveal its links with desire and power.... Speech is no mere verbalization of conflicts and systems of domination ... it is the very object of man's conflicts.[26]

Despite Ricoeur's simplified idealization, and far from being a type of conversation between equals, the discursive situation is more usually like the unequal relation between colonizer and colonized, oppressor and oppressed. Some of the great modernists, Proust and Joyce prominent among them, had an acute understanding of this asymmetry; their representations of the discursive situation always show it in this power-political light. Words and texts are so much of the world that their effectiveness, in some cases even their use, are matters having to do with ownership, authority, power, and the imposition of force. A formative moment in Stephen Dedalus' rebellious consciousness occurs as he converses with the English dean of studies:

> What is that beauty which the artist struggles to express from lumps of earth, said Stephen coldly.
>
> The little word seemed to have turned a rapier point of his sensitiveness against this courteous and vigilant foe. He felt with a smart of dejection that the man to whom he was speaking was a countryman of Ben Jonson. He thought:—The language in which we are speaking is his before it is mine. How different are the words *home, Christ, ale, master,* on his lips and on mine! I cannot speak or write these words without unrest of spirit. His language, so familiar and so foreign, will always be for me an acquired speech. I have not made or accepted its words. My voice holds them at bay. My soul frets in the shadow of his language.[27]

Joyce's work is a recapitulation of those political and racial separations, exclusions, prohibitions instituted ethnocentrically by the ascendant European culture throughout the nineteenth century. The situation of discourse, Stephen Dedalus knows, hardly puts equals face to face. Rather, discourse often puts one interlocutor above another or, as Frantz Fanon brilliantly described the extreme to which it could be taken in *The Wretched of the Earth,* discourse reenacts the geography of the colonial city:

> The zone where the natives live is not complementary to the zone inhabited by the settlers. The two zones are opposed, but not in the service of a higher unity. Obedient to the rules of pure Aristotelian logic, they both follow the principle of reciprocal exclusivity. No conciliation is possible, for of the two terms, one is superfluous. The settlers' town is a strongly-built town, all made of stone and steel. It is a brightly-lit town; the streets are covered with asphalt, and the garbage-cans swallow all the leavings, unseen, unknown and hardly thought about. The settler's feet are never visible, except perhaps in the sea; but there you're never close enough to see them. His feet are protected by strong shoes although the streets of his town are clean and even, with no holes or stones. The settler's town is a well-fed town, an easygoing town; its belly is always full of good things. The settler's town is a town of white people, of foreigners.

The town belonging to the colonized people, or at least the native town, the negro village, the medina, the reservation, is a place of ill fame, peopled by men of evil repute. They are born there, it matters little where or how; they die there, it matters not where, nor how. It is a world without spaciousness; men live there on top of each other, and their huts are built on top of the other. The native town is a hungry town, starved of bread, of meat, of shoes, of coal, of light. The native town is a crouching village, a town on its knees, a town wallowing in the mire. It is a town of niggers and dirty arabs. The look that the native turns on the settler's town is a look of lust, a look of envy; it expresses his dreams of possession—all manner of possession: to set at the settler's table, to sleep in the settler's bed, with his wife if possible. The colonized man is an envious man. And this the settler knows very well; when their glances meet he ascertains bitterly, always on the defensive "They want to take our place." It is true, for there is no native who does not dream at least once a day of setting himself up in the settler's place.[28]

No wonder that the Fanonist solution to such discourse is violence.

Such examples make untenable the opposition between texts and the world, or between texts and speech. Too many exceptions, too many historical, ideological, and formal circumstances, implicate the text in actuality, even if a text may also be considered a silent printed object with its own unheard melodies. The concert of forces by which a text is engendered and maintained as a fact not of mute ideality but of *production* dispels the symmetry of even rhetorical oppositions. Moreover, the textual utopia envisioned each in his own way by T. S. Eliot and Northrop Frye, whose nightmarish converse is Borges' library, is at complete odds with form in texts. My thesis is that any centrist, exclusivist conception of the text, or for that matter of the discursive situation as defined by Ricoeur, ignores the self-confirming will to power from which many texts can spring. The minimalist impulse in Beckett's work is, I think, a counterversion of this will, a way of refusing the opportunity offered to him by modernist writing.

. . .

But where in all this is the critic and criticism? Scholarship, commentary, exegesis, *explication de texte*, history of ideas, rhetorical or semiological analyses: all these are modes of pertinence and of disciplined attention to the textual matter usually presented to the critic as already at hand. I shall concentrate now on the essay, which is the traditional form by which criticism has expressed itself. The central problem of the essay as a form is its *place*, by which I mean a series of three ways the essay has of being the form critics take, and locate themselves in, to do their work. Place therefore involves relations, affiliations, the critics fashion with the texts and audiences they address; it also involves the dynamic taking place of a critic's own text as it is produced.

The first mode of affiliation is the essay's relation to the text or occasion it attempts to approach. How does it come to the text of its choice? How does it enter that text? What is the concluding definition of its relation to the text and the occasion it has dealt with? The second mode of affiliation is the essay's intention (and the intention, presumed or perhaps created by the essay, that its audience has) for attempting an approach. Is the critical essay an attempt to identify or to identify with the text of its choice? Does it stand between the text and the reader, or to one side of one of them? How great or how little is the ironic disparity between its essential formal incompleteness (because after all it is an essay) and the formal completion of the text it treats? The third mode of affiliation concerns the essay as a zone in which certain kinds of occurrences happen as an aspect of the essay's production. What is the essay's consciousness of its marginality to the text it discusses? What is the method by which the essay permits history a role during the making of its own history, that is, as the essay moves from beginning to development to conclusion? What is the quality of the essay's speech, toward, away from, into the *actuality*, the arena of nontextual historical vitality and presence that is taking place simultaneously with the essay itself? Finally, is the essay a text, an intervention between texts, an intensification of the notion of textuality, or a dispersion of language away from a contingent page to occasions, tendencies, currents, or movements in and for history?

A just response to these questions is a realization of how unfamiliar they are in the general discussion of contemporary literary criticism. It is not that the problems of criticism are undiscussed, but rather that criticism is considered essentially as once and for all by its secondariness, by its temporal misfortune in having come after the texts and occasions it is supposed to be treating. Just as it is all too often true that texts are thought of as monolithic objects of the past to which criticism despondently appends itself in the present, then the very conception of criticism symbolizes being outdated, being dated from the past rather than by the present. Everything I tried earlier to say about a text—its dialectic of engagement in time and the senses, the paradoxes in a text by which discourse is shown to be immutable and yet contingent, as fraught and politically intransigent as the struggle between dominant and dominated—all this was an implicit rejection of the secondary role usually assigned to criticism. For if we assume instead that texts make up what Foucault calls archival facts, the archive being defined as the text's social discursive presence in the world, then criticism too is another aspect of that present. In other words, rather than being defined by the silent past, commanded by it to speak in the present, criticism, no less than any text, is the present in the course of its articulation, its struggles for definition.

We must not forget that the critic cannot speak without the mediation of writing, that ambivalent *pharmakon* so suggestively portrayed by Derrida as the constituted milieu where the oppositions are opposed: this is where the interplay occurs that brings the oppositions into direct contact with each other, that overturns oppositions and transforms one pole into another, soul and body, good and evil, inside and outside, memory and oblivion, speech and writing.[29] In particular the critic is committed to the essay, whose metaphysics were sketched by Lukacs in the first chapter of his *Die Seele und die Formen*. There Lukacs said that by virtue of its form the essay allows and indeed is the coincidence of inchoate soul with exigent material form. Essays are concerned with the relations between things, with values and concepts, in fine, with significance. Whereas poetry deals in images, the essay is the abandonment of images; this abandonment the essay ideally shares with Platonism and mysticism. If, Lukacs continues, the various forms of literature are compared with sunlight refracted in a prism, then the essay is ultraviolet light. What the essay expresses is a yearning for conceptuality and intellectuality, as well as a resolution to the ultimate questions of life. (Throughout his analysis Lukacs refers to Socrates as the typical essayistic figure, always talking of immediate mundane matters while at the same time through his life there sounds the purest, the most profound, and the most concealed yearning—*Die tiefste, die verborgenste Sehnsucht ertönt aus diesem Leben.*)[30]

Thus the essay's mode is ironic, which means first that the form is patently insufficient in its intellectuality with regard to living experience and, second, that the very form of the essay, its being an essay, is an ironic destiny with regard to the great questions of life. In its arbitrariness and irrelevance to the questions he debates, Socrates' death perfectly symbolizes essayistic destiny, which is the absence of a real tragic destiny. Thus, unlike tragedy, there is no internal conclusion to an essay, for only something outside it can interrupt or end it, as Socrates' death is decreed offstage and abruptly ends his life of questioning. Form fills the function in an essay that images do in poetry: form is the reality of the essay, and form gives the essayist a voice with which to ask questions of life, even if that form must always make use of art—a book, a painting, a piece of music—as what seems to be the purely occasional subject matter of its investigations.

Lukacs' analysis of the essay has it in common with Wilde that criticism in general is rarely what it seems, not least in its form. Criticism adopts the mode of commentary on and evaluation of art; yet in reality criticism matters more as a necessarily incomplete and preparatory process toward judgment and evaluation. What the critical essay does is *to begin* to create the values by which art is judged. I said earlier that a major inhibition on critics is that their function as critics is often dated and circumscribed for them by the past, that is, by an already created work of art or a discrete occasion. Lukacs acknowledges the inhibition, but he shows how in fact critics appropriate for themselves the function of starting to make values for the work they are judging. Wilde said it more flamboyantly: criticism "treats the work of art as a starting point for a new creation."[31] Lukacs put it more cautiously: "the essayist is a pure instance of the precursor."[32]

I prefer the latter description, for as Lukacs develops it, the critic's position is a vulnerable one because he or she prepares for a great aesthetic revolution whose result, ironically enough, will render criticism marginal. Later, this very idea will be converted by Lukacs into a description of the overthrow of reification by class consciousness, which in turn will make class itself a marginal thing.[33] Yet what I wish to emphasize here is that critics create not only the values by which art is judged and understood, but they embody in writing those processes and actual conditions in the *present* by means of which art and writing bear significance. This means what R. P. Blackmur, following Hopkins, called the bringing of literature to performance. More explicitly, the critic is responsible to a degree for articulating those voices dominated, displaced, or silenced by the textuality of texts. Texts are a system of forces institutionalized by the reigning culture at some human cost to its various components.[34] For texts after all are not an ideal cosmos of ideally equal monuments. Looking at the Grecian urn Keats *sees* graceful figures adorning its exterior, and also he actualizes in language (and perhaps nowhere else) the little town "emptied of this folk, this pious morn." The critic's attitude to some extent is sensitive in a similar way; it should in addition and more often be frankly inventive, in the traditional rhetorical sense of *inventio* so fruitfully employed by Vico, which means finding and exposing things that otherwise lie hidden beneath piety, heedlessness, or routine.

Most of all, criticism is worldly and in the world so long as it opposes monocentrism, a concept I understand as working in conjunction with eth-

nocentrism, which licenses a culture to cloak itself in the particular author-
ity of certain values over others. Even for Arnold, this comes about as the
result of a contest that gives culture a dominion that almost always hides its
dark side: in this respect *Culture and Anarchy* and *The Birth of Tragedy* are
not very far apart.

NOTES

1   Paul Ricoeur, "What Is a Text?: Explanation and Interpretation," in David
    Rasmussen, *Mythic-Symbolic Language and Philosophical Anthropology: A
    Constructive Interpretation of the Thought of Paul Ricoeur* (The Hague, 1971),
    p. 138. For a more interesting distinction between oeuvre and text, see Roland
    Barthes, "De l'Oeuvre au texte," *Revue d'esthethique* 3 (1971): 225–32.

2   I have discussed this in chapter 4 of *Beginnings: Intention and Method* (New
    York, 1975).

3   Michael Riffaterre, "The Self-Sufficient Text," *Diacritics* 3 (1973): 40.

4   This is the main polemical point in this tract, *Ar-rad'ala'nuhat*, ed. Shawki Daif
    (Cairo, 1947). The text dates from 1180.

5   Roger Arnaldez, *Grammaire et théologies chez Ibn Hazm de Cordoue* (Paris,
    1956), p. 12. There is a clear, somewhat schematic account of Ibn Ginni, Ibn
    Mada', and others in Anis Fraiha, *Nathariyat fil Lugha* (Beirut, 1973).

6   Arnaldez, *Grammaire et théologies*, p. 12.

7   Arnaldez, *Grammaire et théologies*, p. 69.

8   Arnaldez, *Grammaire et théologies*, p. 77.

9   *The Journals and Papers of Gerard Manley Hopkins*, ed. Humphry House and
    Graham Storey (London, 1959), p. 195.

10 Hopkins, *Journals and Papers*, p. 129.

11 *The Poems of Gerard Manley Hopkins*, ed. W. H. Gardner and N. H. Mackenzie
    (London, 1967), p. 90.

12 *The Letters of Gerard Manley Hopkins to Robert Bridges*, ed. Claude Colleer
    Abbott (Oxford, 1955), pp. 51–52.

13 Quoted in Anthony Bisshof, S. J., "Hopkins' Letters to his Brother," *Times Literary
    Supplement*, 8 December 1972, p. 1511.

14 *The Poems of Gerard Manley Hopkins*, p. 108.

15 *The Artist as Critic: Critical Writings of Oscar Wilde*, ed. Richard Ellmann (New
    York, 1970), p. 386.

16 *Complete Works of Oscar Wilde*, ed. J. B. Foreman (London, 1971), p. 335.

17 Oscar Wilde, *De Profundis* (New York, 1964), p. 18.

[18] Wilde, *De Profundis*, pp. 80, 61.

[19] Wilde, *De Profundis*, pp. 34–35.

[20] George Eliot, *Middlemarch*, ed. Gordon S. Haight (Boston, 1956), p. 302.

[21] Joseph Conrad, *Lord Jim* (Boston, 1958), p. 161.

[22] Conrad, *Lord Jim*, p. 161.

[23] Karl Marx, *Der Achtzehnte Brumaire des Louis Bonaparte* (1852; Berlin, 1947), p. 8.

[24] Nietzsche's analyses of texts in this light are to be found everywhere in his work, but especially in *The Genealogy of Morals* and in *The Will to Power*.

[25] See in particular Ernst Renan, *Histoire générale et système compare des langues sémitiques*, in *Ouevres completès*, ed. Henriette Psichari (Paris, 1947–61), vol. 7, pp. 147–57.

[26] Michel Foucault, "The Discourse in Language," in *The Archaeology of Language*, trans. A. M. Sheridan Smith (New York, 1972), p. 216.

[27] James Joyce, *A Portrait of the Artist as a Young Man* (New York, 1964), p. 189.

[28] Frantz Fanon, *The Wretched of the Earth*, trans. Constance Farrington (New York, 1964), pp. 31–32.

[29] Jacques Derrida, "La Pharmacie de Platon," in *La Dissémination* (Paris, 1972), pp. 145 and passim.

[30] Georg Lukacs, *Die Seele und die Formen* (1911; reprint Berlin, 1971), p. 25.

[31] Wilde, *The Artist as Critic*, p. 367.

[32] Lukacs, *Die Seele und die Formen*, p. 29.

[33] See Georg Lukacs, *History and Class Consciousness: Studies in Marxist Dialectics*, trans. Rodney Livingstone (London, 1971), pp. 178–209.

[34] See the discussion of this point in Richard Poirier, *The Performing Self: Compositions and Decompositions in the Languages of Everyday Life* (New York, 1971).

IN TRANSIT: THEORIZING CULTURAL APPROPRIATION IN MEDIEVAL EUROPE

CLAIRE SPONSLER

In the 1980 South African film *The Gods Must Be Crazy*, by Janie Uys, a !Kung bushman in the Kalahari encounters technology for the first time, in the shape of a Coca-Cola bottle that falls from the sky. As the film unfolds, we watch the bushman take the talismanic object back to his tribe, where it is put to many uses and acquires a quasicultic status. When people start to fight over the bottle, however, the dark side of the talisman is revealed; to put a stop to its disruptions, Xixo (played by N!xau) decides to throw the evil object over the edge of the earth. This transformation of the detritus of Western commodity culture into a valuable object is popular cinema's treatment of the phenomenon known to anthropologists as the *cargo cult*, a term coined by anthropologists to describe the refashioning by Pacific islanders of worthless detritus washed ashore from Western shipwrecks, a refashioning that converted flotsam into potent cultic symbols.[1] With its radical actions of seizure and reshaping, the cargo cult offers an extreme example of cultural appropriation in which the source item is stripped of its original meaning and function in order to be given an entirely new use and significance.

The specific version of the cargo cult portrayed in *The Gods Must Be Crazy*, with its nostalgic handling of cultural contact in which the Coke bottle becomes a symbol of evil Western technology and the bushman, voyaging to the ends of the earth to save his people from its destructive

From *Journal of Medieval and Early Modern Studies* 32.1 (Winter 2002): 17–39; reprinted with permission of Duke University Press.

influence, an image of the noble savage, is more complex than one might at first suspect. For, in its own slapstick way, the film sketches a compelling moral critique of Western commodity culture, as the bushman tries to grapple with the effects of the cargo on his traditional tribal culture. Particularly within the context of South Africa's struggles in the 1970s and 1980s to appropriate Western business models, the film's rejection of the tangible signs of that culture has to be seen at one level as a principled stand against commodification, a stand that is grounded in a moral no longer available in the West, so the film suggests.

Along with this incipient critique of the culture of consumption and more central to the concerns of this essay, the film also offers a capsule portrait of the *mise en abyme* nature of appropriation. The Coke bottle falls from the sky and is appropriated by the bushmen who then turn it briefly into an object of veneration before expelling it from their world. The film appropriates the Coke bottle as a sign of evil technology and the bushman as noble savage. I, as critic, appropriate the film as an example of the dynamics of appropriation. You, as reader, appropriate my essay for purposes that remain to be discovered. Cargo cults, filmmakers, critics, and readers, linked in this chain of appropriation, usefully foreground some of the intricacies of cultural transmission and hence make a good starting point for considering cultural appropriation in medieval Europe and modern reflections on it.

The politics not just of appropriation but of theorizing about it are complex and have a loaded history, which includes, among other things, an intersection with the marxist critique of ideology that has given it a lingering left-leaning connotation. Although a thorough discussion of that history is beyond the scope of my essay, a brief consideration of the etymology of the term seems warranted. The word *appropriate*, "to make one's own," comes to us from the Latin *proprius*, "proper," or "property," which points to a system of objects within which valued artifacts circulate and are given meanings and underscores the way in which appropriation is an act of possessing—of ideas, objects, texts, beliefs. In the twentieth century, this understanding of appropriation as property management surfaces in the writings of Baudrillard, among others. In his analysis of the deployment of objects within the modern capitalist West, Baudrillard has insisted on the way that all categories of meaningful objects, including those marked off as great works of art and literature, circulate within a coherent system of symbols and values.[2] The work of collectors, scholars, and critics helps to create value and ensures that a meaningful deployment and circulation of artifacts is maintained.

To a significant extent, appropriation theory has become a well-established analytical tool in many areas of cultural studies broadly understood. Contemporary theories of interpretation have, for better or for worse, by now shifted attention away from traditional concerns with the origin or source, looking instead at appropriation as a key event in the creation of meaning. Particularly in ethnography and in those cultural studies influenced by it, appropriation has become a central concern, as scholars increasingly often critique the ideological forces structuring the appropriation of one culture by another, of art objects by collectors, of whole peoples by ethnographers.[3] In a refinement of prevailing models of cultural transmission and of older notions of appropriation, which have often seemed too unilateral, too monolithic, and too smooth, scholars have turned to notions such as improvisation, revision, translation, citation, and parody to describe how new meanings are given or added to already-existing objects, events, and texts.

Although acts of appropriation of all kinds of things—of metaphors, of images, of ideologies, of power and authority, of ideas, of ritual objects, of texts, of performances, of musical phrases—were integral aspects of cultural production in the societies of medieval Europe, scholarly attention has tended not to confront them as acts, but to concentrate instead on the things being appropriated. For most of its history, the study of medieval Europe has been a recuperative project preoccupied with beginnings, sources, and the recovery of lost origins. Beginning with sixteenth-century antiquarians, those casting their eyes back on the medieval past were primed to save whatever remnants of it could be rescued. This bent was intensified following the medieval revival of the later eighteenth and nineteenth centuries when medieval studies became a specialized discipline, and scholars involved in projects as diverse yet fundamentally related as the Early English Text Society, the Society of Antiquaries, and the Rolls Series in England, the Monumenta series published by the Institute for Research on the German Middle Ages in Berlin, or the Société des Anciens Textes Français and L'École des Chartes in Paris made it their life's work to locate and preserve as much of the medieval past as possible.[4]

The tendency of medieval scholars to approach their task as one of salvage has privileged the "artifact" as the focal point of study rather than the "process" of cultural creation and transmission.[5] This despite the fact that both written texts and visual artifacts from medieval Europe usually exist in multiple and often divergent copies that make any search for an originary text difficult. What can be taken as the original, canonical, or definitive text or image, when authorship is often anonymous, and even when the creator is known a work exists in numerous copies from different countries, copies which in some cases the creator or an assistant was responsible for altering over a number of years?

Since source studies have fallen into disrepute in recent years—not always with good cause—and scholarly interest has shifted toward study of the cultural artifact in its synchronic historical context, there continues to be a dearth of work focused on the diachronic process whereby artifacts moved through culture until winding up where we now find them, with an accretion of attached meanings and values (which can of course always be lost or revised). To cite one example from the field of medieval drama, the sole surviving copy of the Croxton *Play of the Sacrament* is now in Trinity College, Dublin, MS F.4.20, fols. 338r–56r, in a compilation once owned by John Madden (d. 1703), a man who in the late seventeenth century was president of the Royal College of Physicians of Ireland. The worn condition of the outer pages of the play suggest that it originally existed separately from the Trinity compilation for some period of years (this copy of the play appears from its handwriting and watermarks to have been made in the mid-sixteenth century, although the date of composition was probably earlier, sometime after 1461, a date mentioned near the close of the play).[6] Given that one of the central scenes of the Croxton *Play of the Sacrament* is the attempted healing of the Jew Jonathas, whose hand has been torn off after it becomes stuck on a eucharistic wafer he has bought from a Christian merchant, by a quack doctor, Master Brundiche of Brabant, there would appear to be an interesting story linking Madden the physician and the play. Yet almost all of the most vibrant and energetic recent work on the play has been focused on fixing the play in a time and place—various sites in late fifteenth-century East Anglia—with an aye to unpacking its cultural work within that locale. Valuable though such studies are, another story has been overlooked, one in which the play is removed over the course of a hundred or so years from East Anglia, from the hands of the touring players by whom it was probably originally performed, into Ireland, into a "book," and into the possession of a man whose chief interest in the play may have less to do with doctrinal issues, conversion of the Jews, or religious orthodoxy—all meanings that scholars have ascribed to the play—less to do even with drama and performance, than with the pleasure of reading about a quack doctor. To suggest that we should look to a physician owner's interest in a play about a quack doctor as evidence of appropriation is of course to say that all reading is an act of appropriation, since once a text is published, even in the limited terms of publication available in a manuscript culture, it becomes a form of property and thus is opened to readers' varied ways of owning it. We cannot know for certain why Madden possessed this manuscript, what the Croxton play meant to him, or even whether he read it, but surely his ownership of it should at least be recalled when we attempt to reconstruct the play's historical meanings.

If it can be assumed that whether in the form of scribal copying of a manuscript, the translation of relics from one shrine to another, the co-opting of a ceremonial role, the redrafting of an iconographic image, or the reading of a text, medieval cultural productions were to a remarkable degree in transit, then the challenge for scholars, so often confronted with the seemingly static end-product—finished manuscript, enshrined relic, enacted performance, or completed painting—is to find a way of accessing the shifting processes of appropriation that produced those results now apparently fixed in ink or paint or stone.

The remainder of this essay looks at four different acts of appropriation, pairing them with four different ways of theorizing appropriation. The examples are familiar—manuscript transmission, the circulation of relics, the representation of pictorial images, and theatrical performance—a list of artifacts and theories that is not intended to be exhaustive or even exemplary, but instead aims to offer a representative sampling. My purpose in presenting these examples is to suggest what focusing on the processes of appropriation, rather than on the finished product or the source material where attention is more often directed, can reveal that might otherwise be hidden about the functioning of these cultural productions within their specific social contexts.

MANUSCRIPT TRANSMISSION
AND BRICOLAGE

My first example is that of manuscript transmission and the theory of appropriation known as *bricolage*. In his influential treatment of subculture studies, *Subculture: The Meaning of Style*, published in 1979 in Methuen's New Accents series, Dick Hebdige broadened the scope of British cultural-studies accounts of the textual struggle for meaning to encompass the material form of subcultural style, by examining the representational codes (particularly of dress, music, and behavior) of specific urban youth subcultures in 1970s Britain. Hebdige's ethnographic study deploys semiotics and techniques of literary studies to analyze how British working-class urban subcultures used commodity culture to mark the subculture off from dominant cultural formations.[7]

Hebdige draws on earlier work such as the introduction to *Resistance through Rituals*, in which Stuart Hall and Tony Jefferson argue that culture is not monolithic but instead composed of competing, overlapping, and sometimes conflicting smaller groups that create their own patterns of life and define themselves through their distinctive institutions, beliefs and customs, social relations, and uses of objects, thus developing symbolic systems that give expressive form to their social and material life-experiences.[8] Hebdige's analysis expands on Hall and Jefferson's understanding of the "maps of meaning" that constitute the subculture, doing so by engaging the subculture largely at the level of signs and signification, through an innovative focus on "the contradictions displayed . . . at the profoundly superficial level of appearance: that is, at the level of signs."[9] For Hebdige, style is "pregnant with significance," and the task of the critic is "to discern the hidden messages inscribed in code on the glossy surfaces of style, to trace them out as 'maps of meaning' which obscurely represent the very contradictions they are designed to resolve or conceal."[10]

In Hebdige's reading, British punks rejected the consumption patterns associated with middle-class propriety, adorning themselves in their own distinctive style, one crafted out of mass-market commodities, a process of appropriation Hebdige analyzes by turning to Claude Lévi-Strauss's notion of bricolage.[11] Although the subculture's stylistic interventions are limited to the raw materials offered by the marketplace, the subculture in Hebdige's reading is not forced to accept the meanings usually attached to those materials, but instead is free to improvise with the materials it acquires from the marketplace, giving them new meanings and uses. An ordinary domestic item such as the safety pin, for instance, coded by mainstream culture as benign and protective, becomes, after subcultural appropriation, dangerous and grotesque when it is used not to hold together diapers but to pierce flesh. For Hebdige, what marks the subculture off from more orthodox cultural formations is the way in which commodities are used.

In *The Savage Mind*, Lévi-Strauss shows how the magical systems of primitive peoples (myth, sorcery, superstition) present their users with coherent systems of connection between things by means of which people can understand the world around them. One reason these systems of connection work is because their parts can be played with: the basic elements of the system are flexible enough that they can be used in a variety of improvised

combinations to create new meanings. The improvisational aspect of brico-
lage is underscored in Lévi-Strauss's definition of it as the tinkering around
of an amateur handyman, or the art of making do with what's at hand. This
definition assumes the possession of a stock of materials or rules of thumb
that are fairly extensively available throughout the culture, though not fixed
in any immutable sense—in other words, multiple and open to manipula-
tion, but at the same time limited and not completely random. The defini-
tion also assumes the ability of cultural agents continually to rearrange that
stock of materials in new or different patterns and configurations. For the
bricoleur, Lévi-Strauss says, "the rules of the game are always to make do
with 'whatever is at hand,' that is to say with a set of tools and materials
which is always finite and is also heterogeneous because what it contains
bears no relation to the current project, or indeed to any particular project,
but is the contingent result of all the occasions there have been to renew or
enrich the stock or to maintain it with the remains of previous construc-
tions or destructions."[12] Bricolage thus can open up the world, especially the
world of objects, to new and oppositional readings.

Similar acts of appropriation in which cultures and communities are seen
as *bricoleurs* have been described by theorists of postcolonial social forma-
tions like Paul Gilroy. Gilroy's *The Black Atlantic*, which continues his project
of dislodging the cultural nationalism of British cultural studies (a project
begun in his *There Ain't No Black in the Union Jack* [1987]) while at the same
time challenging constructions of race that are dominated entirely by eth-
nicity, explicitly rejects the structures of the nation-state and the location of
a black diasporic identity in an African source or original.[13] Instead, Gilroy
demonstrates that the black settler communities of the Atlantic rim have
forged hybrid or compound cultures by tinkering with material offered by
both the dominating and dominated source cultures in ways that the tra-
ditional terms for cultural melding, *creolization* and *syncretism*, are inade-
quate to explain. This ingenious tinkering with the material at hand, Gilroy
shows, whether deliberately subversive or not, shares a common refusal to
be limited by whatever form or meaning the source material initially bears.
Bricolage, then, as deployed by the subjects studied by Hebdige and Gilroy,
suggests the possibility of resourceful ways of refashioning cultural material
to fit whatever needs are at hand. Although the notion of bricolage has usu-
ally been applied to subcultural activities, where it is obviously apt, it need
not be limited to those uses, as the example of the Lancastrian appropriation
of Chaucer's *Canterbury Tales* demonstrates. In an essay called "A Language
Policy for Lancastrian England," John Fisher points to the link between the

date at which manuscripts in English began to multiply and the date of the Lancastrian usurpation of the throne of England in 1399.[14] Before 1400, as Fisher observes, we have virtually no manuscripts of poetry in English that were commercially prepared and intended for circulation. Yet after 1400, the manuscripts of Gower, Chaucer, and other fourteenth-century writers, as well as the works of Lydgate, Hoccleve, Scogan, and emerging fifteenth-century authors, begin to proliferate. Fisher argues that this burst of literary effort was not a matter of simple linguistic evolution attributable to the rise of English, but was deliberately encouraged by the Lancastrian kings Henry IV and Henry V. The outburst of copying and composing in English that took place after 1400 can be explained, Fisher asserts, as a consciously instigated policy designed to gain support for a questionable usurpation of the throne and to lay the groundwork for the political actions of 1416 to 1422. The Lancastrian decision to push English as a national language and to give it prestige was thus politically inspired. The publication of Chaucer's writings and his enshrinement as the father of English poetry were central parts of this effort.

Fisher argues that a circle of powerful Lancastrians and their supporters—John Lydgate, Thomas Chaucer, and Thomas Hoccleve—acted, in essence, as *bricoleurs* (though he doesn't use that term), on two levels, first by seizing on available cultural material—that is, writings in English by a handful of authors—and cobbling it together into a national literature; and second, and perhaps more interestingly, by putting together out of the hodgepodge of Chaucer's writings—multiple yet limited—left in disarray at his death a bricolage text of the *Canterbury Tales*. Certain facts support Fisher's claim. There are no extant manuscripts of Chaucer's poems dating before his death in 1400, not even any presentation copies, even though Chaucer was a court poet and his poetry must have been in oral circulation for at least thirty years. Fisher ascribes this situation to the fact that although everyone spoke English, official and polite writing took place in the nonnative prestige languages of Latin and French, offering no openings for the publication of written versions of Chaucer's poems. The coincidence of Richard II's deposition in 1399, Chaucer's death one year later, and the survival of his unpublished writings offered the chance for the Lancastrian *bricoleurs* to appropriate and shape Chaucer's writings, especially the *Canterbury Tales*, to their own ends. Norman Blake has given a persuasive account of the various stages of this act of bricolage applied to the text of the *Canterbury Tales* from the initial effort to make sense of the foul papers in the Hengwrt manuscript to the fully edited text of the sumptuous Ellesmere manuscript. To see the Lancastrians as *bricoleurs* tinkering with the hodgepodge of materials left behind by Chaucer and turning it into the *Canterbury Tales* that we read today is to see the unfinished and unpublished tales Chaucer had written being transformed into an authoritative text with a veneer of completeness, a text appropriated for political purposes.

The relationship between Margery Kempe and the male scribes who produced her *Book* can be thought of as a similar work of bricolage, in which the scribes select from and appropriate Kempe's oral narrative, refashioning it into a written text.[15] Or think of Book I of Jean Froissart's *Chroniques*, which relies heavily on, which is to say appropriates, Jean le Bel's account of the reigns of Edward II and III, and which Froissart himself revised and changed a number of times.[16] Froissart in Book I performs a similar act of bricolage, in this instance one that involves tinkering with his own material. In all these cases, the *bricoleur*'s role is that of the handyman appropriating and reworking the material at hand. As Hebdige's analysis of British punks suggests, however, the *bricoleur*'s work is far from meaningless, and, in fact, as the role of Margery Kempe's scribes indicates, is itself a generative and creative activity.

It is also worth stressing that as an act of appropriation bricolage is not random; on the contrary, as Lévi-Strauss stresses, it is motivated by the necessity of the moment, and insofar as it works, it does so because it makes sense and is homologous with larger structures and concerns. Hebdige argues that the bits and pieces of commodity culture reassembled by punks made sense, because what was produced was homologous with the concerns, activities, group structure, and collective self-image of the subculture: in other words, the pieces fit together in a meaningful way.[17] A similar intersection of homology and bricolage can be seen in the Lancastrian tinkering with Chaucer's *Canterbury Tales*: the choice of the *Tales* as vehicle for Lancastrian propaganda made sense for a number of reasons, not least their various features of style, structure, and content. For instance, Chaucer's tendency to end his social critique well short of wholesale attack on major institutions or his representation of a spectrum of English society that carefully avoids the extremes of deep poverty and overweening wealth must have sounded the right note, one homologous with a desired Lancastrian representation of what "the English" were like.

To pay attention on to textual bricolage, then, is to notice the handyman's active role in constructing the text and its meanings, a role that can be as important as that of the original producer of the text. Focusing more directly on what happens when *bricoleurs* in the form of copyists, editors, and even authors themselves tinker with texts fills the gap between lost original and extant end-product, while also redirecting interpretive efforts away from finished products and toward processes of textual production.

CIRCULATION OF RELICS AND
CONSUMPTION AS PRODUCTION

My second example of appropriation theory focuses on the circulation of relics and the theorization of culture as consumption, which differs from bricolage chiefly in its scope. Moving beyond the notion of the relatively singular and infrequent work of the *bricoleur*, recent theories of cultural consumption have argued that most if not all consumption by all consumers is a form of production, capable of creating ways of using cultural materials that cannot be limited to the intentions of those who produce them.[18] This perspective gives a central place to the "art of doing" and "doing with," as Michel de Certeau has argued in *The Practice of Everyday Life*, and gives cultural consumption a new status, no longer seeing it as passive, dependent, and submissive, but as creative, and even powerful enough to resist suggested or imposed models of meaning.[19] Even though most subordinated social groups cannot control the means of production, they can exert control over consumption, which de Certeau, like most cultural critics who follow him, tends to see as subversive.

De Certeau suggests that although patterns of consumption remain to some extent dominated by forces of social control, consumers nonetheless have the ability to take charge of the consumer items they are usually assumed to ingest passively, exerting a bottom-up power that can be evasive or even resistant. Even though consumption has usually been taken as the domain of inertia and passivity, de Certeau stresses that consumers can poach on and appropriate the items of consumption that mass culture offers for their ingestion. The kinds of consumer practices open to appropriation include cooking, shopping, reading, and even renting a place to live, which in de Certeau's view "transforms another person's property into a space borrowed for a moment by a transient"; through the act of leasing, renters insinuate themselves into another person's place, making it temporarily their own and actively serving their own rather than the landlord's ends. Shopping is similarly open to restructuring of buyer and seller relationships, since even if the economic advantage remains with sellers, buyers can concoct their own uses for the products they acquire. In so doing, they, and other consumers of culture, refashion to their own ends the objects, images, and ideas they receive, although they will always do so, de Certeau concedes, under the dominating influence of forces of cultural control.

In *Culture and Consumption*, a book that shares an obvious affinity with de Certeau's work even if that affinity is not explicitly acknowledged, Grant McCracken presses the notion of active consumption even further, proposing an alternate approach to the usual understanding of consumer goods as carrying and communicating cultural meaning.[20] The limitation of the traditional understanding of consumption, McCracken argues, is that it fails to observe that the cultural meaning of goods is constantly in motion, flowing to and from its several locations in the social world, aided by the efforts of designers, producers, advertisers, and consumers. Meaning may begin in the culturally constituted world, that is, the world of everyday experience in which "the phenomenal world presents itself to the senses of the individual, fully shaped and constituted by the beliefs and assumptions of his or her culture," but then it is "unhooked" by product designers, advertisers, marketers, and journalists and transferred to the consumer object.[21] As consumers, we then fetch this meaning out of goods for our own purposes in the construction of our own worlds. We accomplish this, McCracken says, through such mechanisms as exchange rituals, which map social relations onto goods through gift-giving and other systems of exchange; possession rituals that personalize the goods; grooming rituals that coax attributes out of perishable goods such as clothes, make-up, or hair products, and attach them to the consumer; and divestment rituals that either allow the new owner of a previously possessed good to divest it of its pre-owned meanings or help erase old meanings from a good that is being given away. Thus, McCracken claims, in a formulation far wider-reaching and diffuse than the much more focused notion of bricolage, all of us employ consumption as a source of cultural meaning and use it in the construction of our individual and collective worlds.

Although McCracken's study begins with what he identifies as the "consumer revolution" that begins in Elizabethan England, his analysis of person-object relations and his mapping of the complex processes of appropriation that drive the manufacture and movement of meaning in the world of goods can aptly be applied to medieval culture and particularly to the circulation of relics. As Patrick Geary has argued in *Living with the Dead in the Middle Ages*, relics are perhaps best understood precisely as commodities circulating within a transactional culture.[22] This transactional culture was structurally diverse, as Geary shows, encompassing a variety of mechanisms of exchange. Drawing on the work of economic historians, Geary argues that trade was not the only or even the usual means by which commodities changed hands in medieval Europe. Much of the exchange network probably operated by barter rather than sale, and gift-giving and theft were more basic forms of property circulation in the early Middle Ages than trade, and enjoyed more prestige. Ritual exchanges of goods and services formed the normal means of distributing wealth acquired from plunder or agriculture. And goods exchanged served to create bonds between giver and recipient, however much they may also have been desired for themselves.

As commodities, relics of saints circulated in similar fashion, Geary asserts, acquiring value and meaning as they entered into circulation. Whether in the form of particles of clothes or parts of bodies or objects associated with the saint, relics had no intrinsic value apart from a set of shared beliefs and were of no practical use. In order for relics to become valuable, they had to undergo a social and cultural transition from ordinary objects and human remains to venerated mementos of a saint. In McCracken's terms, relics thus had to enter into the processes of meaning-manufacture engineered by distributors, other mediators, and consumers in the world of goods. In the case of relics, such processes included the public ritual of discovery or *inventio* of the saint's remains, authentication of the remains, translation to an appropriate site for veneration, and identification of miraculous interventions of the saint that proved the relics efficacious. Once relics had achieved recognition, their continued significance and value depended on their continued performance of miracles and their relative power compared with that of other relics. In other words, continued public use of the relics was necessary for them to remain valuable and to retain their meaning as sacred objects.

Corresponding to the intermediaries McCracken describes—the advertisers, marketers, and journalists who play a role in the appropriation of goods and the distribution of meanings to them—were the clerics responsible for promoting a specific cult; the writers of propaganda and devotional literature or of pilgrimage accounts, which aided in turning shrines into tourist attractions and created interest in the cult; and the patronage networks by means of which relics were donated, either by the pope or a lesser donor, and moved from the "production centers" of Rome, the Near East, and the areas of Spain and Gaul that had been part of the Roman Empire in late antiquity to other local sites.

Once acquired, relics had to undergo processes of reconstruction of value similar to the rituals described by McCracken. Since the very act of transfer of the relic removed it from the cultural structure in which it had originally acquired value, it arrived in the new community as an unproven object; hence, the relic had to undergo a process of social negotiation within the new community. This negotiation was made easier by the fact that the construction of value and the mode of circulation often overlapped: acquiring the relic gave it value because it was worth acquiring, and acquisition, because often so difficult, was evidence that the relics were genuine. Thus, circulation not only gave value to, but created, the commodity being circulated.

In the case of relics, then, consumption becomes production, with the value and indeed even the identity of the object being conferred in an act of consumption that transforms mere human bones into sacred commodity. By appropriating the relic, the community acquiring it creates its value and its identity. As Geary notes, that value was by no means permanent but had to be recreated continually as the relic was used. Only so long as the relic was repeatedly consumed and appropriated, made over into a powerful ritual object, did it retain its value. By appropriating the saint's relic, a community thus produced that cult object. Without consumption, the relic would remain just bits of dust, or cloth, or bones.

If we think of consumption as a method of appropriation whereby cultural objects of all kinds are used, put into motion, and created as symbolic goods, then, as McCracken argues, we also have to recognize how highly mobile not just those objects but also their meanings are. "Meaning," as McCracken states, "is constantly flowing to and from its several locations in the social world,"[23] hence any investigation of meaning and meaning-making has to pay attention to movement, movement that is linked to social change. The object-code at any given historical moment serves as an instrument of both change and continuity. It offers a means for a society to encourage change by helping social groups establish ways of seeing themselves that stand outside and in opposition to existing social structures, but it also provides a way for society to absorb change and limit its destabilizing potential. The role of consumers in this process is thus as transporters of both innovative, transgressive cultural meanings and conservative, status quo-preserving ones. In either case, the role of consumers is a productive one in that they actively shape cultural meanings.

PICTORIAL IMAGES AND DISCOURSE FLOW

My third example looks at pictorial images and appropriation from the perspective of discourse analysis. McCracken's analysis of person-object relations shows that transactions of object-exchange and meaning-making don't stop at the borders of discourses, but instead move across them, with advertising offering one example of such discursive flow. But theories of consumer appropriation, including de Certeau's and McCracken's, tend not to play up the importance of discourse crossing, in large part because of their focus on consumers as agents of cultural meaning-making. The processes of appropriation that take place as a result of discourse flow are perhaps best approached by focusing less on individual agents and more on relatively impersonal structures of the sort embodied in discourse analysis.

In part as a result of the impact of Gramsci's sophisticated reformulation of the notion of ideology, which has solved a number of problems that seemed to hamper applications of other theories of ideology, including Althusser's, textual analysis has become more aware of the ways in which signs and signification are combined within historically and culturally specific discourses.[24] The term *discourse* itself points to socially produced groups of ideas that are manifested in individual cultural objects but are also tied to larger historical and social relations. Perhaps the most important figure for discourse analysis within cultural studies has been Foucault, who in works like *Discipline and Punish* (1979) examined how discourses shape the operation of power, or, more specifically, how institutions like prisons established practices that regulated the experience of those under its control.[25] Foucault's focus on discourses has been taken up by cultural studies in a wide range of analyses of institutions (the Hollywood star system, for example), cultural formations (the heritage industry), and cultural definitions (of the body and sexuality in particular).[26]

In 1434, Jan van Eyck painted a portrait of the Italian merchant Giovanni Arnolfini and his wife Giovanna Cenami to commemorate their wedding. The *Arnolfini Portrait* depicts the merchant and his bride, sedately yet sumptuously dressed, holding hands in the center of a richly detailed bedchamber as they exchange marriage vows. Behind the swelling figure of Giovanna and the lushly cascading folds of her gown, we see a large canopied bed upholstered in red, ornamented with a carving of St. Margaret, patroness of childbirth. An elaborate gold chandelier hangs overhead while on the wall beyond them we see their images reflected in an intricately framed, round mirror. At their feet are a pair of casually kicked-off shoes and a small dog, a creature traditionally associated with lust and carnality, as Erwin Panofsky notes.[27] Off to the side, oranges lie on a wooden chest, while outside the window a fruit-laden cherry tree can be glimpsed. The artist has put his name in a prominent position on the picture with the

Latin words "Johannes de eyck fuit hic" ("Jan van Eyck was here"). In the mirror at the back of the room we see the whole scene reflected from behind, and there, so it seems, we also see van Eyck's own tiny self-portrait, accompanied by another man who may have been the official witness to the ceremony. The carved frame of the mirror is inset with ten miniature medallions depicting scenes from the life of Christ, a subtle co-opting of religious imagery for this bourgeois marriage.

As Margaret Carroll has recently argued, this insertion of the merchant into a domestic setting charged with the imagery of family, fertility, sexuality—and, we might add, Christianity—constitutes a potent act of cross-discourse appropriation.[28] In Carroll's reading, van Eyck's painting appropriates early-fifteenth-century Franciscan discourse about the morality and ethics of late medieval capitalism, transferring into pictorial form the themes of sermons addressing how merchants and tradesmen might accumulate wealth without risking damnation. These sermons were preached in the context of centuries of suspicion about usury, which had rendered mercantile activities socially and morally suspect. Most late medieval commentaries on trade, in fact, betray a lingering disdain for individuals engaged in commerce and anxiety about whether merchants can live lives free from sin. Interestingly, those fears, and the reassurances used to allay them, were often couched in the imagery of the family and sexuality. The Franciscan preacher Bernardino of Siena, for instance, warned that merchants traveling in foreign lands were in danger of falling into carnal sin and sodomy; to help avoid that possibility, he urged merchants' wives to accompany their husbands on their trading journeys.

Given such attitudes, the domestic imagery of van Eyck's portrait offers reassurances not only about Arnolfini's sexual probity, Carroll argues, but also about his methods of acquiring wealth, which came primarily from moneylending and capital investment. From Aristotle through Aquinas and on, a distinction was persistently made between lending money at interest, which was considered illicit, and investing in land or goods or a partnership, which was permissible.[29] Significantly, this distinction was explained using the imagery of sexuality and procreation: since money could not bear children, interest charged on a loan must be condemned as the unnatural progeny of money. Conversely, investing in a partnership was likened to marriage, with the money invested being described as the fertile seed or semen, and the profits said to be "born" from it being called fruits or offspring. The allusions in the *Arnolfini Portrait* to permissible marital sexuality, to fecundity, to the abundance of nature, and to childbirth are,

Carroll claims, the imagery not just of honorable marriage but of respectable capitalism as well.

This transdiscursive act of appropriation in the *Arnolfini Portrait*, which takes imagery deriving from scholastic and popular theological discourses, as Carroll demonstrates, and uses it within a visual medium to present Arnolfini as an ideal type of contemporary merchant, involves relatively little reshaping of the appropriated material but manages to tap into a powerful cluster of related themes, all of which play a role in sanctifying, witnessing to, and legitimating bourgeois marriage. But transferal is not always so simple. In a discussion of the Mashpee Wampanoag trials held in Massachusetts in the late 1970s, James Clifford raises to the surface some of the complexities of such acts of transferal from one discursive frame to another. Clifford observes how a whole range of discourses came to bear on this trial—a trial whose purpose was to rule on whether or not the Mashpees constituted a "tribe" and hence could sue in federal court to regain lands alienated from them more than two centuries ago. To mention just two instances, Clifford notes that a central tension in the trial derived from the conflicting perspectives of the anthropologists and historians called as expert witnesses by each side. While the prevailing discourses of the anthropologists envisioned cultural identity as a shifting and complex thing, the discourses of the historians encouraged a search for a point of historical origin that would identify the present-day members of the tribe once and for all as Indians or not.[30] In another instance, Clifford observes that one of the problems facing the Mashpees was that they did not look "Indian," that is, they did not match up with received images—such as those derived from Edward Curtis's sepia-tinted photographs of stoic-faced warriors—of how Indians should look. The lack of fit between mainstream cultural images of Indianness and the appearance of the Mashpees in the courtroom undermined their efforts to present themselves as a distinctive cultural group, revealing that the transferal of cultural material from one discourse to another in this case did not work as readily as it did in the *Arnolfini Portrait*.

Moments of blockage at which appropriation across discourses is halted deserve as much attention as moments of cross-discursive flow, since they can be analogous to ideological gaps and silences within texts and discourses. Like such gaps, blockages might signal ideological impasses that impose limits on the dispersal of cultural material and suggest points of friction or resistance that provide an opening for glimpsing the larger, obdurate discourses in which they are enmeshed. Whether blocked or free-flowing, however, cross-discursive appropriation reminds us that cultural objects, texts, and events, are not free-standing units but rather are caught up in webs of social and discursive relations whose operation we need to beware of if we hope to understand the meaning or function of any specific cultural object.

THEATRICAL ROLES AND CULTURAL POACHING

My fourth and final example takes up theatrical performances and appropriation in the form of cultural poaching. In his *Chronicle*, Edward Hall describes the following incident involving Henry VIII in 1509, the first year of his reign. One morning, accompanied by twelve other noblemen, Henry burst suddenly into the queen's chamber. According to Hall, Henry and his men were "all appareled in shorte cotes, of Kintishe Kendal, with hodes on their heddes, and hosen of the same," all carrying bows and arrows and sword and buckler, like outlaws or Robin Hood's men. The effect on the queen and her ladies was such that they were "abashed, as well for the straunge sight, as for their sodan commyng."[31] This odd little escapade, which has recently been discussed by Peter Stallybrass, invites us to examine cultural poaching in operation as these royal gentlemen appropriate the popular outlaw hero Robin Hood, well known for at least three centuries from plays, games, and ballads.[32] Andrew Ayton claims that by the 1260s the name *Robin Hood* was recognized as a nickname for fugitives from the law and by the fifteenth century was widely associated with collective criminal activity in the greenwood, associations that seem also to have informed Henry's playacting.[33]

Stallybrass suggests that King Henry's playing at outlawry constitutes an elaborate aristocratic sex fantasy. That seems plausible. But this playacting might also have allowed Henry to envision himself as a transgressive hero, one who boldly breaches the barricades not just of the queen's bedroom but also of norms of royal behavior by adopting the pose of criminality, however transient and artificial. Tellingly, this wasn't the only occasion on which Henry poached off of popular culture. Another royal co-optation of Robin Hood with more overtly political purposes took place a few years later in 1515, when Henry VIII and his court rode out to Shooter's Hill, the woodland outside London that was a site for popular games. According to Hall's *Chronicle*, there they were "ambushed" by two hundred "yeomen" clothed in green and led by "Robin Hood," who invited the king and queen to come into the greenwood and see how the outlaws lived. The royals accepted his offer and were served venison by "Robin" and his men; soon afterwards, Hall adds, Henry "took his progress Westwards" and heard complaints from his countrymen, and wherever he rode he hunted and liberally gave away venison, thus playing the role of Robin Hood before his subjects. In Henry's progress through his realm we can already see the beginnings of the transformation of Robin Hood from rough yeoman outlaw into the figure of gentlemanly largesse and aristocratic patronage he would become in the sixteenth and seventeenth centuries.

As with bricolage, acts of cultural poaching are usually associated with a descent down the social or power scale, as for instance in carnival plays or inversionary festivities such as boy-bishop performances, when the relatively powerless poached the roles of those in power, temporarily seizing them for their own ends. But Henry's playing at Robin Hood suggests that cultural poaching could move up the social hierarchy as well. Bourdieu's theorization of the connections between aesthetic taste and social class in his book *Distinction: A Social Critique of the Judgement of Taste* helps explain why.[34]

Arguing that taste is the product of upbringing and education, which are linked in turn to class and economic positions, Bourdieu is chiefly interested in exposing the ways in which aesthetic response is class-determined and constructed rather than spontaneous and natural (what Bourdieu refers to as "the ideology of charisma"). Appreciation of art is thus not an act of empathic recognition of the art object's beauty but rather the implementation of cultural codes of perception that have been acquired through schooling or in the home. What the relation to cultural products reproduces, Bourdieu insists, are the social relations under which individuals live.

Bourdieu's analysis focuses primarily on the ways in which dominated groups are excluded from cultural as well as economic capital. But his analysis also suggests that dominant social groups rich in economic and symbolic capital by virtue of their control of wealth and institutions may also at times find it desirable to raid the cultural store of dominated groups. In Bourdieu's economy, one reason cultural poaching can be attractive for elites is that it provides a way for them to add cultural assets to their already existing stock of economic and symbolic wealth. In the case of Henry VIII, the powerful symbolism of popular culture and misrule were valuable cultural assets, coins he could trade on in constructing a particular kingly persona for himself and in solidifying political power.

As Bourdieu's ideas imply, the work of signification is a social accomplishment, whose outcome does not flow in a strictly predictable or necessary manner from a given reality. In other words, there is no necessary or inevitable reason why Henry should have chosen to play Robin Hood, nor is there any reason to assume his subjects would respond as he wished them to. More importantly, as Volosinov reminds us in *Marxism and the Philosophy of Language*, the work of signification involved in an act of appropriation such as Henry's poaching of medieval popular culture is part of a social struggle. Volosinov comments that in every ideological sign—in this case Robin Hood—there is an intersection of differently oriented social interests, with the result that the sign becomes an arena of class struggle. Moreover, this "social multi-accentuality" of the sign is crucial to the sign's existence: a sign that is withdrawn from the pressures of the social struggle inevitably loses force, degenerating into allegory, no longer the object of a live social intelligibility.[35] Volosinov thus suggests that Henry's act of cultural poaching, which appropriated the sign of Robin Hood, should be seen as part of a social struggle that gave life and meaning to that sign. There is, then, a reciprocal relation between the act of poaching and the cultural role that is poached: the cultural meanings of the stolen role are conferred on the poacher, but at the same time the act of poaching gives renewed meaning to that cultural role. Henry's theft of the outlaw not only allowed some of the outlaw's power to flow to him, but also kept the outlaw alive as a vital ideological sign. Once again, as with the circulation of saints' relics, appropriation becomes a creation and a way of making the sign signify.

. . .

By way of conclusion, it is useful briefly to consider two implications of these four examples of appropriation. What is it they say to us as medievalists working in our various disciplines, searching for the meanings of events and objects from the distant past? First of all, because at their most fundamental level all of these examples view every instance of use of a cultural item—whether in the form of reading or viewing or worshipping or performing—as an act of appropriation and hence of creation, they make it difficult to look for any immediately and unmediatedly available meaning located in the source or original. They thus point away from intentionalist theories of interpretation which seek to discover the meaning that the author or artist *put into* the cultural item; they would thus tend to undermine the E. D. Hirsch style of hermeneutics that distinguishes between meaning and significance, the former given to the text by its author, the latter imposed by readers.

More importantly, given that intentionalist theories hold less sway these days than they once did, these examples also imply that meaning can't be fixed in the text or object itself without knowledge of its uses, which is to say, knowledge of its various appropriations. This creates problems for the semiotician, for if there are no sacred signifiers how can we discern the values and meanings of objects? Consider another incident from near the end of the Mashpee trial. A teenager named Chiefy takes the stand wearing a bandanna. The judge, obviously eager for a definitive sign of "Indianness" at last, tries to get Chiefy to say that the bandanna signifies precisely that. Chiefy, however, refuses to cooperate, stating flatly that he bought the bandanna in the local five-and-dime, the same way anybody could, and wears it to keep his hair out of his eyes, as anyone might. Pity the poor judge: if we can't say what a sign or object means, then how can we interpret it? Vexing though the message of Chiefy's bandanna may be, it nonetheless points to the user's powerful role in assigning—or denying—meaning through the appropriation of an object.

The relevance of both of these implications to medievalists—that meaning can't be grounded in the intent of the producer nor in the sign itself—is nicely demonstrated by Roger Chartier, in an essay appropriately entitled "Culture as Appropriation," which discusses popular cultural uses of printed books in early modern France.[36] Arguing that the determination to impose cultural models does not guarantee the way in which they are received and used, and noting that the circulation of cultural models or objects cannot be controlled so as to keep them out of the hands of unauthorized users, Chartier proposes that what distinguishes cultural worlds are different kinds of use and different strategies of appropriation. Using seventeenth-century France as an example, Chartier argues that "popular printing" in that country during that century has a complex meaning based on its recovering and reuse for a new public of texts that once belonged to an elite culture before they fell from fashion, which at the same time stigmatizes those texts, in the eyes of the cultured, as unworthy reading, because these texts belong to the popular classes. Hence what marks popular culture off from elite culture is not the intent of producers nor the cultural items exclusive to each group, but rather the functions, uses, and values each group assigns to those items—functions, uses, and values that are open to continual change.

Finally, what these examples of various acts of appropriation in medieval culture perhaps most strongly underscore is the logic of James Clifford's claim that the history of cultures is less a story about unbroken continuity than about "complex historical processes of appropriation, compromise, subversion, masking, invention, and revival."[37] Difficult though it may be, to scrutinize processes of appropriation—rather than fixed texts, objects, and events—lets us glimpse that history being written.

NOTES

[1] For recent studies of the phenomenon, see Martha Kaplan, *Neither Cargo nor Cult: Ritual Politics and the Colonial Imagination in Fiji* (Durham, N.C., 1995); and Harvey Whitehouse, *Inside the Cult: Religious Innovations and Transmission in Papua New Guinea* (Oxford, 1995).

[2] Jean Baudrillard, *Le Système des objets* (Paris, 1968).

[3] Key texts for appropriation studies include Homi Bhaba, *The Locations of Culture* (New York, 1994), which emphasizes the importance of going beyond originary narratives to focus on moments of cultural engagement; James Clifford and George E. Marcus, ed., *Writing Culture: The Poetics and Politics of Ethnography* (Berkeley, 1986), which critiques the appropriation practices of ethnographers; Sally Price, *Primitive Art in Civilized Places* (Chicago, 1989), which examines the collecting of "primitive" art by Western connoisseurs; and Janice Radway, *Reading the Romance: Women, Patriarchy, and Popular Literature* (Chapel Hill, 1984), which analyzes how women readers appropriate mass cultural texts.

[4] For accounts of nineteenth-century scholarly medievalism in England, Germany, and France, see Joan Evans, *A History of the Society of Antiquaries* (Oxford, 1956); William R. Keylor, *Academy and Community: The Foundation of the French Historical Profession* (Cambridge, Mass., 1975); Dom David Knowles, *Great Historical Enterprises* (London, 1964), which discusses both the Monumenta and Rolls series; and Peter H. Reill, *The German Enlightenment and the Rise of Historicism* (Berkeley, 1975).

[5] For a discussion of the salvage impulse in anthropology, see James Clifford, "Of Other Peoples: Beyond the Salvage Principle," in *Discussions in Contemporary Culture*, ed. Hal Foster (Seattle, 1988), pp. 121–50. For its impact on medieval studies, see my "Medieval Ethnography: Fieldwork in the Medieval Past," *Assays* 7 (1992): 1–30.

[6] For information about the provenance and date of the Croxton *Play of the Sacrament* as well as about the Trinity manuscript, see Norman Davis, ed., *Non-Cycle Plays and Fragments*, EETS s.s. 1 (Oxford, 1970); and John C. Coldewey, "The Non-Cycle Plays and the East Anglian Tradition," in *The Cambridge Companion to Medieval English Theatre*, ed. Richard Beadle (Cambridge, Eng., 1994), pp. 189–210.

7 Dick Hebdige, *Subculture: The Meaning of Style* (London, 1979).

8 Stuart Hall and Tony Jefferson, ed., *Resistance Through Rituals: Youth Subcultures in Postwar Britain* (London, 1976).

9 Hebdige, *Subculture*, p. 17.

10 Hebdige, *Subculture*, p. 18.

11 Hebdige's use of the notion of bricolage, implicit throughout *Subculture*, is directly discussed on pp. 102–106.

12 Claude Lévi-Strauss, *The Savage Mind* (Chicago, 1966), p. 17.

13 Paul Gilroy, *The Black Atlantic: Modernity and Double Consciousness* (Cambridge, Mass., 1993). Gilroy's examination of the hybridity of the African diaspora and the instability and immutability of identities foregrounds the relationship between ethnic sameness and differentiation, arguing for what Gilroy calls "a changing same" (p. xi).

14 John F. Fisher, "A Language Policy for Lancastrian England," *PMLA* 107 (1992): 1168–80.

15 *The Book of Margery Kempe*, ed. Sanford Brown Meech and Emily Hope Allen, EETS 212 (London, 1940). Scholarship has tended to downplay the role of scribes, but see John C. Hirsh, "Author and Scribe in *The Book of Margery Kempe*," *Medium Aevum* 44 (1975): 145–50.

16 Jean Froissart, *Chroniques de J. Froissart*, ed. S. Luce et al., 15 vols. (Paris, 1869–1975). For a discussion of the various redactions of the *Chroniques* and Froissart's habits of tinkering, see Peter Ainsworth, *Jean Froissart and the Fabric of History: Truth, Myth, and Fiction in the "Chroniques"* (Oxford, 1990), pp. 219–25 and passim; and J.J.N. Palmer, "Book I (1325–78) and Its Sources," in *Froissart: Historian*, ed. J. J. N. Palmer (Woodbridge, Eng., 1981), pp. 7–24.

17 Hebdige, *Subculture*, pp. 113–17.

18 For a discussion of consumption from the perspective of symbolic anthropology, see Mary Douglas and Baron Isherwood, *The World of Goods* (New York, 1979), which argues that consumption is "the very arena in which culture is fought over and ordered into shape" (p. 57). For studies of late medieval consumption, see Fernand Braudel, *Capitalism and Material Life, 1400–1800*, trans. Miriam Kochan (New York, 1973) and R. H. Britnell, *The Commercialization of English Society, 1000–1500* (Cambridge, Eng., 1993).

19 Michel de Certeau, *The Practice of Everyday Life*, trans. Steven F. Rendall (Berkeley, 1984).

20 Grant McCracken, *Culture and Consumption: New Approaches to the Symbolic Character of Consumer Goods and Activities* (Bloomington, 1988), pp. 71–92.

21 McCracken, *Culture and Consumption*, pp. 72–73.

[22] Patrick Geary, *Living with the Dead in the Middle Ages* (Ithaca, N.Y., 1994), pp. 194–218.

[23] McCracken, *Culture and Consumption*, p. 71.

[24] Among the important aspects of Gramsci's understanding of ideology are that he historicizes ideology, looking at specific historical constructions of power, and that he offers a less mechanistic notion of determination and ruling-class control than is found in someone like Althusser, arguing, for example, that change is built into the ideological system and that individual agents have power because the determining structure that produces individuals also produces a range of possibilities for them. See Louis Althusser, "On Ideology and Ideological State Apparatuses," *Lenin and Philosophy and Other Essays*, trans. Ben Brewster (New York, 1971), pp. 121–73; and Antonio Gramsci, *Selections from the Prison Notebooks*, ed. and trans. Quintin Hoare and Geoffrey Nowell-Smith (London, 1971). Althusser's marxism and its influence have been analyzed by Alex Callinicos, *Althusser's Marxism* (London, 1976). For a useful analysis of Gramsci's impact on cultural studies, see David Harris, *From Class Struggle to the Politics of Pleasure: The Effects of Gramscianism on Cultural Studies* (London, 1992).

[25] Michel Foucault, *Discipline and Punish: The Birth of the Prison*, trans. Alan Sheridan (New York, 1977).

[26] For representative studies, see Richard Dyer, *Heavenly Bodies: Film Stars and Society* (London, 1986); Patrick Wright, *On Living in an Old Country: The National Past in Contemporary Britain* (London, 1985); and Teresa de Lauretis, *Technologies of Gender: Essays on Theory, Film, and Fiction* (Bloomington, 1987).

[27] Erwin Panofsky, "Van Eyck's Arnolfini Portrait," *The Burlington Magazine* 64 (1934): 127.

[28] Margaret D. Carroll, "'In the Name of God and Profit': Jan van Eyck's *Arnolfini Portrait*," *Representations* 44 (1993): 96–125.

[29] See Toon van Houdt's recent analysis of the evolution of scholastic thought in response to emerging commercial practices of lending and credit in "Tradition and Renewal in Late Scholastic Economic Thought: The Case of Leonardus Lessius (1554–1623)," *Journal of Medieval and Early Modern Studies* 28 (1998): 51–73, especially p. 56 ff. This special issue, "Markets and Novelty," offers other examples of appropriation, including the Netherlandish appropriation of images for a newly expanding middle class.

[30] For a cogent discussion of the intersection of history and anthropology in medieval studies, with an eye to its importance for popular culture, see John

Ganim, "The Literary Uses of the New History," in *The Idea of Medieval Literature: New Essays on Chaucer and Medieval Culture in Honor of Donald R. Howard*, ed. James M. Dean and Christian K. Zacher (Newark and London, 1992), pp. 209–26. Ganim notes that one result of this intersection is an increased awareness of the literary text as "a site for cultural events, some of which are evident as powerful traces, and others of which may just be forming themselves in new combinations and reactions" (p. 225).

[31] Edward Hall, *Hall's Chronicle* (1547; reprint London, 1809), p. 520.

[32] Peter Stallybrass, "'Drunk with the Cup of Liberty': Robin Hood, the Carnivalesque, and the Rhetoric of Violence in Early Modern England," in *The Violence of Representation: Literature and the History of Violence*, ed. Nancy Armstrong and Leonard Tennenhouse (London, 1989), pp. 45–76.

[33] Andrew Ayton, "Military Service and the Development of the Robin Hood Legend in the Fourteenth Century," *Nottingham Medieval Studies* 36 (1992): 143.

[34] Pierre Bourdieu, *Distinction: A Social Critique of the Judgement of Taste*, trans. Richard Nice (Cambridge, Mass., 1986).

[35] V. N. Volosinov, *Marxism and the Philosophy of Language* (New York, 1973), p. 23.

[36] Roger Chartier, "Culture as Appropriation: Popular Cultural Uses in Early Modern France," in *Understanding Popular Culture: Europe from the Middle Ages to the Nineteenth Century*, ed. Steven Kaplan (Berlin, N.Y., 1984), pp. 229–53.

[37] James Clifford, "Identity in Mashpee," *The Predicament of Culture: Twentieth-Century Ethnography, Literature, and Art* (Cambridge, Mass., 1988), p. 338.

BEOWULF AND THE
ANCESTRAL HOMELAND

NICHOLAS HOWE

W hether remembered as cautionary tale from the past or as exodus to a promised land or as impetus for missionary work, the ancestral migration from continent to island stood as a founding event in the ecclesiastical history of the Anglo-Saxons. Their vigorous Christianity owed much to this persistence of memory because it taught that they had reached both the land of conversion and the possibility of salvation through a migratory journey. By setting this memory of the pagan past within Christian history, Bede and others transformed it into a myth of the culture. When the continental past of the Anglo-Saxons was interpreted biblically, it could be remembered without risk of theological error.

For some Old English poets, however, the pagan past could not be accommodated quite so directly. Rather than providing a warrant for action, it forced memories of distant places and figures—some no more than names—onto their consciousness. Other OE poets, notably Cynewulf, found another sense of the past in Christianity and avoided direct engagement with ancestral history. But for the poets of *Beowulf*, *Widsith*, and *Deor*, to name the most obvious, the past could not be separated from the pre-

From *Migration and Mythmaking in Anglo-Saxon England* (1989; reprint Notre Dame, 2001), pp. 143–79; reprinted with permission of Notre Dame University Press. The only alterations to the original have been to remove references Howe makes in the body of the essay to other sections of the book in which this essay originally appeared, and to convert the original "works cited" method of reference to endnotes. Translations of some Old English passages have also been added.

Christian homeland. For each, history becomes "the obligation of his art."[1] While these poets name places and give some sense of relative location, they think of Germania less as a region to be mapped than as one to be evoked. Germania endures for us as a distinct place because it is there that the historical imagination of these OE poets flourished. In a memorable essay, Eudora Welty explains the allure of place in fiction: "Location is the crossroads of circumstance, the proving ground of 'What happened? Who's here? Who's coming?'—and this is the heart's field."[2]

Germania as the "crossroads of circumstance" is evoked most hauntingly in the catalogues of rulers and tribes that make up *Widsith*. Here the greatness of the poet-figure as the embodiment of his people's history is celebrated through the dimension of geography. The fictional Widsith tells us that he has mastered the past and can salvage it from oblivion because he has traversed the northern world during his impossibly long life. The belief that from journeys comes knowledge serves as the governing poetic fiction of *Widsith* and also of *The Fates of the Apostles*, as Cynewulf designates the place where each of the twelve died in the course of enlarging Christendom. Whether used to demarcate the setting of sacred or legendary history, this fiction transforms the past into a territory the poet can master only by traversing it. Since the *Beowulf* poet must set the life of his hero into a narrative, he cannot cross the northern world as daringly as does the *Widsith* poet. Rather than use the *Widsith* poet's formula of X ruled Y, he must relate what happens when a king rules a people, and then must depict how that rule affects the life of his hero. In a brilliant essay on the poet's sense of history, Roberta Frank reminds us that Beowulf is not isolated in any one corner of Germania: "The *Beowulf* poet does his best to attach his pagan champion to as many peoples as possible—Danes, Geats, Swedes, Wulfings, and Wægmundings—as if to make him the more authentically representative of the culture and traditions of central Scandinavia: an archetypal Northman."[3] The poet does not achieve this wider geographical scope only through the life of his hero; he moves to other places and times in the northern world indirectly through extensive and artfully developed digressions.[4] Either way, the poet reveals the same impulse to evoke the north as his setting and ranges far more widely across Germania than would be necessary if he sought only to retell Beowulf's life.

The setting of this most English of Old English poems in the Scandinavian regions of Germania has often been noted.[5] Its hero is a Geat who performs his great deeds first among Danes and then among his own people. Although the Hengest of *Beowulf* may be the Hengest who led the Anglo-

Saxon migration, and the Offa of the poem may allude to the Offa who ruled Mercia, the poet offers no explicit connections between the world of his poem and that of his audience.[6] Most decisively, he does not name *Englalond*. The migration myth exists in the very texture of his poem, that is, in his use of geography as a narrative convention. We should remember that there is no surviving OE poem that relates the ancestral migration as explicitly as the *Aeneid* narrates the founding of Rome. Moreover, if such a poem ever existed, it has left no discernible traces in extant works.[7] While admitting the randomness of manuscript survival, I suspect no migration epic was ever composed in Anglo-Saxon England precisely because Bede had preempted the subject in his *Historia*. His vision of the migration and its effects on the culture was at once so encompassing and accessible that it left little room for another version of the story. A poet who knew more about the event than he found in Bede might have shaped a narrative from this myth. But there is no reason to credit an OE poet, of any period, with such knowledge about the mid-fifth century.

What remained for a great poet was the more audacious vision of recreating the northern world in the century or so after the traditional date for the Anglo-Saxon migration.[8] Beowulf belongs to the sixth century; he becomes king of the Geats some years after Hygelac's ill-fated raid into Frisia of ca. 521. The *Beowulf* poet saw that the history of the continental homeland did not end when the Angles, Saxons, and Jutes migrated to Britain. The events he relates were compelling because they were set in or near the old tribal regions. Since we are uncertain about the homelands for some of the tribes in *Beowulf*, it would be rash to argue precise geographical correspondences between poem and migration. The Geats, to cite the obvious example, have been placed in the north of Jutland and, alternatively, in the south of Sweden.[9] The Danes present less grave problems of localization. Still, as Gwyn Jones cautions, "He would be a man supremely bold or learned who claimed to know the exact relationship, habitat, or even identity, of Danes, Jutes, Eruli, Heathobards, and Angles."[10] For the reader of *Beowulf*, these problems are not fatal. The relation between ancestral and poetic geography is adequate to carry the poem's historical burden. The Danes and Geats were sufficiently akin in culture and location to serve in an OE poem that recreated the region left behind in fact but not in memory. Rather than impose our cartographical sense of geography on the poet and his audience,[11] we must recognize that, in spirit at least, Boniface's description of the continental Saxons holds also for the peoples of *Beowulf*: They are of the same blood and bone as the Anglo-Saxons. Whenever the poem was composed, its audience would have been alert to its setting; connections between continent and island—ranging from peaceful trading to violent raiding—kept alive ties with the place of the past.

The poet's choice of a Geatish hero may seem an oblique way of commemorating the ancestral homeland. Why did he not celebrate a figure from the premigratory past of the Angles or Saxons or Jutes? Did he choose Beowulf simply because he knew more about him than some more suitable hero? To ask such questions is to mistake the poet's purpose. He has no antiquarian curiosity about events before migration; he has a culturally imposed concern with the continuing history of the pagan north because it offers some vision of what the Anglo-Saxons might have become had they not made their exodus. The poet did not write a local poem but ventured into the territory and past of tribes other than the Geats. Most of his forays are so beautifully controlled by the thematic needs of the narrative moment that they do not seem intrusive.[12] His skill can lead us, then, to slight his evocation of a northern world not far distant from that of his ancestors.

The setting of *Beowulf* may be understood as the homeland before conversion. While thoroughly pagan, it is viewed through the sympathetic eyes of a Christian poet.[13] His sympathy does not lead him to cast the figures of his poem as Christians in all but the name of their belief. There is nothing sentimental about his vision; some Geats and Danes are virtuous in ways that Christians may honor, but none are Christian.[14] Yet the poet rarely condemns them as pagans. Those who believe a Christian poet would write of pagans only to censure them[15] might argue that his audience would pass that judgment for themselves. The belief that the poet and his audience would maintain an absolute distinction between pagan and Christian is crudely reductive, however, because it denies to both any knowledge of their past. Regardless of when we date the poem, both poet and audience would have known that they were descended from pagans who had been brought, by God's grace, to the true faith. And unless we put the poet very early, before 700, he could also have known of Anglo-Saxon missions to the continent. There is every reason to credit the poem with a historically informed and even charitable vision of pagans.[16] As Fred Robinson observes of the poet, "He wants [his audience] to accept the heathenism of the men of old and to join him in regretting it, but then he wishes to take his audience beyond this recognition of their spiritual status to a sympathetic evaluation of them for what they were."[17] To condemn these pagans would be to betray the past of the English and also their historically imposed duty to lead other peoples into Christendom. Stories about the Danes and the Geats could serve as a powerful reminder of the Anglo-Saxons' origins, both geographically and religiously.

The *Beowulf* poet found his warrant for this vision of the past in the Old Testament. All of his explicit biblical references are pre-Mosaic; he evokes a Genesis-like story of Creation for the *scop* at Heorot and places Grendel among the race of Cain. Morton Bloomfield has argued that the pagans of *Beowulf* live in a state much like that which prevailed until Moses handed down the New Law from Mount Sinai. He adds that this vision of the Old Law was "one way converted pagans could accept the New Law and still maintain pride of ancestry."[18] Something more vital than "pride of ancestry" was at stake, however, for this ancestral memory preserves the essential stage before conversion in a people's ecclesiastical history. Bloomfield rightly sets the poem's paganism in a past like that of the Old Law but does not recognize that, in both the Bible and in *Beowulf*, the Old Law held in places from which Israelites and Anglo-Saxons made their exodus. The New Law was given to each because it began a journey to its promised land. As in the OE *Exodus*, Germania was not Egypt; Bede's Angles, Saxons, and Jutes were not in bondage to pharaoh. Nonetheless, the north could be seen as a place of spiritual bondage from which these tribes had to flee if entry into Christendom were to be possible for a later generation.

When *Beowulf* is set beside the story of migration as found in Gildas, Bede, and *Exodus*, its use of time and place becomes deeply compelling. As these sources make clear, the continental homeland was a pagan place. That the migration of the Anglo-Saxons was an exodus—a divinely ordained journey—was manifested first by their role as God's agents for purging the island of British sinners and then by their conversion beginning in 597. The Christianity of the *Beowulf* poet is mediated by an informed sense of what is religiously possible in a given time and place. By seeing conversion as a process that begins with paganism, he could write of Germanic tribes that had not been converted because they lived beyond the frontiers of Christendom. Like book I of Bede's *Historia*, *Beowulf* locates the place of paganism in the religious history of the Anglo-Saxons.

· · ·

From the start, we hear that "the heart's field" of *Beowulf* is at once another time and another place. The opening of the poem creates a vivid sense of elsewhere and yet also enforces a sense of connection with the native land:

Hwæt! We Gar-Dena in geardagum,
þeodcyninga þrym gefrunon,
hu ða æþelingas ellen fremedon! (lines 1–3)[19]

Yes, we have heard of the glory of the Spear-Danes' kings in the old days—
how the princes of that people did brave deeds. (Donaldson, p. 1)

The phrase *in geardagum* and the preterite *fremedon* declare the pastness
of these noble deeds. The poet sets these deeds in a more complex sense of
the past by reminding his listeners that they have already heard—more ex-
actly, have already learned—about them. John D. Niles makes the necessary
point: "The sophisticated knowledge that the narrator assumes on the part
of the audience concerns not scriptural history but Germanic lore."[20] As the
most common verb in OE to denote memorial transmission, *gefrignan* ("to
hear") identifies the poem's substance as traditional.[21] The double allitera-
tion linking both elements of *Gar-Dena* and *gear-dagum* welds time and
place into the twin dimensions of the poet's narrative. One other connection
in this passage is so obvious that it may escape notice; *we gefrunon* unites
not only poet and audience, but also English audience and Danes, who, we
come to appreciate, represent a larger Germania.[22] The joining of insular au-
dience and continental history requires no act of translation but rather can
be accommodated by the vernacular. Unlike the *Exodus* poet who strained
his vernacular to assimilate the Israelites, the *Beowulf* poet worked within
the conventions of Germanic poetry. *Beowulf* never rises to the metaphoric
intensity or stylistic energy of *Exodus* because its poet did not need to re-
make his language to evoke the alien world of a distant people.

After reading *Beowulf*, one may see that its opening establishes the dy-
namic of the poem; it links the narrative moment (*we gefrunon*) with the
past (*in geardagum*) of another place (*Gar-Dena*). Fascinated by his cre-
ation of a past extending beyond the span of his hero's life, we slight his
creation of a setting that extends beyond the borders of his hero's home-
land.[23] Yet the poet is as digressive in his geography as in his chronology.
Most of the digressions about Beowulf and all of the digressions about
Germanic figures extend beyond the narrow confines of Geatland. The
poet is notably more precise in specifying the locale of these digressions
than in stating their date. From the start, he refuses to confine himself
to any one area of the north. He opens his poem about a Geatish hero
with an extended genealogy for the Danish royal house culminating with
Hrothgar and the crisis among the Danes. The temporal movement from

Scyld Scefing to his great-grandson Hrothgar is also a movement to the setting of Beowulf's first achievement. The opening reference to the Danes is thematically appropriate, but it also signals the geographical dimension of the poem. A sense of motion from one place to another runs throughout *Beowulf*. This is vividly apparent from the prefatory encomium for Scyld; he comes to Denmark as a child from across the sea and is given back to the sea after his death (lines 4–52).[24] Whatever mythic value may attach to his mysterious appearance and equally mysterious destination, his life establishes the pattern of movement by which the hero weaves tribal regions into a larger cultural homeland. Scyld's status as ancestor figure in the genealogies of both Anglo-Saxon and Danish kings provided the audience of *Beowulf* with a clear imperative to link the history and culture of the two regions.[25]

The ordering of *Beowulf* through an outwardly expanding and more encompassing sense of place depends heavily on its digressions. The first excursus into Germanic legend portrays Sigemund, the great dragon-slayer of the north. As it follows Beowulf's defeat of Grendel, this story seems beautifully integrated into the narrative.[26] As it looks forward to the third and final combat in the hero's life, it gains a prophetic weight. The joining of narrative and digression is masterful, but the poet's artistry expands beyond the thematic because this initial digression, when understood fully, sets a course for reading those that follow. Notice that Hrothgar's *scop* sets the parallel between Sigemund and Beowulf and in turn expands the narrative beyond its immediate setting. By endowing this fictional character with his own impulse to enlarge the poem's range, the poet suggests that his concern with the dimensions of the northern world is culturally determined and not idiosyncratic. In praising Sigemund's great deeds, the *scop* specifies among them his *wide siðas* ("wide journeys," line 877b).[27] These journeys are not described; that they were made seems a sufficient measure of renown. The poet has his *scop* portray Sigemund as the figure who embraces all of the legendary north. This portrait defines the hero as the man who is known throughout the world because of his deeds. Only at the poem's end, when Beowulf is mourned by his people, do we fully appreciate this insistence on measuring renown through geography.

The poet anticipates this definition of heroism in the lines immediately before the Sigemund digression. Here, too, he speaks through the words of his characters. As the Danes and Geats return from Grendel's mere, they celebrate Beowulf's fame with a kind of geographical hyperbole:

> Đær wæs Beowulfes
> mærðo mæned; monig oft gecwæð,
> þætte suð ne norð be sæm tweonum
> ofer eormengrund oþer nænig
> under swegles begong selra nære
> rondhæbbendra, rices wyrðra. (lines 856b–61)

There was Beowulf's fame spoken of; many a man said—and not only once—that, south nor north, between the seas, over the wide earth, no other man under the sky's expanse was better of those who bear shields, more worthy of ruling. (Donaldson, pp. 15–16)

All of this seems hopelessly imprecise: What are these seas? How far do these measures of north and south extend? If these seas are taken as the North and the Baltic, "be sæm tweonum" means "east and west" and completes "suð ne norð." To quibble about these seas or to limit these measures, however, would be to misread the poet's geography. In *Beowulf*, the hero's valor must be compared to that of men as they live across the world because renown is measured more resonantly in space than in time.[28] Just as Sigemund's *wide siðas* make him famous, so too Beowulf's fame will journey widely.

The Sigemund story validates the praise given to Beowulf by those returning from the mere because the deeds of the two heroes correspond. The offering of praise during the course of a journey looks forward, within the poem, to the outward spread of Beowulf's fame *ofer eormengrund* ("over the wide earth"). For it has already spread beyond Heorot, the site where it was won. Geography as the measure of fame offers the firmest connection between narrative and digression here because it establishes a principle for reading other such junctures in *Beowulf*, regardless of theme. Geography is implicated yet more deeply as the Sigemund story opens out to include Heremod:

> Se wæs wreccena wide mærost
> ofer werþeode, wigendra hleo,
> ellendædum—he þæs ær onðah—,
> siððan Heremodes hild sweðrode,
> eafoð and ellen. (lines 898–902a)

He [Sigemund] was adventurer most famous, far and wide through the nations, for deeds of courage—he had prospered from that before, the protector of warriors—after the war-making of Heremod had come to an end, his strength and his courage. (Donaldson, p. 16)

That the poet introduces this transition by again citing the wide journeys and fame of Sigemund suggests he intended a more complex opposition than beneficent hero and evil king.[29] The heroically wide-ranging Sigemund, who has no home, is set against the evil Heremod, who rules badly in the *eþel Scylding* ("Danish land," line 913).[30] Heremod's misrule is located among one people; Sigemund's renown spreads across many nations. Events and individuals acquire meaning as they exist within a sense of place. In relating Heremod's ill-fated life, the poet identifies his realm and says that he met his end elsewhere, *mid Eotenum* (line 902b). Whether this phrase means "among giants" or "among Jutes" has been much debated.[31] Linguistic evidence does not invalidate the reading of Jutes, and context favors it. For while this passage describes combat against monsters, it does so within a very human sense of place. Beowulf's valor in *eþel Scyldinga* leads the poet to speak of Sigemund and then of Heremod as figures who exist within the world of human beings. The digression is prompted by monster-slaying, but here, as elsewhere in *Beowulf*, an act is to be judged by its consequences for those who live in a given time and place.

The reference to *eþel Scyldinga* locates Heremod's crimes and also honors the eponymous Scyld. Within the history of this place, there are both negative and positive figures of kingship. Their meaning is stated explicitly in the famous speech Hrothgar directs at the triumphant Beowulf to warn him against youthful promise gone bad:

> Ðu scealt to frofre weorþan
> eal langtwidig leodum þinum,
> hæleðum to helpe. Ne wearð Heremod swa
> eaforum Ecgwelan, Ar-Scyldingum;
> ne geweox he him to willan, ac to wælfealle
> and to deaðcwalum Deniga leodum .... (lines 1707b–12)

You shall become a comfort, whole and long-lasting, to your people, a help to warriors. So was not Heremod to the sons of Ecgwela, the Honor-Scyldings. He grew great not for their joy, but for their slaughter, for the destruction of Danish people. (Donaldson, p. 30)

Although Hrothgar will narrate Heremod's crimes in detail (lines 1713–22a), he begins by setting them among the sons of Ecgwela, the Honor-Scyldings, the Danish people. Variation functions as geographical demarcation; by any of these names, the people now ruled by Hrothgar and rescued from monsters by Beowulf was once tyrannized by Heremod. The naming of this tribe for its heroes stands as a judgment against Heremod. For his people do not honor him by bearing his name. Hrothgar stresses the didactic value of Heremod's story by concluding with an imperative to Beowulf that he learn from it and be generous to his *folc*, "Ðu þe lær be þon, / gumcyste ongit!" ("Teach yourself by him, be mindful of munificence," lines 1722b–23a).

If one takes Hrothgar's speech as an implicitly Christian sermon, his portrait of Heremod may be read as an attempt to inculcate virtue in Beowulf. While this is partly true, it flattens Heremod into an abstract figure of evil by denying him his place in the north. If, instead, one believes that Hrothgar's words bear the heavy weight of history and his experience as ruler of the Danes, one may see that the geographical references associated with Heremod establish him as the figure of misrule in the history of the *eþel Scyldinga*. Hrothgar offers this portrait of Heremod to Beowulf, as he prepares to return to Geatland, to signal his vision of the hero's responsibility: He must not betray his youthful accomplishment among the Danes when he becomes king in another place across the sea.

In retelling Beowulf's deeds among the Danes, the poet names that people with various epithets. Some characterize their lineage, especially *Scyldingas*, and others emphasize their martial character, especially *Gar-Dene*. He offers another type of epithet in order to measure their homeland: *West-Dene* (line 383), *East-Dene* (line 392), *Suð-Dene* (line 463), and *Norð-Dene* (line 783). F. P. Magoun has argued that the poet used these terms to satisfy the demands of alliteration.[32] Since these epithets do not name groups of Danes, but rather the Danes as a whole,[33] it is risky to assign any value to individual uses. When all four are registered, however, these terms designate the range of the Danish homeland in the north. Just as Beowulf's fame is measured both south and north, east and west, so the Danes are registered with the four cardinal points. By setting events in their geography, the poet establishes that they occur in the world as it is demarcated and comprehended by the human imagination. Only as history is grounded in geography can it inform the hero's moral education.

The history of the Danes is Hrothgar's most generous gift to Beowulf for slaying Grendel and his mother. Knowledge of events in another region of the northern world is more precious than gold or horses, for it is the one good of the pagan world not subject to death and decay. Hrothgar offers, in Robinson's words, "a kind of natural, universal wisdom that any noble heathen might share with a Christian."[34] His lesson depends on a belief in the prudential value of the past. Heremod's tragedy teaches that glorious deeds may signal the hero's promise but can offer no assurance of future conduct. In relating Beowulf's stay among the Danes, the poet emphasizes the hero's deeds. As a public good, killing of monsters need not be explained; it is enough that it offers release from constant terror. As an event in a hero's life, however, such a triumph must be set in the larger ethical and legendary community presented through the digressions. When Beowulf returns to his *epel*, he knows far more about the north than he did when he set off for Heorot and may thus better understand his own deeds. Following Hrothgar, I have stressed the lesson of Heremod in the *epel Scyldinga*. But Beowulf's education ranges further afield.

While with the Danes, he learns about other regions and peoples of Germania. Most obviously, he hears about the journey of Hnæf and his Danish retinue to Finnsburg in Frisia. As it illustrates the inevitability of feuds, this episode offers a sobering counterpoint to the celebration at Heorot. Like others in the poem, this feud portrays the conflict of two distinct peoples inhabiting two different regions. The slaughter in Finn's hall is set in motion by Hnæf's presence in Frisia, but its roots run deep in the history of Danes and Jutes. We hear that Hnæf makes this journey to visit his sister Hildeburh, who has been married to Finn in the hope of weaving a peace and settling the old enmity between the two tribes. The characters in this episode seem more than usually ready to quarrel with one another. As the first sustained portrayal of a feud in *Beowulf*, the Finnsburg episode presents an anatomy of society in the north as it is fragmented by the persistence of the past.[35] The feud is particularly horrible because, when winter comes, Hengest and the surviving Danes cannot return home after Hnæf has been slain and a truce declared.[36] Even in truce, the tribes of this world cannot live together. Only geographical distance allows for some uneasy measure of stability. When spring arrives and the feud reaches its bloody end, Hengest and his followers journey home over the sea with Hildeburh: "Hie on sælade / drihtlice wif to Denum feredon, / læddon to leodum" ("They brought the noble woman in the sea-journey to the Danes, led her to her people," lines 1157b–59a). The digression ends artfully by returning to the narrative setting among the Danes and their queen, Wealhtheow.

The feud at Finnsburg is not the first such event retold in *Beowulf*.[37] Hrothgar is quick to note that Beowulf's visit to the Danes may be traced to a feud begun by his father, Ecgtheow. After killing Heatholaf of the Wylfings, Ecgtheow must flee Geatland and take refuge among the Danes when Hrothgar is a young king. Hrothgar thus interprets Beowulf's desire to slay Grendel as a delayed but no less welcome return for taking in his homeless father. As this story suggests, feuds have a geographical dynamic because they drive men and tribes beyond the confines of the homeland. The story of Ecgtheow and Hrothgar is atypical only because some good does come of an old conflict. In contrast, Finnsburg renders the true horror of feud by recording the breakdown of social cohesion. Within the narrative, it is the first sustained treatment of the "theme of the precarious peace."[38] The theme is first set elsewhere, far from the Danish homeland, because this distance echoes the terrible isolation that results from feuds. Each time this theme recurs, it enlarges the poem's portrayal of the northern world. Most poignantly, it will define Beowulf's particular greatness as the king who rules his own homeland well and imposes peace on the world around him until his death. Beowulf never forgets his education among the Danes, for his reign is the poet's only persuasive evidence that Finnsburg need not be inevitable.

That Beowulf carries this knowledge of other places back with him across the sea, that he has in some sense been rendered a Dane through Hrothgar's gift of history, establishes a model for the poem's audience: what happened elsewhere in Germania speaks to their own homeland. Events take place far afield, but their significance may be comprehended wherever people hear of them. Although these digressions move the narrative beyond the Geatish homeland, they display no taste for the strange or exotic. Unlike *The Wonders of the East* or *Alexander's Letter to Aristotle*, its companions in the manuscript, *Beowulf* never enters regions of the fabulous.[39] Even its monsters seem conventional when set beside the sideshow freaks reported by travelers to Asia.[40] Neither the poet nor his characters describe life elsewhere as being categorically different from that among the Geats or Danes. Swedes and Frisians may be ferocious enemies to the Geats, but they are not said to practice barbaric customs or worship alien gods. Feuds are never born in differences of belief. As the stories of Sigemund, Heremod, and Finnsburg extend the poem's territory, they also establish a certain consistency of behavior and belief among the various tribes of Germania.[41]

During the Danish section of the poem, each of the digressions is set within the narrative as a formal speech delivered by a character, whether it be Hrothgar or a nameless performer. Each is heard by Beowulf and becomes part of his education about the dimensions of his northern world.

As the poet recounts Beowulf's return to Geatland and later events, he enlarges the poem's territory in different ways. Now the stories about elsewhere are offered by the poet or, in a signal of his newly won status, by the hero himself. This change in technique is immediately evident in the poet's description of Beowulf's return to Geatland. As he follows Beowulf from his beached ship to Hygelac's hall, the poet adds two references to the north where Beowulf figures as hero. He speaks first of Thryth and Offa and then of Ongentheow.

The presence of Hygd, the generous queen, in the hall of the Geats prompts this reference to her counterpart, the enigmatic and haughty Thryth.[42] The comparison flatters Hygd for her graciousness and also evokes a pleasing memory of that other gracious queen, Wealhtheow.[43] While Hygd plays a role in Beowulf's ascension to the throne, the purpose of the Thryth digression emerges from the poet's statement that she changed for the better after her marriage to Offa. The reference to Offa brings yet another region and people, the continental Angles, into the orbit of the poem. This king had an immediately topical value for the poem's audience because he was honored as the noblest continental ancestor of the insular Angles.[44] The movement from Hygd to Thryth proves ultimately to be an occasion for praising Offa and evocatively linking the poem's audience and ancestral subject. Offa is described in terms that the poet has already used; he is "þone selestan bi sæm tweonum / eormencynnes" ("the best of mankind between the seas," lines 1956–57a) because he "wisdome heold / eðel sinne" ("he held his homeland with wisdom," lines 1959b–60a). The use here of *bi sæm tweonum* as a geographical measure of fame echoes its application to Beowulf (line 858), Æschere (line 1297), and Hrothgar (line 1685). The phrase may be formulaic, but the poet reserves it for deserving figures. His use of it after Beowulf's return to Geatland demonstrates its value as a measure of heroism for uniting figures from the Danish and Geatish sections of the poem. The phrase denotes the geography of the north and stresses its cultural uniformity. Its application to Offa allows us to understand the earlier statement that Beowulf's fame will spread between the seas. For this reason, Offa must be held in reserve until Beowulf is back among the Geats.

As Beowulf nears Hygelac's hall, the poet describes the Geatish king as the slayer of Ongentheow (*bonan Ongenþeoes*, line 1968). While this epithet for Hygelac is not literally accurate, it does allude darkly to later events in Geatish history. Through Ongentheow, this epithet designates the Swedes, who will pose the greatest danger to the Geatish homeland during the rest of the poem. Yet the poet does not need the allusions to Offa and

Ongentheow to move Beowulf from his ship to his lord's hall. For a man who has just slain two monsters, this action seems too trivial to mention. That it should prompt references to a larger legendary community marks it as more than the mere crossing of Geatish ground. The presence of Beowulf demands stories of other heroes and other places because he can no longer be contained only within the history of his own land. The cluster of allusions elevates Beowulf's passage to the hall into the ceremonial homecoming of the newly emergent hero.[45] As the scene illustrates, tribal identity in an oral culture is defined by "the body of tradition into which the individual and his deeds must be fitted."[46] The reference to Offa predicts the nature of Beowulf's mature achievement, and that to Ongentheow names the region from which it will be threatened.

When Beowulf enters Hygelac's hall and relates his stay among the Danes, he does not merely narrate what he has accomplished. He speaks as the hero who must understand his experience as it embraces both action and history. Although he is typically modest in stating that he slew Grendel and his mother, he shows surprising authority in speaking of the Danes. As he praises the high ceremonial style of Heorot, he emphasizes the grace of Wealhtheow and her daughter, Freawaru. Beowulf's memory of these two women passing the cup among the assembled warriors is perhaps the most moving depiction of peace and harmony in the poem. With this speech, Beowulf evokes the counterpoint of feud more powerfully than any other speaker in the poem. He also expresses his fear that the proposed marriage of Freawaru and Ingeld will fail to set a peace between Danes and Heathobards. In doing so, he does not mechanically repeat predictions of disaster he has heard elsewhere. Instead, he himself imagines a feud in the hall between Danes and Heathobards. As the two come together, the Danes display arms that had been won from the Heathobards in the past and that stand as brutal tokens of their defeat. The Heathobards will thus be driven, Beowulf predicts, to avenge their earlier losses, and the marriage of Freawaru and Ingeld will collapse.

Beowulf's prediction is the slaughter at Finnsburg reset in the land of the Heathobards. Roberta Frank describes this scene as "a fine display of chronological wit,"[47] but it is more immediately a fine display of geographical wit. The transposition of a Jutish story is possible because feuds occur throughout the north. Beowulf can shape his prediction about Freawaru and Ingeld into a dramatic event because of his education among the Danes. That a tale learned in a foreign place about a foreign people can be brought home and reset in yet another place demonstrates the larger cohesiveness of the

north. The bonds of that world are fragile and break at the slightest provo-
cation. Yet the stories told of that breakage endure and give some measure
of coherence to the north. Beowulf's recasting of the Finnsburg episode is
an exemplary act of cultural history because it demonstrates that the past
of another place speaks to the present. The *Beowulf* poet shrewdly used
the Ingeld story to illustrate this form of storytelling because, as Arthur
Brodeur notes, versions of the story were known in Anglo-Saxon England.[48]
The audience could recognize that its own knowledge of the Ingeld story
resulted from a comparable act of cultural transmission from continent to
island. Although listeners of *Beowulf* could hardly emulate the hero by slay-
ing monsters, they could do so by transferring a story from one setting to
another. In doing so, they would be likely to conclude that the various tribes
in *Beowulf* are remarkably similar despite their proclivity for feuding; and
yet all of them are radically different from the Anglo-Saxons because they
are pagan.[49]

In the first 2200 lines of the poem, until the dragon comes, we are held
by the figure of Beowulf. His deeds demand admiration and his wisdom
respect. To slight the narrative of monster-slaying and focus on the digres-
sions, as I have done, may seem myopic, until one considers that the poet
demarcates the world in which Beowulf's fame will resound by placing him
in the company of Sigemund and Offa. We do not keep count because of the
poet's art, but we have been introduced to Danes, Geats, Wylfings, Wendels,
Frisians, Goths, Brondings, Helmings, Angles, Swedes, and Heathobards.
Each tribe figures in the education of Beowulf before he becomes king of
his own land. And many of these tribal stories carry the same burden of a
broken peace. Germania, as Beowulf learns of it, seems a region of old en-
tanglements that smolder until they ignite into feuds.[50]

When Beowulf becomes king of the Geats, the focus of the poem shifts
from abroad to home. The poet continues to digress in his geography, but
his excursions speak directly to events in Beowulf's life and to the condition
of the Geats as a people. The poet's handling of narrative in the last third of
the poem is highly artful; he creates a present moment depicting Beowulf's
fight against the dragon while interweaving references to the past to explain
what will happen to the Geats in the future after Beowulf dies in that fight.
The poet must alter his opening strategy by depicting the outside world as a
threat to the homeland rather than as a proving ground for the hero.

As the poet moves from the young to the old Beowulf, he omits the whole
of his mature life. His disregard for biography is breathtaking. He dismisses
a fifty-year reign with the laconic remark that Beowulf was "ða frod cyning,

/ eald eþelweard" ("the wise king, the old guardian of the homeland," lines 2209b–10a). Since we read with expectations learned from later narratives, we may fail to recognize that the artfulness of this transition rests on a sense of place rather than time. We last see the young Beowulf in the Geatish hall exchanging treasure with Hygelac. Fresh from his return home, the hero offers some of Hrothgar's gifts to Hygelac, and the king reciprocates with his father's sword and a grant of land in the Geatish nation. With this scene, the direct portrayal of Beowulf's foreign exploits reaches its end. Having returned from his journey as a hero, he is given land where he may settle and assume his rightful place among the Geats. He will journey again, most notably with Hygelac to Frisia, but he goes as a proven retainer rather than as a free-willed youth out to win renown.

Beowulf never seems more open with possibility than during this exchange of gifts between Beowulf and Hygelac. The generous peace of the Geatish hall is deeply moving because, as Martin Stevens observes, treasure in all its forms "assures the continuity of civilization."[51] In their provenance, the gifts exchanged in Hygelac's hall may testify to ancient feuds, but they also assert the presence of the larger outside world of heroes. By setting this ceremony in Geatland, the poet creates a moment of repose between recounting the deeds Beowulf accomplishes abroad and in his own *eþel*. Just when the poem seems most evocative of a larger world, however, it abruptly narrows. After returning Beowulf to his home, the poet rapidly traces the developments by which he assumes the Geatish throne. Later, in flashbacks, he will fill out these events; now he seeks only to establish the fact of Beowulf's reign:

> Eft þæt geiode ufaran dogrum
> hildehlæmmum, syððan Hygelac læg,
> ond Hear[dr]ede hildemeceas
> under bordhreoðan to bonan wurdon,
> ða hyne gesohtan on sigeþeode
> hearde hildfrecan, Heoðo-Scilfingas,
> niða genægdan nefan Hererices—:
> syððan Beowulfe brade rice
> on hand gehwearf. (lines 2200–08a)

Afterwards it happened, in later days, in the crashes of battle, when Hygelac lay dead and war-swords came to slay Heardred behind the shield-cover when the Battle-Scylfings, hard fighters, sought him among his victorious

nation, attacked bitterly the nephew of Hereric—then the broad kingdom
came into Beowulf's hand. (Donaldson, pp. 38–39)

In summary, the poet tells us that first Hygelac and then Heardred dies—at
which point Beowulf becomes king. There is a sequence of rulers here but
no count of the years between Hygelac's gift of land and Beowulf's acces-
sion to the throne. We hear only that Beowulf ruled for fifty years, so round
a number it may mean no more than "for a long time." The transitional
passage concerns events set in time, but it organizes its larger meaning by
commemorating where Hygelac and Heardred die.

Hygelac falls amid the wreckage of his raid into Frisia, far from his
homeland. After this debacle, Beowulf, having won in battle thirty suits of
armor, returns across the water to Geatland. While these spoils cannot re-
deem Hygelac's death, they do testify to Beowulf's deeds in a distant land.
Within this transition, the death of Hygelac encapsulates the poem's first
section by registering once again the geographical pattern of the hero re-
turning home after winning fame abroad. There is also a difference because
this foreign episode will affect the Geats as a people. Beowulf's return is at
best the salvaging of personal heroism from communal disaster. In con-
trast with Hygelac, Heardred is slaughtered in the Geatish *eþel* where he has
been hunted down by avenging Swedes. The Swedish incursion alters the
geographical focus of the poem. Now the outside world becomes the source
of danger to the Geatish *eþel*. The transition from Hygelac to Heardred re-
capitulates the large movement in Beowulf from the hero in distant lands to
the hero in his homeland. Since the first of these failed kings indulges in for-
eign adventurism,[52] and the second proves unable to protect his *eþel* when
he is slain by Swedish raiders, this transition has a darkly ominous tone. As
kings gone wrong, however, Hygelac and Heardred cannot be classed with
Heremod; instead, they form the background for Beowulf's rise to kingship
and the present crisis of the dragon.

The attack of the dragon becomes the great, defining event of Beowulf's
reign. The dragon is an escapable danger; it burns Beowulf's hall and rav-
ages his land:

> Þa wæs Biowulfe broga gecyðed
> snude to soðe, þæt his sylfes ham,
> bolda selest brynewylmum mealt,
> gifstol Geata. (lines 2324–27a)

> Then the terror was made known to Beowulf, quickly in its truth, that his own home, the best of buildings, had melted in surging flames, the throne-seat of the Geats. (Donaldson, p. 41)

Throughout the poem, monsters are depicted as terrifying because they destroy the hall and with it all possibility of communal life.[53] Attacks by monsters are the domestic equivalent of tribal feuds; each fractures the social order in ways that only the hero—the man of force—can repair. If Beowulf was free earlier to seek out the monstrous at a safe distance in Heorot, now he must confront its ravages in his own hall. By locating this combat in Geatland, the poet defines the hero's responsibility to his own community. Edward Irving observes that "the defender of the hall [is] the embodiment of a profound kind of courage even beyond ordinary heroism."[54] The dragon fight balances the earlier fights with Grendel and his mother; as Beowulf wins his fame by combat with the nonhuman, so he dies in combat with the nonhuman. When read as the course of his life, *Beowulf* has a beautiful rhythm. J. R. R. Tolkien's description of this rhythm has never, to my mind, been bettered: "In its simplest terms [the poem] is a contrasted description of two moments in a great life, rising and setting; an elaboration of the ancient and intensely moving contrast between youth and age, first achievement and final death."[55] Yet *Beowulf* goes beyond the life of its hero to portray a common culture held together by both shared values and tribal feuds. The rhythm of home and abroad provides the poem with its sense of causality. Beowulf wins glory by venturing beyond Geatland; Geatland enjoys peace with the outside world because of Beowulf's glory.

Since the poem derives its coherence from this rhythm of the heroic world, the story of Beowulf's stand against the dragon presents the poet with an aesthetic dilemma. By foregrounding this event in Geatland, he risks losing the sense of a larger world he created earlier in the poem. Although he must portray Beowulf's death in painful detail, he cannot allow his poem to degenerate into a local episode or a tale of dragons. After stating that Beowulf's fame has spread *ofer eormengrund*, he must portray his death as an event that will fragment the political geography of the north.

The poet maintains this larger resonance by interrupting his account of the dragon fight with digressions set elsewhere in the north. These stories differ from earlier ones because Beowulf need no longer be defined through Sigemund or Offa. Instead, the poet presents stories about the Geats set in Frisia and Sweden to fill the lacunae of the transitional passage at line 2200. Many of these episodes are cast as the memories or speeches of Beowulf himself. After the dragon makes known his terrible presence, Beowulf falls into despair and accuses himself of breaking the Old Law:

wende se wisa, þæt he Wealdende
ofer ealde riht ecean Dryhtne
bitre gebulge; breast innan weoll
þeostrum geþoncum, swa him geþywe ne wæs. (lines 2329–32)

The wise one supposed that he had bitterly offended the Ruler, the Eternal Lord, against old law. His breast within boiled with dark thoughts—as was not for him customary. (Donaldson, p. 41)

It is significant that the poet's only portrayal of a despairing Beowulf should concern the *ealde riht*, the natural, or pre-Mosaic, code of law.[56] Beowulf's attempt to explain the violence of the dragon by charging himself with a violation of the Old Law brings the poem's undercurrent of religious belief to the surface. In his despair, Beowulf relates the peril facing the homeland to his individual transgression of an *ealde riht*, which is not to be confused with Christianity. The Old Law has meaning as a concept only from the retrospective position of the New Law of the Old Testament or the Gospels of the New Testament. Before the dispensation of the New Law, no one who held to the Old Law would designate it as such: it was simply the Law. By using *ealde*, the poet clarifies for his Christian audience which Law it is that Beowulf, as a pagan, believes himself to have transgressed.[57] The poet does not smuggle Beowulf into the poem as a latent Christian—a concept so anachronistic that it would have been beyond his comprehension.[58] Instead, he holds to a precise sense of time and place by using *ealde riht*, for that was the law honored in the pagan homeland before the exodus to the promised land. This use of *ealde riht* reveals his vision of conversion as a process that begins with a sense of spiritual life and transgression. He never details the substance of this life, perhaps because he did not know enough about the old gods to recreate pagan theology, or perhaps because he felt such material would disturb his audience. It was sufficient to characterize the pagan north as holding to the *ealde riht*.

Beowulf's sense of transgression explains the ritualistic preparations he undertakes before setting off to fight the dragon.[59] He orders an iron shield to be built because he knows the usual lindenwood cannot protect him against fire: *lind wið lige* (line 2341).[60] More crucial, he prepares himself by remembering the battles he has fought across the north after purging Hrothgar's hall. He thinks of Hygelac's raid into Frisia and the old entanglement between Swedes and Geats that led to Heardred's death and his own rule. His memories are set largely in other regions of the north, but they press most insistently on him as he readies himself to meet the dragon in his own land. The tie between the homeland and distant regions seems inescapable because of this pressure of memory. Beowulf turns to the past at this moment because he knows that his triumphs abroad are at best temporary stays against the invasion of Geatland.

Stories about Frisia or Ravenswood begin as digressions because they interrupt the account of dragon-fighting. But unlike digressions about Sigemund and Heremod, Beowulf's memories of his earlier life are not distanced from the narrative. The fight at Finnsburg lacks the dramatic immediacy of that at Ravenswood precisely because Beowulf hears and assimilates it as a coherent story told about another place. He does not need to interpret this feud because the *scop* does so through the act of telling the story. Ravenswood is more problematic because Beowulf must determine for himself how it will shape his fate and that of his people. The poet does not present the history of the Swedish-Geatish feud in a single, chronologically ordered passage, but rather returns to it on several occasions during the last third of the poem. The Swedish-Geatish feud is harder to understand than the Finnsburg episode precisely because it is not offered as a set piece performed by the *scop* in the hall. More precisely, this feud is harder to understand—for hero and audience—because it has yet to reach its conclusion.

In complicating the narrative of the dragon fight with Beowulf's memories of his earlier life, the poet follows the sequence laid down in the transitional passage at line 2200: first Hygelac and then Heardred. To name these kings is to evoke their enemies—first the Frisians and Franks, then the Swedes—and to bring them into the orbit of Geatish history. Whether we take the passage beginning at line 2384 to be the poet's summary or Beowulf's memories, it says very little about the hero's deeds in Frisia except that few of the Hetware returned home after encountering him there.[61] The poet displays a curious reticence here, as if seeking not to implicate Beowulf too deeply in Hygelac's folly.[62] It seems enough that Beowulf should survive the debacle in Frisia and return home with trophies to prove that he fought well.[63] Still, the poet's version of the Frisian raid seems ominous because it lacks the focused power and closure of the Finnsburg episode. We know enough about the dynamics of a feud to recognize that the poet offers a shadowy account of the Frisian episode so that he may suggest its significance lies not in the raid itself but in its consequences for the next generation. The Geats and Beowulf have left enemies behind in Frisia who will not forget this incursion into their homeland.

In relating Beowulf's guardianship of the young Heardred, the poet re-asserts the presence of a larger northern world by explaining more about the feud between Swedes and Geats. At this moment in the dragon fight, the poet does not identify the ultimate cause of this feud or trace its tortu-ous sequence of events. He says only that Heardred took in Eanmund and Eadgils, the sons of Othere, when they were driven out of Sweden after Onela usurped the throne. In turn, Onela tracked them down in Geatland, slew Eanmund as well as Heardred, and left Beowulf to rule over the king-dom before returning home. Again, the poet displays a curious reticence about Beowulf. We do not know if he, as Heardred's counselor, agreed with his policy of sheltering Eanmund and Eadgils. Nor do we learn why Onela should later have entrusted the Geatish kingdom to the most formidable of all Geats, to a man who had already proven his prowess across the northern world.[64] Far from being a puppet ruler, Beowulf will avenge the death of Heardred by supporting Eadgils when he overthrows Onela. As in the poet's account of the Frisian expedition, it seems enough that Beowulf should sur-vive Onela's incursion and come to the throne so that he may be brought, as *eþelweard*, into combat with the dragon. Here, too, the partial presentation of a foreign entanglement suggests that the feud of the Geats and Swedes cannot be completed in the narrative because it has not yet been complet-ed in history. This technique is not the poet's artful attempt at suspense because his audience is presumed to know the story being told. Instead, the poet unfolds the Geatish-Swedish entanglement stage by stage—in the midst of the dragon fight—to heighten the sense of inevitability. Beowulf will fall, and enemies will come.

As the poet returns to the narrative present and describes Beowulf chal-lenging the dragon, he does not leave the Geatish past behind. Beowulf himself cannot resist speaking further of the Swedish entanglement. As he sits on the headland near the dragon's barrow, he addresses his band of Geats and tells them of Hrethel, Hæthcyn, and Hygelac. Through this line of Geatish kings, Beowulf traces the Geatish-Swedish feud to earlier genera-tions so that he might offer something like its origin. Although this feud's full genealogy can be related only after his death, Beowulf does explain to his retinue that Hygelac came to the throne after Hæthcyn died in battle with the Swedes. By setting this feud deeper in the past, Beowulf reveals his awareness that it will erupt after his death when Swedes from across the wa-ter will attack the Geats. Significantly, it is Beowulf himself who establishes the larger geographical dynamic of this feud:

> Þa wæs synn ond sacu Sweona ond Geata
> ofer wid wæter wroht gemæne,
> herenið hearda, syððan Hreðel swealt,
> oððe him Ongenðeowes eaferan wæran
> frome fyrdhwate, freode ne woldon
> ofer heafo healdan, ac ymb Hreosnabeorh
> eatolne inwitscear oft gefremedon. (lines 2472–78)

Then there was battle and strife of Swedes and Geats, over the wide water a quarrel shared, hatred between hardy ones, after Hrethel died. And the sons of Ongentheow were bold and active in war, wanted to have no peace over the seas, but about Hreosnabeorh often devised awful slaughter. (Donaldson, p. 43)

The conflict between the two tribes extends over "the wide water" because the sons of Ongentheow would hold no friendship "over the sea." The conviction that nothing can keep feuds from touching the homeland is rendered tellingly by the reference to Hreosnabeorh. By designating this hill, one of the few features of Geatish topography named in the poem, Beowulf localizes the death of Hæthcyn in his own *eþel*. When we note that first Hæthcyn and then Heardred are killed by Swedes who have crossed to Geatland, we may better appreciate that the dynamic of home and abroad is not a narrative convention; it is the rhythm of history in the pagan north as reconstructed by the Anglo-Saxon poet. His vision of political geography may be reduced to a single axiom: life in the north changes because individuals or tribes cross the sea to attack other tribes. The poet's vision has in *Beowulf* a powerful simplicity that identifies the recurrent pattern of history.

After recounting Hæthcyn's death at Hreosnabeorh, Beowulf speaks with quiet force of his loyalty to Hygelac. He says that he repaid him for his gifts by doing battle and, invoking the most resonant of all OE tropes, understatement, adds that Hygelac had no need to search among the Gifthas or Danes or Swedes to buy a worse warrior. Even as he deprecates his status, Beowulf cannot restrict himself to the borders of Geatland; he must resort to a larger geography. Although acknowledging his loyalty to Hygelac, he asserts his primacy among the Geatish retinue: "symle ic him on feðan beforan wolde, / ana on orde" ("I would always go before him in the troop, alone in the front," lines 2497–98a). To be "alone in the front" is to strike a perfect balance between the role of hero and the status of retainer—a balance appropriate for Beowulf while he serves Hygelac. And yet this has always been true of him.

Whether he leads his retinue to Heorot as a young hero or to the dragon's barrow as an old king, he is always alone in the front. At this moment, he speaks also of his victory, achieved without weapons, over the Frankish warrior Dæghrefn. Although Beowulf's speech may be read as an attempt to inspire his men with a loyalty like that he displayed to Hygelac, it has the more evocative value of revealing his own recognition of his power in the north.

As Beowulf prepares to defend his homeland against the dragon, he cannot resist wandering through the scenes of his earlier heroism. There is nothing here of worldly vanity. All that Beowulf says is beautifully modulated by understatement. He remembers his life across the larger northern world because he knows that the tribes he names—Frisians, Franks, Swedes—have suffered losses at his hand that they will remember and avenge on the Geats. As he prepares to fight the dragon, Beowulf looks forward to a series of events that have little to do with the dragon and everything to do with his own death.[65] His life has taught him that the homeland is never isolated from other lands, that the wide sea can and will be crossed by those intent on repaying old injuries. The persistence of feuds proves that there is no defense against the memory of those who live in the north. Indeed, history seems the curse inflicted on the pagan north. Its inhabitants remember in order to avenge.

Beowulf himself cannot bring us all the way back in the Geatish memory to the scene of Ravenswood. That is left for the messenger to do after the king lies dead. The consequences of the stories told by Beowulf in his last hours can be apprehended only after his death. Each of the tribes he names will reappear in the prediction of disaster offered by the Geatish messenger. As he tells the Geats, once the death of the *eald epelweard* becomes known in the north, then Frisians, Franks, and Swedes will attack Geatland. He offers his prediction by summarizing the stories of feuds that Beowulf has just retold:

> Nu ys leodum wen
> orleghwile, syððan underne
> Froncum ond Frysum fyll cyninges
> wide weorðeð. Wæs sio wroht scepen
> heard wið Hugas, syððan Higelac cwom
> faran flotherge on Fresna land,
> þær hyne Hetware hilde genægdon,
> elne geeodon mod ofermægene,
> þæt se byrnwiga bugan sceolde,
> feoll on feðan . . . . (lines 2910b–19a)

71

> Now may the people expect a time of war, when the king's fall becomes wide-known to the Franks and the Frisians. A harsh quarrel was begun with the Hugas when Hygelac came traveling with his sea-army to the land of the Frisians, where the Hetware assailed him in battle, quickly, with stronger forces, made the mailed warrior bow; he fell in the ranks. (Donaldson, p. 51)

The predictive force of this speech depends on the repetition of *syððan* in two rather different senses; the first use refers to the future, when the Franks and Frisians will hear of Beowulf's death, and the second to a past, when Hygelac invaded Frisia. Through this repetition, the speaker establishes the causal relation between past and future. There is also an unstated sense of *syððan* here that looks further into the future: when Franks and Frisians arrive, disaster will come to the Geats. This same conviction of impending destruction, as it is rooted in past events, colors the words of the messenger when he speaks of the Swedes:

> Ne ic te Sweoðeode sibbe oððe treowe
> wihte ne wene, ac wæs wide cuð,
> þætte Ongenðio ealdre besnyðede
> Hæðcen Hreþling wið Hrefnawudu,
> þa for onmedlan ærest gesohton
> Geata leode Guð-Scilfingas. (lines 2922–97)

> Nor do I expect any peace or trust from the Swedish people, for it is wide-known that Ongentheow took the life of Hæthcyn, Hrethel's son, near Ravenswood when in their over-pride the people of the Geats first went against the War-Scylfings. (Donaldson, p. 51)

This speech is framed through the measure of space rather than time; its predictive force depends on the messenger's statement that Ongentheow's killing of Hæthcyn is widely known. The messenger will go on to deliver the poem's only full account of the battle at Ravenswood, for now that Beowulf lies dead its significance must be directly addressed. Speaking of Hrethel's death, which occurs at another stage in the Swedish-Geatish feud, Irving remarks, "It is typically a king's death that releases such anarchic savagery."[66] Seen in another way, such a death unleashes the ferocity of history. For then a tribe must admit that its safety and even its identity have rested on its king's reputation for martial valor.

72

The messenger's speech is the most explicit statement in *Beowulf* about the hero's power to stay anarchy through personal authority. As I shall argue, this statement is crucial to the poem as it enfolds the pagan north into its narrative. For the moment, one must stress that the messenger is portrayed anonymously as the voice of the Geats. Precisely because he has no identity, his prediction cannot be dismissed as his own fear. His voice could belong to any Geat with an historical imagination. A few lines later, the poet affirms the substance of the messenger's prophecy:

> Swa se secg hwata secggende wæs
> laðra spella; he ne leag fela
> wyrda ne worda. (lines 3028–30a)

> Thus the bold man was a speaker of hateful news, nor did he much lie in his words or his prophecies. (Donaldson, p. 53)

The poet hardly needs to confirm the messenger's speech, for its validity is deeply rooted in the stories told about the Geats' feuds with Frisians, Franks, and Swedes. He intervenes in these lines to set another, more necessary perspective on Geatish history, that of a Christian Anglo-Saxon. With these lines, the poet signals to his audience that they must withdraw from the narrative and ponder its meaning. He restates his vision of the pagan north: There is nothing to end the relentless dynamic of the feud as it fragments that world from one generation to the next. The poet's moral and historical vision is not invalidated by the fact that the Geats did not disappear with Beowulf's death but rather survived for several more centuries.[67] The poet uses Beowulf's death to consign the Geats to the margin of history. The meaning of this fate is voiced most eloquently by the series of anonymous speakers who appear throughout the last third of the poem: the "Last Survivor," who bequeaths his people's treasure to the earth (lines 2247–66); the messenger, who announces the impending end of the Geats (lines 2900–3027); and the woman who keens over Beowulf's body as he is buried (lines 3150–55a).[68] None can be remembered by name; each speaks from the margin.

The Geats as a people are given final closure; they exist only in the poet's re-creation of the pagan north. They have no direct descendants to commemorate them in their own homeland. They survive only as they are remembered by Anglo-Saxons who could trace their ancestry to the exodus of the mid-fifth century. Finally, this explains the poet's choice of a Geatish hero for his epic of the ancestral homeland. Unlike such continental peoples as Franks, Frisians, or Saxons, the Geats had no role in the insular history of the Anglo-Saxons. Later events did not disprove the poet's vision of their extinction. Most urgently, there was no tradition of a Geatish conversion led by English missionaries. For the Anglo-Saxons, the Geats as a people lived and died in Egypt and were remembered only by those who had reached Canaan.

This English perspective on continental history validates the complicated matter in which the poet tells of the Frisians and Swedes. At first, the narrative power of the dragon fight makes us impatient of these digressions. We are held rapt by the depiction of Beowulf's final stand and pass over earlier events set in distant regions of the north. Finally, we do register these digressions because they demarcate the reach of Beowulf's authority as he rules the Geats and also because they establish his achievement of holding the north in peace. In a passage of astonishing majesty, Beowulf states the meaning that he must set to his lifework before he dies:

> Ic ðas leode heold
> fiftig wintra; næs se folccyning,
> ymbesittendra ænig ðara,
> þe mec guðwinum gretan dorste,
> egesan ðeon. Ic on earde bad
> mælgesceafta, heold min tela,
> ne sohte searoniðas, ne me swor fela
> aða on unriht. (lines 2732b–39a)

> I held this people fifty winters. There was no folk-king of those dwelling about who dared approach me with swords, threaten me with fears. In my land I awaited what fate brought me, held my own well, sought no treacherous quarrels, nor did I swear many oaths unrightfully. (Donaldson, p. 48)

To keep foreign kings at bay to avoid feuds at home is to counter the dangers of the outside world and of the *eþel*.[69] The digressions in the final one thousand lines prove the difficulty of holding this balance, for they name no other king who could attach a similar value to his life. Beowulf has wielded his reputation for heroism as a weapon to keep the peace at home and abroad. He alone holds the world around him from the chaos of feuds because he alone perceives that heroism extends beyond personal fame and can become a form of political stability. Even the manner of his death expresses this vision. He is spared the ignoble end of a Hygelac and also emerges undiminished by human defeat. While he ruled, no enemy could stand against him and the Geats; only a battle with the dragon, the emblem of this world's darkness,[70] can provide a fitting end for the hero who kept the peace throughout the north. The unavoidable irony of this pagan culture is that Beowulf, the only figure in the poem with this vision of a larger world, should die defending the *eþel* against a monster.

Beowulf's tragedy is to apprehend the limits of individual heroism in a pagan world. For it is his fame that has spread *ofer eormengrund* and imposed peace on a recalcitrant world. The realpolitik of the north is brutally simple: Tribes without a famous warrior king are open to attack. The winning of heroic reputation need not be seen as *vanitas*; rather it serves as a bulwark against outsiders while its bearer survives to wield weapons and preserve the integrity of the homeland.[71] In remembering his life, Beowulf draws no easy distinction between hero and king; the great deeds he accomplishes abroad while a youth insure his authority when he rules as the old king of the Geats.[72] As for the objection that an old king should not play the young hero by taking on the dragon alone, the poet tells us that, as Beowulf seems about to fall, only Wiglaf joins him in combat. Ultimately, the hero is alone in his mortality before both the dragon and the suspended threat of feud: *ana on orde.*

If Beowulf attempts the impossible, it is not in fighting the dragon by himself but rather in holding to some vision of peace across the north. For there is neither the force of national identity nor the authority of religious belief to maintain peace after his death. In this pagan world, violence exists unrestrained by any sense of ethical or political good. Only the hero can hold feuds in abeyance, and he is constrained by his own mortality. Whether Beowulf dies beside the dragon or gently in his sleep, the world will collapse around his people because the past cannot be erased. He cannot leave behind what he has struggled all his life to create. With profound insight, the poet allows him to die without an heir.[73] There runs through *Beowulf* an implicit, but radical, critique of individual heroism as limited by morality.[74] Even the noblest heroic achievement is transient. The poet is far too aware of the historical distance between himself and his subject, however, to direct this critique of heroism at Beowulf. As a man, he does far better than anyone can expect of him. Instead, the poet directs his critique at the fatally limited world in which his hero must move, for it holds to no faith or higher vision of life by which to preserve peace across the turn of generations. Finally, Beowulf does not represent his world as, we are told, epic heroes should do. Instead, his world betrays his achievement by succumbing to feuds as soon as he is dead. In portraying the heroic ethos of the north, the *Beowulf* poet forces us to recognize that its emphasis on physical strength, courage, and loyalty is ultimately to no avail. There is no sense of sacred or earthly justice to insure that such virtues will be placed in the service of the good. For every Beowulf, there is at least one Heremod.

Although he exerts his authority to keep the peace, Beowulf cannot reshape his world of fragmented tribes and kingdoms; he is not a sixth-centuty Bismarck or even a Charlemagne. Rather, Beowulf holds out some brief hope that the geography of the north need not be demarcated by feuding parties but by beneficent voyagers such as he was as a youth. He offers this vision in his dying request that his funeral barrow be made into a beacon to guide journeyers across the sea:

> Hatað heaðomære hlæw gewyrcean
> beorhtne æfter bæle æt brimes nosan;
> se scel to gemyndum minum leodum
> heah hlifian on Hronesnæsse,
> þæt hit sæliðend syððan hatan
> Biowulfes biorh, ða ðe brentingas
> ofer floda genipu feorran drifað. (lines 2802–08)

> Bid the battle-renowned make a mound, bright after the funeral fire, on the sea's cape. It shall stand high on Hronesness as a reminder to my people, so that sea-travelers later will call it Beowulf's barrow, when they drive their ships far over the darkness of the seas. (Donaldson, p. 49)

As a beacon to guide sailors over the darkness of the waters, this monument honors the visionary hope Beowulf has offered to the pagan north.[75] The poet's description of this monument as *beadurofes becn* ("a beacon for the bold in battle," line 3160) is a powerful reminder that Beowulf could impose peace because he was bold in battle. Beowulf must set his vision in stone because of his fear that this hope will not survive in a Geatland soon to be consumed by feuds. That his choice for a memorial seems at best emblematic—and at worst quixotic—only proves its urgency.

The symbolic intent of Beowulf's memorial testifies to his exceptional nature in the north, for it is the rarest of heroic warriors who turns his strength to peace rather than to conquest. In his singularity, Beowulf is the appropriate hero for an Anglo-Saxon poem about the continental homeland. Through him, the poet can reveal and indict the limits of this pagan culture. In a Germania unsanctified by conversion, the Christian good of peace can be achieved only by the strong man and then only for a brief time. For an Anglo-Saxon poet, Beowulf has the great virtue of being a warrior of peace rather than a killing machine: "He is heroic and pious, a pagan prince of peace."[76] If this distinction seems anachronistic, remember that it lies at the heart of *The Dream of the Rood*. Yet to name this poem is to appreciate why Beowulf is not a type of Christ; his achievement must be ephemeral in a pagan warrior culture that is not nourished by some shared theology of peace.

To interpret *Beowulf* as a critique of the pagan culture that survived in the homeland is to read the poem through the perspective of Anglo-Saxon England. This reading is not shaped entirely by religious difference, although the poem's informing Christian voice must not be forgotten. Equally important is the memory of cultural continuity between continent and island. The poet fills his narrative with geographical movement to establish that the relation of homeland and larger world provides the necessary principle for understanding history. While it would seem crucial to know something about where the poem was composed, history tells us little about the English milieu of *Beowulf* that cannot be deduced from its language. To belabor the point, this poem about Geats and Danes was composed in the vernacular of Anglo-Saxon England. More vitally, its language bears no mark of translation. One can offer much the same thematic reading of *Beowulf* from its use of language as from its use of history and geography.

Such a reading of the poem's language has been provided by Fred C. Robinson in *Beowulf and the Appositive Style*. At the risk of distorting his subtle argument, I quote the following passage as a summary of his interpretation:

> The poet of *Beowulf* attempts to build a place in his people's collective memory for their lost ancestors. This lofty and challenging theme requires for its expression an appositive style, a style more suggestive than assertive, more oblique than direct. A poet who, in a deeply Christian age, wants to acknowledge his heroes' damnation while insisting on their dignity must find and exercise in his listeners' minds the powers of inference and the ability to entertain two simultaneous points of view that are necessary for the resolution of poignant cultural tensions.[77]

Robinson traces this appositive style through key terms in the poem, especially those that refer both to the paganism of the continental Geats and the Christianity of the insular Anglo-Saxons. The semantic range of *metod* to name a pagan and a Christian deity is perhaps the clearest illustration of this method. When a character in the poem speaks of *metod*, we must understand a pagan creator but must also set this sense in a complementary relationship with *metod* as it names the Christian deity.

Since the language of *Beowulf* is characteristically appositive, it makes continuous demands on its audience. The frequency of apposition means that one cannot discard older, pagan meanings in favor of newer, more comfortable meanings unique to Christianity. At a lexical level, apposition forces listeners to hold two meanings at the same moment; at an interpretative level, it forces listeners to accept ambiguity and understand that history cannot be reduced to a single dimension. Robinson argues that apposition is a "habit of mind" by which to accept historical complexity.[78] In its range of meanings, for example, *metod* contains the essential stages of Anglo-Saxon religious history. The poet can balance these meanings because of the historical conversion, which unites the varieties of experience necessary to sustain apposition.[79] Dorothy Whitelock has said that the *Beowulf* poet "was composing for Christians, whose conversion was neither partial nor superficial."[80] It follows, she argues, that the audience required no explanation of the poet's biblical allusions. But it also follows that the audience understood the cultural meaning of conversion. One may develop Robinson's argument by noting that the older meanings carried by the poem's central religious terms—those that are pagan and potentially dangerous—are neutralized by the poet's geography. For he establishes through the narrative that the pagan reference of *metod* and similar terms held not merely in the past but also in another place: a region of the *ealde riht*, distanced by the literal geography of the North Sea and the symbolic geography of exodus. To speak figuratively, *Beowulf* has an appositive geography in which one term is explicit (the pagan north) and the other is implicit (Christian England). The poet's practice of portraying his characters' journeys and also of setting his digressions in distant places creates a pattern of response for his audience. For only as they make this imaginative journey back to the continental homeland can they appreciate how conversion altered their condition as a Germanic people.

The poet enforces this response on his audience through his dextrous handling of geography. Although he has a keenly defined sense of the past, he works it into his narrative chiefly through the measure of place. The past may be a construction of chronology, but there is also a geographical sense of the past, especially in cultures that possess an enduring myth of migration. For the significant act rendered by this myth is movement from a place of origin to a place of new beginnings. As the myth of the American West demonstrates, the vital past of the United States is located in a pattern of movement from the settled regions of the east to the frontier of the west. Although this myth draws on events from the nineteenth century, its value lies in a metaphorically liberating sense of place. If the past can exist most enduringly as a place in a literate culture with a precise chronology, then it may well have done so even more strongly in Anglo-Saxon England, where chronology had not yet become a universal convention. Although Bede was the first to master the system of *anno Domini* for an extended work, the opening book of his *Historia* integrates geographical myths of origin with a Christian measure of chronology. As he knew, geography captures better than chronology the distinctions between continent and island. Moreover, the Book of Exodus showed that geography as a means for ordering a people's religious experience had a reassuringly ancient status.

The geographically ordered narrative of *Beowulf* may be read as a model to apprehend and interpret the historical process by which Anglo-Saxon culture was transformed from its origin in pagan Germania to its converted state in Christian England. The *Beowulf* poet, unlike such masters of place in modern fiction as Hardy or Faulkner, does not immerse us so deeply in Geatland that we forget the world beyond its borders. Geatland differs from Wessex or Yoknapatawpha County because it serves as the place of origin for the narrative. From that corner of the Germanic world, the poem moves outward to embrace the pagan north and then, by the force of apposition, England. The poet's piety for the place of the past remains firmly in the service of a larger piety. The meaning of his poem holds within the literal and symbolic geography of Christendom. For only the memory of exodus and then of conversion can justify the poet's retelling of stories about pagans. No other extant work from Anglo-Saxon England makes the meaning of the fifth-century migration as vividly powerful as does *Beowulf* because no other work demands that its audience make a return migration to the continent. That this journey must be imaginary rather than actual underscores the social value of poetry, for few individuals of the time could venture back to the continent as missionaries.[81] In a profound sense, the *Beowulf* poet demands of his listeners that they imitate the poetic fiction of the traveling *scop*. Like the speakers of *Widsith* or *The Fates of the Apostles*, they must traverse the geography of the past in order to understand the meaning of their religious history and their faith as Christians.

If *Beowulf* is set beside Wulfstan's *Sermo Lupi ad Anglos*, its use of the migration myth may seem implicit to the point of invisibility. Obvious differences of purpose and genre, however, make any comparison between the two misleading; the poet did not intend to write a hortatory work to rally his fellow Anglo-Saxons to moral reform.[82] Nothing about the poem indicates that it was composed during a moment of crisis.[83] The deeply absorbed quality of the migration myth in *Beowulf* suggests that the poet sought to explore its larger significance for the Anglo-Saxons. His digressive use of geography demonstrates that a past set in many places can serve as a coherent body of knowledge about a culture's origins and current state. Indeed, through his act of composition, the poet teaches a method for comprehending and ordering the past. He displays a reflective quality, a willingness to envision the pagan world as a complex and necessary subject. For this reason, we must resist interpreting the poem as meaning "There but for the grace of God, go we Anglo-Saxons." While this might render the meaning of a sermon, it does not respond to the imagined reality of *Beowulf*—to its careful and distantly admiring evocation of another world.[84]

Beowulf survives today as poetry because the relation between island audience and continental subject is set implicitly into the texture of its narrative. The poet had no need to announce this relation because he could trust to the Anglo-Saxon myth of migration. He saw himself as complementing, perhaps even completing, that myth by venturing back to Geatland, Denmark, Frisia, and Sweden. As modern readers, we must reconstruct the poet's intent in depicting the pagan north because we do not feel the animating power of the migration myth. While it flourished, however, the poet could evoke the place of his poem and trace the journeys of heroes across the north without explaining his method. To cite a parallel, Americans required no explanation to feel in their bones the mythic value of a political appeal for a New Frontier.

The *Beowulf* poet's judgment of the pagan north is conditioned by yet one further factor. As he portrays life among the various pagan tribes, he works from the perspective of a larger communal group. His vision that peace in the pagan world is ephemeral and dependent on the power of individual heroes is sharpened by his membership in a more enduring society. To claim that he belonged to a nation, as we use the term, would be foolish.[85] To suggest he had historical reasons for believing the English were a more unified people than any of the ancestral northern tribes would not be entirely misleading. The poet wrote during the long and difficult transition from tribe to nation. The time of Beowulf was already in the past. If this transition had yet to be completed, it was set inexorably in motion. Although the poet could think of his people as a Christian *folc*, that vision encouraged a larger identification with Christendom rather than with the unique circumstances of Anglo-Saxon history. He required a vision by which to set the place of the English as a people within the larger dimensions of Christendom. For this purpose, the migration myth stood unchallenged in its historical and theological power.

• • •

The myth of migration gave the English as a *folc* a common identity by teaching them that they were descended from those who had made the exodus of the mid-fifth century. In the absence of the political cohesiveness offered by nationhood, a myth of origin provides a people with some means for determining its organic status as a group. When that myth of origin may be envisioned through a central story from the Bible, such as Exodus, then it acquires the necessary theological warrant to locate the place of a people within Christendom. Indeed, the continuing vitality and diversity of the migration myth in Anglo-Saxon England can be explained only by this theological warrant. The vision of historical and contemporary events that we find in Wulfstan and Alcuin, Gildas and Bede, the OE *Exodus* and *Beowulf* is too multifaceted to be explained by any single abstract principle of history. Instead, this diversity must be explained by the grounding of the migration myth in the history of the Israelites as a chosen people. For just as their history embraced danger and triumph, faith and sin, so it was with the history of the Anglo-Saxons in that long stretch from 449 to 1014 and beyond.

NOTES

[1] Gwyn Jones, *Kings, Beasts, and Heroes* (London, 1972), p. 41.

[2] Eudora Welty, *The Eye of the Story: Selected Essays and Reviews* (New York, 1979), p. 118.

[3] Roberta Frank, "The *Beowulf* Poet's Sense of History," in *The Wisdom of Poetry: Essays in Early English Literature in Honor of Morton W. Bloomfield*, ed. Larry Benson and Siegfried Wenzel (Kalamazoo, 1982), p. 64. For the setting of the poem of the shores of the Kattegat, see Frank, "Skaldic Verse and the Dating of *Beowulf*," in *The Dating of "Beowulf*," ed. Colin Chase (Toronto, 1981), pp. 129–30.

[4] I use "digressions" here and elsewhere because it belongs to the established terminology for *Beowulf*, and also because it suggests that an episode has a different setting from that of the narrative. As for the poet's artistry, I agree with Eric Stanley that "far from being intrusions or excrescences [the digressions] are the result of his directness of expression" ("*Beowulf*," in *Continuations and*

Beginnings: Studies in Old English Literature, ed. Eric G. Stanley [London, 1966], p. 133).

5 For surveys of English-Scandinavian relations during the Anglo-Saxon period, see Nicolas Jacobs, "Anglo-Danish Relations, Poetic Archaism and the Date of *Beowulf*," *Poetica* (Tokyo) 8 (1977): 23–43; Alexander Callander Murray, "*Beowulf*, the Danish Invasions, and Royal Genealogy," pp. 101–11 and R. I. Page, "The Audience of *Beowulf* and the Vikings," pp. 113–22, both in Chase, *The Dating of "Beowulf"*; and Robert T. Farrell, "*Beowulf* and the Northern Heroic Age," in *The Vikings*, ed. Robert T. Farrell (London, 1982), pp. 180–216.

6 The evidence for determining whether these two Hengests are one and the same is presented by, among others, A. Van Hamel, "Hengest and His Namesake," in *Studies in English Philology: A Miscellany in Honor of Frederick Klaeber*, ed. Kemp Malone and Martin Ruud (Minneapolis, 1929), pp. 159–71; J. E. Turville-Petre, "Hengest and Horsa," *Saga-Book of the Viking Society for Northern Research* 14 (1953–57): 287–89; and Brian D. Joseph, "Using Indo-European Comparative Mythology to Solve Literary Problems: The Case of the Old English Hengest," *Papers in Comparative Studies* 2 (1982–83): 177–86. The description of Hengest seems to encourage this identification; he is said to be eager to sail across the sea (lines 1127b–35a) and is often associated with sea journeys (e.g., *sælad*, lines 1139, 1157). Yet this evidence is not conclusive, precisely because of the dynamic of sea journeys within the narrative of *Beowulf*. The relation between the two Offas is discussed later in this essay.

7 Ritchie Girvan, *"Beowulf" and the Seventh Century* (London, 1935) states, "If there were Anglo-Saxon lays about the conquest of England we know nothing of them" (p. 3). See also Alistair Campbell, "The Use in *Beowulf* of Earlier Heroic Verse," *England Before the Conquest: Studies in Primary Sources Presented to Dorothy Whitelock*, ed. Peter Clemoes and Kathleen Hughes (Cambridge, Eng., 1971), pp. 283–92. For a suggestive comparison of *Beowulf* and the *Aeneid* as "focused on the adventures of a new hero," see Frank, "The *Beowulf* Poet's Sense of History," p. 64. Theodore Andersson makes a claim for direct influence in *Early Epic Scenery: Homer, Virgil and the Medieval Legacy* (Ithaca, N.Y., 1976), pp. 145–59.

8 Stanley observes, "Perhaps there is a deeper reason why *Beowulf* is satisfactory. The Christian poet chose to write of the Germanic past" ("*Beowulf*," p. 137).

9 For studies of the Geats in history and literature, see Kemp Malone, "The Identity of the *Geatas*," *Acta Philologica Scandinavica* 4 (1929–30): 84–90; Jane Acomb Leake, *The Geats of "Beowulf": A Study of the Geographical Mythology of the Middle Ages* (Madison, 1967), and the important response by George V. Smithers, "The Geats in *Beowulf*," *Durham University Journal* 63 (1971): 87–103; and Robert T. Farrell, *Beowulf, Swedes, and Geats* (London, 1972).

[10] Gwyn Jones, *A History of the Vikings*, rev. ed. (Oxford, 1984), p. 48.

[11] See William W. Lawrence, *"Beowulf" and the Epic Tradition* (Cambridge, Mass., 1928), p. 32.

[12] On the relation between narrative moment and digression, see Claire Kinney, "The Needs of the Moment: Poetic Foregrounding as a Device in *Beowulf*," *Studies in Philology* 82 (1985): 311.

[13] The pagan elements of *Beowulf* have been discussed by virtually every critic. For a judicious summary of recent opinion, see Fred C. Robinson, *"Beowulf" and the Appositive Style* (Knoxville, 1985), pp. 9–14.

[14] For the paganism of Hrothgar's Danes and the important phrase *hæþenra hyht* ("the hope of heathens," line 179), see Arthur G. Brodeur, *The Art of "Beowulf"* (Berkeley, 1959), pp. 206–08; Eric G. Stanley, "Hæthenra Hyht in *Beowulf*," in *Studies in Old English Literature in Honor of Arthur G. Brodeur*, ed. Stanley B. Greenfield (Eugene, 1963), pp. 136–51, especially p. 150; and Karl P. Wentersdorf, "*Beowulf*: The Paganism of Hrothgar's Danes," *Studies in Philology* 78 (1981): 91–119.

[15] See W. F. Bolton, *Alcuin and "Beowulf": An Eighth-Century View* (New Brunswick, N.J., 1978), pp. 175–77.

[16] See Brodeur, *The Art of "Beowulf*," p. 210, and Derek Pearsall, *Old English and Middle English Poetry* (London, 1977), p. 11.

[17] Robinson, *"Beowulf" and the Appositive Style*, p. 11.

[18] Morton Bloomfield, "Patristics and Old English Literature: Notes on Some Poems," in Greenfield, *Studies in Old English Literature*, p. 39. See also Charles Donahue, "*Beowulf*, Ireland and the Natural Good," *Traditio* 7 (1949–51): 275 and "*Beowulf* and the Christian Tradition: A Reconsideration from a Celtic Stance," *Traditio* 21 (1965): 80–85.

[19] All references to *Beowulf* are from Fr. Klaeber, ed., *"Beowulf" and the Fight at Finnsburg*, 3rd ed. with supplements (Lexington, Mass., 1950). All translations are from E. Talbot Donaldson, trans., *Beowulf* (New York, 1966), and all references to such will be made parenthetically by page number.

[20] John D. Niles, *"Beowulf": The Poem and Its Tradition* (Cambridge, Mass., 1983), p. 207.

[21] See Jacobs, "Anglo-Danish Relations," p. 28; on *Beowulf* as "heroic history," see Robert W. Hanning, "*Beowulf* as Heroic History," *Medievalia et Humanistica*, n.s., 5 (1974): 77–102. My reading on *Beowulf* has been deeply shaped by Hanning's discussion of the poet's sense of the past.

[22] Robinson, *"Beowulf" and the Appositive Style*, pp. 9–10.

[23] For a sensitive exploration of the *Beowulf* poet's use of time, see Niles, *"Beowulf": The Poem and Its Tradition*, pp. 179–96. His claim that the poem "does not achieve epic fullness through geographic comprehensiveness (for the action is

narrowly localized)" (p. 195) is true if one defines epic by the standards of the *Odyssey* or the *Aeneid*. Yet if one considers the *Beowulf* poet's use of historical and legendary materials, then one may conclude that his geography of the Scandinavian world is as inclusive, albeit on a smaller absolute scale, as Homer's geography of the Mediterranean world.

[24] On the motif of the sea journey in *Beowulf*, see Lee C. Ramsey, "The Sea Voyages in *Beowulf*," *Neuphilologische Mitteilungen* 72 (1971): 51–59.

[25] See Murray, "*Beowulf*, the Danish Invasions, and Royal Genealogy," pp. 103–09, and Frank, "Skaldic Verse and the Date of *Beowulf*," pp. 126–29.

[26] See Adrien Bonjour, *The Digressions of "Beowulf"* (Oxford, 1965), pp. 47–48.

[27] See Campbell, "The Use in *Beowulf* of Earlier Heroic Verse," p. 289.

[28] This geographical measure of fame is invoked frequently in the poem. Wealhtheow tells Beowulf that he will be praised "efne swa side swa sæ bebugeð" ("as wide as the seas surround the shores," line 1223); and he says of journeying: "feorcyþðe beoð / selran gesohte þæm þe him selfa deah" ("far countries are well sought by him who is himself strong," lines 1838b–39).

[29] On the skaldic treatment of these two heroes, see Frank, "Skaldic Verse and the Date of *Beowulf*," p. 131; on the use of names to strengthen this distinction, see Robinson, *"Beowulf" and the Appositive Style*, p. 22.

[30] The manuscript's use of the runic letter ᛟ rather than the word *eþel* here may be a touch of the exotic—a reminder of the continental setting of this homeland. This could, of course, be appreciated only by those reading the manuscript.

[31] See N. F. Blake, "The Heremod Digressions in *Beowulf*," *Journal of English and Germanic Philology* 61 (1962): 278–87; R. E. Kaske, "The *Eotenas* in *Beowulf*," in *Old English Poetry: Fifteen Essays*, ed. Robert P. Creed (Providence, R.I., 1967), pp. 285–310; and C. L. Wrenn, ed., *Beowulf*, rev. ed. W. F. Bolton (London, 1973), p. 131.

[32] F. P. Magoun, "Danes, North, South, East, and West, in *Beowulf*," in *Philologica: The Malone Anniversary Studies*, ed. Thomas A. Kirby and Henry B. Woolf (Baltimore, 1949), p. 24.

[33] Lawrence, *"Beowulf" and the Epic Tradition*, p. 34.

[34] Robinson, *"Beowulf" and the Appositive Style*, p. 33.

[35] See Martin Carmago, "The Finn Episode and the Tragedy of Revenge in *Beowulf*," *Studies in Philology* 78 (1981): 132.

[36] See John F. Vickrey, "The Narrative Structure of Hengest's Revenge in *Beowulf*," *Anglo-Saxon England* 6 (1977): 102.

[37] In his essay "*Beowulf* and the Margins of Literacy," Eric John notes, "There are twenty-five references to feuds [in *Beowulf*] according to my calculation: the poet is obsessed by them" (*Bulletin of the John Rylands University Library* 56 [1975]: 411).

[38] Bonjeur, *The Digressions in "Beowulf,"* p. 61.

[39] Kenneth Sisam's witty description of Cotton Vitellius A.xv as "Liber de diversis monstris, anglice" (*Studies in the History of Old English Literature* [Oxford, 1953], p. 96) is convincing if taken to designate the manuscript compilation. It should not be taken to mean that the various works in the manuscript display the same sense of the monstrous.

[40] See Stanley, *"Beowulf,"* pp. 105–08, and Smithers, "The Geats in *Beowulf,"* p. 88.

[41] The differences between the tribes noted by Roberta Frank ("The *Beowulf* Poet's Sense of History," p. 55) are noteworthy but not so significant as to affect this claim; the Swedes and Geats are, as she says, "more authentically primitive, more pagan in outlook and idiom, than the Danes," but all three tribes are indisputably pagan.

[42] See Norman E. Eliason, "The 'Thryth-Offa Digression' in *Beowulf,"* in *Franciplegius: Medieval and Linguistic Studies in Honor of Francis Peabody Magoun, Jr.*, ed. Jess B. Bessinger and Robert P. Creed (New York, 1965), pp. 124–38, for a useful discussion of the continental Offa.

[43] The connection between these two women is signaled by Beowulf when he gives Hygd the necklace given him by Wealhtheow (lines 2172–73). See Bonjour, *The Digressions in "Beowulf,"* pp. 53–55.

[44] See Jacobs, "Anglo-Danish Relations," pp. 41–43. As has been suggested by various critics (Stanley, *"Beowulf,"* pp. 133–35, and Chambers, *"Beowulf": An Introduction to the Study of the Poem*, 3rd ed., rev. C. L. Wrenn [Cambridge, Eng., 1967], pp. 31–40), the poet's praise of the continental Offa may have been meant to flatter Offa of the Mercians (d. 796?). Although this suggestion requires that we date *Beowulf* no earlier than the end of the eighth century, it is attractive because the Anglo-Saxon Offa was famous for his continental ties, especially with Charlemagne (see J. M. Wallace-Hadrill, *Early Medieval History* [Oxford, 1975], pp. 155–80). On Offa, see Edith Rickert, "The Old English Offa Saga," *Modern Philology* 2 (1904–05): 1–48 and *Modern Philology* 3 (1905): 1–56, and Whitelock, *The Audience of "Beowulf,"* pp. 57–64.

[45] *Sæ-Geatas* appears twice in the poem: in Hrothgar's last speech to Beowulf as he prepares to leave the Danes (1ine 1850), and in the description of his return to Geatland and Hygelac (line 1986). The use of *sæ* in this compound alludes to both the journey by which Beowulf wins fame and the geographical dimension of heroic fame.

[46] Robert W. Hanning, *The Individual in Twelfth-Century Romance* (New Haven, 1977), p. 143.

[47] Frank, "The *Beowulf* Poet's Sense of History," p. 55.

[48] Brodeur, *The Art of "Beowulf,"* p. 175.

[49] On the audience's Christian and English perspectives, see Marijane Osborne, "The Great Feud: Scriptural History and Strife in *Beowulf*," *PMLA* 93 (1978): 978–80.

[50] In this regard, at least, *Beowulf* seems a reasonably accurate mirror of conditions in the north: "Also, the early petty kingdoms [in Denmark], however entitled, were subject to vicissitude. By conquest, inheritance, coalescence, or act of god, their fortunes and boundaries changed" (Jones, *A History of the Vikings*, p. 51).

[51] Martin Stevens, "The Structure of *Beowulf*: From Gold-Hoard to Word-Hoard," *Modern Language Quarterly* 39 (1978): 227.

[52] In this interpretation of Hygelac, I follow R. E. Kaske, "The Sigemund-Heremod and Hama-Hygelac Passages in *Beowulf*," *PMLA* 74 (1959): 490; for a more laudatory view, see G. N. Garmonsway, "Anglo-Saxon Heroic Attitudes," in Bessinger and Creed, *Franciplegius*, pp. 140–41. On Hygelac as meaning "instability of mind," see Fred C. Robinson, "The Significance of Names in Old English Literature," *Anglia* 86 (1968): 57.

[53] Niles, *"Beowulf": The Poem and Its Tradition*, p. 233.

[54] Edward B. Irving Jr., *A Reading of "Beowulf,"* (New Haven, 1968), p. 40.

[55] J. R. R. Tolkien, "*Beowulf*: The Monsters and the Critics," *Proceedings of the British Academy* 22 (1936): 271.

[56] Bloomfield, "Patristics and Old English Literature," pp. 36–43.

[57] See Frank, "The *Beowulf* Poet's Sense of History," p. 55.

[58] On the Anglo-Saxon belief that "salvation without conversion was impossible," see Robinson, *"Beowulf" and the Appositive Style*, p. 13. For a very different reading of *ealde riht*, see Charles Moorman, "The Essential Paganism of *Beowulf*," *Modern Language Quarterly* 28 (1967): 3–18.

[59] See Garmonsway, "Anglo-Saxon Heroic Attitudes," pp. 143–45.

[60] See Irving, *A Reading of "Beowulf,"* p. 217.

[61] See Walter Goffart, "*Hetware* and *Hugas*: Datable Anachronisms in *Beowulf*," in Chase, *The Dating of "Beowulf,"* pp. 83–100.

[62] See Stanley B. Greenfield, "Geatish History: Poetic Art and Epic Quality in *Beowulf*," *Neophilologus* 47 (1963): 213.

[63] That Beowulf must survive if there is to be a poem about his rule negates Moorman's claim that "we should have expected Beowulf to have died at Hygelac's side, and it may well be that his flight is the violation of an *ealde riht* of the *comites* which he recalls and laments at the end of his life" ("The Essential Paganism of *Beowulf*," p. 15). See Greenfield, "Geatish History," p. 213.

[64] See Norman E. Eliason, "Beowulf, Wiglaf, and the Wægmundings," *Anglo-Saxon England* 7 (1978): 99–101.

[65] See Brodeur, *The Art of "Beowulf,"* p. 77.

[66] Irving, *A Reading of "Beowulf,"* p. 181.

[67] On the survival of the Geats after the time of Beowulf, see Farrell, *Beowulf, Swedes, and Geats,* pp. 29–43, and Frank, "Skaldic Verse and the Date of *Beowulf,*" pp. 125–26. Any discussion of this matter must be guided, as Farrell notes, by the claims of poetry rather than history: that the Geats will be wiped out makes for an "ethically satisfying narrative" even if historically inaccurate (p. 1).

[68] On the woman who keens over Beowulf's body, see Irving, *A Reading of "Beowulf,"* p. 198.

[69] On this passage, see Thomas D. Hill, "The Confessions of Beowulf and the Structure of the *Volsung Saga,*" in Farrell, *The Vikings,* pp. 165–79. Beowulf's defence of the homeland is all the more remarkable because Geatland, unlike Denmark, is not "an island nation with natural boundaries" (Kathryn Hume, "The Theme and Structure of *Beowulf,*" *Studies in Philology* 72 [1975]: 16).

[70] See Daniel G. Calder, "Setting and Ethos: The Pattern of Measure and Limit in *Beowulf,*" *Studies in Philology* 69 (1972): 35.

[71] In "Social Structure as Doom: The Limits of Heroism in *Beowulf,*" in *Old English Studies in Honor of John C. Pope,* ed. Robert B. Burlin and Edward B. Irving (Toronto, 1974), pp. 37–79, Harry Berger Jr., and Marshall Leicester Jr. argue that Beowulf performed too well: "What he fashioned and gave with such generosity was himself. And in so doing, he unwittingly but unavoidably took something too: his unique and charismatic being made reciprocity impossible—worse, it made reciprocity unnecessary" (p. 64).

[72] A fatal contradiction between Beowulf as hero and as king has been argued by John Leyerle in two articles, "Beowulf: The Hero and the King," *Medium Ævum* 34 (1965): 89–102, and "The Interlace Structure of *Beowulf,*" *University of Toronto Quarterly* 37 (1967): 1–17, and also by Margaret E. Goldsmith in her book *The Mode and Meaning of "Beowulf"* (London, 1970), pp. 222–28. For challenging responses to this view, see Hume, "The Theme and Structure of *Beowulf,*" pp. 1–27; Colin Chase, "Beowulf, Bede, and St. Oswine: The Hero's Pride in Old English Hagiography," in *The Anglo-Saxons: Synthesis and Achievement,* ed. Douglas J. Woods and David A. E. Pelteret (Waterloo, 1985), pp. 37–48; and Stanley B. Greenfield, "Beowulf and the Judgment of the Righteous," in *Learning and Literature in Anglo-Saxon England: Studies Presented to Peter Clemoes,* ed. Michael Lapidge and Helmut Gneuss (Cambridge, Eng., 1985), pp. 393–407.

[73] See Eliason, "Beowulf, Wiglaf, and the Wægmundings," pp. 102–05.

[74] See John Halverson, "The World of *Beowulf,*" Journal of *English Literary History* 36 (1969): 593–608, and Berger and Leicester, "Social Structure as Doom."

[75] See Irving, *A Reading of "Beowulf,"* p. 234, and Peter Clemoes, "Action in *Beowulf*

and Our Perception of It," in *Old English Poetry: Essays on Style*, ed. Daniel G. Calder (Berkeley, 1979), p. 167.

[76] Frank, "The *Beowulf* Poet's Sense of History," p. 62; also, Frank, "Skaldic Verse and the Date of *Beowulf*," p. 133.

[77] Robinson, *"Beowulf" and the Appositive Style*, pp. 13–14.

[78] Robinson, *"Beowulf" and the Appositive Style*, p. 80. Robinson writes, "Amid the historically determined ambiguities of his Cædmonian formulas, the poet finds a place in his people's mind and language where their ancestors can remain, not with theological security, but with dignity," (p. 59). Roberta Frank speaks of the poet's use of language "to conquer a remoteness, the space between himself and the sixth-century world he wanted to portray" ("'Mere' and 'Sund': Two Sea-Changes in *Beowulf*," in *Modes of Interpretation in Old English Literature: Essays in Honor of Stanley B. Greenfield*, ed. Phyllis Rugg Brown et al. [Toronto, 1986], p. 165).

[79] I must acknowledge my debt throughout this chapter to Patrick Wormald's illuminating essay, "Bede, *Beowulf*, and the Conversion of the Anglo-Saxon Aristocracy," in Bede and Anglo-Saxon England, ed. Robert T. Farrell, *British Archaeological Reports* 46 (1978): 32–95.

[80] Whitelock, *The Audience of "Beowulf*," p. 5.

[81] For a sensitive exploration of possible relations between Beowulf and the continental missions, see Larry D. Benson, "The Pagan Coloring of *Beowulf*," in Creed, *Old English Poetry: Fifteen Essays*, pp. 193–213.

[82] See Brodeur, *The Art of "Beowulf*," p. 185.

[83] This statement should not be taken as evidence for the date of *Beowulf*. While this matter remains very much in doubt, recent studies have had the great virtue of destroying the old orthodoxy that the poem could not have been composed during the Danish occupation of England (Whitelock, *The Audience of "Beowulf*," pp. 24–26). See the studies on Anglo-Scandinavian relations by Jacobs, "Anglo-Danish Relations"; Kevin S. Kiernan, *"Beowulf" and the "Beowulf" Manuscript* (New Brunswick, N.J., 1981), pp. 15–23; Murray, "*Beowulf*, the Danish Invasions, and Royal Genealogy"; Page, "The Audience of *Beowulf* and the Vikings"; Eric G. Stanley, "The Date of *Beowulf*: Some Doubts and No Conclusions," in Chase, *The Dating of "Beowulf*," pp. 197–211; and Frank, "Skaldic Verse and the Date of *Beowulf*" and "The *Beowulf* Poet's Sense of History." I would add only that the Anglo-Saxons hardly needed contact with Danes or Vikings to be interested in their continental ancestry; that subject was very much a part of the migration myth from Bede to Wulfstan. It is, however, quite possible that the Danish occupation of England served to renew stories about the Scandinavian homeland among the English. (Much the same may be said also of the OE

Exodus, if one assumes that it was written after the Scandinavian settlements of the ninth century.) In this matter, it is salutary to quote Alain Renoir: "I readily confess that I should be at a loss to tell when, where, by whom, and under what circumstances, this greatest of all early-Germanic epics was composed" ("Old English Formulas and Themes as Tools for Contextual Interpretation," in Brown et al., *Modes of Interpretation in Old English Literature*, p. 68).

[84] Frank puts it well: "The *Beowulf* poet pondered his northern heathens and northern heroes, and raised to their memory a monument far more Christian and, at the same time, far more Scandinavian, than the mound at Sutton Hoo" ("Skaldic Verse and the Date of *Beowulf*," p. 139).

[85] On this point, see Jacobs, "Anglo-Danish Relations," pp. 30–34.

WRITING THE
UNREADABLE *BEOWULF*

ALLEN J. FRANTZEN

HOMER AND *BEOWULF*

I n an early scene in *The Caxtons: A Family Picture*, the novel published by Edward Bulwer-Lytton in 1850, Augustine Caxton is mulling over the effects of textual criticism on Homer. The precise nature of Homer's achievement, in particular the probability that the poem had been written in a form different from that in which it had been composed, had been a subject of scholarly controversy for nearly three centuries. But the "marriage" between textual and literary criticism that was needed to reveal the historical Homer as an origin, as a center from which one could chart the history of the epics in antiquity, was first realized in the work of the German scholar F.A. Wolf, who published the *Prolegomena ad Homerium* in 1795. Wolf attempted to discover the original form of the *Iliad* by defining detailed criteria that helped reconstruct the state of the text as it had been transmitted century after century; he explained how revisers had altered the poem as it passed from oral to written culture, and in so doing he successfully attacked the unity of the text and the status of its author.[1] As Caxton reads, his

From *Desire for Origins: New Language, Old English and Teaching the Tradition* (New Brunswick, 1990), pp. 168–200; reprinted with permission of Rutgers University Press. The only alterations to the original have been to remove references Frantzen makes in the body of the essay to other sections of the book in which this essay originally appeared and to amplify material in footnotes for the sake of clarity.

wife interrupts to ask what they shall name their newborn son; she assumes "Augustine," after the father, but he objects and suggests "Samuel" instead, a name his young wife abhors. Caxton continues to read; his wife continues to ask about the baby's name. Suddenly he bursts out, "'Pisistratus!,'" the name of the Athenian tyrant (600–528 B.C.) credited by some scholars with having fixed the oral text of Homer that the rhapsodists recited at the Panathenaic festival held every four years at Athens.[2] "'Pisistratus Caxton," says his wife. "'Thank you, my love: Pisistratus it shall be.'" "'Do you contradict me?'" he replies to her unexpected response. "'Do you side with Wolfe and Heyne, and that pragmatical fellow, Vico? Do you mean to say that the Rhapsodists—.'" His wife hastens to assure him that she does not contradict him (nor, indeed, does she know what he is talking about). Caxton, a shy man who hates ceremonies, contrives to miss the baby's christening; he learns to his horror that his son, at his own suggestion, has been named after a sixth-century Greek "enslaver of Athens and disputed arranger of Homer."[3]

Bulwer (1803–1873) was a member of Parliament and a prolific novelist. Although he is not taken seriously by critics of the novel, his historical fiction was as influential in interpreting the Middle Ages for nineteenth-century readers as were the novels of Sir Walter Scott. Bulwer historicized aspects of medieval culture that modern criticism has only begun to notice. One of his historical novels, *Rienzi: Last of the Roman Tribunes*, published in 1835, recounts the life of the fourteenth-century revolutionary Cola di Rienzo. Revolution does not seem to be an obvious subject for an M. P. raised to peerage in 1866, but Lord Bulwer was radical in his politics, and the interest in revolution, heavily sentimentalized, is not so out of place as one might expect. *Rienzi* was translated into German in 1839 and made its way into the hands of a writer with a considerably keener interest in revolutions, Richard Wagner, who fashioned it into his first successful opera, *Rienzi, der Letzte der Tribunen*, staged in Dresden in 1842.[4]

Just as he historicized the Middle Ages, Bulwer helps us to historicize his contemporaries. *England and the English*, published in 1833, surveys the national character, educational apparatus, and social structure with the shrewd observations that are also engaged in his fiction.[5] *The Caxtons* is not in Bulwer's historical vein, although the great fifteenth-century printer, William Caxton, supposedly stands at the foot of this family tree. The novel's mild satire on pedantry historicizes textual criticism of the professional, "Germanic" type, as well as publishing and printing, in the context of armchair scholarship still traditional in the middle of the century. Bulwer's joke requires little more than that his audience recognize the importance of Homer and the affront to common sense created by German criticism's attempt to dismantle his identity.

Wolf's work appeared when the foundations of textual criticism and modern scholarship were taking form in German universities. Philology and classical and biblical scholarship were all part of his achievement, and were in turn all deeply influenced by it.[6] Wolf's thesis about Homer influenced Karl Lachmann and, through Lachmann, generations of scholars who contemplated the origins of *Beowulf*. Karl Müllenhoff, one of Lachmann's students, proposed multiple authorship for *Beowulf* in 1869. Müllenhoff's *Liedertheorie* ("song theory") posited the origin of *Beowulf* in folk lays, where Lachmann had placed the origin of the *Niebelungenlied*. Just as the songs of the wandering minstrels were the supposed origins of the *Iliad*, folk songs were the supposed origins of *Beowulf*. One of Müllenhoff's inspirations was John Mitchell Kemble, who published the first English edition of *Beowulf* in 1833 (corrected and reissued in 1835), with translation and commentary following in 1837.[7] But when Augustine Caxton contemplated Homer, *Beowulf* was still too obscure to have been a subject for public humor.

That much has changed. Woody Allen advises students not to take "courses where they make you read *Beowulf*"[8] and *Beowulf* and the *Canterbury Tales* are the only English texts before Shakespeare to merit a place in Maurice Sagoff's *ShrinkLits: Seventy of the World's Towering Classics Cut Down to Size*, which boils the epic down to 26 lines: "Monster Grendel's tastes are plainish. / Breakfast? Just a couple Danish."[9] *Beowulf* survives in the *Norton Anthology of English Literature*, a partner to Bede's *Ecclesiastical History* and the episode of Cædmon in shaping impressions of Anglo-Saxon culture for the undergraduate audience. *Beowulf* is the only Old English text to exist in a *Norton Critical Edition* (although in translation),[10] and it is the only Old English text to merit one of the MLA's "approaches" volumes.[11]

No other Old English text has attained such status, nor is another likely to challenge the position of *Beowulf*. Its reputation among general readers is, of course, dreadful, but this is less the fault of the text than of those who teach it and those who interpret its editorial and textual tradition. Yet, at the levels of reading and instruction discussed in relation to "Cædmon's Hymn," *Beowulf* can be understood as a complex and important cultural event rather than an obscurity people of sense will seek to avoid.

The *Approaches to Beowulf* collection offers an instructive review of attitudes towards the poem. Useful though individual essays are, the collection has three major weaknesses that characterize *Beowulf* scholarship more generally. First, there is, apart from a single essay on women's perspectives, no attempt to address contemporary critical theory, although the importance of philology (never seen as theoretical) is frequently asserted, as if it were in danger of being left out. Second, none of these essays makes integral use of the history of the poem's reception, a matter of great importance, since much was added to and some taken away from *Beowulf* as it emerged in the nineteenth century; nothing at all is made of the poem's reception history before the late nineteenth century. Third, a remarkable degree of consensus prevails, which may also be seen as a lack of dissent over issues that have always animated *Beowulf* criticism and that today are especially controversial. These issues include the date of the poem, which has been confidently placed in the seventh and eleventh centuries, and in all centuries between, and the reliability of the manuscript as an indication of the poem's age, authorship, and historical value.

Controversial issues are usually argued with fierce finality in *Beowulf* criticism, as if they could be settled once and for all. To argue either that the manuscript can plainly support an eleventh-century date for the poem—the position of Kevin S. Kiernan—is no more helpful than maintaining that it "has nothing to tell us about the date of the poem," the position of one of his more hostile reviewers.[12] The meaning of such disagreement is frequently lost. *Beowulf* is an incomplete text, incompletely attested, and it will always be controversial. Its incompleteness is not only a conceptual problem: it is also an event.

BEOWULF IN SURVEY CLASSES

The first step in making a classicized text eventful is to break the anthology's hold on the text, to explain how its assertions about Anglo-Saxon culture are selective and even stereotypical and to show that the text itself offers characterizations of early English culture that the criticism ignores. I see the *Norton Anthology* as a register of received opinions about early English culture; as such, it is worth taking seriously. By challenging what the *Norton* claims about Anglo-Saxon literary culture, we reopen issues that the anthology presents as settled. We see these issues as sites of controversy rather than as given truths, and thereby open *Beowulf* to a discussion of fresh ideas about the historical reception of Anglo-Saxon culture, and the connection of that culture to our own.

Familiar issues provide the framework for expanding our idea of *Beowulf*: translation, which includes translating Old English poetry into modern prose, and transmitting an ancient Germanic text through a Christian culture; historical perspective, and how it is affected by using a poem whose dating is highly controversial to characterize any and all phases of Anglo-Saxon culture; and incompleteness in the text, gaps or defects in the manuscript and silences in the narrative. These issues help us concentrate on the "not Old English" element of the Anglo-Saxon tradition, on "culture" rather than "documents," and on meaning as well as method. A review of the editorial history of *Beowulf* reveals how method developed to produce in the poem a cultural meaning that already existed outside it, a horizon consisting in part of Homeric epic and textual practices that, to Caxton's distress, were being applied to it.

Whether teaching *Beowulf* in a survey course or a course in Old English, one is invariably frustrated by the problem of translation. Translation is interpretation; the translation of *Beowulf* by E. Talbot Donaldson in the *Norton* is an interpretation of the text. Since editors must interpret, editors of *Beowulf* who confront its numerous ambiguities are doing what editors are supposed to do. They are making informed choices for their readers. That they make different choices at different points in history—that editions are "timely" in the sense of "bound by time"—is a positive rather than a negative feature of the tradition, and it is easily addressed in an introductory class in which the poem is read in translation. One need only produce a few pages of other translations—early translations in both Latin and English, for example—to demonstrate that translations differ and to explain why they do. When one compares a translation to a glossary, one sees that the glossary sometimes becomes the translator's gospel.

Examples in *Beowulf* are numerous. The best demonstration I have seen comes from a high-school English literature survey, *England in Literature*, in which four translations of a single short passage—ranging from J. Duncan Spaeth's 1921 version to Michael Alexander's translation published in 1973—are arranged on the page so that students can see how diverse in tone and effect the poem can become in the hands of different translators.[13] Students can be encouraged to explore the source of these differences, the editors' glossaries, which show them that a single word can hold quite different meanings and that the editor's choice is his or her own. For example, in the standard edition of *Beowulf* by Frederick Klaeber, *ellen* can mean "courage, valor, strength, zeal," and "deeds of valor" (p. 322); *nið* can mean "(ill-will, envy), violence, hostility, persecution, trouble, affliction," and "battle, contest" (p. 380); *dollic* can mean "foolhardy, audacious, daring" (p. 316). Again, a few photocopied pages—even paragraphs—are sufficient to make the point that editors unavoidably rewrite and interpret the poems they publish.

Teaching translations "against" each other does not cause students to despair at the arbitrariness of editors and translators; instead, it arouses interest in the flexibility of the Old English vocabulary and helps them to see that a translation, and even an edition, is the result of a hermeneutic process. This approach also alerts students to the power of editions they use or will use in other courses. Placing the "definitive" translation in historical context—one can use early as well as recent translations—prepares students to assess the "definitive edition," that institution whose powerful implication of objective editorial standards they will encounter often.

But editors respond to texts, and to manuscripts, as if they were univocal, speaking in one voice only, rather than in several voices at once, some mute, some muddled. The implications of the multiple layers of the manuscript for approaches to narrative in *Beowulf* are too frequently missed because the choices of editors and translators are allowed to stand in place of manuscript and cultural contexts. An obvious, and probably the most important example in *Beowulf*, as in "Cædmon's Hymn," is the mixture of pagan and Christian perspectives. It is usually approached as a compromise between a Christian world view, with its promise of redemption, and the fated universe of Germanic paganism. But this cultural theme is an event; it becomes a conclusion, the solution to a conceptual problem, only through the lexical process of determining how words, including references to fortune, fate, and divinity, will be translated. As Fred C. Robinson has shown, editors and translators juggle the balance of these elements according to the version of Anglo-Saxon culture they have chosen. Pagan or Germanic definitions predominate in some views, while references to the Christian God prevail in others. Often what conveys the decision is an arbitrary use of capitalization: Old English *ælmihtig* ("almighty") becomes *Ælmihtig* ("Almighty") and a term with an important ambiguity is reduced to simple statement.[14] Students using translations have no way of knowing, if their teachers are not alert, what is afoot.

This cultural controversy is settled in the *Norton Anthology*, where *Beowulf* is seen as a repository of some of the most important institutions of Germanic culture. The introduction to the Old English period in the *Norton* is a veritable digest of myths about Anglo-Saxon England. There we learn that the "heroic ideal had a very practical bearing on the life of the people whom the king ruled," although there is very little evidence about the lives of those who were ruled, as opposed to those who ruled; and that the Germanic people "never tired of hearing the deeds of their folk heroes," so that "the immortality that the old heroes had sought was achieved through poetry, and poetry in turn gave inspiration to later men in leading their own lives." Men in the meadhall seldom relaxed and wore armor all the time in case Fate should call, and so forth.[15] Thus stereotypes about Anglo-Saxon culture are passed on uncritically, with no thought to the cultural origins of these stereotypes in nineteenth-century criticism. Anglo-Saxonists probably brush aside such characterizations of *Beowulf* and Anglo-Saxon culture as amateur or unspecialized, but students and other readers should be encouraged to question these views on grounds of their exclusivity. The two-part valorization in the *Norton* is doubly deadly: it not only characterizes aesthetic response ("never tired of hearing") but asserts a direct relation between hearing poetry and leading an inspired life. Bulwer would have approved, but how are readers who are aware of postmodern possibilities to regard such assessments? We should regard them with skepticism, I believe, and with the awareness that they are the product of desire.

One of the strongest desires evident in *Beowulf* criticism is the wish to invoke the historical perspective of ancient Germanic institutions as background to the poem. The view of Anglo-Saxon culture taken in the *Norton* is not Anglo-Saxon at all; it is drawn from Tacitus's *Germania*, written in the first century. Tacitus was a Roman historian, but his influence over Anglo-Saxon literary history is great. Klaeber observes that the poem is "a veritable treasure-house of information on 'Germanic antiquities,' in which we seem at times to hear echoes of Tacitus' famous *Germania*."[16] Thus Tacitus looms large in the *Norton* introduction, and has been cited in a long list of Anglo-Saxon literary histories: C. L. Wrenn's portrait of the heroic in Anglo-Saxon literature;[17] the assessment of Stanley B. Greenfield and Daniel G. Calder;[18] and Margaret Goldsmith's view.[19] Tacitus too has to be interpreted before he can be used to interpret, and scholars needing a pure Germanic past for *Beowulf* have invented it in *Germania*, treating Tacitus as an objective reporter of Germanic customs and applying his fragmentary analysis of a first-century culture wholesale to Anglo-Saxon culture six centuries later. Rare is the caution of Milton McC. Gatch, who, unlike so many who write about the Germanic roots of Anglo-Saxon culture, hesitates to take Tacitus at face value and instead portrays him as a cynical observer of urban Roman culture who found in the provincial north a rustic culture to romanticize.[20] Tacitus has become a beginning for *Beowulf* earlier than English culture; not unexpectedly, he is a classical and Roman point of reference, an anchor to antiquity, a link between the wilds of the North and the civilized pursuits of Anglo-Saxon culture. Once such views of Tacitus have been repeated and asserted enough times, they become institutionalized; readers of *Beowulf*—especially students pondering this long and confusing text as the first masterpiece of English literature—automatically integrate institutionalized ideas into their view of the text. Those received ideas are little more than conventional wisdom; they are readily dislodged by discussion of the text's reception, which, instead of dishing up fixed assessments, asks readers to use their own experience as a point of entry into the text: in other words, to identify a shared horizon, and work from it.

One can offset these traditional, institutional assertions about *Beowulf* by historicizing the function of the poem as a version of English history. Early scholars saw *Beowulf* as a record of English Germanic origins and mined it for evidence of the heroic civilization that distinguished the Anglo-Saxon past. This view has been out of fashion ever since J. R. R. Tolkien challenged the historical approach in an essay widely accepted as the starting point (i.e., the beginning) of literary criticism of *Beowulf*.[21] Thereafter, almost any historical approach to the text, as opposed to a literary critical approach, seemed antiquated. But the poem's historical function, as I see it, is not only its account of the Anglo-Saxon era, but its reception in the nineteenth century, when it mirrored world views of its editors and translators and thus helped to shape the course of Anglo-Saxon studies.

Tolkien asserted powerfully, for the first time, that *Beowulf* was a text no less worthy of "literary criticism" than any other. Part of Tolkien's task was celebratory. He lamented the prominence given to the poem as history, as witnessed, for example, in the view of Archibald Strong, published in 1921, that *Beowulf* is "the picture of a whole civilization, of the Germania" of Tacitus, when Tolkien himself wished its poetry to overshadow its historical function. Tolkien asserted that more than one modern poem was inspired by *Beowulf* since "*Beowulf* escaped from the dominion of students of origins to the students of poetry."[22] Here is a dichotomy worth analysis: poetry, or literary merit, as defined by aesthetics, set in opposition to history as expressed in a search for origins. Tolkien functioned as a gatekeeper in the history of *Beowulf* criticism, not only because he made a case for the poem as literature but because he felt it necessary to rescue *Beowulf* from historians to whom it was "a quarry of fact and fancy" rather than "a work of art."[23]

Tolkien dismissed the idea that *Beowulf* is a "quarry of fact and fancy," but as a work of art it is, of course, just that. Rather than see the *poem* as a "quarry," however, we can apply that concept to the *manuscript* and subject it to Foucauldian archaeology, a study of all that has grown up around the manuscript and that filters the text and conditions its reception. We can undertake this pursuit with the *Beowulf* manuscript rather than the poem because the poem was discovered long after the manuscript (London, British Library, Cotton Vitellius A.xv). The first readers of *Beowulf* did not know what an Anglo-Saxon poem was. They had no horizon of Old English verse into which to insert it. Tolkien put an end to the "old historicism" of those who wanted to use the poem in positivist historical ways; but without realizing it, he handed *Beowulf* over to New Criticism, which developed as the "literary" channel for "higher criticism," while philology continued to direct the flow of "lower criticism." Together the two came to constitute the "traditional" approach to medieval studies, Anglo-Saxon studies included.

The alternative to this neat pair of New Criticism and old history is not "New Historicism,"[24] but a historicism that attempts to understand earlier editors and readers and to establish a sympathetic perspective in which their work is valued rather than dismissed. Like any damaged ruin, *Beowulf* must be restored before it can be understood. But what one era "appreciates" and so reconstitutes in the poem is, in a later era, a layer through which one must seek the monument. One makes this point by showing students that between the *Beowulf* manuscript and us are many layers of emendations, solutions to cruces, proposed by these scholars. The editorial and critical history of *Beowulf*—its reception—is not a process of removing error or late accretions in order to disclose a pristine Ur-text; rather, it is a process of adding to such accretions, layer upon layer. The manuscript history is an archive of the development of Anglo-Saxon studies. The oldest layer of that archive, the manuscript, already comprises several layers of data: corrections, erasures, a palimpsest, damaged and rebound pages. Surrounding this text is a long and contentious history of transcripts, translation, editions, and critical analysis or literary interpretation. This accumulated body of evidence attests to the cultural significance of *Beowulf* and to its power to command scholarly attention and readership. Placed at the center of our understanding of the poem, the manuscript shows us not how *Beowulf* was created, but how we have created it, making and remaking not just its literary meaning, but its language.

Anyone who sees a facsimile of a few of the manuscript's badly damaged pages knows why editing *Beowulf* amounts to writing it. Dealing with defects has always been a necessary part of its reception, as we see in the facsimile edited by Julius Zupitza for the Early English Text Society,[25] Joseph Tuso's well-presented facsimile page in the *Norton* critical edition, which contains a transcription and an edited version of the text,[26] or Kiernan's several pages reproducing the manuscript. Incompleteness of this sort is, as I have said earlier, a feature of many Anglo-Saxon texts. Teaching that engages this aspect of the text can illustrate how scholars, as a necessary condition of their work, help to shape their subject by restructuring textual evidence.

BEOWULF IN INTRODUCTORY OLD ENGLISH CLASSES

We can raise the questions of translation, historical reception, and incompleteness when teaching *Beowulf* in translation in a survey course. All these issues raise themselves in introductory Old English courses, when students learn about the condition of manuscripts and the nature of textual emendations, although rarely from *Beowulf,* which modern introductory Anglo-Saxon textbooks seldom include. The omission is due to the traditional format for presenting Anglo-Saxon in the curriculum in a two-course sequence; the first course consists of grammar, taught chiefly through prose, and the second course consists of *Beowulf.* But older texts include excerpts from *Beowulf* as a matter of routine. *The Elements of Old English*, by Samuel Moore and Thomas A. Knott, includes several early episodes: Grendel's raids, Beowulf's arrival at Heorot, and his fight with the monster.[27] Henry Sweet chose several parts of the poem in *First Steps in Anglo-Saxon*, inserting his own subheads (in Old English, no less), to introduce each excerpt.[28] In *The Threshold of Anglo-Saxon* (an interesting response to Sweet's title), A. J. Wyatt managed to incorporate the whole poem, interspersing excerpts with the summary of William Morris.[29] R. C. Alton's *An Introduction to Old English* includes a few sections only.[30] The two most popular introductory texts, *A Guide to Old English*, by Bruce Mitchell and Fred C. Robinson, and *Bright's Reader*, edited by F. G. Cassidy and Richard N. Ringler, omit *Beowulf* entirely.[31] My survey is not systematic (such a survey would be useful), but it is apparent even from a brief accounting that *Beowulf* has left the middle ground of Anglo-Saxon studies and can be found chiefly in introductory surveys and in seminars for those who have already studied some Old English.

The values formerly attached to *Beowulf* in introductory courses can be seen in Sweet's *Anglo-Saxon Reader*, first published in 1876 and revised many times. It includes the episode in which Beowulf fights with Grendel's mother (lines 1251–1651), which he calls "one of the most vivid parts of the poem." Sweet believed that the "poet's Christian intention is shown by the unequivocal claim that Beowulf owed his victory over Grendel to his faith in God."[32] Sweet's choice of episodes reveals his view of the poem as a Christian epic and his expectation that vivid action, on the level of an adventure tale, is an important aesthetic consideration. His capitalization illustrates the Christian perspective he claims for the poem; *anwalda*, meaning "ruler," appears as *Anwalda*, indicating the Christian God (line 1272), and *alwalda*, meaning "omnipotent one," appears as *Alwalda*, meaning "God" (line 1314).[33] That the capitalization is an interpretation of the manuscript readings—a Christianizing of them—is left for the student to determine; in his prefatory note apparently explaining all, Sweet is silent on this count.

The relationship of translation to interpretation is the very subject of an introductory course in Old English. Equally important is the linking of interpretation to incompleteness. Students learn about incompleteness by another name, the *crux*, a term designating not only "a difficult problem, a puzzling thing," but also "a critical moment, a crucial point," even "the essential or most important point."[34] This word, *crux*, and this concept in Anglo-Saxon scholarship, like so many other fundamental notions of textual criticism, come to us from the Latinate vocabulary of early textual critics and classicists. It is a fascinating term, meaning "cross," coming from *crucio*, "to crucify," to torture or to torment. Alexander Pope was one of the eighteenth-century writers for whom the link between antiquarian study and pointless pain was already clear; *The Dunciad* scoffs at those who "Old puns restore, lost blunders nicely seek, / And crucify poor Shakespear once a week."[35]

For Anglo-Saxonists, a crux is traditionally seen as a riddle or a puzzle that can be solved by the proper application of critical and scholarly ingenuity to the linguistic facts at hand. The crux usually involves a manuscript reading that does not fit its context. Cruces are sometimes generated by the expectation that *Beowulf* must set a standard for grammatical usage and meter. Since *Beowulf* is not only the earliest English literature, but also the only medieval epic in English, the poem is expected to preserve the earliest forms of Anglo-Saxon language and art—the primary data for the analysis of meter, vocabulary, and even style. Metrical restorations seek to present the poem in strict conformity with the rules of Old English meter as they were formulated in the nineteenth century; *Beowulf* is used to test other Old English poetry for metrical regularity, thereby setting the standard for all Old English verse. Just one of many possible examples is the comment by T. P. Dunning and A. J. Bliss, in their edition of *The Wanderer*, that "The meter of *The Wanderer* conforms in general with the strict standards of the *Beowulf* poet."[36] Ashley Amos characterized the "proper rules for the meter of *Beowulf*" as the "classical" meter of Old English poetry, but notes disagreement on the application of these rules to other poems.[37]

But some cruces are related to a different kind of unreadability. They may involve not only missing letters and difficult readings, but also style and subject matter—not cruces, in the narrow sense, but aesthetic defects that can be seen wherever the epic does not meet the expectations of editors and critics. For *Beowulf* is a repository of literary and linguistic institutions, including poetic style, type scenes, and lexicography. Expectations appropriate to *Beowulf* as the earliest example of these features create the unreadability they seek to remedy; they are only academic notions, critical conventions of what an Anglo-Saxon epic poem ought to be. It ought to be highly serious, universal, unified, correct, and *complete*. To demand completeness of a poem essentially incomplete is, of course, unwise, since the manuscript makes the physical fact of incompleteness apparent, and since the poem periodically fails strict metrical or grammatical criteria. The poem's incompleteness, manifest in fragmentary episodes and occasional defects in meter, has something important to tell us about the text and about how its gaps guide our teaching and scholarship, our reading and writing of *Beowulf*.

THE POEM AND SCHOLARLY EDITING

Desire for a complete *Beowulf*—for *Beowulf* as a pure point of origin—has inspired editors to create its wholeness by writing supplements to fill the gaps in the text. These gaps, or cruces, are of two kinds: literal gaps, where the text cannot be read and where important information is suppressed, leaving the plot incomplete; and figurative gaps, where the text can be read, but not to the satisfaction of metrical standards or other criteria that scholarship imposes on the manuscript. The first kind of gap requires editors to emend the manuscript and publish their emendations simply as *Beowulf*; they indicate their changes with brackets or italics, as tradition dictates, but their corrected text, not the manuscript of *Beowulf*, is the one put before the reading public. The second kind of gap requires that we "write," meaning "interpret," whenever we undertake to make a text conform to our image of it, our concept of its possibilities. The narrative gaps must be addressed when *Beowulf* is taught in translation, so I begin with them.

The most notorious of the textual episodes, usually referred to as "digressions," are the obscure fight at Finnsburg (lines 1068–1159b), the Sigemund digression (lines 874b–897b), the complex sequence about

Onela at the end of the poem (lines 2345–2509b, 2910–2998b), and the account of Beowulf's later years as king, including the conditions that surround the appearance of the dragon (lines 2210b–2231a, 2669–2820b) who ends the hero's life. These episodes prevent us from knowing what we need to know to make the poem complete. The incompleteness of the poem is evident in what it does not discuss; what *Beowulf* leaves unsaid, including the thoughts of most of its women characters, must be spoken for when the poem is spoken about. Attention called to this function of the poem's incompleteness—its stimulus to speaking—complicates and enriches a student's introduction to it. Gillian R. Overing's link between women and death in *Beowulf* describes the feminist and semiotic possibilities of the poem's silences and omissions powerfully.[38] The gaps are untold parts of the story; they unsettle its telling.

These gaps remind us that *Beowulf* exists in the form of a copy, not an original. Kiernan's recent arguments that the poem was partially rewritten in the eleventh century is only the latest version of a position that the poem is a copy.[39] Indeed, the widely accepted view that *Beowulf* is an ancient poem reworked in later cultures, which has been the standard paradigm of its reception, altered only by Kiernan's argument that the poem was revised in the eleventh century, poses a model for narrative study based on the existence of gaps (their presence), rather than on the usual scholarly response of filling them in (their absence).

The narrative and textual gaps in *Beowulf* are intertexts, distinct but interactive "sign systems" or narrative units. My argument about these intertexts and the poem's intertextuality is a return to the premise of the *Liedertheorie*, but it is not the *Liedertheorie* made new. The thesis that *Beowulf* is composed of separate *Lieder* is only a claim for the existence of texts within the text and for the creation of *Beowulf* through the interplay of these individual textual voices. The merits of this claim, as the *Liedertheorie* advances it, have not been welcome, even though the "unity" of *Beowulf* has always been controversial. Kiernan sees the poem as a conflation of two texts brought together for the first time by an author, who created neither poem, in the eleventh century. He argues for two authors for *Beowulf* but rejects the *Liedertheorie* because it is an "impotent assault on the artistic integrity of the poem"; he maintains that the poem has descended to us in "unquestionably unified" form, but not everyone agrees.[40] Tolkien argued that *Beowulf* is composed of separate texts not entirely happily joined. Explicitly theological parts of the poem—an early passage condemning the monsters and the later passage absurdly known as "Hrothgar's sermon"—were, he thought, liable to have been expanded or revised; they had a "ring" unlike the rest of the poem.[41] C. L. Wrenn proposed moving some lines to eliminate inconsistencies in tone (i.e., unwarranted Christian references).[42]

Anglo-Saxonists become understandably impatient when the issue of multiple authorship is raised in *Beowulf*, not wanting the problems of a poem with more than one author (or one reader?) written in more than one century. But a contemporary critical model, such as M. M. Bakhtin's "dialogized imagination," and a contemporary concept of authorship, such as Michel Foucault's idea of "the disappearance of the author," offer complex and divergent models that actually demand, rather than merely allow for, historical perspective.[43] These more complex narrative models do not disregard the "hard" evidence of manuscript tradition and editorial practice. Foucault wrote about narrative in the novel, not in the epic; and though Bakhtin discusses the epic, he positions its narrative qualities in contradistinction to the "dialogic" qualities of novelistic narrative. Nevertheless, their concepts are more fluid and precise ways to discuss "inner history" than Anglo-Saxonists have yet explored. Bakhtin's concept of a "dialogized" text—a text with several voices—or Said's concept of a repressive text whose hidden melodies can still be heard, is a far more promising model than the tradition of "the poet" and "the *Beowulf* poet," the Anglo-Saxon counterpart to Homer, whose nonexistence, should anyone dare to proclaim it, would, at the end of the twentieth century, provoke a reaction not too different from Augustine Caxton's a century and a half earlier.

It is not surprising that, today, few dare to advocate origins for *Beowulf* in several poems composed by different authors; nor, as a result, is it surprising that another plausible idea—that *Beowulf* generates meaning through the interplay of individual textual voices generated by its external and internal readers—has likewise gone unobserved. We are too busy admiring the poet and correcting his language in our search for a unified literary experience. Our obsession with the need for a pure, complete origin in *Beowulf* has inspired criticism to focus on the unities and achievements of the text rather than its gaps and fissures. "Gaps" and "fissures" are, to some medievalists, irritatingly contemporary terms, synonymous with that urge in contemporary criticism to look at what is not in the text and claim for it as much significance as what traditional criticism has put there. Let us recall that it is a function of history to invent origins. When we see how origins of various kinds have been invented for *Beowulf*, by which I mean the set of traditions surrounding the poem, we can, in a sense probably more literal than he meant it, second Edward Irving's statement that "*Beowulf* is the product of centuries"[44]—not centuries preceding the poem, however, but, the centuries that have come after it.

Gaps of two kinds, both textual and narrative, can serve (and have served) as sites for reading and writing; these activities align the horizons of characters in the poem, the scribes who copied it, and the early nineteenth-century scholars who recovered the poem.[45] My focus on reading and writing *Beowulf* has two sides: the manuscript itself and what must be written to make it readable; and the interpretive act, what must be written about *Beowulf* in order to interpret it. I shall take issue with the extent to which "writing" in the form of reconstruction of physical evidence has been permitted, and will encourage the conception of criticism as another kind of writing. The ways in which the poem's incompleteness can contribute to its effectiveness are to be found in the history of its reception.

An act of reception in the poem that all critics recognize is Hrothgar's welcome to Beowulf and his entourage when they arrive in Heorot. At folio 138v, lines 8-11, of the original manuscript, Hrothgar tells his messenger, Wulfgar, to make haste in admitting the visitors to the king's presence:

"Gesaga him eac wordum þæt hie sint wilcuman
Deniga leodum." Word inne abead:
"Eow het secgan sigedrihten min...."[46]

"Say to them in words that they are welcome to the people of the Danes."
He spoke the words within: "I am commanded to tell you that my glorious leader...."

The half-lines of the second line do not alliterate. They should do so, and in 1857 Christian W. M. Grein wrote two more half-lines, as follows, to supply alliteration for the a-verse of the second line, making the existing half-line into the b-verse of the next line:[47]

"Gesaga him eac wordum þæt hie sint wilcuman
Deniga leodum." (Ða wið duru healle
Wulfgar eode.) worde inne abead:
"Eow het secgan sigedrihten min...."

"Say to them in words that they are welcome to the people of the Danes."
(Then Wulfgar went to the door of the hall.) He spoke the words within: "I am commanded to tell you that my glorious leader...."

All editors follow suit, but most change the text, as did Klaeber, from "Wulfgar eode" to "widcuð hæleð" ("widely known warrior").[48] Thus *Beowulf* acquired an entire line to remedy a metrical defect.

A restoration on the most badly damaged folio (179r) solves a crux that is not even recognized as an emendation but that instead has been regarded as a manuscript reading. At line 2221 of the poem, two manuscript readings, one obscure, one plain, are involved. The second word in the line cannot be read; Zupitza suggested *mid*:

> Nealles mid gewe(a)ldum wyrmhord a(b)ræ(c)
> sylfes willum. . . .

> Not deliberately, for his own desires, did he break into the dragon's
> hoard. . . .

The consequence of Zupitza's reading is that the sentence lacks a verb, and this in turn necessitated the rewriting of *cræft* ("strength" or "skill"), which is perfectly plain in the manuscript, to *abræc* ("break into"). Neither Klaeber nor Wrenn-Bolton marks *mid* as a restoration, and Birte Kelly, in a long, two-part discussion of editorial emendations, does not list it either.[49] The rewriting of *cræft* at least merits a note in Klaeber and Wrenn-Bolton. Seeking to keep the manuscript reading, Kiernan suggests *næs* for Zupitza's *mid*:

> Nealles næs geweoldum wyrmhorda(n) cræft
> sylfes willum. . . .

But that this line *is* a crux only Kiernan seems aware.[50] *Cræft* became *abræc* in the hands of Max Kaluza, a metricist who suggested the emendations to Ferdinand Holthausen, through whose two-volume edition of the poem, *Beowulf nebst dem Finnsburg-Bruchstück* (1905–06), it passed into the poem. Here we have, then, three cruces; two of them are pseudo-cruces, and one is a crux that is not even recognized as such. There are other examples.

Editorial emendation is sometimes a necessary rewriting. I wish to look at another kind of rewriting that *Beowulf* forces on its readers. Sometimes when we write *Beowulf*, we add something to the poem, not to restore or emend its meter and grammar, but to voice its silences. I want us to consider as a crux what is said about writing and reading in the poem. "Intertextuality" has a wide semantic range; it revives and redefines the concept of an "inner history" of *Beowulf* and likewise alters our concept of the poem's readability. Eugene Vance describes it as the relationship "between a single text and the network of *other* texts that constitutes its cultural horizon."[51] Julia Kristeva introduced the term to French criticism in *La Révolution du langage poétique* to describe "transposition of one or more *systems* of signs into another, accompanied by a new articulation of the enunciative and denotative position."[52] The "other texts" or systems I shall discuss in intertextual relation to *Beowulf* are the incomplete episodes of *Beowulf*, its "digressions." They appear in narratives of the *scop* in Hrothgar's court, in recollections by the poet of *Beowulf*, and on the hilt of a sword. Taking a cue from a pun on "writing" and "cutting through," I shall also identify a story "written" by Beowulf when he pierces the dragon.

The intertextual relationship between the writing instruments and their carving action is clarified in Michael Riffaterre's definition of intertextuality through *syllepsis*, "the trope that consists in understanding the same word in two different ways at the same time," one meaning being literal or primary, the other figurative, with the second meaning "tied to the first as its polar opposite," as the two sides of a coin are joined. The relationship of the suppressed subtext to the text of the poem is intertextual because "the intertext is partly encoded within the text and conflicts with it because of stylistic or semantic incompatibilities." In "intratextual" intertextuality, Riffaterre says, "the syllepsis symbolizes the compatibility, at the significance level, between a text and an intertext incompatible at the level of meaning."[53]

I propose that we see *writan* and the element *writan* in *forwritan* as a *syllepsis*, as a structure joining writing and death in a pun on opposite meanings. Jonathan Culler discusses such words as "points of condensation," when "a single term brings together different lines of argument or sets of values."[54] Intertexts, I propose, can be identified in references to writing and reading as acts that surround texts, recognizing and receiving them. Some intertexts are created by critics and by editors whose technical practices govern our knowledge of *Beowulf*, intercepting the manuscript and writing the poem for us. Reading and writing also occur *within Beowulf*, and this I will demonstrate by examining these key words, *writan* and *forwritan*, words which pun on "to write" and "to carve" and represent analogues for "to interpret."

Writan, "to write," occurs only once in *Beowulf* (line 1688b), where the word is, with a nice irony, now only partially written; it survived as *writen* in the early nineteenth century, however, as recent work shows.[55] We may be surprised to find it in a poem said to reflect an oral rather than a written culture, a poem transmitted in oral form and about stories transmitted orally rather than in writing. I will juxtapose this word with another that occurs only once in *Beowulf* and that, in addition, appears only here in all of Old English, *forwritan* (line 2705a), meaning "to cut through" or "to cut in two." Given the choices possible for describing this very common action of hewing or cutting, this word too seems unexpected. Both words are linked to weapons. In line 1688b, *writen* (past participle) refers to a story about monsters engraved on the hilt of a magic sword taken from the cave of Grendel's dam; I quote the passage at some length.

> Hroðgar maðelode—hylt sceawode,
> ealde lafe, on ðæm wæs or written
> fyrngewinnes, syðþan flod ofsloh,
> gifen geotende giganta cyn
> frecne geferdon; þæt waes fremde þeod
> ecean Dryhtne; him þæs endelean
> þurh wæteres wylm Waldend sealde.
> Swa wæs on þæm scennum sciran goldes
> þurh runstafas rihte gemearcod,
> geseted and gesæd, hwam þæt sweord geworht
> irena cyst ærest wære
> wreoþenhilt ond wyrmfah. (lines 1687–98)

Hrothgar spoke—he examined the hilt, the ancient heirloom, on which was written the origins of ancient strife when the flood, the rushing ocean, slayed the race of giants. They suffered terribly, those people alien to [their] god; their ruler sent them their final reward through the surging waters. On the shining metal handle [of the sword] it was marked, set down, and said through secret letters, clearly, by [or for] whom the best of irons first was made, with a twisted hilt and with curved ornaments.

Hrothgar reads a story about the race from which Grendel and his mother descended. He examines the *lafe* ("remnant"), on which is written the origin of ancient strife; this bright gold sword hilt declares "through secret letters" for whom the sword was made. The engraved hilt constitutes a text, not simply a set of pictures, as the usual interpretation of *runstafas* ("runes") implies.

In line 2705a, *forwritan* (preterite, *forwrat*) is used to describe how Beowulf cuts through the middle of the dragon once the monster has been wounded by Wiglaf:

> Ða gen sylf cyning
> geweold his gewitte, wæll-seaxe gebræd
> biter ond beaduscearp, þæt he on byrnan wæg;
> forwrat Wedra helm wyrm on middan. (lines 2702b–05)

The king still controlled his own senses; he drew the belt-knife, pointed and battle-sharp, that he wore on his shirt of mail; he, the protector of the Weders, carved the worm in the middle.

These two weapons accomplish Beowulf's revenge on three monsters. The magic sword is the *bil* that penetrated the dam (line 1567b) and cut off Grendel's head (line 1590b); he retrieves only the hilt from the cave, for the sword itself has mysteriously melted (lines 1615b–17b). The later sword *forwrat* ("cuts through"; line 2705) the fire dragon in the last of the hero's three encounters with monsters.

Hewing and carving align these weapons with instruments for engraving and writing, in the sense of inscribing. *Writan* and *forwritan* derive from the same root, meaning "to cut" or "to carve." But *forwritan* may also translate *proscribere*, meaning "to outlaw" or "to banish"; *forscrifen* (line 106) means "to proscribe," and *scrifan* means "to assign penalty," a secular as well as an ecclesiastical term.[56] Although the second sword's act of carving evokes writing—"forwriting" as it creates death, so to speak—this is not the direction in which the wordplay leads us. *Forwritan* is a *hapax legomenon* (a sole occurrence of a word), but its etymological roots are those of *writan*, and we have no other examples in Old English to contradict or to offset our response to the second element of the compound: *forwritan* means "to cut through" just as *writan* means "to write (by means of carving)." These words suggest that *Beowulf* contains subtextual references to reading and writing as yet uninterrogated; runes may be secret or magic writing, but they are writing nonetheless.[57]

I wish to use *writan* and *forwritan* in their immediate lexical context in *Beowulf* to discuss what I call the suppressed textuality of the poem. By juxtaposing these two words, we connect writing to death. *Runstafas* (line 1695) is a compound for "secret letters." A three-part apposition locates the letters: they were "gemearcod, geseted, and gesæd": *gemearcod* from *mearcian*, "to mark"; *geseted* from *settan*, "to set down"; and *gesæd* from *secgan*, "to say." The textuality of the passage is developed by appositional verbs referring to one act of inscribing in three different but closely similar ways. These three appositives sharpen the link between "marking" and "telling."

We are told this not once, then, but three times—to mark, to set down, to say; only the former pertains exclusively to carving, only the latter exclusively to telling.[58] The "-staf" element appears shortly after this passage at line 1753, in *endestæf*, which occurs only in *Beowulf*. It is usually translated "end," but it means "final letter" in Hrothgar's famous speech in which he says, "in the end," the body will decay. This is a striking reference, coming as it does after the *runstafas* on the sword hilt. What these "secret letters" convey is not conveyed to the reader, nor is it interpreted for us by those who read the runes in the poem.

My immediate concern is with the first sword (line 1688), on which is written a story about the race from which Grendel and his mother descended; this is the only story in *Beowulf* transmitted in written rather than oral form. The magic sword, as a text, has therefore already been "cut through": a "pen" (an engraving instrument) has written on the sword, cutting through the metal to create the text and, in the context of *Beowulf*, cutting through time to record the history of the race of Cain. We remember, of course, as we think about the relationship between swords and monsters, that part of Grendel's power is that such weapons cannot harm him, since he is protected from them (by a magic spell?)—"he sigewæpnum forsworen hæfde" ("he had placed a curse against battle-weapons"; line 804). In any case, Grendel cannot be cut through by a sword, although his mother is not protected in this way.[59]

By juxtaposing *writan* and *forwritan*, I juxtapose the sword as a text, an object that preserves the past and hence serves as a beginning, with the sword as a weapon, an object of destruction and ending. We can thereby juxtapose and relate writing and reading and, by implication, origins and ends. The juxtaposition as framed by writing (*writan*, *forwritan*) is, for us, admittedly coincidental. But coincidence here and elsewhere has the merit of helping us to see the familiar anew. *Beowulf* is about writing as well as about "cutting through," and therefore about the pen as well as the sword, because it is about both storytelling and stories. Frequent references to the *scop* remind us that texts lie within *Beowulf* and that we must view the work intertextually. The so-called digressions prevent us from knowing what they contain, what they narrate. As such, they are stories whose meaning, contained in their details, we will never know. Each episode is a text, a history partially written in *Beowulf* and partially lost. The Sigemund episode is an example.

Certain parallels between the Sigemund episode and Beowulf's own career as a swordsman are arresting. Surrounded with references to story-telling and mystery, the Sigemund episode is the most enigmatic of these tales and the most obvious account of story-telling. Sigemund, like Beowulf, uses his sword to cut through (*þurhwod*; line 890) a dragon. Sigemund is the *scop*'s subject; the *scop* tells everything (*welhwylc*; line 874) he has heard about Sigemund, but also mentions many strange things—feuds and crimes—unknown to men because Sigemund told no one except his nephew, Fitela, about them. What should the reader of *Beowulf* make of this discussion? After all, these exploits are unknown to men, yet they alone preserve Sigemund's great fame. The episode of the sword and Sigemund serves as an example of bravery in battle, and more generally good kingship, of the type Beowulf himself will later demonstrate. This mysterious passage is followed by a perfectly clear one, and one that contrasts sharply with the Sigemund episode: the severely critical summary of Heremod's career as an unworthy king and Sigemund's predecessor. The contrast needs no further comment.

Like the Sigemund digressions, the episode involving Hrothgar and the sword hilt relates an event no one has witnessed. Beowulf uses the sword (*bil*) to kill the dam and sever Grendel's head (the latter at last succumbing to the weapon powerless against him in life). As we have seen, Beowulf retrieves only the hilt from the cave, since the sword itself has mysteriously melted (lines 1615b–17b). The writing on the hilt, not noticed until the feast following Beowulf's victory, is another fragmentary story, told not by the *scop* who tells us about Sigemund, or the poet who tells us so little about Finnsburg. Instead it is read—and not told—by Hrothgar alone. And the reference to the text on the hilt comes at a crucial juncture in *Beowulf*: it is Hrothgar's act immediately before he begins the long narrative known as his "sermon" (lines 1700–84). Criticism of the poem, to the extent that it notices the sword hilt, imagines that Hrothgar's harangue somehow expounds on or constructs an exegesis of the story on the hilt. We have been invited to suppose that the sword hilt and Hrothgar's speech contain the same lesson; I now invite us to suppose that these two texts diverge and that Hrothgar's speech counteracts the text on the hilt. The sword hilt contains only one—a single story not about the heroes, Beowulf, Hrothgar, Hygelac, Sigemund, and others, but about their enemies.

Not all readers agree. James W. Earl, like Margaret Goldsmith, did not consider this passage a crux; both demystified the text on the hilt, saying that it records a story about the race of giants punished by the flood (Genesis 6:4). The sword, according to Earl, reveals a divine judgment on the race of Cain after that judgment has been executed. Earl's link between Grendel, his mother, and the race of Cain is a traditional strategy that implies more than it needs to. This strategy invites us to assume that when Beowulf kills the monsters, the doom of their race, forecast on the sword, has been fulfilled. The hilt, the work of giants, may tell of the origin of the conflict, the "beginning of the ancient warfare"; this may be the flood that supposedly destroyed the race of giants, the fallen angels incestuously joined to daughters descended from Cain.

The sword hilt, therefore, may not depict the end of the race of Cain, but rather the flood that tried unsuccessfully to end that race. There is a large apocryphal literature about the creatures who escaped destruction, creatures who, if not like Grendel and his mother, are at least distantly related to them. The sword hilt is not necessarily a story of endings; it may quite possibly be a story of beginnings. It may tell of the beginning of an evil line, rather than its end, and in *Beowulf* it may serve to establish continuity between the curse of Cain, the descendants of creatures who escaped the flood, and the evil that has escaped Beowulf's own retribution and that will destroy him.

Beowulf's death is exchanged for cultural immortality. His people, the Geats, want to compose poetry at his funeral pyre ("wordgyd wrecan ond ymb w(er) sprecan," or so line 3172 is reconstructed), fittingly praising their leader "when he must [go forth] from his home" (lines 3176–77). The juxtaposition of writing and death—of the writing Beowulf performs, and the writing of *Beowulf*, with the deaths he is responsible for, and with his own death—prompts one to connect the poem to Foucault's essay "What is an Author?" which deploys the notion of a multifaceted "author-function." Foucault maintains that in the modern world writing is linked to death. He contrasts this link to the conception of classical epic (and thus, for Anglo-Saxonists, the epic world of *Beowulf*), which "was designed to guarantee the immortality of a hero," and to the related phenomenon, as witnessed in *The Arabian Nights*, of stories that had "as their motivation, their theme and pretext, this strategy for defeating death"—that is, telling stories to postpone the moment of silence, to avert the unnameable.

Foucault's concern with how we conceptualize the creative consciousness at work in a text poses a challenge to criticism of anonymous texts. What sort of "author-function" do we prescribe for works by unknown hands? An "author-function" is responsible for many procedures that authenticate texts: a uniform level of quality, conceptual or thematic coherence, stylistic consistency, and even historical credibility. Unevenness in the text is "ascribed to changes caused by evolution, maturation, or outside influences."[60] Readers of *Beowulf* have much to think about after reading Foucault. *Beowulf* is an

epic whose hero is "most eager for fame." The price of fame—lasting sig-
nification and heroic reputation—is death; a meaning that outlives time is
purchasable only by death. To be present for eternity, Beowulf must become
absent in the world in which he seeks to be remembered.

But this is not where the reader would expect a desire for origins to lead.
When we turn back to *writan* and *forwritan*, and ask again what difference
it makes that we consider these verbs as puns, we can contemplate a horizon
between readers and writers in the poem, and those outside it reading—and
writing—their vision of history into *Beowulf*. As readers of *Beowulf*, we may
wish to take these references to writing as warnings against rigorous inter-
pretation. No one knows or will ever know what is written on the sword hilt,
what Sigemund told Fitela, or what took place in the Finn episode. We shall
never decipher the hermeneutic role of Hrothgar, whose "sermon," a com-
mentary on a text we cannot read, creates our only textual link to the sword
hilt. Swords supposedly put an end to the monsters, but in fact they did not;
and pens continuously try to put an end to the stories of *Beowulf* by writing
the deeds of the swords. But writing is a subject in the text and of the text,
and so long as we read and write with it in view, the traditional valorization
of the epic as a fixed monument to English culture is an indulgence.

I have tried to demonstrate that the illusive and allusive nature of writ-
ing and reading in *Beowulf* discourages us from acts of closure, and indeed
prevents those acts of interpretation, of "cutting through," sought by con-
ventional criticism. In order to interpret, one has to "cut through," a vio-
lent act that results in "death" in the text—calling a halt to the interplay of
signs and sign systems—so that the critical act can be completed (art must
die in order that criticism, so to speak, may live). There is a difference in
Beowulf between what cannot be understood (i.e., known for certain) and
what cannot be interpreted. Editorial conjecture and critical analysis are
both attempts to understand that produce interpretations, even though the
attempts remain incomplete. Indeed, they produce meaning *because* they
remain incomplete.

BEOWULF IN HISTORY

Linking the study of Anglo-Saxon texts to the history of their reception
requires an initial gesture of defamiliarization. Thinking about intertextu-
ality, writing, and death in *Beowulf* is one means by which I hope to wrest
this text from comfortable interpretive paradigms of which those in the

Norton Anthology are only the most obvious.[61] One reason that we have learned to ignore the history of texts is that philology has become a given of literary interpretation: philology seeks to account for *all* past knowledge of the manuscript, the text, and its language, and hence to constitute the culmination of the past. At this point, we need to recall Hans Robert Jauss's discussion of literary history at the end of the nineteenth century. Just as literary history saw the present as culminating in the past, so philology sees the past of the history of *Beowulf*'s reception culminating in its own mode of analysis. The literary critic uses philological data, which is regarded as factual assessment and which, therefore, stands for history, to mediate the text aesthetically.[62]

This is a profoundly unsatisfactory mode of operation. It reduces the cultural testimony—the reading and writing, the textual experience—of generations of previous readers to documentary evidence. Because their understanding of the text, its date and language, is seen as inferior to our understanding, their experience can be set aside; this demand, generated by the paradigm of progress, has narrowed the interpretive tradition to a process, which, at its worst, amounts to little more than a competition among readings of the texts as various cruces are variously solved in the interest of producing different literary interpretations. Examples in *Beowulf* criticism are numerous: Is *Beowulf* a Christian hero? Is he guilty of avaricious misjudgment at the end of the poem?

A study of the poem's reception is a vigorous alternative to this speculation. If we ask how the text incorporates reading and writing, themselves acts of reception and textual production, we establish a point of common interest between ourselves and characters in the poem, as well as its author and transcribers. Everyone who reads *Beowulf* today does so through a consciously perceived method; a related part of my strategy is to stress hermeneutic self-consciousness, especially on the part of those who have taken to making final pronouncements about *Beowulf* and other texts. *Beowulf* may be a cliché and a joke inside as well as outside the profession, but it is a very young text all the same: it has had readers for barely two hundred years, while Bede's readership is of nearly thirteen hundred years' standing. The emergence of *Beowulf* into literary-historical time reveals the remarkable fact that its first readers, including Sharon Turner, John Josias Conybeare, and Benjamin Thorpe, were both the poem's editors and its translators. That is, the lack of interpretive tradition for the vernacular epic, and the utter unfamiliarity of the text, forced them to translate—to interpret in the language of the day—what they transcribed and edited.[63]

Their hermeneutic mission was obvious, and the experimental nature of their work allowed them to change their minds, to correct their mistakes, and to alter their conclusions with impressive frequency. About the meaning of the poem they had little doubt. They seem to have decided what it meant chiefly by situating it in a horizon of texts constituted by the *Iliad* and the *Aeneid*, two texts often mentioned by early scholars of *Beowulf*. But *Beowulf* did not emerge as epic; it was first seen as romance and first admired by scholars reacting to the classicizing bias of the eighteenth century. In 1826, John Josias Conybeare, who had been the Rawlinson professor of Anglo-Saxon at Oxford from 1809 to 1812, noted, "it may even excite a smile to hear a production so little resembling the purer models of classical antiquity dignified by the name of poetry, or considered an object of criticism." Like Turner and others who, to Tolkien's dismay, admired *Beowulf* as history, Conybeare understood the poem chiefly as "a picture of manners and opinions, and in some measure even as a historical document," although it was in style more like to "the father of the Grecian epic, than to the romancers of the middle ages." The Finnsburg fragment he understood, with *Beowulf*, as "having constituted a portion of a similar historical romance."[64] Romance was an important attribute to document in Anglo-Saxon literature for the simple reason that romance could then no longer be considered a French tradition introduced into Anglo-Saxon culture by the Normans.

Turner's discussion of *Beowulf* indicates some of the prejudice against which Anglo-Saxonists of his generation labored. Referring to the notorious "philologer" Joseph Ritson, Turner remarked, "It was asserted by Mr. Ritson, in conformity with the prevailing opinion of antiquaries, that the Anglo-Saxons had no poetical romance in their native tongue." Ritson's charge was of a piece with the view, common in the eighteenth century, that Anglo-Saxon England was a barbarous place with a barbarous civilization only lifted to respectability by the Norman Conquest. By demonstrating that *Beowulf* was a "poetic romance," Turner was able to claim that the merits of English literature after the Conquest were also evident before the Conquest; it was perhaps the first time that the "literary merit" of Anglo-Saxon texts was asserted in defending the Anglo-Saxon period against charges of barbarism.[65] No doubt the prejudice of Ritson and others against Anglo-Saxon literature had helped to delay the study of *Beowulf*. Turner introduced his summary of *Beowulf* in the 1823 edition of his three-volume *History of the Anglo-Saxons* by observing, "The origin of the metrical romance has been lately an interesting subject of literary research; and as it has not been yet completely elucidated, it seems proper to enquire whether any light can be thrown upon it from the ancient Saxon poetry."[66]

As we would expect of scholars working in the vernacular, Anglo-Saxonists took their methods from the established routines of classical scholars. They knew what *Beowulf* meant, but they had to discover how to explain the certitude of that knowledge, and eventually how to defend it. They reversed the expected relationship between method and meaning. For us, the former creates the latter, but for them, I believe, the latter created the former. They knew what *Beowulf* was: a historical romance, akin to a national epic, and an account of national origins at once historical and mythical. Their pressing need was to explain why they were right. Like "Cædmon's Hymn," *Beowulf* was only rudimentary as poetry; but it contained the seeds of later greatness, and therein lay its value.

There is no record of anyone having read or understood *Beowulf* in the sixteenth or seventeenth century, although the manuscript came to the attention of seventeenth-century readers. These included Richard James (between 1628 and 1638) and Francis Junius (the Dutch scholar and publisher of the "works" of Cædmon, who lived in England from 1620 to 1650).[67] *Beowulf* was, for practical purposes, the discovery of Humphrey Wanley, who was the first Anglo-Saxonist to describe the manuscript, which he did in his catalogue of 1705. An earlier catalogue by Thomas Smith (1696) made no reference to *Beowulf*. Laurence Nowell wrote his name in the manuscript in 1563; Kiernan suggests that he acquired it through Queen Elizabeth's Lord Treasurer William Cecil and that John Bale (1495–1563) might have owned it earlier, but there is no clear evidence of ownership before Nowell. Someone in Nowell's time underlined passages in the manuscript, but the markings are not those of Elizabeth's Archbishop Matthew Parker's assistants.[68] Nearly a hundred years later neither Abraham Wheelock, who held the first professorship in Anglo-Saxon at Cambridge, nor John Milton recognized an Anglo-Saxon poem when they saw it; "Cædmon's Hymn" had no status as a poem apart from sanctioning the use of music to instruct the faithful. Given the importance of ecclesiastical prose texts in sixteenth-century Anglo-Saxonism, one cannot be sure what those who could have read *Beowulf* at that time would have thought of it.

But at the end of the sixteenth century Richard Verstegan and William Camden had begun writing about the continental origins of the English language. The study of "northern antiquities" became a preoccupation of Anglo-Saxonists in the eighteenth century, but even then *Beowulf* went nearly unnoticed and obviously unread. Its syntax made it much more difficult to read than the relatively straightforward prose—for example, the laws, the *Anglo-Saxon Chronicle*, even Bede's *History*—that was the scholars' chief concern. Even in the nineteenth century, Anglo-Saxonists were not sure of the nature or form of Old English poetry. The printed verse form of *Beowulf* fluctuated throughout the nineteenth century, sometimes appearing as individual half-lines (as in Benjamin Thorpe's edition of 1855) rather than the two-part lines modern readers are accustomed to, and sometimes in "long lines," or two full lines printed as one.

Wanley described the poem as an account of "Beowulf the Dane" against the Swedes; his description caught the attention of another reader. An eighteenth-century Danish archivist, Jakob Langebek (1710–1775), noticed *Beowulf* in Wanley's catalogue and wondered why no English scholar had studied this "Poema Anglosaxonicum vestustum & egregium" (Wanley's description). Langebek's notice in turn came to the attention of Grimur Jonsson Thorkelin (1752–1829), an Icelander in the service of the Danish government who went to England to look for manuscripts about Danish history and who became the first editor of *Beowulf*. Thorkelin transcribed the poem and hired a copiest to make another transcript some years later; he published his edition in 1815 with a Latin translation—a gesture reminiscent of many earlier Anglo-Saxonists' work, and a sign that he did not expect a scholarly audience to read Anglo-Saxon.[69]

Thorkelin's edition was ready for the press much earlier, but it was destroyed, in a staggering irony, when his house burned during the British bombardment of Copenhagen in 1807. Two years earlier, Sharon Turner had become the first English scholar to make prominent mention of *Beowulf*. Turner checked Thorkelin's transcriptions. "I have commonly found an inaccuracy of copying in every page," he noted, "but for a first publisher he has been, on the whole, unusually correct." Turner formed his own impressions of the poem; since he knew little Anglo-Saxon, he made numerous errors in describing the poem's events, but his views of 1805 were significantly different when the fourth edition of his *History* appeared in 1823. What Turner said about *Beowulf* would be repeated many times. "It is the most interesting relic of the Anglo-Saxon poetry which time has spared to us," he wrote, "and, as a picture of the manners, and as an exhibition of the feelings and notions of those days, it is as valuable as it is ancient."[70] His views were durable; they find an echo in the *Norton Anthology*.

Turner was asserting the value of Anglo-Saxon literature and history against a prejudice deeper than that concerning literary taste. Thanks to the trend of neoclassicism, the eighteenth century was hostile to Anglo-Saxon antiquities, and Turner and other scholars had much prejudice to combat as they sought to make way for the poem. Turner's view of the history recounted in the text reflects some of this bias; the view that *Beowulf* was a pirate, which I have traced to John Lingard's *The History and Antiquities of the Anglo-Saxon Church* (1806), is a good example. Chauncey B. Tinker attributes some of Turner's misunderstandings to a misplaced page in the manuscript, which led him to an amusing mistake. The misplaced sheet (folio 137) had been inserted to follow line 90 of the poem, with the result that the end of folio 130v, which describes a *scop* singing a "creation hymn" (lines 90–98) that has been compared to Cædmon's, was immediately followed by the account of Grendel's first assault on Heorot after Beowulf has arrived, so that line 91b and line 740a were continuous: "feorran reccan" (line 91b) "feng hraðe forman siðe" (line 740).[71] The result was a jarring juxtaposition of the *scop*'s graceful narrative with a description of a warrior being slain by the monster:

> He who knew
> The beginning of mankind
> From afar to narrate.
> "He took willfully
> By the nearest side
> The sleeping warrior.
> He slew the unheeding one
> With a club on the bones of his hair."[72]

After he published this translation in 1805, Turner realized that a leaf was misplaced early in the codex and corrected his translation. His view of the piratical nature of Beowulf's voyage was not related to this mistake, however, and it appears in both the first and the fourth editions of his work. Turner's view that Beowulf appeared in the poem as "preparing for a warlike or predatory venture," and later, in the court, can be traced to Unferth's challenge to the hero: "Art thou Beowulf, he that with such profit labors on the wide sea, amid the contests of the ocean? There you for riches and for deceitful glory, explore its bays. . . ."[73] Turner directs Lingard's view of the piratical nature of the Saxons at his hero.

The rehabilitation of Anglo-Saxon studies brought about by the study of *Beowulf* was greatly assisted by the next English scholar of the poem, John Josias Conybeare. Conybeare's work was not published until 1826, after his death, and it included studies that he carried out as a pastor after leaving

Oxford. Conybeare's achievements were many. In addition to publishing texts from the *Exeter Book* for the first time, he began the study of Old English meter, and greatly assisted the effort to win recognition for poetry in Old English, correctly perceiving that its value as literature depended on this link. Conybeare asserted that Old English poetry was undervalued and that the fault lay with "our still imperfect knowledge" of the construction of Anglo-Saxon poetry rather than with the poetry itself. Conybeare was conscious of the work of contemporary philologists, and wrote that certain elements in Beowulf "do assuredly bear, if it may be so termed, an oriental rather than a northern aspect," noting that certain scholars were claiming Gothic and Sanskrit "as cognate dialects."[74] He was the first to connect *Beowulf* not only to northern antiquities, but to the Orient. His views of Anglo-Saxon poetry, along with those of Benjamin Thorpe, another translator of *Beowulf* who was working in Denmark, were incorporated by Henry Wadsworth Longfellow, who turned some of Conybeare's text into modern English.[75]

Conybeare's work with meter and his comparative studies (between Old English and Scandinavian poetry) indicated his awareness of the need for method. Method came to nineteenth-century Anglo-Saxon studies in the person of John Mitchell Kemble, who was influenced by Jakob Grimm, and who was nineteenth-century England's most important Anglo-Saxonist. Kemble edited *Beowulf* twice, in a limited edition in 1833 that he improved and corrected and published again in 1835. In 1837 he published his translation and notes, dedicating it to Jakob Grimm. Kemble describes Grimm as the "founder of that school of philology, which has converted etymological researches, once a chaos of accidents, into a logical and scientific system."[76] But it was more than scholarly method that Kemble brought to England; he brought with it historical meaning in the form of a pure, pagan, Germanic origin that would serve as the foundation of scholarly ideas about Anglo-Saxon England for more than a century.

Kemble first believed that *Beowulf* was historical, as did Turner and Conybeare, and dated it to the mid-fifth century, close to "the coming of Hengest and Hors into Britain." He believed that the poem was brought by these settlers and that the manuscript was only a "careless copy" of "an older and far completer poem." The implications of his view for editorial method are considerable. Kemble believed that manuscript readings should be kept rather than emended, since they "serve sometimes as guides and clues to the inner being and spiritual tendencies of the language itself." He lamented the continuing decline of the manuscript, the "progressing evil" of letters falling away.[77] Kiernan estimated that some two thousand letters were lost between the time of Thorkelin's transcripts and the rediscovery of *Beowulf* in the mid-nineteenth century.[78] Kemble rather apologetically made corrections to Thorkelin's transcripts (again, one can compare Kemble to Turner in this regard).

Kemble's 1837 "Postscript" to his earlier preface contained a great deal of backtracking; it declared the 1833 preface "null and void." His view of the historical significance of *Beowulf*, which he attributed to the Danish historian Suhm, Kemble now renounced. *Beowulf* became instead "a confused remembering of heathen myth," and its main character but a "shadow" of the "earlier Beowulf," who was a divinity. Kemble traced extremely elaborate genealogies for Germanic and Scandinavian deities he saw hovering in the text of *Beowulf*. Beowulf's name itself had taken many forms—Beow, Beowine—that connected him to "the Olympus of the North," as John Earle later put it.[79] Kemble showed the capacity of philology to produce extravagant speculation, richly supported by arcane learning, much of it mythological and most of it thoroughly romantic. His preface to his 1835 edition and "Postscript" to that preface in his 1837 translation of the text bristle with learning forced into abstractly perfect patterns, finding, through some very fine differentiation of proper names, twenty-four mythic heroes, "the ancient mythic genealogy of our kings nearly as it was known to our forefathers in the heathen times."[80] Thus the genealogy of the pagan gods did not, in the end, remove *Beowulf* from the scene of national literary history. The poem asserted a direct relation of the past ("our forefathers") to the present ("our kings").

Kemble's two prefaces and "Postscript" illustrate the important consequences of method for meaning. His growing grasp of philological criticism and its relation to mythology caused him, in just two years, to repudiate a whole set of assumptions about the poem and its history. The more "scientific" his method, the more remote and exotic the meaning. Kemble ascended these rather dizzying heights in order to proclaim the greatness of Grimm and the philological method; his speculations are a potent reminder of the fundamental romanticism of Grimm's own thinking about language, myth, and history.

Kemble's most important influence on *Beowulf* came through a scholar inspired by him and by Karl Lachmann, Lachmann's pupil Karl Müllenhoff, who applied Lachmann's *Liedertheorie* to *Beowulf* and so put scholarship of the English epic on the level of that of Homer's. Müllenhoff sent *Beowulf* flying in several directions. Tracing the "inner history" of the poem required some remodeling and house cleaning. In particular, its Christian content had to be identified as added and interpolated, an excrescence to be rejected so that the poem could be newly restored to its original purity. The theory was better received in the next century, when, in 1905, L. L. Schücking endorsed it in *Beowulfs Rückkehr*, and later scholars, including Berendsohn in 1935, and, most prominently in 1950s, Francis P. Magoun, Jr., explored the idea.[81] However, this attempt to recover origins conflicted with emerging claims for the achievement of Anglo-Saxon culture in unifying Christian and pagan worldviews.

But Müllenhoff's was not the most radical scholarship of the poem in the nineteenth century. That distinction, I believe, belongs to one of its Danish scholars, Thorkelin's successor as custodian of the poem, Nikolai F. S. Grundtvig. Although a part of the poem had been translated earlier by Ebenezer Henderson, who used Thorkelin's transcript to translate the *scop*'s songs into English,[82] Grundtvig produced the first full-length paraphrase of *Beowulf*. Discussions of the poem, after Müllenhoff, become notorious for designating certain parts of the poem as interpolations and arguing that they be excised; Grundtvig was the first to make *Beowulf* longer. This he did twice, first in 1820. As his title—*Bjowulfs Drape* ("Beowulf's Burial")—indicates, Grundtvig wrote a conclusion for the poem. In his edition of *Beowulf*, published in 1861, he incorporated the whole of the "Finnsburg Fragment" into the text after line 1160. Thorkelin protested the first addition, as one might expect; Grundtvig's achievement remains underappreciated. What he wrote is no mere continuation of the poem, however, but an account of Beowulf's last words by a Danish *skald*. The poet implores that the "clan of the Angles, now alienated from the North, might remember old Denmark."[83]

Grundtvig's edition of *Beowulf* of 1861 is important for several reasons. Earle considers it the most extreme edition in its incorporation of emendations. In fact, Grundtvig began correcting Thorkelin's transcripts without having seen the manuscript itself. "Almost all his corrections proved to be identical with the reading of the manuscript," Earle reports, and Grundtvig was subsequently accorded "a demonstrated right to correct the manuscript itself."[84] This view corresponds to Kemble's 1837 "Postscript," which claims that a modern edition by a scholar well versed in Anglo-Saxon "will in all probability be much more like the original than the [manuscript] copy."[85]

But Grundtvig mastered details of *Beowulf* that no one before him had understood. His most famous discovery was the identification of Hygelac in *Beowulf* with Chochilaicus, a king mentioned by Gregory of Tours, an important historical connection that Grimm borrowed in his *Geschichte der Deutschen Sprache*.[86] Grundtvig's text—but not his compendious editorial apparatus—was adopted by C.W.M. Grein, whose edition of the poem in 1867 was notable for its conservatism. Grein relied on Grundtvig for the simple reason that Grundtvig had collated Thorkelin's transcripts against the manuscript in England (between 1829 and 1831) and was assumed to have an unparalleled knowledge of it.

Early scholars of *Beowulf* both edited and translated the text, and could not do one without the other. Birte Kelly's recent study notes that over half the emendations of *Beowulf* accepted by editors from 1950 onward had already been proposed by Grein in 1857. Kelly adds—and this is usually forgotten—that numerous errors and inconsistencies were introduced into the text during this same period because, until 1888 and Zupitza's facsimile and edition, no one had yet edited the poem from the manuscript itself: all editors before Grundtvig worked with transcripts only.[87] In other words, over half the emendations of *Beowulf* accepted in modern scholarship are based on the work of editors who never saw the manuscript.

BEOWULF AS HISTORY

What emerges in the early history of *Beowulf* scholarship is not a march of progress, or a transition from one view to another, but a picture of ongoing disputes about method and the poem's meaning. In Denmark, we can compare Thorkelin to Grundtvig; in Germany, we can compare Müllenhoff to Grein; in England, Kemble to Thorpe. The lines dividing scholars were not national, although their scholarship was often intensely nationalistic. Rather, the major arguments were about methods of textual criticism. We can see that the early history of *Beowulf* scholarship is, therefore, relevant to teaching the poem as a record of how the methods of studying Anglo-Saxon poetry were developed, so to speak, in the laboratory of the text—a figure of speech some of the scholars would have approved of. The first phase of reception was historical, as we see in Thorkelin and Grundtvig, both of whom continued a Danish antiquarian tradition for several decades; and in Turner and the Kemble of 1833. The second phase emphasized poetry and mythology, as we see in Conybeare, the Kemble of 1837, and Müllenhoff's application of the *Liedertheorie*, an extension of Kemble.

The history of this scholarship is rich in summary views. That which I have found most useful is Earle's of 1892, sympathetic in regard to early scholars; jaundiced in regard to those who came later, especially to scholars who advocated the *Liedertheorie*, which he called "that passion for discovering the sutures of poetic workmanship which they have excited among themselves through generations of competitive theorizing about Homer."[88] One phrase in particular here leads me to my conclusion: "competitive theorizing." Let me set Earle's disdain for competitive theorizing against a similar sentiment from a highly regarded source, R. W. Chambers, whose great study, *"Beowulf": An Introduction to the Study of the Poem*, is a retrospective on scholarship. After nearly four hundred pages that examine a century's worth of historical evidence, including the consequences of claims for the "inner history" of the poem, Chambers pointed to the synthesis of views in Klaeber's edition, and remarked, "It [the edition] *has* shown that, *if we can agree upon the method to be used,* a good many problems can be settled" (his emphasis). A few paragraphs later he acknowledged differences dividing his views, Klaeber's, and those of several other scholars, and wrote, "The essential thing is the agreement."[89]

Conflict is a meaningful rather than distasteful part of scholarship. Earle's dismay at German competitiveness and Chambers's insistence that shared method would bring agreement are statements from two very different scholars about issues fundamental to my study of Anglo-Saxon scholarship and my views of the profession as it enters its postmodern age. For I believe in teaching conflict rather than endorsing methodological uniformity to obliterate it; and I believe in encouraging a diversity of methods that renews conflict productively and meaningfully. The history of *Beowulf* scholarship demonstrates the effect of reading and writing in *Beowulf* on *Beowulf*. Textual reception and textual production express a desire for origins. Activities exterior to the origin they desire, they themselves constitute the origin, and *Beowulf* scholars, as if unaware of the paradox, pursue each other rather than the epic they claim to study.

NOTES

[1] F. A. Wolf, *Prolegomena to Homer, or Concerning the Original and Genuine Form of the Homeric Works and their Various Alterations and the Proper Method of Emendation* (1795), trans. Anthony Grafton, Glenn W. Most, and James E. G. Zetzel (Princeton, 1985); see the introduction, pp. 1–35, on Wolf's education and his influence.

[2] The tradition, that Pisistratus did fix the text of Homer is "late and untrustworthy," according to Moses Hadas, *A History of Greek Literature* (New York, 1950), p. 27.

[3] Edward Lytton Bulwer, *The Caxtons: A Family Picture* (1850; reprint New York, 1902), pp. 12–13.

[4] See Raymond Mander and Joe Mitchenson, *The Wagner Companion* (New York, 1977), pp. 47–55.

[5] Edward Lytton Bulwer, *England and the English*, ed. Standish Meacham (Chicago, 1970).

[6] For an analysis of Germanic scholarship in this period, see P. H. Reill, *The German Enlightenment and the Rise of Historicism* (Berkeley, 1975); additional bibliography can be found in Grafton et al., *Prolegomena to Homer*, pp. 249–54.

[7] John Mitchell Kemble, ed., *The Anglo-Saxon Poems of "Beowulf," The Traveller's Song, and the Battle of Finnesburh* (London, 1833); the second edition appeared in two volumes, vol. 1 in 1835, with same title as the first edition, and vol. 2, *A Translation of the Anglo-Saxon Poem of Beowulf* in 1837 (both London). See Fr. Klaeber, ed., *Beowulf and The Fight at Finnsburg*, 3rd ed. with supplements (Lexington, Mass., 1953), pp. cxxxix–cxlii, for studies of individual legends related to the poem. All quotations of *Beowulf*, unless otherwise noted, will be taken from this edition, and further references will be given in the text, when not cited in footnotes.

[8] Quoted in James W. Earl, *Thinking About "Beowulf"* (Stanford, 1994), p. 165.

[9] Maurice Sagoff, *ShrinkLits: Seventy of the World's Towering Classics Cut Down to Size* (New York, 1980).

[10] *"Beowulf": The Donaldson Translation, Backgrounds and Sources, Criticism*, ed. Joseph F. Tuso (New York, 1975).

[11] Jess B. Bessinger Jr. and Robert F. Yeager, eds., *Approaches to Teaching "Beowulf"* (New York, 1984).

[12] Kevin S. Kiernan, *"Beowulf" and the "Beowulf" Manuscript* (New Brunswick, N.J., 1981). I quote the review of Kiernan's book by R. D. Fulk, *Philological Quarterly* 61 (1982): 357.

[13] Helen M. McDonnell et al., eds., *England in Literature* (Glenview, Ill., 1985), pp. 22–23.

[14] Fred C. Robinson, *"Beowulf" and the Appositive Style* (Knoxville, 1985), pp. 34–35.

[15] M. H. Abrams et al., eds., *The Norton Anthology of English Literature*, 5th ed., vol. 1 (New York, 1986), pp. 3–5.

[16] Klaeber, *Beowulf*, p. lxiii.

[17] C. L. Wrenn, *A Study of Old English Literature* (New York, 1967), pp. 74–76.

[18] Stanley B. Greenfield and Daniel G. Calder, *A New Critical History of Old English Literature* (New York, 1986), pp. 134–36.

19 Margaret Goldsmith, *The Mode and Meaning of "Beowulf"* (London, 1970), pp. 60–61.

20 Milton McC. Gatch, *Loyalties and Traditions* (New York, 1971), pp. 54–55.

21 J. R. R. Tolkien, "*Beowulf*: The Monsters and the Critics," in *An Anthology of "Beowulf" Criticism*, ed. Lewis Nicholson (1963; reprint Notre Dame, 1980), pp. 51–103.

22 Tolkien, "Monsters and Critics," pp. 53, 65.

23 Tolkien, "Monsters and Critics," p. 52.

24 On the assumptions and assertions of "New Historicism," I recommend Edward Pechter, "The New Historicism and Its Discontents," *PMLA* 102 (1987): 292–303.

25 Julius Zupitza, ed., *"Beowulf": Reproduced in Facsimile from the Unique Manuscript, British Museum MS. Cotton Vitellius A.xv, with a Transliteration and Notes*, 2nd ed., EETS o.s. 245 (1959; reprint London, 1967).

26 Tuso, *"Beowulf": The Donaldson Translation*, pp. 194–96.

27 Samuel Moore and Thomas A. Knott, eds., *The Elements of Old English* (Ann Arbor, 1940), pp. 280–84.

28 Henry Sweet, ed., *First Steps in Anglo-Saxon* (1897; reprint Oxford, 1925), pp. 39–67.

29 A. J. Wyatt, *The Threshold of Anglo-Saxon* (1926; reprint Cambridge, Eng., 1950), pp. 35–59.

30 R. C. Alton, ed., *An Introduction to Old English* (Evanston, Ill., 1961), pp. 109–113.

31 Bruce Mitchell and Fred C. Robinson, *A Guide to Old English* (Toronto, 1982); F. G. Cassidy and Richard N. Ringler, *Bright's Old English Grammar and Reader*, 3rd ed. (New York, 1971). A more recent revision of Mitchell and Robinson's *Guide* includes *Beowulf* excerpts.

32 Dorothy Whitelock, ed., *Sweet's Anglo-Saxon Reader in Prose and Verse* (Oxford, 1967), p. 102.

33 Klaeber capitalizes both words as well; in Sweet, *First Steps in Anglo-Saxon*, see p. 103, line 22, and p. 104, line 64, where Sweet notes that the manuscript reads *alfwalda*.

34 These definitions are from the *Oxford English Dictionary*, 2nd ed., vol. 4 (Oxford, 1989), p. 91.

35 Alexander Pope, *The Dunciad*, in *The Poems of Alexander Pope*, ed. John Butt (New Haven, 1963), p. 363.

36 T. P. Dunning and A. J. Bliss, eds., *The Wanderer* (London, 1969), p. 74.

37 Ashley Crandell Amos, *Linguistic Means of Determining the Dates of Old English Literary Texts* (Cambridge, Mass., 1980), pp. 15, 6–7.

[38] Gillian R. Overing, "Swords and Signs: A Semiotic Perspective on *Beowulf*," *American Journal of Semiotics* 5 (1987): 35–57, and *Language, Sign, and Gender in "Beowulf"* (Carbondale, 1990).

[39] See Klaeber, *Beowulf*, pp. lxxxviii–lxxxix.

[40] Kiernan, *"Beowulf" and the "Beowulf" Manuscript*, p. 250. *Liedertheorie*, or "song theory," as mentioned previously, was developed by the German scholar Karl Lachmann, who also "developed the genealogical method of editing texts, sorting manuscripts into families and using 'genetic' relationships to reconstruct lost archetypes" (Frantzen, *Desire for Origins*, p. 66).

[41] Tolkien, *"Beowulf*: The Monsters and the Critics," pp. 93–95 (concerning Hrothgar) and pp. 101–02 (concerning the monsters).

[42] C. L. Wrenn, ed., *Beowulf*, rev. W. F. Bolton (London, 1973), pp. 62–67 (hereafter referred to as Wrenn-Bolton). E. G. Stanley discusses several of these views in his book *The Search for Anglo-Saxon Paganism* (Cambridge, Eng., 1975), pp. 40–53.

[43] M. M. Bakhtin, *The Dialogic Imagination*, ed. Michael Holquist, trans. Caryl Emerson and Michael Holquist (Austin, Tex., 1981); Michel Foucault, "What Is an Author?" in *Language, Counter-Memory, Practice: Selected Essays and Interviews by Michel Foucault*, ed. Donald F. Bouchard, trans. Donald F. Bouchard and Sherry Simon (Ithaca, N.Y., 1977).

[44] Edward B. Irving, *A Reading of "Beowulf"* (New Haven, 1968), p. 1.

[45] The following discussion is abridged from my essay, "Writing the Unreadable *Beowulf*: 'Writan' and 'forwritan,' the Pen and the Sword," *Exemplaria* 3 (1991): 327–57.

[46] In Klaeber, the passage reads:

> " . . . gesaga him each wordum, þæt hie sint wilcuman
> Deniga leodum." [Þa to dura eode
> widcuð hæleð,] word inne abead:
> "Eow het secgan sigedrihten min, . . ." (lines 388–91)

> " . . . say to them in words, that they are welcome to the people of the Danes."
> [Then the widely-known warrior went to the door,] spoke the words within:
> "I am commanded to tell you that my glorious leader . . ."

[47] Christian W. M. Grein, ed., *Beowulf nebst den Fragmenten Finnsburg und Valdere* (Kassel, 1867).

[48] Klaeber's second supplement has the same second half-line—"Wulfgar eode"— as Grein.

49 Birte Kelly, "The Formative Stages of *Beowulf* Textual Scholarship: Part I," *Anglo-Saxon England* 11 (1983): 247–74, and "The Formative Stages of *Beowulf* Textual Scholarship: Part II," *Anglo-Saxon England* 12 (1984): 239–75.

50 Kiernan, *"Beowulf" and the "Beowulf" Manuscript*, p. 237.

51 Eugene Vance, *From Topic to Tale* (Minneapolis, 1967), p. xxvii.

52 Julia Kristeva, *Desire in Language: A Semiotic Approach to Literature and Art*, ed. Leon S. Roudiez, trans. Thomas Gora, Alice Jardine, and Leon S. Roudiez (New York, 1980), p. 15 (quoted in the editor's introduction). Kristeva's definition is used by Martin Irvine, who defines intertextuality as "the principle that a text presupposes prior texts, forms of expression, modes of signifying and representing, and codes of intelligibility" ("Anglo-Saxon Literary Theory in Old English Poems," *Style* 20 [1986]: 158).

53 Michael Riffaterre, "Syllepsis," *Critical Inquiry* 6 (1980): 629, 627. In addition, see Riffaterre's essay "The Intertextual Unconscious," *Critical Inquiry* 13 (1987): 371–85.

54 Jonathan Culler, *On Deconstruction: Theory and Criticism After Structuralism* (Ithaca, N.Y., 1982), pp. 213–14.

55 Kevin S. Kiernan, *The Thorkelin Transcripts of "Beowulf,"* Anglistica 25 (Copenhagen, 1986), p. 71.

56 I thank James W. Earl for these observations.

57 But see Paul Beekman Taylor, "Grendel's Monstrous Arts," *In Geardagum* 6 (1984): 1–12, for comments which, although brief, do raise the issue of reading and writing in the poem. John Earle related "writing on the sword" to the transition from "heathen magic" to Christianity in *The Deeds of "Beowulf"* (Oxford, 1982), p. 165.

58 Little has been made of these references to writing in *Beowulf*. The Wrenn-Bolton edition notes at line 1696 simply that "the name of the first owner of the sword is carved in runes on the thin gold plating" of the hilt (p. 160). Readers traditionally translate *runstafas* simply as "runes" and the sequence of verbs that I take to designate writing and narrating instead as "set down, said, marked."

59 The spell is disputed, but see Klaeber's notes to line 804 (p. 157) and line 1523 (p. 187).

60 Foucault, "What Is an Author?" pp. 117, 128.

61 For some stimulating remarks on defamiliarization and this poem, see Ian Duncan, "Epitaphs for Æglacan: Narrative Strife in *Beowulf*," in *"Beowulf": Modern Critical Interpretations*, ed. Harold Bloom (New York, 1987), pp. 111–30.

62 Hans Robert Jauss, *Toward an Aesthetic of Reception*, trans. Timothy Bahti (Minneapolis, 1982). For a selective survey of *Beowulf* criticism, see

Douglas Short, *"Beowulf" Scholarship: An Annotated Bibliography* (New York, 1980).

[63] The history of the work's reception is compact but extensive. See Chauncey B. Tinker, *The Translations of "Beowulf": A Critical Bibliography*, with revised bibliography by Marijane Osborne and a foreword by Fred C. Robinson (Hamden, Conn., 1974), and Stanley, *The Search for Anglo-Saxon Paganism*.

[64] John Josias Conybeare, *Illustrations of Anglo-Saxon Poetry*, ed. William Daniel Conybeare (1826; reprint New York, 1964), pp. 79–81. For a good assessment of Conybeare's achievements, see Daniel G. Calder, "The Study of Style in Old English Poetry: A Historical Introduction," in *Old English Poetry: Essays on Style*, ed. Daniel G. Calder (Los Angeles, 1979), pp. 9–13.

[65] See Earle, *The Deeds of "Beowulf,"* pp. xvi–xvii, concerning Ritson and Turner; Earle incorrectly dates Turner's first reference to the poem to 1807, when, in fact, it was 1805.

[66] Sharon Turner, *The History of the Anglo-Saxons: Comprising the History of England from the Earliest Period to the Norman Conquest*, 4th ed., vol. 3 (London, 1823), p. 280. Turner's *History* was originally published in three volumes between 1799 and 1805, with *Beowulf* being treated in the third volume.

[67] On the history of the manuscript, see Kiernan, *"Beowulf" and the "Beowulf" Manuscript*, pp. 65–85.

[68] Kiernan, *"Beowulf" and the "Beowulf" Manuscript*, p. 162 n. 69. On Parker's and other sixteenth-century antiquarians' work with Anglo-Saxon manuscripts in the sixteenth century, see Frantzen, *Desire for Origins*, pp. 35–50.

[69] On Thorkelin's acquaintance with the manuscript, see Kiernan, *The Thorkelin Transcripts of "Beowulf,"* pp. 1–34. See also R. W. Chambers, *"Beowulf": An Introduction to the Study of the Poem with a Discussion of the Stories of Offa and Finn* (Cambridge, Eng., 1959), pp. 419–50. For an early, and lively, account of Danish scholarship concerning Anglo-Saxon England, see Earle, *The Deeds of "Beowulf,"* pp. x–xvii.

[70] Turner, *The History of the Anglo-Saxons*, vol. 3, pp. 280–81, 283, n. 9.

[71] See Zupitza's facsimile of *Beowulf*, pp. 5, 36.

[72] Tinker, *The Translations of "Beowulf,"* p. 12. On Turner's translation, see also Kiernan, *"Beowulf" and the "Beowulf" Manuscript*, p. 137.

[73] Turner, *The History of the Anglo-Saxons*, vol. 3, p. 285, n. 17 (concerning the transposed leaf), p. 283 (concerning Beowulf's motives), and p. 291 (concerning Unferth's speech).

[74] Conybeare, *Illustrations of Anglo-Saxon Poetry*, p. 80.

75 See Henry Bosley Woolf, "Longfellow's Interest in Old English," in *Philologica: The Malone Anniversary Studies*, ed. Thomas A. Kirby and Henry Bosley Woolf (Baltimore, 1949), pp. 281–89.

76 Kemble, Preface, *The Anglo-Saxon Poems of "Beowulf"* (1833), p. xxxii.

77 Kemble discusses *Beowulf* and pagan beliefs in *The Saxons in England: A History of the English Commonwealth till the Period of the Norman Conquest*, vol. 1 (London, 1876), pp. 413–32. Kemble's comments on language and the manuscript are taken from his preface to *The Anglo-Saxon Poems of "Beowulf"* (1833), pp. xix–xxiv.

78 Kevin S. Kiernan, "The Legacy of Wiglaf," *The Kentucky Review* 6 (1986): 28.

79 Kemble, "Postscript to the Preface," *A Translation of the Anglo-Saxon Poem of "Beowulf,"* p. xliv; Earle, *The Deeds of "Beowulf,"* p. xxiv.

80 This material was published by Kemble as "Über die Stammtafel der Westsachsen" in Munich in 1836; Kemble reported that Grimm reviewed the article favorably.

81 For a good summary of this issue, see Kiernan, *"Beowulf" and the "Beowulf" Manuscript*, pp. 250–57; see also Wrenn-Bolton, *Beowulf*, pp. 65–67, and Kemble, "Postscript to the Preface," *A Translation of the Anglo-Saxon Poem of "Beowulf,"* pp. xxviii–xxix, xliv.

82 Ebenezer Henderson, *Iceland, or the Journal of a Residence in that Island*, vol. 2 (Edinburgh, 1818), pp. 329–30.

83 I quote the English translation of the Danish by Fred C. Robinson, distributed at the 1987 meeting of the International Society of Anglo-Saxonists at the University of Toronto. See N. F. S. Grundtvig, *Beowulfes Beorh eller Bjovulfs-Drapen* (Copenhagen, 1861).

84 Earle, *The Deeds of "Beowulf,"* p. xxxvii.

85 Kemble, "Postscript to the Preface," *A Translation of the Anglo-Saxon Poem of "Beowulf,"* p. xxiv.

86 See Franklin D. Cooley, "Contemporary Reaction to the Identification of Hygelac," pp. 269–74, and David J. Savage, "Grundtvig: A Stimulus to Old English Scholarship," pp. 275–80, both in Kirby and Woolf, *Philologica: The Malone Anniversary Studies*.

87 Kelly, "The Formative Stages of *Beowulf* Textual Scholarship: Part II," pp. 246–48.

88 Earle, *The Deeds of "Beowulf,"* p. lii.

89 Chambers, *"Beowulf": An Introduction to the Study of the Poem*, pp. 396, 398.

LOCATING *BEOWULF* IN LITERARY HISTORY

JOHN D. NILES

Faced with the problem of making sense of a poem like *Beowulf*—a poem from a very different epoch, composed according to stylistic criteria that differ markedly from those in fashion today—readers naturally want to ask "What does it mean?" Related to this question is a similar one favored by English professors, who like to take literary machines apart to see how they tick: "How does the poem mean?" Without neglecting either of these questions, neither one of which leads to simple answers, I wish to focus attention on a third one that is not so frequently asked: *"What work did the poem do?"*

Putting the same matter in other words, what I propose to ask is, "What are the cultural questions to which *Beowulf* is an answer?" This perspective involves, among other things, looking upon Anglo-Saxon heroic poetry as a discourse, in Foucault's sense of a corporate means for dealing with a subject and authorizing views of it. Adopting this stance, we can inquire how the poetic tradition of which *Beowulf* is an example served as one important means by which a culture defined itself, validated itself, and maintained its equilibrium through strategic adaptations during a period of major change.

Thanks in part to the impressive formalist scholarship of the past fifty years, we are accustomed to reading *Beowulf* as a superb work of art. The achievement of the broadly philological scholarship that has dominated the

From *Exemplaria* 5.1 (March 1993): 79–109; reprinted with permission of Pegasus Press.

academies within living memory has been to create this poem as an aesthetic object worthy of minute critical inquiry. Structuralist rage for order, patristic source-hunting, and oral-formulaic analyses of patterned phrasing have indeed extended our knowledge of the text, its filiations, and its internal systems of order. Paradoxically, the success of these forms of criticism may also have served to occlude our understanding of *Beowulf* as a socially embedded poetic act. As John Hermann has remarked,

> The problem is that it [i.e., the philological heritage] has been too successful; its very dominance keeps Old English studies from developing in new directions.[1]

Like Hermann and some other youngish scholars, as well as some old-school scholars of an historical bent, I suspect that the issue of understanding a poem of this kind cannot be resolved by philological or aesthetic investigations alone. That is not to say that such inquiries, if well conducted, will not form the basis of our understanding. They will. But the underlying issue is ontological, not aesthetic. To paraphrase Leo Spitzer, what one wants to know is "Why did the phenomenon of *Beowulf* happen at all?"[2]

Answering this question means reading the poem as a literary act with cultural antecedents and consequences. To begin with, we need to reconstruct an Anglo-Saxon context within which the poem and the fact of its textual existence make sense. I am not speaking of a "background," in the repudiated sense, but rather of an historical matrix in which the discourse of heroic poetry took place—whether in oral or manuscript form—and which this discourse had some power to shape, as well. As we proceed along these lines, eventually in the direction of assessing the poem's place in a larger cultural heritage that extends to the present day, we can proceed with indifference to earlier conceptions to the effect that *Beowulf* reflects the mentality of one time or place, or provides a clear window on early Germanic social institutions, or stands as an unambiguous statement of "heroic values," "Christian allegory," or any other monolithic abstraction. Instead, we can begin to read the poem as a site of ideological conflict, a complex work of art that responded to lively tensions, agreements, and disagreements in the society from which it came, just as its text has provoked many conflicting approaches in the last two centuries. Some readers, following Mikhail Bakhtin, have contrasted epic poetry to the novel, seeing the epic as a monologic genre that expresses a kind of party line.[3] This may be true of some epic poems. If so, I have not come across them. Much can be learned about

Beowulf, I believe, by approaching it as a polyphonic work whose messages are contingent and sometimes contrary.

Rather than reflecting the static conditions of a single or simple age, *Beowulf* represents a broad collective response to changes that affected a complex society during a period of major crisis and transformation. To note only the most obvious of these transformations: by the time that this poem was put down in writing,[4] the English-speaking peoples of Britain had turned away from pagan beliefs and had embraced the teachings of Christianity. They had weathered the storm of Viking invasions and had established control of a mixed and somewhat turbulent Anglo-Scandinavian society. They were no longer competing against one another as separate tribes ruled by warlords but had developed a single kingdom, built largely on the Carolingian model and administered through coinage, written documents, and a state bureaucracy. The changes that affected the society to which *Beowulf* pertains were momentous, and by their workings the nation that we call England came into being.

In particular, the society to which *Beowulf* pertains was using writing, and not just oral poetry, to express an ideology capable of persuading people to be governed and rulers to govern well. To an extent that still seems remarkable no matter how familiar one is with this phenomenon, late Anglo-Saxon England excelled in book-making, and much of this book-making was in the vernacular. Whether the literacy that book-making presupposes was ever widespread among the laity, we cannot know with certainty.[5] By the time that *Beowulf* was written down, however, at least some of the secular aristocracy were no longer illiterates, relatively self-sufficient in their isolation from Mediterranean culture and, perhaps, indifferent or even hostile to the values that that culture represented. They were familiar with the use of poetry in English as a vehicle for Christian doctrine and a means of reinventing the Germanic past.

To see how these momentous events affect our reading of *Beowulf*, we should briefly place the poem into relation to the literary tradition that developed in post-Roman Britain once Germanic-speaking kings were in control of the land. I must apologize to my readers if this survey requires me to proceed over some well-worn ground; my only justification for doing so is that I shall find out a somewhat different path than others have taken.

· · ·

When Britain was a Roman colony, many of its inhabitants were familiar with both the arts of literacy and the Christian faith. During the fourth and fifth centuries, for reasons not wholly clear, Roman Britain suffered an economic and administrative collapse that left it cut off from the mother country. Various forms of chaos and regression ensued until, according to tradition, the land was conquered by Germanic-speaking invaders from the North Sea coastal areas. The first of these warriors came as mercenaries. Others then migrated in great numbers, killing or enslaving the inhabitants and establishing their own kingdoms along ancestral lines. This is the account that the people of Anglo-Saxon England gave of their historical origins, at any rate, and most people of later ages have accepted it at its face value.

For archaeologists, the problem with this account is that there is little hard evidence for a large Germanic migration that led to the conquest of Britain. A Roman collapse there was, but a Germanic conquest? Maybe. There is much to be said for Richard Hodges's theory whereby the myriad regions of sub-Roman Britain evolved into the kingdoms of early Anglo-Saxon England rather than being suddenly replaced by them.[6] According to this theory, Roman Britain became progressively more and more Germanized rather than being conquered outright. Eventually a "Myth of Migration" then developed as a way of legitimizing the political interests that emerged in the post-colonial period, when warlords of Germanic stock or aspirations were intent on establishing their hegemony over a mixed population. In short, the Myth of Migration that was one of the Anglo-Saxons' controlling political ideas (as Nicholas Howe has shown) was a projection of a desire on the part of many inhabitants of Britain for a distinguished non-Roman racial past.[7] For better or worse, this desire happens to have been replicated by many people in England, Germany, and North America during the period from the late eighteenth to the earlier twentieth century, when the tide of Western racial consciousness reached its high-water mark in modern times.[8]

As Hodges notes, advocates of his theory must respond to the spiny question of why Latin and the Celtic languages were so fully eclipsed by the English language in Britain. Whether or not the theory is correct, and it will be debated for years to come, it has the attraction of drawing attention to the historicity of history; that is to say, the set of biases that make documents such as Bede's *Ecclesiastical History* and the annals of the *Anglo-Saxon Chronicle* untrustworthy as an account of "what actually happened." The theory is not contradicted by what we know of the human capacity for mythmaking. As Eric Hobsbawm and other historians have pointed out, there are few things more easily invented than a tradition that has existed since time immemorial.[9]

Whatever the right story of the decay and displacement of Roman institutions in Britain may be, the island soon became part of what Hodges calls a North Sea interaction zone. During the fifth, sixth, and seventh centuries, as new trade routes and intertribal connections linked the peoples of Britain with the other peoples fringing the North Sea, paganism of the old Germanic type became increasingly the norm. Latin disappeared as the language of the ruling class. Germanic laws and customs took the place of Roman ones. The power of important leaders was displayed through the circulation of prestige goods as gifts in the context of funerals, such as the spectacular seventh-century grave-sites at Taplow and Sutton Hoo.

Most important for our present concerns, Anglo-Saxon kingship took on insular forms in a land that was once again yielding the impressive agricultural surpluses that translate into cash and loot. By the early seventh century, kings were constructing palaces, such as the one at Yeavering (Northumberland), that served as the focal points of their realms and the most visible expressions of their prestige. In royal milieus of this kind, cultivated poetry could flourish. From this time on, it is fair to surmise, stories relating to the Heroic Age, the half-mythical fourth- and fifth-century Age of Migrations, found a favored place in the repertory of singers vying for aristocratic patronage. Both then and now, people of noble status or ambitions have tended to have a weak spot for questions of lineage. Not only could heroic poetry express the ideology of current regimes, legitimizing structures of power through tales of dead ancestors. It could also satisfy the desire for origins (to use Allen Frantzen's phrase)[10] that anyone in Britain may have felt.

In this formative period, apparently, there developed a firm tradition of heroic poetry of the kind that Alcuin complains about, in his famous letter of 797, and that eventually found complex literary expression in *Beowulf*, *Waldere*, and the *Finnsburg Fragment*. During this period members of the ruling class had little use for books but possessed a well-developed literature without letters. They were familiar with runes but used them for practical rather than literary ends. Instead, in keeping with Old Germanic practice, they patronized songs that skilled poets performed aloud in celebration of kings and heroes.[11]

Too frequently, in the past, the study of the putative oral roots of texts that have come down to us in writing has been undertaken in a spirit of celebration of a golden childhood of the race from which literacy has lamentably cut us off. Work of this odor has a way of provoking an allergic reaction on the part of hard-nosed scholars who value both their own literacy and that of the Anglo-Saxons. Given the history of these debates, it is worth taking a moment to reconsider the oral matrix from which some of our extant texts are likely to derive.[12]

• • •

Understanding the literature that has emerged in a dominantly oral context, whether in the past or the present, is not an easy task. As Brian Stock has aptly remarked, "it may be asked whether, as literates, we understand orality as anything but the opposite of literacy."[13] People whose lives are deeply invested in Western educational institutions naturally tend to understand illiteracy as nothing but deprivation, and this attitude is reinforced by a host of governmental agencies. Today some people even speak of "cultural literacy" as a synonym for broad-based humanistic knowledge of the kind nice white people ought to have, while "cultural illiteracy" is another term for unwashed ignorance. During the past hundred and fifty years, as the disciplines of anthropology and folklore have emerged into their modern forms, the search for the primitive or folk "other" has sometimes been pursued as a foil for the dominant culture's quest for its self-identity. Remnants of once-viable oral cultures have been folklorized to indulge the nostalgia of the dominant society and to swell the pocketbooks of entrepreneurs. Even good anthropological and folkloristic research has sometimes been received in an atmosphere of colonialism or ethnocentrism, so that just by employing the value-laden concepts of literacy and orality, in Stock's view, "we thus run the risk of intellectual imperialism among peoples that do not share our faith in the value of writing."

The fundamental and almost inevitable bias with which we favor the written word can affect our ability to understand a poem like *Beowulf*, which both is rooted in an oral culture and depicts one, in imaginary guise. If we look upon an oral culture as lacking something that it should have in order to be complete, we will not understand it as a working system with its own efficacy and equilibrium.

The active tradition-bearer who is the heart of an oral tradition—its motor, so to speak—is likely to have a recognizable style that sets him apart from other performers.[14] When we look for that hypostatic entity we call "the tradition," in fact, what we find are just such creative individuals, each with his or her own way of speaking or singing. As specialists in established forms of oral expression, these people tend to be known and honored by name in their communities. They are the makers of the tradition, not its slaves, and their creativity is often manifest in a personal style that may include a display of neologisms and original figures of speech, as well as an ability to spin simple tales into complex, highly ornamented verbal displays. The most gifted singer recorded by Milman Parry and Albert Lord in the Balkans, Avdo Međedović of the village of Obrov in eastern Montenegro, was able to hear a song performed by a less skilled person, meditate on it overnight, and perform the same song the next day at nearly three times its earlier length, expanding the story with ornamental details of the kind that were prized in this tradition: catalogs of names, descriptions of men, horses, and weapons, detailed journeys, examples of direct discourse, evocations of personal emotion on the part of actors, flashbacks in time, and the like.[15]

Fieldwork that I have undertaken with Scotland's travelling people in 1984, 1986, 1987, and 1988 reinforces this point. The person whom I have recorded at greatest length, Duncan Williamson of Argyll and Fife, is a connoisseur of oral traditions. He has made a lifetime habit of listening intently to other performers and absorbing their words, so that now, in his mid-fifties, he is a walking encyclopedia of verbal lore that he has learned from family members, crofters, fellow-workers, tramps, and friends. He has a larger repertory of songs and stories than anyone else whom I have encountered. Moreover, he has compiled full versions of songs that he learned from other people only in fragments, and when he learns a new story, he is likely to retell it at length in his own fully ornamented style. When in the company of other singers, he is often able to help them when they falter, and in private he can be a sharp critic of other people's performances.[16] Through active, self-conscious, intelligent tradition-bearers like Međedović and Williamson, an oral culture realizes its full potential.

It would be a mistake to see such performers as isolated geniuses. An active tradition-bearer can only flourish when a community of like-minded individuals shares a body of lore and supports particular forms of verbal expression. The singer or storyteller tends to be a spokesman for accepted wisdom. His or her art is the art of perfecting known modes of expression and familiar themes, not inventing new ones. Gifted performers like these bring established genres to a fine point of expression, to the delight of those listeners who have competence in this medium. Oral literature can thus serve important functions of education and acculturation in the society in which it occurs. It tends to be one of the most important means by which children absorb the values of adult society and learn to pattern their behavior according to accepted norms. For adults, it confirms the grid work of understanding that constitutes their knowledge of history, social structure, and moral action: in short, their culture.

• • •

The culture of early Anglo-Saxon England began undergoing the first of its crises of identity beginning in 597 when, according to Bede, missionaries sent by Pope Gregory the Great arrived in Kent to forge a new kind of colonial relationship between a set of Germanized kingdoms and what was now also a fairly thoroughly Germanized Rome. This missionary activity was both reinforced and threatened by the work of Irish monks in northern Britain. The relative speed with which the rulers of seventh-century Britain came to adopt Christianity—and adopt it systematically, not just as one of a number of competing cults—speaks of their desire for participation in a wider world of power and history than their Myth of Migration could provide.

Anglo-Saxon literature offers abundant evidence of a dynamic and sometimes contradictory accommodation of religious and temporal values during the period after the Conversion.[17] Perhaps more readily apparent than the new religion's effect on ethics was its impact on Anglo-Saxon concepts of identity. The proud pagan kings of sixth- and seventh-century Britain doubtless considered their domains to be "central" and "normal," as people like to do. With the Conversion, they were faced with an alternative perspective whereby they were peripheral members of a larger Christian community whose centers of physical and spiritual power were farther East, in Rome and Jerusalem. In this larger geographical context, purely Germanic customs were potentially aberrant. In like manner, Anglo-Saxon history could come to seem merely insular. One of the effects of the Conversion was to subordinate the Germanic past to the dominant history of the Mediterranean lands. The extended pseudo-genealogy that the West Saxon royal line invented for itself by the time of King Alfred is perhaps the most dramatic single manifestation of this tendency toward accommodation and subordination.[18] According to this new concept of history, the kings of Wessex no longer traced their lineage back to Woden and Geat as divine ancestors. Instead, these figures, now euhemerized, became intermediate links in a grand line of descent from Noah, hence from Adam. The Germanic tribes were thus welcomed to the family of the people of the Book, just as the Anglo-Saxon kingdoms became an outpost of Roman ecclesiastical organization. Germanic, Roman, and Biblical antiquity became three aspects of a single past.[19]

These cultural transformations were made possible through the mastery of writing, or what Jack Goody has called the technology of the intellect.[20] Writing made far-flung ecclesiastical organization possible. In time, it permitted the growth of a state bureaucracy to facilitate large-scale administration and finance. As Seth Lerer has discussed in depth, writing was a linking device that promoted complex cultural connections, as when Bede incorporated written documents such as papal letters into his *History* or when various Anglo-Saxon authors wrote glosses on Scriptural texts, glosses that in turn sometimes inspired later commentary.[21] By permitting knowledge to be accumulated in stable form in books and monastic libraries, the technology of writing fostered the growth of science, in partial displacement of magic. By calibrating time in the form of annals, writing made possible history in something like the modern sense, as opposed to legend or myth. It also allowed for the invention of literature as we know it today, with its allusive and densely intertextual character, as opposed to the poetry that was known only in face-to-face encounters.[22]

As Patrick Wormald has shown in an important attempt to set *Beowulf* within the aristocratic climate of early English Christianity, it would be a mistake to look upon Anglo-Saxon monks as a separate class with no worldly interests.[23] By birth as well as personal outlook, many monks had links with the secular aristocracy. Some noblemen seem to have looked upon certain monasteries as, in essence, their private domains, and abbots and priors were naturally drawn from the ranks of the upper class. Anglo-Saxon *boceras*, the bearers of literary culture, thus comprised an elite not only thanks to their knowledge, with its attendant power, but also through their social connections. This elite class may have had a strong influence in the secular realm from early on. Certainly it did so by the end of the ninth century, once Alfred the Great, following the lead of King Offa of Mercia, had reorganized the West Saxon kingdom on the Carolingian model, with a strong emphasis on piety and the literate arts. By this time, the commonplaces of Latin learning had filtered through to all levels of the vernacular culture. But in the meantime, a major external threat had imperiled the continuity of life and letters in Britain.

· · ·

It is no accident that we know of the defense of southern Britain from Viking marauders chiefly through a literary source, the *Anglo-Saxon Chronicle*, that seems to have been initiated with King Alfred's blessing. Like many canny statesmen, Alfred was aware of the political uses of literacy, and the *Chronicle* could be called the first piece of political propaganda written in English. Its annals for 871 to 896 consistently take a West Saxon perspective and show the king in a sympathetic and indeed heroic light. The same is true of the king's authorized biography, Asser's *Life of Alfred*, a work whose chief literary model was Einhard's *Life of Charlemagne*. Asser's book traces, among other subjects worthy of emulation, Alfred's tenacious efforts to learn to read, and it thereby helps document the revival of English learning and bookmaking for which this king is justly famed. Taken together, the literary translations from Latin into English that Alfred either sponsored, encouraged, or undertook in person represent, with the *Chronicle*, the first literary canon in English. Europe had not seen such a burst of literary activity since the age of Charlemagne.

Unlike Charlemagne, however, Alfred encouraged the growth of a kind of literacy that was previously of little importance in England and was virtually unknown elsewhere in Europe. This was literacy in the vernacular. To the extent that the ambitious program of education in English letters that he announced in the preface to his translation of Gregory's *Pastoral Care* was realized, it broadened the base of the pyramid of learning, making reading and writing less an esoteric exercise on the part of a clerical elite.[24]

Alfred's impressive accomplishments laid the foundations for a period that can justly be called the Tenth-Century Renaissance. This was a time of consolidation and growth in many spheres, not just the literary arts. The story of the Danes in Britain during this period is largely one of accommodation and acculturation, as the Viking inhabitants of the Danelaw intermarried with the English, accepted the Christian faith, and took on positions of responsibility in both Church and state. With due attention to his quasi-imperial stature, as well as to the luster that accrued to him from his triumph at Brunanburh in 937, Alfred's grandson Athelstan styled himself by such honorific titles as *basileus*, *imperator*, and *Angelsaxonum Denorumque gloriosissimus rex*.[25] By Athelstan's reign, for the first time, it was possible to speak of the English nation.

The flowering of literary arts during the tenth and eleventh centuries justifies our speaking of this period as a golden age of vernacular letters. In keeping with the literary program of his immediate predecessors, Athelstan had scribes at his disposal and accumulated an impressive number of manuscripts, which he distributed strategically as gifts.[26] In subsequent years, after old monasteries were reestablished and many new ones founded, all of them affected by the Benedictine Reform that was sweeping Europe during

the second half of the tenth century, scribes produced a wealth of manu-
scripts written in both Latin and English. The great bulk of Old English
writings that have come down to us, including the five great poetic codices
that were inscribed about the year 1000, dates from this tenth- and elev-
enth-century period.[27]

• • •

How does the poem of *Beowulf* relate to these events?

To begin with, we should divide the question into two. First, what is the
probable origin of the discourse, the collective heroic verse-making tra-
dition, that finds textual expression in *Beowulf*? And second, what is the
probable origin of this individual poem, in the shape that we now have it?
Who wrote this text down, approximately when, and for what reasons?

The first question can perhaps be answered more readily than the sec-
ond, and I have already given my thoughts on it in brief. Inasmuch as a
well-defined tradition of heroic poetry was cultivated by the Anglo-Saxon
warrior class, we can probably trace its origins to the period of growth and
consolidation of the Anglo-Saxon kingdoms during the sixth to eighth cen-
turies AD. In its basic formal characteristic, this kind of verse surely goes
back earlier, to the sorts of songs that once circulated among Germanic
tribes on the Continent. These early songs, however, must have differed
markedly from the elaborate heroic poetry that developed in the halls of
Anglo-Saxon kings. Blessed with wealth and occasional leisure, the Anglo-
Saxons of the ruling class transformed memories or fantasies relating to
the Age of Migrations into the stuff of a collective dialogue about history.
They invented the Heroic Age as a legendary counterpart to their own era,
one that chartered their own cherished institutions of kingship, thaneship,
gift-giving, oath-swearing, and vengeance. They peopled this realm with
shadowy chieftans—"Hengest," "Finn," "Offa," "Eormanric," and others, to
cite examples only from *Beowulf*—whose names are attested in various and
shifting ways in the genealogies of Anglo-Saxon kings. To these chieftans
they added other lords and heroes whose names figured prominently in
the oral history of the tribes of the North Sea rim: "Hygelac," "Sigemund,"
"Weland," "Hama," "Ingeld," "Ongentheow," and the like, again to cite ex-
amples only from *Beowulf*, leaving aside the whole panoply of names that
are put on display in *Widsith* and *Deor*, or that figure in the *Waldere* or
Finnsburg fragments and other sources. Verbal portraits of this Age of
Heroes served to express (or, perhaps, put into question) the ideology of a

141

ruling class through a kind of poetry that was not history, but was a form of history. That is to say, this poetry reconstructed in imaginary form that period of the past that was felt to have the most direct influence on the present, or on what people wanted the present to be, or not to be.

As for dating *Beowulf*, we can begin with the certainty that the poem was composed during the three-hundred-year period between the "Cædmonian revolution" of the late seventh century and the time that our copy was written down, about the year 1000. In one sense or another, as part of a general movement by which songs were legible texts, the poem is a product of what German scholars have called *Verschriftlichung*, a noun that sounds better in German than in its English equivalents "literarization" or "textualization."[28] In order to narrow down the limits within which this specific act of textualization took place, let us give brief attention to the time when English poetry was first reified in writing.

· · ·

Like most of the tales embedded in Bede's *History*, the story of Cædmon is a legendary account whose truth should not be confused with fact.[29] Whatever its factual bases may be, and it would be foolish to deny them altogether, the story functions as a myth of the coming of culture. According to widespread belief, important new elements of human culture are not made but given. They are the product of a gifted person's inspiration in a moment of isolation, when contact with divine power is made possible through prayer or dream.[30] The myth lends divine sanction to the cultural form or forms in question. In this instance, Bede's account of Cædmon serves as an origin myth for two related activities: the use of native verse to celebrate Christian themes, and the use of the technology of writing to record vernacular literature.

Although one still sometimes reads authoritative statements to the effect that one of the first tasks of St. Gregory's missionaries was "to destroy non-Christian mythology, along with the heroic poetry that could serve as a rallying point for a cultural tradition outside Christianity,"[31] such claims are fairly empty. Through euhemerizing the Northern gods, the missionaries did indeed manage to destroy them except as a racial memory, but heroic poetry is another matter. By following the example of Cædmon, Anglo-Saxon poets transmuted the medium of Old English verse into an instrument of Christian teaching and mental exploration. At the same time, by continuing to take their subjects from Germanic legendry as well as from Christian history, they salvaged what was salvageable from the historical ideas of their ancestors, not so as to compete with Christian faith but to bring this faith to more perfect expression, in terms that made culturally specific sense.

To begin with, Christian poets had to learn to sing the divine names. This is chiefly what "Cædmon's Hymn" consists of. But songs of praise were just the beginning. In time, poets learned to sing complex stories focusing on characters who shaped their thoughts and actions in accord with both heroic models and Biblical ones. In a poem like the Old English verse paraphrase of *Exodus*, Moses resembles a Germanic warlord. In a tale like *Beowulf*, correspondingly, the hero takes on Moses-like or Christ-like attributes.[32] The poetic tradition thus proved itself resilient, like any deeply entrenched cultural form. Far from being a static repertory of songs insensitive to a changing social and intellectual climate, Old English poetry remained culturally meaningful by adapting to the realities of the hybrid civilization, both Germanic and Mediterranean in its origins, that was now ascendant in Britain.

Literary histories published before the 1980s regularly state that *Beowulf* was composed not long after the Cædmonian revolution and probably during the eighth century, or the period of Bede and Alcuin, some time before the Vikings began their attacks. More recent scholarship has shaken this orthodoxy and has rekindled speculation that the poem derives from the Viking age, much nearer the date of the extant manuscript.[33] Although certainty in this matter may never be possible, I agree that there are good reasons for taking the poem as we have it as the product of the Tenth-Century Renaissance. As far as *Beowulf* studies are concerned, the Anglo-Scandinavian period is an idea whose time has come.

. . .

There are at least seven good reasons for locating *Beowulf* in the period of nation-building that followed the ninth-century Viking invasions. Other scholars may have other reasons for preferring either this date or an alternative one, but these seven points seem to me persuasive when taken together.

1. The role of the Danes. The action of most of the poem is set in Denmark and serves as a showcase for the magnificence of the Danish court. Such an interest in things Danish is understandable after the Danes had settled in England in some numbers, but not before. In addition, the poet depicts the Danes in an ambiguous light. Some of them are admirable, though rather better at talking than fighting. Others practice cursed rites, drink more beer than is good for them, or (like Hunferth) have a way of blustering over-much and stabbing one another in the back. Such an ambiguous portrait of the Danes fits the tenth-century period after the Viking wars had cooled, when many Danes, now converted to the faith, were being assimilated to the dominant culture.[34]

2. The Scylding connection. Near the beginning of *Beowulf*, the poet calls prominent attention to the Danish king Scyld Scefing ("descendant of Scef") and his descendants, while twice, later, he draws attention to a Danish king named Heremod. The poem here either draws on or replicates the expanded West Saxon pseudo-genealogy that the West Saxon kings adopted by the time of King Alfred, under Viking influence. This genealogy included early kings named Scyldwa and Heremod, going back to a still more shadowy king Sceaf, "who was born in Noah's Ark." By the late ninth century, in other words, the genealogies of both Anglo-Saxon and Danish royal lines had been made to converge. The beginning of *Beowulf* thus celebrates an ancestral king of the English, not just of the Danes. The whole Grendel episode is thereby brought into relation to English history, which takes on a pan-Germanic aspect, and the kings of England are legitimized as rulers of both Anglo-Saxons and Danes.[35]

3. Language and rhetoric. With its well-developed vocabulary of religious experience, as well as its assimilation of commonplace Biblical and Latinate learning, the language in which *Beowulf* is composed shows strong affinities to that of other vernacular works that are most plausibly dated to the tenth century or thereabouts. Worth noting here are the vocabulary and rhetoric not only of poems chiefly secular, such as *Wanderer* and *Widsith*, but also of devout works in verse like *Judith*, as well as late prose laws or sermons directed against pagan practices. Scholars who favor an eighth-century date for *Beowulf* have had notorious difficulty in accepting the authenticity of several overtly Christian passages that have a "late" feel to them.[36] The hypothesis of a tenth-century date eliminates this problem. In addition, certain skaldic turns of phrase in *Beowulf*, when taken in connection with the poet's sustained interest in things Scandinavian, suggest Norse influence from the post-Viking period.[37]

4. Virtuous pagans. While the *Beowulf* poet depicts the characters of his poem as pagans, as is historically accurate, he also presents at least some of them as admirable persons. Both Beowulf and Wiglaf are models of courage. The aged Beowulf rules as a *rex justus*, pious and kind, somewhat nearer to the ideal of Augustine and Gregory the Great than one would predict of a Germanic warlord of the Heroic Age.[38] Many characters speak of God and His power, and at one point Hrothgar, another *rex justus*, delivers so sententious an address, couched in familiar homiletic phrases, that many commentators have referred to it as a "sermon." No authors writing in Latin during the eighth century portrayed the ancestral Germanic past in so favorable a light. Bede cast a cloak of silence over early Germanic legendry. Alcuin cried out against its influence in the monasteries. Only with the Alfredian Renaissance do we see authors, writing now in English, seek to rehabilitate the materials of a Germanic legendry for pious or didactic ends, as when Alfred, paraphrasing Boethius on the subject of mutability, laments "Where are now the bones of Weland?" The *Beowulf* poet's interest in virtuous pagans meshes with the Alfredian program of cultural reform, with its stress on the pious laity. The poem pertains to a stage of English culture when pagan Germanic lore no longer represented a threat to Christian spirituality, so that pagan Scandinavia could be used as the setting of a poem that addresses issues of salvation and spiritual evil.[39]

5. *Old Norse analogues.* The only close medieval analogues to the *Beowulf* story are preserved not in English but in Old Norse.[40] *Hrólfs Saga Kraka* tells of the adventures of a certain Boðvarr, son of a person who was a man by night but a bear by day, who travels from Gautland (corresponding to the *Beowulf* poet's Geatland) to Denmark to stay at the court of king Hrólfr Kraki (corresponding to the *Beowulf* poet's Hrothulf, who in Danish tradition takes the place equivalent to Hrothgar's in *Beowulf*). There he humiliates Hrólfr's retainers and takes service with the king, then kills a beast who is described as "the worst of trolls." *Grettis Saga* follows a different plot but includes two passages that are remarkably similar to what we find in the Danish episode in *Beowulf*, once allowances are made for the difference between an aristocratic heroic poem and a domestic Icelandic prose saga. These passages represent the closest parallels to *Beowulf* to be found anywhere. Other Old Norse analogues are found in *Orms Þáttr Stórólfssonar* and *Samsons Saga Fagra*, among other texts. The existence of these parallels is enough to show that the story-pattern that underlies the Danish episode in *Beowulf* was fairly well known in Scandinavian lands during the post-Viking period, although not necessarily in other parts of Germania either then or at other times. The story-pattern could have traveled either way, but its relative popularity in Old Norse literature suggests that some early version of it traveled into England. There the *Beowulf* poet gave it heroic dress and elaborate ornamentation, in keeping with the habits of the kind of verse of which he was a master. Interchange between Danish- and English-speak-

ing inhabitants of England during the ninth or tenth century is not the only way of accounting for this shared story-pattern, but it is the easiest way.

6. *Three probable English allusions.* The poet makes much of three figures whose names would have set bells ringing in the minds of Anglo-Saxons: *Hengest*, the protagonist of a song that is performed to entertain the nobles in Heorot after Beowulf's first victory; *Offa*, king of the Continental Angles, whom the poet goes out of his way to praise in extravagant terms (lines 1945–62); and *Wiglaf*, the young warrior who ventures his life to go to the aid of Beowulf during the fight against the dragon. To take up each of these in turn:

a. The Hengest of the *scop's* song bears the same name as the quasi-historical or pseudo-historical Hengest, who, with his brother Horsa, in an account that goes back beyond Bede and the *Chronicle* to the history ascribed to Nennius, was one of the fifth-century founders of Anglo-Saxon England. This Hengest was honored as the ancestor of the kings of Kent. Apart from these two instances, "Hengest" ("steed") is not an Anglo-Saxon proper name. The fight of the *Beowulf* poet's Hengest against Finn is not datable, but it pertains to that part of the heroic past that shortly precedes the poem's present action. To take this Hengest to be the Hengest of the Migration Myth seems only natural.[41]

b. The *Beowulf* poet's Offa bears the same name as the celebrated English king Offa who ruled Mercia from 757 to 796. In one document this latter Offa styled himself *rex totius Anglorum patriae*, "king of the whole land of the English," the first Anglo-Saxon king to claim so grand a title.[42] Offa of Mercia traced his ancestry back to the Continental Offa, who governed a territory (the old province of the Angles, in Jutland) that eventually fell under Danish rule. In later times the Danes, too, honored Offa as an ancestor and retold stories about him that they may have learned from English sources.[43] The poet's extravagant praise of the earlier Offa thus could serve as a compliment not only to the Mercians (or their political descendants), as has been often remarked, but also to the Danes as inheritors of Jutland and recent immigrants to Britain.

c. The Wiglaf of *Beowulf* has no counterpart in early Germanic legendry. Perhaps significantly, however, he bears the name of an historical English king, the Wiglaf who ruled from 827 to about 840 as the last independent king of Mercia before it fell under West Saxon domination. The *Beowulf* poet ascribes to his Wiglaf a father named Wihstan and another ancestor named Waegmund. The Mercian Wiglaf had a grandson named Wihstan and a son named Wigmund. While the correspondence of names here does not match up in genealogical sequence, it amounts to more than the usual sort of alliterative chime between the names of blood-relations that one finds in poetry and history.[44] The collection of three such names in each of two families, one fictive and one historical, cannot be coincidence. While the quest for allegory in *Beowulf* has always proven vain, the search for culturally significant allusion is another matter. Very possibly, the poet's invention of a conspicuously heroic character named "Wiglaf," with these named ancestors, reinforces the oblique compliment to the royal family of the Mercians that many readers believe to be effected by the allusion to Offa.

If the passage relating to Offa does carry allusive force, then the poem dates from any time after Offa or Mercia stood in high repute. If the Wiglaf passages are allusive as well, then *Beowulf* was composed no earlier than the time of the historical Wiglaf's grandson, or the late ninth century. By this time Mercia had been absorbed into a larger political unity ruled by the West Saxon royal line. When taken together with other criteria for dating, the evidence of the Offa and Wiglaf passages points to (though it does not necessitate) a date for the composition of *Beowulf* during the earlier tenth century. In this connection it is worth remembering that Alfred's successors claimed descent from both Offas, as well as a right to Mercia, through Alfred's marriage to a lady of the Mercian royal line.

7. The role of the Geats. The poet is clear in specifying that the hero of the poem, "Beowulf," like his king, Hygelac, whom he succeeds to the throne, is a Geat. To what cultural questions is this tribal identification an answer? Few scholars have been concerned with this question lately. Editors have accepted that the Old English tribal name *Geatas* corresponds phonologically to the Old Norse tribal name *Gautar* (modern Swedish *Götar*), have noted that in Old Norse sources the Gautar inhabited a region corresponding to the southern part of modern Sweden, and have left the matter at that, with some speculative remarks concerning the date at which the Gautar were or were not absorbed into the Swedish nation and the possible connection of this historical event to the ending of *Beowulf*, with its predictions of tribal dissolution facing the Geats. But this is by no means the end of the matter. According to Bede's influential statement (*Ecclesiastical History* 1:15), Britain was settled by "the three most powerful nations of Germany": the Saxons, the Angles, and the Jutes (Latin *Iuti* or *Iutae*). The first two of these tribal identifications present no difficulty. The third has long been a puzzle, both to modern scholars and, apparently, to the Anglo-Saxons themselves. When Bede's Latin was rendered into Old English during the time of Alfred, the translator renders the name of this latter tribe as the *Geatas*—a name that sounds vaguely like *Iuti* or *Iutae* but means something different. This name, as Jane Leake has pointed out in a book whose impact on *Beowulf* scholarship has not yet been fully felt, is not a miswriting; rather, the translator rationalized Bede's history in the light of current knowledge.[45] His rendering makes sense as an expression of mythical geography, for it is an anglicization of the Latin name *Getae*. The Hygelac who, in *Beowulf*, rules over the *Geatas* and dies at the mouth of the Rhine, appears in the *Liber Monstrorum* under the name of Higlacus; and there (contrary to Gregory of Tours, who calls him a Dane) he is said to have ruled over the *Getae*. In the popular mind, as Leake has shown, the *Getae* were regarded as common ancestors of the Jutes, Danes, Goths, and Gautar. They stood in relation to these various tribes as an *Ur*-Germanic people of remarkable size and prowess. Their homeland was a great place for dragons, among such other marvelous inhabitants as the Amazons, cynocephali, anthropophagi, and sea-serpents who are described in *The Marvels of the East*, a work that directly precedes *Beowulf* in British Library MS Cotton Vitellius A.xv. When Alfred's translator interpreted Bede's *Iuti* or *Iutae* as the *Geatas*—just as when Alfred himself called Jutland *Gotland*, i.e, "land of Goths," when he interpolated into Orosius' *Universal History* a passage that tells of the journey of a Danish sailor past the coast of Jutland—he drew attention to this imagined link between the people of England and the storied tribes of the Scandinavian *heimat*. *Beowulf* thus shows some points of continuity with the historical and geographical writings that formed part of the Alfredian and post-Alfredian canon. By making his hero a Geat, the *Beowulf* poet indirectly shed luster on the English people by shoring up their Germanic ethnic credentials. He also made clear how different the English had become—whether wiser, or simply diminished—from their grand and terrible Northern ancestors.

These then, in brief, are seven reasons for concluding that the orthodox eighth-century dating of *Beowulf* need not be accepted without question. No one of them is conclusive. Taken together, however, they point to a date for the composition of *Beowulf*, as we now have it, not earlier than the reign of Alfred and probably during the reign of one of his immediate successors, possibly Athelstan, who was chosen king by both Mercians and West Saxons in 924.

• • •

The question remains: why did someone, or why did some group of people, decide to go to the trouble and expense of committing to parchment what might seem, by strict devotional standards, a fairly "useless" secular poem like *Beowulf*?[46]

Looking just at the mechanics of writing, there are three chief possibilities: (1) *intervention by an outsider*, or collection of the poem from a poet skilled in the oral tradition by someone who was not the author; (2) *intervention by an insider*, or the writing down of the poem by a poet, skilled in oral composition, who was also trained in the technology of script; and (3) *literary imitation*, or deliberate literary composition in a manner that invokes or replicates certain features of the oral, traditional style. Present scholarly opinion seems to favor either the second or third possibility. I find the third one unattractive for reasons similar to those advanced by Irving, who has shown good stylistic and aesthetic grounds for reading *Beowulf* not as a lettered work sprinkled with oral formulas, but rather as "a most distinguished descendant of a long and skillful oral tradition.[47] Although I would not rule out the second alternative, the manifest differences in subject, style, known sources, authorial voice, and artistic achievement that set *Beowulf* apart from such other Old English works as the signed poems of Cynewulf, who may well have been an author of such dual accomplishments, leave me skeptical of this approach. Instead, I would suggest that the first possibility—the model of Cædmon and the monks of Whitby, transposed to a secular key—may be the most likely. This claim calls for brief justification.

In a society where oral poetry is the norm, those poets who live within the tradition feel little impulse to write their songs or stories down. They do not need to write poems down to preserve them, because they and their audiences preserve them very well, thank you. That is what both they and their ancestors have been doing for years. The impulse to take down poems in writing comes chiefly from outside the oral culture, when another interested party happens upon the scene. The texts that result from this encounter are transmutations of the poetry into a different symbolic code meant for the eyes of people with literary training, and those people then do with such texts what they will. Examples of this kind of intervention into a tradition are to be found throughout the literature of modern anthropology and folklore: in the myths, legends, and charms that Malinowski collected from Trobriand Islanders or Sapir from California Indians, or the prose tales that fieldworkers allied with the Irish Folklore Commission recorded from Gaelic speakers in the west of Ireland, or the words and tunes that Cecil Sharp collected from rural singers in Somerset and the Southern Appalachians. Examples could be multiplied at will. Some epic poetry that has been published in recent years also falls within this category: the Finnish *Kalevala*, the Serbo-Croatian *Wedding of Smailagić Meho*, and *The Mwindo Epic* from central Africa certainly result from such a process of self-conscious collection, combined in the Finnish instance with a significant degree of rewriting and shaping. Some classicists accept that the Homeric epics are the result of a similar process of collection and reworking.[48] However hypothetical this suggestion must remain, it is a plausible one, and the length and artistic excellence of the Homeric poems do not count against it. Texts that result from an outsider's sympathetic engagement with an oral tradition, though highly mediated, are often long and of high quality, for they represent the collaborative efforts of a painstaking collector and the most gifted informants who can be found: the Mededovićs and Williamsons of an oral tradition, as it were. If all goes well, the text that results from oral dictation will be a "best" text that showcases the poet's talents.[49] It is often more complex, or more fully elaborated, or more clear and self-consistent in its narrative line, than a verbatim record of a primary oral performance would be, for it is the result of a purposive effort to obtain an impressive text that literate people will want to read. The editor of *The Mwindo Epic*, Daniel Biebuyek, notes that the version of this poem that he prints in his 1969 edition, and that he recorded from dictation, is not only by far the longest one he heard performed in the country of the Nyanga but also the "most comprehensive, most coherent, most detailed, and most poetic" of them all.[50] This is a version that Biebuyck specially commissioned, to the surprise of the poet, who was not accustomed to singing the episodes of this story as a continuous whole.

If my hypothesis carries weight, and the *Beowulf* poet was indeed a master of the aristocratic oral tradition who happened to be enlisted in an effort to reify this poem in the form of a material text, then what launched the material text into its existence was what can be called an *oral poetry act*. An oral poetry act is what happens when a collector asks a singer to perform a work not in its natural context, but rather in some special setting in the presence of a scribe, a team of scribes, a tape recorder, or some other secondary audience. The collector thus becomes a third factor in shaping the poem, after the poet and the primary oral audience, for he or she too has influence over what is performed. Like Hild and the monks at Whitby, the collector usually has a certain kind of poem in mind and may be indifferent to other, "irrelevant," kinds. He can specify that the poem is to be a summarized or fully elaborated version. He may ask the poet to bring out certain aspects of his work and downplay others. Whether or not the collector has a clear literary agenda, the poet himself naturally wishes to please, especially if he is a professional who expects to be rewarded for his services in money or esteem. Any performer who is not a mere memorizer is used to reshaping materials to suit a particular audience and is unlikely to forego this habit for no good reason.

In these ways and in others, the presence of the collector affects the product of the oral poetry act. At first, this is a "scratch" version of the poem as it can be read by a textual community—that is, a group of readers who may or may not have much competence in the oral tradition, but who participate in an ongoing discourse about books.[51] If, later, a text comes to be distributed more widely, it will naturally be improved in ways that accord with the aims of the collector, the needs or desires of its readers, and the general conventions of written literature in the society in which it will be read. The meter may be smoothed out. Rhyme or other technical features may be made more regular. Non-standard or dialect forms may be replaced with standard ones or may be made more consistent. Gaps in the story may be filled in, errors or inconsistencies corrected, useless fillers deleted. Capital letters and punctuation may be added, lineation imposed, sectional divisions introduced, and so on. From beginning to end of this process of textualization, the collector thus becomes a collaborator in the act of poetry, not just a recorder of it. As the inventor of the text as it can be read in "hard copy," the collector makes myriad choices, whether consciously or unconsciously, that determine the character and readability of the product of his or her intention into the realm of oral performance.

If the view that I am presenting has merit, then we do not have to read *Beowulf* as a literate island in a sea of much inferior oral poetry, as some scholars do, nor as the unmediated gift of an oral poet's inspiration, as some Romantically inclined scholars have done in the past. Rather it is a *tertium quid*: a unique kind of hybrid creation that came into being at the interface of two cultures, the oral and the bookish, through some literate person's prompting. The important thing to keep in mind is that, like all oral poetry recorded before the advent of advanced audio-visual technology, as Goody has reminded us,[52] the text of *Beowulf* would have been taken down outside the normal context of performance, in a situation where one or more outsiders were involved.

It would be vain, however, to speculate as to who wrote down the text, on what occasion. To the question "Why was the text of *Beowulf* written down?" perhaps only one good answer can be given, a negative one: "Why not?" By the end of the seventh century, the technology of writing down long poems was well in place in England. Literary models were there, in the form of Latin works like the *Aeneid* as well as vernacular ones like

Cædmon's Biblical paraphrases. The important question to ask, perhaps, is "By what time did the reasons for *not* writing down a secular poem like *Beowulf* lose their force?"

As Roberta Frank has shown, ecclesiastical opposition to poems about pagan antiquity seems to have cooled by the last years of the reign of Alfred the Great and the early years of the tenth century, roughly speaking.[53] By this time, the climate of opinion about the Germanic past had shifted among monks and clerics to the point that songs about pagan Germanic heroes had ceased to seem either threatening or irrelevant. By this time, if not well before, songs about the pagan past had become infused with Christian values. Once this momentous shift of mentality and literary sensibility had occurred, someone in a position of power saw fit to preserve in writing the poem that we now call *Beowulf*. Whatever exact authority he or she wielded, this patron not only oriented his activities toward a Christian textual community, but also had some awareness of being part of that new political order that we now call the English nation. In company with other like-minded people, the patron knew or intuited that national ambitions could be legitimized in mythic terms through invocation of a common, pseudo-Christian, Anglo-Danish past.

In contemplating the place of *Beowulf* in literary history in terms like these, I do not claim to invalidate other approaches to the questions of date and origins. At most, I only hope to render such alternatives relatively unattractive, so that those scholars who advocate them may perhaps do so with less claim to authority. As Frederic Jameson has remarked, "Only another, stronger interpretation can overthrow and practically refute an interpretation already in place."[54]

One of the tasks of current Old English scholarship is the Jamesonian one of unmasking *Beowulf* as a socially symbolic act. Although its action is set in fifth- and sixth-century Scandinavia, the poem articulates a response to the two great sources of tension in English culture during the late sixth through early tenth centuries: the integration of Germanic culture and Christian faith into a single system of thought and ethics, and the integration of all the peoples living south of Hadrian's Wall and east of Offa's Dyke into one English nation ruled by the West Saxon royal line.

Whether or not literature in general is produced through one or more ideological contradictions, as some modern theorists have held, it seems likely that *Beowulf* is the result of two major conflicts, each one of which was a lively cause of concern to Englishmen of the later Anglo-Saxon period. They can be paraphrased as follows: (1) "Our ancestors were great noblemen; our ancestors are damned." The first attitude could not simply be cast aside when Christian missionaries arrived to teach the need of salvation through Christ. *Beowulf* reveals a profound disquiet in regard to the orthodox doctrine that anyone not baptized into the faith is beyond redemption. (2) "The Danes are murderers and damnable heathens; the Danes are our trusted allies." The first attitude could not die out as soon as the descendents of the Viking invaders began to farm the land in peace, so that the second view could be safely announced. *Beowulf* shows how the impulse to honor the Danes and integrate their traditions with English ones was mingled with memories of a heathen people who had done their best to ravage English society and its centers of religion and learning over a period of some years. The poet's evocations of the magnificence of Hrothgar's court alternate with allusions to the damned rites that some of the Danes practice there (lines 175–88) and to acts of fratricidal violence.

To put the matter a different way, we might say that when viewed in terms of its own culture, *Beowulf* is the projection of two great desires: (1) for a distinguished *ethnic* origin that would serve to merge English and Danish differences into a neutral and dignified pan-Germanism, and (2) for an *ethical* origin that would ally this unified race with Christian spiritual values. No matter that the heroes of Beowulf's day were unbaptized. Of their own free will, exercising the God-given power of reason, they recognized the controlling power of Providence in human affairs and had the wisdom and fortitude to fight against God's enemies on earth—or at least the more enlightened ones among them did, according to the poet's audacious fiction.

If this view is correct—and I must beg forgiveness for repeating this hedging rhetoric, for certainty in such matters must remain beyond our grasp—then for all its fictive and fantastic elements, *Beowulf* was a vehicle for political work in a time when the various peoples south of Hadrian's Wall were being assimilated into an emergent English nation. "Political" is perhaps too narrow a term for the work the poem does. For in reinventing the ancestral past in the light of Christian doctrine and the Danish presence, as well as in articulating a system of values appropriate to this task, the poem is a site where cultural issues of great magnitude and complexity are contested. Some of these issues, particularly the ones that involve the deadly opposition of the hero and the Grendel-kin, doubtless transcend the historical tensions of any one era and connect with bedrock contradictions that underlie civilization itself and its inevitable discontents.

To read *Beowulf* as I am suggesting is to read it as an exemplary specimen of the art of *homo narrans*, an art that has received much scrutiny in recent years. As folklorist and American Studies specialist Jay Mechling has pointed out,

> Many respectable scholars, some of them giants in their specialties, have turned away from positivist and formalist epistemologies to an epistemology that sees reality as created, mediated, and sustained by human narratives. To accept this view is also to see that narratives are emergent, contingent, public, and contested; that they reflect interests (such as class, gender, race, age) and, therefore, that they are ideological and political, even when they seem not to be.[55]

In keeping with this socially embedded way of looking at narrative, I suggest that *Beowulf* did much ideological work in its time. To be precise, we should not speak of this work as being done by the poem, but rather by its discourse, taken as the sum of poetic impulses of this kind. For however valuable *Beowulf* may be as a unique creation, it is still more important as an example—the only one that has happened to survive almost intact—of a type of literature that probably retained cultural centrality until fairly late in the Old English period, bearing the intellectual brunt of such social changes as occurred over time. In any period when philosophy and history function as aspects of poetry rather than claiming (even if speciously) the status of autonomous enterprises, poetry does the collective thinking of a people. Through poetry, issues of common concern in a society are thought through and are resolved in the form of stories. In such a medium, as Umberto Eco has said of the tradition of medieval scholastic thought,

> Innovation came without fanfare, even secretively, and developed by fits and starts until it was eventually absorbed with a free-and-easy syncretism.[56]

A task still facing *Beowulf* scholars is to define more exactly the nature of the syncretistic system of thought that underlies this narrative and lends it ethical and spiritual significance. Doubtless this task will never be complete, for, in attempting it, we are defining our own mentality as much as that of a distant historical period. Much is at stake when it comes to the study of origins, as recent scholarship has made us aware. As Edward Said has remarked,

> there is no such thing as a merely given, or simply available, starting point: beginnings have to be made for each project in such a way as to *enable* what follows from them.[57]

In early English literary history, questions relating to origins are also ones of character and potential use. "Is it oral or literary?" "Is it pagan or Christian?" "Is it Germanic or Latinate?" "Is it a part of English literature, or not?" "Is it *ours* or *theirs*?" One's answers to these questions are likely to reveal as much about one's own cultural investments as they suggest about a society and a literature that are now vanished beyond all power of recall, except in terms that make sense in our own consciousness. Precisely because the effort to understand the place of a work in literary history is itself an historically conditioned enterprise that almost cannot help but be bound up, whether implicitly or explicitly, with the aims of cultural critique,[58] the task should not be abandoned, however recalcitrant it may be.

NOTES

[1] John Hermann, *Allegories of War: Language and Violence in Old English Poetry* (Ann Arbor, 1989), p. 199.

[2] Leo Spitzer, *Linguistics and Literary History: Essays in Stylistics* (Princeton, 1948), pp. 3–4.

[3] M. M. Bakhtin, *The Dialogic Imagination: Four Essays*, ed. Michael Holquist, trans. Caryl Emerson and Michael Holquist (Austin, Tex., 1981), especially the first essay, "Epic and the Novel." For a critique of this aspect of Bakhtin's work as well as of Derridean deconstruction when applied to the realm of orality, see Ward Parks, "The Textualization of Orality in Literary Criticism," in *Vox Intexta: Orality and Textuality in the Middle Ages*, ed. A. N. Doane and Carol Braun Pasternack (Madison, 1991), pp. 46–61.

[4] By "the time that the poem was put down in writing," I mean the time that our unique MS was written down, ca. 1000 AD. Almost everyone agrees that this MS is a scribal copy. What is disputed is how long a poem we can meaningfully call "*Beowulf*" existed before this moment of copying. For reasons explained in this essay, I see no reason to push the date of composition of the poem back before the tenth century, and the following discussion is based on this premise. Early-daters can still perhaps follow along with my discussion, granted that the poem continued in circulation through the tenth century.

[5] The best overview of the subject is C. P. Wormald, "The Uses of Literacy in Anglo-Saxon England and Its Neighbors," *Transactions of the Royal Historical Society*, 5th ser., 27 (1977): 95–114. Wormald sees no reason to think that cultured literacy ever became widespread among the laity, Two recent studies that finesse his conclusions are Susan Kelly, "Anglo-Saxon Lay Society and the

Written Word," pp. 36–62, and Simon Keynes, "Royal Government and the Written Word in Late Anglo-Saxon England," pp. 226–57, both in *The Uses of Literacy in Early Medieval Europe*, ed. Rosamond McKitterick (Cambridge, Eng., 1990).

[6] Richard Hodges, *The Anglo-Saxon Achievement: Archaeology and the Beginnings of English Society* (Ithaca, N.Y., 1989).

[7] Nicholas Howe, *Migration and Mythmaking in Anglo-Saxon England* (New Haven, 1989).

[8] On this topic see Reginald Horsman, *Race and Manifest Destiny: The Origins of American Racial Anglo-Saxonism* (Cambridge, Mass., 1981).

[9] Eric Hobsbawm and Terence Ranger, eds., *The Invention of Traditions* (Cambridge, Eng., 1983), especially Hobsbawm's "Introduction: Inventing Traditions," pp. 1–14.

[10] Allen J. Frantzen, *Desire for Origins: New Language, Old English, and Teaching the Tradition* (New Brunswick, N.J., 1990).

[11] R. W. Chambers briefly reviews this heritage of oral poetry in his essay "The Lost Literature of Medieval England," *The Library*, 4th ser., 5 (1925): 293–321. For the evidence from classical authors bearing on Germanic singers, see Jeff Opland, *Anglo-Saxon Oral Poetry: A Study of the Traditions* (New Haven, 1980), pp. 40–73.

[12] For an overview of issues relating to the understanding of oral poetry see Ruth Finnegan, *Oral Poetry: Its Nature, Significance and Social Context* (Cambridge, Eng., 1977). For a review of recent research in the fields of orality and literacy with particular attention to the medieval connection, and with citations to the relevant work of Eric Havelock, Walter Ong, Jack Goody, Michael Clanchy, Franz Bäuml, and other scholars, see D. H. Green, "Orality and Reading: The State of Research in Medieval Studies," *Speculum* 65 (1990): 267–80. For a critique of Anglo-Saxon orality and textuality from a current theoretical stance, see Martin Irvine, "Medieval Textuality and the Archaeology of Textual Culture," in *Speaking Two Languages: Traditional Disciplines and Contemporary Theory in Medieval Studies*, ed. Allen J. Frantzen (Albany, 1991), pp. 181–210, 276–84.

[13] Brian Stock, *Listening for the Text: On the Uses of the Past* (Baltimore, 1990), p. 9.

[14] The influential concept of active and passive tradition-bearers goes back to the work of C. W. von Sydow, "On the Spread of Tradition," reprinted in his *Selected Papers on Folklore*, ed. Laurits Bödker (Copenhagen, 1948), pp. 12–13.

[15] Albert Bates Lord, "Avdo Meðedović, *Guslar*," *Journal of American Folklore* 69 (1956): 320–30, reprinted in his *Epic Singers and Oral Tradition* (Ithaca, N.Y., 1991), pp. 57–71. See also Meðedović, *The Wedding of Smailagić Meho*,

translated by Lord in *Serbocroatian Heroic Songs*, collected by Milman Parry, vol. 3 (Cambridge, Mass., 1974).

[16] Some of Williamson's stories have been published from transcriptions of his tellings made by his American-born wife Linda: see *Fireside Tales of the Traveller Children* (1983), *The Broonie, Silkies, and Fairies* (1985), *Tell Me a Story for Christmas* (1987), *May the Devil Walk Behind Ye!* (1989), *Don't Look Back, Jack!* (1990), and *Tales of the Seal People* (1992), all published in Edinburgh, and also *A Thorn in the King's Foot* (Harmondsworth, 1987) and *The Genie and the Fisherman and Other Tales from the Travelling People* (Cambridge, 1991). Recordings from my Scottish fieldwork are on deposit in the American Folklife Center at the Library of Congress.

[17] The best study of how this accommodation affected religious poetry remains Michael D. Cherniss, *Ingeld and Christ: Heroic Concepts and Values in Old English Christian Poetry* (The Hague, 1972). Charles J. Donahue, "Social Function and Literary Value in *Beowulf*," in *The Epic in Medieval Society: Aesthetic and Moral Values*, ed. Harald Scholler (Tübingen, 1977), pp. 382–90, offers some brief but stimulating suggestions about how it affected *Beowulf*.

[18] See Kenneth Sisam, "Anglo-Saxon Royal Genealogies," *Proceedings of the British Academy* 39 (1953): 287–346. Michael Lapidge discusses these genealogies carefully in "*Beowulf*, Aldhelm, the *Liber Monstrorum*, and Wessex," *Studi Medievali* 23 (1982): 151–92, where he holds that the extension from Geat back to Sceaf, and eventually to Adam, is a fabrication that "was done with Alfred's consent and arguably at his instigation" (p. 187).

[19] On this synthesis, see Michael Hunter, "Germanic and Roman Antiquity and the Sense of the Past in Anglo-Saxon England," *Anglo-Saxon England* 3 (1974): 29–50.

[20] Jack Goody, *The Interface Between the Written and Oral* (Cambridge, Eng., 1987), p. 59.

[21] Seth Lerer, *Literacy and Power in Anglo-Saxon England* (Lincoln, Nebr., 1991).

[22] On this transformation, see Jeff Opland, "The Impact on English Literature of the Technology of Writing," in *Oral Literature in Context: Ten Essays*, ed. John D. Niles (Cambridge, Eng., 1980), pp. 30–43.

[23] Patrick Wormald, "Bede, *Beowulf*, and the Conversion of the Anglo-Saxon Aristocracy," in *Bede and Anglo-Saxon England*, ed. Robert T. Farrell, British Archaeological Reports 46 (Oxford, 1978), pp. 32–95.

[24] On this process, see D. A. Bullough, "The Educational Tradition in England from Alfred to Aelfric: Teaching *Utriusque Linguae*," in "La scuola nell'occidente latina dell'alto medioevo," *Settimane di studio del Centro Italiano di studi sull'alto medioevo* 19 (1972), 2:453–94.

[25] F. M. Stenton, *Anglo-Saxon England*, 3rd ed. (Oxford, 1971), p. 353.

[26] Simon Keynes, "King Athelstan's Books," in *Learning and Literature in Anglo-Saxon England: Studies Presented to Peter Clemoes on the Occasion of His Sixty-Fifth Birthday*, ed. Michael Lapidge and Helmut Gneuss (Cambridge, Eng., 1985), pp. 143–201.

[27] According to figures provided by Neil R. Ker, *Catalogue of Manuscripts Containing Anglo-Saxon* (Oxford, 1957), pp. xv–xix, of the 189 major manuscripts written in Old English, all but eight are from the tenth century or later.

[28] See Alois Wolf, "Die Verschriftlichung von europäischen Heldensagen als mittelalterliches Kulturproblem," in *Heldensage und Heldendichtung im Germanischen*, ed. Heinrich Beck (Berlin, 1988), pp. 305–28. For a discussion in English of some of the same issues, see Wolf, "Medieval Heroic Traditions and Their Transitions from Orality to Literacy," in Doane and Pasternack, *Vox Intexta*, pp. 67–88.

[29] Bede, *Ecclesiastical History of the English Peoples*, 4:24. For good comments on the story see Donald K. Fry, "The Memory of Cædmon," in *Oral Traditional Literature: A Festschrift for Albert Bates Lord*, ed. John Miles Foley (Columbus, 1981), pp. 282–93.

[30] For some mythic and legendary parallels to Bede's account see Louise Pound, "Cædmon's Dream Song," in *Studies in English Philology: A Miscellany in Honor of F. Klaeber*, ed. Kemp Malone and Martin B. Ruud (Minneapolis, 1929), pp. 232–39.

[31] Northrop Frye, *The Secular Scripture: A Study of the Structure of Romance* (Cambridge, Mass., 1976), p. 20.

[32] The first of the transmutations involved here is discussed well by Cherniss in *Ingeld and Christ*. On the second, note Gernot Wieland, "*Manna Mildost*: Moses and Beowulf," *Pacific Coast Philology* 23 (1988): 86–93.

[33] See the articles collected in Colin Chase, ed., *The Dating of "Beowulf"* (Toronto, 1981), as supplemented by Nicholas Jacobs, "Anglo-Danish Relations, Poetic Archaism, and the Date of *Beowulf*: A Reconsideration of the Evidence," *Poetica* (Tokyo) 8 (1977): 23–43; Kevin S. Kiernan, *"Beowulf" and the "Beowulf" Manuscript* (New Brunswick, 1981); and other articles cited below, among other recent studies.

[34] I have discussed this matter in *"Beowulf": The Poem and Its Tradition* (Cambridge, Mass., 1983), pp. 96–117.

[35] See Alexander Callander Murray, "*Beowulf*, the Danish Invasions, and Royal Genealogy," in Chase, *The Dating of "Beowulf,"* pp. 101–11, and Audrey L. Meaney, "Scyld Scefing and the Dating of Beowulf—Again," *Bulletin of the John Rylands University Library of Manchester* 71 (1989): 7–40.

[36] An example is Dorothy Whitelock, *The Audience of "Beowulf"* (Oxford, 1951), pp. 77–78, following J. R. R. Tolkien, "*Beowulf*: The Monsters and the Critics," *Proceedings of the British Academy* 22 (1936): 294 n. 34.

[37] Roberta Frank, "Skaldic Verse and the Date of *Beowulf*," in Chase, *The Dating of "Beowulf*," pp. 123–39.

[38] This point has been forcefully made by L. L. Schücking, "Das Königsideal in *Beowulf*," *Modern Humanities Research Association Bulletin* 3 (1929): 143–54, translated as "The Ideal of Kingship in *Beowulf*," in *An Anthology of "Beowulf" Criticism*, ed. Lewis E. Nicholson (Notre Dame, 1963), pp. 35–49.

[39] See the important article by Roberta Frank, "The *Beowulf* Poet's Sense of History," in *The Wisdom of Poetry: Essays in Early English Literature in Honor of Morton W. Bloomfield*, ed. Larry D. Benson and Siegfried Wenzel (Kalamazoo, 1982), pp. 53–65, 271–77.

[40] See Fr. Klaeber, *"Beowulf" and the Fight at Finnsburg*, 3rd ed. with supplements (Lexington, Mass., 1950), pp. xiv–xx; R. W. Chambers, *"Beowulf": An Introduction to the Study of the Poem*, 3rd ed. (Cambridge, Eng., 1959), pp. 48–61, 138–92; G. N. Garmonsway, *"Beowulf" and Its Analogues* (New York, 1971), pp. 302–31.

[41] For discussion of the question from two different perspectives, historical and mythological respectively, see Anton Gerard Van Hamel, "Hengest and His Namesake," in Malone and Ruud, *Studies in English Philology*, pp. 159–71, and J. E. Turville-Petre, "Hengest and Horsa," *Saga-Book of the Viking Society* 14 (1953–57): 273–90.

[42] Walter de Gray Birch, ed., *Cartularium Saxonicum*, vol. 1 (London, 1885), p. 302 n. 214; for discussion see F. M. Stenton, "The Supremacy of the Mercian Kings," *English Historical Review* 33 (1918): 433–52.

[43] Robert H. Hodgkin, *A History of the Anglo-Saxons*, vol. 1 (Oxford, 1935), assumes that the Danes, in appropriating the province of Anglia, "took over some of its Anglian folklore" (p. 31); but the Danes' knowledge of traditions concerning Offa could also have come through the Danelaw.

[44] Alois Brandl, "The *Beowulf* Epic and the Crisis in the Mercian Dynasty about the Year 700 AD," *Research and Progress* 2 (1936): 199–203, and George Bond, "Links Between *Beowulf* and Mercian History," *Studies in Philology* 40 (1943): 481–93, both make this connection, but in the context of arguments too speculative to command assent.

[45] Jane Acomb Leake, *The Geats of "Beowulf": A Study in the Geographical Mythology of the Middle Ages* (Madison, 1967), especially pp. 98–133. Leake brings into a new dimension a suggestion that was made by Elis Wadstein, "The *Beowulf* Poem as an English National Epos," *Acta Philologica Scandinavica* 8 (1933): 273–91. The reader is referred to Leake for details of the complex argument that

I accept here in its main features, despite some lingering questions about the Gautar and why Leake is so uninterested in them. There is no reason to refute the objections of G. M. Smithers in his review article, "The Geats in *Beowulf*," *The Durham University Journal* 63 (1971): 87–103, for most of his arguments have no relation to Leake's main point about geographical mythology. Kemp Malone's peremptory dismissal, in his review of Leake's book, on phonological grounds, of any identification of the *Geatas* with the *Getae* (*Speculum* 43 [1968]: 736–39) misses the point. Even if the Anglo-Saxons should not have made this identification, the evidence of *Beowulf* and the *Liber Monstrorum* is that they did so, and so we must reckon with their creativity.

46 The term "secular" is of course not wholly appropriate to a work like *Beowulf* that celebrates a kind of Christian hero, as is noted by Karl Brunner, "Why Was *Beowulf* Preserved?" *Études anglaises* 7 (1954): 1–5. Wormald, "Bede, *Beowulf*, and the Conversion," answers the question of preservation in his own way based on the assumption that *Beowulf* is pre-Alfredian and the work of a fully literate author. Here I present a different possibility based on a hypothesis that Wormald rejects, namely that the text of *Beowulf* has a close relation to the Anglo-Saxon aristocratic oral tradition. This claim rests on evidence (much of it stylistic) that I shall not try to present here. Many insights into the oral context of early Germanic verse are presented by Alain Renoir, *A Key to Old Poems: The Oral-Formulaic Approach to the Interpretation of West-Germanic Verse* (University Park, Penn., 1988). Edward B. Irving, Jr., *Rereading "Beowulf"* (Philadelphia, 1989), especially pp. 1–35, has cast its considerable authority behind the idea of an oral-derived *Beowulf* and uses this idea to make sense of many formal and aesthetic features of the poem.

47 Irving, *Rereading "Beowulf,"* p. 2. Understandably but still perhaps disappointingly, Irving does not engage the issue of how the material text of *Beowulf* came into being.

48 See Albert Bates Lord, "Homer's Originality: Oral Dictated Texts," *Transactions of the American Philological Society* 94 (1953): 124–34, reprinted with slight revisions in his *Epic Singers*, pp. 38–48.

49 The adjective "best" here refers to the collector's perspective, which represents that of a literate society. The collector's best text may be of no use whatever to the original audience.

50 Daniel Biebuyck and Kahombo C. Mateene, ed., *The Mwindo Epic from the Banyanga* (Berkeley, 1969), p. 19.

51 The notion of a textual community is one that I am adapting from Stock, *Listening for the Text*, using "textual" in the narrow sense here to refer to the products of writing. The notion of literary competence, drawn from linguistics, has

been discussed by Jonathan Culler in *Structuralist Poetics* (Ithaca, N.Y., 1975), reprinted in *Reader-Response Criticism: From Formalism to Post-Structuralism*, ed. Jane P. Tompkins (Baltimore, 1980), pp. 101–17. Oral heroic poetry is only a forceful instance of the general phenomenon whereby literature is made intelligible through systems of convention that make understanding possible. For a study of how members of Anglo-Saxon textual communities may have had some competence in oral poetry, see Katherine O'Brien O'Keefe, *Visible Song: Transitional Literacy in Old English Verse* (Cambridge, Eng., 1990).

[52] Goody, *Interface Between the Written and the Oral*, p. xi.

[53] Frank, "The *Beowulf* Poet's Sense of History."

[54] Frederic Jameson, *The Political Unconscious: Narrative as a Socially Symbolic Act* (Ithaca, N.Y., 1981), p. 13.

[55] Jay Mechling, "*Homo Narrans* Across the Disciplines," *Western Folklore* 50 (1991): 43.

[56] Umberto Eco, *Art and Beauty in the Middle Ages*, trans. Hugh Bredin (New Haven, 1986), p. 2.

[57] Edward W. Said, *Orientalism* (New York, 1978), p. 16, summarizing his own argument in his book *Beginnings: Intention and Method* (New York, 1975).

[58] George E. Marcus and Michael M. Fischer, *Anthropology as Cultural Critique: An Experimental Moment in the Human Sciences* (Chicago, 1986), make the same point about ethnography that I am making about literary history, which can resemble a kind of ethnography of the past.

ETHNICITY, POWER AND THE ENGLISH

JOHN MORELAND

"The eternal stream of blood binds us across the ages."[1]

I n his *Travels in Hyperreality*, Umberto Eco suggested that all our contemporary "hot" problems have their source in the Middle Ages, and argued that "we go back to . . . [*the Middle Ages*] every time we ask ourselves about our origin"; that "people started dreaming of the Middle Ages from the very beginning of the modern era."[2] In one such dream, the blood of the *gentes* (peoples) of the early Middle Ages still flows in the veins of their modern kin. The issue of origins is "hot" because there are still people who believe that there is an eternal stream of blood linking them to their "ethnic" ancestors and the "homeland." For many that "blood" flows from the early Middle Ages. They further believe that archaeological and historical evidence can be used to demonstrate this, and can confirm them in their ancestral homelands or show them where those homelands are. In this essay I want to begin a study of the way in which these "dreams" of the Middle Ages have contributed to the construction of the English.[3]

From *Social Identity in Early Medieval Britain*, ed. William O. Frazer and William Tyrell (London, 2000), pp. 23–51; reprinted with permission of The Continuum International Publishing Group. Material cited in endnotes has been augmented for clarity.

As archaeologists and historians we have to investigate these issues be-cause we can *show* that in the Middle Ages—that place to which people so often return in their dream-world—ethnicity was not based on "blood." [4] The "eternal stream of blood" binds neither the English nor any other mod-ern people across the ages to their ethnic forebears.[5] We can *demonstrate* this. It is true that "medieval peoples . . . seem frequently to have *believed* that they belonged to nations (*nationes*) and peoples (*gentes*)," and that "since a people was formed by descent, blood was the vehicle for its consoli-dation and expansion from one generation to the next."[6] However, it is also true that these "peoples" were "imagined communities"[7] bound together by belief in common descent and actual common interests.[8] The *gentes* of the early Middle Ages came to *believe* that they constituted "blood-communi-ties" as a *result* of social and political solidarity.[9] As Richard Jenkins argues, people come to believe that they share a common ancestry as a *consequence* of acting together.[10]

This does not mean that ethnicity did not exist in the early Middle Ages; it did. But it was bound up with other forms of identity, and particularly with relationships of *power* and domination. The imposition of *our* con-cept of a discrete and objective ethnicity on the early Middle Ages may provide the *medieval* concept of ethnicity with a power in the structuring of society and the life of the individual which it never had at the time. The consequence of our imposition is that we ignore or devalue factors which were then of greater importance in the construction of society and the self. An awareness of this provides us with a very different image of the Middle Ages and a very different understanding of the "dreams" we can responsibly draw from it.

It is easy to appreciate the role of ethnicity in the wars that have ripped through the Balkans; many people can, perhaps, come to see the Northern Ireland "Troubles" as an ethnic as opposed to (or as well as?) a religious conflict. However, we have a tendency to see ethnicity not as part of *our* make-up, but as something particular to the "Others."[11] With characteristic forthrightness, Michael Ignatieff states that at the end of his "Journeys into the New Nationalism" he had to confront

> the central conceit which cosmopolitans everywhere, and the British in particular, have about the tide of ethnic nationalism destroying the fixed landmarks of the Cold War world: everyone else is a fanatic, everyone but us is a nationalist.[12]

With these insights in mind, I want to begin digging into the myths of the English. I want to question commonly held ideas about their origins and to counter the implicitly held notion that the emergence of England and Englishness was part of some *inevitable* process.[13] In particular I will question the constitution of the "peoples"—the Angles, Saxons and Jutes—who, largely on the basis of one short paragraph in Bede's *Ecclesiastical History of the English People*,[14] are deemed the ancestors of the English, and assess what kind of identities we can read from their material culture.

One of the strongest and most persistent "myths of the English" is that they are descended from these three Germanic peoples. In the late nineteenth century Francis Gummere argued that "Germanic invaders" provided the foundation of English national life;[15] in the late twentieth century Professor Sir Geoffrey Elton asserted that "the mixed collection of Germanic raiders . . . [became] subsumed under the name of the English."[16] However, one of the conclusions of this essay is that the "English" are not biologically descended from the Germanic stock of Bede's account. The belief that they are is a myth that draws heavily on "dreams" of the Middle Ages. It is a myth that is perpetuated through a misreading of historical and archaeological evidence, and through the imposition of modern concepts of identity onto the Migration Period past. It is a myth that has penetrated to the core of many peoples' beliefs about their "origins," and it is the source of many of the characteristics that they feel to be peculiarly "English."

Of course, historians have questioned the myth, in whole or in part.[17] However, such criticisms have proved unattractive to English historians, since they attack the "English national story."[18] Today, while historians and archaeologists have expressed the belief that they have a sophisticated understanding of the Migration Period, when it comes to the sources for the "English national story" many scholars "still seem far too willing to suspend their disbelief."[19]

In other parts of the world, we can see that "ethnic dreams" of the Middle Ages are of more than academic concern. At a time when the former governing party has been reduced to a purely English heartland; when the people of Scotland and Wales have voted for devolution; when the Labor government is not dependent on Unionist votes in Westminster and the future of Northern Ireland within the Union is again being considered; and when Norman Tebbit has argued that the failure of "minority" cultures to integrate into British/English culture would result in disintegration and the "Balkanization" of Britain,[20] an appreciation of the *constructed* nature of English identity may be timely.

Like many others, Lord Tebbit believes that there is a *single* English culture into which the Others must integrate. However, it is clear that what cultures, languages, and histories there are within England are the product of the history of the *many* peoples who have lived (and fought) there. They are not the product of some mythical, coherent, homogeneous, ancient people called the *English*.

Standing outside the myth of Englishness, I will assess the evidence from England. Throughout this essay, however, I will also draw upon the archaeological and historical evidence from across Migration Period Europe. That is the world from which the supposed ancestors of the English emerged. Further, this information can serve to put the laconic "English" sources into context[21] and can assist in overcoming that insularity of outlook which has dominated early Anglo-Saxon studies, and contributed to assumptions about the "inevitability" of England and the "uniqueness" of the English.

In addition, I will argue that much misunderstanding of Migration Period England is a consequence of the absence of theorization of some of the key concepts we use—in particular of ethnicity, material culture, and the relationship between them. I will therefore attempt to provide such a "theorization," drawing upon recent archaeological, anthropological and sociological theory and on fresh readings of some of the documentary and archaeological evidence.

The aim here is not to destroy the feelings of belonging (and security?) which this story bestows but to show that the English, just like the Others, are constructed through myth; and that the myth of the English, like other national myths, owes more to culture and history than to blood and manifest destiny. In addition, if we deconstruct this story we can produce a history of the English which is more in tune with their heterogeneous past and their multicultural present.

ARCHAEOLOGICAL CULTURES AND "PEOPLES"

Susan Reynolds has suggested that the "most difficult problems of all in what we think of as Anglo-Saxon history come right at its very beginning, with what is traditionally called the Anglo-Saxon settlement."[22] In one of the most powerful "dreams" of the English, this is where they were born.

The problems of studying this period are indeed difficult and are made more so by the inadequate theorization of concepts. The archaeological evidence is comparatively sparse and difficult to interpret. The same can be said of the documentary sources. However, this difficulty in interpretation has not always been recognized and past scholarship is littered with uncritical readings of the historical sources and attempts to situate the archaeological evidence within them.[23] To initiate this discussion, however, we have to go back to Reynolds's "very beginning."

In the early eighth century, Bede, in his *Historia Ecclesiastica Gentis Anglorum*, provided us with an account of the settlement of England by the Angles, Saxons and Jutes:

> the race of the Angles or Saxons, invited by Vortigern came to Britain in three warships. . . . They came from three very powerful Germanic tribes, the Saxons, Angles and Jutes. The people of Kent and the inhabitants of the Isle of Wight are of Jutish origin and also those opposite the Isle of Wight, that part of the kingdom of Wessex which is still today called the nation of the Jutes. From the Saxon country, that is, the district now known as Old Saxony, came the East Saxons, the South Saxons, and the West Saxons. Besides this, from the country of the Angles, that is, the land between the kingdoms of the Jutes and the Saxons which is called *Angulus*, came the East Angles, the Middle-Angles, the Mercians, and all the Northumbrian race (that is those people who dwell north of the river Humber) as well as the other Anglian tribes. *Angulus* is said to have remained deserted from that day to this. Their first leaders are said to have been two brothers, Hengist and Horsa.[24]

This is the account of the Anglo-Saxon settlement which has so beguiled generations of archaeologists, historians, politicians and Churchmen. It provides the historical context within which many archaeologists have sought to situate their evidence. Thus J. N. L. Myres, one of the greatest Anglo-Saxon archaeologists of the twentieth century, began his investigation of the continental background of the "English settlements" with Bede's statement, and argued that it was possible to accommodate this with the archaeology, especially with the cremation pottery to whose study he devoted his life.[25] For Myres, commencing his studies in the 1920s, it appeared natural to use the cremation urns as ethnic signifiers. Much the same approach of matching the pottery and jewelry from English cemeteries with that from northern Germany and southern Scandinavia, and then applying "ethnic names" drawn from the historical sources, has been followed more recently by Martin Welch and (to some extent) John Hines.[26]

These archaeologists write within what is known as the culture-history approach. This kind of archaeology/history is based on the premise that we can link the distribution of clusters of archaeological artifacts with the "peoples" referred to in the historical sources.[27] In culture-history, Archaeology's subservience to History is reproduced, and archaeologists continue to labor under the "tyranny of the historical record."[28] David Austin suggests that "the archaeologist feels bound . . . by the rules of historical practice laid down by documentary historians."[29] Historians set the agenda for the study of the period and when archaeologists have contributed they have tended to "accept unchallenged the 'truth' of [the] documentary information and its interpretations as the unquestioned framework of the discussion."[30] One of the results, says Austin, is that "archaeology has followed for most of this century an ethnocentric, and racial, view of early medieval Britain as the political and cultural product of conquest and colony."[31] I hope that in the course of this essay it will become clear that many historians and archaeologists have indeed constructed a racial and ethnocentric view of early English history. Most, however, are unaware that they have done so.

It is necessary to draw out the implications of the kind of history which culture-history produces:

1. There is a direct relationship between ethnicity and material culture, despite the protestations of archaeologists for at least the last decade.
2. The Angles, Saxons and Jutes existed as discrete groupings in their Continental homelands and remained so in the early period of their settlement in England.
3. Somehow these discrete groupings gradually coalesced or were absorbed to form the nation we know as England and the people we know as the English.

As archaeologists we really should know by now that there is no immediate and direct relationship between ethnicity and material culture. Stephen Shennan tackles this problem head on. He points out that archaeologists have identified what are called "archaeological cultures"—a range of artifacts associated in time and space—and have linked these to the names of peoples given in the written sources. The archaeological cultures are thus regarded as material manifestations of discrete and autonomous ethnic groups, of peoples.[32] The implication is that "peoples" in the past signaled their affinity (and primarily their ethnic affinity) *directly* in the material objects they used, and that we can trace the pattern of movement of these "peoples" through the changing distribution of distinctive artifacts.[33] This is a seriously flawed argument but is one which contributes to the "stream of blood" theories to which I referred earlier. It has to be challenged.

Shennan shows that to link archaeological cultures with historically-recorded (so-called) ethnic groups is mistaken since "we cannot assume that the 'peoples' described in the sources correspond to the *self-conscious identity groups* which are essential to the definition of ethnicity."[34] In addition, if we are fixated with the idea that late antique and Migration Period material culture should be seen only as ethnic group signifiers, we miss other, perhaps more important, meanings which can be read from this material, and ignore the *active* role of material culture postulated by so many post-processual archaeologists. We should also be aware of the parallel arguments concerning the ways in which archaeologists construct "cultures," and especially the fact that "in many instances such entities are purely constructs devised by archaeologists."[35] As Sian Jones further points out, we have to be aware of the "unfortunate implication . . . that archaeologists, and other social scientists, may have developed paradigms to explain that which they have themselves created."[36]

Dominic James has examined the relationship between brooch form and imperial status in late antiquity.[37] He argues that, because of the power of the State—what he calls its "golden clasp"—the aristocracy of the late Empire wore golden cross-bow brooches. These brooches were worn as emblems of allegiance, *regardless* of ethnic affiliation.[38] They relate to the power structures of the late Roman empire rather than to the ethnic identity of their wearers. They bespeak identity, but not ethnic identity. We miss such important insights into the relationship between material culture and *other* forms of collective identity when we assume a direct and inflexible link between it and *ethnicity*. We might examine the "chip-carved" belt fittings from late Roman Britain in the same light.

The documentary sources tell us that Germanic mercenaries were employed in the defense of late- and sub-Roman Britain, and attempts have been made to link these belt-fittings directly with these early "Germanic" settlers.[39] Such objects are found throughout the empire, especially along the Rhine-Danube frontier,[40] and it has been argued that the similarity between those from the latter area and those in England was archaeological evidence for early Germanic occupation.[41] Further it was suggested that this "Germanic" settlement might in fact be "Anglo-Saxon" since "it is . . . assumed that the most likely source for the Germanic *foederati* was the Anglo-Saxon homelands."[42] The "chip-carved" belt fittings thus became early Anglo-Saxon ethnic identifiers.

However, much doubt has now been cast on this interpretation. It has been pointed out that these artifacts are probably from "official issue" belts, which may have been worn by the "officials of the administrative and financial bureaucracies charged with the smooth running of the diocese."[43] Catherine Hills accepts that some types of buckles *may* have been associated with the military, but notes that this is "not the same as accepting that they were worn *only* by Germanic soldiers."[44] Kevin Leahy makes the point that "there has been a tendency to overemphasize their Germanic nature," and argues that "the dolphins that decorate them are more closely related to late Roman, rather than Germanic tastes."[45]

Frequently, these objects are found in the excavation of burials, and A.S. Esmonde Cleary points out that a new burial rite appeared around the middle of the fourth century. Male graves contained belt fittings at the waist, a crossbow brooch at the shoulder and an "offering" by the right foot.[46] In his study of the same phenomenon in northern Gaul, Guy Halsall has pointed out that the burial rite, similar to the one we have been describing—"the standard Roman form of burial but with the addition of more numerous grave-goods, including weaponry and belt-sets for the men and jewelry for the women"— is significantly different from those of Free Germany.[47] Halsall has extracted similar belt fittings from a "Germanic" context and sees them instead as "symbols of authority."[48] He argues that the burials in which they occur took place in the context of challenges to Roman authority at times when that authority was weakened. Importantly, it is argued that while such opposition might come from "Roman" or "German" sources, the people who mounted the challenges were doing so largely within "the accepted imperial idioms of authority."[49] In this context it should come as no surprise that they, and their contemporaries in Britain, also used material symbols of that authority.

There may have been "Germanic" mercenaries in Britain in the fourth century. This would not be unexpected and it need not have taken an "invitation" from Vortigern to bring them. There had been "Germanic" soldiers in Britain in the period of Roman occupation and it is possible that many stayed at the end of empire. It is generally assumed that the Roman army was withdrawn in the early fifth century,[50] but "the only firm evidence we have for troop withdrawals comes in 401/2 . . . [when] Stilicho removed a British legion . . . to help in the defense of Italy against Alaric's invasion."[51] Procopius tells us that after the suppression of the revolt of the "emperor" Constantine in 409, the Romans could no longer maintain their hold on

Britain and it was then ruled by "tyrants." However, as Averil Cameron points out, it is unlikely that Roman rule ended so abruptly.[52]

We might instead imagine a situation in Britain in the late fourth century much like that argued for Italy in the seventh century by Tom Brown. Here the structures of the State remained in place for much longer, but as cash payments to the army became a problem in the late sixth and early seventh centuries, soldiers began to acquire land and live off its produce, a process which "gave troops a major incentive towards the vigorous defense of their own properties and communities."[53]

In Britain, coins (especially silver and gold) are extremely rare from 378.[54] In this context we might see Roman soldiers (Germans and others) immersing themselves in the local power structures of late imperial Britain. Increasingly these were power structures which bore an antagonistic but dependent relationship to the authority of Rome. The onerous late Imperial demands for taxation, among others factors, had eroded the effectiveness of *Romanitas* as a binding mechanism, and the elite increasingly opted out of the State, preferring to develop their "private" powers as landowners and landlords.[55] It is in this context—fragmentation of state authority and con-solidation of private power—that the "chip-carved" belt fittings belong. At this stage the "ethnic" identity of the wielders of this localized power mat-tered little; nor was it to matter for some time. What did matter was the construction of power in and against a relationship with the authority of Rome.

We are therefore now in a position to see these belt sets, and the buri-als in which they are incorporated, in a late Roman and not specifically "Germanic" context. Like the cross-bow brooches studied by Janes, they have connections with the late Roman state. Like the cross-bow brooches, the belts were symbols of collective identity, but not ethnic identity. The belt fittings and cross-bow brooches belong in a world of transition where iden-tities and loyalties were complex and, at times, contradictory. To see them only as symbols of Germanic ethnicity is not only to ignore the evidence while laboring under the "tyranny of the historical record,"[56] it is also to misunderstand the complex web of identities that existed at the time.

Tackling this issue from another direction, we might accept *for the mo-ment* that the material record of the Migration Period in England is indeed a reflection of past ethnicity. If we assume that the Angles, Saxons, and Jutes were bounded, discrete, homogeneous cultural groups who reflected their identity through material culture, we might expect clear distinctions in the archaeology of their respective "settlement areas." While it is the case that there are parts of England where so-called Anglian or Saxon material culture dominates, this is not always true. Hines has noted that in the period up to circa 475 early "Saxon" material is found "across the whole of the area from north of the Humber to Sussex, with the exception of Kent east of the Medway, where Jutish material . . . is predominant."[57] Barbara Yorke suggests that "archaeological evidence suggests that the material culture of the Hampshire Jutes was not strikingly different from that of their Saxon neighbors."[58] On the same theme, Hills points out that in the pagan Anglo-Saxon cemeteries of East Anglia, although there are objects which resemble those from the "continental Anglian areas. . . . There are also applied brooches of Saxon types and bone combs paralleled both in the Elbe-Weser region and further west." She concludes that attempts to locate discrete Anglian, Saxon and Jutish groups in England is fruitless since on the Continent these groups were really "loose confederations drawn from a variety of people."[59]

Usually such "anomalies" to the expected "Bedan" pattern are simply noted and ignored; where explanation is attempted, this is couched in culture-historical terms with all the implications to which I have already referred. For example, Leahy argues that "the people who settled Lindsey during the 5th century were predominantly Angles but with the addition of some Saxons and other elements."[60] From time to time the recognition of such anomalies within the culture-historical framework results in further "anomalies" and necessitates somewhat tortuous explanations. Thus, we are told that the earliest evidence for the presence of "Saxons" in Wessex is at Hod Hill, where they had "arrived by the mid-fifth century." However, it appears that the "Saxon" finds emerge from a "British" context and the strict association assumed between material culture and ethnic group necessitates the conclusion that "the fifth century objects from Hod Hill may have belonged to the families of Saxon warriors in British employ"![61] Bruce Eagles also argues that a particular type of "hand-made organic-, often grass- or chaff-tempered pottery" provides "one of the few pointers to the British population." In essence, it becomes an ethnic identifier for an undifferentiated "British" people. However, we are also told that it was found on "Anglo-Saxon" sites such as Portchester, was associated with "a possible Anglo-Saxon sunken-featured building" at Hucklesbrook, and was "recovered from Anglo-Saxon burials at Ford Petersfinger and Winterbourne Gunner."[62]

Here we should also note the evidence for more localized "material cultures" within the so-called Anglian and Saxon settlement areas. Yorke points out that in the sixth century in Wessex, "no two cemeteries are identical and . . . each community had patterns of burial ritual or dress peculiar to itself."[63] Several scholars have pointed to the existence of differentiation within individual cemeteries.[64] Ellen Pader well illustrates the scale and "proximity" of difference:

> the populations buried at Westgarth Gardens and Holywell Row did not choose to differentiate between children and adults in the same manner or to the same degree. Nor did they always use the same objects (e.g. knives for females). Yet both are on tributaries of the River Lark, are only some 19km apart, and overlap temporally.[65]

However, these are only anomalies if we persist in believing in bounded and homogeneous "ethnic" groups in the past, and if we continue to interpret the archaeological record through the methodologies of culture-history. A fresh look at the evidence, combined with a reconsideration of the nature of ethnicity in the early Middle Ages, suggests that processes other than (as well as?) those of ethnic "signaling" were at work in the fifth- and sixth-century regions of England.

ETHNICITY AND HETEROGENEITY

Contrary to common understanding, it would be a gross error to assume that the Angles, Saxons and Jutes possessed discrete identities in their so-called tribal homelands and maintained them in the early part of their settlement in England. However, in his recent volume on *The English*, Sir Geoffrey Elton tells us that "the Anglo-Saxons did not intermarry with the indigenous population . . . [and] did not mix significantly with the Celts (Britons)."[66] In a similar vein, Welch has "real problems" accepting the idea that the *adventus Saxonum* was in fact made up of

> a small number of well-armed warrior bands . . . [who] married native British women and that they and their *mixed-blood* "Anglo-Saxon" progeny are the occupants of the many so-called Anglo-Saxon burial grounds studied by archaeologists

and argues instead that the invaders brought their wives with them.[67] The same view is implicit in the writings of those who argue for the "separateness" and "distinctiveness" of Anglian and Saxon groups up to the sixth century.[68]

However, some archaeologists and historians now question the assumed racial purity and integrity of Migration Period groups.[69] Thus, Herwig Wolfram reminds us of the vast array of "peoples" in the fourth-century Ostrogothic "kingdom" of Ermanaric. More generally, he argues that "the sources attest the basically polyethnic character of the *gentes*. Archaic peoples are mixed. . . . Their formation . . . is not a matter of common descent but one of political decision."[70] The presence of "Romans," or for-mer "Romans," in these "barbarian" groups should be emphasized.[71] The situation detected by Patrick Amory where small cultivators who joined the army of Theodoric the Great would have *become known as* Goths by 493, was surely more widespread than the areas of Pannonia, Moesia, and northern Italy.[72] In this context we might remember that Orosius, "writing of the irruption of Germans into Gaul and Spain early in the fifth century, could say that some Romans preferred to live among the 'barbarians,' poor in liberty, rather than endure the anxiety of paying taxes in the Roman em-pire."[73] In the changing world of late antiquity, people were making *active* choices, and those choices were no longer (if they ever had been) between Roman and barbarian. With the transformation of Empire, and of the insti-tutional structures which formed it, "people were forced to choose loyalties from among the new smaller communities within which they found them-selves."[74] In addition, it is not at all clear that *ethnic* identity formed the basis of these new communities. In the Burgundian kingdom many members of the Roman elite prospered under the new regime. After the fall of the Burgundian kingdom in 534 some remained prominent under the Franks. Significantly,

> none of them has left any record of feeling different or special due to their *Roman* descent. Their prominence and self-conscious pride were due to their *senatorial* descent, a more specialized category than an ethnic group.[75]

The fact that they remained in position throughout the changes in "ethnic" control in the region suggests that social and economic *power*, rather than ethnic identification or exclusion was an essential element in the construction of their identity—as a people apart. Significantly, it appears that Burgundian or Germanic "ethnicity" was not the most important factor for those mem-bers of the elite with Germanic names. They too lived in and through the structures formed from the political demise of the Roman empire.[76]

Where, then, do the Angles, Saxons and Jutes as coherent peoples fit into this picture of "bewildering heterogeneity" and overlapping identities? Although the prominence given to Bede's statement about the Angles, Saxons and Jutes has foreclosed much discussion of alternatives, the very fact that all Migration Period groups were characterized by fluidity and heterogeneity makes it extremely unlikely that the "ancestors of the English" were any different. Some of the late Antique sources speak of "peoples" other than the Angles, Saxons and Jutes taking part in the "settlement" of England.[77] Hines has suggested that there is archaeological evidence for an undocumented movement of people from "southern and western Norway about the beginning of the last quarter of the fifth century,"[78] although we must be mindful here of slipping into culture-historical arguments. We might also cite the reference that in 527,

> pagans came out of Germany, and occupied East Anglia . . . from where some of them invaded Mercia and waged many wars against the Britons: but because their leaders were many, they have no name.[79]

This is interesting not because it records "another" migration, but because of the implications it has for the structure of the "warbands." "Their leaders were many" might suggest a heterogeneous group made up of individuals attached to their own "warleader." We might envisage a similar structure in the groups which *ultimately* became known as the Angles, Saxons and Jutes. The fact that the latter "had a name" (and that those recorded in 527 did not) may have more to do with the late seventh- and early eighth-century political circumstances in which Bede was writing than with the actual homogeneity of the original group.[80]

In England in the fifth century, we do have evidence for the migration of people from northwestern Europe. It would be perverse to deny this. But it cannot be emphasized strongly enough that these population movements were part of the European pattern of *Völkerwanderungen*, and given the evidence cited for the heterogeneous constitution of the Continental *gentes*, we cannot expect the "people" who *became known* as the Angles, Saxons and Jutes to have been any different. Additionally, we have to understand that the "Bedan" account of the "migration" is likely to represent a condensation in time of a long-term process.[81] The fire and sword scenario painted by many for the *adventus Saxonum* is unlikely to have occurred; there was no confrontation between coherent, homogenous Anglo-Saxons and an equally coherent and homogenous British "people" in a few cataclysmic years.

It is equally important to remember the context into which these "migrants" inserted themselves. This was one of decentralized power held by members of the "Roman" elite, and probably the army, some of whom may have been of "Germanic" extraction. But as already argued, the "ethnicity" of the powerful was not important; power was. And here we must understand the nature of the societies from which the migrants came. These were not the egalitarian, free, Germanic communities of Tacitus's construction. Archaeological evidence from Denmark and northern Germany clearly shows that the communities from which the "Angles," "Saxons" and "Jutes" emerged were hierarchically structured,[82] and there is no reason to believe that they lost this structure in the journey across the North Sea. These were not the free, German, yeoman stock of English mythology.

Nicholas Higham has argued that the archaeological evidence from parts of southern England shows clear links with southern Denmark and northwest Germany, areas which he considers as "not already much affected by cultural contacts with Rome," and "reached Britain unaffected by Romanizing influences."[83] It would appear that such comments are the product of an overly insular perspective. It is well recognized by Danish and other Continental scholars that although Denmark lay well beyond the *lines*, and beyond the "buffer-zone" of "Romanized tribes," its people were profoundly affected by trade and exchange networks and other forms of interaction with "Rome." Some of them had served in the Roman army. These connections resulted in the flow of Roman objects into Denmark. The flow was controlled by Danish elites and the objects, and the control over their distribution, were used in strategies which reproduced and transformed social relations within Danish society.[84] These people were not Romanized, but they used Roman material culture and experience of Rome in the construction of self and society.

It is also apparent from the archaeology that relationships with the Roman Empire were not the only factors in the construction and reproduction of the power of the elites in Denmark. The material culture from Funen, for example, illustrates the especially strong contacts with the peoples of southeastern Europe.[85] The point is that the societies from which the "Germanic" settlers of England emerged were complex and stratified. These were not the "hillbillies" or "backwoodsmen" of the Germanic migrations.[86] The basis of elite power appears to have lain in their control over the acquisition and distribution of objects and knowledge from Other peoples, across a wide geographical area. The recognition of the importance and wide-ranging nature of such relationships should further undermine notions of the existence of discrete and bounded "ethnic" units in the fourth to sixth centuries, and of the archetypal yeoman farmer of English mythology.

What is clear is that we can no longer see the "peoples" of the Migration Period as discrete, homogeneous, autonomous groups. It is fairly depressing to note that this much is recognized, and then ignored, by scholars.[87] Thus John Blair can assert that "it would be anachronistic to envisage separate races with separate cultures . . . or to imagine them colonizing England in large, politically coherent groups which kept their identity in isolation from others,"[88] and can then concur with Tania Dickinson's statement that "the Thames was a major line of communication for the Upper Thames region with *other Saxon* communities"[89]—implying separate communities of Saxons, using Saxon material culture, communicating with each other.[90] As Reynolds observes, many scholars seem able to accept the heterogeneous nature of these groups but still hold to the idea that "each tribe or people that had (or has) a separate name formed some kind of cultural entity."[91]

CONSTRUCTING ETHNICITY

It is clear that there are serious problems in using the culture-history approach as the basis for interpretation, and major deficiencies in our understanding of the nature and composition of "Germanic" groups (both on the Continent and in England). However, it is also apparent from recent work in archaeology, anthropology and sociology that it would be a debilitating step to move from the rejection of a direct and inflexible link between ethnic identity and material culture to argue that there is *no* relationship.[92] As I have already suggested, many of the problems in this area lie in an inadequate theorization (and therefore understanding) of ethnicity and material culture.

If we abandon (as we must) the notion of ethnic groups as unchanging, bounded entities, a minimal definition of ethnicity might be "a collective identification that is *socially constructed* with reference to *putative cultural similarity and difference*."[93] This "putative cultural similarity and difference" is used in a series of social strategies to classify people as belonging (or not), and to define membership (or Otherwise) of a collectivity. As a result "identity is a matter of the *outs* as well as the *ins*"; it is a matter of "social closure."[94] It is one of the strengths of Richard Jenkins's work that he emphasizes the creation of "outsiders" through ethnic closure. However, he does more than this since he argues that *power* is inherent in this relationship,[95] and that the process of closure, of categorization as "outsider," can be used by "outsiders" in the process of constructing their own identity.[96]

Ethnic identity, therefore, is *constructed* through the process of inter-action between people. Cultural traits are implicated and manipulated in this process.[97] Archaeologists understand that material culture was actively drawn upon in the very *creation* and reproduction of relations of power, identity, and gender.[98] It also provided a "basis and resources for ethnic clo-sure";[99] it was the "objectification of cultural difference."[100]

The recognition that ethnic identity is frequently constructed in a pro-cess of categorization which excludes the "Others," and that material culture can be implicated in this process, might allow us to predict the situations in which material symbols of similarity and difference would be brought to the fore (although it should be clear that material culture is not activated as part of the process of ethnic identity construction only in such "contact" situations. The process is continuous and changing).[101] With the *adventus Saxonum* we might expect both the "invaders/settlers" and the "natives" to do just this, since in the still dominant interpretation of the *adventus* we have the remnants of Romano-British society being challenged by mi-grating "peoples" ("Angles," "Saxons" and "Jutes") from continental Europe. The migrants were supposedly confronted by the "British" who were ulti-mately defeated and either killed or driven into the fastness of Wales and the West.[102] Conflict and war with the "barbarian" Other might be expected to enhance significantly the ethnic identity, and the feeling of "Us-ness," among the first generations of "Angles," "Saxons" and "Jutes."

This, however, does not appear to have been the case. The detail of the fifth-century archaeological material from the so-called settlement areas of the Angles, Saxons and Jutes does not suggest that "material symbols of similarity and difference" were being emphasized by "peoples" at this early date. I have already referred to the fact that in the period up to circa 475 "Saxon" material is found across most of England "from north of the Humber to Sussex," with "datable Anglian material . . . [being] largely con-fined to cruciform brooches."[103] Speaking of the "Jutes" of Kent and the Isle of Wight, Hills points out that although this area had a distinctive material culture, this was not in the period of the Migrations as we would expect if "Jutish ethnicity" was being signaled in this period of "contact"; rather it was in the sixth century.[104] Even the architecture of the early "Anglo-Saxon" house is no longer seen as distinctively Germanic.[105]

Given our expectation that in the fifth century, in the context of "contact" with the British Other, if at any time, specific Anglian, Saxon and Jutish identities should be signaled, our failure to find such evidence forces us to reconsider the traditional picture of the *adventus Saxonum*, and the images of conflict, battle and devastation which have played such an important part in explanations for the emergence of the English from Germanic stock.

Arguments for ethnic conflict between homogeneous and coherent "peoples"—Angles, Saxons, Jutes and Britons—leading to ethnic cleansing and decimation are not supported by the archaeological, environmental, or historical evidence. Equally we cannot accept the more "moderate" view which does away with the "fire and sword" imagery but still postulates coherent and discrete "peoples"—Angles, Saxons and Jutes—maintaining their separate and distinctive identities through time to become the English.

We must accept that people constructed their identities through a dialectic between past experience and current social, economic and (in particular) power relationships. We must understand that material culture was actively drawn upon in the construction and reproduction of those relationships. The people who lived in England in the fifth and sixth centuries acted and created within the emerging structures of society. If we examine the sixth-century evidence more closely, we may be able to see how material culture was actively used in the construction of identity at that time. It is surely not coincidental that it is also in the sixth century that we get archaeological and documentary evidence for the emergence of overarching systems of power and authority.

On page 63 of his *Anglo-Saxon England*, Welch provides us with an image of "three women dressed in regional fashions of the sixth century." Ignoring the fact that the women are presented as very much alive while the reconstructions are based on cemetery evidence, we should pay particular attention to the dress of the "Anglian" woman:

> The well-dressed woman in the Anglian regions . . . would be similarly dressed [to the Saxon woman], except that the range of brooches was somewhat different and the undergarment had long tailored sleeves fastened by cuff-link-like fittings called wrist clasps. These small hook-and-eye metal fittings were sewn on either side of a split sleeve and are extremely rare in England outside this region. Keys and mock keys called girdle hangers also play a prominent role in Anglian dress.[106]

The image presented is a static one in which material culture (in life as in death) *reflected* Anglian ethnic identity. In fact, the archaeological evidence shows that such a picture is profoundly misleading. What appears in the sixth century as "Anglian" dress is very much a *construction*, a *creation* of that time. It does not stem from the migration into England of the Angles in the middle of the fifth century, but from the construction of a sense of identity in the particular social and political circumstances of the sixth century in England.

Hines shows how, within a few generations of the *adventus*, a "new, consistent and distinctive Anglian English culture was . . . put together out of a remarkably diverse range of sources."[107] He argues that this material culture assemblage should not be seen simply as an indicator of the extent of Anglian occupation, but rather as "a means by which people could both claim their membership of the new group and promulgate the conditions by which membership was established."[108] Scull has pointed out that not only were many of the known cemeteries established two to three generations after the *adventus*, but also that much of the material culture had by then taken on a "distinctively *insular* character."[109] In other words, by the time we get the emergence of these distinctively regional sets of material culture, some of the objects are the product of a mixture of "traditions." They have been called "Germanic offshoots out of the late-Roman craft tradition."[110]

In the sixth century, material culture was being activated in the construction and signaling of "cultural similarity and difference," not by simply drawing upon a set of fixed ethnic signifiers stemming from a supposed Continental inheritance, but through a mixture of adoption, selection, creativity and continuity.

In a recent reassessment of the cemetery evidence from the Isle of Wight, Chris Arnold has examined the evidence for a supposed "Jutish" settlement of that island from Kent. He points out that when we look at the total assemblages from the graves, few of them have distinctively "Kentish" objects, such as brooches. In those that do, these Kentish objects are rarely associated with other "Kentish" artifacts. In addition many of the objects in the graves are of types which are generic to most of southern England. Arnold concludes that the material evidence may represent "nothing more than the movement of people or objects between families maintaining a traditional link between Kent and the island."[111]

I would go further, and suggest that if this "traditional" link existed, it was incorporated as one element in a series of "traditions," "memories," or "aspirations" which were used in the construction of regional identities in the sixth century. The "memory" or myth of "Jutishness" may have been one aspect of that construction. Detailed analysis, at the regional level, elsewhere in England might show the active construction of similar "material cultures." The possibility of recognizing these, and then interpreting them, is severely hampered by the traditional practice of focusing on the highly diagnostic artifacts ("Anglian," "Saxon," or "Jutish") within individual grave assemblages.[112] A spurious uniformity is thereby imposed on a potentially more heterogeneous and "constructed" assemblage, resulting in an equally spurious reading of the past.

If these regional patterns really are markers of group identity (and I think that they are), then we have to remember that "identity is a matter of the *outs* as well the *ins*"; it is a matter of "social closure."[113] Who then were the "outs"; against whom was the "closure" designed to operate? A conventional response would be the Britons. But then we would have to ask why it took several generations (of conflict?) to produce these strategies and symbols of exclusion. In fact it might be argued that, in the context of the sixth-century Anglo-Saxon world, the Others meant *each other*. Given what I have already said about problems with historical sources such as the early sections of the *Anglo-Saxon Chronicle*,[114] I hardly dare mention that the first strife recorded between the "English" is in the sixth century, 568—"In this year Ceawlin and Cutha fought against Ethelbert, and drove him in flight into Kent."[115]

It can also be argued that the strategies of inclusion and exclusion, in which the material culture we have been considering played a part, were the product of the emergence of regional structures of *power*. I shall return to this later. For the moment I want to emphasize once again that the symbols of group identity in sixth-century England were a product of processes current in sixth-century England. It was in this context that new identities, ethnicities if you like, were *constructed*.

ETHNICITY AND POWER

If we can agree that it is anachronistic to envisage separate races as the basis for a sense of ethnic identity in the early Middle Ages, we have to ask what formed the basis for such identity? Patrick Geary argues that in the early Middle Ages

> one concludes that ethnicity did not exist as an objective category but rather as a subjective and malleable category by which various preexisting likenesses could be manipulated symbolically to mold an identity and a community.[116]

We have a tendency to see ethnicity as discrete and *objective* and as a major force in the construction of individuals and peoples in the past.[117] By contrast, as Jenkins does for the present, so Geary argues that in early medieval Europe ethnicity itself was *constructed*, "molded" in the context of the operation of *power* relationships.[118] Examining the historical sources for the contexts in which an "ethnicity" is appended to named individuals, Geary discovered that very few people are ever so identified.[119] Further, it became clear that "the terms *Franci, Alamanni, Burgundiones, Gothi* and the like appeared in connection with kings and with war."[120] Geary concludes that

> the peoples of the migration period acquired their identity through their adherence to particular royal or ducal families alongside whom they fought and whose traditions they adopted.
>
> The actual circumstances in which ethnic designations seem to have been felt most acutely were largely *political*.[121]

This discussion takes us back to the heart of the question of concepts of ethnicity in the early Middle Ages. We have a tendency to assume that *all* members of a particular social grouping constituted the *ethnos*. In fact it seems likely that such a sense of belonging was more socially circumscribed. Wolfram tells us that "[a]rchaic peoples are mixed; they never comprise all potential members of a *gens*";[122] "the *gens* is the people in arms";[123] "a *gens* is a large group as much as a clan, a fraction of a tribe as much as a confederation of several ethnic units."[124] In the Burgundian law codes, the terms "Roman" and "Burgundian" always refer to the upper ranks of society—"the *nobiles* and *mediocres*. The *coloni* and slaves, whatever their familial origins, do not get ethnic adjectives."[125] More generally, where we can extract "identities" from the Burgundian sources, these are usually constructed on the basis of politics and power, not "blood."[126]

Peter Heather argues that Gothic identity (or "Gothicness") was focused on a caste of "freemen"—"a dominant and restricted social elite: a minority . . . within the total adult male population of groups calling themselves Gothic."[127] He goes on to point out that this obviously left the majority of the population as an "underclass." Their commitment to "Gothicness" cannot really be measured from the historical or archaeological sources, but it is surely noteworthy that when the nobles were killed in battle the rest of the Gothic population simply surrendered.[128] We cannot know the "ethnic allegiance" (if it existed) of the vast majority of the Gothic (or Burgundian) population, but with Amory we can suggest that "for the lowest classes, social role and geographic location were more important defining traits than ethnic identity."[129]

This all suggests that when the historical sources speak of a *gens*—a people like the *gens Anglorum*—they are not referring to *all* the inhabitants of England, or even of any of the "settlement areas." They are referring to an *elite* within that larger entity. We might call this "restricted ethnicity" but ultimately, they are talking about *power*.

This concept of "restricted ethnicity" has important implications for our understanding of the operation of early "English" society. The problem we have in discussing "restricted ethnicity" in the case of Anglo-Saxon England derives, once again, from the nature of the sources. As I have already noted, contemporary English documentary sources for the fifth and sixth centuries do not exist, and later sources must be read with a deep awareness of their context.[130] As Reynolds succinctly puts it,

> we do not know how consistently the Germanic-speaking invaders of Britain behaved like a group or felt themselves to be a group during the fifth and sixth centuries. We do not know what they called themselves, if indeed they had any collective name.[131]

However, Higham argues that there is evidence in Bede for an exclusive understanding of what/who constituted the *gens Anglorum* in the seventh century. Higham shows that there are remarkably few references to the lower orders in Bede's text and argues that they were beneath Bede's attention.[132] He would not have had them in mind when he spoke of the *gens Anglorum*.

Bede tells us that in 679 a battle was fought, "near the river Trent," between the Northumbrian king Ecgfrith and the Mercian king Æthelred during which the former's brother Ælfwine was killed.[133] In the course of the battle, Imma, a *miles* of Ælfwine, was wounded, and after lying for some time among the dead on the battlefield,

> he was found and captured by men of the enemy army, and taken to their lord, who was a *gesith* of king Æthelred. On being asked who he was, he was afraid to admit that he was a thegn; but he answered instead that he was a poor peasant and married; and he declared that he had come to the army in company with other peasants to bring food to the soldiers. The *gesith* took him and had his wounds attended to. . . . When he had been a prisoner with the *gesith* for some time, those who watched him closely realized by his ap-

pearance, his bearing, and his speech that he was not of common stock as he had said, but of noble family.[134]

Higham argues that the deception perpetrated by Imma was designed to prevent his being killed by the Mercians in revenge for the losses they had incurred. More significantly for our purposes, the fact that

> the *miles* was considered by both parties to be an appropriate object of such revenge, but the *rusticus* not, implies that the former, but not the latter, was considered to be a full member of the appropriate *gens* (people)—so vulnerable to a blood feud which that *gens* had incurred *en masse*.[135]

It is also significant that the Mercians eventually recognized Imma to be of noble birth from "his appearance, clothing and speech." We might conclude that such signs distinguished him from the lower orders who supported him in battle, if only by way of bringing provisions to the army.

Such perceptions of the significance of the lower orders were not restricted to Bede. In a letter to Æthelheard, Archbishop of Canterbury, written after the Viking destruction of the monastery at Lindisfarne in 793, Alcuin urges the English to reform themselves so that the same might not happen again. The clergy are reminded of their spiritual duties; those best able to do battle (we might call them the *bellatores*) are to protect the clergy (*oratores*). However, Alcuin "does not name those who labor; they have no role during a time of crisis."[136] These may only be the perceptions of the clergy, but they are reinforced by the evidence of the seventh- and eighth-century law-codes of kings Æthelberht of Kent and Ine of Wessex,[137] and in any case they are the only literary perceptions we have. What they suggest is that in the seventh century the *gens Anglorum* comprised a restricted secular and ecclesiastical elite who exercised extensive power over the vast majority of the population.[138]

In this summary Higham returns us to the link between the "peoples" named in the historical sources and relationships of power and domination— Imma claimed he was a peasant bringing provisions to the Northumbrian *militia*. However, he does so by imposing a crude "ethnic" (in its biological sense) hierarchy on to what is clearly a social/cultural one. Thus he argues that the "*gens Anglorum* was a political, military and cultural elite, atop a community which remained otherwise quite British even up until the early eighth century."[139] I would suggest that the social and political hierarchy was not so clearly constructed on biological grounds.

Higham's argument for a socially restricted sense of *gens Anglorum* is echoed by others.[140] At a different level, Hines, discussing the meaning of named late sixth- and earlier seventh-century political units for their inhabitants, suggests that

> we have little reason to suppose that they expressed in any consensual way the group-identity of most of these inhabitants, and that consequently a group name like the Hæstingas is not to be conceived of as representing some comfortably clannish system in which all the people of Hæst were one as if part of some extended family and thus united by their ethnic identity at least: it could rather be an administrative, *possessive*, *imposed* description—the people who belong to N.[141]

In the past it was thought that these -*ingas* names were evidence for the earliest settlement of England by Germanic families, with the family head providing the prefix (*Hæstingas* = the kin of Hæsta). It is now recognized that they belong to a rather later phase of early English history, one associated with "consolidation and demarcation."[142] Hines's observation removes the assumption of "familiarity" and consensus which has frequently been associated with these names, and places them in the context of developing power relations, which also involved "consolidation and demarcation." The suggestion that it could have been an imposed term also removes the necessity to assume "blood" links between (for example) the members of the *Hæstingas*.

There are, therefore, indications that in the seventh century and later, the term *gens* referred to elite identity. The Continental evidence suggests that it would not be surprising if the concept of restricted ethnicity (in which the membership of a *gens* was socially circumscribed) *did* apply in England in the fifth and sixth centuries. Despite the often cited differences in the economic and political situation in fifth-century Britain and Gaul (for example),[143] and in the "non-Romanized" nature of the "invaders" of England, "it seems implausible that the customs of . . . [the Germanic-speaking settlers of England] differed so much from those of other Germanic-speaking barbarians of northwestern Europe"[144] as to render inappropriate the application of insights drawn from the Continent.

CONCLUSION: GERMANIC KIN?

The material cultures which culture-historians link with the peoples named in Bede's one paragraph on the Germanic ancestors of the English were the product of actions taken in England in the sixth and seventh centuries. They were the product of interactions between emerging regional networks of power, both "Anglo-Saxon" and "British." Their style was determined by late Roman forms associated with the authority of Rome and by memories and myths of a "Germanic" homeland. But the main point is that they were *constructed* in the context of sixth- and seventh-century regional *power* structures. The emergence of such structures is manifest in the archaeology of cemetery and settlement. In the cemeteries there is increasing evidence for stratification and hierarchy in the second half of the sixth century,[145] while in the seventh century this is more clearly marked, especially in the individual barrow burials.[146] The settlements of the fifth and early sixth century are marked by a profound lack of differentiation, both internally and across regions. Richard Hodges points to the contrast between the fortified hill-top centers of western Britain where the scale of refurbishment, the presence of "high status" imports from the Mediterranean, and the nature of some of the structures argue for their occupation by an elite, and the "egalitarian quality of . . . [the] modest farmsteads" of contemporary early Anglo-Saxon England.[147] Just such an apparently egalitarian picture emerges from the excavations of the mid-fifth-century phases of the settlement at Mucking in Essex. Here the "absence of large, 'high status,' or obviously central buildings" and the "lack of any obvious structure or planning within the settlement" were used to argue for "the absence of an overall, regulating authority."[148] There is evidence for differentiation within Anglo-Saxon period settlements, and for the kind of structure and planning so evidently absent at West Stow and the early phases at Mucking, but this appears in the late sixth and seventh centuries;[149] at the same time as we get the construction of distinctive regional material cultures. I would argue that there is an intimate connection between these two phenomena, and that the forms of identity we find expressed in the regional material cultures are those of affiliation and allegiance to regional "aristocratic" elites.

Five generations after the supposed *adventus Saxonum*, the "blood ethnicity" of these elites would have been hard to determine, even if it mattered.[150] Given the lack of evidence for a massive rupture in the countryside of late Roman Britain, however, we must assume that the vast majority of the population was *not* of Germanic origin/descent. Abandoning the notions of homogeneous groups of Anglo-Saxons "invading" and destroying a coherent entity, in favor of a more continuous process of assimilation into the decentralized and personalized power structures of sub-Roman Britain, means that we cannot even assume that the elites were primarily Germanic.[151] What matters is that the heterogeneous peoples of the regions of England came to *see themselves* as having a common identity. They did so as a consequence of collective action and interaction with other British and Anglo-Saxon entities. It *may* be at this time (in the late sixth and seventh centuries) that this identity came to be seen as Anglian, Saxon, etc. but we still have to recognize that we have no idea what the peoples of fifth- and sixth-century England called themselves "if indeed they had any collective name."[152] It *may* be that this sense of identity—of "Anglian-ness," "Saxon-ness," etc.—was restricted to a social elite, and it seems that this concept of "restricted ethnicity" existed by the end of the seventh century.[153] It is probably of some importance that, in the eighth century, succession to the throne was linked to descent from a sixth-century "ancestor."[154] But as we have already noted, a concomitant of ethnicity is *power* and this must be especially true of "restricted ethnicity." The elites of the kingdoms of "Anglo-Saxon" England may have emphasized their Anglo-Saxon origins from the seventh century onwards, drawing upon a common mythical past to promote a common sense of belonging and so create what Shennan has called "the self-conscious identity groups which are essential to the definition of ethnicity";[155] but, as with Heather's Goths, the ethnic identity of the mass of the population is unclear and likely to have been at least ambivalent. The reality for them, as it was for Imma, was economic, social and political subordination.

I dedicate this article to my uncle Sean Ritchie who died while it was being written. While he might not have favored the focus on the English, I hope he would have approved of the sentiments which underpin this work. William Frazer, Andrew Tyrell, and Nicholas Brooks provided invaluable editorial comments. Richard Jenkins, Alex Woolf, Heinrich Härke, Vanessa Toulmin, Richard Hodges and Mark Pluciennik enhanced my perspectives on ethnicity and the English. Participation in the European Science Foundation's Transformation of the Roman World project enabled me to meet and discuss some of the issues with scholars from across Europe. In the light of the problems addressed in this article it seems more than appropriate to thank all those involved in this trans-national venture. My deepest thanks, however, go to Prue for helping me through a very difficult time.

NOTES

[1] H. Reinerth, *Das Federseemoor als Siedlungsland des Vorzeitmenschen* (Leipzig, 1936), p. 5; cited in B. J. Arnold, "The Past as Propaganda: Totalitarian Archaeology in Nazi Germany," *Antiquity* 64 (1990): 468.

2 Umberto Eco, "Dreaming of the Middle Ages," *Travels in Hyperreality* (London, 1987), p. 65.

3 That study will appear in more complete form in my forthcoming book, *Myths of the English*.

4 This is despite the implications of much of the recent work on genetics and archaeology. See Patrick Sims-Williams, "Genetics, Linguistics, and Prehistory: Thinking Big and Thinking Straight," *Antiquity* 72 (1998): 505–27.

5 Walter Pohl, "The Barbarian Successor States," in *The Transformation of the Roman World AD 400–900*, ed. Leslie Webster and Michelle Brown (Berkeley, 1997), p. 47.

6 R. R. Davies, "The Peoples of Britain and Ireland 1100–1400, 1. Identities," *Transactions of the Royal Historical Society*, 6th ser., 4 (1994): 4, 6 (emphasis added).

7 Davies, "The Peoples of Britain and Ireland 1100–1400," p. 4.

8 Patrick Amory, "Names, Ethnic Identity, and Community in Fifth- and Sixth-Century Burgundy," *Viator* 25 (1994): 4.

9 Susan Reynolds, "What Do We Mean by 'Anglo-Saxon' and 'Anglo-Saxons'?" *Journal of British Studies* 24 (1985): 405.

10 Richard Jenkins, *Rethinking Ethnicity: Arguments and Explorations* (London, 1997), p. 10.

11 Jenkins, *Rethinking Ethnicity*, p. 14.

12 Michael Ignatieff, *Blood and Belonging: Journeys into the New Nationalism* (New York, 1994), p. 11.

13 J. G. A. Pocock, "British History: A Plea for a New Subject," *Journal of Modern History* 47 (1975): 609. See also Patrick Wormald, "Bede, the *bretwaldas* and the Origins of the *gens Anglorum*," in *Ideal and Reality in Frankish and Anglo-Saxon Society: Studies Presented to J. M. Wallace-Hadrill*, ed. Patrick Wormald (Oxford, 1983), p. 104.

14 *Bede's Ecclesiastical History of the English People*, ed. Bertram Colgrave and R.A.B. Mynors (Oxford, 1969), I.15 (hereafter referred to as Bede, *HE*; all citations will refer to Bede's book and chapter divisions). See also Michael Hunter, "Germanic and Roman Antiquity and the Sense of the Past in Anglo-Saxon England," *Anglo-Saxon England* 3 (1974): 31.

15 Francis Gummere, *Germanic Origins: A Study in Primitive Culture* (New York, 1892), pp. 1–2.

16 Geoffrey Elton, *The English* (Oxford, 1992), p. 1. The "conquest myth" is examined by Heinrich Harke, "Material Culture as Myth: Weapons in Anglo-Saxon Graves," in *Burial and Society: The Chronological and Social Analysis of Archaeological Burial Data*, ed. Claus Kjeld Jensen and Karen Hoilund Nielsen (Aarhus, 1997), pp. 120–24.

[17] See Patrick Sims-Williams, "The Settlement of England in Bede and in the *Chronicle*," *Anglo-Saxon England* 12 (1983): 1.

[18] Sims-Williams, "The Settlement of England in Bede and in the *Chronicle*," p. 1.

[19] Sims-Williams, "The Settlement of England in Bede and in the *Chronicle*," p. 39.

[20] M. White, "Hague Fury at Tory 'Dinosaurs,'" *The Guardian* 8 Oct. 1997: 1; interview with Lord Tebbit, *Today*, BBC Radio 4, 8 Oct. 1997. See also David Lowenthal, "British National Identity and the English Landscape," *Rural History* 2 (1991): 205–30.

[21] For an assessment of these sources, see David Dumville, "Essex, Middle Anglia, and the Expansion of Mercia in the South-East Midlands," in *The Origins of Anglo-Saxon Kingdoms*, ed. Steven Bassett (London, 1989), pp. 123, 126. See also, Christopher Scull, "Archaeology, Early Anglo-Saxon Society and the Origins of Anglo-Saxon Kingdoms," *Anglo-Saxon Studies in Archaeology and History* 6 (1993): 65–66, and Richard Hodges, *The Anglo-Saxon Achievement* (Ithaca, N.Y., 1989), pp. 22–23.

[22] Reynolds, "What Do We Mean by 'Anglo-Saxon' and 'Anglo-Saxons'?" p. 400.

[23] References and discussion are provided in David Austin, "The 'proper study' of Medieval Archaeology," in *From the Baltic to the Black Sea*, ed. David Austin and Leslie Alcock (London, 1990), pp. 9–42. Many people have now reassessed the historical evidence and we can read it in a more "realistic" fashion. See, among others, Barbara Yorke, "Fact or Fiction? The Written Evidence for the Fifth and Sixth Centuries AD," *Anglo-Saxon Studies in Archaeology and History* 6 (1993): 45–50; David Dumville, "Kingship, Genealogies and Regnal Lists," in *Early Medieval Kingship*, ed. Peter Sawyer and Ian Wood (Leeds, 1977), pp. 72–104; and Sims-Williams, "The Settlement of England." The archaeological evidence is considered by (again, among many others) A. S. Esmonde Cleary, *The Ending of Roman Britain* (London, 1989), pp. 130–87; C. J. Arnold, *The Archaeology of the Early Anglo-Saxon Kingdoms*, 2nd ed. (London, 1997); N. J. Higham, *Rome, Britain and the Anglo-Saxons* (London, 1992); Catherine Hills, "The Archaeology of Anglo-Saxon England in the Pagan Period: a Review," *Anglo-Saxon England* 8 (1979): 297–329; Scull, "Early Anglo-Saxon Society," pp. 65–82; John Hines, "The Scandinavian Character of Anglian England: an Update," in *The Age of Sutton Hoo: The Seventh Century in North-Western Europe*, ed. Martin O. H. Carver (Woodbridge, Eng., 1992), pp. 315–29; and J. N. L. Myres, *The English Settlements* (Oxford, 1986). Language is considered by John Hines in "Philology, Archaeology and the *adventus Saxonum vel Anglorum*," in *Britain 400–600: Language and History*, ed. Arthur Bammesberger and Alfred Wollmann (Heidelberg, 1990), 17–36, and in "The Becoming of the English: Identity, Material Culture and Language in early Anglo-Saxon England," *Anglo-Saxon Studies in Archaeology and History* 7 (1994): 49–59.

24 Bede, *HE* I.15.

25 Myres, *The English Settlements*, pp. 46, 63.

26 Martin Welch, *Anglo-Saxon England* (London, 1992), p. 11. See also Hines, "The Scandinavian Character of Anglian England," in addition to items of Hines's cited in notes 23 above and 78 below; John Blair, *Anglo-Saxon Oxfordshire* (Oxford, 1994), pp. 7–8; and Barbara Yorke, *Wessex in the Early Middle Ages* (London, 1995), p. 44.

27 Some of the problems with the culture-history approach are discussed below, and in Austin, "The 'proper study' of Medieval Archaeology"; Sian Jones, *The Archaeology of Ethnicity: Constructing Identities in Past and Present* (London, 1997), pp. 15–26, 135–44; Stephen J. Shennan, "Introduction: Archaeological Approaches to Cultural Identity," in *Archaeological Approaches to Cultural Identity*, ed. Stephen J. Shennan (London, 1988), pp. 1–32; and Bruce Trigger, *A History of Archaeological Thought* (Cambridge, Eng., 1989), pp. 148–206.

28 Timothy Champion, "Medieval Archaeology and the Tyranny of the Historical Record," in Austin and Alcock, *From the Baltic to the Black Sea*, p. 91.

29 Austin, "The 'proper study' of Medieval Archaeology," p. 12. See also Janet Richards, "Style and Symbol: Explaining Variability in Anglo-Saxon Cremation Burials," in *Power and Politics in Early Medieval Britain and Ireland*, ed. Stephen T. Driscoll and Margaret R. Nieke (Edinburgh, 1988), p. 145; and Hills, "The Archaeology of Anglo-Saxon England in the Pagan Period," pp. 325, 328.

30 Austin, "The 'proper study' of Medieval Archaeology," p. 25. Lotte Hedeager, *Iron Age Societies: From Tribe to State in Northern Europe 500 BC to AD 700*, trans. John Hines (Oxford, 1992), p. 181, has identified the same problem in Danish archaeology.

31 Austin, "The 'proper study' of Medieval Archaeology," p. 15.

32 Shennan, "Introduction: Archaeological Approaches to Cultural Identity," p. 6.

33 For an extreme example, see Volker Bierbrauer, Herman Büsing, and Andrea Büsing-Kolbe, "Die Dame von Ficarolo," *Archaeologia Medievale* 20 (1993): 686.

34 Shennan, "Introduction: Archaeological Approaches to Cultural Identity," p. 15 (emphasis added).

35 Jones, *Archaeology of Ethnicity*, pp. 108–09, 131.

36 Jones, *Archaeology of Ethnicity*, p. 139.

37 Dominic Janes, "The Golden Clasp of the Late Roman State," *Early Medieval Europe* 5 (1996): 127–53.

38 Janes, "The Golden Clasp of the Late Roman State," pp. 146–48.

39 A principal source for this discussion is still Hills, "The Archaeology of Anglo-Saxon England in the Pagan Period."

[40] Hills, "The Archaeology of Anglo-Saxon England in the Pagan Period," p. 298.

[41] Sonia Chadwick Hawkes and G. C. Dunning, "Soldiers and Settlers in Britain, Fourth to Fifth Century," *Medieval Archaeology* 5 (1961): 1–70, and Hills, "The Archaeology of Anglo-Saxon England in the Pagan Period," p. 299.

[42] Esmonde Cleary, *The Ending of Roman Britain*, p. 56.

[43] Esmonde Cleary, *The Ending of Roman Britain*, p. 55. See also Guy Halsall, "The Origins of the *Reihengräberzivilisation*: Forty Years On," in *Fifth Century Gaul: A Crisis of Identity?* ed. John Drinkwater and Hugh Elton (Cambridge, Eng., 1992), p. 200.

[44] Hills, "The Archaeology of Anglo-Saxon England in the Pagan Period," p. 305 (emphasis added). See also Halsall, "The Origins of the *Reihengräberzivilisation*," pp. 200–01.

[45] Kevin Leahy, "The Anglo-Saxon Settlement of Lindsey," in *Pre-Viking Lindsey*, ed. Alan Vince (Lincoln, Eng., 1993), p. 30.

[46] Esmonde Cleary, *The Ending of Roman Britain*, p. 55.

[47] Halsall, "The Origins of the *Reihengräberzivilisation*," p. 202.

[48] Halsall, "The Origins of the *Reihengräberzivilisation*," p. 205.

[49] Halsall, "The Origins of the *Reihengräberzivilisation*," p. 204.

[50] Higham, *Rome, Britain, and the Anglo-Saxons*, p. 215.

[51] Martin Millett, *The Romanization of Britain: An Essay in Archaeological Interpretation* (Cambridge, Eng., 1990), p. 215.

[52] Averil Cameron, *Procopius and the Sixth Century* (Berkeley, 1985), pp. 213–14.

[53] T. S. Brown, *Gentlemen and Officers: Imperial Administration and Aristocratic Power in Byzantine Italy AD 554–800* (London, 1984), p. 88.

[54] Millett, *The Romanization of Britain*, p. 219.

[55] See Chris Wickham, "The Other Transition: From the Ancient World to Feudalism," *Past and Present* 103 (1984): 3–36; Higham, *Rome, Britain, and the Anglo-Saxons*, pp. 213–14; and Scull, "Archaeology, Early Anglo-Saxon Society and the Origins of the Anglo-Saxon Kingdoms," p. 70.

[56] Champion, "Medieval Archaeology and the Tyranny of the Historical Record," p. 91.

[57] Hines, "Philology, Archaeology, and the *adventus Saxonum vel Anglorum*," p. 27.

[58] Barbara Yorke, "The Jutes of Hampshire and Wight and the Origins of Wessex," in Bassett, *The Origins of Anglo-Saxon Kingdoms*, p. 92.

[59] Hills, "The Archaeology of Anglo-Saxon England in the Pagan Period," p. 317. See also Scull, "Archaeology, Early Anglo-Saxon Society and the Origins of the Anglo-Saxon Kingdoms," p. 71.

[60] Kevin Leahy, "The Anglo-Saxon Settlement of Lindsey," p. 37.

[61] Bruce Eagles, "The Archaeological Evidence for Settlement in the Fifth to

Seventh Centuries AD," in *The Medieval Landscape of Wessex*, ed. Michael Aston and Carenza Lewis (Oxford, 1994), p. 27.

[62] Eagles, "The Archaeological Evidence for Settlement in the Fifth to Seventh Centuries AD," p. 18.

[63] Yorke, "The Jutes of Hampshire and Wight and the Origins of Wessex," pp. 44–45. See also Richards, "Style and Symbol: Explaining Variability in Anglo-Saxon Cremation Burials," pp. 145–61.

[64] See Heinrich Harke, "The Shield in the Burial Rite," in *Early Anglo-Saxon Shields*, ed. Tania Dickinson and Heinrich Harke (London, 1992), p. 65; Ellen J. Pader, "Material Symbolism and Social Relations in Mortuary Studies," in *Anglo-Saxon Cemeteries, 1979: The Fourth Anglo-Saxon Symposium at Oxford*, ed. Philip Rahtz, Tania Dickinson, and Lorna Watts (Oxford, 1980), pp. 147–49, 157; C. J. Arnold, "The Anglo-Saxon Cemeteries of the Isle of Wight: An Appraisal of Nineteenth-Century Excavation Data," in *Anglo-Saxon Cemeteries: A Reappraisal*, ed. Edmund Southworth (Sutton, Eng., 1990), p. 168; Jeremy W. Huggett, "Social Analysis of Early Anglo-Saxon Inhumation Burials: Archaeological Methodologies," *Journal of European Archaeology* 4 (1996): 348–58, 362; and Christopher Scull, "Before Sutton Hoo: Structures of Power and Society in Early East Anglia," in Carver, *The Age of Sutton Hoo*, p. 15.

[65] Pader, "Material Symbolism and Social Relations in Mortuary Studies," p. 158. See also Hodges, *The Anglo-Saxon Achievement*, pp. 37–38.

[66] Elton, *The English*, p. 3.

[67] Welch, *Anglo-Saxon England*, p. 11 (emphasis added). See also N. J. Higham, *The English Conquest: Gildas and Britain in the Fifth Century* (Manchester, Eng., 1994), p. 168. For a useful corrective, see Arnold, *The Archaeology of the Early Anglo-Saxon Kingdoms*, p. 24.

[68] See footnotes 88 and 89 below.

[69] See Austin, "The 'proper study' of Medieval Archaeology," p. 16, where he refers to Walter Goffart, *Barbarians and Romans AD 418–584: The Techniques of Accommodation* (Princeton, 1980). See also Edward James, "Burial and Status in the Early Medieval West," *Transactions of the Royal Historical Society*, 5th ser., 39 (1989): 25.

[70] Herwig Wolfram, *History of the Goths*, trans. Thomas J. Dunlap (Berkeley, 1988), pp. 7–8, and "*Origo et religio*: Ethnic Traditions and Literature in Early Medieval Texts," *Early Medieval Europe* 3 (1994): 21. See also Thomas Anderson, Jr., "Roman Military Colonies in Gaul, Salian Ethnogenesis, and the Forgotten Meaning of the *Pactus Legis Salicae*," *Early Medieval Europe* 9 (1995): 136, and Edward James, "The Origins of Barbarian Kingdoms: The Continental Evidence," in Bassett, *The Origins of Anglo-Saxon Kingdoms*, p. 48.

71 See Wolfram, *History of the Goths*, p. 8.

72 Amory, "Names, Ethnic Identity, and Community in Fifth- and Sixth-Century Burgundy," p. 5 (emphasis added).

73 G. E. M. de Ste Croix, *The Class Struggle in the Ancient Greek World: From the Archaic Age to the Arab Conquests* (Ithaca, N.Y., 1981), p. 481.

74 Amory, "Names, Ethnic Identity, and Community in Fifth- and Sixth-Century Burgundy," p. 5.

75 Amory, "Names, Ethnic Identity, and Community in Fifth- and Sixth-Century Burgundy," p. 22.

76 Amory, "Names, Ethnic Identity, and Community in Fifth- and Sixth-Century Burgundy," p. 19.

77 Procopius, *History of the Wars: Books VII (continued) and VIII*, trans. H. B. Dewing (Cambridge, Mass., 1928), VIII.20, records the Frisians as one of the peoples of Britain. For discussion, see E. A. Thompson, "Procopius on Brittia and Britannia," *Classical Quarterly* 30 (1980): 498–507, and Cameron, *Procopius and the Sixth Century*. See also Hines, "The Becoming of the English," p. 50, for the problems with using another comment by Bede (*HE* V.9) as a list of the Migration Period settlers of England.

78 Hines, "Philology, Archaeology, and the *adventus Saxonum vel Anglorum*," p. 29. See also his *The Scandinavian Character of Anglian England in the Pre-Viking Period* (Oxford, 1984) and "The Scandinavian Character of Anglian England: an Update."

79 Cited in Tom Williamson, *The Origins of Norfolk* (Manchester, Eng., 1993), p. 63; Nicholas Brooks (personal communication) reminds me of the rather dubious authority of the original source. For discussion, see W. Davies, "Annals and the Origin of Mercia," in *Mercian Studies*, ed. Ann Dornier (Leicester, 1977), pp. 17–29; Scull, "Before Sutton Hoo," p. 5; and Pauline Stafford, *The East Midlands in the Early Middle Ages* (Leicester, 1985), p. 81.

80 See Barbara Yorke, "Political and Ethnic Identity: A Case Study of Anglo-Saxon Practice," pp. 69–89, and Alex Woolf, "Community, Identity and Kingship in Early England," pp. 91–109, both in *Social Identity in Early Medieval Britain*, ed. William O. Frazer and Andrew Tyrell (London, 2000).

81 See Scull, "Before Sutton Hoo," p. 8. For a parallel situation in early historic Scotland, see Margaret Nieke and Holly Duncan, "Dalriada: The Establishment and Maintenance of an Early Historic Kingdom in Northern Britain," in Driscoll and Nieke, *Power and Politics in Early Medieval Britain and Ireland*, pp. 6–21.

82 See notes 84 and 85 below.

83 Higham, *Rome, Britain, and the Anglo-Saxons*, p. 123 (see also p. 226).

84 These ideas are discussed in detail by Lotte Hedeager, "Empire, Frontier and

Barbarian Hinterland: Rome and Northern Europe AD 1–400," in *Center and Periphery in the Ancient World*, ed. Michael J. Rowlands, Morgans Larsen, and Kristian Kristiansen (Cambridge, Eng., 1987), pp. 125–40, "Kingdoms, Ethnicity and Material Culture: Denmark in a European Perspective," in Carver, *The Age of Sutton Hoo*, pp. 281–82, and *Iron-Age Societies*. See also the papers in *The Archaeology of Gudme and Lundeborg*, ed. Poul Otto Nielsen, Klavs Randsborg and Henrik Thrane (Copenhagen, 1994), and Klavs Randshorg, "Beyond the Roman Empire: Archaeological Discoveries in Gudme on Funen, Denmark," *Oxford Journal of Archaeology* 9 (1990). Malcolm Todd, *The Early Germans* (Oxford, 1992), pp. 88–103, gives some idea of the range of Roman objects which passed into "Free Germany" and beyond.

[85] See Birger Storgaard, "The Arslev Grave and Connections Between Funen and the Continent at the End of the Later Roman Iron Age," pp. 160–68, and Charlotte Fabech, "Reading Society from Cultural Landscape: South Scandinavia Between Sacral and Political Power," p. 178, both in Nielsen, Randsborg, and Thrane, *The Archaeology of Gudme and Lundeborg*.

[86] This is against Higham's view in *Rome, Britain, and the Anglo-Saxons*, p. 226.

[87] See Sims-Williams, "The Settlement of England in Bede and the *Chronicle*," p. 39.

[88] Blair, *Anglo-Saxon Oxfordshire*, p. 7 (see also note 89 below).

[89] Tania Dickinson, *The Anglo-Saxon Burial Sites of the Upper Thames Region, and Their Bearing on The History of Wessex, c. AD 400–700* (Unpublished Oxford DPhil thesis, 1976), pp. 415–17 (emphasis added); cited in Blair, *Anglo-Saxon Oxfordshire*, p. 8. For the same phenomenon see also Arnold, *The Archaeology of the Early Anglo-Saxon Kingdoms*, pp. 23–30.

[90] See also Blair, *Anglo-Saxon Oxfordshire*, pp. 14–16.

[91] Reynolds, "What Do We Mean by 'Anglo-Saxon' and 'Anglo-Saxons'?" p. 400.

[92] See Jenkins, *Rethinking Ethnicity*, and Jones, *The Archaeology of Ethnicity*.

[93] Jenkins, *Rethinking Ethnicity*, p. 75 (emphasis added).

[94] Jenkins, *Rethinking Ethnicity*, pp. 10, 11.

[95] Jenkins, *Rethinking Ethnicity*, pp. 52–63, 71–72.

[96] Jenkins, *Rethinking Ethnicity*, p. 70.

[97] Jenkins, *Rethinking Ethnicity*, p. 10. See also Amory, "Names, Ethnic Identity, and Community in Fifth- and Sixth-Century Burgundy," pp. 4–5, and Jones, *The Archaeology of Ethnicity*, p. 128.

[98] See my "Method and Theory in Medieval Archaeology in the 1990s," *Archaeologia Medievale* 18 (1991): 7–42, and "Through the Looking Glass of Possibilities: Understanding the Middle Ages," in *Die Vielfalt der Dinge: Neue Wege zur Analyse Mittelalterlicher Sachkultur*, ed. Helmut Hundsbichler, Gerhard Jantz, and Thomas Kühtreiber (Vienna, 1998), pp. 85–116.

[99] Jenkins, *Rethinking Ethnicity*, p. 10.

[100] Jones, *The Archaeology of Ethnicity*, p. 120.

[101] Jones, *The Archaeology of Ethnicity*, p. 122.

[102] See Higham, *Rome, Britain, and the Anglo-Saxons*, pp. 2–15, and Sims-Williams, "The Settlement of England in Bede and the *Chronicle*," p. 2. See also Eric John, *Reassessing Anglo-Saxon England* (Manchester, Eng., 1996), pp. 7–8.

[103] Hines, "Philology, Archaeology, and the *adventus Saxonum vel Anglorum*," p. 27–28.

[104] Hills, "The Archaeology of Anglo-Saxon England in the Pagan Period," p. 313. See also Helen Geake, "Burial Practice in Seventh- and Eighth-Century England," in Carver, *The Age of Sutton Hoo*, p. 92, and Sims-Williams, "The Settlement of England in Bede and the *Chronicle*," p. 25. For a European perspective, see Ian Wood, "The European Science Foundation's Program on the Transformation of the Roman World and the Emergence of Early Medieval Europe," *Early Medieval Europe* 6 (1997): 224.

[105] See, among several others, P. Dixon, "How Saxon is a Saxon House?" in *Structural Reconstruction*, ed. P. J. Drury (Oxford, 1982), pp. 275–87, and Simon James, Anne Marshall, and Martin Millett, "An Early Medieval Building Tradition," *Archaeological Journal* 141 (1984): 182–215.

[106] Welch, *Anglo-Saxon England*, pp. 62–64.

[107] John Hines, "Cultural Change and Social Organization in Early Anglo-Saxon England," in *After Empire: Towards an Ethnology of Europe's Barbarians*, ed. Giorgio Ausenda (Woodbridge, Eng., 1995), p. 81.

[108] Hines, "Cultural Change and Social Organization in Early Anglo-Saxon England," p. 81.

[109] Scull, "Archaeology, Early Anglo-Saxon Society and the Origins of Anglo-Saxon Kingdoms," p. 71 (emphasis added). See also Hills, "The Archaeology of Anglo-Saxon England in the Pagan Period," p. 316.

[110] Hines, "Philology, Archaeology and the *adventus Saxonum vel Anglorum*," p. 23. See also Arnold, *The Archaeology of the Early Anglo-Saxon Kingdoms*, p. 192, and C. J. Arnold, *Roman Britain to Saxon England* (Bloomington, 1984), p. 103.

[111] Arnold, "The Anglo-Saxon Cemeteries of the Isle of Wight," p. 170.

[112] Arnold, "The Anglo-Saxon Cemeteries of the Isle of Wight," p. 167.

[113] Jenkins, *Rethinking Ethnicity*, p. 11.

[114] See note 23 above.

[115] *The Anglo-Saxon Chronicle*, trans. and ed. Dorothy Whitelock et al. (London, 1961), p. 13. See also C.J. Arnold, "Wealth and Social Structure: A Matter of Life and Death," in Rahtz, Dickinson, and Watts, *Anglo-Saxon Cemeteries*, p. 84, and Reynolds, "What Do We Mean by 'Anglo-Saxon' and 'Anglo-Saxons'?" p. 402.

[116] Patrick Geary, "Ethnic Identity as a Situational Construct in the Early Middle Ages," *Mitteilungen der Anthropologischen Gesellschaft in Wien* 113 (1983): 16. See also Amory, "Names, Ethnic Identity, and Community in Fifth- and Sixth-Century Burgundy," p. 29.

[117] See Arnold, *The Archaeology of the Early Anglo-Saxon Kingdoms*, p. 21.

[118] Geary, "Ethnic Identity as a Situational Construct in the Early Middle Ages," pp. 24–25. See also Jenkins, *Rethinking Ethnicity*.

[119] Geary, "Ethnic Identity as a Situational Construct in the Early Middle Ages," p. 21 nn. 26–28. See also Amory, "Names, Ethnic Identity, and Community in Fifth- and Sixth-Century Burgundy," p. 3.

[120] Geary, "Ethnic Identity as a Situational Construct in the Early Middle Ages," p. 22.

[121] Geary, "Ethnic Identity as a Situational Construct in the Early Middle Ages," pp. 22–24 (emphasis added).

[122] Wolfram, "*Origo et religio*: Ethnic Traditions and Literature in Early Medieval Texts," p. 21.

[123] Wolfram, *History of the Goths*, p. 7.

[124] Wolfram, *History of the Goths*, p. 11.

[125] Amory, "Names, Ethnic Identity, and Community in Fifth- and Sixth-Century Burgundy," pp. 4, 8.

[126] Amory, "Names, Ethnic Identity, and Community in Fifth- and Sixth-Century Burgundy," p. 3.

[127] Peter Heather, *The Goths* (Oxford, 1996), p. 301.

[128] Peter Heather, *The Goths*, p. 301.

[129] Amory, "Names, Ethnic Identity, and Community in Fifth- and Sixth-Century Burgundy," p. 4.

[130] Dumville, "Essex, Middle Anglia, and the Expansion of Mercia in the South-East Midlands," p 123. See also Sims-Williams, "The Settlement of England in Bede and in the *Chronicle*," pp. 1–41; Scull, "Archaeology, Early Anglo-Saxon Society and the Origins of Anglo-Saxon Kingdoms," pp. 65–66; Hodges, *The Anglo-Saxon Achievement*, pp. 22–23; and Barbara Yorke, *Kings and Kingdoms of Early Anglo-Saxon England* (1990; reprint London, 1997), pp. 1–4 and "The Jutes of Hampshire and Wight and the Origins of Wessex," pp. 84–88.

[131] Reynolds, "What Do We Mean by 'Anglo-Saxon' and 'Anglo-Saxons'?" p. 401.

[132] N. J. Higham, *An English Empire: Bede, the Britons, and the Early Anglo-Saxon Kings* (Manchester, Eng., 1995), pp. 218–19.

[133] Bede, *HE* IV.21.

[134] Bede, *HE* IV.22.

[135] Higham, *An English Empire*, pp. 225–26.

[136] Nicholas Howe, *Migration and Mythmaking in Anglo-Saxon England* (New Haven, 1989), p. 24.

[137] Higham, *An English Empire*, pp. 235–40.

[138] Higham, *An English Empire*, p. 255.

[139] Higham, *An English Empire*, p. 254 (emphasis added).

[140] See, for example, Sims-Williams, "The Settlement of England in Bede and in the *Chronicle*," p. 24.

[141] Hines, "Cultural Change and Social Organization in Early Anglo-Saxon England," p. 82 (emphasis added).

[142] See Blair, *Anglo-Saxon Oxfordshire*, p. 35, and Yorke, *Wessex in the Early Middle Ages*, pp. 40–43.

[143] Many of these differences are summarized in H. R. Loyn, *The Making of the English Nation: From the Anglo-Saxons to Edward I* (London, 1991), pp. 10–17. See also Welch, *Anglo-Saxon England*, p. 104.

[144] Susan Reynolds, *Fiefs and Vassals: The Medieval Evidence Reinterpreted* (Oxford, 1994), p. 325.

[145] See Hodges, *The Anglo-Saxon Achievement*, p. 38.

[146] See J. F. Shephard, "The Social Identity of the Individual in Isolated Barrows and Barrow Cemeteries in Anglo-Saxon England," in *Space, Hierarchy and Society: Interdisciplinary Studies in Social Area Analysis*, ed. Barry C. Burnham and John Kingsbury (Oxford, 1979), pp. 47–79, and Martin O. H. Carver, *Sutton Hoo: Burial Ground of Kings?* (Philadelphia, 1998).

[147] Hodges, *The Anglo-Saxon Achievement*, p. 34. See also Scull, "Archaeology, Early Anglo-Saxon Society and the Origins of Anglo-Saxon Kingdoms," p. 72; David Hinton, *Archaeology, Economy and Society: England from the Fifth to the Fifteenth Centuries* (London, 1990), p. 2; Yorke, *Wessex in the Early Middle Ages*, p. 22; and Leslie Alcock, *Cadbury Castle, Somerset: The Early Medieval Settlement* (Cardiff, 1995), p. 150.

[148] Helena Hamerow, "Settlement Mobility and the Middle-Saxon Shift: Rural Settlements and Settlement Patterns in Anglo-Saxon England," *Anglo-Saxon England* 20 (1991): 8–9, and *Excavations at Mucking, Volume 2: The Anglo-Saxon Settlement* (London, 1993), p. 89.

[149] See Hodges, *The Anglo-Saxon Achievement*, pp. 58–65; Scull, "Before Sutton Hoo," p. 21; and Hinton, *Archaeology, Economy and Society*, p. 27.

[150] Reynolds, "What Do We Mean by 'Anglo-Saxon' and 'Anglo-Saxons'?" pp. 402–03.

[151] This is against Higham, *An English Empire*, p. 254.

[152] Reynolds, "What Do We Mean by 'Anglo-Saxon' and 'Anglo-Saxons'?" p. 401.

[153] See Higham, *An English Empire*, pp. 225–26.

[154] Dumville, "Kingship, Genealogies and Regnal Lists," p. 73.

[155] Shennan, "Introduction: Archaeological Approaches to Cultural Identity," p. 15.

LANDSCAPES OF CONVERSION: GUTHLAC'S MOUND AND GRENDEL'S MERE AS EXPRESSIONS OF ANGLO-SAXON NATION BUILDING

ALFRED K. SIEWERS

Modern scholarship long believed that descriptions of nature in Anglo-Saxon literature tended to be more alienated and distanced in tone and theme than those in neighboring contemporary Insular literary cultures. This judgment was often extended to include differences in their treatment of pre-Christian ancestral traditions associated with natural landscapes. J. R. R. Tolkien in his foundational study of *Beowulf* defined this view most famously when he contrasted Anglo-Saxon lore with "less severe Celtic learning."[1] In a recent examination of the construction of nature in Old English poetry, Jennifer Neville notes more precisely:

> For the Old English poet, the representation of the natural world helps to create the context of helplessness and alienation that motivates the seeking of God. For the Irish poet, the representation of the natural world creates the context of wonder and joy that surrounds the seeking of God.[2]

In this she echoes Margaret Goldsmith's comparison a generation earlier of "creation songs" in early Irish and Old English verse:

> . . . the Irishman shows a typical interest in the small creatures, the birds and the fish, and the domestic creatures, fire and cattle, whereas the English poet sweeps his gaze across the whole earth and the firmament.[3]

From *Viator* 34 (2003): 1–39; reprinted with permission of Brepols Publishers. Some material in the endnotes has been augmented for clarity.

Despite such explication, the underlying consensus has gone relatively unexamined and unexplained since Tolkien's time. Suspicions about romanticized notions of ethnic temperament, doubts about the validity of definitive historical labeling of ethnic identity in Britain,[4] and greater awareness of the heterogeneity of early medieval Insular texts all have tended to shift the focus of discussion away from such issues of alleged cultural difference. At the same time, however, newer ecocritical approaches to texts, foregrounding the background of narrative while contexualizing its expression of cultural attitudes toward nature, now make it possible to acknowledge (and explain) in qualified terms this long-observed difference in emphasis.[5]

In applying ecocritical approaches to early Insular narratives, we can see a distinct (though far from monolithic) emphasis in Anglo-Saxon construction of literary landscape, one supporting the appropriation of nature for nation-building, which is based in the emerging Augustinian theology of western Europe. This ideological project involved a significantly different orientation toward natural landscape overall than was found in the neighboring early literatures of Wales and Ireland, where regional cultures were positioning themselves as native by constructing a more positive engagement with pre-Christian ancestral tradition and nature, amid a different ecclesiastical context.[6]

This study examines the most extensive extant Anglo-Saxon landscape narratives, the Old English poem *Beowulf* and the Anglo-Latin and Old English prose and poetic versions of the *Life* of St. Guthlac, from an ecocritical perspective. In these texts, the mere and monsters in *Beowulf*, and the fens and demons in the Guthlac tales can be seen as landscape narratives both of conquest and possession, and of the formation of cultural identity. They are contemporary literary equivalents of the construction of Offa's Dyke, defining a new cultural pattern of landscape on the island of Britain.[7] They also thus reflect the political and cultural situation of eighth-century Mercia, which as the dominant Anglo-Saxon kingdom was in desperate need of an ethnic identity, given the somewhat shadowy nature of Anglo-Saxon ethnicity in its domain. These landscapes of control also necessarily reflect the theological authority of the Augustinian outlook on nature that was especially pronounced for historical reasons in the Anglo-Saxon church.[8] Augustinian sign theory and views on theophany (related as they were to an emphasis on the fallen nature of the world and the centrality of grace) made it natural to see landscape in what was both a more objectified and allegorical way than was the case with neighboring literatures in Ireland

and Wales. Examination here of two landscape-related motifs in the Anglo-Saxon narratives, that of the battle for the haunted barrow and that of the heroic venture into otherworldly waters, will illustrate how the creative tension between Augustinian otherworldliness and secular nation-building produced a new cultural landscape in both polity and literature for emerging Anglo-Saxon elites. In addition, psychoanalytic critic Julia Kristeva's theory of abjection, as she relates it to medieval Western theology, will be used to help understand this process of cultural differentiation in terms of how constructions of nature relate to development of a new kind of performative subjectivity for cultures and people in the early medieval West.

Somewhat paradoxically, Augustinian theological emphases on the corruption of nature, extended to natural landscape and its ancestral associations with indigenous culture, empowered the Anglo-Saxon ideological project of superimposing a new cultural landscape on Britain's most fertile land areas, in narrative landscapes based on a sense of Anglo-Saxon culture as God-chosen and hegemonic that erased textually the presence of earlier inhabitants as thoroughly as Old English linguistically replaced Romano-Celtic languages in those areas. The presence of indigenous Romano-Celtic linguistic cultures that were Christianized long before those of the Anglo-Saxon realms, and which exerted a large continuing influence on the latter, was thus conveniently erased or subsumed.

In the emergence of this cultural Augustinianism, I will argue, we can see the roots of what W. J. T. Mitchell has called the Western imperial gaze, the objectification and possession of landscape through turning it into a distanced externality to be viewed in linear time as a kind of passing panorama reflecting only the concerns of human society.[9] This contrasts with the more iconographic approach to nature seen in the desert fathers and in Eastern Christian notions of divine energies that were developing in the early medieval period in the Byzantine cultural zone. These were paralleled in emphases of Celtic monasticism and related literary cultures, which were less directly influenced by the developing Augustinianism of the Western church seen in the Anglo-Saxon and Frankish realms.[10]

BEDE'S BRITAIN: TEXT AND LANDSCAPE

The focus in this reading of *Beowulf* and the Guthlacian *Lives* is upon a cultural image of the physical environment that mediates between the human mind and nature, which is what is meant here by the term "landscape."[11]

That word itself, however, entered into modern English from Dutch only as a technical term for visual art that sought to capture the natural environment as object of the human gaze. Yet an earlier cognate, *landscipe*, attested in one instance in the Anglo-Saxon *Genesis B* poem (and thus, because of the poem's origins, really an Old Saxon word), is defined by Bosworth and Toller as "a tract [or region] of land," thus conceptually related to notions of defining land for purposes of control.[12] In *Genesis B*, Satan says of hell, "ic a ne geseah laðran landscipe" ("I never have seen a more hostile landscape," lines 375–76).[13] This utterance could be taken as motto of the problems that the defining of landscape raised for the Anglo-Saxons' new literary culture after the papal mission of 597: How to relate their physical domains to their newly constructed culture as immigrant pagan conquerors who were also God's pilgrim Christian people in earthly exile? That question was answered by the Venerable Bede, at the twin monastic communities of Wearmouth-Jarrow in Northumbria, in his monumental *Historia Ecclesiastica Gentis Anglorum*, around 731.

Bede credited St. Augustine of Canterbury's mission, at the behest of Pope Gregory I, to convert the Anglo-Saxons from a base in Kent with introducing both Christianity and a Rome-centered ecclesiastical system to the Anglo-Saxon cultural zone. Not only was Anglo-Saxon culture then increasingly constructed (proudly) as of foreign extraction (of sturdy Germanic stock), by comparison with that of supposedly decadent native Celts to the north and west (in a motif set by the Romano-Celtic Gildas circa 500 but established in more ethnic terms by Bede),[14] but so too its church was described by Bede and other Anglo-Saxons as purely derived from Rome, in contrast with Celtic churches they saw as having schismatic or even heretical tendencies. In other words, the definition of Anglo-Saxon culture involved a certain distancing from non-Anglo-Saxon ancestral associations with the land in Britain, including native peoples and churches. In many ways, it was the very textualizing of the land of the Anglo-Saxons by Bede that made the Anglo-Saxon church and people a cultural entity. Whatever the real context and impact of the papal mission in 597, Bede made the coming of that mission foundational for the Anglo-Saxon people as a nation, and linked it by parallel structuring in his account to the coming of the Anglo-Saxons to Britain in fulfillment of a destiny as God's chosen people. As Colgrave and Mynors note, "he had one great aim":

> It was to tell the story of the development of God's plan for the conversion of the English people and the building up of one united Church in the land.

He began by painting a background, geographical and historical, picturing the British inhabitants as feeble in time of war and, though Christian in name, vicious in time of peace, easily falling into heresies; but, worst of all, refusing to co-operate in the conversion of the "heathen Saxons." Then he plunges straight into the story of the mission of St. Augustine [of Canterbury] and its arrival in England.[15]

The opening of Bede's history describes in impressively empirical terms, which are yet at times laconically idyllic, a seemingly objective unitary view of Britain as a land awaiting its fulfillment in the arrival of the Anglo-Saxons:

Opima frugibus atque arboribus insula, et alendis apta pecoribus ac iumentis . . . fluuiis quoque multum piscosis ac fontibus praeclara copiosis; et quidem praecipue issicio abundat ei anguilla.

The island is rich in crops and in trees, and has good pasturage for cattle and beasts of burden. . . . It is remarkable too for its rivers, which abound in fish, particularly salmon and eels, and for copious springs.[16]

In part his description is modeled on that of Gildas. However, while Bede's description of the island is longer and appears to be more factual, the realities of the coming of the Anglo-Saxons and the development of Christianity in Britain were in many respects far different from Bede's attempted reconstruction. If Bede's opening analysis of the islands is distinctively objective to modern readers by comparison with early medieval histories from the Irish and Welsh realms, his project is even more distinctive: Constructing a narrative unity of the Anglo-Saxon church and the pagan Anglo-Saxon invaders, Bede's history was itself a type of imposition of cultural landscape on Britain. The process by which his history created a monumental sense of English landscape, a cultural topography embodying the new identity of the Anglo-Saxons as a Christian pilgrim people,[17] is also reflected in the vernacular, ostensibly secular, narrative of *Beowulf*,[18] and in analogous elements of the *Lives* of the Anglo-Saxon St. Guthlac (probably written around the same period as the hero-epic, as argued below). Themes and issues related to landscape being expressed and worked out in these texts—historical, epic, and hagiographic—were similar in essence.

There were two primary and inter-related historical motivations in the constructed relation of Anglo-Saxon culture to its island: political, in terms of the formation of an Anglo-Saxon polity in what is now England; and religious, in terms of development of ideological and ecclesiastical structures that reflected the formative role in Anglo-Saxon culture of the papal mission in 597. Both were in important ways colonial projects. According to revisionist historical and archaeological interpretations in recent years, the Germanic migration to Britain in the preceding invasion era, circa 410–550, was surprisingly small in terms of numbers: roughly 15,000 by one estimate, not more than five percent of the population of the island.[19] Yet Bede in his early eighth-century Anglo-Latin *Historia*, following in part on the ambiguous religious polemic of Gildas circa 500,[20] described this migration two centuries earlier as in effect a series of mass invasions—a notion challenged by recent historians and archaeologists who see the process as involving considerably more complex cultural change.[21] Bede described these pioneering Germanic migrants themselves as an ethnically varied collection of Angles, Saxons, Jutes, Frisians, and Franks; and thus even within his own rather neat depiction there are discrepancies: Other peoples or at least cultural influences besides Anglo-Saxons appear somewhat ambiguously at the start of his account of the founding of the Anglo-Saxon realms, and the archaeological record includes suggestions of influence from Scandinavia, as well as the likelihood again of a largely continuous indigenous population. Anglo-Saxon elites by Bede's time apparently needed to articulate a simpler new cultural landscape to legitimize their expanding regional dynasties.

Here the ideology of the papal missions was also formative. Both Pope Gregory I's focus on the chief Latin father Augustine, and his mission to the Anglo-Saxons, were part of his larger policy "of looking towards the West, towards the Latin world with its new masters, rather than waiting resentfully and often uselessly for help and attention from the Eastern Emperor."[22] That double-barreled project of developing a replacement for Byzantium in the West with a focus on Latin (rather than Greek) patristics continued among many of his successors, culminating in the papal crowning of Charlemagne as emperor in 800. "Augustine's legacy inspired the [Carolingian] period's most fundamental attempts to define a Christian European culture."[23] Moreover, Augustine's downplaying of the role of nature in salvation, and his tendency to place it in an oppositional role with grace, paralleled an apparent desire of Western elites both to distance themselves from the fallen Roman Empire (represented in Britain by indigenous Romano-Celtic peoples and cultures) and to establish a new sense of authority on a spiritual basis that was legitimized by identification with the universal, imperial trappings of Rome as the papal seat.[24]

This new foundation for legitimacy in the West involved the authority of a literary formulation of nature or landscape. The fact that Anglo-Saxon culture was in some ways constructed by Bede and others as a *de novo* creation of the papal mission made it a center for this new ideology, even more so than the Frankish realms, which culturally negotiated establishment of a Westernized Christian culture with the Gallo-Roman remnant culture within their borders.[25] Anglo-Saxon cultural landscape was more hegemonic in original construction. As John Koch wrote: " . . . it is in political and intellectual developments of the seventh century [following the Gregorian mission] that we first see interests decisively polarize along English vs. non-English lines."[26]

Enabling this was the dichotomy of nature and grace that Augustinianism encouraged in the early medieval West, which involved the development of sign theory as a mediator between the two. The basis for this can be seen especially in Augustine's major works, *De Doctrines Christiana*, *De Trinitate*, and *De Civitate Dei*. Theophanies, such as appearances of God in the Old Testament or of the Holy Spirit as a dove in the New, were explained as temporal events, one-time miraculous physical creations that subsequently vanished.[27] Augustine's difficulty in articulating the relationship between nature and grace, and his emphasis on a solely relational role of the Holy Spirit to the other members of the Trinity (in effect subordinating the Spirit to the Son), encouraged a view of signs (including divine manifestations) as not having meaning in themselves, while at the same time paradoxically being objectified by their associations with the physical world.[28] His discussion of the connection between time and grammar also encouraged a systematic distinction of both symbols and creation from the divine,[29] an issue with origins in the pre-Christian Greek philosophy and classical Latin rhetoric that Augustine had studied as a youth. It was in this somewhat autonomous emerging symbolic realm of thought that Western approaches to landscape were forged in Anglo-Saxon and Carolingian courts. In the textualizing, and resulting distancing, of the natural and the spiritual, Augustine's writings helped shape the theme of environmental utilitarianism so important in Western culture,[30] which emerged early in Anglo-Saxon literature for reasons of political ideology.[31]

MERCIA: TEXTUALIZING A LANDSCAPE

The cultural identity of Anglo-Saxon Mercia as a kingdom and as a people was still a work in progress in the eighth century when the *Lives* of Guthlac

were composed under Mercian political hegemony, and this has impor-
tant implications for the literary landscapes associated with it and their re-
lated religious ideology. David Dumville notes that "Mercia seems to have
been by a substantial margin the latest of the major kingdoms [described
in Bede's history of the Anglo-Saxon realms] to come together as a single
unit." The fact that "the political unit came together relatively late may even
help to explain why we have no annals or chronicle for the Midlands. At the
time when such a record might first have been created, there was no sin-
gle Midland unit or dynasty to give coherence or focus."[32] While Nicholas
Higham argues that circumstantial evidence points to continuity of a politi-
cal entity in the Midlands from sub-Roman times,[33] even so Mercia would
have marked the last major area of Anglo-Saxon culture to establish its
identity as such. Its name derived from an Old English word (*myrce*) for
border-land. Under Offa in the late eighth century, it built the dyke that
physically defined the boundary between Anglo-Saxon and Welsh cultures.
It was the last of the major Anglo-Saxon polities to allegedly sport a pagan
king (Penda). Under Offa it also lobbied successfully for its own distinct
ecclesiastical jurisdiction. There are also indications, described below, of a
continuity of identifiable Celtic polities or populations relatively late in the
Midlands region that constituted Mercia, some of them possibly included
in the patchwork of Midlands sub-kingdom lists in the Tribal Hidage. It
was, in short, in many ways the ultimate Anglo-Saxon kingdom *ex nihilo*,
with a recently constructed Germanic and Christian cultural and politi-
cal identity, and forming in its domination of Southumbria the geopolitical
center of what would become modern England. Establishing the identity
of the Mercian land would be an important project of literary narrative in
the realm's passage from borderland to heartland, especially given the links
between Anglo-Saxon elite political circles and monastic establishments
producing literary works, as described by Patrick Wormald.[34]

Felix's Latin *Vita Sancti Guthlaci*, written circa 721–749, is dedicated to
the East Anglian King Ælfwald and favorably depicts the region's contem-
porary Mercian over-king Æthelbald. Felix recounts the life of the warrior
scion of a Mercian noble family who ends up living in the wilds of Middle
Anglia as a Christian holy man. There are a number of landscape-related
analogues between this earliest *vita* of Guthlac and *Beowulf*, which are often
cited in arguments that the latter was also of eighth-century Mercian prov-
enance.[35] In each of these texts, a monumental mound has a climactic role
in marking territory with memory for newcomers, in contrast to the prior
presence of native-dwellers. Fiends attacking Guthlac's mound include

Welsh-speaking spirits, apparently ghosts of the region's indigenous people associated in Felix's text with contemporary Welsh-Mercian battles. They, like the monstrous inhabitants of the mere in *Beowulf*, are labeled by Felix as "sons of Cain." Sam Newton catalogued specific analogues that involve fiendish figures associated with the natural landscape:

> Felix's depiction of Guthlac's demonic opponents shows notable similarities in some respects to the depiction of Grendel and his mother in *Beowulf*. In both works, the heroes exorcise specific places haunted by fen-dwelling demons who are angered initially by a particular type of song. Grendel, who is *eald-gewinna*, "the old enemy" (line 1776a), and *feond moncynnes*, "the enemy of mankind" (line 164b), begins the haunting of the newly-built hall of Heorot after he hears there the sound of the song of Creation (lines 86–101). Similarly, Felix refers to the *antiquus hostis prolis humanae*, "ancient foe of the human race," beginning to trouble Guthlac as he sings psalms and hymns at his newly-built hermitage in a burial-mound on the island of Crowland (chap. 29). Furthermore, the fiends who subsequently attack Guthlac are addressed by the saint as the "seed of Cain" (chap. 31). This reference to fiends as descendants of Cain does not appear in any of the later Old English poetic versions of *Vita Sancti Guthlaci* and yet exactly the same monstrous pedigree is attributed to Grendel and his kind in *Beowulf* (lines 102–114, 1261b–1265a).[36]

The several *Lives* of Guthlac provide a spectrum from literal to more allegorical style in descriptions of the landscape, from the relatively circumstantial Latin account of Felix to the Old English prose version and homily fragment that follow it fairly closely with respect to landscape issues (except as noted below), to the poetic versions A and B, the latter especially evidencing an allegorical emphasis as will be discussed soon.[37] The exact dates and sequences of these texts are not known, however, although the provenance of the Latin version is fairly well established by clues within the text. Writing at a time when, judging by Bede's comments about the British church, ecclesiastical tempers still ran high over perceived Celtic heterodoxy on tonsures and especially the dating of Easter (the Welsh were not in compliance with Rome on that jurisdictionally defining issue until 768), Felix took a stance that, to use Koch's phraseology, decidedly defined himself as "English vs. non-English,"[38] and created an Anglo-Saxon landscape to match. Felix takes care to describe how Guthlac had a Petrine tonsure and later quotes a report of "pseudo-anchoritae" among the Irish (chapters 20 and 46).[39] In addition, he refers in chapter 34 to an attack on Guthlac at the barrow by Welsh-speaking spirits at a time when the Britons, "infesti hostes Saxonici generis," were attacking and pillaging (presumably the Mercian Midlands) during the reign of Coenred of the Mercians. Felix apparently forgot in his heated labeling of them as "implacable enemies of the Saxon race" (Colgrave's translation) that in the days of Coenred's grandfather Penda's hegemony, the Britons had been key allies of developing Mercia.[40] In fact, Penda's alliances with Welsh Christian rulers and his apparent willingness to allow his children to be baptized, together with Bede's general neglect of the presence of the British church,[41] raise the question of whether his alleged paganism itself may have been a smear by later Anglo-Saxon writers due to his association with British Christianity.

At any rate, it is possible that negative attitudes toward the Welsh and Irish in Felix's narrative reflect concerns about Anglo-Saxon national identity among the Mercians related not only to the kingdom's position on the border with Wales, but also to the presence of British populations in Mercia, and the relatively short time in which the realm had been Germanic in character. Early twentieth-century scholars such as the Celticist John Rhys first raised the possibility that, given the cultural milieu of seventh-century Mercia, Guthlac himself (as well as the Mercian royal line of which he was a distant relation) could have been descended from native British populations.[42] Felix gives Guthlac's father's name as Penwall, or Penwalh, a name seeming to have components of the Welsh *pen* (meaning "head" or "chief") plus an ending that could be related to Anglo-Saxon words for native inhabitants that evolved into the word Welsh, meaning originally "alien" or "stranger."[43] Sims-Williams recently suggested that "some British alliance or intermarriage may be implied" by the elements of the name.[44]

The apparent continuation of a Roman-British name for the kingdom of Lindsey (Lincolnshire), along with archaeological evidence for post-Roman survival of a British population in the Lincoln area and a British name in the genealogy of the kings of Lindsey,[45] are all indications of a lingering presence of indigenous culture in the regions neighboring the Mercian-dominated fenlands of Middle and East Anglia. Such indications are also in line with evidence cited by Hope-Taylor, and by Koch, that parts of what became the kingdom of Northumbria were British polities taken over wholesale by Anglo-Saxon warriors, with populations relatively intact, and Higham's theory of possible post-Roman political continuity in the Midlands.[46] Such continuity underlines the constructed nature of Anglo-Saxon (and especially Anglian Mercian) ethnicity (and hence landscape) in this period.[47]

The emergence of the Anglo-Saxon over-kingships described by Bede, however, together with the accompanying ecclesiastical consolidation advanced by Archbishop Theodore in the late seventh century,[48] seem to have led to the more differentiated ethnic consciousness found in Bede's *History*, written circa 731, and in Felix's *Vita*. There is no specific archaeological or place-name evidence indicating the survival of a distinct native British population within the Fens as Arthur Gray and others suggest Felix's account indicates. Yet, as Dumville notes, the Middle Anglians were not cited as a single people in the Tribal Hidage, and seem to have been a "creation by the Mercians in the mid-seventh century of a convenient unit representing an agglomeration of formerly independent peoples of varying sizes and relative importance."[49] Among the neighbors of this "agglomeration," to their north lay Lindsey, again a polity of probable Celtic provenance, and to the southwest, the Hwicce, also potentially Celtic in origin. Guthlac himself is described by Felix as having been an exile among the Britons for a time (chap. 34).

Such issues of ethnicity are relevant to descriptions of the Fens in Felix as a last refuge for the demonic spirits he associates with the Britons, as well as to the description of the landscape of the Fens themselves. In chapter 24, we are told in Virgilian terms:

> Est in meditullaneis Brittanniae partibus immensae magnitudinis aterrima palus . . . nunc stagnis, nunc flactris, interdum nigris fusi vaporis laticibus, necnon et crebris insularum nemorumque intervenientibus flexuosis rivigarum anfractibus, ab austro in aquilonem mare tenus longissimo tractu protenditur.

> There is in the midland district of Britain a most dismal fen of immense size [that] stretches from the south as far north as the sea. . . . a very long tract, now consisting of marshes, now of bogs, sometimes of black waters overhung by fog, sometimes studded with wooded islands and traversed by the windings of tortuous streams.[50]

Then we are told (chap. 25) that Guthlac finds his way with help from a guide who

> scisse aliam insulam in abditis remotioris heremi partibus confitebatur, quam multi inhabitare temtantes propter incognita heremi monstra et diversarum formarum terrores reprobaverant.

declared that he knew a certain island in the more remote and hidden parts of that desert; many had attempted to dwell there, but had rejected it on account of the unknown portents of the desert and its terrors of various shapes.[51]

Guthlac travels (still chap. 25) in a fisherman's skiff with his guide (an image at once a bit reminiscent of classical journeys to Hades, Odinic-guide appearances in Norse literature, and, probably most relevantly here, Andreas's heavenly/disguised boat guide in that saint's Old English hagio-graphical poem),

> per invia lustra inter atrae paludis margines Christo viatore ad praedictum locum usque pervenit; Crugland dicitur, insula media in palude posita quae ante paucis propter remotioris heremi solitudinem inculta vix nota habe-batur. Nullus hanc ante famulum Christi Guthlacum solus habitare colonus valebat, propter videlicet illic demorantium fantasias demonum, in qua vir Dei Guthlac, contempto hoste, caelesti auxilio adiutus, inter umbrosa soli-tudinis nemora solus habitare coepit.

> traveling with Christ, through trackless bogs within the confines of the dis-mal marsh till he came to the said spot; it is called Crowland, an island in the middle of the marsh which on account of the wildness of this very remote desert had hitherto remained untilled and known to a very few. No settler had been able to dwell alone in this place before Guthlac the servant of Christ, on account of the phantoms of demons which haunted it. Here Guthlac, the man of God, despising the enemy, began by divine aid to dwell alone among the shady groves of this solitude.[52]

In *Guthlac A*, we are told that the demonic residents of the barrow-island came there weary to rest for a while, enjoying the temporary quiet granted to them in that wild place (lines 205–16a). While that has explicit parallels to the plight of devils exiled by God (and, as will be discussed later, to that of the Irish Tuatha Dé Danann), the sinister description of the Fens and its inhabitants also bears comparison to the foreboding landscape described by early Pilgrims arriving in New England (i.e., William Bradford's journal). The latter, like the account of Guthlac, recounts "alien" landscape. In fact, one of the ways in which the spirits try to terrorize Guthlac is by telling him that there won't be anyone to feed him in the middle of a bog (line 274), sounding much like the view of wetlands taken by Euro-Americans until recently. The view of the Fens is much how one imagines the perspective of a culture constructing itself as both dominant and imposed, viewing a "backward" indigenous people living in an ecosystem that is not compatible with the emerging polity's imposition of order, and thus not well understood.[53]

Indeed, contrary to a sense of these wetlands as a primeval wilderness, there are archaeological traces in part of the Fens of drainage and dense settlement in Romano-British times.[54] The notion that wetlands could easily have been a place of refuge for indigenous people in early medieval Britain is also suggested later in the purportedly ninth-century biography of Alfred by the Welsh cleric Asser, which tells of Alfred's own exile from the Vikings at a site in the Athelney Marshes of the West Country, described as "surrounded by swampy, impassable and extensive marshland and groundwater on every side," where Alfred later endowed a monastery,[55] and also perhaps by the Old English poem *The Wife's Lament*.[56] Furthermore, the central temptation of Guthlac by the spirits of the place in *Guthlac A* is to tell him that he needs to return to his own people, his own community (line 291).

The central historical conflict that can be seen as roiling the landscape of the different Guthlacian narratives relates to the tension between that new ecclesiastical-political order of the Anglo-Saxons and oppositionally framed indigenous ancestral connotations of the land.[57] In this context, Guthlac's exorcism of the Fens parallels readings of Beowulf's foray into the Grendelcyn's mere as the exorcism of an earlier indigenous culture.[58] Certainly the harsh description of the Grendelcyn mere in *Beowulf* seems to bear comparison to Felix's description of the Fens, and the inhabitants of the mere to Celtic-speaking demons of the fenlands. (Other analogues again, cited by Newton, include the way in which "the heroes exorcise specific places haunted by fen-dwelling demons who are angered initially by a particular type of song" that is biblically related, and how foes are described as descendants of Cain,[59] like the Tuatha Dé Danann of Irish legend stuck between heaven and hell, inhabiting haunted mounds.)

The descriptions of the saint's early home as a barrow in a grove in the Fens in *Guthlac A* (line 429), as a mysterious and inhospitable island grove with a barrow in Felix, and as an island in *Guthlac B* (line 507), are all reminiscent of Insular traditions of sacred islands that parallel pre-Christian Germanic tradition. However, in the Guthlac and *Beowulf* narratives (the latter included if considering the mere cave as a type of otherworldly island), this native cultural landscape is described in hostile, alien terms.[60] Comparing Celtic and Anglo-Saxon poetic approaches to the natural world, Neville notes of the Old English poems on Guthlac:

When the demons come to see *hwæðre him þæs wonges wyn sweðrade*, "whether the joy of that place had dwindled for him" after their assaults, they find that *wæs him botles neod*, "his home was a pleasure to him," rather like the forests and coastlands that often inspired Irish poets. If Guthlac had been commemorated by an Irish poet, it appears likely that the poem would have contained the kind of detailed praise of birds and plants expressed in "Manchán's Wish." *Guthlac*, however, contains almost no description of the land, water, vegetation and animal life that help to make the saint's home so pleasant for him. Old English poets appear not to have been inspired to use the representation of the natural world in the same way as Irish poets, even when describing similar circumstances of comfort and joy. Instead, Old English poets reserve the representation of the natural world for use as a force to oppose and test their saints' resolve and powers of resistance.[61]

It is not as if pre-Christian Germanic traditions did not contain their own pleasant associations with sacred natural areas.[62] But the response of Anglo-Saxon Christian literary culture to such traditions differs greatly in its representation of landscape from Welsh and Irish literary practices. While all the Insular cultures in this period were undergoing to a degree the process of political centralization, the difference for Anglo-Saxon culture, relating directly to construction of landscape, lay again in the latter's need to form a new unified ethnic identity that was also ecclesiastical in nature. Significantly, Felix's account begins by citing Gregory I on the uses and limitations of words, a reminder of the key influence of Augustinian semiotics and cosmology both on the Anglo-Saxon literary world.[63]

Traveling through landscape is traveling through ancestry, and the shadowy ethnic context for Felix's *Vita* is backdrop to the central place of the barrow. Judging by early medieval Irish and Welsh literature, mounds were entry points to the indigenous Otherworld that were also identified with earlier inhabitants of the landscape and with control of the cultural landscape of imagination. Irish legends associate mounds such as the Neolithic Newgrange in the Boyne Valley with earlier inhabitants of the island.[64] In the Welsh *Mabinogi* is found the Mound of Arberth (modern-day Narberth, a name meaning "by the oaks," perhaps originally a reference to a sacred grove), another apparent portal into the Otherworld, where for example Manawydan and friends see the placing of a curse on the landscape, and whence the curse is later lifted.[65]

The Anglo-Saxons, too, seem to have had traditions associating mounds with a mythic Otherworld, although apart from later Old Icelandic descriptions of the World Tree and connecting worlds, we don't have any narratives indicating their pre-Christian cosmology.[66] Yet a pattern of political meaning attached to mounds stretches back apparently to include both pre-*adventus* and Anglo-Saxon examples.[67] John Shephard found that the location of isolated Anglo-Saxon barrows indicated "the burial of an individual, or small group of individuals who were members of a superordinate social rank, the status position being ascribed rather than achieved."[68] The development of such barrows in otherwise flat-grave cemeteries with Germanic-style accoutrements began amid the pagan Anglo-Saxon culture of the mid-sixth century and is described by Shephard as "a means of establishing the social system through the evolution of hierarchic regulators."

In this prehistoric coding of landscape monuments, which in a sense is appropriated and transformed by the Guthlac texts, an isolated barrow such as Guthlac's was a sign that resources were being claimed by a particular heir or family. Shephard relates a pattern of such barrows to development of a strongly centralized manorial system in the medieval Midlands,[69] as contrasted with the *gavelkind*[70] landholding system in Kent where barrows were more commonly grouped in cemeteries. This regional difference is probably another sign of the relative late development of a unified Anglo-Saxon identity for the Mercian polity, as compared with the kingdom of Kent, which with its close ties to the Frankish monarchy was the host of the original Augustinian mission (and whose name probably is of Romano-Celtic origin, indicating a relatively early transition to Anglo-Saxon rule). In any case, scholarship on Anglo-Saxon boundary charters also suggests the use of mounds from various eras as property markers: The *Codex Diplomaticus* includes the description of 150 barrows along the edge of an estate, for example.[71]

While pagan Anglo-Saxons may have derived their limited barrow-building habit from earlier prehistoric examples in the British landscape,[72] the construction of the earliest barrows has in turn been related to an agrarian cultural reorientation of the British landscape:

> The ancestral powers and meanings in the landscape now became actively *appropriated* by individuals and groups through the construction and use of chambered tombs, long cairns and long barrows. . . . Ancestral powers now became double. The tombs presenced and marked out the bones of the ancestral dead in the landscape. In so doing they visibly brought the presence of the ancestral past to consciousness. Their specific morphological characteristics and their landscape settings also served to relate the bones

of previous generations to a more generalized ancestral power embodied in the topography and symbolic geography of place and paths of movements which had already been constructed in the Mesolithic. The location of important points in the external world became captured in the orientation of morphological features of the monuments and their placement in the landscape. Their settings were deliberately chosen to fix a certain vantage point in relation to perception of the world beyond. During the Mesolithic the significance of place was understood in terms of its setting in the landscape. In the Neolithic this was reversed—the landscape was now understood in terms of its relation to the setting of the monuments.[73]

By the eighth century, however, the monuments were being understood in terms of their relation to written texts such as the *vitae* of Guthlac and *Beowulf*. Ancestral powers were in a sense trebled, to extend Christopher Tilley's figure of speech. Earlier they had been extended by the creation of physical monuments with functions as regional landscape markers. Now, in written texts, they were related to a more transcendental system of religion and statehood than that which had been possible in non-literate society, and thus strengthened into a new sense of ethnic identity. There are analogies to the earlier process of conversion described by Barbara Rosenwein in Gaul: "In the ancient world the countryside had been, as people of the time understood it, populated by deities. These were transformed into demons in the early Christian period. But by the end of the sixth century, the countryside had become sacred once again, purged by the presence of dispersed and carefully housed relics of saints."[74] A significant difference between the process in Mercia and in Gaul, suggested by the treatment of landscape in the Guthlac narratives as well as historical and archaeological evidence, is that this process had already occurred much earlier in Britain, only to be layered over by another pattern of Christianization of the landscape. When the Anglo-Saxon establishment of culture occurred, it was done through a centralized organizational vehicle (the papal mission, its Augustinian doctrine, and its royal connections) and in sharp opposition to the already indigenous Christian culture, rather than the complex engagement of Gallo-Romans and Franks in post-Roman Gaul.

Read as part of an examination of the role of the hagiographic genre and its conventions in the textual process of formulating an Anglo-Saxon land and identity in the borderlands of Mercia, early medieval narratives of saints from other Insular cultures—together with the archetypal Life of the Egyptian desert father St. Antony—often present a different approach to landscape than that presented in the Guthlacian tradition. Felix's Anglo-Latin account of Guthlac's life has analogues in both Athanasius's account of Antony's life, which includes the saint's battling with demons in a tomb, and in St. Jerome's description of a hermitage built over a cistern in a shady grove.[75] This, however, makes the differences from Athanasius's descriptions of landscape relative to St. Antony only more striking. In the Egyptian Thebaid, we are told:

> The monasteries in the hills were like tents filled with heavenly choirs, singing, studying, fasting, praying, rejoicing for the hope of the life to come, laboring in order to give alms, having love and harmony among themselves. And in truth it was like a land of religion and justice to see, a land apart. For neither wronger nor wronged was there; nor plaint of tax-gathering; but a multitude of ascetics, all with one purpose to virtue; so that, looking back on the monasteries and on so fair an array of monks, one cried aloud saying (Num. 24.5): *How lovely are thy dwellings, O Jacob, thy tents O Israel; like shady groves, and like a garden by a river, and like tents that the Lord hath pitched, and like cedars beside the waters.*[76]

And when Antony goes to the inner desert to escape the crowds, we are told:

> Antony, as though moved by God, fell in love with the place; for this was the place indicated by the voice that spoke to him at the river-bank. At the beginning he got bread from his fellow-travelers and abode alone on the hill, none other being with him; for he kept the place from then on as one who has found again his own home. The Saracens themselves, who had seen Antony's earnestness, used to travel by that way on purpose and were glad to bring him bread . . . .[77]

Aided by those people of the desert, Antony when in the tomb fights demons that are identified as aerial by nature, not associated with the land. The love he expresses for the land and the successful human community described as part of it during his life stand in contrast to Felix's account of the ex-warrior Guthlac, for whom the landscape comes to bloom after his fight against the demons with their Welsh associations, but is not finally transformed until after his death, when no human community is described there. Guthlac goes to heaven, and the barrow is virtually an empty tomb, a literary cenotaph.

Guthlac's reported background as a plunderer-warrior, in an Anglo-Saxon culture whose most distinctive qualities of historical identification before its conversion had been military, and his Christian war against the demons, relates in martial spirit to the Christian warrior themes in Willibald's late eighth-century Anglo-Latin life of St. Boniface, in which a climactic moment comes when Boniface destroys a giant oak identified with pagan worship.[78] Contrast such Anglo-Saxon hagiographic taking-possession of the landscape with Muirchú's late seventh-century Hiberno-Latin account of St. Patrick, in which the Irish saint obtains possession of the hill at Armagh for a Christian city after the miraculous death of a domesticated horse, followed by Patrick's saving the life of a wild fawn that shows where a church altar would be located (the horse belonged to a villainous lord who would not cede the hill because he kept his prized horse there). Patrick and company ascended the hill after it was given them to survey the land,

> and found there a deer with its little fawn lying in the place where now the altar is. . . . Patrick's companions wanted to catch and kill the fawn, but the saint did not want this to happen and would not permit it. Instead, the saint himself took hold of the fawn and carried it in his arms and the deer followed him like a loving lamb until he set the fawn free in another valley on the northern side of Armagh. There even today, as those who know about these things relate, some signs of his power still remain.[79]

One more example is especially relevant to Guthlac, both because of its apparent influence on Felix's writing and also because it is by an author who was instrumental in developing Anglo-Saxon historical identity in the early eighth century: Bede's life of St. Cuthbert. Catherine Cubitt writes of the narrative's "strongly ideological character" that transformed the seventh-century Cuthbert "from a figure whose sanctity was rooted in Irish practices to one whose *vita* could be used as a vehicle for Romanizing propaganda."[80] Part of this transformation involves a dramatic change in the use of topography and landscape as compared with an earlier anonymous *vita* of the saint by a monk at the Celtic foundation at Lindisfarne. In the earlier work, described by Cubitt as "snapshot" in its relatively non-linear narrative style, incidents "are often very precisely located, naming the villages and regions in which miracles happen."[81] Bede's account uses a framework of a "coherent narrative" with "explanation, causation and context," but omits "virtually all of the geographical material" found in the earlier work.[82] It creates a totalizing narrative overlay.

Cubitt places the context of such Anglo-Saxon hagiography in a line with the didactic approach of its spiritual father, Gregory I, in his famous *Dialogues*. Gregory's allegorization of nature in works such as his commentary on Job was an important influence on Anglo-Saxon literature. It used Augustinian ideas but went further. In an era when Christianity did not face the intellectual challenges of Augustine's time in both late antiquity and the period of the fall of Rome, Gregory did not seem to engage all the theoretical nuances and qualifications found in the writings of his spiritual mentor. Before pursuing analysis of landscape motifs in texts from the Gregorian-influenced Anglo-Saxon literary culture, it is worth considering R. A. Markus's summation of Gregory's allegorizing approach to physical creation:

> Gregory used the Pauline verse "The letter killeth but the Spirit giveth life" (2 Cor. 3.6) only to justify the exegetical freedom to interpret texts allegorically. Augustine, though he had also understood it in this sense, came in later life to be more reserved both about allegory and the use of the verse to justify it. That reserve is altogether alien to Gregory. Much more than Augustine, Gregory is ready to jump from the letter to its spiritual meaning; and equally he is much more ready to make the leap from the material universe to its Maker. Commenting on the verse "Who does not know the hand of the Lord has done this?" (Job 12.9), Gregory wrote: " . . . all proclaim God to be the creator of all. . . . This may also be understood literally [*iuxta solam speciem litterae*]: for each creature when looked at gives as it were its own testimony, [by means of] the very form it has [*ipsam quam habet speciem suam*]. Cattle, birds, the earth or fish, if we ask them while we look, reply with one voice that the Lord made everything. While they imprint their form [*species*] on our senses they proclaim that they are not from themselves. By the very fact that they are created, they proclaim by the form they manifest [*per ostensam speciem*] their creator: [this is] as it were the voice of their confession . . . ." (*Moralia* xi.4.6)

A famous passage of Augustine's *Confessions* is so like Gregory's that it is hard to imagine that Gregory did not have it at the back of his mind: "I asked the sea, the deeps, the living creatures that creep, and they responded: 'We are not your God, look beyond us.' . . . And with a great voice they cried out: 'He made us' (Ps. 99.3). My question was the attention I gave to them, and their response was their *species*" (*Confessions* x.6.9, trans. Chadwick). A comparison, however, quickly reveals a characteristic contrast between the two writers. Augustine immediately catches himself: " . . . the created order speaks to all, but is understood by those who hear its outward voice and compare it with the truth within themselves."

This is something that is altogether missing in Gregory. He does not doubt that it will indeed be evident to all that creatures point to the Creator: for him they are transparent without any need to question and to judge the creatures' response.[83]

Such an approach of allegorization of the physical world commended itself to nascent Christian Anglo-Saxon realms like Mercia on grounds of both ecclesiastical genealogy (traced back by Bede and others to Gregory) and the political necessity of defining a sovereign identity for the state. The basic problem of Mercia and the West at large, in terms of development of a Christian landscape, was threefold: lack of a unifying Christian empire, of historic biblical holy places, and in the Anglo-Saxon realms (among others) the lack of prominent and long-lived ascetic traditions associated with place, such as the Egyptian Thebaid of the desert fathers or the islands of Irish monks.[84] There was also the influence of Augustinian semiotics, in which "the reader" became the dominant model of the "reflective self."[85] The resulting Anglo-Saxon textualized sense of space was oriented not around ancestral monuments and traditions of an Otherworld encompassing nature and the human world both,[86] but around a politically controlled literacy whose linearity cut through native ancestral space with the point of a pen. It is a pattern of cultural seizure of Insular landscape that involves not so much demolition of the indigenous Otherworld that once encompassed it, as a taking possession of that Otherworld in the name of consolidating royal and ecclesiastical power. In this, the process of monumentalizing landscape through text is in line with Pope Gregory I's instructions to his English mission, to ritually cleanse and then re-use pagan sites as needed to convert the English, "not accommodation, but . . . appropriation . . . an effort to claim existing pagan sacred sites for Christianity."[87] In Britain, it could also be an effort to claim indigenous Christian sites for papal Christianity, as in the case of conducting worship in Kent at the site of an old Romano-British church.

The on-the-ground hegemonic effect of Anglo-Saxon appropriation of the landscape is suggested by Stancliffe's interpretation of Gregory's attitude toward the British cult of St. Sixtus. Relics of the Roman St. Sixtus were sent at Augustine of Canterbury's request to discourage the native cult, but were to be enshrined in a different place than that of the British Sixtus's tomb, which was then to be closed to prevent people from venerating "uncertain" remains.[88] Yet perhaps the most potent indicator of the nature of Anglo-Saxon landscape is the dearth, relative to early Irish and Welsh texts, of detailed descriptions of the natural world and its features in extant Old English and Anglo-Latin writings. Cultural topography of emerging Angleland was to be found in texts of Christian Anglo-Saxon culture, in allegorized form. The new literary monumentalizing was ultimately totalizing in intent, seeking as it did to control the narrative of land, ancestry, and identity through written text in which engagement with the physical land became increasingly symbolic and relative to a more transcendent spiritual cosmos and polity.

THE HAUNTED BARROW

The thematic motif of the battle for the haunted barrow in the Guthlac narratives and *Beowulf* can be taken as a metaphor of the Anglo-Saxon literary construction of the landscape of Britain. It is, as noted, an application of a Gregorian papal lesson to the landscape, an appropriation of ancestry. And it is a conquest that takes place in a literate symbolic realm. It is further argued below that the *Guthlac B* poem's discussion of the soul and body represents an extension of the haunted barrow into a more directly Christian allegorical realm, a metaphor for Augustinian church ideology as well.

The image of the haunted barrow itself, specifically the dragon and his hoard found in *Beowulf*, but with analogues in the treasure-raided and demon-infested barrow described by Felix,[89] relates to folkloric associations of barrows with ancestors or earlier (and now supernatural) inhabitants of the land.[90] In Old English poetry, burial mounds with treasure were described as dragon hills.[91] H.R. Ellis Davidson cites Norse analogues in suggesting that the description in *Beowulf* that the dragon had lain in the mound 300 years before a thief arrived "is a rationalization of the idea (which would be repugnant to a Christian audience) that the dead man himself became a dragon."[92] In any case, we do know that there were direct connections in both Celtic and Germanic tradition between standing on a mound, in effect possessing it symbolically, and taking possession of (or alternately, uniting with) the landscape.[93] In the Welsh story of *Pwyll*, the male ruler of the land ascends the mound and thus finds the goddess of the land with whom he mates, a necessity for the fertility of the land also in Irish tradition. Likewise in Norse sagas, a king dispensing justice or claiming his royal inheritance might do so sitting on a burial mound, and in early medieval Wales there are recorded instances of a king granting land to a church while within or on the tomb of a former king.[94]

In the Anglo-Saxon realms, "tumuli were often used, and continued to be used until well on into Christian times, as meeting places for political assemblies and for transacting the business of the Anglo-Saxon hundreds," and thus had ritual associations, and even remained in rural areas "potential locations for the continuation or revival of forbidden pagan practices."[95] Davidson makes the case that Guthlac is assuming the ancestral powers of the mound, whose infesting spirits she describes as reflecting "the pagan tradition of the dead in the grave-mound, and that these creatures are its inhabitants," hence appropriately speaking the British language of the ancients. And although the real estate does not seem choice from Felix's description, Guthlac is envied and the target for an attempted assassination by a priest wishing to take his place on the mound. "There seems little doubt that a man who could keep his place upon the mound . . . would in fact be the Christian successor of those pagan seers who sat upon the mounds for inspiration."[96] Guthlac's own supposed words on this topic, as recorded in the *A* poem, lines 383–86, suggest the situation has some prestige:

> Nis þisses beorges setl
> meodumre ne mara þonne hit men duge
> se þe in þrowingum þeodnes willan
> dæghwam dreogeð.

> The abode on this mountain is not more excellent nor greater than serves for a man who daily in tribulations performs the will of God.[97]

Marking the mound with a cross (lines 179–83) was part of the warrior saint's taking of the landscape, reminiscent of conquistadors later laying claim to a "New World" by erecting crosses (although here the irony is that it was already a Christianized land).

Although in examining the barrow image in the Guthlacian *Lives* we are dealing with a presentation of legendary "fact," there is nothing left on the ground of any barrow at the Crowland site,[98] and the pedigree of such a monument remains a mystery.[99] The presence of a barrow at Crowland would fit the distribution of Romano-British barrows better than that of prehistoric burial chambers. But Glyn Daniel, noting recorded instances of people living in "burial chambers," admits that Guthlac's home conceivably could have been a Neolithic passage tomb as well, given that "it is only in some of the Roman barrows in England that chambers occur."[100]

The approach of the *A* poet to the landscape is more general than Felix's, with no description of the Fens, not even the few details about the cistern and hut and plundered treasure that Felix provides, and no mention of raids by Britons or Celtic-speaking demons. The absence of the latter may be part of the phenomenon of a less critical approach to native traditions in vernacular as opposed to Latin texts,[101] perhaps related to the degree to which clerics identified with a sense of ecclesiastical *Romanitas*, although it also may reflect a later political-ecclesiastical context in which the processes of both allegorization of the landscape and Mercian political hegemony were better established. In any case, the landscape of battle in *Guthlac A* generally seems more formally allegorical than Felix's *Vita*, functioning in what Lawrence Shook calls "the symbolic mode" in which the barrow comes to

> stand for all that is significant in the spiritual life of the good Christian: grace, struggle, the Will of God, temporal perseverance, and eternal salvation. His use of the barrow removes it from the category of a mere geographical appendage to a religious theme and makes it the center of the poem as a poem.[102]

In response, Paul Reichardt sought to use this same argument to argue for a return to the translation of *beorg* as mountain, being more appropriate to the "symbolic mode" of the poem and its setting in "a spiritual landscape as much as a geographical one."[103] Thus the meaning of mountain has important symbolic associations for a monastic readership in relation to biblical imagery. But citing evidence of continued strength of paganism in the medieval English countryside after the time of Guthlac, Karl Wentersdorf argued in response to Reichardt that the centrality of the *beorg* translated as a "barrow" in the poem is appropriate given efforts by the Anglo-Saxon church to follow Gregory's advice to transform pagan sacred sites to Christian uses, in order to help bring the population closer to Christ.[104] The site was a *mearclond* (line 174a) in terms of spiritual as well as human jurisdictional boundaries, "a disputed borderland where the followers of God and Satan clashed,"[105] described in a term used for pagan Mermedonia in the Old English poem *Andreas*. In the poem, Guthlac "intended primarily to establish and visibly demonstrate possession of the barrow for the Church."[106] The appositive meanings of *beorg*, pagan and Christian, were probably part of the intent of a poet whose theme rode a *mearclond* between different British landscapes.[107]

In the response of the natural landscape to the saint's victories over the demons in *Guthlac A* (lines 732b–45a), we can see most clearly the implications of Guthlac's taking possession of the land, and the meaning of this perceptual grid of ownership for the cultural topography of Anglo-Saxon sovereignty:

> Sigehreðig cwom
> bytla to þam beorge. Hine bletsadon
> monga mægwlitas, meaglum reordum,
> treofugla tuddor, tacnum cyðdon
> eadges eftcyne.
>
> . . .
>
> Smolt wæs se sigewong ond sele niwe,
> fæger fugla reord, Folde geblowen;
> geacas gear budon.

> The builder returned triumphantly to the mound; many species of creatures blessed him; with loud songs and signs, swarms of birds in the trees announced his return. . . . Peaceful was his new home on the field of victory and pleasant was the singing of the birds; the earth brought forth flowers, and the cuckoos heralded the spring.[108]

Here we seem to have the equivalent of the lifting of a curse on the landscape, which seems to become more fertile as a result. Yet there is a striking contrast here, in terms of attitudes toward populated landscapes with ancestral associations, with the lifting of the curse on the landscape in the Welsh tale of Manawydan in *The Mabinogi*, as well as with the vernacular Anglo-Saxon term for wasteland used in the poem. In the Welsh story, which seems related to Irish notions of ensuring the fertility of the land through the king's union with the goddess of the land,[109] the cursed landscape seen from the sacred mound is a fertile natural landscape but devoid of people. Analogously, in derivative form, the later Arthurian romances depicted the wasteland of the Fisher King as a place in which the manmade castle or its inhabitants would vanish as the king was ailing. Use of the Old English term *westen* in the Guthlac accounts and elsewhere likewise doesn't necessarily signify a wasteland in the modern sense, as in some kind of arid or poisoned desert, so much as it does an area devoid of people and human improvements. But what happens narratively in the aftermath of Guthlac's victories is not the restoration of people to the landscape, but in effect their expulsion from it, and the poet's description of the phantom beings as woeful refugees at the mound informs our sense of them as related to indigenous ancestral aspects of the landscape.[110]

In a sense, the devilish spirits of the landscape are the spirits of the native population that demographically was still present in the Anglo-Saxon kingdoms, though increasingly being defined as essentially distinct (when not assimilated through marriage and cultural change) by consolidated Anglo-Saxon polities such as Mercia and the centralized ecclesiastical jurisdictions entwined with them. Moreover the landscape itself was, as *Guthlac A* indicates, being cast in allegorical mode. Guthlac's real home was in heaven, not on earth. As he casts out the Welsh-speaking devils in Felix's account, he does so by reciting the opening verse of Psalm 67 (Latin and Greek numbering), which aptly deals with the triumph of God over enemies; this same psalm also contrasts the mountain of God with other wicked mountains that are compared to evil kings. A second transformation of the landscape is described near the end of *Guthlac B* at the saint's departure to the spiritual landscape of his eternal home. There is a similarity here with the ending of *Beowulf*. There the hero lifts a curse on the land by expelling the dragon from the treasure-raided barrow. Yet there too the redeemed landscape is one devoid of human fertility. The hero's eagerness for fame has left him without an heir and the kingdom undefended, its impending doom already known to the poem's readers, only the monument of the beacon-barrow left behind. Monks follow Guthlac to the site, according to later tradition, but this is not explained in the early accounts of his life examined here. If Beowulf is a type of the pagan hero, celebrated with a necessary circumscribed destiny by a Christian writer, Guthlac's reward lies not in worldly fame but in an eternal home.[111]

The image of the haunted barrow receives added significance in *Guthlac B* from the poem's discussion of the death of Guthlac using the image of the body as a house, with the corollary that death involves the unlocking of the house. Here themes of the Fall (such as the motif of Eve's drink as a poison in Creation not antidoted until the Incarnation and Eucharist) and of Guthlac as a healing warrior of God attended by birds in his fight with demons, give way to a discussion by the saint of the upcoming severance of body and soul. The focus of the battle for the haunted barrow has here become almost entirely the mortality of fallen man that is the curse of Eve's disobedience, and the saint's triumph over it through Christ by escaping the haunted barrow that is itself the earthly barrow (and lot) of mortal man. Guthlac tells his faithful companion (presumably Beccel) here of his eagerness for his "dwelling on high" to come, how he is "girt for the journey" in which his "soul struggles forth from the body to lasting joy in bliss."[112] Again and again the emphasis is on his spirit passing from his body, and how this sustains him. In the end, his bodily presence is made to seem almost a phantom existence compared to the life to come. He instructs his follower to bury his "soulless frame" at the barrow mound, "where it shall bide afterwards for a space in its earthly house."[113] He pledges that his friendship with his follower will continue after death, and suddenly it is as if the reader glimpses an answer to the lost ancestral associations of the "native" terrestrial landscape in the intertwining of the living and the dead among the saints of the church. The landscape description is breathtakingly a landscape of death and spiritual rebirth, a rush of perspective adjusting to another world:

> Þa se æþela glæm
> setlgong sohte, Swearc norðrodor
> won under wolcnum, Woruld miste oferteah
> þystrum biþeahte, þrong night ofer tiht
> londes frætwa. Ða cwom leohta mæst,
> halig of heofonum hædre scinan,
> beorhte ofer burgsalu.
> . . .
> Wuldres scima,
> aeþele ymb æþelene, ondlonge niht
> scan scirwered. Scadu sweþredon,
> tolysed under lyfte. Wæs se leohta glæm
> ymb þæt halge hus, heofonlic condel,
> from æfenglome oþþæt eastan cwom
> ofer deop gelad dægredwoma,
> wedertacen wearm. (lines 460–75)

Then the glorious splendor sought its setting; the black northern sky was dark under the clouds; it wrapped the world in mist; covered it with darkness; night came rushing down over the world, over the land's adornments. Then came the greatest of lights in holiness from heaven, shining clearly, radiant over the city-dwellings [or dwellings of that refuge].[114] . . . An excellent glorious light shone bright about the noble man the livelong night; the shadows drew off, dispersed through the air. The gleaming splendor, the heavenly candle, stayed round that sacred house from the dusk of evening till dawn; the glowing sun came from the east over the deep sea path.[115]

The saint, saying, "Now the soul is very ready to leave the body, longing for joys divine," partakes of the eucharist, opens his eyes and looks towards the heavenly kingdom, "towards the reward of grace; and then sent forth his spirit, beauteous by its acts, into the joy of heaven."[116] His departure is more heroic, reminiscent of Christ in *The Dream of the Rood*, than Augustinian in doctrine of salvation. But it is the allegorization of landscape that reflects the Gregorian development of Augustinian world-view. In the end a tower of light is described as going from Guthlac's hermitage into the heavens, brighter than the sun, as angels sing a song of triumph, "the old dwelling of the blessed one filled within with the sound of angels." The angelic song and holy odor on the island, more pleasant than any in the world, is reminiscent of some of the Irish otherworldly descriptions of blessed isles. But it is Guthlac's release from the haunted barrow of the body that has brought the transformation. His companion, afraid, rows away over the waters, lamenting in the style of other Anglo-Saxon poetic themes of water-faring wanderers, the loss of friend and home. The dirge is both a reminder of the old Germanic heroic ethic applied to a Christian context, and an implicit comparison of the empty barrow of Guthlac's island and body with the empty tomb of Christ.

> Ellen biþ selast þam þe oftost sceal
> dreogan dryhtenbealu, deope behycgan
> þroht, þeodengedal þonne seo þrag cymeð,
> wefen wyrdstafun. (lines 530–33)

> Courage is best for him who most often must endure great ills, seriously ponder on grievous parting from a master, when the time comes destined by fate.[117]

While Guthlac's body will be buried on the island, we are told that its time there too is temporary; his new home is in heaven. The landscape and the earth have become the monument of an empty tomb, a marker of the holy man's incorporation of the landscape, and thus synecdochally the incorporation of the landscape by the spiritual authority (the church and perhaps Christian state) that he represents in the narrative.

In the varying Anglo-Saxon accounts of Guthlac's life we can see a sig- nificant orientation of Mercian landscape akin in scope to that described by Tilley in the early Neolithic, and comparable in some ways to the ap- pearance of inscribed stones as boundary markers in western Britain in the fifth to seventh centuries.[118] However, this monumentalization of the landscape is textual and allegoric. The mound-monuments in *Beowulf* and the Guthlac tales mark a map of conceptual control not only over the geo- graphical landscape of their settings (with, in the case of *Beowulf*, analogues to southeastern Britain), but also of the Otherworld of native ancestral as- sociations with the land, including natural forces beyond the immediate cosmos of human community.

INTO THE OTHERWORLDLY WATERS

In both *Beowulf* and the Guthlac narratives, this landscape motif of the haunted barrow is framed by otherworldly waters that express this pro- cess of monumentalizing landscape by textualizing it. Seascapes in par- ticular frame *Beowulf*, a text whose placelessness is paradoxically rooted in ancestral history, with the dragon's barrow in faraway Geatland and the Grendelcyn lair (itself a kind of tomb for both its clan and perhaps for the older giant race whose artifacts are found there) in the midst of the watery mere.[119] Even the seemingly geographic waters of the sea in the poem have metaphoric connotations. "The Anglo-Saxons developed a fondness for lit- eralizing the Augustinian metaphor of alienation," James Earl notes,[120] and the poem maps a literal landscape of alienation, sea-side, that echoes other Old English poetic seascapes but stands in contrast with Irish depictions of the sea as paradisiacal Otherworld (yet extension of the earth), seen in the eighth-century *Imram Brain*.

To the evolving Anglo-Saxon sense of identity, the sea was both an eth- nic historical border and an allegory for the Christian sense of the fleeting nature of mortality. The two are related in the traditional Christian view of baptism as an immersion in waters signifying death followed by new life. *Beowulf* as a retrospectively Christian reconstruction of ancestral pagan heroism is thus appropriately hedged about by descriptions of the sea, as is the Norse cosmology sketched by Snorri Sturluson in thirteenth-century Iceland, but in a way also reminiscent of Bede's description of the parable of the bird flying through the mead hall as an illustration of the immense unknowns bounding human life. The double-bound metaphoric meaning of the sea was appropriate to a culture that in the eighth century was constructing its origins as a pilgrim people, in a sense both spiritually and historically, in exile on British soil, with an Augustinian ideology that emphasized the fallen nature of creation and human beings.

This less-than-solid setting for a landscape of origins is extended metaphorically in descriptions of both Grendel's watery mere and Guthlac's fens. *Beowulf* starts with the mythic tale of Scyld, progenitor of a Danish dynasty to which the poem gives Anglian connections,[121] who appears from the sea and vanishes back into it on a burial boat. The poem ends with the mound erected on the coast as a memorial to Beowulf (a hero who narratively comes from the sea both in a youthful initiation rite and in his arrival to rescue the Danes), a monument to guide seafarers and remind them of his fame.

The sea or the wilds surrounding mere and fenland all divide the reader from the place of the action while implicitly echoing both the religious distance to the spiritual homeland of Christians in the Augustinian tradition especially and the motif of exile/immigrant origin myth as formed fully by Bede for pagan Anglo-Saxon culture. This process parallels thematically the metrical effect of the caesura-break in Old English poetic lines, which Fred Robinson described as stylistically representing the thematic apposition (and separation) of ancestral pagan past and Christian present in *Beowulf*. Of the sea-enclosed end (and beginning) of Scyld, the *Beowulf* poet wrote,

> Nalæs hi hine læssan lacum teodan,
> þeod-gestreonum, þon þa dydon,
> þe hine æt frumsceafte forð onsendon
> ænne ofer yðe umbor-wesende.
> Þa gyt hi him asetton segend gyldenne
> heah ofer heafod, leton holm beran,
> geafon on gar-secg; him wæs geomor sefa,
> murnende mod. Men ne cunnon
> secgan to soðe, sele-rædende,
> hæleð under heofenum, hwa þæm hlæste onfeng. (lines 43–52)

> They decked his body no less bountifully
> with offerings than those first ones did
> who cast him away when he was a child
> and launched him alone out over the waves.
> And they set a gold standard up

high above his head and let him drift
to wind and tide, bewailing him
and mourning their loss. No man can tell,
no wise man in hall or weathered veteran
knows for certain who salvaged that load.[122]

Beowulf's memorial is described in similar terms:

Geworhton ða Wedra leode
hleo on hoe, se wæs heah ond brad,
weg-liðendum wide gesyne,
ond betimbredon on tyn dagum
beadu-rofes becn; bronda lafe
wealle beworhton, swa hyt weorðlicost
fore-snotre men findan mihton. (lines 3156–62)

Then the Geat people began to construct
a mound on a headland, high and imposing,
a marker that sailors could see from far away,
and in ten days they had done the work.
It was their hero's memorial; what remained from the fire
they housed inside it, behind a wall
as worthy of him as their workmanship could make it.[123]

In this seascape frame of *Beowulf* we see an embodiment of both the Anglo-Saxon literary motif of exile and the aforementioned Augustinian metaphor of alienation, in a hero who fights monsters in a foreign land and returns home but never founds a family or a dynasty of his own. His rule is ended by a supernatural monster whom he chooses to fight alone, while his heroic death is cast as leading inevitably to the destruction of his kingdom, even as the hero is eulogized over a pyre and in a memorial mound along the sea. The poem itself, framed by Scyld's appearance from the sea and Beowulf's seaside beacon-barrow, reflects the immensities framing earthly exile between birth and death. As Earl writes, the roots of the "image of the exile in the prison-house" displayed in Old English poems such as *The Seafarer* and *Christ I* (but also arguably in Beowulf's mere and barrow fights, and indeed his whole earthly career), using sea-related imagery, lie in Augustinian theology. While calling such religious influence "distant and subliminal," Earl notes that it shapes the exile theme nonetheless, which "flourishes in these poems independently, because it is the profoundest philosophical expression of the traditional Anglo-Saxon view of the world that is at least compatible with Christianity, if uneasily."[124]

The analogue between this aspect of *Beowulf* and Bede's account of the pagan Northumbrian high-priest Coifi's parable of a sparrow flying through a hall as representing human life is also apparent. The sea-framed exile theme "is something of a compromise, really, between the Adamic myth and the parable of the sparrow-flight, stressing the wretchedness of man's condition more than his sinfulness."[125] In these literary seascapes, the image of the war band member in exile becomes merged with that of the voyage of the Christian depicted in the metaphor of the ship at the end of *Christ II* and Bede's construction of the pilgrim Anglo-Saxon people. This highlights the relation of the poem's landscape to concerns of political power, what Alcuin in his conception of allegory considered a necessary grounding of story in history.[126] Stylistically, the meeting of Christian ideology and Germanic poetic tradition helps to explain the conjunction of "transcendent" and "immanent" imagery that Earl saw as a hallmark of Old English poetry, the stylistic "clarity" of thematically obscure poetry as described by Sara Higley in contrast with early Welsh verse.[127] Herein lies a seeming paradox of Old English narrative, that often it is both realistic and allegorical.[128] Thus, for example, the description of Beowulf's encounter with the sea in his competition with Breca is naturalistic—at least relative to other Insular narrative traditions[129]—while expressing the harsh allegoricized sense of the sea distinctive to Old English poetry:

> Ða wit ætsomne on sæ wæron
> fif nihta fyrst, oþþæt unc flod todraf,
> wado weallende, wedera cealdost,
> nipende niht, ond norþan-wind
> heaðo-grim ondhwearf. Hreo wæron yþa,
> wæs mere-fixa mod onhrered.
>
> . . .
>
> Ac on mergenne mecum wunde
> be yð-lafe uppe lægon,
> sweordum aswefede, þæt syðþan na
> ymb brontne ford brim-liðende
> lade ne letton. Leoht eastan com,
> beorht beacen Godes; brimu swaþredon
> þæt ic sæ-næssas geseon mihte,

windige weallas. Wyrd oft nereð
unfægne eorl, þonne his ellen deah. (lines 544–49; 565–73)

Shoulder to shoulder, we struggled on
for five nights, until the long flow
and pitch of the waves, the perishing cold,
night falling and winds from the north
drove us apart. The deep boiled up
and its wallowing sent the sea-brutes wild.

. . .

Instead, in the morning, mangled and sleeping
the sleep of the sword, they slopped and floated
like the ocean's leavings. From now on
sailors would be safe, the deep-sea raids
were over for good. Light came from the east,
bright guarantee of God, and the waves
went quiet; I could see headlands
and buffeted cliffs. Often, for undaunted courage,
fate spares the man it has not already marked.[130]

The light that is both the sunlight and also signifies the divine presence, at the conclusion of Beowulf's struggle with the sea monsters, is reminiscent of the light in his later mere struggle. Likewise, the threatening nature of the waters here is amplified in the description of the mere at a later, more climactic point in the poem. Here too we see represented a major theme of the poem, that is, the role of the hero in making safe the landscape (in this case seascape) for human use:

þæt syðþan na
ymb brontne ford brim-liþende
lade ne letton. (lines 567b–69a)

. . . so that henceforth they [sea monsters] would never hinder sea-goers in their passage over the deep ocean-crossing.[131]

By comparison, accounts of the sea and watery encounters with sea monsters in Irish writings (the sea tends not to figure largely in the apparently landlocked literary imagination of the Welsh) tend not to be so charged with evil associations and moral concerns related to the fate of human society.[132]

The play of cultural concerns upon the settings of Old English poetry yields seascapes that are expressions of subjectivity,[133] projections of internal mental conditions, while also seeming extraordinarily real to the reader (as in *The Seafarer* or in Beowulf's match with Breca or his struggle in the mere). However, as noted, they also are more distanced from associations with specific Insular physical places than Irish and Welsh landscape narratives. While we often know where on the actual landscape of Ireland and Wales the stories are unfolding, Beowulf is in a far country and even Guthlac's mound is hidden among the fens. This does not mean, however, that these works themselves were distant from the concerns of their audiences. Not fully allegories, they are however allegorized, with their center not in a larger sense of nature or Creation but in human moral concerns. They reflect both the separation between spiritual and earthly realms evident in Augustine's *De Civitate Dei* and Gregory I's influential derivative view of nature as an allegorized mediating space, as seen in his *Moralia in Job*.

In this context, it is no coincidence that Beowulf's fight with Grendel's mother in the mere, the most prominent landscape of the work, lies structurally at the center of the triptych of the warrior's heroic monster battles. The detailed and gloomy description of the mere is a geographical interiorizing of the Anglo-Saxon seascape of exile, representing its transfer to the interior of the countryside (putatively Scandinavian but metaphorically Anglo-Saxon).[134] It advances Mercian hegemony over that interior by supporting the Anglo-Saxon identity myth of supra-landscape authority, vested in both Bede's history and in Augustinian Christianity. It also functions as a backdrop for a type of exorcism of pagan ancestral associations from earlier cultural landscapes[135] (analogous with Beowulf's earlier removal of the sea monsters from the sea lanes during his competition with Breca), in which Grendel and his mother function as stand-ins for residual "native" Celtic populations in areas such as the fenlands, while also displaying analogues with descriptions of Christ's descent into hell and apocryphal visions of the Christian Hades.

> Nis þæt feor heonen
> mil-gemearces, þæt se mere standeð
> ofer þæm hongiað hrinde bearwas;
> wudu wyrtum fæst wæter oferhelmað.
> Þær mæg nihta gehwæm nið-wundor seon,
> fyr on flode; no þæs frod leofað

gumena bearna þæt þone grund wite.
Ðeah þe hæð-stapa hundum geswenced,
heorot homum trum holt-wudu sece,
feorran geflymed, ær he feorh seleð,
aldor on ofre, ær he in wille,
hafelan hydan. Nis þæt heoru stow;
þonon yð-geblond up astigeð
won to wolcnum, þonne wind styreþ
lað gewidru, oðþaet lyft ðrysmaþ,
roderas reotað. (lines 1361b–82)

    A few miles from here
a frost-stiffened wood waits and keeps watch
above a mere; the overhanging bank
is a maze of tree-roots mirrored in its surface.
At night there, something uncanny happens:
the water burns. And the mere bottom
has never been sounded by the sons of men.
On its bank, the heather-stepper halts:
the hart in flight from pursuing hounds
will turn to face them with firm-set horns
and die in the wood rather than dive
beneath its surface. That is no good place.
When wind blows up and stormy weather
makes clouds scud and the skies weep,
out of its depths a dirty surge
is pitched towards the heavens.[136]

Ofereode þa æþelinga bearn
steap stan-hliðo, stige nearwe,
enge an-paðas, uncuð gelad,
neowle næssas, nicor-husa fela.
He feara sum beforan gengde
wisr monna, wong sceawian;
oðþæt he færinga fyrgen-beamas
ofer harne stan hleonian funde,
wyn-leasne wudu; wæter under stod
dreorig on gedrefed. Denum eallum wæs,
winum Scyldinga, weorce on mode

to geþolianne, ðegne monegum,
oncyð eorla gehwæm, syðþan Æscheres
on þam holm-clife hafelan metton.
 Flod blode weol—folc to sægon—
hatan heolfre. Horn stundum song
fuslic fyrd-leoð. Feþa eal gesæt;
gesawon ða æfter wætere wyrm-cynnes fela,
sellice sæ-dracan sund cunnian,
swylce on næs-hleoðum nicras licgean,
ða on undern-mæl oft bewitigað
sorh-fulne sið on segl-rade,
wyrmas ond wil-deor. (lines 1408–30)

So the noble prince proceeded undismayed
up fells and screes, along narrow footpaths
and ways where they were forced into single file,
ledges on cliffs above lairs of water-monsters.
He went in front with a few men,
good judges of the lie of the land,
and suddenly discovered the dismal wood,
mountain trees growing out at an angle
above grey stones: the bloodshot water
surged underneath. It was a sore blow
to all of the Danes, friends of the Shieldings,
a hurt to each and every one
of that noble company when they came upon
Aeschere's head at the foot of the cliff.
 Everybody gazed as the hot gore
kept wallowing up and an urgent war-horn
repeated its notes: the whole party
sat down to watch. The water was infested
with all kinds of reptiles. There were writhing sea-dragons
and monsters slouching on slopes by the cliff,
serpents and wild things such as those that often
surface at dawn to roam the sail-road
and doom the voyage.[137]

 This forbidding watery landscape has, in broad terms, analogues in the Old
Icelandic *Grettissaga*[138] and especially in explicitly Christian writings such as

the Old English Blickling Homily and Irish texts of the *Visio S. Pauli*.[139] The existence of such explicit analogues to descriptions of the Christian hell, in such a detailed description of the backdrop to an heroic act in pagan times, testifies again to the distinctive character of Old English literary landscape, as allegoricized in a fairly objectified style of description. In addition, Frank Battaglia and Richard North have separately analyzed the use of *geofon* ("sea" or "ocean" in Klaeber), a term derived from a Germanic goddess name, in descriptions of watery depths in *Beowulf* and other Old English poetry, as lending remote pagan or demonic associations to the sea for a Christian audience.[140] Hellish aspects of the description of the mere set the hero Beowulf in a role of harrowing hell as a Christ figure, while at the same time forming part of a story about a hero defeating a monstrous demon in a pagan setting. The description elsewhere in the poem of Grendel and his mother as descendants of Cain also place these monsters not only in a biblical context but identify them (unlike Celtic analogues) as human or quasi-human beings with an ancient pedigree in the land.[141] Beowulf's extinction of the Grendelcyn climaxes in his struggle with Grendel's mother, in which the hero finds the mere illumined by divine light as he slays her. The waters boil and their surface seethes with her blood as he shoots back up to the top of the mere. Beowulf, a warrior from across the sea, has slain the quasi-human creatures most identified with the landscape, thus purging the wasteland of evil. This echoes Guthlac's own exorcism of the Welsh-speaking spirits infesting his barrow in the fens in Felix's eighth-century Latin life of the saint.

But again the sense of what defines a wasteland appears to be very different in Celtic and Anglo-Saxon narratives. In both *Beowulf* and the Guthlac tales, a purification of wastelands is marked by an exorcism of quasi-human land spirits, and ultimately by a kind of monolithic (and in twentieth-century terms existential) loneliness of the hero before God that marks cleansing and restoration of the landscape. In Beowulf's final purging of the dragon from his kingdom, the end result is the destruction of his kingdom, leaving only his memorial mound and praise of his heroism. While Guthlac's legacy at Crowland is implicit in his *Lives*, the early English accounts do not describe the creation of a monastic "city" as his legacy. Here the influence of St. Augustine of Hippo's theory of two invisible cities of human history, the "city of God" and "city of man," forged in the fall of the Western empire, is again apparent in the Anglo-Saxon distancing of text from experience of a living landscape.

In Old English literary culture, the sea and its derivatives reflect both a re-imagined Germanic ancestral past and the unredeemed human condition, an insubstantial wasteland that in turn provides the model for nature more generally in Old English poetry.[142] The plots of both *Beowulf* and the *Lives* of Guthlac contrast earthly wastelands with potential spiritual reward. The same contrast implicitly defines older, more indigenously constructed British-Celtic polities as unredeemed, while supporting the land claims of the new more centralized and ecclesiastically allied Anglo-Saxon realms. In Augustinian terms, "True justice can exist only among the citizens of the City of God,"[143] which becomes identified with imperial claims of Western kingship in the Carolingian era. In Beowulf's victorious plunge into the interior sea of the mere can be seen a paradigm legitimizing Mercian hegemony over the English landscape.

The relationship between this literary making of landscape and emerging medieval notions of both monarchy and individuality is suggested by the literary theorist Julia Kristeva's analysis of the role of Augustinian theology in constructing the relation between notions of identity and nature in the West. In this process the Augustinian "dual procession" definition of the Trinity, ascendant in the Anglo-Saxon church as on the Continent in the early Middle Ages,[144] is a key marker. In the West, greater focus on the role of the Son in the Trinity, and lessened emphasis on the Holy Spirit

> had the advantage of providing a basis for the political and spiritual authority of the papacy on the one hand, and on the other for the autonomy and rationality of the believer's person, identified with a Son having power and prestige equal to that of the Father. What had thus been gained in equality and therefore in performance and historicity had perhaps been lost at the level of the experience of *identification*, in the sense of a permanent instability of identity. Difference and identity, rather than autonomy and equality, did on the contrary build up the Eastern Trinity, which consequently became the source of ecstasy and mysticism.[145]

Beowulf's emergence from the mere can be understood in this theological perspective and in Kristevan terms as the establishment of the autonomy of the individual hero (and of his warrior/proto-Christian culture) with respect to the natural landscape, the Subject in relation to the Other. Politically this is paralleled in an emergence of an ideology of individualized, proprietary and patrimonial but national monarchy in the Anglo-Saxon and Frankish realms.[146]

The problem of the lack of stable identification that Kristeva sees in Western definitions of individuality relates to the West's arguably more objectified and oppositional social relations with both nature and ancestry. A literate sense of individual autonomy in Western culture in the early Middle Ages can thus be contextualized as emerging at the intersection of Augustinian Christianity with concerns about forging national identities from populations lacking clear demographic ethnicity. Intensifying this process for the Anglo-Saxons is the defining of native British or Welsh ethnicities, and by extension the native landscape of Britain, as a kind of subhuman Other that is pre-symbolic.[147] In this context the description of the mere can be viewed as the construction of a pre-symbolic place, into which the hero injects the symbolic and himself emerges as a symbol. The differentiation of the Western individual has become a performative act in opposition to nature, as has the formation of nationhood, reflecting the Gregorian notion that nature is a virtual code, devoid of real meaning until read (and hence also written), in which process subjectivity is performed for both individuals and nations.

In a Kristevan landscape analysis, the bloody grime of the mere of Grendel's mother, like menstrual blood, is thus both a reminder of difference and a threat to the social aggregate of patriarchal symbolic order.[148] With the arrival of Beowulf, the entrance of linear temporality "renders explicit a rupture, an expectation, or an anguish which other temporalities work to conceal."[149] Augustine likewise wrote of linear time as related to the grammar of the sentence.[150] Indeed, the runic giant sword taken up by Beowulf in the mere is a literate monumental object, reordering the previously chaotic, non-objectified maternal landscape (and destroying its monstrous inhabitants). In a sense, the hall of the Danes could not exist without the maternal mere defining it from outside by its role as the abject, what Kristeva calls in another context "the horror that they seize on in order to build themselves up and function,"[151] just as the construction of English identity in the seventh and eighth centuries required a defining of the Welsh and other non-English cultures as Other.

Yet Heorot is constructed as an island of civilization (and, analogous to the hall in Bede's sparrow story and Valhalla in paean tradition, a microcosm of Creation as well) even more confined and hemmed in by the powers of chaos than the kingdom of Ulster in the *Táin Bó Cuailnge*, where human society, the landscape, the route of the attack and defense, and the running of the magical bulls, are all less singly focused, and the struggle is ultimately human. If Beowulf ("the bear") shares with the Ulster hero Cúchulainn ("the dog of Culann") an animal name, the Anglo-Saxon hero is throughout his narrative both more distanced from nature and in a sense more isolated from the divine. While both tales have been read as recounting a breaking of the power of a goddess figure, in the Irish cycle there is a sense of both nature and mythic history continuing to run their interlaced course after the narrative's denouement.[152] This is framed in one of the Irish manuscripts by an ongoing argument of colophons in Irish and in Latin over whether this is appropriate literature to be reading (yes says the Irish, no says the Latin). Ulster is saved, and lives on to have more than allegorical meaning for emerging contemporary dynastic concerns. At the end of *Beowulf*, by contrast, we are left in effect with a cenotaph (as in the Guthlacian *Lives*).[153] Integral to the secular poem's conclusion is the foreshadowing of the end of the kingdom. The mourning for the uncertain end of a human hero in a fallen world is a prototype of Anglo-Saxon exile heroes like St. Guthlac, who in a newly constructed land could only hope for entry into the city of God while bringing true Christian rule to benighted British earth. And that is the great theme of Bede's near-contemporary history and its framework cultural landscape: the textually totalizing (and necessarily imperfect) effort to resolve the tension between religious and secular concerns regarding nation-building.

In the Augustinian interpretation of signs and its Gregorian derivative can be found the framework for Anglo-Saxon literary landscape as both more subjectified in the sense of its moral focus and more objectified in its stylistic construction.[154] When the grace of the Holy Spirit is emphasized doctrinally more as an objectified and discrete insertion into creation (as arguably was the case in the Augustinian West, contrasted with the Greek emphases on divine energies in nature), the divine becomes more distanced from the natural, and the natural from the human as God's image. Nature becomes more symbolic than real. Such a monumentalizing of landscape as written text, rather than merely marking a specific physical place with a physical monument as in the prehistoric or earliest Christian landscapes of Britain, is integrally related in the Anglo-Saxon texts examined here to narratives of taking possession of a wilderness land. This is achieved through textually distancing the reader from the physical environment by symbolizing a vista naturalistically, while ironically tending to render the environment in the text lifeless. Here can be seen the apparent paradox that Augustinian emphases on the corruption of nature supported the construction of a new cultural landscape promoting political hegemony, which developed into ultimately more allegoric yet naturalistic Western literary and artistic views of landscape, all the way from the narrative frame of Dante's high medieval cosmic fantasy to virtual realities of our day. The Anglo-

Saxon literary landscape differentiated itself from the iconographic sense of integration with the physical world found in pre-Augustinian notions of synergetic salvation, which helped shape narratives of neighboring Irish and Welsh literary traditions. And in a trend begun in that formative era of early medieval narratives of nation-building, landscape became in the West both a palimpsest for human moral and political concerns, and a cenotaph in its lack of real engagement with larger forces of nature.

NOTES

[1] J. R. R. Tolkien, *"Beowulf": The Monsters and the Critics* (1936; reprint London, 1958), p. 24.

[2] Jennifer Neville, *Representations of the Natural World in Old English Poetry* (Cambridge, Eng., 1999), p. 37.

[3] Margaret Goldsmith, *The Mode and Meaning of "Beowulf"* (London, 1970), p. 44.

[4] Such doubts and suspicions stem both from reinterpretation of archaeological evidence in a way that now suggests that "Germanic" migration to post-Roman Britain was very limited in number and also greater awareness of the politics behind ethnic-defining scholarship: see respectively Michael Jones, *The End of Roman Britain* (Ithaca, N.Y., 1996), and Patrick Sims-Williams, "The Visionary Celt: The Construction of an Ethnic Preconception," *Cambridge Medieval Celtic Studies* 2 (1986): 71–96.

[5] Ecocriticism is a type of literary criticism related to postcolonial theory that seeks to center readings on attitudes toward the natural land in literary texts, in order to analyze implicit cultural attitudes toward nature and related issues of ethnicity and power that might otherwise lie unexamined. The coining of the term is credited to William Rueckert, whose seminal article "Literature and Ecology: An Experiment in Ecocriticism" is reprinted in a basic anthology of ecocritical writings entitled *The Ecocriticism Reader*, ed. Cheryll Glotfelty and Harold Fromm (Athens, Georgia, 1996), pp. 105–23. Cheryll Glotfelty is a founding figure in the movement and of its central journal *ISLE: Interdisciplinary Studies in Literature and Environment*. Lawrence Buell's book *The Environmental Imagination: Thoreau, Nature Writing, and the Formation of American Culture* (Cambridge, Mass., 1995) is a seminal extended scholarly work in the field. In the view of Buell, one of the goals of such criticism should be "to take stock of the resources within our traditions of thought that might help address" modern biases about nature, and thus achieve a more "ecocentric" view of human communities in relation to the environment in the 21st century, based on better understanding of past traditions (p. 21). For

fairly recent approaches to issues of landscape focusing mainly on later periods of English and Western European literature, see also *The Environmental Tradition in English Literature*, ed. John Parham (Aldershot and Burlington, Eng., 2002); Corinne J. Saunders, *The Forest of Medieval Romance* (Cambridge, Eng., 1993); and Paul Piehler, *The Visionary Landscape* (London, 1971). Nicholas Howe has discussed the constructed yet layered nature of early English literary landscapes (and their sense of pilgrim-exile) in his valuable essay "The Landscape of Anglo-Saxon England: Inherited, Invented, Imagined" in *Inventing Medieval Landscapes: Senses of Place in Western Europe*, ed. John Howe and Michael Wolfe (Tallahassee, 2002). For recent studies of physical aspects of Anglo-Saxon landscape, see Delia Hooke, *The Landscape of Anglo-Saxon England* (London, 1998), and Oliver Rackham's works on early English woodlands.

6   Earlier modern scholarship tended to assume some kind of ethnic predisposition or pagan influence involved in "more severe" Anglo-Saxon treatments of nature, rather than approaching more rigorously how cultural values in a formative period of a culture can set patterns of perception, as discussed in anthropological terms by Clifford Geertz among others. See Geertz, *The Interpretation of Cultures* (New York, 1973). The importance of formative ideological emphases is exemplified on a large physical scale by the influence of 18th-century Jeffersonian Enlightenment cosmology on the national landscape of the United States. Much of the American Middle West's topography is now meshed by a right-angled grid of settlement and fanning as a result of Cartesian views of nature encoded in the Northwest Ordinance.

7   As discussed later, I accept the 20th-century scholarly consensus, recently backed by Michael Lapidge's paleographical analysis, that *Beowulf* most likely has an eighth-century provenance, although the issue remains contentious; see Michael Lapidge, "The Archetype of *Beowulf*," *Anglo-Saxon England* 29 (2000): 5–41. My arguments relating issues of ethnic and national identity with landscape in the poem could still apply to a date for the poem in the later Danelaw era, however, in a changed context.

8   "Augustinian" and "Augustinianism," like "Celtic," are broad but needed shorthand terms in relation to the intellectual pedigree of Anglo-Saxon Christianity as traced back through its spiritual father Pope Gregory I, who organized the mission that Bede in his early 8th-century history cast as foundational for Anglo-Saxon identity. The key elements of Augustine of Hippo's influence relating to the subject of this study are his emphases on salvation by grace and not works; on individual transmission of Original Sin; on the procession of the Holy Spirit from the Son and the Father together (a doctrine that became the *filioque* addition to the Nicaean-Constantinopolitan Creed); and on signs as having a

reality apart from that which they symbolize. The combination of these four related emphases is what is meant here by Augustinian. As amplified by Gregory the Great and others, Augustine's writings on these topics greatly influenced literary views of Creation, and thus the portrayal of landscape. Such ideas of course influenced Irish literary culture as well, but because the Romano-British, Pictish, and Irish realms were not convened through Gregory's mission, and did not identify their Christian culture with papal influence to the same extent as the Anglo-Saxons, this influence was not so pronounced. Gregory was revered in both Irish and Greek literary worlds as a holy man and father of the church (to the extent that, in the former, he was claimed to have had an Irish mother!), especially for his *Dialogues*. But in Anglo-Saxon England Gregory's literary role was ancestral in import, and part of a narrowing of the range of patristic influences in the developing Western church. "One of the chief links between Augustine and the Middle Ages," Gregory "owes more to Augustine than to any other individual writer," notes Carole Straw ("Gregory I," in *Augustine through the Ages*, ed. Allan D. Fitzgerald [Grand Rapids, 1999], pp. 402, 404).

[9] W. J. T. Mitchell, "Imperial Landscape," in *Landscape and Power*, ed. W. J. T. Mitchell, 2nd ed. (Chicago, 2002), pp. 5–34.

[10] Many commentators, most recently Michael Herren and Shirley Anne Brown in *Christ in Celtic Christianity* (Woodbridge, Eng., 2002), have sought to define a Pelagian strain in early Irish and Welsh Christianity, although Cassianite better suggests its relative orthodoxy. Irish ascetic and penitential emphasis on a synergy of grace and works was shaped in a "pre-Augustinian" Christian milieu in the British Isles, long prior to Pope Gregory's papal mission to the Anglo-Saxon realms in 597, on the model of the desert fathers, and probably influenced by connections with the Eastern Mediterranean. John Cassian's portrayal in his thirteenth conference of a desert father's implicit criticism of Augustine's emphases on grace and Original Sin was, if not a source for early Celtic literary culture, a parallel expression of prevalent ascetic emphasis. An early Irish elegy to St. Columba suggests the importance of Cassian's writings to that seminal figure in the Irish church; likewise echoes of Cassian's thought are found in the seminal Celtic penitential attributed to Uinniau; see Herren and Brown, *Christ in Celtic Christianity*, pp. 117,124. While Stephen Mercer Lake in "The Influence of John Cassian on Early Continental and Insular Monasticism to ca. A.D. 817" (Ph.D. diss., Cambridge University, 1996) is skeptical of Cassian's direct influence on Western monasticism, he notes apparent affinities of Irish monasticism with the Egyptian monasticism that Cassian promoted (p. 218). Such affinities lie in part behind Michael Richter's statement that the Irish tendency to honor the concept of the "naturally good" and pagan ancestral tradition in a non-Augustinian way

was probably well-established "considerably earlier" than the seventh century: "If the Irish Christian teachers had had a choice between Augustine and others, they chose the others" (*Ireland and her Neighbors in the Seventh Century* [New York, 1999], p. 37). This in turn relates to the wide range of patristic sources for early Irish literary culture, apparently more extensive than that evidenced in the Anglo-Saxon corpus, and compared to a bibliographic "hall closet" distinctive in the early medieval West; see Peter Jeffery, "Eastern and Western Elements in the Irish Monastic Prayer of the Hours" in *The Divine Office in the Latin Middle Ages*, ed. Margot E. Fassler and Rebecca A. Baltzer (Oxford, 2000), p. 100. See also Thomas N. Hall, "Apocryphal Lore and the Life of Christ in Old English Literature" (Ph.D. diss., University of Illinois at Urbana, 1990), and Charles D. Wright, *The Irish Tradition in Old English Literature* (Cambridge, Eng., 1996). A parallel example of inculturation of non-Augustinian Christianity with a developing sense of "native" identity is seen in the encounter of Russian missionaries with Aleuts in Alaska as described by Michael Oleska, *Alaskan Missionary Spirituality* (New York, 1987).

[11] Landscape as a modern term has no commonly used precise equivalent in early Insular literatures—Irish, Welsh, Old English, and associated Latin works. "Creation" instead was the corresponding cultural concept, interwoven with definitions of physical environment. The Anglo-Saxons had terms in their native vocabulary for nature in the sense of character (*cynd*) or creation (*gesceaft*), but not for "the natural world" in the modern Western sense: (see Neville, *Representations of the Natural World*, pp. 1–2). The often-used Latin words *natura* and *physica* (the latter especially rooted in Greek philosophy) carried metaphysical aspects as well. Indeed, conceptions of the physical world had overt ontological meaning in such pre-industrial societies, as the anthropologist and archaeologist Christopher Tilley points out in his definition of traditional cultural constructions of human environments in *A Phenomenology of Landscape: Places, Paths, and Monuments* (Oxford, 1994), p. 26: "A landscape has ontological import because it is lived in and through, mediated, worked on and altered, replete with cultural meaning and symbolism—and not just something looked at or thought about, an object merely for contemplation, depiction, representation and aestheticization."

[12] Joseph Bosworth and T. Northcote Toller, *An Anglo-Saxon Dictionary* (Oxford, 1898), p. 619.

[13] *Genesis B*, ed. A. N. Doane (Madison, 1991).

[14] For a helpful essentially postcolonial take on Bede's writing, and its relation to Gildas's and other early insular histories, see Nicholas Higham's *King Arthur: Myth-Making and History* (London, 2002).

[15] Bede, *Ecclesiastical History of the English People*, ed. Bertram Colgrave and R. A. B. Mynors (Oxford, 1969), p. xxx. All subsequent references to Bede are to this edition, either by page number or by Bede's book and chapter numbers.

[16] Bede, *Ecclesiastical History*, p. 15.

[17] For discussion of the concept of monumentality in cultural ideology and artifacts, see Wu Hung, *Monumentality in Early Chinese Art and Architecture* (Palo Alto, 1995), p. 4 and throughout. Here the terms "monumental" and "monumentalizing" with respect to landscapes are used to express the fixed imposition of a static cultural map or matrix for a realm, involving ideological purposes of control related to issues of defining ancestry and legitimizing authority.

[18] Patrick Wormald has detailed *Beowulf*'s probable monastic context in his essay "Bede, *Beowulf* and the Conversion of the Anglo-Saxon Aristocracy," in *Bede and Anglo-Saxon England*, ed. Robert T. Farrell (Oxford, 1978), pp. 32–95.

[19] Jones, *The End of Roman Britain*, pp. 27, 67.

[20] Gildas, a British Celtic monk who according to tradition ended up in Brittany, in his *De Excidio Britanniae* provided a sketchily near-apocalyptic account of the invasion of the Anglo-Saxons in the context of a jeremiad directed against the immorality of native British kings.

[21] See, for example, Jones, *The End of Roman Britain*; Nicholas Higham, *Rome, Britain and the Anglo-Saxons* (London, 1992); K. P. Dark, *From Civitas to Kingdom* (Leicester, 1994); and C. J. Arnold, *An Archaeology of the Early Anglo-Saxon Kingdoms* (London, 1988).

[22] Veronica Ortenberg, "The Anglo-Saxon Church and the Papacy," in *The English Church and the Papacy in the Middle Ages*, ed. C. H. Lawrence (1965; reprint Phoenix Mill, 1999), p. 34.

[23] John J. Contreni, "Early Carolingian Era," in Fitzgerald, *Augustine through the Ages*, p. 126.

[24] The connection between the Augustinian intellectual pedigree of the papal mission, and the derivative ecclesiastical system of the Anglo-Saxon realms, is symbolized by the direct influence of Augustine of Hippo's writing on the works of their chronicler, Bede, and by the significant and influential presence of Augustinian books both in his library and in that of his mentor Benedict Biscop; see M. L. W. Laistner and H. H. King, *A Hand-List of Bede Manuscripts* (New York, 1943), and Joseph Kelly, "Late Carolingian Era," p. 132 and George H. Brown, "Venerable Bede," pp. 124–29, both in Fitzgerald, *Augustine through the Ages*. Even more pervasive however was the influence of a broader Augustinian perspective on landscape in the "deep structure" of the new Anglo-Saxon culture celebrated by Bede.

[25] Carole M. Cusack, *The Rise of Christianity in Northern Europe, 300–1000* (London, 1999), p. 81.

[26] John Koch, *The Gododdin of Aneirin* (Cardiff, 1997), p. xliii.

[27] Augustine, *De Trinitate*, ed. John Rotelle, trans. Edmund Hill (Brooklyn, 1991), 2.31.

[28] The developing articulation of theophany in Eastern Christianity, as for example in St. Gregory of Nyssa's *Life of Moses*, ed. and trans. Abraham J. Malherbe and Everett Ferguson (New York, 1978), saw revelatory signs as the direct presence of divine energy in Creation.

[29] Brian Stock, *Augustine the Reader* (Cambridge, Mass., 1995), pp. 75–76, 236. Not coincidentally, it was resistance to a standardized literary systematization of time, in terms of a new way of computing the date of Easter, that Bede presented as the primary example of early Irish and Welsh heterodoxy or even heresy.

[30] See Neville, *Representations of the Natural World*, pp. 28–29.

[31] This relates to the crucial distinction of *uti* and *frui* in Augustine's thought, starting early in his career with the first book of *De Doctrina Christiana*, and developed throughout later works. His distinction between enjoyment and use relates to his strong distinction between the eternal and temporal: "Only eternal, unchangeable realities are to be enjoyed, while the rest are to be used" (Raymond Canning, "*Uti/frui*," in Fitzgerald, *Augustine through the Ages*, p. 859). See *De Doctrina Christiana*, trans. R. P. H. Green (Oxford, 1997), 1.22.20.

[32] David Dumville, "Essex, Middle Anglia and the Expansion of Mercia in the South-East Midlands," *The Origins of the Anglo-Saxon Kingdoms*, ed. Steven Bassett (London, 1989), p. 140.

[33] Nicholas Higham, *An English Empire: Bede and the Early Anglo-Saxon Kings* (Manchester, Eng., 1995), p. 148.

[34] Wormald, "Bede, *Beowulf* and the Conversion of the Anglo-Saxon Aristocracy."

[35] Against Kevin Kieman and others who postulate a late date for the poem in the 10th or 11th centuries, both the consensus of early 20th-century *Beowulf* scholarship and later re-examinations of the issue (see Wormald, "Bede, *Beowulf* and the Conversion of the Anglo-Saxon Aristocracy" and Sam Newton, *The Origins of "Beowulf" and the Pre-Viking Kingdom of East Anglia* [Cambridge, Eng., 1993]) point to an eighth-century date as likeliest. The sparse evidence for the original dialect of the poem suggests an Anglian provenance in the Midlands: see Robert Bjork and Anita Obermeier, "Date, Provenance, Author, Audiences," in *A "Beowulf" Handbook*, ed. Robert Bjork and John D. Niles (Lincoln, Nebr., 1997), p. 26. This evidence is reinforced by the central presence in the text of the name of the ancestral Anglian king Offa and analogues between that reference and alleged marital sufferings of the 8th-century Mercian king

Offa: see *"Beowulf" and its Analogues*, trans. G. N. Garmonsway and Jacqueline Simpson (London, 1968), pp. 236–37. Also significant, given the probable role of a religious center as the site of the composition, is the "close connection between the Mercian dynasty, whose ancestors appear in *Beowulf*, and which . . . produced successive kings named Beornwulf and Wiglaf in the early ninth century, and many of the most important religious foundations of the time" (Wormald, p. 54). In addition, there are the poem's analogues with the *Lives* of St. Guthlac and their 8th-century Anglian provenance, apparently under Mercian overlordship. For a recent paleographical argument also supporting an 8th-century date for the poem, see Lapidge, "The Archetype of *Beowulf*."

[36] Newton, *The Origins of "Beowulf" and the Pre-Viking Kingdom of East Anglia*, pp. 142–43.

[37] Quotations from the Old English poetic versions of Guthlac's *Life* that follow are from Bernard Muir, ed., *The Exeter Anthology of Old English Poetry* (Exeter, 1994).

[38] See Koch, *The Gododdin of Aneirin*, p. xliii.

[39] *Felix's Life of St. Guthlac*, ed. Bertram Colgrave (Cambridge, Eng., 1956). Subsequent quotations from Felix's text are from this edition.

[40] By contrast, the undated but later Old English prose version of Felix's *Vita* contains only a positive tribute to Irish spiritual devotion, reminiscent of the way in which the ninth-century Alfredian Old English translation of Bede's history likewise tones down negative references to the Irish, long after either peculiar Irish ways or Welsh arms were seen as real threats to Anglo-Saxon sovereignty.

[41] Bede's history, for example, runs counter to a Welsh tradition of more of a Celtic role in the initial conversion of Northumbria. While the latter tradition is extant in the much later Cambro-Latin *Historia Brittonum*, Nora Chadwick in her article "The Conversion of Northumbria: A Comparison of Sources" (in *Celt and Saxon: Studies in the Early British Border*, ed. Nora Chadwick [Cambridge, Eng., 1963], pp. 138–66) has collected circumstantial evidence for a larger role for the British and Irish churches in the Anglo-Saxon conversion than Bede allowed. Clare Stancliffe has presented an updated study of this issue with similar conclusions in "The British Church and the Mission of Augustine," in *St. Augustine and the Conversion of England*, ed. Richard Gameson (Phoenix Mill, 1999), pp. 107–51.

[42] John Rhys, *Celtic Folklore, Welsh and Manx* (1901; reprint New York, 1980), pp. 676–77.

[43] Arthur Gray, "On the Late Survival of a Celtic Population in East Anglia," *Proceedings of the Cambridge Antiquarian Society* 15, n.s. 9 (1910–11): 45.

[44] Patrick Sims-Williams, *Religion and Literature in Western England, 600–800* (Cambridge, Eng., 1990), p. 26. Rhys, *Celtic Folklore*, pp. 675–77, in a now-dated theory that nonetheless is supported by some aspects of recent archaeological interpretation, also suggested that inhabitants of the Fens of Middle and East Anglia might have preserved communities intact from waves of invasions going back to those by the supposed Belgic Celtic overlords of the late Iron Age. Folkloric evidence for continued British presence in the Fens was catalogued idiosyncratically by Arthur Gray early in the 20th century (see footnote 43 above). Based on revisionist views of post-Roman British history, however, it would be more likely that Britons in the area would not have constituted tribal remnants hiding in the Fens so much as the majority population whose polities would have been seized or acquired through marriage and alliance by Anglo-Saxon warriors. Not mentioned by Gray and Rhys, but fitting the hypothesis of a recrudescent Celtic population in the region of the Middle Anglians, is terminology in the Old English *Guthlac A* poem that, while standard for demons in Old English literature, also conjures up appositive associations of refugee exile for the barrow spirits hidden in the fens (e.g. *wræcsetla*, line 296; *werga gæst*, line 451; and *wræcsiða*, line 509). The second term can refer to either "spirit" or "stranger/guest," depending on the vowel length.

[45] Bruce Eagles, "Lindsey," in Bassett, *The Origins of the Anglo-Saxon Kingdoms*, p. 206.

[46] See Higham, *An English Empire*, p. 148.

[47] See also Dark, *From Civitas to Kingdom*, pp. 86–88, and Higham, *Rome, Britain and the Anglo-Saxons*, p. 149.

[48] Theodore, sent as new archbishop of Canterbury on what was in effect the second papal mission to England in 668 by Pope Vitalian, brought with him in his company not only a returning Biscop augmenting his Augustinian library but also Hadrian of North Africa, who had been the pope's first choice for the job. Bede reports that Theodore, who was from Tarsus and a native Greek speaker, was assigned Hadrian as a companion by the pope "to take great care to prevent Theodore from introducing into the church over which he presided any Greek customs which might be contrary to the true faith" (*Ecclesiastical History*, p. 171). While this charge is thought specifically to relate to the pope's concern about monothelitism in the East, it does also seem to suggest a concern of Bede's with Eastern Otherness similar to his otherized construction of the intransigent Irish and especially native British churches.

[49] See Dumville, "Essex, Middle Anglia and the Expansion of Mercia," p. 134.

[50] Colgrave, *Felix's Life of St. Guthlac*, p. 87.

[51] Colgrave, *Felix's Life of St. Guthlac*, p. 89.

[52] Colgrave, *Felix's Life of St. Guthlac*, p. 89.

[53] For example, the Great Kankakee River Marsh region in Illinois once rivaled the Everglades in size. In the 19th century it was drained by immigrant farmer-settlers, mainly of English and German descent, who considered it a wasteland. But to Native Americans it had been an "ice box," a cornucopia of food supplies, as Jerry Lewis, a Potawatomi historian and former research fellow at the Newberry Library in Chicago, noted to me in an interview.

[54] See Colgrave, *Felix's Life of St. Guthlac*, p. 1.

[55] Asser, *Alfred the Great*, ed. Simon Keynes and Michael Lapidge (Harmondsworth, Eng., 1983), p. 103.

[56] Paul Battles describes parallels between descriptions in this poem and British legend in Layamon's *Brut* in "The Art of the Scop: Traditional Poetics in the Old English *Genesis A*" (Ph.D. diss., University of Illinois at Urbana, 1998).

[57] British-Celtic Christians were described in Bede's *History* as practically reprobates, unredeemed by the reformation of the Irish at the Synod of Whitby in 664, improperly ordaining priests and bishops, and allied with the purportedly pagan Penda of Mercia against Christian Northumbria (*Ecclesiastical History*, 2.2, 2.20, 3.28, 5.23).

[58] See also Frank Battaglia, "The German Earth Goddess in *Beowulf*," *The Mankind Quarterly* 31 (1990–91): 415–46; Robert Bly, *Sleepers Joining Hands* (New York, 1973); Randall Bower, "*Beowulf* and the Bog People," in *Literary and Historical Perspectives of the Middle Ages*, ed. P. W. Cummins et al. (Morgantown, 1982); and Garrett S. Olmstead, *The Gods of the Celts and the Indo-Europeans* (Budapest, 1994), p. 230.

[59] Newton, *The Origins of "Beowulf*," pp. 142–43.

[60] Besides apparently early accounts of magical and sacred islands in Welsh and Irish traditions, there are later widespread traditions of the Isle of Avalon associated with derivative Celtic lore, an island with a grove of apple trees associated with the site of Glastonbury Abbey in the West Country. Referred to as an Irish religious center in the *Sanas Chormaic* circa 900, Glastonbury was also described by "B" in his *Vita S. Dunstani* circa 1000 as "a certain royal island . . . spread wide with numerous inlets, surrounded by lakes full of fish and by rivers, suitable for human use . . . [where] the first neophites of the catholic law discovered an ancient church built by no human skill" (A. Gransden, "The Growth of the Glastonbury Tradition and Legends in the Twelfth Century," *Journal of Ecclesiastical History* 27 [1976]: 343). This welcoming description of the primeval sacred island-marsh landscape of Glastonbury, rooted in tradition influenced by Celtic cultures in west Britain, stands in palpable contrast to the foreboding description of the natural landscape of the Crowland area in the

Guthlac narratives. See Alfred K. Siewers, "A Cloud of Witnesses: The Origins of Glastonbury in the Context of Early Christianity in Western Britain" (M.A. thesis, University of Wales at Aberystwyth, 1994), pp. 74–80, and "Gildas and Glastonbury: Revisiting the Origins of Glastonbury Abbey," in *Via Crucis: Essays on Early Medieval Sources and Ideas*, ed. Thomas N. Hall (Morgantown, 2002), pp. 423–32. Likewise, early Irish voyage narratives often portray islands in otherworldly paradisaic terms; see Charles Wright, "'Insulae Gentium': Biblical Influence on Old English Poetic Vocabulary," in *Magister Regis: Studies in Honor of R. E. Kaske*, ed. Arthur Groos et al. (New York, 1986), on the patristic and Insular theme of islands as churches redeemed from paganism.

[61] Neville, *Representations of the Natural World*, p. 44.

[62] Anglian tradition on the Continent (presumably a precursor to the Anglians who came to dominate Mercia) had a tradition of the otherworldly island that seems analogous with the Celtic theme evident in the Glastonbury tradition—"On an island of the sea stands an inviolate grove . . . holy of holies," sacred to the goddess Nerthus, Mother Earth (Tacitus, *The Agricola and the Germania*, ed. D. H. Mattingly, trans. S. A. Handford [Harmondsworth, Eng., 1975], pp. 134–35). The sacredness of groves to the pagan Anglo-Saxons is also attested by place-name evidence: see David Wilson, *Anglo-Saxon Paganism* (London, 1992), pp. 23–24.

[63] " . . . let [the learned reader] remember the saying of St. Gregory, who considered it to be a ridiculous thing to confine the words of the heavenly oracle within the rules of the grammarian Donatus" (Colgrave, *Felix's Life of St. Guthlac*, p. 61). This is analogous to Augustine's analysis of the Trinity, in which Edmund Hill says he concludes "that it does not matter what word you choose, it is purely a matter of convention and convenience" (*The Trinity* [Brooklyn, 1991], p. 44). As with words, so with natural phenomena: "The divine scriptures then are in the habit of making something like children's toys out of things that occur in creation," Augustine writes, by which to entice our sickly gaze and get us step by step to seek as best we can the things that are above and forsake the things that are below" (*On Christian Teaching*, trans. R. P. H. Green [Oxford, 1997], p. 66).

[64] Proinsias Mac Cana, *Celtic Mythology*, rev. ed. (New York, 1996), p. 63.

[65] *The Mabinogi*, trans. Patrick Ford (Berkeley, 1977), pp. 42, 77, 84.

[66] We do have scraps of references and folklore, for example of Weland, the smith-god, "whose smithy was believed by the men of Wessex to have been in a neolithic Long Barrow on the Berkshire Downs near Uffington Castle" (Alfred Smyth, *King Alfred the Great* [Oxford, 1995], p. 569); see also Jim Hargan, "A Walk Through Time," *British Heritage* (April/May 1999): 48.

[67] D. P. Kirby, *The Earliest English Kings* (London, 1992), p. 128.

[68] John Shephard, "The Social Identity of the Individual in Isolated Barrows and Barrow Cemeteries in Anglo-Saxon England," in *Space, Hierarchy and Society: Interdisciplinary Studies in Social Area Analysis*, ed. Barry C. Burnham and John Kingsbury (Oxford, 1979), p. 70.

[69] Shephard, "The Social Identity of the Individual in Isolated Barrows," p. 77.

[70] A system of land being held by rent or non-military service in which landholdings were subject to equal division among sons after death of the owner. By the mid- or late-Anglo-Saxon period, by contrast, the Midlands led development of "open field" communally allotted holdings and nucleated settlement landscapes, based on archaeological and historical evidence that also suggests a strong system of local lordship (C. J. Bond, "Field Systems," in *The Blackwell Encyclopedia of Anglo-Saxon England*, ed. Michael Lapidge et al. [Oxford, 1999], p. 184; see also Hooke, *The Landscape of Anglo-Saxon England*, pp. 105–38).

[71] H. R. Ellis Davidson, "The Hill of the Dragon," *Folk-Lore* 61 (1950): 173, n. 21.

[72] Ronald Hutton, *The Pagan Religions of the Ancient British Isles* (Oxford, 1993), p. 276.

[73] Christopher Tilley, *A Phenomenology of Landscape*, pp. 202–03.

[74] Barbara Rosenwein, *Negotiating Space: Power, Restraint, and Privileges of Immunity in Early Medieval Europe* (Ithaca, N.Y., 1999), p. 73.

[75] Catherine Cubitt, *Anglo-Saxon Church Councils c. 650-c. 850* (London, 1995), p. 55.

[76] Athanasius, *The Life of St. Anthony the Great* (Willits, Calif., 1980–87?), pp. 64–65; see also *Vita S. Antoni*, trans. H. Ellershaw, in *Athanasius: Select Works and Letters, Nicene and Post-Nicene Fathers*, vol. 4., ed. Philip Schaff and Henry Wace (1892; reprint Peabody, 1999), p. 208.

[77] Athanasius, *The Life of St. Anthony the Great*, p. 69; see also *Vita S. Antoni*, p. 209.

[78] Willibald, *The Life of St. Boniface*, trans. C. H. Talbot, in *Soldiers of Christ*, ed. Thomas F. X. Noble and Thomas Head (University Park, Penn., 1995), p. 126. The ex-soldier St. Martin of Tours also cuts down a pagan-dedicated pine tree with miraculous results in Sulpicius Severus's late fourth-century Gallo-Roman account, but the focus there is not so much on the destruction of the tree as in Boniface's account, where the oak is then triumphantly reused for church timbers.

[79] Quoted in *Celtic Spirituality*, ed. Oliver Davies (New York, 1999), p. 111. In another famous early medieval Irish tradition, Patrick and companions are said to have been transformed into deer to escape persecutors, while the saint evoked what has become known as the breastplate or *lorica* of Patrick, a protective prayer that invokes natural forces as expressions of divine power (Davies, *Celtic*

Spirituality, pp. 118–119). The privileging of wild animal life in connection with a specific place and associated human community mark an attitude toward nature that often distinguishes the approach to landscape in Celtic hagiography from Anglo-Saxon.

[80] Cubitt, *Anglo-Saxon Church Councils*, p. 30.

[81] Cubitt, *Anglo-Saxon Church Councils*, p. 40.

[82] Cubitt, *Anglo-Saxon Church Councils*, pp. 42–43.

[83] R. A. Markus, *Gregory the Great and his World* (Cambridge, Eng., 1997), p. 49.

[84] Note, however, that writings about the holy places of biblical lands by Bede and others were probably attempted literary remedies among the Anglo-Saxons for this situation, as was, apparently, the prominence that Bede gave to the St. Alban's legend early in his history.

[85] See Stock, *Augustine the Reader*, p. 278.

[86] Marie-Louise Sjoestedt, *Gods and Heroes of the Celts*, trans. Myles Dillon (Blackrock, 1994), pp. 1–2.

[87] David Chidester, *Christianity: A Global History* (New York, 2000), p. 166.

[88] Stancliffe, "The British Church and the Mission of Augustine," pp. 121–22.

[89] Dorothy Whitelock, *The Audience of "Beowulf"* (Oxford, 1951), pp. 80–82.

[90] Certainly later British literary tradition in the so-called Nennian writings and those of Geoffrey of Monmouth suggests an association of dragons with control of the landscape, whether through the battling red and white dragons associated with Merlin or the title of the legendary Arthur's father, Uther Pendragon. A similar theme is found in the putative 7th-century Breton-Latin *Vita (Prima) Sancti Samsonis* in which a giant dragon is controlling the landscape from a cave, from which the saint expels him, lifting the curse (B. Lynette Olson, *Early Monasteries in Cornwall* [Woodbridge, Eng., 1989], p. 11). The symbolic power of such a chthonic monster relative to landscape may also have had vernacular mythological precedence, as seen in the world-encircling serpent of Norse tradition; see Ursula Dronke, "*Beowulf* and Ragnarok," in *Saga-Book of the Viking Society for Northern Research* 17 (1969): 302–25.

[91] See Davidson, "The Hill of the Dragon," p. 178.

[92] Davidson, "The Hill of the Dragon," p. 181. For a more recent examination of backgrounds and analogues to the dragon fight, see Charlotte Rauer, "*Beowulf*" *and the Dragon* (Woodbridge, Eng., 2000).

[93] The distinction drawn here between such "taking possession" of the land and monumentalizing it as in the Anglo-Saxon stories is that in the latter the otherworldly realm of the mounds is seized and subsumed both in the plot and in the textuality of the narrative through an allegorizing of it, whereas in the Welsh and Irish stories discussed it implicitly remains outside of human control

and more of a larger-than-life mystery that is nonetheless oddly engaging with humans (as opposed to clearly evil).

94 See Davidson, "The Hill of the Dragon," pp. 174–75. The Christian church in Britain adapted such landscape features to its claims of power as well: "Early Christian churches were sometimes built beside or even over a burial mound" (Davidson, "The Hill of the Dragon," p. 175). The mound at Dowth, near Newgrange in the Boyne Valley of Ireland, likewise became the site of a church, while the one at Knowth became an early medieval dynastic center; see Clare O'Kelly, *Illustrated Guide to Newgrange* (Ardnalee, 1978), p. 80. The ancient ritual and settlement mounds at Emain Macha and Ard Macha also became important early medieval dynastic and religious centers respectively in Ulster; see discussions in N. B. Aitchison, *Armagh and the Royal Centers in Early Medieval Ireland* (Woodbridge, Eng., 1994), and Alfred K. Siewers, "Stories of the Land: Nature and Religion in Early British and Irish Literary Landscapes" (Ph.D. diss., University of Illinois at Urbana, 2001).

95 Karl Wentersdorf, "*Guthlac A*: The Battle for the *Beorg*," *Neophilologus* 62 (1978): 139.

96 Davidson, "The Hill of the Dragon," p. 177.

97 *Anglo-Saxon Poetry*, trans. R.K. Gordon (London, 1954), p. 262.

98 Glyn Daniel, *The Prehistoric Chamber Tombs of England and Wales* (Cambridge, Eng., 1950), p. 23.

99 The absence of the mound in itself is not surprising, given the large numbers of such mounds that have disappeared across the centuries in Britain, judging by records in the historic period of mound sites that no longer exist today. Archaeologists have analyzed the description in chapter 28 of Felix's *Vita*—Colgrave, *Felix's Life of St. Guthlac*, pp. 93, 95—and have concluded that it probably does represent "a plundered chamber barrow" (see Daniel, *The Prehistoric Chamber Tombs*, p. 23).

100 Daniel, *The Prehistoric Chamber Tombs*, p. 23, nn. 3 and 4. It has also been hypothesized to have been a Bronze Age round barrow with stone cistern. An account in 1708 of "concrete" foundation walls and unsewn stone access passages at the base of a demolished chapel on the traditional site of the saint's home may suggest lingering features of a more extensive and older passage tomb (see Colgrave, *Felix's Life of St. Guthlac*, p. 183). In any case, the word *tumulus* in Felix's account is specific in indicating a tomb, and a similarly specific term *hlaw* is used in the Old English prose translation of Felix. Davidson notes of mounds in the charters that when *beorh* or *hlaw* were used, they might be pre-Saxon mounds, later ones often being "identified by the names of the men laid in them" ("The Hill of the Dragon," p. 174). But use of the word *beorg* in *Guthlac*

A aroused scholarly controversy in the 1960s and 1970s as Anglo-Saxonists debated whether the traditional translation of "mountain" (used by Gordon in his translation in *Anglo-Saxon Poetry*) should be replaced by "barrow." Both meanings of the word are attested, but Lawrence Shook cites examples elsewhere in reference to an artificial mound, and proposed that this was correct here, given the relatively flat landscape of the Fens ("The Burial Mound in *Guthlac A*," *Modern Philology* 58 (1960): 4. (The traditional site of Guthlac's retreat is, however, what is now called Anchorite or Anchor Church Hill, a short distance away from the current monastery building.) The *A* poet's description of a *grena wong* forming an *eard* (see lines 746, 477, 256. 428. 745) indicates a clearing among the trees with a mound located somewhere within its circumference," as Shook describes (p. 5).

[101] This seems reminiscent of the odd colophons to the *Táin Bó Cuailnge* in the Book of Leinster in which the Latin message denounces the tales as including "devilish lies . . . for the enjoyment of idiots," while the Irish message reads: "A blessing on everyone who will memorize the *Táin* faithfully in this form" (*The Táin*, trans. Thomas Kinsella [Oxford, 1970], p. 283).

[102] Shook, "The Burial Mound in *Guthlac A*," p. 10.

[103] Paul Reichardt, "*Guthlac A* and the Landscape of Spiritual Perfection," *Neophilologus* 58 (1974): 334.

[104] Wentersdorf, "*Guthlac A*: The Battle for the *Beorg*," pp. 137–38.

[105] Wentersdorf, "*Guthlac A*: The Battle for the *Beorg*," p. 140.

[106] Wentersdorf, "*Guthlac A*: The Battle for the *Beorg*," p. 141.

[107] See Fred C. Robinson, "*Beowulf and the Appositive Style*" (Knoxville, 1985).

[108] See Wentersdorf, "*Guthlac A*: The Battle for the *Beorg*," p. 141.

[109] James MacKillop, *Dictionary of Celtic Mythology* (Oxford, 1998), pp. 344–45.

[110] Charles D. Wright has examined in detail sources and relations of a motif in Anglo-Saxon poetry of the biblical Abel's blood polluting vegetation of the earth with sin. Some read this polluted-wasteland imagery as an expression of direct Augustinian allegory. See Charles D. Wright, "The Blood of Abel and the Branches of Sin: *Genesis A, Maxims I* and Aldhelm's *Carmen de uirginitate*," *Anglo-Saxon England* 25 (1996): 7–19.

[111] See Wentersdorf, "*Guthlac A*: The Battle for the *Beorg*," p. 136, and also *Guthlac A*, lines 150a–51a. Compare these resolutions-by-conquest-and-transcendence of the wasteland with an episode from the early Latin life of the Welsh-Breton St. Samson, purported to date to the seventh century (see Olson, *Early Monasteries in Cornwall*). Samson rids the Cornish countryside of a destructive dragon, after being led to its cave and throwing it down from there to its destruction. He then takes up residence in the cave temporarily as a hermit before moving on

to Brittany. The actual landscape of the cave is described in detail, including a miraculous spring there produced by the saint's prayers. The saint founds a monastery nearby and then moves on. Here there is a casting out of a monster, and a quickening of the landscape in terms of the spring and the founding of the monastery, but the saint does not take personal possession of the site for life. The landscape remains something greater than the saint, more of an external reality than in the Guthlac poems. The victory does not create the empty-tomb-centered landscapes of *Beowulf* and *Guthlac B*. Generally, the mound dwellers of Irish and Welsh stories are not demonic monsters, as in *Beowulf* and the Guthlac accounts, though linked to earlier inhabitants of the land and natural forces.

[112] Gordon, *Anglo-Saxon Poetry*, pp. 273–74; see also Frederick M. Biggs, "Unities in the Old English *Guthlac B*," *Journal of English and Germanic Philology* 89 (1990): 35–51.

[113] Gordon, *Anglo-Saxon Poetry*, p. 275.

[114] *Anglo-Saxon Poetry*, trans. S.A.J. Bradley (London, 1982), p. 281.

[115] Gordon, *Anglo-Saxon Poetry*, p. 277.

[116] Gordon, *Anglo-Saxon Poetry*, p. 277.

[117] Gordon, *Anglo-Saxon Poetry*, p. 278.

[118] See Mark Handley, "The Early Medieval Inscriptions of Western Britain: Function and Sociology," in *The Community, the Family and the Saint: Patterns of Power in Early Medieval Europe*, ed. Joyce Hill and Mary Swan (Turnhout, 1998), pp. 339–61.

[119] Despite efforts by Gillian Overing and Marijane Osborn to retrace physically the routes of the hero Beowulf, and by various scholars to etymologically locate the landscape of Heorot in present-day England, the one extant Old English secular narrative cycle, unlike its Irish and Welsh counterparts, is strangely notable for its lack of connection to any specific Insular physical landscape. See Gillian Overing and Marijane Osborn, *Landscape of Desire: Partial Stories of the Medieval Scandinavian World* (Minneapolis 1994).

[120] James W. Earl, "Transformation of Chaos: Immanence and Transcendence in *Beowulf* and Other Old English Poetry," *Ultimate Reality and Meaning* 10 (1987): 170.

[121] See Newton, *The Origins of "Beowulf*," p. 132.

[122] *"Beowulf": A New Verse Translation*, trans. Seamus Heaney (New York, 2000), p. 5. The Old English text printed alongside Heaney's translation is based on *"Beowulf*," *with the Finnesburg Fragment*, ed. C. L. Wrenn and W. F. Bolton (Exeter, 1988).

[123] Heaney, *"Beowulf": A New Verse Translation*, p. 213.

[124] Earl, "Transformation of Chaos," pp. 177–78.

[125] Earl, "Transformation of Chaos," p. 178.

[126] W. F. Bolton, *Alcuin and "Beowulf"* (New Brunswick, N.J., 1978), pp. 43–44.

[127] Sara Higley, *Between Languages: The Uncooperative Text in Early Welsh and Old English Nature Poetry* (University Park, Penn., 1993).

[128] The Anglo-Saxon tendency toward objectifying landscape in descriptions both allegorized and naturalistic can be glimpsed in a comparison of a text by Gregory familiar to the Anglo-Saxons with an Old English wisdom poem. Translated from the Alfredian version of Gregory's *Pastoral Care* by Earl, Gregory's words (with Virgilian echoes) read: "What is power and rulership but the mind's storm, always tossing the ship of the heart on the waves of thoughts?" (Earl, "Transformation of Chaos," p. 174). In *Maxims I*, part 1, lines 50–60, a parallel moral lesson is expressed in a quasi-realistic description of a sea storm. See Muir, *The Exeter Anthology of Old English Poetry*, p. 253; Earl, "Transformation of Chaos," p. 172; and Bradley, *Anglo-Saxon Poetry*, p. 347.

[129] Anglo-Saxon literature can be termed more detailed in its treatment of landscape than other early Insular traditions in the qualified context of narrative. However the exquisite detail of description in some of the so-called Irish "nature" or "hermit" poetry shows the Irish literary tradition as more than capable of naturalistic description. Similar attention to detail is evident in Irish and Welsh narratives, although often expressionistic and not in the context of creating the impression of a coherent cause-and-effect narrative of action related to landscape. One example is the motif of describing the sight of drops of blood in snow related to the beauty of a beloved in Ulster Cycle and Welsh tales. The distinction here is between a realistic landscape narrative and what could be termed more of a mosaic approach to detail. This mosaic or "snapshot" approach is compatible stylistically with the literal tendency of Irish exegesis, in terms of the latter's frequent attention to literal detail outside of an overall linear narrative form. Stylistic tendencies in the few examples of Old English landscape narrative could be compared by analogy with modern landscape portraits rather than mosaics, or with film as opposed to still photos. Their very scarcity however suggests the triumph of allegory in the formative period of the culture, evident in the apparently progressive allegorizing of landscape in the Guthlac accounts, and in the probable dating of *Beowulf* in the same relatively early era of Anglo-Saxon letters. In *Beowulf* we find landscape depictions that are more realistically naturalistic in overall setting than the often more stylized descriptions of Welsh and Irish narratives, forming a continuous scene of action like a 19th-century panorama. But the Old English narratives about Beowulf and Guthlac again lack the "snapshot" details of nature and engagement with animals and rivers and trees that figure in both Welsh and Irish heroic stories, and specific associations

with Insular topography and named places made in early Celtic narratives. The "snapshot" effect of engagement in the Celtic stories and poetry is similar (and perhaps related in religious worldview as will be explored below) to that which James H. Billington observed in the Eastern iconographic tradition: an "'inverse perspective' that thrusts focal points out at us, while in a seeming paradox "reminding us of our distance from heavenly things" (*The Face of Russia* [New York, 1999], p. 50). This is an aesthetic expression of the non-Augustinian cosmology expressed by St. Basil the Great and later Byzantine writers as the distinction between divine energy and essence: "We know the essence through the energy. No one has ever seen the essence of God, but we believe in the essence because we experience the energy" (quoted in Bishop Kallistos Ware, *The Orthodox Way* [Crestwood, 1999], p. 22).

[130] Heaney, *"Beowulf": A New Verse Translation*, pp. 37, 39.

[131] Gordon, *Anglo-Saxon Poetry*, p. 426.

[132] One exception is the "Death of Fergus Mac Leide," a late addition to the Ulster Cycle (circa 1100 according to Tom P. Cross and Clark Harris Slover, *Ancient Irish Tales* [1936; reprint New York 1996]). Even here, however, with its analogues to *Beowulf*, the Irish tale of monstrous watery conflict is less charged with moral concerns of hubris and community than the Old English narrative. The contrast can also be seen in Irish hagiography, where the most famous encounter with a denizen of the deeps, that of St. Columba with the prototypical Loch Ness monster, ends merely with the saint commanding the monster to return to the depths, the saint having saved a companion in an apparent test of spiritual power with the beast. See Adomnán, *Life of St. Columba*, ed. Richard Sharpe (London, 1991), 2.27. There is no detailed or negative description of the waters or dramatic destruction of the creature as in *Beowulf*. In the story of *Táin Bó Fróech*, often cited as an Irish analogue to Beowulf's struggle in the mere, the hero's fight with the water monster occurs in the context of a wooing challenge, and he is helped by his lover who provides him with a sword, unlike Beowulf's encounter in the mere, where he is alone with the monster and finds the giants' sword in the monsters' hoard. In the Irish story, there is no detailed description of the waters, and no connection of the landscape with either the divine, moral or civilizing concerns. St. Antony's struggle with a watery serpent in Athanasius's Greek hagiography involves no slaying of the monster, which is pacified.

[133] See Howe's discussion of Anglo-Saxon literary landscapes, "The Landscape of Anglo-Saxon England."

[134] The word *fyrgenstream*, used to describe the mere waters, is a sea-related term equated by Kemp Malone with Oceanus. See Goldsmith, *The Mode and Meaning of "Beowulf,"* p. 123.

135 Indeed Friedrich Klaeber in the introduction to his edition of the poem picturesquely referred to how "the brilliant picture of the monsters' mysterious haunt might well remind us of Celtic fancy" (*"Beowulf" and the Fight at Finnsburgh*, 3rd ed. with supplements [Lexington, Mass., 1950], p. xxi).

136 Heaney, *"Beowulf": A New Verse Translation*, pp. 95, 97.

137 Heaney, *"Beowulf": A New Verse Translation*, p. 99.

138 See Klaeber, *"Beowulf" and the Fight at Finnsburg*, pp. xiii–xxi.

139 Wright, *The Irish Tradition in Old English Literature*, pp. 117, 133. Sims-Williams notes that the Greek-Egyptian original of the *Visio*, the *Apocalypse of St. Paul*, evidenced a long popularity in "condemnations by Augustine. Aldhelm, Ælfric and others." This does not mean, however, that such a source outside Augustinian tradition could not be given Augustinian emphasis when drawn upon. Sims-Williams, for example, also describes a prayer of apparent Mercian provenance with analogues to one attributed to the Irishman Columbanus. Different from Columbanus's version was the putative Mercian text's "stress on human dependence, rather than human volition, in accordance with Augustine's teaching on Grace. Although Augustine wrote frequently of man's quest for God, this quest was originally inspired by God's Grace. . . . On the one hand it involves God's legitimate exercise of a terror inspired by love: on the other it co-operates with the innate motivation of the soul" (Patrick Sims-Williams, *Religion and Literature in Western England, 600–800* [Cambridge, Eng., 1990], pp. 249, 309–10).

140 Richard North, *Heathen Gods in Old English Literature* (Cambridge, Eng., 1997), pp. 221–26, and Battaglia, "The Germanic Earth Goddess in *Beowulf*," pp. 415–46. North also noted evidence in *Beowulf* and other Old English works for pagan Anglo-Saxon animism, transformed in the era of Christian literacy into representations of an Odinic cult acting as a kind of symbolic "straw man" for Christian concerns about pagan idolatry. He identifies a kind of double-erasure of pagan animism in Old English literature, in which paganism (like nature) is allegorized.

141 Compare the wholly non-human sea monsters in *Táin Bó Fróech*, St. Columba's encounter at Loch Ness, or St. Antony's encounter with a sea monster in Athanasius's *Vita* of the desert father. The portrayal of landscape in this scene also departs significantly from the landscapes of the Welsh and Irish stories already discussed.

142 See Neville, *Representations of the Natural World*, p. 38.

143 R. W. Dyson, Introduction, in Augustine, *De Civitate Dei (The City of God Against the Pagans)*, trans. R. W. Dyson (Cambridge, Eng., 1998), pp. xxiii.

144 There are indications the Irish were less enthusiastic. For example, while the Anglo-Saxon scholar Alcuin was a strong advocate of the *filioque*, following

Theodore of Canterbury, the Irish Eriugena did not advocate it. The Stowe Missal suggests a later addition of the *filioque* to a text of the Nicaean Creed in use in Ireland that earlier did not feature the change.

[145] Julia Kristeva, "Dostoevsky, the Writing of Suffering, and Forgiveness," *Black Sun*, trans. Leon S. Roudiez (New York, 1989), p. 211.

[146] A prototype of Western feudal monarchy differentiated from traditional conceptualizations of cosmic empire and civic space, as in for example Byzantine ideology.

[147] See Carole M. Cusack, *The Rise of Christianity in Northern Europe, 300–1000* (London, 1999), p. 81.

[148] Julia Kristeva, *Powers of Horror: An Essay on Abjection*, trans. Leon S. Roudiez (New York, 1982), p. 71.

[149] Julia Kristeva, "Women's Time," in *Critical Theory Since 1965*, ed. Hazard Adams and Leroy Searle (Tallahassee, 1986), pp. 472–73.

[150] Stock, *Augustine the Reader*, pp. 76–77. The emerging Augustinian-Gregorian conception in the early medieval West of an objectified phenomenal world is again theologically related to the developing notion of grace as created (see J. Patout Burns, "Grace," in Fitzgerald, *Augustine through the Ages*, p. 396), and of theophany as mainly mediated through created objects, all expressed in allegorical artistic styles.

[151] Kristeva, *Powers of Horror*, p. 210.

[152] Comparison of the differing frameworks of time and space in Anglo-Saxon and Celtic narratives of landscape yields analogues too in comparative studies of hagiography in seventh- and eighth-century Frankish realms. Those saints' lives that were "Irish-inspired," according to Pierre Riché, involved the sense that "The saint has been freed from the ordinary human condition that results from man's Fall and rediscovers the harmony of paradise. In such brief moments the two worlds, which were thought to be separate, have a fleeting reunion." In those accounts influenced less by Irish monasticism on the Continent, miracles were a matter of practical betterment along a linear sense of progression in the physical realm. See Pierre Riché, "Columbanus, his Followers and the Merovingian Church," in *Columbanus and Merovingian Monasticism*, ed. H. B. Clarke and Mary Brennan (Oxford, 1981), pp. 69–70; see also John Carey's connection of non-Augustinian Irish Christian emphases with secular Irish narratives of the Otherworld in his *A Single Ray of the Sun* (Andover and Aberystwyth, 1999).

[153] A monument without a body, such as Beowulf's beacon mound or ultimately Guthlac's mound, the cenotaph as a symbol for mainstream Western views of nature relates also to Kristeva's description of the Augustinian Trinity as an inverted triangle. Its emphasis on God descending into creation, in its special

privileging of both Father and Son together above the Holy Spirit, reaches down to an individual focal point (the crucified Christ, the sense of the soul bound in flesh that is ultimately abandoned by the soul) and does not involve to the same extent (in Kristeva's phrase) the "erotic fusion" of the Athanasian-Cappadocian Trinity—an equilateral triangle, hinged on an upper focal point in the Father, drawing up the broad base of creation in the deification of believers.

[154] Again involving a more distant presence from human life than Welsh and Irish counterparts. Consider as a last example the literary construction of place in two narrative encounters with oak-related themes: Rhiannon's ride past the mound of Arberth (meaning "by the grove," in conjunction with the prehistoric mound likely referring to an oak grove of pre-Christian significance) where Pwyll waits, in the early Welsh First Branch of *The Mabinogi*, and Augustine of Canterbury's waiting for the British-Celtic bishops at the oak named for him, in Bede's Anglo-Latin *History*. The first is a non-linear otherworldly encounter integrative of nature and human activity. The second is an event placed in linear time and distinguishing between "natural" indigenous culture and the new Anglo-Saxon order. There is of course a difference in genre between the two narratives, and the story of Pwyll is later in date than Bede, though based on earlier mythic traditions. However, similar if less dramatic mythic contrasts to Bede's landscape style could be found in early Irish and Welsh mythic "pseudo-histories." And, arguably, *The Mabinogi* is a foundational narrative text of Welsh cultural identity as much as Bede's *History* was for the Anglo-Saxon people. Both descriptions involve places of "real" geographic landscape, associated by name with oaks, a native tree with traditional associations. Both also involve a certain cloaking of cultural as well as natural history in a textual landscape—in the case of Bede, of a full picture of native British Christianity, and in the case of the Welsh story, an explication of Rhiannon's associations with pre-Christian mythology of the horse goddess, although arguably her name and presentation in the story involve these implicitly in a fairly direct way. Indeed the visibility of cultural stratification in the Welsh narrative is part of the difference in approach symbolized by the contrast of the two narrative landscape settings.

BEOWULF AND THE
ORIGINS OF CIVILIZATION

JAMES W. EARL

THE ROLE OF PSYCHOANALYSIS

Here I offer a model for understanding heroic literature, and epic in particular, as an idealization of a certain sort, inviting certain forms of psychological identifications in the audience—socially desirable identifications, to be sure, but necessarily effected in the individual. In the case of *Beowulf*, these identifications are facilitated by vast silences in the text—analogous to the silence of the psychoanalyst, another facilitator of such identifications. In this way, heroic literature produces an analyzable psychological effect in the audience, much as tragedy does with its catharsis.

Also, insofar as *Beowulf* is a Christian poem, I would like to restore the psychological dimension to our discussion of the Anglo-Saxon conversion. The conversion is central to our understanding of Anglo-Saxon culture and literature but is always treated as if it were a purely ideological phenomenon,

From *Thinking about "Beowulf"* (Stanford, 1994), pp. 161–88; originally published in slightly different form in *Speaking Two Languages: Traditional Disciplines and Contemporary Theory in Medieval Studies*, ed. Allen J. Frantzen (Albany, 1991), pp. 65–89, and reprinted here with permission of The State University of New York Press. The only alterations to the original have been to remove references Earl makes in the body of the essay to other chapters of *Thinking About "Beowulf*," and to convert the original "works cited" method of reference to footnotes.

a more or less simple matter of shifting alliances, reforming institutions, and substituting terms. But Christianity, by cultivating the superego in the individual and institutionalizing a cultural superego in the Church, imports its own psychology along with new social structures and doctrines.

This Christian psychology invites psychoanalytic interpretation, so its historical origins in the conversion should be analyzable as well. The notoriously difficult relations between Christian and pre-Christian traditions and values in Anglo-Saxon culture, and in *Beowulf* in particular, can be understood historically and theologically, of course; but they can also—and perhaps even better—be understood psychologically, as an interesting case of ambivalence at the cultural level.

As I read *Beowulf* and other heroic literature, I am led to wonder about the relation of individual to social and cultural psychology. Like Freud, I am tempted to analyze culture as if it were an individual—to speak, for example, of its growth, its mourning, or its ambivalence, or of myths (and to some extent literature) as its dreams. But how can such analogies be defended—how can *psychoanalysis* be defended—among today's competing critical ideologies? Many have renounced both the concept of culture (a "facile totalization" as Frederic Jameson would say, at best only a dominant culture repressing myriad subcultures struggling for expression), and the concept of the individual (a bourgeois fabrication built on a humanistic conception of human nature, the myth of the autonomous ego). And even if those concepts could be retained, could we discover a clear train of linkages between them to account for all their tempting analogies?

I pragmatically dismiss these philosophical objections. Jameson's "political unconscious"[1] might seem to offer a linkage between the insights of psychoanalysis and Marxism, one source of these criticisms, but that concept is as mystical in its Hegelian way as the Jungian collectivities from which it is derived via Northrup Frye, and it cannot be counted as psychoanalytic. Louis Montrose's "politics of the unconscious"[2] is closer, perhaps, but dialogue between psychoanalysis and Marxism is still bound to be uncomfortable at best. At the very least, we will wish to clarify those areas of psychoanalytic theory where the linkages between the individual and the group must lie—the theories of identification and the superego.

Not to forget the text itself (so easy in theoretical discussions like this), I will point to certain passages in *Beowulf* characterized by silence and ambivalence, the psychological signatures of Anglo-Saxon heroic and elegiac poetry. But I am not so much interested in "psychoanalyzing the text" as in understanding how the text, with its deep, uninterpretable silences, might be said to sit in the analyst's place and psychoanalyze its audience—then and now—by acting as a screen for our projections.

This approach hardly replaces earlier approaches to the poem and in fact builds upon them; in the end, psychoanalysis being the omnivorous hermeneutic that it is, it interprets them, and itself, right along with the poem. Psychoanalysis is not inimical to other critical discourses, but it is not exactly complementary either. Psychoanalysis is concerned with all the mental states relevant to the poem and its understanding, and therefore our other critical responses to the poem are an important part of its subject. When I come to grapple with particular problems in the poem, it will be seen how psycho-analytic judgments tend to grow out of philological, textual, literary, and historical analysis, considered along with our more immediate psychological responses to the poem.

Nor can psychoanalysis, at least as I invoke it here, claim to interpret the poem better or more comprehensively than other contemporary approaches. I certainly do not consider psychoanalysis an "ultimate horizon" (Jameson's term again) or a programmatic hermeneutic. I can only claim to address the sorts of psychological questions that the poem prompts in a student of Freud. But these are important, if not ultimate, questions. Primarily they concern origins: not only the origins of civilization but the origins of the poem too, and also the origins of our critical attitudes toward it. All these questions turn out to be related psychologically. The individuality of the author and the reader, I will suggest, is one issue that binds them all into a single problem.

For the philologist, the folklorist, the new critic, the oralist, the postmodernist, and the new historicist—that is, for just about every scholarly reader—the author of *Beowulf* is decentered, erased, ignored, diffused into a web of preexisting traditions and historical forces, or evaporated into the ephemerality of oral culture. On the other hand, if I am right, the author was a highly original genius, a strong poet who helped shape those traditions in large part, at least as we perceive them now. Why is this position, which I find almost inevitable, so at odds with most traditions of *Beowulf* scholarship? What is it about the poem that invites such resistance to the idea of authorship, at least in those who have set about to conquer the poem intellectually?

It is partly because the roots of *Beowulf* scholarship lie in folklore and philology: the idea of an author never had a chance. Today it is orality and ideology. The poem does invite this response, I must admit, by passing itself off as traditional, even though it is demonstrably unique and original in many important respects, and even though there is scant proof of its traditionality outside its own claims and our uncommon willingness to believe them.

These two readings of the poem (the traditional *Beowulf* and the original *Beowulf*) imply not just ideologies but critical psychologies as well; for if the poem sits in place of the analyst, much of our response to questions of origin and authorship will be influenced by our dispositions toward the authority of the text and toward authority in general. The ideology served by our interpretations may be humanism, romanticism, nationalism, Marxism, or feminism; but weighed psychoanalytically, our interpretations will always be to some extent vicissitudes of the family romance, operations of the ego, expressions and sublimations of our own narcissism. We are social beings; but reading the poem here at the desk late at night remains an extremely private, individual act. That individuality is not insignificant, or imponderable, and it might be factored right into our interpretations.

Our attitudes toward authorship and the authority of the text will be the inverse of our attitudes toward the autonomous ego, the self. If these are indeed ideological commitments (Humanism! Marxism!), they still have psychological roots and can hardly be dissociated from our conceptions of ourselves as relatively free individuals, or as members and representatives of groups, or as expressions or victims of historical forces. Such self-representations are largely characterological, hammered out in childhood; as the poem sits in place of the analyst, the analyst ultimately sits in place of our parents. Epic especially may be said to serve with singular devotion that universal (though not ultimate) ideology that Lacan calls the Law of the Father and that Freud explored in his theory of the superego. Both theories are good descriptions of the Anglo-Saxon concept of fate, *wyrd*. Thus our own highly individualized relations to the superego are bound to inform our interpretations of a poem like *Beowulf*.

The role of psychoanalysis in critical thinking today is largely determined by the ideological drift of other schools: its role is to reassert the value and legitimacy of the individual (whether the author or the reader) as a focus of critical attention and the importance of the unconscious and the irrational in interpretation—and in mental life generally. Psychoanalytic readings of texts, psychobiographies of their authors, and psychohistories of their contexts notwithstanding, however, the greatest contributions of psychoanalysis to literary criticism are probably just the internalization of the simplest Freudian insights—unconscious intention, for example, or the overdetermination, condensation, and displacement of meaning, or art as sublimation. Another obvious example is Harold Bloom's realization that literary influence is not just one poet's having learned from another, like a student from a teacher, but more a matter of the deeply "agonistic" relations of parent and child.[3]

The anxiety of influence is not a matter just for poets. Every reader's relation to a text is similarly complex, if we treat reader response responsibly in light of Freud. The common reader's response is also oedipal to a degree. That is the simple insight I would like to internalize here. Psychologically, the suspension of disbelief is not rational or entirely willing; it is a complicated, spontaneous act of projection and identification. That is where we must start; though in the end, projection and identification will lead us, like the Oedipus complex itself, back to the theory of the superego.

As a genre, epic is involved with the task of superego construction at both the individual and the cultural levels. Freud summarizes: "Strengthening of the superego is a most precious cultural asset in the psychological field. Those in whom it has taken place are turned from being opponents of civilization into being its vehicles."[4] That strengthening is one of the tasks of epic, the poetic accompaniment to the birth of civilization.

But the epic cannot discriminate among its audiences: it sets about constructing our superegos as well as its original audience's. So in the case of epic especially, interpretation is likely to express our own invaded psychologies as well as the author's. In this regard, *Beowulf* is an extreme, and therefore an extremely interesting, case.

WHY *BEOWULF*?

Beowulf has a bad reputation: Woody Allen advises English majors, "Just don't take any course where they make you read *Beowulf*." Despite its foreignness and its difficulty, however, and despite its funereal obsession with death, *Beowulf* is now commonly taught to ninth graders, along with the *Iliad* and the *Odyssey*, as if it were an adventure or fantasy story. This trivialization accounts for some of the poem's bad reputation, but not all of it.

Beowulf is a hard text. Its language, style, and values seem as distant and strange as those of Homer and the Greek tragedies. Like them, *Beowulf* opens up a metrical world parallel to our own, different but strangely akin, throwing our ideas and attitudes, some of them unconscious, into new light. But our kinship with the world of *Beowulf*—our perspective in this new light—always remains hauntingly out of focus. Today a good reader of *Beowulf* has to be an expert time traveler and mystery unraveler—an expert scholar and interpreter; but even so, it remains uncertain what we can learn from the poem that is not wholly contingent on our own attitudes and beliefs. It is not at all clear that a "clean" interpretation is possible. This may be true of all texts to a degree, but again, *Beowulf* is an extreme case.

The poet and his first readers already had something of the same problem, however. The world of *Beowulf*, set in the heroic past, was already distant from them, akin to but strangely different from their Christian Anglo-Saxon world. Between the world of the poem and the world of its poet lay not only the gulf of meter but the complex transformations, social and psychological, of the development from tribe to state and of the conversion to Christianity. The relation of the Germanic tribal elements in the poem to Christianity has always been its most notorious crux and the driving force of its criticism. *Beowulf* is an ethical poem of the Christian Anglo-Saxons, but its ethics are not Christian, and its hero is not an Anglo-Saxon; so it is not clear how the poem's ideals might actually have functioned in the actual world of the audience.

Many scholars meditating on this problem have concluded that an Anglo-Saxon audience could not have accepted the poem's non-Christian ("pagan") ideals, so it is commonly argued that the poem's heroic warrior virtues are actually metaphors for Christian ones. Lately it is even commonly said that the poem's greatness may lie precisely in the way it subtly undermines those heroic ideals—in effect, undermines itself. Robert Hanning, for example, argues that the poet "completely reverses all tendencies toward harmony in heroic history, and offers instead a soured, ironic version of what has gone on before, embodying a final assessment of a world without God as a world in which time and history are themselves negative concepts."[5] T. A. Shippey claims "that the poet is demonstrating the inadequacy of heroic society; that he sees this the more forcibly for being a Christian; and that his rejection of overt finger-pointing first gives the pleasure of ironic perception, and second shows the glittering insidiousness of heroism, the way it perverts even the best of intentions."[6] The latest major statement of this position is Bernard Huppé's *Hero in the Earthly City*.[7] These are modern readings of *Beowulf*. They are not entirely false, but they are unlikely simplifications, because they still leave many questions unasked.

A few questions I like to ask are these: (1) How do the psychologies of tribal and civilized societies differ? (2) What are the psychological dynamics of the transition from one to the other, and of religious conversion? (3) How and why do we idealize the past? and (4) How do we identify with and internalize a work of literature? In any case, we can assume from the start that *Beowulf* bore a complex, indirect, and nonmimetic relation to any historical reality, including the Anglo-Saxon *ethos* either before or after the conversion.

I have mentioned our kinship with the poem and also the Anglo-Saxons' kinship with it; but then there is a third kinship, ours to the Anglo-Saxons. We still live in a largely Anglo-Saxon world, and even over a millennium the child is father to the man. Different as we have become from the Anglo-Saxons and from each other, in our cultural origins we still sometimes see stark enlargements of our deepest traits, which otherwise now go unobserved—though they have hardly disappeared for all that. The hall may have become the office, its rituals a system of contracted salaries, duties, and taxes, the wars corporate (or even academic); but the relations of such traditionally male-dominated institutions to women, the family, and religion remain as teasingly unresolved as ever and are still the subject of much of our literature. So too the broken oath, the failed promise, the conflict of loyalties, the silent hero, the alienation of the individual from society, and the problematic roles of women and kinship in social life.

These are the great Germanic themes—Germanic, more than biblical or classical. Our modern English-speaking world is indebted to those three traditions equally, and the Germanic leg of this cultural triad is firmly rooted in *Beowulf*. It is perhaps the oldest, most ambitious, and most deeply resonant text in that tradition; it is the nearly inaudible, Germanic *basso profundo* of English and other Germanic literature. For all its Christian elements, it is still our most pregnant Germanic text. *Beowulf* is not just another poem. It seems to lay bare our Germanic, our Anglo-Saxon origins.

But the investigation of our own origins has to be fraught with all the usual perils of self-reflection—nearsightedness first of all, blindness to what is too close; also ambivalence, denial, avoidance, and vague fears of what might be discovered beneath the mask—in short, anxiety and guilt. As a result, *Beowulf* both reveals and disguises some surprisingly familiar structures of our cultured Germanic, Anglo-Saxon, English-speaking minds—our antifeminism, for example, our repression of affect, our materialism, and our denial of death.

This system of relations—of us to *Beowulf*, of *Beowulf* to the Anglo-Saxons, and of the Anglo-Saxons to us—constitutes the meaning of *Beowulf*. There is not much agreement about this meaning, though the poem's best students do like to claim that *Beowulf* is a poem for our day. But it has always been a poem for the day. That is because silence was a positive virtue to the Anglo-Saxons. Thus *Beowulf*—(like the Old Testament, but unlike the classical epics) has its deep silences—so much is left unsaid!—in which we can hardly help but read our selves, and out of which we draw our in-terpretations. Like the sagas, the poem seldom speaks, for example, of its characters' motivations or feelings; so it is easy to assume they are like us, or like our stereotyped ideas of them. Not only speech but heroic behavior is also typically restrained. Behind this restraint, can we assume great pas-sions are being repressed? Which ones? Fear perhaps, hiding behind all its predictably heroic reaction-formations?

Family and economic life are wholly invisible in the poem too; and the poem's attitudes toward women, and toward themes as fundamental as re-ligion and heroism, are famously ambiguous. The poem might be said not to articulate its themes at all, leaving the reader a very wide range of inter-pretive freedom. Thus the heroic, or the overreaching, or the sinful, or the existential, or the Christian, or the Christlike Beowulf—the folk-Beowulf, the kingly Beowulf, the monastic Beowulf: like *Hamlet*, *Beowulf* supports with its silence whatever reading we most wish, and modern readers seem to wish many things of it.

Interpretation is not a science even in straightforward cases, and *Beowulf* is a rock on which interpretations are easily broken. The history of *Beowulf* scholarship (like Anglo-Saxon scholarship generally) has been a history of the projection of cherished beliefs upon the poem, both individually and collectively. They form the great tradition of Protestant, English, Gothic, pan-Germanic, Romantic, Victorian, and modern readings of Anglo-Saxon culture—a tradition of cherished beliefs that the Anglo-Saxons were really Protestant, or democratic, or noble savages, or Aryan folk, or anxiously self-contradictory existential Christian warriors.

The modern interpretation of *Beowulf* was born in Tolkien's analysis of its martial heroism in 1936, on the eve of World War II: "While the older southern imagination has faded for ever into literary ornament, the north-ern has power, as it were, to revive its spirit even in our own times. It can work, even as it did work with the *goðlauss* viking, without gods: martial heroism as its own end. But we may remember that the poet of *Beowulf* saw clearly: the wages of heroism is death."[8] This is in fact a very wise—and very modern—interpretation, one that genuinely makes *Beowulf* a poem for Tolkien's day; only three years later the great ship-burial at Sutron Hoo was exhumed and immediately reburied to protect it from the Nazis. Tolkien was not in a position to romanticize Germanic heroism or to trivialize it. To him the poem's theme is obvious: the poet saw clearly that the wages of heroism is death. One could say just as easily, however, that the poet saw clearly that the wages of heroism is victory, or glory, or peace.

Unbelievably, only a half-century later, Tolkien's Christian existentialism, which has served so many interpretations well and which is so moving in itself, looks almost sentimental to postmodern eyes, like Churchill's posturing. Tolkien's own fiction is in some measure responsible for the reduction of *Beowulf* to adolescent literature. We await a postmodern *Beowulf*; for surely, poised between holocausts as we sometimes feel ourselves to be, our more complete disillusionment is bound to discover itself in those same poetic silences even more forcefully.

I do not deliver a postmodern *Beowulf*. My theme, the origins of civilization, is Freudian in spirit and therefore distinctly old-fashioned in the postmodern climate. By the suspicious totalization "civilization" I mean a stage in social evolution characterized by cities as well as by literacy, statutory law, and civil government—as opposed to an earlier stage characterized by villages, orality, revenge, customary law, and kinship structures. These are well-worn anthropological concepts, still useful since Freud's day, though they will never be precise enough to resist philosophical attack, because the development from one stage to the other involves large and complex areas of overlap. But is it necessarily reductive or essentialist to define such structures contingently, within the numberless historical accidents we call a society, or the ceaseless flow we call history? Must it always be mean-spirited, patronizing, or romantic to explore the otherness of tribal societies still struggling on the margins of civilization, or explore, as in this case, the deepest roots of our own civilization?

For in our generation we have witnessed this other holocaust too: civilization's eradication of tribal societies everywhere. We are bound to mourn this loss forever. We share this mourning with the *Beowulf* poet, and it is one of our deepest ties to the poem. For now especially, in this generation, the relation of civilizations to the "primitive" societies that preceded them, and from which they developed, remains an urgent issue in the great tradition of Montaigne, Rousseau, and Freud. My focus is the transition in England. For the English-speaking world, and for much of the rest of the world too now, Anglo-Saxon England, along with early Greece and ancient Israel, was one of those formative stages determining the direction of future development. It remains one of our earliest cultural memories, traces of which can still be found deeply embedded in the present.

Interestingly, the Anglo-Saxons themselves, like the Greeks and the Jews before them, once they entered into the stream of civilization, were immediately obsessed with their own origins, with the transition they had just endured. *Beowulf* was not written in the heroic past but about it, and in particular about the trauma of its loss. In large part the poem creates that heroic past retroactively, thematizing cultural origins and the transition to civilization. Like the Pentateuch, and like Homer and the Greek tragedies, *Beowulf* and many of its companion poems in Old English dwell on the origins of civilization, mourning the loss of the prehistoric tribal past, now redefined as a heroic age. This mournful obsession defines the heroic, the epic, and the elegiac generally, and the Anglo-Saxon case with special clarity.

More than my theme is Freudian in spirit. I too am affected, as I think through this mournful obsession, attempt to re-create the audience's psychological relations to that imaginary heroic world, and experience their identification with those consoling idealizations of what has been lost. Criticism too has its psychological component: the greatest inhibitions to interpretation, in literature as well as life, seem to me to be psychological before they are philosophical, and they are barely open to "critical" discussion at all because they occur at the personal (and often unconscious) level, even if collectively. These are the inhibitions Freud called projection, resistance, and transference and countertransference.

I have already mentioned *projection* as a special problem in reading Old English poetry because of the ethical value the Anglo-Saxons placed on silence, as well as our unconscious *resistance* to perceptions that pose a threat to us. *Transference* and *countertransference* are more specifically psychoanalytic terms. The first refers to the projections of the analysand upon the silent analyst; the second refers to the limitations placed on analysis by the analyst's own neuroses, which necessarily cloud and distort interpretation unless he or she is aware of them. That is why the analyst must be analyzed. Countertransference is the specific mechanism of projection and resistance in the psychoanalyst, but the concept might easily be extended to interpretation in general.

In short, who we are means quite a lot to our interpretations, and the best we can do is account for ourselves every step of the way. In this regard, the neuroses I bring to *Beowulf* are neither religious nor heroic; but scholarship has its own neuroses, so it might be pertinent here to report two recent dreams.

Falling asleep recently while thinking about *Beowulf*, I dreamt of a sphinx, not quite buried in the desert sand; in fact, no matter how hard I tried to bury it, one eye always remained uncovered. The sphinx is *Beowulf*, of course, but it is also my superego. I take this as a good sign.

I had the second dream the night before delivering a conference paper on the poem. I dreamt about a little girl who had a fascinating, unusual doll, every part of which—arms, legs, head, torso—seemed to be made from other dolls, all of different colors and proportions. I knew where it had come from: the little girl's brother had collected all the old, broken dolls he could find around the neighborhood, and he had loaded them into his red wagon and pulled them home behind his bicycle; then he had made a single doll out of all their parts, and had given it to his little sister. Far from thinking it was junk, she thought it was beautiful and loved it—first of all because it was unlike any other doll, yet like them all; also because it was so interesting, and because her brother had made it for her and made it so well.

The doll, of course, is *Beowulf*; I am the little girl, and the poet is her brother. In the construction and meaning of the doll may be seen something of my understanding of the poem's genesis, and the relation of its traditions to its originality. Perhaps because I first studied *Beowulf* while also reading Lévi-Strauss, in the dream I represent the poet as a *bricoleur*. When I sleep, it seems, I am still a structuralist.

So I am the little girl; but the dream is in the third person, because I am also the brother, piecing together (like the poet) my own *bricolage*, my effigy of *Beowulf* constructed from past scholarship; and you are the sister I am trying to please. In scholarship as in poetry, practice tells me, originality is still mostly *bricolage*, a new and loving reconstruction of the materials we have inherited from the past. Among other things, the dream tells me that as a scholar I do not identify so much with the hero of the poem as with the poet and with others who have made this identification. I take this as a good sign too.

My double identification in the dream, with both the girl and her brother, illustrates certain features of identification—its shifting ambivalence and overdetermination—which will be important in our interpretation of the poem. The most important of these features is that insofar as I am a reader of *Beowulf* I identify with the girl, but insofar as my reading is itself a creative act, I identify with her brother the artist. This is how overdetermination works.

Actually, the situation is much more complex than that, the images more overdetermined; for the characters in the dream are clearly modeled on my wife and her older brother (she was my *Beowulf* student, he is a craftsman), as well as my earliest memories of me and my own older brother (an inveterate scavenger with his red wagon). My scholarship is never entirely free of even the most intimate themes of my life. Enough said about that.

Like the poem, then, the dream is richly overdetermined and deeply ambivalent. In fact, the neatness of all this splitting makes me think that my ambivalence itself is probably the dream's latent thought, and that *Beowulf* has unconsciously become a symbol of it for me. Thus the ambivalent image of the poem itself: it is only a junk-doll, but a unique, beautiful, and meaningful one.

The dream also brings rather delicate problems of gender to consciousness. *Beowulf* is a markedly antifeminist poem, and making it a gift to the little girl is my attempt at compensation, though necessarily condescending: she is still being strongly marginalized, after all. I do not see any way around that, since the poem so strongly marginalizes the female reader already. My simultaneous identification with her, however, indicates my deep ambivalence about the patriarchal project of the poem and the patriarchal project of its criticism (not to mention the patriarchal structures of professional life, teaching, and marriage). Beyond that, moreover, the bond of love between her and her brother, both of whom I identify with strongly, though in different ways, indicates how far from such ideological criticism my personal responses to the poem really are.

The fulfilled wish of the dream is the harmony of opposites, *concordia discors*. Pursued long enough, the analysis would come to rest in the thought that although I am a child, I am also a parent—a form of the original oedipal paradox: What walks on four legs in the morning, two in the afternoon, and three at night? Much unresolvable conflict and ambivalence is harmonized in the manifest dream, and the junk-doll *Beowulf* is an overdetermined symbol of this harmony.

The ease with which the problem of understanding *Beowulf*, more than other poems, shades into the problem of understanding myself suggests to me (naturally) that the high indeterminacy of the poem provokes strong psychological responses which may well be a clue to its *raison d'être*. Just such an indeterminacy in the Greek tragedies seems intended to provoke catharsis. What does *Beowulf* intend for us in this way? If the overdetermined symbols and vast silences of the poem function like the silence of the analyst, the poem will function as a screen for our projections, which can be manipulated by the plot and predictably drawn toward resolution.

Identification of one sort or another is essential. Our relations to poetry are always highly personal. Even Keats's negative capability is only the heightened ability to make identifications without the interference of transference and countertransference. When statements about art claim to be impersonal, objective, and scientific, we are probably in the presence of resistance. The compulsion to objectivity is both a denial of affect and an exaggerated claim of importance—"my thought, my theory, my method is universal, ultimate, transcendental"—two sides of the same neurotic coin. There is still a lot of positivistic and rationalistic scholarship being produced about *Beowulf*, in a spirit of resistance to the more modest and self-effacing claims of both modernism and postmodernism.

I am finally coming to see the necessity and the value of what Bloom calls a "strong misreading." Thus objectivity is not exactly the goal of my interpretation; objectivity is not what is left when the psychological inhibitions to interpretation are finally overcome. *Disillusionment* strikes me as a more useful, less impersonal concept. This disillusionment is not necessarily negative or morbid; like the reality principle, it is an agent of the ego, something close to an active psychological force. Perhaps it is a version of Freud's death instinct, progressing naturally, though against resistance, from infant narcissism to the bier. Perhaps it would be more comforting to think of it in Socratic terms as the humility that naturally comes with self-knowledge.

Not surprisingly, the silences of *Beowulf* seem to me symptomatic, or proleptic, of even these latest developments in our cultural and personal histories. I see *Beowulf* as an artful, cagey, and defensive last stand against disillusionment with both heroism and religion; affirming and denying the comforts of both those illusions at the same time; post-heroic, Christian but secular. That is not the same as saying that the poem undermines its own ideals, though: ambivalence is not the same as ambiguity. Ambivalence is a psychological term pointing to the attitudes, conscious or unconscious, of the author and the audience, as well as to the poem. Ambiguity is a hermeneutic problem involving the critical faculties. Ambivalence, on the other hand, is a vicissitude of the passions, requiring a certain amount of disillusionment for its appreciation. This is one of the qualities ninth graders do not bring to *Beowulf*.

I suspect that behind the silence and restraint of Germanic heroism there are indeed great passions being repressed, and that there is therefore great ambivalence. The elegies, especially *The Wanderer* and *The Wife's Lament*, tell me so.

> I know for a fact
> in an earl it is always a noble habit
> to seal fast the breast's locker,
> the heart's coffer, think what he may.
> The weary mind cannot withstand fate,
> or a troubled spirit be of assistance.

> Eager for glory then, often the dreary
> he binds fast in his breast's coffer. (*The Wanderer*, lines 11–18)

The Wanderer's psychology is neither Christian nor Roman, nor even consistent. It is easy enough to understand the masculine, stoic, "noble" impulse to lock sorrow away in the silence of the heart, to repress it; it is more difficult to understand that doing so might actually cure the troubled spirit. To the Wanderer, the mind is only weary if its weariness is spoken, but he is certainly a bad advertisement for this assumption. As in the other elegies, his hoarding of language in silence is overfilled and broken even as it is being described and affirmed. Readers cannot decide, therefore, whether the Wanderer is at peace or in despair, whether he awaits God's grace or has already achieved it, or gains it in the course of speaking—or whether the conflicting attitudes in the poem can even belong to a single voice. The poet could have made such issues plain, but rather he invites these questions, perhaps because he cannot answer them, perhaps because he cannot even ask them. We are thrust into his ambivalence regarding them as soon as we accept the irreducibility of the poem to a set of true or untrue statements. Strong arguments for any one of the interpretations I have listed are to some extent, then, projections of the reader's own attitudes, various rationalizations of the same provocative inkblot. And *Beowulf* presents us with an even greater screen than *The Wanderer* on which to project our fears, desires, and ambivalences.

HERO TO HERO

A year after my essay "The Role of the Men's Hall in the Origin of the Anglo-Saxon Ego" first appeared in *Psychiatry*,[9] Colin Chase reviewed it in the *Old English Newsletter*: "Despite his claim that psychoanalytic anthropology is both 'universal and particular,' Earl is quick to dismiss particular literary problems if they clash with his general theory. Having classified Beowulf as an 'ego ideal,' for example, Earl dismisses the question of whether Beowulf's behavior at the end of the poem is in fact ideal as being 'beside the point.'"[10] I would like to answer this criticism by considering the psychoanalytic relationship between the two heroes Beowulf and Byrhtnoth (hero of *The Battle of Maldon*) in some detail. The conceit of this argument will be that Byrhtnoth represents the epic's intended audience, so we might explore his identification with Beowulf as a sort of thought-experiment.

I like to imagine Byrhtnoth as a reader of *Beowulf*. I even like to imagine *Beowulf* inspiring the English at the Battle of Maldon, as Henry Adams (in *Mont-St.-Michel and Chartres*, following William of Malmesbury and Wace) liked to imagine the *Chanson de Roland* inspiring the Normans at the Battle of Hastings. It makes a certain sense, even if it never happened. For all we know, *Beowulf* was written after the Battle of Maldon and was influenced by it. For all we know, *Beowulf* never had any readers at all. But even these possibilities do not detract from the interest of our thought-experiment: how might Byrhtnoth have read *Beowulf*? Not in the sense of W. F. Bolton's question, how Alcuin might have interpreted *Beowulf*,[11] but in psychoanalytic terms, what would the structure of Byrhtnoth's identification with the epic hero have been?

Identification with the hero is not a simple matter, considered philosophically or psychologically. The hero is an idealization, and both idealization and identification are complex areas of psychoanalytic theory.[12] What exactly is the hero an idealization of? Do I identify with him as a representation of my ego?—or what I would like to be, or what I should be, or even (the possibilities are endless) what I most fear or hate? What if the hero, like God, were an idealized parent figure, with all the conflicted feelings *that* could involve? These and other questions suggest themselves. Nor is there any reason the possibilities should not be mixed; as in my dream of the *Beowulf* doll, so with mental representations generally: overdetermination is the rule.

Earlier we defined identification roughly as a failure or refusal to distinguish the self from an object. But which part of the self is being extended in this way, the id, the ego, or the superego? And most important, what results are brought about by such identifications, especially with a literary character? My first thought is that whereas the tragedy aims at relieving, in its oddly negative way, certain feelings in the audience temporarily—like a laxative—the epic is more positively ambitious: it aims at structuring and reinforcing prevailing social relations by creating and maintaining certain shared attitudes in the audience. Identification is the means to this end, but it is indirect and complex; it is certainly not a matter of encouraging everyone in the audience to imitate the hero—for what kind of society would that be?

According to Aristotle, the epic hero (Achilles) is flawed like the tragic hero (Oedipus). The flawed hero—an idealization conspicuously short of ideal in some regard—presents special problems of identification. Our identification implicates us in the hero's flaw and the guilt that it symbolizes. Certainly in the case of the tragic hero, who is being conspicuously punished by the gods for his *hamartia*, identification with him either produces, or is produced by, feelings of guilt in ourselves, the audience. The death of the hero with whom we have identified then brings cathartic relief from these feelings in the form of self-punishment. To some extent at least, we go to the tragedy to punish ourselves and feel the better for it.

I have always resisted the common notion that Beowulf has such a tragic flaw, because I do not want to confuse epic with tragedy or encourage the elucidation of this flaw as the aim of criticism; but Beowulf and Byrhtnoth do raise questions of this sort. There is an especially puzzling contradiction encoded in the Anglo-Saxon version (perhaps the Germanic version generally) of the heroic ideal and in our responses to it. In both *Beowulf* and *The Battle of Maldon* this contradiction appears as a suicidal logic of unresolvable conflicts, complete with easy rationalizations of unarticulated ambivalence. These rationalizations ("the conflict of loyalties," or "Christian versus Germanic," for example) have been the traditional subject of literary criticism, so here we must take a non-psychoanalytic detour.

If we come to *Beowulf* primarily through its Germanic background, we tend to see Beowulf's fateful decision to face the dragon alone as exemplary of Germanic heroism; the dragon evokes the Midgarth-serpent, an apocalyptic symbol of fatality itself. On the other hand, if we come to the poem from a Christian angle, we tend to find Christian wisdom in it; the dragon is a symbol of *malitia*, evoking the Beast of the Apocalypse, and Beowulf's defeat is a flawed moral action: he is brought low in the end by his pride and avarice. Which is only to say, perhaps, that from a Christian point of view, Germanic heroism looks a lot like a combination of pride and avarice.

Whatever our perspective, the result of Beowulf's fateful decision is the same: his people, vigorously berated for abandoning him in the hour of his greatest need (though he did insist on going alone, didn't he?), are certain to be destroyed also, now that he is dead. The messenger predicts,

> So shall the spear be
> many a morning cold fast in fist,
> upheld in hand, no sound of harp
> to wake warriors, but the wan raven
> chattering eagerly over the doomed,
> telling the eagle how he and the wolf
> gulped their food as they stripped the dead. (lines 3025b–31)

After this grim prophecy, Wiglaf delivers his terse summary judgment:

> Often for the will of one, many an earl
> suffers punishment: so it happened to us. (lines 3077–78)

But is this moral judgment, or simple wisdom? The first clause reads like an Old English maxim, almost as matter-of-fact as "frost shall freeze" or "a king shall be on the throne." It is difficult to believe that Wiglaf is actually criticizing the dead Beowulf here; but it is just as difficult to understand how this could not amount to criticism, especially of a king. Did Beowulf insist on going against the dragon alone, or did his men abandon him? Is his heroism exemplary or cautionary? Is the dragon evil, or is the hero cursed for opening the hoard? Is Beowulf wise, over the hill, kingly, proud, or foolish? As with *The Wanderer*, the meaning is very much of our making.

The Battle of Maldon comes with a similar wrinkle. Byrhtnoth's *ofermod* is either "great courage" or "overweening pride,'" depending on your attitude (and your glossary)—much as the word "pride" today has two morally opposed meanings, as a secular virtue and a religious vice. *Ofermod* may be the sin of Satan in the poem *Genesis*, but it is difficult to accuse Byrhtnoth of that. After all, *The Battle of Maldon*'s famous climactic wisdom (again in maxim form), which no one has ever thought to criticize, is "mod sceal þe mare"[13] ("*mod* must be the more," line 313a). But then again, is Byrhtnoth not responsible for the lives of his men? Does he not condemn them by the heroic code's expectation that a warrior will fight to the death when his lord has fallen? This in spite of Rosemary Woolf's demonstration that there is no Germanic tradition of suicidal battle:[14] the ethic of suicidal heroism is so powerful in *Maldon* precisely because it is freely chosen. Even in the eleventh-century the Anglo-Saxon army was motivated by appealing to local ties of lordship rather than national loyalties.[15] Could not Byrhtnoth's men also have complained, "Often for the will of one, many an earl / suffers punishment: so it happened to us"?

The two cases are different, of course. Whereas Beowulf is an entirely fictional character, Byrhtnoth's action is historical and not just literary—though to what extent we will never know. Since Byrhtnoth is a literary hero as well, it is hard to know how to proceed with this thought. It is hard to know if the anachronisms in the poem belong to the hero or the poet. Both *The Battle of Maldon* and *Beowulf* are composed in an archaic style, including an archaic social structure and code of behavior. Did Byrhtnoth really have a *comitatus* like an ancient Germanic warlord? Did tenth-century soldiers really feel the force of the heroic code defined by Tacitus nine hundred years before?

Well, yes and no, in the postheroic, prefeudal tenth century; but to understand Germanic heroism in whatever form it takes, we must always start by going back to Tacitus for the ideal. His famous formula has not yet yielded all its secrets:

> It is shameful for the lord to be excelled in valor, shameful for his companions not to match the valor of the lord. Furthermore, it is shocking and disgraceful for all of one's life to have survived one's lord and left the battle: the prime obligation of the companions' allegiance is to protect and guard him and to credit their own brave deeds to his glory: the lord fights for victory, the companions for the lord. . . . Banquets and provisions serve as pay. The wherewithal for generosity is obtained through war and plunder.[16]

This passage illuminates quite brightly the problem I am raising in our poems, the contradiction in the Germanic heroic code. The heroism of Wiglaf and of Byrhtnoth's companions is self-evident, set as it is in high relief against the flight of others. Their heroism is essentially their obedience—faithfulness to their oath, willingness to die for their lord, no matter what the cause, no matter how hopeless. Byrhtnoth's men die for him and for honor, not for the king, or for England, or Christendom; and their more immediate loyalty (*treow*), which seems to be the chief point of the narrative, is certainly offered as exemplary.

But how do we judge the behavior and the heroism of Beowulf and Byrhtnoth themselves? Their valor and generosity—the only lordly virtues mentioned by Tacitus—are not in question. It is not their *fortitudo* but their *sapientia* we doubt. On this subject Tacitus is curiously silent, as are our poems. The "literary problem"—in Chase's words, "whether Beowulf's behavior at the end of the poem is in fact ideal"—reflects a problem in the heroic ideal itself and cannot be solved.

The most Tacitus offers by way of a motive for lordly heroism is victory, in the pregnant formula, "The lord fights for victory, the companions for the lord." Perhaps if we could hold on to this thought, we could still charge our heroes with entering battle with something other than victory in mind (Pride! Avarice!). But in this little formula, "The lord fights for victory, the companions for the lord," we can see the deeper problem of Germanic heroism: there are two heroic codes, one for the lord and one for his companions; and whereas the ethical principles pertaining to the latter are perfectly clear, even to Christians, no principle at all is educed to explain why a lord fights—except to win, to prove his valor, and to acquire the wealth needed to pay his men. No wonder it looked like pride and avarice to Christians. Even Tacitus saw the self-perpetuating circularity of violence in the structure of Germanic society, for which war was an economic system requiring valor and obedience, but not necessarily nobility of purpose.

Nevertheless, the ideal of the obedient *thegn* prohibits criticism or contradiction of the lord, no matter what—with the result that lordly heroism, in poetry and life, could operate in relative freedom from ethical constraints. Though we would like to derive a consistent code of honor from the behavior of Beowulf and Byrhtnoth, Gunnar and Njal, Sigemund and Sigurth, the most important trait they all share is that like Greek tragic heroes they resist such criticism and analysis. In both our poems the result of this lordly freedom is suicidal annihilation—which pushy Christians like Alcuin might fairly interpret as a moral judgment, but which seems rather to operate more like a law of physics in the secular world of the poems. Heroic action is emphatically not practical action; nor is it necessarily imitable or even ethical, much less moral. Most important, no one tells the hero what to do; he *knows* what to do—and who is to gainsay it?

Now we may return to our psychoanalytic argument. The sort of idealization I have been describing, one that demands obedience and resists criticism—requiring, that is, the submission of the ego—is well known to psychoanalysis. In *Group Psychology and the Analysis of the Ego*, Freud analyzed the military as a typical group and connected it to his "scientific myth" of the ur-group, the "primal horde." In the primitive family, according to this myth, the father tyrannizes his sons, who eventually join together to kill him. Thereafter, their shared guilt for this primal crime holds the group together; that is, the dead father is not really eliminated but is internalized in the members of the group as a tyrannical voice of authority, the ego ideal or superego.

The theory has its problems, to put it mildly; but interpreting it has become something of a glamour area for criticism.[17] For Freud it was a way of illustrating the relations between the Oedipus complex and group psychology. His conclusion, that "the group appears to us as a revival of the primal horde,"[18] lets us take his account of the horde simply as a metaphoric description of strong groups: "A primary group . . . is a number of individuals who have put one and the same object in the place of their ego ideal and have consequently identified themselves with one another in their egos."[19] This insight hardly depends upon the myth.

The myth goes on to suggest that it is the epic poet who first forged the collective ego ideal, in the form of the hero[20]—which is to say, apropos of our argument, that the hero is defined by the audience's shared guilt in relation to him. The heroic ideal, then, is not simply a model of excellence or virtue to be imitated, but is also a forbidden and unattainable desire, highly defended against, sharply distinguished from the ego itself, and highly critical of it.

Mutually exclusive as these two descriptions sound, the superego is definitively both at the same time. "Its relation to the ego," Freud writes, "is not exhausted by the precept: 'You *ought to be* like this (like your father).' It also comprises the prohibition: 'You *may not be* like this (like your father)—that is, you may not do all that he does; some things are his prerogative.'"[21] At the behavioral level, the result of this quite normal ambivalence is a guilt-ridden obedience to the ideal. In a warrior society, where obedience must be instilled as a cardinal virtue, this effect can be amplified by the construction of an artificial superego, to be shared by the group. This is the sort of ideal we are identifying with in the epic hero—or rather, we are identifying with each other in our egos, by means of our shared identification with him as our common superego. Two sorts of identification are involved. Regarding the latter especially, we must not forget that "identification, in fact, is ambivalent from the very first";[22] so the idealization of the hero, which frees him from criticism, is accompanied by self-criticism among his followers—and the audience.

Thus the faithful Wiglaf's speech excoriating the unfaithful companions (lines 2864–91) is not anticlimactic after Beowulf's death, nor is the messenger's speech prophesying the nation's extinction (lines 2900–3027). These speeches have the effect of chastising the audience, whose shared guilt in relation to the hero, it turns out, is one of the most important bonds holding the warrior society together, since it is the basis for the identification of the members of the group with each other. And thus also, Wiglaf's implicit criticism of the hero ("Often for the will of one . . .") remains only implicit. Its restraint, which to us seems an uninterpretable ambiguity, actually masks his (and our) ambivalence toward the hero.

Because the hero is an ideal of this sort, however, he is invulnerable to our criticism. He need not be exemplary to retain his authority. The endless debate over whether Beowulf behaves correctly at the end of the poem is thus beside the point—because, consciously at least, we are expected to identify our ego with the *thegnly*, not the lordly, hero. Our identification with the lordly hero as superego will remain largely unconscious, like so much of the superego's activity, and to that extent be felt only as anxiety or guilt. Prufrock was right after all: "No! I am not Prince Hamlet, nor was meant to be; / Am an attendant lord."

The hero's invulnerability to criticism—including our criticism—has behavioral and psychological repercussions within the poem and critical repercussions for us. Just as we detected two sorts of heroism in Tacitus's account, Freud discovered two psychologies in his account of the group: "From the first there were two kinds of psychologies, that of the individual members of the group and that of the father, chief, or leader. The members of the group were subject to ties just as we see them today, but the father of the primal horde was free. His intellectual acts were strong and independent even in isolation, and his will needed no reinforcement from others."[23] For some reason, *Beowulf* criticism has chosen not to respond to this heroic freedom but to respond instead to the group ties, as if they applied to the hero as well. So critics are always passing judgment on Beowulf, good or bad, which the poet and his world would probably have found presumptuous and irrelevant.

It is easy to see the social function of such an ideal of heroic freedom, for it corresponds not only to fatherhood but also lordship in the real world. In the late tenth century, warriors like Byrhtnoth were eldermen, officials of the king's government, responsible for the well-being of large areas of England. It was obviously in their interest to promote the principle that although the lord is responsible *for* those below him, he is not responsible *to* them. It was to an audience of warrior-aristocrats like Byrhtnoth and his men that heroic poetry was traditionally addressed. This audience certainly promoted this concept generally, in an effort to keep society tightly bound to them by vows of unquestioning obedience.

Most men in this audience, being of the *thegnly* class, would have identified with Beowulf in the first part of the poem, insofar as he is an utterly exemplary *thegn*. Beowulf serves both Hygelac and Hrothgar faithfully, without any ambition to supplant or even succeed them, and totally without consideration of their conspicuous faults. But in the last part of the poem, this audience would probably have shifted their identification—at least in part—to Wiglaf, who comes to occupy the position of the faithful retainer. Beowulf himself, then, at the end of the poem, is a representation not of the ego but the superego—inspiring, but terrifying in his heroic freedom and superiority; revealing by his very existence our inadequacy, and punishing us for our inability to be like him. (Christianity has its own language for the same thought.)

When we consider Byrhtnoth in particular as the audience, the situation is complicated by the fact that he is at once both *thegn* to King Æthelred and lord to his own men. Thus insofar as he is the king's man, he too would shift his identification toward the faithful Wiglaf. The lesson that you defend your lord at all costs, without judging him, had some relevance in the reign of Æthelred the Unready; it has a special self-defeating urgency in the reign of any bad king, when criticism is most tempting. *But it is never your place to criticize your lord*: for by definition that would amount to challenging his lordship, and thus lordship generally, including your own. Unquestioning obedience is essential to the system.

It is not so simple, of course, not to criticize a bad king: "Be Kent unmannerly when Lear is mad!" Byrhtnoth has something of the same problem as Kent, perhaps, and his devotion to the *ideal* of the king could easily be interpreted as criticism of the reality. Accordingly, the focal question in *Maldon* scholarship seems recently to have become whether Byrhtnoth's action praises or criticizes Æthelred. Wiglaf too has something of the same problem: he can help his king only by disobeying him. "Wait on the hill, it's not your adventure," Beowulf had said (lines 2529–31). Thus Byrhtnoth's identification with Wiglaf would have led him to the excruciating outer limits of the ideal of obedience, where it becomes heroic by becoming its opposite.

But insofar as Byrhtnoth himself is a lord, he would also maintain his identification directly with the hero, right through to the end of the poem. That is, his identification would become split—much as in my dream I was able to identify simultaneously with both the girl and her brother, though in different ways. In fact, it is this doubleness of vision in the poem that lay behind the doubleness of the dream; the repeated splitting of identification in the poem became associated in the dream with other nodes of ambivalence, like child-parent, male-female, passive-dominant, and self-other. These may not be neatly parallel, but they all reflect the theme of my individuality in relation to the determining structures of history and society—that is, the relation of the ego to the superego.

(Now suddenly I can see the most surprising, and therefore perhaps the most important meaning of the dream. Not only do I identify with the boy and the girl, but there is a third, more infantile, identification as well. Like the doll, I too am "unlike any other, and yet like them all"—a unique individual as well as a typical member of the group. Insofar as I identify with the doll, then the boy and girl naturally represent my parents. I watch my own children play out their family romances like this with their dolls every day.)

The problem of our individuality in relation to the group cannot be solved; the contradictory relation of our freedom to necessity is a problem that cannot be solved; the ego's relation to the superego is destined to be ambivalent. These are antinomies we learn to live with. Not fortuitously, this lesson is an epic as well as tragic theme, and thus a deep theme in *Beowulf*, which is a hymn to the individual hero as much as to the group he belongs to—and which he transcends, at least in desire. Insofar as I wish to be autonomous (and this wish is indestructible, being infantile)—that is, insofar as I actually wish to *be* the superego rather than be governed by it—I will identify (perhaps unconsciously) with the hero himself; but insofar as I must always remain an agent of history, I will retain my conscious identification with the loyal *thegn*. The end result is guilt, the fuel of obedience. Christianity could only have clarified and deepened this already amplified dynamic.

At the Battle of Maldon, Byrhtnoth stumbled into one of those rare moments of lordship's terrible responsibility, when even in his highly codified world he was free actually to choose between desperate alternatives, to fight or not, to die or not, to commit his men to death or spare their lives, to dare to be more valorous and heroic even than the king. In his freedom, Byrhtnoth could identify with Beowulf himself. That secret infantile wish came true: in the most crucial moment of his life, he finally got to become the superego.

What kind of behavior would such a thrilling identification recommend? What could Byrhtnoth learn from Beowulf? Be generous, be valorous; not much beyond that. It is true that a code of honor, minimal, contradictory, and extremely subtle, can be deduced from heroic poetry. It is seldom articulated, though, because its first rules seem to be silence and restraint. It is a Hemingway heroism of power, generosity, valor, restraint, *treow*, revenge—and occasionally the nobility of spirit to forgo revenge. But this loose, unformulated code provides little guidance at the heroic moment, when unresolvable conflicts arise and a decision must be made, when responsibility and power fall to you. When you are the hero, there is no one to tell you what to do.

In epic, this heroism is usually tested against death, because the real issue of heroic behavior is how to engage necessity with freedom. Epics as diverse as *Beowulf*, *Njalssaga*, and *The Nibelungenlied*, as well as the ancient cycle of poems in the *Edda*, all offer us primarily models of heroic dying. It might fairly be said that in identifying with these heroes Byrhtnoth could have learned little else than how to die well—that is, how to embrace his fate freely and without fear. Students of Freud may wonder at this point how the hero, if he really represents the superego, could actually die. This harsh backlash of the idealization is symptomatically Anglo-Saxon: even the ideal submits to necessity and goes down in this world. Freud always assumed anyway that the id, ego, and superego have buried alliances in the unconscious.

What could Byrhtnoth have learned from Beowulf, then, except to plunge toward death against all odds, without the interference of complicating practical or moral considerations? As Beowulf had said to his companions, "'It's not your adventure, / nor any man's measure but mine alone'" (lines 2531–32). As the French said of the Charge of the Light Brigade, *"C'est magnifique, mais ce n'est pas la guerre."* But as readers—and as *thegnly* readers at that, most of us—ours is not to reason why. The forms of identification these poems invite from us do not invite us to question whether Beowulf and Byrhtnoth behaved correctly or not. Rather, they invite us—try to coerce us—into an identification with our fellows and an unquestioning obedience to the hero's authority.

In the current critical climate, *The Battle of Maldon*, even more than *Beowulf*, is a sitting duck for disquieted critics unwilling to obey or admire this authority; it is a preposterous, excessive illustration of the self-destructive contradictions built into the Anglo-Saxon male master discourse. The feminine is entirely absent from the poem. How I have wished for an image like the one in the medieval battle in Eisenstein's film *Alexander Nevsky*, when the women appear in the night after the battle, walking with their lamps among their slain husbands, sons, and fathers in the icy landscape, a tender pathetic critique of male heroism—not so much valkyries as victims. I see the next generation of critics holding up their lamps to the carnage at Maldon, asking "Why?" and expecting no good answer. The poem's literary values will be irrelevant to such an ideological critique. The poem's coercive, patriarchal demands will fall on deaf ears. Byrhtnoth, we are bound to be told, richly deserved what he got. And those who are still inexplicably moved by the frightening psychodynamics of heroism, the masculine forces at work in heroic literature, will find there is no satisfactory reply to these charges. Nonetheless, on the anniversary of the battle's millennium, I am moved to praise the hero one last time:

> O Byrhtnoth, better had you died in bed,
> Than your descendants in a thousand years
> Should scorn that white, heroic, severed head:
> For who among your judges are your peers?

THE RIDDLE OF *BEOWULF*

I must admit, however, that my interpretation of *Beowulf* and its effects on the audience sits rather uneasily with my own individuality and my own resentful attitudes toward authority. The oedipal failure the poem tries to enforce is intended to socialize us into a radically authoritarian world. It is balanced, thank goodness, by the spectacle of the hero's awesome, if unobtainable, freedom. This freedom may choose to express itself traditionally, but it is still freedom, feeding our most infantile desires even as it punishes us for them. For the reader-as-critic, like us, caught in the poem's thoroughgoing ambivalence, this freedom is the hero's and the poem's freedom from all our reductive interpretations, and their freedom from our demands that they be simpler or other than they are.

One would think modern, if not postmodern, readers would be interested in this freedom from criticism, but no. Not content with stressing the hero's traditionality, his allegiance to established values, or his role as an ethical or moral example, *Beowulf* criticism has proceeded to reduce even the poet to a cultural vector field as well. This common attitude to the poem amounts to a two-pronged attack on its most real authority, the autonomy and authenticity of its author, who created the hero and (as Freud put it) "had in this way set himself free from the group in his imagination." "At bottom," Freud concludes of the epic poet, "this hero is no one but himself."[24] Recent advances in oral theory do not dissuade me of this, at least in the case of *Beowulf*, this most original poem with its invented hero.

The Oedipus complex tempts us to parricide, but that is not its best resolution! Criticism, having too little interest in our unconscious response to the poem, has set out to kill off both the hero and the poet in revenge for their power and superiority. In trying to fulfill this wish, criticism only rebels against the poem's authoritarian intentions like an adolescent, declaring itself victor prematurely. But you can't fool the superego. The poem will survive all our depredations.

And now I see the meaning of my dream of the sphinx whose eye could not be covered. The sphinx is, as I knew immediately, the riddle of *Beowulf*, and the eye is the ever-observant, omniscient superego. They are identified in such a way that the poem looks down through the ages to criticize me, even as I am in the act of criticizing it. My criticism seems, at least when I am asleep, only like so much sand heaved futilely against the truth.

But I am scholar enough to have a second, reflexive association with the sphinx, whose riddle is of course the riddle of Oedipus, the riddle whose answer is Man. I did not yet understand, when I had the dream, that my reading of *Beowulf* could be largely determined by oedipal themes—as I have come to discover. Not only is the reader's relation to the author always oedipal to a degree, in the sense that Bloom suggests; but in the case of *Beowulf* the poem invites a meditation on the unconscious themes of our own individual and cultural origins—invites it with that same silence of the psychoanalyst, who allows us to relive and reformulate our own oedipal dramas, but consciously this time, by loudly plucking the deepest chords of ambivalence within us.

NOTES

[1]   Frederic Jameson, *The Political Unconscious: Narrative as a Socially Symbolic Act* (Ithaca, N.Y., 1981).

[2]   See Louis A. Montrose, "*A Midsummer Night's Dream* and the Shaping Fantasies of Elizabethan Court Culture: Gender, Power, Form," in *Rewriting the Renaissance*, ed. Margaret Ferguson et al. (Chicago, 1986), pp. 109–30.

[3]   See Harold Bloom, *The Anxiety of Influence: A Theory of Poetry*, 2nd ed. (Oxford, 1997).

[4]   Sigmund Freud, *The Future of an Illusion*, vol. 21 of *The Standard Edition of the Complete Psychological Works of Sigmund Freud*, ed. and trans., James Strachey, 24 vols. (London, 1953–74), p. 11.

[5]   Robert W. Hanning, "*Beowulf* as Heroic Poetry," *Medievalia et Humanistica* 27 (1974): 88.

[6]   T. A. Shippey, *Beowulf* (London, 1978), pp. 37–38.

[7]   Bernard Huppé, *The Hero in the Earthly City: A Reading of "Beowulf"* (Binghamton, 1984).

[8]   J. R. R. Tolkien, "*Beowulf*: The Monsters and the Critics," in *An Anthology of "Beowulf" Criticism*, ed. Lewis A. Nicholson (Notre Dame, 1963), p. 77.

[9]   James W. Earl, "The Role of the Men's Hall in the Origin of the Anglo-Saxon Superego," *Psychiatry* 46 (1983): 139–60; reprinted as chapter 4, "*Beowulf* and the Men's Hall," in *Thinking About "Beowulf*," pp. 100–36.

[10] Colin Chase, "Beowulf," in *The Year's Work in Old English Studies*, ed. Rowland L. Collins, *Old English Newsletter* 18 (1984): 96.

[11] W. F. Bolton, *Alcuin and "Beowulf"* (New Brunswick, N.J., 1978).

[12] See, for example, Hans Loewald, *Papers on Psychoanalysis* (New Haven, 1980); Roy Schaefer, *Aspects of Internalization* (New York, 1968); Joseph H. Smith, "Identification Styles in Depression and Grief," *International Journal of Psycho-Analysis* 52 (1971): 259–66; Richard Wolheim, "Identification and Imagination," in *Freud: A Collection of Critical Essays*, ed. Richard Wollheim (New York, 1974); Janine Chasseguet-Smirgel, *The Ego Ideal: A Psychoanalytic Essay on the Malady*

of the Ideal (New York, 1984); and Mikkel Borch-Jacobsen, *The Freudian Subject*, trans. Catherine Porter (Stanford, 1988).

[13] Cited from Elliott Van Kirk Dobbie, ed., *The Anglo-Saxon Minor Poems*, The Anglo-Saxon Poetic Records 6 (New York, 1942).

[14] Rosemary Woolf, "The Ideal of Men Dying with Their Lord in the *Germania* and 'The Battle of Maldon,'" *Anglo-Saxon England* 5 (1976): 65–81.

[15] See Richard Abels, *Lordship and Military Obligation in Anglo-Saxon England* (Berkeley, 1988).

[16] Tacitus, *Agricola, Germany, Dialogue on Orators*, trans. H. W. Bernario (Norman, 1991), p. 47.

[17] See, for example, Derek Freeman, "*Totem and Taboo*: A Reappraisal," in *Man and His Culture: Psychoanalytic Anthropology After "Totem and Taboo,"* ed. Warner Muensterberger (New York, 1970); René Girard, *Violence and the Sacred*, trans. P. Gregory (Baltimore, 1977); C. R. Badcock, *The Problem of Altruism* (Oxford, 1986); Chasseguet-Smirgel, *The Ego Ideal*, pp. 76–93; and Borch-Jacobsen, *The Freudian Subject*.

[18] Sigmund Freud, *Group Psychology and the Analysis of the Ego*, vol. 18 of *The Standard Edition of the Complete Psychological Works*, p. 116.

[19] Freud, *Group Psychology*, p. 125.

[20] Freud, *Group Psychology*, pp. 88–89.

[21] Sigmund Freud, *The Ego and the Id*, vol. 19 of *The Standard Edition of the Complete Psychological Works*, p. 34.

[22] Freud, *Group Psychology*, p. 95.

[23] Freud, *Group Psychology*, p. 125.

[24] Freud, *Group Psychology*, p. 88.

ENJOYMENT OF VIOLENCE AND DESIRE FOR HISTORY IN *BEOWULF*

JANET THORMANN

A s Beowulf prepares for the last of the three great battles with monsters that structure the narrative of the poem, he voices the first of a particular sequence of speeches. Cumulatively, these speeches form what Joseph Harris has analyzed as Beowulf's "death song," composed of an anthology of genres.[1] I want to emphasize here the first speech's concern with history. The speech, lines 2425–2537, culminates in Beowulf's resolve to act as protector of his people, "to seek out the feud" (*fæhðe secan*, line 2513)[2] with the dragon. This final assertion of his heroic will is preceded by an extended act of recollection in which Beowulf, facing his death as a vulnerable, mortal body, speaks as a historian, telling specifically of the death of rulers—more precisely, of Hrethel's death in paralyzed sorrow over his son's fratricide and Hygelac's death in a raid against the Frisians. Because Beowulf is a member of the royal family through his mother and is therefore in the ruling line, his story is simultaneously his autobiography and the tracing of dynastic succession. History here is genealogy and royal biography, the rule of powerful, elite men.[3] It is also the narration of the performance of feud and the death of rulers in feud, as the repetition of the

A grant from the National Endowment for the Humanities for the 2004 Summer Institute on "Anglo-Saxon England" at Trinity College, Cambridge University provided the opportunity to complete this essay. I thank Paul Szarmach for his direction and assistance during the seminar. I am especially grateful to Katherine O'Brien O'Keeffe for a meticulous, helpful review. Eileen Joy's stimulation and generosity were invaluable.

word *fæhþe* in the speech underlines—*fæghðe gebetan* ("to make good the feud," line 2465), *fæhðe ond fyrene* ("feud and crime," line 2480), and *fæhðe secan* ("to seek out the feud," line 2513). At the same time, while his speech memorializes dynastic history, the negative exemplifications of paralyzed fathers in Beowulf's speech demonstrate a crisis of feud that interrupts the history in which he has participated.

Beowulf's initial memorialization of his family's history is one of the several passages surrounding the fight with the dragon that reconstruct the history of the Geats. These passages typically fall under what Adrien Brodeur called the digressions in *Beowulf*.[4] However, the passages add up to an extensive effort at the construction of a Geatish past; rather than constituting digression, this history becomes the focus of the poem's second half. For Beowulf as speaker, the narration of history is prompted by his awareness of his own impending death. The *banhus* ("bone house," or more loosely, "body," line 2508) that previously has been protected by armor and by the strength of physical force is now only flesh, open and vulnerable. Fate is about to touch his body—"wyrd ungemete neah, / se ðone gomelan gretan sceolde" ("fate [was] immeasurably near, that was going to greet the old one," lines 2420b–21)—in a gesture of closeness, of physical intimacy, and Beowulf feels his death upon him: "Him wæs geomor sefa / wæfre ond wælfus . . . no þon lange wæs / feorh æþelinges flæsce bewunden" ("his spirit was sorrowful, uneasy and ready for death . . . not for long was the life of the noble man to be bound up in flesh," lines 2419b–24). The narrator describes Beowulf's anxiety and anticipation of dying, and clearly his approaching death compels him to become a historian.

For Wiglaf, speaking after Beowulf's death, memorialization anticipates the destruction of the realm. Following Wiglaf's speech, the messenger's accounts of feuds—specifically, a feud between the Swedes and Geats related to Wiglaf's and Beowulf's own family, the Wægmundings, and a feud between Geats and Frisians—explain the motivation for the destruction of the Geats' culture that Wiglaf expects. Wiglaf and the messenger, like Beowulf, are personally implicated in the history they tell. In the various accounts of past battles that pile up in the second half of the poem, history is the speaking of memory in personal, familial, and communal encounters with the death of rulers in feud. Together the various accounts demonstrate the poem's desire for a language that would construct a communal history from the speaking of personal memory.

Beowulf, I will try to show, works toward imagining a history that will limit the deadly repetitions of feud. The narratives of the Geats' feuds with the Frisians and the Swedes, because they can lead only to their own repetition, and the crisis in feud exemplified in the two grieving fathers of Beowulf's first speech, who demonstrate the paralysis of action in limit cases of feud, open up the possibility of another history that would be organized by the principle of law. This is to say that the poem, by tracing the limits of its social structure, makes way for an order different from the system of feud that it represents.

My analysis makes use of Lacanian psychoanalytic theory to reveal the dynamics of feud as a system of social exchange supported by an enjoyment of violence. While psychoanalytic practice attends to the vulnerable speaking body, psychoanalytic theory examines the subject immersed in collective forms of exchange and reveals the social operations of violence, reciprocity, the law, and desire in the subject and in discourse. The world of *Beowulf* is governed by what Lacan explains as imaginary processes of rivalry and identification between equals. It lacks a symbolic authority that would assert a law capable of allowing a route of escape from the reciprocity of feud relations and from the enjoyment of violence that supports those relations. In the absence of an authority that is above and outside of feud, the poem cannot imagine such a principle of law. However, when the poem traces the limits of its history, dramatizes the crisis of feud, and points to Beowulf's leadership as an alternative form of rule, it opens on to the potential of a different future. *Beowulf* exceeds the history it works to construct by leaving space for a regime of law under the office of kingship, a public authority that may be filled in by individual rulers but remains detached from the person of the individual ruler. Such an impersonal authority, as was achieved in the Anglo-Saxon kingdom in the tenth century, is capable of restricting the repetitions of violence governing the poem.

I

The poem's desire for a discourse of history under an authority that would control the seemingly continuous repetition of violence issues from a crisis of feud developed at the start of Beowulf's death song. Establishing the royal genealogy of the Geats from Hrethel and his sons, Herebeald and Hæthcyn, and with *Hygelac min* (line 2434), Beowulf inserts his place in the male royal line when his grandfather, Hrethel, becomes his protector. Beowulf recounts the fratricide that inaugurates the genealogical succession of his family:

Wæs þam yldestan ungedefelice
mæges dædum morþorbed stred,
siððan hyne Hæðcyn of hornbogan,
his freawine flane geswencte,
miste mercelses ond his mæg ofscet,
broðor oðerne, blodigan gare. (lines 2435–40)

A death-bed was made wrongfully for the eldest by a kinsman's actions
when Haethcyn killed his lord with an arrow from his hornbow, missed
the mark and killed his kin; one brother [killed] the other with a bloody
arrow.

The words describe the killing in bare, factual terms, and most scholarship
treats Herebeald's death as an accident. But this is an accident with benefits
for the successor, and hence it may well be motivated.[5] As one of the three
fratricides treated in the poem—the other two are Cain's killing of Abel,
initiating the monstrous race of Grendel's genealogy (lines 1040–114), and
Unferth's fratricide (lines 587–89)—Haethcyn's murder of Herebeald is a
limit case of the threat underlying all feuding between neighboring and
related peoples; it enacts the possible, logical end result of any feud. Given
the close relations between tribes and the constant possibility of conflict-
ing loyalties between kin—evident, for example, in Beowulf and Wiglaf as
members of the Wægmundings living among the Geats—tribal feud may
always be fratricidal. Hrethel's case shows that feud is potentially a dead
end, since Hrethel can do nothing, neither kill the murderer who is also his
son nor pay himself compensation. Hrethel's paralysis and grief is a case of
the limits of feud at the personal level.

Exemplification of the limits of feud at what may be designated the po-
litical level follows in the case Beowulf offers immediately after Hrethel's,
the story of the unnamed father who grieves that his young son rides on a
gallows: "Swa bið geomorlic gomelum ceorle / to gebidanne, þæt his byre
ride / giong on galgan" ("So it is miserable for an old man to endure that his
son rides young on a gallows," lines 2444–46a).[6] This case is both like and
unlike Hrethel's: the father shares with Hrethel an obstacle to the compen-
sation of revenge, although the obstacle now is different; that is, hanging as
a punishment for crime. The restriction on personal action here may ema-
nate from a power to punish superseding and obstructing the kin impera-
tive of vengeance. The nameless father cannot act because he is inhibited by
an impersonal authority.

With these two examples of feud devolving to impotence, violence runs up against an internal and external structure of intelligibility: violence without resolution, originating in fratricide, and violence without resolution, subsumed in the power of impersonal punishment. The poem here critiques personal justice, the mechanism of feud that has been its impelling force, by juxtaposing it with a form of public justice, emanating from an impersonal authority removed from and stronger than any private interest. What especially suggests that the two cases mark a crisis of feud and a transition to another form of justice is the formulaic theme of the loss of hall joys that concludes Beowulf's description of the unnamed father, who looks sorrowfully on

> winsele westne, windge reste
> reote berofene,—ridend swefaþ,
> hæleð in hoðman; nis þær hearpan sweg,
> gomen in geardum, swylce ðær iu wæron. (lines 2456–59)

> the empty wine-hall, the windswept resting place, lacking pleasure; the horsemen sleep, heroes in graves, nor is there the sound of harps, joys in the court, as there once were.

Metonymies of absence, of empty place and lack of sound, announce the end of a social world. In an earlier appearance in *Beowulf* in the speech of the lone survivor burying his people's treasure (lines 2244–70), the theme punctuates the dissolution of a culture, and in its revival in the messenger's anticipation of the destruction of the Geats, when the formulaic sounds of the beasts of battle replace the absent sound of the harp, it likewise signals a culture's annihilation:

> nalles hearpan sweg
> wigend weccean, ac se wonna hrefn
> fus ofer fægum fela reordian,
> earne secgan, hu him æt æte speow,
> þenden he wið wulf wæl reafode. (lines 3023b–26)

> Not at all will the sound of the harp stir up warriors but the dark raven, greedy for dead flesh, will say a lot, ask the eagle how he prospered at the meal, when he with the wolf plundered the slaughter.

In this landscape of cultural death, the sounds of birds, ironically given verbs of speech, *reordian* and *secgan*, substitute for the human sounds of speaking and making music. When it exemplifies the impasses of feud and mourns for an anticipated cultural destruction, the poem moves beyond the insistent repetitions of a feud regime that trap the poem's action and looks to the closure of the system of exchange of violence it has represented.[7]

Feud is the primary system of social exchange structuring the world of the poem and the narrative action; the gift giving that cements personal relations, acting as an attempt to forestall feud, depends upon that primary structure of violence. Not only the battles with monsters but warfare between peoples is regularly described as feud: Hygelac raids the Frisians in a feud ("fæhðe to Frysum," line 1207); Beowulf describes the marriage of Hrothgar's daughter Freawaru to Ingeld as an exchange intended to settle a feud, asserting "þæt he mid ðe wife wælfæhða dæl, / sæcca gesette" ("that he should with this wife settle deadly feud, set down conflict," lines 2028–29a) and also relates how Hæthcyn dies in a feud with Ongentheow (*fæhðe*, line 2480), later avenged by Hygelac; the messenger refers to that same battle as a feud stirred up between Swedes and Geats, "ða folc mid him fæhðe towehton" ("the people with them stirred up the feud," line 2948), and anticipates the revival of that feud in a coming Swedish invasion: "Þæt ys sio fæhðo ond se feondscipe" ("That is the feud and the hatred," line 2999). Personal relations may be extensions of feud: Hrothgar saved Beowulf's father, Ecgtheow, a Wægmunding, in a great feud (*fæhðe mæste*, line 459) by settling the feud with the payment of compensation ("fæhðe feo þingode," line 470). That arranged marriages, like Freawaru's or Hildeburh's, may be attempts to obstruct feud through the exchange of women, "peace-weavers," or that compensation may be paid or offered and refused, as seems to be the case (but perhaps only ironically) with Grendel, who, in his evil and feuding ("fyrene ond fæhðe," line 153), will not settle and make peace (lines 154–56), emphasizes how formalized a procedure feud was.[8]

The poem describes the origin of feud in God's punishments of Cain and the monsters descended from Cain. God is the guarantee of the necessity for the reciprocity of violence. If the murder of Abel is the origin of violence in fratricide, murder becomes feud when it is avenged (*gewræc*, line 108) by God; God's vengeance is itself avenged by the revolt of monsters, a revolt continued by Grendel's attacks on Heorot. That is to say, feud is not murder in itself but the reciprocal violence, motivated by a demand for revenge, that acts as a compensation for violence. Feud is a form of reciprocity and exchange. When God's exile of Cain is described as carrying out vengeance—

"þone cwealm gewræc / ece Drihten" ("eternal God avenged that murder," lines 107–08)—vengeance is given divine sanction. As if to emphasize the genealogy of feud from God, the narration provides an alternate origin for feud in God's destruction of monsters, inscribed—written or pictured—on the sword hilt Beowulf brings back from the fight in the mere:

> on ðæm wæs or written
> fyrngewinnes, siðþan flod ofsloh,
> gifen geotende
> . . .
> him þæs endelean
> þurh wæteres wylm Waldend sealde. (lines 1688b–93)

> On it was inscribed the origin of the ancient strife after the flood killed the race of giants . . . the Lord gave them reward for this with the watery surge.

God's vengeance against monsters is an originary violence that carries out justice. The power of the incident as a myth of origins is emphasized by its mysterious presence on the sword appearing almost supernaturally in the underwater cave. The sword thereby metonymically, through proximity, links Grendel and his mother, coming from the race of Cain, and the giants killed in the flood. Since the violence of revenge is initiated by God, feud is legitimated as a form of justice.[9]

Besides serving justice, feud also leads to economic exchange. For the ruler, or war leader, one of the rewards of successful feud is booty to distribute, providing a means for payment for the service of a fighting force and ensuring its loyalty, while conquest of a territory in feud may ensure the stable income of tribute. The warrior who kills in feud may indeed be generously rewarded: Beowulf receives much land and power—"seofan þusendo, / bold ond bregostol" ("seven thousand measures of land, a hall and a ruler's seat," lines 2195b–96a)—from Hygelac when he returns from Heorot, and Eofor is given a bride in recompense for killing Ongentheow (lines 2997–98), a clear example of women being used to facilitate relations between men. The gift giving between groups of men, the rewards for service that secure alliance—the necklace, horses, helmet, saddle, garments, and treasure Beowulf earns at Heorot, for example—is the other side of feud, the occasion for ceremonial generosity. John Hill, in an analysis of both ceremonial gift-giving and the violence subtending it, shows the necessary dependence of the gift economy on violence and hence the systemic character of war: "Indirectly, in its underwriting of just revenge through divinity, king, and hero, *Beowulf* clearly countenances the good of violence in situations where one seeks a justifiable settlement rather than dark pleasures."[10] The "dark pleasures," however, cannot be separated from the legitimate purposes and functions of violence, since it is violence itself that carries those pleasures, even, or especially, when it performs justice. The violence evokes in the narrative's combatants and audience an enjoyment that cannot be divorced from the justice feud is intended to carry out.

An enjoyment of the violence that propels exchange and supplements the performance of justice cements the social system of *Beowulf*. Violence impels the narrative, moving it from battle to battle as a mechanism, a kind of narrative fate or inevitability that ends only when the narrative ends, with Beowulf's death, but continuing into a projected future, anticipated in the poem's concluding moments. The compulsive force of violence is underpinned by a bodily enjoyment that is the inevitable underside of the law of social exchange. Such enjoyment is the materialization of what Lacan describes as the Real. In Seminar VII, Lacan shows that the law produces its proper violation; the commandments (i.e., "Thou shalt not kill") invoke the possibility of transgressive desire just when they establish prohibition.[11] Prohibition is the cause of desire, beginning with the originary prohibition of incest, which, according to Lacan, allows for any desire at all. However, what holds together the social relation is not the prohibition of law but the enjoyment underlying the law. Slavoj Žižek explains that "the most profound tie which 'holds together' a community is thus not so much the identification with the Law which regulates the course of daily, 'normal' communal life, *but rather the identification with a specific form of transgression of the Law, of the suspension of the Law* (in psychoanalytic terms, with a specific form of *jouissance*)," or enjoyment.[12] The superego, in this psychoanalytic theory, is the force proclaiming the injunction, Obey! The superego, then, materializes an enjoyment that is the force of the voice asserting the law. Hence Žižek claims that the "superego is the necessary inverse, underside . . . of the ethical norms founded upon the Good of the community."[13] The body enjoys the violence that, in *Beowulf*, is supported by the norms of social exchange.[14]

Enjoyment is different from pleasure, since pleasure derives from desire, while enjoyment is in excess of desire. Enjoyment therefore is a kind of "unpleasure" that admits pain, anxiety, and discomfort. The repeated scenes of violence enacted upon the body in *Beowulf* are vivid and detailed, conveying an enjoyment of fear or terror. The description of the funeral pyre at

Finnsburg decomposes the body into disparate parts: "hafelan multon, / bengeato burston, ðonnne blod ætspranc" ("heads melted, open wounds burst and blood spurt from them," lines 1120b–21). Grendel takes apart the sleeping Hondscio in a nightmare vision evoking a fear of the body torn into bits and pieces: "bat banlocan, blod edrum dranc, / synsnædum swealh" ("he bit into his joints, he drank blood from his veins, he swallowed up chunks of flesh," lines 742–43a). Beowulf slices at Grendel's mother to break into her body (*banhringas bræc*, line 1567). These episodes are designed to instill a thrill of excitement. Similarly calling up fear and suspense, the account of Ongentheow's dying in battle relates as if in slow motion the kind of blow-by-blow combat with which the poem's audience may well have been familiar:

> Hyne yrringa
> Wulf Wonreding wæpne geræhte,
> þæt him for swenge swat ædrum sprong
> forð under fexe. Næs he forht swa ðeh,
> gomela Scilfing, ac forgeald hraðe
> wyrsan wrixle wælhlem þone,
> syððan ðeodcyning þyder oncirde.
> Ne meahte se snella sunu Wonredes
> ealdum ceorle ondslyht giofan,
> ac he him on heafde helm ær gescer,
> þæt he blode fah bugan sceolde,
> feoll on foldan .... (lines 2964b–75a)

Wulf, son of Wanreding, angrily thrust at him with his weapon, so that blood ran out in streams from under his hair because of the blow. He wasn't scared, the old Scylfing, but right away he gave back a worse exchange for that hit when the leader turned there. The quick son of Wanreding could not offer a response to the old man, but he first cut through the helmet on his head, so that stained with blood he had to collapse; he fell to the earth.

Ongentheow strikes, and Wulf strikes back; Ongentheow retaliates, and Wulf falls to the ground. Streams of blood spring from hair; a helmet shatters; a bloody body collapses. Such realism and immediacy of physical detail, perhaps representing the audience's experiences fighting in hand-to-hand combat, testify to a bodily engagement and enjoyment in excess of the pleasures of language.

The enactment of violence on the body also reminds the audience that the body is vulnerable: it enjoys, but it may also die in, violence. Grendel's slow-motion approach to Heorot incrementally builds an increasing terror, as the repetition of *com* (lines 702, 710, and 720) brings him closer to his prey.[15] The stalking Grendel carries the threat of imminent death, warning the audience of the sleeping troops' vulnerable exposure to danger. Likewise instilling a fear of bodily destruction, the sound of Ongentheow's menacing taunts hovers over the Geatish troops, waiting trapped and defenseless through the night in Ravens' Wood, like the voice of mortality:

> wean oft gehet
> earmre teohhe ondlonge niht,
> cwæð, he on mergenne meces ecgum
> getan wolde . . . . (2937b–40a)

All night long he repeatedly promised harm to the anxious troop; he said he would get them with a sword's blades in the morning.

In the event, the Geats are saved by Hygelac, yet Ongentheow's voice has struck fear into them. Finally, Beowulf's anticipation of death, when he faces his battle with the dragon, emerges from an awareness of the open vulnerability of the body, an awareness that acts as a pressure to account for his life. Facing death, Beowulf responds no longer as the impregnable, solid, and self-mastered ego but as a subject of mortality. The confrontation with the potential death of the self and with the death of others brings the world of sociality home to the audience, whether hearing or reading the poem; the consciousness of the vulnerable body, subject to pain and death, is the beginning of ethics.

The reciprocal relations of feud call on personal obligation and duty; thus men must engage in war to avenge the slaying of kinsmen in war. Feud also produces social solidarity; a ruler keeps the loyalty of his band of warriors by promising the enjoyment of material reward and honor earned in warfare. Violent reciprocity, however, if it structures the social, is as well the opening to the failure of social community because it threatens mutual annihilation. Feud is a reciprocity of the same, a transitivity teetering between identification and rivalry that Lacan identifies with the Imaginary register. In the Imaginary, the ego—not yet a subject structured by language—identifies itself in the image of the other, finding itself as an ego, an individual form, in the other's place. The image of the body—and for Freud, as for

Lacan, the ego is the surface of the body—is formed in the image of the mirroring other that unifies the separate bits and pieces of the body into cohesion, as corporal form and as ego. But since the other giving the unifying image is in the place of the ego, the other must be destroyed to make room for the ego. This is a see-saw movement, a dialectic of identification and aggression alternating repeatedly between amity and enmity.[16] So feud carries out the economy of the imaginary register of the ego. Honor and status are asserted, and the ego is strengthened; the other is cleared out, but the ego may conversely be destroyed by the other.[17] The Imaginary produces what Juliet Flower MacCannel describes as "the regime of the brother," a group of equal and necessarily opposed egos lacking a superseding authority.[18]

If the register of the Imaginary is one of opposed forms—the opposition of bodies and egos that allows for identification and leads to rivalry—the register of the Symbolic is for Lacan a structure of difference between the signifiers of language. In the Symbolic, the subject is constructed in language; it is given a solid identity by a name and by master signifiers defining its traits. For example, Beowulf is recognized by name when Unferth challenges him: "Eart þu se Beowulf, se þe wið Brecan wunne" ("Are you the Beowulf who struggled with Breca?" line 506), and Beowulf responds by displaying the traits—strength, courage, self-control, and courtesy—that define a heroic subject. The subject, however, has only the property of a void, a lack the subject constantly tries to avoid by filling it in with an enjoyment that provides an illusion of substance. The Symbolic reduces enjoyment by inserting it into language; this is what castration is for Lacan. In language, enjoyment of the body becomes the pleasure of desire. The subject, however, resists giving up on enjoyment and settling for desire, and so clings to the idea of the Real in the form of a symptom, a fantasy of fulfillment, or an overwhelming drive. Contemporary ideologies use the citizen's wish for enjoyment to induce social cohesion, whether through rabid nationalism, hatred of a foreign enemy, envy and debasement of a racial other and abjection of the poor, or the thrills of popular culture and glamour of consumerism.

The law in and of language is instituted and upheld by the authority of the Father who must be dead for that authority to operate; the law must remain outside of potential rivalry and equality. The Father, then, is the Name-of-the-Father, a function that is a place any actual father may take up. Language and social community constitute, in contrast to the equal imaginary others of identification and rivalry, the big Other in which the subject is constructed. This Other is necessarily more than the sum of individual egos or subjects. It is guaranteed by the empty principle of the Name-of-the-Father that a particular individual will occupy; the principle operates as an authority detached from its embodiment.

No social reality can exist outside of the Symbolic, if only because human bodies use language and speak and thereby enter into the social exchange of signifiers (where "saying," however, can never be directly equivalent to "meaning"). Nevertheless, any social system may be more or less governed by the imaginary rivalries of competition and warfare and by the imaginary meanings of ideology that give meaning to violence. The social world of *Beowulf* seems to be ruled largely by the register of the Imaginary in which kings maintain power by means of violence rather than by a disinterested legal code that will develop, for example, in tenth-century England. Vertical succession, following from the Name-of-the-Father, is not firmly established in the poem: brother replaces brother in the Geatish line, although Beowulf encourages patrilineal succession when he allows Heardred, Hygelac's son, to succeed before him; Onela takes the Swedish kingship from his brother's sons, Eanmund and Eadgils, before they can inherit it. But the poem, by thinking through the limits of its world, in the crisis of feud explored in Beowulf's final speech and in its efforts to construct what might be called a "whole," redemptive history, allows for the potential of a different future in which personal vengeance is controlled under the authority of impersonal law.

The enjoyment subtending the violence of *Beowulf* is an excessive Real. It is what is excluded from the Symbolic and retroactively posited by symbolic language as what precedes it. At the same time the Real runs through language as the enjoyment at which desire aims, and it subsists outside language. Beyond the Symbolic, what is real is the death of the body, my own death I cannot speak or comprehend, and the other's death, the body that resists any speech except the deictic, the indication of a "this." The Real is the trauma of violence and the bodily enjoyment violence produces, what supports the system of feud in *Beowulf*. It is the horror of genocide and the disappearance of peoples. But real enjoyment may be pacified by language and reduced, leaving a hole in the Symbolic, an empty space as a potential awaiting fulfillment.

Touching on the limits of its history in feud, *Beowulf* opens onto an absence that allows a desire for history to emerge. The critic Gerhard Richter, writing about the German artist Anselm Kiefer's use of history in his work, suggests a way of accounting for the intervention of an historical discourse in *Beowulf* when he describes "the rupture that removes the artwork from its historical embeddedness in a way that permits the specific forms of this rupture to spell the work's history. What is truly historical—rather than merely mimetic—about a work is inseparable from what within it exceeds its history."[19] The historical in *Beowulf* lies in its effort to bring the past into language, to represent the contradictions of the history it narrates as taking place in the past to be a crisis of feud in the present of the narrative. History emerges as a discourse when Beowulf is compelled, facing death, to account for his past, and he becomes an authority whose name and reign potentializes an unknown future. The narration figures that authority as a void, an excess that is an externality internal to the narrative. As Richter describes, "By being exposed to its own excessiveness, the historical returns again and again not simply as a normative question, but, more importantly, as an open question."[20] The future opened as a hole in the narrative is the space for the transition from a social system governed by imaginary relations to one under the control of symbolic Law.

II

If language reduces the excess of enjoyment, *Beowulf's* effort to narrate feud is itself an attempt to limit the enjoyment of feud. If what happens in *Beowulf* is feud, what appears in the historical discourse it works to produce is a desire to make sense of feud, to put into language what compels repetition and so escapes control and, by speaking and signifying the compulsion to repeat violence, to reduce it. As it becomes a work of history, *Beowulf* closes upon its own history and thereby permits the institution of a different social symbolic under the authority of law.

Beowulf is historical in the sense that it transmits certain traditional legends and celebrates (if ambiguously at times) the values of a commemorative Germanic past, and perhaps also represents the ideology of the present of its audience, whoever and wherever that audience was,[21] and in so doing it may have contributed to the work of constructing a national identity.[22] The poem is historical as well in the sense that history is itself a concern of the narration and increasingly its subject. However, history is developed in the poem in several different discourses: a referential discourse, in which words refer to things; a narrative discourse, explaining character motivation and the causation of action whose context may be history; and a historical discourse, composed of what linguists call "constative statements," in which words refer only to other words. The several treatments of Hygelac's raid on the Frisians can exemplify these different discourses.

The first allusion to the raid is connected to Beowulf's receipt in Heorot, after his fight with Grendel, of the gift of the neck-ring, which the poet claims is "healsbeaga mæst / þara ic on foldan gefrægen hæbbe" ("the greatest neck-ring I ever heard of on the earth," lines 1195–96):

Þone hring hæfde Higelac Geata,
nefa Swertinges nyhstan siðe,
siðþan he under segne sinc ealgode,
wælreaf werede; hyne wyrd fornam,
syþðan he for wlenco wean ahsode,
fæhðe to Frysum. He þa frætwe wæg,
eorclanstanas ofer yða ful,
rice þeoden; he under rande gecranc.
Gehwearf þa in Francna fæþm feorh cyninges,
breostgewædu, ond se beah somod;
wyrsan wigfrecan wæl reafedon
æfter guðsceare, Geata leode
hreawic heoldon. (lines 1202–14a)

Hygelac of the Geats, the nephew of Swerting, had that neck-ring on his last venture when he guarded treasure under the battle standard, guarded the spoil of battle; fate took him when out of pride he went looking for trouble in a feud with the Frisians. He, the powerful prince, wore the jewelry, the precious stones, over the sea. He fell dead under his shield. The life of the king, as well as the breast-armor and the ring, passed to the possession of the Franks; worse fighters stripped the corpse after the slaughter; they kept the battlefield from the leader of the Geats.

History is told here as the history of a material object. The neck-ring is first given by Wealhtheow to Beowulf as a gift, honoring his victory at Heorot, and as a security, intending to forge an alliance between Beowulf and her sons, the Danish princes. Beowulf presents it to Hygd when he returns home; in the passage above we are told it will be worn by Hygelac when he dies raiding the Frisians, and it becomes booty when Frisian warriors strip it from Hygelac's corpse (*wæl reafedon*, line 1212). The neck-ring compresses the moments of its ownership in an enduring materiality, so that it becomes a reification of time as it migrates from person to person. Time's passage inheres in the concrete persistence of the object, while the object's possessor and the circumstances of its possession change.

This is history as a mimetic discourse that attaches meaning to things.[23] In such a discourse, the material thing is treated as a sign pointing to human activity; the object works like an element of language, and even as narration itself. Mimetic discourse is most obvious in the several instances in the first part of the narrative in which a body part functions as a *tacen*, a sign. Grendel's hand, arm, and shoulder compose a clear sign (*tacen sweotol*, line 833) of Beowulf's victory, and it is hung under the roof of Heorot to signify that victory. Likewise, Beowulf brings back from the mere the head of Grendel's mother as a sign of his victory (*tires to tacne*, line 1654) in the fight in her den. The head of Æschere, posted on the path to the mere, is read by the thanes as a horrifying announcement of continuing feud: it was a "weorce on mode / to geþolianne . . . oncyð eorla gehwæm" ("an anxiety in the spirit to suffer . . . a horror to each man," lines 1418b–20a), signaling a continuing threat. Finally, carrying an ambiguous reference, Grendel's campaign of violence is itself treated as a sign: "ða him gebeacnod wæs, / gesægd soðlice sweotlan tacne" ("it was signaled to them, truly said with a clear sign," lines 140b–41), indicating, perhaps, that Grendel "signals" his hatred with the dead bodies of murdered thanes.

Referentiality to materiality—and mimetic discourse is reference: it is language referring to a hard, material reality—is supposed to root history in a demonstrable world. The concrete certainty of reference is an illusion, of course, since at the minimum, the object could never have been literally present to the poem's audience and only ever really exists in the poem's language. Moreover, objects become meaningful only in the context of the language that "signifies" them.

A different kind of discourse builds the narrative present of the poem. This discourse is illustrated in the second reference to Hygelac's Frisian raid. The narrative function of the raid is to motivate the action that will lead to Beowulf's succession: "Eft þæt geiode ufaran dogrum / hildehlæmmum, syððan Hygelac læg" ("Afterwards it happened in later days, after Hygelac lay dead in battle," lines 2200–01). After Hygelac's death, Heardred became king, and following Heardred's death, Beowulf will rule: "Beowulfe brade rice / on hand gehwearf" ("the broad kingdom passed into Beowulf's control," lines 2207–08a). Passages retelling legend and history in the first part of the poem most often function as elaborations of the narrative present, as many analyses have shown: building character (e.g., the story of Sigemund, lines 874–97, elevating Beowulf's stature); presenting didactic example (e.g., the story of Heremod, lines 1709–24, serving as a negative example in Hrothgar's instruction of Beowulf); providing analogies to present situations (e.g., the story of Hildeburh in Finnsburg, lines 1071–1159, spelling, through analogy, the fate of Freawura's coming marriage to Ingeld). The fourth reference to Hygelac's raid, lines 2501–08, performs similarly with narrative purpose: when Beowulf tells of his fight with Dæghrefn before his escape from Frisia, he establishes his heroic commitment to encounter the dragon, at the same time as he implies his vulnerability in age in contrast to the strength of his youth.[24]

Another discourse develops from the third elaboration of the Frisian raid, lines 2354–79, which, while it also relates Beowulf's escape from danger, is followed by an account of an episode in the Swedish feud, and then in the fifth elaboration presented by the messenger, lines 2910–21, anticipates the future after Beowulf's death. These passages build up a properly historical discourse as the context of Beowulf's final battle and ultimate death. They compose a historical discourse insofar as their language refers to other language, to their speakers' memories that can exist only as language; they are not attached to material objects nor is their purpose to motivate or explain character, except to the extent that character is engaged as agency in public action with dynastic consequence. The insistent repetitions of episodes from the Frisian and Swedish wars; their fragmentary, segmented, often allusive structure; and the absence of chronological order in their delivery are symptoms of the narration's effort to construct a history. Such a history would move the poem beyond the feud regime that it dramatizes and from which it derives.

The poem's desire to compose a discourse of history comes up against the absence of an organizing principle different from the repetitive exchange of feud, a linguistic authority that would align the separated memories of the past in a sequence or a chronology. The speaking of memory does not in itself compose a discourse of history, for history must be ordered by a principle and directed by a meaning with social significance. Yet even in the absence of an evident ordering, the separate segments of Beowulf's and Wiglaf's personal memories, together with the messenger's retellings and anticipation of future wars, add up to a history of the Geats that must be constructed in the minds of the poem's audiences through a purposeful connection and ordering of the separate segments of language. In other words, lacking a principle that would relate the episodes in a narrative chronology, the time sequence of the feuds is not given in the poem but must be reconstructed, as it were, from the outside, by the audience in the past who would have known the events as inhering in a cultural memory or by contemporary readers who must piece them together into a recognizable narrative.[25] The poem thereby invites the work of a desire for the Symbolic, for the making of a discourse of history. No history is ever more than a symbolic construction, more than language relating only to other language (or, to real events that can only be represented, nevertheless, in language), nor may history be ethical before it recognizes itself to be only language and hence acknowledges its limits while also reaching for the Real (of both the past and the future).[26] Only in language does the vulnerable body appear—not the real, indestructible enjoying body or the imaginary, fortified ego of the young warrior, but the subject without certainty, absolute control, or secure foundation.

Coming out of the narration's circular, seemingly compulsive repetitions, emerging as a leftover from the narration's desire for history, is the excess that Lacan calls *the Real* and Richter terms *historicity*. The excess of historicity emerges from an absence in the text of *Beowulf*, the gap of Beowulf's reign that is its ethical core. Springing out of the narration in two and a half lines and sinking back into its momentum, Beowulf's reign quickly appears and disappears: "siððan Beowulfe brade rice / on hand gehwearf; he geheold tela / fiftig wintra" ("then the broad kingdom came into Beowulf's control; he held it well for fifty years," lines 2207–09a). Fifty years come and pass as in a fairy tale, like magic. That gap of fifty years is in the past of the narrative's present, yet it is also in the future, what never entered the narrative but remains buried within it to be resurrected when the present looks back and makes its own history. This calls to mind Walter Benjamin's "messianic" historicism, in which the present redeems what in the past was desired but was not able to actually enter into time.[27] For despite the messenger's and the Geatish mourner's prophecies at the end of the poem, and despite our knowledge of the doom-laden endings of Germanic legend, *Beowulf* does not set down the conclusion of its history, perhaps because feud has no conclusion. Beowulf's absent rule is the possibility of a different future, in which the law of a centralized authority replaces the perpetual repetitions of feud. Beowulf dies, and a future becomes possible in his name.

III

The poem gives little to fill in the fifty-year gap of Beowulf's rule, but what it does indicate is sufficient to suggest an alternative to the regime of feud. Beowulf provides peace for his people, and his strength is a protection against violent reciprocity, holding its return in abeyance. He does not lead a feud; notably he protects Eadgils from Onela, and if he supports Eadgil's campaign against Onela, he does not act in it. He also protects Wiglaf from any repercussions of his father's, Weohstan's, help in Onela's elimination of Eadmund as a threat to the Swedish throne. His own summation of his rule (lines 2732–43) points to his pride in keeping the peace, and remarks in particular on his avoidance of quarreling—"ne sohte searoniðas" ("I did not seek out insidious quarrels," line 2738a)—and of the murder of kinsmen, which he recognized from the start as a danger of feud: "me witan ne ðearf Waldend fira / morðorbealo maga" ("the Lord of men need not judge me for the murder of kin," lines 2741–42a). He encourages the patrilineal descent of kingship, refusing to rule until Hygelac's son, Heardred, is dead, and thereby sponsors stable, hierarchical authority.[28] His death transforms Beowulf from a person to a principle, "the Name-of-the-Father" that authorizes lawful rule. A concern for peace, control over feud, and the strengthening of centralized authority: the achievements of Beowulf's absent rule are congruent with the concerns of the laws promulgated between the years of Alfred and Edmund for a centralized Anglo-Saxon kingship. These laws strengthen the position of kingship as an office, filled in by individual rulers, with the power to subordinate violence to the direction of public authority.

The codes of Ine and Alfred are bound together in a tenth-century manuscript that also includes the earliest surviving text of the Anglo-Saxon *Chronicle* (Corpus Christi College, Cambridge, MS 173), likely composed and promulgated under the sponsorship of Alfred (871–899),[29] and taken together, as they were intended to be by Alfred, they progressively assert the power of kingship over feud. The presence of these codes alongside the first vernacular history of England is clear evidence of the relation between the efforts to record history and to formulate law in the late ninth century. Already the laws of Ine (688–694) that preface Alfred's laws witness a concern with keeping peace and with an intention to control private violence.[30] Yet at the same time, the codes allow for the continued practice of traditional forms of customary law and legislate only certain specific forms of violence; for example, they seem to take for granted and build upon the practice of remitting *wergild* ("man-payment") and, in most cases, the assessment of *wergild*.

Ine's laws lay out concerns that Alfred will later develop in greater detail and length:[31] to penalize fighting in the king's house and in public places (6 and 6.4); to fine those who commit forcible entry into the houses of the nobility, including the king's residence (45), or who harbor thieves in their houses (36); to allow for sanctuary (5); and to force remission of a portion of *wergild* to the king in the case of the slaying of foreigners (23). Further, Ine's laws distinguish between the compensation that is to be paid to those harmed in a feud and the fine that is to go to the king. So, for example, in law 23 (mentioned above), "the king shall have two-thirds of his [the slain foreigner's] wergild, and his son or relatives one-third."[32] Ine's laws also stipulate certain instances when a kin-feud is not allowed to be instigated; so, in law 35, "He who kills a thief shall be allowed to declare with an oath that he whom he has killed was a thief trying to escape, and the kinsman of the dead man shall swear an oath to carry no vendetta against him. If, however, he keeps it [the homicide] secret, and it afterwards comes to light, then he shall pay for him."[33] Ine's laws thereby assert the interest of a public system of justice in regulating, adjudicating, and curbing violence, and they also penalize what they frame as the violation of public order.

Alfred's law codes, appended to Ine's in the *Chronicle*, and other laws promulgated throughout the tenth century are continuing evidence of what Patrick Wormald characterizes as "the kings' aggressive intervention in the dialogue of dispute."[34] Alfred's laws repeat provisions for the king's peace (7), and they develop the right of sanctuary with greater detail and nuance (2, 2.1, and 5–5.4) than did Ine's decrees. Rights of sanctuary are significant legally, not only because they extend the domain of peace and safety for individuals, but because they also allow for a cooling-off period, during which violence may be negotiated. For example, in law 5, it is stipulated that "if a man, attacked by enemies, reaches it [a church] either on foot or on horseback, he shall not be dragged out for seven days, if he can live despite hunger, and unless he [himself comes] out [and] fights."[35] As well, Alfred formulates penalties and procedures for dealing with pursuit and murder by bands of men (26, 27, and 28.1). The most significant evidence of the king's "intervention in the dialogue of dispute" are provisions addressing the payment of *wergild* by maternal kinsmen (30) or payments by those without kin (30.1 and 31) that are to go to the king. II Æthelstan (924–939)[36] extends the state's control of feud by laying out elaborate judicial procedures for bringing suit for *wergild* that demands the presence of witnesses and the taking of oaths. Such procedures suggest that the requirement of obedience to legal authority is devolving to a complex administration of justice.

The climax of the state's continuing concern with feud is II Edmund (939–946), which is devoted entirely to the means of its settlement. The code is prefaced by a statement of the king's intention to legislate continuing violence: "I myself and all of us are greatly distressed by the manifold illegal deeds of violence which are in our midst."[37] A series of detailed provisions account for the liability of kin and associates in acts of violence, imposing fines and forfeiture as punishment, and, importantly, allowing kin to remove support and participation in feud. For example, in laws 1 and 1.1, it is stipulated that,

> if anyone slay a man, he shall himself [alone] bear the vendetta, unless with the help of his friends he pay compensation for it, within twelve months, to the full amount of the slain man's wergild, according to his inherited rank. If, however, his kindred abandon him and will not pay compensation on his behalf, it is my will that, if afterwards they give him neither food nor shelter, all the kindred, except the delinquent, shall be free from vendetta.[38]

Wormald's summary of these provisions shows that II Edmund "allows kin to opt out of their duty to help their members in feud or compensation. . . . Edmund has reduced the liability of an offender's associates for the harm he does."[39] Traditional practices are subsumed under the authority of the law and are standardized: II Edmund, law 7, asserts, "The authorities[40] must put a stop to vendettas. First, according to public law, the slayer shall give security to his advocate, and the advocate to the kinsmen [of the slain man], that [the slayer] will make reparation to the kindred." The effect of such legislation is to isolate the criminal outside the protection of kinship relations, since the criminal must face a disinterested public justice (*æfter folcrihte*) on his own.

Taken together, the tenth-century law codes bear striking testimony to Anglo-Saxon kings' efforts to define violence as having a detrimental public impact and to establish the power of a central, political authority to intervene in feud.[41] By imposing financial penalties on a murderer, the king not only standardizes a *practice* of the compensation of *wergild*, but also enters into feud in a public capacity in order to assert the law of the state over kin relations. The law acts without personal motive, but perhaps with some monetary interest. *Wergild* is allowed to compensate for harm to status or for injury, and allows for a personal interest in feud. But in addition, a penalty, paid to the king, is imposed as a punishment; the penalty recognizes that feud is a crime against the public interest, under the impersonal authority of the ruler. The law codes also begin to distinguish between crime and tort, or civil law, which Paul Hyams traces in the development of English law—that is, the difference between a transgression against the public good, which is punished in criminal prosecution, and action resulting in personal wrong, such as the loss of honor or shame, which may require compensation.[42] The significant transition in the late ninth and first half of the tenth century, then, is from personal to political justice, which also ushers in the separation between individual, personal power and political authority, and the regulation of personal interests by the law. The authority of public law steps into feud, treating it as a crime against order and demanding a share of compensation because of a now public interest in justice. Hyams discovers in the tenth century the strengthening of "Downwards Justice backed by royal power with afflictive penal sanctions," and states that, "under Alfred and his successors a sharp shift of emphasis from a largely private enterprise system of compensation for wrong to one more focused on prosecution and punishment in the king's name and justified by the interests of the Christian community."[43] Feud does not disappear, but it is increasingly controlled by legal authority.

The rule of law is feasible only when backed by a strong, centralized political authority, and conversely the law contributes to the power and centralization of that authority. Wormald suggests that the strength of a developing English legal system was an indication of the strength of an English state: "inasmuch as pre-Conquest England had kings who did in fact punish even their greatest subjects for what they identified as crime, and in the name of the whole community they ruled, it fulfilled one of the main criteria of statehood."[44] The power of the Christian governing authority is obvious in the remarkable confidence and command with which IV Edgar (962–963) refers to a common nation, *eallum leodscype*: "The following measure, however, shall apply generally to the whole nation—to the English, Danes, and Britons in every part of my dominion—to the end that rich and poor may posses what they have lawfully acquired."[45] Acting as an agent of Christian justice, Edgar conceives of his territory as a nation uniting several peoples ruled by law.

Wormald argues that it is a feature of English law from the start that it responds to immediate social problems: "West Saxon kings are thus seen to legislate in writing on tensions as and when experienced by the society they ruled. . . . [T]hese were situations coming up from the ground and forcing themselves on the legislator's attention."[46] The very attempt to legislate violence indicates a continuing problem; feud never really disappeared from Anglo-Saxon England. Simon Keynes insists on the difficulties that royal authorities had throughout the century in enforcing the law: "It is abundantly clear . . . that the tenth-century kings experienced considerable difficulties in maintaining the rule of law and order. . . . It would be mistaken to imagine that the tenth-century kings were wholly successful in achieving their purpose."[47] Citing a charter of king Æthelred, Keynes discusses at length the case from the end of the century of a certain Wulfbald, who illegally seized others' property and also refused to obey Æthelred four times, and whose "wergild was assigned to the king" on each occasion of disobedience; for Keynes, the case shows that as late as 996 private feud competed with public justice and that the authority of the state was not completely secure. Kinship and the ties created by marriage continued to exert powerful claims: after Wulfbald "was dead, on top of all this, his widow went, with her child, and killed the king's thegn Eadmær, the son of Wulfbald's father's brother, and fifteen of his companions, on the land at Bourne which Wulfbald had held by robbery despite the king."[48] Æthelred's charter gives a dramatic narrative of late-tenth-century social relations still permeated by feud, but Keynes argues that, even in the early tenth century, "King Æthelstan seems to have been confronted with men so rich or belonging to so powerful a kindred that they could not be restrained from crime or prevented from harboring criminals."[49] Æthelred's confrontation with Wulfbald, then, is evidence of an ongoing problem for royal authority during the tenth century.

The history of medieval England, and of much of Europe as well, is from a certain perspective the attempt of the king to assert himself against and above other, often equal and sometimes more powerful, noble men. The conflict between Æthelred and Wulfbald takes place in the specific context of late-tenth-century rule and may be a local manifestation of the broader problem of the exertion of royal authority. Adding complexity to the context of Wulfbald's case, Pauline Stafford notes that numerous charters from Æthelred's reign in the 990s adjudicate claims of aristocratic inheritance, in large part because Æthelred made extensive use of forfeiture, for both his own profit and that of the church. Noble families then came in conflict with the crown and the church over rights to the possession of land. Stafford argues that forfeiture "was deeply inimical to kinship values," and that the final years of the tenth century were a period in which there was no sharp distinction between "a public political world and a private one of kinship and family."[50] However, contradicting Stafford's description, the law codes give powerful evidence that the public authority of law did take great pains to separate itself from, and also preside over, the private world of kinship feud. Certainly the power of centralized authority could have broken down somewhat during Æthelred's rule, especially under the pressure of Viking invasions, and loyalty to the king could be weak. In addition, the boundaries between, as well as the meanings of, public and private are continually redefined and shift over time, and given that kingship in medieval England was always attached to kinship and frequently would lead to conflict between kin, public authority would continue to be a familial matter. Likewise, under any regime, private interests may manipulate or control public authority. Nevertheless, the weaknesses of centralized authority under Æthelred can be seen, I would argue, as an exception to the prevailing tendency during the century for the royal centralization of the administration of law.

The growth of the Anglo-Saxon nation from Alfred through Edgar was made possible only by the strengthening and extension of public power and the implementation of that power through law. The law codes make it clear that feud did become subject to the king's justice and that public power was increasingly consolidated under law, reaching a high point with Edgar in the alliance of the king's office with the monastic reform movement.[51] In contrast, *Beowulf*'s world of violent feud makes impossible any centralized authority independent of the person of the king, nor can it impose a principle of order beyond physical power (as Hrothgar's failure indicates). When it dramatizes the deadlocks of the feud regime that structures its system of social exchange and when it articulates a desire for a discourse of history that might "make whole what has been smashed,"[52] the poem exposes the limits of its world. Because it is so thoroughly conscious of the history in which it is immersed, *Beowulf* opens a space for the future.

NOTES

[1]   Joseph Harris, "Beowulf's Last Words," *Speculum* 67.1 (1992): 1–32.

[2]   All quotations of *Beowulf* are from Fr. Klaeber, ed., *"Beowulf" and The Fight at Finnsburg*, 3rd ed. with supplements (Lexington, Mass., 1950). Translations are my own.

[3]   Clare A. Lees discusses *Beowulf*'s focus on action in a "male aristocratic heroic world" structured by patrilineal genealogy in "Men and *Beowulf*," in *Medieval Masculinities: Regarding Men in the Middle Ages*, ed. Clare A Lees (Minneapolis, 1994), pp. 129–48, and reprinted in this volume. Gillian R. Overing focuses on the place of women in the poem's "masculine economy" in *Language, Sign, and Gender in "Beowulf,"* (Carbondale, 1990), especially pp. 68–107. David N. Dumville, in "The Ætheling: A Study in Anglo-Saxon Constituional History," *Anglo-Saxon England* 8 (1979): 1–33, traces succession to kingship in the Anglo-Saxon kingdoms, concluding that, "In the Anglo-Saxon period as a whole we see how eligibility for the throne deriving from descent from the fifth- or sixth-century founder of the kingdom, probably through a direct male line, changed

into an eligibility limited to perhaps a three-generation group" (p. 32). He shows that as late as the West Saxon kingdom primogeniture was not secure, since brothers and half-brothers could succeed and even a cousin could threaten to succeed. I thank Katherine O'Brien O'Keeffe for calling my attention to this article, as well as for pointing out how significant it is that Beowulf allows Heardred to succeed after Hygelac's death. Beowulf is, according to Dumville's terms, an "ætheling" and therefore in line for the succession, but his support of Heardred is at the same time support of vertical succession from the father. Such parallels between succession in *Beowulf* and the Anglo-Saxon kingdoms open up the problem of the poem's date. While it is not the purpose of this essay to suggest a date for *Beowulf*, my argument does have implications for dating the poem. In the view I propose here, the original composition and transmission of the poem would have long preceded our existing manuscript version, which everyone agrees is dated circa 1000 C.E., where its preservation in writing would likely have furthered the effort to build an emerging national culture under the expanding rule of an Anglo-Saxon "nation." On this last point, see John D. Niles, "Locating *Beowulf* in Literary History," *Exemplaria* 5 (1993): 79–109, and reprinted in this volume.

4   Adrien Bonjour, *The Digressions in "Beowulf"* (Oxford, 1965).

5   Treating the killing as a murder is consistent with reading the passage as participating in the crisis of feud. Envy or resentment of an older brother would exacerbate ordinary sibling rivalry in cultures practicing horizontal inheritance, since displacement of the brother would lead to power. Moreover, the fact that this killing is one of several instances of fratricide in the poem suggests that this fratricide is not an extraordinary, isolated, or completely unmotivated accident.

6   The identity of the unnamed father is disputed, with many scholars identifying him with Hrethel and the entire passage as a continuation of the previous one, and others treating him as a separate, different character. In his translation of the poem, Roy M. Liuzza writes that the passage is typically viewed as "a kind of epic simile, comparing Hrethel's grief over his son's death—a death beyond the scope of vengeance—to the grief of a criminal's father, who cannot claim compensation for the execution of his son" (*"Beowulf": A New Verse Translation* [Ontario, 2000], p. 128 n. 1). Since the point of the first passage is that Haethcyn can *not* be punished for killing Herebeald, it would seem that that unnamed father and son are not Hrethel and Haethcyn.

7   In "King Hrethel's Sorrow and the Limits of Heroic Action in *Beowulf*," *Speculum* 62.4 (1987): 829–50, Linda Georgianna provides a sensitive analysis of the paralyzed fathers and of the deadlocks of feud, although she reads the poem as a Christian condemnation of pre-Christian culture. What she describes as

"the limits of heroic action and perhaps of heroic narratives as well" (p. 830) are ultimately ascribed to the poem's exposure of the "hopelessness of the heathens" (p. 848): a Christian perspective reminds "a Christian audience of the gulf separating even noble pagans from Christians" (p. 850). Thus she finds that the passages surrounding the dragon fight enforce a distance from Beowulf and create "confusions and ambiguity" in the narrative (p. 841). Without approaching the vexed issue of the Christian context of *Beowulf*, my essay tries to show that Beowulf's subjectivity is developed intimately, and is therefore not distanced, as he prepares for his final battle, and that the poem, rather than being confused or ambiguous, is fully in control of its material.

[8] The systemic character of feud is treated in fine detail by John M. Hill in *The Cultural World of "Beowulf"* (Toronto, 1995). Hill uses ethnographic evidence to discuss feuding as "a legal response" (p. 37) that can "be good and jurally definitive (p. 29). Hill returns to this subject in his article "The Ethnopsychology of In-Law Feud and the Remaking of Group Identity in *Beowulf*: The Cases of Hengest and Ingeld," *Philological Quarterly* 78 (1999): 97–123, which is reprinted in this volume. Harry Berger Jr. and M. Marshall Leicester, in "Social Structure as Doom: The Limits of Heroism in *Beowulf*," in *Old English Studies in Honor of John C. Pope*, ed. Robert B. Burlin and Edward B. Irving Jr. (Toronto, 1974), pp. 37–79, also show that feud is a structure, necessarily imbricated in the social system. Thomas L. Wymer and Erin F. Labbie discuss the difference between "uncontrolled rage" and "controlled rage," which in their view is useful in the development of social relations in the poem, in "Civilized Rage in *Beowulf*," *The Heroic Age* 7 (2004), available at http://www.heroicage.org/issues/7/labbie&wymer.html.

[9] In "Cain's Monstrous Progeny in *Beowulf*: Part II, Post-Diluvian Survival," *Anglo-Saxon England* 9 (1981): 182–97, Ruth Mellinkoff addresses the confusion over Cain's descendants and the monsters who were supposed to be killed in the Flood, and argues that the *Beowulf* poet "had a clear-cut notion that, whereas some of Cain's monstrous progeny had drowned in the Flood, others had not" (p. 184). Seth Lerer, in "Hrothgar's Hilt and the Reader in *Beowulf*," *Literacy and Power in Anglo-Saxon Literature* (Lincoln, Nebr., 1991), pp. 158–94, and reprinted in this volume, discusses the inscription of the Flood story on the sword hilt as the poem's dramatization of "differing forms of literary communication" (p. 182), seeing it as an example of writing through which the poem questions narrative authority and the differences between orality and textuality. My discussion of feud as a system of exchange supported by an enjoyment of violence draws upon and elaborates material from my essay "Beowulf and the Enjoyment of Violence," Literature and Psychology 43.1-2 (1997): 65-76.

¹⁰ Hill, *The Cultural World in "Beowulf,"* p. 33. What Lacan gets at through the theorizing of "enjoyment" is explained by the dynamics of Kleinian psychoanalysis in Hill's earlier article, "Revenge and Superego Mastery in *Beowulf,"* *Assays* 5 (1989): 3–38, much of which is incorporated in chapter 5 of *The Cultural World of "Beowulf."*

¹¹ Lacan's seminar of December 23, 1959 (Seminar VII), in *The Seminar of Jacques Lacan. Book I: The Ethics of Psychoanalysis, 1959–1960,* ed. Jacques-Alain Miller, trans. Dennis Porter (New York, 1992), reaches this conclusion: "The dialectical relationship between desire and the Law causes our desire to flare up only in relation to the Law" (pp. 83–84).

¹² Slavoj Žižek, "L'image sublime de la victime," *Lignes* 25 (1995): 233 (my translation).

¹³ Slavoj Žižek, *The Metastases of Enjoyment* (London, 1994), p. 69.

¹⁴ James Earl's essay, "*Beowulf* and the Men's Hall," in his book *Thinking About "Beowulf"* (Stanford, 1994), pp. 100–138, employs a Freudian psychoanalytic theory, together with an approach to Anglo-Saxon history informed by anthropology, to understand *Beowulf* "as an act of cultural mourning" depicting "the death of the old heroic world, thereby clarifying the culture's renunciation of its own pagan past" (p. 133). According to this Freudian reading, the Christian Church, acting "in the culture as the superego does in the individual, was established in England by the same mechanism through which the individual superego is formed—the turning back of aggression upon the self" (p. 127). The superego, like the church, is accordingly an agent of civilization, allowing for "an orderly and moral society" (p. 127). Clearly, Earl is concerned with many of the issues developed in this paper, in particular, with what he calls the opposition between kinship and lordship, reexamined here as the opposition between private vengeance and public legal authority, which he sees playing out "in the laws, which document the solidification of political power and the gradual erosion of the rights and duties of kinship in legal matters" (p. 110). He emphasizes the need to eliminate feud, or "self-perpetuating violence," which can only be satisfied "by a central legal authority that guarantees vengeance in the name of the state" (p. 111). I acknowledge a debt to his work, while at the same time I would stress that institutions of state law do not pursue vengeance but, rather, impersonal justice, which is why capital punishment is banned in most legal systems today. Likewise, Anglo-Saxon law does not further "an attack on the right of kindred" (p. 113) so much as it attempts to regulate vengeance in order to mediate and control that violence and to administer justice and thereby extend its authority. The distinction between Freudian and Lacanian psychoanalytic theory is apparent in their differing characterizations of the

superego. For Earl, following Freud, the superego is a civilizing force. For Lacan the superego is a voracious call to enjoyment. The Symbolic, not the superego, civilizes the human being by submitting it to language and reducing enjoyment to desire. Aggression is not turned back on the self, as it is in Freud, but pacified in speech when it is taken out of the Imaginary. Above all, there is no story of progress in Lacan. Any human subject is a structure, a peculiar knotting of three registers—Imaginary, Symbolic, and Real—held together by the symptom, the particular individual's form of enjoying an object. By way of briefly explaining how Lacan deployed these three terms, the Imaginary is a mainly visual, pre-verbal, and pre-Oedipal register that comes before the Symbolic, which is the register of discourse, where the self undergoes a process of alienation (because, even though there can be no "subject" outside of language, language is always provisional and creates a continual *displacement* of meaning along endless chains of signification—i.e., "saying" can never be directly equivalent to "meaning"), and the Real is what always lies beyond language and can only be experienced through a mediation between the Imaginary and the Symbolic. Lacanian psychoanalysis is a structural, not a developmental, model of the subject.

[15] See Alan Renoir, "Point of View and Design for Terror in *Beowulf*," *Neuphilologische Mitteilungen* 63 (1962): 154–67, for an analysis of Grendel's approach to Heorot. See also Michael Lapidge, "*Beowulf* and the Psychology of Terror," in *Heroic Poetry in the Anglo-Saxon Period: Studies in Honor of Jess B. Bessinger, Jr.*, ed. Helen Damico and John Leyerle (Kalamazoo, 1993), pp. 373–402.

[16] See Jacques Lacan, "The Mirror Stage as Formative of the Function of the I," *Écrits*, trans. Alan Sheridan (New York, 1977), pp. 1–7, and Seminar I, in *The Seminar of Jacques Lacan. Book I: Freud's Papers on Technique, 1953–1954*, ed. Jacques Alain-Miller, trans. John Forrester (New York, 1988).

[17] Lacan distinguishes between "other" (with a small "o")—a specific, individual "other," or "others," by whom the individual is faced (and with whom he might feel identification or opposition)—and "Other" (with a capital "O"), which is "Otherness" is general (or, the larger alterity that is always threatening to subsume and destroy the individual ego).

[18] Juliet Flower MacCannell, *The Regime of the Brother: After the Patriarchy* (London, 1991).

[19] Gerhard Richter, "History's Flight, Anselm Kiefer's Angels," *The Connecticut Review* 24 (2002): 114.

[20] Richter, "History's Flight," p. 123.

[21] Nicholas Howe, "The Uses of Uncertainty: On the Dating of *Beowulf*," in *The Dating of "Beowulf*," ed. Colin Chase (1981; reprint Toronto, 1997), pp. 113–20, reviews attempts to date the poem and comes to the modest conclusion that

"Anglo-Saxonists must accept a burden of ignorance about matters of authorship and chronology that would be, I think, intolerable to those who work in most other periods of literary history" (p. 113). Howe argues that, in the absence of a firm date for *Beowulf*, the task of interpretation and of critical self-consciousness is both more difficult and more urgent.

22 On the subject of the poem as concerned with what might be called "nation-building," see Roberta Frank, "The *Beowulf* Poet's Sense of History," in The Wisdom of Poetry: Essays in Early English Literature in Honor of Morton W. Bloomfield (Kalamazoo, 1983), pp. 53–65; John D. Niles, "Locating *Beowulf* in Literary History" and *Homo Narrans: The Poetics and Anthropology of Oral Literature* (Philadelphia, 1999), pp. 120–45; Robert L. Kellogg, "The Context for Epic in Later Anglo-Saxon England," in Damico and Leyerle, *Heroic Poetry in the Anglo-Saxon Period*, pp. 139–56; and Peter Richardson, "Making Thanes: Literature, Rhetoric, and State Formation in Anglo-Saxon England," *Philological Quarterly* 78.1–2 (1999): 215–32. Kathleen Davis, "National Writing in the Ninth Century: A Reminder for Postcolonial Thinking about the Nation," *Journal of Medieval and Early Modern Studies* 28.3 (1998): 611–37, looks at the formation of a Christian, English people under Alfred, and Sarah Foot, "The Making of *Anglecynn*: English Identity Before the Norman Conquest," in *Old English Literature: Critical Essays*, ed. R. M. Liuzza (New Haven, 2002), pp. 51–79, studies Alfred's "promotion of the *Anglecynn* as a people with a shared past united under West Saxon rule," enabling "the creation of a . . . national consciousness" (p. 66). For the contributions of the law codes to a developing sense of Anglo-Saxon nationhood, see Mary P. Richards, "The Manuscript Context of the Old English Laws: Tradition and Innovation," in *Studies in Earlier Old English Prose*, ed. Paul E. Szarmach (Albany, 1986), pp. 171–92, and in "Anglo-Saxonism in the Old English Laws," in *Anglo-Saxonism and the Construction of Social Identity*, ed. Allen J. Frantzen and John D. Niles (Gainesville, 1997), pp. 40–59. Earl, *Thinking About "Beowulf,"* p. 113, and Richardson, "Making Thanes," pp. 220–21, both refer to the laws' restrictions on kin relations.

23 Edith Wyschogrod, *An Ethics of Remembering: History, Heterology, and the Nameless Others* (Chicago, 1998), pp. 1–40, distinguishes a mimetic, referential discourse from a more properly historical discourse in which language refers only to other language. Further, she writes, "From the commonsense point of view, events that have gone by are imprinted on a surface or stored in a repository in the forms of words and images that can be accessed over and over again, remembered. On this view, to re-member is to bring back, to re-present, what was previously encoded. The commonsense view conflates the major models of memory that have governed Western thought, that of inscription, incising

upon a surface, and that of a storehouse into which one can reach to fetch up some particular of the past. According to the last of these views, what is brought back is either raw material to be worked up into a coherent narrative or detritus to be shunned and cast back into, as Augustine would put it, the great belly of memory. If remembering is a species of representation as the everyday view implies, the epistemic difficulty that pertains to representation . . . is reinstated: language about the past is second-order discourse without any first-order level to which definitive appeal can be made. Even if, hypothetically, some original 'scene' could be replicated [mimesis], the gap that opens between first and later occasions creates an unsurpassable difference" (pp. 174–75). Gillian Overing, in "Swords and Signs: Dynamic Semeiosis in *Beowulf*," *Language, Sign, and Gender in "Beowulf*," pp. 33–67 (reprinted in this volume), discusses what is here termed "mimetic" discourse under the heading of the "index," which she illustrates with reference to material objects, such as the giant sword hilt Beowulf comes across when he is fighting Grendel's mother in the mere, as well as detached body parts. In "Grendel's Glove," *ELH* 61 (1994): 721–51, Seth Lerer also reads the fragmented body parts in the poem as "signs and symbols, figures for a violence that has gone on long ago. . . . They exemplify the symbolic itself" (p. 741). Although Lerer places these "figures" within an Indo-European cultic and mythological context, he understands those figures as material signs in a discourse that signify "the idea of representation itself" (p. 741).

24 See Edward B. Irving Jr., *A Reading of "Beowulf"* (New Haven, 1968) for an analysis of the prominent contrast between youth and old age in the poem, among many other contrasts that structure the poem.

25 Stanley B. Greenfield, "Geatish History: Poetic Art and Epic Quality in *Beowulf*," in *Interpretations of "Beowulf": A Critical Anthology*, ed. R. D. Fulk (Bloomington, 1991), p. 121, reconstructs the history of the Geatish-Swedish wars, as does Liuzza in *"Beowulf": A New Verse Translation*, pp. 157–58. G. N. Garmonsway and Jacqueline Simpson, in *"Beowulf" and Its Analogues, ed. Garmonsway and Simpson* (London, 1965), give relevant source material for the Swedish wars, pp. 212–221, and for the Heathobards, pp. 238–250. Briefly, the dynastic history is as follows: The eldest son in the Geatish ruling family, Herebeald, is accidentally killed by the second brother, Hæthcyn, who becomes king, and their father, Hrethel, dies of grief. When Hæthcyn attacks the Swedes, in retaliation for when the sons of Ongentheow, Othere and Onela, attacked the Geats, he is killed by Ongentheow; Ongentheow is killed in the continuing battle by Wulf and Eofer, and Hygelac becomes king of the Geats, with Othere becoming king of the Swedes. Hygelac is killed in Frisia on a raiding mission and his son, Heardred, succeeds to the kingship, with Beowulf's acquiescence. Onela then usurps the

Swedish throne, displacing Eanmund and Eadgils, the sons of Othere, who escape into Heardred's protection. Going after the fugitive sons, Onela murders Heardred and, acting for Onela, Weohstan (father of Wiglaf) kills Eanmund. Beowulf becomes king and supports Eadgils, who apparently chases down Onela and kills him and also, presumably, becomes king of Sweden.

[26] In *An Ethics of Remembering*, Wyschogrod writes that "the past is not part of the world's density in that it can never be brought back materially but only as word or image. 'It was' *is* an unsurpassable negation that enters the world's materiality and, as such, whose material return is precluded" (p. 173).

[27] See Walter Benjamin, "Theses on the Philosophy of History," *Illuminations: Essays and Reflections*, ed. Hannah Arendt, trans. Harry Zohn (New York, 1969), pp. 253–64.

[28] In "Beowulf as Peacekeeper" (unpublished paper), Lisa Darien analyzes Beowulf's role as protector of his people, although her main interest is in complicating the conventional understanding of gender in the poem. In Darien's view, when Beowulf acts as a "peace-weaver," he performs what is characteristically viewed as a female social function. Wymer and Labbie everywhere emphasize Beowulf's concern to promote social order by controlling the enjoyment of violence (what they call "rage") and promoting peace during his rule in "Civilized Rage in *Beowulf*."

[29] The placement of the various law codes in diverse manuscripts is laid out by Mary P. Richards in "The Manuscript Contexts of the Old English Laws."

[30] It is important to note here, as Dorothy Whitelock does, that "[w]e owe the survival of the laws of the West Saxon king, Ine . . . solely to their being added as a supplement to the laws of Alfred, who expressly mentions his use of them. . . . It is not, however, safe to assume that we have them complete, for King Alfred may have copied only such as were useful for his purpose, and have ignored any which time had made a dead letter" (*English Historical Documents, c. 500–1042*, ed. Dorothy Whitelock [New York, 1955], p. 364). At the same time, Whitelock also cautions that "it must not be assumed that there was a widespread practice of modernization, for the presence of much archaic diction and syntax [in our copy of Ine's laws] proves that in general that the text was rendered much as it stood" (p. 328). The laws of Ine, then, can be seen as part and parcel of Alfred's legal system, as well as an historical precursor.

[31] All citations of law codes are, for Ine, Alfred, and Æthelstan, from *The Laws of the Earliest English Kings*, ed. and trans., F. L. Attenborough (1922; reprint New York, 1963), and for Edmund and Edgar, from *The Laws of the Kings of England from Edmund to Henry I*, ed. and trans. A. J. Robertson (Cambridge, Eng., 1925). Both volumes also provide, with facing translations, the original

text of Felix Liebermann's edition of the law codes, *Die Gesetze der Angelsachsen*, 3 vols. (Halle, 1903–1916). References to specific laws will be to the king and numbering provided in the volumes cited above. In some cases, translations of specific laws will also reference Attenborough's and Robertson's editions.

[32] Attenborough, *The Laws of the Earliest English Kings*, p. 43.

[33] Attenborough, *The Laws of the Earliest English Kings*, p. 47.

[34] Patrick Wormald, *Legal Culture in the Earl Medieval West: Law as Text, Image and Experience* (London, 1999), pp. 194–95.

[35] Attenborough, *The Laws of the Earliest English Kings*, p. 67. See also Paul Hyams, "Feud and the State in Late Anglo-Saxon England," *Journal of British Studies* 40 (2001): 1–43, especially p. 27.

[36] According to Whitelock, for the reign of Æthelstan, there are six codes and a brief ordinance on almsgiving, and "II Æthelstan" refers to laws written "at Grateley" (*English Historical Documents*, p. 332). In the original text, the code of II Æthelstan is concluded with the statement that, "All this was established at the great assembly at Grateley, at which Archbishop Wulfhelm was present, with all the nobles and councilors whom King Æthelstan had assembled" (Attenborough, *The Laws of the Earliest English Kings*, p. 143).

[37] Robertson, *The Laws of the Kings of England from Edmund to Henry I*, p. 9.

[38] Robertson, *The Laws of the Kings of England from Edmund to Henry I*, p. 9.

[39] Wormald, *Legal Culture in the Early Medieval West*, p. 337.

[40] The original text reads *witan* where Robertson has "the authorities," and Whitelock translates with "leading men," but she also notes that "*witan* 'wise men' seems here to be used more widely than its usual meaning of 'councilors'" (*English Historical Documents*, p. 392 n. 4).

[41] As regards the issue of establishing a "central" authority through the law codes, Whitelock writes that "many copies [of the law codes] must have been circulated, in order that the decisions should become known to all whose concern they were. One of Edgar's codes gives instructions about the circulation of copies 'in all directions' by the ealdormen in their individual provinces, while among the legal texts that survive from an earlier reign, that of Æthelstan, one is a reply from the bishops and other councilors of Kent accepting and putting into force the measures enacted by the king and his councilors, and another shows how the Londoners proposed to apply in detail to the area of their own jurisdiction the general injunctions they had received on the maintenance of the peace" (*English Historical Documents*, pp. 327–28).

[42] Paul Hyams, "Does It Matter When the English Began to Distinguish Between Crime and Tort?" in *Violence in Medieval Society*, ed. Richard W. Kaeuper (Woodbridge, 2000), pp. 107–28. According to Hyams, however, the distinction

between crime and tort does not appear in English law until the second half of the twelfth century, during the reign of Henry II. In his book *Rancor and Reconciliation in Medieval England: Conjunctions of Religion and Power in the Medieval Past* (Ithaca, N.Y., 2003), pp. 71–110, Hyams traces the development of Old English legal categories in great detail. See also the debate over the institution of "public justice" between Hyams, "Nastiness, Wrong, Rancor, Reconciliation," pp. 195–218, and Charles Donahue Jr., "The Emergence of the Crime-Tort Distinction in England," pp. 219–28, both in *Conflict in Medieval Europe: Changing Perspectives on Society and Culture*, ed. Warren C. Brown and Piotr Górecki (Burlington, 2003).

[43] Hyams, "Does It Matter When the English Began to Distinguish Between Crime and Tort?" pp. 133, 117.

[44] Wormald, *Legal Culture in the Early Medieval West*, p. 352.

[45] Robertson, *The Laws of the Kings of England from Edmund to Henry I*, p. 33.

[46] Wormald, *Legal Culture in the Early Medieval West*, p. 191.

[47] Simon Keynes, "Crime and Punishment in the Reign of King Æthelred the Unready," in *People and Places in Northern Europe 500–1600: Essays in Honor of Peter Hayes Sawyer*, ed. Ian Wood and Neils Lund (Woodbridge, Eng., 1991), pp. 69, 71.

[48] The charter is quoted from Whitelock, *English Historical Documents*, p. 532.

[49] Keynes, "Crime and Punishment in the Reign of King Æthelred," p. 70.

[50] Pauline Stafford, "Political Ideas in Late Tenth-Century Charters," in *Law, Laity and Solidarities: Essays in Honor of Susan Reynolds*, ed. Pauline Stafford, Janet L. Nelson, and Jane Martindale (Manchester, Eng., 2001), pp. 79, 76.

[51] Katherine O'Brien O'Keeffe, "Body and Law in Late Anglo-Saxon England," *Anglo-Saxon England* 27 (1998): 209–32, elaborates on the decisive development in the character of Anglo-Saxon law when a sense of guilt is internalized within the subject of state power. Between 970 and 1035, "produced by a synergism of monastic and royal concerns for regulation," legal punishment "extends the power of the law (previously satisfied by external compensation) inward into the criminal's soul" (p. 230).

[52] Benjamin, "Theses on the Philosophy of History," p. 257. In this essay, Benjamin meditates on a Paul Klee painting, "Angel Novus," which "shows an angel looking as though he is about to move away from something he is fixedly contemplating." Benjamin sees in this image "the angel of history.... Where we perceive a chain of events, he sees one single catastrophe which keeps piling wreckage upon wreckage and hurls it in front of his feet. The angel would like to stay, awaken the dead, and make whole what has been smashed" (p. 257).

THE ETHNOPSYCHOLOGY OF IN-LAW FEUD AND THE REMAKING OF GROUP IDENTITY IN *BEOWULF*: THE CASES OF HENGEST AND INGELD

JOHN M. HILL

n *Beowulf* the clearest instances of groups reforming themselves, other than Wiglaf's remaking of the Geatish wartroop, are those involving either feud between in-laws or strife within dynastic houses. Principally, dynastic strife occurs in the Swedish house, although for many readers the poet also hints at such strife in Heorot for the Danes (regarding Hrothgar's nephew, Hrothulf, and Hrothgar's sons). Because of the dramatically coherent, although compressed narratives involved—in contrast both to the scattered remarks about actual dynastic strife among the Swedes and the possible intimations of strife among the Danes—this essay will only explore the two stories of in-law feud in *Beowulf*. Those scenarios become especially provocative as the poet's sketches, given one incident or another, open up to the revival of bitter memories and the renewal of slaughter. The resulting narratives, however, while usually understood as typical Germanic instances of heroic loyalties either in conflict or else overcome through the imperatives of blood revenge, do more than confront us with dismaying violence.

In their own ways they are socially acute meditations on the prospects for settlement, for accomplished and extended community, between groups who bring histories of past strife to their efforts at composing a feud. They are also meditations on the dynamic of group reformation—a dynamic that involves what for us are archaic social conceptions and an ethnopsychology of loyalty, honor and retainer identity—once lethal violence under-

From *Philological Quarterly* 78.1/2 (Winter 1999): 97–123; reprinted with permission of *Philological Quarterly*.

cuts a prior accommodation. In short, the stories of Finn, Hildeburh, and Hengest, of Danes and Ingeld's Heathobeards—these are much more than object lessons regarding kinship loyalties caught up in what, to modern commentators, has too often seemed a matter simply of doom brought on by the intractable imperatives of revenge. Indeed, those episodes have so dismayed modern commentators that they have been almost universally interpreted as springboards for a general critique of revenge feud on the poet's behalf. Yet, while kinship loyalties, retainer and lordship loyalties, and acts of revenge figure centrally in these stories, the significance of those loyalties and acts prove, upon ethnopsychological inspection, to be other than the grounds for an indictment of revenge. When a bitter Hengest—having lost his lord, Hnæf, in a storm of Frisian and Jutish terror—accepts and then wields a retributive sword, he disentangles the Half-Danes from their winter alliance with Finn (Hnæf's slayer, in effect). In doing so, he breaks off a carefully balanced arrangement that is, in effect, deeply shameful. The retributive outcome is this: Hengest and his Danes annihilate Finn's group, killing Finn; they then sack Finn's hall and retrieve Hildeburh, Hnæf's sister, who is also Finn's queen. This seems grim enough. But what becomes apparent only in an ethnopsychological perspective is that the Danes through blood *rightly* reassert their honor and identity while taking back Finn's queen, Hildeburh, their princess. She returns to her people, to a reintegration with her patriline.

The prospective redefining and violent reassertion of Heathobeardic honor in Beowulf's story about the marriage between Freawaru and Ingeld involve similar issues but in a very different situation. Here we begin with accommodations of honor possible between two contending peoples, this in a new "peace-kin" alliance through marriage, Hrothgar's hope for the redirection, indeed the settlement, of recent feuding between Danes and Heathobeards. However, in anticipation of what is likely to happen during the wedding process, Beowulf foresees a fracturing of relationships between Danes and Heathobeards when an old Heathobeard sees how a Danish warrior in the bride's entourage wears the sword of a defeated Heathobeard. Beowulf supposes that the old warrior will repeatedly goad a young Heathobeard, pointing out that sword to its previous owner's son. Most readers focus on that goading and thus see bitter revenge need as the guiding light here. But as far back as 1911, thematic emphasis in the story has been seen otherwise. Vilhelm Grønbech notably considered this event and thought of the Danes as boastful, both implicitly and as the old Heathobeard warrior characterizes them.[1] That kind of reading is one that

Kemp Malone later elaborates fancifully as involving the deliberate provocation of a failed (Danish) suitor for Freawaru.[2]

That point aside, the prompted Heathobeard is much like Hengest in that he is urged to reassert his and his group's honor or else retreat ignominiously. The psychological and social force of this prompting is one reason why Beowulf does not think much will come of Hrothgar's efforts at peace kinship in this case. After the revenge slaying of the young Dane, Ingeld reacts against the Danes, his hatred increasing and his love for his bride cooling. At this point the old Heathobeard warrior has, in effect, disentangled the groom from his in-law alliance with the Danes (an alliance Saxo Grammaticus will much later treat as a species of luxurious gluttony, a gluttony unmindful of ancestral values.[3] Similarly, the Danes in the Finn episode disentangle both themselves and the bride-queen, Hildeburh, from her grievously tainted life with Finn and his Frisians. After killing Finn, they bring Hildeburh home to her people. These are symmetrical stories, then, when seen from kinship and group reformation points of view. Violence resumes in each case shortly after a peace—a shameful peace of the hall in the one case and a fragile wedding alliance, too short-lived in the face of a terrible history of strife to establish anything, in the other.

Regarding the Danes and Heathobeards, Frederick Klaeber has imagined both a story line and a chronological expanse for this narrative: Ingeld's father, Froda, slays Hrothgar's father, Healfdene. Heorogar, Hrothgar, and Halga reply, slaying Froda in their attack on the Heathobeards. Twenty years later, Hrothgar tries to compose the feud through marriage. Thus the old Heathobeard warrior who remembers the strife, remembers back a good long time; yet the *Beowulf* narrative does not suggest anything like this scenario, which indeed depends upon inferences inspired by much later Danish analogues. Beowulf, without saying anything about who in the past killed whom, makes it seem that only a short time has passed since warfare and calamity befell the people; and the old Heathobeard simply remembers it all, the spear-death of men. The totality of the slaughter is vivid for him. As these facts come into focus for us, we need to reassess Klaeber's thematic conclusions about the episode also: does this narrative actually highlight a central, tragic motive, "the implacable enmity between two tribes, dominated by the idea of revenge which no human bonds of affection can restrain?"[4] While the issues of honor are complicated, the presence of something like "implacable enmity" is socially unlikely. But let's look closely at these matters, beginning with the case of attempted marriage-alliance—Hrothgar's way of trying to settle (legislatively) a history of strife. That beginning, at the least, should be noted. It suggests that enough has changed in the relation-ships between the two peoples so that Hrothgar could propose and Ingeld honorably receive a marriage proposal in the first place. Clearly we are not dealing here with implacable enmity—at least not yet, and perhaps never.

Beowulf begins his story in the course of answering Hygelac's reception speech in Hygelac's hall. Sitting beside his nephew (sister's son), kinsman with kinsman, Hygelac has courteously questioned Beowulf about how he fared on his suddenly resolved upon journey, given the strife he sought. Did he improve matters regarding the famous, widely known suffering of Hrothgar? Hygelac immediately follows this question with a revelation of his deep concern for Beowulf, of how in a state of surging sorrow and care he had not trusted his beloved warrior's journey and that he long urged Beowulf not to greet that slaughter spirit. Let the South-Danes do battle against Grendel themselves. But he thanks God that he now sees Beowulf sound and safe.

Beowulf has to address Hygelac's implied but powerful rebuke here, espe-cially as it has been so movingly couched in an intimate seating arrangement between two near equals (at the kinship level, kinsman sitting beside kins-man). He needs to respond to an implicit, although lovingly anxious con-cern about getting mixed up in someone else's feud with a slaughter spirit. What has happened? Has Beowulf compromised his Geatish loyalties while helping or in some sense perhaps even serving Hrothgar in the Grendel affairs (there are implications in this world to repeated service—after all, Hrothgar did some time ago recruit Beowulf's father by settling a feud on his behalf)? And how has Beowulf, despite hailing Hygelac in an ethically ap-propriate way—he is said to have greeted Hygelac "loyally," *hold* being part of the reciprocal vocabulary of the warband—changed or not since entering into what for anyone else would have been a fool's bloody disaster?[5]

We can read the story of Hrothgar's prospects regarding the Heathobeards as Beowulf's indirect reply to the hovering of such unstated questions. His scenario does more than simply exhibit his sense of how the world goes (a common reading of his motive for digressing in this way); I think his story obliquely answers Hygelac's exposure of past and (implicitly) continuing concern. It is as though Beowulf is reassuring Hygelac here, after the fact, that he knows that some Danish feuds are not likely to be easily or happily settled. Indeed, Beowulf will end his scenario regarding Ingeld by conclud-ing that because of what he has reviewed as a likely series of events, he does not count much on firm Heathobeardan friendship regarding the Danes. This is a way of saying, "Dear Lord and Uncle, I'm not a fool, not when I went to Heorot and not now, not in any sense in the flush of my triumph. Feud settlements are not cheaply or easily achieved." But in contrast, some feuds are open, it seems, to happy settlement given vigorous effort. Hygelac is right not to trust in happy outcomes, but the Grendel affair did turn out well, even though Grendel's mother came the next night and Beowulf, because Hrothgar implored him by Hygelac's name (something Beowulf says, falsely), sought revenge on the mother also.[6] At the end of his long speech he says that Hrothgar's great gifts were given to him, into his own keeping, as though alienated from Hrothgar and bespeaking no continuing ties to him (which is what is important about telling Hygelac that Hrothgar invoked Hygelac's name). Indeed, they belong to Hygelac, to whom Beowulf wishes to offer them, saying that all his joys still depend on Hygelac. Thus, implicitly, he too is very happy to see Hygelac. He, Beowulf, is unwaveringly loyal to his uncle and lord. There was no need to mistrust the Grendel affair, either as a feud to settle or as an avenue into Danish orientations and thus a shift in loyalties.

With this overview regarding possibly changed loyalties, we have at least one of Beowulf's motives for telling the story of a young, gold-adorned Freawaru betrothed to the shining, glorious son of Froda ("gladum suna Frodan," line 2025b). Efforts to compose compensatory patterns, new loyalties that is, can break down for a combination of reasons. With that in mind we should now probe the psychological and social dimensions of the scenario itself. The subject of this betrothal preoccupies Beowulf as he hits upon a probable line of development between Danes and Heathobeards. Although the initial opening for the match suggests possibilities, even glitters with promise, something is likely to undermine it, doing so despite that advice or counsel (*ræd*) Hrothgar considers: to wit, that through Freawaru he will settle this portion of slaughter-feud, the fighting between Danes and Heathobeards.

While fighting can be a way of settling a feud, as when Beowulf thinks of Grendel approaching Heorot (line 600), it is of course counsel opposed to fighting that Hrothgar acts upon in this prospective peace-kinship between Danes and Heathobeards. The hope involved in that action may seem foolish in retrospect, given the way Beowulf supposes matters will turn. Yet, on the face of it, marriage alliances can work in Beowulf's world; this one at least gets off the ground enough so that Danes and Heathobeards undertake the opening rituals of wedding festivity, with the Heathobeards *graciously* receiving Freawaru and her entourage of young warriors (the initial quality of that reception matters—a quality apparent in "gladum suna Frodan" ("gracious son of Froda," line 2025b) and in the entertaining of the Danes (*duguða biwenede*, line 2035b). But in Beowulf's opinion, apparently, the connotations of *wælfæhð* are forbidding. Can "murderous slaughter," can "slaughter-feud," be easily composed short of violence? Obviously some slaughters require vigorous reprisal, as against Grendel, his mother, and the dragon, and also when the Geats, as we learn late in the poem, reply aggressively to Swedish ambushes. Is there here, however, in the Freawaru and Ingeld story, a case of murderous feud potentially rectifiable by less than bloody means, or do we in fact have, on the poet's part, the beginning of an implicit critique of heroic institutions, as Harry Berger and Marshall Leicester once argued?[7] The latter does seem possible given Beowulf's view of what will likely develop. But I do not think his scenario carries with it a fundamental critique of revenge feud from the poet's perspective. I will attempt to support my view below.

That feud can be composed or settled through reprisal is clear enough in other places in the poem's dramatic action as well as in background information. God, for example, punishes Cain's feud against Abel (line 109). Grendel feuds criminally against the Danes (line 153), wanting no peace, kinship (*sibbe*) or settlement. Then Hrothgar says that Grendel's mother has killed Æschere because of Beowulf's feud-settlement with Grendel (line 1333), but that he, Hrothgar, will settle rewards on Beowulf should Beowulf take up the feud with Grendel's mother (line 1380). Finally, we should not forget that Hrothgar settles a feud non-violently on Edgtheow's behalf (Beowulf's father) with the Wilfings (line 470) and that Geats and Danes, now friends, once "engaged in," that is, exchanged enmities ("inwitniþas, þe hie ær drugon," line 1858).

As feuds can be settled, marriage alliances can succeed. We do not know whether past feuds occurred between Danes and Wealhtheow's people, only that Wealhtheow and Hrothgar are nobly and functionally wed; likewise, Hrothgar's sister seems a successful bride among Onela's Swedes, Hygd among the Geats, and Thryth among Offa's people (one of the warriors Thryth had slain may have been kin to Offa, although he is nonplussed by her past actions and reputation as a princess). These groups, interrelated by marriage at one time or another, may well have fought each other also at one time or another, fulfilling an ethnological adage if so: those one fights may also include those one marries in group relations characterized by exogamy (where women marry out, living with their husbands and in-laws).

Of course, we do not know just how Heathobeards and Danes have been connected or not (or who the Heathobeards were exactly), just as we do not know what relations Frisians and Danes and Frisians and Geats have had in the past, aside from the feuds the poem recalls. Perhaps Danes, Swedes, and Geats form a more tightly linked network of alliances (although hardly barring feud) than is the case for Danes and Frisians or for Geats and Frisians (and Merovingians) and Danes and Heathobeards. These may be peoples with whom the central grouping of three has looser and even more fractious ties. Still, on the face of it, a splendid marriage alliance between previously feuding peoples may not be inevitably doomed—unless the feud has been too bitter too recently, or unless the settlement itself falls in the beginning to cutting insult and afflicted feeling. Unfortunately both of these conditions obtain in the case Beowulf sketches out.

Beowulf indicates Hrothgar's legislative kingship in Hrothgar's counseled effort at settlement. The "friendly lord" of the Scyldings, the guardian of the kingdom, has considered good counsel. Nevertheless, seldom anywhere after *leodhyre*, the fall of a people—a phrase that applies also to the Geats later, following the Swedish King Onela's attack in pursuit of his nephews, during which Beowulf's king, Heardred, dies—does the slaying-spear, for more than a little while, remain submissive. This probability would arise even though the bride is good (and the match a strong one in an effort at fostering community and kinship). The converse of this is that it would take a long time to overcome the festering enmity consequent upon such a calamity for the side that bore the greater slaughter (as seems the case with the Heathobeards). So, this is what Beowulf thinks. But ethnopsychologically, how does this state of affairs arise in Beowulf's world?

Apparently, Beowulf's answer would be that the prodding of personal and group honor would work otherwise than for a kinship peace in such circumstances. Beowulf proposes that the lord of the Heathobeards, Ingeld, and each of his thanes, may well be displeased (*ofþyncan*, line 2032) when young Danish warriors walk with the bride into the hall, are as a group well-attended to (*biwenede*, line 2035). Despite that attention the Danes apparently, quite naturally and unthinkingly, sport weapons taken from Heathobeards killed in losing battle, battle during which the Heathobeards fought for as long as they could. The combinations here of terror in the past befalling a people, of brave struggle in a losing effort, and then of grievous insult in the reception hall—these clearly enough render the Heathobeards initially as the rightly aggrieved party.

In other Old English literature, the word for displeasure here expresses a precondition for martial and often civil strife, when one party seriously dislikes the actions of another. This is the case between Roman consuls in *Orosius*, 5.9; or among subject peoples, the Persians, who opposed the dominion of the Medes (*Orosius*, 1.12); or, in Xerxes' case, his frustration that a small army should slaughter a much larger one (*Orosius*, 2.5). This "displeasure" regarding a group of people, is a prelude to killings and warfare, much as it also expresses hostile ambivalence toward one's new in-laws. In a sense the Heathobeards might feel that they have in some compensatory sense triumphed over the Danes by accepting or figuratively stealing their woman, a woman one wants without being beholden to the giver. For their part, the givers, obliquely or even "accidentally" through their emissaries, may give while taunting sexually—as in the wearing of weapons taken from the slain (read "castrated") fathers of their new in-laws.

Beowulf characterizes the Heathobeardic weapons worn by Danes favorably. He notes the conditions under which they were lost and effectively identifies their significance. Those weapons are ancient heirlooms, hard and ring-marked, the treasure of Heathobeards who gave them up reluctantly, who wielded them for as long as they could. Those Heathobeards then finally led themselves and their companions into that shield-play that killed them. Seeing those ancient, bitterly yielded weapons shining on the persons of hospitably received Danes must then be doubly galling, doubly shameful. So far, Beowulf tells this story from the point of view of aggrieved Heathobeards, who have agreed to the wedding and who have indeed honorably received young warriors attending the bride, warriors who are the sons of their former enemies. Beowulf then conjures up an old spear-warrior who speaks at the beer-feast, one who sees a (formerly Heathobeardan) treasure ring on a young Dane, one who remembers all, the spear death of men. To him is the spirit grim.

That old warrior begins, sad in mind, to try (*cunnian*, a verb having to do with depths) a young warrior's heart, to sound out and fathom, to know the thought of the young man's breast and there "kindle the baleful affliction of war" (*wigbealu weccean*, line 2046a). *Wigbealu* suggests something tainted in that "balefulness" and "affliction" in *Beowulf* usually await or need remedy (as the Danes await some remedy in the Grendel case). But the old warrior has been stirred up to grim remembrance and present counsel by the sight of those ancient heirlooms worn either in amazing ignorance by the bride's attendants or in no subtle despite of the Heathobeards. The former seems most incredible. The latter possibility is not, as though in wearing those appropriated weapons the young Danes are saying this: "we may give you our princess, Freawaru, to wed and thus to penetrate sexually, but we wear the emblems of your fathers' castrations—those fathers of yours that our fathers killed."

Something like this is the probable content, psychologically considered, of the insult Vilhelm Grønbech long ago noted in this passage and which other readers have at least superficially registered. Swords in relation to weddings can only mean trouble of some sort, embroiling all in a subliminal drama of rape or castration or both. John Hermann has developed a similar point regarding Judith's prayer to the God of Simeon in the *Liber Iudith*, with Simeon in turn taking us to the story of Sichem's rape of Dina. Her brothers, Jacob's sons, while pretending reconciliation with Sichem and the Sichimites, demand that the Sichimites be circumcised; three days after the circumcisions, Dina's brothers, without asking Dina, avenge her dishonor by slaughtering all of the apparently weakened as well as ritually lulled Sichimite males.[8]

In "Reflections on the Notion of Kinship," Georges Devereux speculates that essentially the marriage rite does much more than create a bond between husband and wife and an alliance between the two families. By proclaiming an alliance, the marriage rite affirms "an understanding so as to avoid a brawl, to substitute peace for war."[9] This, of course, is Hrothgar's great hope, following the advice he has taken and given that war between Danes and Heathobeards has been much more than figurative. But Devereux goes on to offer the story of Sichem and Dina that Hermann discusses as one of the most striking for revealing the "latent hostility of the 'givers of women'"[10] and for establishing the ostensibly anthropological fact that marriages principally concern relationships between men. Those relationships, for Devereux, are in part disguised as such reciprocal practices as brideprice and morning gifts seem to put women at the center.[11] Some such disguise is necessary, Devereux would add, because the relationships he has in mind finally reveal or in some way express "the threatening specter of latent homosexuality,"[12] a fantasy of coitus on the part of the taker of the woman with the giver. That fantasy needs to be repelled in some way.

It is interesting in this connection to recall that the poem's most stable tie between two groups said to have exchanged enmity—the ongoing, mutual alliance between Geats and Danes—does not involve an exchange of women. Still, I do not quite see the "specter of homosexuality" operating in the Ingeld episode, or even generally in *Beowulfian* marriage exchanges. Primitive libido may well be "homosexual," "narcissistic," or "bisexual," as Freud and others would aver; and certainly in *Beowulf* homosocial libido has something to do with the making and maintaining of relationships within the warband. That libido, however, is drawn up into the formation of conscience instead of expressed nakedly or else in barely deflected forms.

Moreover, in a war-lord world like Beowulf's and Hygelac's, the formation of conscience comes to involve strong identifications with the martial needs of one's father or else uncle and lord.

The stories of conflict reveal ambivalence, competition, and hostility at that level primarily, although Grendel's exclusive life with, one might say possession of, his mother may take us deeper. So, in *Beowulf*, at any rate, we have little of the "specter" of homosexuality to deal with. Rather, we are always potentially in a world of masculine triumph (or at least fantasies of it) over the lord who gives. Giving is, after all, a gesture of superiority. That fantasy would operate on the part of the lord who receives, the receiver being implicitly in the position of inferior. In this kind of fantasy, the receiver would rather, I am supposing, be seen as a taker. For his part, the generous giver (Hrothgar in this effort regarding Ingeld) might well wish to hoard or else be a taker himself underneath the very act of giving. This could account in part for the element of taunt in the weapons Danes carry to the wedding festivities. Of course, the entire, overtly articulated moral world of the poem stands opposed to these possible, inglorious wishes. The giver who takes instead of giving would be a King Heremod for Hrothgar, given Hrothgar's sententious words after seeing the great sword hilt Beowulf retrieves from Grendel's mere. Hrothgar pointedly notes that despite great, God-given success and worldly power, Heremod grew bloody-mined and niggardly—"not at all did he give gifts to the Danes in pursuit of glory" ("Hwæðere him on ferhðe greow / breosthord blodreow; nallas beagas geaf / Denum æfter dome," lines 1718b-20a).

Even if we do not accept the presence of homophobia here, normal marriage exchanges are likely to be rife enough with ambivalence regarding the givers of women, which is Devereux's more general suggestion. As that is so, such exchanges within a context of bitter, recent strife between the parties will certainly reflect the kind of highly intensified ambivalence sketched above in analogy with the revenge Dina's brothers took on the weakened and no doubt surprised Sichimites. Moreover, the hostile ambivalence of givers is likely to have its counterpart in the latently ungrateful triumph of takers, who now have someone else's woman and would, subliminally, prefer to triumph in every way over the woman's men. For the Heathobeards, this need would be particularly strong—however ameliorated for a time by the compensatory ritual of marriage exchange—in relation to Danes who apparently carried the day in the still remembered slaughter between the two peoples.

The old Heathobeard begins his probing of a young warrior by referring directly to that warrior's father. He notes the precious iron that by right should be the young warrior's. Beginning by addressing the young Heathobeard as "my friend" or "lord," thus establishing or else preparing for an identification between the two of them as friendly lord and loyal man, he asks the warrior whether or not he (the warrior) recognizes the sword the warrior's father wore to battle? The father wore the precious iron there where the Danes slew him and controlled the slaughter place after Wiðergyld (the name even suggesting payment or repayment) lay dead, after brisk Scyldings destroyed Heathobeard warriors.[13]

This direct reference to the warrior's father reinforces a sense of close ties and of identity, of inheritance and warrior to warrior transmission, now lost, but which should have been the young Heathobeard's. That reference sets up the crucial observation that follows. "Now here a son or whatever of one of the killers, exulting in treasure, walks in the hall boasting of that murder and bearing that treasure which by right should be your (wartime) counsel" (lines 2053–56). This is very different counsel (*ræd*) from that Hrothgar accepted earlier when he thought to settle a portion of deadly slaughter through a wedding alliance between himself and Ingeld. This is the counsel of borrowed identity and of inherited identity both, of the warrior self as derived from the twin sources of father and lord, sharply, lethally emblematized in the sword that should by right, by law of descent, be the young warrior's wartime counsel. In effect, the old spear-warrior notes that the young *cempa* is hardly a warrior or champion yet—that he has indeed been cheated out of rightful inheritance and thus out of his rightful identity. As Beowulf puts it, the old warrior urges on and admonishes the young one, sorrowfully doing so many times. Eventually he will have recalled so many bitter things to mind, repeatedly, that then the proper time for retribution will have arrived. Then one of the bride's attendants, because of what the attendant's father had done, will sleep blood-stained after the sword-edge's bite, having forfeited life as though he were criminal and in need of punishment (note *ealdres scyldig*, line 2061a, a phrase that applies also to Grendel, line 1338). A similar end, by the way, "sword-bale," awaits Finn when the Danes in that tale avenge their shame on Finn and his remaining Frisians. But, to return, the Heathobeard warrior escapes, knowing the country well as he does. The especially interesting point about the old warrior's urging is that the young warrior does not think about the matter independently. He does not even appear to accept or receive the old warrior's admonishments. It is as though the repeated urgings themselves simply produce the happy slaying by forming the young warrior's mind, the warrior himself only being the agent of death. Crime has been requited. A previous slaughter and a current taunt now have been rectified. The juridical warrior in Beowulf sees nothing wrong with this.

In ethnopsychological terms, as Georges Devereux and Gillian Gillison might have put it were they to look at this scene, we here would have a breakdown of figurative coitus (alliance) regarding the bride's father (Hrothgar) on the part of the son-in-law (Ingeld).[14] Instead, we have the enactment of a lethal substitute from the side of the taker, that enactment of course being a response to the mutely displayed hostility of the givers. The young warrior is both agent and weapon, while the old warrior stands in for Ingeld, their mutually gestated violence directly arousing Ingeld's hate. In this view, the sword is a coital sword, with which the bride's father (or stand-in brother or retainer—note, *fæmnan ðegn*, "thane of young woman," for the Danish warrior, line 2059a) is penetrated. So much for a marital settling of dire feud.

This urging of revenge for both current and past injury is juridical. That is, the old warrior's urging has legal or customary respectability and seems to have Beowulf's sympathies, given his almost Heathobeardic interest in the ancient heirlooms, in how they were surrendered in a losing battle in which dear comrades and warrior-lords died. Moreover, the old warrior's claim that these weapons and treasures are worn as insults, as goads and boasts regarding the deaths of their former owners—this interpretation is entirely plausible. However, that the young Heathobeard warrior should need repeated urgings, while suggesting the latent formation over time of a righteously violent state of mind, does indicate a degree of restraint, of how much the compensatory wedding bond can at least temporarily deflect transactional passion. This latter possibility deserves notice because it must play some part in those marriage exchanges that work successfully toward alliance rather than brawl.

After this slaying, the sword-oaths of great warriors are broken on both sides, once-deadly hate (compare with Nebuchadnezzar's deadly hatred of the Israelites, *Daniel*, line 46) wells up in Ingeld—a hatred referred to earlier in the poem (line 85), in an anticipatory aside about sword-hate between sworn in-laws and the burning of Heorot. For Ingeld now, however, the immediate result is a complete rupture of the proposed alliance when a slaughter-hate surges up within him and his wife-love cools after rising sorrow. The "care-wellings" here are elsewhere found only with Hrothgar, in Beowulf's speech to the frontier guard, when Beowulf says (lines 277b-82b) that he might be able to offer good advice about overcoming Grendel, if reversal shall ever come for Hrothgar and his cares cool or subside. Placing

Ingeld in this position makes his wife-love a kind of care entangled in misery, for which remedy is sought.

This afflicted mixture reappearing between two peoples who have feuded bitterly is finally what destroys Hrothgar's marriage effort—an effort that is almost amazing both in the face of what it would settle and that it is nearly consummated. Therefore, whereas Hrothgar once considered the giving of Freawaru in marriage as a good way to settle deadly feud, Beowulf does not reckon on, without deceit or crime, the reciprocal favoring of the Heathobeards with the Danes. He does not expect firmness in the noble kinship established between them, the firmness of the friendship. This matter of favoring, friendship, and noble kinship without deceit is almost juridically phrased. *Unfæcne*, "without deceit," appears in Ethelbert's laws (no. 77) regarding honest bride payment: "Gif man mægð gebigeþ ceapi, geceapod sy, gif hit unfacne is"[15]—one is not to buy a bride, that is, exchange cattle or goods for her, with anything else (presumably "buy" could include promise or perhaps even seizure, capture). It appears in those laws again (no. 30) regarding honest *wergeld* ("Gif man mannan ofslea, unfæcne feo gehwilce gelde"). And it appears in the laws of Hlothere and Eadric (n0.16) regarding a Kentish man's need for two or three honest *ceorls*, or else the king's town reeve, to witness his purchases in London.[16]

But why does Beowulf raise the question of deceit now, at the end of his scenario? Has he suddenly considered an alternative unfolding, one in which the Heathobeards do not soon reply to Danish insults? Probably he now supposes that unless they are deceitful they will react as he has projected—that is, honestly, openly, in the manner recommended by the laws. They will violently reply to that stinging mockery—a mockery enacted in the very hall where they graciously received their wedding guests. Beowulf does not amplify this matter, although he pitches his closing remark as an assessment of Heathobeardan infirmity in friendship given this in-law kinship and alliance. We might say that Heathobeardan griefs are still too fresh and the Danish wedding party too boastful for us to trust long in Heathobeardan peacefulness: certainly not after a prodded warrior has shown the way. Ingeld's hatred will rise and he will reassert old honor by re-cognizing Heathobeardan identity, seeking reversal for the sexual entanglement with others that love for his bride signifies. Thus the problem here is not in revenge itself, for revenge is not indicted in this complex situation. Nor is the point that in-law kinship and peace are somehow inexorably doomed—after all Wealhtheow is a peace-kin (*friðusibb*, line 2017) for the peoples brought together by her marriage to Hrothgar (as is Hygd among the Geats, Hrothgar's sister among the Swedes, and Thryth among Offa's people). Rather the situation is primed to explode in violence as the Heathobeards eventually regroup, reasserting righteously by the prompted sword their old identities not entangled in alliance with the Danes. Of this Beowulf does not seem to disapprove, although he does apparently think that Hrothgar's hope in this alliance is not well founded, given both the past bitterness of the feud and the likelihood of semiconsciously provocative display by the Danes. The counsel Hrothgar received was not thoughtful enough in the face of all that. Correspondingly, Heathobeardic passions, as well as their frustrated sense of subliminal triumph, are perhaps too intense, although by now, I hope, more than understandable.

Apparently something more than minimal receptivity has to precede a wedding in this case, something that diminishes feelings and weakens unhappy memories on both sides. Perhaps the following is the kind of counsel Hrothgar should have received: first, regularize relationships carefully through exchanges of goods and visits over time by groups whose weapons are not goads and sad reminders; then look to the second generation for a development of ties that are of blood rather than alliance only. Something like this has happened in the Finn and Hildeburh story, although the episode itself, as the poet presents it, simply begins with terrible violence, with deadly catastrophe.

Something terrible happens during a visit by Hildeburh's brother and his retinue. The narrative begins with a two-part summary: Finn's sons are overcome by fear and disaster (*fær*, line 1068b) in the course of events. In this their fate parallels the fate of the Egyptians in *Exodus* (line 452). Yet, unlike the Egyptians, they suffer terror unjustly, for the connotative purview of *fær* in *Beowulf* almost exclusively involves either monstrous attack or monstrous habitat (compare with *færgryre*, line 174; *færnið*, line 476; *færgripe*, line 738, the sudden appearance of stunted trees near Grendel's mere; and *fær begeat*, line 2230, possibly a sudden emotion overtaking the thief in the dragon's barrow). The only exception is Beowulf's "sudden" resolve to seek out Hrothgar regarding the Grendel affair (line 1988). Thus, in most cases, and obliquely in the exceptional one, *fær* has shocking, unsettling, monstrous affects. This is truly a terror-imbued disaster. Hnæf of the Scyldings, the champion of the Half-Danes, had to fall in initial, Frisian slaughter. The narrative then focuses extensively and with deep sympathy on Hildeburh, the Danish princess who is Finn's queen and thus queen of the Frisians. We learn that she has no need to praise the fidelity and good faith of the Eotens (Jutes, or perhaps even connotatively "giants," given possible confusion between inflected plural forms of *eoten*—giant—and *Eotan*, Jute, a "confusion" perhaps poetically assured by the reverberations of *fær*). Finn's hall-troop seems mixed, containing both Frisians and Jutes. If we accept a connotative hint of "giant" inside the inflected, plural forms of *Eotan*, only a bitterly ironic negative remark follows. Insofar as "giant" can only have negative connotations in *Beowulf*—elsewhere a noun or adjective form refers to or implies Grendel twice, sea monsters once, three times a gigantic or else giant-made sword, and twice one of the species of things that arose in some way from Cain—the "Giants" whose fidelity (*treow*) Hildeburh need not praise can only suggest Terror. Among the Frisians they are the perpetrators of slaughter and death—a slaughter that takes in all the Frisians and Half-Danes, save a small remnant on each side eventually.

The fidelity of Jutes indeed is not praise-worthy. That kind of "fidelity," a commitment to terror, must be opposed. In some way terror in this world must always be definitively answered: so much is a true warrior's juridical responsibility. But we do not reach this point immediately. First the dreadful, initial outcome of this terror is dwelled upon through Hildeburh's suffering. Hers is truly a grievous, even criminal disaster as she suffers "the murder-bale of kinsmen," an horrendous crime of which Beowulf much later says God cannot accuse him (line 2742). She loses both her son and brother (who thus are uncle and sister's-son to each other, the most tender of cross-group ties in *Beowulf*). We are told that not without cause does Hildeburh, here called Hoc's daughter to emphasize her patriline, mourn the decree of fate in the morning. She sees under the heaven's expanse (global implication) nothing but the murder of kinsmen there where previously she had had her greatest, worldly joy—a joy only recently burst forth if we accept Rolf Bremmer's speculation that her son has come with her brother, Hnæf, being a member of Hnæf's warband.[17] That crime calls out, implicitly, for justice—a terrible crime perpetrated by terror-Jutes, inside whose name there is, possibly, a hint of terror-giant.

But then this awful emptying of possibly recent joy from the world is held in suspension for a considerable time as the narrative in mid-line turns to Finn's losses; he too has lost greatly, so much so that his survivors are too few in number to press the battle against Hengest, Hnæf's thane. That certainly is one reason why Finn and his men offer a settlement, announce terms or outcomes (*geþingo*, line 1085b). Both sides shall share a hall and high-seat together, and he, Finn, the son of Folcwalda, will honor the Danes through ring and treasure giving just as he honors Frisians in the beer hall. Thus Finn will become the evenhanded lord for a dangerously mixed group of aggrieved Half-Danes and aggressively edgy, if weakened, Frisians. His offer of settlement, bound together prospectively through his promise of reciprocal honoring of both parties, needs now the ratification of oaths on both sides. This happens, we learn, as each side pledges a firm peace-agreement (*frioðwær*, line 1096a).

The term here for peace is a weak indicator of loyalty—more a beginning contract or contact, as in the case of the exile who steals an ornate cup from the dragon's barrow and asks for a compact with Beowulf, proffering the cup as his offering (line 2282b). Thus Hengest accepts perhaps mainly because his group of warriors has been greatly diminished. But the whole compact must rankle, as Finn is well aware. For how can a loyal retainer, whose essential identity is on loan, in effect, from his lord, and who has thus internalized his lord's violent needs as his own, follow truly his lord's and so, in a sense, his own slayer? He cannot for long, given the psychology discussed above in the Heathobeard case.

In the face of such a psychology, and with the advice of counselors, Finn nevertheless would settle this affair, this slaughter, by the further stipulation that he would hold Hengest and his men in such reciprocal honor (*ar*) that no man should by word or deed break off the peace-agreement. Nor shall anyone through enmity ever complain, even though the Danes follow their ring-giver's slayer, lordless, as to them was so needful (dictated by circumstance). A malicious Frisian might well gloat over this fact—a shameful fact unless somehow ameliorated. If then any Frisian through audacious or dangerous speech should recall that murderous hatred to mind, then the sword's edge will end it. The legislative sword is the guarantee here of peaceful words and actions; moreover, generous ring giving and hall and treasure sharing should ameliorate an otherwise nearly unbearable compact for the Danes, necessitated by their greatly reduced numbers. As Hrothgar did, Finn here hopes to settle his part of deadly slaughter through this oath-borne, ring-cemented alliance. The reciprocal honor Finn offers is genuine, I think. He would—and this is the amazing, even wondrous proposal at the heart of this episode—be foster-lord for Hengest and the surviving Danes, if only he could now make his need for composition of the feud theirs also. But, as in Hrothgar's case, recollected or else aroused grief will unsettle this tenuous peace; eventual retribution will make of Finn something of a tragic character.

While these elaborate conditions are worked out and sworn to over the course of thirty-four and a half lines, we lose sight of Hildeburh and thus of her dark disaster especially (not just what has befallen both Frisians and Danes in general). Presumably the oath making and giving of gold from

Finn's hoard prepares the way now to see to the dead. The last rites might in fact bring the two groups together in joint sorrow and feeling for mutually suffered losses. But that does not seem the case here. First we hear that the Scylding champion (Hnæf), the best of warriors, was laid on the pyre. On that pyre it was easy to see the bloody shirt of mail, the swine image in gold, the boar hard as iron of many a chieftain. Many had fallen in the fight. But does this mean that, after peace-oaths and now with Hnæf, all has been laid to rest? No, for just here Hildeburh dramatically and, I believe, strategically reappears for her final eleven lines (she had nine and a half earlier). In commanding fashion, she takes over this sad ritual made bitter by the unrelieved disaster she has suffered: "Het ða Hildeburh æt Hnæfes ade / hire selfre sunu sweoloðe befæstan, / banfatu bærnan, ond on bæl don / eame on eaxle" (lines 1114–17a). On her own behalf now, Hildeburh orders that her own son, "hire selfre sunu"—the possessive separating him from Finn—be placed on the pyre beside Hnaef, his *eam* ("mother's brother"). Beside them both she mourns this bitter "family reunion," as Edward B. Irving, Jr. calls it.[18] Their bone-cases burn; willfully and powerfully, perhaps aggressively, she laments them in song.[19]

Most commentators have overlooked Hildeburh's intense *purposefulness* here.[20] Most of us have simply been overwhelmed by her losses, the disaster she suffers, indeed, by the fact that she seems here only to suffer unendingly—although for sheer dramatic elaboration she is not the focal point of this episode: Finn's efforts at hall peace and Hengest's temporary acquiescence are. Nevertheless, given how she suffers, we understandably come to see her as pure victim. We then unwisely extend that perspective, especially in recent commentary, to include almost all of the women characters in the poem. Aside from Thryth or else Modthryth, sublimed in her marriage to Offa, and perhaps Grendel's mother (if seen as a woman), the female lot in *Beowulf* has come for many to be that of futile, hapless "peace-weaving." Narrowly, however, this particular term only applies directly to Modthryth, doing so ironically regarding her cruel practice of binding and executing men who gaze upon her. The idea of peace-weaving in relationship to bloody outbreaks of violence leads us to see irony and pathos on behalf of actual and prospective queens in *Beowulf*. We are, in part, beguiled by a misplaced sense of compassion as well as by a mistaking of queenly roles: peace-weaving by way of the cup-bearing ritual occurs in the hall, as Wealhtheow demonstrates amply and successfully in Heorot, in her moments. Of course no such weaving guarantees the future or, in fact, establishes relationships between unstably accommodated peoples. That happens through the bride as a "peace-kin," a necessarily ambivalent but hardly fateful role for all queens in the poem.[21] As this is so, we need to reformulate the kinds of judgments that Jane Chance, Joyce Hill, and Gillian Overing, for example, come to when they contemplate Hildeburh's place in the poem. Joyce Hill does notice that Hildeburh acts when she has her son placed side by side with Hnæf on the funeral pyre. But this act is seen in contrast to the acts of male warriors; "it has only a backward-looking symbolic value in emphasizing the intertribal loyalties that could have been and which are now felt in a purely personal capacity by Hildeburh alone."[22] She has a "still dignity in mourning" but nothing more as she is carried back to Denmark, "the supreme victim, reduced to the status of an object, as if she were part of the booty of war."[23] Joyce Hill is right to see the uncle-nephew bond here as betokening inter-group loyalties. More than loyalty, however, that connection in those persons (sister's brother and sister's son) is the closest kind of kinship tie between two groups dramatized in the poem. It is felt strongly both personally and socially, and it is a tie now horribly ruptured in this case. As that is so, why think of Hildeburh's action as a retrospective one only? It is certainly a grimly bitter action in the moment, at a given point in the episode. And its purport can be seen as ongoing, as urging action in the very image, mentally searing, of bursting heads and bodies. That action finally occurs when Hengest takes up the sword: in that regard he could be seen as his countrywoman's active double. Moreover, given her in-between role as peace-kin between Danes and Frisians, her family loyalties are still strongly Danish: she is identified as Hoc's daughter and she is called noble when taken home, returned to her people—hardly reduced to a trophy of war.

True, as Gillian Overing points out, Hildeburh has lost husband, brother, and son—a nasty game in which it seems "Queen loses all"[24]—but not to a self-emptying extent: her identity, indeed her legal place in the world, has always remained in part with her people, the Half-Danes. Because of her ties to different kin-groups, she has options in her loyalties and mobility if she needs it. Think too what she might be feeling during the long winter of Hengest's discontent: could not her love cool toward this husband of hers (as Ingeld's does for his wife) and toward his infamous, violent Jutes? If so, in the final retribution, when her husband dies, she might well feel this, strongly: what to her is a (foreign) husband, who has killed her brother, after all, in comparison to that same brother and her dead son? Though it must be mixed in feeling, Hengest's revenge is a good for her in this world: both something urged mutely by the ghastly funeral pyre she commands and part of the Danish instauration to which she belongs.

Jane Chance, while noting rightly that Hildeburh unjustly (*unsynnum*, line 1072) loses her Danish brother and Frisian son, misses Joyce Hill's concession to action. She does this especially when claiming that "all [Hildeburh] does, this sad woman (*geomuru ides*, line 1075), is to mourn her loss with dirges and stoically place her son on the pyre."[25] Indeed, for Chance, Hildeburh can do nothing because she is "caught in the very web she has woven as peace-pledge, a passive role precisely because the ties she knots bind *her*—she *is* the knot, the pledge of peace."[26] When her brother, son, and husband die, she fails as a peace-pledge, her identity gone. This reification of the peace-pledge as Hildeburh herself has no social warrant, whatever loyalties Hildeburh should have to her husband (and no doubt she has some). The Finn story contradicts such a metamorphosis in both emphasizing her patriline and her return, as noble, to her people. Recall that we can think of these marriage alliances as made between men; yet the women involved occupy an ambivalent space between two kindreds and might well maneuver in that space to suit themselves. Also, clearly enough, Hildeburh has not failed here; others (Jutes) have terribly failed *her*, and the peace-kinship between two peoples has failed just when it has begun to bear fruit (given the second generation).

Gillian Overing rightly dislikes this notion that Hildeburh is passive, a pawn merely in an economy of male to male relationships. Hildeburh's "absence," her lack of a voice, feels like a *différance*, not merely something subsumed into a male polarity of active versus passive. While Overing's Derridean formulations are opaque, her intuition here is sound: the silence Hildeburh "creates" is an affront, but expressive of her; and her story does create "a paralysis of understanding" regarding the modern reader, but not as Overing would have it and not as a point of paradox.[27] In Hildeburh's case, the affront is deep, sharp, and wordlessly burned into everyone's consciousness through her command over the pointedly grim funeral pyre— that image, potentially, of incendiary rage as the fire brutally consumes the bursting heads and bodies of the two dearest kinsmen for any queen in this aristocratic world (brother and son). Compared to those kinsmen, what is a husband? We only with difficulty come to understand this because we are not comfortable with the urgent, dark feelings of those who take their revenge from the margins, through others (Hildeburh in this case, the old shield warrior in the Heathobeard case).[28]

We should now go in closer: there will be no purgative knitting through funeral rites here. Instead the terrible image of dear uncle and nephew burning side by side on the funeral pyre intensifies. The funeral fire rises to the heavens (perhaps a sign of the battle warrior's innocence) as the great slaughter fire resounds; heads melt, wounds burst open, blood springs out of hateful body bites ("hafelan multon, / bengeato burston," lines 1120b-21a). The language here, followed by the notion that fire, the greediest of spirits, swallowed up all of both peoples taken by war ("Lig ealle forswealg," line 1122b) is essentially Grendelian: intense greed fits the mother, complete swallowing fits Grendel (in Beowulf's account of Hondscio's death, "lic ealle forswealg," line 2080b); the mother is also "sword-greedy," ravenously greedy (*heorogifre*, line 1498a). This is the dreadful outcome: a funeral of terror as the glory of everyone on the pyre burns, but most notably that of Hildeburh's brother and son. These graphically hostile images should by now be seen to reflect Hildeburh's bitter grief—an intense, angry grief that must cry out for revenge, for retribution regarding disaster, crime, and terror.

We learn next that many Frisians depart, leaving their dead comrades behind. Finn stays on, as does an unhappy and constrained Hengest, who thinks of going home but who is winterbound in Finn's land. This fact of ice-bondage is more than a weather report; it reflects his bondage entirely in his situation. His ties to Finn are unhappy ones—ties to a lord that can only remind him of his personal lordlessness and of the terror that had recently overtaken him and his men. With the advent of spring comes thought of revenge more than of a sea-journey, thought of an aggrieved, angry meeting through which he might show that he still had in mind the sons of Jutes. So Hengest does not refuse the widely accepted counsel when Hunlafing places the best of swords, the battle-light, in his lap (with "light" and a figure for sword suggesting the glory of Tiu, the ancient god of war as law, as settlement).[29] This, then, is the juridical sword of retribution, accepted world-wide (and originally having divine warrant) as an invitation to settle one's grievances.

Much as the old Heathobeard urges the young warrior, so Hunlafing urges Hengest, making a gesture that cannot rightly or nobly be refused. Moreover, the sudden-terror-bringing Jutes, we are told, were quite familiar with the edge of that sword. The perpetrators of terror have already felt its edge, so it is especially fitting to use it legislatively now, not in defense, but in retributive attack. Establishing and carrying through with this moment takes thirty-three and a half lines, in the course of which we finally learn that Finn experienced cruel sword-bale in his own home—a wording that expresses the poet's localized sympathy for this tragic king—after Guthlaf and Oslaf join in. They thus repeat Hunlafing's kind of urging when they recall their path of misery. Unable to *restrain* restless feelings in his heart, Hengest acts much as Wiglaf will later in the poem when impelled to aid a fire-encompassed Beowulf. Although already long ago incinerated, Hengest's lord, Hnæf, now receives his due support through Hengest's reformation of himself and the Danes in their recommitment through retributive violence. His situation is more complex than Ingeld's, but that complexity characterizes rather than undermines the force of the general principle. Terror must be answered, definitively, if possible. That Finn, in part, ends up a victim of Jutish terror matters in the bloody moment of his death, but not juridically for the episode as a whole. I think we have overemphasized the place Hildeburh has in this episode—she matters in only twenty-two percent of the lines—and grossly under-read the great extent to which the episode focuses on Finn's need to reconcile and Hengest's eventual need to act. We have also, as I have argued above, underestimated the extent to which Hildeburh's bitter appropriation of the funeral pyre is a mute demand for retribution.

Again, we need to note that nothing in this narrative suggests the inherent instability of peace-kin arrangements through wedding alliances. In both this story and in the scenario regarding Freawaru's marriage to Ingeld, neither the violence before nor the goading and terror that comes makes for a situation too volatile to settle peacefully for long. In-law ties are weak to begin with; only in the next generation, through sister's-son fosterage, do two peoples come close together, perhaps even ideally close. But this tie is terribly destroyed when in the Finn episode Hildeburh loses both her son and her brother, placing the two, in a bitterly angry gesture, side by side on the funeral pyre. All that is left now is this: wait for an opportunity to punish the terror-Jutes definitively, extract Hildeburh from their implicit possession of her, and reform Danish honor and community through a definitive, bloody settlement with Finn.

NOTES

[1] See Vilhelm Grønbech, *Culture of the Teutons*, 3 vols., trans. William Worster (Oxford, 1931).

[2] Kemp Malone, "The Tale of Ingeld," in *Kemp Malone: Studies in Heroic Legend and in Current Speech*, ed. Stephan Einarsson and Norman E. Eliason (Copenhagen, 1959), p. 74.

[3] For a convenient summary, see G. N. Garmonsway and Jacqueline Simpson, trans., *"Beowulf" and Its Analogues* (London, 1968), pp. 243–47.

4 Fr. Klaeber, ed., *"Beowulf" and the Fight at Finnsburg*, 3rd ed. with supplements (Lexington, Mass., 1950), p. xxxvi. For the seminal account of that warband vocabulary, see D. H. Green, *The Carolingian Lord: Semantic Studies in Four Old High German Words: Balder, Fro, Truhtin, Hero* (Cambridge, Eng., 1965).

5 Beowulf has various motives for the several turns his "retelling" of events in Heorot takes. Many have noticed these turns, usually putting differences between the narrative of the Grendel fights as we have them and Beowulf's later accounts to Hygelac down to the local inconsistencies that can arise in extended, perhaps originally oral composition. Or else we allow Beowulf to add detail harmlessly, detail the poet might have included originally but overlooked. A few readers, however, have seen political purpose or performative purpose in Beowulf's work here. See John M. Hill, *The Cultural World in "Beowulf"* (Toronto, 1995), pp. 104–06; Seth Lerer, *Literacy and Power in Anglo-Saxon Literature* (Lincoln, Nebr., 1991), pp. 182–84; George Clark, "Poetry in Heorot" (unpublished essay, 1995). Lerer nicely thinks of Beowulf's work in this retelling as transforming "the terror of his experience into a form of social entertainment" as in a kind of punning when naming Hondscio [glove] and describing Grendel's dragon-skin pouch or glove (p. 184). Clark follows suit approvingly, adding that if "Beowulf makes Grendel and Grendel's mother seem unfrightening in Hygelac's hall, he also makes himself unthreatening." Turning the Danish adventure into a marvelous entertainment makes that affair unthreatening also, thus indirectly allaying Hygelac's concern both about the adventure and about what kind of Beowulf it is who has returned. This leads to various other maneuvers of Beowulf's in the course of delivering up his great gifts, moves that cumulatively reassert his absolute loyalty still to Hygelac, his only lord and great kinsman (see Hill, *The Cultural World in "Beowulf"*).

6 Compare Peter Clemoes, *Interactions of Thought and Language in Old English Poetry* (Cambridge, Eng., 1995), p. 193: "Exploration of the issue through narrative led him to an opinion different from Hrothgar's own." That is, Beowulf comes to his opinion by considering general truths in relationship to particular situations that actualize them. For Edward B. Irving, Jr., however, the contrast here is mainly one of a sapient Beowulf and a Hrothgar whose political wisdom has lapsed disastrously. See his *Rereading "Beowulf"* (Philadelphia, 1989), p. 61.

7 Harry Berger, Jr. and H. Marshall Leicester, Jr., "Social Structure as Doom: The Limits of Heorism in *Beowulf*," in *Old English Studies in Honor of John C. Pope*, ed. Robert B. Burlin and Edward B. Irving, Jr. (Toronto, 1974), pp. 37–79.

8 For a summary, see John P. Hermann, *Allegories of War: Language and Violence in Old English Poetry* (Ann Arbor, 1989), pp. 183–84.

9 Georges Devereux, *Ethnopsychoanalysis: Psychoanalysis and Anthropology As Complementary Frames of Reference* (Berkeley, 1978), p. 197.

[10] Devereux, *Ethnopsychoanalysis*, p. 197.

[11] In this connection, Gillian Overing, "The Women in *Beowulf*" in *"Beowulf": Basic Readings*, ed. Peter S. Baker (New York, 1995), p. 224, would not be wrong to follow Giles Deleuze and Felix Guattari, *Anti-Oedipus: Capitalism and Schizophrenia*, trans. Robert Hurley, Marke Seem, and Helen R. Lane (Minneapolis, 1985), p. 165, here indebted certainly to Devereux in thinking that marriage is an alliance of men (a tie involving primary homosexuality). Women are the visible tokens of that alliance and, of course, do not undertake their own marriages in *Beowulf*. But this view hardly relegates peace brides to a nothingness (Overing's Lacanian and even Derridean view). Indeed, ethnologically considered, they are more likely to be *present* threateningly, given their ambivalent status, loyalties, and rights between two kindreds, which might create space for a kind of independence (as we see in Wealhtheow); compare with also, albeit in a clan context, Marilyn Strathern, *Women in Between: Female Roles in a Male World: Mount Hagen, New Guinea* (1972; reprint Boston, 1995), pp. 285–305. Where are their primary allegiances? Clearly the burden in Beowulf's account is such that we do not face this issue with Freawaru; Hildeburh's case is a different story altogether. See, further, Alexandra Hennessey Olsen, "Gender Roles," in *A "Beowulf" Handbook*, ed. Robert E. Bjork and John D. Niles (Lincoln, Nebr., 1997), pp. 311–24, for insights on Hildeburh's possible family obligations: urging revenge for her brother, mourning aggressively.

[12] Devereux, *Ethnopsychoanalysis*, p. 211.

[13] Wiðergyld's name, taken as "payback," or "requital," becomes part of Craig Davis's argument for an inexorable revenge impulse here, especially given that in-law ties are weak, that an old warrior's resentment will deepen, and that the pride of kings like Ingeld is a "touchy, tinder-box" business. All of this constitutes "the fatal volatility of the kin-feud system" (*"Beowulf" and the Demise of Germanic Legend in England* [New York, 1966], p. 101). My disagreements are many, as indicated in this essay; primarily, they rest on the assumption that feud between neighboring and competing groups is not in principle interminable or genocidal for the *Beowulf*-poet. There are distinctions to be made, settlements to celebrate, and countervailing pressures.

[14] Gillian Gillison, "Symbolic Homosexuality and Cultural Theory: The Unconscious Meaning of Sister Exchange Among the Gimi of Highland New Guinea," in *Anthropology and Psychoanalysis: An Encounter through Culture*, ed. Suzette Healde and Ariane Deluz (London, 1994), pp. 210–14.

[15] Joseph Bosworth, *An Anglo-Saxon Dictionary*, ed. and enlarged by T. Northcote Toller (Oxford, 1898).

[16] For handy contexts, see Dorothy Whitelock, *English Historical Documents, 500–1042* (Oxford, 1955), pp. 392, 393, 395.

[17] Rolf H. Bremmer, Jr., "The Importance of Kinship: Uncle and Nephew in *Beowulf*," *Amsterdamer Beitrage zur Alteren Germanistik* 15 (1980): 21–38, especially p. 33.

[18] Edward B. Irving, Jr., *A Reading of "Beowulf"* (New Haven, 1968), p. 136.

[19] See George Clark, *Beowulf* (Boston, 1990), p. 80, for a sense of Hildeburh's active role here—a parallel peace move Clark thinks. That could be so, although Hildeburh does not express her feelings for us. Yet the immediately following account of bursting heads and bodies on the pyre suggests considerable bitterness on Hildeburh's behalf, which in turn can shift the psychology of mourning toward anger (possible connotatively in *bemearn*—note its use in the context of Heremod's excesses, line 907, for which his Danes betray him, requiting his terror).

[20] The exception would be Clark, *Beowulf*.

[21] Larry L. Sklute, "Freoðuwebbe in Old English Poetry," in *New Readings on Women in Old English Literature*, ed. Helen Damico and Alexandra Hennessey Olsen (Bloomington, 1990), pp. 204–10, would collapse the two terms, *freoðuwebbe* and *friðusibb*, for lack of clear corroboration regarding their differences in *Beowulf*, although the one is used for Modthryth (who as princess does not behave as a peace-weaver) and the other for Wealhtheow in the passage that directly concerns Freawaru—Hrothgar's hope for a marriage alliance with the Heathobeards. Compare in this connection *dryhtsib* (line 2068a). The first element in Sklute's compounds concerns peace or protection alike; the point for distinction is the second element—weaving concord in contrast to kinship peace alliance. As a link between two peoples, Wealhtheow is obviously the latter; as a personage in the hall she is the former. Compare also Michael J. Enright, *Lady with a Mead Cup: Ritual, Prophecy, and Lordship in the European Warband from La Tene to the Viking Age* (Dublin, 1996), p. 2, for the queen's roles as both carrier of alliance and maker of harmony in the hall.

[22] Joyce Hill, "*Þæt wæs geomuru ides!* A Female Stereotype Examined," in Damico and Olsen, *New Readings on Women in Old English Literature*, p. 241.

[23] Hill, "*Þæt wæs geomuru ides!*" p. 241.

[24] Overing, "The Women in *Beowulf*," p. 231.

[25] Jane Chance, "The Structural Unity of *Beowulf*: The Problem of Grendel's Mother," in Damico and Olsen, *New Readings on Women in Old English Literature*, p. 251.

[26] Chance, "The Structural Unity of *Beowulf*," p. 251.

[27] Overing, "The Women in *Beowulf*," p. 235.

[28] See William I. Miller, *Bloodtaking and Peacemaking: Feud, Law, and Society in Saga Iceland* (Chicago, 1990), pp. 211–13, and Hill, *The Cultural World of "Beowulf*," p. 28.

[29] Working in an Indo-European context, Georges Dumezil comments on Tiu and on his loss of his hand (legend has him lose his hand when Fenris, the cosmic wolf, eats it after the gods successfully bind him—Tiu having placed his hand in Fenris wolf's mouth as a trick pledge that the gods would not imprison Fenris wolf): "the sovereign administration of the world is divided into two great provinces, that of inspiration and prestige [Odin's], that of contract and chicanery [Tiu's], in other words, magic and law" (*Gods of the Ancient Northmen*, trans Einar Haugen [Berkeley, 1973], p. 46). Thus Tiu would be the wargod of law, of warfare as rightful settlement and the drawing of boundaries. Both gods were known in England. The runic mark for Tiu was carved on weapons presumably to ensure victory. Tiu is probably the original All-Father and Sky-god, his name coming to mean light and glory either by itself or as part of a compound. See Brian Branston, *The Lost Gods of England* (New York, 1957), pp. 74–75; Gale R. Owen, *Rites and Religions of the Anglo-Saxons* (London, 1981); and Hill, *The Cultural World of "Beowulf,"* pp. 61–67.

THE RUINS OF IDENTITY

JEFFREY JEROME COHEN

The body doesn't lie. . . . Maps whose territories are named in languages which are no longer understood show where the passions are hidden. —Kathy Acker[1]

FOUNDATIONAL MOMENTS

An the most celebrated essay in Anglo-Saxon studies, J. R. R. Tolkien liberated Old English literature from its monsters. The opinion of philologists such as W. P. Ker had long held sway: *Beowulf* was a poem valuable for the historical allusions that limn its periphery, worthless for the three battles against monsters that form its narrative heart. This fascination with grotesque bodies is the poem's "radical defect, a disproportion that puts the irrelevances in the center."[2] In 1936 Tolkien delivered the Gollancz Memorial Lecture to the British Academy and challenged Ker's dismissive summation. "*Beowulf*: The Monsters and the Critics" argues that the cannibalistic giant Grendel, his vengeful mother, and the fiery dragon are beneath their lurid flesh ethical allegories. The dragon is "a personification of malice, greed, destruction";[3] Grendel is an adversary of the soul; the poem is about

From *Of Giants: Sex, Monsters, and the Middle Ages* (Minneapolis, 1999), pp. 1–28; reprinted with permission of University of Minnesota Press. The only alteration to the original has been to convert the original "works cited" method of reference to footnotes.

pietas. By translation from Old English into Latin, the monsters become "not an inexplicable blunder of taste" but "fundamentally allied to the underlying ideas of the poem, which give its lofty tone and high seriousness."[4]

Beowulf had once been difficult to place, confusingly hybrid, *monstrous*; now it was a safely canonical object of New Critical, *humanistic* inquiry. Whereas Tolkien believed that the literary remnants of Anglo-Saxon culture may be studied in spite of its monsters, more recent critics have asserted that the corpus deserves critical analysis because of its monstrous content.[5] Writers and artists in early medieval England were fascinated by the grotesque and the marvelous. Their literature, historiography, manuscript illustration, and plastic arts reveal a cultural obsession with the malleability of the human form. *Wonders of the East,* a text with which *Beowulf* is bound in monstrous affiliation, is crammed with bodies transfigured and deformed. One magnificent illustration (British Library, MS Cotton Tiberius B.v, folio 83v) makes real the Donestre, a fabulous race described in the legends of Alexander. These strange creatures embody a monstrosity that is both corporeal and linguistic. Because they know all human languages, the Donestre are able to hail foreigners with familiar speech, convincing them that they know their kinsmen and homeland. They then devour the body of their victims except for the head, over which they sit and weep.[6]

The illustration in Cotton Tiberius B.v consists of three successive scenes, read clockwise starting at the top. This Donestre is a fleshy, naked man with a lion's head. His curly mane sweeps the curve of his shoulder, and with a sad frown and huge, watery eyes, he commiserates with a traveler. The foreigner gesticulates widely, perhaps in the midst of relating some story about his distant home to his sympathetic auditor. The patient monster extends an enormous hand to touch the speaker, a reassuring gesture. Below and to the right is the next episode of the pictorial narrative: the Donestre, having heard enough, is busy devouring the traveler. His naked body is directly on top of the man, pinning him to the earth. The final scene, in the lower left corner, finds the Donestre looking melancholic. He holds his hands to furry ears, frowns miserably, and stares at the bodiless head of his victim, the only remnant of the gruesome feast.

When read chronologically, the Donestre's body undergoes a revealing transformation. At first more virile than bestial, the monster's animal head is fully anthropomorphized to give an empathetic look. His hands, calves, and chest bulge with muscles. His genitalia, painted a vibrant red, are prominently displayed. Compared to this hypermasculine body, the traveler's form is thin, stooped, ill proportioned. As the Donestre ingests his victim, he becomes more leonine: he is on all fours, as if he has just pounced; his nose and lips form a snout; his eyes suddenly lack whites. An oral, animal ecstasy characterizes the second scene as the monster—bare buttocks arched above the prone foreigner's hips—devours the man's erect arm. That this combination of violence, eroticism, and transgression is difficult to contain in the illustration is indicated by the Donestre's very human left foot, which steps out of the picture and into the frame—the only part of the illustration to violate the demarcative power of its border. The last segment of the tripartite story finds both bodies much reduced. The traveler has vanished, replaced by the peacefully oblivious head. The monster is an indistinct collection of curved lines that center around a trembling hand, a dark eye, and a tight frown.

The material incorporation of one body into the flesh of another, cannibalism condenses a fear of losing the boundary that circumscribes identity and produces discrete subjects. The illustration from *Wonders of the East* uses anthropophagy to explore selfhood's limits. Its polyglot and hybrid monster is a cultural, linguistic, sexual other who seems to be intimate (he knows you, he can talk about your relatives, he can share in your *mal du pays*) but in fact brutally converts an identity familiar and secure into an alien thing, into a subject estranged from its own body. In the last scene of the narrative, the traveler has been completely transformed. The severed head is an empty point of fascination that directs the viewer's gaze back to the alienating form in which the traveler is now contained, at the monster he has now become; he ponders what he once was from the outside, *as a foreigner*. The Donestre transubstantiates the man, making him realize through a somatic conversion that he was always already a stranger to himself, despite his attachment to—his self identification by means of—*home*. The Donestre-traveler stares at the mute, lifeless head with such affective sadness because at this moment of plurality he sees the fragility of autonomous selfhood, how much of the world it excludes in its panic to remain selfsame, singular, stable.

The monster exposes the *extimité*, the "extimacy" or "intimate alterity" of identity: its inescapable self-estrangement, the restless presence at its center of everything it abjects in order to materialize and maintain its borders. To be fully human is to disavow the strange space that the inhuman, the monstrous, occupies within every speaking subject. To succeed on a mass scale, this disavowal requires two things: a degree of cultural uniformity and relative social calm. England in the centuries before the Norman Conquest was a heterogeneous collection of peoples who were constantly forced to examine who they were in relation to a shifting array of alterities. "Anglo-Saxon England" is a blanket term that hides more than it reveals.

In a real sense, there were no Anglo-Saxons, only scattered groups of varied ancestry in growing alliances who were slowly building larger political units.[7] "England" existed as an ambiguous region of a large island and was very much in the process of being invented as a unifying geography, as a nation capable of transcending the differences among those bodies it collects beneath its name. The various Germanic peoples who sailed to England beginning in the fifth century were culturally diverse. As they settled the island they intermingled with the Celts (some Romanized, some not) and with each other. The Latin church colonized in successive waves, offering a European lingua franca to restructure their northern epistemological systems. In 835, the Vikings began their violent incursions, forcefully reminding the *gens Anglorum* of northern heuristics. Yet to speak of Latin, northern, and Celtic culture is to pretend that these were monolithic and discrete, when each was composed of often competing ideologies, dialects, mythologies—like "Anglo-Saxon England" itself. These various languages and discourses combined into fragmentary epistemes, as unstable and amalgamative as the many little kingdoms that formed and were absorbed into larger ones. The history of Anglo-Saxon England is a narrative of resistant hybridity, of small groups ingested into larger bodies without a full assimilation, without cultural homogeneity: thus the realms of Hwicce, Sussex, Kent, Lindsey, Surrey, Essex, East Anglia, Northumbria, Mercia, and Wessex were sutured over time into progressively larger kingdoms; but although they were eventually unified in political hegemony, these areas retained enough force of heterogeneity to remain dialect regions that persist to the present day.

Anglo-Saxon England is not so very different from the Donestre by whom it was fascinated: familiar and strange, hybrid rather than homogenous, an amalgamative body that absorbs difference without completely reducing or assimilating it. Because of its diversity and because of its permeable, perpetually transgressed borders, Anglo-Saxon England was relentlessly pondering what it means to be a warrior, a Christian, a hero, a saint, an outlaw, a king, a sexed and gendered being. If there is a generalization under which such a long and varied time period can be gathered without doing reductive violence to its expansiveness, it is simply that during the span of years now designated by the rubric "Anglo-Saxon England," the limits of identity were under ceaseless interrogation because they were confronted by almost constant challenge. It is not surprising, then, that the monster became a kind of cultural shorthand for the problems of identity construction, for the irreducible difference that lurks deep within the culture-bound self.

THE WORK OF GIANTS

The mythology of the medieval European north, of which the literary re-
mains of Anglo-Saxon England form a part, was fascinated by the giant.[8]
When the various Germanic tribes that are now called the Anglo-Saxons
arrived in the land now called England, they encountered towering struc-
tures of ancient stone that made them feel like small children as they stood
beside them. They described this alien architecture as *enta geweorc*, "the
work of giants." Some of these structures were the great monoliths, dolmens,
and stone circles such as Stonehenge built by the mysterious pre-Celtic
peoples, who have left no other trace of their sojourn. Other monumen-
tal edifices were built by the Romans during that period when the Eternal
City could see all the way to the hinterland of Great Britain. The aqueducts
and temples of Bath, for example, had written Roman civility across a resis-
tant wilderness, transforming the Celts into imperial subjects and the land
into the empire's dominion. But the memory of these builders (prehistoric
and cloaked in mystery, Roman and clothed in history) had fragmented
by the time the Angles, Saxons, and Jutes sailed in their war boats from
Scandinavia, early in the fifth century. Since these Germanic tribes built
their homes, sheep sheds, and mead halls exclusively from wood, stone in
their sign system was associated with the primitive and the inert. Wood was
a living substance to be carved and joined, the raw material of community;
stone was recalcitrant and dead, good for etching runes but otherwise im-
possible to transform. Like their forebears, the Anglo-Saxons contrasted
wood's modernity with the ancient, elemental harshness of stone. Men built
with wood. Giants, the vanished race who had ruled the earth in its larger-
than-life, Paleolithic days, were architects of stone.

The Bible only confirmed what their native mythology already told
them, a story that the legends of the conquered Celts corroborated: hu-
manity was a secondary race of creatures, belated, the gods' afterthought.
Northern myth held that giants had been the first race to inscribe their
identity into the earth's landscape, and that the human body was a continu-
ation and reduction of that *figura*.[9] Gargantuan amalgams of appetite and
strength, these giants were thought to live at civilization's periphery, often
in a specially realized geography (Geirrodstown, Glasisvellir, Jotunheim).
Creatures of the world's First Order, they were so close to nature that they
were linked to meteorological phenomena—to the storms, lightning, fog,
and blizzards that terrified northern explorers with their violent unpredict-
ability. Unlike their counterparts in Latin tradition, Germanic giants could
also at times be female; biblical, classical, and later medieval giants were

relentlessly gendered masculine. The northern giants married freely with gods and men, as often representing a middle step between the human and the divine as an inferior genus between man and animal. The Aesir, the most powerful gods of the Norse pantheon, were descended from giants.[10] As elemental, perhaps autochthonous beings, giants were inextricable from the earth and stone they worked, so they gained an explanatory function as creators of landscape, ancient ruins, and mysterious architecture.

The Old English poem that most vividly captures this wistful genealogy of the giants' stone leavings is *The Wanderer*.[11] The poem is spoken by a home-less exile (*anhaga*) who treks through a bleak, frozen landscape and meditates on the cruelty immanent in this world where the price of subjectivization is loss. Each morning he voices his sorrow as a way of coming to understand a painful history that haunts his present with spectral remembrances. This transformation of the past into poetic language enacts a fantasy of inhabiting it again as if it were a place, a blissful space-time before the trauma of separa-tion irrupted. The Wanderer (*eardstapa*, "earth-walker") imagines that he is with his beloved lord once more, that his "gold-friend" (*gold-winne*) kisses and clasps him, that he lays his head to rest on his protector's lap, "swa he hwilum ær / on gear-dagum gief-stoles breac" ("as he did once in days now lost, when he enjoyed the gift-stool," lines 43–44). He achieves in this gesture of conjoining a profound peace. Þegnscipe ("thaneship"), his homoerotic sur-render to the word, agency, and body of his master, is absolute.

The dream breaks. The Wanderer awakens to find that he remains among hoarfrost and frigid waves. Seabirds perform their insensate rituals ("baþian brim-fuglas, brædon feþra," line 47) while snow and hail swirl: a cold, inhu-man world oblivious to the sorrow that wells within him. In this winterscape, "sorg biþ geniewod" ("sorrow freshens," line 50). This *sorg* of separation is written across the interior of his body, as a wound that scars his heart ("þonne beoþ þy hefigran heortan benna," line 49); his ache for his beloved (*swæsne*), the dead lord, has not been reduced through a life spent wandering.

In early northern European culture, the mead hall (*meduheall*) was the center of community, the materialization into concrete public space of he-roic group identity. By the time *The Wanderer* was written, probably in a monastery, this heroic age and its glorious halls were images from a history receding into myth. The elegy is doubly nostalgic. Quiet yearning for a van-ished past is voiced once by the narrator of the poem, for whom that past is proximate, and secondarily by the writer(s) of the lines, for whom that past is almost wholly imaginary. *The Wanderer* asks what it is like to suffer the trauma of loss and discovers that what seemed a dissolution of wholeness is actually its reconfiguration into a diminished, bleak, and lonely state of autonomy. The text arrives at this insight by imagining an originary moment before the subject was alienated within the symbolic order that grants his meaning-in-being. Lacanian psychoanalysis, embedded in class- and time-specific ideals of familial structuration, dreams of an originary trauma that attends the separation from the mother, when the entrance into a paternal language occurs; the presymbolic bliss of *The Wanderer* is a bit queerer and resides in the complete union of two male bodies, materialized in the gesture of the embrace and lost through the violence of other men. Like Lacan, like *The Seafarer* (lines 12–19), the elegy imagines a prehistory during which the subject could feel at home in his own body, at home in the world.

At home, or at hall. Architecture articulates identity: in the time of wholeness, in the time before loss and lack, the Wanderer resided with his lord in *sele-dreamas* ("hall-joys," line 93). In the submissive tableau of being embraced, laying head upon lap, the Wanderer knew plenitude. The narrator rejoices not in his individuality (he is not even named) but in full contiguity; in the dependency of thane upon lord, he finds his full bliss. This primal enjoyment, frozen in time and frozen as place, is rendered possible through the hall, the structure that demarcates warm, communal Inside from frigid, solitary Exterior. Under the protective wood of the hall's steep gables, fires blaze and feasting resounds. Men drink and sing and exchange the gold rings that serve as material articulations of the system of relations that bind them like brothers, like circles of a closed chain. The exiled Wanderer is *sele-dreorig*: not homesick, but hall-sick (line 25).

Outside the hall, an inimical geography sprawls: ice-laden winds, tempest-troubled seas, dark promontories, the habitations of monsters. The danger of a happy hall is that one of these lone monsters will hear the sweet music that escapes from the windows, will rise from the dark mere, and will burst through the door like the giant cannibal Grendel and devour the place of home.

"BEING INSISTS IN SUFFERING"

You never look at me from the place from which I see you. —Jacques Lacan[12]

The door splinters at the giant's touch, and Grendel strides into the hall. The men still sleep. He seizes Hondscio, the nearest warrior, and guts him as he dreams. The giant rips the body to pieces, "bat ban-locan, blod edrum dranc,

/ synsnædum swealh" ("bit into muscles, swilled blood from veins, tore off gobbets, " lines 742–43a).[13] The giant eats the sleeper alive, everything, "fet ond folma" ("even hands and feet," line 745a). The fear that animates this gory evisceration is that all that is rhetorically outside, incorporated into the body of the monster, will suddenly break through the fragile architecture of the hall, which is the fragile identity of the subject, and expose its surprised inhabitants to what has been abjected from their small world to make it livable.[14] Like the sleeping, peaceful, unspeaking Hondscio, the traumatized subject will be ingested, absorbed into that big Other seemingly beyond (but actually wholly within, because wholly created by) the symbolic order that it menaces.

In *The Wanderer*, these monstrous anxieties cannot find expression in fleshly form. Instead they are written across the landscape, becoming no less potent for not having found a body to inhabit. The world itself comes to life. Anthropomorphized, it acts as one malevolent body (lines 101–06). The cold ocean, the bitter winds, the bare trees, and the frozen hills all stir under the compulsion of a vaguely malevolent animism. Even the "rough hail" (*hreo haegl-farue*) has its inscrutable but inimical intentions ("norðan onsendeþ / hreo hægl-fære, hæleþum on andan," lines 104–05). What house or hall can stand when the very earth turns against it? Deep in sadness, the Wanderer turns to the stone ruins he sees before him and projects his story of persecution by a giant, unknowable Other onto this wreckage of an alien city, making his private history a palimpsest for History writ large. This big Other (Lacan's *grand autre*) is a fantastic, "personal" incorporation of the symbolic order by means of which the chaos of the world is organized into linguistic and epistemological coherence. As the desperate projection into place of a meaning in no way immanent there, this ghostly giant obscures the fact that meaning does not reside in any "there"—in any space, architecture, or geography—only in the structures by which it is organized, the monsters in which it is embodied.

The Wanderer's willful historiography occurs within a meditation upon homelessness. The motion that is his desire begins as a search for another hall in which to dwell, another lord under whom to serve, and culminates when his hopeless journey brings him to the ruins of an unknown city, broken stonework as cold as the bathing seabirds that conduct their animal rituals outside the realm of human meaning, of human feeling. A silent testament to the destructive inevitability of time, the windswept remains are described as "eald enta geweorc idlu stodon" ("the old work of giants, standing abandoned," line 87). For all of its stock character, the allusion fits tightly into the poem's obsession with unrecoverable loss. Associated with a race defined simultaneously by its terrible power and its ancient vanishing, the time-broken architecture becomes a living elegy. The Wanderer, alienated from his origin, projects this estrangement upon the ruins, estranging them from *human* origin.

Having given to the lifeless ruins a monstrous derivation, the Wanderer begins the process of rebuilding them, of anthropomorphizing their history to place in their center the warmth of human meaning. A barren landscape is imagined to encircle what it has shattered in defeat (lines 85–93). At least four temporal frames intersect here: the distant past when the city was constructed out of stone by mythic giants; a nearer past when men lived and died; the bitter present of the Wanderer, whose melancholic state of mind is interjected into that past; and the timeless moment of the wise observer who moralizes on the remains. The city's giant builders are conflated with eulogized warriors who perished in a lost, bloody history; they in turn are linked with the recent plight of the *anhaga* (the solitary one, the homeless Wanderer), and his fate provokes a consideration of universal end. The poem is a condensed narrative of cycles of fall in which the passing of the giants, the Old Order of the world, is linked with the necessary passing of humanity. This somber dissolution is then doubled back into a monstrous prehistory for the city of man. The crumbling of the dwelling is like the banishment from Eden, or the devastating loss of the hall, or (to place the loss in the familial terms that the Wanderer would not have understood) the loss of the (m)other's body at the forced differentiation that entrance into the symbolic order demands. No place can ever be as certain, as paradisal, or as full as the imaginary left behind. To be human, the poem insists, is to be homeless. The primal dwelling has crumbled, and the world has crashed inside. This loss of a secure place to inhabit is constitutive of identity, of becoming a speaking subject (one who can voice elegy, one who can speak grief). Self-consciousness occurs once the mead hall is a ruin, when plenitude is a distant memory: "Eall is earfoþlice eorðan rice" ("In the earth-realm all is crossed," line 106]. The price of subjectivity is to become eternally *anhaga*, *eardstapa*, a Wanderer.

Another poem from the Exeter Book, *The Ruin*, opens with a similar apostrophe to the time-blasted leavings of giants: "Wrætlic is þes wealstan, wyrde gebræcon; / burgstede burston, brosnað enta geweorc" ("Wondrous is this stone wall, smashed by Fate; the city is broken to pieces, the work of giants has crumbled," lines 1–2). Something of a ruin itself because of the poor condition of the manuscript, the poem describes what appears to be Roman remains through fragments of fallen stone and the ghostly presence of vanished inhabitants. As in Norse writings, the giants here suggest an alienating presence that predates humanity. In the uncertain past constructed by the sagas, the giants are encountered only in the waning of their race and are knowable in the author's present from the monstrous traces their bodies have etched into the landscape. Giants represent the unassimilated remnant of a past that, although it eludes the complete historical memory of the recorder, is integrally bound to the process of giving that history an identity. The vanished builders of *The Ruin* are also associated with a culture of idolatry (line 25), the sin of embodying in all too human form the gigantic might of the divine. The connection derives from the Book of Enoch, an apocryphal book of the Bible that seems to have exerted great influence on Anglo-Saxon gigantology.[15]

Enta geweorc (the work of giants) and its variants (*enta ærgeweorc, giganta geweorc*)[16] are somewhat formulaic descriptions, useful for completing a poetic half line quickly, but always something more than stock quotations. These phrases are fairly widespread in Old English literature, nearly always referring to ancient stone buildings or walls (*Andreas*, line 1492; *Maxims*, 2.1; *Elene*, line 30). A cognate phrase (*wrisilic gewerc*) even appears in Old Saxon. In *The Wanderer* and *The Ruin*, the elegiac resonance invoked through citation of the ancient giants fits perfectly the poems' cycle of loss and vanishing at the hands of fate (*wyrde*) and time. From a less literary viewpoint, stone ruins are logically *enta geweorc* not only because of the great size of the ruined architecture but also because of the elemental connection of giants with the earth and masonry in northern mythology.[17] Recent decades have produced theories that the Egyptian pyramids, pre-Columbian ruins, and geometric patterns in English wheat fields are the work of ancient aliens, carried from the margins of space in their chariots of the gods. The existential melancholy that drives such etiologic narratives arises because these more-than-human beings have abandoned humanity to itself, leaving enigmatic traces of a joyful proximity never to be regained.

ORIGINARY FANTASIES

The giant must dwell in the fen, alone in the land.—Cotton Gnomic Verses, 42–43

The giant builds the home (the ruins are *enta geweorc*, the work of giants), but the giant destroys the home, too: Grendel bursts the door from its hinges and devours the sleepers inside. Such is the vexing duality of the monster, especially in northern tradition. The giant is simultaneously the origin of the world and its greatest enemy. According to the surviving Norse cosmogonies, giants predate the material universe, which itself was fashioned from the corpse of the ur-giant Ymir:

> Of Ymir's flesh the earth was shaped
> the barren hills his bones;
> and of his skull the sky was shaped,
> of his body the briny sea.[18]

The monster's body becomes the raw material of cosmogenesis. To read the giant into the landscape as creator of topography, builder of strange architecture, or (as in Vafþrúðismál) as the constitutive first matter of the earth is to partake of that philosophical category called the sublime, in which the (male) human body is projected across the land as its organizing principle. The landscape becomes corporeal as "the male individual makes over aspects of himself—particularly the bodily component he fears may be alienable, the phallus—to nature" and "one's words undergo translation into images."[19] The giant, the human body introjected into the world, throws the land into tumult by smashing its mountains or making toys of its stones; or the giant erects huge and mysterious structures that dwarf human achievement, that threaten to overwhelm with their size and phallic power. The giant's spatial and temporal passing is registered only in the aftermath of the sublime, in the eerie ruins of his achievements, when his footprints have filled with water and become lakes—when words have returned to the observer, emotion can be harnessed, and speech can describe his path through the landscape, or through time. The earth and its altered features (mountains, bodies of water, the ruins of ancient cities) are the giant's story, a source of quiet wonder and contemplative sadness after sudden, cosmic fear.

This process of projecting a history upon the land is the mirror image of the process of identity formation outlined by the French psychoanalyst Jacques Lacan. In his originary essay "The Mirror Stage," Lacan established a new identity for psychoanalysis, reading the vast, fragmentary body of Freudian thought through Saussurian linguistics.[20] Lacan argues that the subject initially experiences itself as *un corps morcelé*, a body in pieces. By looking into a mirror or seeing itself mimicked in the actions of another, the subject receives its selfhood, a gestalt that confers a unity while radically estranging subjectivity from somaticity. Identity for Lacan is predicated upon a fundamental misrecognition (*méconnaissance*). The subject takes a specular, exterior image to be what it inside *is*. This misconstruction is a kind of teratogenesis: "The child, itself so recently born, gives birth to a monster: a statue, an automaton, a fabricated thing."[21] This specular monster is anything but the giant. For the giant is a body that is always in pieces, since within a human frame, he can be perceived only synecdochically, never as a totality. The giant is the prehistory of the body, standing at that origin point before it metamorphoses from one kind of monster (*le corps morcelé*) to another (the "fabricated thing"): from monstrous birth to monstrous becoming. Lacan's originary nightmare never loses its power to haunt. A Boschian giant reappears in nightly visitations as "*imagos of the fragmented body*."[22] *Le stade du miroir* becomes the arena in which the subject is persecuted by the fragmentary body of the giant, the monstrous being that is undeniably both human and something Other (prehuman, posthuman).

Time, body, and place tumble together in Lacan's originary myth, leaving the self without a permanent architecture under which to find rest. The Wanderer best speaks this restless, radical alienation that is homelessness (*wræclast*, "the path of exile"):

> þeah-þe he mod-cearig
> geond lagu-lade lange scolde
> hreran mid handum hrim-cealde sæ,
> wadan wræc-lastas. Wyrd biþ full aræd. (lines 2b–5)

> though he must traverse tracts of sea, sick at heart,—trouble with oars, ice-cold waters, the ways of exile—Wierd [Fate] is set fast.

Compare this Anglo-Saxon quest for a warm hall to Lacan's description of the subject's battle for a coherent "I." Embodiment occurs when an insubstantial image is materialized as the self. Because this image is exterior to the subject, a gap opens that cannot be bridged or filled, only temporarily allayed: the life of the *anhaga* who roams the "marshes and rubbish-tips" of the world in search of a "fortress, or stadium" or gabled hall in which to be at home. The Lacanian unconscious is a place, an imaginary geography in every way parallel to the wintry wastes and churning seas over which the Anglo-Saxon exile wanders.[23]

Lacan's creation myth is persuasive but, when read beside the giant-driven Norse cosmogony, lacks something. Vafþrúðismál suggests that constructing an identity for the subject and composing a history for the world are two versions of the same process. The giant is the fragmented body written across the landscape to provide *its* prehistory, its identity. The world coheres only after the body has been projected across its contours, arranging rivers, valleys, and mountains into a geography that gigantizes the somatic. Identity proceeds by both introjection (cannibalism) and projection (expulsion, abjection). The exterior delineates the body, while the body is written across the exterior. This doubled movement, this entwined and generative flux, ensures that identity and place are mutually constitutive. The *corps morcelé* of the land becomes the "alienated identity" of the map. Ymir becomes the earth, and even if his skull, corpse, and blood are recognizable in sky, soil, and water, it is because he cannot be gazed upon whole. To render the world an imaginary body makes it delusionarily coherent, just as to embody a subject in its specular image is to make that subject similarly an illusory, lacking whole: "We continually project the body into the world in order that its image might return to us."[24]

This spectacular integrity is always temporary. The integral body (of the land, of the subject) is always about to become, once more, the body in pieces: a dream intervenes, and the giant reappears.

HOMELESSNESS

If the giant is simultaneously exterior and interior to embodiment, a fragmentary whole (*enta geweorc*) at the origin of human identity and a projection from its full form, then the home has already been invaded, and that timeless place of rest (the Wanderer's longed-for hall, Lacan's distant fortress) is neither pure nor safe. Perhaps there is no reason for Grendel to burst the door from its iron hinges and invade the warmth that the walls of Heorot enclose. Perhaps the giant is already there, at the foundation.

Gaston Bachelard succinctly speaks the name of "the chief benefit of the house": "The house protects the dreamer, the house allows one to dream in peace."[25] His reverie over the integrative powers of this quintessential modern structure is rapturous, impossible, enticing. Like the Wanderer, Bachelard offers through his verbal conjuration a moment of repose for a world doomed to homelessness. The passage is worth lingering over:

> In the life of a man, the house thrusts aside contingencies, its councils of continuity are unceasing. Without it, man would be a dispersed being. It maintains him through the storms of the heavens and through those of life. It is body and soul. . . . Life begins well, it begins enclosed, protected, all warm in the bosom of the house.[26]

357

Bachelard's domestic reverie is suffused with nostalgia. He imagines a time when the subject was at peace, when the storms and tempests of the world did not "knock like a rifle-butt against the door," when the monster remained safely outside.[27] But nostalgia is always a yearning for a space-time that has never been. Nostalgia constructs a naive Other whose gaze we temporarily inhabit to look upon the scene for us so that we can believe in it, even though we know its paradisal simplicity to be impossible. The subject's relation to such temporal utopias is therefore "always divided, split between fascination and ironic distance: ironic distance toward its diegetic reality, fascination with its gaze."[28] The impervious Bachelardian house that "thrusts aside contingencies" is mythic, unreal, a Platonic form locked in heaven; in the true house, the vinyl-sided kind one finds by the million gridded across the suburban landscape, the storm has broken through the window, the giant is already within.

The door splinters at the giant's touch, and Grendel strides into the hall. In the Anglo-Saxon *heall*, the mighty structure that tames a formless wilderness into representability by establishing a structurating principle at its middle, the giant is already nearby, in some secret place (*healh*) not far from the threshold. Again, the problem of origins arises, the collapse into duality precipitated by the body of the monster, the hybrid nature of human identity. Which came first, the giant or the architecture he threatens? The safety of the primal dwelling, or the frightening presence of the Real, the monster or the tempest at the door? Do fantasies of buildings or embodiments that "thrust aside contingencies," whose "councils of continuity are unceasing," exist to protect humanity from becoming, like Hondscio, a "dispersed being"? Or does the monster's threat of fragmentation and ingestion intrude only after the strong walls of the hall have been erected, only after Grendel has heard drifting over his mere the maddeningly sweet, infuriatingly exclusive music of the hall?

Psychoanalysis offers another way of formulating the same question of origins and then suggests a resolution: Who came first, the Father of Prohibition or the Father of Enjoyment? These two paternal figures haunt the myth and history of the West because they arise from the same formal necessity, through the very process of symbolization. As origin incarnate, the two fathers suggest why in Anglo-Saxon England the monster is the necessary prehistory and intimate exterior of human identity. The Father of Prohibition initiates the law through the prohibition of incest and therefore stands at the mythic origin of culture. His primal "NO" hurls the child into language, the system that orders the wilderness of experience by taming it via the laws of syntax into coherent signification. The Father of Prohibition embodies the way in which, after the mirror stage has worked its optical magic, language estranges the subject from itself again. In the movement from the realm of visual phenomena (the Lacanian imaginary order) into verbal interaction with the laws of signification (the symbolic order), the subject becomes divided against itself by that same linguistic indoctrination that makes self-consciousness possible. Self-presence is predicated upon self-estrangement, just as words (signifiers) are phenomenologically distinct from the things they signify. The structures and strictures of language are *constitutive* of selfhood at the same time as they remain intimately *alien*.[29]

The Father of Enjoyment delights in being prior, and therefore exterior, to the law. This "primal father" of Freud's *Totem and Taboo* is the mythic and pre-Oedipal figure who must once have possessed the plenitude of enjoyment now barred the speaking subject. Yet this myth of origins is not so chronologically straightforward as it seems. These two paternal figures are ultimately one and the same. Freud's Father of Enjoyment does not know bodily limits and is therefore outside of the law (full enjoyment is his alone); but through his prohibitions, he differentiates the other members of the primitive horde, who then know themselves as sons, daughters, and wives only by virtue of the familial grammar he institutes and the access to enjoyment he withholds. These two fathers, Prohibition and Enjoyment, are as intertwined as speech and loss. "*Jouissance* is forbidden to him who speaks, as such":[30] if it is true that enjoyment is rendered impossible because of the estranging effect of language (that is, if it is true that the price of linguistic subjectivization is the barring of the full enjoyment symbolized by such fantasies of presymbolic bliss as the mother's body, the wanderer's hall, the dreamer's fortress, all those impossible visions of a lost, untroubled home), then the two fathers are part of the same retroactive fantasy by which the subject imagines a plenitude it never had in order to understand the *extimité* of its present selfhood.[31] The myth of the two fathers arises because if enjoyment is only *lost* rather than *impossible*, then the chance exists that it can be regained. In other words, the Father of Enjoyment is conjoined with the Father of Prohibition to confer "the form of a symbolic *interdiction*" upon a structural *impossibility* (no speaking subject can have unmediated access to *jouissance*).[32] The "problem of origins" arises as a formal effect of symbolization. The severe father who prohibits, and the obscene father who enjoys; the Bachelardian house, and the "storms of the heavens" that hurl themselves at its windows; the gabled hall that renders a frigid wilderness a cradled warmth, and the monster who shatters its primal unity: these visions of the world that teeter between "oceanic oneness" and a horrifying disaggregation are all versions of a retroactive fantasy by which the fragments of the past are sutured into a coherent, teleological history whose culmination is the homeless, self-estranged subject, the Wanderer. The fantasy materializes for the subject a continuous identity, a past that makes sense of the present's fragility. Further, by representing enjoyment as lost rather than impossible, the subject gains a future—if only a nomadic life spent searching for the hall or home where *jouissance* could be possessed again, where a giant has not yet risen from his distant mere in jealous hatred of communal songs.[33]

In the long postcolonial moment that occurred on the island as the Roman church extended the sphere of its epistemological hegemony, *Christianitas* was continuously promulgated as a unifying principle, as a point of identification strong enough to overcome the constituent differences that kept Anglo-Saxon England fragmentary, to effect a newly totalizing identity.[34] The two fathers become part of an ideological fantasy that covers over the radical alterity, the incommensurability, of the northern (pagan) and Latin (Christian) worldviews—a difference in symbolization so fundamental that it extends all the way to their foundational myths, their cosmogonies. Under the new regime of signs, the Father of Prohibition becomes the divinity who reconfigures the symbolic order through his resounding "NO," the father who cuts off access to the riches of heaven by immuring behind strong walls what treasure it holds. The Father of Enjoyment, on the other hand, is he for whom enjoyment was once possible, the one prior to, or outside of, this foundational Law, celebrant of the flesh and the enemy of the divine. Conveniently, that figure is the giant in both traditions, and so this monster was a natural point at which to begin the translation of early northern myth into the exegetical *lingua Christianitatis*.[35] Within the new symbolization of the *ordo mundi* precipitated by the meeting of the Latin and northern cosmogonies, both Anglo-Saxon fathers became coincipient, mutually constitutive. Since God and the giants were entwined in a new moment of origin, both figured within a widespread cultural narrative of how the world received its primal ordering. In fact, whenever a problem of origins is approached in early medieval England, the giant lurks nearby, never far from the threshold of whatever architecture is being built to erect an interiority against a wilderness, to give a human form to history.

Late in the ninth century, King Alfred the Great reworked Boethius's sixth-century philosophical treatise *De Consolatione Philosophiae* (*The Consolation of Philosophy*) into Old English prose, the first of two English monarchs to translate the Latin work. His contemporaries may well have found the *consolatio* promised by the title as they read the work in its new vernacular edition. Medievalists are apt to value it more highly, however, for the insights contained in the numerous glosses to what Alfred considered difficult or obscure passages. For example, the somatic transformations worked by a sorceress in the *Odyssey* are connected in a short Boethian meter to inner morality and outward appearance. The Latin speaks obliquely of *dux Neritii* (Ulysses) and *pulchra dea solis edita semine* (Circe). In the course of explaining the second allusion, Alfred writes:

> Þa wæs þær Apollines dohter Iobes [Jove's] suna; se Iob was hiora cyning, and licette þæt he sceolde bion se hehsta god; and þæt dysige folc him gelyfde, for þaðe he was cynecynnes; and hi nyston nænne oðerne god on þæne timan, buton hiora cyningas hi weorþodon for godas. Þa sceolde þæs Iobes fæder bion eac god; þæs nama wæs Saturnus; and his suna swa ilce ælcne hi hæfdon for god. Þa was hiora an se Apollinis þe we ær ymb spræcon. Þæs Apollines dohtor sceolde bion gydene, þære nama wæs Kirke.[36]

> At that time there was a daughter of Apollo, son of Jupiter; this Jupiter was their king and had pretended that he was the highest god; and that foolish people believed him, because he was of royal blood; and they knew no other god in that time, but worshipped their kings as divine. Thus Saturn, the father of Jupiter, had likewise to be a god, as well as each of his sons. One of these was Apollo, whom we just mentioned. This Apollo's daughter had to be a goddess; her name was Circe.

The explanation does more than elucidate a difficult Latin phrase. It provides a myth of origin for the gods of classical antiquity. The pagan divinities are dismissed as prideful, all too human monarchs and their families, for whom deification is something of a fad: once the man named Jupiter succeeds in convincing his credulous subjects of his immortal blood, his father, sons, and even granddaughter insist upon their place in the new pantheon. The story validates *Christianitas* over pagan error while explaining to the curious how anthropomorphic pseudodivinities entered the world.

The linking of the deities of classical mythology to mortal or demonic impersonators is a commonplace in early theological writing. Justin Martyr in the *Apologia* and Augustine in *De civitate dei* were among the many patristic writers to reiterate the belief. Isidore of Seville summarized this exegetical tradition in his influential *Etymologiae* (8.xi), "De diis gentium":

> Those whom the pagans worship as gods were once human and lived among men, such as Isis in Egypt, Jupiter in Crete, and Faunus in Rome.

... They were formerly mighty heroes [*viri fortes*], founders of cities; when they died, images were erected to honor them. . . . Persuaded by demons, posterity esteemed these men gods, and worshiped them.[37]

These deceiving *viri fortes* were first described by the church fathers as fallen angels; then, with a shift in the exegesis, they became powerful, evil men, often said to be descended from either fratricidal Cain or Noah's mocking son, Cham. In Anglo-Saxon England, the *viri fortes* became *gigantes*. Oliver Emerson argues that the early Christian writers precipitated this myth by building on the conflation of the giants of Genesis with the classical stormers of Olympus by the Jewish historian Josephus.[38] No doubt this conjoining was enabled through the moralizing of the biblical giants already well under way by the time of the Jewish apocrypha. The Book of Wisdom characterizes these monsters as corporeal signifiers of overbearing pride, destroyed as a rebuke to that primal sin: "From the beginning when the proud giants perished, the hope of mankind escaped on a raft and . . . bequeathed to the world a new breed of men" (14:6). The biblical passage underscores the giants' historicity: these monsters predate the flood, which was sent to cleanse the earth of the evils they embody. By simultaneously reading the body of the giants as allegory, however, the Book of Wisdom suggests a continuity with the giants of classical tradition, likewise condemned as monstrously prideful in their failed attempt to pile Ossa on Pelion to steal from the gods the immortal home of Olympus.[39]

After describing the demise of the giants, the passage from Wisdom explains how later in world history "tyrants" devised idols to deny the fact of the body's mortality (14:15–21). The story entwines loss (a father mourns his dead son with an image that others worship as a god), pride (despots [*tyranni*] thinking themselves greater than human order their statues venerated), the alluring power of the visual (the idols elicit awe because of their "ideal form," an artistically induced numinousness), and the reifying power of the law (the longer the idol is worshiped, the more natural such action appears, so that through repetition a reality is materialized for divinity). As in the Lacanian mirror stage, a jubilant image becomes a trap for the gaze, a lure that catches the unwary subject in an estranging identification—here, one that produces a false deity rather than an embodied ego.

In the Latin church, wicked men rather than inhuman monsters were invariably held to be those *tyranni* responsible for the sin of embodying divinity within human corporeality. For Anglo-Saxon writers, however, these primordial deceivers were always the giants.[40] The Book of Wisdom unites the giants and the "despotic princes" only by narrative proximity, but in early medieval England, the two episodes in salvation history (the destruction of the giants, the promulgation of idols) became conjoined into a newly hybrid foundational narrative that bridged classical, biblical, and northern traditions. The homilist Ælfric explicates this myth of origin in the "Passio Apostolorum Petri et Pauli," as an elucidation of why Peter should have called Jesus "son of the living God":

> [Petrus] cwæð "þæs lifigendan Godes," for twæminge ðæra leasra goda, ða
> ðe hæðene ðeoda, mid mislicum gedwylde bepæhte, wurðodon. Sume hi
> gelyfdon on deade entas, and him deorwurðlice anlicnyssa arærdon, and
> cwædon þæt hi godas wæron for ðære micelan strencðe e hi hæfdon; wæs
> ðeah lif swiðe manfullic and bysmurfull.[41]

> Peter said "of the living God" to distinguish the lesser gods, who deceived
> the heathens with various heresies. Some believed in dead giants, and raised
> up precious images, and said that they were gods because of their great
> strength; nevertheless their lives were very sinful and unclean.

The giants are an ancient, vanished race whose fossilized remains are not mysterious bones or odd topography but the lingering worship of their iniquity. The references to constructing idols and deifying the sun and moon that follow make it clear that Ælfric has both biblical and classical deities in mind. By describing the genesis of the false, mortal divinities of the Greeks and Romans (along with those of the Babylonians, Canaanites, and wayward Israelites), Ælfric is repeating a connection frequently made in Old English literature between the opprobrious giants of Christian tradition and the gods of classical mythology.

Etiologic myths linking biblical exegesis with Greek and Roman literature were a favorite of erudite Latin culture throughout the Middle Ages. Yet there is something distinctly Anglo-Saxon about this fascination with giants conjoined to the formation of alienated, human identities. In the course of one of the many homilies collected by Napier, a discourse on the early power of the devil over humanity leads to an excursus amounting to a full creation myth for the numerous gods of old:

> Se deofles man rixað on middanearde, and swa lange he winð ongean
> god and godes þeowas; and he ahefð hine sylfne ofer ealle, þa ðe hæðene
> men cwædon, þæt godas beon sceoldan on hæðene wisan; swylc swa wæs

Erculus se ent and Apollinis, þe hi mærne god leton; Þor eac and Owðen, þe hæðene men heriað swiðe.[42]

The devil ruled men on earth, and he strove against God and God's people; and he raised himself over all, so that the heathens said that the gods were their heathen leaders; such a one was the giant Hercules and Apollo, who left the glorious God; Thor also and Odin, whom the heathens greatly praise.

Apollo, the classical pantheon, and even the semidivine Greek hero Hercules are not the only divinities invented by megalomaniacal giants. Thor (Þor) and Odin (Owðen), the most familiar gods of northern provenance, also become originary *entas*. Even after the Vanir and Aesir had been replaced by Christian monotheism, traditions of giants lingered. As erudite culture displaced the more indigenous, heathen tradition, this old order of giants became conflated with the vanished gods whom they had aided and battled so that both could then be denigrated as deceivers and impersonators, validating the superiority of *Christianitas* as a homogenous, erudite, right-thinking culture. The northern mythographic propensity to use giants in a drama of etiology was adapted to the formation of a new scholastic myth through which the Germanic cosmology could be restructured and subordinated beneath a new set of master signifiers.

The giants of the homilists are the ancient, primal, but *dead* Fathers of Enjoyment who committed every sin, including the institution of embodied divinity. The *deus pater* of Christian tradition is the second aspect of this originary paternal dyad: his Word is a speech act ("Let there be light, and there was light"), his prohibition the foundation of Law. Outside this regulation, because he is its creator, this Father does not enjoy because he is likewise outside of sexuality (the origin of which is coincipient with the origin of law). The Father of Prohibition is autogenous, creating without the aid of female agency, without the aid of any kind of body at all. God guarantees the sanctity of the symbolic order by expelling the giants and the sins of their obscene enjoyment from its center.

The Book of Genesis relates that in the days after the banishment from Eden, several rebellious angels copulated with human women and engendered a *genus gigantum*: "Giants were on the earth in those days [*Entas wæron ofer eorþan on þam dagum*],[43] when the sons of God [angels] had intercourse with daughters of men and begot children [the giants] upon them" (6:4). According to the dominant exegesis of this passage, God sent the Flood to cleanse these monsters and the stain of their sins from the earth. The eradication of the giant is contemporaneous with the establishment of the law that delineates exogamy and endogamy, for the giants are the organic realization of a primal miscegenation: angels mix with humans, and the purely spiritual touches flesh. The giants arise and are destroyed to demonstrate that the word of the Father institutes and then controls sexuality. This instantiation of desire is the Oedipal moment: God the Father decrees through divine fiat the proper relations among sexed subjects, and the giants vanish. The Flood heralds the dawn of a new order, the postdiluvian age that extends to the present day, for humanity is as much descended from Noah and his wife as from Adam and Eve. Destruction becomes a kind of creation. The problems of origin are swept away by a world-purging deluge.

The same process of destructive birth or violent cleansing is enacted through the very Christianization that gives Anglo-Saxon England this new originary myth. The Oedipal Father of Christian tradition replaces the nonfamilial, nonautogenous, anthropomorphic deities of the Norse pantheon. Where once blurred boundaries and contiguity reigned, the church instituted a new model of relations based upon the almighty Father, who is originless and origin-incarnate. The pagan gods, who are no different from the giants (being descended from them, in both traditions), are made to vanish, rendered as good as dead. The giants perish with them, for who can withstand such an exegetical flood?

When Beowulf defeats Grendel's mother in her lair by means of a conveniently discovered *ealdsweord eotenisc* ("old giants' sword," line 1558), a weapon so large that it is, like the ruins that the Wanderer beholds, *giganta geweorc* ("the work of giants," line 1562), it is impossible to say exactly which tradition of giants is supposed to be responsible for having forged the blade. That this *enta ærgeweorc* ("ancient work of giants," line 1679) is also *wundorsmiþa geweorc* ("wrought by wonder-smiths," line 1681) points to an association with the giants of northern tradition, renowned for their skill as smiths. Yet Hrothgar sees that depicted on the hilt is "fyrngewinnes, syðþan flod ofsloh, / gifen geotende giganta cyn, / frecne geferdon" ("that ancient strife, when the flood, the rushing sea, slew the giants, who suffered terribly," lines 1689–91). If the story depicted is that of the biblical deluge, sent by God to destroy the giants, who, then, made the sword? The same giants it depicts being destroyed? The death by water carved upon the weapon's hilt could also represent the flood caused by the letting of Ymir's blood by the Norse gods, an act that was supposed to have drowned all the remaining giants of the world except Bergelmir and his spouse. In either case, the originary relationship of metalsmith to depicted subject, and of these giants to Grendel and his mother, is impossible to disentangle.

This *ealdsweord eotenisc* serves well as an emblem for the impure identity of the Anglo-Saxon giants and their entanglement in narratives of *human* origin. In Latin tradition, in Norse mythology, and in psychoanalytic myth, the Fathers of Enjoyment vanish so that the reign of the Father of Prohibition can begin. The giant represents access to that lost enjoyment that *must* at one time have been possible, access to a lost sense of oneness with the world that explains a contemporary feeling of estrangement. That the giant is a monster suggests the danger that a return to *jouissance* represents to a symbolic order founded upon its impossibility, to a subjectivity made possible only through its occlusion. In the end, what matters is not from where the giants derived, but what origin they enable.

In both Christian and Germanic tradition, a flood destroys the giants. More importantly, in both traditions, *the giants return*. Despite the primordial catastrophe depicted on the sword's hilt, Grendel haunts his mere and prompts the men he besieges to revert to the worship of idols. The Hebrew Bible overflows with stories of postdiluvian giants: Og of Bashan, the aboriginal inhabitants of Canaan, David's mighty nemesis, Goliath. Only Noah and the contents of his ark were supposed to survive God's celestial wash cycle, and yet giants were still walking the earth after the divinity purged its dirtied landscape. Some theologians speculated that these monsters survived by climbing the tallest mountains and thrusting their nostrils above sea level for forty days and forty nights, or that one of them, Og, had simply ridden atop the roof of the ark. But the myth of the two fathers and its relation to the Anglo-Saxon giants suggests a very different conclusion. The giants endured because they have always already lurked at the threshold of the house of God, in the haunted *healh* against which his holy *heall* stands. His rule begins with a founding Word that simultaneously excludes the giants and makes them a structural necessity: no prohibition without mythic enjoyment, no God without monsters. To abject the giant and everything his body encodes from cultural meaning is to ensure that the monster will haunt the periphery that abjection constructs, because a signification based upon exclusion depends upon the continued presence (if only a presence in death) of the thing it exiles. When northern mythology met Christian epistemology, the resultant clash of meaning systems led to a new systemization of belief, one in which the giants and the instantiation of Christian divinity were coincipient, coconstitutive. The fate of the giants of the Bible was alloyed, like the metal of Beowulf's sword, to the fate of the giants of northern cosmogony: both became part of a symbolic structure that condensed around a new Father, a Christian father, one who could banish the giants with a flood and transport the enjoyment they embodied from the past into the future, as the promise of heaven.

THE LETTER KILLETH

John Hunter, the father of British surgery, was just as happy to have the bones of the giant James Byrne as to study him alive. Similarly, Frederick I of Prussia, attempting to kidnap a giant named Zimmerman, smothered him in a coffin, yet was just as satisfied with his skeleton.—Susan Stewart[44]

If the symbolic order—the landscape through which the speaking subject treads "the paths of exile" in a doomed search for permanent place of repose—is already a dead order, structured as much around the primal absence of gods as the presence of a transcendent divinity who stands outside as its guarantee of meaning, then why fear the giant? Perhaps because he embodies a pronouncement heretical to voice: the system through which subjects are formed and through which they gain their self-consciousness is inhuman, monstrous, alive in death—like language itself.[45] To master language is to be mastered by language, since language is structured around prohibitions; it is also to be torn apart, made a collection of things with an autonomous existence quite separate from the self that is supposed to unify them. Slavoj Žižek writes in a characteristically Hegelian mode of how "word is murder of a thing," how "the word 'quarters' the thing, it tears it out of the embedment in its concrete context, it treats its component parts as entities with an autonomous existence."[46] The entrance into the linguistic system is thus also the Oedipal moment, when the father's "NO" precipitates a mutilating, exclusionary form of embodiment that renders the subject aware both of its fragility and its constitutive lack. To be Oedipalized, to become a speaking subject, is both to be born (as a unified being) and to die (be torn apart, become monstrous). Identity is constituted by the tumbling together of both terms.

The giant lurks here, even at this entry into language.

In Dante's *Inferno*, as the narrator prepares to descend into the ninth circle of hell, he sees in the distant fog what he believes are enormous towers that encircle the vast pit of Malebolge. From his wise guide Vergil, the narrator learns that these warding structures are living giants, buried in the earth from the navel down. The fiercest of the monsters bellows at hell's two tourists: "Rafel mahee amek zabi almit!" These enigmatic, indecipherable sounds provoke Dante's guide to declare, "His very babbling testifies the wrong / he did on earth: he is Nimrod, through whose evil / mankind no longer speaks a common tongue" (31.76–78).[47] Medieval exegesis held that the giant Nimrod had been the architect of the Tower of Babel, "the first great collective effort of pride against God," so that his punishment is the somatic reification of his traditional sin.[48] Nimrod is even more deadly, transgressive, and anarchic than the classical giants Ephialtes, Briareus, Tityos, Typhon, and Antaeus—the other infernal "towers."

Genesis makes no reference to Nimrod's size, labeling him during his brief appearance in an extended genealogy only a "mighty hunter before the Lord," a grandson of Cham, and the founder of the kingdom of Babel, in Shinar (10:8–10). The Plains of Shinar are, by chance, the very place where the Tower of Babel was constructed (Genesis 11:2), so that Nimrod eventually became its putative builder in various exegetical works, both Jewish and Christian.[49] The Septuagint had used the Greek word for "giant" to describe Nimrod. Philo and Orosius followed, promulgating the idea. According to Walter Stephens, Augustine "bequeathed to the Latin Middle Ages this idea that Nimrod was . . . a 'mighty hunter *against* the Lord' ('gigans uenator *contra* Dominum Deum')," mainly because of his use of a pre-Vulgate text drawn from the Septuagint.[50] Further, even the word *venator* (hunter) amplified Nimrod's gigantism for Augustine, signifying "deceiver, oppressor, and murderer of the earth's animals."[51]

Nimrod's giant body becomes the transgressive architecture that he aspired to build, a living and speaking *enta geweorc*. The Tower of Babel is an affront to the house of God that would bring divinity down to earth. God's punishment against the tower's human builders is to render them wanderers who must circle the earth, speaking new languages that ensure they will never by one another be fully understood:

> Once upon a time all the world spoke a single language and used the same words. As men journeyed in the east, they came across a plain in the land of Shinar. . . ."Come," they said, "let us build ourselves a city and a tower with its top in the heavens, and make a name for ourselves; or we shall be dispersed all over the earth." Then the Lord came down to see the city and tower which mortal men had built, and he said, "Here they are, one people with a single language, and now they have started to do this; henceforward

nothing they have a mind to do will be beyond their reach. Come, let us go down and confuse their speech, so that they will not understand what they say to one another." So the Lord dispersed them all over the earth.[52] (Genesis 11: 1–9)

A community united by their transparent communication seeks a permanent (celestial) place of rest and is punished by confusion of tongues and perpetual motion. *Babel* ("gate of the gods," a city in which to dwell like an unmoving divinity) becomes *balal* ("to babble," to be compelled to search for steadfast meanings). Linguistically and geographically, the architects of Babel lose their home and become nomads; henceforth, no place of union will exist, no city, tower, or hall will stand.

Like the giant erector of the Aesir's citadel Asgarðr or the rebellious giants who in Greek myth piled Pelion on Ossa to attain Olympus, Nimrod is stopped just as his subversive architecture nears completion; the act is always memorialized in its incompletion, to testify to some final, monstrous inadequacy. According to James Dean, "Nimrod's name in medieval writings is synonymous with perversion, that is, with a turning away from old paths toward something novel, with a change for the worse."[53] Again at a point of origin and human identity the giant is lurking. Anglo-Saxon exegesis multiplied the authors of Nimrod's heaven-bent construction, attributing the tower not to one lone giant but to an entire race. The homily *De falsis deis* declares that "Nembroð and ða entas worhton þone wundorlican stypel æfter Noes flod" ("Nimrod and the giants constructed a marvelous tower after Noah's Flood").[54] Ælfric's homily "For the Holy Day of Pentecost" gives a fuller account. He counterpoints the speaking in tongues awarded the apostles at Pentecost and the moment of linguistic unity it created with the expulsion into opaque signification embodied by the giants:

> Hit getimode æfter Noes flode, þæt entas woldon aræron ane burh, and ænne stypel swa heahne, þæt his hrof astige oð heofon. Êa wæs an gereord on eallum mancynne, and þæt weorc wæs begunnen ongean Godes willan. God eac forði hi tostencte, swaþæt he forgeaf ælcumðæra wyrhtena seltcuð gereord, and heora nan ne cuðe oðres spræce tocnawan. Hiða geswiconðære getimbrunge, and toferdon geond ealne middangeard; and wæron siððan swa fela gereord swaðæra wyrhtena wæs.[55]

It happened after Noah's Flood, that the giants wanted to erect a city and a tower so high that its roof would touch heaven. At that time all humanity had one language, and that work was undertaken against God's will. God therefore scattered them, so that each worker had his own language, and they did not comprehend each other's speech. Then they wandered away from their edifice, and dispersed throughout the earth; and there were then as many languages as there had been workers.

The building of the tower is a parable of a second Fall: the one language in which signifier and signified were not separated by any gap gives way to a new, Saussurian linguistics in which words connect only randomly to things. The old language given by God loses its pure signifying power under the giant's influence, replaced by a gibberish that has to be reanalyzed as new languages to reachieve communication. *Rafel mahee amek zabi almit*: a chaotic system of arbitrary signification and linguistic difference reigns where unmediated understanding had once obtained. Radical estrangement becomes the fate of all who enter the symbolic by learning to speak. Their words are not them, are not anything, and yet the words themselves speak, make meanings articulated beyond intention or control. Language, which had been a bond of absolute union, ensures now only distance, removal, loss.

ON REACHING THE GIANT'S HOME

The giant threatens the secure place of home, imagined as a stable core for identity as well as a geographical locus. In Norse myth, the monsters of Jotunheim so menace the god's heavenly abode of Asgarðr that a giant is tricked into immuring its towers and then is destroyed; this mythic association of giants and the building of primal architectures is kept alive in the Old English phrase *enta geweorc*, which transforms ancient human ruins into monstrous history. In classical myth, the primal sons of the earth uproot mountains and assail celestial Olympus, that *arduus aether* (high heaven) might be no safer than the earth.[56] Jupiter strikes down the rebellious monsters with his divine thunderbolts, and from the scattered gore of the fallen giants, a newly monstrous birth arises, spawned of incest (the *gigantes* are the sons of that maternal earth whom they in death impregnate): not giants but men, "sons of blood."[57] According to the Bible, giants are the progeny of humans and devils. They are likewise leaders in the revolt against divinity, the architects of the tower that would have taken heaven away from God. All three myths intertwine monsters, homelessness, and the barring of the subject from full enjoyment (in Christian terms, from union with the divine). Human identity and restless nomadism become inextricable.

Yet none of these myths quite capture the melancholic fascination of Anglo-Saxon England with the giant as figure both of origin and of loss. The monster's connection to human identity received its fullest consideration in the myths the Anglo-Saxons wove for themselves as they tried to make a hybrid past cohere, as they tried to discern why history had placed an intimate stranger at the heart of subjectivity. Grendel, the most famous monster of Old English literature, embodies this Anglo-Saxon fascination with *extimité* well. The giant intrudes into the narrative just as Hrothgar's *scop* is singing, Cædmon-like, of the creation of the world—a bright song that begins with the shaping of the earth (lines 91–92) and ends at its populating (lines 97–98), before the introduction of original sin. Hrothgar's warriors are by conjunction immediately brought into this antediluvian golden age ("Swa ða drihtguman dreamum lifdon," "So the men lived in joy," line 99), until Grendel suddenly intervenes. The monster hates their music, a dynamic metaphor of their communal harmony; this enmity places him outside the realm of the social and aligns him with everything abjected from the warmth of Heorot in order to render it a livable world.

The parallel to the biblical advent of the giants and their promulgation of evil among humanity in the days before the Flood is subtle but unmistakable. Grendel is immediately linked with Cain, who is in turn the progenitor of the very giants of the Book of Enoch and of Genesis whose deeds Grendel is repeating: "Swylce gigantas þa wið Gode wunnon / lange þrage" ("such giants that fought against God for a long time," lines 113–14).[58] Grendel exists in an uncanny (*unheimlich*) narrative temporality that is simultaneously before the deluge (in its biblical time frame) and after it (in its "historical" setting).[59] The attachment of northern monsters ("eotenas ond ylfe ond orcneas," line 111) as Grendel's brethren in Cain's genealogy further complicates the temporal frame, merging these heterogeneous fragments of history into some uncertain, monstrous past that they suddenly share. This manifold history is quietly defined against the Christian present of the poet throughout the narrative. Its point of vanishing is the interlocked deaths of Beowulf and the dragon at the close of the work.

Grendel's relation to the *comitatus* of Heorot is one of illustrative antithesis.[60] He disperses the unity of the war band with an eruption of misdirected violence. He supplants Hrothgar as ruler of the hall through senseless, jealous slaughter. The maintenance of order in a warrior society is achieved only by the repression of those impulses Grendel embodies. *Wergild*, for

example, the system that disallows blood vengeance when a legally bind-
ing sum of appeasing gold has been offered to a victim's family, works well
at defusing violent action only so long as a people can be made to abide
by its strictures. Grendel represents a cultural Other for whom conformity
to societal dictates is an impossibility because those dictates are not com-
prehensible to him; he is at the same time a monsterized version of what a
member of that very society can become when those dictates are rejected,
when the authority of leaders or mores disintegrates and the subordina-
tion of the individual to hierarchy is lost. Grendel is another version of the
wrœcca or *anhaga*, as if the banished speaker of *The Wanderer* had turned
in his exile not to elegiac poetry but to the dismemberment of that cultural
body through which he came to be.[61]

If the Wanderer and Grendel are merely different figurations of the same
symbolic role, another point of human origin has found a giant lurking
both without and within. By way of conclusion, it is perhaps worth ven-
turing to the home that the monster inhabits, to see what relation it bears
to Heorot before its violation, to Bachelard's protective house or Lacan's
distant fortress, to the Wanderer's eternally lost but incessantly beckoning
hall. The *Beowulf* poet describes the submarine cave that Grendel and his
mother share in horrifying terms: fen locked and frost bound, the lake that
bubbles above the cave is overhung with dead trees that "clutch" as if alive.
Its violent waters burn with mysterious fire, and "No man alive, though old
and wise, knows the mere-bottom" (lines 1356–67). The giant's den is a ter-
rifying locus of epistemological uncertainty. Of Grendel's descent, Hrothgar
warns Beowulf, "no hie fæder cunnon, hwæþer him anig wæs ær acenned
dyrnra gasta" ("no one knows of his father, whether any was ever begot-
ten for him among the dark shapes," lines 1355b-57a).[62] This inability to
name a progenitor from which to trace descent condenses all the problems
of origin the giant embodies. Although Grendel has no father to compel
him through some primal prohibition to leave the body of his mother, this
union could hardly be described as presymbolic bliss (*jouissance*). The giant
dwells in a land that is an extension of the same signification system that
distorts his monster's flesh: it is an inhuman realm that offers only dissolu-
tion and death. Æschere's lifeless head is dropped on the cliff by the mere,
a mute testament to monstrosity that recalls the Donestre's desubjectifying
cannibalism.

This monstrous realm is also a gendered place: here Beowulf meets,
fights, and is almost crushed to death by a giantess, a protective *mother*.
Grendel's devoted parent, supposedly less fierce than her son (lines 1282–

84), is in fact more terrible and figures within the poem's homosocial milieu the "vortex of summons and repulsion" that Julia Kristeva has called abjection.[63] In this horrifying, fascinating space, repulsion curves into desire, and everything thought to be "ejected beyond the scope of the possible, the tolerable" is revealed as residing deep within the architecture of selfhood. Kristeva allies abjection specifically with the maternal, with everything that the Wanderer's wished-for embrace excludes.[64] Grendel's unnamed mother, his companion on the paths of exile (lines 1347–48), violently reinscribes into a masculinist account of heroic self-fashioning the bodies, origins, and possibilities that narrative excludes; it is a tribute to the complexities of the poem that it accomplishes this reinsertion by demonstrating that the abjected realm of the monster is also a roofed hall (*hrofsele*) "described in human, almost homey terms"[65]—just another version of Heorot—where Beowulf plays the role Grendel previously enacted. As the dragon will prove again later, the difference between foe (*feond*) and defender (*stearcheort*, "stouthearted one") is a question of perspective, with each term forming the secret interior of the other.[66]

Like Hrothgar in Heorot, Grendel's mother lives for fifty years undisturbed in her hall. Yet her habitation is at once *hrofsele* (roofed hall) and *niðsele* (hateful hall), both beautiful and frightening. This home, which is something less than Bachelard's integrative vision of domesticity, is worth comparing to a more modern version of Beowulf's descent into the mere, this time as described by a critic of the poem who determined to find in modern Scandinavia the exact topography of the Old English narrative:

> When we arrived at the lakeside, I found the grassy sward so inviting and the lake so blue and calm that while Randy went back alone for the car I dozed off in the sun, exactly . . . where Grendel and his mother were wont to roam. Even more disconcerting, or pleasing, depending on one's level of irony, a sanitarium with serene and well-kept grounds now stands "in the very place" where those two monsters used to rage and tear apart their victims for dinner.[67]

In the daylight, the place of monsters is transformed. What was for Beowulf a "place between two deaths" where giants cannibalized their victims becomes a grassy hill that invites dreamy reminiscence. Grendel's lair is not so very different from the Wanderer's hall after all. This duality of signification characterizes what psychoanalysis labels the place of *das Ding*, "the real-traumatic kernel in the midst of symbolic order."[68] *Das Ding* is Freud's appropriately Germanic word for a "sublime object" that is as numinous and inviting as it is horribly alien; *das Ding* is both a longed-for home and the dwelling of the monster. This Thing that is an extimate trauma lurks at the center of subjectivity, ensuring that the process of becoming human is also the process of becoming monstrous: "As soon as brute, pre-symbolic reality is symbolized/historicized, it 'secretes' the. . . 'indigestible' place of the Thing."[69] As Grendel and the Donestre demonstrate, the human body is quite *ingestible*—that is, human subjectivity and human embodiment are historicizable phenomena with a recoverable cultural specificity. What escapes this process of symbolizing the body of the past, however, is its monstrous component, its intimate alterity: there always remains within the subject something "more than itself," something that lurks like a familiar stranger at the threshold of the hall. *Das Ding* is the guarantee of the inadequacy of history, the reason it cannot fully explain the non-contradictory coincidence of what appear on their face to be antithetical extremes.

Beowulf celebrates the death of the giant; the *Liber monstrorum* (c. 650–750), composed by someone familiar with the *Beowulf* tradition, opens with a nostalgic reflection on the dwindling space of the monstrous in the modern world, then fills the gap opened by the triumph of the human (*humanum genus*) over *monstra* by offering a long catalog of unfailingly disturbing hybrid bodies, many of whom are giants.[70] Anglo-Saxon England knew well the inhuman presence that stands at both the origins and the ruins of identity and had the perfect term for this haunting: *enta geweorc*, the work of giants.

NOTES

[1] Kathy Acker, *In Memoriam to Identity* (New York, 1990), p. 6.

[2] W. P. Ker, *The Dark Ages* (London, 1904), pp. 252–53; cited in J. R. R. Tolkien, "*Beowulf*: The Monsters and the Critics," *The Proceedings of the British Academy* 22 (1936): 9.

[3] Tolkien, "*Beowulf*: The Monsters and the Critics," p. 17.

[4] Tolkien, "*Beowulf*: The Monsters and the Critics," p. 19. Tolkien's use of Christian allegory is far more complex than that of later, more reductive readings of medieval literature. Tolkien argues that the poem's power derives from its admixture of Latin piety with northern marvels: "At this point new Scripture and old tradition are ignited," forming a "universal tragedy of man" that Clare A. Lees has critiqued well in its gendered specificity ("Men and *Beowulf*," in

Medieval Masculinities: Regarding Men in the Middle Ages, ed. Clare A. Lees [Minneapolis, 1994], pp. 130–35).

5   The bibliography on monstrousness in Old English texts is too long to reproduce here, but see, most recently, Andy Orchard, *Pride and Prodigies: Studies in the Monsters of the "Beowulf"-Manuscript* (Cambridge, Eng., 1995).

6   Cotton Tiberius B.v is a hybrid version of *The Wonders of the East*, written in Latin and Old English; it has been reproduced in an excellent facsimile (*An Eleventh-Century Anglo-Saxon Illustrated Miscellany: British Library Cotton Tiberius B.v, Part I: Together With Leaves from British Library Cotton Nero D.II*, ed. Patrick McGurk et al. [Copenhagen, 1983]). An Old English version of *Wonders* is bound with *Beowulf* in Cotton Vitellius A. xv. Recent and thorough discussions of *Wonders of the East* may be found in Mary Campbell, *The Witness and the Other World: Exotic European Travel Writing, 400–1600* (Ithaca, N.Y., 1988), pp. 47–86, and Orchard, *Pride and Prodigies*, pp. 175–203.

7   See Nicholas Howe, *Migration and Myth-Making in Anglo-Saxon England* (1989; reprint Notre Dame, 2001), and Sarah Foot, "The Making of *Angelcynn*: English Identity before the Norman Conquest," *Transactions of the Royal Historical Society*, 6th ser., 6 (1996): 25–49.

8   Old English contains four nouns carrying the modern signification of "giant": *ent*, *eten*, *eoten*, and *gigant*; *þyrs* could also be used, but it has the wider denotation of "large monster" (see Alexandra Hennessey Olsen, "'Thurs' and 'Thyrs': Giants and the Date of *Beowulf*," *In Geardagum* 6 [1984]: 35–42]. The etymology of most of these words is unclear, though *eten* may be related to *etan* ("to eat"), and *eoten* is probably cognate with Old Norse *jotunn*; compare even the formulaic phrase for "race of giants" (*iotna ætt* in the *Edda* and *eotena cyn* in *Beowulf*). *Gigant* is taken directly from the oblique forms of Latin *gigas*. *Ent* is by far the most common designation. The glossary in Ælfric's *Grammar* supplies *ent* for Latin *gigas* ("Additional Glosses to the Glossary in Ælfric's *Grammar*," *Dictionary of Old English* transcript), and Aldhelm provides it for *ciclopum* ("Ænigmata," in *Anecdota Oxiensia: Old English Glosses, Chiefly Unpublished*, ed. Arthur S. Napier [1900; reprint New York, n.d.]). Any discussion of the Anglo-Saxon conception of the giant is necessarily indebted to a triad of scholarly works: Oliver F. Emerson, "Legends of Cain, Especially in Old and Middle English," *PMLA* 21 (1906): 831–929, and Robert E. Kaske, "The *Eotenas* in *Beowulf*," in *Old English Poetry: Fifteen Essays*, ed. Robert P. Creed (Providence, 1967), pp. 285–310, and "*Beowulf* and the Book of Enoch," *Speculum* 46.3 (1971): 421–31. I acknowledge them at the outset because the influence of their writing is pervasive in what follows.

9   The discussion that follows is based in large part on the giants of the following texts:

Edda, die Lieder des Codex regius nebst verwandten Denkmälern, ed. Gustav
Neckel and Hans Kuhn (Heidelberg, 1962); *Edda Snorra Sturlusonar,* ed. Finnur
Jónsson (Copenhagen, 1931); *Fornaldar Sögur Norðurlanda,* ed. Guðni Jónsson
(Reykjavik, 1959); *Islendinga Sögur,* ed. Guðni Jónsson (Reykjavik, 1968); and
John R. Broderius, *The Giant in Germanic Tradition,* PhD diss., University of
Chicago, 1932.

[10] The primordial cow Audumla creates Buri, whose son Bar marries the giantess
Bestla; their sons are Odin, Vili, and Vé, who in turn slay the world-giant Ymir
and begin the war of the gods against the giants, a kind of civil war.

[11] Quotations of *The Wanderer* are from R. F. Leslie, ed., *The Wanderer* (Manchester,
1966); translations are by Michael Alexander, *The Earliest English Poems*
(London, 1977), with some slight modifications.

[12] Jacques Lacan, *The Four Fundamental Concepts of Psycho-Analysis,* ed. Jacques-
Alain Miller, trans. Alan Sheridan (New York, 1981), p. 104

[13] All modern English translations of *Beowulf* are from Howell D. Chickering, Jr.,
"Beowulf": A Dual Language Edition (New York, 1977), unless otherwise noted;
quotations of the Old English are from Fr. Klaeber, ed., *"Beowulf" and the Fight
at Finnsburgh,* 3rd ed. with supplements (Lexington, Mass., 1950).

[14] On abjection and the construction of a zone of uninhabitability, see Judith Butler,
Bodies That Matter: On the Discursive Limits of "Sex" (New York, 1993), p. 3.

[15] See Kaske, *"Beowulf* and the Book of Enoch."

[16] *Beowulf,* lines 1679 and 1562, respectively.

[17] To cite one familiar example, an unnamed hill giant builds a stone citadel safe
from the attacks of Jotunheim for the Aesir to inhabit in the popular tale told in
the *Gylfaginning* of Snorri Sturluson (XLII) and perhaps mentioned in the older
Poetic *Edda* (but see J. Harris, "The Master Builder Tale in Snorri's *Edda* and
Two Sagas," *Arkiv for Nordisk Filologi* 91 [1976]: 66–101).

[18] "Vafþrúðismál," *The Poetic Edda,* trans. Lee M. Hollander, 2nd ed. (Austin, 1962),
p. 46.

[19] Paul Coates, *The Gorgon's Gaze: German Cinema, Expressionism, and the Image of
Horror* (Cambridge, Eng., 1991), p. 84.

[20] Jacques Lacan, "The Mirror Stage as Formative of the Function of the I," *Écrits: A
Selection,* trans. Alan Sheridan (New York, 1977), pp. 1–7.

[21] Malcolm Bowie, *Lacan* (Cambridge, Mass., 1991), p. 261.

[22] Jacques Lacan, "Aggressivity in Psychoanalysis," *Écrits,* p. 11. Lacan lists these
images as "castration, mutilation, dismemberment, dislocation, evisceration,
devouring, bursting open of the body" (p. 11).

[23] Lacan insists that topographical metaphors for the unconscious are misleading
(see his "Seminar on *The Purloined Letter,*" trans. Jeffrey Mehlman, *Yale French*

Studies 48 [1973]: 39–72), though he will continue to use topographical language and schematics throughout his writing.

24 Susan Stewart, *On Longing: Narratives of the Miniature, the Gigantic, the Souvenir, the Collection* (Baltimore, 1984), p. 125.

25 Gaston Bachelard, *The Poetics of Space*, trans. Maria Jolas (1969; reprint Boston, 1994), p. 6.

26 Bachelard, *The Poetics of Space*, pp. 6–7.

27 The quotation is from Wallace Stevens, "The Auroras of Autumn," in *The Collected Poems of Wallace Stevens* (New York, 1982), p. 414—another poetic meditation on loss, homelessness, and the fragility of identity.

28 Slavoj Žižek, *Looking Awry: An Introduction to Jacques Lacan through Popular Culture* (Cambridge, Mass., 1992), p. 112. Žižek argues the psychoanalytic structure of nostalgia at greater length than I have space to account for here.

29 See Jacques Lacan, "The Signification of the Phallus," p. 284, and "The Agency of the Letter in the Unconscious, or Reason since Freud," p. 148, both in *Écrits*.

30 "But we must insist that *jouissance* is forbidden to him who speaks as such, although it can only be said between the lines for whoever is subject of the Law, since the Law is grounded in its prohibition. Indeed, the Law appears to be giving the order, 'Jouis!,' to which the subject can only reply 'J'ouis' (I hear), the *jouissance* being no more than understood" (Jacques Lacan, "The Subversion of the Subject and the Dialectic of Desire in the Freudian Unconscious," *Écrits*, p. 319).

31 That this fullness is never more than a retroactive fantasy is clear from the fact that no subject exists *until* this entry into language; the plenitudinous past that the subject creates is a back-formation, a projection into an inaccessible time of a present desire. For the same reason, the identifications of the mirror stage are not so clearly differentiated from this second set; Lacan describes the three orders (Imaginary, Symbolic, Real) as entwined within a Borromean knot rather than as stages of a bodily progress.

32 See Žižek, *Looking Awry*, where he writes, "The point is . . . to acknowledge that part of enjoyment is lost from the very beginning, that it is immediately impossible, and not concentrated 'somewhere else,' in the place from which the agent of prohibition speaks. . . . It is precisely this dependence of the Oedipal father—the agency of symbolic law guaranteeing order and reconciliation—on the perverse figure of the Father-of-Enjoyment that explains why Lacan prefers to write *perversion* as *père-version*, i.e., the version of the father. Far from acting only as a symbolic agent, restraining pre-oedipal 'polymorphous perversity,' subjugating it to the genital law, the 'version of,' or turn toward, the father is the most radical perversion of all" (pp. 24–25).

[33] Here the third pun inherent in Lacan's *nom-du-père* becomes evident: *les non-dupes errent*, exactly caught in the English phrase "the non-duped err." Because fantasy materializes identity and history—because fantasy is not some dreamy mist that gets in the way of seeing reality "as it really is" but instead that which solidifies the ground beneath one's feet—there is no way to "do without fantasy," to stop positing myths of origin such as the two fathers. "Those in the know are lost": to think that one has gained distance on this fantasy is another way of participating in it, of allowing it to make real the world.

[34] Bede, for example, worried endlessly about the proper dating of Easter and the variations between Roman and regional liturgical practice. On the engendering of the medieval category *Christianitas* as a foundational category and the violence to difference that its institution enacts, see Kathleen Biddick, "Genders, Bodies, Borders: Technologies of the Visible," *Speculum* 68 (1993): 390, 392–93, 402–09. On the creation and sustenance of the "identity of a given ideological field beyond all possible variations of its positive content," see Slavoj Žižek, *The Sublime Object of Ideology* (New York, 1989), pp. 87–129 (quotation from p. 87).

[35] Thus, when both Bede and Alcuin gloss the meaning of *gigantes*, they characterize the monster as a large body endowed with excess physicality: "Gigantes dicit homines immensis corporibus editos ac potestate nimia preditos" (Bede, *Libri quatuor in principium Genesis*, p. 100); "homines immenso corpore . . . moribus inconditi" (Alcuin, *Interrogationes et Responsiones in Genesin*, XCVI, in *Patralogia Latina*, ed. J.P. Migne, 221 vols. [Paris, 1844–64; hereafter referred to as *PL*], 100 c.526). Orchard treats both passages in *Pride and Prodigies*, pp. 78–79.

[36] *King Alfred's Old English Version of Boethius' "De Consolatione Philosophiae,"* ed. Walter John Sedgefield (Oxford, 1899), pp. 115–16. A portion of the quotation appears in Emerson, "Legends of Cain," who points out that the Old English poetical version of the *Metres of Boethius* contains a similar gloss in its translation of the same verses (p. 908).

[37] *PL* 82, c.314. Augustine makes a similar statement in his *Confessions*, 1.17. Compare with the explanation of idolatry found in the Book of Wisdom (14:14–20).

[38] Emerson, "Legends of Cain," p. 905.

[39] The writer(s) of the Book of Wisdom no doubt knew the Greek myth of the gigantomachia, recorded as early as 600 B.C.E. on vase paintings and frequently allegorized in poetry and literature thereafter. Anglo-Saxon England would have known the myth from the Roman fascination with its political symbolism. Vergil refers to the storming of Olympus twice (*Georgics*, 1.277–83; *Aeneid*, 6.578–84)

(in *Virgil*, ed. H. Rushton Fairclough [Cambridge, Mass., 1973]), and Ovid related the myth at length in his *Metamorphoses* 11.128–621 (ed. G.P. Goold [Cambridge, Mass., 1984]).

[40] There are, in fact, two brief references connecting giants to pagan deities in the Eastern church: Justin Martyr's *Apologia* (1.190) and *The Instructions of Commodius* (chap. 3). It is likely that this tradition and the Old English one were separate, both arising directly from independent knowledge of the Book of Enoch and its giants.

[41] *The Homilies of the Anglo-Saxon Church: The First Part Containing the Sermones Catholici, or Homilies of Ælfric in the Original Anglo-Saxon*, ed. Benjamin Thorpe (1844; reprint New York, 1971), 1:366.

[42] *Homilies for Unspecified Occasions*, ed. Arthur S. Napier (Berlin, 1883), no. 42, p. 144. The reference is taken from Antonette di Paolo Healey and Richard L. Venezky, *A Microfiche Concordance to Old English* (Newark, 1980).

[43] Translated by Ælfric from the Vulgate ("gigantes erant super terram in diebus illis," "giants were on the earth in those days") in the course of a sermon; Joseph Bosworth, *An Anglo-Saxon Dictionary*, ed. and enlarged by T. Northcote Toller (1898; reprint London, 1964), p. 252.

[44] Stewart, *On Longing*, p. 111

[45] For a detailed argument of this point, see David L. Clark, "Monstrosity, Illegibility, Denegation: *The Martyrology* after de Man," in *Monster Theory: Reading Culture*, ed. Jeffrey Jerome Cohen (Minneapolis, 1996), pp. 40–71.

[46] Slavoj Žižek, *Enjoy Your Symptom! Jacques Lacan in Hollywood and Out* (London, 1992), p. 51.

[47] Dante, *The Inferno*, trans. John Ciardi (New York, 1954), p. 260.

[48] Walter Stephens, *Giants in Those Days: Folklore, Ancient History, and Nationalism* (Lincoln, Nebr., 1989), p. 86.

[49] Josephus (*Antiquities*), Augustine (*De civitate dei*), Orosius, and Isidore (*Etymologiae*) all mention the architect Nimrod.

[50] Stephens, *Giants in Those Days*, p. 358.

[51] Augustine, *De civitate dei*, 16.4; cited by James Dean, "The World Grown Old and Genesis in Middle English Historical Writings," *Speculum* 57.3 (1982): 565, who also points out that Peter Comestor later interpreted Nimrod as a hunter of men.

[52] History repeats itself: "Probably the observation of vast temple ruins elicited this theological explanation [for the abandoned city] by those to whom this culture was alien" (*The New English Bible with the Apocrypha* [New York, 1976], p. 11 n. 9). The translation quoted is likewise from this edition; I have used this version rather than the Vulgate because it better gives the passage its folkloric feel.

53 Dean, "The World Grown Old," p. 565. Dean provides an excellent overview of the appearances of Nimrod in Middle English literature, including a reference to the legend that Nimrod built the Tower because he suffered from hydrophobia and was afraid of another giant-destroying Flood (p. 566). The encyclopedic Hereford mappamundi (1290 C.E.) depicts dog-headed giants near Babylon, where the rubric announces "Nimrod the giant built it," but connecting Nimrod to the giants began to grow rather rare by the thirteenth century. Even though Augustine, Hrabanus Maurus, and Peter Comestor all asserted that Nimrod had been a giant, theological interest in his gigantic nature dwindled as the days of Anglo-Saxon England and its cultural mania for giants came to a close.

54 *Wulfstan: Sammlung der ihm zugeschriebenen homilien nebst Untersuchungen über ihre Echtheit*, ed. Arthur S. Napier (Berlin, 1883), p. 105; quoted by Robert J. Menner, *The Poetical Dialogues of Solomon and Saturn* (New York, 1941), p. 122 (where it is wrongly attributed to Ælfric). For an informed discussion on the abundant Old English variations of Nimrod's name, see Menner, *The Poetical Dialogues*, p. 124.

55 Ælfric, *The Homilies of the Anglo-Saxon Church*, p. 318.

56 Ovid, *Metamorphoses*, 1.151–62.

57 Compare with Hesiod, *Theogony*, trans. Norman O. Brown (Indianapolis, 1953), p. 58.

58 The manuscript has *cames*, a reading that seems to be a confusion of Cain and Cham. A derivation from Cham is more logical, but descent from Cain fits the thematic associations better. It seems likely that an original reading of Cain was later imperfectly emended.

59 It might be useful here to distinguish the Freudian *unheimlich* from Lacanian *extimité*. Whereas extimacy is a phenomenon of structuration (related to the ex-centricity of an excluded something), the uncanny is mainly an aesthetic experience and primarily *affective*. The uncanny is caused by the return of the repressed and so has a way of warping temporality; extimacy is not an experience but a description of a structural state that may have various affects connected to it, but such affects are secondary to the phenomenon itself. See Elizabeth Wright, *Feminism and Psychoanalysis: A Critical Dictionary* (Cambridge, Mass., 1993), pp. 436–40.

60 The use of the word *comitatus* (a Latin term, from Tacitus) to describe the organization of Germanic tribes of later periods has been questioned; I use it here in the loosest possible way, as an equivalent to the term "Männerbund." See Joseph Harris, "Love and Death in the *Männerbund*: An Essay with Special Reference to the *Bjarkamál* and *The Battle of Maldon*," in *Heroic Poetry in the Anglo-Saxon Period: Studies in Honor of Jess B. Bessinger, Jr.*, ed. Helen Damico and John Leyerle (Kalamazoo, Mich., 1993), pp. 77–114.

61 What the invasion of Heorot would seem from the monster's point of view is well conveyed by *Grettis saga*, in which the hero is rightfully mistaken for a troll as he bursts into a house and kills its inhabitants (*Grettis saga Asmundarsonar*, ed. Guðni Jónsson [Reykjavik, 1936], pp. 130–31).

62 Compare with Avitus 4.88–93 ("*De diluvio mundi*"): "Nor is it lawful to utter from what seed they were sprung. As to their mother, men spoke of an origin common to all [of the giants]; why this offspring, whence the fathers, mystery shrouds from disclosing" (in *Monumenta Germaniae Historica, Auctores Antiquissimi* [Berlin, 1883]; cited by Kaske, "The *Eotenas* in *Beowulf*," p. 304).

63 Julia Kristeva, *Powers of Horror: An Essay on Abjection*, trans. Leon S. Roudiez (New York, 1982), p. 1.

64 Abjection might be thought of as a specifically gendered kind of *extimité*, and the same kind of structural effect, even though Kristeva never makes that connection herself. The problem with Kristeva's formulation of abjection is one that many feminist critics have pointed out as a problem in her work as a whole: the maternal and the feminine are problematically conflated.

65 Orchard, *Pride and Prodigies*, p. 30.

66 Orchard traces the interrelation of dragon and hero well in *Pride and Prodigies*, pp. 29–30.

67 Gillian R. Overing and Marijane Osborn, *Landscape of Desire: Partial Stories of the Medieval Scandinavian World* (Minneapolis, 1984), p. 22.

68 Žižek, *The Sublime Object of Ideology*, p. 135. On the relation of *das Ding* to originary fantasies and medieval studies, see Gayle Margherita, *Romance of Origins: Language and Sexual Difference in Middle English Literature* (Philadelphia, 1994), pp. 153–61.

69 Žižek, *The Sublime Object of Ideology*, p. 135.

70 That the author of the *Liber monstrorum* knew some version of the Beowulf tradition is indicated by a reference to *Higlacus, rex Getarum* (Hygelac, king of the Geats). Orchard offers a thorough discussion of the relation of the *Liber* to *Beowulf*, as well as an edition of the Latin text (Orchard, *Pride and Prodigies*, pp. 86–115, 254–317).

REGARDLESS OF SEX: MEN, WOMEN, AND POWER IN EARLY NORTHERN EUROPE

CAROL J. CLOVER

In chapter 32 of *Gísla saga*, two bounty hunters come to the wife of the outlawed Gísli and offer her sixty ounces of silver to reveal the whereabouts of her husband. At first Auðr resists, but then, eyeing the coins and muttering that "cash is a widow's best comfort," she asks to have the money counted out. The men do so. Auðr pronounces the silver adequate and asks whether she may do with it what she wants. By all means, Eyjólfr replies. Then:

> Auðr tekr nú féit ok lætr koma í einn stóran sjóð, stendr hon síðan upp ok rekr sjóðinn með silfrinu á nasar Eyjólfi, svá at þegar støkkr blóð um hann allan, ok mælti: "Haf nú þetta fyrir auðtryggi þína ok hvert ógagn með. Engi ván var þér þess, at ek mynda selja bónda minn í hendr illmenni þínu. Haf nú þetta ok með bæði skǫmm ok klæki. Skaltu þat muna, vesall maðr, meðan þú lifir, at kona hefir barit þik. En þú munt ekki at heldr fá þat, er þú vildir." Þá mælti Eyjólfr: "Hafið hendr á hundinum ok drepi, þó at blauðr sé."[1]

In George Johnston's translation:

> Aud takes the silver and puts it in a big purse; she stands up and swings the purse with the silver in it at Eyjolf's nose, so that the blood spurts out all over him; then she spoke: "Take that for your easy faith, and every harm

From *Speculum* 68 (1993): 363–87; reprinted with permission of The Medieval Academy of America.

with it! There was never any likelihood that I would give my husband over to you, scoundrel. Take your money, and shame and disgrace with it! You will remember, as long as you live, you miserable man, that a woman has struck you; and yet you will not get what you want for all that!"

Then Eyjolf said: "Seize the bitch and kill her, woman or not!" [literally, "Seize the dog (masculine) and kill (it), though (it) be *blauðr*"].[2]

Eyjólfr's men hasten to restrain him, noting that their errand is bad enough as it is without the commission of a *níðingsverk* (rendered by Johnston as "a coward's work").

The adjective *blauðr* poses a translation problem.[3] Cleasby-Vigfusson's entries under it and its antonym *hvatr* read as follows:

BLAUÐR, adj. Properly means *soft*, *weak*, answering Latin *mollis*, and is opposed to *hvatr*, "brisk, vigorous"; hence the proverb, *fár er hvatr er hrörask tekr, ef í barnæsku er blauðr* [few are *hvatir* in action who are *blauðir* in childhood]. Metaphorically *blauðr* means "feminine," *hvatr* "masculine," but only used of animals, dogs, cats, fishes; *hvatr-lax = hæingr = salmo mas*; [the feminine noun] *bleyða* is a "dam," and metaphorically "a coward, a craven." *Blauðr* is a term of abuse, a "bitch, coward." . . .

HVATR, adj. "Bold, active, vigorous." II. "Male," opposed to *blauðr*, "female," of beasts.[4]

Attested in both poetry and prose, *blauðr* occurs most conspicuously in verbal taunts toward or about men, and in such cases it is typically rendered in English as "coward" (earlier "craven"), as in Hallgerðr's remark in chapter 38 of *Njáls saga*, "Jafnkomit mun á með ykkr, er hvárrtveggi er blauðr" (translated in the Penguin edition, "The two of you are just alike; both of you are cowards"), directed to her pacifist husband and his equally pacifist friend Njáll, a man who not only favored Christianity but was unable to grow a beard.[5] When *blauðr* is used in reference to women or female animals, however (as in the *Gísla saga* passage above), it is rendered "woman" or "female"; clearly "coward" will not do in the *Gísla saga* passage. The need in English for two words ("coward" and "female") where Norse uses one (*blauðr*), and Cleasby-Vigfusson's brave, but on the face of it hopelessly bedeviled, effort to distinguish "metaphoric" from presumably "real" or "proper" usages, and human from animal, hint at the aspect of early Scandinavian culture, and perhaps Germanic culture in general, that this essay is about: a sex-gender system rather different from our own, and indeed rather different from that of the Christian Middle Ages.

Certainly the *Gísla saga* passage seems a snarl of gender crossings. If her sex qualifies Auðr as *blauðr*, bloodying the nose of a person qualifies her as *hvatr*; and if being a man qualifies Eyjólfr as *hvatr*, having his nose bloodied qualifies him as *blauðr*, and having his nose bloodied by a creature he himself wishes to designate as *blauðr* by virtue of her sex qualifies him as *blauðr* in the extreme—which is, of course, the point of Auðr's reminder that he has been not only struck in the nose, but struck in the nose by a *woman*. When Eyjólfr calls out his order to have her seized despite the fact that she is *blauðr*, he acknowledges that whatever properties are assumed to attach to her bodily femaleness have been overridden by her aggressive behavior. She wants to be *hvatr*, she gets treated accordingly. And when his men restrain him, saying that they have accumulated enough shame without committing a *níðingsverk*, they in effect redefine her as *blauðr*.[6] It could be argued that the scene, particularly the focus on wifely loyalty, has Christian resonances (like all the Icelandic sagas, this one has roots in the pagan era but was written down during the Christian one), and that some part of its confusion stems from what I shall suggest are different gender paradigms.[7] But the real problem, I think, inheres in the *hvatr/blauðr* term set (presumably ancient) and the inability of the modern languages, and modern scholarship, to apprehend the distinction.

. . .

When commentaries on Viking and medieval Scandinavian culture get around (most do not) to the subject of "women" or "sex roles" or "the family," they tend to tell a standard story of separate spheres.[8] Woman's, symbolized by the bunch of keys at her belt, is the world *innan stokks* ("within the household"), where she is in charge of child care, cooking, serving, and tasks having to do with milk and wool. Man's is the world beyond: the world of fishing, agriculture, herding, travel, trade, politics, and law. This inside/outside distinction is formulated in the laws and seems to represent an ideal state of affairs. It is no surprise, given its binary quality, and also given the way it seems to line up with such term sets as *hvatr/blauðr*, that modern speculations on underlying notions of gender in Norse culture should be similarly dichotomous. As labor is divided, in other words, so must be sexual nature: thus we read, in the handbooks, of the "polarity" of the sexes, of an "antithesis between masculine and feminine," of male-female, "complementarity," and so on.[9]

But is it that simple, and, more to the point, is it that modern? Let me begin an interrogation of this sexual binary on the female side. From the outset of the scholarly tradition, readers have been startled and not infrequently appalled by the extraordinary array of "exceptional" or "strong" or "outstanding" or "proud" or "independent" women—women whose behavior exceeds what is presumed to be custom and sometimes the law as well. No summary can do them justice, not least because paraphrase (indeed, translation in general) forfeits the tone of marvelous aplomb, both social and textual, that is such a conspicuous and telling aspect of their stories. But for those unfamiliar with the field, the following list should give a rough idea of the parameters. Heading it is the formidable Unnr in djúpúð-ga. The overwhelming majority of Iceland's founding fathers (the original land claimants) were fathers indeed, but a handful—thirteen, according to *Landnámabók*[10]—were women, and one of these was Unnr, who, fearing for her life and fortunes in Scotland after the death of her father and son, had a ship built in secret and fled, taking all her kin and retinue with her, to Orkney, then the Faroes, and finally Iceland, where, in about the year 900, she took possession of vast lands and established a dynasty.[11] ("In every respect," Preben Meulengracht Sørensen observes, "she has taken over the conduct and social functions of the male householder and leader.")[12]

In Scandinavia as in the Germanic world in general, men preceded women as heirs, but women did inherit, and a variety of evidence confirms that women could, and a not-insignificant percentage did, become considerable landholders.[13] They could also become traders and business partners. One of the main Scandinavian ventures on the North American continent was significantly bankrolled by a woman—a woman who moreover betook herself on the journey. (During the American winter, she is said to have driven her husband to murder several companions while she herself took an axe to their wives.)[14] It may well be that even that most macho of early Scandinavian business activities, organized piracy ("viking" in the proper sense of the term), was practiced by women. *The War of the Gædhil with the Gaill* refers twice to a "red girl" who headed up a viking band in Ireland and invaded Munster in the tenth century, and as any reader of the literature well knows, there are many other such legends of "fierce and imperious women"—legends so numerous and so consistent that, as Peter Foote and David Wilson sum it up, they "must certainly have some basis in reality."[15] More mundane but no less telling, given the "overwhelming maleness" of the enterprise, is the existence of a handful of women skalds.[16] More generally, the sources tell of a number of women who prosecute their lives in gen-

eral, and their sex lives in particular, with a kind of aggressive authority un-
expected in a woman and unparalleled in any other European literature.[17]

Nor was government the exclusive turf of men. It was in principle a male
matter, but in practice, if we are to believe the sagas, women could insinuate
themselves at almost every level of the process. One source claims that until
the year 992, when they were debarred, women in Iceland could bring suit.[18]
Normally women were not allowed to serve as witnesses—but exceptions
could be made. Likewise service as arbitrators; it was a male business, but
we know of at least one woman who "was formally empowered by the dis-
putants to act as an arbitrator in a case."[19] Normally and ideally households
were headed by men, but the laws provide for the female exception, and
although the female house-holder was in principle subject to the authority
of male guardians, the sagas give evidence, as William Ian Miller puts it,
that "women were more than mere title holders with managerial powers
lodged solely with men."[20] Women were, in theory, exempt from feud vio-
lence, but there are cases of their being specifically included together with
able-bodied men as targets of vengeance.[21] In Iceland, not just men but also
women were subject to the penalties of outlawry and execution. Only a man
could *be* a *goði*, but it was technically possible for women to *own* the office.[22]
A woman's control over whatever property she might technically own was
less a function of her sex than her marital status: an unmarried and un-
derage girl had none; a married woman, little; a widow, however (as Foote
and Wilson sum it up), "could have charge of her own property, no matter
her age, and administer that of her children; she also had more say in ar-
rangements that might be made for another marriage."[23] Certainly women's
role, in blood feud, in "choosing the avenger" involved them centrally in
the family politics of honor and inheritance, theoretically male terrain.[24]
Normally women were buried with "female" grave goods (e.g., spinning
implements), but there are enough examples of female graves with "male"
objects (weapons, hunting equipment, carpentry tools) to suggest that even
in death some women remained marked as exceptional.[25]

The examples could be multiplied, but even this summary list should
suffice to prompt the paradoxical question: just how useful is the category
"woman" in apprehending the status of women in early Scandinavia? To
put it another way, was femaleness any more decisive in setting parameters
on individual behavior than were wealth, prestige, marital status, or just
plain personality and ambition? If femaleness could be overridden by other
factors, as it seems to be in the cases I have just mentioned, what does that
say about the sex-gender system of early Scandinavia, and what are the im-

plications for maleness? I have no doubt that the "outstanding" women I enumerated earlier were indeed exceptional; that is presumably why their stories were remembered and recorded. But there is something about the quality and nature of such exceptions, not to say the sheer number of them and the tone of their telling, that suggests a less definitive rule than modern commentators have been inclined to allow. Certainly between women's de jure status and de facto status (as it is represented in literary and even historical texts) there appears to have been a very large playing field, and the woman (especially the divorced or widowed woman) sufficiently ambitious and sufficiently endowed with money and power seems not to have been especially hindered by notions of male and female nature.[26]

The slippage is not only between law and life. It is also between law and law (regional variations pointing to a degree of relativity in the importance of sexual difference), and it is also, on some points, within one and the same law. I turn here to the portion of *Grágás* known as *Baugatal*. A schedule of compensation for slayings, *Baugatal* (literally "ring count") divides the kindred into four tiers depending on their relationship to the slain person. The first tier is composed of near kinsmen of the slain person (father, son, brother, etc.), who are required to pay (if they are defendants) or collect (if they are plaintiffs) the main "ring" or major share of the *wergild*. Then comes the next tier, made up of less immediately related kinsmen with a lesser share of the *wergild*, and so on. The extensive list, which explores all possible permutations of payers and receivers, consists exclusively of men, with one exception:

> Sú er ok kona ein er bæði skal baugi bœta ok baug taka ef hon er einberni. En sú kona heitir baugrygr. En hon er dóttir ins dauða, enda sé eigi skapþiggjandi til hǫfuðbaugs en bœtendr lifi, þá skal hon taka þrímerking *sem sonr*, ef hon tók eigi full sætti at vígsbótum til þess er hon er gipt; enda skulu frændr álengr taka. Nú er hon dóttir veganda, en engi er skapbœtendi til bœtendi til hǫfuðbaugs, en viðtakendr sé til, þá skal hon bœta þrímerkingi *sem sonr* til þess er hon kømr í vers hvílu; en þá kastar hon gjǫldum í kné frændum.[27]

There is also one woman who is both to pay and to take a wergild ring, given that she is an only child, and that woman is called "ring lady." She who takes is the daughter of the dead man if no proper receiver of the main ring otherwise exists but atonement payers are alive, and she takes the three-mark ring *like a son*, assuming that she has not accepted full settlement in compensation for the killing, and this until she is married, but thereafter kinsmen take it. She who pays is the daughter of the killer if no proper payer of the main ring otherwise exists but receivers do, and then she is to pay the three-mark ring *like a son*, and this until she enters a husband's bed and thereby tosses the outlay into her kinsmen's lap.

In other words, when the slain man has no male relatives in the first tier (no son, brother, or father) but *does* have a daughter (unmarried), that daughter shall function as a son. So compelling is the principle of patrilineage that, in the event of genealogical crisis, even a woman can be conscripted as a kind of pinch hitter. Better a son who is your daughter than no son at all.

That the "surrogate son" provision is of some antiquity in Scandinavia is suggested by the presence of similar statutes on the mainland.[28] It is worth noting that its implications go beyond the matter of *wergild*, for insofar as a *wergild* list ranks an individual's kinsmen according to their degree of relatedness to the slain person, it is also assumed to reflect the schedule of inheritance as well. It is moreover assumed to reflect the schedule of actual feud—the order in which the survivors are obliged to take retaliatory action. Thus the law itself contemplates a situation in which, in the genealogical breach, a woman becomes a functional son, not only in the transaction of *wergild*, but also in the matter of inheritance and also, at least in principle, in the actual prosecution of feud. (That she must revert to female status upon marriage further underscores the expectation that gender will yield, as it were, to the greater good of survival of the line.) Just where and when and how completely the surrogate son clause obtained we have no idea, although the ubiquity of "maiden warrior" legends—legends of unmarried, brotherless daughters who on the death of their fathers become functional sons, even dressing and acting the part—suggests that the idea was very much alive in the public mind.[29] In either case, what concerns us here is not so much historical practice as legal contemplation—the plain fact that even within one and the same law, the principle of sex is not so final or absolute that it could not be overridden by greater interests. *Baugatal* and similar surrogate son provisions not only allow but institutionalize the female exception. Again, to judge from the presence of "male" objects in the occasional female grave, not even death necessarily undid such exceptionality.

I have hesitated over such terms as "femaleness" and "masculinity" in the above paragraphs, for they seem to me inadequate to what they mean to describe. The modern distinction between sex (biological: the reproductive apparatus) and gender (acquired traits: masculinity and femininity) seems oddly inapposite to the Norse material—in much the same way that Cleasby-Vigfusson's distinction between literal and metaphoric seems oddly inapposite to the semantic fields of the words *blauðr* and *hvatr*. What can be the meaning of biological femaleness in a culture that permits women to serve as juridical men? If biological femaleness does not determine one's juridical status, what does it determine—and indeed what does it matter? Is this a culture in which "sex" per se is irrelevant and "gender" is everything? Or is it a culture that simply does not make a clear distinction but holds what we imagine to be two as one and the same thing? Something of the sort would seem to be the lesson of the *blauðr/hvatr* complex. Cleasby-Vigfusson proposes (in effect) that the word *blauðr* refers to "sex" when applied to a sex-appropriate being (thus to call Auðr *blauðr* is merely to call her female) but to "gender" when applied to a sex-inappropriate being (thus to call a man *blauðr* is to call him cowardly); but the fact that one word does for both (both "sex" and "gender," or in Cleasby-Vigfusson's terms both "proper" and "metaphoric") would seem to suggest that in Old Norse there is no "both" in the modern sense, but a single notion. That this single notion corresponds, at least in the case of the female, more closely to our sense of gender than to our sense of sex (though I shall suggest later that the Scandinavian sense of "gender" wreaks havoc with the concept of gender as we understand it) is clear from the examples of "exceptional" or "outstanding" women I enumerated above. "Woman" is a normative category, but not a binding one. If a woman is normally *blauðr*, she is not inevitably so, and when she is *hvatr*, she is thought unusual, but not unnatural.

Unusual for the better. Although the woman who for whatever reason plays life like a man is occasionally deplored by the medieval author,[30] so she is more commonly admired—sometimes grudgingly, but often just flatly. Certainly *Laxdæla saga* is unequivocal about Unnr in djúpúðiga: "Hon hafði brott með sér allt frændlið sitt, þat er á lífi var, ok þykkjask menn varla dœmi til finna, at einn kvenmaðr hafi komizk í brott ór þvílíkum ófriði með jafnmiklu fé ok fǫruneyti; má af því marka, at hon var mikit afbragð annarra kvenna" ("She took with her all her surviving kinsfolk; and it is generally thought that it would be hard to find another example of a woman escaping from such hazards with so much wealth and such a large retinue; from this it can be seen what a paragon amongst women she was").[31] So too Auðr in the same saga, who assumes male dress and arms and goes off to exact the revenge her brothers refused to take on her behalf; although the saga does not say so in so many words, it is clear that her actions are approved of, legal injunctions against transvestism notwithstanding.[32] Lest we doubt the gender implications of such women's exceptional behavior, it is spelled out for us in the application to them of that most privileged of epithets, *drengr* (*drengiligr*, *drengskapr*, etc.). Defined by Cleasby-Vigfusson as a "bold, valiant, worthy man," *drengr* is conventionally held up as the very soul of masculine excellence in Norse culture.[33] Yet Njáll's wife Bergþóra is introduced as "kvenskǫrungr mikill ok drengr góðr ok nǫkkut skaphǫrð" ("a women of great bearing and a good *drengr*, but somewhat harsh-natured").[34] Even Hildigunnr, whose goading of Flosi fuels a feud that might otherwise have calmed down, is so designated: "Hon var allra kvenna grimmust ok skaphǫrðust ok drengr mikill, þar sem vel skyldi vera" ("She was the sternest and most hard-minded of women but a great *drengr* when need be").[35] This is a world in which "masculinity" always has a plus value, even (or perhaps especially) when it is enacted by a woman.[36]

. . .

If the category "woman" is a movable one, what of the category "man"? Is maleness, too, subject to mutation and "exception," or is it alone clear and fixed? Much has been said—though far more could be said—about Norse notions of masculinity. On the assumption that readers are generally familiar with the ideal, let me proceed directly to that long and broad streak in the literature—a streak that runs through poetry (both mythological and heroic) and prose, Latin and vernacular, legend and history and even law—in which manliness is most garishly contested: the tradition of insulting.

Although insults are most concentrated in those literary set pieces we call *flytings* (*senna* and *mannjafnaðr*), they can crop up in just about any venue.[37] In terms more or less formal and more or less humorous, the insulter impugns his antagonist's appearance (poor or beggardly); reminds him of heroic failure (losing a battle, especially against an unworthy opponent); accuses him of cowardice, of trivial or irresponsible behavior (pointless escapades, domestic indulgences, sexual dalliance), or of failings of honor (unwillingness or inability to extract due vengeance, hostile relations with kinsmen); declares him a breaker of alimentary taboos (drinking urine, eating corpses); and/or charges him with sexual irregularity (incest, castration, bestiality, "receptive homosexuality"). (Once again, although most insults are traded between men, there are also women in the role of both insulter and insultee—though a woman in either role usually faces off against a man, not another woman, and although she may score lots of direct hits, in the end she always loses. The most fre-

quent charges against women are incest, promiscuity, and sleeping with
the enemy.)[38]

Of these, the most spectacular is the form of sexual defamation known
as *níð*. Very likely part of the Germanic legacy, *níð* was prohibited by law.
The following passages give a sense of the term.[39] The first is from the
Norwegian Gulaþing Code and follows the rubric "If a person makes *níð*
against someone":

> Engi maðr scal gera tungu nið um annan. ne trenið. . . . Engi scal gera yki
> um annan. æða fiolmæle. þat heiter yki ef maðr mælir um annan þat er eigi
> ma væra. ne verða oc eigi hever verit. kveðr hann væra kono niundu nott
> hveria. oc hever barn boret. oc kallar gylvin. þa er hann utlagr. ef han verðr
> at þvi sannr.[40]

> Nobody is to make *tungu níð* [verbal *níð*] about another person, nor a *tréníð*
> [wooden *níð*].[41] . . . No one is to make an *ýki* [exaggeration] about another
> or a libel. It is called *ýki* if someone says something about another man
> which cannot be, nor come to be, nor have been: declares he is a woman
> every ninth night or has born a child or calls him *gylfin* [a werewolf or un-
> natural monster?]. He is outlawed if he is found guilty of that. Let him deny
> it with a six-man oath. Outlawry is the outcome if the oath fails.

The second also comes from the Gulaþing Code, in the passage under the ru-
bric *fullréttisorð* (verbal offenses for which full compensation must be paid):

> Orð ero þau er fullrettis orð heita. þat er eitt ef maðr kveðr at karlmanne
> ǫðrum. at hann have barn boret. þat er annat. ef maðr kveðr hann væra
> sannsorðenn. þat er hit þriðia. ef hann iamnar hanom við meri. æða kallar
> hann grey. æða portkono. æða iamnar hanom við berende eitthvert.[42]

> There are certain expressions known as *fullréttisorð* [words for which
> full compensation must be paid]. One is if a man says to another that he
> has given birth to a child. A second is if a man says of another that he is
> *sannsorðinn* [demonstrably fucked]. The third is if he compares him to a
> mare, or calls him a bitch or harlot, or compares him with the female of any
> kind of animal.

The corresponding provision in the Icelandic *Grágás* establishes lesser out-
lawry (three years' exile) for *ýki* and *tréníð*, but full outlawry (exile for life)

for the utterance of any of the words *ragr, stroðinn*, or *sorðinn*. Indeed, for these three words one has the right to kill.[43]

The legal profile of *níð* is richly attested in the literature. Two examples suffice to give the general picture: Skarpheðinn's taunting suggestion, in *Njáls saga*, that Flosi would do well to accept a gift of pants, "ef þú ert brúðr Svínfellsáss, sem sagt er, hverja ina níunda nótt ok geri hann þik at konu" ("if you are the bride of the Svínafell troll, as people say, every ninth night and he uses you as a woman")[44] and Sinfjǫtli's claim to Guðmundr in the eddic *Helgakviða Hundingsbana I*, "Nío átto við / á nesi Ságo / úlfa alna, / ec var einn faðir þeirra" ("Nine wolves you and I begot on the island of Sága; I alone was their father").[45] As the latter example in particular indicates (and there are many more), what is at stake here is not homosexuality per se, for the role of the penetrator is regarded as not only masculine but boastworthy regardless of the sex of the object.[46] The charge of *níð* devolves solely on the penetrated man—the *sorðinn* or *ragr* man. This architecture is a familiar one in the early world and in certain quarters of the modern one as well, but it surely finds one of its most brazen expressions in the Norse tradition of *níð*.

To what extent sodomy, consensual or otherwise, was practiced in early Scandinavia is unknown. What is clear from a survey of *níð* examples is that the charges to that effect are "symbolic" (as Folke Ström would have it) or "moral" (as Meulengracht Sørensen prefers) insofar as they refer not to an act of sex but rather to such "female" characteristics as "a lack of manly courage," "lack of prowess," or "'unmanliness' in both its physical and its mental sense," or "certain mental qualities, not to mention duties that were considered specifically female."[47] Meulengracht Sørensen distinguishes three meanings of the word *argr/ragr* as it refers to men: "perversity in sexual matters" (being penetrated anally), "versed in witchcraft," and "'cowardly, unmanly, effeminate' with regard to morals and character." The second and third meanings derive from the first, in his view, by the logic that "a man who subjects himself to another in sexual affairs will do the same in other respects; and fusion between the notions of sexual unmanliness and un-manliness in a moral sense stands at the heart of *níð*."[48]

Symbolic or no, the *níð* taunts figure the insultee as a female and in so doing suggest that the category "man" is, if anything, even more susceptible to mutation than the category "woman." For if a woman's ascent into the masculine took some doing, the man's descent into the feminine was just one real or imagined act away. Nor is the "femaleness" of that act in doubt. Anal penetration constructed the man who experienced it as whore, bride, mare, bitch, and the like—in whatever guise a female creature, and as such subject to pregnancy, childbirth, and lactation. In the world of *níð* (male) anus and vagina are for all imaginary purposes one and the same thing. Men are sodomizable in much the way women are rapable, and with the same consequences. The charge may be "symbolic," but its language could hardly be more corporeal, and although, as I shall suggest below, the separate status of the female body is far from secure, there is no doubt that the body of the *ragr* man looks very much like that of a woman.

But is *níð* really the fundamental truth of early Scandinavian sexual attitudes? It is not surprising that modern scholarship has reified it as such, given its special status in the laws and also given the way, thanks to its occlusion in the scholarly tradition, it has been handed to modern critics as a kind of blank slate.[49] But it is important to remember that *níð* insults are by no means the only sort of Norse insult; that they are typically found interspersed, as if on roughly equal footing, with insults not immediately sexual; and that in this larger context, *níð* insults seem part and parcel of a shame system in which the claim of femaleness is an especially striking, but by no means the only, element.

Men call each other poor or beggardly—and in quite stinging terms—as often as they call each other women. They call each other slaves and captives. They accuse one another of having fled from danger or having failed to take action to protect themselves and their kin. A great number of insults occur in alternation with boasts and turn on some standard oppositions: action vs. talk, hard life vs. soft life, adventurer vs. stay-at-home, etc. In a particularly grandiose flyting from *Örvar-Odds saga*, the legendary Örvar-Oddr brags of having explored warfare when all the insultee explored was the king's hall; of having fought the Permians while the insultee was safely ensconced at home between linen sheets; of having razed enemy strongholds while the insultee was "chattering with girls"; of having slain eighteen men while the insultee was staggering his way to a bondwoman's bed; of having brought down an earl while the insultee was "at home wavering between the calf and the slave girl." Similar is the claim in the eddic *Helgi Hundingsbana I* that while the "flight-scorning prince" Helgi was off feeding the eagles, Sinfjǫtli was "at the mill kissing slave girls." Insofar as home-staying (especially when it amounts to combat avoidance) is coded as effeminate (even though the accused may be an active "phallic aggressor"[50] within the realm of the household), these insults, too, are haunted by gender, and they indeed on occasion tip over into *níð*, as in the following stanza from *Örvar-Odds saga*: "Sigurðr, vart eigi, / er á Sælundi felldak /

bræðr böðharða, / Brand ok Agnar, / Ýsmund, Ingjald, / Álfr var inn fim-
mti; / en þú heima látt / i höll konungs, / skrökmálasamr, / skauð hernumin"
("Sigurðr, you weren't on Zealand when I felled the battle-hard brothers
Brandr and Agnarr, Ásmundr and Ingjaldr, and Álfr was the fifth—while
you were lying at home in the king's hall, full of tall stories, a *skauð hernu-
min*").[51] The participial *hernumin* here means "battle-taken" and suggests
the sort of victimization to which a prisoner of war was subject. The femi-
nine noun *skauð* means "sheath" and is a word for a fold or crack in the
genital area—used in practice to refer to the female genital and to the fold
of skin into which a horse's penis retracts.[52] If *skauð hernumin* defies precise
translation, its general sense is clear. The insultee is trebly accused: of being
a draft dodger, of being a prisoner of war and hence subject to whatever
abuse that condition may entail, and of having either no penis or one so soft
and hidden—so *blauðr*—that it is useless as such.

Whatever else they may be, these are insults preoccupied with power—or,
more to the point, with powerlessness under threat of physical force. That
sexual difference is deeply imbricated in this concern is clear. The ques-
tion is which, if either, is primary. Is power a metaphor for sex (so that the
charge of poverty boils down to a charge of femaleness), as Meulengracht
Sørensen argues, or is sex a metaphor for power (so that the charge of *níð*
boils down to a charge of powerlessness)? Modern scholarship has tended
to assume the former. I incline toward the latter, or toward a particular ver-
sion of the latter. The insult complex seems to me to be driven, not by the
opposition male/female per se, but by the opposition *hvatr/blauðr*, which
works more as a gender continuum than a sexual binary. That is, although
the ideal man is *hvatr* and the typical woman is *blauðr*, neither is necessarily
so; and each can, and does, slip into the territory of the other.

• • •

If the human body was once taken as the one sure fact of history, the place
where culture stopped and biological verities began, it is no longer. Not in
the academy, in any case, in which there has arisen a virtual industry of in-
vestigating the ways conceptions of bodies, above all sexed bodies, are his-
torically contingent. Of particular interest for students of early Scandinavia
are the implications of what Thomas Laqueur calls the "one-sex" or "one-
flesh" model of sexual difference that he argues obtained in western Europe
from the Greeks through the early modern period.[53] Unlike the "two-sex"
or "two-flesh" model, which emerged in the late eighteenth century and

which construes male and female as "opposite" or *essentially* different from one another, the "one-sex" model understands the sexes as inside-vs.-outside versions of a single genital/reproductive apparatus, differing in degree of warmth or coolness and hence in degree of value (hot being superior to cool) but essentially the same in form and function and hence ultimately fungible versions of one another. The point here is not that there is no notion of sexual difference but that the difference was conceived less as a set of absolute opposites than as a system of isomorphic analogues, the superior male set working as a visible map to the invisible and inferior female set—for the one sex in question was essentially male, women being viewed as "inverted, and less perfect, men."[54]

So the official story, the one told by medical treatises. Popular mythologies were (and to a remarkable degree still are) rather more fluid in their understanding of which parts match which. A millennially popular "set" equates the (male) anus with the vagina—not a correspondence authorized by the medical treatises, but one that proceeds easily from the one-sex body as a general proposition. (The word *vagina* itself, meaning "sword sheath," was also used in Latin sources to refer to the anus.[55] Certainly, Norse words or periphrases for the vagina are typically usable for the anus, and it is indeed with deprecating reference to the male that such terms are conspicuously attested.)[56] What is of particular interest for present purposes is not so much the system of homologues per se, but the fluidity implied by that system. This is a universe in which maleness and femaleness were always negotiable, always up for grabs, always susceptible to "conditions." If "conditions" could go so far as to activate menstruation in men or a traveling down of the sexual member in women (eventualities attested by medical authorities throughout the early period), then "conditions" could easily enable gender encroachments of a more moderate sort.[57]

A systematic account of the Norse construction of the body, including the sexed body, remains to be written. I presume that the Scandinavians in the early period had some one-sex account of bodily difference—the conflation of anus and vagina and the charges of male pregnancy point clearly in that direction—but no treatise spells out the terms. I also presume that in the same way that the thirteenth-century authors were cognizant of other medical learning (the theory of humors, for example), they were cognizant of the learned hot/cool model of sexual difference—but they did not insinuate that model into the "historical" texts. One can think of several reasons for this: because they preferred to let tradition overrule science, because for narrative purposes strength stood as the objective correlative of heat, because it is the nature of sagas to naturalize learning. But it may also, and above all, be because the medieval authors knew that in the very social stories they had to tell, actual genitals were pretty much beside the point. The first lesson of the foregoing examples is that bodily sex was not that decisive. The "conditions" that mattered in the north—the "conditions" that pushed a person into another status—worked not so much at the level of the body, but at the level of social relations.

The second lesson has to do with the attenuated quality of the category "female." The fact that "femaleness" is so frequently invoked with reference to men (far more often than to women, I suspect), the absence of a language for and lack of concern with features exclusive to women, and the consignment of anything that might qualify as women's sphere to a position virtually outside of history would seem to suggest that what is at stake here is not "femininity" in any modern sense, but simply "effeminacy" or, more to the point, "impotence"—the default category for the person of either sex who for whatever reason fell outside normative masculinity. Scholars who try to distinguish the feminine from the effeminate by suggesting that the female role was ignominious only when it was assigned to a man and that women and female activities as such were not held in contempt are on shaky ground, for the sources point overwhelmingly to a structure in which women no less than men were held in contempt for womanishness and were admired—and mentioned—only to the extent that they showed some "pride" (as their aggressive self-interest is repeatedly characterized in modern commentaries).[58] Again, it seems likely that Norse society operated according to a one-sex model—that there was one sex and it was male. More to the point, there was finally just one "gender," one standard by which persons were judged adequate or inadequate, and it was something like masculine.

What finally excites fear and loathing in the Norse mind is not femaleness per se, but the condition of powerlessness, the lack or loss of volition, with which femaleness is typically, but neither inevitably nor exclusively, associated. By the same token, what prompts admiration is not maleness per se, but sovereignty of the sort enjoyed mostly and typically and ideally, but not solely, by men. This is in any case not a world in which the sexes are opposite or antithetical or polar or complementary (to return again to the modern apparatus). On the contrary, it is a world in which gender, if we can even call it that, is neither coextensive with biological sex, despite its dependence on sexual imagery, nor a closed system, but a system based to an extraordinary extent on winnable and losable attributes. It goes without saying that the one-sex or single-standard system (in the sense I have out-lined it here) is one that advantaged men. But it is at the same time a system in which being born female was not so damaging that it could not be offset by other factors. A woman may start with debits and a man with credits, but any number of other considerations—wealth, marital status, birth order, historical accident, popularity, a forceful personality, sheer ambition, and so on—could tip the balance in the other direction. (When Hallgerðr of *Njáls saga*, who acted herself so forcefully into history, says to her father that "Pride is something you and your kinsmen have plenty of, so it's no surprise that I should have some too," she articulates perfectly the economy of the one-sex model, in which, however unequal, men and women are, or can be, players in the same game.)[59] More to the point, because the strong woman was not inhibited by a theoretical ceiling above which she could not rise and the weak man not protected by a theoretical floor below which he could not fall, the potential for sexual overlap in the social hierarchy was always present. The frantic machismo of Norse males, at least as they are portrayed in the literature, would seem on the face of it to suggest a society in which being born male precisely did *not* confer automatic superiority, a society in which distinction had to be acquired, and constantly reacquired, by wresting it away from others.

• • •

Let me take this a step further and propose that to the extent that we can speak of a social binary, a set of two categories into which all persons were divided, the fault line runs not between males and females per se, but be-tween able-bodied men (and the exceptional woman) on one hand and, on the other, a kind of rainbow coalition of everyone else (most women, chil-dren, slaves, and old, disabled, or otherwise disenfranchised men). Even the most casual reader of Norse literature knows how firmly drawn is that line, for it suggests itself all over the lexical and documentary map, including in the laws themselves, which distinguish clearly and repeatedly between *úmegð* (singular *úmagi*), "dependents" (literally, those who cannot main-tain themselves: "children, aged people, men disabled by sickness, paupers, etc."), on one hand, and "breadwinners" (*magi/megð*) on the other.[60] What I am suggesting is that this is *the* binary, the one that cuts most deeply and the one that matters: between strong and weak, powerful and powerless or dis-empowered, swordworthy and unswordworthy, honored and unhonored or dishonored, winners and losers.[61] Insofar as these categories, though not biological, have a sexual look to them, the one associated with the male body and the other with something like the female one, and insofar as the polarity or complementarity or antithesis that modern scholarship has brought to bear on maleness and femaleness applies far more readily, and with less need for qualification, to the opposition *hvatr/blauðr* or *magi/úmagi*, they might as well be called genders. The closest English comes to the distinction may be "spear side" and "distaff side"—a distinction which, although it is clearly (now) welded to sexual difference, is nonetheless one derived from roles (rather than bodies) and hence at least gestures toward gender (insofar as men are in principle able to spin and women to do battle).

To observe that some such binary is a familiar feature of premodern societies (and at the popular level in modern ones as well) should not detract from its decisive importance in Old Norse.[62] Nor is (for example) the Greek distinction between *hoplites* and *kinaidoi* as it has been outlined in recent scholarship quite apposite to the Scandinavian one between *magi* and *úmagi*, for the gender traffic in Norse involves not only men, but women, and conspicuously so. What Winkler calls the "odd belief in the reversibility of the male person, always in peril of slipping into the servile or the feminine," is matched, in Norse, by the odd belief in the reversibility also of the female person, under the right conditions capable of ascension into the ranks of those who master, and that fact has grave consequences for the male side of the story.[63] Not only losable by men, but achievable by women, masculinity was in a kind of double jeopardy for the Norse man. He who for whatever reason became a social woman stood, to put it crudely, to find himself not just side by side with woman, but under her, and, again, it may be just that ever-present possibility that gives Norse maleness its desperate edge. The literature is in any case rich with scenes, both historical and legendary, that turn on male humiliation or defeat at the hands of women—including, as a relatively gentle example, the encounter between Auðr and Eyjólfr with which this essay began.[64]

Let me turn to a stream in the downward gender traffic that I have not yet mentioned, though it is especially privileged in the documents: men once firmly in category A who have slid into category B by virtue of age. In a literature not given to pathos and little interested in the old, these moments—in which former heroes are shown doddering about, or bedridden, or blind and impotent—stand out in strong relief.[65] We tend to understand the poignancy of such scenes rather straightforwardly in terms of the past, as a kind of northern sounding of the *ubi sunt* or *sic transit gloria* themes so richly developed in Old English verse. Certainly they are that, but with a spin that strikes me as if not uniquely Norse, then characteristically so. For in the Norse examples it is not just the ruination of the once-heroic body that is at stake, but the second-class company such a body is forced to keep.

Consider, for example, just how many of the scenes of Egill Skallagrímsson's old age are played out in the company of women—who cajole, tease, laugh at, advise, and humor him, both figuratively and literally pushing him around. His story could have been told, as others are, with fewer (or indeed none) of these scenes; certainly the preceding 230-odd pages of that text are as woman-free as the Icelandic sagas get. The effect of this cluster of women at the end, I think, is to suggest that Egill has in a sense become one of them—no longer a man of the public world, but a man *innan stokks*. Viewed in this context, his composition, on the death of his son(s), of the lament *Sonatorrek* ("Loss of My Sons")—thought by many the most magnificent poem in the language—takes on a new dimension. To judge from the extant literature, emotional lamentations of this woe-is-me sort are very much the business of women in early Scandinavia, so much so that they seem tantamount to a female industry.[66] Thematically, metaphorically, and lexically, Egill's poem resembles nothing so much as Guðrún's lament in the eddic *Hamðismál* and *Guðrúnarhvǫt*,[67] and although his composition is commonly assumed to be prior, the fact that it is the only male-composed lament of the woe-is-me type in early Scandinavia, and that it is produced so emphatically *innan stokks* (not only within the house but within the bedchamber, where he lies mourning) and so specifically in the company of women (his daughter induces him to compose it, and the audience for its premier performance consists of "Ásgerðr, Þorgerðr, and the household") leads me to wonder whether some part of its original pathos did not have to do with the gendered circumstances of its production.[68] To pose it as a question: is it possible that some of *Sonatorrek*'s contemporary force derived from its point of issue on the distaff side and its coding as a "woman's" form?

By way of steadying this suggestion about *Sonatorrek*, let me turn to two proverbs that explicitly link the condition of old men with femaleness. One, which in fact turns on public speech, occurs in a scene in *Hávarðar saga Ísfirðings* in which a woman named Bjargey urges a husband too old for battle to take up the role of whetter. "Þat er karlmannligt mál," she moralizes, "at hann, er til engra harðræðanna er fǫrr, at spara þá ekki tunguna at tala þat, er honom mætti verða gagn at" ("It is manly for those unfit for vigorous deeds to be unsparing in their use of the tongue to say those things that may avail").[69] The saying is doubly telling. It acknowledges the equivalence of old men and women, for tongue wielding (whetting, egging) is a conspicuously female activity.[70] But it also acknowledges the commensurability of the tongue and the sword. The homology of physical and verbal dueling is a familiar theme in the literature, cropping up in such phrases as "war of words," "to battle with the voice," "to wound with words," or, to reverse the formulation, "quarrel of swords" (= battle). Saxo's *Gesta Danorum* similarly describes Ericus Disertus (Eiríkr inn málspaki or Eric the Eloquent) as an "argument athlete" (*altercationum athleta*) who is as "valorous in tongue as in hand," and Gotwar as a woman for whom "words were weapons," someone who "could not fight" but "found darts in her tongue instead."[71] The tongue may be a lesser weapon, the "sword" of the unswordworthy, but it is a weapon nonetheless, and one whose effects could be serious indeed (as the legal injunctions against *tunguníð* attest). And like the sword it is less than, the tongue is subject to bold use or cowardly unuse, so that even within the category of unswordworthy persons, conspicuously women and old men, the politics of *hvatr* and *blauðr* play themselves out. "It is *manly*," Bjargey says, for the unswordworthy to use their tongues to make things happen. Better to wield the sword than the tongue, in short, but better to wield the tongue than to wield nothing—in both cases whether one is a man or a woman.

Egill himself states the equation in a pithy half-stanza lamenting the effects of age: "my neck is weak," he says; "I fear falling on my head; my hearing is gone; and *blautr erum bergis fótar borr*."[72] The line in question translates something like: "soft is the bore [= drill bit] of the foot/leg of taste/pleasure," the bore referring to tongue if one takes *bergis fótar* to mean "head," but to penis if one takes the kenning to mean "leg or limb of pleasure."[73] If one assumes, as I do, that the art of the line lies precisely in its duplicity and that *both* meanings (penis *and* tongue) inhere in it (skaldic verse is nothing if not a poetry of the double entendre), and if one hears the harmonic "sword" that inevitably sounds over these two tones (for penises and tongues are repeatedly figured as weapons),[74] and finally if one takes in the sense of effeminacy/femaleness that attaches to the word *blautr*, "soft" (a word that rhymes both sonically and semantically with *blauðr*), one has in this five-word verse the full chord: when not only one's sword and penis go limp but also one's tongue, life is pretty much over. This is not the first we have heard of Egill's tongue, of course. *Sonatorrek* itself opens with a complaint about the difficulty of its erection ("Mjǫk erum tregt / tungu at hrœra / eðr loptvæi / ljóðpundara," "It is very hard for me to stir my tongue or the steel-yard of the song-weigher");[75] and although there is no question of an overt sexual or martial meaning here, the wider system of tongue/sword/penis correspondences invites us to just such associations, which serve in turn to confirm our sense that this poem stems from a point very far down the gender scale—a point at which sword and penis have given way to the tongue, and even the tongue may not be up to the task. (The one-sex reasoning behind the sword/penis/tongue construction, and the value of the categories relative to one another, could hardly be clearer. Worth remembering, on the distaff side, is the figure used to characterize the maiden warrior Hervör's shift from the female to the male role: she trades the needle for the sword.)[76] Egill's *Sonatorrek* sounds like a female lament, in short, because in some deep cultural sense it *is* one.

The second proverb is untranslatable, and in its untranslatability is crystallized the problem on which this essay turns. It occurs in *Hrafnkels saga* and is invoked by a serving woman in an effort to rouse Hrafnkell from bed as enemies approach the farm: "Svá ergisk hverr sem eldisk," "Everyone becomes *argr* who [or: as he/she] gets older."[77] Like the entry under *blauðr*, Cleasby-Vigfusson's entry under *argr* (the banned "a" word of the laws) tries to solve the problem by distinguishing a literal meaning ("emasculate," "effeminate") from a figurative one ("wretch," "craven," "coward"). If we elect the latter, we get something along the lines of "Sooner or later, we all end up cowardly" (E. V. Gordon) or "The older the man, the feebler" (Hermann Pálsson), a choice that occludes the sense of gendered degradation that the term *argr* carries with it.[78] If we elect the former, we get something like "Sooner or later, we all end up effeminate." It is clear why translators would prefer "cowardly" here, for "effeminate" jolts: what can it mean if every man eventually becomes it, and do women become it, too? I would argue that (although neither choice is good) "effeminate" is preferable for two reasons: because it captures so succinctly the default social partnership of old men and typical women, and because it reveals in no uncertain terms that, for all its associations with the female body, the word *argr* (*ergi, ergjask, ragr*, etc.) finally knows no sex. Again, the problem is that Modern English has no language for a system in which the operative social binary *looks* sexual (i.e., is figured in terms of male and female bodies) but is in practice *not* sexual, that is to say, neither exclusively nor decisively based on biological difference (or for that matter *any* inborn characteristic, with the presumable exception of natal defects). What the proverb "Svá eldisk hverr sem eldisk" boils down to is that sooner or later, all of us end up alike in our softness—regardless of our past and regardless of our sex.

It is beyond the scope of this already too synthetic essay to probe the impact on the northern periphery of "medievalization" (the conversion to Christianity and the adoption of European social forms), but by way of ending let me hazard some general propositions. The documentary sources, dating as they do from the Christian period, are notoriously slippery, but no reader of them can escape the impression that the new order entailed a radical remapping of gender in the north. More particularly, one has the impression that femaleness became more sharply defined and contained (the emergence of women-only religious orders is symptomatic of the new sensibility), and it seems indisputably the case that as Norse culture assimilated notions of weeping monks and fainting knights, "masculinity" was re-zoned, as it were, into territories previously occupied by "effeminacy" (and other category B traits). (This expansion of the masculine was presumably predicated on the fixing of the female and her relocation at a safe distance.) It may be, as Laqueur argues on the basis of the medical tradition, that the one-sex model of sexual difference did not fully yield to a two-sex one until the late eighteenth century with the invention of a separate femaleness with its own organs and characteristics, but that does not mean that the one-sex era was monolithic or static or that the two-sex model did not have its conceptual harbingers. In the northern world, at least, the social organization of Christian Europe must have been perceived as entailing a profoundly different sex-gender system—one that despite its own stories of real and imagined gender crossings (particularly within religious discourse) drew a line of unprecedented firmness between male and female bodies and natures. The new dispensation would by the same token appear to have blurred the line between able-bodied men and aging men: the portrait of Njáll in that most Christian of sagas seems a conscious attempt to recuperate for Christian patriarchy a man under the old order dismissable by virtue of age, and indeed openly accused of effeminacy by his pagan neighbors. (Egill, on the other hand, born just two decades earlier and hence dead before the conversion, can be construed by his medieval biographer as having missed out.) What I am suggesting is that there are one-sex systems and one-sex systems; that early northern Europe "lived" a one-sex social logic, a one-gender model, to a degree unparalleled elsewhere in the west; and that the medievalization of the north entailed a shift of revolutionary proportions—a shift in the direction of two-sex thinking, and one therefore in kind not unlike the shift Laqueur claims for Europe in general eight hundred years later.[79]

It should by now be clear that the problems of translation with which this essay has been preoccupied are not just unrelated lexical glitches, but cognate symptoms of a larger problem of conceptual translation. Whether the early Scandinavian model is as I have outlined it here—I am aware of having barely scratched the surface—is not clear. What is clear is that their system and ours do not line up and that the mismatch is especially obvious, and especially alien, where women and the feminine are concerned. From the outset, scholars have speculated on what unusual notion of womanhood might account for such startlingly strong female figures in a culture that seems otherwise to hold femaleness in such contempt. (It is a speculation that extends all the way back to Tacitus.) I mean in this essay to turn the question inside out and ask whether the paradox—extraordinary women, contempt for femaleness—may not have more to do with the virtual absence of *any* notion of "womanhood" than it does with the existence of some more spacious or flexible notion than our own. The evidence points, I think, to a one-sex, one-gender model with a vengeance—one that plays out in the rawest and most extreme terms a scheme of sexual difference that at the level of the body knows only the male and at the level of social behavior, only the effeminate, or emasculate, or impotent. The case could be made, particularly on the basis of the mythic narratives, that Norse femaleness was a more complicated business than Laqueur's model would have it,[80] but the general notion, that sexual difference used to be less a wall than a permeable membrane, has a great deal of explanatory force in a world in which a physical woman could become a social man, a physical man could (and sooner or later did) become a social woman, and the originary god, Óðinn himself, played both sides of the street.

NOTES

[1] *Gísla saga Súrssonar*, in *Vestfirðinga sǫgur*, ed. Björn K. Þórólfsson and Guðni Jónsson, Íslenzk fornrit [henceforth cited as ÍF] 6 (Reykjavík, 1958). Translations of Old Norse passages throughout are my own unless otherwise indicated.

[2] *The Saga of Gisli*, trans. George Johnston with notes by Peter Foote (Toronto, 1963), p. 51.

[3] Friedrich Ranke has, "Ergreift den Hund und schlagt ihn tot, wenns auch eine Hündin ist!" (*Die Geschichte von Gisli dem Geächteten* [Munich, 1907], p. 85, and [Düsseldorf, 1978], p. 64); Hjalmar Alving has, "Lägg hand på den djävulen och slå ihäl henne, fast hon är kvinnfolk" (*Isländska sagor* 2 [Stockholm, 1936], p. 66); Vera Henriksen has, "Ta fatt i den bikkja og drep den, selv om det er en tispe!"(*Gisle Surssons saga* [Oslo, 1985], p. 85); George Webbe Dasent has, "Lay hands on

and slay her, though she be but a weak woman" (*The Story of Gisli the Outlaw* [Edinburgh, 1866], p. 98); Preben Meulengracht Sørensen has, "Grib hunden og dræb den, selv om den er af hunkøn" (*Norrønt nid: Forestillingen om den umandige mand i de islandske sagaer* [Odense, 1980], p. 94), which translator Joan Turville-Petre renders, "Lay hands on the hound and kill it, even though it is female" (*The Unmanly Man: Concepts of Sexual Defamation in Early Northern Society* [Odense, 1983], p. 76); and Richard Cleasby and Gudbrand Vigfusson, *An Icelandic-English Dictionary* [Oxford, 1957]; hereafter referred to as Cleasby-Vigfusson) has, under the entry *blauðr*, "take the dog and kill it, though it be a bitch."

4   I have abbreviated and edited the entries. (The definition of the noun *bleyða* as "a craven" comes from the separate entry under that word.) So too Johan Fritzner, *Ordbog over det gamle norske sprog*, 4th ed. (Oslo, 1973). On *blauðr* (*bleyði*, etc.) see also Margaret Clunies Ross, "Hildr's Ring: A Problem in the *Ragnarsdrápa*, Strophes 8–12," *Mediaeval Scandinavia* 6 (1973): 75–92.

5   *Brennu-Njáls saga*, ed. Einar Ól. Sveinsson, ÍF 12 (Reykjavík, 1954), chap. 38. *Njal's Saga*, trans. Magnus Magnusson and Hermann Pálsson (Harmondsworth, Middlesex, 1960).

6   "Þá er fǫr vár helzti ill, þó at vér vinnim eigi þetta níðingsverk, ok standi menn upp ok láti hann eigi þessu ná" ("Our errand has been bad enough without our committing this *níðingsverk*; up, men, don't let him try it!").

7   The relation of the thirteenth-century written sources, especially the Icelandic sagas, to pre-conversion social history is a long-standing point of debate. I am here as elsewhere proceeding on the neotraditionalist assumption that although the written sources may exaggerate or fabricate at some points, there is a large grain of truth in their collective account. For a survey of the relevant literature up to 1964, see Theodore M. Andersson, *The Problem of Icelandic Saga Origins* (New Haven, 1964), and from that date through 1983, my "Icelandic Family Sagas (*Íslendingasögur*)," in *Old Norse-Icelandic Literature: A Critical Guide*, ed. Carol J. Clover and John Lindow (Ithaca, N.Y., 1985), pp. 239–315. On the problem in myth, see John Lindow, "Mythology and Mythography" also in Clover and Lindow, *Old Norse-Icelandic Literature*, pp. 21–67.

8   Two recent full-length studies that go some way in redressing the scant attention paid to women in the literature of the Viking Age are Birgit Sawyer's *Kvinnor och familj i det forn- och medeltida Skandinavien* (Skara, 1992) and Judith Jesch's *Women in the Viking Age* (Woodbridge, Suffolk; and Rochester, N.Y., 1991). Both contain useful bibliographies. See also Roberta Frank, "Marriage in Twelfth- and Thirteenth-Century Iceland," *Viator* 4 (1973): 473–84, and Peter G. Foote and David Wilson, *The Viking Achievement* (London, 1974), especially pp. 108–16. The fullest modern explorations of the sex-gender system (as

opposed to women's status) are Meulengracht Sørensen, *The Unmanly Man* and *Fortælling og ære: Studier i islændingesagaerne* (Århus, 1993); and Clunies Ross's suggestive studies of textual cruces in the mythic tradition in "Hildr's Ring," "An Interpretation of the Myth of Þórr's Encounter with Geirrøðr and His Daughters," in *Speculum Norroenum: Norse Studies in Memory of Gabriel Turville-Petre*, ed. Ursula Dronke et al. (Odense, 1981), pp. 370–91, and, less directly, "The Myth of Gefjon and Gylfi and Its Function in *Snorra Edda* and *Heimskringla*," *Arkiv för nordisk filologi* 93 (1978): 149–65. Because of the synoptic nature of this essay, I have restricted citations to immediately relevant scholarly sources and those recent books and articles that contain more complete and specific bibliographic information. I owe special thanks to Roberta Frank and William Ian Miller for help in need.

9   Meulengracht Sørensen writes, for example: "Fordi kønnet altid er en del af individet og fra naturens hånd er knyttet til så vigtige dele af menneskelivet, og fordi det seksuelle køn er skabt som en komplementaritet, der så umiddelbart indbyder til fortolkning som både modsætning og helhed, er kønnet måske den mest dynamiske kulturelle kategori. . . . Ikke blot i biologisk og fysisk forstand skal en mand være mand og en kvinde kvinde; han og hun skal også efterleve de idealer, som kulturen sætter for deres køn" (*Fortælling og ære*).* See also Sawyer, *Kvinnor och familj*, p. 75. [*This work was forthcoming when Clover originally wrote her essay; therefore, her citations do not contain page numbers.—Eds.]

10   *Landnámabók*, ed. Jakob Benediktsson, ÍF 1 (Reykjavík, 1968). The calculation is Judith Jesch's (*Women in the Viking Age*, pp. 81–83).

11   *Laxdæla saga*, ed. Einar Ól. Sveinsson, ÍF 5 (Reykjavík, 1934), chap. 4. The account is borne out in *Landnámabók*, in which she is called Auðr (pp. 136–46 and passim).

12   In full: "[Unnr] acted as a man because the men who should have acted on her behalf were dead. This was in accordance with the law, which conferred authority on her in this situation, but it became a literary motive too; specifically in *Laxdæla saga* in her role as the revered and authoritative head of the family, when in every respect she has taken over the conduct and social functions of the male householder and leader" (*The Unmanly Man*, p. 22). On the "transsexualization" of women for legal purposes, see the discussion of the *Baugatal* passage below.

13   So suggest place-names and, in eastern Scandinavia, runic inscriptions. See especially Birgit Sawyer, *Property and Inheritance: The Runic Evidence* (Alingsås, 1988) and Barthi Guthmundsson, *Origin of the Icelanders* (Lincoln, Nebr., 1967), pp. 36–40 (translation of *Uppruni Íslendinga* [Reykjavík, 1959]).

14   *Grænlendinga saga*, in *Eyrbyggja saga*, ed. Einar Ól. Sveinsson and Matthías Þórðarson, ÍF 4 (Reykjavík, 1935), chap. 8.

[15] Foote and Wilson, *The Viking Achievement*, pp. 110–11. For further bibliography, see my "Maiden Warriors and Other Sons," *Journal of English and Germanic Philology* 85 (1986): 35–49.

[16] Jesch, *Women in the Viking Age*, p. 161; the following pages detail the women's poetic production. On women's participation in the production of literature more generally, see Else Mundal, "Kvinner og dikting: Overgangen frå munneleg til skriftleg kultur—ei ulykke for kvinnene?" in *Förändringar i kvinnors villkor under medeltiden: Uppsatser framlagda vid ett kvinnohistoriskt symposium i Skálholt, Island, 22.-25. juni 1981*, ed. Silja Aðalsteinsdóttir and Helgi Þorláksson (Reykjavík, 1983), pp. 11–25; also Helga Kress, "The Apocalypse of a Culture: *Völuspá* and the Myth of the Sources/Sorceress in Old Icelandic Literature," in *Poetry in the Scandinavian Middle Ages*, Proceedings of the Seventh International Saga Conference (Spoleto, 1988), pp. 279–302, and "Staðlausir stafir: Um slúður sem uppsprettu frásagnar í Íslendingasögum," *Skírnir* 165 (1991): 130–56.

[17] The locus classicus is the account of al-Ghazal's embassy to what would appear to be a Scandinavian court and his encounter there with a sexually forward queen who claims, in effect, that her people practice open marriage. The historicity of the text is questioned, but as Jesch's prudent point-by-point analysis concludes, "in spite of the literary tricks, there is nothing that is totally incredible in this account and some of it fits with what we already know of Scandinavian society in the Viking Age.... If Arabists reject the story of al-Ghazal's embassy as a fiction, this cannot be because of its inherent improbability as a reflection of royal viking life in the ninth century" (*Women in the Viking Age*, pp. 92–96). The sagas famously present a number of women who arrange their sex lives to their own satisfaction, and the theme of female promiscuity and erotic aggression in the legendary sources confirms the sense that the woman with enough social power was not particularly hindered by the usual sexual constraints. The admiration, grudging or plain, extended to these women conflicts with the scholarly claim, based on the handful of *níð* insults applied to women, that promiscuity in women was the shameful equivalent of effeminacy in men (see notes 38 and 59 below).

[18] *Eyrbyggja saga*, chap. 38.

[19] William Ian Miller, *Bloodtaking and Peacemaking: Feud, Law, and Society in Saga Iceland* (Chicago, 1990), p. 351. The case in question is recounted in *Þórðar saga kakala*, in *Sturlunga saga*, ed. Jón Jóhannesson, Magnús Finnbogason, and Kristján Eldjárn, ÍF 1 (Reykjavík, 1946), chap. 8.

[20] Miller, *Bloodtaking and Peacemaking*, p. 27.

[21] Miller, *Bloodtaking and Peacemaking*, pp. 207–08.

[22] *Grágás: Islændernes lovbog i fristatens tid, udgivet efter det Kongelige Bibliotheks haandskrift*, ed.Vilhjálmur Finsen (1852; reprint Odense, 1974), 1a:142. *Grágás*

1a:1–217, trans. Andrew Dennis, Peter Foote, and Richard Perkins, *Laws of Early Iceland: Grágás* (Winnipeg, 1980). See also Miller, *Bloodtaking and Peacemaking*, p. 24.

[23] Foote and Wilson, *The Viking Achievement*, p. 110. See also Miller, *Bloodtaking and Peacemaking*, especially p. 27.

[24] William Ian Miller, "Choosing the Avenger: Some Aspects of the Bloodfeud in Medieval Iceland and England," *Law and History Review* 1 (1983): 159–204, and *Bloodtaking and Peacemaking*, pp. 211–14; and my "Hildigunnr's Lament," in *Structure and Meaning in Old Norse Literature*, ed. John Lindow, Lars Lönnroth, and Gerd Wolfgang Weber (Odense, 1986), pp. 141–83.

[25] The lively discussion of grave goods and sex is nicely summarized in Jesch, *Women in the Viking Age*, pp. 21–22, 30; see also my "The Politics of Scarcity: Notes on the Sex Ratio in Early Scandinavia," *Scandinavian Studies* 60 (1988): 147–88 (reprinted in *New Readings on Women in Old English Literature*, ed. Helen Damico and Alexandra Hennessy Olsen [Bloomington, 1990]), especially pp. 165–66.

[26] The discrepancy between women's two "statuses" (in the laws and in the narrative sources) is much discussed. See in particular Rolf Heller, *Die literarische Darstellung der Frau in den Isländersagas* (Halle, 1958); Jenny Jochens, "The Medieval Icelandic Heroine: Fact or Fiction?" *Viator* 17 (1986): 35–50, and "Consent in Marriage: Old Norse Law, Life and Literature," *Scandinavian Studies* 58 (1986): 142–76; and my "Politics of Scarcity," especially pp. 147–50 and 182.

[27] *Grágás* 1a:200–201. Translation from Dennis, Foote, and Perkins, *Laws of Early Iceland*, p. 181 (my italics).

[28] See my "Maiden Warriors and Other Sons" for the passages from the *Gulaþing* and the *Frostaþing* laws (p. 46 n. 30) and for an inventory of the relevant literary passages and a bibliography. On the politics of women's becoming "men" in early Christianity, see especially Elizabeth Castelli, "'I Will Make Mary Male': Pieties of Body and Gender Transformation of Christian Women in Late Antiquity," in *Body Guards: The Cultural Politics of Gender Ambiguity*, ed. Julia Epstein and Kristina Staub (New York, 1991), pp. 29–50.

[29] In nineteenth- and early-twentieth-century Albania (a blood feud society remarkably similar to that of saga Iceland), such surrogate sons did indeed assume the male role (taking up pants, rifles, cigars and moving in the male sphere). For a summary discussion of the theme, with relevant bibliography, see my "Maiden Warriors and Other Sons."

[30] Hallgerðr of *Njáls saga* is perhaps the only "exceptional" female figure who is more or less roundly condemned by her author, whose voice is the most consistently misogynist in Icelandic literature. See Helga Kress, "Ekki hǫfu vér

kvennaskap: Nokkrar laustengdar athuganir um karlmennsku og kvenhatur i Njálu," in *Sjötiu ritgerðir helgaðar Jakobi Benediktssyni 20. júli 1977*, ed. Einar G. Petursson and Jónas Kristjánsson (Reykjavík, 1977), pp. 293–313, and, for a more moderate view, Ursula Dronke, *The Role of Sexual Themes in "Njáls Saga,"* The Dorothea Coke Memorial Lecture in Northern Studies (London, 1980). English-speaking readers of that saga should be aware that Hallgerðr comes off rather worse in translation than she does in the original.

31 *Laxdæla saga*, chap. 4. Translation from Magnus Magnusson and Herman Pálsson, *Laxdæla Saga* (Harmondsworth, 1969). The word *afbragð*, here rendered as "paragon," means a superior, exceptional, surpassing person. Although *Landnámabók*'s more historical account of Auðr/Unnr does not comment on her character, its length and detail confirm the esteem in which she was held. *Laxdæla saga*'s interest in (and approval of) "strong" women has long been noted, and Helga Kress has argued that it demonstrates "en kvinnelig bevissthet" that may point to female authorship ("Meget samstavet må det tykkes deg," *Historisk Tidskrift* [1980], p. 279). There is no doubt that *Laxdæla*'s representation of women is extraordinary, but I would suggest that the claim of "feminine (or female) consciousness" for that text is compromised by the fact that it is their exceptional (that is, ideally masculine) qualities that qualify its women for history, as it were. What does it mean to speak of "feminine consciousness" in a world in which femininity is for all practical purposes synonymous with effeminacy? The same question may be asked of Foote and Wilson's suggestion that "Outstanding women, real or legendary, must have done something to lift the status of women in general" (*The Viking Achievement*, p. 111).

32 *Laxdæla saga*, chap. 35. See Meulengracht Sørensen, *The Unmanly Man*, p. 22.

33 Cleasby-Vigfusson derives the word from *drangr*, "jutting rock," "cliff," or "pillar." See Foote and Wilson's discussion of the term and concept in *The Viking Achievement*, pp. 105–8, 425–26, with bibliography.

34 *Njáls saga*, chap. 20, my translation. Magnússon and Pálsson have, "She was an exceptional and courageous woman, but a little harsh-natured."

35 *Njáls saga*, chap. 95, my translation. Magnússon and Pálsson have, "She was harsh-natured and ruthless; but when courage was called for, she never flinched."

36 The "masculine ideal" that underwrites such attitudes is often noted (see, for example, Meulengracht Sørensen, *The Unmanly Man*, pp. 20–22, and Sawyer, *Kvinnor och familj*, pp. 74–75). In her "Forholdet mellom born ok foreldre i det norrøne kjeldematerialet" (*Collegium medievale* 1 [1988]: 2–28), Else Mundal proposes that it is the belief in bilateral genetic inheritance (that is, the belief that the child, regardless of sex, stands to get as much of its character from the mother as from the father) that accounts for the approval the "strong" woman

seems to enjoy: her "masculinity" can be seen as an investment for unborn sons of the future (see especially p. 24). In my "Maiden Warriors and Other Sons," I speculated similarly that "the idea of latent or recessive features, physical or characterological, was undeveloped [in early Scandinavia]; inherited qualities seem to manifest themselves in some degree in every generation. The qualities that Angantýr now bestows [on his daughter Hervör] as the 'legacy of Arngrím's sons,' *afl* and *eljun* [strength and powerful spirit], are emphatically 'male' qualities. They may ultimately be 'intended' for Hervör's future sons and their sons on down the line . . . but in the meantime they must assert themselves in Hervör herself (as indeed they already have)" (p. 39). The very notion that, say, passivity can be inherited from the father and martial propensities from the mother bespeaks a far more tenuous connection between sex and gender than modern ideology would have it.

[37] On the *flyting*, see Joseph Harris, "The *Senna*: From Description to Literary Theory," *Michigan Germanic Studies* 5 (1979): 64–74; my "The Germanic Context of the Unferth Episode," *Speculum* 55 (1980): 444–68, and "Hárbárðsljóð as Generic Farce," *Scandinavian Studies* 51 (1979): 124–45; and Karen Swensen, *Performing Definitions: Two Genres of Insult in Old Norse Literature* (Columbia, S.C., 1991), which contains an especially useful bibliography.

[38] Applied to a woman, the noun *ergi* (adjective *ǫrg*) "is virtually synonymous with nymphomania, which was a characteristic as much despised in a woman as unmanliness was in a man," according to Folke Ström (*Níð, Ergi and Old Norse Moral Attitudes* [London, 1973], p. 4); for Meulengracht Sørensen, the female use means that she "is generally immodest, perverted or lecherous" (*The Unmanly Man*, pp. 18–19). The fact that charges toward women to this effect are so few and far between would seem to suggest that the female use is a secondary formation and a rather unstable one at that. Nor, although space does not permit me to make a full argument here, am I convinced that the *ǫrg* female is as fundamentally different from the *argr* male as these scholars suggest; again I suspect a modern contamination (see note 17 above).

[39] For a detailed account of these and other legal references, see Bo Almqvist, *Norrön niddiktning: Traditionshistoriska studier i versmagi*, 2 vols. (Uppsala, 1965–74), especially pp. 38–68. See also Kari Ellen Gade, "Homosexuality and the Rape of Males in Old Norse Law and Literature," *Scandinavian Studies* 58 (1986): 124–41. On *níð* generally, see (in addition to Meulengracht Sørensen, *The Unmanly Man* and Almqvist, *Norrön niddiktning*) Ström, *Níð, Ergi, and Old Norse Moral Attitudes*; Erik Noreen, "Om niddiktning" in his "Studier i fornvästnordisk diktning II," in *Uppsala Universitets årsskrift: Filosofi, språkvetenskap och historiska vetenskaper* 44 (1922): 37–65; and Joaquín Martínez Pizarro, "Studies

on the Function and Context of the *Senna* in Early Germanic Narrative," Ph.D. dissertation, Harvard University, 1976.

[40] *Norges gamle love indtil 1387*, ed. R. Keyser, P. A. Munch, G. Storm, and E. Herzberg (Christiania, 1846), 1:57. Translations from the laws pertaining to *níð* are adapted from Meulengracht Sørensen's *The Unmanly Man*, pp. 14–32.

[41] *Tréníð* is the plastic equivalent of *tunguníð* (tongue *níð*). The classic example is the carved effigy in *Gísla saga* of one man sodomized by another (chap. 2), but the term may also refer to a pole of the sort described in *Egils saga Skallagrímssonar*, ed. Sigurður Nordal, ÍF 2 (Reykjavík, 1933), chap. 57. For a fuller discussion, see Meulengracht Sørensen, *The Unmanly Man*, especially pp. 51–61; Ström, *Níð, Ergi, and Old Norse Moral Attitudes*, pp. 10–14; and Almqvist, *Norrön niddiktning*, passim.

[42] *Norges gamle love*, 1:70.

[43] *Grágás (Staðarhólsbók)*, 2a:392.

[44] *Njáls saga*, chap. 123. Meulengracht Sørensen notes, "Nobody has suspected Flosi of being homosexual. The charge is symbolic" (*The Unmanly Man*, p. 20). Virtually the same insult occurs in two other sources (*Þorsteins saga Síðu-Hallssonar* and *Króka-Refs saga*).

[45] Strophe 38, in *Edda: Die Lieder des Codex Regius nebst verwandten Denkmälern*, 1: *Text*, ed. Gustav Neckel, 5th ed., rev. Hans Kuhn (Heidelberg, 1983).

[46] On this pattern in cultures present and past, and on the distinction between person and act, there is an abundant literature. See especially David M. Halperin, "One Hundred Years of Homosexuality," in *One Hundred Years of Homosexuality and Other Essays on Greek Love* (New York, 1989), especially the bibliography on p. 159 n. 21, and p. 162 n. 52; and, for another perspective (and for the most up-to-date bibliography on the discussion), David J. Cohen, *Law, Sexuality, and Society: The Enforcement of Morals in Classical Athens* (Cambridge, Eng., 1991), especially chap. 7, "Law, Social Control, and Homosexuality in Classical Athens." Mention should be made, on the Norse side, of the passage in chap. 22 of *Bjarnar saga Hítdœlakappa* (ed. Sigurður Nordal and Guðni Jónsson, in *Borgfirðinga saga*, ÍF 3 [Reykjavík, 1938]), which suggests that the position of the aggressor may have been rather more compromised than tradition would have it.

[47] Ström, *Níð, Ergi, and Old Norse Moral Attitudes*, p. 17.

[48] Meulengracht Sørensen, *The Unmanly Man*, pp. 19–20.

[49] The first full-fledged treatment of the subject was an anonymous essay entitled "Spuren von Konträrsexualität bei den alten Skandinaviern," in *Jahrbuch für sexuelle Zwischenstufen unter besonderer Berücksichtigung der Homosexualität* 4 (Leipzig, 1902), pp. 244–63.

411

50 Meulengracht Sørensen, following T. Vanggaard (*Phallos* [Copenhagen, 1969], translated by the author as *Phallos: A Symbol and Its History in the Male World* [London, 1972]), sees in "phallic aggression" the organizing principle of the early Scandinavian sex-gender system (*The Unmanly Man*, especially pp. 27–28).

51 In *Fornaldar sögur Norðurlanda 2*, ed. Guðni Jónsson (Reykjavík, 1959).

52 Horse genitalia, both male and female, loom large in the obscene literature of Old Norse, and the pattern is presumably Germanic. See especially Martínez Pizarro, "Studies on the Function and Context of the *Senna* in Early Germanic Narrative." The sense of *skauð* is echoed in the noun *hrukka* ("fold" or "wrinkle," referring also to the female genital), related to the verb *hrøkkva* ("fall back, recoil, retreat, cringe"); see Zoe Borovsky, "Male Fears, Female Threats: Giant Women in Old Norse-Icelandic Literature," paper delivered at the annual meeting of the Society for the Advancement of Scandinavian Study, May, 1991. See also Torild W. Arnoldson, *Parts of the Body in Older Germanic and Scandinavian* (1915; reprint New York, 1971), p. 175, and Meulengracht Sørensen, *The Unmanly Man*, esp. pp. 58–59.

53 Thomas Laqueur, *Making Sex: Body and Gender from the Greeks to Freud* (Cambridge, Eng., 1990).

54 Laqueur, *Making Sex*, p. 26. More particularly, penis and vagina are construed as one and the same organ; if the former happens to extrude and the latter to intrude (in an inside-out and upward-extending fashion), they are physiologically identical, and the same words did for both. Likewise testes (the male ones outside and the female ones inside, again with the same words doing for both), and so too genital fluids (menstrual and seminal emissions being cooler and hotter versions of the same matter).

55 On the correspondence, see Laqueur, *Making Sex*, pp. 159 and 270 n. 60. According to psychoanalysis, the one-sex model is alive and well in the unconscious—in the form, for example, of penis envy on the part of females and, on the part of males, fantasies of anal intercourse, pregnancy, and birth. In my book *Men, Women, and Chain Saws: Gender in the Modern Horror Film* (Princeton, 1992), I have argued that the one-sex model is also alive and well in popular culture; it is in any case an obvious feature of horror movies, which commonly turn explicitly or implicitly on the idea that males and females are essentially the same, genitally and otherwise.

56 On the conflation of vagina and (male) anus, see Clunies Ross, "Hildr's Ring," and for a discussion of the equivalence in the modern context, see Leo Bersani, "Is the Rectum a Grave?" *October* 43 (1989): 194–222. For lexical listings, see Arnoldson's *Parts of the Body in Older Germanic and Scandinavian* and William Denny Baskett's *Parts of the Body in the Later Germanic Dialects* (Chicago, 1920).

Unavailable to me is the unpublished manuscript "Verba Islandica obscaena," by Ólafur Davíðsson (Reykjavík, Landsbókasafn Íslands, MS 1204, 8vo).

[57] Laqueur, *Making Sex*, pp. 122–34 and passim.

[58] For example: *Níð* "did not require that women or female activities were held in contempt as such, of course, no more than was a woman's sexual role or her maternal capacity. The female role was ignominious when it was assigned to a man" (Meulengracht Sørensen, *The Unmanly Man*, p. 24).

[59] Compare with Meulengracht Sørensen's claim (in the chapter entitled "Mænds og kvinders ære" in *Fortælling og ære*) that men's and women's honor systems were essentially different. His construction proceeds to a considerable extent from the evidence of *níð* insults, which seem to bespeak a double standard (men are accused of being women, women of being promiscuous). As I have suggested above, a reading of *níð* in context (both the context of other insults and the context of praise- and blameworthy deeds in general) leads to a rather different conclusion—a conclusion buttressed by the paucity and apparent instability of references to female *níð* (see also notes 17 and 38 above). The "one-sex" argument in this and the preceding sections was presented in short form in my review of Meulengracht Sørensen's *Norrønt nid* in the *Journal of English and Germanic Philology* (1982): 398–400.

[60] Cleasby-Vigfusson, entry under *úmagi*. Related terms (also deriving from *mega* "to have strength to do, avail") are *úmeginn* "impotent," *úmegin* "unmight, a swoon," *úmætr* "worthless, invalid," and *úmætta* "to lose strength, faint away"— as opposed, on the positive side, to terms like *megin, megn* "strong, mighty."

[61] The equation of women and old men is also evident in the norms governing the appropriateness of the vengeance target in feud. "The underlying idea," writes Miller, "is that people not socially privileged to bear arms were excused from having arms brought to bear on them" (*Bloodtaking and Peacemaking*, p. 207).

[62] See especially John J. Winkler, "Laying down the Law: The Oversight of Men's Sexual Behavior in Classical Athens," in his *Constraints of Desire: The Anthropology of Sex and Gender in Ancient Greece* (New York, 1990). "The logic of a zero-sum calculus underlies many of the most characteristic predicates and formulae that were applied to issues of sex and gender," Winkler writes. "Thus, not to display bravery (*andreia*, literally 'manliness') lays a man open to symbolic demotion from the ranks of the brave/manly to the opposite class of women" (p. 47).

[63] Winkler, *The Constraints of Desire*, p. 50.

[64] For example, Egill, mocked and pushed around by women in his old age (*Egils saga*, chap. 85); Þorkell, tongue-lashed into submission by his wife Ásgerðr (*Gísla saga Súrssonar*, chap. 9); Þórðr Ingunnarson, assaulted in bed by his angry,

pants-wearing former wife with a short sword—a gesture loaded with sexual meaning and one that had permanent effect (*Laxdæla saga*, chap. 35); and, of course, any number of heroes' battles with giantesses and warrior women in the *fornaldarsögur* and related traditions. Along different but not unrelated lines, Clunies Ross notes the special ability of women in the mythological sources to humiliate men. The passages she analyzes "reveal the conviction that a dominant woman was more to be feared than a man, for she was able to strengthen herself magically in order to usurp male roles and reduce the men in her power to physical and mental debility, to make them *ragr*. . . . The insult of showing the 'ring' to Hǫgni is a verbal equivalent to Hildr's destructive and debilitating powers, for it accuses him of weakness and effeminacy. It is particularly vicious that, having adopted a masculine role herself, she should accuse her own father of having lost his manhood" ("Hildr's Ring," p. 92).

[65] For a new account of emotional expression in Norse literature, see William Ian Miller, *Humiliation and Other Essays in Social Discomfort* (Ithaca, N.Y., 1993). On the social place of aging men, see Miller, *Bloodtaking and Peacemaking*, pp. 207–10.

[66] For a discussion of female lamenting and its role in feud, see my "Hildigunnr's Lament," with notes.

[67] Common features include (in addition to the characteristic mix of lament and revenge) the theme of the withering family line and, in that connection, the use of the extremely rare word *þáttr* (in the meaning "strand," as of a rope); the elegiac conceit of a tree as an image of human growth and ruin; the "chain-of-woes" construction; the self-pitying woe-is-me tone; the ecstatic "now I die" conclusion; and the final authorial remarks on the cathartic effects of lamenting. See Ursula Dronke, *The Poetic Edda, 1: Heroic Poems* (Oxford, 1969), pp. 183–89, and my "Hildigunnr's Lament," pp. 153–62. The "difference" of *Sonatorrek* in the context of Egill's other poetry is often noted. E. O. G. Turville-Petre, for example, writes that the poem "gives a clear insight into the mind of Egill in his advancing years, showing him as an affectionate, sensitive, lonely man, and not the ruffianly bully which he sometimes appears to be in the Saga" (*Scaldic Poetry* (Oxford, 1976], p. 24).

[68] Worth remembering in this connection is the unnamed old man to whom the *Beowulf* poet compares the old king Hrethel, father of a fratricide (lines 2441–65). Overcome by grief, and unable to take revenge, old Hrethel can do no more than the "old man" who "goes to his bed, sings his cares over (*sorh-leoð*, 'sorrow song'), alone, for the other" and then dies. Again we seem to have a male whose lamentation is precisely the effect of disabled masculinity; the other two funeral-lamenters in *Beowulf* are both women (lines 1117–18 and 3150–55). Text and

414

translation from Howell D. Chickering, Jr., *"Beowulf": A Dual-Language Edition* (Garden City, N.Y., 1977). For an especially useful and bibliographically detailed discussion of elegy and death lament (especially reflexive) in the Germanic tradition, see Joseph Harris, "Elegy in Old English and Old Norse: A Problem in Literary History," in *The Vikings*, ed. Robert T. Farrell (London, 1982), pp. 157–64, as well as his article "Beowulf's Last Words," *Speculum* 67 (1992): 1–32.

69 *Hávarðar saga Ísfirðings*, ed. Björn K. Þórólfsson and Guðni Jónsson, ÍF 6 (Reykjavík, 1943), chap. 5.

70 See Miller, "Choosing the Avenger" and *Bloodtaking and Peacemaking*, pp. 212–14. The synonyms *hvetja* and *eggja* mean "whet" in both senses (to sharpen or put an edge on a blade, and to goad or egg on a person).

71 See my "Germanic Context of the Unferth Episode," especially pp. 451–52, for a more complete list and source references.

72 "Vals hefk vǫǫfur helsis; / váfallr em ek skalla; / blautr erum bergis fótar / borr, eo hlust es þorrin" (*Egils saga*, chap. 85).

73 See Noreen, "Studier i fornvästnordisk diktning II," pp. 35–36; and *Egils saga*, p. 294, note on stanza 58. Roberta Frank points out that the duplicitous reading has medieval authority in the "Third Grammatical Treatise" of Óláfr hvítaskáld, who observes that Egill's *bergis fótar borr* works both as a penis kenning and a tongue kenning (*Old Norse Court Poetry: The Dróttkvætt Stanza* [Ithaca, N.Y., 1978], p. 162). The author of the "head" interpretation of *bergifótr* is, of course, Finnur Jónsson, who thought it "en af Egils dristige kenningar" (*Lexicon poeticum* [1931; reprint Copenhagen, 1966]). For other examples of such wordplay, see Kari Ellen Gade, "Penile Puns: Personal Names and Phallic Symbols in Skaldic Poetry," *Essays in Medieval Studies: Proceedings of the Illinois Medieval Association* 6 (1989): 57–67.

74 "Vápn þat er stendr milli fóta manna heitir suerð" ("That weapon which stands between a man's legs is called a sword"), Snorri declares (*Snorra-Edda*, ed. Rasmus Rask [Stockholm, 1818], p. 232, line 19). For literary examples and a discussion of the sword/penis figure, see Meulengracht Sørensen, *The Unmanly Man*, pp. 45–78, and Clunies Ross, "Hildr's Ring." As for the tongue: "Tvnga er opt kavllvð sverþ mals e(ða) mvnz" ("Tongue is often called sword of speech or of mouth," *Edda Snorra Sturlusonar*, p. 191). Consider, for example, *góma sverð* ("sword of the gums") and *orðvápn* ("word-weapon"); see Rudolf Meissner, *Die Kenningar der Skalden: Ein Beitrag zur skaldischen Poetik* (1921; reprint Hildesheim, 1984), pp. 133–34.

75 Text and translation from Turville-Petre, *Scaldic Poetry*, pp. 28–29.

76 *Saga Heiðreks ins vitra/The Saga of King Heiðrek the Wise*, trans. and ed. Christopher Tolkien (London, 1960), p. 10.

77 *Hrafnkels saga*, in *Austfirðinga sǫgur*, ed. Jón Jóhannesson, ÍF 11 (Reykjavík, 1950), chap. 8. The word *ergisk* is the middle-voice verbal form of the adjective *argr* ("to become *argr*"). The word *hverr*, "everyone," is a masculine pronoun usable for a male entity or for the universal person.

78 E. V. Gordon, *An Introduction to Old Norse*, 2nd ed., rev. A.R. Taylor (Oxford, 1957), p. 342 (under *ergjask*); and Hermann Pálsson, trans., *Hrafnkel's Saga and Other Stories* (Harmondsworth, Middlesex, 1971), chap. 17.

79 That the older system did not die at once, but lived in odd ways well into the Christian era, is suggested by, for example, the anomalous practice of priest marriage in Iceland, a practice that suggests the tenacity not only of the clan system but also of certain pre-Christian notions of masculinity. Miller writes, "Sexuality and marriage were a part of the world of manly honor and no one thought to mention that divinity and dalliance need be sundered until the episcopate of Thorlak Thorhallson (1178–93). Thorlak zealously attempted to enforce ecclesiastical strictures dealing with sexual practices, but even he did not tackle clerical celibacy, confining himself instead to separating priests and spouses who had married within the prohibited degrees . . . or who kept concubines in addition to their wives" (*Bloodtaking and Peacemaking*, pp. 37–38; see also his bibliographic references). Consider, too, such historical details as the one recorded in *Jóns saga helga* to the effect that the cathedral school at Hólar in the year 1110 saw fit not only to admit a girl, one Ingunn, but to permit her to tutor her fellow pupils in Latin (*Jóns saga helga*, chap. 27, in *Byskupa sögur*, ed. Guðni Jónsson, 2nd ed. [Akureyri, 1953], 2:43, p. 153.

80 Especially important in this connection is the work of Clunies Ross, especially "An Interpretation of the Myth of Þórr's Encounter with Geirrøðr and His Daughters." See also Borovsky, "Male Fears, Female Threats." That the bodies in question are female (e.g., menstruating giantesses) is clear. What is less clear is what femaleness means in a world in which (at least in the learned tradition) the female body and its fluids were regarded as deformations of male ones (e.g., in which menstrual fluid was construed as cooled-down semen); see Laqueur, *Making Sex*, especially pp. 35–43.

MEN AND *BEOWULF*

CLARE A. LEES

He is a man, and that for him and many is sufficient tragedy.
　　　　　—J. R. R. Tolkien, "*Beowulf:* The Monsters and the Critics"[1]

We certainly do not need feminist theory to tell us that Beowulf *is a profoundly masculine poem.*
　　　　　—Gillian R. Overing, *Language, Sign and Gender in "Beowulf"*[2]

eowulf is an Anglo-Saxon poem about men—male heroes, warriors, kings—and yet the vision and limits of this world as a masculine one have rarely been examined. From the perspective of either feminist or nonfeminist criticism, the question of what it means to call the poem masculine, or its hero male, seems too obvious to merit attention. The foregoing comments from J. R. R. Tolkien and Gillian R. Overing invite assent, not investigation. The masculinity of *Beowulf*, in other words, forms a point of departure—a beginning—that is rarely factored into our interpretations.[3] I wish to turn our critical gaze back onto this beginning and pose two related questions: First, how does *Beowulf* criticism use masculinity as a beginning for interpretation? And second, in what ways can the poem's masculinity be understood?

From *Medieval Masculinities: Regarding Men in the Middle Ages*, ed. Clare A. Lees (Minneapolis, 1994), pp. 129–48.

The insight that informs my own perspective is one fundamental to theories of gender: that the categories of "man," "maleness," and "masculinity" need to be deconstructed in ways similar to those of "woman," "female," and "femininity" (even "feminist"). Gender studies addresses the demystification of the social, cultural, and historical relations between the sexes in order to lay bare the ideological workings that underpin the terms *man* and *woman* at any given historical moment. Neither category exists outside history or culture as a timeless universal, and both are subject to continual redefinition and reinterpretation. Theories of gender, in tandem with much recent materialist criticism, lead me to examine the assumptions of a view that is presented as natural and consensual, and to question whether a particular ideology might be operating instead.[4] In the case of *Beowulf*, we can investigate its so-called self-evident masculinity by inquiring whether "masculinism," as Arthur Brittan usefully puts it, that is to say the "ideology of male power that justifies and naturalizes male domination," has created this effect of self-evidence in its critical reception.[5]

I begin this project of demystification in relation to *Beowulf* and its critical reception by examining in some detail J. R. R. Tolkien's "*Beowulf*: The Monsters and the Critics." First published in 1936, Tolkien's essay remains justifiably influential, and offers an example of how ideologies of masculinism empower and promote a New Critical view of the poem. By contrast, two more recent works by James W. Earl and by Gillian R. Overing propose radically different perspectives. Earl's "*Beowulf* and the Origins of Civilization" demonstrates how psychoanalytic criticism can offer a strong model of readerly identification with the poem, one that appears to carry with it the promise that patriarchy—like masculinism—will remain hegemonic.[6] Overing's *Language, Sign, and Gender in "Beowulf,"* on the other hand, suggestively exposes masculine desire in the poem from the perspective of a feminist reader, and invites, for me at least, a reexamination of how patriarchy and masculinity operate in the internal thematics of the poem itself. Both arguments help me to suggest how the concepts of masculinity and patriarchy inform our understanding of *Beowulf* in the second part of this essay.

These issues of masculinity and patriarchy differ from those addressed by other recent feminist criticism, either on the poem or on Old English literature in general. Work by, for example, Jane Chance or Helen Damico, primarily addresses text-internal issues and is prompted by a desire to reclaim and map out roles for the female in the poem in view of the anti-feminist tradition of much of its critical reception.[7] One limiting feature of this kind of feminist approach is that emphasis on the female figures—vital though it is as an intervention in critical writing on *Beowulf*—has left unexplored and, in some cases, reified the male figures. The trap, of course, is essentialism—one of the targets of the feminist agenda. While building on such feminist work, my own differs in two respects. First, I see the critical reception of the poem as part of the continuing history of its meaning; second, I argue that gender—as one mediating element in this history—implies a reexamination of the interplay between masculine *and* feminine issues, both internal and external to the poem.[8] The poem's readers, after all, are men and women, however much they present themselves as disinterested, objective, or ungendered.

TOLKIEN'S NEW CRITICAL READER

But in the centre we have an heroic figure of enlarged proportions.
J. R. R.Tolkien, "*Beowulf*: The Monsters and the Critics"[9]

In a brilliant riposte to an earlier generation of critics such as W. P. Ker, who viewed *Beowulf* as fundamentally flawed, Tolkien's "*Beowulf*: The Monsters and the Critics" defends the poem's integrity on three fronts: aesthetically, structurally, and thematically. The essay is grounded on, and framed by, an assertion of the poem's right to be read as poetry rather than as poetic historical document: this is, in other words, an early and important example of New Criticism in Anglo-Saxon studies.[10] Tolkien was fully aware of his intervention in mainstream *Beowulfiana*, and prefaces his analysis with a brief apologia, the real force of which is to demonstrate that the poem still awaits its critic: "*Beowulf* has been used as a quarry of fact and fancy far more assiduously than it has been studied as a work of art" (Tolkien, p. 5).

It is clear both from the title of Tolkien's article, with its delightful ambiguity, and from these prefatory remarks that Tolkien offers himself as the poem's (New) literary critic. Appropriately enough, then, his own account of the poem's reception is cast not simply in terms of a brief historical survey (6–14), but also metaphorically or, as Tolkien puts it, "allegorically":

> As it set out upon its adventures among the modern scholars, *Beowulf* was christened by Wanley Poesis—*Poeseos Anglo-Saxonicæ egregium exemplum*. But the fairy godmother later invited to superintend its fortunes was Historia. And she brought with her Philologia, Mythologia, Archaeologia, and Laographia. Excellent ladies. But where was the child's name-sake? Poesis was usually forgotten; occasionally admitted by a side-door; sometimes dismissed

upon the door-step. "*The Beowulf*," they said, "is hardly an affair of yours, and not in any case a protégé that you could be proud of. It is a historical document. Only as such does it interest the superior culture of today." (p. 6)

This extended metaphor is followed by a second that reinterprets the first and prefaces Tolkien's own reading of the poem:

> A man inherited a field in which was an accumulation of old stone, part of an older hall. Of the old stone some had already been used in building the house in which he actually lived, not far from the old house of his fathers. Of the rest he took some and built a tower. But his friends coming perceived at once (without troubling to climb the steps) that these stones had formerly belonged to a more ancient building. So they pushed the tower over, with no little labour, in order to look for hidden carvings and inscriptions, or to discover whence the man's distant forefathers had obtained their building material. Some suspecting a deposit of coal under the soil began to dig for it, and forgot even the stones. They all said: "This tower is most interesting." But they also said (after pushing it over): "What a muddle it is in!" And even the man's own descendants, who might have been expected to consider what he had been about, were heard to murmur: "He is such an odd fellow! Imagine his using these old stones just to build a nonsensical tower! Why did he not restore the old house? He had no sense of proportion." But from the top of that tower the man had been able to look out upon the sea. (pp. 7–8)

The difference between these two narratives registers Tolkien's distance from prevailing critical approaches as well as his desire to forge an alternative reading. Unlike earlier critics, who read *Beowulf* as history and respond to it with historical analysis, Tolkien reads the poem as art and prefaces his response to this artistry with his own narratives. Both merit careful attention for the ways in which gender is deployed by this "new" critic.

In the first, Tolkien recasts the earlier critical tradition (what we might now call the philological school of Anglo-Saxon studies) as symbolically feminine by treading the well-worn path of personification allegory. The kernel of the allegory is self-evident: the poem has been ill served by its historical critics. But look again. Humfrey Wanley, eminent early Anglo-Saxonist, with the full weight of paternal authority as godfather to *Beowulf* and cataloger of the manuscript, recognizes the document as poetry (*Poesis*). On the other hand, the fairy godmother (or is it wicked step-mother?) *Historia*, supported by her grammatically feminine relatives (philology, myth, archaeology, and folklore), forgets, dismisses, and even abandons her adopted child, poetry. Godfather and godmother play asymmetric, nurturing roles to the orphaned and authorless poem, and it is clear where Tolkien's sympathies lie: the godfather (Wanley) empowers *Beowulf* as poetry; the godmother (*Historia*) disables it.

Tolkien rewrites the first allegory in his second and modifies this binarism by rejecting—rather than simply devaluing—the symbolically feminine and the maternal. There are no godmothers here, only men, fathers, forefathers, descendants, and friends interwoven through time in a genealogy of conflict and misunderstanding. This second narrative restores to the poem its filial critic and its fatherly author—both of whom, though criticized for their lack of proportion, are able to look out upon the sea, unified in one perspective. In fact, critic and author come perilously close to being the same figure: the "man" in the allegory can be read as both poet and critic; the tower as both poem and critical interpretation, capable of construction, destruction, and reconstruction. Poet and critic use the tower to empower their transcendental gaze: they look out *upon* the sea, not *at* the object of their construction, the tower/poem/interpretation. No longer the abandoned child of the first allegory, the poem is now a collection of old stones, perhaps ultimately a barrow, certainly a house or hall (which mirrors Heorot), and, above all, a tower. Like the poet, critics are builders, excavators, and miners. In short, Tolkien's condemnatory view of *Beowulf* as a "quarry of fact and fancy" is redeployed to symbolize the poem as a man-made artifact in which lived experience is generated (the house/hall/tower). This view of the poem as artifact or object is, of course, one of the founding premises of New Criticism and resurfaces time and again in Tolkien's subsequent interpretation.

Only in relation to the first allegory can the second be interpreted as symbolically masculine. Tolkien works through the feminine—the older school of philology—in order to erect his own interpretation. That interpretation, which is allied with the poet's own vision by the figure of the tower (the poem, the masculine, the Phallus), looks out upon the sea (the Other, the feminine, the past). Historical criticism, in Tolkien's eyes, fails at least in part for reasons associated with gender: both the "feminine" and the "masculine" allegory have the potential to destroy, or rather deconstruct, the poem. At the same time, and in both allegories, Tolkien casts the poem's "true" defenders as male (Wanley, the poet, and the critic). The second allegory offers Tolkien a means of reconstructing the poem's aesthetics, replacing philological criticism with the New Critical universality of the transcendental gaze. The masculinism of this second allegory, in other words, offers a beginning for literary criticism.

The structures of gender are more complex, therefore, than the binarism female/male suggests, for it is only the second allegory that carries with it the promise of masculinism—creating both an artifact and a criticism to transcend gender. Small wonder that Tolkien's own reading of *Beowulf* expels the female even more dramatically than does the poem. As is well known, Tolkien's monsters are Grendel (the monstrous son) and the dragon; Grendel's mother and other female characters are not mentioned.

"Man" in Tolkien's essay emerges as the liberal humanist construct of the universal male; "we," the unifying perspective of masculinism. Read in the light of these two allegories, Tolkien's comment on the hero Beowulf, "He is a man, and that for him and many is sufficient tragedy" (p. 18), takes on quite a different light. Gender, or more precisely the unifying discourse of masculinism, mediates between the critic's metacritical commentary (the two allegories) and his practice of criticism, his reading of the text. In the remainder of "The Monsters and the Critics," Tolkien sets out to rebuild the poem, and finally, poem, poet, and reader are united in a climactic defense of aesthetics. *Beowulf*, built from the "masonry" of its lines (p. 30), transcends its historical moment as "we" look on: "At the beginning, and during its process, and most of all at the end, we look down as if from a visionary height upon the house of man in the valley of the world" (p. 33). In such a reading, the poem, the poet, and the critic transcend time, conquering it as does the hero, Beowulf, at the moment of his death.

Part of Tolkien's critical project is to reconceptualize the significance of Beowulf to demonstrate that he is indeed a hero worthy of a place in the pantheon of the heroes of classical epic, even if (especially if) he fights monsters. There is no gainsaying that, at least in conventional literary critical terms and certainly in Tolkien's time, epic heroes are men, and his analysis demonstrates how masculinity, maleness, becomes an index of humanity. In fact, Tolkien concentrates on the hero's humanity—as man—and the universality of his experience as a shared and representative focus for all readers—or men.[11] Beowulf, for Tolkien, is a man faced with the inevitable consequences of his knowledge "that man, each man and all men, and all their works shall die" (23). In such a reading, the monsters are a very real presence that signifies the limits of the male world: Beowulf's encounters with Grendel and the dragon thematize the hero's will to death, or his struggle against "Time" (p. 18). The poem's power to generate affect is thus inextricably linked to the temporal humanity of the hero or, in gender terms, his masculinity: "that for him and many is sufficient tragedy" (p. 18).

Beowulf's humanity, moreover, becomes a trope for the vexed question of structure: the two halves of the poem are read metonymically as the rise and fall of one man's life. In the process, Beowulf the man (fighting Grendel) becomes Beowulf the hero (fighting the dragon). Enter the dragon, enter the hero: or, as Tolkien puts it "that first moment, which often comes in great lives, when men look up in surprise and see that a hero has *unawares* leaped forth" (p. 32; emphasis added). This is the classic matrix from which many subsequent interpretations of *Beowulf*—the *great* poem—and Beowulf—the man and hero—emerge. But this transformation of Beowulf from man to hero simultaneously provokes a response in Tolkien the reader, who moves from identification to admiration. There is little the critic can do once this stage has been reached: Tolkien's admiration for "an heroic figure of enlarged proportions" (p. 31), which echoes the laudatory final lines of the poem, signifies distance and closure, and "The Monsters and the Critics" ends shortly after.[12] But, judging from the lengthy appendices attached to the essay, Tolkien's resolution was far from satisfactory; yet the article itself heralded a new generation of critics, all anxious to assign a role to Beowulf (the heroic warrior, the young man, the wise/old/proud king), to enlarge, as it were, Tolkien's preliminary analysis.

What does it mean to call Beowulf a man? Tolkien does not explicitly pose this question (nor should we expect him to—this essay is very much a product of its time), but nevertheless the answer is inextricably linked to the project of New Criticism: Beowulf is a representative of all men and is every man's hero. In the process of analysis, masculinity is pressed into the service of masculinism, and the feminine is expelled from the unified gaze, the shared perspectives of poet, hero, and reader. To put it another way, Tolkien's Beowulf is not simply a man. I do not wish to be too critical of the fact that Tolkien does not address questions of gender; my reinterpretation of Tolkien's essay from just such a perspective, however, reveals the extent to which his argument rests on the untheorized assumption that all his readers will read, as he does, as "men." [13]

GENDER AND INTERPRETATION

By contrast, James W. Earl's "*Beowulf* and the Origins of Civilization" offers a more self-conscious model for reading that examines the poem's patriarchy in psychoanalytic terms. Patriarchy here becomes the key to understanding the poem's, and the hero's, unique power to generate ambivalence in the poem and in the reader. As a result, Earl addresses the very issues that remain implicit and unfocused in Tolkien's essay. To examine the relationship between the hero and the reader in terms of identification, Earl reads Tacitus's well-known comment on the two heroic codes of warrior society ("The lord fights for victory, the companions for the lord"; cited by Earl, p. 81) from the stance of a creative Freudian psychoanalysis. Earl adapts Freud's theory of the group to explicate how the poem enforces a radically authoritarian patriarchy in its readers by splitting identification between Beowulf as heroic ideal or superego and Wiglaf (the loyal retainer) as brother of the group or *comitatus*. The fact that Tolkien admires or idealizes the hero and thereby defends him from criticism is thus precisely the point: "The heroic ideal, then, is not simply a model of excellence or virtue to be imitated but is also a forbidden and unattainable desire, highly defended against, sharply distinguished from the ego itself and highly critical of it" (Earl, p. 83). As ideal, the hero is defended from the reader's criticism in much the same way as Tolkien's hero "unawares leaped forth" (Tolkien, p. 32).

The ambivalence felt by readers is a direct result of their admiration of the hero, "the idealization of the hero, which frees him from criticism, is accompanied by self-criticism among his followers—and the audience" (Earl, p. 83). The catch, of course, is that the poem's ability to continue to produce these ambivalent effects demands that the reader uncritically occupy a subject position *within patriarchy*. As a symbol of the superego, Beowulf is, of course, the Father. Earl's theory is thus defended more sharply than Tolkien's against the perspective of an Other reader (female or feminist, e.g.), who may have a different investment in patriarchy. As with Tolkien, the process by which Earl arrives at this conclusion has considerable implications for our understanding of the interrelationship of gender and interpretation. In place of Tolkien's two allegories, Earl offers two dreams, both of which use female figures. The (female) sphinx in the first dream symbolizes the riddle of *Beowulf* (read as the riddle of Oedipus), which occupies the position of the superego (like Beowulf in the latter part of the poem) and silently analyzes its readers as they seek to analyze it.[14] In the second dream, the poem itself is a fabulous doll:

> I dreamed about a little girl who had a fascinating, unusual doll, every part of which—arms, legs, head, torso—seemed to be made from other dolls, all of different colors and proportions. I knew where it had come from:

the little girl's brother had collected all the old, broken dolls he could find around the neighborhood, and he had loaded them into his red wagon, and pulled them home behind his bicycle; then he had made a single doll out of all their parts and had given it to his sister. Far from thinking it was junk, she thought it was beautiful, and loved it—first of all because it was unlike any other doll, and yet like them all; also because it was so interesting, and also because her brother had made it for her, and because he had made it so well. (Earl, pp. 73–74)

This dream is brilliantly analyzed by Earl himself, who, however, never identifies the doll—or poem—as female, yet there are some suggestive hints: in the splitting identifications of the dream, Earl as reader is female as well as male ("Insofar as I am a reader of *Beowulf* I identify with the girl"; p. 74), and the reader to whom the gift of the doll is made is also identified as female ("You are the sister I am trying to please"; p. 74) I freely admit that this is a somewhat partial view of Earl's own analysis of his over-determined dream (which also concentrates on his identification with the poet), but it heuristically foregrounds the problem of gender in his two dreams. In both, the poem is read as symbolically female. Earl explains the second dream as follows:

The dream also brings rather delicate problems of gender to consciousness. *Beowulf* is a markedly antifeminist poem, and making it a gift to the little girl is my attempt at compensation, though necessarily condescending: she is still being strongly marginalized, after all. I do not see any way around that, since the poem so strongly marginalizes the female reader already. My simultaneous identification with her, however, indicates my deep ambivalence about the *patriarchal* project of the poem and the *patriarchal* project of its criticism (not to mention the *patriarchal* structures of professional life, teaching, and marriage). Beyond that, moreover, the bond of love between her and her brother, both of whom I identify with strongly, though in different ways, indicates how far from such ideological criticism my psychoanalytic responses to the poem really are. (pp. 74–75; emphasis added)

Who is marginalizing the female here: Earl the dreamer or Earl the analyst? The dream itself focuses on the female—the little girl and the beautiful doll—as much as it does on her brother, whereas the analysis admits to, and attempts to compensate for, a desire to marginalize her. The deep divide between Earl's psychoanalytic response to the patriarchal structures of the poem and his resistance to the ideology of patriarchy as an institution of gender relations (note the number of times "patriarchal" is repeated in the above quotation) leads me to suggest that what is still being avoided is gender. Indeed, his essay skirts the "delicate problems of gender" posed by the poem while simultaneously promoting the Law of the Father. The result is that for Earl, reading as one man, patriarchy and its psychic structures are presented as hegemonic, and gender highly defended against: "I do not see any way around that," Earl says (p. 74).

At the heart of Earl's analysis lies a vital contribution to *Beowulf* criticism, namely, the role of identification and transference in eliciting and constructing interpretation. Whether or not the poem marginalizes the female reader (as opposed to the evident marginalization of women *in* the poem), many women do read it, and Earl's analysis of his own dreams points to an understanding of identification that can include us. It is obvious enough to suggest that women readers may identify differently with the poem and its hero—Freud's insistence on primary bisexuality, for example, allows for a broad range of oedipal conflicts, resolutions, and, hence, identifications across the sexes. The poem, in other words, may attempt to enforce an authoritarian patriarchy upon its readers, male or female, but there is no guarantee it will succeed as Earl suggests. In spite of this, patriarchy here assumes the same conceptual status that liberal humanism (as New Criticism) does in Tolkien's essay: it is, as Earl implies, a transhistorical and universal theory of the relationship of the individual to the group, of the rule of the Father. The way around this problem may be to consider a second (nonpsychoanalytic) interpretation of patriarchy as a social system of *dominance of men over women*.[15] This definition of patriarchy enlightens Earl's anxieties, as his resistance is not to the female (as is clear in his second dream) but to his own interpretation of her, which produces an analysis of how men maintain dominance, not simply in the poem, but in the project of its criticism. As Earl himself says, he is deeply ambivalent about the patriarchy of the poem and of its criticism: his dreams attempt to compensate for the marginalization not simply of the woman, but also the man, whose identification with the poem might usher in a male oedipal failure and an identification with an authoritarian patriarchy.[16]

We can demystify Earl's project of patriarchy in ways similar to my reading of Tolkien's project of New Criticism. The parallels between the two essays, though clearly not intentional, are nevertheless notable. Like Tolkien, Earl uses gender (his gendered dreams) as a beginning—this time for a psychoanalytic reading. Again, the symbolically female is replaced by the symbolically male, this time to provide a sophisticated account of the structures of patriarchy in *Beowulf* with considerable power to explain the psychological process-es whereby obedience is enforced and maintained within a necessarily male warrior class (Earl, p. 84). In the process, Earl targets the ambivalence that the poem itself expresses toward this patriarchal project—a point to which I shall return later. If Tolkien reads the poem from the perspective of the universal "man," however, Earl reads more self-consciously as just one "man."

It is precisely in opposition to reading as a "man" that the first wave of feminist criticism on *Beowulf* is produced. Part of a widespread feminist project that seeks to reclaim the female, its critical insights are frequently purchased at the price of remaining firmly tied to gendered binary assump-tions. The ideological underpinning of criticism in general remains un-questioned by these moves: to Beowulf the hero is added Chance's *Woman as Hero*; to the male warrior figure is added Helen Damico's valkyrie; to the male roles of hero and king are added the female roles of peace-weaver and queen; and so forth. These analyses are conducted with varying degrees of sophistication, but they are based on a conception of binarisms as equal and opposite rather than asymmetric, and they offer little explanatory power with which to analyze the patriarchy of the poem or the patriarchal assump-tions of much of its criticism, including their own. The feminist gaze on the poem remains firmly on the female, which has the curiously unfeminist ef-fect of leaving the question of the male protected and hidden. We could say that such readings stem from the same masculinist assumptions as Tolkien's allegories: the critical gaze looks beyond the artifact of its own creation.

By contrast, Earl's analysis of the reader urges the importance of examin-ing our critical constructs (and their unconscious motivations), and a simi-lar position is adopted in Gillian R. Overing's *Language, Sign, and Gender in "Beowulf,"* which examines the patriarchy of *Beowulf* from an Other, femi-nist perspective to demonstrate how its perceived hegemony is neither con-sistent nor without consequences. Overing starts with a premise similar to Earl's—that the text may be said to invent its readers (Overing, p. xiii)—but she theorizes *Beowulf*'s patriarchy using a feminist semiotic and psychoana-lytic understanding of desire: "Who wants what in *Beowulf* and who gets it?" (p. 69) thus usefully contrasts with Earl's questions of identification. Casting desire as the centerpiece of the symbolic economy of the poem (read as mas-culine), Overing suggests that the male characters of the poem cast their ob-jects of desire as Other and, through subjugation and appropriation, main-tain their own Sameness (xxiii, pp. 69–70). Women, the feminine, thus have no position from which to signify—nameless, silent, or even resistant, as use-objects within this economy they can have little investment in it. Though marginalized, women may usurp their position of Other by hysteria. They disrupt, displace, and deflect what Overing calls the dominant masculine desire of the poem—revealing it and, at the same time, intersecting with the process of its drive toward death. The problem of the marginal female is fully addressed as a critical issue, and what is presented as a source of anxiety in Earl is given centrality by Overing, who, by acknowledging the asymmetry of the binarisms—man/woman; active/passive; silent/speech—resists recuperation of the female by making her the Same as him.

As we have seen, Earl's analysis clears the ground for an understanding of readerly identification that is ostensibly male but need not exclude the female while pointing to the poem's manipulation of patriarchal structures. Equally important, Earl concentrates on the poem's, and the reader's, idealization of the hero. Overing suggests a similar idealization but approaches it from the Other's direction—Beowulf, in his speech community of one, is potentially the male hysteric of the poem (p. 84):

> Beowulf forms a speech community of one, however, he is judge and jury. His heroism demands a degree of self-absorption that closes the social circuit of language; he creates his separate relation to reality. (p. 93)

From the position of Other (which can be occupied by both female and male subjects), Overing deliberately unsettles the reader with her comments on Beowulf as hysteric: to her, Beowulf is not the universalized hero but man-as-scapegoat, as Other. The power of the masculine hero as analytic construct, which is used to unify the critical perspectives on the poem by Tolkien and Earl, is therefore severely tested. Following Hélène Cixous and Catherine Clément, Overing suggests that the appropriation of the role of Other can be used to unsettle and challenge the hold of patriarchy.[17] From this position as Other, it is possible to return our gaze onto the masculine economy of the poem and use Overing's emphasis on the female to rethink Earl's emphasis on the male. We can ask what it means to be a signifying subject in *Beowulf*, what it means to be a man, bearing in mind the problems of essentializing the categories of either man or woman.

PATRIARCHY, MASCULINITY, *BEOWULF*

Beowulf creates an almost exclusively male world, as I said at the beginning of this essay, but, in spite of Tolkien's assertions, it does not claim to be a poem about men or masculinity in general. Rather, as both Earl and Overing imply but do not develop, it is a poem about a particular group of men, associated by their aristocratic rank, their kin, and their lords. It is also a poem that directs much of its attention to one man, Beowulf, of the same class, similar family structure, and lords. What unifies these two groups—Danes and Geats—is the ethic of warrior behavior: only warriors from this rank act to become heroes, leaders, kings. As is often remarked, this world is further circumscribed: women are markedly marginal, as are the family and domestic relations between the sexes—institutions that might be expected to parallel the world of the warrior. There are, in other words, deliberate constraints on this masculine poetic world that can be understood in terms of their relationship with the ideological institutions of rank, family, and ethical (or cultural) norms. By examining the social matrix of such constraints in the poem, we can modify and complement Earl's insights into their psychological components.

Contemporary social theorists have observed similar matrices that underpin masculinity and patriarchy, which can be usefully tested against a reading of the poem, despite radical differences in time and subject. Sylvia Walby, for example, argues that the principal sites for the contestation of patriarchy, understood as a social system of gender inequalities that enforces male dominance over women, are waged work, culture, housework, sexuality, violence, and the state.[18] Each of these sites will necessarily vary from culture to culture and period to period as patriarchy is reconstructed and remodified, but they have some usefulness as the beginnings of analysis. As Arthur Brittan reminds us, ideologies of power such as masculinism (male domination of other men) and patriarchy (male domination of women) are never simply givens imposed on any particular society, but are contested by individuals within particular institutions.[19]

Beowulf is a poem in part about history, but it is not a work of historiography: if we wish to understand more fully the patriarchal structure of Anglo-Saxon society, this poem will give us only notoriously limited answers. The subject of the poem is not Anglo-Saxon England and, as is well known, critics cannot even agree on its date and place of production.[20] *Beowulf* as a poem is, nevertheless, part of this culture's social formation and, given its careful construction of a particular kind of masculine world, it is reasonable to consider just what kind of perspective on men in what kinds of institutions *Beowulf* offers. We can extend the insights of Earl and Overing into the relationship between gender and interpretation by reexamining the poem's re-presentation of patriarchy and of masculine values.

The patrilineal family is a useful place to start and broadens Earl's focus on the *comitatus* while complementing Overing's concentration on the marginalized position of the female figures within the family. The poem opens with the patrilineal family of the Scyldings—the ruling family of motherless Danes—and the ruling dynasties, whether Danish or Geatish, form one of its fundamental preoccupations. What is immediately striking is the severe pressure under which these motherless families operate. Scyld's glorious founding family is in radical stasis within three generations (and many fewer lines), with the twelve-year persecution of Hrothgar's hall by Grendel. Intimations of future discord between his nephew, Hrothulf, and his sons Hrethric and Hrothmund haunt Beowulf's successful slaughter of Grendel's mother (lines 1180b–91). Similarly, Beowulf's own father, Ecgtheow, was indebted to the Danish family because of feuding (lines 459–72) and plays an extremely curtailed role in his son's life, who is far more closely identified with his uncle Hygelac and his grandfather Hrethel, of the Geatish ruling family. The Geats, too, are beset with problems of kingly succession, partly as a result of feuding with the Swedish ruling family. By the end of the poem, the Geats are lordless, without an obvious successor because Beowulf leaves no direct heir, as he himself acknowledges (lines 2729–32a). While praising these dynasties, the poem leaves us in no doubt of their tenuous hold on life in the hall. The maintenance of patrilineal genealogy is no easy thing.

In fact, *Beowulf* concentrates on what we might call the crucial sites in genealogical or patrilineal succession. The poem opens with a fatherless father whose past is unknown, Scyld, and closes with the death of a childless son, Beowulf. Patrilineal relationships cement strong bonds between a father and a son—the family of Scyld is a matter for praise and memory—and yet they are also fragile ones. The memory of Ecgtheow is similarly conflicted—the father of Beowulf found himself in need of Danish assistance. Succession within the same family leads as often to conflict, as in the case of Hrothgar, as it does to relative stability, as in the case of his grandfather, Beowulf Scyldinga (lines 12–19). Relationships between uncle and nephew, brother and brother, are equally tense: Beowulf is the loyal nephew of Hygelac, who ends up the most famed king of the Geats, but it was the accidental slaying of Hygelac's own brother, Herebeald, by his other brother, Hæthcyn, that brought Hygelac to the throne (lines 2435–40). Indeed, the most potent bonds between man and man are not necessarily those of father and son but those of lord and noble retainer. The poet uses such bonds to underscore the symbolic conflict between kinship ties and rank affiliations that can always erupt into literal violence. Significantly, the poet reserves his most emotional language to express these displaced bonds. Hrothgar becomes a metaphoric father in his speeches to Beowulf and weeps at his parting (line 1872b); Hrethel before him (lines 2426–34) and Hygelac after him both treat Beowulf as a son. By contrast, the most stigmatized though equally poignant relationship in the poem is that of the father living on alone after the unavenged death of his son, as Beowulf laments in one of the most sustained metaphors in the entire poem (lines 2444–61a).

The focus on patrilineal genealogy therefore provides the poem with a particularly conflicted set of male relationships. The attitude of the poem toward these relationships is deliberately ambivalent: the institution cannot guarantee the continuity of kingly life, but it is the only institution available. The poem's focus is therefore on individual men who sustain, interact with, and reinterpret this institution. It is perhaps no accident that Beowulf dies in battle with the only major figure in the poem without a genealogy: the dragon. Genealogy offers the ambiguous promise of male succession; how this power is managed by men forms one aspect of the broader patriarchal dynamics of the poem. The focus on genealogy, however, is a narrowly circumscribed one, defined by the interests of the ruling families as measured in kinship bonds or loyalty ties. Accordingly, social power is always concentrated in a few male hands.

Patriarchy is most commonly defined as a system of gender inequalities by which men preserve their dominion over women, and, as Overing indicates, this is certainly the case in *Beowulf*. The poem, however, is arguably as much preoccupied with the ways in which aristocratic warriors dominate other men as they do monstrous Others. This is expressed in terms of the language of masculinism: *Beowulf* ritualizes aggression both physically *and* verbally[21] to enforce obedience of the dominated to the dominant. Aggression is central to the maintenance of power in the ruling families and is formulated throughout the poem in terms of a heroic ideology, or code. Most of the events enacted or recited in the poem are attempts to control or resolve violent situations. Violence may be implicit in the structure of warrior society and therefore man-made—as represented in the complex clashes of kinship and revenge in the Finnsburh episode (lines 1068–1159a)—or represented by the challenges of the alien or the Other—clashes of man and monster, man and woman (the example of Modthryth springs to mind).

Beowulf is a bloody poem. It dwells on death and lingers on the tearing of vertebrae, the severed arm, the burnt body. Grendel relishes blood:

> Ne þæt se aglæca yldan þohte,
> ac he gefeng hraðe forman siðe
> slæpendne rinc, slat unwearnum,
> bat banlocan, blod edrum dranc. (lines 739–42)

Nor did the monster think to delay, but on the first occasion he quickly seized a sleeping warrior, tore without hindrance, bit bone-links, drank blood from veins.

So too does the poem, as the description of Grendel's mortal wound makes plain:

> Licsar gebad
> atol æglæca: him on axle wearð
> syndolh sweotol; seonowe onsprungon,
> burston banlocan. (lines 815b–18a)

The terrible monster experienced body-pain: a huge wound gaped on his shoulder; sinews sprung apart, bone-links burst.

But Grendel is not alone in desiring blood, the ethos of the heroic world demands it. There is, however, a crucial difference between Grendel's desire for aggression and that of the heroic world he attacks. Grendel's desire is channeled into the production of death; warriors, too, produce death, but their desires are channeled into a social ethos that ritualizes desire as heroic choice, thus ensuring the preservation of that ethos.[22] The institution of the warrior caste encodes the desires of its members, and warriors choose death as a means of its reproduction—the warriors fight on even after the death of their lord, as Earl reminds us. At the same time, however, the poem tells us that this institution does not guarantee success, and its reproduction is fragile.

Deeds of aggression are therefore necessarily as praiseworthy as the patriarchal family—they too are the matter of memory and of song. Good deeds and bad are preserved in the communal songs of *Beowulf*. As a good king and one who demands loyalty and tribute, Scyld Scefing acts forcefully, rules through territorial expansion and subjugation, and leaves a son: "þæt wæs god cyning!" (line 11b). To be a good king is also to be a dead one. The parameters of the poem's masculine heroic world are inscribed in the opening lines (lines 4–11) and are subject to redefinition and reinterpretation throughout. The leader comes from elsewhere, from the unknown, reinstates order through aggression, rules successfully (as measured by the assent of his subjects and poets), and dies, returning to the unknown. Continuity is ensured in two ways—through the memory of his actions and through his sons—but neither is reliable. The heroic actions of the past are not predictable guides to those of the present or future: "þæt wæs god cyning!" is statement, not advice. Scyld Scefing's line will be threatened by Grendel and destroyed by feuding.

The actions of dead kings and dead heroes, however, provide the only guides for interpreting action in *Beowulf*. After Beowulf's battle against Grendel, his actions are celebrated with a song about two other heroic men: Sigemund and Heremod (lines 874b-906). The successful slaying of one monster prompts the recall of another famous monster-slayer, Sigemund, and it would appear that Beowulf's present actions are to be analogically interpreted via this song. But Beowulf is not Sigemund. Beowulf has killed Grendel and will later kill a dragon, but he will die in the encounter, unlike Sigemund, who survived. In the song, Sigemund is contrasted with the ignoble Heremod, who does not fulfill his early promise as a good king. Later Hrothgar too urges Beowulf to contemplate the lesson of Heremod (lines 1709b-22). But Beowulf, unlike Heremod, lives out the promise of the heroic ethos and the institution of kingship. Although the poem invites us to measure man against man, the coordinates of the past offer only superficial parallels. As with genealogy, patriarchal power within the institution of the warrior class is managed and tested by its individual male members.

Beowulf, as a result, is as much about the limits of aggression in this male aristocratic heroic world as it is about its successes. By resting its gaze on Beowulf, the poem gives us a man who exposes the workings of these institutions—that is to say, an example of how one man (the hero) manages its obligations to maintain power in the male hands of ruling dynasties. It is with the representation of this one man that the poem images the ambiguous functions of the masculine world, which can produce an Unferth and a Beowulf: hence, Beowulf's power to unsettle and disturb critical thought as hero, which all the best commentators on the poem have understood. Beowulf is the only warrior in the poem not fully sanctioned by a legendary or mythical lineage. His own line has ambiguous overtones because of his father's earlier feuds, and his earlier life is subject to challenge and redefinition. Beowulf is therefore only partially assimilable to the heroic world of either Danes or Geats. Associated with the Danes via his father's debt to Hrothgar as well as his heroic actions, he is seen as a threat to the ruling family by at least one member (Wealhtheow), whereas Hrothgar views him as a promising candidate for the throne of the Geats (lines 1844–53a), and perhaps too for the Danes. In his own country, however, Beowulf comes to power only as a result of the interminable Swedish-Geatish wars. Beowulf, moreover, refutes the promise of genealogical succession by dying without a son, even while making alternative arrangements for Wiglaf to succeed him (lines 2800a-2801b).

In terms of the management of aggression, Beowulf occupies a privileged position as the only successful warrior in Denmark. But, as Tolkien, Earl, and Overing all note, Beowulf is the outsider as hero, like Scyld before him. Unlike Scyld, however, Beowulf demonstrates that the successful management of events is not a matter simply of actions but of words. As Overing says, Beowulf is "a speech community of one" (p. 93). In the series of highly ritualized encounters that mark Beowulf's advance from the seashore to Heorot, Beowulf progressively reveals in speech his own past until that past is climactically appropriated by Hrothgar (lines 372–76). In fact, he is always the privileged speaker in the poem and the poem becomes in part *his* narrative. We hear his rhetorical mastery of personal memory in combat with communal memory represented by Unferth's challenge, when he exposes the illusions of the Danes, whose best riposte is discord, and whose best account of Breca is Unferth's (lines 506–28). Beowulf triumphs in words before he defeats Grendel, and succeeds not because his version of the contest is "true" (that truth is unverifiable by those in the present), but because his words carry the authority of one who has rhetorically restructured the past to best suit the present. This restructuring continues throughout the poem. Beowulf retells of his struggles against Grendel and Grendel's mother time and again, on each occasion reformulating the account to mold it to present circumstances (lines 958–79, 1652–76, 2069b-2143). He relates to Hygelac his interpretation of the political situation in Denmark (lines 2020–69a), foregrounding the internal dynastic feuds that were simply allusions earlier in the poem. And he shares with the narrator the stories of the Swedish~Geatish wars that precipitate his rise to power (lines 2426–2509). Beowulf speaks as both warrior and king from the privilege of both personal and communal experience. The successful manipulation of patriarchal power, therefore, rests on one discourse, as well as on one body.

As the poem repeatedly emphasizes, power is played across the bodies of individual men: desire, channeled through the institutions of heroism and family, comes to rest in the dead body of Beowulf as he himself reminds us in his penultimate speech (lines 2729–51). Here, Beowulf laments the absence of an heir to his body ("lice gelenge"; line 2732a) to whom he could present his war-gear. Beowulf is a great king but even he cannot resist the dragon. He comes into the poem from across the seas (like Scyld), from the unknown, and is buried looking out upon the sea. Finally, he is only one more dead but praiseworthy man—warrior and king: the only good hero, after all, is a dead one.

CONCLUSION

Concepts such as gender mediate in our interpretations of *Beowulf*, and my own position has been to illustrate how the patriarchal project of *Beowulf* criticism (to paraphrase Earl) can create a reading of the poem that naturalizes gender and thereby promotes masculinism. We need only turn to Earl and Overing to see how crucial the concepts of patriarchy and gender are to reading. As both suggest, the masculinity of *Beowulf* may be self-evident, but its construction—how masculinity works in the poem—is by no means transparent. The construction of this masculine world is bought at a huge price: women, men, and monsters are all sacrificed to an artistic vision that focuses on the desires of a very narrowly defined warrior class. The ideologies of patriarchy and masculinism help define the matrix of this circumscribed world by attending to the relationship between the patrilineal aristocratic family and the institutionalized aggression of its warrior class, by whom it maintains power. The poem does not condemn these warriors, but its patriarchal gaze is simultaneously appreciative *and* critical. The challenge readers face is how to explore the difference, or alterity, of this poetic world without falling into glib and easy statements about its apparent celebration of male violence. Although *Beowulf* is a poem that is frequently cast in a sentimental light, there is nothing sentimental about its ambiguous and ambivalent gaze on men.[23]

To James W. Earl and Gillian R. Overing, I owe a special debt for the patience and generosity with which they responded to my questions about their work and read my own. In addition, I thank Thelma Fenster and Julian Weiss for their insightful comments and productive criticism.

NOTES

[1] J. R. R. Tolkien, "Beowulf: The Monsters and the Critics," Proceedings of the British Academy 22 (1936): 245-95, reprinted in *The Monsters and the Critics and Other Essays*, ed. Christopher Tolkien (London, 1983), pp. 5-48, at p. 18. Page numbers for Tolkien's essay are from the 1990 reprint. All subsequent references to this work are by page number and author, when relevant.

[2] Gillian R. Overing, *Language, Sign, and Gender in "Beowulf"* (Carbondale, 1990), p. xxiii. All subsequent references to this work are by page number and author, when relevant.

[3] The theoretical distinction between beginnings and origins is applied to the discipline of Anglo-Saxon studies in general by Allen J. Frantzen, *Desire for Origins: New Language, Old English, and Teaching the Tradition* (New Brunswick, 1990), pp. 1–26, especially pp. 23–24.

[4] An interesting and broadly materialist study of masculinity is that by Arthur Brittan, *Masculinity and Power* (Oxford, 1989); see also Toril Moi's pertinent comments in "Men against Patriarchy," in *Gender and Theory: Dialogues on Feminist Criticism*, ed. Linda Kaufman (Oxford, 1989), pp. 181–88. One of the best introductions to materialist criticism generally is Raymond Williams, *Marxism and Literature* (Oxford, 1977).

[5] Brittan uses the term *masculinism* to distinguish the ideology of masculine power from the concept of masculinity, that is to say, those aspects of male behavior that are subject to change over time and that suggest that (male) identity is fragile; see *Masculinity and Power*, pp. 3–4.

[6] James W. Earl, "*Beowulf* and the Origins of Civilization," in *Speaking Two Languages: Traditional Disciplines and Contemporary Theory in Medieval Studies*, ed. Allen J. Frantzen (Albany, 1991), pp. 65–89. All subsequent references to this work are by author and page number.

[7] Jane Chance, *Woman as Hero in Old English Poetry* (Syracuse, 1986); Helen Damico, *Beowulf's Wealhtheow and the Valkyrie Tradition* (Madison, 1984). See also Helen Damico and Alexandra Hennessey Olsen, eds., *New Readings on Women in Old English Literature* (Bloomington, 1990). For a survey of feminist approaches to Old English literature, see Helen T. Bennett, "From Peace Weaver to Text Weaver: Feminist Approaches to Old English Studies," in *Twenty Years of the "Year's Work in Old English Studies,"* ed. Katherine O'Brien O'Keeffe, *Old English Newsletter*, Subsidia 15 (1989): 23–42; and, more briefly, Helen T. Bennett, Clare A. Lees, and Gillian R. Overing, "Gender and Power: Feminism and Old English Studies," *Medieval Feminist Newsletter* 10 (Fall 1990): 15–23.

[8] Gender is, of course, only one such mediation; others would be race and gender, for example, Williams, *Marxism and Literature*, pp. 95–100, offers a useful discussion of the concept of mediation. For another discussion of mediation,

directly related to Old English, see Frantzen, *Desire for Origins*, pp. 103–5.

9   Tolkien, "*Beowulf*: The Monsters and the Critics," p. 31.

10 As Frantzen notes; *Desire for Origins*, p. 79.

11 Whereas, according to Frantzen, the poem itself distinguishes *only* Beowulf's behavior as an index of human behavior, superior to other men (and women); see his "When Women Aren't Enough," in "Studying Medieval Women: Sex, Gender, Feminism" (special issue), ed. Nancy F. Partner, *Speculum* 68 (1993): 445–71. I am grateful to Professor Frantzen for letting me read and refer to this essay prior to its publication.

12 Fr. Klaeber, ed., *"Beowulf" and the Fight at Finnsburg*, 3rd. ed. (Lexington, Mass., 1950), lines 3180–82. All subsequent references to *Beowulf* are to this edition, by line number. All translations are my own.

13 For an introductory discussion of the concept of gendered reading, see Patrocinio P. Schweikart, "Reading Ourselves: Toward a Feminist Theory of Reading," in *Gender and Reading: Essays on Readers, Texts, and Contexts*, ed. Elizabeth A. Flynn and Patrocinio P. Schweikart (Baltimore, 1986), pp. 31–62. Overing applies the concept to Old English literature in "On Reading Eve: *Genesis B* and the Readers' Desire," in Frantzen, *Speaking Two Languages*, pp. 35–64.

14 "Falling asleep recently while thinking about *Beowulf*, I dreamed of a sphinx, not quite buried in the desert sand; in fact, no matter how hard I tried to bury it, one eye always remained uncovered. The sphinx is *Beowulf*, of course, but it is also my superego" (Earl, p. 73).

15 As Juliet Mitchell says, "Psychoanalysis is not a recommendation *for* a patriarchal society, but an analysis *of* one" (*Psychoanalysis and Feminism* [Harmondsworth, Middlesex, 1975], p. xv). A useful discussion of feminist approaches to psychoanalytic theory remains Michèle Barrett's, *Women's Oppression Today: The Marxist/Feminist Encounter* (London, 1980, rev. 1988), pp. 42–83.

16 This passage into patriarchy is assessed by Earl, who offers this strongly marked compensation cast in terms of his own gaze on the poem: "I must admit that my pleasure with this understanding of *Beowulf* and its effects on the audience sits rather uneasily with my own individuality, and my own resentful attitudes toward authority. The oedipal failure the poem tries to enforce is intended to socialize us into a radically authoritarian world. It is balanced, thank goodness, by the spectacle of the hero's awesome, if unobtainable, freedom" (p. 87).

17 Hélène Cixous and Catherine Clément, *The Newly Born Woman*, trans. Betsy Wing (Minneapolis, 1986).

18 Sylvia Walby, *Theorizing Patriarchy* (Oxford, 1990), p. 21. Anthropological studies of men also indicate some transcultural similarities in the construction of male identities; see, for example, Stanley Brandes, *Metaphors of Masculinity: Sex*

and Status in Andalusian Folklore (Philadelphia, 1980) and David D. Gilmore, *Manhood in the Making: Cultural Concepts of Masculinity* (New Haven, 1990).

[19] Brittan, *Masculinity and Power*, pp. 19–45.

[20] See, for example, Kevin S. Kiernan, *"Beowulf" and the "Beowulf" Manuscript* (New Brunswick, 1981); David M. Dumville, "Beowulf Come Lately: Some Notes on the Palaeography of the Nowell Codex," *Archiv für das Studium der neueren Sprachen und Literaturen* 225 (1988): 49–63; and the essays in Colin Chase, ed., *The Dating of "Beowulf"* (Toronto, 1981).

[21] As Ward Parks reminds us in *Verbal Dueling in Heroic Narrative: The Homeric and Old English Traditions* (Princeton, 1990).

[22] These brief comments on desire as a psychoanalytic mechanism for production have been stimulated by Klaus Theweleit's analysis of fascism, *Male Fantasies*, vol. 1, trans. Stephen Conway in collaboration with Erica Carter and Chris Turner (Minneapolis, 1987), pp. 215–28. Theweleit also draws some suggestive parallels between the fascist male and men in general: "I don't want to make any categorical distinction between the types of men who are the subject of this book and all other men. Our subjects are equivalent to the tip of the patriarchal iceberg, but it's what lies beneath the surface that really makes the water cold" (p. 171).

[23] See, for example, Fred C. Robinson, *"Beowulf" and the Appositive Style* (Knoxville, 1985).

BEOWULF'S TEARS OF FATHERHOOD

MARY DOCKRAY-MILLER

Virginia Woolf's oft-quoted remark about the equation of women with sex—"sex—woman, that is to say"—seems no longer appropriate in gender studies.[1] While we still read and study in a world where libraries shelve history books into "history" and "women's history" sections, men and masculinity are being legitimately studied as gendered entities rather than as quasi-neutral universals. The examination of women prompted by the feminist movement of the seventies and eighties has led us to an examination of men as well, in history, in literature, in culture at large.

The figure of Hrothgar, aging king of the Danes, forces an analysis of the relationships among age, maleness, and masculinity in *Beowulf*. Masculine characters, while enacting the poem's complex reciprocities and social transactions in the hall and on the battlefield, accrue status and power through assertions of control and dominance, through knowledge and use of the rituals of hierarchy, and through manipulation of the variety of relationships that exists in the social world of *Beowulf*. The complexities of masculine assertion of power go beyond simple won/lost lists in the innumerable battles detailed or alluded to in the poem, although fighting prowess stands at the top of the list of masculine attributes.

Two specific incidents within the text exhibit Hrothgar's growing inability to exert power over others and to enact this masculine heroic ethos. The first is heterosexual, a departure to and return from his wife's bed; the

From *Exemplaria* 10 (1998): 1–28; reprinted with permission of Pegasus Press.

second is homosocial, his leave-taking of Beowulf. While this second instance is actually a scene in which Hrothgar tries to assert masculine power, Hrothgar's masculinity is undermined as he oversteps the bounds of heroic society. The emotional and homoerotic nature of the farewell scene shows that the "normal" male-male relationship of the *comitatus*, with which the Danes have been having so much trouble since Grendel's coming, has broken down to the point where Hrothgar cannot find an unambiguously masculine gesture of parting from the younger man.

In psychoanalytic terms, Hrothgar must renounce his Fatherhood, without even the consolation of death made complete by knowledge that he struggled to maintain his masculine, patriarchal power to the end. In psychoanalytic theory, the Father has become a signifier, a metaphor, or a Law-wielding phallus discussed only in relation to the child. However, to be Father to a child with a resolved Oedipus complex necessarily imparts a good deal of phallic power to the Father. This psychoanalytic model of generational power informs Hrothgar's relationship with Beowulf; Hrothgar *tries* to be Beowulf's Father (I capitalize to indicate the psychoanalytic associations of the word), and his failure in that role indicates that he does not have the power of the phallus. Hrothgar, the proto-masculine great king, is actually *losing* masculine status within the social networks and battles of the poem because he does not wield power and dominate others in the manner that Beowulf can. In *Beowulf*, Hrothgar does not die; he just fades away.

Masculinity in pre-Christian Scandinavia, and in *Beowulf* in particular, has been the subject of much recent critical attention. Carol Clover, Allen Frantzen, and Clare Lees have each discussed this inextricable relationship between masculinity and power in early Scandinavian culture; Lees and Frantzen comment specifically on *Beowulf*. A meeting of Clover's more general analysis of a gender continuum in early Scandinavian cultures and the gendered politics of *Beowulf* allows an interpretation of masculinity, in the world of the poem, as power and the social status that power engenders. Within Clover's rubric, stereotypical oppositions such as masculine/feminine or dominant/dominated evaporate so that the poem can be read within an economy of masculinity: to be more powerful, both socially and militarily, is to be more masculine. As Lees puts it, "*Beowulf* ritualizes aggression both physically *and* verbally to enforce obedience of the dominated to the dominant";[2] both parties, in this situation, are usually male.

In her analysis of the sex or gender system constructed in the Norse sagas, Clover describes a system in which "there was finally just one 'gender,' one standard by which persons were judged adequate or inadequate, and it was something like masculine."[3] Drawing on the one-sex model of Thomas Laqueur, Clover uses incidents from the sagas to show that while men had inherent advantage in Norse heroic society, there superiority was by no means assured. Women were frequently lauded for the way in which they wielded power, men frequently ridiculed for their lack of power. Along this continuum of power, biological sex did not fix a subject's place; as Clover says:

> [G]ender, if we can even call it that, is neither coextensive with biological sex, despite its dependence on sexual imagery, nor a closed system, but a system based to an extraordinary extent on winnable and losable attributes.[4]

Women who settled feuds, controlled land, defended themselves, and went on Viking raids, were "masculine," while men who stayed home to dally with servant girls were not. Clover attributes the "frantic machismo of Norse males" to this cultural system "in which being born male precisely did *not* confer automatic superiority."[5] Masculinity, and its power, had to be earned.

The relationship between gender and power is one of Frantzen's subjects in his essay "When Women Aren't Enough," in which he argues that men and masculinity in medieval texts must be investigated just as women and femininity have been.[6] Frantzen disparages those critics who ostensibly write about gender but have ignored men and masculinity because "to write about men was unnecessary, for everything already written was about them."[7] To read Clover with Frantzen is illuminating; Frantzen's brief analysis of Hrothgar as a "manly man" places him (Hrothgar, that is) at the most masculine, most powerful point of Clover's continuum. The poet calls Hrothgar's actions *manlice* (line 1046);[8] Frantzen's analysis of editors' equation of "manly" with "nobly" or "generously" shows that "Hrothgar seems to define the word 'manfully' rather than to be described by it."[9] While Frantzen prefers to read *manlice* as a reference to class, *manlice*, via Clover, lexically places Hrothgar at the pinnacle of masculine power: high in status by virtue of class *and* gender.

Hrothgar's designation as a "manly man," like many of the poet's epithets that describe the aging king, belies the inherent weakness of his position within the narrative. Clover discusses the weakness that comes, inevitably, with old age for those "men once firmly in category A who have slid into category B by virtue of age."[10] Hrothgar is just such a man, though Clover, in her only citation of *Beowulf*, refers to the lament of the old man who must

441

watch his son die on the gallows rather than to Hrothgar as an example of a man "whose lamentation is precisely the effect of disabled masculinity."[11] Hrothgar's frequently cited grief for the horrors in Heorot is another *Beowulf*ian example of this "disabled masculinity," a gender construction defined by lack of previously exerted power. His grief is almost always presented in indirect narrative rather than in direct, spoken statement; for example, "Swa ða mælceare maga Healfdenes / singala seað" ("Thus the son of Healfdane continually brooded over the time-sorrow," lines 189–90).[12] Hrothgar does not speak his own grief, except at line 473, when he tells Beowulf, "Sorh is me to secganne on sefan minum / gumena ængum" ("It is a sorrow to me to tell [what is] in my heart to any men," lines 473–74). More usually, the narrator speaks Hrothgar's emotions for him.[13]

Lees looks at "Men and *Beowulf*" (the title of her essay) as well as men in *Beowulf* as she examines the way that male and female critics have read *Beowulf* in the last sixty years, taking Tolkien specifically as an example of a male critic who assumes an ideal, implicitly male reader for the poem: "'Man' in Tolkien's essay emerges as the liberal humanistic construct of the universal male."[14] This assumption of masculinity has impeded examination of the text's male characters; Lees proceeds with just such an examination, showing how the poem exposes the inherent weakness of male-based patrilineal genealogy, though such genealogy "is the only institution available."[15] According to Lees, the strongest male-male bonds in the poem are those of lord and retainer, not of father and son, so that the weakest of bonds forms the basis of society.

Lees is correct when she points out that patrilineal succession is the ideal in *Beowulf*, although it is not firmly achieved by any of the major characters.[16] She does not address, however, the strong male-male bond exhibited in the poem by uncle and nephew, when the nephew is the son of the sister. While this bond is also that of lord to retainer (Hygelac and Beowulf, possibly Beowulf and Wiglaf), it privileges specific kinship over the more general *comitatus*.[17]

But these variations of the male-male relationship, with kin or not, expose the fragility of masculinity in the text, for those bonds are inevitably broken by forces within or without the tribe. Ultimately, for Lees, "power is played across the bodies of individual men" in a struggle that is necessarily fruitless since "desire, channeled through the institutions of heroism and family, comes to rest in the dead body of Beowulf . . . the only good hero, after all, is a dead one."[18] Only a dead hero can rest with his reputation, and hence his masculinity, intact. Lees sees *Beowulf* as a poem primarily about power relations between men: how they dominate each other, how they define their masculinity through ritualized aggression.

• • •

Within the context of these three readers, Clover, Frantzen, and Lees, I undertake my own exploration into masculinity in *Beowulf*, specifically into the figure of Hrothgar, the man too old to be a man. Critical judgment about Hrothgar, especially before 1985, tends to fall into one of two categories: one group sees Hrothgar as wise old king, the other as weak old king. No matter which category these critics fall into, however, almost all agree that Hrothgar's main function in the poem is to provide some sort of foil for Beowulf.

Those critics who see Hrothgar as prudent and explicitly celebrated are best represented by John Leyerle, who in 1965 argued that Hrothgar's choice not to fight Grendel himself is an example of kingly prudence.[19] The duty of kings is to protect their people; had Hrothgar fought Grendel (and inevitably lost), his people would be leaderless, much as the Geats are after Beowulf's fight with the dragon.[20]

Another interpretation of Hrothgar as wholly good and praiseworthy focuses on his act of creation in the building of Heorot, a symbol of harmony in a civilized world.[21] Critics also tend to praise Hrothgar's diplomatic expertise.[22] For example, at Beowulf's arrival in Denmark (lines 457–72), Hrothgar makes it clear to Beowulf that he views Beowulf's offer not so much as a godsend but as a requital for a debt Beowulf owes him through Ecgtheow, Beowulf's father; he lets Beowulf know that Beowulf owes Hrothgar, not the other way around.

All of these critics and others like them rely on the voice of the poet, who continually tells the audience that Hrothgar is *god cyning*, *helm scyldingas*, or *mære þeoden* (a "good king," "protector of the Scyldings," "a great lord").[23] Most of the critics who fall in the opposite camp, arguing that Hrothgar is weak, read these epithets somewhat ironically: how can Hrothgar be "protector of the Scyldings" if Scyldings are routinely being eaten by a monster?[24] Even critics who admit Hrothgar's basic weakness but praise his wisdom have to grapple with his ineffectuality; Robert Kaske points out that the supposedly wise Hrothgar makes some very bad decisions: marrying Freawaru to Ingeld, letting Hrothulf stay at his court, and forgetting to tell Beowulf that there was a second monster after the first one had been killed. These decisions undermine his reputation for wisdom, as well.[25]

Finally, Hrothgar has been accused of that worst of medieval Christian vices, pride. Much of the critical discussion of Hrothgar centers on his "sermon" (or "harangue" as Klaeber and others have called it), in lines 1700–84, usually interpreted as a lesson to Beowulf about the pitfalls of kingship and power.[26] Critics have alternately discussed the patristic sources of this speech and affirmed its inherently secular nature.[27] Critical focus on the speech suggests that it is, as Stephen Bandy says, "the ethical center of the poem." [28] With examples and gnomic statements, Hrothgar warns Beowulf about the sin of pride, and there is a veritable critical industry that focuses solely on whether Beowulf took that advice (an industry to whose products I am not going to add here).

More recently, the decline of structuralism and the rise of post-structuralist criticism have led to an acceptance of ambiguity rather than opposition in textual analysis; rather than Hrothgar being weak and old (or prideful) in opposition to Beowulf's strong youth, critics in the late eighties and early nineties have viewed Hrothgar as a source of tension in the poem. That tension, I contend, comes from his faltering masculinity.

Most representative of this sort of argument is Edward Irving's determination that there is no one definitive identity for Hrothgar; Irving sees "contempt as well as respect" for the figure of the old king in literature (he discusses Priam, Nestor, and Charlemagne in addition to Hrothgar).[29] Like most critics, Irving sees Hrothgar as a foil to Beowulf; Irving sees this contrast working in two ways: Hrothgar as a foil for Beowulf the young hero and for Beowulf the fighting old king. Hrothgar's passivity contrasts with Beowulf's action as an old man; where Hrothgar waited, Beowulf acts. The ambiguity stems from the results of that action and inaction: in the end, both the Danes and the Geats are torn apart by feud, the Danes from within, the Geats from without.

Critics like Irving[30] are taking *Beowulf* criticism in the direction described and taken by Gillian Overing in *Language, Sign, and Gender in "Beowulf."* Overing notes in her introduction that "Teaching this poem can be in itself a deconstructionist exercise in dismantling hierarchical oppositions"; among the oppositions that need to be dismantled is "whether Hrothgar is weak or strong."[31] Overing's reading of the many layers of signs in the "sermon" does not just dismantle but goes beyond the opposition weak/strong to examine "the remarkable and multifaceted prism of sign interaction" throughout the scene: not just the words Hrothgar speaks, but the signs carved on the hilt of the sword and the hilt itself.[32]

Although Overing's discussion of gender ultimately focuses on the feminine, her discussion of the "masculine economy" of *Beowulf* provides a vocabulary for my analysis of Hrothgar's fading masculinity. In Overing's terms:

> In the masculine economy of the poem, desire expresses itself as desire for the other, as a continual process of subjugation and appropriation of the other. The code of vengeance and the heroic choice demand above all a *resolution* of opposing elements, a decision must always be made.[33]

For Overing, masculinity in *Beowulf* entails dominance and resolution; no ambiguity—of hierarchy, of gender, of decision—is permissible. She continues:

> A psychoanalytic understanding of desire as deferred death, of the symbolic nature of desire in action, is often not necessary in *Beowulf*; death is continually present, always in the poem's foreground: the hero says "I will do this or I will die." Resolution, choice, satisfaction of desire frequently mean literal death.[34]

Men in *Beowulf*, for Overing, live in a world of absolutes: they will fight the monsters or die, they will avenge a death or die. Overing reads Beowulf himself as a figure to trouble this absolute assertion, but acknowledges that the absolute resolution is intact even at the end of the poem. The masculine characters define themselves against an unfavorable Other: men are strong, noble, generous (recalling the definitions of *manlice*, discussed by Frantzen, which I noted above); the Other is weak, ignoble, miserly—and might as well be dead, for within the masculine economy of this poem, those attributes have no value.[35]

In Clover's terms, Hrothgar's masculinity is slipping away from those positive values of strength, nobility, and generosity towards effeminacy, towards Otherness. In a world where masculinity is defined by power, control, and assertion of status, he asserts his status only through gift-giving—one aspect, but not the most important one, of presentation of himself as a *manlice* king. He cannot control Grendel, as is obvious from the events of the poem, and, while he tries to control Beowulf, he does not succeed even partially.

The poet continually reminds us, throughout the Danish sections of the poem, of the tenuousness of Hrothgar's kingdom. As the feast celebrating Grendel's defeat begins, the poet remarks that "nalles facenstafas / Þeod-Scyldingas þenden fremedon" ("Then the Scylding princes did not perform treacheries," lines 1018–19), implying that there would be treachery in the

future; similarly, in the introduction of Hrothgar and Heorot, the poet notes
that Heorot will burn in a feud among kin:

Sele hlifade
heah ond horngeap; heaðowylma bad,
laðan liges; ne wæs hit lenge þa gen,
þæt se ecghete aþumsweoran
æfter wælniðe wæcnan scolde. (lines 81b–85)

The hall towered high and wide-gabled; it waited for hostile flames, for
hateful fire; nor was it still long [to wait] then, that the sword-hate among
in-laws would awaken on account of deadly hostility.

Hrothgar's hall, the scene of much of his masculine status-building—in gift-
giving, diplomacy, and advising—will fall, and the poet never lets Hrothgar
relax, as it were, as lord of Heorot; we can never forget the feuds that follow
his death and end in the destruction of his legacy.

Hrothgar's hall does not and cannot make, in Overing's terms, the ul-
timate masculine statement—I will defeat the monster or die—no matter
how *manlice* he is in his distribution of gifts or in the building of alliances.
The richness of his gifts betokens his status as a kingly gift-giver, but per-
haps the greatness of those gifts is an attempt, on some level, to make up
for his inability to kill the monster himself. In two scenes that have received
surprisingly little critical attention, these slips in his masculinity become
apparent: his departure to and return from Wealtheow's bed, and his fare-
well to Beowulf. Both scenes underscore the weakness of Hrothgar's subject
position in a society where men assert their masculine status through the
complex power structures of their relationships with other men.

• • •

The first of these scenes is actually two scenes separated by the fight with
Grendel, and is explicitly heterosexual, unusual in a poem that tends to
avoid any mention of sexual relationships. Overing notes and expands
upon Fred Robinson's observation that there is very little romantic love in
Beowulf:

Robinson has noted the absence of "love" or "romantic passion between
the sexes" in *Beowulf* . . . the secondary nature of the emotional marital

bond provides a possible explanation for the hero's apparent celibacy. While scholars have pondered over Beowulf's marital status, Robinson suggests that the poet might simply have considered that "Beowulf's marital status was of insufficient interest to warrant mention in the poem."[36]

For Overing, "marriage is valued as an extension of this larger emotional context," the context of male-male relations, cemented by a marriage alliance.[37] But Hrothgar's marriage is a complex exception to this lack of attention to domesticity in *Beowulf* and other Old English poetry. In the poem, only Hrothgar obviously (even ostentatiously) goes to the women's quarters to find a woman (Wealtheow). Rather than assert the bond between the lord and warrior by sleeping in camaraderie with his men, Hrothgar chooses to sleep with the queen.

The entrance and exit, in which Hrothgar leaves Heorot and then returns the following morning, frame Beowulf's fight with Grendel:

> Ða him Hroþgar gewat mid his hæleþa gedryht,
> eodur Scyldinga ut of healle;
> wolde wigfruma Wealhþeo secan,
> cwen to gebeddan. (lines 662–65a)

Then from him [Beowulf] Hrothgar went with his troop of heroes, the prince of the Scyldings, out of the hall; the war-chief wished Wealhtheow to seek, the queen as a bed-companion.

>   Eode scealc monig
> swiðhicgende to sele þam hean
> searowundor seon; swylce self cyning
> of brydbure, beahhorda weard,
> tryddode tirfæst getrume micle,
> cystum gecyþed, ond his cwen mid him
> medostigge mæt mægþa hose. (lines 918b–24)

Many a man went valiant to the high hall to see the curious wonder [Grendel's arm]; just so the king himself from the bride-bower, the guardian of the ring-hoard, stepped glorious with a great troop, known for excellence, and his queen with him traversed the mead[hall] path with a troop of maidens.

This exit and entrance are juxtaposed with Beowulf's fight, which Overing would term an ultimately masculine action in that Beowulf has asserted that he will kill Grendel or die trying.

An initial sense that perhaps Hrothgar's "grand" departure and subsequent entrance here are less than heroic is strengthened by John Niles's reference to the Danes' sleeping quarters during Grendel's twelve-year control of Heorot. In the process of documenting the decline of the Danish line ("The glories of the Danes are now past"),[38] Niles notes that when the Danes leave Heorot to Grendel, they probably go to sleep in the women's quarters:

> Faced with the sudden loss of thirty of his thanes, Hrothgar simply sits, immobilized by his sorrows. None of his surviving retainers offers to challenge the monster, and the aged king is unwilling or incapable of undertaking the task himself. The only thought his retainers have seems to be to find themselves a more secure place to sleep *æfter burum*, "among the bedchambers" (line 140a), presumably among the women's quarters.[39]

Grendel is not interested in the women's quarters (Niles points out that the surest way to avoid being eaten is simply to leave Heorot).

The change in sleeping locale is obviously a reduction in masculine, heroic status for the men; to sleep in the same space as women, rather than merely to have sex with them and then go sleep in the hall with other men, is to taint oneself with effeminacy, with cowardice. Sleeping in the hall, dressed for battle, is an expression of masculinity, a form of "male bonding" in the poem that affirms the heroic ethos. The Danes regain some of this masculinity associated with sleeping in the hall after the fight with Grendel:

> Reced weardode
> unrim eorla, swa hie oft ær dydon.
> Bencþelu beredon; hit geondbræded wearð
> beddum ond bolstrum. Beorscealca sum
> fus ond fæge fletræste gebeag.
> Setton him to heafdon hilderandas,
> bordwudu beorhtan; þær on bence wæs
> ofer æþelinge yþgesene
> heaþosteapa helm, hringed byrne,
> þrecwudu þrymlic. Wæs þeaw hyra,
> þæt hie oft wæron an wig gearwe,
> ge æt ham ge on herge, ge gehwæþer þara

efne swylce mæla, swylce hira mandryhtne
þearf gesælde; wæs seo þeod tilu. (lines 1237b–50)

A countless number of earls occupied the hall, as they often had done be-
fore. They bore the bench-planks; it [the hall, the benches] was over-spread
with bedding and bolsters. One of the beer-drinkers ready and fated [for
death] sank into hall-rest. They set for themselves at their heads the battle-
shields, the bright board-wood; there on the bench was for the nobles eas-
ily visible the battle-towering helmet, the ringed byrnie, the strength-wood
[spear] magnificent. It was their custom that they often were ready for bat-
tle, whether at home or in the army, each of them, even at such of times as
need befell their man-lord.

Even in this scene, however, the Danes' preparedness does them little good.
Grendel's mother, frightened by their drawn swords, still does manage to
seize Æschere, probably the "one" referred to in line 1240. But the lengthy
description of the preparations here indicates their importance to the con-
struction of a warrior's masculinity; the loving description of the weapons
and clothes of war of the sleeping troop affirms that sleeping in the hall
with comrades is an assertion of masculinity. One may infer that repeatedly
sleeping in the women's quarters is definitively not.

Hrothgar's noted departure for the women's quarters on the eve of battle,
then, highlights a lack of masculinity in his choices rather than affirming
some sort of masculine, sexual prowess. His chosen relationship on this
night is with a woman, not another man or group of men. In both of these
passages there are some evident ironies. Hrothgar the "war-chief" is seek-
ing his queen, not a valiant battle; indeed, he and his "troop of heroes" are
very conspicuously *leaving* the scene of battle, calling into question, by their
actions, the veracity of these epithets.

In the following passage describing Hrothgar's return to the hall, the poet
uses a form of exaggeration that accentuates Hrothgar's lack of masculinity
as he returns to his hall that (he thinks) has been purged for him. Why does
Hrothgar need a "great troop, known for excellence" when he is going only
from one place of safety (the women's quarters) to another (daylit Heorot)?
How *tirfæst*, glorious, can he be when another man has succeeded in mak-
ing the ultimately masculine statement—I have killed the monster—that
Hrothgar was unable to make?

Raymond Tripp argues that the diction and structure of this return to the
hall conveys "an implication that Hrothgar returns like a cock with his flock

449

of hens."[40] Tripp comments on the relatively large number of hapax legomena (most notably *brydbure*, bride-bower, which Tripp also reads as, pun-like, bird bower) to show that there is humor, specifically "avian humor" in this scene that presents Hrothgar as an Anglo-Saxon Chanticleer. While Tripp relies on some shaky connections with much later Middle English words for his argument, I think he is correct in asserting the humor of this scene. What Tripp does not see is that the humor of this scene is at Hrothgar's expense. If Hrothgar is something of an Anglo-Saxon Chanticleer, then just as Chanticleer is a figure of exaggerated, pompous masculinity in Chaucer, Hrothgar here becomes a ridiculous, randy old man. Hrothgar and his Danes, although they have repeatedly tried to purge their hall of Grendel, have failed; Beowulf has done what they could not. Hrothgar might sleep with the queen, but he does not fight the monster or die, and as such his masculinity is imperiled rather than affirmed by his obvious and unique heterosexual relations in the poem.

The final irony in this scene is that Hrothgar's sexual activity has failed to produce a son of the correct age, old and strong enough to continue Hrothgar's line. Hrothgar's age and the relative youth of his sons (too young to defend themselves against their cousin Hrothulf) suggest that he has had some trouble in conceiving sons. His sons were probably not born until he was already past his prime. The poet refers to the boys as *byre* ("sons," "boys," line 1188) and bearn (children, sons, line 1189); both words indicate childhood or a lack of maturity. Wealhtheow calls them *geogoðe* (line 1181) and the poet refers to them as *giogoð* (line 1190); the translation of "youths" (Klaeber's), implies that while they might be considered more than children, they are still inexperienced.

In an ideal Beowulfian world, Hrothgar's sons would "now" be the same age as Hrothulf (definitely full grown) and ready to take over most of Hrothgar's duties (including, presumably, monster-fighting). Instead, they are still in need of protection. His daughter Freawaru is old enough to be married to Ingeld the Heathobard, suggesting that she is the eldest of his children even if not dramatically older than her brothers.

The notion of a paternal masculinity that is strengthened by the births of sons and weakened by the births of daughters is assumed in a poem notoriously interested in paternity, in "patrilineal geneaology" (to use Lees's term) of father and son. While the agnatic kinships of brothers (like Hrethel's three sons) or the previously mentioned sister's son-mother's brother kinships are important, the father-son relationship is sustained as the most prominent and idealized relationship. Beowulf is referred to as Ecgtheow's son fourteen times in various formulations.[41] In contrast, he is called Hygelac's thane or kinsman only eight times.[42] Daughters, as critics from Eliason to Overing have noted, usually do not even appear as names in genealogical lists. A daughter does not increase a man's masculine prestige in the way the son does. Hrothgar, unlike Ecgtheow, has not produced a warrior-son who can increase the father's own masculine prestige.

Many critics have written about Hrothgar's attempted adoption of Beowulf: "Nu ic, Beowulf, þec, / secg betsta, me for sunu wylle / freogan on ferhþe" ("Now, Beowulf, best of men, I wish to love you like a son in spirit," lines 946–48).[43] This attempt begins a series of speeches and actions representative of the complex transactions that take place in Heorot and indicate the fluctuating status and power relationships among the hall's occupants. Hrothgar follows his offer of adoption with kingly gifts: fine armor, eight superb horses, and a rich saddle fit for a king. He could be "setting up" Beowulf as a son by giving him the royal family heirlooms.

The social power in the hall continues to shift after Hrothgar's gift-giving. After the interlude of the song of Finn—an exercise in the problems of exogamy and peace-weaving—Wealtheow presents Beowulf with a rich necklace and indicates through her speeches that she is attempting to protect the rights of her sons to inherit the kingdom; she asks Beowulf to look after their interests (which presumably would exclude accepting Hrothgar's offer and usurping their kingdom).

I find Beowulf's lack of response to these speeches and gifts the most startling part of this entire sequence. Beowulf's only speech during these lines is a regret to Hrothgar that he did not kill Grendel right there (lines 958–79). He does not acknowledge the offer of adoption, of kingly power; he does not even thank Hrothgar and Wealtheow for their gifts. The dynamics of power in this scene revolve around Beowulf: giving him gifts, making him offers, waiting for him to respond. I would like to suggest that Hrothgar's attempted adoption of Beowulf may be a strategy of Hrothgar's to recoup some of the power and status of masculinity that he no longer commands: by adopting a powerful, strong, intelligent, adult son who does make the absolutist, masculine statements that Hrothgar no longer can, a son who can kill the monster.

This lure of a powerful, prototypically masculine son colors all of Hrothgar's dealings with Beowulf. Their relationship, even more than Hrothgar's physical relationship to his queen, determines his slip away from masculinity on Clover's continuum. Not only does Hrothgar sleep with the women, he no longer can dominate men in the way a *man-dryhtne* ("man-lord," line 1249) should. In the relationship between Beowulf and Hrothgar, Beowulf is un-questionably the one with the power, both physical and emotional.

• • •

Nowhere in the text is this power made more apparent than in the second scene under discussion, the farewell scene before Beowulf and his Geats go back to their boat. Beowulf has affirmed the alliance between the Geats and the Danes, promising to return if Hrothgar is ever again in need and promis-ing Hrethric, Hrothgar's son, a warm welcome should Hrethric ever venture to Geatland (lines 1818–39). In this speech, Beowulf's offer of allegiance, through future hospitality to the king's son, may indicate his gratitude and esteem for Hrothgar and the gifts the Danish king has bestowed upon him.

However, the speech also makes the formal leave-taking into an asser-tion of Beowulf's masculine power and status. Somewhat arrogantly, he as-serts that he will come save the Danes again should they ever need him to make again that ultimate masculine statement that they cannot: I will kill the monster or I will die. Next, he offers a friendly place of safety for the young traveling prince, implying that the Geatish hall offers what the Danish hall cannot: protection from monsters and other foes.

In response to these offers, Hrothgar says goodbye to the hero. In these lines, his thoughts and his actions reveal his lack of emotional control; this lack is yet another instance, like the Grendel-kin attacks, in which Hrothgar's lack of control shows his waning masculinity. In this scene, Beowulf is in control, and as such is the dominant male in a situation that Hrothgar wished to construct so that he as Father would dominate and ac-crue power from Beowulf as Son:

> Gecyste þa cyning æþelum god,
> þeoden Scyldinga ðegn betstan
> ond be healse genam; hruron him tearas
> blondenfeaxum. Him wæs bega wen
> ealdum infrodum, oþres swiðor,
> þæt h[i]e seoðða[n] [no] geseon moston,
> modige on meþle. Wæs him se man to þon leof,
> þæt he þone breostwylm forberan ne mehte;
> ac him on hreþre hygebendum fæst
> æfter deorum men dyrne langað
> beorn wið blode. Him Beowulf þanan,

guðrinc goldwlanc græsmoldan træd
since hremig; (lines 1870–82a)

> Then the king kissed the good nobleman, the prince of the Scyldings took the best thane by the neck; tears fell from him, the grey-haired one. In him, old and wise, was the expectation of two things, the other more strong, that they might not see [each other] afterwards brave in counsel.
>
> The man was by him so loved that he could not forbear the breast-welling; but for him in his spirit (with heart-bonds fast because of the dear man) *secretly the man [Hrothgar] longed with blood.*[44]
>
> Away from him Beowulf thence, the warrior gold-adorned, trod the greensward, exulting in treasure.

This passage spans folios 170v and 171r.[45] Much of the edge of folio 171 has crumbled away, probably due to damage in the 1731 fire as well as age, but most of the words or parts of words now missing[46] were recorded in one of the Thorkelin transcripts or are visible in part (like the *w* of *wæs*, line 1876).[47] None of the words in this passage is in question, as far as manuscript presentation goes, though I will below take issue with some editors' choices in grammatical definitions. Frantzen refers to "the ways in which Anglo-Saxon editors have used glossaries to shape translations from their editions";[48] editors and critics, especially Thomas Wright (the only critic to comment on this scene at length), have interpreted this part of the text in such a way that it glosses over the homoerotics of the scene. The emotional and physical presentation of Hrothgar's farewell underscores the fragility of Hrothgar's masculinity as he tries to assert himself as a Father figure but ends up positioning himself as an effeminate Other.

The erotics in the farewell scene are intense beyond the norm of male-male social relations (the *comitatus*). Lees notes that the lord-thane bond is actually the strongest of bonds in the poem,[49] and the Geats epitomize that bond throughout the poem. The troop attending Beowulf waits on the bank of the mere after the Danes have given up; Beowulf demonstrates unwavering loyalty to his lord Hygelac and Hygelac's son Heardred; even at the end, as most of the Geats run away, Wiglaf shows Beowulf the kind of loyalty demanded in this male-male bond. Beowulf has made it clear to Hrothgar that his primary loyalty lies with Hygelac (most especially in his pre-battle boasts, lines 435, 452–54, 1482–88). However, Hrothgar seems almost desperate to have some sort of primary bond with Beowulf; his attempted "adoption" indicates this desire. Lees refers to the farewell scene in her assertion that "the poet reserves his most emotional language to express these displaced bonds [between father and son]",[50] and Howell D. Chickering goes so far as to say that "it almost seems as though the language of erotic poetry were being misapplied to a father's love for a son."[51] The unusual physical and emotional description in the scene highlights this desire as well.

The first word of the farewell scene, *gecyste*, might seem to set an erotic tone for the scene, but kissing in surviving Old English texts is not necessarily erotic; indeed, more often than not, it is religious. Saints kiss their followers, kisses of peace seal treaties.[52] The combination of the kiss and the embrace (*he healse genam*), however, suggests that scene is more emotionally charged than the usual goodbye; when Hrothgar starts to cry (*hruron him tearas*), that suggestion is confirmed. While Chickering says that the emotion of this scene "asks us to widen our conception of the pattern of feelings in heroic life,"[53] I contend that the scene shows that Hrothgar's actions are outside the bounds of "heroic life," that to cry, embrace, and kiss at a farewell are distinctly non-heroic gestures that indicate desperation rather than resolution. Nowhere else in Old English poetry do men display such overt emotion towards each other.[54]

A lexical analysis of *blondenfeax*, "grey-haired," a word used repeatedly to describe Hrothgar, confirms this teetering masculinity I see in the beginning of the farewell scene. *Blondenfeax* is used only in poetry, never in prose.[55] Within *Beowulf*, it refers to Hrothgar (three times) and to the Swedish king Ongentheow (once). The contrast between Ongentheow and Hrothgar, lexically linked through their grey hair, emphasizes Hrothgar's incapacity as he strives for the power of the Father in the farewell scene.

Ongentheow is the sort of old king who does everything Hrothgar does not. He is called *blondenfexa* as he dies in battle:

> Þær wearð Ongenðiow ecgum sweorda,
> blondenfexa on bid wrecen,
> þæt se þeodcyning ðafian sceolde
> Eafores anne dom. (lines 2961–64a)

> There was the grey-haired Ongentheow brought to bay by the edges of the sword, so that the people-king must submit to the sole judgment of Eofor.

Ongentheow dies in battle, enacting Overing's ultimate masculine statement: "I will triumph or I will die." Ongentheow has already killed Haethcyn, Hygelac's brother, at Ravenswood; Eofor continues the feud by killing Ongentheow to avenge Haethcyn's death. Though *blondenfeax*, Ongentheow is not passive, feeble, crying, or sleeping with women. He preserves his masculinity intact until the end of his life, showing that, in *Beowulf*, a man's advancing age does not necessarily mean a movement away from masculinity on Clover's continuum.

In contrast to heroic and grey-haired Ongentheow, the three references to Hrothgar as *blondenfeax* occur at key moments when he is acting in a manner that undermines his masculinity, defined as his ability to make absolute statements or to exert his power and status over other men. The last of these is the use in the farewell scene, to which I will return in a moment; the others occur at Hrothgar's departure from the shore of the mere when the Danes think Beowulf has probably been killed and at one of Hrothgar's retirements to his bed (discussed above as a feminizing action):

> Blondenfeaxe,
> gomele ymb godne ongeador spræcon,
> þæt hig þæs æðelinges eft ne wendon,
> þæt he sigehreðig secean come
> mærne þeoden; (lines 1594b–98a)

The grey-haired ones, old [knowledgeable] about goodness, together said that they did not expect again this hero, who had come victorious to seek the famous lord.

> wolde blondenfeax beddes neosan,
> gamela Scylding. (lines 1791–92a)

The grey-haired one wished to seek his bed, the ancient Scylding.

In the first of these passages, the word *blondenfeaxe* is plural, referring not only to Hrothgar but to all the Danes who lack the faith in Beowulf that the Geats (who remain by the shore) demonstrate. The second reference occurs the night before Beowulf's departure; again, Hrothgar has deliberately absented himself from the place of battle and the place of male bonding, where warriors sleep in the hall together, ostensibly prepared for battle.[56] Thus, Hrothgar is *blondenfeax* and ineffectual, in contrast to Ongentheow, who is *blondenfeax* and heroic and super-masculine.

The emotional tone of the farewell scene, wherein Hrothgar is also termed *blondenfeax*, has elicited relatively little critical comment. Even in editions of *Beowulf,* notes on the scene tend to focus on the odd construction "him wæs bega wen" (line 1873) or on the lost letters in the manuscript rather than the unusual content.[57] Chickering devotes a section of his commentary to "Hrothgar's Tears," noting that the emotion in this passage can be appreciated only by parents who have watched children depart.[58] In 1967 Thomas Wright analyzed the scene in detail and managed to interpret the scene in such a way that the tension of emotion and desperation disappear.[59] Wright not only "contorts familiar formulas,"[60] but reads Hrothgar and Beowulf as representational ideas rather than characters, conveniently dismissing the discomfort the scene produces in the reader.

Wright begins by questioning a reading of the passage that "turns him [Hrothgar] from a stalwart if tragic king to a sentimental ancient whose concern for his own mortality is neither admirable nor Teutonic."[61] Wright is unabashedly in favor of interpreting Hrothgar as an active participant in the heroic ethos; he refers to his "interest in restoring Hrothgar to the good eminence he deserves as a vigorous and exemplary figure in the epic." Wright also discusses at length "him wæs bega wen," in his translation removing the emendation of *no* in line 1875 so that Beowulf and Hrothgar *do* (rather than do not) expect that they will see each other again. This reading begins Wright's argument that the poet "is at pains to justify and explain Hrothgar's emotional outburst." Wright's use of the word "justify" is illuminating; the emotion of the scene obviously unsettles him and needs to be accounted for.

The second half of Wright's reading focuses on the last three lines of the farewell scene, and he restructures the grammar of the scene in a manner of which I thoroughly approve. Most editors read *langað* as a noun ("longing") and *beorn* as a verb ("burned"); they translate lines 1879–80, in effect, "secret longing burned within his blood." Like Wright, I reverse the grammatical usages, so that *langað* is a verb ("longs, desires") and *beorn* is a noun ("a warrior, a man").

Wright does not address the lexical precedents for such translations, so I shall do so here. Although Dobbie attempts to cite some precedent uses of *beorn* (third-person-singular preterite indicative of *byrnan*) as a verb in Old English poetry, none of them are unproblematic.[62] Dobbie's references to *Guthlac* (lines 938, 964, 980) are actually to the word *born*; *born* occurs in *Beowulf,* as well, as a third-person-singular preterite indicative of *byrnan* (line 2673). Dobbie's citation of *beorn* in *Christ I* (line 540) is actually to a "corrected reading" of *b-orn* with an erasure between the *b* and the *o*; however, in their edition of the *Exeter Book,* Krapp and Dobbie suggest the erased letter is an *i,* not an *e.*[63] *Beorn*'s usage as a verb in *Beowulf* at line

1880, if accepted, is unique within the poem and most likely within the poetic corpus; editors can produce no substantive evidence of *beorn* as a verb elsewhere. In contrast, forms of *beorn* mean "man, warrior" ten times in *Beowulf* alone. Lexical evidence in the text and in the corpus points to a reading of *beorn* as a noun meaning "warrior."

Langað occurs seven times in the Old English corpus; all six of the other uses are third-person-singular verb forms.[64] If *langað* is a noun, it is the only usage of the word in that way; concordance evidence points to Wright's and my grammatical interpretation, that *langað* is a verb rather than a unique noun form. The usual grammatical construction de-personalizes the "longing" and lessens the emotional effect: "the longing burned." The more active, immediate translation of "the warrior desires" conveys a more subject, emotional intensity.

At this grammatical juncture Wright and I part company, however. Wright reads the last lines of this scene within a "generalizing intent of the poet" and sees in the tears not sorrow at Beowulf's departure but joy in "the continuity of valor."[65] For Wright, Hrothgar is "submitting to tears that acknowledge, not gratitude and regret, but fellowship and a sense of destined succession." His tears show "a bond well known among men who have shared combat together and discovered in their mutual strength unsuspected kinship." Wright seems untroubled that Hrothgar and Beowulf have very specifically *not* shared combat, that they have no "mutual" strength (Beowulf conducted both battles alone), and that Beowulf has rejected Hrothgar's offer of kinship by asserting his ties to Hygelac.

Wright's translation of these lines, translating *langað* as the emotionally neutral "belongs to," reads:

> for in his heart he held him fast
> in the custom that belongs to dear men
> as a warrior of the same blood.

My translation emphasizes rather than neutralizes the emotion of the scene:

> but in his [Hrothgar's] spirit (with heart-bonds fast because of the dear man) the man secretly longed for him [Beowulf] with blood.

Where Wright sees a generalized heroic bond, I see an emotional power struggle. Wright's translation puts Hrothgar and Beowulf on relatively even ground;

they are each powerful as well as ingratiatingly indebted to the other. His reading depends, however, on ignoring the faltering masculinity and power of Hrothgar that has been constructed in the text previous to the farewell scene; rather than a bonded camaraderie, the farewell scene bespeaks emotion wherein the aging male longs not just for Beowulf's approval and acceptance, but for the power implicit in becoming the father of the powerful son.

Beowulf is unmistakably the masculine figure of power in this scene, as throughout the poem. His response to Hrothgar's outburst of emotion is the same as his response to the offer of adoption: he ignores it, thinking about his gain, his treasure, and not about its source. In a striking change of tone, after the poet tells us that Hrothgar is longing for Beowulf in his blood, Beowulf simply walks away ("him Beowulf þanan," "away from him Beowulf thence," line 1880). He is thinking not about the man he has just left, the alliance he has forged, or the ties he has formed. Instead, he is "since hremig" ("exulting in treasure," line 1882), gloating about the gifts he received and the greatness they signify in him. His power over Hrothgar is absolute, just like everything else about him.

The syntax of one of John Hill's sentences makes Beowulf's absolute control of the situation clear: "He has come to love this great warrior as a son, to hope for a kinship and a continuing relationship in any connection Beowulf might want or allow."[66] Beowulf has the power to "allow" Hrothgar to have a relationship with him. Later in that essay, Hill defines Hrothgar's love for Beowulf as "anxious."[67] Similarly, Irving comments on the power Beowulf demonstrates in this scene:

> Hrothgar's deep love for Beowulf . . . evident . . . in his outburst of tears when Beowulf leaves to return to his own people, is wholly justified and genuinely touching—but it betrays a terrible dependence.[68]

Irving's sense of Hrothgar's dependence here confirms that, in the farewell scene, Hrothgar does not "move up" on the continuum of masculinity. Rather than a shared masculine bond, his inability to control his emotions and Beowulf's neglect of their expression show him to be a figure of impotence, crying while Beowulf walks away.

• • •

Hrothgar's attempt to adopt Beowulf is another strategy that fails; had he succeeded, he would have become the Father to Beowulf the powerful Son and as such accrued power through his implicit domination of the son. A brief foray into psychoanalytic theory and psychoanalytic readings of *Beowulf* reveals that fatherhood, as Lees has intimated, is a fragile institution in *Beowulf*, and Beowulf chooses Hygelac, rather than Hrothgar, as the Father to whom he submits himself in his Oedipal drama.

The Oedipus complex is one of the primary concepts in twentieth-century psychoanalytic theory. The Oedipal narrative describes the process by which "the child," implicitly male, grows into a contributing member of society who obeys and accrues status from its laws. The resolution of the Oedipus complex, first described by Sigmund Freud and refined by (among others) Jacques Lacan, is a form of socialization. For Freud, children wish to be able, like Sophocles's Oedipus, to kill their fathers and have sex with their mothers. He says of a spectator of Sophocles's play:

> He reacts as though by self-analysis he had recognized the Oedipus complex in himself and had unveiled the will of the gods and the oracle as exalted disguises of his own unconscious. It is as though he was obliged to remember the two wishes—to do away with his father and in place of him take his mother to wife—and be horrified at them.[69]

Lacan's expansion of Freud determines, partially through linguistics,[70] that the resolution of the drives represented in the Oedipus complex is the child's entrance into language, the Symbolic. This resolution implicitly requires acceptance of the Law of the Father. As the child acquires language, he no longer wants to kill his father and have sex with his mother; the Father becomes a revered figure of power, power in which the child can share, while the mother, the Other without the phallus, is renounced as object.

For Lacan, the phallus and the paternal are entwined. The power to create and regulate language depends on both: the phallus "is a signification that is evolved only by what we call a metaphor, in particular, the paternal metaphor."[71] Lacan links "the signifier of the Father, as author of the Law, with death";[72] in a Lacanian analysis, powerful concepts of death, the phallus, signification, and Law meet in the figure of the Father.

If we are looking for Oedipal Fathers in *Beowulf*, we might compare Hrothgar and the other *blondenfeax* man in *Beowulf*, Ongentheow, who is killed by the younger Eofor in an inter-tribal feud that also spans generations within the tribes of Swedes and Geats. As such, Ongentheow could be read as Father in an Oedipus complex in which the son or younger man *succeeds* in killing the Father and (possibly) having sex with the

Mother—Ongentheow's wife was abducted by the Geats before the battle of Ravenswood. Indeed, Ongentheow is defined specifically as a father, his wife specifically as a mother, in the description of the battle:

> Sona him se froda fæder Ohtheres,
> eald ond egesfull ondslyht ageaf,
> abreot brimwisan, bryd ahredde,
> gomela iomeowlan golde berofene,
> Onelan modor ond Otheres; (lines 2928–32)

> At once the wise father of Ohthere, old and terrible, returned the onslaught, cut down the sea-king, rescued the bride, the old woman bereft of gold, the mother of Onela and Ohthere.

Appropriately enough, Eofor marries Hygelac's daughter as part of his reward for Ongentheow's death, receiving a highly suitable bride for his efforts on the (Oedipal?) battlefield. Although dead, Ongentheow, the old and terrible Father, dies with his masculinity and position as Father intact (as Lees says, "The only good hero . . . is a dead one").[73] Hrothgar, in contrast, has to live as a rejected Father, his masculinity faltering.

Psychoanalytic readings of *Beowulf*, like Lacan and Freud, tend to focus on the son, on Beowulf. For example, James Earl argues that readers and listeners of *Beowulf* identify with Beowulf in his position as thane only in the first half of the poem; as Beowulf becomes more of a "superego" in the second half, the reader transfers that identification to Wiglaf.[74] Hrothgar receives some attention as a father-figure who gives Beowulf advice,[75] but the focus is rarely on him. One exception is Strother Purdy, who reads Grendel as Hrothgar's dream, a creation of his unconsciousness: Hrothgar and Grendel never appear together because they are, in some way, the same.[76]

Another exception is John Miles Foley, whose essay "*Beowulf* and the Psychohistory of Anglo-Saxon Culture" argues that the poem "transmits the story of the psychological development of individual and of culture."[77] Foley's analysis takes an odd turn when he reads Hrothgar and Grendel as the good and the terrible fathers that Beowulf must face in his psychological development. For Foley, "the benevolent, positive aspect of the archetype is projected in the character of Hrothgar, under whom the hero-ego Beowulf must serve his heroic apprenticeship";[78] at the same time, Hrothgar is "a symbolic projection of the ego's successful adjustment to maleness."[79] While Hrothgar and Beowulf as father and son is nothing new, Grendel as Father strikes me as bizarre. Since Grendel has a mother, he is defined in the poem as a son, not a parent. Grendel functions more as a bad son to Hrothgar or an evil double of Beowulf (as suggested by Hill)[80] than as a "terrible father" whom Beowulf must castrate.[81]

These critics seem not to notice that Beowulf implicitly rejects Hrothgar's Fatherhood in a number of ways. He walks away with no comment after Hrothgar's emotional farewell embrace (Hill refers to "the world of a young man who has yet to meet and lose someone dear to him").[82] He does not respond to Hrothgar's offer of adoption in his speech that follows the offer (lines 958–79); he does not respond to the "sermon" or "harangue" either, except to sit down and continue feasting (lines 1785–89). He repeatedly affirms his loyalty to Hygelac, *Hygelac min*, his uncle. Hrothgar is a father-figure in the eyes of *Beowulf* critics, but not in the eyes of Beowulf. Hygelac, not Hrothgar, is Beowulf's Father.

Within the terms of Lacanian psychoanalysis, if Hrothgar is *not* the Father, he does not have the phallus. He does not determine signification or metaphor. He does not control the Law, the imposition of cultural norms. He can see himself in the position of powerful masculinity, in the position of Fatherhood, but is not actually there. The last scene in which we see Hrothgar is the farewell scene, his last-ditch attempt to assert masculinity by playing the role of Father to Beowulf as son. If Beowulf had responded at all to Hrothgar's emotion, his tears, the longing in his blood, it would have been an acknowledgement that Hrothgar held some sort of power over him. But he does not respond. Hrothgar is left at the veritable bottom of Clover's continuum, crying as the hero walks away without speaking.

The two scenes I have discussed, Hrothgar's exit from and entrance to Heorot and the farewell scene, show that Hrothgar's masculinity is in jeopardy in this poem that constructs the masculine, as Overing defines and problematizes it, in oppositional absolutes. Neither through heterosexual relations with his wife nor through paternal, quasi-erotic relations with Beowulf can Hrothgar regain his once vital, now fading masculine power. Just as in the medieval Scandinavia that Clover describes, masculinity is an achievable or losable quality in *Beowulf*, and Hrothgar is losing it, despite his pretensions to the contrary. As such, he functions in the text as a warning to other masculine figures about the fragility of that masculinity; perhaps, at some level, Beowulf faces the dragon so that he will be like Ongentheow and die with his masculinity intact rather than, like Hrothgar, fade into effeminate irrelevance.

NOTES

[1] Virginia Woolf, *A Room of One's Own* (1929; reprint New York, 1957), p. 27.

[2] Clare Lees, "Men and *Beowulf*," in *Medieval Masculinities: Regarding Men in the Middle Ages*, ed. Clare Lees (Minneapolis, 1994), p. 142 (emphasis hers). This essay is reprinted in this volume.

[3] Carol Clover, "Regardless of Sex: Men, Women, and Power in Early Northern Europe," *Speculum* 68 (1993): 379. This essay is reprinted in this volume.

[4] Clover, "Regardless of Sex," p. 379.

[5] Clover, "Regardless of Sex," p. 380 (emphasis hers).

[6] Allen Frantzen, "When Women Aren't Enough," *Speculum* 68 (1993): 445–71.

[7] Frantzen, "When Women Aren't Enough," p. 449.

[8] Citations of the poem are from Fr. Klaeber, ed., *"Beowulf" and the Fight at Finnsburg*, 3rd ed. with supplements (Lexington, Mass., 1950), by line number.

[9] Frantzen, "When Women Aren't Enough," p. 461.

[10] Clover, "Regardless of Sex," p. 381.

[11] Clover, "Regardless of Sex," p. 383 n. 68.

[12] Translations are my own, and are as literal as I have been able to make them.

[13] See similar constructions in lines 129–30, 146–49, and 170–71.

[14] Lees, "Men and *Beowulf*," p. 133.

[15] Lees, "Men and *Beowulf*," p. 142.

[16] The only king in the poem who passes his kingdom intact to his son is Offa, father of Eomer and husband of the enigmatic Modthryth.

[17] Rolf Bremmer shows that the relationship between sister's son and mother's brother is an important one throughout most cultures; in *Beowulf*, Bremmer argues, that relationship is often mutually satisfying, while the father's brother-brother's son relationship is fraught with tension. See Rolf Bremmer, Jr., "The Importance of Kinship: Uncle and Nephew in *Beowulf*," *Amsterdamer Beitrage zur Alteren Germanistik* 15 (1980): 21–38.

[18] Lees, "Men and *Beowulf*," p. 145–46.

[19] John Leyerle, "Beowulf the Hero and the King," *Medium Ævum* 34 (1965): 89–102.

[20] For a similar reading see A. E. C. Canitz, "Kingship in *Beowulf*," *Mankind Quarterly* 27 (1986): 97–119.

[21] See, for example, John Halverson, "The World of *Beowulf*," *ELH* 36 (1969): 593–608; Michael Swanton, *Crisis and Development in Germanic Society 700–800: "Beowulf" and the Burden of Kingship* (Goppingen, 1982); Raymond Tripp, "The Exemplary Role of Hrothgar and Heorot," *Philological Quarterly* 56 (1977): 123–29.

[22] Most recently discussed by John Hill, "Hrothgar's Noble Rule," in *Social Approaches to Viking Studies*, ed. Ross Samson (Glasgow, 1991), pp. 169–78,

and by Stephanie Hollis, "Beowulf and the Succession," *Parergon* n.s. 1 (1983): 39–54.

23 For similar praises of Hrothgar as good if not ideal king, see Malcolm Brennan, "Hrothgar's Government," *Journal of English and Germanic Philology* 84 (1985): 3–15; John Gardner, "Fulgentius's *Expositio Vergiliana Continentia* and the Plan of *Beowulf*: Another Approach to the Poem's Style," *Papers on Language and Literature* 6 (1970): 227–62; Marie Nelson, "It is More Honorable to Give . . . ," *Neuphilologische Mitteilungen* 74 (1973): 624–29; and Levin Schücking, "The Ideal of Kingship in *Beowulf*," in *An Anthology of "Beowulf" Criticim*, ed. Lewis Nicholson (Bloomington, 1963), pp. 35–49 (originally "Das Koenigsideal im *Beowulf*," *Modern Humanties Research Association Bulletin* 3 [1929]: 143–54).

24 For recent analyses of Hrothgar as a weak king, see John Niles, *"Beowulf": The Poem and its Tradition* (Cambridge, Mass., 1983); Edward B. Irving, Jr., "What to Do with Old Kings," in *Comparative Research on Oral Tradtions*, ed. John Miles Foley (Columbus, 1987), pp. 259–68; René Derolez, "*Hrothgar* King of Denmark," in *Multiple Worlds, Multiple Words*, ed. Hena Maes-Jelinek et al. (Liège, 1987), pp. 51–58.

25 Robert Kaske, "*Sapientia* and *Fortitudo* and the Controlling Theme of *Beowulf*," *Studies in Philology* 55 (1958): 435.

26 Klaeber outlines the speech into four divisions: an introduction (lines 1700–09), the Heremod section (lines 1709–24), "the 'sermon' proper," (lines 1724–68), and the conclusion (lines 1769–84). Most critics have followed these divisions in their analyses of the speech.

27 For the classic exegetical reading, see Margaret Goldsmith, *The Mode and Meaning of "Beowulf"* (London, 1970); for secular or heroic analyses, see Michael Cherniss, *Ingeld and Christ: Heroic Concepts and Values in Old English Christian Poetry* (The Hague, 1972), and Robert Kindrick, "Germanic *Sapientia* and the Heroic Ethos of *Beowulf*," *Mediaevalia et Humanistica* 10 (1981): 1–17.

28 Stephen Bandy, "*Beowulf*: The Defense of Heorot," *Neophilologus* 56 (1972): 91.

29 Irving, "What to Do with Old Kings," p. 260.

30 Sara Highley also discusses the ambiguity of Hrothgar's status in "*Aldre on Ofre*, or the Reluctant Hart: A Study of Liminality in *Beowulf*," *Neuphilologische Mitteilungen* 87 (1986): 342–53.

31 Gillian Overing, *Language, Sign, and Gender in "Beowulf"* (Carbondale, 1990), p. xv.

32 The sign systems of the giantish sword are also discussed by Allen Frantzen, "Writing the Unreadable *Beowulf*: 'Writan' and 'Forwritan,' the Pen and the Sword," *Exemplaria* 3 (1991): 327–57, and by Richard Schrader, "The Language

on the Giant's Sword Hilt in *Beowulf*," *Neuphilologische Mitteilungen* 94 (1993): 141–47.

[33] Overing, *Language, Sign, and Gender in "Beowulf*," p. 70 (emphasis hers).

[34] Overing, *Language, Sign, and Gender in "Beowulf*," p. 70.

[35] In an interesting breakdown of binarism, the two most obvious examples of the miserly Other in *Beowulf* are masculine, not feminine: Heremod, the king who perished in exile because of his closed-handedness, and the Dragon, whose treasure becomes useless because it is not used in an economy of exchange.

[36] Overing, *Language, Sign, and Gender in "Beowulf*," pp. 73–74. Overing is quoting Fred Robinson, "Teaching the Backgrounds: History, Religion, Culture," in *Approaches to Teaching "Beowulf*," ed. Jess Bessinger and Robert Yeager (New York, 1984), pp. 118–19.

[37] Overing, *Language, Sign, and Gender in "Beowulf*," p. 74.

[38] Niles, *"Beowulf": The Poem and its Tradition*, p. 108.

[39] Niles, *"Beowulf": The Poem and its Tradition*, p. 108.

[40] Raymond Tripp, *"Beowulf 920b–24: Avian Humor and Hrothgar's Approach to Heorot," Literary Essays on Language and Meaning in the Poem Called "Beowulf"* (Lewiston, 1992), p. 61.

[41] All but two of the uses of Ecgtheow's name in *Beowulf* are genitive compounds with *bearn*, *sunu* or *maga*. See Klaeber, *Beowulf*, p. 434.

[42] Klaeber, *Beowulf*, p. 438.

[43] For analyses of the legal and emotional action of this scene, see John Miles Foley, "*Beowulf* and the Psychohistory of Anglo-Saxon Culture," *American Imago* 344 (1977): 133–53; Elaine Tuttle Hansen, "Hrothgar's Sermon in *Beowulf* as Parental Wisdom," *Anglo-Saxon England* 10 (1982): 53–67; John Hill, "Hrothgar's Noble Rule"; Hollis, "Beowulf and the Succession"; and Irving, "What to Do with Old Kings."

[44] See below for an explanation of my unconventional translation of this half-line.

[45] The foliation of the *Beowulf* manuscript, Cotton Vitellius A.xv, is a matter of some dispute; I am following what E. V. K. Dobbie, in *"Beowulf" and "Judith*," Anglo-Saxon Poetic Records 4 (New York, 1953), terms the "old" foliation since I am working with the Zupitza facsimile, the only facsimile readily available: Julius Zupitza, ed., *Beowulf*, 2nd ed., rev. Norman Davis, Early English Text Society o.s. 245 (1959; reprint Oxford, 1967).

[46] Missing are the end of *seoððan* (line 1875), *wæs* (line 1876), "breost" from *breostwylm* (line 1877), *on* (line 1878), "deo" from *deorum* (line 1879), and "lo" from *blode* (line 1880). The *no* at 1875 is an emendatory addition.

[47] Zupitza, *Beowulf*, p. 86.

[48] Frantzen, "When Women Aren't Enough," p. 461.

[49] Lees, "Men and *Beowulf*," p.142.

[50] Lees, "Men and *Beowulf*," p. 142.

[51] Howell D. Chickering, *"Beowulf": A Dual Languge Edition* (New York, 1977), p. 348.

[52] There are over 150 uses of *cyssan* and *gecysan* listed in *A Microfiche Concordance to Old English*, ed. Antonette di Paolo Healy and Richard Venezky (Newark, 1980). I will reference the *Concordance* by letter and fiche number; for instance MCOE G017 refers to fiche 17 of the letter G.

[53] Chickering, *Beowulf*, p. 348.

[54] One possible exception could be the fantasy of the narrator of *The Wanderer*, who imagines laying his head in his lord's lap (lines 41–44); this emotionally charged moment, however, exists only in the narrator's mind, while the farewell scene occurs within the textual "reality" of *Beowulf*. Another possible exception could be the end of *The Battle of Maldon*, as the thanes prepare to follow their leader into death, an intensely emotionally charged moment. These men, however, are shaking their spears and flinging javelins, not crying and embracing each other.

[55] MCOE B015. Outside *Beowulf*, *blondenfeax* refers to Sarah and Lot, both in *Genesis A*. Sarah is called grey-haired (line 2343a) when the poet affirms that one day she will bear a son for Abraham; Lot is called grey-haired when his daughters ply him with drink and commit incest with him to continue his line after the destruction of Sodom (line 2602b). It is interesting that the other *blondenfeax* characters, like Hrothgar, have trouble conceiving or begetting heirs.

[56] It should be noted that Beowulf does not sleep in Heorot on the night of Grendel's mother's attack—"næs Beowulf ðær / ac wæs oþer in ær geteohhod / æfter maþðum-gife mærum Geate" ("Beowulf was not there but other [accommodation] was previously assigned to the noble Geat after the treasure-giving," lines 1299–1301). Beowulf, however, was *assigned* those quarters, while Hrothgar always actively *seeks* his bed.

[57] See, for example, the editions of Dobbie and Klaeber (both cited above) and of C.L. Wrenn and W.F. Bolton, eds., *"Beowulf," with the Finnesburg Fragment*, rev. ed. (Exeter, 1988).

[58] Chickering, *Beowulf*, p. 347.

[59] Thomas Wright, "Hrothgar's Tears," *Modern Philology* 65 (1967): 39–44.

[60] Chickering comments that Wright's conclusions come "at the cost of contorting a number of familiar formulas" (*Beowulf*, p. 348).

[61] I am following Wright's argument, "Hrothgar's Tears," pp. 39–41.

[62] Dobbie, *"Beowulf" and "Judith,"* p. 211.

[63] *The Exeter Book*, ed. G. P. Krapp and E. V. K. Dobbie, Anglo-Saxon Poetic Records 3 (New York, 1936), p. 18.

[64] MCOE L002. Other uses of *langað* are as follows: (1) *Genesis*, lines 495–97a, when the devil asks Adam if he *desires* to be with God; (2) *Soul and Body I*, lines 152–54a, when the soul *longs* for the body to realize its afflictions; (3) Ælfric's *De temporibus anni* 4.44, when the day *lengthens*; (4) *Byrhtferth's Manual*, when the night *lengthens* at midwinter; (5) Psalm 81:5 (82:5 in the King James version), when the sinners *languish*; (6) *Durham Proverbs* 9, when men *long* most eagerly for love.

[65] Wright, "Hrothgar's Tears," p. 43; all quotations in this paragraph are from this page.

[66] Hill, "Hrothgar's Noble Rule," p. 175.

[67] Hill, "Hrothgar's Noble Rule," p. 176.

[68] Irving, "What to Do with Old Kings," pp. 263–64.

[69] Sigmund Freud, "The Development of the Libido and the Sexual Organizations," in *Introductory Lectures on Psychoanalysis*, trans. James Strachey (New York, 1966), p. 331.

[70] Jacques Lacan, "The Meaning of the Phallus," in *Feminine Sexuality*, ed. Juliet Mitchell and Jacqueline Rose, trans. Jacqueline Rose (New York, 1982), p. 78.

[71] Jacques Lacan, "On the Possible Treatment of Psychosis," in *Écrits: A Selection*, trans. Alan Sheridan (New York, 1977), p. 198.

[72] Lacan, "On the Possible Treatment of Psychosis," p. 199.

[73] Lees, "Men and *Beowulf*," p. 146.

[74] James Earl, "*Beowulf* and the Origins of Civilization," in *Speaking Two Languages: Traditional Disciplines and Contemporary Theory in Medieval Studies*, ed. Allen J. Frantzen (Albany, 1991), pp. 84–85.

[75] See, for instance, Hansen, "Hrothgar's Sermon."

[76] Strother Purdy, "Beowulf and Hrothgar's Dream," *Chaucer Review* 21 (1986): 267–68.

[77] Foley, "*Beowulf* and the Psychohistory of Anglo-Saxon Culture," p. 135.

[78] Foley, "*Beowulf* and the Psychohistory of Anglo-Saxon Culture," p. 138.

[79] Foley, "*Beowulf* and the Psychohistory of Anglo-Saxon Culture," p. 140.

[80] John Hill, *The Cultural World of "Beowulf"* (Toronto, 1995), p. 123.

[81] Foley, "*Beowulf* and the Psychohistory of Anglo-Saxon Culture," p. 150.

[82] Hill, "Hrothgar's Noble Rule," p. 177.

VOICES FROM THE MARGINS: WOMEN AND TEXTUAL ENCLOSURE IN *BEOWULF*

SHARI HORNER

I n an article published in 1960, Paull F. Baum speculated (jokingly) that *Beowulf* was written by a woman, perhaps an educated abbess such as Hild.[1] According to Baum, "feminine authorship would account for many things in the poem" (p. 358), including its relative lack of graphic violence, its sympathy for underdogs (including women), its moderate descriptions of victory celebrations ("with none of the grosser indulgences"), and its "extraordinary amount of talking and the tendencies to 'digress'" (p. 359). Baum himself seems not to subscribe to this theory, but asserts that such speculations "do no harm if they are not taken too seriously" (p. 359).

Though his language seems laughable today and his speculation is, at any rate, unverifiable, Baum's theory of female authorship for *Beowulf* nonetheless creates a useful starting point for thinking about the women of *Beowulf*. Based on twentieth-century essentialist views of femininity, his suppositions that women are typically unconcerned with gore and battles, sympathetic to other women's plights, and given to talking too much—simply because they are women—are of course cultural constructions; yet they reflect the belief that women behave certain ways due to biology rather

From *The Discourse of Enclosure* (Albany, 2001), pp. 65–100; reprinted with permission of State University of New York Press. The only alterations to the original have been to remove references Horner makes in the body of the essay to other sections of the book in which this essay originally appeared, and to amplify material in footnotes for the sake of clarity.

than to social conditioning. Recent feminist theory has taught us that such essentializing notions are not only wrong-headed but counterproductive, because they obscure the cultural conditions that produce "women" and "men" (themselves constructed categories) within a given culture. Thus analyzing the women—or men—of *Beowulf* according to modern standards will produce an unsatisfactory understanding, partial at best, of how Anglo-Saxon culture viewed its women and men. Rather than evaluate (as Baum unwittingly suggests) the gender dynamics of the poem according to anachronistic guidelines, we would do better to approach such an analysis by reconstructing (as much as possible) the cultural, social, and historical contexts in which the poem was written.[2]

In this essay, I will consider how models of female enclosure operate in *Beowulf*. Unlike Baum, I will not speculate on either the sex or provenance of the author. In examining the ways that *Beowulf* contains its female characters, I do not mean to suggest any literal or historical connection between the poem and female monasticism, though of course the poem has long been recognized to document, however implicitly, a Christian world-view.[3] Yet because *Beowulf* is foundational for any study of Old English literature, its female characters are regularly the standards by which other women in Old English literature are examined. Thus it is important to investigate the extent to which the cultural and rhetorical trope of enclosure shapes and defines the women of *Beowulf*.

I have suggested in other writings that the enclosure model in female monasticism functions on a physical, material level by literally confining and isolating female speakers. This model serves to maintain monastic imperatives including regulating the female body and its desires, reducing the threats of female sexuality and female authority, and attempting (though not successfully) to silence the female voice. I shall argue here that the control of women in *Beowulf* is analogous to that of women in early medieval monastic culture, and that reading the poem's women in terms of enclosure reveals the broad cultural theme of female containment—and its corollary, the danger of escape—that mark much of early English literature. We shall see that the women in *Beowulf* are enclosed literally (within physical space), textually (within the poem's narrative structures), and symbolically (within the poem's cultural conceptions of femininity and within kinship structures). Even the text itself works to maintain control of its female characters in terms of both plot and structure. Within the poem, women's stories frame and are framed by each other, functioning intratextually to construct a *Beowulf*ian concept of conventional femininity.

It is important to note at the outset that a study of the discourse of female enclosure in *Beowulf* will not simply reconfirm traditional models of Anglo-Saxon femininity as passive and long-suffering.[4] Instead, examining *how* the stories of women are told and retold will offer insight into the rhetorical practices of the poem. Feminist scholars such as Jane Chance, Helen Damico, and Gillian Overing have demonstrated that the women of *Beowulf* are not incidental but integral—indispensable—to the poem's plot, narrative structure, and meaning. Examining the tellings and retellings of these women's stories, I will suggest, allows us to better understand the poem's constructions of (and the limits it imposes on) femininity. The rhetorical model of female enclosure is, I will argue, fundamentally linked to the poem's narrative operations.

Recent studies of *Beowulf*—long examined for its oral properties—demonstrate that the poem is, to a significant extent, conditioned by a textual or literate consciousness.[5] Late twentieth-century readers have increasingly seen *Beowulf* as a story about story-telling, a text that both constructs and contains many other kinds of texts—histories, sermons, lyrics, and so forth—told for the edification and entertainment of the poem's internal and external audiences alike. John Niles summarizes the correspondences between orality and literacy that likely shaped the *Beowulf* audience's response to the poem:

> [T]he society to which *Beowulf* pertains was using writing, and not just oral
> poetry, to express an ideology capable of persuading people to be governed
> and rulers to govern well. . . . They were familiar with the use of poetry in
> English as a vehicle for Christian doctrine and a means of reinventing the
> Germanic past.[6]

Similarly, the stories told within *Beowulf*, while orally transmitted by its various characters, imply a familiarity or resonance with other medieval textual traditions. Certain of these stories in fact resonate with the early medieval ideology of female enclosure. *Beowulf*'s reinvention of the Germanic past through poetry, as Niles puts it, means that we need not automatically assume that female enclosure is a Christian "overlay" added to the poem. Instead, the enclosure of women (possibly a tradition preserved from the poem's Germanic past, but certainly a feature of late Anglo-Saxon religious life) offers us a more complex way of reading the poem's treatment of women within the context of late Anglo-Saxon Christianity. *Beowulf*'s stories of women build upon and echo each other, so that these "texts" function intratextually to inform and revise themselves. According to Fred Robinson, this continual retelling is an integral feature of the poem: "That the poet was emphasizing that his poem is a retelling is suggested by the fact that he includes so much retelling within *Beowulf*. Repeatedly we are asked to listen to one account of an event and to compare it with another."[7]

Beowulf's stories about women form one cohesive set of "retellings." To show that the interdependent narrative threads of these stories all stem from the same source, I will suggest an analogy to a traditional medieval textual practice: each retelling functions as a gloss or commentary on the previous one and signals an interpretive act on the part of the teller. Like glosses on a manuscript page, the poem's stories about women are marginal yet integral to its meaning. To anticipate my argument briefly: we shall see that the originary story of Hildeburh, evidently familiar to the poem's internal and external audiences, represents the *scop*'s version of the traditional "peace-weaver" narrative (discussed below). This is the first telling within the poem (and although the Finn episode seems elliptical to us, it must have been well-known to the *Beowulf* audience). After the *scop* completes his song, Wealhtheow picks up the narrative and rewrites it, mingling Hildeburh's story with her own and revealing her dissatisfaction with the story's inevitable outcome. Following the intervention of Grendel's Mother, the narrator rewrites the story again in his linked accounts of Hygd and Modthryth. Finally, Beowulf himself concludes the story-telling with predictions about Freawaru that indict the peace-weaving system. Thus the poem contains (encloses) its female characters (and femininity more generally) as it tells and retells their stories. Out of the "text" of Hildeburh an intratextual system develops that both glosses and interprets the roles available to women in the poem. The tropes and thematics of female enclosure govern femininity in *Beowulf* as much as in the female elegies or in more overtly religious literature.

The dominant critical model for women in *Beowulf* has typically been the peace-weaver, *freoðuwebbe*.[8] The metaphor refers to a woman's arranged marriage to a member of a hostile tribe, as a means of securing peace between feuding factions. Such peace might be the result of either childbearing or verbal diplomacy. In either event, the peace-weaver is framed symbolically between two groups of men, confined by a strict kinship system, enclosed by and exchanged between the groups. Ironically, as Chance and Overing have shown, the peace-weaver inevitably fails; the peace rarely lasts for long and peace-weaving often produces death.[9] Yet at the same time, peace-weaving is productive—if only temporarily. Both childbirth and diplomacy (even if short-lived) are creative acts: the peace-weaver produces a "text" that rewrites history, either her own or that of the two tribes. Among the products of peace-weaving are the new stories that develop out of what is already known.

I return, then, to the analogy of the medieval gloss and the textual operations of the commentary tradition. In Martin Irvine's definition, the medieval gloss "is essentially an interpretive supplement, a set of expressions that attempts to disclose some latent or suppressed meaning in an earlier set of expressions." The gloss supplements the source text by providing "an interpretation that is itself a text." [10] The textual activity of glossing works two ways: a gloss looks back to, indeed is dependent upon, the source text from which it derives its meaning. And it looks ahead, insofar as it creates new meaning, a new interpretation of the source. In Michael Clanchy's useful description, "[t]he successive series of glosses around a central text show, like tree rings, the proliferation of written record over generations of scholars."[11]

The etymological links between weaving and textuality have long been recognized.[12] According to Mary Carruthers,

> The Latin word *textus* comes from the verb meaning "to weave" and it is in the institutionalizing of a story through *memoria* that textualizing occurs. Literary works become institutions as they weave a community together by providing it with shared experience and a certain kind of language. . . . Their meaning is thought to be implicit, hidden, polysemous and complex, requiring continuing interpretation and adaptation. . . .
>
> In the process of textualizing, the original work acquires commentary and gloss; this activity is not regarded as something other than the text, but is the mark of textualization itself.[13]

Within *Beowulf*, a story such as the Finn episode provides precisely the sort of institutionalizing effect Carruthers identifies: it knits the community at Heorot together through its shared knowledge of the events at Finnsburg. We can trace the process of textualization as the story of Hildeburh—the peace-weaver's story—threads its way through the stories of women told throughout the poem. Each woman's story glosses (that is, reinterprets) the original peace-weaving narrative of the Finn episode. The poem's feminine texts offer a series of readings and rewritings that find closure, finally, through the hero's own indictment of the system they narrate.

AT THE CENTER: HILDEBURH AS FOUNDATIONAL TEXT

Hildeburh, the originary site of feminine textuality in *Beowulf*, is arguably the most fully enclosed woman in Old English literature. She is not technically a player in the main plot of the poem, but is instead a character in a lay sung by Hrothgar's *scop* during the victory banquet following Beowulf's defeat of Grendel. Her tragic story is so fragmentary and elliptical that we can only assume it was well-known to the poem's internal and external audiences. The *scop* tells of the legend of Finnsburg, specifically of a breakdown in the alliance formed between the Danes and the Frisians. Hildeburh, the daughter of the former Danish king and sister to the present king, was given in a peace-weaving marriage to Finn, king of the Frisians. When a violent quarrel broke out between the two sides, Hildeburh's brother and son (by Finn) were killed. She ordered a joint funeral pyre for her brother and son, and we are told that she mourned their deaths with song. Following a temporary peace settlement, the hostilities erupted again, Finn was killed, and Hildeburh was transported (along with the other battle spoils) back to her people, the Danes. As the *scop* finishes his song, festivities at Heorot resume.

The lay begins and ends by focusing closely on Hildeburh; it is obviously her story, and she frames the narrative. At the same time, she is framed by it: this episode of approximately 90 lines (1067–1159) locates Hildeburh at its beginning (lines 1071–74), its midpoint (lines 1114–18), and its end (lines 1157–59).[14] Her story is also enclosed (framed) by the two appearances of Wealhtheow (lines 612b–41 and 1162b–91). As Pauline Head has recently demonstrated, framing devices (or ring structures) in Old English literature and art act as interpretive aids to readers or viewers, enabling more nuanced readings of the text within the frame:[15]

> Frames participate in the construction of the reading process. The decorative borders of Anglo-Saxon manuscript illuminations relate to the images they contain in ways that complicate interpretation. . . . [T]hey draw attention to themselves (so that the reader lingers in enjoyment of them and is aware of the text as something that has been crafted), and then, often, they overlap with the image, suggesting that the limit they have traced can be transgressed. The framing devices of Old English poetry construct a similar reading process, drawing attention to themselves and overlapping semantically with the passage they have defined. Like all frames, those of

Old English poetry guide the reader's interpretation of the text (mediate between the readers and text), telling her or him that this linguistic unit exists within a larger context, yet is in some way distinct from its surroundings (so they also mediate between general and specific).[16]

The Finn episode, then, draws attention to itself by both enclosing (framing) and being enclosed by (framed by) Hildeburh; this complex structural enclosure is further framed by the two appearances of Wealhtheow, which, as Head's discussion suggests, overlap with and guide our interpretation of Hildeburh's story.

Hildeburh's reported speech ordering the funeral pyre occurs at the precise midpoint of the episode, that is, 45 lines into this 90-line passage. Though we do not hear her voice, and though many critics have found her to be hopelessly passive throughout the episode, the moment at which she orders the funeral pyre is, rather, a moment of intense narrative, textual, and sensory power. She orders a visual symbol of the destroyed peace accord, and the pyre signals not only the breakdown in the alliance at Finnsburg, but also the impossibility of creating peace out of hostility. She, as much as Beowulf will do later, indicts the system through this gesture.[17] And like the speakers of the female elegies, she *geomrode giddum* ("mourns with songs," line 1118) from deep within the confines (literal and textual) of her enclosure.

Whereas the speakers of the female elegies, however, found means of self-expression within their enclosures, Hildeburh's voice is silenced within the poem, because the litotes introducing her actually removes the possibility of her speech:

Ne huru Hildeburh herian þorfte
Eotena treowe; unsynnum wearð
beloren leofum æt þam lindplegan
bearnum ond broðrum. . . . (lines 1071–74a)

Nor indeed had Hildeburh need to praise the faith of the Frisians; she was blameless, deprived of her loved ones, her son and her brother, at the shield-play.

The rhetorical figure plays its usual part in providing emphasis through understatement, yet in this case it also silences Hildeburh, denying the audience the opportunity to hear her condemnation of the Frisians. Nevertheless, the narrator absolves her of responsibility for the failed alliance by describing her as *unsynnum*, "blameless"; although some critics, such as Overing, have tended to see Hildeburh as a "failure" at peace-weaving, the breakdown in peace between the Danes and the Frisians is not attributed to her within the poem.

When Hildeburh does speak, however, as reported by the *scop*, she orders the ritual that displays the failed peace:

> Het ða Hildeburh æt Hnæfes ade
> hire selfre sunu sweoloðe befæstan
> banfatu bærnan, ond on bæl don
> eame on eaxle. (lines 1114–17a)

> Then Hildeburh commanded her own son [to be] entrusted to the flames on Hnaef's pyre, put on the pyre by his uncle's side, their bodies [to] burn.

Symbolically she continues to weave together the two sides of her family in an alliance—though here the alliance, on the funeral pyre of her brother and son, is a gruesome parody of the peaceful alliance her marriage was to have ensured. The burning bodies on the pyre are described in bloody and graphic terms:

> .... hafelan multon,
> bengeato burston, ðonne blod ætspranc,
> lað bite lices. (lines 1120b-22a)

> Their heads melted, their wounds burst open, the blood sprang out from their bodies' wounds.

By joining her son's body to that of her brother, Hildeburh symbolically "writes" the violent and deadly results of the hostilities between the two tribes. Not only is the body of her son a kind of "text" she has produced through the creative processes of peace-weaving, but the pyre, too, is her production, her text. When Hildeburh orders the funeral pyre, she performs her own textualizing act. The pyre serves as her commentary or gloss on a peace-weaving system that is, as Overing and others have noted, destined to self-destruct.[18]

The Finn episode is intensely physical. The funeral pyre requires us to focus on the burning bodies of Hildeburh's son and brother. Similarly, Hildeburh's peace-weaving role highlights the functions of her body within the narrative: her social roles as wife and mother are also necessarily physical ones. The narrative asks that we think about Hildeburh in spatial and sensory terms: symbolically framed by groups of men, she views the bodies of her dead relatives *under swegle* ("under the sky," line 1079a). When she mourns at the funeral pyre, she is not silently weeping, but rather audibly *geomrode giddum* ("lamenting with songs," line 1118a). At the end, she is physically removed from Finn's hall: when the Danes finally seek revenge for Hnaef's death, Finn is killed "ond seo cwen numen" ("and the queen taken," line 1153b). The Danes take Finn's treasures for themselves, and Hildeburh, too, is carried back to the Danes' homeland as part of the spoils:

> Sceotend Scyldinga to scypon feredon
> eal ingesteald eorðcyninges,
> swylce hie æt Finnes ham findan meahton
> sigla searogimma. Hie on sælade
> drihtlice wif to Denum feredon,
> læddon to leodum. (lines 1154–59a)

> The warriors of the Scyldings carried to the ship all the king's house-property, such as they could find at Finn's home, jewels and precious gems. They carried the noble woman to the Danes on a sea-journey, led her to [her?] people.

The verb *feredon*, "carried," describes the Danes' actions in transporting both the treasures and the woman, thus marking Hildeburh as a valuable commodity, one of Finn's treasures. This final mention of Hildeburh either requires us to view her as an object, similar to treasure, or at least reminds us that the Danes view her as such. Either way, she remains firmly under male control, so that leaving Finnsburg to return to her own people does not free her from either physical or social containment.

Even the elements of Hildeburh's name signal her confined social position: *hild* signifies "battle"; *burh* or *burg* means "fortified place," according to Klaeber. The battle that results when the peace-weaving alliance fails (that is, the battle between the two male kinship groups that frame her) is contained within her very body. She embodies the unsuccessful peace, both as the mother of a dead son who was born of that alliance, and as the agent (the peace-weaver) who originally bound the hostile sides together. As a peace-weaving mother, her body once enclosed the "text" of that peace, and that body, *burh*, becomes the site of the battle, *hild*—she is the fortified place where the tribes met and fought. Hildeburh's is the first story we are told in *Beowulf*, and the most deeply embedded structurally. It is, in a sense, the foundation (the fortified place) of feminine textuality in the poem. As a peace-weaver, Hildeburh is enclosed between two groups of men. She is likewise enclosed textually, within the lay of Finnsburg, and framed by Wealhtheow's two appearances. Hildeburh's fragmentary story presumably does not originate with the *scop*; in retelling the canonical text, he glosses, provides commentary, on that story. His emphasis on Hildeburh's role may suggest his awareness of one important female listener, Wealhtheow.[19]

FRAMING THE TEXT: WEALHTHEOW RESPONDS

H. Ward Tonsfeldt has shown that the Finn episode is a tightly structured ring composition, with events extending outward in either direction from the central moment when Hildeburh orders the funeral pyre.[20] His schematic opens and closes with the narrator's warning, at lines 1017 and 1163, that the peace between Hrothgar and Hrothulf, his nephew, will be short-lived, and this warning is amplified through the account of the tragic events at Finnsburg. Yet extending this ring structure outward (beyond Tonsfeldt's schematic) reveals that the narrator's warnings and the story of Hildeburh at Finnsburg are further enclosed by the two appearances of Wealhtheow, at lines 612–41 and 1162–1232. As we have seen, frame structures in Old English poetry act as interpretive aids, guiding readers' understanding of both the framed text and the frame itself. When Wealhtheow frames the narrative of Hildeburh at Finnsburg, we can see a semantic overlap: the story of Hildeburh may anticipate what Wealhtheow (or any peace-weaver) can expect to be her own fate. But Wealhtheow does not simply replicate Hildeburh's role—she revises it, offering her own interpretation of events at Heorot filtered through her perception of events at Finnsburg.

Wealhtheow's first appearance (lines 612–41) establishes normative peace-weaving behavior, and thus conventional femininity for the poem. Her ceremonial cup-bearing serves to solidify relations between Hrothgar, his retainers, and Beowulf, and she passes the cup to each man in a strictly choreographed scene.[21] Her movements figuratively bind the men and their retainers together. Beowulf's treatment of Wealhtheow suggests that her role is not simply ceremonial, however; in response to her greeting and exhortation he offers his binding resolution to defeat Grendel or die trying. The narrator emphasizes the fact that Wealhtheow's response matters by stating, "Ðam wife þa word wel licodon" ("the woman liked those words very much," line 639). Yet although Wealhtheow figures prominently in this opening frame, she remains fully conventional, and her words and actions seem only to represent Hrothgar's desires. After listening to Beowulf's pledge, she returns to Hrothgar's side (line 641b).[22]

Wealhtheow's second appearance completes the narrative frame that encloses the story of Hildeburh, and she glosses or interprets that story. Although her actions and speech in this second scene suggest the possibility of subversion, of a woman's expression beyond her enclosure, the possibility is short-lived. Wealhtheow's ability to influence events beyond her enclosure is stopped short by the narrative intervention of Grendel's Mother. We shall see that any prospect of an unenclosed peace-weaver in the poem is forestalled with this monstrous reminder of the dangers of unconfined femininity.

In this second appearance, Wealhtheow weaves her way, gold-adorned, among the warriors, but here the similarities to her first appearance end:

> Þa cwom Wealhþeo forð
> gan under gyldnum beage þær þa godan twegen
> sæton suhtergefæderan; þa gyt wæs hiera ætgædere,
> æghwylc oðrum trywe. . . .
>
> Spræc ða ides Scyldinga:
> (lines 1162b-64, 1168b; emphasis added)

> *Then* Wealhtheow came forward, walking under a golden crown to where the two good men sat, nephew and uncle; their peace was as yet unbroken, each true to the other. . . . *Then* the woman of the Scyldings spoke.

Wealhtheow's first speech follows the *scop*'s tale of Finnsburg almost immediately, and the temporal adverbs (lines 1162b, 1168b) that bring her forward and introduce her speech may signal a causal connection between her words and the story of Hildeburh. Wealhtheow seems compelled to respond to the lay. She must, in particular, offer up her interpretation to the two people most directly implicated by it: Hrothgar and Hrothulf. Whereas in her first appearance her indirect discourse seemed a mere extension of Hrothgar's wishes, the direct discourse of her two speeches marks a change. She resists the unsatisfactory fate of Hildeburh by trying to ensure that events in her own community unfold differently. Her speeches offer up her interpretation of the Finnsburg episode as well as her attempts to revise the ending.

Wealhtheow's first speech, as Helen Damico has shown, is controlled by
imperative verbs, directed toward Hrothgar:[23]

> Onfoh þissum fulle, freodrihten min,
> sinces brytta! Þu on sælum wes,
> goldwine gumena, ond to Geatum spræc
> mildum wordum, swa sceal man don!
> Beo wið Geatas glæd, geofena gemyndig,
> nean and feorran þu nu hafast.
> Me man sægde, þæt þu ðe for sunu wolde
> hereri[n]c habban. Heorot is gefælsod,
> beahsele beorhta; bruc þenden þu mote
> manigra medo, ond þinum magum læf
> folc ond rice, þonne ðu forð scyle
> metodsceaft seon. (lines 1169–80a)

Take this cup, my noble lord, giver of treasure. Be joyful, gold-friend of
men, and speak kind words to the Geats, so should one do. Be gracious with
the Geats, mindful of the gifts near and far that you now have. Someone has
told me that you would have the warrior [Beowulf] for your son. Heorot,
the bright ring-hall, is cleansed; make use of your many rewards while you
can, and leave to your kinsmen the people and kingdom when you shall go
forth to see the decree of fate.

Through her strategic use of syntax, Wealhtheow's peace-weaving words
("Onfoh þissum fulle" [line 1169a]; "Þu on sælum wes" [line 1170b]; etc.)
actually cushion her harsher intent: to tell Hrothgar that his pledge to make
Beowulf his adopted son and heir is not acceptable. She will, instead, promote
their nephew Hrothulf as heir to the throne, thereby ensuring the eventual
succession of her own sons.[24] Having just witnessed the strife that can oc-
cur when the peace pledge fails, she seems to be deliberately trying to avoid
Hildeburh's fate. Thus she creates a new version of the traditional peace-weav-
ing text, a new ending; rather than passively accepting events as they unfold
(as the men determine them), she wishes to shape the future herself. Her
commentary on Hildeburh's story is likewise seen in her optimistic prediction
that Hrothulf will treat her sons well; she is trying to write a happier ending
for her sons than that suffered by Hildeburh's son. By asserting that women
can surmount the passive peace-weaver role in order to influence political
and dynastic decisions, Wealhtheow actively rewrites the story of Hildeburh.

Her commentary thus locates creative "textual" production at the site of fe-male enclosure. Even as her appearances encircle Hildeburh within the nar-rative, her "reading" of Hildeburh grows outward from, and surrounds, that unsatisfactory peace-weaving narrative by offering a new ending.

The short passage (lines 1192–1214) that is textually framed between Wealhtheow's two speeches also revises the peace-weaver's role. In particu-lar, it revises Wealhtheow's first appearance. Just as the Finn episode opened up for Wealhtheow a space to speak within the poem, after her first speech she has a new acting role, since she no longer appears to participate in the cupbearing ritual seen previously. Rather, beginning with line 1192, the ac-tions of cupbearing are described with passive verbs.[25] The agent of these actions is invisible, written out of the picture syntactically:

> Him wæs ful boren, ond freondlaþu
> wordum bewægned, ond wunden gold
> estum geeawed, earm[h]reade twa,
> hrægl ond hringas, healsbeaga mæst
> þara þe ic on foldan gefrægen hæbbe. (lines 1192–96)

> The cup was carried to him and friendship offered with words, and twisted gold courteously presented [to him]. Two arm ornaments, a corselet, and rings, [and] the greatest of neck-rings I have ever heard about on earth.

Whereas in the first cupbearing scene, Wealhtheow was the subject of the verbs ("Eode Wealhtheow forð," "Wealhtheow went forth," line 612b; "þa freolic wif ful gesealde," "the noble woman gave the cup," line 615; "grette Geata leod," "she greeted the man of the Geats," line 625; etc.), the agent of the passive verbs in this second passage is unspecified. If the agent were Wealhtheow, the poet would presumably have used syntax similar to that of the first cupbearing scene. Perhaps the cupbearer now is Freawaru, who we later learn also performed this activity during Beowulf's stay at Hrothgar's court. If Wealhtheow's main function is to initiate and perform the cup-bearing ritual, as Michael Enright has recently argued, what happens when she stops serving?[26] Her transformation from a silent cupbearer to a com-manding speaking presence is a rewriting of the peace-weaver's role and a disruption of it as well. By reprimanding Hrothgar and abandoning the cer-emonial tasks of the peace-weaver, Wealhtheow unsettles (unweaves) the relationship he is attempting to build with Beowulf, even as she works to bind Hrothgar more closely to his own kin.

The narrative lingers only briefly on this cupbearing activity, but it keeps Wealhtheow firmly in mind as it describes the gifts bestowed on Beowulf and makes the first of several allusions to the death of Hygelac, Beowulf's king, in a fatal raid on the Frisians. John Leyerle has explained the structural operations of these allusions:

> The poem interlaces these episodes to achieve juxtapositions impossible in a linear narrative. In the first episode the gift of a precious golden torque to Beowulf for killing Grendel is interrupted by an allusion to its loss years later when Hygelac is killed. Hygelac's death seeking Frisian treasure foreshadows Beowulf's death seeking the dragon's hoard. The transience of gold and its connection with violence are obvious.[27]

Perhaps not so obvious, but no less present, are the connections this scene establishes between Wealhtheow and Hygd, both of whom try to determine political and familial succession via the conduit of Beowulf. The narrator's allusion to Hygelac's fate is prompted by the neck-ring, an object that later in the poem links Wealhtheow to Hygd. Wealhtheow's two speeches frame this digression, and, as usual, the framing device both illuminates and is illuminated by the text it frames. Her first speech exposes the potential instability that could result from Hrothgar's rash promise of his kingdom to Beowulf and thereby anticipates the later predicament of Hygd, who likewise will try to determine political succession after Hygelac's death. The neck-ring symbolically links the two events. Stephanie Hollis has argued that Hygd's offer "endorses, *in principle*, the rectitude of Wealhtheow's involvement in determining the succession of the throne that she shares."[28] Yet however "right" we may see their actions to be, the poem does not permit Wealhtheow or Hygd to leave off being peace-weavers in order to become independent political thinkers. Peace-weaving, as an enclosed social role, does not allow them to operate outside of their frame of reference, to shape events independently from their husbands. In both cases, when Wealhtheow and Hygd try to shape political events, they are juxtaposed with a socially threatening female counterpart: Grendel's Mother and Modthryth, respectively, exemplars of the dangers of uncontrolled feminine power.

Following the neck-ring digression, Wealhtheow again becomes the agent of the active verbs as she begins her second speech. This speech, too, is governed by imperative verbs that signal her appropriation of an active political role. Paradoxically, although we might today read her actions as positive examples of feminine assertiveness, within the poem they represent the incipient disintegration of society: by reprimanding Hrothgar, she undermines his authority.[29] Likewise, when she uses imperative verbs to address Beowulf, her act of commanding revises the passive peace-weaving role. Elaine Tuttle Hansen has shown that this type of "instructional" discourse, governed by imperative verbs, is typical of wisdom literature, which for Old English poetry often meant a father's instructions for his son, as in the Old English *Precepts*. The imperative mood, according to Hansen, "marks an utterance with the assumption of an authority that needs no justification for its right to command and expect obedience."[30] Thus, only when Wealhtheow appropriates a specifically masculine form of syntax is she able to participate discursively. In her speeches she revises and transcends the conventionally silent, acquiescent peace-weaving role (as exemplified by Hildeburh) and assumes a masculine guise. We will see in the discussion of Grendel's Mother below that the transgression of gender boundaries is one of the most threatening acts of the poem. When Wealhtheow adopts the language of a masculine genre for her own purposes, both her actions and her speech signal her desire to change the story, to revise the Hildeburh model, to write a new ending.

Yet in response to Hildeburh's firmly enclosed status, Wealhtheow offers only a partial possibility of release from the social and material bonds that confine the peace-weaver. Following her two speeches, Wealhtheow is silent, seen only once more as she (along with other members of Hrothgar's court) gazes silently at the head of Grendel that Beowulf has brought back from the mere. In this last image she is again subordinated to the more active males:

Þa wæs be feaxe on flet boren
Grendles heafod, þær guman druncon,
egeslic for eorlum ond þære idese mid,
wliteseon wrætlic; weres on sawon. (lines 1647–50)

Then Grendel's head was carried by its hair over the floor to where the men drank, terrible for the warriors, and the woman with them, a wondrous sight. The men looked at it.

Here Wealhtheow is fully marginal, included almost as an afterthought among the group gazing on the monstrous head. Like Hildeburh, she ends up nameless and inactive. This final "containment" of Wealhtheow is linked to our initial view of her, so that her active speaking role is framed by two scenes where she is passive and silent. The display of Grendel's head, of course, follows Beowulf's defeat of Grendel's Mother, who is paired with Wealhtheow in an instructive way. Grendel's Mother teaches us about the dangers of feminine power and authority and how to control them; thus it is no coincidence that Wealhtheow is framed between two mourning mothers, Hildeburh and Grendel's Mother, each—like Wealhtheow—seeking power in her own right, yet each powerless in the end.

WITHIN THE MERE: READING GRENDEL'S MOTHER

Grendel's Mother is undoubtedly the least enclosed woman in Old English literature. She and Hildeburh frame Wealhtheow in what appears to be a strictly regulated continuum moving from containment to release; Wealhtheow tries to move towards Grendel's Mother's end, but finally becomes more like Hildeburh. In the case of all three women, and in early English literature more generally, female escape from enclosure is undesirable. Within a system that deeply values female enclosure, it is precisely because Grendel's Mother is able to transgress boundaries that she is especially dangerous.

What makes Grendel's Mother so monstrous? She poses a real threat to Beowulf, of course, but the narrator diminishes her power early on by stating that she was less terrible than her son just as women are less powerful than men (lines 1282b-87). Thus her gender is foregrounded and linked to her actions. Although her species has been a matter of critical debate, it is legitimate to read her as a woman; not only are many of the epithets that describe her also used for other women in the poem, but descriptions of her thoughts and actions personify her.[31] She is, for example, *yrmþe gemunde*, "mindful of misery" (line 1259b), her adventure is *sorhfulne*, "sorrowful" (line 1277a), and her action vengeful (line 1278). I suggest that her position within (or more accurately, outside of) the society of the poem is so monstrous because she is a woman. Given that we will probably never come to a definitive understanding of such fundamental characteristics as her gender and species, we should consider instead the effect of not defining them. Nameless, indescribable, and illimitable, Grendel's Mother likewise stands outside of the institutional enclosure that governs the other women in the poem. Significantly, she is contained, named, and made known by the hero himself.

Grendel's nameless Mother occupies a substantial portion of the poem—roughly 400 lines. She is identified only by her biological function of having given birth to Grendel (a role that links her to nearly all the other women in the poem). Her namelessness defines her place in the poem's symbolic order: if naming one's enemies is a form of controlling them, this particular enemy is initially beyond control. According to Seth Lerer's recent analysis, one role of the act of naming in *Beowulf* is to diffuse anxiety.[32] Such naming becomes part of the larger project of story-telling, which instructs and entertains, and thus disempowers the named character or object by placing it within the familiar frame of language. Yet one fundamental threat goes unnamed: uncontrolled feminine power and sexuality in the form of the uncontained Grendel's Mother. She alone remains outside of the peace-weaving economy of exchange, and thus outside of any kind of physical or cultural enclosure.

The uncontainability of Grendel's Mother is mirrored neatly by the lexical ambiguities of her descriptions—neither male nor female, human nor animal. Yet the language used to describe her is centrally concerned with the thematics of enclosure we see informing all representations of women in *Beowulf*. In the case of Grendel's Mother, this means references to movement, space, boundaries, and borders—or the lack thereof. Both she and Grendel are *micle mearcstapan* ("huge border-wanderers," line 1348a), who *moras healden* ("keep to the moors," line 1348b); she goes on a *sorhfulne sið* ("sorrowful journey," line 1278a) to avenge her son's death. Her attack on Æschere is marked by rapid movement: "Heo wæs on ofste, wolde ut þanon, / . . . hraðe heo æþelinga anne hæfde / fæste befangen, þa heo to fenne gang" ("she was in haste, wanted to get out of there. . . . Quickly she firmly grasped one of the noblemen, then she went to the fen," lines 1292a-95b).

When Hrothgar describes this event to Beowulf, he emphasizes her mysteriousness and her mobility by calling her *wælgæst wæfre* ("wandering murderous spirit," line 1331). *Wæfre* ("wandering") is a word associated with death in *Beowulf*; its two other occurrences (at lines 1150 and 2420) describe the events leading up to the final battle at Finnsburg and Beowulf's fight with the dragon, respectively. In both of these cases, however, the adjective describes a wandering or fluctuating set of thoughts. Before Beowulf fights the dragon, his mind is sorrowful, restless, and ready for death: "Him wæs geomor sefa, / wæfre and wælfus" (lines 2419–20). Similarly, in recounting the Danes' final revenge on Finn, the narrator explains, "ne meahte wæfre mod / forhabban in hreþre" ("The restless spirit could not remain in the breast," lines 1150–51). Both other occurrences describe a mental or emotional condition, but when *wæfre* describes Grendel's Mother it specifies her physical movement.[33]

Moreover, Hrothgar's account of the mere concerns its lack of limits: "No þæs frod leofað / gumena bearna, þæt þone grund wite" ("There is no one of the sons of men wise [enough] who knows the bottom," lines 1366b-67). The rich descriptions mystify, rather than explain the mere:

> Hie dygel lond
> warigeað wulfhleoþu, windige næssas,
> frecne fengelad, ðær fyrgenstream
> under næssa genipu niþer gewiteð,
> flod under foldan. Nis þæt feor heonon
> milgemearces, þæt se mere standeð;
> ofer þæm hongiað hrinde bearwas,
> wudu wyrtum fæst wæter oferhelmað.
> Þær mæg nihta gehwæm niðwundor seon,
> fyr on flode. (lines 1357b–66a)

They dwell in a secret land, the wolf-slopes, the windy headlands, the perilous fen-paths, where the mountain stream goes downwards under the headlands' mist, water under the earth. It is not far from here, in terms of miles, that the mere stands; frost-covered groves hang over it, the root-bound woods hang over the water. Each night one may see there a fearful wonder, fire on the water.

Thus the space occupied by Grendel's Mother is really indescribable: it is secret, dangerous, under darkness, under the earth, a wonder. It can only be reached via a narrow and unknown path. As Hrothgar reminds Beowulf, "Eard git ne const, / frecne stowe, ðær þu findan miht / sinnigne secg; sec gif þu dyrre!" ("You do not yet know the region; the terrible place, where you might find the sinful one; seek [her] if you dare!" lines 1377b–79).[34] Beowulf's response begins the process of confining Grendel's Mother:

> Ic hit þe gehate: no he on helm losaþ,
> ne on foldan fæþm, ne on fyrgenholt,
> ne on gyfenes grund, ga þær he wille! (lines 1392–94)

I promise you this: [s]he will not escape into protection nor into the bosom of the earth, nor in the mountain woods, nor on the bottom of the sea; go where [s]he will.

Beowulf limits the possibilities of her mobility. His own discourse begins to contain Grendel's Mother; his battle and eventual beheading of her will finish the task.

So far we have seen two ways that Grendel's Mother blurs convention-al gender boundaries: at the level of language, she is described as both *wif* ("woman") and *secg* ("man"); and at the level of plot, she is the only woman to wander outside her allotted space, the mere. Her third transgression of gender boundaries is social: she avenges the death of her son, a masculine action. As Jane Chance has argued, "it is monstrous for a mother to 'avenge' her son . . . as if she were a retainer, he were her lord, and avenging more important than peace making." Grendel's Mother is physical, not verbal, and she uses violence rather than language to achieve her goals. She is thus unenclosed both literally and figuratively; after Grendel's death, no "imprisoning" male relatives gov-ern her actions. Her environment is not a male-controlled enclosure, such as Heorot, but a fluid, bloody, feminized space that suggests as well the mysteries of the female body and the (perceived) dangers that lurk therein.[35]

In his battle with Grendel's Mother, Beowulf dominates and destroys the feminine threat.[36] The battle embodies both the disruption and the righting of *Beowulf*ian gender boundaries. When Beowulf enters the mere, Grendel's Mother recognizes the violation (lines 1497–1500) and seeks to reverse it by attempting to penetrate his armor with her fingers, but: "hring utan ymb-bearh, / þæt heo þone fyrdhom ðurhfon ne mihte, / locene leoðosyrcan la þan fingrum" ("his ring-mail protected him from without, so that she could not penetrate that war-dress, the linked mailshirt, with her hateful fingers," lines 1504b-05). His armor is impenetrable. The most dramatic moment in the action comes when the sword fails Beowulf, when it looks as though Grendel's Mother may overwhelm him. The ensuing struggle plays out anxi-eties about female sexuality: she again tries to penetrate his armor, this time with her blade, and she again fails (lines 1545–49). Her failure is mandated by the principles of female enclosure which do not permit women to breach boundaries. Grendel's Mother, destined to exist on the borders of society, cannot cross the border of that society's most representative body. Beowulf's armor acts as both a literal and social barrier that she cannot cross.

Of course, at this moment, Beowulf spies the ancient sword and plunges it into Grendel's Mother's body (thereby reversing the rape imagery), killing her: "bil eal ðurhwod / fægne flæschoman" ("the blade went through the doomed body," lines 1567b-68a). He then cuts off Grendel's head, bringing both it and the sword-hilt back to Hrothgar as his battle-spoils. Both of these prizes can be read as the "texts" of Grendel's Mother, subsuming her into the peace-weaving paradigm. The "texts" woven by the peace-weavers in *Beowulf* are their sons. In this respect, Grendel, as her product, is a failed attempt at perpetuating her lineage. Like the speaker of the female elegy "Wulf and Eadwacer," and like Hildeburh, Grendel's Mother is contained by a system that leaves her alone to mourn the death of her son.

Lest this message of female containment be lost on the various audiences within and outside of the poem, Beowulf himself offers a re-telling of his fight with Grendel's Mother when he returns to Hygelac's court. Grendel's Mother, Beowulf tells Hygelac, carried Æschere's body away to a spot *(un)der firgenstream* ("under a mountain stream," line 2128b), here the sole descriptor of a place that previously took several lines to describe. He similarly downplays his entry into the mere:

> Ic ða ðæs wælmes, þe is wide cuð
> grimne gryrelicne grundhyrde fond
> Þær unc hwile wæs hand gemæne;
> holm heolfre weoll, ond ic heafde becearf
> in ðam [guð]sele Grendeles modor
> eacnum ecgum; unsofte þonan
> feorh oðferede. . . . (lines 2135–41a)

> I then found the guardian of the deep water, the grim terror as is now widely known. For a while we shared hands [in battle]; the sea welled with blood, and with a powerful sword-edge, I cut off the head of Grendel's Mother in the battle-hall; with difficulty I went from there with my life.

Thus the bloody and bottomless pit has become simply "the deep water" and the horror of Grendel's Mother is reduced to a single half-line, *grimne gryrelicne* ("the grim terror," line 2136a). The dangerous battle is made to seem roughly equitable until Beowulf prevails. Most importantly, the horror of Grendel's Mother "þe is wide cuð" ("is now widely known," line 2135b), contained and unfrightening.

[EN]CLOSING THE LOOP: READING HYGD, MODTHRYTH, AND FREAWARU

Following the intervention of Grendel's Mother, three final stories about women in *Beowulf*—Hygd, Modthryth, and Freawaru—serve to interpret

and supplement those stories already told.[37] Structurally, these stories con-
form to a tightly regulated pattern. The stories of Hygd and Modthryth, in-
tertwined in the manuscript, present interpretations of the two paradigms
of women seen thus far in the story. Just as Beowulf was responsible for both
destroying Grendel's Mother and reducing the anxiety she provoked by tell-
ing a greatly diminished version of her story, so too the narrative accounts
of both Hygd and Modthryth offer diminished and contained versions of the
poem's two models of femininity (passive and active). Beowulf's predictions
about the future of Freawaru—a text which itself is deeply embedded within
other women's texts—effectively ends the story-cycle by normalizing her
story, asserting the peace-weaver's failure as the inevitable order of things.

The stories of Hygd, Modthryth, and Freawaru are significant both
structurally and thematically. Structurally, these stories form a ring com-
position or multiple framework of the sort that has often been identified
as a governing structural principle within the poem, and that we have seen
operating with some regularity in the stories of *Beowulf*'s women. Like the
frames discussed earlier, ring structures invite readers' attention and par-
ticipate in the construction of meaning. John Niles has usefully defined ring
composition as

> a chiastic design in which the last element in a series in some way echoes
> the first, the next to the last the second and so on. Often the series centers
> on a single kernel, which may serve as the key element. . . . The poet uses
> ring composition as a means of traveling from the immediate reality . . . to
> an "other" legendary reality that is used as a point of comparison . . . then
> back again to the present reality.[38]

This is precisely the design of the three final women's stories in *Beowulf*.
A brief summary of how this pattern governs these three stories will be
helpful before going into a more detailed analysis of how each revises prior
"texts" and how the passage overall establishes the peace-weaving paradigm
as one of firm and stable enclosure.

The initial description of Hygd, linked to the later passage in which she
receives Wealhtheow's gift of a neck-ring, opens the frame for these final
stories. This frame encompasses, within only 150 lines, five stories about
women. Structurally, the stories are precisely balanced:

A. initial description of Hygd (lines 1926–31a, ca. 5 lines)
B. description of Modthryth (lines 1931b–62, ca. 30 lines)

C. Beowulf's prediction of Freawaru's future (lines 2016b–69a, ca. 50 lines)

B¹. Beowulf's description of Grendel's Mother (lines 2115–44, ca. 30 lines)

A¹. Beowulf gives Hygd the neck-ring (lines 2172–76, ca. 5 lines)

The opening and closing descriptions of Hygd firmly identify her as a conventional peace-weaver, and the final passage links her to Wealhtheow through the exchange of the neck-ring. Likewise, the story of the evil Modthryth is symmetrically balanced with Beowulf's narration of his fight with Grendel's Mother. Embedded deep within frames A and B, A¹ and B¹, is Beowulf's prediction (C) about the inevitable failure of Freawaru's peace-weaving alliance, the lengthiest of the stories at roughly fifty lines. Thus the accounts of Hygd enclose the two stories of tamed feminine aggression and transgression; these in turn enclose the doomed peace-weaver of the future, Freawaru.

The narrator's first mention of Hygd explicitly recalls that of Wealhtheow—both passages catalogue queenly behavior. Though young, Hygd is *wis welþungen*, "wise and accomplished" (line 1927). She is generous and kind, "næs hio hnah swa þeah / ne to gneað gifa" (lines 1929b–30a), and like Wealhtheow she distributes *maþmgestreona*, "treasures" (line 1931a). Like the other peace-weavers, Hygd is married and thus confined symbolically. The descriptive language encloses her as well: she is *under burhlocan* ("under or within the castle-enclosure," line 1928), so that her world, like Wealhtheow's, does not extend beyond the walls of her husband's court. Later the narrator makes the connection between the two women explicit:

Hyrde ic þæt he ðone healsbeah Hygde gesealde,
wrætlicne wundurmaððum, ðone þe him Wealhðeo geaf,
ðeod(nes) dohtor, þrio wicg somod
swancor ond sadolbeorht; hyre syððan wæs
æfter beahðege br[e]ost geweorðod. (lines 2172–76)

Then I heard that he [Beowulf] gave the neck-ring to Hygd, the splendid, wondrous jewel that Wealhtheow gave him; [gave it] to the king's daughter, [and] three horses also, supple and saddle-bright; afterwards, her breast was adorned on account of receiving the neck-ring.

This five-line passage, which closes the frame around the women's stories, is itself a brief ring composition, with the neck-ring literally encircling the passage (*healsbeah*, line 2172, and *beahðege*, line 2176) and encircling also Hygd herself, embedded in the passage as *ðeod(nes) dohtor*, surrounded by descriptions of bright treasure. The circular image of the neck-ring is perfectly appropriate for joining and circumscribing (both literally and figuratively) these two idealized women. Thus Hygd's story is a solid link in the intratextual chain, and lest we miss its significance, the narrator evokes the image of Hygd's breast, adorned with the neck-ring. The grammatical construction of the passage is curiously passive; the neck-ring itself seems to be the true agent of the action, or rather, perhaps, the vehicle through which Beowulf transacts the exchange between women.

The account of Modthryth, as has often been noted, marks a surprising intervention into Hygd's story.[39] Modthryth is notable in part because her story is one of the few in Old English poetry that actually uses the term *freoðuwebbe*, "peace-weaver" (line 1942a)—here used to define what Modthryth is not. The possibly faulty manuscript does not permit us to know whether the relationship between Hygd and Modthryth is deliberate, or even if such a relationship existed, but the contrast between the behavior of the two women is explicit.[40]

In telling Modthryth's story, the narrator rewrites the text of Grendel's Mother by filtering it through the lenses of Hildeburh, Wealhtheow, and Hygd. Through this interpretive act, the anti-peace-weaver is tamed and reconfigured to fit the poem's own social values. Modthryth initially resembles Grendel's Mother: violent, unviewable in daylight, fatal for men to encounter. In *Language, Sign, and Gender*, Overing writes:

> Modthryth causes a temporary shudder of discomfort, followed by a generalized sigh of relief that the disorder she threatens has been contained and that things are once more under the control of the masculine economy.

The "shudder of discomfort" must certainly stem from Modthryth's evocation of Grendel's Mother and Beowulf's close call with her. Like Grendel's Mother, Modthryth seizes with *wælbende*, "deadly bonds" (line 1936a), any man who dares to penetrate her personal domain. For Grendel's Mother, that domain was a physical space, the mere. For Modthryth, the domain is more ephemeral, but no less personal: she demands that any man who dares to look at her be killed (lines 1932–40a). Death in both scenes is determined by sword, and it seems likely that the shudder Modthryth evokes is the glimpse into what could have been Beowulf's fate. The Modthryth passage leaves ambiguous just what exactly (that is, whose death) is settled by sword—presumably the death of those men who stare at her. Yet we have already seen the outcome of one such sexual battle, when feminine aggression was tamed through the death of Grendel's Mother. The symmetry of these two stories links and compares the two "texts." Modthryth's story revises that of Grendel's Mother and proposes an alternate ending, as Modthryth is transformed into a model queen.

Like Grendel's Mother, Modthryth temporarily subverts normative gender paradigms in the poem, even as her story illustrates the process by which a woman moves from outside to inside; that is, it narrates the process of her enclosure or domestication.[41] We can see this as a kind of "reading process" in which the poem reads the stories of earlier women into its account of Modthryth's behavior. The audience evaluates that behavior based on what they (and we) know about the roles open to women in the poem. To diffuse the disruptive feminine threat, Modthryth is tamed, confined within a marriage, after which, we are told, she becomes a good queen, conforming to the models we have already seen of Wealhtheow and Hygd.[42]

Regardless of the extent, however, to which Modthryth is able to subvert normative gender, the lesson of her story is that enclosure within the social structure of marriage is essential for conventional femininity. A woman outside the system must be contained. Her unconventional (unpeace-weaver-like) behavior clearly meets with the narrator's disapproval: "Ne bið swylc cwenlic þeaw / idese to efnanne, þeah ðe hio ænlicu sy, / þætte freoðuwebbe feores onsæce / after ligetorne leofne mannan" ("That was not a queenly custom for a woman to perform, though she be beautiful, that a peace-weaver should deprive a dear man of life after a pretended injury," lines 1940b–43). Once she is contained by marriage, Modthryth's threat is diffused as her story is appropriated and retold by ale-drinking men: "ealo-drincende oðer sædan" ("ale-drinkers told another story," line 1945). Once married, they say, Modthryth became famous for her goodness: "ðær hio syððan well / in gumstole, gode mære, / lifgesceafta lifigende breac" ("There on the throne she was afterwards famous for generosity, while living made use of her life," lines 1951b–53).[43] The words contain her both spatially (on her throne) and narratively, rejecting her violent behavior. Female characters in *Beowulf* are most threatening when they produce death; peace-weaving can only signify as a creative act. When women cannot be identified as mothers, or when mothers produce death, the social order perceives its greatest threat. The threat is controlled through the poem's readings and revisions of both of these dangerous women, as their stories are framed by the normative accounts of peace-weavers.[44]

The final woman's story in *Beowulf* is that of Freawaru, Hrothgar and Wealhtheow's daughter. Beowulf himself tells this story, as a revised version of the stories he has heard (or seen) so far. In short, he predicts that the marriage Hrothgar has arranged for his daughter with Ingeld is doomed to failure, because the presence of Freawaru and her retainers at her husband's court will painfully remind the Heathobards of their long-standing feud with the Danes (lines 2024b–69a). Such a situation is ripe for violence, Beowulf asserts, "þeah seo bryd duge" ("though the bride be good," line 2031b). Beowulf's story interprets texts he knows already: the story of Hildeburh, the resulting political negotiations at Heorot, the facts he has evidently learned there about Freawaru's impending marriage. He turns the story into an explicit commentary on the shortcomings of tribal warfare and the resultant impossibility of weaving a permanent peace between hostile factions—which leads, ironically, to the impossibility of permanent female enclosure. The transient settlements achieved through peace-weaving alliances can ensure female enclosure only temporarily, and thus the threat of unenclosed women can never be fully eradicated.

Beowulf's commentary on peace-weaving establishes, finally, textual production in the poem as a masculine act. Put in a somewhat complicated way: Freawaru's story is Beowulf's reading of Wealhtheow's reading of the *scop*'s reading of Hildeburh. Freawaru's story is Hildeburh's, at several removes, filtered through every other woman's story, including those of Grendel's Mother, Hygd, and Modthryth. In Beowulf's prediction, the old Heathobard will incite the young warrior to break the peace with the Danes, because in Hildeburh's story, men's language created violence and death. Likewise, the old Heathobard's speech will destroy Freawaru's peace-weaving. The containment of feminine textuality in the poem is thus realized when Beowulf interprets known texts to "write" Freawaru's future.

The story of women in *Beowulf* effectively ends when the narrator interprets Beowulf's reading of Freawaru in a passage that essentially sums up the hero's lesson about the hopelessness of the heroic ideal:

> Swa sceal mæg don
> nealles inwitnet oðrum bregdon
> dyrnum cræfte, deað ren(ian)
> hondgesteallan. (lines 2166b–69a)

So should kinsmen do, not weave nets of malice for each other through secret skill, [nor] prepare death for their companions.

The narrator's weaving imagery recalls the distinction made earlier by Beowulf between women's and men's acts. One ought not to use weaving to create violence, because weaving is a feminine craft through which women attempt to ensure peace. Once again, the poem foregrounds the dangers of transgressing gender boundaries.

The structural embeddedness of Freawaru's story is significant, but its greater message, I would argue, lies in the fact that Beowulf himself tells the story. We have seen a wide variety of female transgressions, both corporeal and textual, in the poem, ranging from Wealhtheow's appropriation of masculinist discourse to the death-producing acts of Grendel's Mother and Modthryth. Beowulf's final act of narrative containment limits the multiplying textual links between women in the poem and ensures that no further interpretations are possible (a point confirmed by the fleeting descriptions of Grendel's Mother and Hygd that close the frame). Beowulf's narrative achieves closure: except for a brief mention of Hygd (lines 2369–72, in a passage reminiscent of Wealhtheow), no other named women appear in the poem.

In effect, *Beowulf* produces its category of "the femmine" through its ever-expanding repetition and interpretation of the enclosed peace-weaver motif. The hero himself sets the limits for this expansion. In this way, *Beowulf* illustrates Judith Butler's concept of gender performativity:

> Gender is . . . *a set of repeated acts within a highly rigid regulatory frame* that congeal over time to produce the appearance of substance, of a natural sort of being. A political genealogy of gender ontologies, if it is successful, will deconstruct the substantive appearance of gender into its constitutive acts and locate and account for those acts *within the compulsory frames set by the various forces that police the social appearance of gender.*[45] (emphasis added)

Examining the women's stories in *Beowulf* as discrete yet interdependent strands of the same fabric permits us to analyze the poem's gender operations in the way Butler proposes. A rhetoric of enclosure "frames" women in the poem (and in Old English literature more generally) so that the condition of being framed or enclosed produces femininity. When enclosure (seen in a variety of social and textual structures) begins to be seen as normative or "natural" for the women of *Beowulf*, any divergence from that norm—that is, any escape or release from enclosure such as we see to varying degrees in nearly all the women in the poem—is necessarily unnatural, unfeminine. The condition of enclosed femininity is, in this formulation, one of the forces that determines "the social appearance of gender."

The textual and rhetorical enclosure of women in *Beowulf* illustrates the broad sociocultural conventions of female enclosure at work in early medieval England. *Beowulf*, a text that, regardless of its site of production, is hardly likely to be directly concerned with issues of female monasticism, nevertheless displays the cultural thematic of enclosure as an identifying mark of the feminine. Structurally, framing devices and ring patterns can be found throughout the poem, of course; they are not exclusive to its treatment of women. But when women are treated by the poem, framing devices are ubiquitous—all women in *Beowulf* frame and are framed by each other, and both the frames and the framed texts (the enclosures and the enclosed) are mutually interpretive entities. By separating the monolithic figure of the peace-weaver into its individual acts, or stories, and by examining how each appearance interprets and develops each prior and each subsequent woman's story, we can better understand how *Beowulf* normalizes and regulates femininity.

NOTES

[1] Paull F. Baum, "The *Beowulf* Poet," *Philological Quarterly* 39 (1960): 389–99, reprinted in *An Anthology of "Beowulf" Criticism*, ed. Lewis E. Nicholson (Notre Dame, 1963), pp. 353–65. References to the 1963 version will be provided parenthetically in my text.

[2] I use the term "written" rather than "composed" or "originated" because I am primarily interested in the late Anglo-Saxon Christian culture that preserved the poem in the manuscript form that we have today. The debate surrounding the date of the poem continues, and I will not engage that debate here. For my purposes, I will consider the date of the poem to be the date of the manuscript. For a recent and cogent overview of the dating controversy, see Roy Michael Liuzza, "On the Dating of Beowulf," in *"Beowulf": Basic Readings*, ed. Peter S. Baker (New York, 1995), pp. 281–302.

[3] The relationship between *Beowulf* and Christianity has, of course, long been a matter of critical debate; scholars now largely agree that the poem as it is preserved in the manuscript has been shaped by the cultural manifestations of Christianity in Anglo-Saxon England, and thus represents a fusion of pre-Christian Germanic and Christian Latinate cultures. For a general overview of the relationship, see Fred C. Robinson, "*Beowulf*," in *The Cambridge Companion*

to Old English Literature, ed. Malcolm Godden and Michael Lapidge (Cambridge, Eng., 1991), pp. 142–59. In *"Beowulf" and the Appositive Style* (Knoxville, 1985) Fred C. Robinson discusses the poem's deliberate ambiguity as an attempt to reconcile its own Christian present with the pre-Christian past of its characters (pp. 42–43). As Dorothy Whitelock explains, "if a heathen poem on this subject once existed, it must have been very different from the work that has come down to us. As has often been pointed out, the Christian element is not merely superimposed; it permeates the poem . . . an acceptance of the Christian order of things is implicit throughout the poem. It pervades the very imagery" ("The Audience of *Beowulf," From Bede to Alfred* [London, 1980] pp. 3–4).

4 The "passive" Anglo-Saxon woman has long been a critical commonplace. For representative views, see Alain Renoir, "A Reading Context for 'The Wife's Lament,'" in *Anglo-Saxon Poetry: Essays in Appreciation,* ed. Lewis E. Nicholson and Dolores Warwick Frese (Notre Dame, 1975), pp. 224–41, and Richard Schrader, *God's Handiwork: Images of Women in Early Germanic Literature* (Westport, 1983). For useful critiques of this view of passive femininity, see Helen Bennett, "The Female Mourner at Beowulf's Funeral: Filling in the Blanks/Hearing the Spaces," *Exemplaria* 4.1 (1992): 35–50, and Gillian Overing, *Language, Sign, and Gender in "Beowulf"* (Carbondale, 1990), pp. 76–81. Helen Damico rejects the passive model altogether, seeing Wealhtheow, especially, as an active, war-minded valkyrie figure. See *Beowulf's Wealhtheow and the Valkyrie Tradition* (Madison, 1984).

5 Among the recent studies investigating the "textuality" of Old English poetry are Allen Frantzen, *Desire for Origins: New Language, Old English, and Teaching the Tradition* (New Brunswick, 1990); Overing, *Language, Sign, and Gender in "Beowulf"*; Katherine O'Brien O'Keeffe, *Visible Song: Transitional Literacy in Old English Verse* (Cambridge, Eng., 1990); Seth Lerer, *Literacy and Power in Anglo-Saxon England* (Lincoln, Nebr., 1991); and Martin Irvine, *The Making of Textual Culture: "Grammatica" and Literary Theory 350–1100* (Cambridge, Eng., 1994), especially Chapter 9, "The implications of grammatical culture in Anglo-Saxon England." Several of these studies discuss at length the long-standing scholarly debates surrounding *Beowulf,* including its oral origins, its composition, and its date—issues I will not engage here. My reading of the poem is based not on its oral foundations but rather on its preservation in the manuscript, that is, as a textual artifact, governed by what Walter Ong has called the "restructured consciousness" of literacy: see Ong, *Orality and Literacy: The Technologizing of the Word* (London, 1982), especially Chapter 4, "Writing Restructures Consciousness." For a good recent overview of the orality-literacy debate, see Carol Braun Pasternack, *The Textuality of Old English Poetry* (Cambridge, Eng.,

1995), especially Chapter 1. On the relationship of *Beowulf* to literate Latinity, see also, among others, Eric John, "*Beowulf* and the Margins of Literacy," *Bulletin of the John Rylands University Library of Manchester* 56 (1973–4): 388–422, reprinted in Peter Baker, ed., "*Beowulf*": *Basic Readings* (New York, 1995), pp. 51–77, and John Niles, "*Beowulf*": *The Poem and its Tradition* (Cambridge, Mass., 1983), pp. 66–95.

[6] John Niles, "Locating *Beowulf* in Literary History," *Exemplaria* 5.1 (1993): 81–82.

[7] Robinson, "*Beowulf*" *and the Appositive Style*, p. 25.

[8] Because the model is by now well-known, I will not include a lengthy definition or explanation here. See Jane Chance, *Woman as Hero in Old English Literature* (Syracuse, 1986), pp. 1–11, for a good cultural analysis of the peace-weaver in Old English literature and Anglo-Saxon culture; for a detailed lexical analysis, see L. John Sklute, "*Freoðuwebbe* in Old English Poetry," in *New Readings on Women in Old English Literature*, ed. Helen Damico and Alexandra Hennessey Olsen (Bloomington, 1990), pp. 204–10. While Chance sees peace-weaving as a passive and tragic role (p. 10), Sklute argues that peace-weavers are diplomats, actively working to reduce hostilities and promote peace. Although the role of the peace-weaver is now familiar to Anglo-Saxonists, the term appears only three times in Old English poetry, once in reference to a male angel, once for comparative purposes to describe why a woman's behavior is not appropriate (this is Modthryth, in *Beowulf*, discussed below), and only once (in *Widsith*) to describe a woman who has been given in marriage as a token of peace between hostile tribes—the standard definition. The social structure represented by this practice is, however, quite common.

"Peace-weaving" as an anthropological system transacts women as commodities within a homosocial economy. The homosocial bond between male reader and "masculine" spiritual meaning is enabled through the feminine letter of the text. Similarly, the female peace-weaver joins (weaves) a variety of male social groups. See Gayle Rubin, "The Traffic in Women," in *Toward an Anthropology of Women*, ed. Rayna B. Reiter (New York, 1975), pp. 157–210, for the now-classic feminist anthropological reading of this phenomenon. On women as objects of exchange in *Beowulf*, see Christopher Fee, "Beag & Beaghroden: Women, Treasure, and the Language of Social Structure in *Beowulf*," *Neuphilologische Mitteilungen* 97 (1996): 285–94.

[9] See Overing, *Language, Sign, and Gender*, p. xxiv, and Chance, *Woman as Hero*, pp. 3, 106, and passim.

[10] Martin Irvine, "Medieval Textuality and the Archaeology of Textual Culture," in *Speaking Two Languages: Traditional Disciplines and Contemporary Theory in Medieval Studies*, ed. Allen J. Frantzen (Albany, 1991), pp. 192, 193.

[11] M. T. Clanchy, *From Memory to Written Record: England 1066–1307*, 2nd ed. (Oxford, 1993). Clanchy is referring here to twelfth-century manuscripts, but the practice and principle are the same for earlier texts. For a general discussion of the functions of the marginal gloss in Anglo-Saxon texts, see Michael Lapidge, "The Study of Latin Texts in late Anglo-Saxon England I: The Evidence of Latin Glosses," pp. 99–140, and R.I. Page, "The Study of Latin Texts in late Anglo-Saxon England II: The Evidence of English Glosses," pp. 141–65, both in *Latin and the Vernacular Languages in Early Medieval Britain*, ed. Nicholas Brooks (Leicester, 1982).

[12] See John Leyerle, "The Interlace Structure of Beowulf," *University of Toronto Quarterly* 37 (1967): 1–17; see also Chance, *Woman as Hero*, pp. 4–5 and passim, where she links peace-weaving to the material practices of weaving in Anglo-Saxon England.

[13] Mary Carruthers, *The Book of Memory: A Study of Memory in Medieval Culture* (Cambridge, Eng., 1990), p. 12.

[14] Throughout this essay, all references to *Beowulf* are from Fr. Klaeber, ed., *"Beowulf" and the Fight at Finnsburg*, 3rd ed. with supplements (Lexington, Mass., 1950). Internal citations will refer to line numbers. Unless otherwise noted, translations are my own.

[15] In addition to Pauline Head's recent book, cited in note 16 below, there is a substantial body of scholarship showing the structural and aesthetic functions of framing devices, envelope patterns, and ring structures in Old English poetry. See, among others, Adrien Bonjour, *The Digressions in "Beowulf"* (Oxford, 1950); Adeline Courtney Bartlett, *The Larger Rhetorical Patterns in Anglo-Saxon Poetry* (New York, 1935); John Niles, *"Beowulf": The Poem and Its Tradition* (Cambridge, Eng., 1983); Constance B. Hieatt, "Envelope Patterns and the Structure of *Beowulf*" *English Studies in Canada* 1 (1975): 249–65; Ward Parks, "Ring Structure and Narrative Embedding in Homer and *Beowulf*" *Neuphilologische Mitteilungen* 89 (1988): 237–51; H. Ward Tonsfeldt, "Ring Structure in *Beowulf*" *Neophilologus* 61 (1977): 443–52. In general, these studies have shown the various ways that such narrative techniques intensify or illuminate poetic themes by drawing attention to relationships between the framed text (often called a "digression") and the "main" text. In addition, the framing device itself may help to show the relationship between texts within and outside of the frame. For example, the appearances of Wealhtheow that frame the Finn episode prompt the audience to consider the similarities between her situation and Hildeburh's.

[16] Pauline Head, *Representation and Design: Tracing a Hermeneutics of Old English Poetry* (Albany, 1997), p. 66.

[17] See Overing, *Language, Sign, and Gender*, pp. xxiv, 81.

[18] It is interesting to note that the moment when Hildeburh mourns beside the funeral pyre is the most fully embedded moment in the episode. In "Ring Structure in *Beowulf*," Tonsfeldt has shown that the Finn episode is a tightly structured ring pattern, with five levels of events leading into and out of this precise moment (especially pp. 448–52).

[19] The connections between Hildeburh and Wealhtheow, either as parallel figures or as diametrically opposed, have often been noted; see Chance, *Woman as Hero*, pp. 99–101; Damico, *Beowulf's Wealhtheow*, pp. 19–20; and Robinson, *"Beowulf" and the Appositive Style*, p. 26.

[20] Tonsfeldt, "Ring Structure in *Beowulf*," pp. 449–51.

[21] The peace-weaver's duties have been discussed at length in recent scholarship. See Chance, *Woman as Hero*, pp. 1–11; Damico, *Beowulf's Wealhtheow*, pp. 8–9; and Michael J. Enright, *Lady With a Mead-Cup: Ritual, Prophecy, and Lordship in the European Warband from La Tène to the Viking Age* (Dublin, 1996), pp. 1–37.

[22] Damico shows that structurally Wealhtheow's first appearance is governed by an envelope pattern, in which the sounds of celebration that immediately precede her appearance are matched by nearly identical descriptions following it. Thus this first Wealhtheow episode, the first structural component in the narrative frame surrounding Hildeburh's story, is itself textually enclosed (*Beowulf's Wealhtheow*, pp. 9–11).

[23] Damico, *Beowulf's Wealhtheow*, p. 8. See also Overing, *Language, Sign, and Gender*, pp. 95–97.

[24] See Damico, *Beowulf's Wealhtheow*, pp. 127–32, for a lengthy discussion of Wealhtheow's support of Hrothulf. See also Edward B. Irving, Jr., *Rereading "Beowulf"* (Philadelphia, 1989) for a discussion of Wealhtheow's inability to transcend the boundaries of her role, in spite of the potential this scene would seem to offer for just such a transcendence (p. 74).

[25] Like other Germanic languages, Old English has no synthetic passive, but forms passive voice (for the most part) through the use of "to be" verbs, as in this passage. See Bruce Mitchell and Fred C. Robinson, *A Guide to Old English*, 5th ed. (Oxford, 1992), p. 111.

[26] See Enright, *Lady With a Mead Cup*, pp. 5–8.

[27] Leyerle, "The Interlace Structure of *Beowulf*," reprinted in R. D. Fulk, ed., *Interpretations of "Beowulf": A Critical Anthology* (Bloomington, 1991), p. 152.

[28] Stephanie Hollis, *Anglo-Saxon Women and the Church* (Woodbridge, Suffolk, 1992), p. 154, Hollis's emphasis.

[29] See Irving, *Rereading "Beowulf*," p. 61; Damico, *Beowulf's Wealtheow*, pp. 127–32.

[30] Elaine Tuttle Hansen, *The Solomon Complex: Reading Wisdom in Old English Poetry* (Toronto, 1988), p. 47.

[31] See Chance, *Woman as Hero*, p. 38. A recent article by Melinda Menzer deals convincingly with the issue of Grendel's Mother's humanity by showing that the latter element in the compound *aglæcwif* consistently refers in Old English to a female human; that is, *wif* is not simply a gender marker, but more specifically is a marker of gendered personhood. See Melinda J. Menzer, "*Aglæcwif* (*Beowulf* 1259A): Implications for -*Wif* Compounds, Grendel's Mother and Other *Aglæcan*," *English Language Notes* 34 (September 1996): 1–6. In addition, several scholars have attempted through lexical means to evaluate the "inherent nobility" of Grendel's Mother; see Keith P. Taylor, "*Beowulf* 1259a: The Inherent Nobility of Grendel's Mother," *ELN* 31 (1994): 13–25; Kevin Kiernan, "Grendel's Heroic Mother," *In Geardagum* 6 (1984): 25–27; and Christine Alfano, "The Issue of Feminine Monstrosity: A Reevaluation of Grendel's Mother," *Comitatus* 23 (1993): 1–16.

[32] Lerer, *Literacy and Power in Anglo-Saxon Literature*, p. 192.

[33] It may contain a pun. *Wæfre* is not etymologically linked to the Old English verb *wefan*, "to weave," but several of the verb forms have homophonic correspondences. The OE word for spider, *gangelwæfre*, or sometimes *wæfregange* (Bosworth-Toller defines this as a "ganging weaver, spider") suggests a close correlation between Grendel's Mother and the poem's other "weavers." There may also be an echo here of that other non-peace-weaver, Modthryth, who is likewise described in the language of weaving.

[34] On the "topographical uncertainty" of the mere, see Niles, *"Beowulf": The Poem and Its Tradition*, pp. 16–19. Later in his study, Niles asks, "Why does the poet emphasize that the path to Grendel's mere was 'unknown' (line 1410b) when just the day before, men from far and near had traced Grendel's track to the same pool (lines 841–856a)?. . . . It is one thing to fight a known enemy in known surrounding, as the hero had done with Grendel, and quite another to risk one's life in an unknown territory that is equated with the very source of evil. Each landscape fits its scene like the same vista seen first by day and then by night, when even familiar surroundings seem strange" (pp. 170–71).

[35] Chance, *Woman as Hero*, pp. 101, 103–04.

[36] See Chance's cogent analysis of this scene, which she reads as a pseudo-rape scene (*Woman as Hero*, pp. 102–04).

[37] A fourth possible woman, the "geatisc meowle" (line 3150b), may or may not appear briefly at Beowulf's funeral to mourn his death with her songs. The manuscript is faulty at this point and has been the subject of numerous speculative reconstructions. Currently most scholars consider the "geatisc

meowle" emendation to be the most plausible. For a feminist interpretation of the problematic nature of this reconstruction, see Bennett, "The Female Mourner at Beowulf's Funeral."

38 Niles, *"Beowulf": The Poem and Its Tradition*, pp. 152–53.

39 My understanding of Modthryth has been greatly enhanced by the recent analyses of Gillian Overing, in *Language, Sign, and Gender*, and Mary Dockray-Miller, "The Masculine Queen of *Beowulf*," *Women and Language* 21(1998): 31–38. I am grateful to Mary Dockray-Miller for allowing me to see an earlier version of her article.

40 Donaldson suggests that "a transitional passage introducing the contrast between Hygd's good behavior and Modthryth's bad behavior as young women of royal blood seems to have been lost" (in *"Beowulf": The Donaldson Translation*, ed. Joseph Tuso [New York, 1975], p. 34 n. 2). See also Klaeber's notes on Modthryth for a thorough discussion of the "Thryth-Offa" digression (pp. 195–200) and Paul E. Szarmach, "The recovery of texts," in *Reading Old English Texts*, ed. Katherine O'Brien O'Keeffe (Cambridge, Eng., 1997), pp. 124–45, especially 134–137.

41 Overing constructs this model somewhat differently:

> Modthryth offers a variation on Hildeburh's silent declaration of paradox; she reveals the trace of something that we know cannot exist in the world of the poem: the trace of a woman signifying in her own right. Her initial gesture is strikingly alien, incomprehensible, until translated into the binary language of the masculine economy (*Language, Sign, and Gender*, p. 106).

Until the translation occurs, however, Overing shows that Modthryth "escapes, however briefly, the trap of binary definition" (p. 106). In other words, she escapes the demands of female enclosure, but not for long; the poem's project is to contain her.

42 However, Mary Dockray-Miller argues persuasively that rather than conforming, Modthryth is unconventional precisely because she succeeds at marriage where all other women in the poem fail or are expected to: "The cornerstone of Modþryðo's unconventionality is her success in the role in which the others fail. . . . Unlike the other marriages described in the poem Modþryðo's succeeds both emotionally and politically. . . . Modþryðo's supposed acquiescence to the status quo actually undermines it; her success as a queen (not a peace-pledge) defies the system that devalues yet necessitates the woman as peaceweaver" ("The Masculine Queen of *Beowulf*," p. 36). Socially and politically, however, as Offa's queen (or as peace-pledge), Modthryth has been metaphorically contained by a system outside of which she once stood.

43 *"Beowulf": The Donaldson Translation*, p. 34.

44 This is not to say that peace-weaving leads to peace, just the opposite, as Overing
has shown. But the normalizing functions of the role cannot be underestimated;
even Beowulf knows the limitations of this compulsory system.

45 Judith Butler, *Gender Trouble: Feminism and the Subversion of Identity* (New
York, 1990), p. 33.

WHAT IS AN AUTHOR?

MICHEL FOUCAULT

The coming into being of the notion of "author" constitutes the privileged moment of *individualization* in the history of ideas, knowledge, literature, philosophy, and the sciences. Even today, when we reconstruct the history of a concept, literary genre, or school of philosophy, such categories seem relatively weak, secondary, and superimposed scansions in comparison with the solid and fundamental unit of the author and the work.

I shall not offer here a sociohistorical analysis of the author's persona. Certainly it would be worth examining how the author became individualized in a culture like ours, what status he has been given, at what moment studies of authenticity and attribution began, in what kind of system of valorization the author was involved, at what point we began to recount the lives of authors rather than of heroes, and how this fundamental category of "the-man-and-his-work criticism" began. For the moment, however, I want to deal solely with the relationship between text and author and with the manner in which the text points to this "figure" that, at least in appearance, is outside it and antecedes it.

Beckett nicely formulates the theme with which I would like to begin: "'What does it matter who is speaking,' someone said, 'what does it matter who is speaking.'" In this indifference appears one of the fundamental ethical principles of contemporary writing [*écriture*]. I say "ethical" because

From Josué V. Harari, ed., *Textual Strategies: Perspectives in Post-Structuralist Criticism* (Ithaca, 1979), pp. 141–60; reprinted with permission of Cornell University Press.

this indifference is not really a trait characterizing the manner in which one speaks and writes, but rather a kind of immanent rule, taken up over and over again, never fully applied, not designating writing as something completed, but dominating it as a practice. Since it is too familiar to require a lengthy analysis, this immanent rule can be adequately illustrated here by tracing two of its major themes.

First of all, we can say that today's writing has freed itself from the dimension of expression. Referring only to itself, but without being restricted to the confines of its interiority, writing is identified with its own unfolded exteriority. This means that it is an interplay of signs arranged less according to its signified content than according to the very nature of the signifier. Writing unfolds like a game [*jeu*] that invariably goes beyond its own rules and transgresses its limits. In writing, the point is not to manifest or exalt the act of writing, nor is it to pin a subject within language; it is rather a question of creating a space into which the writing subject constantly disappears.

The second theme, writing's relationship with death, is even more familiar. This link subverts an old tradition exemplified by the Greek epic, which was intended to perpetuate the immortality of the hero: if he was willing to die young, it was so that his life, consecrated and magnified by death, might pass into immortality; the narrative then redeemed this accepted death. In another way, the motivation, as well as the theme and the pretext of Arabian narratives—such as *The Thousand and One Nights*—was also the eluding of death: one spoke, telling stories into the early morning, in order to forestall death, to postpone the day of reckoning that would silence the narrator. Scheherazade's narrative is an effort, renewed each night, to keep death outside the circle of life.

Our culture has metamorphosed this idea of narrative, or writing, as something designed to ward off death. Writing has become linked to sacrifice, even to the sacrifice of life: it is now a voluntary effacement which does not need to be represented in books, since it is brought about in the writer's very existence. The work, which once had the duty of providing immortality, now possesses the right to kill, to be its author's murderer, as in the cases of Flaubert, Proust, and Kafka. That is not all, however: this relationship between writing and death is also manifested in the effacement of the writing subject's individual characteristics. Using all the contrivances that he sets up between himself and what he writes, the writing subject cancels out the signs of his particular individuality. As a result, the mark of the writer is reduced to nothing more than the singularity of his absence; he must assume the role of the dead man in the game of writing.

None of this is recent; criticism and philosophy took note of the disappearance—or death—of the author some time ago. But the consequences of their discovery of it have not been sufficiently examined, nor has its import been accurately measured. A certain number of notions that are intended to replace the privileged position of the author actually seem to preserve that privilege and suppress the real meaning of his disappearance. I shall examine two of these notions, both of great importance today.

The first is the idea of the work. It is a very familiar thesis that the task of criticism is not to bring out the work's relationships with the author, nor to reconstruct through the text a thought or experience, but rather to analyze the work through its structure, its architecture, its intrinsic form, and the play of its internal relationships. At this point, however, a problem arises: "What is a work? What is this curious unity which we designate as a work? Of what elements is it composed? Is it not what an author has written?" Difficulties appear immediately. If an individual were not an author, could we say that what he wrote, said, left behind in his papers, or what has been collected of his remarks, could be called a "work"? When Sade was not considered an author, what was the status of his papers? Were they simply rolls of paper onto which he ceaselessly uncoiled his fantasies during his imprisonment?

Even when an individual has been accepted as an author, we must still ask whether everything that he wrote, said, or left behind is part of his work. The problem is both theoretical and technical. When undertaking the publication of Nietzsche's works, for example, where should one stop? Surely everything must be published, but what is "everything"? Everything that Nietzsche himself published, certainly. And what about the rough drafts for his works? Obviously. The plans for his aphorisms? Yes. The deleted passages and the notes at the bottom of the page? Yes. What if, within a workbook filled with aphorisms, one finds a reference, the notation of a meeting or of an address, or a laundry list: is it a work, or not? Why not? And so on, ad infinitum. How can one define a work amid the millions of traces left by someone after his death? A theory of the work does not exist, and the empirical task of those who naively undertake the editing of works often suffers in the absence of such a theory.

We could go even further: does *The Thousand and One Nights* constitute a work? What about Clement of Alexandria's *Miscellanies* or Diogenes Laertius' *Lives*? A multitude of questions arises with regard to this notion of the work. Consequently, it is not enough to declare that we should do without the writer (the author) and study the work in itself. The word "work" and the unity that it designates are probably as problematic as the status of the author's individuality.

Another notion which has hindered us from taking full measure of the author's disappearance, blurring and concealing the moment of this effacement and subtly preserving the author's existence, is the notion of writing [*écriture*]. When rigorously applied, this notion should allow us not only to circumvent references to the author, but also to situate his recent absence. The notion of writing, as currently employed, is concerned with neither the act of writing nor the indication—be it symptom or sign—of a meaning which someone might have wanted to express. We try, with great effort, to imagine the general condition of each text, the condition of both the space in which it is dispersed and the time in which it unfolds.

In current usage, however, the notion of writing seems to transpose the empirical characteristics of the author into a transcendental anonymity. We are content to efface the more visible marks of the author's empiricity by playing off, one against the other, two ways of characterizing writing, namely, the critical and the religious approaches. Giving writing a primal status seems to be a way of retranslating, in transcendental terms, both the theological affirmation of its sacred character and the critical affirmation of its creative character. To admit that writing is, because of the very history that it made possible, subject to the test of oblivion and repression, seems to represent, in transcendental terms, the religious principle of the hidden meaning (which requires interpretation) and the critical principle of implicit significations, silent determinations, and obscured contents (which gives rise to commentary). To imagine writing as absence seems to be a simple repetition, in transcendental terms, of both the religious principle of inalterable and yet never fulfilled tradition, and the aesthetic principle of the work's survival, its perpetuation beyond the author's death, and its enigmatic *excess* in relation to him.

This usage of the notion of writing runs the risk of maintaining the author's privileges under the protection of writing's a priori status: it keeps alive, in the grey light of neutralization, the interplay of those representations that formed a particular image of the author. The author's disappearance, which, since Mallarmé, has been a constantly recurring event, is subject to a series of transcendental barriers. There seems to be an important dividing line between those who believe that they can still locate today's discontinuities [*ruptures*] in the historico-transcendental tradition of the nineteenth century, and those who try to free themselves once and for all from that tradition.[1]

• • •

It is not enough, however, to repeat the empty affirmation that the author has disappeared. For the same reason, it is not enough to keep repeating (after Nietzsche) that God and man have died a common death. Instead, we must locate the space left empty by the author's disappearance, follow the distribution of gaps and breaches, and watch for the openings that this disappearance uncovers.

First, we need to clarify briefly the problems arising from the use of the author's name. What is an author's name? How does it function? Far from offering a solution, I shall only indicate some of the difficulties that it presents.

The author's name is a proper name, and therefore it raises the problems common to all proper names. (Here I refer to Searle's analyses, among others.[2]) Obviously, one cannot turn a proper name into a pure and simple reference. It has other than indicative functions: more than an indication, a gesture, a finger pointed at someone, it is the equivalent of a description. When one says "Aristotle," one employs a word that is the equivalent of one, or a series of, definite descriptions, such as "the author of the *Analytics*," "the founder of ontology," and so forth. One cannot stop there, however, because a proper name does not have just one signification. When we discover that Rimbaud did not write *La Chasse spirituelle*, we cannot pretend that the meaning of this proper name, or that of the author, has been altered. The proper name and the author's name are situated between the two poles of description and designation: they must have a certain link with what they name, but one that is neither entirely in the mode of designation nor in that of description; it must be a *specific* link. However—and it is here that the particular difficulties of the author's name arise—the links between the proper name and the individual named and between the author's name and what it names are not isomorphic and do not function in the same way. There are several differences.

If, for example, Pierre Dupont does not have blue eyes, or was not born in Paris, or is not a doctor, the name Pierre Dupont will still always refer to the same person; such things do not modify the link of designation. The problems raised by the author's name are much more complex, however. If I discover that Shakespeare was not born in the house that we visit today, this is a modification which, obviously, will not alter the functioning of the author's name. But if we proved that Shakespeare did not write those sonnets which pass for his, that would constitute a significant change and affect the manner in which the author's name functions. If we proved that Shakespeare wrote Bacon's *Organon* by showing that the same author wrote both the works of Bacon and those of Shakespeare, that would be a third type of change which would entirely modify the functioning of the author's name. The author's name is not, therefore, just a proper name like the rest.

Many other facts point out the paradoxical singularity of the author's name. To say that Pierre Dupont does not exist is not at all the same as saying that Homer or Hermes Trismegistus did not exist. In the first case, it means that no one has the name Pierre Dupont; in the second, it means that several people were mixed together under one name, or that the true author had none of the traits traditionally ascribed to the personae of Homer or Hermes. To say that X's real name is actually Jacques Durand instead of Pierre Dupont is not the same as saying that Stendhal's name was Henri Beyle. One could also question the meaning and functioning of propositions like "Bourbaki is so-and-so, so-and-so, etc." and "Victor Eremita, Climacus, Anticlimacus, Frater Taciturnus, Constantine Constantius, all of these are Kierkegaard."

These differences may result from the fact that an author's name is not simply an element in a discourse (capable of being either subject or object, of being replaced by a pronoun, and the like); it performs a certain role with regard to narrative discourse, assuring a classificatory function. Such a name permits one to group together a certain number of texts, define them, differentiate them from and contrast them to others. In addition, it establishes a relationship among the texts. Hermes Trismegistus did not exist, nor did Hippocrates—in the sense that Balzac existed—but the fact that several texts have been placed under the same name indicates that there has been established among them a relationship of homogeneity, filiation, authentification of some texts by the use of others, reciprocal explication, or concomitant utilization. The author's name serves to characterize a certain mode of being of discourse: the fact that the discourse has an author's name, that one can say "this was written by so-and-so" or "so-and-so is its author," shows that this discourse is not ordinary everyday speech that merely comes and goes, not something that is immediately consumable. On the contrary, it is a speech that must be received in a certain mode and that, in a given culture, must receive a certain status.

It would seem that the author's name, unlike other proper names, does not pass from the interior of a discourse to the real and exterior individual who produced it; instead, the name seems always to be present, marking off the edges of the text, revealing, or at least characterizing, its mode of being. The author's name manifests the appearance of a certain discursive set and indicates the status of this discourse within a society and a culture. It has no legal status, nor is it located in the fiction of the work; rather, it is located in the break that founds a certain discursive construct and its very particular mode of being. As a result, we could say that in a civilization like our own there are a certain number of discourses that are endowed with the "author-function," while others are deprived of it. A private letter may well have a signer—it does not have an author; a contract may well have a guarantor—it does not have an author. An anonymous text posted on a wall probably has a writer—but not an author. The author-function is therefore characteristic of the mode of existence, circulation, and functioning of certain discourses within a society.

. . .

Let us analyze this "author-function" as we have just described it. In our culture, how does one characterize a discourse containing the author-function? In what way is this discourse different from other discourses? If we limit our remarks to the author of a book or a text, we can isolate four different characteristics.

First of all, discourses are objects of appropriation. The form of ownership from which they spring is of a rather particular type, one that has been codified for many years. We should note that, historically, this type of ownership has always been subsequent to what one might call penal appropriation. Texts, books, and discourses really began to have authors (other than mythical, "sacralized" and "sacralizing" figures) to the extent that authors became subject to punishment, that is, to the extent that discourses could be transgressive. In our culture (and doubtless in many others), discourse was not originally a product, a thing, a kind of goods; it was essentially an act—an act placed in the bipolar field of the sacred and the profane, the licit and the illicit, the religious and the blasphemous. Historically, it was a gesture fraught with risks before becoming goods caught up in a circuit of ownership.

Once a system of ownership for texts came into being, once strict rules concerning author's rights, author-publisher relations, rights of reproduction, and related matters were enacted—at the end of the eighteenth and the beginning of the nineteenth century—the possibility of transgression attached to the act of writing took on, more and more, the form of an imperative peculiar to literature. It is as if the author, beginning with the moment at which he was placed in the system of property that characterizes our society, compensated for the status that he thus acquired by rediscovering the old bipolar field of discourse, systematically practicing transgression and thereby restoring danger to a writing which was now guaranteed the benefits of ownership.

The author-function does not affect all discourses in a universal and constant way, however. This is its second characteristic. In our civilization, it has not always been the same types of texts which have required attribution to an author. There was a time when the texts that we today call "literary" (narratives, stories, epics, tragedies, comedies) were accepted, put into circulation, and valorized without any question about the identity of their author; their anonymity caused no difficulties since their ancientness, whether real or imagined, was regarded as a sufficient guarantee of their status. On the other hand, those texts that we now would call scientific—those dealing with cosmology and the heavens, medicine and illnesses, natural sciences and geography—were accepted in the Middle Ages, and accepted as "true," only when marked with the name of their author. "Hippocrates said," "Pliny recounts," were not really formulas of an argument based on authority; they were the markers inserted in discourses that were supposed to be received as statements of demonstrated truth.

A reversal occurred in the seventeenth or eighteenth century. Scientific discourses began to be received for themselves, in the anonymity of an established or always redemonstrable truth; their membership in a systematic ensemble, and not the reference to the individual who produced them, stood as their guarantee. The author-function faded away, and the inventor's name served only to christen a theorem, proposition, particular effect, property, body, group of elements, or pathological syndrome. By the same token, literary discourses came to be accepted only when endowed with the author-function. We now ask of each poetic or fictional text: from where does it come, who wrote it, when, under what circumstances, or beginning with what design? The meaning ascribed to it and the status or value accorded it depend upon the manner in which we answer these questions. And if a text should be discovered in a state of anonymity—whether as a consequence of an accident or the author's explicit wish—the game becomes one of rediscovering the author. Since literary anonymity is not tolerable, we can accept it only in the guise of an enigma. As a result, the author-function today plays an important role in our view of literary works. (These are obviously generalizations that would have to be refined insofar as recent critical practice is concerned.)

The third characteristic of this author-function is that it does not develop spontaneously as the attribution of a discourse to an individual. It is, rather, the result of a complex operation which constructs a certain rational being that we call "author." Critics doubtless try to give this intelligible being a realistic status by discerning, in the individual, a "deep" motive, a "creative" power, or a "design," the milieu in which writing originates. Nevertheless, these aspects of an individual which we designate as making him an author are only a projection, in more or less psychologizing terms, of the operations that we force texts to undergo, the connections that we make, the traits that we establish as pertinent, the continuities that we recognize, or the exclusions that we practice. All these operations vary according to periods and types of discourse. We do not construct a "philosophical author" as we do a "poet," just as, in the eighteenth century, one did not construct a novelist as we do today. Still, we can find through the ages certain constants in the rules of author-construction.

It seems, for example, that the manner in which literary criticism once defined the author—or rather constructed the figure of the author beginning with existing texts and discourses—is directly derived from the manner in which Christian tradition authenticated (or rejected) the texts at its disposal. In order to "rediscover" an author in a work, modern criticism uses methods similar to those that Christian exegesis employed when trying to prove the value of a text by its author's saintliness. In *De viris illustribus*, Saint Jerome explains that homonymy is not sufficient to identify legitimately authors of more than one work: different individuals could have had the same name, or one man could have, illegitimately, borrowed another's patronymic. The name as an individual trademark is not enough when one works within a textual tradition.

How, then, can one attribute several discourses to one and the same author? How can one use the author-function to determine if one is dealing with one or several individuals? Saint Jerome proposes four criteria: (1) if among several books attributed to an author one is inferior to the others, it must be withdrawn from the list of the author's works (the author is therefore defined as a constant level of value); (2) the same should be done if certain texts contradict the doctrine expounded in the author's other works (the author is thus defined as a field of conceptual or theoretical coherence); (3) one must also exclude works that are written in a different style, containing words and expressions not ordinarily found in the writer's production (the author is here conceived as a stylistic unity); (4) finally, passages quoting statements that were made, or mentioning events that occurred after the author's death must be regarded as interpolated texts (the author is here seen as a historical figure at the crossroads of a certain number of events).

Modern literary criticism, even when—as is now customary—it is not concerned with questions of authentication, still defines the author the same way: the author provides the basis for explaining not only the presence of certain events in a work, but also their transformations, distortions, and diverse modifications (through his biography, the determination of his individual perspective, the analysis of his social position, and the revelation of his basic design). The author is also the principle of a certain unity of writing—all differences having to be resolved, at least in part, by the principles of evolution, maturation, or influence. The author also serves to neutralize the contradictions that may emerge in a series of texts: there must be—at a certain level of his thought or desire, of his consciousness or unconscious—a point where contradictions are resolved, where incompatible elements are at last tied together or organized around a fundamental or originating contradiction. Finally, the author is a particular source of expression that, in more or less completed forms, is manifested equally well, and with similar validity, in works, sketches, letters, fragments, and so on. Clearly, Saint Jerome's four criteria of authenticity (criteria which seem totally insufficient for today's exegetes) do define the four modalities according to which modern criticism brings the author-function into play.

But the author-function is not a pure and simple reconstruction made secondhand from a text given as passive material. The text always contains a certain number of signs referring to the author. These signs, well known to grammarians, are personal pronouns, adverbs of time and place, and verb conjugation. Such elements do not play the same role in discourses provided with the author-function as in those lacking it. In the latter, such "shifters" refer to the real speaker and to the spatio-temporal coordinates of his discourse (although certain modifications can occur, as in the operation of relating discourses in the first person). In the former, however, their role is more complex and variable. Everyone knows that, in a novel narrated in the first person, neither the first person pronoun, nor the present indicative refer exactly either to the writer or to the moment in which he writes, but rather to an alter ego whose distance from the author varies, often changing in the course of the work. It would be just as wrong to equate the author with the real writer as to equate him with the fictitious speaker; the author-function is carried out and operates in the scission itself, in this division and this distance.

One might object that this is a characteristic peculiar to novelistic or poetic discourse, a "game" in which only "quasi-discourses" participate. In fact, however, all discourses endowed with the author-function do possess this plurality of self. The self that speaks in the preface to a treatise on mathematics—and that indicates the circumstances of the treatise's composition—is identical neither in its position nor in its functioning to the self that speaks in the course of a demonstration, and that appears in the form of "I conclude" or "I suppose." In the first case, the "I" refers to an individual without an equivalent who, in a determined place and time, completed a certain task; in the second, the "I" indicates an instance and a level of demonstration which any individual could perform provided that he accept the same system of symbols, play of axioms, and set of previous demonstrations. We could also, in the same treatise, locate a third self, one that speaks to tell the work's meaning, the obstacles encountered, the results obtained, and the remaining problems; this self is situated in the field of already existing or yet-to-appear mathematical discourses. The author-function is not assumed by the first of these selves at the expense of the other two, which would then be nothing more than a fictitious splitting in two of the first one. On the contrary, in these discourses the author-function operates so as to effect the dispersion of these three simultaneous selves.

No doubt analysis could discover still more characteristic traits of the author-function. I will limit myself to these four, however, because they seem both the most visible and the most important. They can be summarized as follows: (1) the author-function is linked to the juridical and institutional system that encompasses, determines, and articulates the universe of discourses; (2) it does not affect all discourses in the same way at all times and in all types of civilization; (3) it is not defined by the spontaneous attribution of a discourse to its producer, but rather by a series of specific and complex operations; (4) it does not refer purely and simply to a real individual, since it can give rise simultaneously to several selves, to several subjects—positions that can be occupied by different classes of individuals.

• • •

Up to this point I have unjustifiably limited my subject. Certainly the author-function in painting, music, and other arts should have been discussed, but even supposing that we remain within the world of discourse, as I want to do, I seem to have given the term "author" much too narrow a meaning. I have discussed the author only in the limited sense of a person to whom the production of a text, a book, or a work can be legitimately attributed. It is easy to see that in the sphere of discourse one can be the author of much more than a book—one can be the author of a theory, tradition, or discipline in which other books and authors will in their turn find a place.

These authors are in a position which we shall call "transdiscursive." This is a recurring phenomenon—certainly as old as our civilization. Homer, Aristotle, and the Church Fathers, as well as the first mathematicians and the originators of the Hippocratic tradition, all played this role.

Furthermore, in the course of the nineteenth century, there appeared in Europe another, more uncommon, kind of author, whom one should confuse with neither the "great" literary authors, nor the authors of religious texts, nor the founders of science. In a somewhat arbitrary way we shall call those who belong in this last group "founders of discursivity." They are unique in that they are not just the authors of their own works. They have produced something else: the possibilities and the rules for the formation of other texts. In this sense, they are very different, for example, from a novelist, who is, in fact, nothing more than the author of his own text. Freud is not just the author of *The Interpretation of Dreams* or *Jokes and their Relation to the Unconscious*; Marx is not just the author of the *Communist Manifesto* or *Capital*: they both have established an endless possibility of discourse.

Obviously, it is easy to object. One might say that it is not true that the author of a novel is only the author of his own text; in a sense, he also, provided that he acquires some "importance," governs and commands more than that. To take a very simple example, one could say that Ann Radcliffe not only wrote *The Castles of Athlin and Dunbayne* and several other novels, but also made possible the appearance of the Gothic horror novel at the beginning of the nineteenth century; in that respect, her author-function exceeds her own work. But I think there is an answer to this objection. These founders of discursivity (I use Marx and Freud as examples, because I believe them to be both the first and the most important cases) make possible something altogether different from what a novelist makes possible. Ann Radcliffe's texts opened the way for a certain number of resemblances and analogies which have their model or principle in her work. The latter contains characteristic signs, figures, relationships, and structures which could be reused by others. In other words, to say that Ann Radcliffe founded the Gothic horror novel means that in the nineteenth-century Gothic novel one will find, as in Ann Radcliffe's works, the theme of the heroine caught in the trap of her own innocence, the hidden castle, the character of the black, cursed hero devoted to making the world expiate the evil done to him, and all the rest of it.

On the other hand, when I speak of Marx or Freud as founders of discursivity, I mean that they made possible not only a certain number of analogies, but also (and equally important) a certain number of differences.

They have created a possibility for something other than their discourse, yet something belonging to what they founded. To say that Freud founded psychoanalysis does not (simply) mean that we find the concept of the libido or the technique of dream analysis in the works of Karl Abraham or Melanie Klein; it means that Freud made possible a certain number of divergences—with respect to his own texts, concepts, and hypotheses—that all arise from the psychoanalytical discourse itself.

This would seem to present a new difficulty, however: is the above not true, after all, of any founder of a science, or of any author who has introduced some important transformation into a science? After all, Galileo made possible not only those discourses that repeated the laws that he had formulated, but also statements very different from what he himself had said. If Cuvier is the founder of biology or Saussure the founder of linguistics, it is not because they were imitated, nor because people have since taken up again the concept of organism or sign; it is because Cuvier made possible, to a certain extent, a theory of evolution diametrically opposed to his own fixism; it is because Saussure made possible a generative grammar radically different from his structural analyses. Superficially, then, the initiation of discursive practices appears similar to the founding of any scientific endeavor.

Still, there is a difference, and a notable one. In the case of a science, the act that founds it is on an equal footing with its future transformations; this act becomes in some respects part of the set of modifications that it makes possible. Of course, this belonging can take several forms. In the future development of a science, the founding act may appear as little more than a particular instance of a more general phenomenon which unveils itself in the process. It can also turn out to be marred by intuition and empirical bias; one must then reformulate it, making it the object of a certain number of supplementary theoretical operations which establish it more rigorously, etc. Finally, it can seem to be a hasty generalization which must be limited, and whose restricted domain of validity must be retraced. In other words, the founding act of a science can always be reintroduced within the machinery of those transformations that derive from it.

In contrast, the initiation of a discursive practice is heterogeneous to its subsequent transformations. To expand a type of discursivity, such as psychoanalysis as founded by Freud, is not to give it a formal generality that it would not have permitted at the outset, but rather to open it up to a certain number of possible applications. To limit psychoanalysis as a type of discursivity is, in reality, to try to isolate in the founding act an eventually restricted number of propositions or statements to which, alone, one grants a founding value, and in relation to which certain concepts or theories accepted by Freud might be considered as derived, secondary, and accessory. In addition, one does not declare certain propositions in the work of these founders to be false: instead, when trying to seize the act of founding, one sets aside those statements that are not pertinent, either because they are deemed inessential, or because they are considered "prehistoric" and derived from another type of discursivity. In other words, unlike the founding of a science, the initiation of a discursive practice does not participate in its later transformations.

As a result, one defines a proposition's theoretical validity in relation to the work of the founders—while, in the case of Galileo and Newton, it is in relation to what physics or cosmology *is* (in its intrinsic structure and "normativity") that one affirms the validity of any proposition that those men may have put forth. To phrase it very schematically: the work of initiators of discursivity is not situated in the space that science defines; rather, it is the science or the discursivity which refers back to their work as primary coordinates.

In this way we can understand the inevitable necessity, within these fields of discursivity, for a "return to the origin." This return, which is part of the discursive field itself, never stops modifying it. The return is not a historical supplement which would be added to the discursivity, or merely an ornament; on the contrary, it constitutes an effective and necessary task of transforming the discursive practice itself. Re-examination of Galileo's text may well change our knowledge of the history of mechanics, but it will never be able to change mechanics itself. On the other hand, re-examining Freud's texts modifies psychoanalysis itself just as a re-examination of Marx's would modify Marxism.[3]

What I have just outlined regarding the initiation of discursive practices is, of course, very schematic; this is true, in particular, of the opposition that I have tried to draw between discursive initiation and scientific founding. It is not always easy to distinguish between the two; moreover, nothing proves that they are two mutually exclusive procedures. I have attempted the distinction for only one reason: to show that the author-function, which is complex enough when one tries to situate it at the level of a book or a series of texts that carry a given signature, involves still more determining factors when one tries to analyze it in larger units, such as groups of works or entire disciplines.

• • •

To conclude, I would like to review the reasons why I attach a certain importance to what I have said.

First, there are theoretical reasons. On the one hand, an analysis in the direction that I have outlined might provide for an approach to a typology of discourse. It seems to me, at least at first glance, that such a typology cannot be constructed solely from the grammatical features, formal structures, and objects of discourse: more likely there exist properties or relationships peculiar to discourse (not reducible to the rules of grammar and logic), and one must use these to distinguish the major categories of discourse. The relationship (or nonrelationship) with an author, and the different forms this relationship takes, constitute—in a quite visible manner—one of these discursive properties.

On the other hand, I believe that one could find here an introduction to the historical analysis of discourse. Perhaps it is time to study discourses not only in terms of their expressive value or formal transformations, but according to their modes of existence. The modes of circulation, valorization, attribution, and appropriation of discourses vary with each culture and are modified within each. The manner in which they are articulated according to social relationships can be more readily understood, I believe, in the activity of the author-function and in its modifications, than in the themes or concepts that discourses set in motion.

It would seem that one could also, beginning with analyses of this type, re-examine the privileges of the subject. I realize that in undertaking the internal and architectonic analysis of a work (be it a literary text, philosophical system, or scientific work), in setting aside biographical and psychological references, one has already called back into question the absolute character and founding role of the subject. Still, perhaps one must return to this question, not in order to re-establish the theme of an originating subject, but to grasp the subject's points of insertion, modes of functioning, and system of dependencies. Doing so means overturning the traditional problem, no longer raising the questions "How can a free subject penetrate the substance of things and give it meaning? How can it activate the rules of a language from within and thus give rise to the designs which are properly its own?" Instead, these questions will be raised: "How, under what conditions and in what forms can something like a subject appear in the order of discourse? What place can it occupy in each type of discourse, what functions can it assume, and by obeying what rules?" In short, it is a matter of depriving the subject (or its substitute) of its role as originator, and of analyzing the subject as a variable and complex function of discourse.

Second, there are reasons dealing with the "ideological" status of the author. The question then becomes: How can one reduce the great peril, the great danger with which fiction threatens our world? The answer is: One can reduce it with the author. The author allows a limitation of the cancerous and dangerous proliferation of significations within a world where one is thrifty not only with one's resources and riches, but also with one's discourses and their significations. The author is the principle of thrift in the proliferation of meaning. As a result, we must entirely reverse the traditional idea of the author. We are accustomed, as we have seen earlier, to saying that the author is the genial creator of a work in which he deposits, with infinite wealth and generosity, an inexhaustible world of significations. We are used to thinking that the author is so different from all other men, and so transcendent with regard to all languages that, as soon as he speaks, meaning begins to proliferate, to proliferate indefinitely.

The truth is quite the contrary: the author is not an indefinite source of significations which fill a work; the author does not precede the works, he is a certain functional principle by which, in our culture, one limits, excludes, and chooses; in short, by which one impedes the free circulation, the free manipulation, the free composition, decomposition, and recomposition of fiction. In fact, if we are accustomed to presenting the author as a genius, as a perpetual surging of invention, it is because, in reality, we make him function in exactly the opposite fashion. One can say that the author is an ideological product, since we represent him as the opposite of his historically real function. (When a historically given function is represented in a figure that inverts it, one has an ideological production.) The author is therefore the ideological figure by which one marks the manner in which we fear the proliferation of meaning.

In saying this, I seem to call for a form of culture in which fiction would not be limited by the figure of the author. It would be pure romanticism, however, to imagine a culture in which the fictive would operate in an absolutely free state, in which fiction would be put at the disposal of everyone and would develop without passing through something like a necessary or constraining figure. Although, since the eighteenth century, the author has played the role of the regulator of the fictive, a role quite characteristic of our era of industrial and bourgeois society, of individualism and private property, still, given the historical modifications that are taking place, it does not seem necessary that the author-function remain constant in form, complexity, and even in existence. I think that, as our society changes, at the very moment when it is in the process of changing, the author-function will disappear, and in such a manner that fiction and its polysemic texts will once again function according to another mode, but still with a system of constraint—one which will no longer be the author, but which will have to be determined or, perhaps, experienced.

All discourses, whatever their status, form, value, and whatever the treatment to which they will be subjected, would then develop in the anonymity of a murmur. We would no longer hear the questions that have been rehashed for so long: "Who really spoke? Is it really he and not someone else? With what authenticity or originality? And what part of his deepest self did he express in his discourse?" Instead, there would be other questions, like these: "What are the modes of existence of this discourse? Where has it been used, how can it circulate, and who can appropriate it for himself? What are the places in it where there is room for possible subjects? Who can assume these various subject-functions?" And behind all these questions, we would hear hardly anything but the stirring of an indifference: "What difference does it make who is speaking?"

NOTES

[1] For a discussion of the notions of discontinuity and historical tradition see Foucault's *Les Mots et les choses* (Paris, 1966), translated as *The Order of Things* (New York, 1971).—Ed., *Textual Strategies*.

[2] John Searle, *Speech Acts: An Essay in the Philosophy of Language* (Cambridge, 1969), pp. 162–74.—Ed., *Textual Strategies*.

[3] To define these returns more clearly, one must also emphasize that they tend to reinforce the enigmatic link between an author and his works. A text has an inaugurative value precisely because it is the work of a particular author, and our returns are conditioned by this knowledge. As in the case of Galileo, there is no possibility that the rediscovery of an unknown text by Newton or Cantor will modify classical cosmology or set theory as we know them (at best, such an exhumation might modify our historical knowledge of their genesis). On the other hand, the discovery of a text like Freud's "Project for a Scientific Psychology"—insofar as it is a text by Freud—always threatens to modify not the historical knowledge of psychoanalysis, but its theoretical field, even if only by shifting the accentuation or the center of gravity. Through such returns, which are part of their make-up, these discursive practices maintain a relationship with regard to their "fundamental" and indirect author unlike that which an ordinary text entertains with its immediate author.—Ed., *Textual Strategies*.

THE TEXTUALITY OF OLD ENGLISH POETRY

CAROL BRAUN PASTERNACK

The modern reader knows Old English poetry as a discrete number of poems, each of which has a title (in all cases, inserted by modern editors), a definite beginning (even if it has been lost), a middle and an end (which may again be lost but which still exists as a supposed structural element). We may read such a poem in its own little book, accompanied by scholarly introduction, glossary and relevant appendices of sources or analogues, or we may read it in a collection, such as John C. Pope's *Seven Old English Poems*, or in a volume with other poems all from the same manuscript, as in the Anglo-Saxon Poetic Records series. In all of these manifestations, the editors present the poems in a manner comparable to modern poems: not only giving each poem a title, printed above the text, but also presenting it in lines that visually mark units defined by rhythm and alliteration, in periods punctuated as modern sentences, and in verse-paragraphs as well. Even when a text is printed with others from the same manuscript, its separateness appears in the visual signs of a preceding blank space, a centered title which becomes a running title at the top of each page, and numbered lines which begin at the start of each "poem." This manner of presentation interrelates with certain beliefs about

From *The Textuality of Old English Poetry* (Cambridge, Eng., 1995), pp. 1–26; reprinted by permission of Cambridge University Press. The only alterations to the original have been to remove references Pasternack makes in the body of the essay to other sections of her book in which this essay originally appeared. Material in footnotes has also been augmented for clarity.

the creation of poems, their subsequent existence, and what and how they communicate.

It follows that modern scholars have been using the same questions to interpret Old English verse that they would apply to modern poems. The questions, then, shape the interpretation: they begin with the assumption that the text has a definite structure, a specific author, date when it was composed and so on, and then look for the evidence to support these assumptions. They ask what the meaning of a text is and in doing so expect to know exactly *what* the text is (where it begins and ends and what is in between). They ask about the date of composition and the associated historical context. They ask about the author's distinctive style and whether other texts have the same style and author. They ask about the influence of one text on another. These questions have remained vexed, not because the reasoning is circular but because the circle does not take into its compass certain important facts.

I would attempt to construct a different hermeneutic circle which is truer because it takes into account the format of the verse as it exists in the manuscripts, the formulaic quality of the diction and the structure that the words convey aurally. These features contribute in essential ways to the poetry's textuality; that is, to the conventions and codes through which the Old English poetic texts communicate with readers. Their textuality differs from that of both oral and printed compositions. I would use the term "inscribed" to discuss these texts, since they inherit significant elements of vocality from their oral forebears and yet address the reader from the pages of manuscripts. I do not use the term "written," because that word has implied a textuality in which not only is the poet absent from the text's performance but, in addition, the reader constructs an authorial voice through the text, identifying the thoughts and the particular words with the author. The reader's construction of such a relationship between the English vernacular text and the author may have begun in Chaucer's time, but it was not fully realized before the development of copyright law, three centuries after the invention of the printing press.[1]

My work, then, contributes to a discussion about the territory between the oral and the written that has been carried on by M. T. Clanchy, A. N. Doane, John Miles Foley, Katherine O'Brien O'Keeffe, Ursula Schaefer and Brian Stock, among others. In 1979 Clanchy undertook to present "the growth of a literate mentality" that, he argued, happened in England between the Norman Conquest in 1066 and the demise of Edward I in 1307.[2] In doing so, he took the important step of distinguishing between the production of written documents, including the ability of certain people to make them and read them, and reliance on those documents over and against "oral recollections of old wise men."[3] Literacy, as he described it, was a social and cultural as much as an individual phenomenon and one which developed very gradually. Brian Stock similarly described literacy as a social phenomenon that developed in England and Europe in a complex pattern over centuries. In his analysis, earlier in the Middle Ages orality and literacy co-existed, "sometimes working together, sometimes working in separate spheres of thought and action." But gradually, beginning in the second half of the twelfth century, "a new hermeneutic environment emerged in Western Europe" that included oral performances but was characterized by references to written texts.[4] Literacy, in this way of thinking, is defined not by the presence or absence of texts made up of letters on pages but by the uses made of texts.

A number of scholars have been attempting to locate Old English poetic texts on the spectrum between the oral and the written texts of full literacy. Placing them at one end, A. N. Doane characterizes most Old English poetry as "writing at the interface" with orality: "That it is writing at all is accidental, extrinsic to its main existence in ongoing oral traditions; hence it was never intended to feed into a lineage of writing."[5] Furthermore, he contends, contemporary audiences would have received the texts as oral: "The fiction operative for the semiliterate audience of secondary orality, the audiences within the oral/written interface, is that the text, now in writing, whether derived from a real oral performative situation or a feigned one, is oral and stems from telling and action, not from writing or imagination."[6] Arguing for the other end are Martin Irvine and Seth Lerer. Irvine acknowledges that "Old English poems belong to two cultural archives simultaneously, orally based poetic tradition and Latin textual culture,"[7] but he emphasizes the textual culture, claiming that the textuality of the poetry "inscribes an orally based social past, but both constructs the written image of orality and cancels its pretextual valence in the act of inscribing it."[8] Lerer goes one step further, venturing that "What we have come to think of as the inherently 'oral' quality of early English poetry—its origins in formulaic composition or its transmission in the public contexts of instruction or entertainment—may . . . be a literary fiction of its own."[9] I locate it in the middle because, on the one hand, the readers decipher letters on pages, and, on the other hand, they need to listen to the rhythms, syntax and meaning of the words to perceive the verse's structure. All in all, they construe meaning through a dynamic that is more clearly seen through orality than through writing. The texts themselves, I would argue, indicate how they operate, through the predominance of aural over visual cues, the absence of the author, the presence of implied tradition and the use of language common to many texts. They do not function in the same ways as printed texts, and they share enough with oral practices to make hypothesizing oral ancestors and oral cousins worthwhile. I therefore put orality in my circle of reasoning as an influence on the poetry's textuality.

The attempt to analyze functional aspects of texts that are neither fully oral nor fully written raises certain questions, fundamental to defining their textuality, that some scholars have been attempting to address. In "Hearing from Books," Ursula Schaefer grapples with the question of how someone accustomed to oral performances could decipher a text without the presence of the poet and his or her gestures and intonations. She believes that although the verse necessarily presented words cut off from the poet's voice by writing, it maintained from orality the significance of the voice; as a result, the poet had to supply a "vicarious voice" by fictionalizing a speaker.[10] This invention of a fictional first person supplied the first step toward fully written discourse in which texts are more "autoreferential," supplying what the readers needed to decipher their meanings, than they are extrareferential, as they were in oral discourse, requiring familiarity with relevant traditions.[11] In *Visible Song*, Katherine O'Brien O'Keeffe examines the physical appearance of Old English verse in its manuscripts, both its visual display and differences between versions of the same text. She addresses the questions of whether these texts required from readers different kinds of knowledge or the employment of different codes and conventions from those used to decipher fully written texts, and of what role the scribe played in relation to the poet or author. O'Keeffe argues "that early readers of Old English verse read by applying oral techniques for the reception of a message to the decoding of a written text"[12] and that scribes drew on their familiarity with oral-formulaic methods of composition, recomposing the verse as they copied it. The "collaborative" nature of the verse, as O'Keeffe points out in her conclusion, throws into question the issue of "authorial intention"[13] and thereby our accustomed goals of interpretation.

The fundamental nature of these questions incites controversy and concern similar to the critical turmoil stirred up in the earlier debate about whether Old English verse was oral. Francis P. Magoun, Jr., began the debate in 1953 with his article on "The Oral-Formulaic Character of Anglo-Saxon Narrative Poetry," in which he asserted that "the recurrence in a given poem of an appreciable number of formulas or formulaic phrases brands the latter as oral, just as a lack of such repetitions marks a poem as composed in a lettered tradition."[14] The "formulaic character" of the poetry could hardly be denied, but scholars did debate whether formulaic language was necessarily linked to orality. Larry D. Benson demonstrated that texts connected with a "lettered tradition,"[15] such as *The Phoenix* and *The Meters of Boethius*, could have a high density of formulas and urged that "we should assume written composition" for texts connected with "written sources" and "poems, such as *Beowulf*, with qualities contrary to what oral composition might lead us to expect . . . the sophistication of its diction and structure."[16] Among the issues at stake were aesthetics and originality. An oral performance might be polished by the succession of previous performances of that poem or one of similar themes,[17] but could it express the original thought and artistic sensibility which literary critics were accustomed to seek in analyzing texts, or did the strength of tradition in formulaic language dilute the individuality of composition and poet? As Stanley B. Greenfield demonstrated as early as 1955, the traditionality of formulaic language provided its own richness of reference. He explained: "the associations with other contexts using a similar formula will inevitably color a particular instance of a formula so that a whole host of overtones springs into action to support the aesthetic response."[18] Interested as Greenfield was in analyzing the conventions distinctive to Old English poetry, such as formulaic language and variation, he only reluctantly allowed the possibility—but not the proof—of the poetry's orality, and he disputed the need, in discussing *Beowulf* (and similarly well-wrought texts), "for abandoning standard critical techniques in analyses of its poetic meanings and values."[19] Greenfield still desired, however, to preserve the virtues of individuality and originality, and he argued that some poets used formulas more artistically than others, venturing the theory that "originality in the handling of conventional formulas may be defined as the degree of tension achieved between the inherited body of meanings in which a particular formula participates and the specific meaning of that formula in its individual context."[20] In identifying tension as the key to originality, his definition valued difference from the tradition. In contrast, a scholar of orality, such as John Miles Foley, recognizes that each singer and each performance differs from all others but is more comfortable stressing the "many-layered" quality of a traditional production,[21] in which, as in a filo pastry, one poet's "layer" can hardly be separated from those that underlie and support it.

The same values influence the debate about inscribed verse. Concerns about individuality and originality inform Douglas Moffat's critique of

O'Keeffe's book. He is willing to accept as "not . . . false" her theory that Old English manuscript verse is a collaborative production in which the scribes participate, drawing on their familiarity with the techniques of formulaic composition, but objects that "it is not so widely applicable as one might be led to believe while reading O'Keeffe's work."[22] The vocabulary of his subsequent discussion, however, shows that he is concerned most of all that scribes did not preserve the purposes and excellences of the authors whose texts they were supposed to be copying. The difficulties, as he sees them, are that some scribes were "not especially sensitive and competent"[23] and that some changes which they made may have come "from misapprehensions"[24] or may produce a meaning "at odds with" that in the exemplar,[25] among other problems that a less competent scribe might introduce. Furthermore, Moffat contends, "the scribes whose productions we happen to possess could well have had other 'agendas' that, in fact, ran counter to our desires" to preserve aesthetically pleasing verse,[26] and a scribe (his example is the scribe who copied the Vercelli version of *Soul and Body*) "may . . . have been unconcerned to transmit exactly what the poet created, or his exemplar read."[27] In sum, Moffat is very concerned about "the possibility . . . that [Old English poetic texts] are composite products of two, or very likely more, minds which were not necessarily working toward the same end" and that because most verse exists in only one copy we may not be able "to detect skillful or even competent interpolation"[28] and as a result may not be able to perform "conventional literary analysis" on these texts.[29] I have quoted Moffat at length because his concerns illuminate how crucial is the idea of the author in our evaluation of Old English poetic manuscripts and what they represent. He is apparently able to accept the possibility of the scribes as "quasi-poets"[30] only if the scribe's purposes and skills match the poet's or author's—if he or she does not, in effect, take on the work of a poet by remaking the text in any significant way. In other words, one person functions as author and creates a determinate text, which we call a "poem," and others who alter that text trample on that territory, which the critic must restore before he or she can analyze it properly.

Michael Lapidge similarly supports O'Keeffe's argument that scribes "were familiar enough with the system of oral formulas from which the verse was composed to enable them to improvise while copying" and that "Old English poems were not regarded as 'fixed.'"[31] In fact, in his discussion of Insular Latin texts, he points out that there were "certain classes of medieval text" that a scribe "altered" as a matter of course to suit "his (or his institution's) requirements"[32] so that, as with the Old English poetic texts, "the text is not fixed and . . . each scribe is in effect the author of the redaction or 'scribal version' he is copying."[33] But Lapidge preserves the idea of the author for Old English verse. He defines textual criticism as "the process of ascertaining and reproducing what an author wrote"[34] and accordingly criticizes the modern reluctance to emend Old English verse, asserting that "in their concern with manuscripts and scribes, modern editors of Old English poetry may risk doing a disservice to their authors."[35]

I would argue, in agreement with O'Keeffe, that the nature of the Old English poetic texts requires an idea of the poet different from the idea of the author that modern critics have been accustomed to employ. By examining structural and stylistic aspects of the poetry, as well as basic elements in its presentation in the manuscripts, it can be demonstrated that this inscribed verse lays itself open to recomposition by subsequent poets and that, in certain respects, scribes and readers could function as poets themselves. In addition, by considering from a theoretical perspective the idea of the author and how readers perceive the author in a text, it can also be demonstrated that while Old English verse was composed, it was not authored, and that while the manuscripts present some very fine poetry, the texts are better described as verse sequences constructed in discrete movements than as poems. These elements in the textuality of the verse are related to their being inscribed rather than being oral or written.

VOCALITY AND INSCRIPTION

Old English verse was inscribed to be read aloud. Certainly all poetry and a great deal of prose benefit from being read out loud, and it has become a commonplace in discussions of medieval textuality that people were taught to read all texts out loud rather than silently as we are today.[36] Even so, in comparison to printed texts, Old English verse was considerably more dependent on the ear than on the eye. In printed poetry, especially free verse, we rely on the eye more than on the sounds of the words to scan rhythms and structures: indeed, the voice follows the eye, which watches for capitals, line divisions and punctuation. In the manuscripts of Old English verse, however, words fill the page from left to right margin, and the reader must hear the alliterative and stress patterns to sense the verse units and the syntactic rhythms to sense the clauses and periods.[37] This method of layout requires that the reader be familiar with aural patterns and be prepared to interpret the structures of the texts.

Malcolm Parkes's discussion of changes in the uses of punctuation from antiquity to the Middle Ages maps out an inverse relationship between a readership's familiarity with the rhythms and literary structures of texts and the amount of punctuation provided in a text, such that more elaborate punctuation in early manuscripts indicates, practically speaking, that the intended readers were for some reason unable to hear the significant rhythms. He points out that the *scriptio continua* of antiquity required readers whose "literary training and . . . habitual aural response to the written word" would direct their analyses of the text, and who knew "the metrical patterns of verse, and the rhythms of the *clausulae* in prose."[38] By the fourth century, punctuation had become more common as the reading public needed more direction, with the rise of new wealthy and powerful classes who wanted to become literate in classical texts but did not have the same literary training as the previous elite, and with the concern of certain Christian writers that their more plebeian devotees should understand sacred and dogmatic texts properly.[39] However, when monastic practice advocated that readers meditate on the meaning of texts, the insertion of punctuation in manuscripts became much less prevalent.[40] Although the practice for inscribing verse in antiquity was to give each verse its own line, when in the Middle Ages readers were familiar with verse rhythms of hymns from recurring melodies, scribes customarily wrote each stanza in the form of a prose paragraph, rather than separating the verses on individual lines.[41] Consequently, some pre-Carolingian Latin poetry was inscribed filling the page in the manner of prose.

Evidently, that familiarity with the rhythms and melodies of Latin hymnody did not last past the eighth century in England, and by the time that the Old English poetic manuscripts were produced there was a greater demand for punctuation in Latin than in Old English inscriptions of verse. As O'Keeffe points out, after the eighth century in England Latin verse was presented complete with "a set of conventional visual cues" which "regularly distinguished verse from prose," placed individual verses on separate lines, and generally used space, capitalization and punctuation to assist the reader in decoding the text.[42] Old English verse in tenth-century manuscripts, on the other hand, has for the most part only light punctuation, which, as Parkes says, "indicates only the largest semantic units."[43] This form of text required readers to be quite familiar with the rhythms of verse form and syntax. The Junius manuscript, with its fuller pointing of verses, is the exception. Parkes believes that the pointing "was inserted after the text was copied, partly by the scribe and partly by a later corrector" and that "these additions suggest that the texts were being prepared for reading aloud" since the pointing "seems to divide each text into declamatory units."[44] But the effect on the finished manuscript is, as O'Keeffe argues, to make the text appear more like "important Latin poetic texts," complementing its elaborate program of illustrations, and she calls the manner of punctuation "bookish metrical pointing."[45] Even with these features, the text provides few directives. Occasionally a small capital helps the reader to note a semantic unit. A large capital and fitt number marks the beginning of a major section of verse and heavy punctuation and space mark the end. But there are no titles or incipits such as a more bookish text would supply.

At the structural level, as at the level of verse and sentence, the readers had to employ their knowledge of aural and semantic cues, interpreting the material on the page. Although at the structural level, space, points and capitals occasionally instruct the reader where to pause and where to consider that something is ending or beginning, for the most part sounds and meanings of words define larger units of sense. These units, which for the most part range in length from ten to twenty-five pairs of verses, I call "movements."

To articulate these "movements," inscribed verse draws on some of the same techniques for defining structure that oral compositions do. We can find in Old English texts some of the key features of oral poetry that Albert B. Lord described in his seminal work, *The Singer of Tales*.[46] Oral poets build their performances out of structural units called "themes," which present a narrative scene or exposition of wisdom according to a conventional set of elements and structure. These units have, according to Lord, "a semi-independent life of their own."[47] Although poets adapt them to their present work, they draw them from a repertoire of scenes that exist in their memories and in the repertoires of other poets, and the poets maintain the distinctiveness of the units through acoustics. According to Lord, oral poets use assonance, alliteration, syntax and rhythm to create patterns that unify a movement either by developing a series of parallel and balanced lines or by developing a pattern different from those of the previous and following units.[48] They also create patterns that mark the beginning and end of the unit. For example, a singer may end a descriptive unit with a "last line, beginning with a shout and sung in a different and cadential rhythm."[49] The separate shapes and identities of movements facilitate composition, assist the memory and connect the performance to community traditions.[50]

The sorts of patterns that Lord describes as marking off the oral theme delineate inscribed verse as well, the texts communicating, as do their oral cousins, via the ear rather than the eye.[51] An aural pattern, or a set of semantic cues, or both help to define a unit of thought by marking it as a formally distinct, semi-independent unit, contrasting in style or content with the text that precedes and follows it. In some cases, highly figured patterns involving parallel word order and repeated sounds delineate movements;[52] in some cases, one syntactic structure dominates a section defining it as a movement; and in some cases, aural and semantic effects mark the borders of a movement. In a considerable number of instances, multiple cues define movements. Readers of inscribed verse hear these cues as they voice the words.

POET, AUTHOR AND TRADITION

In many respects, inscribed texts function without authors: the poet, oral or stylus-in-hand, has left the scene, a scribe has intervened, and the language of the texts conveys the imprint of tradition rather than of an author. A significant, if ironic, aspect of these "traditional" rather than "authored" texts is their openness to new constructions of texts by subsequent poets, performers or scribes, and to varied constructions of meaning by readers. This openness derives in part from the way in which the texts couple features of the oral and the written.

If we are right to imagine that inscribed verse bears the marks of its oral relatives, then its most distinctive feature may be the poet's absence from the received text. Of course, there were poets who made crucial contributions to Old English inscribed verse, but their presence is not implied in the texts. Their absence characterizes this verse almost as much as the poet's physical presence characterizes oral productions.

In oral compositions, poets inflect traditional material with their own voices and gestures. Not only can they make their performances longer or shorter in response to an audience's interests, elaborating on favored topics and omitting what seems unwanted, but the intonations and rhythms of their delivery clarify any syntactic ambiguities. Also, the poet's very presence suggests that there are relationships among the movements of a composition, which might otherwise perhaps seem so discrete as to belong to different performances. A fully written text compensates for the absence of the poet in a number of ways. Punctuation and layout eliminate many ambiguities in sentence and verse structure. Diverse styles or topics are assigned to different speakers or different narrative situations. In addition, a written narrative provides a fictional narrator to stand in for the poet.

The need for some kind of poet-figure seems to have been felt very early, on the way from oral to written composition. As Franz H. Bäuml suggests, because of the author's absence from the written text, "the public . . . must 'constitute' a narrator on the basis of the text"; a fictional narrator is the "inevitable" result.[53] By the twelfth century we see "the narrator explicitly posing as author," showing that writers by this time were aware of "the inevitable fictionality of the narrator."[54] Schaefer sees an incipient form of this gesture in Old English poetry in what she calls a "conditional fictionality" and argues that it arises directly from a desire to "abide by the semiotic rules of vocal communication." As a result, some texts "staged" the performing poet with "a first-person singular *I*, or even more fictitiously merging in the communal *we*"—not that an oral poet might not use these pronouns but that in those instances the "I" or the "we" is not fictional.[55] We see this staged "I" in *The Dream of the Rood*, *The Wanderer*, *The Seafarer*, Cynewulf's epilogue to *Elene* and other poetry as well.[56] The "staged I," however, has not yet fully become a fictional narrator: the language remains formulaic rather than shaped to imply a particular subjectivity, and the "I" seldom dominates more than a movement or two of a verse sequence.

In addition, no name of a poet claims that the text expresses that person's sensibility. In oral performances, the poet is present, body, voice and name. In printed texts, the name typically appears at the beginning of the text, marking its separateness and distinctiveness from the rest of the world, including the readers' own sensibilities. But in Old English inscribed poetry, no name appears either at the commencement or at the end of a text to mark that separation and identify certain verses with a certain consciousness. Cynewulf's so-called signatures are not an exception. Although four texts incorporate runes that can be decoded to identify "Cynewulf" as the person who made the verses, only one, *The Fates of the Apostles*, points to the runes as indicating "hwa þas fitte fegde" ("who this fitt joined," line 98a). More important here, the runes do not visually mark the beginning or end of a verse sequence, the place where a signature would appear in a more modern text, but are embedded in the text from half-a-page to a page-and-a-half before the texts' ending cues (*FINIT* signals the end of *The Fates of the Apostles* sequence; *AMEN* the ends of *Juliana* and *Elene*; heavy punctuation the ends of *The Ascension* and *Juliana*).[57] Without a poet's body or name, the text stands open for the taking by others—poet, reader or scribe.

In fact, the texts do not present a poet's own text, but one mediated by manuscript compiler and scribe. We can see the effects of that mediation in the few cases in which related versions of poetic texts have survived.[58]

Although substantial sections present the same narration of story or idea and most of the time the same words, the versions differ in the contexts provided for the common movements, and from time to time in the formulas used to fill out a verse or express an idea. For example, the text in Junius that we call *Daniel* incorporates in a much longer narrative a version of the one we call *Azarias*, in the Exeter Book; the Vercelli *Soul and Body* couples to a version of the Exeter text movements on heavenly bliss, presenting a text one-third longer; and the Ruthwell Cross bears on one of its sides a version of the crucifixion narrative that also appears as one-third of *The Dream of the Rood* in the Vercelli Book. In the sections that the versions share, according to O'Keeffe's studies of *Cædmon's Hymn* and *Solomon and Saturn I*, it was normal for particular formulas to vary from one inscription to another. O'Keeffe theorizes that the scribes introduced their own "'formulaic' guesses into the written text."[59] Roy Michael Liuzza, in summarizing the differences between the two versions of *Riddle 30*, points out that some changes that a scribe might introduce alter the sense of the text: "substituting familiar words for unfamiliar ones, inserting conjunctions or particles to clarify the assumed sense, or rearranging syntax and grammar, not always at the expense of the meter."[60] Because cumulatively these changes "could alter the rhetorical structure, and hence the style of a passage," he contends that the scribe functions "as an 'editor'" and is "in a very real sense . . . the shaper, not merely the transmitter, of Old English poetry."[61] But because of the formulaic nature of the language and the absence of the poet, I find it difficult to make such a clear-cut distinction between poet and editor.

The degree to which the scribe reshapes the text in re-presenting it can be understood through the model of the oral poet. So some scholars contend that these texts vary in much the same way as oral compositions do, the scribe "performing" the verses he or she has inherited, altering the text where occasion or desire dictates. O'Keeffe views the scribe's formulaic substitutions as "an accommodation of literacy, with its resistant text, to the fluidity of the oral process of transmission."[62] Doane characterizes *Daniel* and *Azarias* as products of "different performative situations."[63] Tim William Machan argues that even in the later Middle Ages "a variety of the conscious alterations effected by scribes as they 'copied' texts are similar to the changes made by oral poets as they re-create songs—that a model of improvisation can describe the performance qualities of both oral poets and scribes."[64] Like oral performances, these manuscript texts are a single instance in a multitude of possible versions, each of which will diverge from the others and be legitimate within its context.[65]

530

Whether or not one accepts the model of the oral poet, scribal practices make it difficult to say who authored a particular text and which version is the authored work. As Paul Zumthor says about thirteenth-century texts, the poetry "escape[s] from the orbit of the original poet."[66] As it is transmitted, those involved in that process freely make changes. Zumthor points out that the "very conditions of transmission, producing minor variants in words and odd phrases of the written text; more important variants, by which considerable stretches of text may be added, suppressed, modified, or transposed; and major variants in the number and order of structural elements of the text, could not but conspire to prevent the early formation of the idea of the work as something complete in itself,"[67] something that an author has created and which therefore should not be changed. Instead of considering that one author created a determinate text that others have emended, Zumthor suggests that "each version of a text . . . be treated . . . as deriving from the reuse of materials; that is, as a new creation" and speaks of the related texts as being "by successive 'authors' (singers, reciters, scribes)."[68] The case is somewhat more difficult to make for Old English poetry since so much verse survives in only one copy, but the poetry's traditional language and composition in movements also indicate that poetic texts were always subject to remaking and to re-use, one "poet" freely borrowing from another.

This blurring of categories interrelates with the fact that the textuality of Old English poetry does not employ an idea of the author but rather an idea of tradition. The virtual absence of poets' names signifies the author's insignificance. The author's name is not simply a bit of knowledge that is readily lost and potentially discoverable. It performs a function within a culture of classifying texts and designating certain texts as products of one person's mind rather than any other's and thereby as owned by that person.[69] But one cannot own texts in a discourse with such a high degree of formulaic language, or in which the remaking of verse sequences is so freely executed. Old English verse does not convey the sense that a poet produces his or her own discursive constructs and that these have a very particular mode of being. As Irvine says, "the Old English poem is produced from within, and merges into, the dominant cultural discourses"[70] and the boundaries blur, making it ambiguous which expression belongs to which specific text and therefore to which poet's voice. According to Michel Foucault's explanation, the author "is a certain functional principle by which, in our culture, one limits, excludes, and chooses; in short, by which one impedes the free circulation, the free manipulation, the free composition, decomposition, and recomposition of fiction,"[71] operations which characterize the construction of Old English poetry.

In addition, the author is something that, in the absence of the poet's voice and body, readers must construct from the text (or a group of texts that are signed with the same name or characterized by the same style). As those addressed by the text, readers derive their idea of the author from the text's subjectivity as it is constituted by its narrative and characters.[72] But the language of Old English verse does not suit that kind of analysis. No subjectivity makes its mark throughout a text defining it as its own. As mentioned above, a few texts propose a first-person speaker and a couple of them even sustain the "I"—*The Wife's Lament, The Dream of the Rood*—but they follow convention in that they do not develop and sustain a subjectivity through their language. First of all, the language is formulaic and therefore by its nature open to any voice; but, more important, the convention of structuring verse sequences in discrete movements inhibits any such development. In fact, stylistic contrasts between movements are so prominent at times that the critical histories of many texts have been riddled with questions about their unity and authorship. When a text has a strong narrative line, such as we find in those that are versions of Latin narratives, critics have been relatively comfortable with its unity. But for texts that do not take their structure from Latin narratives, shifts in style have seemed more problematic. Consequently, such scholars as Bruce Dickins and Alan S. C. Ross and Rosemary Woolf have doubted that the second half of the *Dream* is by the same poet;[73] others have questioned the unity of *The Seafarer, The Wanderer* and many other texts. These doubts arise from sensitive readings of style which register the absence of a single subjectivity that would relate these movements in the manner that we are accustomed to call "authorship."

Instead of implying an author, Old English verse implies tradition. Formulaic echoes and patterns that are frequently used to express an idea function as a code that readers can interpret as "tradition." In doing so, they recognize the present text's place in a network of expressions and thought: the movement-structure frees the reader from thinking of the text as an entity that is indissolubly whole, and the language points the reader away from the present text toward similar expressions of the same idea that may be spoken or inscribed in any number of other texts.[74] Tradition is coded through intertextual relationships that are characterized by the formulaic nature of the poetry's language.[75] In modern literature, readers are apt to be alerted to intertextual resonances by what Michael Riffaterre calls "intratextual anomalies" and "ungrammaticalities,"[76] constructions that are undecipherable until one recognizes the repressed meaning expressed in an external intertext, which may be a specific work or a specific way of meaning, such as slang or some other sociolect.[77] In traditional texts, in contrast, the formulaic sound of the language, the very expectedness of an idea's expression, elicits intertextual resonances. Those who do not hear the echoes may make perfectly acceptable sense out of the traditional expression, though the meaning will be flat instead of multidimensional. Very often, however, even with the limited amount of verse now extant, the formulaic echoes resound and imply thereby that the verses are generated from and sanctioned by tradition. Yet, because by its nature formulaic language appears in many places instead of being specific to one context, people hearing the echoes may bring to their experiences diverse intertexts. It follows that, though the language announces the conservativeness of the text, it does not require the reader to conform to a certain interpretation.

The openness of the text to diverse readings also derives from the very nature of the intertextuality that implies tradition. The intertextuality of traditional texts shares with that of modern texts an interplay of meaning that the echoes themselves facilitate. As Julia Kristeva writes with regard to the intertextuality of novels, an intertextual term has "two significations," from the present text and the intertext, and so is "ambivalent" in meaning, the doubleness deriving from the "joining of two sign-systems."[78] Traditional intertextuality generates a similar play of meaning in which a word or phrase derives multivalent significations from the indefinite number of sign systems in which it might participate. Hence, even while the intertexts label the text as part of the community's traditions in that it expresses similar thoughts in similar language, and thereby sanction it as "true," the doubleness of the language, together with its multiplicity of possible associations, opens the text to varieties of interpretation.[79] The multiplicity comes from the continuance of formulaic language from oral composition into inscribed verse.

THE READER

These texts necessitate an active reader who will take on the text and produce it in a manner analogous to an oral poet, who performs a text learned from a previous performer. As mentioned above, readers physically face a text divided simply into parts by initiating capital letters, closing punctuation and blank space. Especially since every poetic manuscript manages punctuation differently,[80] readers must constantly evaluate what they see, engaging in a kind of dialogue with the format of a manuscript, questioning it as to the meaning of capitals, punctuation and space, looking for answers in the inscribed words, and constructing the poems themselves through this engagement with the physical and semantic dimensions of the text. At times the meanings of the words combine with the graphics to make evident that a certain point begins or ends a narrative or sequence of thought, but in many cases the text opens itself to more than one interpretation. If these readers heard an oral performance of such a text, the performer's voice would convey the sentences without structural ambiguities and the performance itself would have a certain beginning and end. But in the absence of an oral poet or performer, the readers must decide the ambiguities and modulate their own voices accordingly. Physical features of the inscribed text make it possible for readers to take possession of the text to a degree not possible for readers of modern printed books.[81] The printed text divides itself from the reader and the world with the initial designation of author's name and text's title, the title designating what follows as a particular, nameable entity and the author's name identifying it with patterns of thought and expression customarily connected with that name. Lacking such a designation and identification, the inscribed text can become the reader's. The absence of an implied author further facilitates the reader's appropriation. In addition, the inscriptions have taken the place of the oral poet's voice and gestures, eliminating that physical subjectivity and leaving a yawning gap for readers to color the words with their own gestures and inflections, introducing their own subjectivity.[82] The reader's voice, then, assumes the role of the poet's.

The structure of the poetry encourages still more the reader's appropriation of the text. As mentioned above, the verse presents itself to the reader as a sequence of discrete movements, often juxtaposed without any narrative connection. The inscribed text does provide the reader with some directions for reading these movements. It presents them in a particular sequence: although one movement does not develop into the next, they have a kind of interdependence in which a movement takes on meaning from those that precede and follow it. That contextualization transpires simply from the fact of the sequence. In addition, the text incorporates verbal echoes that readers might use to spin out lines of association among movements. Often the first movement of a sequence will include terms that do not make sense on the literal level, peculiarities or oddities in expression— what Riffaterre would call "ungrammaticalities." They make sense, however, in light of comparable expressions in other movements, which function as "intratextual intertext[s]":[83] the oddity of their usage calls attention to them as terms, and they become resonant throughout the sequence, highlighting contradictory and complementary relationships between the narrative events or assertions that the movements propose. This kind of intertextual relationship is possible, as Riffaterre says, for "any unit of significance that can be identified as the narrative unfolds, any segment of that narrative that can be isolated without cognitive loss, . . . if the latter has features in common with the former"[84]—and Old English verse, I am arguing, is composed of such units. The units, then, function as "homologues" of each other, one modifying the reader's thinking on the others.[85] This reading counteracts the temporal or causal progression of a sequence, "offering a nonsequential and nonnarrative reading of the chain of events, or of selected links in that chain."[86] But though the echoes suggest that readers associate certain narrative events or assertions, the associations themselves remain ambiguous within the text.

The text then opens itself to a certain amount of play, giving the reader the choice of leaving the ambiguities open, at play, or resolving them through interpretation. What the text does not do is dictate to its readers a single meaning, orthodox or otherwise. As Gillian R. Overing writes, drawing on Derrida, Barthes and Lacan, "The contiguous dyadic alignment of metonymic phrases or ideas resists the interpretive closure of metaphor."[87] In metaphor, as she continues, "meaning is construed, governed, by a third element, a collocating reader or the poet's contextual directive."[88] While Overing contends that Old English poetry is insistently metonymic, refusing interpretative closure, I think that we can only know that the poet does not provide in the text a directive for closure. The reader, nevertheless, is left the possibility of collocating the metonymically related movements, if he or she so desires, into the metaphoric resolution that his or her textual and other experiences suggest is true. In fact, a structure that does not dictate a single interpretation encourages the reader's own interpretation.[89] Overing herself cites Lacan's theory that interpretation and desire are driven by a "metonymic remainder . . . an element necessarily lacking, unsatisfied, impossible, misconstrued (*méconnu*)."[90] In the verse's structure, the movements are juxtaposed without a syntactic connection which would designate their relationship and provide a full supply of information necessary to produce whatever meaning the poet wished to designate. The missing element of syntactic connection drives the reader to interpret, to supply the lack, to close the openness of the text. The absence of syntactic connection implies some sort of equivalence or metaphorical relation.[91] But the drive toward metaphoric resolution, in which each of the movements and the entire sequence are understood as a substitute for the referent, does not eliminate the play, nor does it direct readers toward a definitive meaning, since each reading will attempt the resolution in a different way, perhaps including readings which refuse any resolution (although such readings would contradict Lacan's analysis of desire and interpretation).

Approaching the problem of Old English poetic structure through Roland Barthes's theoretical paradigm, we might say that the reader is "a producer of the text" rather than merely a passive "consumer."[92] According to Barthes, certain texts are "writerly" in character (a term ironically at odds with the vocality of Old English verse). "The writerly text," as Barthes defines it,

> is a perpetual present . . . the writerly text is *ourselves writing*, before the infinite play of the world . . . is traversed, intersected, stopped, plasticized by some singular system (Ideology, Genus, Criticism) which reduces the plurality of entrances, the opening of networks, the infinity of languages. The writerly is the novelistic without the novel, poetry without the poem, the essay without the dissertation, writing without style, production without product, structuration without structure.[93]

Old English verse inscriptions similarly present "poetry without the poem . . . structuration without structure." The verse's openness, or "plurality of entrances," counteracts the conservative force of its traditionality. The formal beginnings and endings of movements limit their assertions, the absence of connectors prevents those assertions from building one into another, and the differences in style among the movements imply various understandings rather than a definitive statement. Thus, these structural characteristics of the verse require that each reader produce his or her own poem from the poetry that the manuscript presents.

NOTES

[1] On the relationship between printer, author and text in the eighteenth century and the idea of the author, see Mark Rose, "The Author as Proprietor: *Donaldson v. Becket* and the Genealogy of Modern Authorship," *Representations* 23 (Summer 1988): 51–85.

[2]   M. T. Clanchy, *From Memory to Written Record: England, 1066–1307*, rev. ed. (Oxford, 1993), p. 2.

[3]   Clanchy, *From Memory to Written Record*, p. 3.

[4]   Brian Stock, *The Implications of Literacy: Written Language and Models of Interpretation in the Eleventh and Twelfth Centuries* (Princeton, 1983), p. 10.

[5]   A. N. Doane, "Oral Texts, Intertexts, and Intratexts: Editing Old English," in *Influence and Intertextuality*, ed. Eric Rothstein and Jay Clayton (Madison, 1991), p. 86.

[6]   Doane, "Oral Texts," p. 82.

[7]   Martin Irvine, "Medieval Textuality and the Archaeology of Textual Culture," in *Speaking Two Languages: Traditional Disciplines and Contemporary Theory in Medieval Studies*, ed. Allen J. Frantzen (Albany, 1991), p. 185. See also Irvine's *The Making of Textual Culture: "Grammatica" and Literary Theory, 350–1100* (Cambridge, Eng., 1994), in which he presents his argument in greater detail and a fuller context.

[8]   Irvine, "Medieval Textuality," p. 196.

[9]   Seth Lerer, *Literacy and Power in Anglo-Saxon Literature* (Lincoln, Nebr., 1991), p. 4. See also Kevin Kiernan, "Reading Cædmon's 'Hymn' with Someone Else's Glosses," *Representations* 32 (Autumn 1990): 157–74, who argues that Cædmon's "Hymn," as it is transmitted in the (Alfredian) Old English translation of Bede's *Historia ecclesiastica* and in subsequent modern editions, is itself a kind of fiction, a translation from Bede's Latin prose into Old English poetic form that began as a marginal gloss of the Latin rather than as an oral remnant written into the margins of Latin manuscripts.

[10] Ursula Schaefer, "Hearing from Books: The Rise of Fictionality in Old English Poetry," in *Vox Intexta: Orality and Textuality in the Middle Ages*, ed. A. N. Doane and Carol Braun Pasternack (Madison, 1991), p. 124.

[11] Schaefer, "Hearing from Books," p. 120.

[12] Katherine O'Brien O'Keeffe, *Visible Song: Transitional Literacy in Old English Verse* (Cambridge, Eng., 1990), p. 21.

[13] O'Keeffe, *Visible Song*, p. 193.

[14] Francis P. Magoun, Jr., "The Oral-Formulaic Character of Anglo-Saxon Narrative Poetry," *Speculum* 28 (1953): 446–47.

[15] Larry D. Benson, "The Literary Character of Anglo-Saxon Formulaic Poetry," *PMLA* 81 (1966): 334.

[16] Benson, "The Literary Character of Anglo-Saxon Formulaic Poetry," p. 340.

[17] See Benson, "The Literary Character of Anglo-Saxon Formulaic Poetry," who expresses the concern that the "poet who composes extemporaneously . . . cannot be held to the same aesthetic demands that we make of a poet who composes in the

literary way on parchment in his cell" (p. 337). This sense that poetry composed during performance is not as polished is answered by R. F. Lawrence, in an essay published in 1966, the same year as Benson's: "The Formulaic Theory and its Application to English Alliterative Poetry" (in *Essays on Style and Language*, ed. Roger Fowler [London, 1966], pp. 166–83). He points out that oral poetry "is progressively developed and refined by a succession of oral poets" and through this process "could achieve a perfection of form and a density of utterance perhaps even beyond the capacity of written literature" (p. 173).

[18] Stanley B. Greenfield, "The Formulaic Expression of the Theme of 'Exile' in Anglo-Saxon Poetry," *Speculum* 30 (1955): 205.

[19] Stanley B. Greenfield, *The Interpretation of Old English Poems* (London, 1972), p. 31.

[20] Greenfield, "The Formulaic Expression of the Theme of 'Exile,'" p. 205; see also Greenfield, *The Interpretation of Old English Poems*, pp. 30–59.

[21] John Miles Foley, "Tradition and the Collective Talent: Oral Epic, Textual Meaning, and Receptionalist Theory," *Cultural Anthropology* 1 (1986): 217.

[22] Douglas Moffat, "Anglo-Saxon Scribes and Old English Verse," *Speculum* 67 (1992): 810.

[23] Moffat, "Anglo-Saxon Scribes," p. 823.

[24] Moffat, "Anglo-Saxon Scribes," p. 815.

[25] Moffat, "Anglo-Saxon Scribes," p. 816.

[26] Moffat, "Anglo-Saxon Scribes," p. 824.

[27] Moffat, "Anglo-Saxon Scribes," p. 825.

[28] Moffat, "Anglo-Saxon Scribes," p. 826.

[29] Moffat, "Anglo-Saxon Scribes," p. 827.

[30] Moffat, "Anglo-Saxon Scribes," p. 814.

[31] Michael Lapidge, "Textual Criticism and the Literature of Anglo-Saxon England," *Bulletin of the John Rylands University Library of Manchester* 73 (1991): 41–42.

[32] Lapidge, "Textual Criticism," pp. 28–29.

[33] Lapidge, "Textual Criticism," p. 30.

[34] Lapidge, "Textual Criticism," p. 17.

[35] Lapidge, "Textual Criticism," p. 41.

[36] See Jean Leclercq, *The Love of Learning and the Desire for God*, 3rd ed., trans. Catharine Misrahi (New York, 1982), pp. 15 and 72–73, for a discussion of monastic methods of reading; see also, Malcolm B. Parkes, *Pause and Effect: An Introduction to the History of Punctuation in the West* (Berkeley, 1993), p. 9; and Irvine, *The Making of Textual Culture*, pp. 69–72.

[37] *Deor* is the apparent exception in that the text is presented in verse paragraphs which range in length from two lines on the page to nine, each beginning with

a large capital and ending with a cluster of punctuation and part of the line left blank. But here, too, aural patterns convey the verse units and syntax, and even the paragraphs that the scribe displays are also delineated by the easily heard refrain, "þæs ofereode, þisses swa mæg" ("that has passed on, so can this," lines 7, 13, 17, 20, 27, 42).

38 Parkes, *Pause and Effect*, p. 11.

39 Parkes, *Pause and Effect*, pp. 13–17.

40 Parkes, *Pause and Effect*, p. 18.

41 Parkes, *Pause and Effect*, pp. 97–98.

42 O'Keeffe, *Visible Song*, p. 3.

43 Parkes, *Pause and Effect*, p. 111.

44 Parkes, *Pause and Effect*, p. 111.

45 O'Keeffe, *Visible Song*, p. 186.

46 Although a great deal of valuable work has been done in the thirty years since Albert Bates Lord published *The Singer of Tales* (Cambridge, Mass., 1960), his discussion of theme and its relation to song is still widely accepted. Useful overviews of oral theory can be found in Walter J. Ong, *Orality and Literacy: The Technologizing of the Word* (London, 1982), and John Miles Foley, *Oral Formulaic Theory and Research: an Introduction and Annotated Bibliography* (New York, 1985).

47 Lord, *The Singer of Tales*, p. 94. In *The Singer of Tales*, Lord discusses movements that structure narrative scenes (an assembly, a battle, a marriage), which he calls "themes." Donald K. Fry, in "Old English Oral-Formulaic Themes and Type-Scenes," *Neophilologus* 52 (1968): 48–54, contributes the useful term "type-scene" to distinguish between the set structures of certain scenes and the broader concept to which we more commonly refer by the term "theme." I am using the musical term "movement" because I wish to refer more broadly to any structural unit that has a distinct formal and semantic structure, whether its content is narrative or expository. For discussion of such units in oral or orally based poetry, see Lord, *The Singer of Tales*; Fry, "Old English Oral-Formulaic Themes and Type-Scenes"; and Alain Renoir, *A Key to Old Poems: The Oral-Formulaic Approach to the Interpretation of West-Germanic Verse* (University Park, 1988).

48 Lord, *The Singer of Tales*, pp. 55–58.

49 Lord, *The Singer of Tales*, p. 55.

50 See Foley, "Tradition and the Collective Talent," for a discussion of ways that the recognition of a "theme" or "type-scene" enables a reader's or listener's interpretation of the "gaps" in "oral literature."

51 I say "cousin" in order to make explicit that oral poetry and manuscript poetry can co-exist and can interchange expressions, stories and wisdom. (Oral poetry

is not a parent who dies after the birth of writing.) See Alois Wolf's discussion of Germanic and Roman texts in "Medieval Heroic Traditions and Their Transitions from Orality to Literacy," in Doane and Pasternack, *Vox Intexta*, pp. 67–88.

52 See Adeline Courtney Bartlett's *Larger Rhetorical Patterns in Anglo-Saxon Poetry* (Morningside Heights, 1935), as well as handbooks of Latin rhetoric. I include in this group principally patterns that color a series of lines, such as anaphora and other figures involving parallelism. There has been considerable discussion as to whether the many figures present in Old English poetry derive from familiarity with Latin handbooks or the usage of Germanic oral poets. Essential articles in the argument include Joshua Bonner, "Toward a Unified Critical Approach to Old English Poetic Composition," *Modern Philology* 73 (1976): 219–28; Jackson J. Campbell, "Learned Rhetoric in Old English Poetry," *Modern Philology* 63 (1966): 189–201 (including specific discussion of *The Wanderer*) and "Knowledge of Rhetorical Figures in Anglo-Saxon England," *Journal of English and Germanic Philology* 66 (1967): 1–20; James E. Cross, *Latin Themes in Old English Poetry* (Bristol, 1962) and "Ubi Sunt Passages in Old English—Sources and Relationships," *Vetenskaps-Societetens i Lund Årsbok* (1956): 25–44. Since the rhetorical handbooks are codifications of oral techniques, it seems likely that Germanic and Latin methods overlapped considerably.

53 Franz H. Bäuml, "Varieties and Consequences of Medieval Literacy and Illiteracy," *Speculum* 55 (1980): 253.

54 Bäuml, "Varieties and Consequences," p. 252.

55 Schaefer, "Hearing from Books," p. 125.

56 At times scholars have tried to create an author out of these movements and have employed the concept to reject those parts of the texts which, because of their content and style, did not provide such an opportunity. On this rationale critics have dismissed the homiletic movements of *The Dream of the Rood*, *The Wanderer* and *The Seafarer*, among others. See Bruce Dickins and Alan S. C. Ross, eds., *The Dream of the Rood* (New York, 1966), pp. 17–19. Since we have become more influenced by modernist art and theory, our acceptance of multivoiced, authorless texts has grown, and those movements have been brought back into the fold.

57 *Elene*, in fact, displays a "FINIT" at the end of the narrative, which divides the narrative from the movement in which an "I" steps forward to identify himself as the one who *wordcræftum wæf* ("wove with word-skills," line 1237), after *wisdom onwreah* ("wisdom revealed," line 1242), the knowledge.

58 Four pairs of closely related compositions are still extant: the Junius *Daniel* and Exeter *Azarias*, the Ruthwell Cross poem and the Vercelli *Dream of the Rood*, the Vercelli and the Exeter versions of *Soul and Body*, and the two

versions of *Solomon and Saturn I* in Cambridge, Corpus Christi College 41 and Cambridge, Corpus Christi College 422. In addition, the four early manuscripts of *The Anglo-Saxon Chronicle* present versions of *The Battle of Brunanburh* and the five other *Chronicle* poems, *Cædmon's Hymn* appears in fourteen manuscripts (see O'Keeffe, *Visible Song*, p. 24) and the Exeter Book's *Riddle 30* appears twice in that manuscript.

59 O'Keeffe, *Visible Song*, p. 46.

60 R. M. Liuzza, "The Texts of the Old English Riddle 30," *Journal of English and Germanic Philology* 87 (1988): 14.

61 Liuzza, "The Texts of the Old English Riddle 30," p. 14.

62 O'Keeffe, *Visible Song*, p. 46.

63 Doane, "Oral Texts, Intertexts, and Intratexts" p. 86. See Jones, "*Daniel and Azarias*," for the argument that *Daniel* and *Azarias* are related oral productions.

64 Tim William Machan, "Editing, Orality, and Late Middle English Texts," in Doane and Pasternack, *Vox Intexta*, pp. 229–45, at 237. John Dagenais, "That Bothersome Residue: Toward a Theory of the Physical Text," in Doane and Pasternack, *Vox Intexta*, pp. 246–59, suggests a more general "analogy" between oral performances and manuscripts: "that most ephemeral of literary events, an oral performance, comes closest to imitating that solidly physical text we seek: in its uniqueness, in the impossibility of its iteration, in its vulnerability to accidents of time and environment" (p. 255).

65 Lord writes: "Any particular song is different in the mouth of each of its singers. If we consider it in the thought of a single singer during the years in which he sings it, we find that it is different at different stages in his career." There is no "ideal text" or "original" but "an ever-changing phenomenon" (*The Singer of Tales*, p. 100). In fact, "the words 'author' and 'original' have either no meaning at all in oral tradition or a meaning quite different from the one usually assigned to them" (*The Singer of Tales*, p. 101).

66 Paul Zumthor, *Toward a Medieval Poetics*, trans. Philip Bennett (Minneapolis, 1992), p. 47.

67 Zumthor, *Toward a Medieval Poetics*, p. 46.

68 Zumthor, *Toward a Medieval Poetics*, p. 47.

69 On the connection between the "author-function" and ownership of the text, see Michel Foucault, "What Is an Author?" in *Textual Strategies: Perspectives in Post-Structuralist Criticism*, ed. and trans. Josue V. Harari (Ithaca, N.Y., 1979), p. 148; this essay is reprinted in this volume. M. B. Parkes's work on "the development of the book" shows how much the idea of the author was a part of the reforms in thought and textual organization that evolved with

scholasticism. Scholastics began to compile "fat volumes embracing as many as possible of the writings of a single *auctor*" ("The Influence of the Concepts of *Ordinatio* and *Compilatio* on the Development of the Book," in *Medieval Learning and Literature: Essays Presented to Richard William Hunt*, ed. J. J. G. Alexander and M. T. Gibson [Oxford, 1976], p. 123). They also distinguished the roles of the scribe, the compiler, the commentator and the author (pp. 127–28).

[70] Martin Irvine, "Anglo-Saxon Literary Theory Exemplified in Old English Poems: Interpreting the Cross in *The Dream of the Rood* and *Elene*," *Style* 20 (1986): 159. Although I find this description apt, Irvine's project differs from mine. He is concerned with the relationship between Old English poems and "Latin literary culture" and attempts to demonstrate that *The Dream of the Rood* and *Elene* "are to be read as interpretive readings or rewritings of Latin texts and Latin forms of literary representation" (p. 157).

[71] Foucault, "What is an Author?" p. 159.

[72] See Julia Kristeva, "Word, Dialogue and Novel," in *The Kristeva Reader*, ed. Toril Moi (New York, 1986), p. 45.

[73] Dickins and Ross, *The Dream of the Rood*, pp. 18–19; Rosemary Woolf, "Doctrinal Influences on *The Dream of the Rood*," *Medium Ævum* 27 (1958), p. 153 n. 34.

[74] John Miles Foley describes the echo as a part of the tradition that refers to it "*pars pro toto*" so that "the traditional idiom resonates with 'extratextual' meaning, makes necessary (because institutionalized) reference to situations, characters, and deeper strata shared with other poems" ("Orality, Textuality, and Interpretation," in Doane and Paternack, *Vox Intexta*, p. 42). I am reluctant to assert that formulaic reference is "necessary" because I believe that different readers will be familiar with different texts and therefore make formulaic associations with somewhat different situations, etc., even if the situations are in some way versions of each other. For related discussions, see also Foley, "Tradition and the Collective Talent" and his discussion of formula in "Genre(s) in the Making: Diction, Audience and Text in the Old English *Seafarer*," *Poetics Today* 4 (Jerusalem) (1983): 683–706, and Renoir on type-scenes in *A Key to Old Poems*. In *A Key to Old Poems*, Renoir writes, "With oral-formulaic rhetoric . . . the statement calls to mind a paradigmatic situation whose conscious or unconscious evocation informs our interpretation of the immediate context: it is not any specific work but rather the general associations attached to the statement which affect our reaction to the work in which it occurs" (p. 89). Doane denies altogether the idea that formulas refer. He asserts: "the relation of productive speech

to this precedent material is of something generated, not something to be referred to. Rather than intertextual relations to a pre-text, we might rather conceive of an infratext, the invisible structuration that organizes any actual manifestation of speech, the pre-spoken, always drawn from deep structural recesses of the mind and always recursive, unified within the flow of the voice" ("Oral Texts, Intertexts, and Intratexts" p. 102).

[75] Kristeva coined the term "intertextuality," using it to refer to a general principle, "that every signifying practice is a field of transpositions of various signifying systems (an intertextuality)," such that a word, phrase, sentence, dialogue in a text is transposed from another sign system. Hence, no one ever writes anything original, and a text is necessarily a composition from previous texts and exists as an intertextual construction. It is not, however, the same as the other texts because transposition alters the significance of the material: it "demands a new articulation of the thetic—of enunciative and denotative positionality" ("Revolution in Poetic Language," in Moi, *The Kristeva Reader*, p. 111). In many texts, this construction is naturalized so that most of the time the reader does not consider the text as "a field of transpositions"; however, in some modernist and postmodern texts, intertextuality "appears as such," the structure of the writing communicating the play between texts. In any case, the intertext carries meaning from its present use and previous use, or "intertext." Rather than focusing on the general principle that Kristeva enunciated, some other important theorists have been particularly interested in specific instances of intertexts in which the reader must decipher the intertextual relationship in order to understand the meaning of the text. Michael Riffaterre, for example, has written extensively about the operation of these constructions.

[76] Michael Riffaterre, "Syllepsis," *Critical Inquiry* 6 (1980): 627.

[77] Michael Riffaterre, "The Intertextual Unconscious," *Critical Inquiry* 13 (1987): 374–75.

[78] Kristeva, "Word, Dialogue and Novel" pp. 43–44.

[79] For another discussion of intertextuality in Old English verse, see Irvine, "Anglo-Saxon Literary Theory Exemplified in Old English Poems," pp. 157–81.

[80] O'Keeffe, *Visible Song*, pp. 186–87.

[81] The textuality of Old English poetic manuscripts shared with that of early Latin manuscripts this contrast with print textuality. As Irvine writes about the "grammatical theory" underlying early Latin manuscripts, "nothing pre-existed the reader's production of the text; that is, a text, as an object of knowledge, did not exist in some positive state prior to being read and

constructed as a piece of articulate, significant discourse, as if its sense and meaning were already given in the script. To become *sermo*, discourse, the silent written signifiers required the human voice, and every reading was, in an important sense, a performance, a production of meaning, and a reactivation of memory deferred in writing" (*The Making of Textual Culture*, pp. 69–70).

[82] See Paul Zumthor, "The Text and the Voice," *New Literary History* 16 (1984): 67–92.

[83] Riffaterre, "The Intertextual Unconscious," p. 380.

[84] Riffaterre, "The Intertextual Unconscious," p. 380.

[85] Riffaterre, "The Intertexual Unconscious," pp. 380–81. The term "homologue" points to the similarity in structure or to the elements that the units have in common, such that they are seen as versions of the same statement, each contributing to the reader's understanding of the other.

[86] Riffaterre, "The Intertextual Unconscious," p. 381. See also Riffaterre, "Syllepsis," and Allen J. Frantzen's discussion of *Beowulf*, using Riffaterre's concepts, "Writing the Unreadable *Beowulf*," *Desire for Origins: New Language, Old English, and Teaching the Tradition* (New Brunswick, 1990), p. 184; this essay is reprinted in this volume.

[87] Gillian Overing, *Language, Sign, and Gender in "Beowulf"* (Carbondale, 1990), p. xvii; this essay is reprinted in this volume. "Metonymic" here stresses the principle of contiguity that underlies the figure of speech called metonymy. It refers to the perception that elements placed side by side are related by association rather than equivalence, whether they be grammatical units or thematic units. The horizontal thrust of the metonymic mode contrasts with the vertical thrust of the metaphorical mode, which resolves diverse elements in an overriding abstraction, asserting the equivalence or resemblance of the elements. Overing's use of metaphor and metonymy as modes of discourse differs in some respects from Roman Jakobson's seminal discussions of the distinction. Jakobson identifies the metonymic with contiguity and the metaphoric with equivalence, as does Overing, but in his discussions metonymy refers to a syntactical sort of structure in which subject leads to verb to object, or, as in the realistic novel or film, one action leads into the next, and in non-fiction prose, points are made in a logical sequence. In addition to Jakobson's "Two Aspects of Language and Two Types of Aphasic Disturbances," in *Fundamentals of Language*, ed. Roman Jakobson and Morris Halle (The Hague, 1956), pp. 55–82, see his "Closing Statement" in the same volume, and David Lodge, *The Modes of Modern Writing: Metaphor, Metonymy, and the Typology of Modern Literature* (London, 1977), pp. 73–93. Overing

and I were evidently working on the concepts of metonymic structure and disjunction or movement-structure at the same time: she includes my article, "Stylistic Disjunctions in *The Dream of the Rood*" (*Anglo-Saxon England* 13 [1984]: 167–86) in her discussion of metonymy and points quite rightly to the fact that her view, like mine, "allows, in fact insists on, the metonymic irresolution of the experience of the text" but that we differ in that I recognize in the poetry's content a turn toward the divine, representing a desire for a final unity not possible in the world of human expression and perception. I do wish, however, to step back somewhat from the too encompassing and thoughtlessly gendered assertion with which I concluded that article, "For medieval man the whole truth resides in God. . ." (p. 186). While many verse sequences conclude by expressing a desire for a part in cosmic unity, they do not all do so, and the prominence of that desire in the manuscript poetry has, I assume, something to do with the monastic production of the manuscripts rather than a universal concurrence in that ideology.

88 Overing, *Language, Sign, and Gender in "Beowulf,"* p. xvii.

89 Jakobson contends that in poetry the juxtaposition of two units always implies that they form to some degree a metaphorical equivalence: "In poetry where similarity is superimposed upon contiguity, any metonymy is slightly metaphorical and any metaphor has a metonymical tint" (Jakobson, "Closing Statement," p. 370).

90 Jacques Lacan, *The Four Fundamental Concepts of Psycho-Analysis*, ed. Jacques-Alain Miller, trans. Alan Sheridan (New York, 1981), p. 154; Overing, *Language, Sign, and Gender in "Beowulf,"* p. xxi.

91 See also the discussion of "gaps" by Wolfgang Iser, "The Reading Process: a Phenomenological Approach," *New Literary History* 3 (1972): 279–99 (reprinted in *The Implied Reader: Patterns of Communication in Prose Fiction from Bunyan to Beckett* [Baltimore, 1974], pp. 274–94): "Whenever the flow is interrupted and we are led off in unexpected directions, the opportunity is given to us to bring into play our own faculty for establishing connections—for filling in the gaps left by the text itself." "Modern texts," as he says, "frequently exploit" this quality (p. 280). One part of the reading dynamic that they encourage is "the process of grouping together all the different aspects of a text to form the consistency that the reader will always be in search of. . . . By grouping together the written parts of the text, we enable them to interact, we observe the direction in which they are leading us, and we project onto them the consistency which we, as readers, require" (pp. 283–84). Fred C. Robinson, *"Beowulf" and the Appositive Style* (Knoxville, 1985), discusses gaps as an aspect of what he calls *Beowulf*'s "appositive style," but he seems

to believe that the relationship the audience must figure out is singular and specific. Discussing the variation in lines 2596–97 as one aspect of this style, he expands and subordinates parts, asserting, "This rendition of the poet's logically reticent paratactic sentence into an elaborately explicit hypotactic version is not entirely arbitrary; it is, I believe, implied in the selection of the two terms in apposition" (p. 4).

[92] Roland Barthes, *S/Z*, trans. Richard Miller (New York, 1974), p. 4.

[93] Barthes, *S/Z*, p. 5.

SWORDS AND SIGNS: DYNAMIC SEMEIOSIS IN *BEOWULF*

GILLIAN R. OVERING

A sign is something by knowing which we know something more.
Charles Sanders Peirce

INTERLACE, TEXT, AND SIGN

My chapter, "Language: An Overview in Process," in my book *Language, Sign, and Gender in "Beowulf,"* suggests that we can understand the interpretive impulse toward, or resistance against, making parts into wholes in terms of metonymic or metaphoric principles motivating the text or the reader.[1] *Beowulf* and *Beowulf* scholarship represent a curious disjunction in this regard—the poem stubbornly resists the impulse, while its critics have persistently enacted it. The essentially non-Aristotelian narratological structure of the poem has usually been viewed as a problem to be solved, and the impulse to unify its disparate parts has pervaded

From *Language, Sign, and Gender in "Beowulf"* (Carbondale, 1990), pp. 33–67; reprinted with permission of Southern Illinois University Press. The only alterations to the original have been to remove or augment references Overing makes in the body of the essay to other sections of the book in which this essay originally appeared, and to convert the original "works cited" method of reference to footnotes. Some material in the footnotes has also been emended and/or augmented for clarity.

Beowulf scholarship in many guises. When Klaeber described the structure of *Beowulf* in terms of "lack of steady advance," he pinpointed, somewhat euphemistically, the problem facing readers searching for unity. If the author "does not hesitate to wander from the subject," by what means can the reader identify that subject clearly, or trace a coherent line of progress along the poem's "rambling, dilatory path?"[2] Klaeber's question puts the burden of responsibility on the reader for discovering a whole out of these unruly parts, but it does not call attention to the possibility that the desire for unity originates and terminates within the reader.

The search for unifying structural principles in *Beowulf* has gone hand in hand with an overall critical desire to legitimate its equally unruly subject matter. And both desires, Allen Frantzen points out, belong to the reader and not to the poem; they are part of the process by which critics have "written" the poem for themselves.[3] Tolkien's enormously influential essay on monsters and critics begins this dual push for legitimization: After Tolkien, argues Frantzen, a *Beowulf* without thematic coherence became as unthinkable as a *Beowulf* without dignified subject matter.[4] It instigated one of the most prevalent structural and thematic constructions of the poem's unity, a dualistic vision of the poem as a series of contrasts and oppositions. Tolkien summarizes this point of view in his response to Klaeber: "But the poem was not meant to advance, steadily or unsteadily. It is essentially a balance, an opposition of ends and beginnings. In its simplest terms it is a contrasted description of two moments in a great life, rising and setting; an elaboration of the ancient and intensely moving contrast between youth and age, first achievement and final death."[5]

Tolkien's view of opposition as a structural principle has been recast and expanded by Fred C. Robinson's discussion of the appositive style in *Beowulf*.[6] Robinson's argument asserts that the appositive dyad—which characterizes the smallest elements of grammatical structure on through to the broadest thematic elements—resolves into a third entity, a "meaning" collocated by the reader and implied by the poet. To interpret the first two elements, a third comes into play; opposition, or apposition, is resolved or encompassed, a process adumbrated by Tolkien in his notion of "balance." The dynamics of opposition/apposition recast metonymic and metaphoric principles in terms of binarism, a principle of identifying and hierarchizing binary oppositions. Pieces of the poem have been occasionally contorted or distorted to comply with the logic of this binary mode, whose inherent demand for resolution and completion reflects another facet of the impulse to make parts into wholes.

We can resist this impulse, or replace it, by positing a nonteleological, nonhierarchical coexistence of the metaphoric and metonymic modes. The semiotic argument of this essay offers a means of concretizing this abstract interpretational principle, a means of conceptualizing the process in which one and two are not inevitably three, nor must one be chosen over two, but one and two exist in a dynamic correlation. The notion of dyadic resolution, moreover, cannot address or encompass the dynamism of the poem as successfully as the concept of the triadic production of meaning, which, as we shall see, is central to Charles Sanders Peirce's theory of signs.

Putting aside the question of a possible overview, or final resolution of the poem's oppositional or appositional elements, in the reader's immediate engagement with the text such resolution is temporary, even mercurial. The narrative progression of the poem foils logical or linear attempts to sum up, to stand back and conclude that *this*, after all, meant *that*. The poem is essentially nonlinear, describing arcs and circles where persons, events, histories, and stories continually intersect. This poem requires a critical confrontation with difference. *Beowulf* is a text that invites a challenge to assumptions about the possibility and desirability of a structural overview. The quicksilver nature of its structure, where individual elements persist, dissolve, and expand in a continuum of resonance and association, questions the notion of textual boundaries as a form of resolution and suggests instead the infinitude of the text. To match the mode of the poem, it may be necessary to postulate and accept the text as without limit, to begin by "infinitizing the totality."[7]

To allow the text to be infinite is to weave the web of *différance*, to "allow the different threads and lines of sense or force" to come together or separate freely; and it is a kind of permission that need not result in a sea of indeterminacy. I want to use two related approaches that help to image this process of weaving, and to construct a critical apparatus that can more specifically describe the operation of the web. Much of this essay will be devoted to constructing this critical apparatus, and I shall take up implicit questions of textual infinitude, and of the reader's connection to it, explicitly in the final section. The first approach, that of visual analogy and interartistic comparison, will be familiar to Anglo-Saxonists; the second, a semiotic critical approach, is one that is just beginning to gain some recognition.

More organic critical approaches to *Beowulf*, which view its structure as cyclical and cumulative, and as an analogue of Anglo-Saxon art, have opened up far-reaching and fruitful areas of investigation into the nature of poetic structure.[8] The most pervasive characteristic of Anglo-Saxon art, found in all art forms from work in precious metal to manuscript illumination, is the use of interlace technique. The term refers to an intricate mode of decoration "having as its main characteristics the absence of any visual center, luxuriant and coiling repetitions, an elusive patterning which defies attempts to perceive the whole design at once."[9] Interlace technique possesses an "inherent power of expansion. . . . Never at rest, it has an elasticity for expansion or contraction so that, like liquid in a container, it is able to adapt itself to the passages it must fill, if necessary changing shape from one design to the next."[10] In a manner that recalls the immediate impact of the metonymic mode in language, interlace produces an experience—a dynamic, essentially kinetic, effect.

In his discussion of the interlace structure of *Beowulf*, John Leyerle argues that the interweaving of themes and motifs in the poem is a poetic structural analogue of interlace design, as elaborate, painstaking, and complex as the most sumptuous carpet page of an illuminated manuscript. Contemplation of the poem's design also provides an experience of its particular dynamic, and a reflexive examination of the contemplative exercise itself yields these insights: "This design reveals the meaning of coincidence, the recurrence of human behavior, and the circularity of time, partly through the coincidence, recurrence, and circularity of the medium itself—the interlace structure."[11]

Interlace as reflective of the poem's nonlinear progression also describes "an organizing principle closer to the workings of the human imagination proceeding in its atemporal way from one associative idea to the next than to the Aristotelian order of parts belonging to a temporal sequence with a beginning, middle and end."[12]

Leyerle and other critics have done much in Old English criticism to help dissolve perceptual barriers, enabling us to see one cultural artistic sign, a design or a painting, in terms of another, a text. Critical objections to discussing poetry in artistic terms, most recently voiced by Morton Bloomfield in his analysis of the inadequacy of the term "interlace" to describe Old English poetry, are based on the premise that a text is unavoidably and inevitably *not* a painting. Bloomfield asserts that we can never break "the iron rule of narrative that two lines of action cannot be *presented to the reader or listener at the same time*."[13] The simultaneity possible in visual art has no parallel in verbal art, and hence the interlace analogy must always, to an extent, fail. A semiotic viewpoint, and especially that of Charles Sanders Peirce, attenuates this impasse. While my emphasis is less on the perspective of simultaneity than on the kinetic affinity of these visual and textual media, the important point here is that a semiotic perspective does not seek to identify one sign system with another but to look at how the systems connect with and inform each other. Jonathan Evans reminds medievalists of the value of an important basic principle of modern semiotics: "if culture is an array of signs or of sign-systems . . . then no semiotic phenomenon can be fully comprehended in an analytical theory that assumes discreteness between the various systems of signs in a culture."[14] Moreover, if we are prepared to accept that "the interartistic comparison inevitably reveals the aesthetic norms of the period,"[15] we may learn a great deal about sign-functioning in the world evoked by the Old English poem by pursuing and extending the domain of the comparison.

In the following discussion I extend the domain of the artistic to include that of the artifact, and I talk about the sign-function of material objects— primarily swords—in *Beowulf*. It should be noted that most of the objects in *Beowulf*, and especially the swords, would have been, according to external and internal evidence, highly sophisticated works of art in their own right. The sword functions as many signs—physical, visual, and linguistic—within the poem: it is a gorgeous treasure prized for its beauty, a symbol of love or loyalty or shame, a reminder of the past, an incitement to future revenge, and much more. The sword signs are both inter- and extratextual, anchored within the narrative as linguistic signs, but evolving through their interrelationship and reverberating without and beyond the text. The nature of the interaction of linguistic signs in the poem mirrors the kinetic dynamic of interlace; it translates our relation to the text into a more visual, physical, material connection with it, one that possesses the immediacy of fact, feeling, or action. Examining how these kinds of sword signs cohere within the text can provide a means of describing the mercurial movement of the text in a manner that matches and retains the regenerative irresolution and visual infinitude of interlace. A semiotic approach also helps to explain one facet of this poem's extraordinary density and power.

The sign for "sword," it may be at once objected, must always be a linguistic one: that is, the Old English word for sword or one of the many descriptive epithets used in its place. And language must always be at one or several removes from reality and experience. Moreover, any good poem is larger than the sum of its signs; it will reverberate within our minds, possibly even change them, in an equally dynamic way. But the extended visual, material domain I am claiming for the linguistic sign in *Beowulf* will depend for its validation on a gradual process of semiotic analysis and reconstruction; it will require permission from the reader, a suspension of judgment, and a temporary dissolution of word/object boundaries, until I arrive at a consideration of how signs cohere in this text.

PEIRCE'S CONCEPT OF SIGN

Semiotic criticism is gradually gaining recognition from medievalists, and there have been several attempts to incorporate sign theory in discussions of Old and Middle English literature.[16] Although there have been some specifically Peircean analyses of medieval texts,[17] the "semeiotic" (a spelling Peirce introduced and one that I will use when referring specifically to Peirce's theories), or philosophical, mathematical, and logical system of sign analysis of Peirce often appears by implication only, these ideas having been so profoundly and pervasively influential that they now form the bases of general principles in modern semiotics. I want to return to Peirce's original hypotheses, and will use some of the formulas of Peirce's system because of their value in constructing a specific critical apparatus.

There are several compelling reasons to use Peirce's system of sign analysis; its comprehensiveness and flexibility make it especially appropriate to the kind of argument I am constructing about levels of cross-signification in *Beowulf*. Peirce's semeiotic encompasses far more than just language; we can interpret all experience in terms of semeiosis, as Peirce states in a well-known letter to Lady Welby: "It has never been in my power to study anything,—mathematics, ethics, metaphysics, gravitation, thermodynamics, optics, chemistry, comparative anatomy, astronomy, psychology, phonetics, economics, the history of science, whist, men and women, wine, metrology, except as a study of semeiotic."[18]

Peirce defines the sign itself in very broad terms:

> A sign, or *representamen*, is something which stands to somebody for something in some respect or capacity. (2.228)[19]

> I define a Sign as anything which is so determined by something else, called its Object, and so determines an effect upon a person, which effect I call its Interpretant, that is the latter is mediately determined by the former.[20]

The effect of the sign, or its interpretant, may itself be a sign that determines another interpretant. Semeiosis involves continual translation, growth, and expansion:

> A sign is not a sign unless it translates itself into another sign in which it is more fully developed. (5.594)

> . . . a sign is something by knowing which we know something more.[21]

Also important to my argument is that Peirce's conception of sign, and his trichotomous divisions of sign categories, are fundamentally connected to his phenomenological categories. The analysis and interpretation of signs always imply a concurrent analysis and interpretation of experience, and of the process of cognition. When applied to a text Peirce's terminology is particularly useful in describing connections, not only within the text, but between words and things, between the language of the text and the subject's experience of the text.

The focus on expansion and continual movement in sign interaction is one important aspect of Peirce's sign theory that matches the mode of *Beowulf.* The connection to experience also distinguishes Peirce's system in that it accounts for a subject and includes a role for the interpreter of signs. One of the limitations of contemporary semiotic theory, according to Teresa de Lauretis and Kaja Silverman, is that it does not fully address the role of the subject and the operations of desire.[22] Peirce's system "greatly complicates the picture in which a signifier would immediately correspond to a signified"[23] by replacing a Saussurean dualism with the more complex notion of triadic sign production. Umberto Eco asks the question, "What is, in the semiotic framework, the place of the *acting subject* of every se-miosic act?"[24] De Lauretis points out that his answer engages the producer of signs, "the subject of enunciation or of a speech act, not its addressee or receiver; not the reader but the speaker/writer."[25] Peirce engages the user of signs. The sign has an effect "upon a person": "it stands to somebody for something. . . . It addresses somebody, that is, it creates in the mind of that person an equivalent sign, or perhaps a more developed sign" (2.228).

The triadic production of signs takes place on many levels; Peirce's system divides and subdivides in ways that are too complex to enumerate here. I propose instead to establish some working definitions for my purposes and to refer the reader to the extensive research on Peirce for more detailed explication.[26] I shall be referring primarily to the phenomenological categories of Firstness, Secondness, and Thirdness, to his best-known sign trichotomy, that of icon, index, and symbol, and to the division of types of interpretants—a very small fraction of Peirce's total system. The phenomenological categories are especially important because they provide an overarching perspective on all semeiosis:

> My view is that there are three modes of being. I hold that we can directly observe them in elements of whatever is at any time before the mind in any way. There are the being of positive qualitative possibility, the being of actual fact, and the being of law that will govern facts in the future. (1.23)

> It seems, then, that the true categories of consciousness are: first, feeling, the consciousness which can be included with an instant of time, passive consciousness of quality, without recognition or analysis; second, consciousness of an interruption into the field of consciousness, sense of resistance, of an external fact, of another something; third, synthetic consciousness, binding time together, sense of learning, thought. (1.353)[27]

The categories of Firstness, Secondness, and Thirdness underpin Peirce's other triadic divisions, including the second trichotomy of signs, which describes the sign in relation to its object (icon, index, symbol) and the classes of interpretant (Immediate, Dynamic, Final).[28] Here I refer to Shapiro's useful and straightforward summary of these sign types: "the relation between sign and object may be one of iconic resemblance (such as a portrait and the person portrayed), of indexical contiguity and dynamic interaction (smoke and fire), or of symbolic law (a habit, such as an item of language)."[29]

The last set of definitions that will figure prominently in my discussion of *Beowulf* involves the interpretant, "the cognition produced in the mind" (1.372), the effect that the sign determines in the mind of the interpreter:

> My Immediate Interpretant is implied in the fact that each sign must have its peculiar interpretability before it gets any Interpreter. My Dynamical Interpretant is that which is experienced in each act of interpretation and is different in each from that of any other; and the Final Interpretant is the one Interpretative result to which every Interpreter is destined to come if the Sign is sufficiently considered. The Immediate Interpretant is an abstraction, consisting in a Possibility. The Dynamical Interpretant is a single actual event. The Final Interpretant is that towards which the actual tends.[30]

Throughout most of this discussion, my primary focus will be on the second element of these various triadic structures; I shall argue that in *Beowulf* we enter a world characterized largely by Secondness, by Dynamical Interpretants, where indexicality is the dominant mode of signification and the compulsion of the *hic et nunc* claims and engages the reader. By this I do not mean to imply that there is an absence of synthesis, characterized by Thirdness or symbolicity. Just as metonymy may predominate without precluding the presence of metaphor, so too may the compulsion and dynamism of Secondness predominate without excluding the reflective, synthesizing consciousness of Thirdness—an analogue for the metaphorizing reader who collocates and resolves meaning. The coexistent dynamic of Secondness and Thirdness, and of metonymy and metaphor, are both means of examining the nature and possibility and extent of resolution in this text. Silverman notes that the commutability of the signified revealed in Peirce's notion of the interpretant parallels Derrida's "freeplay"[31]; both concepts image the web of *différance*, the process of weaving. Peirce's terminology, however, in addition to offering a means of questioning literal or thematic textual boundaries, also engages the role of the subject in that process of questioning.

WORDS, THINGS, AND THE SPACE BETWEEN

Within the text the sign for sword is a linguistic one—that is, the occurrence of a word. Strictly speaking according to Peirce's first trichotomy of signs describing signs in relation to themselves (qualisign, sinsign, legisign), a word is a legisign, a third, instantiated in a particular instance by a sinsign, a second. Words fit most easily into the first trichotomy, and things, like swords, fit into the second trichotomy of icon, index, and symbol. A word will not have the iconic or indexical presence of an object, visual or material; it is not a picture, a pointing finger, or a billow of smoke. Though words can quite comfortably be symbols (it is possible to conflate the trichotomies), they always lack a "feeling of presence," the difference insisted on by Steiner in her discussion of textual and visual affect.[32] The closest linguistic analogy to the pointing finger would be a pronoun: "all words are legisigns, although the indexical relation predominates over the symbolic in deictic words such as pronouns."[33] Peirce in one instance exemplifies an index in terms of the moods of speech: "Icons and indices assert nothing. If an icon could be interpreted by a sentence, that sentence must be in a 'potential mood,' that is, it would merely say 'Suppose a figure had three sides,' etc. Were an index so interpreted, the mood must be imperative, or exclamatory, as 'See there!' or 'Look out!'" (2.291).

It is precisely this imperative mode, this quality of fixing and riveting attention, that I claim for the sign-functioning of the sword and other objects in *Beowulf*, for the linguistic signs for these objects. This is not really unusual; words often develop extreme indexical properties depending on our level of familiarity with them, or the associations that develop over a period of time (for example, ice cream points to good, delicious; anchovy points to tasty or revolting, according to your point of view). Our relation to a word can determine its degree of symbolicity or indexicality.

The interwoven networks of indexical connotations surrounding the term "sword" in *Beowulf* are dense and complex; interpreting these networks, even tracing their outline, involves an effort, a shift in vision that is in tune with the poem. Again, the interartistic comparison helps the reader to do this; if we allow the text to work upon us in the manner of interlace design, we can more easily follow the interplay of linguistic signs; we can begin to trace the interwoven networks of association and experience their indexical connective force. As with any poem, we build as we read what Peirce calls "collateral experience" of the objects of signs. "The sign can only represent the object and tell about it. It cannot furnish acquaintance with or recognition of that object" (2.231). "It can only indicate [the object] and leave the interpreter to find out by collateral experience" (8.314), which is "previous acquaintance with what the sign denotes" (*NE* 3.842). We may understand the meaning of a word by simple differentiation within a language system, but its actual use is discovered and developed through collateral observation, or increased understanding of its context. The poem is the context for our collateral observation of sword signs, but this context might legitimately be expanded beyond the text.

So far I have been hovering (perhaps precariously) in a space between words and things. The swords, or other objects in the poem, are not, of course, present in front of our eyes to scan like a picture (I do not intend to become fully embroiled in controversy about temporal-spatial divisions in art and poetry), nor would they have been for an Old English reader, or audience of the poem. But we can assume that the familiarity with the sword sign and its visual and semantic connotations would have been far greater for the contemporaneous reader or listener. This familiarity, Caroline Brady suggests, was both esthetic and practical; the audience of *Beowulf* "knew also about their weapons, their strengths and weaknesses, but above all about their swords upon the quality of which their lives depended."[34] Much the same principle of reconstruction applies to our understanding of the historical and mythological allusions in the poem. We can piece together a broader context, to inform ourselves and come closer to that contemporary familiarity and recognition, and so build our collateral experience.

The following brief and necessarily partial reconstruction of "sword lore" might help to establish the connection between sign and object, between swords and beautiful objects and their relation to words.

Most of the surviving artifacts of outstanding artistic merit in this period are illuminated manuscripts, but these, art historian C. R. Dodwell insists, were not what the Anglo-Saxons cared for most. In fact precisely because books were less valued did they survive the plundering and pillage of successive Viking invasions. More highly valued was work in precious metals, which better reflected the Anglo-Saxon "love of resplendence"; objects like jeweled drinking cups, neck- and arm-rings of twisted gold, gold-filigreed helmets and war gear, the damascened blades and decorated hilts of swords—the clank and gleam of which pervade *Beowulf*. There is ample evidence that the poetic descriptions of these objects easily matched the reality: "the poets were not dreaming up gilded visions but delineating the tastes of the world around [them]."[35] The love of resplendence is everywhere reflected. Evidence of Anglo-Saxon wills shows that swords were usually decorated with gold, as were spurs, musical instruments, and ships' prows.[36]

"In any unsettled society art treasures never lose their connotation of accessible wealth,"[37] and the material worth of these objects is often emphasized in the poetry. The minstrel in *Widsith*, Dodwell points out, knows the precise value of Eormanric's gift of an arm-ring.[38] That treasures were relished and enjoyed as well, forming a kind of currency, is especially evident in *Beowulf*. John D. Niles calls attention to this parallel investiture of functional and esthetic significance: "In his sermon, Hrothgar could have made much of the vanity of earthly goods. Instead, he stresses the danger of a king's bottling up wealth. Rather than exhort his audience to forego material goods, time and again the poet dwells lovingly on the beauty or value of precious objects and speaks of the honor they lend their possessors."[39]

Elsewhere the poet lists and describes with care just how many treasures and of what kind Beowulf receives as payment or reward for his services. As Niles points out, the treasures comprise a moral, emotional currency as well: they express the sentiments of the giver, and transmit honor to the receiver. They approve Beowulf's actions and complement his courage.[40] The drinking cup acquires meaning in its ritual of passing from one warrior to another. Treasure acquires significance through its distribution.[41] This central part of the heroic ethos is reflected in the poem's vocabulary: the lord is *goldwine gumena* ("gold-friend to men," line 1602), a *beag-gyfa* ("ring-giver," line1102), who distributes treasure in a *goldsele* ("gold hall," line 715).

Precious objects were often invested with human significance; this is seen not only in the pervasive use of personification in *Beowulf*, but is well attested outside the context of the poem, and is especially true of swords: "Germanic and Old English poetic convention as well as Anglo-Saxon laws and beliefs encouraged the belief that a sword metonymically inherited and participated in the qualities, attainments, excellences as well as defects of its original owner and transmitted these almost magically to its wielder."[42] The sword might even substitute for its owner. In the Sutton Hoo burial no body was found;[43] the placement of grave goods, however, suggests that the sword was laid in its place.[44]

The esthetic and nonesthetic values of the object are closely linked; the more carefully decorated and ornate are his sword hilt and blade, the better the warrior. Michael Cherniss points out that Anglo-Saxon warriors would not have worn campaign ribbons or medals, but would acquire increasingly more valuable (more highly decorated) war gear.[45] The sword of good quality, one with a low carbon content to make it steely and flexible, would be judged according to the complexity and delicacy of its decorative pattern.[46] The blade pattern was produced by damascening or pattern-welding, a painstaking process of welding strips of iron and wires together technically outlined by H. E. Davidson; the effect, however, is best described in her translation of Cassiodorus's fifth-century letter sent to thank another ruler for the present of several swords:

> So resplendent is their polished clarity that they reflect with faithful distinctness the faces of those who look upon them. So evenly do their edges run down to a point that they might be thought not shaped by files but molded by the furnace. The central part of their blades, cunningly hollowed out, appears to be grained with tiny snakes, and here such varied shadows play that you would believe the shining metal to be interwoven with colors.[47]

Many of the swords in *Beowulf* are similarly designed. The use of *mæl* in compounds is a likely reference to pattern-welded blades, as in *brogdenmæl* ("ornamented with a wavy pattern," line 1667), *sceadenmæl* ("branch-patterned," line 1939) and *hringmæl* ("ring-marked," line 2037).[48]

The sword hilt would have been even more elaborately decorated, often displaying serpentine interlace motifs and occasionally inscribed with runes (as is the case with the giant sword in *Beowulf*), thereby intensifying its talismanic significance. The hilt of a king's sword also had special significance, forming part of a ceremony where retainers would pledge their allegiance. Historical evidence shows that the sword was an important heirloom, passed on from one generation to another, given, in some cases, at birth along with a name, or later as a token of manhood.[49] The "sword lore" of this period is extensive and makes for a fascinating study in its own right, but I shall finish this general reconstruction at this point and rely on the poem to extend and support it. Brady's comprehensive study has amply demonstrated that the poem is a mine of specific and practical information about weaponry in general, and swords in particular. A. T. Hatto's earlier study draws attention to the "niceties of sword lore, which the poet is so careful to observe,"[50] and Davidson also believes that the *Beowulf* poet may be trusted for his accuracy: his descriptions of swords "imply considerable detailed knowledge of swords and their appearance."[51]

A sense of what the poem's objects look like and connote should provide some support for my occupation of the space between words and things, and examining the extent of the concept of personification offers a further means of demarcating this space. In a discussion of the ubiquitous device of personification in *Beowulf*, N. D. Isaacs suggests that each object possesses "a living, moving spirit of its own."[52] The sword may metonymically share human attributes, or the sword or other war gear may replace the warrior: when Beowulf and his men first arrive on the shores of Denmark, the suspicious coastguard sees not men approaching, but *beorhte randas* ("bright shields," line 231), or—a more important substitution—in the dragon fight, it is the sword that fails, and not Beowulf's strength (lines 2584–85 and 2680–82).[53] Swords can also sing grim battle songs (lines 1521–22).[54] The notion of interchangeability of objects and persons also extends to words and deeds. The hero's words, or boast, must be tantamount to deeds; deeds, in turn, are equated with treasures as reward; deeds of the past are embodied by objects in the present; the appearance of an object in the present may incite future action.[55] And so we might go round in circles. Like the moving, intersecting spirals of interlace, it is not possible to think of all these exchanges and associations at once.

We cannot simply exchange or simultaneously identify sign systems; words are not deeds, and poems are not paintings, but we can look at the ways that these systems intersect. The poem is a continuum, an echo chamber, where we experience a continual crisscrossing of temporal-spatial values and relations, where the physical world subsumes the mental and vice versa, and where the linguistic sign develops its peculiar palpability, resonance, and kinetic power.

I want to briefly note here another theoretical framework that provides a context for this notion of the palpability of the linguistic sign (or viscerality). The sign, especially the object sign, in *Beowulf* participates to some extent in the power of the primitive sign, as this is designated by Gilles Deleuze and Felix Guattari in their historicized account of the development of representation. In a text such as *Beowulf*, which embodies several coexistent cultural descriptions (oral and literate, pagan and Christian, "barbaric" and civilized society), the cultural and political context of sign development helps to further describe the nature of the sign-object relation and to demarcate words, things, and the space between.

In Deleuze and Guattari's formulation, there are two orders of "graphism," or inscription, which roughly correspond to barbarian and imperial modes of representation. In the barbarian, primitive system of representation, the sign is associated with physical territorial reality, and the violence and cruelty of the "inscription in the flesh"; it retains a vital, interactive, but unsubordinated connection with voice: "primitive societies are oral not because they lack a graphic system but because, on the contrary, the graphic system in these societies is independent of the voice; it marks signs on the body that respond to the voice, react to the voice, but that are autonomous and do not align themselves to it."[56] As the state develops and imposes "imperial" representation, this autonomy disappears; in the second order of graphism (a term that encompasses all systems of representation, legislative, bureaucratic, financial), writing supplants the voice by becoming subordinate to it and makes way for arbitration, control, and resolution: "the voice no longer sings but dictates, decrees; the graphy no longer dances, it ceases to animate bodies, but is set into writing on tablets, stones, and books; the eye sets itself to reading."[57]

The first order of graphism or representation involves the visceral immediacy and self-referentiality allied with the metonymic mode. The primitive sign is "self-validating; it is a position of desire in a state of multiple connections. It is not a sign of a sign or a desire of a desire. It knows nothing of linear subordination . . . it is rhythm and not form, zig-zag and not line, artifact and not idea, production and not expression."[58]

Both sign orders coexist in *Beowulf*; here I want to point out that the concept of primitive sign also returns us to an emphasis on process and experience, and to a construction of interpretation *as* desire, whereas the "imperial" sign mirrors the symbolic metaphorizing function. As the metonym functions within, and also is a function of, the metonymic fabric of the whole text, so the sign in *Beowulf* accrues its visceral and primitive power in dynamic association, in a series of interwoven networks, verbal sign patterns that follow the twists, turns, and recursions of interlace.

THE WEB OF SIGNS

Using Peirce's terminology, I will trace a partial outline of the poem's indexically connected networks, limiting my discussion to four representative strands of interrelation.[59] The first two strands involve cups and rings, the second two focus on swords. In unraveling separate strands of the poem in this fashion one could just as easily start at the end or the middle and work backward, but I shall initially adopt the arbitrary clarity of linear progression.

Beowulf has arrived at Hrothgar's court, has offered his assistance and made his heroic boast; he has inspired a measure of confidence and cheered the beleaguered Danish court to the point where a celebratory feast takes place. Hrothgar takes up the narrative; he recalls the recent past in which his own retainers drank and boasted over their ale-cups that they could defeat Grendel. After a gruesome description of their failure (mead hall and benches dripping with blood, lines 484–87), Hrothgar exhorts Beowulf to enjoy the present feast. This is ceremonially affirmed by a servant who circulates around the company pouring the shining drink (*scir wered*, line 496) from a decorated ale-cup (*hroden ealowæge*, line 495). Following Unferth's hostile challenge to Beowulf—which undercuts the image of hall unity implicit in ale-sharing—Wealhtheow introduces a more festive note when she appears with a ritual drinking cup and passes it around. The gold-adorned queen offers the precious vessel (*sincfato*, line 622) to Beowulf. The cup next appears in the narrative after Beowulf has fought Grendel, and there is a great celebration in Heorot where Hrothgar and his nephew Hrothulf feast together and share *medoful manig* ("many a mead-cup," line 1915).

There follows the extremely sobering tale of Finn and Hengest, and of Hildeburh, the "peace-weaving" woman caught in the middle of their enmity, which is recounted as entertainment by Hrothgar's court poet. Gold-adorned Wealhtheow brings forth another ceremonial drinking cup and makes a speech that is a remarkable mixture of ceremonial affirmation of peace and unity, justifiable political paranoia, and controlled desperation. In an attempt to look out for her two sons, she issues a public reminder/admonition to her husband who has acted rather rashly in offering to adopt Beowulf as his son when he already has two of his own. Her speech also encourages the now proven hero to declare his support for her sons in front of

Hrothulf, the potentially treacherous nephew who might usurp the Danish throne before her sons come of age. (Wealhtheow's situation might also recall the position of the hapless "peace-weaver" Hildeburh, the wife of Finn.) She carries the cup to Beowulf and gives him more precious objects. But thereby hangs another thread.

Let me stop here and gather up this thread so far. These several drinking cups are not important or famous in themselves; they do not have names or histories, but these objects denote and develop a series of indexically connected associations. The different linguistic signs for cup are indexical sinsigns that compel attention to the object and determine a series of dynamic interpretants that are in turn indexical signs. A kind of chain reaction is set up. The indexical connections can be traced more clearly by means of diagrams, although in the diagrams that follow one point should be emphasized. The broken arrow lines connecting the triangles should be understood as indicating accumulation rather than contingency; that is, the sign accrues meanings, so that each successive triangle incorporates the preceding ones and thus represents a varied accumulation of meanings.

Figure 1 shows how the linguistic signs grow and develop each time they are interpreted; the text provides an overall network wherein each interpretation (a dynamic interpretant, which receives a particular instantiation in the text) becomes another index, dynamically, inevitably pointing to its interpretant. Each time the sign appears in the narrative, it may trigger this succession and become part of a chain reaction.

The linguistic sign for the object accumulates an indexical presence parallel to more obvious or literal narrative indices in the poem, like Grendel's claw nailed to the entrance of Heorot as a victory advertisement, and the inevitable sequel, the head of Aeschere, Hrothgar's beloved advisor, displayed on the path to the mere—an index to both Grendel's mother's past revenge and to Beowulf's future retaliation. Or the sword placed on Hengest's lap, which triggers his retaliation against Finn; and the ancestral sword of the Heathobards worn by a young warrior, the simple sight of which starts a fight in memory of the history of its acquisition.

Taking up another strand in the poem, one can trace a similar sign function for objects with a specific history evoked by the narrative. As Wealhtheow approaches Beowulf with the ritual drinking cup, she also rewards him with treasures:

Him wæs ful boren, ond freonðlaþu
wordum bewægned, ond wunden gold

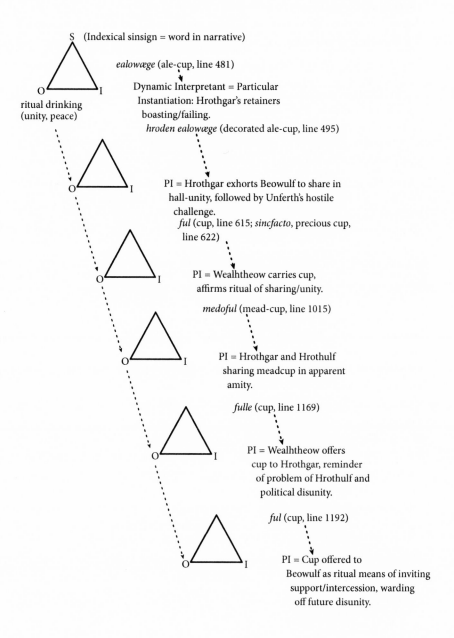

S (Indexical sinsign = word in narrative)

ealowæge (ale-cup, line 481)

O————I

ritual drinking
(unity, peace)

Dynamic Interpretant = Particular
Instantiation: Hrothgar's retainers
boasting/failing.

hroden ealowæge (decorated ale-cup, line 495)

O————I

PI = Hrothgar exhorts Beowulf to share in
hall-unity, followed by Unferth's hostile
challenge.
ful (cup, line 615; *sincfacto*, precious cup,
line 622)

O————I

PI = Wealhtheow carries cup,
affirms ritual of sharing/unity.

medoful (mead-cup, line 1015)

O————I

PI = Hrothgar and Hrothulf
sharing meadcup in apparent
amity.

fulle (cup, line 1169)

O————I

PI = Wealhtheow offers
cup to Hrothgar, reminder
of problem of Hrothulf and
political disunity.

ful (cup, line 1192)

O————I

PI = Cup offered to
Beowulf as ritual means of inviting
support/intercession, warding
off future disunity.

Figure 1

estum geawed, earmhreade twa,
hrægl ond hringas, healsbeaga mæst
þara þe ic on foldan gefrægen hæbbe. (lines 1192–96)

> The cup was carried to him, and friendship offered with words, and twisted gold bestowed with good will, two arm-ornaments, a corselet and rings, the greatest neck-ring that I ever heard tell of.

The poet, however, *does* know of another, even greater, such treasure, and singles out the neck-ring for further comment. It was matched in the past by the legendary Brosings' necklace, acquired amid feuding, treachery, and death. Moving back into the present, the poet forecasts the future of Beowulf's gift: it will be worn by Hygelac (to whom Beowulf, loyal retainer that he is, will turn over all acquired treasures upon his return home) on a reckless raid in which he will die, and the treasure will fall to *wyrsan wigfrecan* ("worse warriors," line 1212), the Franks. Back in the present in the narrative, Wealhtheow exhorts Beowulf to enjoy his treasure ("Bruc ðisses beages," line 1216). This sequence is illustrated in Figure 2. Note also in this sequence how cup and ring linguistic signs/indexes intersect beautifully when Hygelac carries the precious treasure on his raid "ofer yða ful" ("over the cup of the waves," line 1208).

The irony in the Figure 2 sequence is palpable; the gorgeous neck-ring weighs like a millstone on the narrative, but the ornament also fixes a continuum, where past, future, and present reflect, imply, and indexically connect with each other. Niles argues that the complex sense of time in *Beowulf* is one of its most distinguishing elements and adds another dimension to the possibilities for sign interaction; the poem crisscrosses both literal and imaginary time zones:

> Mythic time, legendary time and historical time are all present simultaneously *in potentia* from the beginning of the poem to the end. At any moment, as a way of making the involutions of the text more dense, the poet may allude to persons or actions that pertain to any of these three modes of time. Thus a given moment is not exactly a narrative event, for nothing much may happen in it to advance the plot. It is rather a kind of narrative "crossroads" for the intersection of lines drawn from significant points in and out of time.[60]

I am also suggesting that this kind of "crossroads" can occur at the level of the linguistic sign for objects, whichever time zone we enter. During the

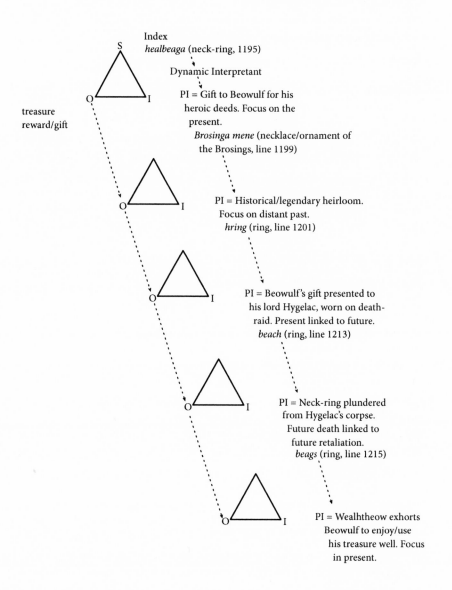

Index
healbeaga (neck-ring, 1195)

Dynamic Interpretant

PI = Gift to Beowulf for his
heroic deeds. Focus on the
present.
Brosinga mene (necklace/ornament of
the Brosings, line 1199)

PI = Historical/legendary heirloom.
Focus on distant past.
hring (ring, line 1201)

PI = Beowulf's gift presented to
his lord Hygelac, worn on death-
raid. Present linked to future.
beach (ring, line 1213)

PI = Neck-ring plundered
from Hygelac's corpse.
Future death linked to
future retaliation.
beags (ring, line 1215)

PI = Wealhtheow exhorts
Beowulf to enjoy/use
his treasure well. Focus
in present.

treasure
reward/gift

Figure 2

dragon fight, Wiglaf's sword acquires a similar repercussive density, functioning also as a narrative index, in that the poet breaks off in the middle of the fight to talk about the sword.[61] The result is an expansion of the simultaneity of perspective, which can also operate at the phraseological level. In *Beowulf* the indexical sword sign holds past, present, and future perspectives before us in a process of inevitable and dynamic coalition. Without further paraphrase, Figure 3 should illustrate this series of connections.

In interpreting these sword signs, which engage a temporal perspective, an important question arises: To what extent are we "binding time together," moving from the dynamism of Secondness into the reflective synthesis of Thirdness? This is a question that I must partially address before examining the fourth, most complex sword sequence in the poem. I have emphasized the indexical quality of the object signs in the poem and therefore the quality of Secondness, "found in action, resistance, facticity, dependence, relation, compulsion, effect, reality, and result."[62] Shapiro's list in many ways provides an accurate general characterization of the world of the poem. The action-packed, dynamic aspect of the narrative is part of its resonance and power. It is not surprising that the popularity and appeal of *Beowulf* persists in, and translates easily into, comic-book form. In this regard, it is important to remember that Peirce differentiated two kinds of index, exemplified by demonstrative and relative pronouns:

> While demonstrative and personal pronouns are, as ordinarily used, "genuine indices," relative pronouns are "degenerate indices"; for though they may, accidentally and indirectly, refer to existing things, they directly refer, and need only refer, to the images in the mind which previous words have created. (2.305)

> If the Secondness is an existential relation, the Index is *genuine*. If the secondness is a reference, the Index is degenerate. (2.274)

The difference might be simply stated as having something pointed out to you initially, or being reminded rather insistently that it is already there. Broadly speaking, we could parallel these two kinds of connections to the difference between modern and medieval standards and definitions of artistry. The genuine index is more prized in the modern view; creative artistry lies in the surprise and innovation of connection, in the breaking up and remaking of possibly complacent patterns of habitual association. In the world of *Beowulf*, however, the power and effect of the index accumulate

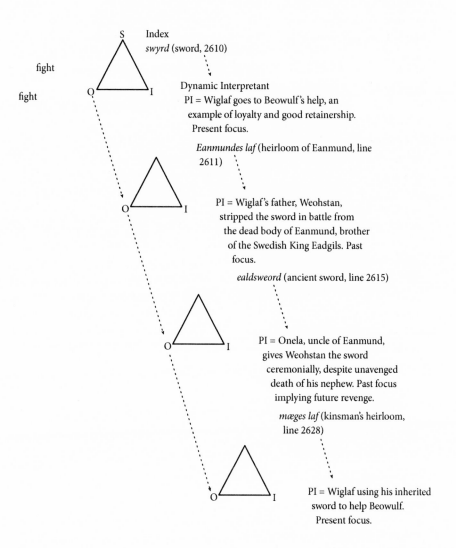

fight

fight

S   Index
     swyrd (sword, 2610)

     Dynamic Interpretant
     PI = Wiglaf goes to Beowulf's help, an
        example of loyalty and good retainership.
        Present focus.

     Eanmundes laf (heirloom of Eanmund, line
        2611)

     PI = Wiglaf's father, Weohstan,
        stripped the sword in battle from
        the dead body of Eanmund, brother
        of the Swedish King Eadgils. Past
        focus.

     ealdsweord (ancient sword, line 2615)

     PI = Onela, uncle of Eanmund,
        gives Weohstan the sword
        ceremonially, despite unavenged
        death of his nephew. Past focus
        implying future revenge.

     mæges laf (kinsman's heirloom,
        line 2628)

     PI = Wiglaf using his inherited
        sword to help Beowulf.
        Present focus.

Figure 3

through the very inevitability of connection, the very predictability of reference. Using conventional poetic diction and formulas, the Old English poet might not appear to be a maker or remaker of language and hence perception, but a reshaper, a reemphasizer of familiar experience using familiar language. This means that we pay ever closer attention to the same things—honor, shame, feuds, loyalty, decision making, sorrow, loss and, above all, death. Instead of enlargement or expansion, the process is one of increasingly minute and inescapable focus.

The psychological action of the index, Peirce says, does not depend "upon intellectual operations" (2.305). To what extent, then, is the poem locked into a world of Secondness, a world devoid of synthesis and reflection, or of interpretation in the hermeneutic sense? What is the place of Firstness and Thirdness, of icons and symbols? Is the poem a series of dynamic interpretants that never become, or even point toward, a Final interpretant? The simple repetitive operation of dynamic interpretants can stop semeiosis, the continual translation and expansion of signs:

> Dynamic interpretants, being finite bounded events, bring semeiosis to a terminus. A simple additive sequence of actions without cumulation into a pattern of habit remains, according to Peirce, at the level of dead Secondness. It is powerless to register the significance of a sign, or to be the sign of some object by signifying yet another sign of the same object. For this reason, Peirce concludes, there must be principles, norms, and laws that guide the interpretation of signs beyond the endless mechanical repetition of identical patterns of behavior.[63]

It should be obvious at this point that I think that the Secondness of *Beowulf* is far from "dead." The lines of indexically connected triangles I have been tracing may eventually connect and become a circle. What Lewis Nicholson says of themes and motifs is also true of signs in the poem: "Just as the spirals of Anglo-Saxon ornament move forward to form intricate patterns and then return to themselves uninterrupted, so one may compare the intricacies of the poetic text where a theme or motif returns to itself like a snake with its tail in its mouth."[64] The drinking cup resurfaces at the end of the poem as the provocation of the dragon's wrath. An unhappy exiled slave steals it from the dragon's hoard as a peace offering to his lord; the gesture toward reconciliation arouses the hatred and vengeance of the sleeping dragon.

Another cup gleams in the pile of treasures next to the dragon's dead body (lines 3047–48), and might easily be one of the many treasures of twisted gold that are burnt on Beowulf's funeral pyre; which funeral might justifiably, if not indexically, recall that of Scyld Scefing at the beginning of the poem—a king's body pushed out to sea surrounded by a pile of gleaming treasures (lines 36–40). Or the "earmbeaga fela / searwum gesæled" ("many arm-rings cleverly twisted," lines 2763–64) that Beowulf stares at (some have said greedily) when he first surveys the dragon's magnificent hoard connect in our minds with the gifts Beowulf leaves to Wiglaf as he dies:

> Dyde him of healse hring gyldenne
> þioden þristhydig, þegne gesealde
> geongum garwigan, goldfahne helm,
> beah ond byrnan, het hyne brucan well. (lines 2809–12)

> The bold-minded king took from his neck the golden ring, and gave to the thane, young spear-warrior, gold-adorned helmet, collar and corselet, bade him use them well.

We cannot help recalling Wealhtheow's ill-fated gift and her words to the young Beowulf earlier in the poem. And so the signs of the poem indexically connect and form intersecting circles. But these are not the vicious and entrapping circles of "dead" Secondness; like the recursions of interlace, they gather and spiral in a process of inherent expansion.

THE GIANT SWORD HILT: A PATH OUT OF SECONDNESS

The last sign-sequence, or thread, that I will trace through the poem provides an especially appropriate forum for some recurrent questions and also returns the discussion to the role of the subject, or interpreter of signs. To ask how or if we move from the dynamic indexicality of Secondness to the synthesizing symbolicity of Thirdness is to raise questions of teleology once more: To what extent is there resolution of meaning in the poem, or is the text infinite? And how is the reading subject involved in either the marking out or dissolution of textual boundaries?

To frame answers to these questions I turn to Peirce's views on teleology and the subject as a context for the analysis of the final sequence. Semeiosis is a teleologically motivated process for Peirce, but he places considerable emphasis on the aspect of process. A sign may determine any number of dynamic interpretants, but possesses only one final interpretant; this is arrived at through "sufficient consideration" of the sign, but it does not need to be actualized in order to exist as a potential goal—"a being *in futuro* will suffice" (2.92). For Peirce, the process of sufficient consideration is itself teleological:

> The idea of a final interpretant presupposes that of a goal of interpretation. For apart from such a goal, "consideration" of a sign would not lead the interpreter to any "destined" conclusion: regardless of the amount of consideration made, any conclusion would remain just as good. But if each sign has a unique final interpretant, then each sign is the sign that it is in relation not only to a ground but also to a goal of interpretation. It is clear, then, that Peirce conceived of semeiosis as a teleological process and of signs as being what their potential role in semeiosis makes them to be.[65]

If, as T.L. Short suggests, signs are what their role in semeiosis makes them to be, then the process of sign interaction itself—the progress toward the Final interpretant—is an important factor in the construction of meaning. And the user or interpreter of signs as a part of the process of triadic sign interaction is also implicated in the construction of meaning. The "meaning" of a sign, its interpretant, is a "cognition produced in the mind," which is yet another sign, but "perhaps a more developed one." Semeiosis, in both text and reader, is an ongoing and reciprocal process, one that engages self and text, inner and outer worlds.[66] The importance of process is well described in the concept of Thirdness: "By the third, I mean the medium or connecting bond between the absolute first and last. The beginning is first, the end second, the middle third. . . . Continuity represents Thirdness almost to perfection. Every process comes under that head. . . . The positive degree of an adjective is first, the superlative second, the comparative third" (1.337).

In this view teleology is a function of continual translation. Peirce adds a new dimension here to a metonymic/metaphoric framework; his concept of Thirdness overcomes the closure of metaphoricity and describes a dynamic relational coexistence of the two modes, and, moreover, this is a dynamic in which the reader thoroughly participates. If we are "spoken" by the metonymic text, or claimed by the compulsion of Secondness, it is with a permission that itself represents the mediating presence of Thirdness. Our permission is here an acknowledgment of and a participation in semeiosis as process.

In Peirce's view, the self is also in process, continually in production as a user and producer of signs; it is, itself, a sign, a point I shall return to at the conclusion of this essay. Subjectivity is an ongoing construction, and halting semeiosis or deciding on final meaning may itself only be a function of what Peirce calls habit or what de Lauretis redefines as "experience . . . a complex of habits resulting from the semiotic interaction of 'outer world' and 'inner world,' the continuous engagement of a self or subject in social reality."[67] The reader who is collocating meaning, achieving the overview of metaphoricity, must beware the trap of Secondness, the lure of the superlative. "In the hierarchy of signs relative to their final interpretants, the highest or ultimate purpose is reached in the dominance of critical control over habits and beliefs."[68] The interpreter of signs must continually reassess the habit of interpretation: meaning, or a truly "living definition," can be created only by "the deliberately formed, self-analyzing habit—self-analyzing because formed by the aid of analysis of the exercises that nourished it" (5.491).

Although Peirce insists on the goal-directed nature of all semeiosis, the potential for hermeneutic circularity and subjectivity in interpreting poetic signs is attenuated in several ways.[69] The interpreter's awareness and self-questioning matches the ever-developing, teleological determinacy of the sign under interpretation, suggesting an isomorphic developmental relation between reader and text. Signs become clearer: "the symbol is essentially a purpose," writes Peirce, "that is, a representation that seeks to make itself definite, or seeks to produce an interpretant more definite than itself" (*NE* 4.261). As Paul Ricoeur points out in his reevaluation of the hermeneutic circle,[70] the process or result of interpretation need not reflect merely circular reasoning or understanding; teleology in Peirce's system may be understood not in terms of circularity, but rather, in Shapiro's view, "it is more precisely a spiral, consisting of organically successive complementary links."[71] Shapiro's terminology describes the conjunctive development of reader and text in semeiosis, while it also recalls the expansive coils of interlace and the connecting triangles of object signs, both means of imaging the semiotic construction of meaning in *Beowulf*.

I conclude this brief overview of Peirce's thinking on teleology and subjectivity, and return to the poem, approaching this final sign-sequence with several Peircean questions in mind. To what extent, for example, does the increasing determinacy of the signs of the poem define a path out of Secondness? The very insistence of Secondness, the networks of reinforcements of a particular mode, might in themselves point to Thirdness. In his study of interlace in *Beowulf,* Nicholson concludes that the recurrence inherent in the interlace technique, while it may not provide directionality, may still be an insistent and subtle way of raising "the great questions of the poem."[72] How far does the sign interaction of the text itself go toward shaping those questions, or defining a path out of Secondness, and how does the reader also shape and discover this path?

I have argued that the dynamic, indexical mode of sign interaction predominates in *Beowulf,* but that this predominance by no means precludes the possibility of the synthesizing force of Thirdness. The signs of the poem achieve such synthesis par excellence on occasion; although, as we shall see, the continual translation of signs precludes stasis or resolution—a Final interpretant remains *in futuro*—Hrothgar's so-called sermon (lines 1700–84) is a remarkable and multifaceted prism of sign interaction. Beowulf has defeated Grendel and his mother and is about to return home; Hrothgar warns the young hero of the dangers of pride and reminds him of his own mortality. The "sermon" is inspired as Hrothgar gazes on the hilt of the giant sword from Grendel's cave (the blade has dissolved in the poisonous blood of the monsters). This, and Grendel's head—another powerfully literal index in the poem—were the only "treasures" that Beowulf carried home as spoils.

At this point in the narrative, the sword hilt may be seen as several signs—icon, index, and symbol. It is a gorgeous, gleaming esthetic object, one of the many objects in the poem whose visual and physical presence is strongly evoked. The iconicity, the quality of Firstness, of precious objects emerges as a result of the rich vocabulary attached to them, the many epithets and descriptive compounds that often extract and focus on a single quality, a gleam, or pattern. A sword may be a *beaduleoma* ("battlelight," line 1523) as it flashes in battle; it may be *brunecg* ("brown-edged," line 1546) or *grægmæl* ("gray-colored/marked," line 2682) according to the bronze or silvery metallic cast of the gleam of its blade; it may be *swate fah* ("stained/colored with blood," line 1286) or *since fage* ("adorned with treasure/jewels," line 1615). The icon, or image, can flicker and change, like the cross in the *Dream of the Rood,* as the poet exploits the several meanings and forms of *fag/fah* ("colored," "stained," "decorated," "variegated"). He describes Hrunting, the sword given to Beowulf by an apparently repentant Unferth, as *atertanum fah* ("gleaming/stained with venom-twigs," line 1459), an "excellent kenning for serpents," Davidson suggests, and an "imaginative way of describing the serpentine patterns on the blade which caught the fancy of Cassiodorus long before."[73] The metonymic quality and context of the descriptive compound also contributes to the visual presence, the present impact of the object's iconicity, the evocation and intimation (which cannot be actualized) of the idea of pure quality and feeling that is Firstness. The gorgeous hilt of the giant sword gleams within, reflects, the narrative:

Swa wæs on ðæm scennum sciran goldes
þurh runstafas rihte gemearcod,
geseted ond gesæd, hwam þæt sweord geworht,
irena cyst ærest wære,
wreoþenhilt ond wyrmfah. (lines 1694–98)

On the sword-guards of shining gold it was rightly marked out in runestaves, set down and told, for whom that sword, best of irons, was first made, with twisted hilt and serpentine markings.

In a narrative and thematic context, the giant sword hilt is one of the most significant objects in the poem, and its iconicity is comprehensive. Lewis Nicholson points out that the description of the artifact in some instances "suggests the texture of the poetry itself,"[74] and this is certainly true of this highly sophisticated icon, a kind of portrait of the poem. It functions in much the same way as a diagram, or an algebraic equation that "*exhibits* . . . the relations of the quantities concerned" (2.274), which are the visual and textual (narrative) structure. The hilt could be seen as an icon of the text, which Hrothgar takes up as *the text* for his sermon, and which he then *reads* and *interprets* within the text.

This remarkable prism of sign interaction and apparent synthesis has even more facets. Is Hrothgar actually *reading* the sword as text, or is he making it his own text, or are we as readers claiming it as our text? James Earl argues that the appearance of the magical giant sword hilt and Hrothgar's "reading" of it represent one of the "few clearly symbolic portions of the narrative" that the poet explicates for us.[75] It "announces its own role in the poem . . . it is an iconographic commentary upon the destruction of the race of Grendel, which Beowulf has just accomplished."[76]

Frantzen, on the other hand, calls attention to the fact that the story on the hilt is one of beginnings, not endings: "the sword hilt may not depict the end of the race of Cain, but rather the flood that tried unsuccessfully to end that race."[77] One of the main purposes of Frantzen's thought-provoking argument is to show how the story on the hilt is actually a textual *aporia*, one of the poem's many gaps and puzzles, one of the several untold stories in the poem awaiting telling, and one that tempts the reader to take over and finish the poet's task. From the point of view of sign interaction, however, let me first postulate that when Hrothgar "interprets" the sword hilt the icon becomes translated into a symbol. We can read the sermon as an assemblage of many of the possible dynamic interpretants of the sword signs; the hilt is an epitomizing, encapsulating icon, while it also seems to clear a pathway through and out of the grip of Secondness into Thirdness.

The hilt initially retains, like so many of the other objects in the poem, a powerful indexical function: not only do the rune staves "spell out" the origin and history of ancient strife (*fyrngewinnes*, line 1689), the presence of the hilt operates as Hrothgar's cue to speak. But Hrothgar interrupts the indexical pointer to combat, breaks the chain reaction and makes the hilt itself an object; his speech is an associative, connecting flow of dynamic interpretants over which Hrothgar apparently assumes control because he allows, in fact insists upon, the symbolicity of the object. Again, a diagram (see Figure 4) may be a clearer way to describe how the speech works from a semeiotic standpoint, although my rough paraphrases of this powerful speech should be understood as merely functional, shortcut references to one of the most complex and debated passages in the poem.

Returning to the issues of teleology, of directions and goals, and of the reader's contribution to constructing meaning, I am left with more questions and the emerging presence of paradox. Perhaps all Hrothgar has done in his famous sermon is to contribute his own collateral experience to our ongoing interpretation of the sword signs in the poem. Perhaps we have made the king make connections that simply are not there. Frantzen suggests that we cannot read a story that is not told, nor interpret a text that simply is not there: "the episode involving Hrothgar and the sword hilt relates an event no one has witnessed," and Hrothgar does not, as some believe, construct "an exegesis of the story on the hilt."[78] Or perhaps, on the basis of the comprehensive symbolicity and temporal synthesis of his interpretation, the king has at least succeeded in defining a trajectory for the sword signs and we may identify, or tentatively assign a Final interpretant to, a definitive meaning, for the sword sign. This might be something like change, or death, or transience, or mortality—the kind of interpretant that rarely acknowledges "sufficient consideration" and does not lend itself to finite, tidy resolution.

The speech is certainly a multifaceted point of sign synthesis—regard-

Hrothgar's sermon: 1700-1784

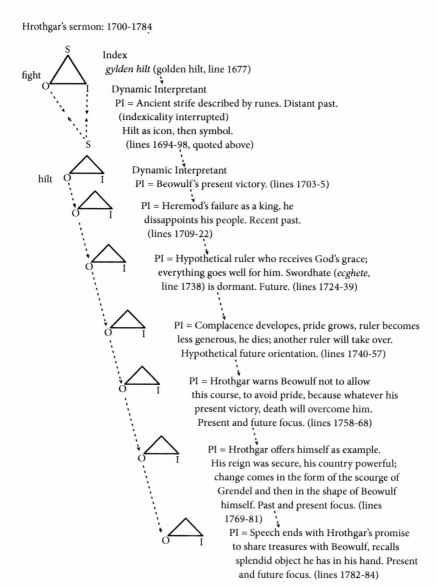

Index
gylden hilt (golden hilt, line 1677)

fight

Dynamic Interpretant
PI = Ancient strife described by runes. Distant past.
(indexicality interrupted)
Hilt as icon, then symbol.
(lines 1694-98, quoted above)

hilt

Dynamic Interpretant
PI = Beowulf's present victory. (lines 1703-5)

PI = Heremod's failure as a king, he
dissappoints his people. Recent past.
(lines 1709-22)

PI = Hypothetical ruler who receives God's grace;
everything goes well for him. Swordhate (*ecghete*,
line 1738) is dormant. Future. (lines 1724-39)

PI = Complacence developes, pride grows, ruler becomes
less generous, he dies; another ruler will take over.
Hypothetical future orientation. (lines 1740-57)

PI = Hrothgar warns Beowulf not to allow
this course, to avoid pride, because whatever his
present victory, death will overcome him.
Present and future focus. (lines 1758-68)

PI = Hrothgar offers himself as example.
His reign was secure, his country powerful;
change comes in the form of the scourge of
Grendel and then in the shape of Beowulf
himself. Past and present focus. (lines
1769-81)

PI = Speech ends with Hrothgar's promise
to share treasures with Beowulf, recalls
splendid object he has in his hand. Present
and future focus. (lines 1782-84)

Figure 4

less of who is doing the synthesizing and why—but its symbolic, contemplative stasis is essentially temporary. Whether we contemplate textual exegesis or textual *aporia*, the convergence of the coils of interlace generates the embryo of the continuing pattern as it also leads back to whence it came. We stand at Niles's narrative "crossroads." We can finish the poet's task and tell an untold story for ourselves (always an option). We can either move on to hear Beowulf's version of events as he reports them to his lord Hygelac, a speech wherein the sword sign regains its bloody indexicality as the hero forecasts the failure of Hrothgar's attempts at peaceweaving occasioned by the sight of an old sword (lines 2032–69). Or we can move back to Wealhtheow's speeches and the irresolvable ambiguity they engender.

In fact, Hrothgar's speech offers several possibilities: a path out of, or back into, Secondness, the option of continuing to engage in the reciprocal semeiosis enacted between reader and text, or of finishing the tale, stopping the journey. The path is neither straight nor circular, but a self-generating spiral always on the move. The Secondness in the poem is far from "dead"; "the fork in the road," writes Peirce, "is a third, it supposes three ways" (1.337).

The nature of object-sign interaction, indeed sign interaction in general, in *Beowulf* demonstrates one of the ways in which this poem rests on the horns of a critical dilemma, or perhaps sits squarely on the fence between Secondness and Thirdness, between the dynamic viscerality of the index and the collected synthesis of the symbol, between the thing and the word, between experience and language.[79] The text neither fully succumbs to the self-presence, appropriation, or resolution—albeit temporary—of the hermeneutic endeavor, nor to the deconstructionist freeplay of substitutions in the closure of a text as "finite ensemble." The object signs are always expanding, cross-referring, resonating, accruing, and continually translating meaning, breaking the boundaries of the text as the spirals of interlace spill over the page. The dynamic semeiosis in the poem, paralleling the metonymic mode of its language, resists resolution and finitude, resists withdrawal into expression and a subsequent recourse to, and privileging of, the subject. If we posit continual semeiosis, a text without apparent end, to what extent must we abandon Peircean teleology, or the attempt to answer "the great questions of the poem"?

The poem offers its own solution, or rather, a mode of persistently shaping its own questions. Suppose we were to accept Hrothgar's interpretation of the sword sign, or decide upon it as our own, there remains a curious isomorphism of mode and meaning in *Beowulf*, which I think may be one reason for the fascination it so persistently retains for readers. We can choose to assign a definitive meaning, a Final interpretant to the sword sign, and are then faced with elusive notions of death and transience. Broadly speaking, the signs of the whole poem add up to a similarly elusive total: we are back on Klaeber's "rambling, dilatory" path. The repetitions, convolutions, and wanderings of theme and structure might suggest that the entire poem is "about" process—the nature of change, social, moral, and mortal—perhaps a form of continual questioning and examination of values, heroic and Christian.

In one sense, then, the signs of this text are self-referential, in that their form, the sign interaction, is best characterized by the process of, even *as* a process of, questioning, revaluing—in effect, translation. The kinetic signs of this text display the same "inherent power of expansion" and restless energy reflected so clearly elsewhere in the period in the art form of interlace, where continuity inheres in the pattern.

If the signs of the poem are "about" process, however, Peirce would insist that we as interpreters of signs are a part of that process, that as subjects we too are in process. Peirce's assertion that the self is a product of signs is itself a sign within the continuum of semeiosis (5.313), and anticipates more contemporary views on the problematic of self. In a letter to Lady Welby quoted earlier in this essay, he comments: "I define a Sign as anything which is so determined by something else, called its object, and so determines an effect upon a person, which effect I call its Interpretant, that the latter is mediately determined by the former. My insertion of 'upon a person' is a sop to Cerberus, because I despair of making my own broader conception understood."[80]

Short argues for the comprehensive breadth of Peirce's concept of semeiosis and demonstrates that intentionality and significance are not dependent on human, conscious thought: "Peirce wished to analyze the human mind as a special case of semeiosis, rather than semeiosis as a special application of mind."[81] The notion that we are "in meaning," and not vice versa, surfaces again. The important distinguishing characteristics of human semeiosis may be a "higher degree of self-correctiveness" and "the goal-directed creation and manipulation of signs as well as their goal-directed interpretation,"[82] but the potential for teleological rigidity, as we have seen, is attentuated by Peirce's pragmatism; definitive meaning is a function of the habit of interpretation: "the most perfect account of a concept that words can convey will consist in a description of the habit which that concept is calculated to produce" (5.491). The "limits" of subjectivity are duly acknowledged, engaged, incorporated, one might say programmed into the semeiotic dynamic, as human semeiosis is also defined particularly in terms of change. In Shapiro's words, "Change as an aspect of continuity in human culture thus arises as a concomitant of the teleology of function in all semeiosis."[83]

Peirce's theory of signs comes close to the goal of all semiotics, which, according to Kristeva, should be to establish a kind of science of process, a descriptive methodology that engages but does not privilege the subject. Semiotics must continually postulate the heterogeneity of all types of systems without making pronouncements about them. As long as the speaking subject is itself understood as the subject of a heterogeneous process, Kristeva asserts that "semiotics can lead to a *historical typology of signifying practices* by the mere fact of recognizing the specific status within them of the speaking subject,"[84] a typology that might fulfill the promise of dialectics that Peirce envisioned.[85] If we also see Kristeva's "speaking subject" or producer of signs as "spoken" or as a receiver, we are once more contemplating the problematic of self and the nature of desire: "As we use or receive signs, we produce interpretants. Their significate effects must pass through each of us, each body and each consciousness, before they produce an effect or an action upon the world. *The individual's habit as a semiotic production is both the result and the condition of the social production of meaning*."[86]

Peirce's theory of signs does not venture into psychological or psychoanalytic domains. Although the classes of interpretants cover an individual's emotions, physical energies, and logical capacities, de Lauretis reminds us that Peirce never "so much as suggests what kind of body it is, or how the body is itself produced as a sign *for* the subject."[87] The forces shaping our habits of interpretation or determining the angle of our collateral observation are not directly addressed in Peirce's semeiotic. What it *can* offer directly is, above all, a nonreductive, creative approach to analyzing and more clearly perceiving experience—linguistic, artistic, and otherwise. His concept of sign offers a means of heterogenizing systems, a way of avoiding—or re-creating—categories, like those of words and things, for example, or in the case of *Beowulf*, of swords and signs.

Peirce's semeiotic reveals how the signs of the poem work, how they can work upon us, how we translate and are translated by them, how we are "spoken" by permission. It offers a vocabulary and a means of discovery, as it crosses and conflates our categories of experience, and as it addresses those qualities of the poem that have been previously perceived in art. Peirce's semeiotic can conjure the persistent regenerative energy of movement and the restlessness of dialectic—a preoccupation of the Anglo-Saxon artist tracing the spirals of interlace.

Although Peirce's system stops short of addressing the nature of the production of the self-sign, his concepts of interpretant and of semeiosis as ongoing, expansive process are central to the problematic of desire and gender in that they "usher in a theory of meaning as a continual cultural production that is not only susceptible of ideological transformation, but materially based in historical change."[88] The sociocultural moorings of semiotic meaning add the strands of culturally engendered desire operating within text and reader to the web of interpretation reciprocally enacted/created by text and reader, and so engender both the web of *différance* and the activity of weaving.

NOTES

[1] Overing, *Language, Sign, and Gender in "Beowulf,"* pp. 1–32.

[2] Fr. Klaeber, ed. *"Beowulf" and the Fight at Finnsburg,* 3rd ed. with supplements (Lexington, Mass., 1950), p. lvii.

[3] Frantzen gives several examples of editors' emendations changing or creating meaning in the poem in "Writing the Unreadable *Beowulf*," *Desire for Origins: New Language, Old English, and Teaching the Tradition* (New Brunswick, 1990), pp. 168–200. See also Allen J. Frantzen and Charles L. Venegoni, "The Desire for Origins: An Archaeology of Anglo-Saxon Studies" *Style* 20.2 (1986): 142–56, for an overview of the ideological assumptions that have shaped the course and nature of scholarship in both poetry and prose.

[4] Frantzen, *Desire for Origins*, pp. 79, 175.

[5] J. R. R. Tolkien, "*Beowulf*: The Monsters and the Critics," in *An Anthology of "Beowulf" Criticism*, ed. Lewis E. Nicholson (Notre Dame, 1971), p. 81.

[6] Fred C. Robinson, *"Beowulf" and the Appositive Style* (Knoxville, 1985).

[7] Julia Kristeva, "The Novel as Polylogue," *Desire in Language: A Semiotic Approach to Literature and Art*, ed. Leon S. Roudiez, trans. Thomas Gora, Alice Jardine, and Leon S. Roudiez (New York, 1980), p. 175.

[8] Studies of art and poetry in the Anglo-Saxon period include John Leyerle, "The Interlace Structure of Beowulf," *University of Toronto Quarterly* 37 (1967–68): 1–17; Lewis E. Nicholson, "The Art of Interlace in Beowulf," *Studia Neophilologica* 52 (1980): 237–50; Peter R. Schroeder, "Stylistic Analogies between Old English

Art and Poetry," *Viator* 5 (1974): 185–97; Jackson J. Campbell, "Some Aspects of Meaning in Anglo-Saxon Art and Literature," *Annuale Mediaevale* 15 (1974): 5–45; and Richard A. Lewis, "Old English Poetry: Alliteration and Structural Interlace" *Language and Style* 6 (1973): 196–205. John D. Niles discusses the cumulative and cyclical aspects of *Beowulf* in "Ring Composition and the Structure of *Beowulf*," *PMLA* 94 (1979): 924–35, where he sees his study as a continuation of Leyerle's work on interlace (p. 933). See also the "Style and Structure" section of Niles's *"Beowulf": The Poem and its Tradition* (Cambridge, Mass., 1983). For an extended discussion of artistic and literary structural principles in several Old English poems, see Bernard F. Huppé, *The Web of Words* (Albany, 1970). Ruth Mellinkoff looks at some connections between serpentine imagery in manuscript illumination and biblical texts in "Serpent Imagery in the Illustrated Old English Hexateuch," *Modes of Interpretation in Old English Literature*, ed. Phyllis Rugg Brown, Georgia Ronan Crampton, and Fred C. Robinson (Toronto, 1986), pp. 51–64.

[9]   Thomas Shippey, *Old English Verse* (London, 1972), p. 28.

[10] Carl Nordenfalk, *Celtic and Anglo-Saxon Painting* (New York, 1977), pp. 18–19.

[11] Leyerle, "The Interlace Structure of *Beowulf*," p. 8.

[12] Leyerle, "The Interlace Structure of *Beowulf*," p. 14. This view both recalls and reiterates the argument of my chapter "Language: An Overview of Process" (in *Language, Sign, and Gender in "Beowulf"*), where the predominance of the metonymic mode of language allows a greater primacy and closeness to actual cognition.

[13] Morton W. Bloomfield, "'Interlace' as a Medieval Narrative Technique with Special Reference to *Beowulf*," in *Magister Regis: Studies in Honor of R. E. Kaske*, ed. Arthur Groos (New York, 1986), p. 52.

[14] Jonathan Evans, "Episodes in Analysis of Medieval Narrative," *Style* 20.2 (1986): 129.

[15] Wendy Steiner, *The Colors of Rhetoric* (Chicago, 1982), p. 18.

[16] For an overview, see Jonathan Evans, "Medieval Studies and Semiotics: Perspectives on Research," *Semiotics 1984*, ed. John Deely (New York, 1985), pp. 511–21. The 1986 volume of *Style* (20.2) is devoted to a variety of articles on medieval semiotics; see especially Martin Irvine, "Anglo-Saxon Literary Theory Exemplified in Old English Poems: Interpreting the Cross in *The Dream of the Rood* and *Elene*," pp. 157–81, and Evans, "Episodes in Analysis of Medieval Narrative," pp. 126–41. For specific reference to *Beowulf* see Evans's "Irony and Ambiguity in the Medieval Dragon Code," *Semiotics 1982*, ed. John Deely and Jonathan Evans (New York, 1983), pp. 141–50. All volumes of *Semiotics* since 1984 contain a separate section on medieval narrative and sign theory, and the 1987 volume of *Semiotica* is a

special medieval studies issue. See also Eugene Vance, *Mervelous Signals: Poetics and Sign Theory in the Middle Ages* (Lincoln, Nebr., 1986), and Paul Zumthor, *Speaking of the Middle Ages*, trans. Sarah White (Lincoln, Nebr., 1986).

[17] See, for example, John Mahoney's dissertation, "The Monodramatic Structure of *Beowulf*" (Auburn, 1975), which applies Peircean models to the poem.

[18] Charles S. Hardwick, ed., *Semiotics and Significs: The Correspondence between Charles Peirce and Victoria Lady Welby* (Bloomington, 1977), pp. 85–86.

[19] References to Peirce's work are from several sources: *The Collected Papers of Charles Sanders Peirce*, 8 vols., ed. C. Hartshorne and P. Weiss (vols. 1–6), and A. Burks (vols. 7–8) (Cambridge, Eng., 1931–58). References to the *Collected Papers* will follow the standard notation of volume and paragraph number, e.g., 5.591. References to Peirce's *The New Elements of Mathematics*, 4 vols., ed. Carolyn Eisele (The Hague, 1976) will be prefaced by *NE*, e.g., *NE* 1.343.

[20] Quoted in Hardwick, *Semiotics and Significs*, pp. 80–81.

[21] Quoted in Hardwick, *Semiotics and Significs*, pp. 31–32.

[22] See Kaja Silverman, *The Subject of Semiotics* (Oxford, 1983), pp. 14–25, and Teresa de Lauretis, "Semiotics and Experience," *Alice Doesn't: Feminism, Semiotics, Cinema* (Bloomington, 1984), pp. 172–81. For a discussion of Peirce's concept of subjectivity and its implications for literary criticism, see Walter Benn Michaels, "The Interpreter's Self: Peirce on the Cartesian 'Subject,'" *Reader-Response Criticism*, ed. Jane P. Tompkins (Baltimore, 1980), pp. 185–200.

[23] De Lauretis, *Alice Doesn't*, p. 172.

[24] Silverman, *The Subject of Semiotics*, p. 314.

[25] Umberto Eco, *A Theory of Semiotics* (Bloomington, 1976), p. 168.

[26] For one of the best introductions to Peirce, which gives a particularly lucid overview and an explanation and breakdown of Peirce's categories and terminology, see Michael Shapiro, "Peirce's Semeiotic," *The Sense of Grammar: Language as Semeiotic* (Bloomington, 1983), pp. 25–72. Another useful introduction is Max H. Fisch, "Peirce's General Theory of Signs," in *Sight, Sound, and Sense*, ed. Thomas A. Sebeok (Bloomington, 1978), pp. 31–70. Silverman and de Lauretis (cited above) discuss Peirce's connections to contemporary semiotic theory and the applications of his sign theory. See also John K. Sherriff, "Charles S. Peirce and the Semiotics of literature," in *Semiotic Themes*, ed. Richard T. de George (Lawrence, 1981), pp. 51–74.

[27] Peirce's further definitions of the phenomenological categories include the following: "Firstness is the mode of being of that which is such as it is, positively and without reference to anything else. Secondness is the mode of being of that which is such as it is, with respect to a second but regardless of any third. Thirdness is the mode of being of that which is such as it is, in bringing a second and third into relation to each other" (quoted in Hardwick, *Semiotics and Significs*, p. 24).

[28] Here is a sampling of Peirce's definitions of icon, symbol, and index:

"An *Icon* is a sign which refers to the Object that it denotes merely by virtue of characters of its own, and which it possesses, just the same, whether any such Object exists or not" (2.243).

"The icon has no dynamical connection with the object it represents; it simply happens that its qualities resemble those of that object" (2.299).

"A pure icon can convey no positive or factual information. . . . But it is of the utmost value for enabling its interpreter to study what would be the character of such an object in case any such did exist. Geometry sufficiently illustrates that" (4.447).

"Of a completely opposite nature is the kind of representamen (sign) termed an *index*. This is a real thing or fact which is a sign of its object by virtue of being connected with it as a matter of fact and also by forcibly intruding upon the mind, quite regardless of its being interpreted as a sign" (4.447).

"Indices . . . direct the attention to their objects by blind compulsion" (2.306).

"Because compulsion is essentially *hic et nunc*, the occasion of the compulsion can only be represented to the listener by compelling him to have experience of that same occasion. Hence it is requisite that there should be a sign which shall act dynamically upon the reader's attention. . . . Such a sign I call an *Index*" (2.336).

"It [the index] is in dynamical (including spatial) connection both with the individual object, on the one hand, and with the senses or memory of the person for whom it serves as a sign, on the other hand" (2.305).

"A Symbol is a representamen [sign] whose representative character consists precisely in its being a rule that will determine its Interpretant" (2.292).

"A Symbol is a law, or regularity of the indefinite future" (2.293).
"The being of a symbol consists in the real fact that something surely will be experienced if certain conditions be satisfied. Namely, it will influence the thought and conduct of its interpreter" (4.447).

[29] Michael Shapiro, *The Sense of Grammar: Language as Semeiotic* (Bloomington, 1983), p. 40.

[30] Quoted in Hardwick, *Semiotics and Significs*, p. 111.

[31] Jacques Derrida, *Speech and Phenomena*, trans. David B. Allison (Evanston, 1973), p. 38.

[32] Steiner, *The Colors of Rhetoric*, p. 21.

[33] Shapiro, *The Sense of Grammar*, p. 45.

[34] Caroline Brady, "'Weapons' in *Beowulf*: An Analysis of the Nominal Compounds and an Evaluation of the Poet's Use of Them," *Anglo-Saxon England* 8 (1979): 108–09.

[35] Charles R. Dodwell, *Anglo-Saxon Art: A New Perspective* (Ithaca, N.Y., 1982), p. 30.

[36] See Dodwell's chapter, "Anglo-Saxon Taste," in *Anglo-Saxon Art*, pp. 24–43, where he repeatedly refers to and demonstrates this "love of resplendence." In this chapter, and throughout the book, Dodwell provides an impressive, extensive collection of examples of the variety of objects customarily adorned with gold or silver.

[37] Dodwell, *Anglo-Saxon Art*, p. 25.

[38] Dodwell, *Anglo-Saxon Art*, p. 24.

[39] Niles, *"Beowulf": The Poem and its Tradition*, p. 223.

[40] In an argument that affirms the positive connotations of treasure, Niles dismisses the notion that Beowulf displayed greed for treasure at the end of the poem. Such a supposition "starts from the premise that all treasure is evil, a point of view that was not common in England and that the poet did not share" (*"Beowulf": The Poem and its Tradition*, p. 220); the treasure buried with the hero is simply "*lof* made visible" (p. 222).

[41] See Michael D. Cherniss, "Treasure: The Material Symbol of Human Worth," *Ingeld and Christ: Heroic Concepts and Christian Values in Old English Christian Poetry* (The Hague, 1972).

[42] S. Viswanathan, "On the Melting of the Sword: *Waelrapas* and the Engraving on the Sword-Hilt in *Beowulf*," *Philological Quarterly* 58 (1979): 360.

[43] See R. L. S. Bruce-Mitford, *The Sutton Hoo Ship Burial* (London, 1968), pp. 19 and 34–35, for a discussion of the missing body in the Sutton Hoo burial.

[44] Bruce-Mitford, *The Sutton Hoo Ship Burial*, p. 53.

[45] Michael D. Cherniss, "The Cross as Christ's Weapon: The Influence of Heroic Literary Tradition on *The Dream of the Rood*," *Anglo-Saxon England* 2 (1973: 245.

[46] H. E. Davidson, *The Sword in Anglo-Saxon England* (Oxford, 1962), pp. 21–23.

[47] Davidson, *The Sword in Anglo-Saxon England*, p. 106.

[48] For a detailed discussion of these and other descriptive epithets for swords, see Caroline Brady's comprehensive study, "'Weapons' in *Beowulf*: An Analysis of the Nominal Compounds and an Evaluation of the Poet's Use of Them," *Anglo-*

Saxon England 8 (1979): 79–141. See also A. T. Hatto, "Snake-swords and Boarhelms in *Beowulf*," *English Studies* 38 (1957): 145–60.

[49] Davidson, *The Sword in Anglo-Saxon England*, pp. 211–12.

[50] Hatto, "Snake-swords and Boarhelms in *Beowulf*," p. 148.

[51] Hatto, "Snake-swords and Boarhelms in *Beowulf*," p. 147.

[52] N. D. Isaacs, "The Convention of Personification in *Beowulf*," *Old English Poetry: Fifteen Essays*, ed. Robert Creed (Providence, 1967), p. 216.

[53] Taylor Culbert discusses these passages in detail in "The Narrative Function of Beowulf's Swords," *Journal of English and Germanic Philology* 59 (1960): 13–20.

[54] See also Robinson's comments on this passage and personification in *Beowulf* in *"Beowulf" and the Appositive Style*, p. 73.

[55] It should be noted that the interchangeability of words, deeds, and things forms a system of circulation, a chain of signification, in which the women of the poem do not participate.

[56] Gilles Deleuze and Felix Guattari, *Anti-Oedipus*, trans. Robert Hurley, Mark Seem, and Helen R. Lane, (New York, 1977), p. 202.

[57] Deleuze and Guattari, *Anti-Oedipus*, p. 205.

[58] Deleuze and Guattari, *Anti-Oedipus*, p. 202.

[59] This kind of analysis has been attempted before, especially in the art/poetry discussions cited in note 8 above, where themes, motifs, and recurrent patterns are examined. As far as I am aware, there has been no attempt to analyze sign interaction in specifically Peircean terms. I have come across one dissertation, "The Monodramatic Structure of *Beowulf*" by John Mahoney (cited in note 17 above), which applies the icon/index/symbol trichotomy to larger structural patterns and rhetorical modes but not to the individual signs in the poem.

[60] Niles, *"Beowulf": The Poem and Its Tradition*, p. 195.

[61] R. E. Kaske, "Weohstan's Sword," *Modern Language Notes* 75 (1960): 465–68, and Adrien Bonjour, "Weohstan's Slaying of Eanmund," *English Studies* 27 (1946): 14–19, present two divergent points of view about the primary significance of this "digression." Kaske sees it as a way to illustrate the ideal of good retainership, whereas Bonjour sees it as a way of connecting all the events associated with the sword. A Peircean model of sign interaction, however, can accommodate both points of view; it can encompass the variety of the sword signs' connotations and account for their dynamic interaction.

[62] Shapiro, *The Sense of Grammar*, p. 30.

[63] Shapiro, *The Sense of Grammar*, pp. 55–56.

[64] Nicholson, "The Art of Interlace," pp. 245–46.

[65] T. L. Short, "Semeiosis and Intentionality," *Transactions of the Charles S. Peirce Society* 17 (1981): 214.

[66] De Lauretis, *Technologies of Gender*, p. 40.

[67] De Lauretis, *Alice Doesn't*, p. 182.

[68] Shapiro, *The Sense of Grammar*, p. 58.

[69] For a longer discussion of Peirce, teleology, and artistic semeiosis, see Michael Shapiro, "Remarks on the Nature of the Autotelic Sign," *Georgetown University Roundtable on Languages and Linguistics* 1982 (Washington, D. C., 1982), pp. 101–11.

[70] See my chapter "Language: An Overview of Process," *Language, Sign, and Gender in "Beowulf,"* p. 11.

[71] Shapiro, *The Sense of Grammar*, p. 10.

[72] Nicholson, 'The Art of Interlace," p. 250.

[73] Davidson, *The Sword in Anglo-Saxon England*, p. 130.

[74] Lewis E. Nicholson, "Hunlafing and the Point of the Sword," in *Anglo-Saxon Poetry: Essays in Appreciation for John C. McGalliard*, ed. Lewis E. Nicholson and Dolores Warwick Frese (Notre Dame, 1975), p. 57.

[75] James W. Earl, "The Necessity of Evil in *Beowulf,*" *South Atlantic Bulletin* 44 (1979): 81.

[76] Earl, "The Necessity of Evil," p. 84.

[77] Frantzen, *Desire for Origins*, p. 188.

[78] Frantzen, *Desire for Origins*, pp. 187–88.

[79] As the poem is poised between Secondness and Thirdness, it is also poised between correlated types of interpretants, dynamic and final. I have referred only to Peirce's second trichotomy of interpretants, immediate/dynamic/final; this overlaps with the first trichotomy, emotional/energetic/logical, to produce some much finer cross-distinctions, which might also describe this "fence" or place between experience and language that the poem can inhabit. Peirce's categories minutely and repeatedly intersect, making for subtleties of definition that I have not been able to address in this short study. One can have a dynamic logical interpretant, or "Firstnesses of Firstness, of Secondness and of Thirdness" (Shapiro, *The Sense of Grammar*, p. 53). For further discussion of these distinctions, I again refer the reader to Shapiro, "Remarks on the Nature of the Autotelic Sign," and to Short, "Semeiosis and Intentionality," pp. 197–223.

[80] Quoted in Hardwick, *Semiotics and Significs*, pp. 80–81.

[81] Short, "Semeiosis and Intentionality," p. 203.

[82] Short, "Semeiosis and Intentionality," p. 220.

[83] Shapiro, *The Sense of Grammar*, p. 212.

[84] Julia Kristeva, "The System and the Speaking Subject," *The Kristeva Reader*, ed. Toril Moi (New York, 1986), p. 32.
[85] Kristeva, "The System and the Speaking Subject," p. 31.
[86] De Lauretis, *Alice Doesn't*, p. 173.
[87] De Lauretis, *Alice Doesn't*, p. 183.
[88] De Lauretis, *Alice Doesn't*, p. 172.

HROTHGAR'S HILT AND THE READER IN BEOWULF

SETH LERER

Fighting with Grendel's mother at the bottom of the mere, Beowulf seizes an enormous sword and runs its patterned blade through the monster. Turning to the dead Grendel, he cuts off his head and soon realizes that the sword's blade has melted clean away in the heat of his blood. Taking only the hilt and the head as his treasures, Beowulf returns to shore and to Heorot and presents the relics of his fight to Hrothgar.

> Hroðgar maðelode, hylt sceawode,
> ealde lafe. On þæm was or writen
> fyrn-gewinnes, syðþan flod ofsloh,
> gifen geotende, giganta cyn;
> frecne geferdon; þæt wæs fremde þeod
> ecean Dryhtne; him þæs ende-lean
> þurh wæteres wylm Waldend sealde.
> Swa wæs on ðæm scennum sciran goldes
> þurh run-stafas rihte gemearcod,
> geseted ond gesæd, hwam þæt sweord geworht,
> irena cyst, ærest wære,

From *Literacy and Power in Anglo-Saxon England* (Lincoln, Nebr., 1991), pp. 158–94. Reprinted by permission of the University of Nebraska Press. The only alterations to the original have been to remove references Lerer makes in the body of the essay to other sections of the book in which this essay originally appeared, and to convert the original "works cited" method of reference to footnotes.

wreoþen-hilt ond wyrm-fah. Ða se wisa spræc,
sunu Healfdenes—swigedon ealle—: (lines 1687–99)[1]

> Hrothgar spoke—he looked on the hilt, the old heirloom on which was writ-
> ten the origin of ancient strife, when the flood, rushing water, slew the race
> of giants—they suffered terribly: that was a people alien to the Everlasting
> Lord. The Ruler made them a last payment through water's welling. On the
> sword-guard of bright gold there was also rightly marked through rune-
> staves, set down and told, for whom that sword, best of irons, had first been
> made, its hilt twisted and ornamented with snakes. Then the wise man
> spoke, the son of Healfdene—all were silent. (Donaldson, p. 30)

This passage has most often been the object of primarily archeological
and grammatical questions. Is the hilt inscribed solely in runes, or does
it offer a mix of runic and pictographic signs? Does it represent a species
of historical object—whether from early Scandinavia or Anglo-Saxon
England—or is it an imaginative fiction of the poet? What are the origins
of its unique vocabulary, and what is the purpose of the jarring break in
the narrative of Hrothgar's speechmaking? The answers to these and to the
many other more specific questions that have been proposed over the last
century provide the background for my own reassessment of the sword-
hilt's physical archaeology and literary history.[2] My concern, however, is
not only to identify the hilt, but to affiliate it with the traditions of crypti-
cally inscribed objects. The hilt confronts the reader with an alien set of
signs; it challenges the viewer to interpret and explain; and it impresses the
beholder as a work of artifice, whose intricate and possibly otherworldly
workmanship reflects on the techniques of verbal craft that shape its literary
presentation.

My purpose here is to understand the hilt scene in the context of the other
scenes of reading which appear in Anglo-Saxon narratives as loci for reflec-
tions on the reader's own relationship to texts, to authors, and to Christian
culture generally. My purpose, too, is to place the episode within the poem's
governing dramatic structure as a way of reconceiving *Beowulf*'s thematic
interest in the forms of making. These lines counterpoint the *scop*'s song of
Creation at the poem's opening, offering a written document of destruction
in contrast to an oral narrative of origins. The vision of the hilt also plays
against the many wondrous works of human and inhuman artifice that fill
the story, most notably Heorot itself and Grendel's glove. Taken together,
these scenes frame the presentation of the hilt and its inscription as a mo-

ment of poetic self-reflection. They invite the audience to understand the place of literature within the human community and to attempt to come to terms with the fantastic or the mythological within that literature.

Moving from the specific to the general, I hope first to explicate some features of the scene's verbal structure, its dramatic quality, and its potential source material in Scandinavian epigraphy. Second, I intend to offer ways of understanding Hrothgar as a type of reader and to suggest an approach to his so-called sermon as a vocalized response to the hilt's text. Third, I claim that in the hilt itself we may find a figure for the poem as a whole. Its inscribed, mythic text comes to represent the larger document of history and marvel that is the narrative of *Beowulf*. To comprehend the ways in which the poem, in effect, represents itself, I turn to Beowulf's narration of the fight with Grendel offered on his homecoming to Hygelac's court. Here, in what I take to be critical retelling of the poem to this point, the hero becomes his own poet. His performance contrasts with the professional accounts of both *scop* and rune master, and read together, they inform us of the poem's governing conceptions of narrative authority, social recitation, and textual interpretation. To speak, then, of the "literacy" of *Beowulf* is to speak of the poet's familiarity with runes, Hrothgar's hermeneutic skills, Beowulf's heroic eloquence, and the status of the poem itself as a text in need of critical interpretation.

Throughout the nearly three centuries of *Beowulf*'s reception, that need for critical interpretation has been focused on a set of issues dealing primarily, though not exclusively, with dating, history, and Christian content.[3] Traditionally, the relationship between the poet and his material has been seen in terms of these three issues and as questions in the varying degrees of knowledge he and his sources, or his characters, share. The poet and his audience, for example, "know" about God and Creation in ways that Beowulf and his companions do not; or, from a different angle, the poem's allusive fragments of Swedish history testify to a knowledge of events that the poet does not share with his imagined characters or their historical forebears. The critical adjudication of problems of this nature depends on many, often tacit, assumptions about the poem's date and mode of composition, the constitution of its audience, and the circumstances of its transcription.[4] The myriad confusions that surround the *Beowulf* manuscript itself, and the interpretations silently enshrined in printed editions that use modern punctuation and capitalization, only add to any insecurities attending a reader of the poem.[5]

Without denying the importance of these current scholarly conundrums, I hope to realign the terms of their investigation. The contrast between the pagan credence in the magic of the letter and the Christian faith in the word as symbol may point to a new way of phrasing the Christian quality of *Beowulf*. Notions of language and its relation to political power come to play in the heroic eloquence of king and hero. The techniques of riddling, and the fascination with the works of verbal and plastic artifice that informs the Exeter Book collection, governs *Beowulf*'s presentation of wrought objects and their understanding. And the notion of the literacy of the self-conscious narrator, and the conception of vernacular poetry as a visualized object, finds an application here in relation to the work of Charles Segal.[6] His arguments on the place of literacy in the construction of poetic authority work in tandem with his understanding of the presence of the oral poet and the absence of the writer in early Greek literatures. Both provide the bridge to my concluding speculations on *Beowulf* and the *Odyssey* as romances whose heroes tell and retell stories of their past.

· · ·

Taken first in isolation, the hilt scene achieves its effects through a complex pattern of rhetorical envelopes, a unique and highly specific vocabulary, and a jarring break in the narrative continuity of the story. It begins with the announcement of Hrothgar's speechmaking, only to break off that speech before it begins. The verbs of its first line shift abruptly from speaking to looking, from the assertion of a verbal performance to the mute apprehension of a thing. The king "looked upon the hilt" (*hylt sceawode*, line 1687), and in this action Hrothgar comes initially to be affiliated with the uncomprehending warriors who, throughout the poem, gaze in wonder at the relics of an alien kingdom. Upon confronting Grendel's severed arm in Heorot, for example, men can only "behold the marvel" (*wundor sceawian*, line 840). When Hrothgar's men idly spear a sea creature at Grendel's mere, they mutely stare at its beached form ("weras sceawedon / gryrelicne gist," lines 1440–41). Faced with such remnants of the other world, the Danes are left speechless. They see that world only through the dead or dismembered creatures who no longer can inhabit it. They differ both from hero and from king in that none of them confronts directly or recounts in words their own experience. Whereas Beowulf can swim through Grendel's mere or Hrothgar can tell legends of its origin, these men see the monstrous only as an object or a relic. They offer up a kind of negative model for the poem's audience, as their visions spark neither word nor action. In contrast, then, to this expected response, Hrothgar's moment with the hilt differs in both its specificity of detail and its provocation of advice. This is an object with a definite history and story of its own. That story, we are told, appears inscribed upon the hilt, and that inscription may contain the stimulus for Hrothgar's following advisory account of moral action and heroic life. It also, I argue, stimulates our own responses to the nature of writing in the epic and to the place of mythic narrative in the construction of a civilized readership. While thus beginning in a manner seemingly familiar to the poem's audience, the episode soon challenges their expectations, and it is my plan in what follows to chart the details of that challenge.

The inscription in particular, and the episode as a whole, works through a series of paired oppositions. The two parts of the hilt's description pivot on the word *swa*, "also," and it is at the very least clear that in this structure, the poem juxtaposes monstrous strife and divine retribution against the physical craft and individual commission that produced the sword. The alienation of the giants contrasts with the rightful possession of the sword; the power of the Ruler opposes the skill of the rune carver. Both halves, in a sense, tell the same story of control and power, the one divine, the other artistic. But, of course, they frame their stories in perhaps the most dissimilar of worlds: the flood and the forge, the ancient past and recorded memory, the collection of giants and the sword's single owner. These verbal contrasts build in the course of the passage until Hrothgar reappears, now ready to speak as the hall falls silent. The poet's second announcement, "Ða se wisa spræc" ("Then the wise man spoke," line 1698b), returns us to his initial phrasing, "Hroðgar maþelode" ("Hrothgar spoke," line 1687a), and these two half-lines set off the hilt and its inscription from the ongoing flow of the narrative. They bracket the entire scene and frame within its larger envelope the more detailed and complicated contrasts between the two parts of the inscription. By concentrically enclosing its *run-stafas* ("rune-staves," line 1695a) with announcements of speechmaking and descriptions of verbal and pictorial ornament, the poet's lines envelop the hilt's text. His poem mimes the function and the vision of the hilt itself, making a verbal construct on a par with this metallic one. The affirmations of divine control, or the rune carver's ability, reflect upon the poet's skills as well, for like the hilt's inscription his words, too, are "rihte gemearcod, / geseted ond gesæd" ("rightly marked, set down and told," lines 1695b-96a). Set as they are in proper order, these words call attention to the poet's own command of traditional poetic technique at the very moment of his representation of a crafted, mythic text.

The patterns I have identified here, patterns of ring-composition or interlace, operate in the hilt episode according to the conventions John Niles has seen as the controlling form for many of the poem's dramas. "Ring composition," he states, "enables the poet to ease into and out of a picture of past terrors," and following the narrator's vision, we do just that, easing into and out of the giants' threat and God's retribution while remaining secure in Hrothgar's hall.[7] The repetitions of Hrothgar's speechmaking will form the points of entry and of exit into that "past terror." They break the poem's story so that the poet may recount *another* story, and in so doing, sustain two simultaneous narratives. This structure helps facilitate what Niles calls "traveling from immediate reality . . . to an 'other,' legendary reality that is used as a point of comparison . . . and then back again to the present reality."[8] Here, that immediate reality includes the scene of presentation in Heorot, with its rituals of fealty and ideals of lordship. Posed against it is the legendary reality of the war of the giants, and later, that of the sword's original owner and its fall into another giant's possession. Ring-composition in this passage helps create, delineate, and frame an alternate world against whose terrors we may measure the benign power of Hrothgar's rule and the comfort of the hall's community of men.

It has long been noticed that these rhetorical manipulations shift not only our sense of space within the poem, but our sense of time, as well. The breaks in continuity they foster have most recently been compared with what Erich Auerbach has labeled the "retarding element" in Homeric narrative. Implicit in Marijane Osborn's reading of the episode is a comparison with Auerbach's conception of the Homeric excursus, a device by which "a newly introduced character, or even a newly appearing object or implement . . . is described as to its nature and origin."[9] The effect of this technique, Auerbach states, is "to represent phenomena in a fully externalized form, visible and palpable in all their parts, and completely fixed in their spatial and temporal relations."[10] Osborn, I think, is right to pull away from a complete mapping of this view of the Homeric style on to the style of *Beowulf*; but instead of couching this critical contrast in the terms of history and scripture, as she does, I would favor a relationship based on reader response. Throughout the poem, narrative time elapses in what might be called the time of telling. The half-day of the hero's swim through Grendel's mere, or more extremely, the generations that trace the history of Denmark from Scyld through Hrothgar, are all, of course, compressed within the narrator's brisk recitation. The gap between the time sequence of telling and the time sequence of fictional events is, as in a variety of literatures, a wide one.[11] Time sequences are not real or mimetic in the poem, save at the moment of the hilt's appearance. The poet's rhetorical bracketing shifts our apprehension of elapsed time from the period it takes to narrate action to the time it takes to read a text. The narrator's account of what is on the hilt is, as everyone has noticed, not a complete verbatim transcript of its text.[12] Rather, it offers an indirect description whose length and detail mime the time and level of attention of the hilt's reader. As it moves from the description of the giants' war to the runic name, it traces the movements of the reader's eye. It is an isolated moment of what may be labeled reader's time: sustained narration that elapses in precisely the same time-frame of the reader's world.

This notion of a reader's time helps clarify the nature of Hrothgar's vision of the hilt and our own relationship to Hrothgar as a figure for the reader. Unlike the epic retardation and the foregrounding of Homeric style, *Beowulf*'s technique here moves us not between moments in history but between moments of interpretation. What Auerbach calls the "absolute" quality of the Homeric foreground, its "local and temporal present,"[13] is absent from the Old English epic in favor of a more fluid and perhaps ambiguous present, one that simultaneously affiliates and differentiates the poem's characters from its audience. Osborn begins in this direction when she asserts that, during the period Hrothgar gazes on the hilt, "considering what to say, the poet tells *us* what is written on it. . . . But we are not told that Hrothgar reads what he is looking at."[14] The purpose of the pause, in her account, is to separate the audience from the king and to provide them with a body of information he cannot have: in her terms, a "scriptural context" for the strife narrated on the hilt. "He gazes upon the hilt, and the information which the poet provides *us* during this pause gives a scriptural context for the wisdom that Hrothgar subsequently reveals about the recurrent feud with mankind's enemy within the human breast."[15]

Osborn is certainly right that pagan king and Christian audience differ in their understanding of a text possibly resonant with scriptural allusion and moral force. Certainly, the mention of the giants and the affirmations of the *ecean Dryhten* ("everlasting Lord," line 1692a) send the Christian reader to specific Bible texts and traditions. But I think that what is at stake here, and what defines the audience's relationship to the king, is less an issue in the text's doctrinal content than a problem in its rhetoric.[16]

The poet tells us what is written on the hilt both to associate us with the king as readers and to distinguish us as a different kind of reader from him. By showing what is on the hilt and by parceling out that showing in the space of what I have called reader's time, the poet makes his audience experience the object in the same time-frame as Hrothgar does. Our sequence of events precisely matches his, as we are drawn into the narrative time of the poem's fiction. Put somewhat loosely, we could say that the poet imaginatively takes us "inside" Hrothgar's mind, making us see the hilt with his eyes. Put more precisely, we may say that the poet has deferred a full description of the hilt until it comes into Hrothgar's hands, so that the reader and the king come face to face with the inscription all at once. We have known nothing of the hilt's message until the king sees it. In Grendel's mother's den, the narrator calls attention only to the sword's size, adornment, and craftsmanship—that is, only those characteristics Beowulf himself would notice, as its glimmer and enormity catch his glance (lines 1557–69). Unlike the Homeric narrator, the poet does not give the genealogy of "a newly appearing object or implement, though it be in the thick of battle."[17] Instead, we have to wait until the hilt comes to Hrothgar, and neither the narrator nor his heroes notice the inscription until it comes into his possession. Within the drama of the presentation, Hrothgar's apprehension of the writing stops his speech even before it starts. It is as if the king, about to speak, suddenly sees the inscription, and pausing in silence, delays his response until the text is grasped. Then, having absorbed its meaning, Hrothgar can resume his initial response and begin to speak. The poet's narrative technique is thus mimetic of his character's actions, as he suspends time to enable the audience and the king to meditate together on the object and its meaning.

But where those meditations lead are two different places, and it is in the nature of their responses, rather than the simple fact of reading or of doctrine, that the pagan king and Christian audience part company. If we may say that Hrothgar "reads" a text, he does so as a pagan: that is, in the terms of the response to writing and the attitudes toward texts which center on the power of the letter and the marvelous quality of writing itself. If the audience of Christians and the Christian poet are to "read" the text, then they are to see it as a symbolic account of higher power and the possibility of miracle. The question of the pagan or Christian *content* of the hilt is thus a question of its inherent verbal ambiguity. Its vocabulary encodes two sets of references to two different interpretive answers. Of course, the ambiguities of such terms as *dryhten* ("lord") and *wealdend* ("ruler") are obvious, and modern editions that capitalize these words only obscure what Robinson and others have identified as their inherently bivalent nature. The reference to the *gigantas* ("giants"), moreover, can be as much a reference to scriptural history in Genesis as it can be to classical mythology filtered, for example, through the *Consolation of Philosophy*.[18] But where the locus of the Christian/pagan split lies, I think, is in the terms of rune carving and the ordering of the inscription itself. This scene offers what I take to be a pointed set of references to a tradition of pagan, Scandinavian writing found not on swords or hilts, but on stories. It is a tradition of runology that makes both Hrothgar and the hilt participants in an old, Continental system of memorial communication and that grounds the poem's fiction all the more firmly in a Scandinavian setting. My purpose in identifying sources for the poem's diction is not so much to posit its unique literary or archaeological referent, nor is it to deny the plain fact that this is a sword-hilt and that, as recent researches have shown, it does bear similarities to recovered hilts and swords inscribed with runic names or formulas. My claim is that the poet synthesizes information from a variety of artistic sources to construct his picture of this object. He offers an evocative assemblage of traditions to portray a pre-Christian, commemorative runic text and to make the verbal presentation of that text unique within the poem as a whole.

. . .

By drawing upon formulas from runic memorial inscriptions, the *Beowulf*-poet describes a cryptic text or an alien writing in terms of contemporary arcana, thereby alluding to writing of restricted usage and professional skill. But *Beowulf* deploys the language not of *runica manuscripta* (the traditions of scriptorial reflection and runic cryptography), but of runestones, and he embeds his references in the habits not of trained scribes but of rune masters. In particular, it is the poet's use of *writan* and the claim that the owner's name was cut "þurh run-stafas rihte gemearcod / geseted ond gesæd" ("through rune-staves rightly marked, set down and told," lines 1695–96a) which ground his language in the conventions of Scandinavian runology. The verb *writan* appears only here in *Beowulf*, and, like its usage throughout Old English poetry, it connotes the act of runic incision. Etymologically, as well as contextually, *writan* suggests a specific epigraphic system at work in the hilt's first inscription—a suggestion reinforced by the concluding characterization of the owner's name.[19] The poet's phrasing here contains within it all the key terms of the runic signatory formulas. Rune, rightness, and inscription (literally, "setting") all appear as an assertion, not of the hilt's beauty or its form, but of the carver's own adherence to the conventions of his craft. Its verbs of writing, *gemearcod* and *geseted*, hark back to formulaic uses of the signature in Scandinavian monuments. "En Asmund markaði," for example, is but one instance of the Old Norse verb *marka* meaning to cut or carve.[20] In Old English, the past participle *gemearcod* glosses the Latin *signatus*, and together with the Old Norse cognates, such evidence strongly suggests the verb's use as a term of signing and its appearance in *Beowulf* as part of a system of signatory formulas.[21] The other verb of writing, *geseted*, recalls such phrases as Old English "on gewrit settan" ("to put in writing"), and the Old Norse cognate *setja* used in runestones to describe the writing of the letters (as well as the setting up of the stones).[22] As Ann Trygstad notes in her study of Upplandic runography, the form of the verb *sætia*, used in such phrases as *sætia runaR rett* ("to write correct runes") or *sætia runaR rettaR* ("to write runes correctly"), offers "a very special use [of the word] in a very old formula in the writing of runes."[23] This verb, together with the terms for runes and for correctness in the signatory formulas, appears in phrases that distinguish the rune carver's assertions of his talent. They resonate with the vocabulary of the Old English poem, and I would posit that they constitute a purposeful allusion to a specific runic tradition.

As Trygstad and Claiborne Thompson have shown, such a tradition centers on assertions of the carver's skill and the invitations for the reader to match talents with the writer. The claims for right writing, first and foremost, call attention to the problems of orthography in cutting runes. The spelling, spacing, and the very letter-shapes of words were rarely fixed; the sixteen-character Norse *futhorc* precluded the phonetic representation of the spoken word, and "each carver, using a knowledge of orthographic conventions and prevailing speech patterns, had to decide how to represent the sounds of each word or phrase that was to appear on the stone."[24] Armed with an inherently ambiguous writing system, rune carvers would have no doubt felt compelled to assert their mastery of form and figure. The runes that they set rightly are the runes that they claimed to intend, and thus whatever indeterminacies the reader may discern cannot be blamed on the writer. Instead, these carvers challenge their readers to produce correct interpretations. One text, for example, enjoins, "May that man who is wise about runes interpret the runes which Balle carved."[25] Another commands, "Interpret the runes correctly—Tolir had [the runes] carved [correctly]."[26] Runestones may tout the pride of their carver, as the one that claims its creation by "the best runester on the west side of the sea."[27] Or they may associate the carver's mastery of the craft with the possibility of correct interpretation in a causal way, as in a Swedish gravestone: "Brand cut correctly, thus one can interpret."[28]

These, and many other examples collected by Trygstad and Lucien Musset, imply that runic writings often take as one of their subjects the methods of their own encryption and decipherment.[29] They recognize that reading and writing are both individual and social skills, for by challenging the reader to match talents with the carver, these texts foster a community of understanding. They call attention to the codes and formulas through which historical information, biographical data, or moral claims can be exchanged and learned. For not only must the readers know the shapes of letters; they must know the standard formulas of the inscriptions: the words and their order to interpret their referents successfully. Trygstad has classified these formulas into a tripartite sequence of memorial, prayer, and signature. She notes that the memorial inscriptions "typically . . . have three parts . . . the name of the person or persons sponsoring or raising the stone, the act or acts of commemorating, and the name of the person commemorated and his relation to the sponsors."[30] Within this conventional organization, individual rune carvers exercised a certain amount of freedom; in Trygstad's view, whatever departures from epigraphic norms can be found could be variations that are "meaningful" only against the foil of formula. The hilt's description in *Beowulf*, too, may be assessed against the norms of the commemorative sequence. As in a runestone, the hilt conveys memorial information about a people's fate, here the giants killed in the flood. It celebrates the rightful power of a deity in a manner consistent with the prayers and invocations offered on the stones. Finally, by postponing mention of the hilt's ownership until the end of the passage, the *Beowulf*-poet follows the formulas of the inscriptions, for there, the name of carver or of dedicatee comes only after the commemorative statement.

In these attentions to the specific words and formal order of runic inscriptions, the poet imaginatively reproduces what was on the sword. His remark that the runes were carved and set correctly is not a value judgment on his part, but rather resembles an indirect quotation of the kind of phrasing used to sign runic texts. Together with the issues of orthography, the notion of "correctness" (in the Old Norse *rett* or *rettaR*, or the Old English *rihte*) implies adherence to a whole tradition of communication. Such correctness, too, becomes a function of the rune stone's visual appearance—the complex and artistic patterns on the rock face which contribute to the aesthetic impact of the text. In their presentation of inscriptions in interlocking bands or loops, their zoomorphic design, and their overall pictorial effect, the Scandinavian stones would have appeared as visually striking objects. They exemplify a sensibility governed by the harmonious blend of text and picture, letter and interlace. Thompson's classification of the styles of the Upplandic stones, together with the work of earlier accounts of other Scandinavian traditions, points to a sense of structure which can integrate figural representation with more abstract serpentine adornment.[31] What Trygstad calls the "correlation of form and content" which motivates the self-consciousness of the rune carver's work also informs the many other works of Scandinavian artistry that would have been familiar to an English audience. On swords and sword-hilts, such details as filigree decoration, interlacing zoomorphic patterns, and runic inscription often point to Scandinavian workmanship or inspiration. Such objects as the Chessel Down sword, recently compared with the hilt in *Beowulf*, show these features at work in an early piece of military metalcraft, and they form part of a tradition of adornment which found its later expression both in the Swedish runestones and in the *wreoþen-hilt* and *wyrm-fah* ("twisted hilt" and "snake-ornamented," line 1698a) appearance of the poem's description.[32]

At the heart of my associations of the hilt with these artistic forms is the belief that the poet uses Scandinavian formulas to create the impression of an inscribed object whose ordered words and visual appearance are controlled by an aesthetic of the rune. Whatever differences of subject matter we may distinguish, the first and second halves of the hilt's inscription are, I think, overshadowed by the overall impression that the entire inscription is in runes. Such a belief, I recognize, is controversial. Scholars have long debated the nature of the inscription, arguing for blends of runic, alphabetic, and pictorial representation. Osborn summarizes the debate, and compromises: "What is written about the ancient fight suggests that the poet has in mind a combination of runic and nonrunic inscriptions."[33] This split in form, as I have mentioned earlier, is signaled in the text by a shift in grammar. The word *swa* has often been taken as a signal of the differing forms of inscription. Klaeber's glossary translation "also" can imply that, in addition to a nonrunic or pictographic inscription, there was *also written in runes* the name of the dedicatee. But I would argue that the *swa* can work as the coordinating conjunction in a list: that there was *also* written in runes the name of the dedicatee, with the implication that the previous text was also written in runes.[34] My point in this grammatical excursus is to enhance an apprehension of the hilt as a unified whole, to argue that the inscription is wholly runic, and that its elements of decoration complement the writing and evoke the intricate elaborations of a runic monument or Scandinavian metalcraft.

What Hrothgar "sees," then, are these Continental, pagan representations of memorial inscription and interlace design. His vision of the hilt, much like Beowulf's earlier sighting of the entire sword, is conditioned by the moral and dramatic frameworks in which it appears. Just as the hero did not notice the runic inscription in the heat of battle, so Hrothgar sees only those things his environment permits him to see. To a Danish king in a pre-Conversion court, the hilt will come as a familiar object of memorial epigraphy. That we too "see" the hilt through his eyes means that we are granted an appreciation of the techniques of its making and a feel for its appearance. But the poet has provided us with information that the king cannot grasp. In his allusions to what many scholars have identified as scriptural history, the poet provides his Christian readership with an interpretive framework for appreciating the hilt's story. Hrothgar may read the hilt, but what he reads are the memorial conventions of the rune master. We, too, may read the hilt, but what we read are the biblically flavored accounts of a war in heaven. The ambiguities incised within its words, then, do not simply turn on pagan ignorance and Christian knowledge. They hinge, rather, on the differing conventions of interpretation, and the various allusions to a Scandinavian writing and a Christian scripture which, in their synthesis, make the hilt a touchstone for the hermeneutic interests of whoever sees it.

• • •

To this point, I have tried to present two contexts in which to place the hilt: one, within the verbal patterns garnered from a close reading of the episode, the other, in a structure of allusions to a form and a vocabulary outside the poem's fiction. Taken together, they may help reformulate the character of Hrothgar's response to the inscription and the dramatic function of the so-called sermon immediately following it. To say that Hrothgar's sermon is in any sense a "reading" of the hilt or an oration "inspired" by its text might, at first glance, seem misleading.[35] Although there are parallels between his speech and the hilt's writing, the controlling relationship between the two depends on structural comparisons to other narratives. *Beowulf* presents Hrothgar's admonitory speech after the viewing of a cryptic text and offers no formal account of the inscription or its meaning, nor does the poet transcribe into direct discourse the exact words of the text. Instead, the poet offers an indirect report of what I would call *run*: specifically runic, or at the very least mysterious writings. He follows these reports with direct speech, with the *ræd* of his idealized characters. This apposition of text and voice, *run* and *ræd*, enacts what I see as an ancient pairing of the forms of discourse. It is preserved throughout alliterative poetry in the associations of the two words within single lines.[36] The Exeter Book *Maxims* transforms this pairing into an injunction: "Ræd sceal man secgan, rune writan" (line

138). At the most basic level, *ræd* is what is spoken, *run* is what is cut. But more than presenting simple definitions, the line suggests as well a place for speech and writing in society. It avers that advice is public, that it grows from the responses to the life lived, and that it may contain interpretations of the written texts of secret or of learned instruction. *Run* demands *ræd* as a text demands a reading, and the etymologies of *ræd* and "read" should not be overlooked.[37] The early pairings of the forms of **writan* and **reðan* in the runic traditions point to the need for right interpretations of texts.[38] "Rad þu," commands an early runestone[39] and the force of this command survives in those riddles that enjoin the solver to interpret (*rædan*) enigmatic codes. If the hilt presents, figuratively speaking, a kind of riddle, then it is a riddle on a par with the inscribed chalice of Riddle 59, or more generally, with the self-conscious "reading" riddles.[40] We might do well, therefore, to consider Hrothgar's sermon as a solution to the riddle of the hilt.

Within this framework, the sermon solves the hilt by answering its enigmatic story of a war with a precise account of a divinely governed peace. Hrothgar's moral tone, rhetorical control, and historical allusions, long noticed by the critics, make his speech a set piece of address.[41] They also come to represent the governing thematic concerns of the oration. They complement the king's preoccupation with order and control, his vision, in Osborn's words, "of giving as a kind of stability in the world of change."[42] In this concern with governance, the speech answers the hilt's story of strife and challenge. It posits a political and moral world where everything turns toward God's will (lines 1738–39) and where the success of the king's own temporal rule echoes the benign power God wields over mortals. It is a speech that opens with a meditation on the distant past ("feor eal gemon," line 1701), tells tales of vengeance, and gives thanks to an eternal Lord for ending "old strife" ("eald gewin," line 1781). In its emphases, the speech responds to the report of challenge and retribution written on the hilt. To speak more generally, both the text and the speech address problems in the order of the world and in the place of social remembrance in the reverence of divinity. A god who overpowers giants, a runesmith who rightly sets his text, a king who wisely governs his own and his people's impulses—these are the interests that yoke together the *run* and the *ræd* and which render Hrothgar's sermon an informed response to the specifics of the hilt.

But if, as I am suggesting, Hrothgar is a type of reader, and if, in part, he is a model or a foil for *Beowulf*'s own audience, what then is the conception of literature envisioned by the poem? Just what *is* being read, and what is the function of the audience in shaping a social place for poetry?

We have here not the formulaic terms of oral poetry—terms of song-shaping, word-weaving, and the like—but the specific terms of writing and interpretation.[43] We have here not the presentation of a public performance but the controlled evocation of a private reading. Unlike the scenes of oral recitation that appear throughout the poem, and in which most modern scholars have found *Beowulf*'s modeling of its mode of composition and transmission, this scene posits a view of discourse as written and private. It suggests that mythic narrative exists in written documents as well as within oral lore, and that the audience for such accounts can be a reader alone as much as a listener among many. To explore the implications of this argument, and to examine the ways in which the poem defines itself within the narrative, I turn to larger, structural comparisons between the hilt scene, the *scop*'s song of Creation, and Beowulf's own account of Grendel and his wondrous glove.

Within the poem's story as a whole, the hilt scene counterpoints the opening performance of the *scop* in Heorot. The two create an envelope pattern in which the central events of *Beowulf*'s Danish narrative transpire. At the beginning, the audience approaches Heorot through the account of its construction and its social celebrations. The hall appears first as a conception in Hrothgar's mind, and then as a created object named and governed by a king who rules with words. The poet interrupts his report, as he often does, with reference to his own reception of the story of the hall: "Ða ic wide gefrægn . . ." ("Then I have widely heard . . . ," line 74). Conventional though this remark may be, when read in tandem with his characterization of the king as verbal ruler and his following report of poetic performance, it contributes to the concerns of this entire block of narrative as focusing on terms of words and power. Hrothgar names the hall, and in so doing comes to stand as something of a Danish Adam, giving name and nature to the creatures of *his* world. That he will rule through the "power of his words" (*wordes geweald*, line 79) contributes, too, to an impression that language is a source of power for the poem. In the voicings of the king's command we find an earthly equivalent to a divine and a poetic power over experience—a power to be illustrated in the poem's following lines. The sound of the harp and the words of the *scop* celebrate the story of Creation, whereas immediately afterward the poem's narrator frames Grendel's entrance in a post-Edenic genealogy. The force of this entire episode thus hinges on our recollection of a God whose word is His deed, of a first man who names the creatures of the world, and of a first sin in which murder finds its natural ally in the spoken lie.[44]

The point that I would stress is that within this human, verbal world, Grendel enters as a creature of mute anger. His marginality in this scene— his banishment from the hall and from all human, daily life, his relegation to the border lands (in the appellation *mearc-stapa*, line 103)—grows as much from his silence as from his lineage. For here, Grendel cannot participate in the shared experience of verbal oath, poetic history, or social discourse. Hrothgar can name his own hall and the *scop* can sing of *se Ælmihtiga*, but only men can christen Grendel ("Wæs se grimma gæst Grendel haten," "The grim spirit was called Grendel," line 102), a fact Hrothgar will make explicit in his later account of the monster's origins: "Þone in gear-dagum 'Grendel' nemdon / fold buende" ("Then long ago men called him 'Grendel,'" lines 1354–55). As a creature named by men, Grendel participates in this strange mix of biblical and mythic stories of creation as a kind of anticreature, one whose semihuman form belies his deeply inhuman nature. That he himself cannot speak, save to cry incomprehensibly during Beowulf's attack, renders him the antithesis of a hero who can name himself on his first entry in the court: "Beowulf is min nama" (line 343).

I have dwelled on these accounts of naming, and on what I take to be the theme of verbal power, as a way of preparing the contrast between the opening performance of Creation with the hilt scene at the poem's middle.[45] Both focus on the relationship of naming and control, and both offer an account of divine action shaped within the figures of human craft. At the penultimate moment of the Danish narrative—before Beowulf leaves for Hygelac's court—we see the hilt and "hear" the sermon and return to the ideals of a heroic eloquence posed at *Beowulf*'s opening. But at this point, it is a text of devastation that recalls a lay of origins. The war against the giants, the flood, and God's retribution invert the ideals of order stated in the *scop*'s song.

> þær wæs hearpan sweg,
> swutol sang scopes. Sægde se þe cuþe
> frumsceaft fira feorran reccan,
> cwæð þæt se Ælmihtiga eorðan worhte,
> wlite-beorhtne wang, swa wæter bebugeð:
> gesette sige-hreþig sunnan ond monan
> leoman to leohte land-buendum,
> ond gefrætwade foldan sceatas
> leomum ond leafum; lif eac gesceop
> cynna gehwylcum, þara ðe cwice hwyrfaþ. (lines 89b–98)

There was the sound of the harp, the clear song of the scop. There he spoke who could relate the beginning of men far back in time, said that the Almighty made earth, a bright field fair in the water that surrounds it, set up in triumph the lights of the sun and the moon to lighten land-dwellers, and adorned the surfaces of the earth with branches and leaves, created also life for each of the kinds that move and breathe. (Donaldson, p. 3)

In sharp distinction to the *scop*'s tale of calm waters and an Edenic origin, the hilt writes of a violent flood. The "wlite-beorhtne wang, swa wæter bebugeð," which the *scop* describes, contrasts with the "wæteres wylm" ("water's welling") through which God enacts his punishment in the hilt's text (line 1693). Instead of relating the beginning of things, the hilt records an ancient strife and the death of a race. But more pointed, too, are the comparisons between creators. In the *scop*'s song it is *se Ælmihtiga* who makes the earth and who adorns its surfaces with limbs and leaves. There is only a brief mention of the *scop*'s own skill in relating all this, save that he is knowing and his song is clear (*swutol*). In the report of the hilt's text, however, much of its concern is with the human maker and the human owner. Its text is well cut, its owner's name correctly inscribed, its overall appearance intricate and striking. These are the references that close the hilt scene and bridge the link to Hrothgar's speech. The drama of the *scop*'s song, though, is radically different. There, the narrator moves from a statement of Hrothgar's power, to a comment on the *scop*, a précis of his song, and a review of the biblical genealogy of Grendel and his kin. By moving from the king, to singer, to Creation, to monsters, this opening directs the audience from present human life to the past origins of both our own and the other world. It traces a pattern exactly opposite from that of the hilt scene, where we move from ancient strife and runic skill to Hrothgar's present performance of what the narrator had considered his ability to rule in words.

Where the hilt and song part company, as well, is in their use of naming. The poem's opening attentions to the names of man and monster, and the details of its references to Cain and Abel, to the genealogies of Grendel and the *eotenas*, *ylfe*, and *orcas*, and to *se Ælmihtiga* are all missing from the comparably vague report on the hilt's text. There, the maker of the sword is unnamed, and the sword and patron remain equally anonymous. This is not "Welandes geweorc," nor is it christened with a meaningful identity like Hrunting or Nægling.[46] The vagueness of this hilt contrasts with the specificity of the opening, rendering it all the more ambiguous and alien.

At the poem's start, the narrator supplies all the information we need to understand, frame, and appreciate the making of the hall, the skill of the *scop*, and the nature of God and Grendel. But in the hilt scene, we are provided with no such data. Who are the giants, who made the sword, and how did it come into the possession of the hoard of Grendel's mother? These are questions scholars long have asked, and I would claim that these are questions that the text itself invites. To understand the hilt, the audience must go outside the poem to explore its origin. Whether we see it in the archeological details of early metalwork, or the runology of Scandinavian commemoration, we are provoked to find a context. Our own interpretive insecurity with the passage is only heightened by its unique vocabulary. Even though scholars may alleviate that insecurity through philological analysis or textual comparison, for any reader of the poem, medieval or modern, the passage seems to alienate itself verbally from the rest of the text. Set off by its rhetorical brackets, full of odd words and strange idioms, the hilt scene is itself an almost indigestible nugget of description. It is itself a poetic text that demands interpretation—in short, a kind of riddle whose expected solution now rests not with Hrothgar and his men, but with the reader of *Beowulf*.

Such a solution, I would posit, will concern not just the specifics of the sword's origin and appearance. It will concern the nature of literature itself and the place of poetry in human society. The opening of *Beowulf* suggests an answer, dramatizing a poetic performance and offering firm grounding in the frameworks of myth and history that make sense of its account. Its very specificity complements the publicly shared experience of literature. What unites the poet's audience into a culture is a shared belief in the workings of a God and their appreciation of His acts. The references to Cain and Abel, or to the genealogies of kings and monsters, give voice to those shared beliefs. It is information offered *us*, not necessarily the poem's characters: information we can situate within the body of remembrances that make a Christian audience for poetry. But what unites the people within the poem's fiction is their status as an audience for song. The *scop*'s performance brings them into a community of listeners for whom art is a public and a social act. In the appreciation of that act, moreover, lies an invitation to participate in rituals that mark a civilized society. Such rituals have little to do with the observance of a Christian rite, and as Osborn and others have illustrated, it is these differing "levels of knowledge" or belief that separate the poem's fictional and historical audiences.

Nonetheless, these audiences share a common goal. The power both of the *scop's* song and of the poet's poem lies in its ability to recognize the place of literature in culture. By defining mankind as an audience, they alert us to our own shared humanity—a humanity, pointedly, which Grendel cannot gain. For Grendel's life is marked not only by sin or evil, but by silence. More than just a picture of the demon or the alien, the figure of Grendel exiled from Heorot affirms the power of poetry to exclude as well as include. If it brings people together to instruct them in their heritage, then it is poetry that exiles Grendel. He cannot be an audience for literature, nor can he share in the lineage such literature contrives for us. As Cain's kin or the descendant of giants, Grendel is by his nature excluded from the literary history articulated by the *scop*.

The vision of the past encoded on the hilt, however, implies a much different version of literature and its audience. Instead of offering the sure landmarks of name and heritage, the hilt speaks in anonymous generalities. Instead of uniting the court into a community of listeners, it separates Hrothgar as a lone reader. Instead of relegating monsters and their kin to the outskirts of Creation, it makes them the center of its story. Now, only when they have been safely and irrevocably killed, can monsters be admitted into Heorot. Grendel's head may terrify the viewer (lines 1647–50), but for Hrothgar it is little more than a trophy of God's grace (lines 1780–81). The sword may have killed Grendel's mother, but its blade is gone. In bringing these treasures into the hall, Beowulf brings the king face to face with the written history and disembodied head of his enemy. Unlike the physical appearances of Grendel and his mother, striking men dead while Hrothgar slept apart, now in their textual appearance the race of giants comes only to the king's eyes. It forces him (and us) to find a context for an understanding, a "reading" of the hilt. Now, in its vague anonymities, the hilt remains a text to be interpreted, a text whose meaning is to be sought *not* in the shared responses of a listening community, but in the individual interpretations of the reader alone.

As a counterweight to the *scop's* song of Creation, the hilt invites a private reading rather than a public performance. It narrates destruction rather than creation, types instead of names. It takes as its subject the history of a race exiled not only from the hall but from the matter of hall poetry. Their history, in consequence, is not expressible within the public songs of hall life, but in cryptic documents. The text is made accessible, in part, to Hrothgar and to us so that we may together try to understand the mythic origins of the terror we have seen and to realize that, in the end, we can only live with monsters and their kin in writings: works that are as impotent as a bladeless sword or a bodiless head. Those monsters now are like the hilt itself. Both come as a written tale, able to enter the hall and hurt no one, to sit silently like a souvenir of an alien kingdom.

. . .

My argument about the place of writing in *Beowulf*, and about its place in "oral" literature more generally, may find its more precise articulation in the terms Charles Segal has provided for the study of early Greek poetry. Broadly put, Segal's work proposes two interrelated consequences of the rise of social literacy and the representation of writing in narratives marked by a growing authorial self-consciousness. In his work on Pindar, Segal claims that written composition fosters a new sense of poetry as craft: of the poetic artifact as intricately worked object, and of the poet as an artisan of words. The self-consciousness of literary representation—that is, the ways in which the poet figures himself in his crafty heroes or elaborate displays of verbal technique—develops in tandem with rising literacy. These claims inform my conception of the *Beowulf*-poet's attentions to craft and to performance, but in my present analysis I turn to the second of Segal's claims for writing. In his studies of Greek tragedy, he suggests that in the representations of reading and writing lie the authors' meditations on the relationship between private and public that inform the tragic impulse. What he calls the "graphic space" of writing "becomes a convenient metaphor for making visible the hidden realm of emotional life,"[47] and he continues:

> At least two factors aid this association of writing and emotional interiority: the tendency in an oral culture to connect writing with private, secret, or deceitful communication . . . and the importance that writing gives to vision. . . . This graphic space . . . corresponds to the tragedians' new self-consciousness about what is going on behind and beneath, about what cannot be shown visually in the scenic action (the self as inner and hidden) and in the scenic language (the written text).[48]

For *Beowulf*, what cannot be shown visually is the terror of destruction visited upon the warring giants: the ancient myth now confined to a written object. Segal's arguments that writing offers baleful or restricted forms of communication—as, for example, in the *semata lugra* of the *Iliad*, the suspect documents of Thucydidean history, or the letters exchanged throughout Greek tragedy—fits the apprehension of the sword-hilt.[49] Writing enables, here, the private sharing of old knowledge. It shows the king, and us, something about the awesome power of a God and those who challenge Him. It shows us, too, an object whose own origins are cloaked in mystery. Its quasi-marvelous appearance and its own possibly mythic origins render it a thing not only alien but ominous.

In tandem with this sense of written objects as a challenge to the expectations of character or audience, Segal intuits an approach to the poet's own self-presentation. In the traditional oral media of exchange, social and literary contact go on face to face. Gesture and vision work together to inform the speakers of themselves, their lineage, and their motives. The formal conversations in *Beowulf* serve to affirm the ways in which spoken communication is immediate and visual. In the performance of poetry, it is the living presence of the *scop* that vivifies the literary exchange. Poetry, in *Beowulf*, is an occasion, whether it develops from the celebrations of the hall, the praise of Beowulf's heroics, or the more reflective moments of social enjoyment. In the variety of scenes of *scop*-craft, *Beowulf* revels in the spontaneity of verse making. Poetry grows from the rhythm of the moment; it responds to and can provoke action and further speech. It is, as many of its critics have concluded, a performance in the full sense of the term.[50] As Segal puts it, synthesizing a tradition of its study, oral poetry

> gives us the sensation of the full presence of events: we feel that we have all the necessary details and that we possess that immediacy of foreground eloquently described by Erich Auerbach in the famous first chapter of *Mimesis*. Tragedy, based as it is on a written text, is full of elusive details, missing pieces, unexplained motives, puzzling changes of mood, decision, or attitude. Instead of the oral poet who tells us in person of the will of Zeus, we have the absent poet who has plotted out every detail in advance.[51]

This difference between oral and written poetry, and the attendant differences between knowledge and ignorance, specificity and ambiguity that mark it, I find dramatized in the hilt episode itself. Unlike the immediate and shared experience of bardic eloquence, the hilt offers a text that breaks the poem's narrative and separates the king from his companions. Unlike the vision of a present *scop*, the hilt records a long-dead and anonymous runester. In the song of Creation we do feel, I think, that "we have all the necessary details" to appreciate the singer's craft and grasp the moral function of his story. The scene at Heorot, as I have illustrated, fills itself

607

with names and genealogies. But, much like Segal's version of the written text, the hilt episode "is full of elusive details, missing pieces, unexplained motives." We are not granted access to the history of the giants' war, nor can we garner the motivations of their strife. God acts, in this brief story, not in the historical framework of an Adamic curse or a Noachic promise, but simply *as God*. His retribution and his acts are absolute. We are not invited to explore *His* motives or their implications. Similarly, we know nothing of the sword's creation or its transmission to Grendel's mother. Even the details of its physical appearance and its fluid grammar leave us wondering about the proper meaning of its words and their relationships.

The hilt's inscription, in the terms Segal offers, will present itself as the recorded work of a now absent maker. Its ambiguities are those of written words themselves. Its strange allusions are the reminiscences of other texts and contexts long past. It comes to represent the nature of all writing and the need for an interpreter to make sense of the works of the dead. Without the presence of the *scop*, and without the authority his living audience will grant him, the story on the hilt cannot be quickly grasped. Instead, its understanding requires meditation. Gone is the immediacy that characterizes face-to-face performance. In its place is the slow reading and the attendant break in narrative assurance which, as I have argued, characterize the hilt scene's place within the poem's drama as a whole. That break gives to both Hrothgar and the poem's audience the time to see and to digest this strange text. The move from what I have called narrative time to reader's time may now be rephrased as a move from listening to reading. To appropriate the vocabulary of Segal's inquiry, *Beowulf* represents a move from presence to absence as it dramatizes differing forms of literary communication and response.

If my appropriation of Segal's words appears to render my own arguments a seemingly formulaic rephrasing of current critical interests, I want to stress that such interpretive issues as poetic authority and reader response are made the subject of the literature itself. The presence of the *scop* is celebrated throughout *Beowulf*, and in the absence of a named authority, the hilt's text does challenge the conventions of communication it has been the business of the poem to establish. What I wish to claim, as well, is that the poem reconceives the relationships of narrator and audience as it effectively "rewrites" the earlier reports of monstrous beings and marvelous objects. In Beowulf's own recitation before Hygelac's court of his exploits at Heorot, the poet offers what I consider a humorous critique of tale-telling, and another reassessment of the nature of narrative authority. In the hero's extended description of Grendel's glove, moreover, we may find a strange revision of the terms of craft and power, artifice and culture, which have governed the poem's heroics to this point.

. . .

On his return to Hygelac's court, Beowulf responds to his king's eager requests for an account of the adventure. He recalls the events at Heorot, digresses on the moral implications of heroic action through historical allusions, and narrates in detail the story of his fights with Grendel and his mother. The sequence of events will be familiar to the poem's audience, and in his autobiographical performance, Beowulf appears to fit the model of the returning romance hero who, in turning past action into present words, offers a display of verbal prowess to be judged and rewarded. By transferring the physical ordeal into the conventions of heroic eloquence, Beowulf confirms his reentry into the civilized world after his sojourn in the wilderness, and part of my purpose is to explore the function of that verbal reentry. But everything that Beowulf says will not be familiar to the audience, and part of my purpose, too, is to distinguish what is new about it. Whatever the conventional nature of his speech, he proffers information on his fight with Grendel that neither the poem's characters nor its audience seem to know. In his naming of the first Geat killed, Hondscio, and his description of Grendel's glove, Beowulf offers a revision of the tale and a potential recasting of its central themes. The method of his narrative returns us to the techniques of naming and the emphasis on artifice that were established in the *scop*'s song and the hilt's description. Read in tandem with these earlier moments, the narrative of Grendel's glove affirms an understanding of interpretation as a form of power in the poem.

Beowulf announces, "Ic sceal forð sprecan / gen ymbe Grendel" ("I shall speak forth further about Grendel," lines 2069–70), and then goes on to tell the story of his fight. His phrasing, at first, seems wholly conventional, with its references to the *heofenes gim* which *glad ofer grundas* (the "heaven's jewel" which "glided over the earth," lines 2072–73) and its reminiscences of the vocabulary that described Grendel's approach earlier: "gæst yrre cwom" ("the angry spirit came," line 2073).[52] Immediately thereafter, however, he tells us the name of the first Geat killed, and as James Rosier noticed long ago, the abrupt announcement of Hondscio's name calls into question his place in the narrative.[53] The first two times this warrior appeared, he was a nameless *slæpende rinc* ("sleeping man," line 741) and the one (*þone anne*) for whom Hrothgar orders payment (lines 1053–54). In these scenes, he participates in the communal sense of loss shared by the Geats; we need not know his name at either moment, for he is simply a representative of a dramatic fact (the first to be killed) or a social convention (the payment of *wergild*). In Beowulf's retelling, though, Hondscio's name becomes, in Rosier's words, "artistically relevant" to the moment at hand. The etymologies of his name and the immediate surrounding mention of Grendel's glove suggest the use of wordplay here: a man whose name means "glove" dies just before we see the monstrous glove in which Grendel keeps his victims.[54] As Rosier puts it:

> [The poet's] use of the words *hand* and *glof* in turn suggested, as he realized the appropriateness of particularizing Beowulf's lost companion, a germanic equivalent—a form of *hantscuoh*—which he decided to adapt as a personal name, since as a compound it contributes to the hand motif and in a sense picks up or puns upon the allusion to the glove.[55]

Rosier is right to note the punning effect of the man's name and the creature's glove; but he does not, I think, go far enough in exploring the artistic relevance of the pun. Part of that relevance hinges on the technique of deferred naming I have mentioned earlier. At this moment, the poem's audience learns Hondscio's name, and it can interpret rightly his thematic function in the poem.[56] As an individual, rather than a nameless figure in the group, the Geat has a meaningful place in the present drama. That place, now, is not part of a moral allegory or a precise historical reference in the way that, for example, Unferth's name or references to Scandinavian kings operate. Instead, its place is with play and humor. "Hondscio" is a joke, a contribution to the tame and reassuring retelling of Beowulf's story. Far from Denmark, and distanced from his exploits, Beowulf transforms the terror of his experience into a form of social entertainment. The play on name and glove effectively dramatizes the horror of the Geat's death and the monster's appetite. It makes the story an acceptable social performance, one that will not—as Grendel's own disembodied head did—frighten men and queen (lines 1647–50).

In Grendel's glove itself we may find the sustained expression of that verbal playfulness:

> Glof hangode
> sid ond syllic, searo-bendum fæst;
> sio wæs orðoncum eall gegyrwed,
> deofles cræftum ond dracan fellum. (lines 2085b-88)

His glove hung huge and wonderful, made fast with cunning clasps; it had been made all with craft, with devil's devices and dragon's skins. (Donaldson, p. 36)

All the terms of artifice that had been building in the poem come together here. Laced up, *searo-bendum fæst*, it recalls the human works of skill (*searo-þonc*, line 775) which kept Heorot together, bound fast in iron bands during the fight with Grendel:

> ac he þæs fæste wæs
> innan ond utan iren-bendum
> searo-þoncum besmiþod. (lines 773b-75)

but it (i.e., the hall) was so firmly made fast with iron bands, both inside and outside, joined by skillful smith-craft. (Donaldson, p. 14)

As a work of personal artifice, the glove recalls as well the near-magical armor whose locked rings kept Beowulf safe (the *searo-fah* mail shirt, line 1444) or the *searo-net* that clothed his men (line 406). It also recalls Grendel's severed head itself, the *searo-wundor* at which Hrothgar and his men stare (line 920). The glove's ornamented features further resonate with the vast adornments that accompany both men and their creations throughout the poem. But as a work of *deofles cræftum*, made with dragon skin, Grendel's glove presents a counter-instance of the works of artifice that fill the world of men. It stands as lone exception to the social norm, as Fred Robinson has put it, of artifice as "reassuring" in the face of a malevolent nature.[57] For here, we have a grim work of horrific craft, a thing whose *orðonc* ("craft") exemplifies neither the ingenuities of men nor the inherent artistry of God's Creation.

The description of the glove in general, and the mention of the word *orðonc* in particular, renders the passage as a whole a kind of negative riddle. It is an object far unlike the crafted things that populate the Exeter Book, mediating between the divine order, human handiwork, and verbal performance. Not only is it something not of this world; not only is it a work of the devil. It is a powerful inversion of the social and artistic norms that it had been the purpose of the riddles to celebrate. The riddles' patterns of verbal finesse, interlace structure, and paranomasia all contribute to a form of literature that humorously explores the relationships between human language and interpretation and the signs of the created world. The word *orþoncbendum* in the Cock and Hen Riddle signifies the ways in which the material culture of the reader's life—here, the techniques of book-making—can enclose both the facts of the barnyard and the imaginations of the mind. The play of ambiguities, here and throughout the riddles, is the play of human understanding. On occasion, though, the riddler takes as his subject his own enterprise. Some of the extant riddles may have "language," "speech," or "riddling" itself as their solutions, and Krapp-Dobbie 39[58] is perhaps the most fully developed, and the most puzzling, of such meditations. "Þæt is wrætlic þing to gesecganne," that is a marvelous thing to say, or in Craig Williamson's felicitous translation, "speaking is a marvelous thing." To speak of the riddle's solution is, the poem avers, a long story.[59]

> Long is to secganne
> hu hyre ealdorgesceaft æfter gongeð—
> woh wyrda gesceapu. Þæt is wrætlic þing
> to gesecganne. (lines 22b–25)

> It takes a long time to say how its state goes afterwards—the obscure destinies of words. Speaking is a marvelous thing.

The myriad verbal ambiguities in these lines have been classified by Williamson, and explicit in his reading of the riddle is the notion that the poem's play on multiple meanings and self-reference offers us a meditation on the nature of language itself.[60] The destinies of words are hard to chart, and rather than to speak much longer on the subject, Riddle 39 quickly ends with an injunction to find "true words" for the solution.

Beowulf's story shares many of this riddle's idioms and emphases, but offers in the end a much different celebration of the possibilities of language. The full account of his fight with Grendel is, for the purposes of his narration, too long:

> To lang ys to reccenne, hu ic ðam leod-sceaðan
> yfla gehwylces ondlean forgeald (lines 2093–94)

> It is too long to tell how I repaid the people's foe his due for every crime. (Donaldson, p. 37)

His interruption breaks off a more detailed account of the fight, the blow-by-blow description that the audience knows from lines 710–836. But it also playfully returns us to the hero's announcement that had started this story: "Ic sceal forð sprecan." Taken together, these two announcements bracket Beowulf's retelling of the tale of Grendel within two self-conscious references to speechmaking. They tell us, in effect, that its enclosed twenty-odd lines will inform us less about the struggle than about Beowulf's own skills at personal narration. The details we remember of that fight and the ones the poet highlighted (e.g., the handgrip and wrestling lock, the voracity of Grendel, the strength of the hall, the tumult of the encounter) are all elided here in favor of two seemingly irrelevant and newly offered details. And yet, it is in these details that Beowulf presents what *he* apparently thinks was important about the battle; or, to put it more precisely, what the poem at this point wishes to stress about the appropriate forms of social narration and the decorous skills of the heroic narrator. Beowulf's speech responds to certain social demands, and in so doing, gives us a creative retelling of the story that we know. It rephrases the central interests of the poem into pun and wordplay. It takes the techniques of riddling and gives us a solution without an enigma: names and things with little challenge to interpret them. It is as if Beowulf gives voice to answers to the unasked questions: who was the first to die, and what did Grendel do with the bodies of the men he killed? Such questions now become the province of heroic wordplay. We are not offered a moral interpretation of the fight in the gnomic terms the poet, or Hrothgar, had earlier presented. Instead, we get an entertainment, a self-conscious display of Beowulf's abilities at *sprecan* and an ironic finish when he knows he may have spoken for "To lang."

Two complementary analogues from other European literatures may help to clarify my view of Beowulf's narration as a critical retelling of the poem's central actions. The first is to the *Odyssey*: to its relationship to the matter of the *Iliad*, and to its presentations of Odysseus himself as poet of his life. What James Redfield has called the "collapse of epic distance" in the *Odyssey* illuminates the ways it juxtaposes the heroic ideals of Iliadic history with the ironies of everyday life or the fantasies of romance.[61] He explains that, in the *Odyssey*,

> a naturalistic background is made to accommodate figures from epic and fantasy. Thus it happens that Odysseus can listen to the bard tell his own story; it is as if Octavius, in *Antony and Cleopatra*, should attend a performance of *Julius Caesar*. There is much that is playful in the ironies of the *Odyssey* and much that is serious: the poet inquires into the meaning of the heroic by testing it against the world familiar to his audience. That is, the

> poet, by collapsing the epic distance, allows the two worlds to comment on
> each other. He often appears, further, to be making a comment on his own
> work as an epic poet.[62]

The "collapse of epic distance" outlined here appears to work, in miniature, in the account of Beowulf's performance. To call the hero's speech comic or humorous is not to say that it is funny or critical in any narrow or sportive way. Rather, it is to say that both the tone and purpose of his narrative differ from those of the poet's own version of the fight with Grendel. It is to say, too, that Beowulf is here a kind of critic of the poem, much like the poet of the *Odyssey* has been considered a critic of the *Iliad*.[63] His speech calls attention to the many problems inherent in narrative artistry. There is the selection of detail, the patterning of rhetorical emphasis, and the precise gauging of anticipated audience response. Scholars have seen these issues at work in the presumed transmission of the Finnsburh material, for example.[64] What, many have asked, are the criteria for narrative emphases in lay and epic? What distinguishes the handling of what must have been familiar stories in contexts shaped by formal recitation or social exchange? For the Finnsburh story, we have only *Beowulf*'s embedded performance and the separate, and textually difficult, fragment. Whatever judgments critics make on its appropriations must be based on the conjectures about missing elements of plot or deeply obscure allusions. For *Beowulf*, however, we have the complete story before the hero's own retelling. The poet has already given us the information against which we may both measure and query Beowulf's telling, and he invites us to appreciate his hero's performance as a critical and personal response.

If Beowulf appears, in these lines, to be something of his own poet, then he parallels, in what may be a more precise way, the figure of Odysseus himself. Critics of the *Odyssey* have long noticed how Odysseus habitually presents himself through forms of verbal and physical disguise. His self-naming, his stories, and his own responses to the tales of Troy told by court bards or Sirens have been seen as the examples of a Homeric reflection on the nature of mimetic art.[65] As Sheila Murnaghan has argued, "Odysseus's successive experiences of acting as his own poet . . . are expressions of just how rare and complete his success in the *Odyssey* is."[66] He is unique among heroes, for he is able both to be the subject of heroic song, and to survive heroic exploits in order to tell his own story. Beowulf, too, survives to tell his tale, and like Odysseus, he too will make explicit the link between his recitation and the public performance of poetry. Immediately following his story of the fight with Grendel, Beowulf tells of his rewards at Heorot and of the social customs that gave pleasure to the men:[67]

> Þær wæs gidd and gleo; gomela Scilding,
> fela fricgende, feorran rehte;
> hwilum hilde-deor hearpan wynne,
> gomen-wudu grette, hwilum gyd awræc
> soð and sarlic, hwilum syllic spell
> rehte æfter rihte. (lines 2105–10)

> There was song and mirth. The old Scylding, who has learned many things, spoke of times far-off. At times a brave one in battle touched the glad wood, the harp's joy; at times he told tales, true and sad; at times he related strange stories according to right custom. (Donaldson, p. 37)

What interests Beowulf are not the details of the songs performed at Heorot. We find no mention of their content in the way that we had been informed of the *scop*'s opening song of Creation. Instead, Beowulf focuses solely on form and quality. The songs are true, sad, strange, and rightly or traditionally put. His concept of the singer's role is clearly as the teller of true things and the transmitter of social custom. Song is more a ritual than an art for Beowulf, and I think his characterization of this performance reflects back on his own narrative goals. Beowulf, too, has seemed to offer a story true and sad, a strange one, but at the same time, one told in accordance with the formulas of recitation and the conventions of public performance. Hondscio's death and Grendel's glove form the two poles of his report: the one *soð and sarlic*, the other *syllic*. His own verbal rectitude is signaled by his two announcements of speech-making and the good sense he shows in keeping the story short. Like the performances at Heorot, Beowulf himself speaks *rehte æfter rihte*, and much like the idioms of correctness in the hilt scene, these ideals of verbal control reflect, as well, on the *Beowulf*-poet's own command of narrative technique.

My second literary analogue comes from the heroes of the later European romances. Beowulf exemplifies in his performance what R. Howard Bloch has called the victor's return "in order to tell the story of his *avanture*."[68] What Bloch sees as "the conversion of the adventure . . . into verbal account once a knight reenters the limits of organized society"[69] is classed, in his story, with legal forms of disputation and the shape of the Arthurian material. The hero's urge to tell, however, has a more general function in the typologies of return that characterize all romance forms. It appears as early as the *Odyssey*, in which Odysseus's sure homecoming is signaled by his story to Penelope.[70] His recapitulation of the marvelous events of his journey finds a willing and receptive audience, while at the same time canonizing, in Murnaghan's words, "the fantastic version of what he was doing between his departure from Troy and his return."[71] The urge to tell accompanies the events of Bede's holy histories, where for example, Imma comes home to tell his brother "a full account of all his troubles and the comfort that had come to him in those adversities," and Cædmon comes back from the cow-shed to tell his masters of the marvel.[72] In *Andreas*, too, the romance homecoming finds its voice in the speeches that frame the apostles' return and the poet's own announcement of the need to chronicle his own literary journey through history and texts (lines 1478–91).[73]

In Beowulf's case, we do not hear the details of the story as we know them, but we get what Bloch calls "a mediated version of his adventures in the form of a verbal record."[74] It is mediated, in this sense, by the demands of a listening court, and more generally, by the governing literary need to tame the violence of the hero's past adventure. If the job of Beowulf has been to cleanse Heorot and return triumphant to his court, then it lies in the nature of that cleansing to remove the possibility of any future horror. To come home only to astound and scare his audience would serve little purpose. To come home as a hero *and* an entertainer serves a great purpose. It makes, I think, a profound statement about the place of fantastic narrative in court life. The exploits become a story, and like Hrothgar's hilt—which codes the legend of the gigantic war—Beowulf's tale renders the fantastic safe and palatable. Moreover, in his playful and controlled verbal performance, Beowulf comes to represent a certain model of narration itself. In Bloch's words, "The hero is, in essence, one who becomes capable, through his accomplishments, of telling the tale which we read."[75] In *Beowulf*'s terms, the hero is the one who can combine historical account with entertaining story to tell *us* something of the function of literature in civilization.

That function, as I have suggested throughout this essay, is the bringing together of an audience into a shared community and the demystification of the alien and supernatural. By opening the poem with a sequence of names and genealogies, appellations and poetic recitations, the *Beowulf*-poet grounds both the very old and the very odd in a precise interpretive framework. We know exactly who Grendel is, what *se Ælmihtiga* did, and where Hrothgar lives. These acts of naming are the features of a literature of performance—the face-to-face encounters between present teller and his audience. In a similar way, Beowulf identifies the human and the other-worldly for the first time. Hondscio's name and the account of Grendel's glove eliminate our uncertainties in the precision of description. That the result of such naming is to defuse anxiety or offer wordplay means that Beowulf sees part of his narrative purpose as a form of entertainment. Like the *scop* at Heorot, Beowulf demystifies the fight with Grendel. He renders it a verbal game, a clash of words, not hands. By painting Grendel's glove in the familiar terms of artifice, he renders the monstrous and the mythical domestic. Of course it is bizarre; but like the vision of the hilt, it is bizarre only in contrast to the other objects that have been described in the same way. That both scenes, too, should draw on Scandinavian sources—the formulas of runecarving or the legends of troll-gloves—further affirms the poet's techniques of alienation. It would appear that when he seeks to describe the oddness of another world, he resorts to a non-English set of referents.

But where the story of the glove and the legend of the hilt differ most fundamentally is in the issue of the name and in the presence of the teller. In the anonymities of the hilt are the mysteries of origin. In its refusal to name sword or maker, or the specific actors of the story, the hilt presents an ambiguous text. Its long-dead maker is not here to tell us—or the Danes—just who is who or where the meaning of *his* story lies. But Beowulf *is* there at Hygelac's court, carefully manipulating both the matter and the manner of his story. His emphases on the precision of detail and the correctness of his own and of the *scop*'s earlier performances are fully in keeping with the vision of the young hero we had first seen entering Heorot. There, he had announced and named himself, corrected Unferth's unflattering rendition of the swimming match, and recalled for public approval the histories of his and Hrothgar's families. The young Beowulf enters and leaves the poem as an authorial and authorizing figure. In these scenes, he does more than set the record straight. He does nothing less than recreate his own past, and the audience's trust in Beowulf's narrative authority stems as much from his imposing bearing as it does from the pervasive associations between the hero and the *scop*. Beowulf effectively has conquered twice: first, by physically ridding Denmark of the monsters; second, by verbally transforming those actions into an entertaining and compelling story.

What, then, remains the place of "literacy" in *Beowulf*? For much of this essay, I have addressed the forms of speaking, rather than writing, and have attended to the broad homologies between the poem's presentations of performance and the features of ancient Greek or medieval European romance. My answer would be that these scenes of verbal prowess frame themselves in contrast to the enigmatic text at the poem's center. The clear definitions and familiar narratives of *scop* and hero take on new and purposeful effects when understood against the foil of the anonymous, inscribed hilt. My purpose in suggesting analogues or sources from Scandinavian runology for that hilt has been to show, among other things, that this is an allusive and, perhaps, willfully obscure passage. The *Beowulf*-poet's description of the hilt trades on half-remembered myths or learned arcana. But just who is remembering these myths or learning runic esoterica? Arguments about the historical audience of *Beowulf* are naturally more speculative than those for Bede's *History*; nonetheless, there are representations of a variety of audiences in the poem, and as I have assumed throughout this essay, such representations may tell us of the poem's own conception of the role of literature in culture and the nature of poetic response.

With these assumptions in mind, I would conclude by offering that *Beowulf* presents two versions of itself. In scenes of bardic narrative or of heroic reminiscence, it shows us a world of oral literature in action. It emphasizes the presence of the live performer, the specifics of historical detail or thematic content that characterize his verse, and the importance of communal sharing of a literary inheritance. In what I now will call the scene of reading, *Beowulf* presents a cryptic text that Hrothgar sees or "reads" alone. It shows us what mythic narrative can become when written down and read long after both its makers and its audience have died. Whether *Beowulf* once existed as a string of oral tales before its commission to manuscript, or whether it was first "composed" in writing by a lettered poet is not my primary concern. What is my concern is that the poem itself imaginatively anticipates this scholarly debate. It shows us oral literature and written texts, and in so doing, asks us to reflect on what it may be like to hear the songs or read the poem.

What may be called the "literacy" of *Beowulf* may now be said to be the way in which it imagines its own reading public—the way in which it shows us that to read the legends of the past is to read by ourselves. Faced with the absence of an author or the vague allusiveness of texts, we are left only to interpret. Hrothgar's sermon may have nothing to do with the hilt's inscription; and yet, in the dramatic sequence of the *run* and his *ræd*, it may come to seem a personal interpretation of the vision of the hilt. Similarly, Beowulf's retelling of the fight with Grendel has little to do, in detail, tone, or length, with the "original" account we know; yet, it too is an interpretation of the story, retold for a new audience in a new setting. And in the end, when Beowulf is dead and his pyre is aflame, people will speak about the king, recount his deeds, and praise his valor. In so doing, they make a literature of Beowulf himself, and tell us, in the process, that the king's fame rests in the retelling and rereading of his poem.

NOTES

[1] All citations of *Beowulf* are from C. L. Wrenn, ed., *"Beowulf," with the Finnesburg Fragment*, 3rd ed., rev. W. F. Bolton (New York, 1973). All translations are from *"Beowulf": The Donaldson Translation*, ed. Joseph F. Tuso (New York, 1975), with some modifications of my own where noted. References to Donaldson will be made parenthetically by page number.

[2] For a summary of early interpretations, see the notes in Fr. Klaeber, ed., *"Beowulf" and the Fight at Finnsburgh*, 3rd ed. with supplements, (Lexington, Mass., 1950), pp. 189–90; and more recently, Marijane Osborn, "The Great Feud: Scriptural History and Strife in *Beowulf*," *PMLA* 93 (1978): 973–81, and Johann Köberl, "The Magic Sword in *Beowulf*," *Neophilologus* 71 (1987): 120–28. For archaeological parallels to the sword, see Rosemary Cramp, "*Beowulf* and Archaeology," *Medieval Archaeology* 1 (1957): 57–77; A. T. Hatto, "Snake-Swords and Boar-Helms in *Beowulf*," *English Studies* 38 (1957): 145–60; and Sonia Chadwick Hawkes and R. I. Page, "Swords and Runes in South-East England," *Antiquaries Journal* 47 (1967): 210–19. For parallels in Celtic myth, see Martin Puhvel, "The Deicidal Otherworld Weapon in Celtic and Germanic Mythic Tradition," *Folklore* 83 (1972): 210–19. For critical interpretations of the episode within the poem as a whole, see Osborn's overall account, and the remarks in Edward B. Irving, Jr., *A Reading of "Beowulf"* (New Haven, 1968), pp. 121–24, 145–47; Margaret Goldsmith, *The Mode and Meaning of "Beowulf"* (London, 1970), pp. 88–90, 120–23; Gillian Overing, "Swords and Signs: Dynamic Semeiosis in *Beowulf*," *Language, Sign, and Gender in "Beowulf"* (Carbondale, 1990), pp. 33–67 (and reprinted in this volume). After this essay was completed, I became aware of Allen Frantzen's essay, "Writing the Unreadable *Beowulf*," *Desire for Origins: New Language, Old English, and Teaching the Tradition* (New Brunswick, 1990), pp. 168–200 [and reprinted in this volume]. Our arguments share several points of detail and interpretation, and Frantzen's treatment of the hilt scene happily confirms my own intuitions of its importance to the poem as a whole. It is my pleasure to acknowledge his generosity in sharing this essay with me before its publication.

[3] This is not the place to review exhaustively the scholarly debate on the Christianity of *Beowulf*, but the following studies may offer guides to the

competing interpretations: Dorothy Whitelock, *The Audience of "Beowulf"* (Oxford, 1951); Goldsmith, *The Mode and Meaning of "Beowulf"*; Michael Cherniss, *Ingeld and Christ* (The Hague, 1972); Alvin A. Lee, *The Guest-Hall of Eden* (New Haven, 1972); Robert W. Hanning, "*Beowulf* as Heroic History," *Medievalia et Humanistica* n.s. 5 (1974): 77–102; John D. Niles, *"Beowulf": The Poem and Its Tradition* (Cambridge, Mass., 1983); and Edward B. Irving, Jr., "The Nature of Christianity in *Beowulf*," *Anglo-Saxon England* 13 (1984): 7–21. A concise review of the relationship of Christian doctrine to Germanic diction appears in Stanley Greenfield and Daniel G. Calder, *A New Critical History of Old English Literature* (New York, 1985), pp. 134–57.

[4] On the varying opinions of the poem's date and mode of composition, see the studies collected in Colin Chase, ed., *The Dating of "Beowulf"* (Toronto, 1981) and the revisionary account in Kevin Kiernan, *"Beowulf" and the "Beowulf" Manuscript* (Ann Arbor, 1981).

[5] On the manuscript and its history, see Kiernan, *"Beowulf" and the "Beowulf" Manuscript*. On editing and punctuation, see Bruce Mitchell, "The Dangers of Disguise: Old English Texts in Modern Punctuation," *Review of English Studies* 31 (1980): 385–413, and the responses in Fred C. Robinson, *"Beowulf" and the Appositive Style* (Knoxville, 1985), pp. 18–19.

[6] Charles Segal, "Greek Tragedy: Writing, Truth, and the Representation of the Self," *Interpreting Greek Tragedy: Myth, Poetry, Text* (Ithaca, N.Y., 1986).

[7] Niles, *"Beowulf": The Poem and Its Tradition*, p. 153.

[8] Niles, *"Beowulf": The Poem and Its Tradition*, p. 153.

[9] Erich Auerbach, *Mimesis: The Representation of Reality in Western Literature*, trans. W. R. Trask (Princeton, 1953), p. 5. See Osborn, "The Great Feud," especially p. 977 and n. 14, although she does not quote directly from Auerbach's study.

[10] Auerbach, *Mimesis*, p. 6.

[11] My discussion in this and the following paragraphs of the differing levels of time in the poem draws on a number of distinctions from recent narrative theory. For a formalist approach to distinguishing between reader "clock-time" and "fictional" chronology, see A. A. Mendilow, *Time and the Novel* (New York, 1972), pp. 63–73. For the concept of a "temporal stance," which embraces both "the pace of the narrative and the temporal distance between the moment of telling and the moment when the narrated events take place," see Susan Snaider Lanser, *The Narrative Act* (Princeton, 1981), pp. 198–201.

[12] See, for example, Goldsmith, *The Mode and Meaning of "Beowulf"*, pp. 88–89, and Osborn, "The Great Feud," pp. 977–98. For an argument that the "name" inscribed on the hilt is that of Heremod, see Köberl, "The Magic Sword in *Beowulf*."

13 Auerbach, *Mimesis*, p. 7.

14 Osborn, "The Great Feud," pp. 977–78 (emphasis hers).

15 Osborn, "The Great Feud," p. 978 (emphasis hers).

16 For a reading of the passage that stresses such doctrinal content, see Goldsmith, *The Mode and Meaning of "Beowulf,"* pp. 88–90, 183.

17 Auerbach, *Mimesis*, p. 5.

18 On the polyvalence of *dryhten, wealdend* and other terms of lordship, see Robinson, *"Beowulf" and the Appositive Style*, pp. 29–59. On the referents of *gigantas*, see Goldsmith, *The Mode and Meaning of "Beowulf,"* pp. 45–46, who adduces Genesis 6.4–7, Job 26.5, and Wisdom 14.6, along with Gregory's remarks in the *Moralia in Job* (citing the edition in the *Patrologia Latina*, 76:24), that "all these biblical giants [are] symbols of those who are damned through the sin of pride" (p. 46; see too, pp. 120–23). For the story of the giants as the myth of the war against the Titans, see Boethius, *Consolation of Philosophy*, chapter 3, par. 12, where Lady Philosophy refers to the fables of which the Prisoner must have heard: "'Accepisti,' inquit, 'in fabulis lacessentes caelum Gigantas.'" In the Alfredian translation the passage reads: "Hwæt ic wat þ ðu geherdest oft reccan on ealdum leasu[m] spellum þte Iob Saturnes sunu sceolde bion se hehsta god ofer ealle oðre godu,] he sceolde bion þæs heofenes sunu,] sceolde ricsian on heofenu[m];] sceolden gigantes bion eorðan suna,] ða sceolden ricsian ofer eorþan;] þa sceolden hi bion swelce hi wæren geswysterna bearn, fordæmþe he sceolde beon heofones sunu,] he eorðan.] þa sceolde þæm gigantum ofþincan þ he hæfde hiera rice" (W. J. Sedgefield, *King Alfred's Old English Version of Boethius* [Oxford, 1899], pp. 98–99).

19 On the etymologies of *writan*, and its resonances with runic epigraphy, see my discussion in chapter 4 of my book *Literacy and Power in Anglo-Saxon England*, pp. 126–57. Klaeber glosses the word simply as "cut, engrave," permitting an argument for nonlettered, pictorial illustration on the hilt. Bosworth-Toller cites few instances of the verb outside the context of incising or writing letters, for example, "Writ ðysne circul mid ðines cnifes orde on anum stane," from *Leechdom*, I.395.3. Other citations refer to the meaning "to draw a figure," such as a horse or cross. Whereas other poetry (notably *Daniel*, line 726, *Maxims I*, line 138) associates *writan* with some form of *run* or *run-stafas*, later religious poetry appropriates the verb as a general term of nonrunic writing (see *Andreas*, line 13, and *Seasons for Fasting*, "on bocstafum [i.e., alphabetic letters] breman and writan"). For the Old Norse cognate *rita* as the verb used to define rune carving, see Claiborne W. Thompson, *Studies in Upplandic Runography* (Austin, 1975), pp. 19–21, and the phrasing in *Atlamál in Groenlenzko*, "Runar nam at rista" ("She [i.e., Gudrun] set about cutting runes," 4.1), "Red ik þær runar,

/ er reist in systir" ("I have read the runes that your sister carved," 11.5–6) and "skyldi vilt rista" ("to cut the runes wrongly," 12.4).

[20] "And Asmund cut [this stone]," the standard conclusion to inscriptions made by Asmund Karasun, an eleventh-century rune carver from Uppland in Sweden. On this figure in particular and on Upplandic runology in general, see Ann Trygstad, "The Järsta Stone," *PMLA* 100 (1985): 9–19, and Thompson, *Studies in Upplandic Runography*. On Old Norse *marka* as "cut" or "carve" in the signatory formulas, see Trygstad, "The Järsta Stone," pp. 12–13 and Thompson, *Studies in Upplandic Runography*, pp. 19–21. More generally, see Richard Cleasbey and Guðbrandr Vigfusson, eds., *An Icelandic-English Dictionary*, 2nd ed. (Oxford, 1957), s.v. *marka*, II, "to sign," and F. Jonsson, ed., *Lexicon Poeticum Antiquiore Linguae Septentiornalis* (Copenhagen, 1966), s.v. *marka*, "cut," and the citation "marka hvitum staf" (to cut a white letter or rune stave) from *Merlinspá*, II, 63, m. A citation in A. Zoega, ed., *A Concise Dictionary of Old Icelandic* (Oxford, 1910), offers the phrase, "ok merkja a nagli nauð," and mark the *nauð*-rune (i.e., the letter N) on one's nail (s.v. *merkja*).

[21] See John Bosworth and T. Northcote Toller, eds., *An Anglo-Saxon Dictionary* (London, 1898), s.v. *gemearcod*. For the gloss, see Arthur S. Napier, *Old English Glosses* (Oxford, 1900), number 3899; the lemma, *signatus*, is from Aldhelm's *De laudibus virginitatis*, Bodleian Library MS Digby 146, fol. 64b, 54,14.

[22] See Bosworth-Toller, *settan*, XIII, "to compose a book," offering this quotation from the Old English Bede, "Ic ðas boc wrat and sette . . . ic sette feower boc," and the phrasing cited from the Laws of Alfred, "On gewrit settan," "to put into writing," which may itself be a translation of the Latin idiom *litteris mandare* ("to put into writing"). For Old Norse *setja*, "to compose a book," see Cleasbey and Vigfusson, s. v. *setja*, and the citations to the phrase *setta saman* from the works of Snorri Sturlusson.

[23] Trygstad, "The Järsta Stone," p. 18.

[24] Trygstad, "The Järsta Stone," p. 15.

[25] "Raði drængR þar rynn se runum þæim sum Balli risti," quoted and translated in Trygstad, "The Järsta Stone," p. 17. Although Trygstad calls attention to this and many other signatures that "mention both raising the stone and carving the runes as significant aspects of the commemoration" (p. 17), she does not explore the relationship between carver and audience as one of challenge or invitation.

[26] "raþu runaR rít lit rista toliR," quoted and translated in Trygstad, "The Järsta Stone," p. 18, to which she offers an alternate translation: "Interpret the runes—Tolir had (the runes) carved correctly."

[27] "þisar runar rist sa þaþr er runstr er fyrir uæstan haf," one of three twelfth-century inscriptions on a stone found in the Orkneys. Printed in Lucien Musset,

Introduction à la Runologie (Paris, 1965), pp. 440–41 (no. 159), and described as part of "un exercise de virtuosité littéraire et runologique" by an Icelandic carver in the Orkneys (p. 441). For a similar and even more hyperbolic assertion of the rune carver's skill, see Trygstad, "The Järsta Stone," p. 17, who quotes an Upplandic inscription: "Iak veit Hæstain, þa Holmstæin broðr, mænnr rynasta a Miðgarði" ("I know the brothers Hastæin and Holmstæin were among men the most knowledgeable about runes in Midgard," i.e., on earth).

[28] "brantr riti iak þu raþa khn," the concluding section of what is probably an eleventh-century inscription from Oland. Printed in Musset, *Introduction à la Runologie*, p. 409 (no. 95), with the note that *khn* is an error for *kan*.

[29] For other examples of the rune carver's challenge to the reader, see the inscriptions quoted in Trygstad, "The Järsta Stone," pp. 16–18, and the following selection from Lucien Musset, "Anthologie runique," in *Introduction à la Runologie*: nos. 48, 67, 95, 106, 159.

[30] Trygstad, "The Järsta Stone," p. 16.

[31] See Thompson, *Studies in Upplandic Runography*, pp. 22–32, and the responses to earlier work cited therein.

[32] See the remarks in Hawkes and Page, "Swords and Runes in South-East England," on an "unusual feature of the Chessel Down hilt": "the little rectangular gold plate, decorated with tiny filigree rings inside a beaded border, which now adheres to the corroded iron tang. . . . Such ornaments are rare on sword handles, and this one at once recalls the gold filigree mountings on a well preserved horn and hilt from an unknown province in Cumberland" (p. 12). Hawkes and Page argue that this form of filigree ornamentation is Scandinavian in origin and workmanship: "That it is Scandinavian in origin seems overwhelmingly probable. Fine ring-filigree is not a characteristic of Anglo-Saxon goldwork, whereas in Scandinavia filigree of comparable delicacy is relatively common, particularly on jewelry of the late fifth and early sixth centuries" (p. 12).

[33] Osborn, "The Great Feud," p. 977.

[34] See Mitchell, *Old English Syntax*, 2 vols. (Oxford, 1985), 1:718, quoting Eston Everett Ericson, *The Use of 'Swa' in Old English* (Baltimore, 1932), p. 19, that "initial *swa* may serve as a mere transitional link between clauses or at the head of a sentence. In such examples, the modal signification is so low that the *swa* approximates 'and.'" My understanding of this remark implies that *swa* may link two items in a list, both of which are equal in value or referent: thus, two inscriptions of the same kind.

[35] Most recent critics believe that there is at least some relationship between the hilt and the sermon. For Irving, both function in the governing drama of heroic advice (*A Reading of "Beowulf*," pp. 145–53). Goldsmith's intuition that "both the

engraving of the antediluvian war upon the sword-hilt and the central thought of the admonition [in the sermon] . . . must have something to do with each other," becomes her argument: "The sermon was written as a key to the interpretation of the story" (*The Mode and Meaning of "Beowulf,"* p. 183; see also her chapter 6, "Hrothgar's Admonition to Beowulf," pp.183–209).

36 For *run* (counsel, secret, mystery, text) and *ræd* (advice, interpretation) as an alliterative pair, see *Beowulf*, line 1325, where Hrothgar says of Æschere, "min *run*-wita and min *ræd*-bora" ("my speaker of wisdom and my bearer of counsel"), and *Beowulf*, lines 171–72, regarding the Danes in counsel, "monig oft gesæt / rice to rune, ræd eahtedon" ("Many a noble sat often in council, sought a plan"). See, too, the pairing in *Seasons for Fasting*, "rincum to *ræde* and him *runa* gescead" (line 6), and in *Exodus*, "*run* bið gerecenod, *ræd* forð gæð," (line 526). For Old Norse parallels, see *Atlamál in Groenlenzko* 11.5, Kostbera to Hogni, "Red ek þær *runar*" (in Ursula Dronke, *The Poetic Edda*, vol. 1 (Oxford, 1969). In stanza 9, while Kostbera knows the meaning of runes (*runa*), she is unable to "construe" (*raða*) their mutilated inscription. Although its meaning is still subject to debate, the phrasing at the close of Riddle 58 may sustain the pairing of the two words: "Þry sind in naman / ryhte runstafas, þara is rad forma" (lines 14–15). For a summary of solutions and discussion of the meaning of *rad* here, see Craig Williamson, *The Old English Riddles of the Exeter Book* (Chapel Hill, 1977), pp. 311–12, who prints the word with a capital, *Rad*, implying that it is the name of the R-rune. This pairing may also survive in *Sir Gawain and the Green Knight*, when Arthur's counselors decide to give Gawain the beheading game: "Ryche togeder con roun, / And syþen þay redden alle same" (lines 362–63).

37 See *Oxford English Dictionary*, s.v. *read*, which remarks that "the sense of considering or explaining something obscure or mysterious is also common to the various [Germanic] languages, but the application of this to the interpretation of ordinary writing, and to the expression of this in speech, is confined to English and ON, in the latter perhaps under Eng. influence."

38 See Musset, *Introduction à la Runologie*, pp. 89–90, and Richard L. Morris, "Northwest-Germanic *Run*—'Rune': A Case of Homonomy with Go. *Runa*, 'Mystery,'" *Beiträge zur Geschichte der deutschen Sprache und Literatur* 107 (1985): 347–48.

39 Musset, *Introduction à la Runologie* pp. 380–81 (no. 48).

40 The chalice riddle presents a carved object in which the *wunda* (wounds) apparently cut into it are "letters or icons that inspire faith and that enable the dumb creature to 'speak' of Christ before the congregation" (Williamson, *Old English Riddles*, p. 313). The riddle concludes with an injunction to explain or interpret the function of such "wounds": "Ræde se þe wille" (line 15). At the

close of the helmet or shirt riddle (Krapp-Dobbie 59), the solver is enjoined, "Ræd hwæt ic mæne."

41 The clearest exposition of the sermon, with attentions to its rhetorical control and generic affiliations in the wisdom literature, is Elaine Tuttle Hansen, "Hrothgar's Sermon in *Beowulf* as Paternal Wisdom," *Anglo-Saxon England* 11 (1982): 53–67, later reworked into her book, *Solomon Complex* (Toronto, 1988), pp. 55–67.

42 Osborn, "The Great Feud," p. 978.

43 On the traditional metaphors for oral-poetic composition, and the shifts attendant on the introduction of writing in Anglo-Saxon England (exemplified in Cynewulf's poetry), see Jeff Opland, "From Horseback to Monastic Cell: The Impact on English Literature of the Introduction of Writing," in *Old English Literature in Context*, ed. John D. Niles (Totawa, 1980), pp. 30–43.

44 I am not arguing for a specific set of references to religious doctrine or patristic exegesis, although much of what I am saying here did form the subject of early medieval speculations on language, and in particular in commentaries on Genesis from Augustine to Bede. For a survey of these traditions, see Marcia Colish, *The Mirror of Language*, 2nd ed. (Minneapolis, 1985). For a review of the impact of Adam's naming of creatures (Genesis 2.19) on later exegetical theories of the sign, see R. Howard Bloch, *Etymologies and Genealogies: A Literary Anthropology of the French Middle Ages* (Chicago, 1983), pp. 39–45, especially p. 40 (on Adam as first namer and the implications of "this founding linguistic moment" to later rhetorical, theological, and grammatical speculation) and p. 45 (on the centrality of this gesture to later medieval "strategies of origin"). Some specific texts relevant to these intuitions include Augustine, *De Genesi Litterarum* 10.12.20–22, and Isidore, *Etymologies* 12.1–2. For a reading of *Beowulf* through the exegetical understanding of Cain and his descendants, see David Williams, *Cain and Beowulf* (Toronto, 1980).

45 My treatment of naming in the poem, and its attentions to the ways in which names are announced or deferred, derives from the suggestive remarks in Patricia Parker, *Inescapable Romance: Studies in the Poetics of a Mode* (Princeton, 1979). Her argument, in brief, is that the nature of the romance quest involves the hero's and the reader's search for meaning and closure. By deferring the naming or identification of key figures in the narrative, romance poets place the reader on the quest for understanding. Working, in part, from the theoretical reformulations of Fredric Jameson, Parker states that romance "necessitates the projection of an Other, a *project* which comes to an end when that Other reveals his identity or 'name'" (citing Fredric Jameson, "Magical Narratives: Romance as Genre," *New Literary History* 7.1 [1975]: 161). See, further, her remarks at

pp. 61-69, 99, and 127. For an exemplary discussion of an analogous use of names and name-play in the *Odyssey*, see Norman Austin, "Name Magic in the *Odyssey*," *California Studies in Classical Philology* 5 (1972): 1–19. Although I do not concentrate on its approaches or attend primarily to its conclusions, the influential work of Fred Robinson should be mentioned as well. See his "The Significance of Names in Old English Literature," *Anglia* 86 (1968): 14–58, and "Some Uses of Name-Meanings in Old English Poetry," *Neuphilologische Mitteilungen* 69 (1968): 161–71.

[46] Beowulf describes his armor as "Welandes geweorc" at line 455 (see Klaeber, *Beowulf*, p. 145, for sources and parallels). *Hrunting* is the name of Unferth's sword, which fails Beowulf in battle with Grendel's mother (lines 1459, 1490, 1659, and 1807). *Nægling* is Beowulf's sword, which breaks during the fight with the dragon (line 2680). It may be significant that the only sword which does not fail in the poem is the unnamed gigantic sword which Beowulf finds lying in Grendel's hall, whereas the named and known swords cannot harm the monsters. For a recent reassessment of the nature and function of swords in the poem, see Overing, "Swords and Signs."

[47] Charles Segal, "Greek Tragedy," p. 81.

[48] Segal, "Greek Tragedy," pp. 81–82.

[49] Segal, "Greek Tragedy," pp. 93–94, discussing the *semata lugra* encoded on the tablets Bellerophon carries and which inscribe his death (*Iliad* 6.168); the account in Thucydides of the "Spartan Pausanias' illicit dealings with the Persian king, [where] letters are the mark of his secrecy" (Thucydides 1.133); and the associations between "writing, trickery, concealed love, and female desire as all related distortions of the truth" in Sophocles' *Trachiniae* and Euripides' *Hyppolytus*. See, further, Segal's remarks on the ways in which "textual self-consciousness" provokes a "concern with the hidden, private, inner space"—that is, with the representation of interior, emotional states and the presentation of action in enclosed, domestic spaces (p. 99).

[50] For a review of scholarship on oral poetry, and a reformulation of the dynamics of performance and reception using analogues from South African literatures, see Jeff Opland, *Anglo-Saxon Oral Poetry* (New Haven, 1980), especially his remarks on pp. 80–85 concerning "the social character of an oral performance: the performance is part of an event, it consists of actions by the performer and interactions with the audience" (p. 83). Note that I am not concerned here with the question of oral composition as represented in *Beowulf* or as governing Old English poetry generally; rather, I am concerned with the notion of performance and the social norms that govern its reception. For arguments about the nature of the transmission of oral poetry, and its mediations by writing, see Katherine

O'Brien O'Keeffe, "Orality and the Developing Text of Caedmon's *Hymn*," *Speculum* 62 (1987): 1–20.

51 Segal, "Greek Tragedy," p. 79.

52 *Brunnanburh*, lines14b-15: "mære tungol, / glad ofer grundas Godes condel beorht." Beowulf's words, "gæst yrre cwom," echo the poet's earlier description of Grendel approaching Heorot, "Ða com of more under mist-hleoþum / Grendel gongan Godes *yrre* bær" ("Then from the moor under the mist-hills Grendel came walking, wearing God's anger," lines 710–11), and the appellation, earlier, "Wæs se grimma *gæst* Grendel haten" ("The grim spirit was called Grendel," line 102).

53 James L. Rosier, "Uses of Association: Hands and Feasts in *Beowulf*," *PMLA* 78 (1963): 11.

54 Rosier, "Uses of Association," shows that the name "Hondscio," unique in Old English, does appear in Old and Middle High German, and is close to the Modern German *Handschuh*, "glove" (p. 11, n. 14).

55 Rosier, "Uses of Association," pp. 11–12.

56 Compare Parker's remarks on Spenser's technique: "Editions which provide the reader with the identity and name of each character as he appears could not be further from the phenomenology of Spenser's poem, where 'identity' is less an endpoint than a process of discovery. 'Meaning' is deferred in order to leave room for the crucial act of reading, which does not necessarily lead to a single end" (*Inescapable Romance*, p. 99). In *Beowulf*, Hondscio's name is withheld, in a similar way I think, in order to defer the reader's recognition of its meaning and make the hero himself the one who confers "identity" on this previously nameless soldier.

57 Robinson, *"Beowulf" and the Appositive Style*, pp. 71–74.

58 Krapp-Dobbie refers to George Philip Krapp and Elliott Van Kirk Dobbie, eds., *The Exeter Book*, The Anglo-Saxon Poetic Records 3 (New York, 1936). The numbers refer to their numbering of the Old English riddles in the Exeter manuscript.

59 I quote from the edition of Williamson, *Old English Riddles*, who numbers this Riddle 37, and I rely on his explications of these puzzling lines. Their ambiguities, for Williamson, produce two equally plausible translations; one I offer in my text, the other being: "It takes a long time to say how its state goes afterwards— the twisted (or obscure) destinies of events." Both translations, together with commentary, are on pp. 263–64 of his edition.

60 See Williamson's extended interpretation of this riddle in *Old English Riddles*, pp. 258–61.

61 James Redfield, *Nature and Culture in the Iliad: The Tragedy of Hector* (Chicago, 1975), pp. 35–41.

[62] Redfield, *Nature and Culture in the Iliad*, p. 37.

[63] Redfield, *Nature and Culture in the Iliad*, p. 39.

[64] Debate on the nature of the Finnsburh Fragment and Episode has often centered on the reconstruction of an earlier, lost narrative, and on the ways in which the performance of the story at Heorot exemplifies both the techniques and subject matter of oral composition. For a summary account of the arguments and findings, see Donald K. Fry, *Finnsburh: Fragment and Episode* (London, 1974).

[65] Among the most recent readings of the *Odyssey* along these lines, see Pietro Pucci, *Odysseus Polutropos* (Ithaca, N.Y., 1987), especially pp. 76–109; Sheila Murnaghan, *Disguise and Recognition in the Odyssey* (Princeton, 1987), especially pp. 143–75; and Jenny Strauss Clay, *The Wrath of Athena: Gods and Men in the Odyssey* (Princeton, 1983).

[66] Murnaghan, *Disguise and Recognition in the Odyssey*, p. 152.

[67] For an analysis of the many problems of syntax and vocabulary in this passage, and the apparently vague relationship between singer and king, see Opland, *Anglo-Saxon Oral Poetry*, pp. 199–201. In my quotation of the passage, and my abbreviated use of Donaldson's translation, I break at line 2110a, before the appearance of the "rumheort king," who, as Opland illustrates, may or may not be equated with the singer in this episode.

[68] R. Howard Bloch, *Medieval French Literature and Law* (Berkeley, 1977), p. 199.

[69] Bloch, *Medieval French Literature and Law*, p. 199.

[70] Murnaghan, *Disguise and Recognition in the Odyssey*, pp. 166–75 and the bibliography cited therein.

[71] Murnaghan, *Disguise and Recognition in the Odyssey*, p. 173.

[72] "Replicauit ex ordine cuncta, quae sibi aduersa, quaeue in aduersis solacia prouenissent" (*Bede's Ecclesiastical History of the English People*, ed. Bertram Colgrave and R. A. B. Mynors [Oxford, 1969], pp. 404–05). Caedmon first goes "to the reeve who was his master, telling him of the gift he had received" ("Veniensque mane ad uilicum, qui sibi praeerat, quid doni percepisset indicauit"); he is then taken to the scholars of the abbey where "he was then bidden to describe his dream in the presence of a number of the more learned men and also to recite his song" ("multis doctoribus uiris praesentibus, indicare somnium et dicere carmen") (*Ecclesiastical History*, pp. 416–17).

[73] For a discussion of the poet's review of the story, and his reflections on the relationships of source and history, present purpose and future readerships, see James W. Earl, "The Typological Structure of *Andreas*" in Niles, *Old English Literature in Context*, pp. 68–69.

[74] Bloch, *Medieval French Literature and Law*, p. 201.

[75] Bloch, *Medieval French Literature and Law*, p. 202.

"AS I ONCE DID WITH GRENDEL": BOASTING AND NOSTALGIA IN *BEOWULF*

SUSAN M. KIM

This essay reads *Beowulf*'s presentation of both what threatens and what establishes human language, and thus human identity. Because language works by difference, by alienation of the sign as thing and the sign as meaning, but also of sign from sign, the very process of identification in language inscribes alienation within human identity. On one level, this is the alienation of the self understood as the body and the self represented in language. In *Beowulf* this alienation is literalized in the identification of Beowulf with the monster and the establishment of the severed arm as a "sign" of Beowulf's triumph over the monster. Given the poem's literal construction of language as dislocation from a body equally the hero's own but made monstrous to him, the work of the poem becomes the negotiation of ways to use language so conceived: as Beowulf shifts from boasting as his identifying mode of speech to the nostalgia which marks his final words, the poem manipulates the alienation internal to human identity so that it can be articulated not as horror but as potential. This essay locates the poem's representations of linguistic performance in the context of early medieval linguistic theory and, within this context, treats the engagements with linguistic performance as negotiations of concepts of personal identity. This essay also examines how these negotiations are treated in the poem's modern reception and in light of contemporary fascinations with the monstrous other and with nostalgia.

From *Modern Philology* 103.1 (August 2005): 4–27; reprinted with permission of The University of Chicago Press.

In *Beowulf*, the monsters and the violence associated with them surface first in the modes of speech through which men define themselves: the *scop* song and boasting. Grendel appears in the poem and the world of Heorot when the *scop* sings his song of creation. As J. R. R. Tolkien observes, "Grendel is maddened by the sound of harps."[1] The *scop* is "se þe cuþe/ frumsceaft fira feorran reccan" ("he who knew how to relate from far back the origin of men," lines 90–91).[2] His song of creation is about the divine construction of the human world. Grendel's terror is thus paired with the presentation of a stock narrative of human origin. Hrothgar's later description of Grendel's terror, however, does not locate its cause in the *scop* song that the text suggests is its provocation. When Hrothgar tells Beowulf about the horror Grendel has worked in the hall, he elides the attack. He can't seem to say the words; as he puts it,

> Sorh is me to secganne on sefan minum
> gumena ængum, hwæt me Grendel hafað
> hynðo on Heorote mid his heteþancum,
> færniða gefremed. (lines 473–76a)

> It is a sorrow for me in my heart to say to any men what Grendel with his hateful thoughts has brought about for me of harm in Heorot, of sudden attacks.

Instead, he describes first his men boasting and then the devastation in the morning:

> Ful oft gebeotedon beore druncne
> ofer ealowæge oretmecgas,
> þæt hie in beorsele bidan woldon
> Grendles guþe mid gryrum ecga.
> Ðonne wæs þeos medoheal on morgentid,
> drihtsele dreorfah, þonne dæg lixte,
> eal bencþelu blode bestymed,
> heall heorudreore. (lines 480–87a)

> Very often having drunk beer, warriors boasted over ale-cups that they wished to await Grendel's warfare in the beer-hall with the terrors of sword-edges. Then in the morning was this mead hall, the noble hall, stained with blood, when day shone, all the bench-planks wet with blood, the hall with battle-blood.

Hrothgar's elision not only contrasts the boasts and the ensuing reality. It also locates Grendel's terror, albeit by a kind of *post hoc ergo propter hoc* logic, *within* the warriors' boasting speeches: the warriors boast, and in the morning the hall is wet with blood. This representation of horror embedded in the modes of boasting and the *scop* song suggests that the figuration of the monstrous violence of the text is, among other things, a literalization of the function of its language.

Vivien Law has demonstrated that scholars from late antiquity through the Middle Ages theorized language through models of human identity.[3] She argues, "We cannot think about language without making some assumptions about the nature of man. Usually implicit, as often as not unconscious, our picture of the human being rebounds upon our view of language, shaping it to conform to our mental image of its speakers."[4] Hence, she argues that Augustine's comparison of the sounds of language to the body of man and of the meaning to his soul relies upon a model, largely dominant throughout the period, of human identity as a relationship of body and soul.[5] The very compelling evidence Law marshals, however, also suggests a corollary: if "we cannot think about language without making some assumptions about the nature of man," the nature of man is also implicated in our understanding of language.

Language, for Augustine, operates through dislocation, or difference, between the sign and its meanings. In *On Christian Doctrine*, Augustine defines the sign as "a thing which causes us to think of something beyond the impression the thing itself makes on the senses."[6] In his distinction between natural signs, such as smoke and animal tracks, and the conventional signs of language, Augustine emphasizes the necessary absence of a natural connection between linguistic signs and their meanings as the linguistic sign transfers meaning between speakers. Similarly, in his distinction between literal and figurative readings, Augustine stresses the function of difference: literal signs, as linguistic signs, work by "bringing forth and transferring to another mind the action of the mind in the person who makes the sign,"[7] but figurative signs, because they "occur when that thing which we designate by literal sign is used to signify something else," require an additional level of transfer and difference.[8] Thus, because figurative signs are different from other linguistic signs not so much in kind as in degree, the dangers which Augustine represents in the failure to read figurative signs correctly as such speak directly not only to the dangers in reading figurative signs, but also to the dangers in using language. Augustine explains that

when that which is said figuratively is taken as though it were literal, it is un-
derstood carnally. Nor can anything more appropriately be called the death
of the soul than that condition in which the thing which distinguishes us
from beasts, which is the understanding, is subjected to the flesh in pursuit
of the letter. He who follows the letter takes figurative expressions as if they
were literal and does not refer the things signified to anything else.[9]

As Law's analysis has suggested, for Augustine human identity is a
relationship of the soul, here associated with reason, and the flesh, or the
body; mapping that relationship in the theorizing of reading reveals much
about the construction of both soul and body: the devaluation of the body and
its association with death, the conception of not simply the soul but reason as
"that which distinguishes us from beasts." However, the fact that here *linguistic*
failure, the failure to recognize difference, to transfer meaning from the literal
to the figurative, is the condition which causes "the death of the soul" also
suggests that human identity is maintained *through* language; *like* language, it
requires difference, difference from the literal, the carnal, the body.

Given such a conception of language and human identity, one might
expect to find in *Beowulf* a representation of the relationship between
language and body characterized, for example, by heroic efforts to resist
embodiment or to identify the self with language rather than body. Sheila
Murnaghan locates just such relationships in Greek epic and early Greek
tragedy. In Murnaghan's argument, the violence catalogued in the *Iliad*, for
example, represents the ultimate embodiment of death, embodiment the
hero is always ready to risk but also always resists, particularly through his
identification with forms of language such as the boast, which replace or
at least delay physical combat.[10] However, in *Beowulf*, the same modes of
language, the *scop*'s poetry and the heroic boast, register rather than replace
violence and literal, bodily dislocation in the form of the monster Grendel.

As Michael Lapidge has argued, although Grendel is named and thus
rendered familiar if not precisely identifiable, in his approach to Heorot,
Grendel's physical appearance is almost entirely obscured. For Lapidge, this
obscurity creates terror both within the poem and for the audience.[11] Yet
Grendel's monstrosity is manifest in several ways: he has a big body, he is a
voracious cannibal, and he never speaks. The terror he represents is clearly
the terror of the speechless body, the terror of losing oneself to that body, of
falling into it, being eaten by it. At the same time, however, the Danes' terror
at the approach of Grendel is also, and perhaps more immediately, the terror
of *losing* the body, of the body being eaten by something alien to it. *Beowulf*

embeds this double terror in both the *scop* song and boasting because both modes of speech make a claim to the alignment of word and deed, like that of language and body. The impossibility of that alignment makes the potential for slippage from human identity monstrously apparent.[12]

The poem flags the problem of boasting's claim to the alignment of word and deed as soon as Beowulf sets foot in the land of the Danes. The coast guard warns Beowulf, as the Geats' most prominent boaster, "Æghwæþres sceal / scearp scyldwiga gescad witan, / worda ond worca, se þe wel þenceð" ("The sharp shield-warrior, who thinks well, must understand the difference of each of words and deeds," lines 287–89). As T. A. Shippey points out, the literal translation of this maxim, on the level of the plot, doesn't make much sense. As he says, "Any fool can tell the difference between words and deeds," and the maxim should probably read, on this level, something like "The sharp shield-warrior must be able to judge everything, words as well as deeds."[13] The maxim does make sense, however, literally, in the context of the poem's concern with human identity as the negotiation between the self understood as the body and the self represented in language. Understanding the difference between words and deeds means understanding the impossibility of the claim to their alignment that underlies the boast.

Beowulf, however, does not seem to respond to the coast guard's warning. After an extended boasting session in Hrothgar's court, Beowulf fights Grendel: he literalizes his boasting speech by fighting with grips, by physically holding on to the monster, in the same way that he is attempting to hold his body to his words.[14] The problem that he thus faces is that to uphold his boast, to purge (*fælsian*) and protect Heorot, he also has to fail in his grip. To purge Heorot, he has to rid it of Grendel permanently. To be human, he has to both speak and be in human form: he has to hold together the self he represents in language and the self he inhabits as his body. But to speak, even in boasting, he has to maintain the difference between the sign as thing and the sign as meaning and that between his body and the self he represents in language. That Grendel's body is also Beowulf's own becomes explicit during the fight, when, as Katherine O'Brien O'Keeffe points out, the bodies of the two *æglæcan* are literally joined.[15] Beowulf is trapped by the demands of his boast, by the relationship that that mode of speech forces him to take not with an external opponent, but with himself.

O'Keeffe argues that the poem's exploration of the limits of the human draws both the hero and the monster to a boundary where the distinction between them blurs. O'Keeffe defines the human on the level of the social rather than the personal.[16] Her argument, however, applies to the problem which Beowulf's mode of speech presents. O'Keeffe concludes that the geographic distancing of Grendel from human society is an effort to reassure, because "Grendel is at his most terrifying not in the marches but in the place of men. When he opens the door of the hall, our horror is a horror of recognition."[17] Although for O'Keeffe Grendel is a parody of the human, her own account suggests that, at least in the moment of confrontation, Grendel is literally inseparable from Beowulf; that is, as Jeffrey Jerome Cohen has more recently argued, Grendel *is* Beowulf, and thus Beowulf fights paradoxically both to defeat and to hold on to him, to preserve him.[18]

As Beowulf finds himself compelled by his boast to attempt to align his words and deeds identically, he confronts the monster Grendel; that is, he faces both his own body, which he alienates from himself, and the horror of losing that body, which is equally himself, through that alienation. Beowulf, heroically, tries to hold on to Grendel but cannot. He tells Hrothgar,

> Ic hine hrædlice heardan clammum
> on wælbedde wriþan þohte,
> þæt he for mundgripe minum scolde
> licgean lifbysig, butan his lic swice;
> ic hine ne mihte, þa Metod nolde,
> ganges getwæman, no ic him þæs georne ætfealh,
> feorhgeniðlan; wæs to foremihtig
> feond on feþe. Hwæþere he his folme forlet
> to lifwraþe last weardian,
> earm ond eaxle; (lines 963–72a)

> I intended to twist him quickly with hard grips on a bed of death, so that he because of my handgrip had to lie down, struggling for life, except his body escaped; I could not, when the creator did not wish, separate him from his going, by no means did I hold to him, to the life-enemy so eagerly; he was too strong, the enemy, in his going. Nevertheless, he left his arm behind, as a life-protection, his arm and shoulder.

Beowulf cannot purge Heorot in the same way that he cannot hold his body to his words as his boasting speech requires. He insists that he tried, "except his body escaped." Beowulf means Grendel's body here, but he is also talking about his own. Beowulf hasn't exactly failed, however. As he says, Grendel has left behind a literal trace of himself which acts *to lifwraþe*, "as a life-protection." The arm is a "life-protection" for Beowulf because it allows him to uphold, for the moment, the premise of his boasting speech, but it also allows him to escape, for the moment, from his boast's impossibly contradictory demands.

As a "clear sign," a *tacen sweotul* (line 834), the arm is graphically met-onymic, a literal dislocation from the monstrous body. Gillian Overing argues that *Beowulf*'s use of metonymic rather than metaphoric language affirms the ambiguity and play of language and counters the binarism of the masculine economy of violence.[19] Beowulf's violent establishment of the literally metonymic sign of Grendel's arm, however, not only positions the metonymic within the violent economy and the binarism of the mode of boasting; it also counters Overing's assertion that

> the aspect of self, or presence as determiner of meaning in any degree, is ab-sent, simply not required, in a purely metonymic structure. As an instance of the Saussurean system of internally referential differences, or of Derrida's field of infinite substitutions the poem requires that the subject be a func-tion of language, and not the other way around. The nature and function of the self are identified and determined by the nature and function of the system, whether this be language in general or its specific instantiation in a poem. . . . [An] Old English poem encourages, even demands that the reader be "in language"; the metonymic impact of the poem originates in the thrilling and freeing experience of being "spoken."[20]

While the metonymic sign of Grendel's arm is raised as a triumph in the poem, as a remedy to the terror in Heorot, it remains a literal dislocation: the same physicality which makes the arm as sign literally metonymic also in-sists on its presence, its existence—and Beowulf's—as not language but body. The arm as sign is also the remainder of a self identified as presence, or as exactly what lacks language. The sign of the arm suggests not a celebration of absorption by language, but a rejection of the alienation of word and body demanded by language. Beowulf's establishment of the sign of Grendel's arm is already marked by desire for a relationship to language which would allow for the identification of the self otherwise than through its dislocation.

The contingency of Beowulf's solution, however, is evident. As a "clear sign," the arm is evidence of the separation, or difference, from the mon-strous body. But it is a metonymic sign, in the most literal way. Its substitu-tion for the potency of the whole body ("þær wæs eal geador / Grendles grape," "there was, altogether, Grendel's grip," lines 835–36) is proof of Beowulf's successful escape from the impossible task of both holding on to and driving out the monster, or holding the body to his words. At the same time, however, the clearly metonymic sign is also evidence of Beowulf's failure. Beowulf has possession of it, but it is still Grendel's grip (line 836). It is the monstrous body's literal remainder, a trace, and, like spoor, or the footprints that people come from near and far to look at, it is a "leaving," which will track back to the monster whose demise it is celebrating. The arrival of Grendel's mother is already implicit.

Grendel's mother is not just another monster. As the monster's mother, she is literally of his body, as he is of hers. She is called into the poem, however, by his dismemberment and death. Coming as she does to avenge her son's death, her monstrous appearance in the poem is a reformulation not of his whole body, but of his trace, his "last," or the sign which Beowulf has made out of him. As a reformulation of the "clear sign" of Grendel, Grendel's mother appears as a representation, not just a monstrous and speechless body, but *idese onlicnes*, "in the likeness of a woman" (line 1351). In his fight with Grendel's mother, Beowulf is struggling with the result of his fight with Grendel. Accordingly, he finds his way to the mere by following the bloody and obvious tracks: "lastas wæron / æfter waldswaþum wide gesyne, / gang ofer grundas" ("The tracks were seen far along the forest-paths, the track over the plains," lines 1402–04). He goes to the mere, that is, by reading the sign he has made.[21]

Grendel's arm calls forth Grendel's mother because the "clear sign" of the arm clearly locates the body at the same time that it makes that body alien to it, as both its issue (the monster it summons) and its antecedent (the monster's mother).[22] The arm as sign also literalizes the mechanics of boasting on another level. Boasting requires the identification of the present self as a uniform continuity of narratives of past heroism with a promised future.[23] The alternative to fulfilling the boast, matching word and deed on one level, aligning the past stories of heroism with the promised future on another, is death. In order to be Beowulf, Beowulf has to be both the self understood as the body and the self represented in language, as well as both "that Beowulf who competed with Breca and won" and "that Beowulf who will fight with Grendel and win." The problem for Beowulf with this identification is that he must lay claim to a past which he will prove by his future performance and that he will use to justify the promise of his future performance. This past, however, is not simply his as he lived it. The past that he requires in order to justify his promised future is a narrative, and a public one, and thus is not stable, concrete, indisputable, or inalienable.

Beowulf is confronted by the alienability of his past in his *flyting* match with Unferth.[24] Unferth begins,

Eart þu se Beowulf, se þe wið Brecan wunne,
on sidne sæ ymb sund flite,
ðær git for wlence wada cunnedon
ond for dolgilpe on deop wæter
aldrum neþdon? (lines 506–10a)

Are you that Beowulf who contended with Breca, competed in swimming
on the broad sea, where you two because of pride made a trial of the water,
and because of foolish boasting risked your lives in deep water?

He concludes his challenge,

Ðonne wene ic to þe wyrsan geþingea,
ðeah þu heaðoræsa gehwær dohte,
gimre guðe, gif þu Grendles dearst
nihtlongne fyrst nean bidan. (lines 525–28)

Then I expect from you worse things, although you were strong on every
occasion in storms of battle, in grim battle, if you dare to wait for Grendel
nearby for a nightlong space of time.

Beowulf can and does contradict Unferth with his own accounts of both
the swimming match with Breca and his promised outcome for the fight
with Grendel. Nothing in his account, however, makes that account more
recognizable as fact—as Beowulf's actual experience—for all that he might
"consider it truth."[25] Beowulf recognizes his alienation from his own iden-
tifying narrative: his recognition becomes clear when Beowulf both denies
that he is boasting and escalates the *flyting* with his charge of fratricide.
Beowulf concludes his version of the match against Breca,

Breca næfre git
æt heaðolace, ne gehwæþer incer,
swa deorlice dæd gefremede
fagum sweordum—no ic þæs [fela] gylpe—,
þeah ðu þinum broðrum to banan wurde,
heafodmægum; þæs þu in helle scealt
werhðo dreogan, þeah þin wit duge. (lines 583b–88)

Breca never yet, nor either of you, accomplished such bold deeds at battle with decorated swords—by no means therefore do I boast much—although you became a murderer to your brothers, to near kinsmen; for that you must endure punishment in hell, although your wit is strong.

In order to carry his boast, Beowulf asserts that he is not really boasting. In effect, he claims that his narrative is simply true. Beowulf attempts to anchor his narrative in experience that is widely recognizable but that he can also claim as indisputably his own. The anxiety attendant upon this attempt, however, is manifest in Beowulf's turn immediately after making this claim to his charge of fratricide and his manipulation of a narrative of Unferth's past.[26] Beowulf recognizes that he cannot simply counter Unferth's charge with the identifying story of his own "true" past, because the mere fact of Unferth's accusation presents the inevitable alienability of that past and thus the impossible instability of the identity he constructs by boasting.

Beowulf's establishment of the arm as sign literalizes the dislocations inherent for Beowulf in his identification through boasting. The literalness of the arm as sign poses a temporary solution to the problems of identification that it also reveals. This literalness articulates the desire for revision, not only of the alienated relationship of the self represented in language and the self understood as the body, but also that of the alienability of the self constructed as the continuity of its past and promised future. Beowulf himself proposes this desired revision when he revises his story on his return to Higelac's court.

· · ·

In his re-telling, Beowulf introduces two significant details into the story of the fight with Grendel: the name of the warrior Hondscio and the description of Grendel's fabulous glove. Beowulf tells Higelac,

> þær wæs Hondscio hild onsæge,
> feorhbealu fægum; he fyrmest læg,
> gyrded cempa; him Grendel wearð
> mærum maguþegne to muðbonan
> leofes mannes lic eall forswealg.
> . . . . Glof hangode
> sid ond syllic, searobendum fæst;
> sio wæs orðoncum eall gegyrwed

deofles cræftum ond dracan fellum.
He mec þær on innan unsynningne,
dior dædfruma gedon wolde
manigra sumne; hyt ne mihte swa,
syððan ic on yrre uppriht astod.
To lang is to reccenne, hu i(c ð)am leodsceaðan
yfla gehwylces ondlean forgeald. (lines 2076–94)

There was the battle fatal to the doomed Hondscio, a deadly evil; he, girded
warrior, lay dead first; to him, to the famous young retainer, Grendel be-
came a slayer with the mouth, swallowed up entirely the body of the dear
man. . . . A glove hung roomy and strange, fast with cunning bands; it was
all adorned with skills, crafts of the devil and the skins of a dragon. He, the
fierce doer of (evil) deeds wished to put me, guiltless, inside there, one of
many, but could not do it thus, after I in anger stood upright. It is too long in
the telling, how I paid that enemy of the people the requital of each evil.

Seth Lerer argues that by naming Hondscio and constructing the image of
the glove, Beowulf significantly revises the earlier account.[27] Lerer takes the
name "Hondscio" as punning evidence of Beowulf's transformation of the
episode into a joke, a reassuring social performance. Lerer also focuses on
the glove as a key image in the poem's representation of "the act of imagina-
tive representation itself."[28] He reads the episode as evidence of Beowulf's
self-conscious wordplay and humor, which places the episode with Grendel
in the context of "the great myths of communal ingestion and bodily break-
age" as well as traditions of poetic presentation. Although he looks close-
ly at the glove as a suggestive image of both hand and devouring mouth,
both body and "horrific craft,"[29] Lerer does not note the link between the
hand, which the poem presents as a literal "sign," and the glove as evidence
of Beowulf's skill at poetic transformation. The pairing of the dead man's
name, Hondscio, and the description of Grendel's glove in the context of
his narration of the establishment of the sign of Grendel's arm, suggests not
humor but a different kind of horror, through which Beowulf represents
not only his skill with language, but also his recognition and refusal of the
consuming absence with which this language threatens him.

The terror in the retelling is of being, like Hondscio, snatched away and
eaten. As Lerer argues, Grendel, depicted as grasping hand and bloody
mouth, is thus neatly represented as the glove, "a hand-shaped cavity that
swallows men" (line 735), and Beowulf's self-conscious interjection, "To

lang is to reccenne" ("it is too long to tell," line 2094), emphasizes his recognition of his own skill at linguistic manipulation.[30] However, the juxtaposition of the image of the glove with the sign of the arm, both in the earlier textual presentation and as the "swaðu" in Beowulf's retelling, prevents the simple transformation of this terror into edification or entertainment: the literalness and presence of the arm as sign speaks exactly to the danger of Beowulf's linguistic facility, the danger of being swallowed by the absence necessary to using language. The monstrousness of the glove is thus not only its association with the bodiliness of Grendel, but also its representation as language; as such, the glove also represents the consuming absence at the center of Beowulf's own narrative.[31]

This absence is, as I have argued, in part the absence necessary to using language conceived as founded on the alienation of the sign as thing and the sign as meaning. The absence figured by the glove also suggests, however, the revision of the mode of speech through which Beowulf has chosen to represent himself. Before he fights Grendel's mother, Beowulf offers Hrothgar the maxim, "Ne sorga, snotor guma! Selre bið æghwæm, / þæt he his freond wrece, þonne he fela murne" ("Don't grieve, wise man! It is better for every man that he avenge his friend, than that he mourn much," lines 1384–5). Explicitly, in the context of his boast of a reversal for Hrothgar, Beowulf privileges the action of revenge over mourning. In his retelling, however, Beowulf's language no longer makes the claim of certainty with respect to events in the world. The self-consciousness of Beowulf's language in the retelling is also a deliberate dissociation of the narrative of the past from accountability to events in the past or future. The absence figured by the glove is also recognition that this dissociation involves loss, the loss of exactly the claims to alignment, presence, and continuity that the mode of boasting sustains. This loss is not simply loss, however, because articulating the experience of the loss becomes a means of generating a present identity: the mode of speech which Beowulf is developing around this figured absence is nostalgia.

In nostalgia, the mourning that Beowulf eschews in the confidence of his boasting becomes central, but with the difference that the loss that is lamented is itself recognized as narrative. In her book, *On Longing*, Susan Stewart argues,

> Nostalgia is a sadness without an object, a sadness which creates a longing that of necessity is inauthentic because it does not take part in lived experience. Rather, it remains behind and before that experience. Nostalgia,

like any form of narrative, is always ideological: the past it seeks has never existed except as narrative, and hence, always absent, that past continually threatens to reproduce itself as a felt lack. Hostile to history and its invisible origins, and yet longing for an impossibly pure context of lived experience at a place of origin, nostalgia wears a distinctly utopian face, a face that turns toward a future-past, a past which has only ideological reality. This point of desire which the nostalgic seeks is in fact the absence that is the very generating mechanism of desire.[32]

The absence at the center of the glove, which Beowulf constructs as a metaphor for his own narrative of past achievements, also figures the loss of boasting's claim to alignment of word and deed and continuity of past and future identity. At the same time, it represents the absence essential to the nostalgia through which Beowulf revises the mode of boasting: the absence of the authentic origin which is longed for; the absence of the present moment in an account which defines that moment with respect to a self-consciously inauthentic past.

The poem presents Beowulf's nostalgia as nostalgia explicitly for the mode of boasting. Before Beowulf faces the dragon, the poem draws out the pathos of his imminent death. Beowulf speaks his characteristic boasting words apparently "for the last time" ("niehstan siðe," line 2510) and "for the last time" (*hindeman siðe*, line 2518) greets each of his dear companions. He then claims,

> Nolde ic sweord beran,
> wæpen to wyrme, gif ic wiste hu
> wið ðam aglæcean elles meahte
> gylpe wiðgripan, swa ic gio wið Grendle dyde;
> ac ic ðær heaðufyres hates wene,
> [o]reðes and attres; forðon ic me on hafu
> bord on byrnan. (lines 2518b–23)

I would not wish to carry a sword, a weapon to the worm, if I knew how else against the worm I could fight with grips according to boast, as I once did with Grendel; but I there expect battlefire, hot breath and venom; therefore I have on me shield and armor.

The poem here presents the pause between what Tolkien sees an "opposition of ends and beginnings" or of "two moments in a great life, rising and setting; an elaboration of the ancient and intensely moving contrast between youth and age, first achievement and final death."[33] The appearance of balance and contrast of this sort, however, is not sustained. Beowulf boasts for what the poem promises is the "last time," then claims to have given up boasting, then *boasts,* with a formulation nearly identical to that of his earlier boasts, "Ic mid elne sceall / gold gegangan, oððe guð nimeð, / fearhbealu frecne frean eowerne!" (I with courage shall win gold, or battle, terrible deadly evil will take your lord!" lines 2535–37). What is articulated here as the loss of youth, physicality, and the power of boasting, for both Beowulf and the poem, cannot be simply loss: Beowulf, after his statement of loss, is in fact as able as he was before, and he proves it, immediately, by boasting. The desire implicit in Beowulf's regret ("Ic *nolde* sweorde beran. . . .") becomes manifestly not simply desire for potency that has been lost, but also desire for that potency to be located in the past, so that it *can* be lost and regretted. At the same time, Beowulf's ability to boast again, immediately after his assertion of loss and regret, suggests that his nostalgia is also generative: Beowulf uses his nostalgia not only to dissociate himself from the fullness, the loss of which he laments, but also to reposition himself in his present moment as potentially in possession of that fullness.

Beowulf needs only to mention fighting "as I once did with Grendel" to evoke that fight. It has already been presented to the reader once by the narrator and once by Beowulf; it is already an old story. The effect of Beowulf's evocation is to position him in his present moment with respect to the past moment of his fight with Grendel. Beowulf's desire here is explicitly the nostalgic longing for a past moment of origin, which is full, is fixed, and can be held on to in the way that Grendel could be and which is thus experienced only within the nostalgic narrative of loss: the episode with Grendel has already been represented within the poem as Beowulf's own narrative. Beowulf thus positions himself in a present moment defined by the loss of a past moment; he knows, by the very gesture of its evocation as already an old story, that this is an impossible origin, a self-conscious narrative rather than a lived experience. His present moment, constructed in this way, is not surprisingly an absence in his account. Beowulf moves from his regret, that he cannot now fight as he once did with Grendel, to his expectation of fire and poison from the dragon.

The nostalgia of Beowulf's evocation, with its corresponding absence of an account of his present moment, is weighted. It cannot be simply personal because Beowulf carries the burden of history within the poem. As Laurence de Looze points out, Beowulf's fight with the dragon is "profoundly linked" to the Swedish-Geatish wars, and his defeat will mean the final disintegration of the Geats.[34] Beowulf, both the hero fighting the monster and the king fighting for the survival of a nation, must articulate narratives that are at once personal and historical. De Looze suggests that Beowulf, struggling with the conflicting demands of his situation (knowledge that he must act and answer the dragon's provocation, confounded by the knowledge that his probable death will leave the Geats open to attack by human enemies), uses the technique of "fictional projection" in order to "distance himself from the clash of obligations facing him, to examine them more objectively."[35]

De Looze takes lines 2287–2508 (and following) as a series of narrative shells surrounding Beowulf's extended metaphor of the lamenting father (lines 2444–62). Dragon feud episodes (lines 2287–349, 2508b, and following) surround Swedish-Geatish war episodes (lines 2349b–99a, 2472–508a) which surround the Hæthcyn episodes (lines 2425–43, 2462b–71) which encase the Father's Lament (lines 2444–62a). In de Looze's reading, Beowulf, unable to find a model for solving his dilemma in history, turns finally to fiction, which enables him to return with a resolution to his present problem. More than providing "an excellent example of creative problem solving," however, the location of Beowulf's extended metaphor at the center of the narratives of personal and historical confrontation argues for the centrality of "fictionalizing" to these modes of discourse.[36] This is not to say that the historical in *Beowulf* is reducible to personal fiction, but rather to suggest that the stake in the poem's presentation of the historical narratives of tribal disintegration is a version of that in Beowulf's metaphors of personal loss.[37]

The lament metaphor focuses on the centrality not only of the father's loss, but also of his consciousness of the loss and on the relationship of both loss and consciousness of loss to his own singing and recitation, to his own "fictionalizing":

> Swa bið geomorlic gomelum ceorle
> to gebidanne, þæt his byre ride
> giong on galgan; þonne he gyd wrece,
> sarigne sang, þonne his sunu hangað
> hrefne to hroðre, ond he him helpe ne mæg
> eald ond infrod ænige gefremman.
> Symble bið gemyndgad morna gehwylce
> eaforan ellorsið; oðres ne gymeð
> to gebidanne burgum in innan

yrfeweardas, þonne se an hafað
þurh deaðes nyd dæda gefondad.
Gesyhð sorhcearig on his suna bure
winsele westne, windge reste
reote berofene,—ridend swefað,
hæleð in hoðman; nis þær hearpan sweg,
gomen in geardum, swylce ðær iu wæron.
Gewiteð þonne on sealman, sorhleoð gæleð
an æfter anum; þuhte him eall to rum,
wongas ond wicstede. (lines 2444–62a)

Thus it is sad in the experiencing for an old man, that his son swings young
on the gallows; then he recites a tale, a mournful song, when his son hangs
as a joy to the raven, and he, very old and wise, cannot provide any help to
him. Always he is reminded, on each of mornings, of his son's journey else-
where; he does not care to await another heir in the stronghold, when he
alone has, through death's compulsion, experienced evil deeds. Sorrowful,
he sees in his son's dwelling a deserted winehall, a windy resting-place be-
reft of joy,—the riders sleep in death, the heroes in the grave; there is not the
sound of the harp, sport in the yards, as there once was. He goes then to the
bed, sings a sorrow-song, one alone for the one; to him everything seemed
too roomy, the plains, and the dwelling-place.

The pathos of the metaphor is in the father's tortured recognition of his
impotence. His son hangs on the gallows and there is nothing he can do to
help him. This information is presented tersely in the first six lines of the
metaphor. The remaining thirteen lines dwell on the father's psychology, on
what the world seems like to him after he experiences his son's death. The
present world exists for the father only inasmuch as it can remind him, or
direct him to the world which he considers now lost to him. He won't al-
low his present to be populated; he doesn't heed what is actually there, the
possibility of another heir and life in the stronghold, so that he can occupy
a vacancy, the "deserted wine-hall." This vacancy is not, however, exactly
empty: the father responds to his loss with song. He "recites a tale, a mourn-
ful song," (lines 2445–46) when his son is on the gallows and "sings a sor-
row-song, one alone for the one" (lines 2460–61) from his bed.

The two descriptions of the father moved to song essentially frame the
metaphor, so that the father's loss is presented as not only generative of his
lament, but also contained by it. The father's loss is the life of his son, but

his son is a version of himself, as is clear from the description of the lament, "an æfter anum" ('one after one"). This phrase erases any difference between father and son except for the temporal or causal difference carried by *æfter*, again emphasizing the problem that the father's longing is also for his past self.[38]

In the same way that Beowulf evokes his past and longed-for potency, the father here summons in the "deserted wine-hall" a past that is overtly fictionalized, populated by the stock features of happy life in the hall—riders, heroes, and harpsong—and contained by his "mournful song." Klaeber notes the similarity of the father's lament to the elegy at lines 2246–66.[39] These lines, particularly lines 2262–67, most clearly set up the father's riders, heroes and harpsong as stock, as already figures from a tradition for representing loss.[40]

> Næs hearpan wyn,
> gomen gleobeames, ne god hafoc
> geond sæl swingeð, ne se swifta mearh
> burhstede beateð. Bealocwealm hafað
> fela feorhcynna forð onsended!

> There was not the joy of the harp, or the mirth of the gleewood, nor does the good hawk fly through the hall, or the swift horse tramp the castle court. Evil death has sent forth many of the race of men!

The recognition of this fictionalizing at the center of the narrative shells surrounding the metaphor cuts the narratives of genealogical and tribal disintegration from any perception of their anchoring in a full and tangible origin. At the same time, it makes the experience of that dislocation itself generative of these narratives.

The absence that Beowulf figures by the glove is the absence, or vacancy, of the present moment in the nostalgic narrative, the willful vacancy of the lamenting father's empty wine hall or the aged Beowulf's elision as he moves from the memory of his past potency in the fight with Grendel to the expectation of disintegration. For the older Beowulf, his fight with Grendel and his struggle to uphold the claims of his boasting speech become the focus of his nostalgia; the recognition of their unavoidable failure and repetition, already articulated in the episode, generates his nostalgia, this longing to read the fight as a moment of authenticity and origin. Susan Stewart argues,

> The nostalgic dreams of a moment before knowledge and self-conscious-
> ness that itself lives on only in the self-consciousness of the nostalgic narra-
> tive. Nostalgia is the repetition that mourns the inauthenticity of all repeti-
> tion and denies the repetition's capacity to form identity. . . . The inability of
> the sign to "capture" its signified, of narrative to be one with its object, and
> of genres of mechanical reproduction to approximate the time of face-to-
> face communication leads to a generalized desire for origin, for nature, and
> for unmediated experience that is at work in nostalgic longing.[41]

Beowulf's story about his fight with Grendel according to boast stages "the
inability of the sign to 'capture' its signified, of narrative to be one with its
object." That is, it represents the crisis which in Stewart's account motivates
nostalgia's desire for origin. Beowulf's locating of this episode as the mo-
ment of origin, or fullness, or past potency is thus recognition that that
origin is already a fiction, an absence, a story that can only generate other
stories. But at the same time, by making the "crisis of the sign" just another
story of origins, Beowulf is also denying the tangible reality of that crisis. In
a similar move, in the retelling episode, Beowulf introduces Hondscio and
the glove in order to figure his own narrative construction. After spelling
out the glove's "broad and strange" capaciousness as language, as well as the
monster's desire to put him inside of it, an undifferentiated "one of many,"
Beowulf narrates his refusal to enter the glove, and re-presents the arm as
sign.

Beowulf's re-presentation of the arm as sign is less a viable revision than
evidence of his self-conscious rejection of his understanding of the way his
narrative works. He cannot sustain his rejection. Although Beowulf escapes
the glove in the retelling of the fight with Grendel, he ends torn apart by
the force of his own language: "oð þæt wordes ord / breosthord þurhbræc,"
("until the force of the word broke through the breasthord," lines 2791–92),
and transformed, at his own request, into "the sign of the one brave in bat-
tle" (*beadurofes beacn*, line 3160).[42] The story of Beowulf's absorption into
the language of the poem cannot, however, be read as a straightforward
account of Beowulf's loss to his language, because the poem establishes that
loss as generative, not only of its own dislocations, but also of the potential
for the fullness that is being lamented as lost.

Beowulf dies in the end of the poem. However, by posing through nos-
talgia the potential for an identity not understood as dislocated or alien-
ated from itself, he also poses his nostalgia as a response to the deathliness
of that alienation. Allen Frantzen argues, through his reading of a pun on

the words "forwritan" and "writan," that *Beowulf* juxtaposes writing and death, or the interplay of signs in language and the closure of analysis.[43] He sees the textual conflict reproduced in both the critical discourse and in editorial emendation. He argues that "desire for a complete *Beowulf*—for *Beowulf* as a pure point of origin—has inspired editors to create its wholeness by writing supplements to fill the gaps in the text."[44] Attempts to close the text's literal or figurative gaps with emendation or interpretive certainties reproduce processes represented within the text as violence, "cutting through," and death.[45]

Frantzen does not, however, acknowledge that his own rhetoric of the "restocking" or "recovery" of cultural significance through the histories of textual reception participates inevitably in "revision" or the closure of analysis. His rhetoric thus reinforces his argument that the poem stages the processes of writing and reading and their association with death and in doing so enforces its readers' participation in those processes.[46] Although Frantzen claims that Anglo-Saxon studies "are a way to recall what our cultural memory has begun to forget, and a way to recover connections that have been weakened," he distances himself explicitly from nostalgia ("nostalgia is not my interest") in favor of his consideration of the history of Anglo-Saxon studies and their modern critical contexts.[47] *Beowulf*'s manipulation of nostalgia, however, presents an alternative to the death that Frantzen both reads within the text and its scholarship and reproduces with his rhetoric of the "recovery" of its history. Beowulf's use of his nostalgia before the dragon fight is enabling because it establishes his present moment as an absence of physical potency, an absence that he regrets, but with the same gesture desires ("Ic *nolde* sweorde beran. . . .") because it is proof of his identification through language and thus of his human identity. At the same time, however, his nostalgic evocation renders that potency *potential*, because it reads the story of loss as just a story, a fiction rather than an event in the tangible world and hence a possibility rather than an actual and thus irretrievable loss. This is why Beowulf can counter the image of the glove with that of the arm as sign and why he can boast after lamenting the loss of the physical confidence which enabled him to grapple with Grendel.

The nostalgia of *Beowulf* as a whole works in a similar way. *Beowulf* uses its nostalgia to read its own dislocations not as horror or death, but as generative and potential. Tolkien argues that

> when new, *Beowulf* was already antiquarian, in a good sense, and it now produces a singular effect. For it is now to us itself ancient and yet its maker

was telling of things already old and weighted with regret, and he expended his art in making keen that touch upon the heart which sorrows have that are both poignant and remote. If the funeral of Beowulf moved once like the echo of an ancient dirge, far-off and hopeless, it is to us as a memory brought over the hills, an echo of an echo.[48]

In Stewart's account, "the antiquarian searches for an internal relation between past and present which is made possible by their absolute disruption," and thus the condition of his search is the death of the past that he seeks to revitalize.[49] This is to some extent the project that Tolkien reads in *Beowulf*'s nostalgia, and his focus on Beowulf's funeral is particularly apt, because it plays out the hostility of the antiquarian poet towards the past he portrays. Tolkien's discomfort with his characterization of the poem as such is evident, however, in his rush to modify it. The poem, he explains, is not simply antiquarian, but "antiquarian, in a good sense." He claims that it acquires its power less through disruption than through sameness with the modern reader's experience. The funeral in *Beowulf* is not a funeral, the actual disposal of the dead hero; it is already "the echo of an ancient dirge, far-off and hopeless," which comes to its modern readers as "an echo of an echo." Its loss is not its own, but already a story of loss in the self-conscious past of its "days of yore." Because of this distance, the poem, Tolkien argues, gains its special powers to move through sorrows "that are both poignant and remote."

The nostalgia internal to the poem, however, counters its own "remoteness" by the literalness of its representation of that loss and by the self-conscious manipulation of that representation that makes loss fiction and presence thus potential. Tolkien's own description of the poem as "from a pregnant moment of poise, looking back into the pit,"[50] provides another metaphor for the absence through which the nostalgic poem represents its present moment. At the same time, it suggests, in the reader-poet's stake in the "inevitable ruin" of the past, the death Stewart sees in antiquarianism and Frantzen reads as associated with writing or interpretation in the poem. The "pregnancy" of this "moment of poise," however, also suggests the poem's insistence, on one level, on the bodiliness of identity even in the recognition of the consuming absence necessitated by identification through language. This is the insistent "bodiliness" that emerges in Beowulf's presentation of the arm as sign.

On another level, the "pregnant moment of poise" also figures *Beowulf*'s rejection of the nostalgic absence of an account of its own present moment as present. The poem represents its hero as an old man looking back into the dragon's pit. Beowulf witnesses before he dies the start of the emptying of this pit; the poem ends with its treasure buried in the barrow, "eldum swa unnyt, swa hit æror wæs" ("as useless to men as it was before," line 3168), and the lament of the Geatish survivors. Unlike the father's lament, in which the father chooses the deserted wine-hall and his lamenting over the possibilities of life in the present, the final lament of the poem places the body of Beowulf and all of the treasure he has won from the dragon literally in its center:

> þa ymbe hlæw riodan hildedeore,
> æþelinga bearn, ealra twelfe,
> woldon (care) cwiðan, [ond] kyning mænan,
> wordgyd wrecan, ond ymb w(er) sprecan; (lines 3169–72)

> Then those brave in battle, the sons of princes, twelve in all, rode around the barrow, wished to lament in sorrow, and to speak of the king, to compose an elegy and to talk about the man.

The poem thus literally fills the lament with the excavated treasure and with Beowulf's body. The core of the lament cannot be read in any straightforward way as only the stock figures of old stories of loss, because these figures are a literal presence.[51] Beowulf's solution of the arm as sign can only be temporary; his body is torn apart and absorbed by language, and he has to die in order for his body's remains to fill the language of the lament. The fullness of the lamenting language at the close of the poem, however, produces the "singular effect" not of loss alone, but also of the effort of, and potential for, survival.

Many thanks to Modern Philology's *anonymous reviewer for generous and insightful criticism and to Christina von Nolcken for invaluable guidance.*

NOTES

1. J. R. R. Tolkien, "*Beowulf*: The Monsters and the Critics," in Lewis E. Nicholson, ed., *An Anthology of "Beowulf" Criticism* (Notre Dame, 1963), pp. 51–104, 88; reprinted from *Proceedings of the British Academy* 22 (1936): 245–95.
2. All quotations from the poem are from Fr. Klaeber, ed., *"Beowulf" and the Fight at Finnsburg*, 3rd ed. with supplements (Lexington, Mass., 1950). Translations

are my own. Hereafter cited parenthetically in the text by Klaeber's line number only.

3   Vivien Law, *Wisdom, Authority and Grammar in the Seventh Century: Decoding Virgilius Maro Grammaticus* (Cambridge, Eng.,1995).

4   Law, *Wisdom, Authority and Grammar*, p. 57.

5   Law, *Wisdom, Authority and Grammar*, p. 57. Law quotes from *De quantitate animae*: "Since the word consists of sound and meaning and sound pertains to the ears whereas meaning pertains to the mind, don't you think that in the word, as in any living creature, the sound is the body and the meaning the soul of the sound, as it were?" (p. 57). The development of Anglo-Saxon models of the mind in particular is discussed in Malcolm R. Godden's seminal article, "Anglo-Saxons on the Mind," in *Learning and Literature in Anglo-Saxon England: Studies Presented to Peter Clemoes on the Occasion of his Sixty-Fifth Birthday*, ed. Michael Lapidge and Helmut Gneuss (Cambridge, Eng., 1985), pp. 271–98.

6   Augustine, *On Christian Doctrine*, trans. D. W. Roberston (New York, 1958), p. 34. I discussed these passages in relation to other texts of the *Beowulf* manuscript in "Bloody Signs: Circumcision and Pregnancy in the Old English *Judith*," *Exemplaria* 11.2 (1999): 285–307, 290–91.

7   Augustine, *On Christian Doctrine*, p. 35.

8   Augustine, *On Christian Doctrine*, p. 43.

9   Augustine, *On Christian Doctrine*, p. 84.

10 Sheila Murnaghan, "Body and Voice in Greek Tragedy," *The Yale Journal of Criticism* 1.2 (Spring 1988): 23–43.

11 Michael Lapidge, "Beowulf and the Psychology of Terror," in *Heroic Poetry in the Anglo-Saxon Period: Studies in Honor of Jess B. Bessinger*, Jr., ed. Helen Damico and John Leyerle (Kalamazoo, 1993), pp. 373–403. Lapidge notes that although the naming of Grendel assures a certain familiarity, the name "Grendel" itself conveys little information: "In any case, if the poet wished to avoid communicating anything of the monster's nature, he chose an ideal name for it, for the etymology and meaning of the name Grendel are unknown" (p. 378).

12 While there is much to be said about the *scop* song and its relationship to the written text which both contains it and laments its loss, I will focus here on the poem's similar treatment of the related mode of boasting, in which Beowulf locates his lost and youthful potency, and Hrothgar locates Grendel's terror.

13 T. A. Shippey, *Beowulf* (London, 1978), pp. 12–14.

14 Ian Duncan argues that "the excellence of Beowulf is that he is able to join wordas and worcas [*sic*] in transparent, performative unity, by carrying out his boasts." "Epitaphs for Æglæcan: Narrative Strife in *Beowulf*," in *Modern*

Critical Interpretations: "Beowulf," ed. Harold Bloom (New York, 1987), pp. 111–130, 123.

15 Katherine O'Brien O'Keeffe, "*Beowulf*, Lines 702b–836: Transformations and the Limits of the Human," *Texas Studies in Language and Literature* 23.4 (1981): 489. Norma Kroll adds that while these fingers "which burst and crack in the struggle become anatomical emblems of personal and social disjunction," still, "interdigitation" can "represent affiliation." "Beowulf: The Hero as Keeper of Human Polity," *Modern Philology* 84.2 (1986): 126.

16 O'Keeffe, "Transformations and the Limits of the Human," p. 491.

17 O'Keeffe, "Transformations and the Limits of the Human," p. 492.

18 Jeffrey Jerome Cohen uses the Lacanian concept of "extimité" to discuss the figure of the monster in the Middle Ages: the monster, the intimate stranger, "reveals the limits of selfhood, reveals that identity is intersubjective, ex-centric, suspended across temporalities, as historically contingent as it is monstrously incomplete" (*Of Giants: Sex, Monsters, and the Middle Ages* [Minneapolis, 1999], p. xv).

19 Gillian Overing, *Language, Sign, and Gender in "Beowulf"* (Carbondale, 1990).

20 Overing, *Language, Sign, and Gender in "Beowulf,"* pp. 13–14.

21 That Beowulf is reading, traveling a conceptual rather than literal distance, is suggested by Hrothgar's explanation that the mere is not far from Heorot, in miles: "Nis þæt feor heonon / milgemearces, þæt se mere standeð" ("It is not far from here in miles that the mere stands," lines 1361–62). The distance from Heorot to the mere is a matter less of physical miles than of conceptual distance.

22 In Cohen's argument, "the giant is at once abjected from human signification and installed deep within the structure of subjectivity, as both its limit and its history in eternal return" (*Of Giants*, p. xvii).

23 Michael Murphy in "Vows, Boasts and Taunts, and the Role of Women in Some Medieval Literature," *English Studies* 66.2 (1985): 105–112, argues for a distinction between the boast, which recounts past deeds, and the vow, which promises future deeds. Murphy acknowledges, however, that the two are often classed together "because the activities are closely related, and because Old English words like *gilp* and *beot* and their derivatives are not distinguished with the precision we would like" (p. 105).

24 In "Flyting and Fighting: Pathways in the Realization of the Epic Contest," *Neophilologus* 70.2 (1986): 292–305, and "The Flyting Speech in Traditional Heroic Narrative," *Neophilologus* 71.2 (1987): 285–95, Ward Parks examines *flyting* in *Beowulf*, and the "Battle of Maldon," as well as several classical texts. Parks's interest is in structural or "microstructural" description ("Flyting

Speech," p. 285), but he also discusses *flyting* as a means of establishing identity "agonistically yet within a contractual framework" ("Flyting Speech," p. 292).

25 Carol J. Clover observes that Beowulf's own retelling of the adventure with Breca changes only few of the "facts" though of course revises the interpretation: "What is remarkable about Beowulf's reply [to Unferth], after all, is that it concedes the issue. His own additions to the story are minor, more by way of clarification. The disagreement lies not in the facts, which are mutually acknowledged, but in their interpretation" ("The Germanic Context of the Unferth Episode," *Speculum* 55 (1980): 444–68, 462).

26 Clover makes the persuasive argument that accusations of kinship crimes characterize *flytings* in Norse tradition. She claims that "it is a rare *flyting* that does not exhibit at least one such accusation" (p. 463). In the context of Clover's observations, Beowulf's charge of fratricide is not in itself an escalation of the *flyting*. But Clover also suggests that most *flyting* matches are won not by the most offensive insults, but by truest: "It is not, however, the most flamboyant provocations that win the *flyting*, but the most accurate ones" (p. 454). Even if the charge of fratricide does not settle the contest, nonetheless, the very suggestion that Beowulf's narrative of Unferth's fratricide can be somehow more true, more accurate, than Unferth's—or perhaps even Beowulf's—narrative of Beowulf's fight with Breca also dramatically underscores the alienability of such narratives.

27 Seth Lerer, *Literacy and Power in Anglo-Saxon Literature* (Lincoln, Nebr., 1991), p. 183.

28 Seth Lerer, "Grendel's Glove," *The Journal of English Literary History* 61.4 (1994): 721–49, 726.

29 Lerer, "Grendel's Glove," p. 734.

30 Lerer, "Grendel's Glove," p. 735.

31 Michael Near, in "Anticipating Alienation: Beowulf and the Intrusion of Literacy," *PMLA* 108:2 (1993): 320–32, also associates Grendel's monstrosity with the language of the poem. Near suggests that Grendel figures the psychological interiority which he sees as both the reflection of and the condition necessary for literacy; Grendel's alien presence figures the privacy and absence constitutive of literacy. Near's point is that "implicit in the poem's involvement with language is a marked and persistent hostility toward the epistemological foundation underpinning the practice of literacy" (p. 321). Beowulf's construction of Grendel's glove reinforces Near's reading of Grendel on the point of Grendel's association with the absence, withdrawal, or alienation constitutive of literacy. However, because Grendel's glove appears in the poem only within Beowulf's own very self-conscious re-telling of the fight, it becomes clear that this alienation is

already recognized by the "completely public, unhesitatingly articulate Beowulf" as also his own (p. 326).

32 Susan Stewart, *On Longing: Narratives of the Miniature, the Gigantic, the Souvenir, the Collection* (Durham, N.C., 1993), p. 23.

33 Tolkien, "The Monsters and the Critics," p. 81.

34 "Beowulf's death in the fight with the dragon will mean a resumption of the Swedish-Geatish conflict and the near annihilation of the leaderless Geatish nation," Laurence N. de Looze, "Frame Narratives and Fictionalization: Beowulf as Narrator," in *Interpretations of "Beowulf": A Critical Anthology*, ed. R. D. Fulk (Bloomington, 1991), pp. 242–50, 243; this essay originally appeared in *Texas Studies in Language and Literature* 26 (1984): 145–56.

35 De Looze, "Frame Narratives," p. 243.

36 De Looze, "Frame Narratives," p. 248.

37 The historical fate of the Geats is not at all clear. Kenneth Sisam argues that "there is not evidence anywhere for the virtual annihilation of the Geats by the Swedes and much against it," and cites evidence both external and internal to the text (Sisam, *The Structure of "Beowulf"* [Oxford, 1965], pp. 55–59). Robert T. Farrell similarly argues that the absence of historical evidence of the annihilation of the Geats in no way contradicts the poem's presentation of relations between the Swedes and the Geats: the Swedes and Geats "engage in a series of battles, with victories on either side. Quite naturally, once they have lost a strong ruler, the Geats fear incursions from without—but there is no mention of tribal destruction in *Beowulf*, and none in history" (*"Beowulf": Swedes and Geats* [London, 1972], pp. 41–43). The impulse to read *Beowulf* as a narrative of national disintegration may reflect less the treatment of the actual fate of the Geats within the poem than the poem's nostalgia, explicit from the beginning in its location of this story of the Geats in the "geardagum" of a lost and heroic past.

38 E. Talbot Donaldson translates the phrase as "one alone for one gone." E. Talbot Donaldson, trans., "Beowulf," in *"Beowulf": The Donaldson Translation, Backgrounds and Sources, Criticism*, Joseph F. Tuso, ed. (New York, 1975), p. 43. Klaeber notes Leonard's translation, "the lone one for the lost one" and finds the phrase "strikingly expressive of the father's solitary state" (p. 214). Klaeber's reference is to William Ellery Leonard, *"Beowulf," a New Verse Translation* (New York, 1923).

39 Klaeber, *Beowulf*, p. 209.

40 The similarity of these passages to the language of the *Exeter Book* laments, most clearly "The Wanderer" (especially lines 91–96) and "The Seafarer," further suggests self-conscious evocation of a genre, or a mode of speech, rather than relation to the experience of the event in the world.

41 Stewart, *On Longing*, pp. 23–24.

42 Fred Robinson observes, "The noun *becn* used of the monument in line 3160 lends it a numinous quality, since *becn* means 'sign, portent, idol,' and it is used in Christian times to refer to the Cross and to Christ's miracles. It can designate memorial stones (especially in the inscriptions written on such stones) but never refers to a tomb in Old English." Fred C. Robinson, *The Tomb of Beowulf* (Cambridge, Eng., 1993), pp. 17–18.

43 Allen J. Frantzen, *Desire for Origins: New Language, Old English, and Teaching the Tradition* (New Brunswick, N.J., 1990). "By juxtaposing 'writan' and 'forwritan,' I juxtapose the sword as a text, an object that preserves the past and hence serves as a beginning, with the sword as a weapon, an object of destruction and ending. We can thereby juxtapose and relate writing and reading and, by implication, origins and ends" (p. 187). Frantzen's larger argument is that reading is ideological and that critical readings of Anglo-Saxon texts have been concerned as much with establishing points of national and cultural origin as with their more explicit agendas.

44 Frantzen, *Desire for Origins*, p.179.

45 In *Desire for Origins*, Frantzen writes, " 'Forwitan' is a hapax-legomenon (. . .), but its etymological roots are those of 'writan,' and we have no other examples in Old English to contradict or to offset our response to the second element of the compound: 'forwritan' means 'to cut through' just as 'writan' means 'to write (by means of carving)'" (p.186).

46 In his preface, e.g., Frantzen explains that his chapters on Bede's *Ecclesiastical History* and *Beowulf* aim "not to 'read' or interpret them, but to *recover*, in the history of their reception, their cultural significance for earlier ages, and to suggest their cultural implications for our own" (p. xiv) and that his own work is an attempt "not so much to take stock of this discipline but to *restock* it with its history . . ." (p. xvi—emphases mine).

47 Frantzen, *Desire for Origins*, p. xvi.

48 Tolkien, "The Monsters and the Critics," p. 88.

49 Stewart, *On Longing*, p. 143.

50 Tolkien, "The Monsters and the Critics," p. 73.

51 Eric Jager, in his discussion of "pectorality" in Old English poetry, argues that Beowulf concludes with the barrow as an image of Beowulf's chest, that part of his body most associated with his capacity to speak ("Speech and Chest in Old English Poetry: Orality or Pectorality?" *Speculum* 65.3 [July 1990]: 845–59, 853).

POST-PHILOLOGY

MICHELLE R. WARREN

P hilology has been more often irrelevant than controversial within mainstream critical debates. With the expansion of electric technologies and the fragmentation of the nationalist disciplines that first nurtured philology, its demise may seem more certain than ever. Indeed, Roberta Frank has pointed out that some dictionaries boldly declare that the word is no longer in use. Many, it would seem, have taken to heart René Wellek's advice "to abandon" philology altogether. Frank, however, still wonders about the future and concludes with a question that has interested me since I first faced the prospect of teaching a graduate course in philology (traditionally a technical course for specialists in medieval studies) for students primarily interested in modern literatures: "Does Philology, backward looking to her core, have a future tense?"[1] My experiences with "Introduction to Romance Philology" led me to formulate the question in terms specific to current critical debates: can philology reach the next "post" along with the "modern" and the "colonial"? How can a discipline devoted to meta-narratives about language cope with critiques of the unity of both language and subjectivity? And how can a discipline fostered in the midst of nineteenth-century European colonialisms engage critiques of that history and its legacies?

In partial answer to these questions, this essay outlines several forms of what I will call *post-philology* in the hope that philology and contemporary

From Patricia Clare Ingham and Michelle R. Warren, eds., *Post-Colonial Moves: Medieval through Modern*, (New York, 2003), pp. 19–45; reprinted with permission of Palgrave Macmillan.

literary and cultural studies remain (or become) vigorous allies. *Post-philology* does not designate a move beyond or against philology: it refers rather to philological practices that entangle themselves with postmodern and postcolonial studies, either implicitly or explicitly. The first part of this essay, then, surveys the problems of definition that beset all three terms. The second part turns to philology's overt encounters with postmodernism since the 1980s, the third to various interactions between philology and postcolonial studies. The examples I adduce witness the already lively practice of post-philology: by outlining a definition I mean less to call for the creation of something new than to render visible the shared implications of these practices.

DEFINITIONS

Philology, *postmodern*, and *postcolonial* are linked first and foremost by their respective identity crises: numerous publications expose definitional controversies. Etymologically, philology designates a potentially infinite range of activities conducted for "the love of language." Disciplinarily, the range is only slightly less broad, and includes historical linguistics, textual editing, literary analysis, and the study of national cultures.[2] In practice, usages that limit *philology* to a set of technical engagements function in tension with this virtually limitless epistemological potential. Indeed, in the Modern Language Association of America's *Introduction to Scholarship in Modern Languages and Literatures*, which includes chapters on composition, rhetoric, literary theory, language acquisition, feminism, and border studies among others, it is classified under a single descriptor: "Philology, Modern—Research."[3] *Philology* thus mediates between the broadest understanding of text-based knowledge and the most specialized techniques for producing texts. Partly for this reason, it is at once ubiquitous and invisible.

From a philological perspective, *postmodern* seems relatively straightforward: it refers to what comes after *modern*.[4] At a first level, then, *postmodern* designates a historical period, although there is little agreement about its parameters (when did *modern* end? did it end in the same way in all cultural fields? can the postmodern also end?). The temporal value of *post*, however, is weakened by postmodernism's aesthetic definitions, which refer to artistic representations that disturb linear and hierarchical relations: they are characterized by fragmentation, lack of reference, pastiche, contingency, simulacra (copies without originals), and meta-fictions. Postmodern aesthetics betray a crisis of representation felt in contrast to modernism's supposedly confident affirmations of the accessibility of truth—and since these affirmations continue, postmodernism contests the modern but does not actually leave it behind.[5] This aesthetic crisis is closely related to a broader cultural crisis, since the critique of origins and referentiality implies a dissolution of modernism's master narratives and thus of established forms of social and political legitimation. Postmodernism calls into question the autonomy and unity of the human subject, as the conditions of knowledge in general are radically de-centered.

Postcolonial presents a similarly double relationship to history: it indicates both a break with colonial pasts and an ongoing engagement with their legacies and renewals. And like *postmodern*, *postcolonial* refers to both historical and aesthetic conditions. For Arif Dirlik, the term's reference is threefold: the formerly colonized societies now existing as independent nation-states, the global condition after the modern period of colonialism, and discourses on the preceding two conditions. Laura Chrisman divides the field somewhat differently: the formerly colonized societies now existing as independent nation-states, intellectual and aesthetic products of colonization, and an individually chosen subject position.[6] Although other variants on this basic split between geo-politics and representation could surely be added, a fundamental political engagement subtends all connotations of *postcolonial*, such that its status as an academic field of study in the universities of former imperial powers is itself suspicious. Indeed, for some critics the globalizing aspect of postcolonial discourse renders it a new form of colonialism that overlooks cultural and class differences.[7]

Even from these superficial sketches, *philology*, *postmodern*, and *postcolonial* appear to share a number of traits as disciplinary practices (besides widespread use by people who freely admit their conceptual inadequacies). Both *postmodern* and *postcolonial*, for example, critique totalizing or universalizing gestures: Kwame Anthony Appiah notes that postmodernism rejects "claim[s] to exclusivity," while Dirlik affirms that postcolonial discourse repudiates master narratives. Both concepts entail what Appiah calls "challenges to earlier legitimating narratives," maintaining what John Frow calls a "difficult and ambivalent resistance to modernity."[8] For postcolonial studies, this relationship is so difficult that it can receive nearly opposite formulations: for Dipesh Chakrabarty modernism is part of European colonialism, while for Benita Parry and Homi Bhabha colonialism is constitutive of European modernity.[9] In either case, the relationship is both historical (in relation to nineteenth- and twentieth-century Europe) and aesthetic (in relation to realist representation). This double engagement, as Chrisman points out, "allows, or implies, the interchangeability of material (geographical, political, and economic) with aesthetic and interpretative processes."[10] As a result, both *postmodern* and *postcolonial* remain in conflict with themselves, divided between significant ideological interventions and solipsistic self-reference.

In theoretical terms, postmodern and postcolonial studies share a debt to poststructuralism and the ways in which deconstruction enables a general dismantling of meaning systems. Indeed, Victor Li gives a definition of postcolonial theory that could apply equally to postmodernism: "A central characteristic of postcolonial theory is its exertion of a certain historical vigilance, a wariness of all monocultural discourses and their colonizing imperative. Postcolonial theory's suspicion of Western narratives of enlightenment and progress is matched equally by its resolve to not be taken in by imagined or invented national allegories of native authenticity. Postcolonial theory's critical vigilance, moreover, is directed against itself, such that its institutional and geopolitical locations, locutions, and interests are all brought into question."[11] Postmodern theory is equally wary of unifying discourses and the powers they subtend, equally critical of teleologies of progress, and equally engaged in self-reflexive critique. In terms of representational strategies, works identified by either label often share narrative modes (e.g., metafiction and irony) and themes (e.g., marginality). Both, then, reconfigure history—which brings them into dialogue with philology, itself a set of methods for constituting history through language.

At first glance, philology seems remote from postmodern and postcolonial studies. Jacques Derrida's critiques of logocentrism, for example, would seem to sound the death knell of a discipline in love with the logos.[12] Yet philology not only continues, it continues to pursue master narratives of legitimation. Rupert Pickens affirms, for example, that "[p]hilological writing embraces a rhetoric not of rupture, but of continuity; it seeks not to destroy, not to subvert, not therefore to renovate."[13] Post-philology takes place somewhere between these two extremes, where the philological fetish for detail makes master narratives difficult. Like the postmodern and the postcolonial, then, philology maintains a difficult relationship with its modernist past. Philology's potential for conflating historical and aesthetic concerns also links it with postmodern and postcolonial criticisms, for while philology claims to establish objective linguistic facts, the visibility of these facts often depends on their satisfying particular aesthetic assumptions about language and meter. Finally, philology is equally implicated in poststructuralism, in the sense that both turn on the materiality of language. Indeed, Paul de Man suggested that deconstruction is nothing more than a form of philology, "an examination of the structure of language prior to the meaning it produces"; Jonathan Culler has recently sustained this alliance with deconstruction. And Peggy Knapp has proposed a "recycled philology" that makes a similar claim: that "mere reading" at the lexical level can disturb critical and historical assumptions.[14] This kind of reading makes philology an active participant in the disruption of hegemonic discourses, and thus of power. Indeed, Edward Said has made philology integral to his critique of empire (albeit often as a counter to postmodernism).[15] Thus, philological, postmodern, and postcolonial criticisms all share engagements with history, methods for confronting relationships between universals and particulars, and challenges to hegemony. Their disciplinary histories, moreover, are all linked to nineteenth-century European colonialisms, their presents to metropolitan academic institutions.

Many other things, of course, distinguish these three terms, including oppositional politics, ludic sensibility, and scientific ambition. If the relationship between philology and postmodernism has been contentious (as I discuss below), that between the postmodern and the postcolonial has been more so. Although the common "post" indicates that both react to antecedents, it alone does not suffice to align these two concepts. For while postmodernism dismantles the binary structures that subtend colonial domination and offers potentially corrosive tools of cultural and political critique, its perceived amorality and ahistoricism have profoundly troubled those attentive to the material demands of resistance and emancipation. Postmodernism's denials of individual agency and subjectivity, moreover, seem to give license to neo-colonial exploitation and to evacuate the possibility of intentional resistance. And more than one critic has noted the pernicious irony of a Western philosophical disavowal of the human subject's effectivity at a time when subjugated peoples were exerting their independence from colonial regimes.[16]

Despite these and other very real differences, the recent history of critical debates within universities has brought *philology, postmodern,* and *postcolonial* together. Since the 1980s, philology and postmodernism have been thrown together explicitly. These debates coincided with the consolidation of postcolonial studies in universities in the United States and the United Kingdom. Philology in the present, then, cannot help but engage the *posts* that currently shape literary and cultural studies.

POSTMODERN

Philology has been under renovation since its origins, as witnessed by the controversies voiced by Plato and other authors of antiquity.[17] In the early history of the modern university, "new philology" designated a distinction from classical philology, institutionalized in the founding of the journals *Neuphilologische Mitteilungen* (1899), *Neophilologus* (1915), and *Studia Neophilologica* (1928). In this same period, Italian scholars formed their own "new philology."[18] And in the 1950s, the Spaniard José Ortega y Gasset formulated his "Axioms for a New Philology," likening "old" philology to a gruesome spectacle of dismemberment: "[it] quarters the reality [of language] and retains only one of its members."[19] In the late 1960s, Robert Dyer claimed "new philology" as the union of linguistics and literary analysis; about a decade later, Mary Speer cast her review of new editing guides as philology's "defense."[20] The "always already" aspect of these repeated declarations of rupture and resistance makes *philology* and the practices it designates almost ideal targets of postmodern analysis. Indeed, in reformulating "new philology" in 1990, Stephen Nichols claimed postmodernity as its distinguishing feature: "It is . . . manuscript culture that the 'new' philology sets out to explore in a postmodern return to the origins of medieval studies."[21] While interest in manuscripts may seem innocuous, even expected, Nichols's "new philology" sparked bitter reactions from editors who perceived an attack on the basic validity of their intellectual projects.[22] Here, however, I am more interested in the seemingly antithetical conjoining of "postmodern" to a "return to origins."

Although the adjective and noun *postmodern* (and its cognates *postmodernism*, *postmodernist*, and the like) are never explicitly defined in the debates about philology, their application has been generally consistent with the semantic field defined by general theoretical discussions. *Postmodernism*, for example, consistently designates a historical period, which extends from the end of modernism (whenever that was) to the present or to some recent past.[23] In this usage, "postmodern philology" means simply the ways in which philology is currently practiced, regardless of the ideology of the practitioner. In similarly objectifying terms, postmodernism is also referred to as a new "climate."[24] This geophysical metaphor locates postmodernism as a presence outside of individual practices: it is not a discourse or a theory, but rather like global warming—something that is happening to us that feels utterly beyond our direct control.

The present climate, in fact, seems to impose the term against critics' will. From its earliest uses in philological discussions, dissatisfaction with the term is one of its most striking aspects. *Postmodern* is applied "loosely and for convenience sake," "to follow current custom," and makes some critics "uncomfortable."[25] (Philology likewise has the power to make critics "uneasy.")[26] In this sense, the postmodern functions as a nondescriptive category, at once inapplicable and obligatory (emptied of meaning, it can even serve as the equivalent of *modern*). [27] Its usage thus designates a disciplinary crisis in which critics no longer define the terms of their own practice but are instead subjected to external forces of an indeterminate nature.

In the absence of a clearly defined disciplinary narrative (the kind of master narrative challenged by postmodernism), the nature of knowledge changes radically. It follows, then, that the nature of what can be known about texts has also changed. This new state of epistemology, characterized by indeterminacy, is called "postmodern."[28] In this sense, postmodernism refers to a necessity to rethink our knowledge of the past; some might even say that it represents a denial of history *per se*.[29] The result of this rethinking is a "methodological questioning," also described as postmodern.[30] One answer to this questioning is a substitution of traditional methodologies with poststructuralism.[31] In these instances, *philology* and *postmodern* designate two poles of an opposition between technique and theory. Another answer is the substitution of traditional methodologies with historicism. This historicism has two main characteristics. First, it focuses on manuscripts, "the study of medieval artifacts in their historic and cultural materiality."[32] Second, this historicism is called ironic, such that hierarchies are dismantled and binary oppositions become simply "difference."[33] In both cases, *postmodernism* refers to the antidote to whatever is perceived as inadequate in past or present criticism. *Postmodern* thus emerges as a brand of either value or illegitimacy depending on critics' presuppositions.

This postmodern "new philology" responded in large part to the practices of philology developed under nineteenth-century modernism, and which were perceived as enduring in the late twentieth century. For modernist philology, as both Nichols and R. Howard Bloch have demonstrated, manuscripts functioned primarily, if not exclusively, as sources for texts—texts needing the clarification offered by modern printing.[34] Joseph Bédier could declare, for example, that all surviving works should be published "ne serait-ce que pour s'en débarasser et pour qu'il soit possible à l'avenir d'en faire table rase" ("if only so that we can be rid of them and so that it might be possible in the future to make a clean sweep of them").[35] Reactions against this philological history were derived in part from the perception that literary criticism in general continued to overlook the relevance of medieval literature. In principle at least, the dismantling of modernist aesthetic values placed medieval texts on equal footing with more recent literature. Even traditional Latinists, for example, imagined that the new criticism of the 1960s could inspire a revival of classical letters and philology.[36] Despite this potential, however, the modernist rubrics of periodization remained largely untouched (due in part to the influence of Michel Foucault's *The Order of Things*), and medievalists came to complain of enduring marginalization within the larger literary field.[37] Most important for philology, textuality itself remained modernist, in the sense that editions continued to function as more or less adequate representations of archival artifacts.

In contrast to this modernist tradition, 1990s "new philology" is defined as postmodern and focused on manuscripts (Nichols later explicitly excluded editions and print culture in general).[38] Yet, the underlying principle of this methodology, which privileges "originality," is far from postmodern. The critique of originality is well developed in aesthetic criticism, most influentially in Walter Benjamin's "The Work of Art in the Age of Mechanical Reproduction."[39] Inspired by Benjamin, Rosalind Krauss has circumscribed originality in explicitly postmodern terms. Krauss argues that the continuation of modernist values in a postmodern world leads critics and artists alike to "[cling] to a culture of originals which has no place among the reproductive mediums." This nostalgia resembles the privileging of original textual artifacts over the various reproductions made possible by photographic and digital technologies. For Krauss, if modernism is characterized by a "discourse of originality" that implies an unauthentic copy as its condition, then postmodernism is characterized by a "discourse of the copy."[40] Postmodern aesthetics thus imply a dispersal of the originary moment and the displacement of the privilege accorded by modernism to both originality and authenticity.

Postmodernism entails a critical revaluing of all cultural artifacts. This revaluing is not a reordering of the hierarchies that have traditionally structured historical understanding but a dismantling of them in favor of heterodoxy or eclecticism (which has in fact been the valence of the several philological analyses that take their inspiration directly from the 1990 "new philology").[41] This is not merely the margins returning to haunt the center, but the dispersal of the centripetal metaphor altogether. To the extent, then, that 1990s "new philology" seeks to replace copies with originals, it is more modern than postmodern. The "desire to return to the medieval origins of philology," "to turn our attention back to the manuscript culture of the Middle Ages," "to the foundations of medieval expression," to prescribe the "center of our effort," bespeaks of a fundamentally modernist perception of history, one that seeks an originary moment distinct from all that precedes or follows.[42] This hierarchical valuation of method is particularly problematic for the practice of "ironic historicism" because the discipline itself does not become the focus of irony.[43] Desire in criticism is perhaps inherent to its practice, but the desire for origins, as Allen J. Frantzen has shown for Anglo-Saxon studies, is particular to modernist modes of criticism.[44] Ultimately, even though philology practiced as a postmodern inquiry informed by historicism pays valuable attention to the historical artifact,[45] the privileging of the manuscript, and particularly the illuminated one, as the authentic artifact of medieval culture cannot constitute a postmodern gesture—precisely because postmodernism necessarily disturbs notions of authenticity.

A philology consonant with postmodernism, which is to say a post-philology, articulates instead the multifarious mediations of historical desires. Post-philology goes beyond the quest for origins, dispersing the evaluative hierarchy whereby studies of the "original materials"—viewed "from the post-modern orientation of material philology" (as Nichols later renamed the "new philology")[46]—are valued more highly than studies addressed to editions.[47] In fact, post-philology's displacement of originality validates the products of earlier philologies as objects of study. This demystification of the artifact, of whatever temporal provenance, enables a historiography from multiple positions.[48] For while it is valuable to investigate the ideological stakes of particular editorial products, such as Linde Brocato's critique of the hidden hermeneutics of P. E. Russell's *Celestina*, for post-philology the purpose of such critiques must go elsewhere than to the judgment of "better" editions:[49] post-philology entails much more than a critique of positivist aspirations.

To the extent that philology means studying manuscripts—in and of themselves and for the purpose of publishing editions—post-philology implies several kinds of practice. It means, for example, reconfiguring the various hierarchies that often govern the interpretation of relationships among texts, images, and other nonlinguistic elements found in manuscripts.[50] In the classification of manuscripts for editorial purposes, post-philology extends the process initiated by Bédier's critique of the practice of establishing "family" relationships with a view to determining the oldest version of a surviving text.[51] While Bédier denounced the reconstruction of "originals," his favoring of a single "best" manuscript effectively turns the medieval manuscript into an analog of the printed book and perpetuates a hierarchical ordering of "best" and "worst."[52] With post-philology, by contrast, young, incomplete, and mangled artifacts become as intriguing as old and lavishly illustrated ones. Even printed and electronic editions become objects of study.[53] While new media cannot claim greater "accuracy,"[54] neither are they inferior to older materials; in post-philology, media of all kinds offer valuable representations of cultural history: the critical challenge is to define the nature of that history.

Post-philology also includes various dialogues between textual criticism and postmodernism. On the one hand, this means theoretically inflected textual criticism,[55] from Paul Zumthor's *mouvance* to Derridean *critique génétique*.[56] As Pickens has pointed out, Zumthor's theory of textuality is consonant with postmodern aesthetics in the sense that *mouvance* legitimizes multiple versions of a text and discards the centripetal notion of "variants" to a supposedly secure original.[57] Pickens's own edition of Jaufré Rudel's poetry exemplifies a "[p]ostmodern account of [medieval] experience," precisely because it refuses to value any version of a poem as original—as more authentic or more close to authorial intention than any other.[58] On the other hand, post-philology means submitting postmodernism to textual criticism. Indeed, Linda Hutcheon all but calls for an alliance between philology and postmodernism when she identifies "the textuality of the archive and the inevitable intertextuality of all writing" as key issues for a postmodern "problematics."[59] The archive's textuality is nothing less than philology's most traditional domain—and an area of increasingly broad critical interest.[60] All of philology's technical methods are needed to continue the dismantling of modernist narratives; likewise, all of postmodernism's theoretical powers are needed to dismantle philological scienticity. Each can productively modify the other, keeping each other "problematic."

Linguistic manuals also interpret textual representations. For historical linguistics, then, post-philology grapples with the consequences of the theoretical dissolution of metalanguage: how can one tell the history of language when there is no "language beyond language"?[61] If philology is the discipline that expertly produces meta-narratives about language, then post-philology tries to tell linguistic histories without assuming the coherence of language systems and with attention to hybrid rather than normative processes. Suzanne Fleischman argued, for example, that descriptions of Old French are often grammatical fictions that respond to modern concepts of usage rather than to historical data. She points out that Gaston Paris regularized noun cases in editing texts—texts subsequently used as illustrations in historical grammars. In the process, linguists sustained a myth of monoglossia that overlooked the hybrid forms of actual texts.[62] In a similar spirit, Roger Wright notes that all synchronic states of a language include both archaic and innovative elements, thereby undermining assumptions of systemic coherence.[63] The modernist ideology of coherence is maintained partly through metaphors—figures that can become the objects of post-philological study. For example, "contamination," "lack of unity," "confusion," "abnormality," "suffering," and the like all cast language itself as a locus of loss and incompletion.[64] In contrast, the asterisk (*), used to indicate words that may have existed, or logically should have existed, holds the place of plenitude: it signifies the fantasy of a coherent system.[65] It can also be understood as the sign of a "Derridean supplement": the asterisked word is both outside the known linguistic system and necessary for its completion.[66] These kinds of critical perspectives on meta-narrative strategies blur the traditional distinction between "internal" linguistics (i.e., morphology, phonology, and the like) and "external" linguistics (i.e., formal grammars, language policy, and the like). Roger Sell refers to the deconstruction of this binary as "postdisciplinary philology":[67] it can just as easily be called "post-philology."

The crisis of textual representation, of representing texts from the past, is a specifically postmodern crisis, and cannot be resolved by simply rejecting the problematic representations (editions, historical grammars, and the like). They condition the scholarship of everyone involved in text-based studies, and can be integrated into theoretical discourse, philological criticism, and our understanding of past and present. Philology engaged with postmodernism, then, can deviate from the quest for origins and commit to more precarious balancing acts.

POSTCOLONIAL

Post-philology is not limited to aesthetics or the critical recuperation of editions as objects of study. It includes a postcolonial engagement, and for several reasons. First, philology collided with postmodernism in academic contexts (in the United States at least) at about the same time that postcolonial studies became a visible and influential academic discourse: this coincidence suggests that philology and postcolonialism are bound for a similar collision. Second, in cultural criticism if not in all cultures, postcoloniality is intimately bound to postmodernity, whether it is a "child" or "offshoot" as Dirlik posits, or a category that "subsumes" the postmodern:[68] a discussion of "posts" that begins with modernism is therefore not complete without colonialism. Indeed, for Walter Mignolo, the difference between the postmodern and the postcolonial is one of location, not kind: "[They] are alternate processes of countering modernity from different colonial legacies and in different national or neocolonial situations."[69] Just as postmodernism moves beyond foundational logics, then, postcolonial studies formulate "post-foundational" histories.[70] Finally, as many critics have noted, philology itself gained force within European universities as a companion to nationalisms[71]—nationalisms that themselves often vigorously supported European colonial expansionism. In some senses, philology's postcolonial moment now seems like a nearly predictable consequence of its birth within nineteenth-century colonizing states.

Philological engagement with postcolonialism has a less obvious record than postmodernism, but one that nonetheless stretches surprisingly far. In the early 1970s, Brian Stock observed that philology ("scientific study") and postcoloniality ("the appearance of new nations") together had shaped medieval studies after World War II.[72] Around the same time, anthropologists countering the colonial legacies of their own discipline turned to philology. Clifford Geertz drew first an analogy between reading manuscripts and reading cultures, and then implied that anthropology should trade colonialism for philology: "Cultural analysis is (or should be) guessing at meanings, assessing the guesses, and drawing explanatory conclusions from the better guesses, not discovering the Continent of Meaning and mapping out its bodiless landscape."[73] By 1980, Alton Becker had gone further, claiming philology ("the unified study of language and text") as essential to "survival in a multilingual world of diminishing resources"; for Becker, philology negotiates a crucial realignment of cultural relations since it means to "give up one's world and let the other emerge from the text."[74] Philology continues to concern those attendant to contemporary colonial and postcolonial dynamics. Indeed, Mignolo has brought philology within postcolonial studies as yet another "new philology": "Transnational languaging processes demand a theory and philosophy of human symbolic production predicated on languaging and transnational and transimperial categories, on a new philology, and on a pluritopic hermeneutics that will replace and displace 'the' classical tradition in which philology and hermeneutics were housed in the modern period."[75]

Despite these and other mutual engagements, metaphors congenial to colonialist ideologies surface in various philological discussions. On the side of "traditional" philology, ideologies of continuity prevail, such that

Pickens denies the very possibility of newness: "[T]here could never be a *new* philology. What would call itself so has already denied philology's basic principles."[76] By identifying philology itself with the impossibility of rupture, this conception places philology on the side of hegemonic power. This totalizing ambition has pernicious potential in that it promises to repress disruptive differences in the name of coherent meta-narratives of linguistic truth. Elsewhere, philological practice is explicitly aligned with maneuvers of domination: A. G. Rigg casts himself as heir to Samuel Champlain, a colonial cartographer exploring the record of medieval Latin literature rather than the coast of Canada; James O'Donnell describes the manuscript cataloguer "like a nineteenth-century explorer back from a remote continent"; Siân Echard refers to manuscripts as "foreign territory" (albeit while exposing the power dynamics that determine "citizenship").[77] Examples of the scholar as explorer could certainly be multiplied: this and similar metaphors, as Bruce Holsinger has also observed, carry unexamined colonialist baggage.[78] Critics associated with postmodernist methodologies carry similar baggage. Jeffrey Jerome Cohen, for example, aligns philology with violent aggression when he writes of medievalists "armed with philology."[79] And Bloch has drawn an unsettlingly celebratory parallel between contemporary medieval studies and Dante's *imperium*: "[T]here has never been a moment more ripe for the teaching of the works of philosophers, historians, and poets who themselves imagined the possibility of what Dante termed the *Imperium*, the known world unified under one rule. Medievalists should exploit the development of the European community to press upon the university curriculum the universalizing aspects of medieval culture."[80] This passage seems to predict, and approve, the triumph of a world government—the political arm of what economic globalization is currently establishing in many postcolonial regions. Here, however, the power of neo-imperialism is concentrated in Europe. Taking the European as universal, this vision of expansionist medievalism places philology directly in the service of neo-colonial capitalism and the political alliances that sustain it.

In disciplinary terms, post-philology would instead address the complex relationships among political, linguistic, and literary histories. In relation to European nationalism, post-philology in this sense is well established. A number of studies have identified philology's national interests in the period of modern colonialism, while others have developed colonial engagements more specifically.[81] Joseph Duggan, for example, has argued that nineteenth-century French interest in the *Chanson de Roland* derived not only from nationalist rivalries with Germany but also from colonialist engagements in Algeria (especially after 1870). Although Bédier's edition and translation of the epic in the early twentieth century reputedly broke with the spirit of this nationalist tradition, his own formation in a Creole family from Ile de la Réunion makes for complex relationships among medievalism, orientalism, and colonialism.[82] The history of medieval studies in Spain is similarly bound to colonial histories, partly because 1898 marks the loss of the last American colony at the same time that it defines the generation of modernist scholars whose philological practices remain influential.[83]

In textual terms, post-philology exposes the ideological engagements of editions and translations. In fact, for David Greetham (as for Mignolo), postcolonial philology will be another form of "new philology," one that articulates the place of institutions, editors, and texts in relation to national and colonial politics.[84] Practices around annotation, for example, establish networks of power over and around textuality. Nichols foregrounds the Roman imperial origins of annotation itself, identifying some of the specifically aggressive implications of both excising manuscript annotation from editions and writing annotations around edited texts.[85] Post-philology also includes critical studies of editions of texts about colonization and colonialism. Textual criticism of narratives of European transatlantic expansion is particularly pertinent, given the complexities of the manuscript materials and enduring ideological investments in this history on both sides of the Atlantic. David Henige, for example, has shown the interpretive fallacies that arise from uncritical editions, while Margarita Zamora has analyzed marginal commentaries in order to elucidate sixteenth-century manipulations of the meaning of "discovery."[86]

Through postcolonial studies, post-philology thus finds another reason to valorize older editions: they can bear witness to expansionist histories and ideologies of domination. Some nineteenth-century philologists actually envisioned editing and translating as colonial interventions. Jean-Bernard Mary-Lafon, for example, offered his translation of the epic *Fierabras* as a literal aid to North African colonization:

> Pourquoi ne montrerait-on pas dans cette épopée chevaleresque la grande figure de Charlemagne aux Arabes d'Afrique, dont le coeur bonderait de joie au récit des grands coups portés par Fierabras, et qui verraient probablement, avec leur foi fataliste, un arrêt prématuré de Dieu et le doigt d'Allah dans la soumission et le baptême du plus brillant de leurs héros? . . . Dans ce fait si étrangement remarquable, du Fierabras de la légende s'agenouillant

aux pieds de Charlemagne et de l'Abd-el-Kader de l'histoire s'agenouillant devant Napoléon, n'y a-t-il pas de quoi frapper des imaginations moins impressionnables que celles des Arabes? . . .

Why wouldn't we show in this chivalric epic the great figure of Charlemagne to the Arabs of Africa, whose hearts would leap with joy at the narrative of the great blows given by Fierabras, and who would probably see, with their fatalist belief, a premature decree of God and the finger of Allah in the submission and baptism of the most brilliant of their heroes? . . . In this fact, so strangely remarkable, of the Fierabras of legend kneeling down at Charlemagne's feet and of the Abd-el-Kader of history kneeling before Napoleon, isn't there enough to strike imaginations less impressionable than those of the Arabs?

Mary-Lafon concludes with the hope that his translation be translated into Arabic, "[pour] redire en Orient et en Afrique, sous la tente et sous le kiosque, les gestes héroïques de nos pères" ("to repeat in the Orient and in Africa, under the tent and under the kiosk, the heroic feats of our fathers").[87] Mary-Lafon's translation, along with the one he imagines, witness the agency of language in colonial ambition. Indeed, translation studies have well established the multifarious ways that languages shape colonial power and resistance.[88] Mary-Lafon's own resistance to the ideology of French unity, born of partisanship for the enduring autonomy of regional cultures that predate the Frankish invasion of Gaul,[89] draws his expansionist rhetoric within an especially complex logic of internal and external colonial legacies. Critics should therefore be wary of the "myth of progress" by which a "good" edition or translation renders its predecessors obsolete.[90] This myth fosters potentially damaging colonial amnesia. And since the only published edition of the French verse *Fierabras* dates from 1860, just a few years after Mary-Lafon's translation, these pasts may still circulate in various unexamined ways.[91] Post-philology, thus, addresses the ideological values of the products of nineteenth-century philology, even when, or perhaps especially when, they are not "reliable" in current philological terms.

In historical linguistics, post-philology means foregrounding the relationships between language change and colonial maneuvers. For the romance languages, Roman imperial history and subsequent European expansionisms shape linguistic histories embedded in coercive bilingualism and diglossic power relations. Nichols, for example, exposes the racial politics that shaped Émile Littré's history of the romance languages in the 1850s.[92]

Post-philology can also mean historical linguistics practiced in relatively recent colonial contexts.[93] Similarly, critical analyses of the category of "prestige" as an agent for or against language change, combined with theoretical analyses of the subjectivity of multilingual speakers in situations of differential diglossia, can elucidate colonialism's linguistic incursions.[94] How, for example, does a "dominant" language become a dialect?[95] Narratives of linguistic history themselves become subjects of critical postcolonial analysis. Monoglossia, for example, is as much a product of colonialist and nationalist desire as of modernist positivism. Anthony P. Esp"sito, for example, deconstructs a myth of monoglossia in Spanish linguistics through analyses of hybrid texts in medieval Catalonia, and in the process decouples language from nation. Likewise, Iris Zavala has shown how early interpreters of Garcilaso turned his text into a monolingual fiction, producing an imperial text in the midst of heteroglossia and heterogeneity. Finally, in the broadest terms, the colonial legacies of the term "Indo-European" call for a questioning of the most basic assumptions about the histories of language, culture, and domination.[96]

The history of explicit linguistic codification and commentary likewise reveals intensive and varied colonial engagements. The earliest grammars of both Spanish and French, for example, testify to expansionist desires. Antonio Nebrija produced a grammar of Spanish dedicated to Queen Isabel ("arbitrio de todas nuestras cosas," including language), designed explicitly to serve the interests of empire, and in a small, portable format convenient for travel. Nebrija opens his text with the famous observation that "siempre la lengue fue compañera del imperio" ("language has always been the companion of empire"). Although this phrase is often cited to imply that language contributes to making an empire, Nebrija's examples of the history of Hebrew, Greek, and Latin demonstrate rather that language reflects imperial development: it grows to perfection and falls into decadence and then oblivion unless codified. Writing in 1492 just after the conquest of Granada and with the prospect of African expansion, Nebrija envisioned Spain as having reached an imperial pinnacle: with a written grammar, the language would reflect this political and military achievement.[97] The text will not only help Spaniards learn Latin more quickly, but will facilitate the necessary spread of Spanish law to newly conquered peoples as well as to all foreigners who have need to communicate with Spain.[98] In New Spain, however, where friars were more interested in grammars of Amerindian languages, Nebrija's Latin grammar was far more influential: the Spanish grammar was not reprinted until 1744, and then not again until 1893, while the Latin grammar has been almost continuously in print since1481.[99] Meanwhile, in the nineteenth century, Nebrija's grammar formed the basis of Andrés Bello's nationalist grammar of Latin American Spanish, leading Mignolo to point out a historical irony of real post-philological import: "the grammar that Nebrija had intended to serve the expansion of the Spanish empire in fact served as a tool to help build the nations that arose from the liberation of the Spanish colonization."[100] In contemporary Spain and Latin America, language and postcolonial politics remain intertwined.[101]

The first grammar of French, by contrast, is a large and unwieldy book, written not by a "native" speaker but by John Palsgrave, "Angloys, natyf de Londres et gradue de Paris." Like Nebrija, Palsgrave offers the vernacular language to his royal sovereign (Henry VIII). But whereas Spanish was codified as an object of export, French is imported. And the "foreigners" Palsgrave addresses will gain, not lose, sovereignty by acquiring French: Henry is called "kynge of Englande and of France," and his wife Mary ("douagere of France") is Palsgrave's most important student. Palsgrave, moreover, praises Henry for procuring the French tongue for his subjects, in a sense adding it to his already "ample dominions" in Europe.[102] In subsequent colonial efforts in the Americas, French was also not exported: in the seventeenth century, Raymond Breton produced a dictionary and grammar of Caraibe—not to teach French to the inhabitants of Guadeloupe but to teach the indigenous language to missionaries and merchants.[103] After the French Revolution, however, internal colonialism proceeded as a primarily linguistic enterprise, with Abbé Grégoire reporting to the new government "Sur la nécessité et les moyens d'anéantir les patois et d'universaliser l'usage de la langue française" ("On the necessity and means of destroying the dialects and universalizing the use of the French language").[104] Current linguistic politics remains a mixture of internal and external colonialism, as France continues to refuse to sign the European "Charte des langues" (which promises support for regional and minority languages) while promoting "La francophonie" worldwide.[105]

The problematics of textual representation—of representing texts—saturate postcolonial studies just as they do postmodernism. The fact that colonial situations shape textual and linguistic forms, and that such forms sometimes legitimize expansionist ambitions or foster resistance, compels renewed philological attention to these histories. Even the metaphors used to describe these histories, such as "marginality," bear philological scrutiny. For while Sylvia Söderlind has considered the concept's relation to typography (and typographical "justification" in relation to power justifications),[106] modern typography did not originate textual spatialization or graphical representations of power: manuscript rulings, lettering, scrolls, and the like, all offer visual tropes of boundary assertion—and unlike the printed book, manuscript margins often bear the marks of intervention (i.e., reader commentary, drawings, corrections, and so on). Post-philology, then, can identify with historical precision the dynamics of oppressive and resistant power that traverse language and text systems. Harnessed to political and ideological critique, philology contributes the corrosive effects of its fetish for detail to significant postcolonial moves.

AROUND THE NEXT POST

At the turn of a century whose intellectual terrain is littered with aftereffects (postwar, postmodern, postfeminist, postcolonial, post-communist . . .), it is time to think of post-philology—that is, of a philology informed by the aesthetic order of postmodernity as concerns originality, and the political order of postcoloniality as concerns figures of domination. The postmodern gesture of philology lies in removing the idea of a privileged center from conceptions of critical practice and in analyzing the symptoms of desires for original artifacts—desires that permeate philology, modernist aesthetics, and colonial power relations alike. Post-philology thus addresses manuscripts along with various kinds of copies, translations, and editions: they all have something to offer to cultural criticism when we are imaginative enough to press them with questions they can answer. When also conceived through postcolonial studies, post-philology focuses on the power dynamics that shape these representations. Post-philology thus attends to local phenomena, while articulating the ideological investments of nationalist and universalist claims; it brings into focus the colonialist overtones of rhetoric of continuity and purity.

Post-philology does not make philology obsolete, any more than postmodernism actually ended "history" or postcolonialism the oppressive legacies of expansionism. As Hutcheon says of the postmodern, it only exposes the constructedness of history and the textual condition of knowledge[107]—and thus their provisionality. Like other *posts*, the *post* of post-philology disarticulates a particular practice or condition from historical teleologies. It identifies and associates practices from various periods or disciplines through their shared methods, even, or especially, when their overt ideologies conflict: Pickens, for example, usefully observes the similarities between some of the methodologies proposed by Karl Uitti (a "traditional philologist") and Cerquiglini (a radical "new philologist").[108] Post-philology also narrows the perceived gap between textual materiality and hermeneutics.

One of the further values of post-philology lies in the opportunity to reconceive of "expertise" and the "experts" who possess it. The philological production of meaning has depended on expert guarantors of objectively true data—that is, on an authoritative unitary subject.[109] Both postmodernism and postcolonial theory destabilize this subject as well as the *logos* itself as a love-object. The result is what Bill Readings and Bennet Schaber have called "a competence beyond expertise." They describe the modernist expert as a "foreigner who is at home everywhere" (implying colonial connections), while identifying the postmodern historian as "a writer who feels the past as a certain 'foreignness at home' . . . , a stranger in the house of modernity."[110] Here, the loss of temporal stability (in postmodern terms) dissolves cultural and geographic unities (in postcolonial terms). The implications of "foreignness at home," or of what Abdul JanMohamed has called "homelessness-as-home," disperse the power of expertise among all citizens of the "empire of the Ps" (Culler's term for the aggressive breadth attributed to philology).[111]

The deconstruction of the expert as a master of discourses and techniques gives material history (i.e., manuscripts, editions, and the like) the same theoretical force as critical narrative: each can modify the other. This does not mean that just anyone can edit manuscripts or write linguistic histories: technical knowledge is indispensable. It does mean, however, a generalized responsibility to account for the power of technique within literary and cultural analyses. The practice of criticism in all fields often depends on repressed power relations with experts and the products of their expertise. And what is left to the "experts" can easily be objectified as admirable or obsolete, urgent or arcane: in any case, it need not concern the public at large. But if it is easy to dismiss philology, who could work without it? (This is of course not to say that philology precedes interpretation: it can be fundamental without being preliminary.)[112] Postmodern and postcolonial studies can thus contribute to a philology cognizant of its epistemological and ideological implications, while philology itself can contribute to the theorization of the material conditions of textuality that shape scholarship across the humanities. This "post-philology" can aspire to perform transactional relationships between material culture and cultural studies at large.

If philology is the art of reading slowly, as Roman Jacobson is reputed to have repeated,[113] then post-philology is reading that can give you a headache: centers constantly shift, parallels meet, origins disperse, politics weighs heavily. And since post-philology remains philology to some degree, its history continues to impose. One of the most influential aspects of that history is Martianus Capella's fifth-century allegory of the organization of human knowledge, *De nuptiis Philologiae et Mercurii* (*The Marriage of Philology and Mercury*). Martianus, it turns out, is an exemplary figure for rethinking the practice of philology in "post" terms. A pagan North African based in Carthage (*Afer Carthaginiensis*),[114] Martianus "authored" medieval Christian education, European humanism, and, distantly, the modern liberal arts. His popularity in Carolingian schools was largely promulgated by immigrant scholars from Ireland; today, his humanist legacies remain contested by various post-criticisms.[115]

In the marriage allegory, Philology must be transmuted from mortal to immortal before the wedding can take place: she thus ensures historical continuity while embodying the potential for rupture. Her hand-maiden Geometry is of particular interest for post-philology, for she is the "Earth measurer" (*geo-metria*), a "tireless traveler" (*viatrix infatigata*) of masculine bearing (*iure ut credatur mascula*) who describes the entire known world.[116] Her description of the world, moreover, follows the legacy of expansionist Rome in making Europe a minor geographical force—quite literally "provincial."[117] Geometry is joined by Arithmetic, Music, and Astronomy to form the *quadrivium*, and by Grammar, Rhetoric, and Logic who form the *trivium*. Philology and her maidens thus bring all the raw materials to the union, while Mercury's role is to interpret them. From this allegory, Western criticism has inherited the metaphors of active, masculine hermeneutics and passive, feminine presentation. Modern criticism, moreover, has often acted as if philology and hermeneutics had long divorced, having nothing to do with each other as each pursued mutually exclusive purposes. Perhaps now we can imagine a transgressive reunion: multiracial and married again (institutions and traditions still delimit critical practices to a degree), Philology sleeps around while Mercury prefers dresses. They are not always happy with each other, but their children are beautiful.

In fond memory of Suzanne Fleischman, who encouraged me in the love and labor of philology.

My comments on the 1990 "new philology" were first presented at the 1994 meeting of the Modern Language Association: I am grateful to David Hult for the invitation to speak, and to Stephen Nichols and William Paden for their enthusiastic responses.

Thanks are also due to my colleagues Jane Connolly and Rebecca Biron for conversations about Spanish, the graduate students of "Introduction to Romance Philology" in Fall 1998, my undergraduate research assistant Angelique Ruhi, and the Honors Program of the University of Miami for sponsoring her research.

NOTES

1 Roberta Frank, "The Unbearable Lightness of Being a Philologist," *Journal of English and Germanic Philology* 96 (1997): 490, 513; René Wellek, *Theory of Literature* (New York, 1949), p. 29.

2 Erich Auerbach, *Introduction aux études de philologie romane* (Frankfurt am Main, 1949); Evelyn S. Firchow, "Today's Definition of Philology," *Monatshefte* 63 (1971): 147–56, 242–6; Margaret E. Winters and Geoffrey S. Nathan, "First He Called Her a Philologist and Then She Insulted Him," in *The Joy of Grammar: A Festschrift in Honor of James D. McCawley*, ed. Diane Brentari, Gary N. Larson, and Lynn A. MacLeod (Amsterdam, 1992), pp. 351–67.

3 Joseph Gibaldi, ed., *Introduction to Scholarship in Modern Languages and Literatures* (New York, 1992).

4 Jean-François Lyotard, *La condition postmoderne: rapport sur le savoir* (Paris, 1979); Fredric Jameson, *Postmodernism, or, the Cultural Logic of Late Capitalism* (Durham, N,.C., 1991); Hans Bertens, *The Idea of the Postmodern: A History* (London, 1995).

5 Linda Hutcheon, "A Postmodern Problematics," in *Ethics/Aesthetics: Post-Modern Positions*, ed. Robert Merrill (Washington, D. C., 1988), pp. 1–10.

6 Dirlik, "Postcolonial Aura: Third World Criticism in the Age of Global Capitalism," *Critical Inquiry* 20 (1994): 332; Laura Chrisman, "Inventing Postcolonial Theory: Polemical Observations," *Pretexts* 5 (1995): 210.

7 Compare Chrisman, "Inventing Post-Colonial Theory," pp. 205–8; Makarand Paranjape, "Theorising Postcolonial Difference: Culture, Nation, Civilization," *Span* 47 (1998): 1–17.

8 Kwame Anthony Appiah, "Is the Post- in Postmodernism the Post- in Postcolonial?" *Critical Inquiry* 17 (1991): 342, 353; Dirlik, "Postcolonial Aura," pp. 334–36; John Frow, "What Was Post Modernism?" in *Past the Last Post: Theorizing Post-Colonialism and Post-Modernism*, ed. Ian Adam and Helen Tiffin (Calgary, 1990), p. 139.

9 Dipesh Chakrabarty, "Postcoloniality and the Artifice of History: Who Speaks for 'Indian' Pasts?" *Representations* 37 (1992): 23; Benita Parry, "The Postcolonial: Conceptual Category or Chimera?" in *The Politics of Postcolonial Criticism*, ed.

Andrew Gurr, *The Yearbook of English Studies* 27 (1997): 17; Homi Bhabha, *The Location of Culture* (London, 1994), pp. 196, 246.

[10] Chrisman, "Inventing Post-Colonial Theory," p. 210.

[11] Victor Li, "Towards Articulation: Postcolonial Theory and Demotic Resistance," *Ariel* 26 (1995): 171.

[12] Mark D. Johnston, "Philology in the Epoch of the Cogito," *Criticism* 25 (1983): 109–22.

[13] Rupert T. Pickens, "The Future of Old French Studies in America: The 'Old' Philology and the Crisis of the 'New,'" in *The Future of the Middle Ages: Medieval Literature in the 1990s*, ed. William D. Paden (Gainesville, 1994), p. 73.

[14] Paul De Man, "Return to Philology," in *Resistance to Theory* (Minneapolis, 1986), p. 24; Jonathan Culler, "Anti-Foundational Philology," *Comparative Literature Studies* 27 (1990): 49–52; Peggy Knapp, "Recycling Philology," *ADE Bulletin* 106 (1993): 13–16. David Greetham, however, rightfully criticizes both De Man and Culler for treating philology as pre-hermeneutic, in his essay "The Resistance to Philology," in *The Margins of the Text*, ed. D. C. Greetham (Ann Arbor, 1997), pp. 9–24.

[15] Edward Said, "Islam, Philology and French Culture: Renan and Massignon," in *The World, the Text, and the Critic* (London, 1984), pp. 268–90; Tim Brennan, "Places of Mind, Occupied Lands: Edward Said and Philology," in *Edward Said: A Critical Reader*, ed. Michael Sprinker (Oxford, 1992), pp. 74–95, especially 77–81, 91–92.

[16] Simon During, "Postmodernism or Postcolonialism?" *Landfall* 39 (1985): 366–80; Helen Tiffin, "Post-Colonialism, Post-Modernism and the Rehabilitation of Post-Colonial History," *The Journal of Commonwealth Literature* 23 (1988): 169–81; Arun P. Mukherjee, "Whose Post-Colonialism and Whose Postmodernism?" *World Literature Written in English* 30.2 (1990): 1–9; Ella Shohat, "Notes on the 'Post-Colonial,'" *Social Text* 10 (1992): 99–113; Bhabha, *Location of Culture*, pp. 171–97; E. San Juan Jr., *Beyond Postcolonial Theory* (New York, 1998); Walter Mignolo, *Local Histories/Global Designs: Coloniality, Subaltern Knowledges, and Border Thinking* (Princeton, 2000), pp. 172–214.

[17] Lee Patterson sketches this history in "The Return to Philology," in *The Past and Future of Medieval Studies*, ed. Tom Van Engen (Notre Dame, 1994), pp. 233–34. R. Howard Bloch considers some of the modern vagaries of "renovation" in "New Philology and Old French," *Speculum* 65 (1990): 38–39.

[18] Michele Barbi, *La nuova filogia e l'edizione dei nostri scrittori da Dante a Manzoni* (Florence, 1938).

[19] José Ortega y Gasset, "The Difficulty of Reading," trans. Clarence E. Parmenter, *Diogenes* 28 (1959): 2, 17.

20 Robert R. Dyer, "The New Philology: An Old Discipline or a New Science?" *Computers and the Humanities* 4 (1969): 53–64; Mary B. Speer, "In Defense of Philology: Two New Guides to Textual Criticism," *Romance Philology* 32 (1979): 335–44.

21 Stephen G. Nichols, "Introduction: Philology in a Manuscript Culture," *Speculum* 65 (1990): 7.

22 Keith Busby, ed., *Towards a Synthesis? Essays on the New Philology* (Amsterdam,1993); Karl Stackmann, "Neue Philologie?" in *Modernes Mittelalter: Neue Bilder einer populären Epoche*, ed. Joachim Heinzle (Frankfurt am Main, 1994), pp. 398–427; Werner Schröder, "Die 'Neue Philologie' nod das 'Moderne Mittelalter,'" *Jenaer Universitätsreden* 1 (1996): 33–50; Martin-Dietrich Glessgen and Franz Lebsanft, eds., *Alte und neue Philologie* (Tübingen, 1997).

23 Suzanne Fleischman, "Philology, Linguistics, and the Discourse of the Medieval Text," *Speculum* 65 (1990): 19; Lee Patterson, "On the Margin: Postmodernism, Ironic History, and Medieval Studies," *Speculum* 65 (1990): 87; Allen J. Frantzen, "The Living and the Dead: Responses to Papers on the Politics of Editing Medieval Texts," in *The Politics of Editing Medieval Texts*, ed. Roberta Frank (New York, 1993), p. 164; William D. Paden, "Is there a Middle in this Road? Reflections on the New Philology," in *Towards a Synthesis?*, p. 122, and "Scholars at a Perilous Ford," in *The Future of the Middle Ages*, p. 8; Pickens, "The Future of Old French Studies in America," p. 72; David Hult, *Nouvelle philologie ou nouvelle imposture? Manuscript Study in the Postmodern Era* (panel title, Modern Language Association meeting, 1994).

24 Fleischman, "Philology, Linguistics, and the Discourse of the Medieval Text," p. 19; Gabrielle Spiegel, "History, Historicism, and the Social Logic of the Text in the Middle Ages," *Speculum* 65 (1990): 59.

25 Stephen G. Nichols, "Editor's Preface," *Romanic Review* 79 (1988): 1; Fleischman, "Philology, Linguistics, and the Discourse of the Medieval Text," p. 19; Paden, "Is there a Middle in this Road?" p. 124.

26 Stephen G. Nichols, "Deeper into History," *L'esprit createur* 23 (1983): 91; Firchow, "Today's Definition of Philology," p. 243.

27 Pickens speaks of Paul Zumthor's work on textual variance as informed by a "modernist/post-modernist perspective" in "The Future of Old French Studies in America," p. 61.

28 Fleischman, "Philology, Linguistics, and the Discourse of the Medieval Text," p. 19; Paden, "Reflections on 'The Past and Future of Medieval Studies,'" *Romance Philology* 50 (1997): 311; Spiegel, "History, Historicism, and the Social Logic of the Text," p. 59.

[29] Keith Busby, "Doin' Philology While the -isms Strut," in *Towards a Synthesis?*, p. 91; Pickens, "The Future of Old French Studies in America," p. 72.

[30] Nichols, "Editor's Preface," p. 1; see also Fleischman, "Philology, Linguistics, and the Discourse of the Medieval Text," p. 19.

[31] Mary B. Speer, "Editing Old French Texts in the Eighties: Theory and Practice," *Romance Philology* 45 (1991): 16, 19.

[32] Nichols, "Introduction: Philology in a Manuscript Culture," p. 1.

[33] Patterson, "On the Margin," p. 90.

[34] Nichols, "Introduction: Philology in a Manuscript Culture," pp. 1–7; Bloch, "New Philology and Old French," pp. 39–47.

[35] Joseph Bédier, "La Société des anciens textes français," *La Revue des deux mondes* 121 (1894): 910.

[36] Henry Bardon, "Philologie et Nouvelle Critique," *Revue belge de philologie* 48 (1970): 5–15. This is precisely the outcome of Kathleen Biddick's imagined postcolonial encounter between the Venerable Bede and a feminist Chicana professor: the professor implies that her students might be willing to learn Latin if sufficiently engaged by the similarities between Bede's linguistic traumas and their own: "Bede's Blush: Postcards from Bali, Bombay, Palo Alto," in *The Past and Future of Medieval Studies*, pp. 30–34.

[37] Patterson at one point poses the "problem" explicitly in terms of the failed promise of a postmodern academy ("The Return to Philology," p. 242).

[38] Stephen G. Nichols, "Philology and Its Discontents," in *The Future of the Middle Ages*, p. 139 n. 14.

[39] Walter Benjamin, *Illuminations*, ed. Hannah Arendt, trans, Harry Zohn (New York, 1968), pp. 219–53.

[40] Rosalind E. Krauss, "The Originality of the Avant-Garde," in *The Originality of the Avant-Garde and Other Modernist Myths* (Cambridge, Mass., 1985), pp. 156, 162, 170.

[41] Willard J. Rusch, "Philology and the Dynamics of Manuscript Glossing," in *Interdigitations: Essays for Irmengard Rauch*, ed. Gerald F. Carr, Wayne Harbert, and Lihua Zhang (New York, 1998), pp. 219–29; Thomas Farrell, "Philological Theory in 'Sources and Analogues,'" *Medieval Perspectives* 15.2 (2000): 34–48.

[42] Nichols, "Introduction: Philology in a Manuscript Culture," pp. 1, 8, and "Editor's Preface," p. 3; Patterson, "On the Margin," pp. 91–101, 107; Nichols, "Why Material Philology?" *Zeitschrift für Deutsche Philologie* 116 supplement (1997): 12–13. Louise Fradenburg has also interpreted the call for a return to origins as a problematic repetition of very old paradigms: "'So That We May Speak of Them': Enjoying the Middle Ages," *New Literary History* 28 (1997): 218–19, 223–24.

[43] Richard R. Glejzer criticizes a similar oversight in the broader program of a "new medievalism" in "The New Medievalism and the (Im)Possibility of the Middle Ages," in *Medievalism and the Academy II*, ed. David Metzger (Cambridge, Eng., 2000), pp. 104–19.

[44] Allen J. Frantzen, *Desire for Origins: New Language, Old English, and Teaching the Tradition* (New Brunswick, 1990).

[45] Nichols, "Philology and Its Discontents," p. 137 n. 5.

[46] Nichols, "Philology and Its Discontents," p. 118; "Why Material Philology?" especially pp. 13, 16–17. See also the variant "materialist philology" in Nichols's Introduction in *The Whole Book: Cultural Perspectives on the Medieval Miscellany*, ed. Stephen G. Nichols and Siegfried Wenzel (Ann Arbor, 1996), pp. 1–2. Nichols's conceptualization seems quite close to Jerome McGann's "materialist hermeneutics" in *The Textual Condition* (Princeton, 1991), p. 15; the term also has a history among Italian philologists—see, for example, R. Antonelli, "Interpretazione e critica del testo," in *Letteratura italiana, IV: L'interpretazione*, ed. Alberto Asor Rosa (Torino: Giulio Einaudi, 1985), pp. 141–23.

[47] Fradenburg similarly laments the message that denies that "those who do not possess philological skills do possess worthy ways of remembering the past, because they are forced to rely on the now-discredited, dead, humanistic 'text' instead of on the living exuberance of medieval 'textuality'" ("'So That We May Speak of Them,'" p. 224).

[48] I develop the positionality of reading more extensively in "Interpreting Codicology: Re-visions of the 'Divine Comedy' in the Codex Altona," *Mosaic* 28.4 (1995): 13–37.

[49] Linde M. Brocato, "Leading a Whore to Father: Confronting 'Celestina,'" *La corónica* 24 (1995): 41.

[50] For example Mary B. Speer, "Editing Old French Texts in the Eighties: Theory and Practice," *Romance Philology* 45 (1991): 30–41; Michael Camille, *Image on the Edge: The Margins of Medieval Art* (Cambridge, Mass., 1992); Stephen G. Nichols, "Picture, Image, and Subjectivity in Medieval Culture," *Modern Language Notes* 108 (1993): 617–37.

[51] Cesare Segre, "La critica testuale," in *Atti: XIV Congresso internazionale di linguistica e filologia romanza, 1974*, vol. 1 (Naples, 1978), pp. 493–9; Germán Orduna, "Hispanic Textual Criticism and the Stemmatic Value of the History of the Text," in *Scholarly Editing: A Guide to Research*, ed. D. C. Greetham (New York, 1995), pp. 486–503; Mary R. Speer, "Old French Literature," in *Scholarly Editing*, pp. 382–416.

[52] Nichols, "Introduction: Philology in a Manuscript Culture," pp. 5–7; Lenora D. Wolfgang, "Chrétien's Lancelot: Love and Philology," *Reading Medieval Studies*

17 (1991): 3–17; David Hult, "Lancelot's Two Steps: A Problem in Textual Criticism," *Speculum* 61 (1986): 845.

53 Donald H. Reiman, "'Versioning': The Presentation of Multiple Texts," *Romantic Texts and Contexts* (Columbia, 1987), pp. 167–80; Robert S. Sturges, "Textual Scholarship: Ideologies of Literary Production," *Exemplaria* 3.1 (1991): 126–30; Roy Rosenstein, "*Mouvance* and the Editor as Scribe: *Trascrittore traditore?*" *Romanic Review* 80 (1989): 157–71; Ross G. Arthur, "On Editing Sexually Offensive Old French Texts," in *The Politics of Editing Medieval Texts*, ed. Roberta Frank (New York, 1993), p. 63; George Bornstein and Theresa Tinkle, eds., *The Iconic Page in Manuscript, Print, and Digital Culture* (Ann Arbor, 1998).

54 Bernard Cerquiglini, *Éloge de la variante: Histoire critique de la philologie* (Paris, 1989), pp. 150–61; Sturges, "Textual Scholarship," p. 130; J. David Bolter, *Writing Space: The Computer, Hypertext, and the History of Writing* (Hillsdale, 1991).

55 For example Jerome J. McGann, *A Critique of Modern Textual Criticism* (Chicago, 1983); Jonathan Goldberg, *Writing Matter: From the Hands of the English Renaissance* (Stanford, 1990); John Dagenais, "That Bothersome Residue: Toward a Theory of the Physical Text," in *Vox Intexta: Orality and Textuality in the Middle Ages*, ed. A. N. Doane and Carol Braun Pasternack (Madison, 1991), pp. 246–59; George Bornstein and Ralph G. Williams, eds., *Palimpsest: Editorial Theory in the Humanities* (Ann Arbor, 1993); David Greetham, *Theories of the Text* (Oxford, 1999), especially pp. 10–11, 86–89.

56 Paul Zumthor, *Essai de poétique médiévale* (Paris, 1972); Pierre-Marc de Biasi, Michel Contat, and Daniel Ferrer, eds., *Pourquoi la critique génétique? Méthodes, théories*, (Paris, 1998).

57 Pickens, "The Future of Old French Studies in America," p. 61.

58 Rupert T. Pickens, ed., *The Songs of Jaufré Rudel* (Toronto, 1978); Paden, "Is there a Middle in this Road?" p. 124. Speer analyzes other editorial projects with similar aspirations, while also arguing that Pickens' printed text visually maintains an authorial center and thus actually perpetuates modernist editorial values ("Editing Old French Texts in the Eighties," pp. 9–10, 25–30).

59 Hutcheon, "Postmodern Problematics," p. 6.

60 For example "The Status of Evidence," *PMLA* 111.1 (1996): 21–31.

61 Bill Readings and Bennet Schaber, ed., *Postmodernism Across the Ages: Essays for a Postmodernity that Wasn't Born Yesterday* (Syracuse, 1993), p. 23.

62 Suzanne Fleischman, "Medieval Vernaculars and the Myth of Monoglossia: A Conspiracy of Linguistics and Philology," in *Literary History and the Challenge of Philology*, ed. Seth Lerer (Stanford, 1996), pp. 92–104.

63 Roger Wright, "Metalinguistic Change in Medieval Iberia," *Early Ibero-Romance* (Newark, 1994), pp. 31–44.

[64] For example Peter Rickard, *A History of the French Language* (London, 1989), pp. 186, 188, 190; Ralph Penny, *A History of the Spanish Language* (Cambridge, Eng., 1991), pp. 216, 218.

[65] For example Roger Wright, "The Asterisk in Hispanic Historical Linguistics," *Early Ibero- Romance* (Newark, 1994), pp. 45–64; Salvatore Claud Sgroi, "L'asterisco nella linguistica italiana, francese e spagnola," in *Italica et Romanica: Festschrift für Max Pfister*, Günter Holtus, Johannes Kramer, and Wolfgang Schweickard, eds., vol. 3 (Tübingen, 1997), pp. 441–47; Javier Elvira, "Sobre reconstrucción lingüística: Uso y abuso del asterisco en gramática histórica," *Boletín de la Real Academia Española* 79 (1999): 425–43.

[66] This observation is inspired by the analyses of Sylvia Söderlind, although she does not discuss the linguistic asterisk *per se*: "Margins and Metaphors: The Politics of Post-***," in *Liminal Postmodernisms: The Postmodern, the (Post-)Colonial, and the (Post-)Feminist*, ed. Theo D'Haen and Hans Bertens (Amsterdam, 1994), pp. 35–54.

[67] Roger Sell, "Postdisciplinary Philology: Culturally Relativistic Pragmatics," in *English Historical Linguistics 1992*, ed. Francisco Fernandez, Miguel Fuster, and Juan José Calvo (Amsterdam, 1994), pp. 29–36.

[68] Dirlik "The Postcolonial Aura," p. 348, and *The Postcolonial Aura: Third World Criticism In the Age of Global Capitalism* (Boulder, 1997), p. 1; Vijay Mishra and Bob Hodge, "What is (Post)-Colonialism?" *Textual Practice* 5 (1991): 412.

[69] Walter Mignolo, *The Darker Side of the Renaissance: Literacy, Territoriality, and Colonization* (Ann Arbor, 1995), p. xii.

[70] Gyan Prakash, "Writing Post-Orientalist Histories of the Third World: Perspectives from Indian Historiography," *Comparative Studies in Society and History* 32 (1990): 398.

[71] Hans Ulrich Gumbrecht, "'Un soufflé d'Allemagne ayant passé'": Friedrich Diez, Gaston Paris, and the Genesis of National Philologies," *Romance Philology* 40 (1986): 1–37; Nichols, "Introduction: Philology in a Manuscript Culture," p. 1; Fradenburg, "'So That We May Speak of Them,'" p. 219; Pascale Hummel, *Histoire de l'histoire de la philologie: Étude d'un genre épistémologique et bibliographique* (Geneva, 2000).

[72] Brian Stock, "The Middle Ages as Subject and Object: Romantic Attitudes and Academic Medievalism," *New Literary History* 5 (1973–74): 527.

[73] Clifford Geertz, "Thick Description: Toward an Interpretive Theory of Culture," *The Interpretation of Cultures* (New York, 1973), pp. 10, 20.

[74] Alton Becker, "Modern Philology," *Forum Linguisticum* 7 (1982): 27, 34.

[75] Walter Mignolo, "Linguistic Maps, Literary Geographies, and Cultural Landscapes: Languages, Languaging, and (Trans)nationalism," *Modern Language Quarterly* 57 (1996): 183; revised in *Local Histories*, p. 220.

76 Pickens, "The Future of Old French Studies in America," p. 79.

77 A. G. Rigg, *A History of Anglo-Latin Literature, 1066–1421* (Cambridge, Eng., 1992), p. 1; James J. O'Donnell, "Retractations," in *The Whole Book: Cultural Perspectives on the Medieval Miscellany*, ed. Stephen G. Nichols and Siegfried Wenzel (Ann Arbor, 1996), p. 172; Siân Echard, "House Arrest: Modern Archives, Medieval Manuscripts," *Journal of Medieval and Early Modern Studies* 30.2 (2000), p. 195.

78 Bruce Holsinger, "The Color of Salvation: Desire, Death, and the Second Crusade in Bernard of Clairvaux's 'Sermons on the Song of Songs,'" in *The Tongue of the Fathers: Gender and Ideology in Twelfth-Century Latin*, ed. David Townsend and Andrew Taylor (Philadelphia, 1998), pp. 156–57.

79 Jeffrey Jerome Cohen, "Introduction: Midcolonial," in *The Postcolonial Middle Ages*. ed. Jeffrey Jerome Cohen (New York, 2000), p. 4.

80 R. Howard Bloch, "The Once and Future Middle Ages," *Modern Language Quarterly* 54 (1993): 73.

81 For example Gumbrecht, "'Un soufflé d'Allemagne,'" in *Medievalism and the Modernist Temper: On the Discipline of Medieval Studies*, ed. R. Howard Bloch and Stephen G. Nichols (Baltimore, 1995), pp. 439–71.

82 Joseph Duggan, "Franco-German Conflict and the History of French Scholarship on the 'Song of Roland,'" in *Hermeneutics and Medieval Culture*, ed. Patrick J. Gallacher and Helen Damico (Albany, 1989), pp. 97–106; Michelle R. Warren, "*Au commencement était l'île*: The Colonial Formation of Joseph Bédier's 'Chanson de Roland,'" in *Translating Cultures: Postcolonial Approaches to the European Middles Ages*, ed. Ananya J. Kabir and Deanne M. Williams (Cambridge, Eng., 2005).

83 For example Dámaso Alonso, "Menéndez Pidal y la generación del 98," *Revista de Letras* 1 (1969): 209–28; Catherine Brown, "The Relics of Menéndez Pidal: Mourning and Melancholia in Hispanomedieval Studies," *La corónica* 24 (1995): 15–41; Peter Linehan, "The Court Historiographer of Francoism?: 'La leyenda oscura' of Ram"n Menéndez Pidal," *Bulletin of Hispanic Studies* 73 (1996): 437–50.

84 David Greetham, *Theories of the Text*, p. 428.

85 Stephen G. Nichols, "On the Sociology of Medieval Manuscript Annotation," in *Annotation and its Texts*, ed. Stephen A. Barney (Oxford, 1991), pp. 43–73.

86 David Henige, "Tractable Texts: Modern Editing and the Columbian Writings," in *Critical Issues in Editing Exploration Texts*, ed. Germaine Warkentin (Toronto, 1995), pp. 1–35; Margarita Zamora, *Reading Columbus* (Berkeley, 1993).

87 Jean-Bernard Mary-Lafon, *Fierabras, légende nationale* (Paris, 1857), pp. xiii, xiv. Janine Dakyns mentions Mary-Lafon in relation to the imperial medievalizing

of Louis Napoleon in *The Middle Ages in French Literature, 1851–1900* (Oxford, 1973), p. 33.

88 Lawrence Venuti, ed., *Rethinking Translation: Discourse, Subjectivity, Ideology* (London, 1992); Gayatri Chakravorty Spivak, "The Politics of Translation," in *Outside in the Teaching Machine* (London, 1993), pp. 179–200; Ruth Evans, "Translating Past Cultures?" in *The Medieval Translator, IV*, ed. Roger Ellis and Ruth Evans (Exeter, 1994), pp. 20–45; Douglas Robinson, *Translation and Empire: Postcolonial Theories Explained* (Manchester, 1997); Susan Bassnett and Harish Trivedi, eds., *Post-Colonial Translation* (London, 1999).

89 On Mary-Lafon's defense of the Midi, see Michael Glencross, "La littérature française du moyen âge dans la critique littéraire sous la Monarchie de Juillet," *Zeitschrift für französiche Sprache und Literatur* 103 (1993): 252.

90 Anne McClintock, "The Angel of Progress: Pitfalls of the Term 'Postcolonialism'" in *Social Text* 31–32 (1992): 84–98, rpt. in *Colonial Discourse/Postcolonial Theory*, Francis Barker, Peter Hulme, and Margaret Iversen, eds., (Manchester, 1994), pp. 253–66; Arthur, "On Editing Sexually Offensive Old French Texts," pp. 21, 59.

91 *Fierabras*, ed. Auguste Kroeber and Gustave Servois (Paris, 1860). Editions have been prepared, but not published, by G. A. Knott (Ph.D., University of Cambridge, 1954) and André de Mandach (1981; CH-3065 Habstetten près Berne, Switzerland).

92 Stephen G. Nichols, "Modernism and the Politics of Medieval Studies," in *Medievalism and the Modernist Temper*, pp. 34–40.

93 For example "Documenting the Colonial Experience, with Special Regard to Spanish in the American Southwest," special issue, ed. Barbara de Marco and Jerry R. Craddock, *Romance Philology* 53 (1999).

94 Penny's *History of the Spanish Language* represents a linguistic history rather closer to a post-philological spirit than Rickard's *History of the French Language*.

95 Manfred Görlach, "Colonial Lag? The Alleged Conservative Character of American English and Other 'Colonial' Varieties," *English World-Wide* 8.1 (1987): 41–60, especially 56.

96 Anthony P. Espósito, "Bilingualism, Philology and the Cultural Nation: The Medieval Monolingual Imaginary," *Catalan Review* 9 (1995): 125–39; Iris M. Zavala, "The Art of Edition as the Techné of Mediation: Garcilaso's Poetry as Masterplot," in *The Politics of Editing*, ed. Jenaro Talens and Nicholas Spadaccini (Minneapolis, 1992), pp. 52–73; Veena Naregal, "Language and Power in Pre-Colonial Western India: Textual Hierarchies, Literate Audiences and Colonial Philology," *The Indian Economic and Social History Review* 37 (2000): 259–94.

97 Eugenio Asensio underscores the retrospective qualities of Nebrija's judgments in "La lengua compañera del imperio: Historia de una idea de Nebrija en España y Portugal," *Revista de filología española* 43 (1960): 406–7. Mignolo, while recognizing that Nebrija could not have had Western expansionism in mind, nonetheless interprets the grammar mainly from the perspective of later centuries (*The Darker Side*, pp. 41 and following).

98 Antonio de Nebrija, *Gramática castellana*, ed. Galindo Romeo and Ortiz Muñoz (Madrid, 1946), pp. a.ii, a.iiii.

99 *Bibliografía Nebrisense: Las obras completas del humanista Antonio de Nebrija desde 1481 hasta nuestros días*, ed. Miguel Angel Esparza Torres and Jans-Josef Niederhee (Amsterdam, 1999), especially pp. 302–5; Mignolo, *The Darker Side*, pp. 49–56.

100 Andrés Bello, *Gramática de la lengua castellana: Destinada al uso de los americanos* (1847), ed. Ramón Trujillo (Santa Cruz de Tenerife, 1981); Mignolo, *The Darker Side*, p. 67.

101 Kathryn A. Woolard, *Double Talk: Bilingualism and the Politics of Ethnicity in Catalonia* (Stanford, 1989); Carmen Silva-Corvalan, ed., *Spanish in Four Continents: Studies in Language Contact and Bilingualism* (Washington, D. C., 1995).

102 John Palsgrave, *Lesclarcissement de langue francoyse, 1530* (Menston, 1969).

103 *Dictionnaire caraibe-francais* (1665; reprint Paris, 1999); *Grammaire caraibe* (Auxerre, 1667). See Doris Garraway, *The Libertine Colony: Creolization in the Early French Caribbean* (Durham, N.C., 2005).

104 Augustin Gazier, *Lettres à Grégoire sur les patois de France, 1790–1794* (Paris, 1880); Michel de Certeau, Dominique Julia and Jacques Revel, *Une politique de la langue: La Révolution française et les patois* (Paris, 1975).

105 Audrey Gaquin, "Les langues minoritaires de France et la nouvelle Europe," *The French Review* 73 (1999): 94–107; Jean-Louis Calvert, "French Language Policy and Francophonie," in *Language, Legislation and Linguistic Rights*, ed. Douglas A. Kibbee (Amsterdam, 1998), pp. 310–19.

106 Söderlind, "Margins and Metaphors," p. 39.

107 Linda Hutcheon, "Beginning to Theorize Postmodernism," *Textual Practice* 1 (1987): 10–31.

108 Pickens, "The Future of Old French Studies in America," pp. 70–71.

109 Hult, "Lancelot's Two Steps," pp. 852–53; Johnston, "Philology in the Epoch of Cogito."

110 Readings and Schaber, *Postmodernism*, pp. 19, 20.

111 Abdul R. JanMohamed, "Wordliness-without-World, Homlessness-as-Home: Toward a Definition of the Specular Border Intellectual," in *Edward Said: A Critical Reader*, pp. 96–120; Culler, "Anti-Foundational Philology," p. 49.

[112] Jerome McGann develops this useful distinction in "The Monks and the Giants: Textual and Bibliographical Studies and the Interpretation of Literary Works," in *Textual Criticism and Literary Interpretation*, ed. Jerome J. McGann (Chicago, 1985), pp. 180–99.

[113] Calvert Watkins couches his report in mystificatory terms that take philology out of history: "Let me include the definition of philology that my teacher Roman Jakobson gave (who got it from his teacher, who got it from his): 'Philology is the art of reading slowly'" ("What is Philology?" *Comparative Literature Studies* 28 [1990]: 25). James McCawley offers a variant memory: "Philology is the art of careful reading" (cited in Winters and Nathan, "First He Called Her a Philologist," p. 351). Other reminiscences include De Man "Return to Philology," and Patterson, "The Return to Philology," p. 236.

[114] William Harris Stahl et al., *Martianus Capella and the Seven Liberal Arts* (New York, 1971–77), 1: 12.

[115] William Harris Stahl, "The *Quadrivium* of Martianus Capella: Its Place in the Intellectual History of Western Europe," in *Arts libéraux et philosophie au moyen âge* (Montreal, 1969), p. 959; Emily Bauman, "Re-dressing Colonial Discourse: Postcolonial Theory and the Humanist Project," *Critical Quarterly* 40.2 (1998): 79–89.

[116] "De nuptiis Philologiae et Mercurii," in *Martianus Capella*, ed. James Willis (Leipzig, 1983), pp. 204, 206, 250; Stahl, *Martianus Capella and the Seven Liberal Arts*, 2: 218, 220, 263.

[117] Stahl, *Martianus Capella and the Seven Liberal Arts*, 1: 131–36.

READING *BEOWULF* WITH ORIGINAL EYES

JAMES W. EARL

Some things I have an ability to see without feeling much previous history, al-
most like birds or dogs that have no human condition but are always living in the
same age, the same at Charlemagne's feet as on a Missouri scow or in a Chicago
junkyard. . . . And sometimes misery came over me to feel that I myself was the
creation of such places. How is it that human beings will submit to the gyps of
previous history while mere creatures look with their original eyes?
Saul Bellow, *The Adventures of Augie March*[1]

Augie March is one of my heroes, for saying things like that. Hardly
postmodern, much less a *Beowulf* scholar, he manages here to cap-
ture the essence of postmodern criticism as I see it. For me, post-
modernism in the literary field means first and foremost the stripping away
of comforting historical meta-narratives from long-inherited texts like
Beowulf. How I wish I could read the poem with Augie's "original eyes."

The odds are against it, though. *Beowulf* comes to us already heavily
dressed, proudly playing major and minor roles in a number of narratives:
among other things *Beowulf* is (1) the epic of Anglo-Saxon England, not
equal to but at least analogous to Homer; (2) *fons et origo* of English literary
history, its dark root, *terminus ab quo*, first chapter in the anthology and
first week of the survey course; (3) *locus classicus* of oral poetry and pre-
history as they are embedded in writing, of Germanic myth and folklore
as they are embedded in Christian narrative, of traditional society as it is
memorialized at the birth of civilization in England; and (4) chief exem-
plar of Germanic heroism, an inextinguishable theme ever after, from *The*

Battle of Maldon to *Henry V*, the Light Brigade, the American West, and *Law & Order*. In all these grand narratives, and others, *Beowulf* carries a lot of weight. And let us not forget (5) the slightly less grand narrative of the poem's own critical history, unfolding in a sort of Hegelian progress from Thorkelin and Thorpe to Ker and Klaeber, from Malone and Magoun to Irving and Orchard, from Napier to Niles, Tolkien to tomorrow.

The postmodern project of stripping away these and other narratives allows us to belong to them and build beyond them simultaneously. Periodically a generation grants itself license to see everything afresh, with original eyes if possible, and this seems to be one of those times. We may bid farewell to the positivism and the aesthetics of the Modern forever—but it remains to be seen if just saying so will have a lasting impact on *Beowulf* studies. In a case like *Beowulf*, isolated as it is from the onrush of cultural change, marginalized in the slower streams of scholarship, the "gyps of previous history" may long outlast us; and in the end, postmodernism may turn out to be just another gyp in the series.

Still, the question is good: What would *Beowulf* look like if we really could see it "without feeling much previous history"? What would it look like stripped of everything we have been taught about it, as if it had just washed up onto our shore and we were reading it for the very first time? Why should it be so hard to see the poem with original eyes, anyway? That is the way most first readers come to it, with little or no understanding of all these grand narratives (except perhaps an intuitive feel for the fourth, the now Americanized heroic tradition). That is how American pop-culture versions of *Beowulf* always begin, by tearing it out of history and casting it as archetypal myth, science fiction, or teen fantasy, loosely draped in pseudo-Viking images off the back lot.

The comforting grand narratives we are trying so hard to jettison were constructed in the first place largely from literature, so it is no surprise that *ipso facto*, like self-fulfilling prophecies, they provide *Beowulf* with such highly satisfying and meaningful contexts. The fact that they are so widely shared is part of their satisfaction, too—so widely shared that they have become obvious, and therefore unquestioned, unremarked, even unconscious. They are ideological by definition, that is, which explains why even teen readers and viewers who know nothing at all about them are by no means free of them. The past speaks through them, in the voice of Tradition.

The scholar's response should be a little more thoroughgoing and critical, however. Most of us are not looking to find adventure in *Beowulf*, much less the meaning of life. What we are looking for at this moment is the sort of knowledge that might proceed from a radical defamiliarization of this far-too-familiar text, setting it free from centuries of encrusted ideologies. In the case of *Beowulf*, I think, such a radical defamiliarization will reveal a radical strangeness in the poem. Freed from its roles in all our grand narratives, *Beowulf* stands apart, an unexpected singularity. It is, not to put too fine a point on it, *weird*.

In any case, without these narratives to guide our responses to *Beowulf*, we need new bearings. We cannot do entirely without bearings. So, inevitably we find ourselves reading *Beowulf* in one of two new ways, and sometimes both at once: more personally than ever before, in idiosyncratic, largely unshareable terms; or more impersonally than ever before, in relatively ahistorical theoretical ones.

READING MORE PERSONALLY

Without the grand narratives of history to guide us, we almost inevitably fall back on the un-grand narratives of our own lives—which can hardly be avoided in any case, but now at least we can do it in full awareness. In this primary-process criticism we find ourselves mostly ignoring the *Beowulf* of history and scholarship, and observing instead the connections that the poem establishes with ourselves and our present world. Putting aside all our laboriously acquired professional tools—history, philology, grammar, poetics, bibliography, exegesis—we find ourselves asking reflectively: Why does it tax our attention so? How has it woven itself into the present world (the one outside the library)? And, What kind of present are we in, anyway?

We have always responded to literature "personally." We have favorites and least favorites, tastes and distastes. Taken seriously, these are the subject of *belles lettres*, not scholarship. We cannot help worrying, then, if our private responses are critical, shareable, or even worth analyzing. Of our most private responses we are largely unaware, however, even as behind the scenes they guide our most public ones; so an examination of them can in fact be tough critical work. We work to bring to consciousness our unconscious relations to the poem. But is there anything especially postmodern about this process? What distinguishes it from psychoanalysis, which is quintessentially modern?

I will not try to answer that question in relation to literature in general, but in relation to *Beowulf* and some other ancient and medieval literature the answer takes a very interesting turn. Finding ourselves engaged with a text written well before the appearance of modern subjectivity in the twelfth century (and especially after Descartes in the seventeenth), we feel it reaching out to us in unexpectedly alien, non-subjective terms. It is not at all like reading Saul Bellow. For example, the poem actively encourages its readers to be socialized in strong male groups, groups organized by a leader's heroic autonomy and his followers' ethical obedience. The poem clearly appeals to its original audience with this idea, and modern readers fond of the idea are drawn to the poem. Its masculinist, fascist appeal is a disturbing side of the poem.

Not only is the poem insistently social, it repels individualism. For example, it is almost impossible to identify closely with *Beowulf*'s characters, because they have virtually no inner lives, no psychologies to which we might connect our own. They are like Greek tragic characters declaiming their lines—no matter how moving—through rigid, larger-than-life masks. They are less personal and more thoroughly social than even Homer's characters. The subtlety of the poem's representations and human interactions reminds us how unnecessary our anguished and conflicted modern interiority might be to the smooth functioning of a highly ethical society.

Nota bene: although we are now considering the "more personal" form of criticism, we are not dealing in individual subjectivity of the modern sort. Rather, the question is how we respond as modern subjects to a text that does not even try to treat us as modern subjects, a text that cannot even imagine a modern subject. The answer is that we are not really modern subjects when we come to *Beowulf*, especially if we come to it with postmodern questions in mind. When we jettisoned the grand narratives of modernity, our modern subjectivity went out the window with them. The internal psychodramas of our modern selves are not the only personal narratives we can invoke in order to structure our responses to the poem; we are immersed as well in huge historical and cultural dramas of a very external nature. A poem like *Beowulf* reaches out to those also, evoking responses in our social-historical as well as our psychological being. It is quite possible, then, culture-to-culture, to identify with *Beowulf* personally, but not subjectively.

Here is one personal narrative. When I was ten I almost died. In 1955, in my neighborhood at least, boys carried knives and played with them daily. One day a game of mumbledy-peg, which involved the throwing of knives close to each other's feet, turned into a wrestling match. My opponent pinned me down, sat on me and put his knife to my throat, imitating a scene we had watched in scores of movies about pioneers, explorers, cow-boys, gangsters, detectives, soldiers, and monsters. I grabbed his wrist, and as I pushed up, he pushed down. I realized immediately, even at ten, that if I did not push harder, and then even harder, this little game could be curtains for me. I escaped, of course, but furious that my would-be killer had not at all appreciated the danger I was in. In the fifty years since, that little mo-ment of childhood terror has come back many times, an unwelcome "spot in time," a viscerally felt metaphor for the always-near presence of death. Heidegger probably has a precise German term for it.

Seven years later the same thing happened again, but this time on a global scale. This spot of time I share with many my age. One night the president announced on television that if the Russians did not turn back in twenty-four hours, nuclear war would result. Those were not his exact words, but those were the words we heard. At school the next day, we all shook hands and said goodbye, not knowing if we would see each other again. I walked home, past the bomb shelter being displayed on the town-hall lawn, my head filled with scenes of Armageddon. Most of those scenes took the form of fantasies of being the last survivor of an atomic holocaust, a popular theme in films of the period, starting with *On the Beach*.

The Russians turned back the next day, but a year later the president was assassinated. In the meantime, I had gone off to college, which in 1963 meant being steeped in existentialism, the *lingua franca* of all my professors. The first public lecture I ever attended was on the subject "Was Plato an Existentialist?" Plato's Cave was presented to the freshmen as a figure of the human world, and, if we choose to make the connection with Kierkegaard and Sartre, a site of alienation. We discussed our alienation in late-night bull sessions.

That was the year, even as the president was being buried and the nation was in mourning, that *Beowulf* finally washed up on my shore. It seemed to be singing a very familiar song. Looking back, I am not surprised it caught me by the throat.

Twenty years later, at a cocktail party on Martha's Vineyard, I met a judge who had managed one of JFK's early campaigns. When I told him I was a *Beowulf* scholar, he told me the following story. One day he went to the Capitol to meet Kennedy for lunch, but the Senate was still in session; so he went up to the gallery to wait, and looking down into the Senate chamber he saw Kennedy, feet up on his desk reading a book. Later he asked him what the book was, and Kennedy held up a copy of *Beowulf*. Now the judge asked me: "Why *Beowulf*?" To me it seemed obvious. I said, "This is the man who wrote *Profiles in Courage*, the hero of PT 109. He was studying to be a hero and a leader. *Beowulf*'s a classic on the subject."

Little in this narrative of mine is really "subjective." The experience of the knife was a private trauma, but it cathected itself to many other events. On reflection, many of the crisscrossing cathexes in my mind are really only the traces of the external world passing through me. Now when I lecture on *Beowulf*, nearly every episode in the poem evokes strings of associations like these, moments when I registered the sharp impacts of the world—even world-historical events.

Having grown up modern, not postmodern, the language of the previous paragraph does make me a little uncomfortable, though. My subjectivity, formed when it was, remains unshakably modern, not postmodern. My first response to externals is usually to defend my individual free will and the dignity of my emotional life, no matter how feeble or illusory they are. Although there are things in *Beowulf* that appeal strongly to this modern subjectivity of mine—its existentialism, for example—there is also much in the poem's premodernism that appeals strongly to our collective postmodernism.

READING MORE IMPERSONALLY

I can fix my memory down to an ant in the folds of bark or fat in a piece of meat or colored thread on the collar of a blouse. Or such discriminations as where, on a bush of roses, you see variations in heats that make your breast and bowel draw at various places from your trying to correspond. . . . The human heat that circulates and warms, when it's piled at any bar or break, burns inward or out with typical embers or sores, and makes a track of fever or fire whose corresponding part is darkness and cold gaps. . . . It's rare to find us without these breaks and interferences.[2]

That is how Augie March describes those original eyes that can see through "the gyps of previous history." And that is how I would like to read *Beowulf*, with a phenomenological intensity alert not only to details but to the "darkness and cold gaps," the "breaks and interferences" in our primary, seemingly natural responses.

I suggested above that *Beowulf*'s premodernism may appeal to our postmodernism, and might allow us to escape our modern subjectivism. Let us subject that idea to a test, by focusing on the passage in the poem that most approximates modern interiority, a moment of intense private emotion described in terms of individual psychology, to which we inevitably respond with an easy personal identification. There are a few such moments in the poem. Students have a keen eye for them, finding them welcome oases of familiar (i.e., modern) humanity in a generally confusing and impersonal narrative. Perhaps the most memorable is the scene of Hrothgar's tears at Beowulf's departure, lines 1826–80. Orchard calls this "a touchingly depicted scene," a "moving image" by which "the sensitive reader cannot but feel disturbed"; "a strong sense of foreboding seems only natural."[3] But is there a "cold gap" between this seemingly natural response and what the text actually says?

First Beowulf makes a speech of fourteen lines. It is all formality, a series of public pledges: he promises to bring a great army to Hrothgar's aid if he is ever attacked, repeats the promise in Hygelac's name, and offers Geatish protection to Hrothgar's son Hrethric if he should ever need it. Hrothgar replies with a speech of twenty-four lines. He praises Beowulf's speech as wise beyond measure, predicts that the Geats will choose Beowulf king after Hygelac dies, declares that Beowulf has brought peace between the Danes and Geats, and finishes by promising future gifts to the Geats. Then come fourteen lines describing Hrothgar's emotional hugging, kissing, weeping farewell. Given the public nature of the previous exchange, the interiority of the feelings described in these last lines is quite startling.

The whole passage is relatively free of textual issues and perennial cruxes, but there are plenty of surprises and problems in it typical of the whole poem. Beowulf's opening lines may at first seem straightforward:

> "Gif ic þæt gefricge ofer floda begang
> þæt þec ymbsittend egesan þywað
> swa þec hetende hwilum dydon
> ic ðe þusenda þegna bringe
> hæleþa to helpe." (lines 1825–30a)[4]

> "If ever I learn over the ocean's way
> that those surrounding you threaten you with terror
> as often before your foes have done
> I will bring thousands of thanes to you
> heroes to help."

But who are these *hetende* ("enemies") who have on occasion (*hwilum*) brought terror to the Danes? All we have ever been told about Hrothgar's martial exploits is, "Ða wæs Hroðgare heresped gyfen" ("Then was Hrothgar given success in war," line 64). Could Beowulf be referring to the Grendels, then? But they are not *ymbsittend* ("neighboring peoples," literally "around-sitters"), at least in the memorable sense of line 9 ("æghwylc þara ymbsittendra ofer hronrade," "each of those sitting around across the whale-road"), and they are hardly like (*swa*) an invading army, calling for thousands of men. The parallel is very weak. If he is not referring to the monsters, though, to what past *hetende* could he be referring? One possibility, although we have certainly not heard a word about it in the poem, is the Geats themselves: for in just a few lines, Hrothgar will make a very puzzling reference to past enmity between the Danes and Geats, which has now been put to rest by Beowulf.

Let us just admit that the *hetende* in this passage are a "loose end." *Beowulf* has hundreds of such loose ends. Some of them seem to connect to other loose ends, as this one might connect to Hrothgar's immanent reference to Geatish enmity. Auerbach says of Homeric narrative that it is all foreground: "[N]ever is there a form left fragmentary or half-illuminated, never a lacuna, never a gap, never a glimpse of unplumbed depths." On the other hand, he says, biblical narrative is "fraught with background": "everything remains unexpressed."[5] *Beowulf* is radically different than both: it is fraught with loose ends, hinting (but only hinting) at a rich background, teasing us with scraps and shards of backstories.

Beowulf ends his speech with a puzzling promise, a shard of a backstory-to-be:

> "Gif him þonne Hreþric to hofum Geata
> geþingeð þeodnes bearn he mæg þær fela
> freonda findan· feorcyþðe beoð
> selran gesohte þæm þe him selfa deah." (lines 1836–39)

> "If Hrethric then to the home of the Geats
> the prince should appeal he may there many
> friends find; distant friends
> a man who would save himself had best seek."

Here he is predicting that Hrethric will go into exile after Hrothgar's death and Hrothulf's accession, and is offering (on behalf of Hygelac) to help him. The scholarship on this Hrothulf backstory is very thick, and unfortunately out of fashion. Orchard wisely tips his hat to it in commenting on these lines;[6] Heaney ignores it, and translates weakly, "If Hrethric should think about traveling as a king's son"[7]—as if a vacation were in order. There is some evidence that Beowulf keeps this promise, if we can trust the much-debated remark made about him at the end of the poem,

> . . . ðe ær geheold
> wið hettndum hord ond rice
> æfter hæleða hryre hwate Scildingas, . . . (lines 3005b–07)

> . . . who earlier held
> against enemies hoard and kingdom
> after the fall of heroes bold Scyldings, . . .

Mitchell and Robinson take this remark too (unconvincingly) as a reference to the Grendels, and see other suggestions as "misguided." An older speculation is that both passages refer to an intervention by Beowulf when Hrothulf assumes the throne—more loose ends that might connect. Klaeber, who shares Auerbach's view that good narrative is either classical or biblical, says of Kemp Malone's reconstruction of these backstories, "It is doubtful whether such a procedure on the part of the poet would have been fair to the readers"[8]—hardly a trenchant critique by today's standards.

Beowulf's speech ends with a maxim. The whole speech has been strikingly impersonal, in the sense of public and formal, although personal in the sense of forging personal commitments. Perhaps the maxim he ends with really is as impersonal as "travel is good for you," as gnomic analogues might suggest;[9] but in this context it might also be poignant advice for an exiled prince: "a man who would save himself had best seek distant friends."

Now Hrothgar replies:

> "Þe þa wordcwydas wigtig drihten
> on sefan sende · ne hyrde ic snotorlicor
> on swa geongum feore guman þingian ·
> þu eart mægenes strang ond on mode frod,
> wis wordcwida · . . ." (lines 1841–45a)

> "Those spoken words did the wise Lord
> send into your mind. Never more wisely
> have I heard a man settle things in such a young life.

You are strong in might and in mind prudent,
in spoken words wise. . . ."

But what has Beowulf said that deserves such lavish praise? How did his
speech, which consisted of no more than pledges of support to Hrothgar
and his son, qualify as *snotor*, *wis*, *frod*, and even divinely inspired? The
word *þingian* suggests an answer: Beowulf does not speak wise thoughts
like a philosopher or a contemplative, as Hrothgar sometimes does; rath-
er, he simply knows how to manage and settle affairs wisely. His wisdom,
which Hrothgar obviously cannot praise highly enough, is entirely practical
in nature, one might even say political, engaged not with ideas or beliefs but
with making arrangements in the external world.

Now we come to Hrothgar's surprising suggestion, referred to above,
that Beowulf has established peace between the Danes and Geats:

> "Me þin modsefa
> licað leng swa wel, leofa Beowulf
> hafast þu gefered þæt þam folcum sceal
> Geata leodum ond Gardenum
> sib gemæne ond sacu restan,
> inwitniþas þe hie ær drugon,
> wesan þenden ic wealde widan rices
> maþmas gemæne, manig oþerne
> godum gegretan ofer ganotes bæð · . . ." (lines 1853b–61)

> "I like your mind,
> the longer the better, beloved Beowulf.
> You have brought it about that to tribes shall,
> to the Geatish people and the Gar-Danes,
> peace together and strife cease,
> malicious attacks which they earlier suffered,
> be while I wield the wide kingdom,
> mutual gifts many another
> to greet with goods over the gannet's bath. . . ."

After the startlingly contemporary phrase "I like your mind," the syntax
grows extraordinarily difficult. I have tried not to disguise that fact in my
translation. The *sceal* in line 1855 governs three infinitives, one of them
six lines away, and the three resulting clauses ("sib gemaene sceal wesan,"

"sacu sceal restan," and "maþmas sceal gegretan") are very oddly interwoven. It is not enough for an editor simply to say "supply *sceal*" before *restan* and *gegretan*. The delay of *wesan* by two lines after its subject *sib* results in the apparently contradictory "þam folcum sceal . . . sib gemæne ond sacu restan" ("for those peoples . . . peace together and war shall rest"). Can *restan* mean both "cease" ("come to rest") and "remain" ("stay at rest") at the same time? Or is it that war shall cease, and peace (after some delay . . .) be? The sentence is very strained: literally it says, "shall mutual peace (and war cease, malicious attacks which they earlier suffered) be. . . ." That is as clotted a syntax as we will find anywhere in the poem. One is reminded of Gerard Manley Hopkins, who could write sentences like,

> I see
> The lost are like this, and their scourge to be
> As I am mine, their sweating selves.[10]

The syntax of that one is clear enough if you work at it long enough, but the poet is obviously taking delight in the difficulty of his style. The difficulty of the syntax in the *Beowulf* passage actually distracts us from the larger problem of the passage: what malicious attacks (*inwitniþas*) could Hrothgar be referring to?

At last we come to The Kiss.

> Gecyste þa cyning æþelum god,
> þeoden Scyldinga ðegn betstan
> ond be healse genam · hruron him tearas
> blondenfeaxum · him wæs bega wen
> ealdum infrodum, oþres swiðor ·
> þæt hie seoðða[n no] geseon moston
> modige on meþle · wæs him se man to þon leof
> þæt he þone breostwylm forberan ne mehte
> ac him on hreþre hygebendum fæst
> æfter deorum men dyrne langað
> beorn wið blode. (lines 1870–80a)

> Then kissed the king of good descent,
> prince of the Scyldings, the best thegn,
> and took his neck. His tears did fall
> on his gray hairs. Two hopes he had,

> the old wise one, one the stronger,
> that they would not after see one another
> courageous in council. The man was so dear to him
> he could not forbear the heaving breast
> but fast in his chest in chains of thought
> for the dear man desire in secret
> burned at the blood.

These lines take us deeper and deeper inside Hrothgar: he kisses Beowulf and hugs him; tears fall on his gray hair; two thoughts occur to him, one stronger than the other; his breast, in spite of the bonds imposed on it by his mind, heaves; and a secret desire burns within him. It is certainly a beautiful, delicate conclusion to the scene, but the precise meaning is lost in a syntactic blur.

Let us focus especially on the last five lines. I get caught on *dyrne langað* every time. In Modern English, the word "desires" might be the plural of the noun "desire," or the third-person singular of the verb "desire," i.e., "he desires." Similarly with the Old English word *langað*: it might be the noun "desire" or the verb "desires." *Dyrne* does not help us decide the matter; besides, it might be either an adverb ("secretly desires") or adjective ("secret desire"). If we expand the context to include the next word, *beorn*, the situation only worsens. If it is a relatively rare form of the verb "burned," some of the ambiguity is resolved, because "desires" must then certainly be a noun, and we can read, "he burned with a secret desire." However, *beorn* is also the very common noun "man," either in the nominative or accusative case. Thus "dyrne langað beorn" could mean "secret desire burned" (or alternately "desire secretly burned"), or "the man secretly desires" (alternately "he secretly desires the man").

Let us not overstate the problem; as with the Hopkins example, repeatedly rereading the whole passage does help. The larger the context, the clearer the meaning—to a degree. The long sentence begins with two verbs, *wæs* and *mehte*, both in the preterite tense; so on reflection we probably need to reject *langað* as a verb, because it is in the present tense; and now we can read with relative comfort, "he could not forbear sighing, but secret desire for the dear one burned. . . ." However, just when we think we have it solved, we confront the last two words of the sentence, *wið blode*. "Secret desire burned *wið* blood"? There is no comfortable interpretation of this phrase. The usual translation, "a secret desire burned in his blood," is devoutly to be wished, but would be a unique use of the preposition *wið*, which indicates distinction or opposition, like Modern English "against" or "over against." Nowhere else in the Old English corpus does *wið* occur with the noun *blode*, or with the verb "to burn." If the poet meant "burned in his blood," why would he have used *wið*, when he could simply have used *in*? Once you notice this one anomalous preposition, you notice another: in the previous line, *æfter* is just as odd a choice. "A secret desire *æfter* a dear man"? There is a lot of action in this psychology, if that is what it is, a lot of reaching toward and pushing away.

Let us read through those last lines again.

> . . . he þone breostwylm forberan ne mehte
> ac him on hreþre hygebendum fæst
> æfter deorum men dyrne langað
> beorn wið blode. (lines 1877–80a)

Assuming that *beorn* really is the past tense of "burn," and not "man," the anomalous phrase "beorn wið blode" has an oddly medical feel to it. Hrothgar's burning desire has an oblique relation to the blood. In the Galenic system, blood is hot and moist, but corresponds to air, not fire. The sanguine is associated with desire and happiness, but the point here seems to be that Hrothgar is both happy and sad at the same time, and the sadness wins out. He is weeping, too, so water is a part of the medical picture. How can *langað* burn and yet produce tears? How can *langað* be *æfter* a dear man, but *wið* the blood?

Two lines earlier, the inner contest was described with the image, "him on hreðre hygebendum fæst." Something is being bound fast in the breast by the mind. Might not the subjection of the heart by the mind be described as an effort *wið blode*? The subject of the sentence seems to be *langað*. As modern readers, we instinctively associate longing with blood and fire, but here longing seems instead to be associated with *hyge*, mind or intention, and opposed to blood. This particular longing, fast in its thought-bonds, seems to be not a burning emotion but a burning thought; it is a desire, but in the sense of will or intention, which is in fact busily suppressing an emotion—or trying to, at least, since Hrothgar sighs in spite of himself.

If we look back another two lines, we find the contest described as two contradictory thoughts appearing at the same time, but one stronger than the other: "him wæs bega wen . . . oþres swiðor." What we might "naturally" think of as an emotional upheaval is actually being portrayed as a cognitive struggle, a struggle of two contradictory thoughts, or expectations. It is not unlike the Homeric trope of a man considering two possibilities and then choosing one, except that Hrothgar seems not even to choose, he simply recognizes the stronger. If individual agency is debatable in Homer (and it is still a hot-button issue, as in Bernard Williams's *Shame and Necessity*),[11] it is even more so in *Beowulf*.

Now let us paraphrase the passage in such a way as to bring out these relationships: "Two expectations occurred to the wise old man, the second one the stronger, that they would not see again. . . . He could not suppress a sigh, but in his breast a secret longing after the dear man, bound fast in thought, burned at the blood." If this last phrase still seems awkward, vague, or counterintuitive, we might recall Augie's commentary:

> You see variations in heats that make your breast and bowel draw at various places from your trying to correspond. . . . The human heat that circulates and warms, when it's piled at any bar or break, burns inward or out with typical embers or sores, and makes a track of fever or fire whose corresponding part is darkness and cold gaps. . . . It's rare to find us without these breaks and interferences.[12]

Bellow actually makes a point of telling us that Augie has read Galen, but it is still surprising to hear him describe his love in Galenic terms. The effort to correspond perfectly to the object of his desire produces changes in his body which disturb the circulation of blood; blocked, the blood either releases its heat outward, producing cold within, or inward, producing fever. In either case the response is inversely related to the desired object: cold produces warmth, and darkness fire. The correspondences balance.

The more familiar paradoxes of Petrarchan love can also be seen as effects of the humors:

> Amor che 'ncende il cor d'ardente zelo
> di gelata paura il ten costretto;
> et qual sia più fa dubbio a l'intelletto
> la speranza o 'l temor, la fiamma o 'l gelo.

> Love fires my heart with ardent zeal,
> constricts it too with icy fear;
> and the mind doubts which is greater,
> hope or fear, the flame or frost.[13]

Augie and Petrarch are experiencing romantic love, and Hrothgar paternal love, but the similarities of language and image are striking: bodily effects, a struggle between the mind and the heart, will and blood, burning and tears, heat and cold. All of that fits with the terminology of the humors. We need not believe that the *Beowulf* poet knew anything of Galen, even indirectly, although recent work on Anglo-Saxon medicine makes it seem quite possible.[14]

Of course there are differences. Petrarch is experiencing a conflict of two passions, burning zeal and freezing fear, whereas Hrothgar is experiencing a conflict of two thoughts (*bega wen*). Perhaps he will see Beowulf again, perhaps not, but the latter seems more likely. That saddens him. His sadness is a reasonable result of his thought, which is highly controlled (*hygebendum fæst*), not an upwelling passion that disturbs his mind. Even at its most apparently sentimental, then, *Beowulf* is decidedly non-sentimental, in fact stoic in its hardened rationalism. (Galen was after all a stoic philosopher— although again, no link to stoicism is implied.)

What is being described in the scene of Hrothgar's tears is a premodern psychology which is very easily confused for modern interiority. The closest analogy may in fact be in Homer, for example when Odysseus is tossing and turning in his bed:

> He struck himself on the chest and spoke to his heart and scolded it:
> "Bear up, my heart. You have had worse to endure before this." . . .
> So he spoke, addressing his own dear heart within him;
> and the heart in great obedience endured and stood it
> without complaint, but the man himself was twisting and turning. (*Odyssey* XX, lines 17–24)[15]

PERSONAL LAUNDRY

What do these two ways of looking at the poem have to do with each other? They seem almost incompatible, but they are in fact two sides of the same coin. Anyone who lives long enough with a work of art has at least these two ways of relating to it, and one of them cannot be too much more important than the other. Our "more personal" reflections connect the dots of our experience, seen from the particular path we cut through it, from the point of view we happen to inhabit. We are free to think of our point of view as a unique subjectivity or as a subject position; either way, *Beowulf* has washed up on our shore, grabbed our attention with a message resonant enough to gather our thoughts around it, and laid its various patterns this way and that upon our lives and ideas. Some of the patterns are narrative, some are more abstract.

When Augie turns his original eyes to the larger patterns of his life, what does he see? Toward the end of his *Adventures* he finds himself in an especially intelligent conversation of the "more impersonal" sort. It is his wedding day, but he is about to be shipped off to war; the stakes are high, the meaning of life at hand. "As you listened to this brilliant educational discussion it was somewhat scary too; like catching hold of high voltage." His historical moment, his present world, his life story, and the complete contents of his five-foot shelf of Great Books all overflow their banks and flood through him:

> Declarations, resolutions, treaties, theories, congresses, bones of kings, Cromwells, Loyolas, Lenins and czars, hordes of India and China, famines, huddles, massacres, sacrifices, he mentioned. Great crowds of Benares and London, Rome, he made me see; Jerusalem against Titus, Hell when Ulysses visited, Paris when they butchered horses in the street. Dead Ur and Memphis. Atoms of near silence, the dead acts, that formed a collective roar. Macedonian sentinels. Subway moles. Mr. Kreindl shoving a cannon wheel with his buddies. Grandma and legendary Lausch in his armor cutaway having an argument in the Odessa railroad station the day the Japanese war broke out. My parents taking a walk by the Humboldt Park lagoon the day I was conceived. Flowery springtime.[16]

His catalogue is factual and poetic, precise and comprehensive, concrete and abstract. It contains wars and revolutions, but also Homer and Josephus, as well as his childhood in a Chicago tenement. This is the world as seen through Augie's original eyes. Books are a big part of it, but there is a very conspicuous absence of any grand narrative. It is borderline chaotic and "somewhat scary"—although no more, really, than my bringing together *Beowulf*, Saul Bellow, JFK, cowboy movies and *On the Beach*, Homer, Plato, Galen, Petrarch, Hopkins and Sartre, the Cuban missile crisis, and a knife at my throat.

More important than the resemblance of Augie's catalogue to my own, however, is its resemblance to *Beowulf*'s vision of history. For what is the effect of all the poem's digressions, allusions, puzzles, cruxes, loose ends, and scraps and shards of backstories, if not to deny us any coherent grand narrative? Except for the hero's trajectory from victory to death, history in the poem is as disjointed as Augie's catalogue, each event in the present evoking a loosely associated discrete event or narrative from the past, or sometimes even the future. No wonder it is so easy to detach the poem from its historical context and redeploy it as myth, fantasy, or science fiction.

Consider in particular how the one extended background narrative we do find in the poem, the mini-epic of the Geatish-Swedish wars, has been broken into pieces and rearranged as a collage-like backdrop to the dragon fight. Its episodes are fragments, unchronological and quite hard to reassemble without a chart, not to mention that they are presented in four different voices—the narrator's, Beowulf's, Wiglaf's, and the messenger's. They remind me of the reconstructed windows of Winchester Cathedral, destroyed in 1642 during the Civil War and reassembled randomly in 1660: beautiful, brilliant—and chaotic.

How does one respond to such confusion? As scholars, of course, with as much line-by-line precision as possible; but as Augie says of the scary high-voltage randomness of his own experience, we are always allowed a more personal response: "I thought there was altogether too much of this to live with. Better forget it, in part. The Ganges is there with its demons and lords; but you have a right also, and merely, to wash your feet and do your personal laundry in it."[17]

NOTES

[1] Saul Bellow, *The Adventures of Augie March* (New York, 1953), pp. 356–60.

[2] Bellow, *The Adventures of Augie March*, p. 356.

[3] Andy Orchard, *A Critical Companion to "Beowulf"* (Cambridge, Eng., 2003), p. 218.

[4] All citations of the poem are from Bruce Mitchell and Susan Irvine, *"Beowulf" Repunctuated*, Old English Newsletter, Subsidia 29 (Kalamazoo, 2000). All translations are mine.

[5] Erich Auerbach, *Mimesis: The Representation of Reality in Western Literature*, trans. Willard R. Trask (Princeton, 1968), pp. 6–7, 11–12.

[6] Orchard, *A Critical Companion to "Beowulf,"* p. 217.

[7] Seamus Heaney, trans., *"Beowulf": A New Verse Translation* (New York, 2000), pp. 125, 127.

[8] Fr. Klaeber, *"Beowulf" and the Fight at Finnsburg*, 3rd ed. with supplements (Lexington, Mass., 1950), p. 225.

[9] See Susan Deskis, *"Beowulf" and the Medieval Proverb Tradition* (Tempe, 1996).

10   Gerard Manley Hopkins, "I Wake and Feel," in *Gerard Manley Hopkins*, ed. Catherine Phillips (Oxford, 1986), p. 166.

11   Bernard Williams, *Shame and Necessity* (Berkeley, 1993).

12   Bellow, *The Adventures of Augie March*, p. 356.

13   "*Rime* 182," in *Petrarch's Lyric Poems*, ed. Robert M. Durling (Cambridge, Mass., 1976), p. 329; my translation (see also *Rime* nos. 48, 55, 132).

14   Anne Van Arsdall, *Medieval Herbal Remedies: The Old English Herbarium and Anglo-Saxon Medicine* (New York, 2002), pp. 68–70.

15   *The Odyssey of Homer*, trans. Richard Lattimore (New York, 1965), p. 298.

16   Bellow, *The Adventures of Augie March*, pp. 534–35.

17   Bellow, *The Adventures of Augie March*, pp. 535.

REPRINTED MATERIAL

"Regardless of Sex: Men, Women, and Power in Early Northern Europe," by Carol J. Clover, reprinted with permission from *Speculum: A Journal of Medieval Studies* 68 (1993), Medieval Academy of America, Cambridge, MA.

"The Ruins of Identity," by Jeffrey Jerome Cohen, reprinted with permission from *Of Giants: Sex, Monsters, and the Middle Ages*, University of Minnesota Press, 1994, Minneapolis, MN.

"*Beowulf*'s Tears of Fatherhood," by Mary Dockray-Miller, reprinted with permission from *Exemplaria* 10 (1998), Pegasus Press, Asheville, NC.

"*Beowulf* and the Origins of Civilization," by James W. Earl, reprinted with permission from *Speaking Two Languages: Traditional Disciplines and Contemporary Theory in Medieval Studies*, edited by Allen J. Frantzen, SUNY Press, 1991, Albany, NY.

"What is an Author?" by Michel Foucault, reprinted with permission from *Textual Strategies: Perspectives in Post-Structuralist Criticism*, edited by Josué V. Harari, Cornell University Press, 1979, Ithaca, NY.

"Writing the Unreadable *Beowulf*," by Allen J. Frantzen, reprinted with permission from *Desire for Origins: New Language, Old English, and Teaching the Tradition*, Rutgers University Press, 1990, Piscataway, NJ.

"The Ethnopsychology of In-Law Feud and the Remaking of Group Identity in *Beowulf*: The Cases of Hengest and Ingeld," by John M. Hill, reprinted with permission from *Philological Quarterly* 78.1/2 (Winter 1999), University of Iowa, Iowa City, IA.

"Voices from the Margin: Women and Textual Enclosure in *Beowulf*," by Shari Horner, reprinted with permission from *The Discourse of Enclosure*, SUNY Press, 2001, Albany, NY.

"*Beowulf* and the Ancestral Homeland," by Nicholas Howe, reprinted with permission from *Migration and Mythmaking in Anglo-Saxon England*, University of Notre Dame Press, 1989, Notre Dame, IN.

"'As I Once Did With Grendel': Boasting and Nostalgia in *Beowulf*," by Susan M. Kim, reprinted with permission from *Modern Philology* 103:1 (2005), University of Chicago Press, Chicago, IL.

"Men and *Beowulf*," by Clare A. Lees, reprinted with permission from *Medieval Masculinities: Regarding Men in the Middle Ages*, edited by Clare A. Lees, University of Minnesota Press, 1994, Minneapolis, MN.